America's
Top-Rated Cities:
A Statistical Handbook

Volume 1

2012
Nineteenth Edition

America's
Top-Rated Cities:
A Statistical Handbook

Volume 1: Southern Region

A UNIVERSAL REFERENCE BOOK

Grey House
Publishing

PUBLISHER: Leslie Mackenzie
EDITORIAL DIRECTOR: Laura Mars
EDITOR: David Garoogian

CONTRIBUTING WRITER: Alison Amorello; Allison Blake
RESEARCH ASSISTANTS: Katrina Doyle; Dawn Jenkins
MARKETING DIRECTOR: Jessica Moody

A Universal Reference Book
Grey House Publishing, Inc.
4919 Route 22
Amenia, NY 12501
518.789.8700
Fax 845.373.6390
www.greyhouse.com
e-mail: books @greyhouse.com

Nineteenth Edition
Printed in Canada

Publisher's Cataloging-in-Publication Data
(Prepared by The Donohue Group, Inc.)

America's top-rated cities. Vol. I, Southern region : a statistical handbook.. -- 1992-

v. : ill. ; cm.
Annual, 1995-
Irregular, 1992-1993
ISSN: 1082-7102

1. Cities and towns--Ratings--Southern States--Statistics--Periodicals. 2. Cities and towns--Southern States--Statistics--Periodicals. 3. Social indicators--Southern States--Periodicals. 4. Quality of life--Southern States--Statistics--Periodicals. 5. Southern States--Social conditions--Statistics--Periodicals. I. Title: America's top rated cities. II. Title: Southern region

HT123.5.S6 A44
307.76/0973/05   95644648

4-Volume Set   ISBN: 978-1-59237-857-9
Volume 1   ISBN: 978-1-59237-858-6
Volume 2   ISBN: 978-1-59237-859-3
Volume 3   ISBN: 978-1-59237-860-9
Volume 4   ISBN: 978-1-59237-861-6

Athens, Georgia

Atlanta, Georgia

Austin, Texas

Cape Coral, Florida

Jackson, Mississippi

Jacksonville, Florida

Miami, Florida

Murfreesboro, Tennessee

Nashville, Tennessee

New Orleans, Louisiana

Orlando, Florida

Pembroke Pines, Florida

Plano, Texas

Round Rock, Texas

San Antonio, Texas

Savannah, Georgia

Tampa, Florida

Introduction

This nineteenth edition of *America's Top-Rated Cities* is a concise, statistical, 4-volume work identifying America's top-rated cities with populations of at least 95,000. It profiles 100 cities that have received high marks for business and living from prominent publications, such as *Forbes* and *U.S. New & World Report,* from surveys appearing in over 300 sources, such as *BusinessWeek, Inc. Magazine, Fortune, Men's Health, The Wall Street Journal, Women's Health,* and *CNBC,* and from first-hand visits, interviews and reports.

Each volume covers a different region of the country—Southern, Western, Central and Eastern—and includes a detailed Table of Contents, City Chapters, Appendices, and Maps. Each City Chapter incorporates information from hundreds of resources to create the following major sections:

- **Background**—lively narrative of significant, up-to-date news for both businesses and residents. Each background combines historical facts with up-to-the-minute development, "known-for" annual events, and an annual weather report.
- **Rankings**—fun-to-read, bulleted survey results from 320 books and magazines, such as general (Best Quality of Life Cities), specific (Most Literate Cities), and everything in between (Happiest Cities).
- **Statistical Tables**—118 tables and detailed topics, with several new and expanded topics, offer an unparalleled view of each city's Business and Living Environments. They are carefully organized with data that is easy to read and understand.
- **Appendices**—five in all, follow each volume of City Chapters. These range from listings of Metropolitan Statistical Areas to Comparative Statistics for all 100 cities.

This new edition of *America's Top Rated Cities* includes cites that ranked highest and received the most points, using our unique weighting system. Twenty-four cities have never before appeared as a top-rated city, and 7 cities have shown up again, after a year or more of not making the cut. New cities, by volume, are:

- SOUTHERN: Cape Coral and Pembroke Pines, FL; Clarkesville and Murfreesboro, TN; Round Rock, TX
- WESTERN: Gilbert, AZ; Carlsbad, Roseville, Sunnyvale, and Temecula, CA; Billings, MT; Henderson, NV
- CENTRAL: Olathe, KS; Sterling Heights, MI; Columbia, MO; Broken Arrow and Norman, OK; Kenosha, WI
- EASTERN: Columbia, MD; High Point, NC; Jersey City, NJ; Huntington and Oyster Bay, NY; Chesapeake, VA

Praise for previous editions:

> "...Smartly compiled with an assortment of useful information, libraries that
> have purchased earlier editions will want to continue that tradition..."

—Against the Grain

> "...Users who are thinking of relocating...or who would like to see if their
> businesses have the possibility of thriving in a new location will find...valuable
> information....[S]uitable for large public libraries, academic libraries [with]
> business schools, business libraries, and corporate libraires."

—ARBA

> "...[ATRC] has...proven its worth to a wide audience...from businesspeople and
> corporations planning to launch, relocate, or expand their operations to market
> researchers, real estate professionals, urban planners, job-seekers,
> students...interested in...reliable, attractively presented statistical infomation
> about larger U.S. cities."

—ARBA

BACKGROUND
Each city begins with an informative **Background** that combines history with current events. These narratives reflect changes that have occurred during the past year, and touch on the city's environment, politics, employment, cultural offerings, climate, and often include interesting trivia. For example, Henderson supplied most of the magnesium needed for WWII planes and weapons, both Presidents Franklin and Theodore Roosevelt went to Harvard, Gatorade was invented to hydrate University of Florida's football team (the Gators), and Temecula harvests more than 50 varieties of wine grapes.

RANKINGS

This section has rankings from a possible 320 (up from 289) books, articles, and reports. For easy reference, these Rankings are categorized into 18 topics including Business/Finance, Dating/Romance, and Health/Fitness.

The Rankings are presented in an easy-to-read, bulleted format and include results from both annual surveys and one-shot studies. **Fastest-Growing Wages . . . Best for Having a Baby . . . Most Well-Read . . . Most Playful . . . Most Wired . . . Healthiest for Women . . . Best for Minority Entrepreneurers . . . Most Romantic . . . Safest . . . Best to Grow Old . . . Most Polite . . . Best for Moviemakers . . . Noisiest . . . Most Vegetarian-Friendly . . . Least Stressful . . . Best Sleeping . . . Best to Ride out a Recession . . . Most Sex Happy . . . Most Political . . . Most Charitable . . . Most Miserable . . . Most Tax Friendly . . . Best for Telecommuters . . . Most Road Rage . . . Greediest . . . Gayest . . . Best for Cats . . . Most Tattooed . . . Best for Wheelchair Users . . . and more.**

Sources for these Rankings include both well-known magazines and other media, including *Forbes, Fortune, Inc. Magazine, Working Mother, Popular Science, Prevention, Field & Stream, BusinessWeek, Kiplinger's Personal Finance, Men's Journal,* and *Travel + Leisure,* as well as resources not as well known, such as the *Asthma & Allergy Foundation of America, Christopher & Dana Reeve Foundation, The Advocate, Black Enterprise, National Civic League, The National Coalition for the Homeless, MovieMaker Magazine, Center for Digital Government, U.S. Conference of Mayors, Milken Institue,* and the *Centre for International Competitiveness.*

STATISTICAL TABLES

Each city chapter includes a possible 118 tables and detailed topics—66 in BUSINESS and 52 in LIVING. Nearly 95% of statistical data has been updated. New topics include *Housing Affordability* and *Consumer Fraud.* Expanded topics include the breakdown of Mexican, Cuban and Puerto Rican for *Hispanic Orgin;* the addition of American Indian/Alaska Native and Native Hawaiian to *Race;* and the addition of: PSA Testing and Seniors Receiving Flu Shots to *Health Risks.*

Business Environment includes hard facts and figures on 12 topics, including City Finances, Demographics, Income, Economy, Employment, and Real Estate. *Living Environment* includes 11 topics, such as Cost of Living, Housing, Health, Education, Safety, Recreation, and Sports Teams.

To compile the Statistical Tables, our editors have again turned to a wide range of sources, some well known, such as the *U.S. Census Bureau, U.S. Environmental Protection Agency, Bureau of Labor Statistics, Centers for Disease Control and Prevention,* and the *Federal Bureau of Investigation,* and some more obscure, like *The Council for Community and Economic Research, Texas Transportation Institute,* and *Federation of Tax Administrators.*

APPENDICES
- **Appendix A**—*Counties*
- **Appendix B**—*Metropolitan Area Definitions*
- **Appendix C**—*Chambers of Commerce and Economic Development Organizations*: Addresses, phone, fax, web sites of these resources help readers find more detailed information on each city.
- **Appendix D**—*State Departments of Labor and Employment*: Additional economic and employment data, with address, phone and web site for easy access.
- **Appendix E**—*Comparative Statistics*: City-by-city comparison comprised of 73 tables. All volumes include all 100 cities.

Material provided by public and private agencies and organizations was supplemented by original research, numerous library sources and Internet sites. *America's Top-Rated Cities, 2012,* is designed for a wide range of readers: private individuals considering relocating a residence or business; professionals considering expanding their businesses or changing careers; corporations considering relocation, opening up additional offices or creating new divisions; government agencies; general and market researchers; real estate consultants; human resource personnel; urban planners; investors; and urban government students.

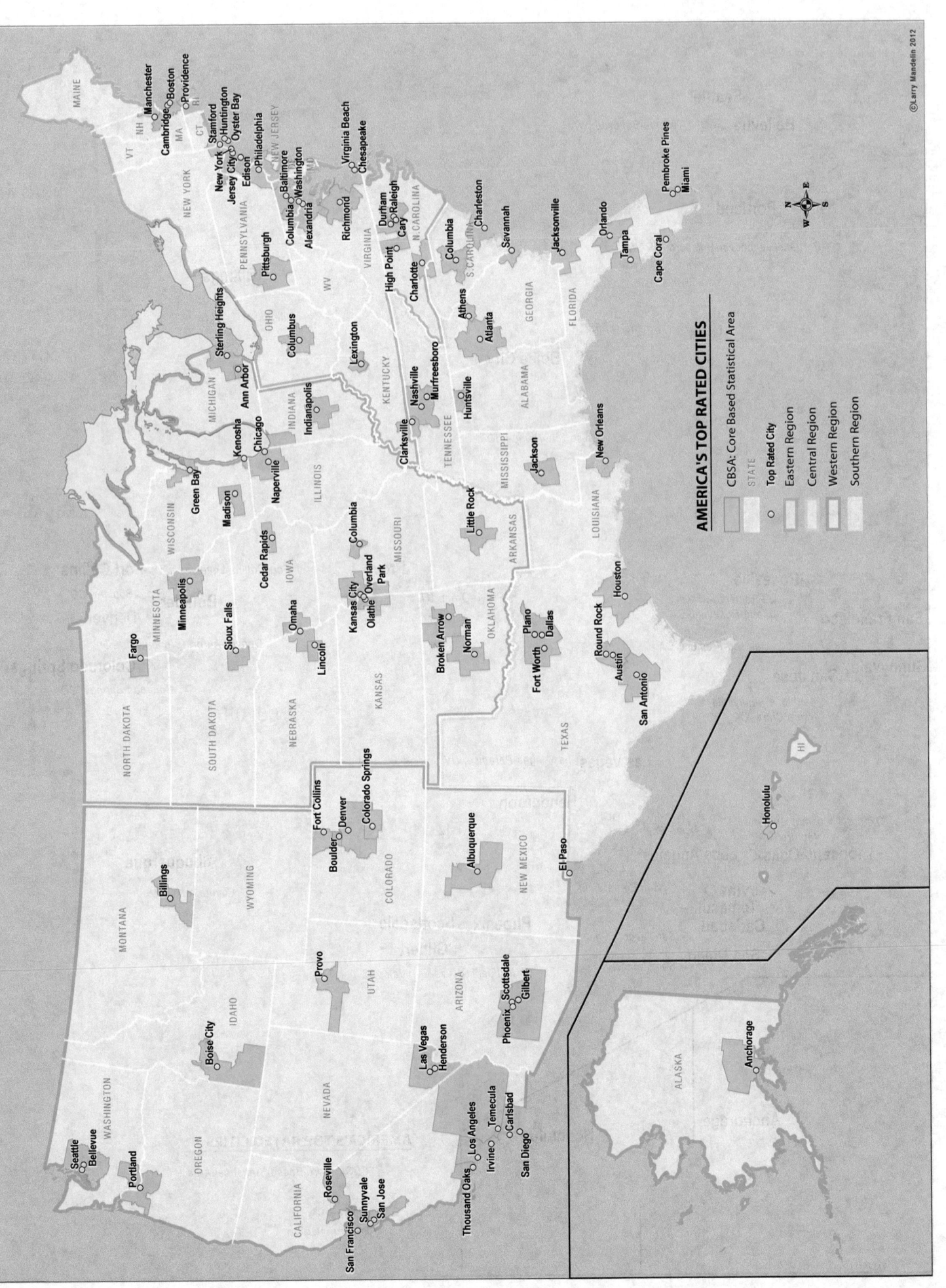

AMERICA'S TOP RATED CITIES

CBSA: Core Based Statistical Area

STATE

○ Top Rated City

Eastern Region
Central Region
Western Region
Southern Region

©Larry Mandelin 2012

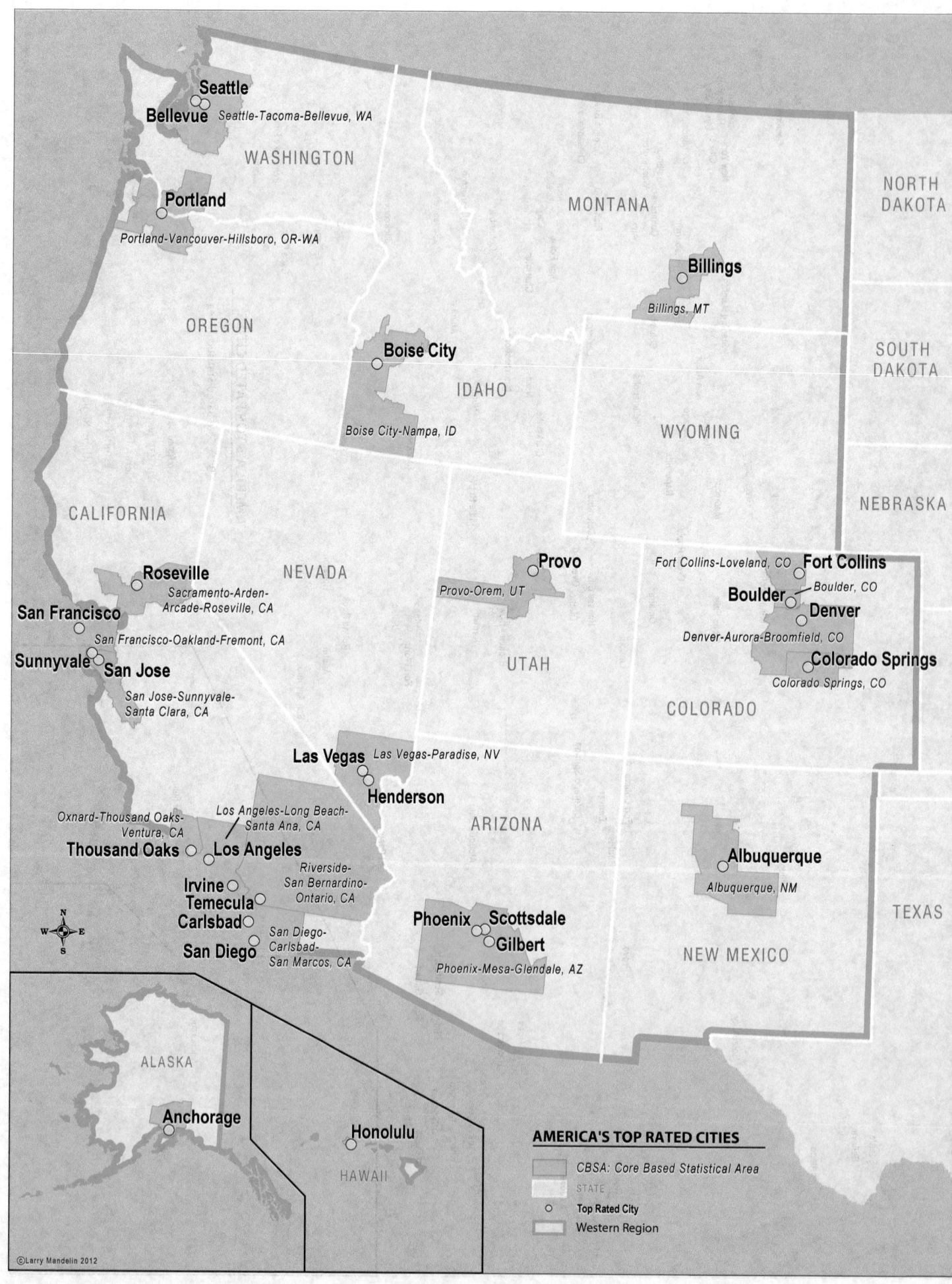

Seattle
Bellevue
Seattle-Tacoma-Bellevue, WA

WASHINGTON

Portland
Portland-Vancouver-Hillsboro, OR-WA

OREGON

MONTANA

Billings
Billings, MT

NORTH
DAKOTA

Boise City
IDAHO
Boise City-Nampa, ID

WYOMING

SOUTH
DAKOTA

NEBRASKA

CALIFORNIA

NEVADA

Roseville
Sacramento-Arden-
Arcade-Roseville, CA

San Francisco
San Francisco-Oakland-Fremont, CA

Sunnyvale
San Jose
San Jose-Sunnyvale-
Santa Clara, CA

Provo
Provo-Orem, UT

UTAH

Fort Collins-Loveland, CO
Boulder, CO
Denver-Aurora-Broomfield, CO

Fort Collins
Boulder
Denver
Colorado Springs
Colorado Springs, CO

COLORADO

Las Vegas
Las Vegas-Paradise, NV
Henderson

ARIZONA

Oxnard-Thousand Oaks-
Ventura, CA
Los Angeles-Long Beach-
Santa Ana, CA

Thousand Oaks
Los Angeles
Irvine
Riverside-
San Bernardino-
Ontario, CA
Temecula
Carlsbad
San Diego
San Diego-
Carlsbad-
San Marcos, CA

Phoenix
Scottsdale
Gilbert
Phoenix-Mesa-Glendale, AZ

NEW MEXICO

Albuquerque
Albuquerque, NM

TEXAS

N
W E
S

ALASKA

Anchorage

Honolulu

HAWAII

AMERICA'S TOP RATED CITIES

CBSA: Core Based Statistical Area
STATE
○ Top Rated City
Western Region

©Larry Mandelin 2012

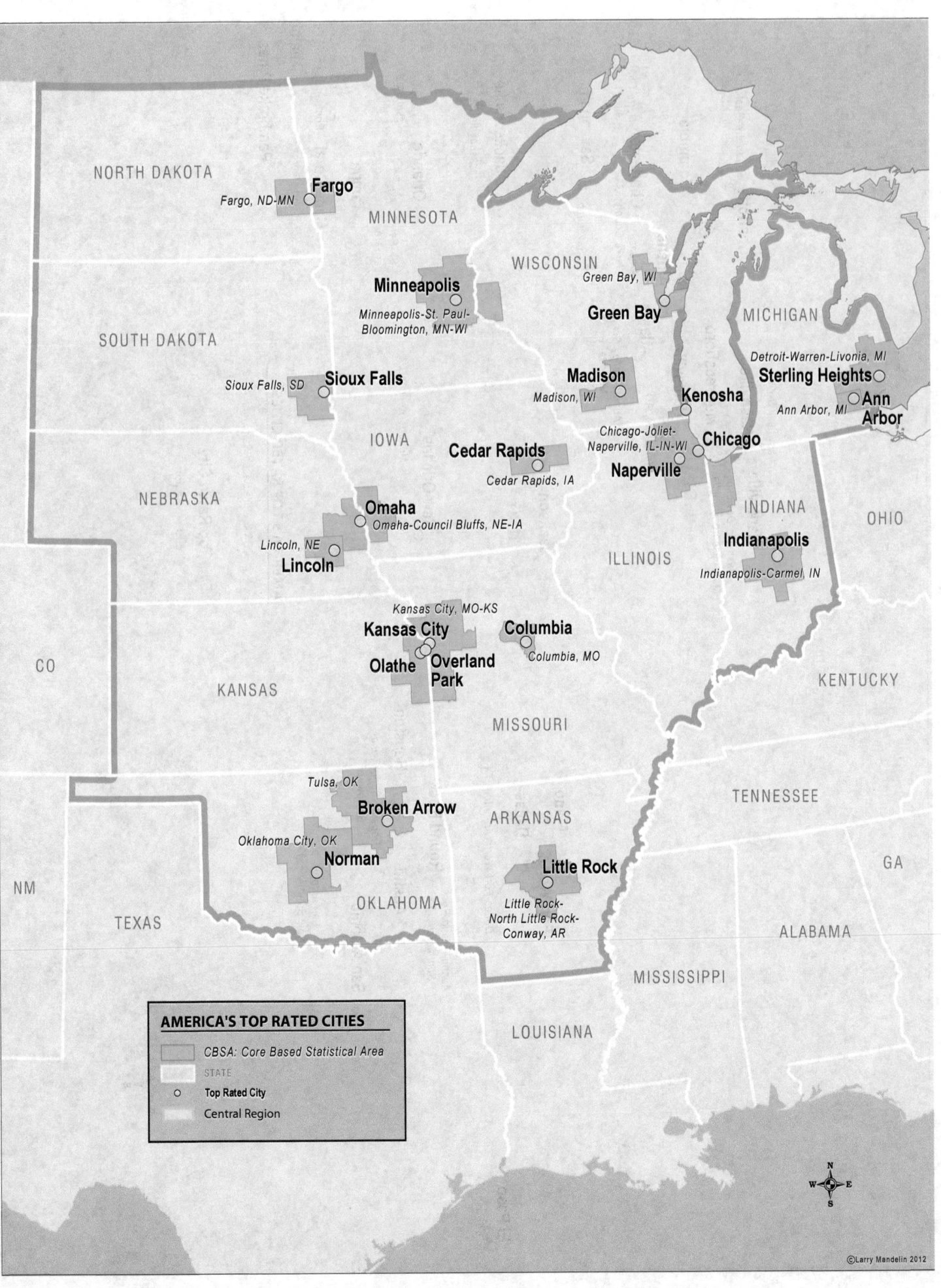

NORTH DAKOTA

Fargo
Fargo, ND-MN ○

MINNESOTA

WISCONSIN

Minneapolis ○
Minneapolis-St. Paul-
Bloomington, MN-WI

Green Bay, WI
Green Bay ○

MICHIGAN

SOUTH DAKOTA

Sioux Falls, SD **Sioux Falls** ○

Madison
Madison, WI ○

Detroit-Warren-Livonia, MI
Sterling Heights ○

Kenosha ○

Ann Arbor, MI **Ann Arbor** ○

IOWA

Cedar Rapids
Cedar Rapids, IA

Chicago-Joliet-
Naperville, IL-IN-WI **Chicago** ○
Naperville ○

NEBRASKA

Omaha ○
Omaha-Council Bluffs, NE-IA

INDIANA

OHIO

Lincoln, NE ○
Lincoln

Indianapolis ○
Indianapolis-Carmel, IN

ILLINOIS

CO

Kansas City, MO-KS
Kansas City ○

Olathe ○ **Overland
Park** ○

Columbia ○
Columbia, MO

KENTUCKY

KANSAS

MISSOURI

Tulsa, OK
Broken Arrow ○

ARKANSAS

TENNESSEE

NM

Oklahoma City, OK
Norman ○

Little Rock ○

GA

TEXAS

OKLAHOMA

Little Rock-
North Little Rock-
Conway, AR

ALABAMA

MISSISSIPPI

LOUISIANA

AMERICA'S TOP RATED CITIES

▭ CBSA: Core Based Statistical Area

▭ STATE

○ Top Rated City

▭ Central Region

N
W ◆ E
S

©Larry Mandelin 2012

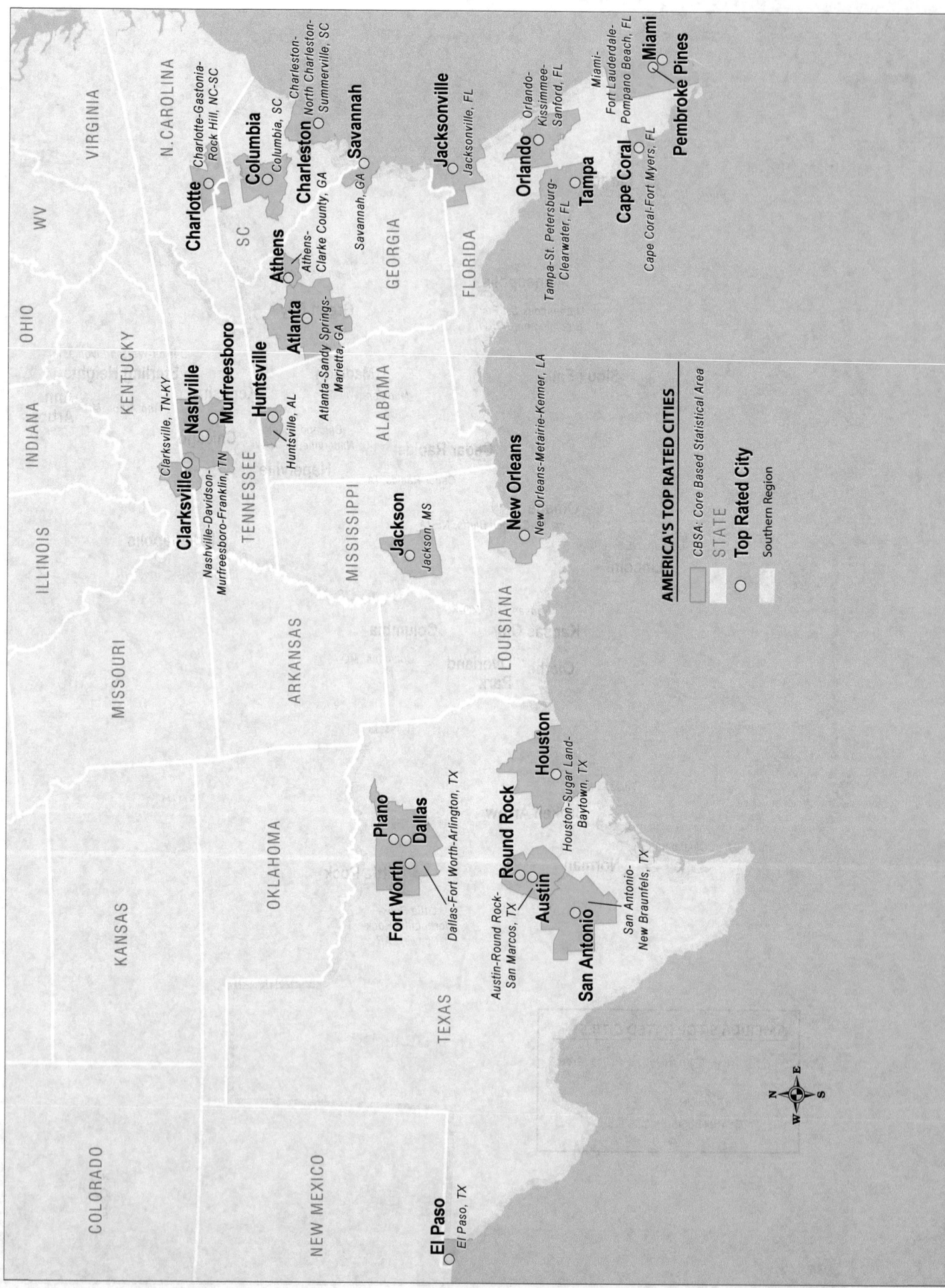

AMERICA'S TOP RATED CITIES

CBSA: Core Based Statistical Area

STATE

○ Top Rated City

Southern Region

Charlotte-Gastonia-Rock Hill, NC-SC

Charleston-North Charleston-Summerville, SC

Columbia, SC

Savannah, GA

Athens-Clarke County, GA

Atlanta-Sandy Springs-Marietta, GA

Jacksonville, FL

Orlando-Kissimmee-Sanford, FL

Miami-Fort Lauderdale-Pompano Beach, FL

Tampa-St. Petersburg-Clearwater, FL

Cape Coral-Fort Myers, FL

Clarksville, TN-KY

Nashville-Davidson-Murfreesboro-Franklin, TN

Huntsville, AL

Jackson, MS

New Orleans-Metairie-Kenner, LA

Houston-Sugar Land-Baytown, TX

Dallas-Fort Worth-Arlington, TX

Austin-Round Rock-San Marcos, TX

San Antonio-New Braunfels, TX

El Paso, TX

Charlotte

Columbia

Charleston

Savannah

Athens

Atlanta

Jacksonville

Orlando

Tampa

Cape Coral

Miami

Pembroke Pines

Clarksville

Nashville

Murfreesboro

Huntsville

Jackson

New Orleans

Houston

Plano

Dallas

Fort Worth

Round Rock

Austin

San Antonio

El Paso

COLORADO

KANSAS

OKLAHOMA

NEW MEXICO

TEXAS

MISSOURI

ARKANSAS

LOUISIANA

ILLINOIS

INDIANA

OHIO

WV

VIRGINIA

KENTUCKY

TENNESSEE

MISSISSIPPI

ALABAMA

GEORGIA

N.CAROLINA

SC

FLORIDA

©Larry Mandelin 2012

N E S W

AMERICA'S TOP RATED CITIES

CBSA: Core Based Statistical Area
STATE
○ Top Rated City
Eastern Region

MAINE

VT

NH

Manchester-Nashua, NH

Manchester

Boston-Cambridge-Quincy, MA-NH

Cambridge

Boston

NEW YORK

MA

RI

Providence

Bridgeport-Stamford-Norwalk, CT

CT

Providence-New Bedford-Fall River, RI-MA

Stamford

New York

Huntington

Jersey City

Oyster Bay

Edison

New York-Northern New Jersey-Long Island, NY-NJ-PA

PENNSYLVANIA

Philadelphia

MICHIGAN

NJ

DE

Philadelphia-Camden-Wilmington, PA-NJ-DE-MD

OHIO

Pittsburgh

Pittsburgh, PA

Baltimore-Towson, MD

Baltimore

Columbus

Columbia

Columbus, OH

Washington

MD

INDIANA

Alexandria

Washington-Arlington-Alexandria, DC-VA-MD-WV

IL

WV

Richmond, VA

Virginia Beach-Norfolk-Newport News, VA-NC

Lexington

Richmond

Lexington-Fayette, KY

VIRGINIA

Chesapeake Virginia Beach

KENTUCKY

Durham-Chapel Hill, NC

Durham

High Point

Raleigh

Greensboro-High Point, NC

Cary

Raleigh-Cary, NC

Charlotte

N.CAROLINA

TENNESSEE

Charlotte-Gastonia-Rock Hill, NC-SC

S.CAROLINA

N
W E
S

MS

ALABAMA

GEORGIA

©Larry Mandelin 2012

Athens, Georgia

Background

Athens, home to the University of Georgia, retains its old charms while cultivating the new. Antebellum homes that grace the city still stand because Gen. William Tecumseh Sherman's March to the Sea took a route that left this northeast Georgia town intact (while burning Atlanta, about 60 miles to the southwest). The Athens Music History Walking Tour, available through the local convention and visitors' bureau, stops at Weaver D's soul food restaurant with the slogan, "Automatic for the People," that went national as the name of locally-grown REM's 1992 album. The college music scene that spawned the B-52s and the Indigo Girls in the 1970s and 1980s, continues to support a thriving music industry. In 2002, the *New York Times* called Athens "Live Music Central."

Present-day Athens started as a small settlement where an old Cherokee trail crossed the Oconee River. In 1785 the state's General Assembly chartered the university, which established a campus here in 1801. Three years later, the school held its first graduation ceremony. The city was named for the ancient Greece's center of learning.

Undoubtedly the major influence in the city and surrounding Clarke County, the University of Georgia is also the area's largest employer. The comprehensive land grant and sea-grant institution offers all levels of degree programs in numerous disciplines. Other educational institutions in Athens are the Navy Supply School, Athens Technical College, and branches of Piedmont College and Old Dominion University.

Other major employers are focused on health care, government, and manufacturing. They include Athens Regional Medical Center and St. Mary's Health Care System, which have enlarged their facilities and specialized in areas including oncology, pediatrics and heart disease. In March 2010, St. Mary's was the first area hospital to implement the next generation of minimally invasive surgery using a hi-tech assistive robot. Manufacturing is a major employment sector; significant employers include poultry producers Pilgrim's Pride and Gold Kist, which operate local processing plants.

The city's official government merged with its home county in 1991, creating the Unified Government of Athens-Clark County.

With its shops, boutiques and restaurants, Athens offers plenty to do. The Georgia State Museum of Art, Museum of Natural History, and the State Botanical Garden here are affiliated with the university. The restored 1910 Morton Theater once hosted Cab Calloway, Duke Ellington, and Louis Armstrong, and now hosts dramatic and musical performances. Undoubtedly the strong presence of young people in Athens has contributed to the burgeoning artistic scene there. The city center is home to bars, galleries, cafes, and music venues that cater to the city's creative climate. The annual AthFest in June, hosts 120 bands to support local education. The city's charms, attractive to all ages, have not gone unnoticed by the media. Athens has been named one of the best places for small business, the best college town for retirees, and the best place to recapture your youth. The city also has a lively bicycle culture, and hosts several annual bicycle races.

The climate is mild, with average temperatures about 20 degrees warmer than the U.S. average. Snowfall is next to nothing, but precipitation is at its highest from January-March. Spring is lovely, with three to four inches of rain, sunshine up to 70 percent of the time starting in April, and temperatures averaging in the 70s.

Rankings

General Rankings

- The Athens metro area was selected one of America's "Best Cities" by *Kiplinger's Personal Finance*. Criteria: stable employment; income growth; cost of living; percentage of workforce in the creative class (scientists, engineers, educators, writers, artists, entertainers, etc.). *Kiplinger's Personal Finance, "Best Cities 2009: It's All About Jobs," July 2009*

Business/Finance Rankings

- Athens was identified as one of "America's Hardest-Working Towns." The city ranked #15 out of 25. Criteria: average hours worked per capita; willingness to work during personal time; number of dual income households; local employment rate. *Parade, "What is America's Hardest-Working Town?," April 15, 2012*

- *American City Business Journals* ranked America's 261 largest cities in terms of their resident's wealth. Athens ranked #190. Criteria: per capita income; median household income; percentage of households with annual incomes of $200,000 or more; median home value. *American City Business Journals, "Where the Money Is: America's Wealth Centers," August 18, 2008*

- The Athens metro area appeared on the Milken Institute "2011 Best Performing Metros" list. Rank: #55 out of 179 small metro areas. Criteria: job growth; wage and salary growth; high-tech output growth. *Milken Institute, "2011 Best Performing Metros"*

Culture/Performing Arts Rankings

- Athens was selected as one of "America's Top 25 Arts Destinations." The city ranked #18 in the mid-sized city (population 100,000 to 499,999) category. Criteria: readers' top choices for arts travel destinations based on the richness and variety of visual arts sites, activities and events. *American Style, "America's Top 25 Arts Destinations," May 2010*

Environmental Rankings

- Athens was selected as one of 22 "Smarter Cities" for energy by the Natural Resources Defense Council. Criteria: investment in green power; energy efficiency measures; conservation. *Natural Resources Defense Council, "2010 Smarter Cities," July 19, 2010*

- Athens was selected as one of "America's 50 Greenest Cities" by *Popular Science*. The city ranked #33. Criteria: electricity; transportation; green living; recycling and green perspective. *Popular Science, February 2008*

- The Athens metro area appeared in *Country Home's* "Best Green Places" report. The area ranked #144 out of 379. Criteria: official energy policies; green power; green buildings; availability of fresh, locally grown food. *Country Home, "Best Green Places," 2008*

- Athens was highlighted as one of the top 25 cleanest metro areas for short-term particle pollution (24-hour PM 2.5) in the U.S. Monitors in these cities reported no days with unhealthful PM 2.5 levels. *American Lung Association, State of the Air 2011*

Real Estate Rankings

- Athens was identified as one of the top 20 metro areas with the lowest rate of house price appreciation in 2011. The area ranked #16 with a one-year price appreciation of -8.3% through the 4th quarter 2011. *Federal Housing Finance Agency, House Price Index, 4th Quarter 2011*

- Athens appeared on *ApartmentRatings.com* "Top College Towns & Cities" for renters list in 2011." The area ranked #34 out of 87. Overall satisfaction ratings were ranked using thousands of user submitted scores for hundreds of apartment complexes located in cities and towns that are home to the 100 largest four-year institutions in the U.S. *ApartmentRatings.com, "2011 College Town Renter Satisfaction Rankings"*

Safety Rankings

- The National Insurance Crime Bureau ranked 366 metro areas in the U.S. in terms of per capita rates of vehicle theft. The Athens metro area ranked #124 (#1 = highest rate). Criteria: number of vehicle theft offenses per 100,000 inhabitants in 2010. *National Insurance Crime Bureau, "Hot Spots," June 21, 2011*

Seniors/Retirement Rankings

- Athens was identified as one of the "100 Most Popular Retirement Towns" by *Topretirements.com* The list reflects the 100 cities (out of 815+ total cities reviewed) that visitors to the website are most interested in for retirement. *Topretirements.com, "100 Most Popular Retirement Towns," February 21, 2012*

Sports/Recreation Rankings

- Athens appeared on the *Sporting News* list of the "Best Sports Cities" for 2011. The area ranked #78 out of 271 cities in the U.S. *Sporting News* takes a 12-month snapshot of each city's sports, putting a heavy premium on regular-season won-lost records (from the most recently completed season). Other criteria include: playoff berths, bowl appearances and tournament bids; championships; applicable power ratings; quality of competition; overall fan fervor (measured in part by attendance); abundance of teams (rewarding quality over quantity); stadium and arena quality; ticket availability and prices; franchise ownership; and marquee appeal of athletes. *Sporting News, "Best Sports Cities 2011," October 4, 2011*

- Athens was chosen as a bicycle friendly community by the League of American Bicyclists. A Bicycle Friendly Community welcomes cyclists by providing safe accommodation for cycling and encouraging people to bike for transportation and recreation. There are four award levels: Platinum; Gold; Silver; and Bronze. The community achieved an award level of Bronze. *League of American Bicyclists, "Bicycle Friendly Community Master List 2011"*

Business Environment

CITY FINANCES

City Government Finances

Component	2009 ($000)	2009 ($ per capita)
Total Revenues	205,815	1,804
Total Expenditures	240,885	2,112
Debt Outstanding	272,457	2,389
Cash and Securities[1]	341,179	2,991

Note: (1) Cash and security holdings of a government at the close of its fiscal year, including those of its dependent agencies, utilities, and liquor stores.
Source: U.S Census Bureau, State & Local Government Finances 2009

City Government Revenue by Source

Source	2009 ($000)	2009 ($ per capita)
General Revenue		
From Federal Government	6,703	59
From State Government	13,031	114
From Local Governments	38,313	336
Taxes		
Property	45,687	401
Sales and Gross Receipts	18,527	162
Personal Income	0	0
Corporate Income	0	0
Motor Vehicle License	0	0
Other Taxes	3,650	32
Current Charges	40,657	356
Liquor Store	0	0
Utility	21,239	186
Employee Retirement	0	0

Source: U.S Census Bureau, State & Local Government Finances 2009

City Government Expenditures by Function

Function	2009 ($000)	2009 ($ per capita)	2009 (%)
General Direct Expenditures			
Air Transportation	1,305	11	0.5
Corrections	12,003	105	5.0
Education	0	0	0.0
Employment Security Administration	0	0	0.0
Financial Administration	4,588	40	1.9
Fire Protection	13,344	117	5.5
General Public Buildings	4,618	40	1.9
Governmental Administration, Other	9,515	83	4.0
Health	11,591	102	4.8
Highways	11,560	101	4.8
Hospitals	0	0	0.0
Housing and Community Development	5,446	48	2.3
Interest on General Debt	64	1	0.0
Judicial and Legal	9,400	82	3.9
Libraries	1,682	15	0.7
Parking	845	7	0.4
Parks and Recreation	8,852	78	3.7
Police Protection	24,281	213	10.1
Public Welfare	569	5	0.2
Sewerage	32,061	281	13.3
Solid Waste Management	7,063	62	2.9
Veterans' Services	0	0	0.0
Liquor Store	0	0	0.0
Utility	47,906	420	19.9
Employee Retirement	0	0	0.0

Source: U.S Census Bureau, State & Local Government Finances 2009

Municipal Bond Ratings

Area	Moody's	S&P	Fitch
City	n/a	n/a	n/a

Rating Systems (shown in declining order of credit quality): Moody's– Aaa, Aa, A, Baa, Ba, B, Caa, Ca, C (numerical modifiers 1, 2, and 3 are added to letter-rating); S&P– AAA, AA, A, BBB, BB, B, CCC, CC, C; Fitch– AAA, AA, A, BBB, BB, B, CCC, CC, C. Ratings may be modified by the addition of a plus or minus sign to show relative standing within the major rating categories.
Notes: n/a Not Available; w/d Withdrawn (1) Not Reviewed; (2) Issuer Rating/No General Obligation; (3) Standard and Poor's Issue Credit Rating (ICR) is a current opinion of an obliger with respect to a specific financial obligation, a specific class of financial obligations, or a specific financial program.
Source: U.S. Census Bureau, 2012 Statistical Abstract, Bond Ratings for City Governments by Largest Cities: 2010

DEMOGRAPHICS

Population Growth

Area	1990 Census	2000 Census	2010 Census	Population Growth (%) 1990-2000	Population Growth (%) 2000-2010
City	86,561	100,266	115,452	15.8	15.1
MSA[1]	136,025	166,079	192,541	22.1	15.9
U.S.	248,709,873	281,421,906	308,745,538	13.2	9.7

Note: (1) Figures cover the Athens-Clarke County, GA Metropolitan Statistical Area—see Appendix B for areas included
Source: U.S. Census Bureau, 2010 Census

Household Size

Area	Persons in Household (%) One	Two	Three	Four	Five	Six	Seven or More	Average Household Size
City	30.6	34.1	15.9	11.9	4.5	1.8	1.2	2.37
MSA[1]	26.5	34.2	16.9	13.7	5.4	2.0	1.3	2.50
U.S.	26.7	32.8	16.1	13.4	6.5	2.6	1.9	2.58

Note: (1) Figures cover the Athens-Clarke County, GA Metropolitan Statistical Area—see Appendix B for areas included
Source: U.S. Census Bureau, 2010 Census

Race

Area	White Alone[2] (%)	Black Alone[2] (%)	Asian Alone[2] (%)	AIAN[3] Alone[2] (%)	NHOPI[4] Alone[2] (%)	Other Race Alone[2] (%)	Two or More Races (%)
City	61.8	26.6	4.2	0.2	0.1	5.0	2.2
MSA[1]	71.4	19.5	3.2	0.2	0.0	3.7	1.9
U.S.	72.4	12.6	4.8	0.9	0.2	6.2	2.9

Note: (1) Figures cover the Athens-Clarke County, GA Metropolitan Statistical Area—see Appendix B for areas included; (2) Alone is defined as not being in combination with one or more other races; (3) American Indian and Alaska Native; (4) Native Hawaiian and Other Pacific Islander
Source: U.S. Census Bureau, 2010 Census

Hispanic or Latino Origin

Area	Hispanic or Latino (%)	Mexican (%)	Puerto Rican (%)	Cuban (%)	Other Hispanic or Latino (%)
City	10.5	6.6	0.6	0.3	3.0
MSA[1]	8.0	5.0	0.4	0.2	2.3
U.S.	16.3	10.3	1.5	0.6	4.0

Note: Persons of Hispanic or Latino origin can be of any race; (1) Figures cover the Athens-Clarke County, GA Metropolitan Statistical Area—see Appendix B for areas included
Source: U.S. Census Bureau, 2010 Census

Segregation

Type	Segregation Indices[1]				Percent Change		
	1990	2000	2010	2010 Rank[2]	1990-2000	1990-2010	2000-2010
Black/White	n/a	n/a	n/a	n/a	n/a	n/a	n/a
Asian/White	n/a	n/a	n/a	n/a	n/a	n/a	n/a
Hispanic/White	n/a	n/a	n/a	n/a	n/a	n/a	n/a

Note: Figures are based on an analysis of 1990, 2000, and 2010 Census Decennial Census tract data by William H. Frey, Brookings Institution and the University of Michigan Social Science Data Analysis Network. In this analysis all racial groups (whites, blacks, and asians) are non-Hispanic members of those races. Hispanics are shown as a separate category; All figures cover the Metropolitan Statistical Area (see Appendix B for areas included); (1) Segregation Indices are Dissimilarity Indices that measure the degree to which the minority group is distributed differently than whites across census tracts. They range from 0 (complete integration) to 100 (complete segregation) where the value indicates the percentage of the minority group that needs to move to be distributed exactly like whites; (2) Ranges from 1 (most segregated) to 102 (least segregated); n/a not available.
Source: www.CensusScope.org

Ancestry

Area	German	Irish	English	American	Italian	Polish	French[2]	Scottish	Dutch
City	9.2	8.6	9.8	8.3	2.2	1.8	1.9	3.6	1.1
MSA[1]	9.2	9.6	11.3	13.2	2.0	1.5	1.7	3.4	1.2
U.S.	16.1	11.6	8.8	6.1	5.7	3.2	3.0	1.9	1.6

Note: Figures are the percentage of the total population reporting a particular ancestry. The nine most commonly reported ancestries in the U.S. are shown. Figures include multiple ancestries (e.g. if a person reported being Irish and Italian, they were included in both columns); (1) Figures cover the Athens-Clarke County, GA Metropolitan Statistical Area—see Appendix B for areas included; (2) Excludes Basque
Source: U.S. Census Bureau, 2008-2010 American Community Survey 3-Year Estimates

Foreign-Born Population

Area	Percent of Population Born in								
	Any Foreign Country	Mexico	Asia	Europe	Carribean	South America	Central America[2]	Africa	Canada
City	n/a	n/a	n/a	n/a	n/a	n/a	n/a	n/a	n/a
MSA[1]	8.1	3.1	2.1	0.8	0.2	0.6	0.6	0.4	0.2
U.S.	12.8	3.8	3.6	1.6	1.2	0.9	1.0	0.5	0.3

Note: (1) Figures cover the Athens-Clarke County, GA Metropolitan Statistical Area—see Appendix B for areas included; (2) Excludes Mexico.
Source: U.S. Census Bureau, 2008-2010 American Community Survey 3-Year Estimates

Marital Status

Area	Never Married	Now Married[2]	Separated	Widowed	Divorced
City	55.9	30.5	2.0	3.7	7.8
MSA[1]	45.2	39.7	2.0	4.3	8.8
U.S.	31.6	49.6	2.2	6.1	10.7

Note: Figures are percentages and cover the population 15 years of age and older; (1) Figures cover the Athens-Clarke County, GA Metropolitan Statistical Area—see Appendix B for areas included; (2) Excludes separated
Source: U.S. Census Bureau, 2008-2010 American Community Survey 3-Year Estimates

Age

Area	Percent of Population							Median Age
	Under Age 5	Age 5 to 17	Age 18 to 34	Age 35 to 49	Age 50 to 64	Age 65 to 79	80 Years and Over	
City	6.0	11.5	47.4	14.4	12.3	6.1	2.3	25.8
MSA[1]	6.0	14.9	35.7	17.7	15.7	7.6	2.5	29.9
U.S.	6.5	17.5	23.2	20.7	19.0	9.4	3.6	37.2

Note: (1) Figures cover the Athens-Clarke County, GA Metropolitan Statistical Area—see Appendix B for areas included
Source: U.S. Census Bureau, 2010 Census

Male/Female Ratio

Area	Males	Females	Males per 100 Females
City	54,781	60,671	90.3
MSA[1]	92,678	99,863	92.8
U.S.	151,781,326	156,964,212	96.7

Note: (1) Figures cover the Athens-Clarke County, GA
Metropolitan Statistical Area—see Appendix B for areas included
Source: U.S. Census Bureau, 2010 Census

Religious Groups

Area	Catholic	Baptist	Non-Den.	Methodist[2]	Lutheran	LDS[3]	Pentecostal	Presbyterian[4]	Muslim[5]	Judaism
MSA[1]	4.4	16.3	2.3	8.4	0.4	0.8	2.8	2.0	0.2	0.4
U.S.	19.1	9.3	4.0	4.0	2.3	2.0	1.9	1.6	0.8	0.7

Note: Figures are the number of adherents as a percentage of the total population; (1) Figures cover the
Athens-Clarke County, GA Metropolitan Statistical Area—see Appendix B for areas included;
(2) Methodist/Pietist; (3) Latter Day Saints; (4) Reformed; (5) Figures are estimates
Source: Association of Statisticians of American Religious Bodies, 2010 U.S. Religion Census: Religious
Congregations & Membership Study

ECONOMY

Gross Metropolitan Product

Area	2007	2008	2009	2010	2010 Rank[2]
MSA[1]	6.1	6.4	6.2	6.4	230

Note: Figures are in billions of dollars; (1) Figures cover the Athens-Clarke County, GA Metropolitan
Statistical Area—see Appendix B for areas included; (2) Rank ranges from 1 to 363
Source: The United States Conference of Mayors, "U.S. Metro Economies: GMP and Employment Forecasts,"
June 2011

Economic Growth

Area	2007-2009 (%)	2010 (%)	2011 (%)	Rank[2]
MSA[1]	-1.6	1.6	3.1	206
U.S.	-1.3	2.9	2.5	–

Note: Figures are real Gross Metropolitan Product growth rates and represent annual average percent change;
(1) Figures cover the Athens-Clarke County, GA Metropolitan Statistical Area—see Appendix B for areas
included; (2) Rank ranges from 1 to 363
Source: The United States Conference of Mayors, "U.S. Metro Economies: GMP and Employment Forecasts,"
June 2011

Metropolitan Area Exports

Area	2005	2006	2007	2008	2009	2010	2010 Rank[2]
MSA[1]	228.5	152.0	182.2	171.4	214.6	194.6	282

Note: Figures are in millions of dollars; (1) Figures cover the Athens-Clarke County, GA Metropolitan
Statistical Area—see Appendix B for areas included; (2) Rank ranges from 1 to 369
Source: U.S. Department of Commerce, International Trade Administration, Office of Trade & Industry
Information, Manufacturing & Services, data extracted April 2, 2012

INCOME

Income

Area	Per Capita ($)	Median Household ($)	Average Household ($)
City	19,023	33,750	51,082
MSA[1]	21,326	40,220	59,125
U.S.	26,942	51,222	70,116

Note: (1) Figures cover the Athens-Clarke County, GA Metropolitan Statistical Area—see Appendix B for areas
included
Source: U.S. Census Bureau, 2008-2010 American Community Survey 3-Year Estimates

Household Income Distribution

Area	Under $15,000	$15,000 -24,999	$25,000 -34,999	$35,000 -49,999	$50,000 -74,999	$75,000 -99,000	$100,000 -149,999	$150,000 and up
City	27.2	14.0	10.2	13.6	15.4	7.2	6.8	5.7
MSA[1]	21.3	12.6	10.3	14.0	16.1	9.5	9.1	7.0
U.S.	13.0	11.0	10.6	14.2	18.5	12.1	12.2	8.4

Note: (1) Figures cover the Athens-Clarke County, GA Metropolitan Statistical Area—see Appendix B for areas included
Source: U.S. Census Bureau, 2008-2010 American Community Survey 3-Year Estimates

Poverty Rate

Area	All Ages	Under 18 Years Old	18 to 64 Years Old	65 Years and Over
City	36.2	36.3	39.1	11.6
MSA[1]	26.8	26.3	29.2	12.4
U.S.	14.4	20.1	13.1	9.4

Note: Figures are percentage of people whose income during the past 12 months was below the poverty level;
(1) Figures cover the Athens-Clarke County, GA Metropolitan Statistical Area—see Appendix B for areas included
Source: U.S. Census Bureau, 2008-2010 American Community Survey 3-Year Estimates

Personal Bankruptcy Filing Rate

Area	2006	2007	2008	2009	2010	2011
Clarke County	2.18	2.66	2.86	3.46	3.54	3.79
U.S.	2.00	2.73	3.53	4.61	4.97	4.37

Note: Numbers are per 1,000 population and include Chapter 7 and Chapter 13 filings
Source: Federal Deposit Insurance Corporation, Regional Economic Conditions, March 9, 2012

EMPLOYMENT

Labor Force and Employment

Area	Civilian Labor Force			Workers Employed		
	Dec. 2010	Dec. 2011	% Chg.	Dec. 2010	Dec. 2011	% Chg.
City	64,416	65,002	0.9	59,484	60,085	1.0
MSA[1]	106,744	107,479	0.7	98,651	99,649	1.0
U.S.	153,156,000	153,373,000	0.1	139,159,000	140,681,000	1.1

Note: Data is not seasonally adjusted and covers workers 16 years of age and older;
(1) Metropolitan Statistical Area—see Appendix B for areas included
Source: Bureau of Labor Statistics, http://stats.bls.gov

Unemployment Rate

Area	2011											
	Jan.	Feb.	Mar.	Apr.	May	Jun.	Jul.	Aug.	Sep.	Oct.	Nov.	Dec.
City	7.8	7.6	7.5	7.1	7.4	8.8	8.2	8.1	8.3	7.7	7.1	7.6
MSA[1]	8.0	7.6	7.3	7.1	7.2	8.3	7.8	7.8	8.0	7.5	6.9	7.3
U.S.	9.8	9.5	9.2	8.7	8.7	9.3	9.3	9.1	8.8	8.5	8.2	8.3

Note: Data is not seasonally adjusted and covers workers 16 years of age and older; All figures are percentages; (1) Metropolitan Statistical Area—see Appendix B for areas included
Source: Bureau of Labor Statistics, http://stats.bls.gov

Projected Unemployment Rate

Area	2010 (%)	2011 (%)	2012 (%)	2013 (%)
MSA[1]	7.9	7.5	7.2	6.7

Note: (1) Metropolitan Statistical Area—see Appendix B for areas included
Source: The United States Conference of Mayors, "U.S. Metro Economies: GMP and Employment Forecasts," June 2011

Employment by Occupation

Occupation Classification	City (%)	MSA[1] (%)	U.S. (%)
Management, Business, Science, and Arts	41.0	38.6	35.6
Natural Resources, Construction, and Maintenance	5.2	8.4	9.5
Production, Transportation, and Material Moving	10.7	11.4	12.1
Sales and Office	22.1	22.8	25.2
Service	21.1	18.7	17.6

Note: Figures cover employed civilians 16 years of age and older; (1) Figures cover the Athens-Clarke County, GA Metropolitan Statistical Area—see Appendix B for areas included
Source: U.S. Census Bureau, 2008-2010 American Community Survey 3-Year Estimates

Employment by Industry

Sector	MSA[1] Number of Employees	MSA[1] Percent of Total	U.S. Percent of Total
Construction	n/a	n/a	4.1
Education and Health Services	n/a	n/a	15.2
Financial Activities	n/a	n/a	5.8
Government	29,100	34.5	16.8
Information	n/a	n/a	2.0
Leisure and Hospitality	7,600	9.0	9.9
Manufacturing	n/a	n/a	8.9
Mining and Logging	n/a	n/a	0.6
Other Services	n/a	n/a	4.0
Professional and Business Services	6,800	8.1	13.3
Retail Trade	9,500	11.3	11.5
Transportation and Utilities	n/a	n/a	3.8
Wholesale Trade	n/a	n/a	4.2

Note: Figures cover non-farm employment as of December 2011 and are not seasonally adjusted; (1) Metropolitan Statistical Area—see Appendix B for areas included; n/a not available
Source: Bureau of Labor Statistics, http://stats.bls.gov

Occupations with Greatest Projected Employment Growth: 2008 – 2018

Occupation[1]	2008 Employment	2018 Projected Employment	Numeric Employment Change	Percent Employment Change
Combined Food Preparation and Serving Workers, Including Fast Food	102,970	134,890	31,920	31.0
Retail Salespersons	156,260	186,090	29,830	19.1
Registered Nurses	66,610	90,440	23,830	35.8
Customer Service Representatives	99,680	122,990	23,310	23.4
Janitors and Cleaners, Except Maids and Housekeeping Cleaners	78,880	95,000	16,120	20.4
Waiters and Waitresses	66,470	82,520	16,050	24.1
Elementary School Teachers, Except Special Education	46,730	61,680	14,950	32.0
Office Clerks, General	86,710	101,420	14,710	17.0
Postsecondary Teachers	36,460	49,930	13,470	36.9
Management Analysts	50,150	62,340	12,190	24.3

Note: Projections cover Georgia; (1) Sorted by numeric employment change
Source: www.projectionscentral.com, State Occupational Projections, 2008–2018 Long-Term Projections

Fastest Growing Occupations: 2008 – 2018

Occupation[1]	2008 Employment	2018 Projected Employment	Numeric Employment Change	Percent Employment Change
Marriage and Family Therapists	260	470	210	80.8
Home Health Aides	11,010	18,230	7,220	65.6
Shoe and Leather Workers and Repairers	290	470	180	62.1
Skin Care Specialists	1,740	2,780	1,040	59.8
Actors	1,150	1,760	610	53.0
Network Systems and Data Communications Analysts	7,800	11,850	4,050	51.9
Makeup Artists, Theatrical and Performance	270	410	140	51.9
Manicurists and Pedicurists	540	810	270	50.0
Mental Health Counselors	1,860	2,730	870	46.8
Physical Therapist Assistants	1,030	1,510	480	46.6

Note: Projections cover Georgia; (1) Sorted by percent employment change and excludes occupations with numeric employment change less than 100
Source: www.projectionscentral.com, State Occupational Projections, 2008–2018 Long-Term Projections

Average Wages

Occupation	$/Hr.	Occupation	$/Hr.
Accountants and Auditors	26.19	Maids and Housekeeping Cleaners	9.19
Automotive Mechanics	19.21	Maintenance and Repair Workers	15.96
Bookkeepers	14.55	Marketing Managers	55.01
Carpenters	16.56	Nuclear Medicine Technologists	n/a
Cashiers	9.40	Nurses, Licensed Practical	17.91
Clerks, General Office	11.01	Nurses, Registered	29.93
Clerks, Receptionists/Information	11.62	Nursing Aides/Orderlies/Attendants	9.02
Clerks, Shipping/Receiving	13.80	Packers and Packagers, Hand	9.63
Computer Programmers	26.38	Physical Therapists	34.06
Computer Support Specialists	17.43	Postal Service Mail Carriers	23.58
Computer Systems Analysts	36.33	Real Estate Brokers	n/a
Cooks, Restaurant	11.61	Retail Salespersons	10.32
Dentists	n/a	Sales Reps., Exc. Tech./Scientific	25.87
Electrical Engineers	34.22	Sales Reps., Tech./Scientific	33.67
Electricians	18.05	Secretaries, Exc. Legal/Med./Exec.	14.86
Financial Managers	59.94	Security Guards	13.95
First-Line Supervisors/Managers, Sales	16.97	Surgeons	107.28
Food Preparation Workers	10.19	Teacher Assistants	9.20
General and Operations Managers	47.10	Teachers, Elementary School	27.60
Hairdressers/Cosmetologists	13.58	Teachers, Secondary School	25.20
Internists	80.48	Telemarketers	10.02
Janitors and Cleaners	11.23	Truck Drivers, Heavy/Tractor-Trailer	18.85
Landscaping/Groundskeeping Workers	9.71	Truck Drivers, Light/Delivery Svcs.	16.62
Lawyers	56.77	Waiters and Waitresses	8.98

Note: Wage data covers the Athens-Clarke County, GA Metropolitan Statistical Area—see Appendix B for areas included. Hourly wages for elementary/secondary school teachers and teacher assistants were calculated by the editors from annual wage data assuming a 40 hour work week; n/a not available.
Source: Bureau of Labor Statistics, Metro Area Occupational Employment and Wage Estimates, May 2011

RESIDENTIAL REAL ESTATE

Building Permits

Area	Single-Family			Multi-Family			Total		
	2010	2011	Pct. Chg.	2010	2011	Pct. Chg.	2010	2011	Pct. Chg.
City	94	84	-10.6	0	87	-	94	171	81.9
MSA[1]	226	240	6.2	0	87	-	226	327	44.7
U.S.	447,311	418,498	-6.4	157,299	205,563	30.7	604,610	624,061	3.2

Note: (1) Metropolitan Statistical Area—see Appendix B for areas included; figures represent new, privately-owned housing units authorized (unadjusted data); All permit data are based on estimates with imputation.
Source: U.S. Census Bureau, Manufacturing, Mining, and Construction Statistics, Building Permits, 2010, 2011

Homeownership Rate

Area	2005 (%)	2006 (%)	2007 (%)	2008 (%)	2009 (%)	2010 (%)	2011 (%)
MSA[1]	n/a	n/a	n/a	n/a	n/a	n/a	n/a
U.S.	68.9	68.8	68.1	67.8	67.4	66.9	66.1

Note: (1) Metropolitan Statistical Area—see Appendix B for areas included; n/a not available
Source: U.S. Census Bureau, Housing Vacancies and Homeownership Annual Statistics: 2011

Housing Vacancy Rates

Area	Gross Vacancy Rate[2] (%)			Year-Round Vacancy Rate[3] (%)			Rental Vacancy Rate[4] (%)			Homeowner Vacancy Rate[5] (%)		
	2009	2010	2011	2009	2010	2011	2009	2010	2011	2009	2010	2011
MSA[1]	n/a	n/a	n/a	n/a	n/a	n/a	n/a	n/a	n/a	n/a	n/a	n/a
U.S.	14.5	14.3	14.2	11.3	11.3	11.1	10.6	10.2	9.5	2.6	2.6	2.5

Note: (1) Metropolitan Statistical Area—see Appendix B for areas included; (2) The percentage of the total housing inventory that is vacant; (3) The percentage of the housing inventory (excluding seasonal units) that is year-round vacant; (4) The percentage of rental inventory that is vacant for rent; (5) The percentage of homeowner inventory that is vacant for sale; n/a not available
Source: U.S. Census Bureau, Housing Vacancies and Homeownership Annual Statistics: 2011

TAXES

State Corporate Income Tax Rates

State	Tax Rate (%)	Income Brackets ($)	Num. of Brackets	Financial Institution Tax Rate (%)[a]	Federal Income Tax Ded.
Georgia	6.0	Flat rate	1	6.0	No

Note: Tax rates as of January 1, 2012; (a) Rates listed are the corporate income tax rate applied to financial institutions or excise taxes based on income. Some states have other taxes based upon the value of deposits or shares.
Source: Federation of Tax Administrators, "State Corporate Income Tax Rates, 2012"

State Individual Income Tax Rates

State	Tax Rate (%)	Income Brackets ($)	Num. of Brackets	Personal Exempt. ($)[1] Single	Personal Exempt. ($)[1] Dependents	Fed. Inc. Tax Ded.
Georgia	1.0 - 6.0	750 (h) - 7,001 (h)	6	2,700	3,000	No

Note: Tax rates as of January 1, 2012; Local- and county-level taxes are not included; n/a not applicable; (1) Married joint filers generally receive double the single exemption; (h) The Georgia income brackets reported are for single individuals. For married couples filing jointly, the same tax rates apply to income brackets ranging from $1,000, to $10,000.
Source: Federation of Tax Administrators, "State Individual Income Tax Rates, 2012"

Various State and Local Tax Rates

State	State and Local Sales and Use (%)	State Sales and Use (%)	Gasoline[1] (¢/gal.)	Cigarette[2] ($/pack)	Spirits[3] ($/gal.)	Wine[4] ($/gal.)	Beer[5] ($/gal.)
Georgia	7.0	4.00	29.4	0.37	3.79	1.51	1.01 (n)

Note: All tax rates as of January 1, 2012 except beer, wine and spirits (September 1, 2011); (1) The American Petroleum Institute has developed a methodology for determining the average tax rate on a gallon of fuel. Rates may include any of the following: excise taxes, environmental fees, storage tank fees, other fees or taxes, general sales tax, and local taxes. In states where gasoline is subject to the general sales tax, or where the fuel tax is based on the average sale price, the average rate determined by API is sensitive to changes in the price of gasoline. States that fully or partially apply general sales taxes to gasoline: CA, CO, GA, IL, IN, MI, NY; (2) The federal excise tax of $1.0066 per pack and local taxes are not included; (3) Rates are those applicable to off-premise sales of 40% alcohol by volume (a.b.v.) distilled spirits in 750ml containers. Local excise taxes are excluded; (4) Rates are those applicable to off-premise sales of 11% a.b.v. non-carbonated wine in 750ml containers; (5) Rates are those applicable to off-premise sales of 4.7% a.b.v. beer in 12 ounce containers; (n) Includes statewide local rate in Alabama ($0.52) and Georgia ($0.53).
Source: Tax Foundation, 2012 Facts & Figures: How Does Your State Compare?

State-Local Tax Burdens

Area	Rate (%)	Rank[1]	Per Capita Taxes Paid to Home State ($)	Total State and Local Per Capita Taxes Paid ($)	Per Capita Income ($)
Georgia	9.1	32	2,411	3,350	36,738
U.S. Average	9.8	-	3,057	4,160	42,539

Note: Figures cover 2009; (1) Rank ranges from 1 to 50 where 1 is highest tax burden
Source: Tax Foundation, State-Local Tax Burdens, All States, 2009

State Business Tax Climate Index Rankings

State	Overall Rank	Corporate Tax Index Rank	Individual Income Tax Index Rank	Sales Tax Index Rank	Unemployment Insurance Tax Index Rank	Property Tax Index Rank
Georgia	34	9	40	12	22	39

Note: The index is a measure of how each state's tax laws affect economic performance. The lower the rank, the more favorable a state's tax system is for business. States without a given tax are given a ranking of 1.
Source: Tax Foundation, Major Components of the State Business Tax Climate Index, FY 2012

COMMERCIAL UTILITIES

Typical Monthly Electric Bills

Area	Commercial Service ($/month)		Industrial Service ($/month)	
	1,500 kWh	40 kW demand 14,000 kWh	1,000 kW demand 200,000 kWh	50,000 kW demand 15,000,000 kWh
City	n/a	n/a	n/a	n/a
Average[1]	189	1,616	25,197	1,470,813

Note: Based on total rates in effect July 1, 2011; (1) average based on 184 utilities surveyed; n/a not available
Source: Edison Electric Institute, Typical Bills and Average Rates Report, Summer 2011

TRANSPORTATION

Means of Transportation to Work

Area	Drove Alone	Car-pooled	Bus	Subway	Railroad	Bicycle	Walked	Other Means	Worked at Home
City	73.2	10.1	3.9	0.0	0.0	1.6	5.1	1.6	4.4
MSA[1]	76.0	10.8	2.4	0.0	0.0	1.0	3.6	1.2	5.0
U.S.	76.0	10.2	2.7	1.7	0.5	0.5	2.8	1.3	4.2

Note: Figures are percentages and cover workers 16 years of age and older; (1) Figures cover the Athens-Clarke County, GA Metropolitan Statistical Area—see Appendix B for areas included
Source: U.S. Census Bureau, 2008-2010 American Community Survey 3-Year Estimates

Travel Time to Work

Area	Less Than 10 Minutes	10 to 19 Minutes	20 to 29 Minutes	30 to 44 Minutes	45 to 59 Minutes	60 to 89 Minutes	90 Minutes or More
City	18.1	51.0	14.2	9.1	2.8	2.9	2.0
MSA[1]	14.9	44.5	18.6	12.8	3.9	3.3	2.0
U.S.	13.9	30.1	20.8	19.8	7.5	5.5	2.5

Note: Figures are percentages and include workers 16 years old and over; (1) Figures cover the Athens-Clarke County, GA Metropolitan Statistical Area—see Appendix B for areas included
Source: U.S. Census Bureau, 2008-2010 American Community Survey 3-Year Estimates

Travel Time Index

Area	1985	1990	1995	2000	2005	2010
Urban Area[1]	n/a	n/a	n/a	n/a	n/a	n/a
Average[2]	1.11	1.16	1.18	1.21	1.25	1.20

Note: Travel Time Index—the ratio of travel time in the peak period to the travel time at free-flow conditions. A value of 1.30 indicates a 20-minute free-flow trip takes 26 minutes in the peak. Free-flow speeds (60 mph on freeways and 35 mph on principal arterials) are used as the comparison threshold; (1) Data for the Athens-Clarke County, GA urban area was not available; (2) average of 439 urban areas
Source: Texas Transportation Institute, Urban Mobility Report 2011, September 2011

Public Transportation

Agency Name / Mode of Transportation	Vehicles Operated in Maximum Service	Annual Unlinked Passenger Trips ('000)	Annual Passenger Miles ('000)
Athens Transit System			
Bus (directly operated)	22	1,779.8	5,385.0
Demand Response (directly operated)	3	9.4	51.7

Source: Federal Transit Administration, National Transit Database, 2010

Air Transportation

Airport Name and Code / Type of Service	Passenger Airlines[1]	Passenger Enplanements	Freight Carriers[2]	Freight (lbs.)
Athens Municipal (AHN)				
Domestic service (U.S. carriers - 2011)	8	1,527	0	0
International service (U.S. carriers - 2010)	0	0	0	0

Note: (1) Includes all U.S.-based major, minor and commuter airlines that carried at least one passenger during the year; (2) Includes all U.S.-based airlines and freight carriers that transported at least one pound of freight during the year
Source: Bureau of Transportation Statistics, The Intermodal Transportation Database, Air Carriers: T-100 Domestic Market (U.S. Carriers), 2011; Bureau of Transportation Statistics, The Intermodal Transportation Database, Air Carriers: T-100 International Market (U.S. Carriers), 2010

Other Transportation Statistics

Major Highways:	CR-82 connecting to I-85 (18 miles)
Amtrak Service:	No
Major Waterways/Ports:	None

Source: Amtrak.com; Google Maps

BUSINESSES

Major Business Headquarters

Company Name	Rankings	
	Fortune[1]	Forbes[2]
No companies listed	-	-

Note: (1) Fortune 500—companies that produce a 10-K are ranked 1 to 500 based on 2010 revenue; (2) all private companies with at least $2 billion in annual revenue are ranked 1 to 212; companies listed are headquartered in the city; dashes indicate no ranking
Source: Fortune, "Fortune 500," May 23, 2011; Forbes, "America's Largest Private Companies," November 16, 2011

Fast-Growing Businesses

According to *Inc.*, Athens is home to one of America's 500 fastest-growing private companies: **PeachMac** (#489). Criteria: must be an independent, privately-held, for-profit, U.S. corporation, proprietorship or partnership; revenues must be at least $80,000 in 2007 and $2 million in 2010; must have four-year operating/sales history. Holding companies, regulated banks, and utilities were excluded. *Inc., "America's 500 Fastest-Growing Private Companies," September 2011*

Minority- and Women-Owned Businesses

Group	All Firms		Firms with Paid Employees			
	Firms	Sales ($000)	Firms	Sales ($000)	Employees	Payroll ($000)
Asian	330	285,670	161	280,037	1,813	40,491
Black	(s)	(s)	(s)	(s)	(s)	(s)
Hispanic	311	22,829	16	11,624	81	2,166
Women	2,687	605,533	366	562,480	4,810	119,645
All Firms	10,181	8,756,927	2,435	8,454,434	48,844	1,391,992

Note: Figures cover firms located in the city; minority- and women-owned business are defined as firms in which the corresponding group own 51% or more of the stock or equity of the company; (s) estimates are suppressed when publication standards are not met
Source: U.S. Census Bureau, 2007 Economic Census, Survey of Business Owners

HOTELS

Hotels/Motels

Area	5 Star		4 Star		3 Star		2 Star		1 Star		Not Rated	
	Num.	Pct.[3]	Num.	Pct.[3]	Num.	Pct.[3]	Num.	Pct.[3]	Num.	Pct.[3]	Num.	Pct.[3]
City[1]	0	0.0	0	0.0	7	20.0	20	57.1	1	2.9	7	20.0
Total[2]	133	0.9	940	6.5	4,569	31.8	7,033	48.9	351	2.4	1,343	9.3

Note: (1) Figures cover Athens and vicinity; (2) Figures cover all 100 cities in this book; (3) Percentage of hotels which have a given star rating; Star ratings are determined by expedia.com and offer an indication of the general quality of a particular hotel.
Source: expedia.com, April 25, 2012

EVENT SITES

Major Stadiums, Arenas, and Auditoriums

Name	Max. Capacity
Sanford Stadium	92,746

Source: Original research

Living Environment

COST OF LIVING

Cost of Living Index

Composite Index	Groceries	Housing	Utilities	Trans-portation	Health Care	Misc. Goods/ Services
n/a	n/a	n/a	n/a	n/a	n/a	n/a

Note: U.S. = 100; n/a not available
Source: The Council for Community and Economic Research, ACCRA Cost of Living Index, 2011

Grocery Prices

Area[1]	T-Bone Steak ($/pound)	Frying Chicken ($/pound)	Whole Milk ($/half gal.)	Eggs ($/dozen)	Orange Juice ($/64 oz.)	Coffee ($/11.5 oz.)
City[2]	n/a	n/a	n/a	n/a	n/a	n/a
Avg.	9.25	1.18	2.22	1.66	3.19	4.40
Min.	6.70	0.88	1.31	0.95	2.46	2.94
Max.	14.30	2.16	3.50	3.18	4.75	6.83

Note: (1) Values for the local area are compared with the average, minimum and maximum values for all 335 areas in the Cost of Living Index; (2) Figures cover the Athens GA urban area; n/a not available; **T-Bone Steak** *(price per pound);* **Frying Chicken** *(price per pound, whole fryer);* **Whole Milk** *(half gallon carton);* **Eggs** *(price per dozen, Grade A, large);* **Orange Juice** *(64 oz. Tropicana or Florida Natural);* **Coffee** *(11.5 oz. can, vacuum-packed, Maxwell House, Hills Bros, or Folgers).*
Source: The Council for Community and Economic Research, ACCRA Cost of Living Index, 2011

Housing and Utility Costs

Area[1]	New Home Price ($)	Apartment Rent ($/month)	All Electric ($/month)	Part Electric ($/month)	Other Energy ($/month)	Telephone ($/month)
City[2]	n/a	n/a	n/a	n/a	n/a	n/a
Avg.	285,990	839	163.23	89.00	77.52	26.92
Min.	188,005	460	125.58	45.39	33.89	17.98
Max.	1,197,028	3,244	339.16	181.97	348.69	40.01

Note: (1) Values for the local area are compared with the average, minimum and maximum values for all 335 areas in the Cost of Living Index; (2) Figures cover the Athens GA urban area; n/a not available; **New Home Price** *(2,400 sf living area, 8,000 sf lot, in urban area with full utilities);* **Apartment Rent** *(950 sf 2 bedroom/1.5 or 2 bath, unfurnished, excluding all utilities except water);* **All Electric** *(average monthly cost for an all-electric home);* **Part Electric** *(average monthly cost for a part-electric home);* **Other Energy** *(average monthly cost for natural gas, fuel oil, coal, wood, and any other forms of energy except electricity);* **Telephone** *(price includes basic monthly rate for a private residential line plus additional local usage charges incurred by a family of four).*
Source: The Council for Community and Economic Research, ACCRA Cost of Living Index, 2011

Health Care, Transportation, and Other Costs

Area[1]	Doctor ($/visit)	Dentist ($/visit)	Optometrist ($/visit)	Gasoline ($/gallon)	Beauty Salon ($/visit)	Men's Shirt ($)
City[2]	n/a	n/a	n/a	n/a	n/a	n/a
Avg.	93.88	81.72	90.54	3.48	32.65	25.06
Min.	60.00	55.33	53.66	3.18	19.78	13.44
Max.	154.98	145.97	183.72	4.31	63.21	46.00

Note: (1) Values for the local area are compared with the average, minimum and maximum values for all 335 areas in the Cost of Living Index; (2) Figures cover the Athens GA urban area; n/a not available; **Doctor** *(general practitioners routine exam of an established patient);* **Dentist** *(adult teeth cleaning and periodic oral examination);* **Optometrist** *(full vision eye exam for established adult patient);* **Gasoline** *(one gallon regular unleaded, national brand, including all taxes, cash price at self-service pump if available);* **Beauty Salon** *(woman's shampoo, trim, and blow-dry);* **Men's Shirt** *(cotton/polyester dress shirt, pinpoint weave, long sleeves).*
Source: The Council for Community and Economic Research, ACCRA Cost of Living Index, 2011

HOUSING

House Price Index (HPI)

Area	National Ranking[2]	Quarterly Change (%)	One-Year Change (%)	Five-Year Change (%)
MSA[1]	291	-3.15	-8.38	-13.77
U.S.[3]	-	-0.10	-2.43	-19.16

Note: The HPI is a weighted repeat sales index. It measures average price changes in repeat sales or refinancings on the same properties. This information is obtained by reviewing repeat mortgage transactions on single-family properties whose mortgages have been purchased or securitized by Fannie Mae or Freddie Mac in January 1975; (1) Metropolitan/Micropolitan Statistical Area—see Appendix B for areas included; (2) Rankings are based on annual percentage change for all metro areas containing at least 15,000 transactions over the last 10 years and ranges from 1 to 306; (3) figures based on a weighted average of Census Division estimates using a purchase only index; all figures are for the period ending December 31, 2011
Source: Federal Housing Finance Agency, House Price Index, February 23, 2012

House Price Valuations

Area	Q4 2005 Price ($000)	Q4 2005 Over-valuation	Q4 2006 Price ($000)	Q4 2006 Over-valuation	Q4 2007 Price ($000)	Q4 2007 Over-valuation	Q4 2008 Price ($000)	Q4 2008 Over-valuation	Q4 2009 Price ($000)	Q4 2009 Over-valuation
MSA[1]	132.7	2.5	138.5	1.3	137.5	-4.4	128.8	-11.8	124.4	-15.9

Note: Figures show the percentage of over- or under-valuation of single family homes relative to statistically normal house values (e.g. a value of 23.6 indicates that house values are 23.6% overvalued). Statistically normal house values are based on house prices, interest rates, household incomes, population densities, and any historical premiums or discounts metropolitan areas have exhibited over time; (1) Figures cover the Athens-Clarke County, GA - see Appendix B for areas included
Source: Global Insight/PNC Financial Services Group, House Prices in America: 4th Quarter 2009 Update

Median Single-Family Home Prices

Area	2009	2010	2011p	Percent Change 2010 to 2011
MSA[1]	n/a	n/a	n/a	n/a
U.S. Average	172.1	173.1	166.2	-4.0

Note: Figures are median sales prices of existing single-family homes in thousands of dollars; (p) preliminary; n/a not available; (1) Metropolitan Statistical Area—see Appendix B for areas included
Source: National Association of Realtors, Median Sales Price of Existing Single-Family Homes for Metropolitan Areas, 4th Quarter 2011

Affordability Index of Existing Single-Family Homes

Area	2009	2010	2011p	Percent Change 2010 to 2011
MSA[1]	n/a	n/a	n/a	n/a

Note: The housing affordability index measures whether or not a typical family could qualify for a mortgage loan on a typical home. The higher the index, the greater the household purchasing power. An index of 100 is defined as the point where a median-income household has exactly enough income to qualify for the purchase of a median-priced existing single-family home, assuming a 20 percent downpayment and 25 percent of gross income devoted to mortgage principal and interest payments; (p) preliminary; n/a not available; (1) Metropolitan Statistical Area—see Appendix B for areas included
Source: National Association of Realtors, Affordability Index of Existing Single-Family Homes, 2011

Median Apartment Condo-Coop Home Prices

Area	2009	2010	2011p	Percent Change 2010 to 2011
MSA[1]	n/a	n/a	n/a	n/a
U.S. Average	175.6	171.7	165.1	-3.8

Note: Figures are median sales prices of existing apartment condo-coop homes in thousands of dollars; (p) preliminary; n/a not available; (1) Metropolitan Statistical Area—see Appendix B for areas included
Source: National Association of Realtors, Median Sales Price of Existing Apartment Condo-Coop Homes for Metropolitan Areas, 4th Quarter 2011

Year Housing Structure Built

Area	2005 or Later	2000 -2004	1990 -1999	1980 -1989	1970 -1979	1960 -1969	1950 -1959	Before 1950	Median Year
City	5.2	13.3	19.9	16.7	18.0	12.4	6.4	8.1	1983
MSA[1]	5.1	12.1	21.9	18.6	17.7	10.4	5.3	8.9	1984
U.S.	5.0	8.6	14.0	14.1	16.3	11.3	11.2	19.6	1975

Note: Figures are percentages except for Median Year; (1) Figures cover the Athens-Clarke County, GA Metropolitan Statistical Area—see Appendix B for areas included
Source: U.S. Census Bureau, 2008-2010 American Community Survey 3-Year Estimates

HEALTH

Health Risk Data

Category	MSA[1] (%)	U.S. (%)
Adults who have been told they have high blood pressure[2]	n/a	28.7
Adults who have been told they have high blood cholesterol[2]	n/a	37.5
Adults who have been told they have diabetes[3]	n/a	8.7
Adults who have been told they have arthritis[2]	n/a	26.0
Adults who have been told they currently have asthma	n/a	9.1
Adults who are current smokers	n/a	17.3
Adults who are heavy drinkers[4]	n/a	5.0
Adults who are binge drinkers[5]	n/a	15.1
Adults who are overweight (BMI 25.0 - 29.9)	n/a	36.2
Adults who are obese (BMI 30.0 - 99.8)	n/a	27.5
Adults who participated in any physical activities in the past month	n/a	76.1
Adults 50+ who have ever had a sigmoidoscopy or colonoscopy	n/a	65.2
Women aged 40+ who have had a mammogram within the past two years	n/a	75.2
Men aged 40+ who have had a PSA test within the past two years	n/a	53.2
Adults aged 65+ who have had flu shot within the past year	n/a	67.5
Adults aged 18–64 who have any kind of health care coverage	n/a	82.2

Note: Data as of 2010 unless otherwise noted; n/a not available; (1) Figures cover the Athens-Clarke County, GA—see Appendix B for areas included; (2) Data as of 2009; (3) Figures do not include pregnancy-related, borderline, or pre-diabetes; (4) Heavy drinkers are classified as males having more than two drinks per day or females having more than one drink per day; (5) Binge drinkers are classified as males having five or more drinks on one occasion or females having four or more drinks on one occasion
Source: Centers for Disease Control and Prevention, Behaviorial Risk Factor Surveillance System, SMART: Selected Metropolitan/Micropolitan Area Risk Trends, 2009, 2010

Mortality Rates for the Top 10 Causes of Death in the U.S.

ICD-10[a] Sub-Chapter	ICD-10[a] Code	Age-Adjusted Mortality Rate[1] per 100,000 population	
		County[2]	U.S.
Malignant neoplasms	C00-C97	172.8	175.6
Ischaemic heart diseases	I20-I25	76.3	121.6
Other forms of heart disease	I30-I51	67.0	48.6
Chronic lower respiratory diseases	J40-J47	33.6	42.3
Cerebrovascular diseases	I60-I69	41.9	40.6
Organic, including symptomatic, mental disorders	F01-F09	35.7	26.7
Other degenerative diseases of the nervous system	G30-G31	19.7	24.7
Other external causes of accidental injury	W00-X59	20.1	24.4
Diabetes mellitus	E10-E14	20.2	21.7
Hypertensive diseases	I10-I15	21.8	18.2

Note: (a) ICD-10 = International Classification of Diseases 10th Revision; (1) Mortality rates are a three year average covering 2007-2009; (2) Figures cover
Source: Centers for Disease Control and Prevention, National Center for Health Statistics. Underlying Cause of Death 1999-2009 on CDC WONDER Online Database, released 2012. Data for year 2009 are compiled from the Multiple Cause of Death File 2009, Series 20 No. 2O, 2012, Data for year 2008 are compiled from the Multiple Cause of Death File 2008, Series 20 No. 2N, 2011, Data for year 2007 are compiled from Multiple Cause of Death File 2007, Series 20 No. 2M, 2010.

Mortality Rates for Selected Causes of Death

ICD-10[a] Sub-Chapter	ICD-10[a] Code	Age-Adjusted Mortality Rate[1] per 100,000 population	
		County[2]	U.S.
Assault	X85-Y09	*Unreliable	5.7
Human immunodeficiency virus (HIV) disease	B20-B24	*Unreliable	3.3
Influenza and pneumonia	J09-J18	10.7	16.4
Intentional self-harm	X60-X84	13.6	11.5
Malnutrition	E40-E46	*0.0	0.8
Obesity and other hyperalimentation	E65-E68	*0.0	1.6
Transport accidents	V01-V99	14.2	13.7
Viral hepatitis	B15-B19	*0.0	2.2

Note: (a) ICD-10 = International Classification of Diseases 10th Revision; (1) Mortality rates are a three year average covering 2007-2009; (2) Figures cover; (*) Unreliable data as per CDC
Source: Centers for Disease Control and Prevention, National Center for Health Statistics. Underlying Cause of Death 1999-2009 on CDC WONDER Online Database, released 2012. Data for year 2009 are compiled from the Multiple Cause of Death File 2009, Series 20 No. 2O, 2012, Data for year 2008 are compiled from the Multiple Cause of Death File 2008, Series 20 No. 2N, 2011, Data for year 2007 are compiled from Multiple Cause of Death File 2007, Series 20 No. 2M, 2010.

Distribution of Physicians and Dentists

Area[1]	Dentists[2]	D.O.[3]	M.D.[4]				
			Total	Family/ General Practice	Pediatrics	Medical Specialties	Surgical Specialties
Local (number)	54	12	268	22	11	88	85
Local (rate[5])	4.8	1.0	23.3	1.9	1.0	7.6	7.4
U.S. (rate[5])	4.5	1.9	18.3	2.5	1.4	6.8	4.1

Note: Data as of 2008 unless noted; (1) Local data covers Clarke County; (2) Data as of 2007; (3) Doctor of Osteopathic Medicine; (4) Includes active, non-federal, patient-care, office-based Doctors of Medicine; (5) rate per 10,000 population
Source: Area Resource File (ARF). 2009-2010 Release. U.S. Department of Health and Human Services, Health Resources and Services Administration, Bureau of Health Professions, Rockville, MD, August 2010

EDUCATION

Public School District Statistics

District Name	Schls	Pupils	Pupil/ Teacher Ratio	Minority Pupils[1] (%)	Free Lunch Eligible[2] (%)	IEP[3] (%)
Clarke County	22	12,456	12.1	80.6	70.7	12.3

Note: Table includes school districts with 2,000 or more students; (1) Percentage of students that are not non-Hispanic white; (2) Percentage of students that are eligible for the free lunch program; (3) Percentage of students that have an Individualized Education Program.
Source: U.S. Department of Education, National Center for Education Statistics, Common Core of Data, Local Education Agency (School District) Universe Survey: School Year 2009-2010; U.S. Department of Education, National Center for Education Statistics, Common Core of Data, Public Elementary/Secondary School Universe Survey: School Year 2009-2010

Highest Level of Education

Area	Less than H.S.	H.S. Diploma	Some College, No Deg.	Associate Degree	Bachelors Degree	Masters Degree	Profess. School Degree	Doctorate Degree
City	16.9	21.4	16.5	4.6	21.5	10.5	3.6	4.9
MSA[1]	18.5	24.5	17.6	4.9	18.1	9.2	3.4	3.8
U.S.	14.7	28.4	21.3	7.6	17.6	7.2	1.9	1.2

Note: Figures cover persons age 25 and over; (1) Figures cover the Athens-Clarke County, GA Metropolitan Statistical Area—see Appendix B for areas included
Source: U.S. Census Bureau, 2008-2010 American Community Survey 3-Year Estimates

Educational Attainment by Race

Area	High School Graduate or Higher (%)					Bachelor's Degree or Higher (%)				
	Total	White	Black	Asian	Hisp.[2]	Total	White	Black	Asian	Hisp.[2]
City	83.1	87.7	73.2	94.8	43.7	40.5	52.6	11.1	82.1	13.1
MSA[1]	81.5	84.9	68.6	96.0	43.8	34.5	39.8	10.3	79.8	13.3
U.S.	85.3	87.5	81.4	85.5	61.6	28.0	29.3	17.8	50.2	13.0

Note: Figures shown cover persons 25 years old and over; (1) Figures cover the Athens-Clarke County, GA Metropolitan Statistical Area—see Appendix B for areas included; (2) People of Hispanic origin can be of any race
Source: U.S. Census Bureau, 2008-2010 American Community Survey 3-Year Estimates

School Enrollment by Grade and Control

Area	Preschool (%)		Kindergarten (%)		Grades 1 - 4 (%)		Grades 5 - 8 (%)		Grades 9 - 12 (%)	
	Public	Private	Public	Private	Public	Private	Public	Private	Public	Private
City	67.7	32.3	81.3	18.7	90.5	9.5	88.0	12.0	94.4	5.6
MSA[1]	61.0	39.0	85.4	14.6	89.5	10.5	87.7	12.3	92.8	7.2
U.S.	55.4	44.6	87.1	12.9	89.4	10.6	89.5	10.5	90.4	9.6

Note: Figures shown cover persons 3 years old and over; (1) Figures cover the Athens-Clarke County, GA Metropolitan Statistical Area—see Appendix B for areas included
Source: U.S. Census Bureau, 2008-2010 American Community Survey 3-Year Estimates

Average Salaries of Public School Classroom Teachers

Area	2010-11		2011-12		Percent Change 2010-11 to 2011-12	Percent Change 2001-02 to 2011-12
	Dollars	Rank[1]	Dollars	Rank[1]		
Georgia	52,815	22	52,938	23	0.23	20.10
U.S. Average	55,623	-	56,643	-	1.83	26.8

Note: (1) State rank ranges from 1 to 51 where 1 indicates highest salary.
Source: National Education Association, Rankings & Estimates: Rankings of the States 2011 and Estimates of School Statistics 2012, December 2011

Higher Education

Four-Year Colleges			Two-Year Colleges			Medical Schools[1]	Law Schools[2]	Voc/ Tech[3]
Public	Private Non-profit	Private For-profit	Public	Private Non-profit	Private For-profit			
1	0	0	1	0	0	0	1	1

Note: Figures cover institutions located within the city limits and include main campuses only; (1) includes schools accredited by the Liaison Committee on Medical Education and the American Osteopathic Association's Commission on Osteopathic College Accreditation; (2) includes American Bar Association-accredited law schools; (3) includes all schools with programs that are less than 2 years.
Source: National Center for Education Statistics, Integrated Postsecondary Education System (IPEDS) Peer Analysis System, 2011-12; Association of American Medical Colleges, Member List, April 23, 2012; American Osteopathic Association, Member List, April 23, 2012; Law School Admission Council, Official Guide to ABA-Approved Law Schools Online, April 23, 2012

According to *U.S. News & World Report*, the Athens-Clarke County, GA is home to one of the best national universities in the U.S.: **University of Georgia** (#62). The indicators used to capture academic quality fall into a number of categories: assessment by administrators at peer institutions; retention of students; faculty resources; student selectivity; financial resources; alumni giving; high school counselor ratings of colleges; and graduation rate. *U.S. News & World Report, "America's Best Colleges 2012"*

According to *U.S. News & World Report*, the Athens-Clarke County, GA is home to one of the best law schools in the U.S.: **University of Georgia** (#34). The rankings are based on a weighted average of 12 measures of quality: peer assessment score; assessment score by lawyers/judges; median LSAT scores; median undergrad GPA; acceptance rate; employment rates for graduates; placement success; bar passage rate; faculty resources; expenditures per student; student/faculty ratio; and library resources. *U.S. News & World Report, "America's Best Law Schools 2013"*

According to *Forbes*, the Athens-Clarke County, GA is home to one of the best business schools in the U.S.: **Georgia (Terry)** (#42). The rankings are based on the return on investment that graduates of the Class of 2006 received (median salary five years after graduation). *Forbes, "Best Business Schools," August 3, 2011*

PRESIDENTIAL ELECTION

2008 Presidential Election Results

Area	Obama	McCain	Nader	Other
Clarke County	64.8	33.6	0.1	1.5
U.S.	52.9	45.6	0.6	0.9

Note: Results are percentages and may not add to 100% due to rounding
Source: Dave Leip's Atlas of U.S. Presidential Elections, www.uselectionatlas.org

EMPLOYERS

Major Employers

Company Name	Industry
Agricultural Research Service	Regulation of agricultural marketing
Athens Regional Medical Center	General medical and surgical hospitals
Athens-Clarke County, Unified Govt of	Executive offices, local government
Athens-Clarke County, Unified Govt of	Air, water, & solid waste management, county govt
Carrier Corporation	Refrigeration equipment, complete
Certainteed Corporation	Insulation: rock wool, slag, and silica minerals
Flowers	Gifts and novelties
Georgia Power Company	Electric services
Island Apparel	Men's and boy's trousers and slacks
McLane/Southeast	Groceries, general line
Power Partners	Power, distribution and specialty transformers
St. Mary's Health Care System	General medical and surgical hospitals
The University of Georgia	Colleges and universities
The University of Georgia	University
The University of Georgia	Vocational schools
The University of Georgia	Educational services
United States Postal Service	U.s. postal service
University of Georgia Athletic Assn	Athletic organizations
Wal-Mart Stores	Department stores, discount

Note: Companies shown are located within the Athens-Clarke County, GA metropolitan area.
Source: Hoovers.com, data extracted April 25 2012

PUBLIC SAFETY

Crime Rate

Area	All Crimes	Violent Crimes				Property Crimes		
		Murder	Forcible Rape	Robbery	Aggrav. Assault	Burglary	Larceny -Theft	Motor Vehicle Theft
City	4,698.2	4.4	25.7	97.5	201.2	1,182.1	2,923.3	264.1
Suburbs[1]	3,503.9	4.0	10.6	30.4	398.7	773.6	2,088.6	198.0
Metro[2]	4,218.5	4.2	19.6	70.5	280.5	1,018.0	2,588.1	237.5
U.S.	3,345.5	4.8	27.5	119.1	252.3	699.6	2,003.5	238.8

Note: Figures are crimes per 100,000 population; (1) All areas within the metro area that are located outside the city limits; (2) Metropolitan Statistical Area—see Appendix B for areas included
Source: FBI Uniform Crime Reports, 2010

Hate Crimes

Area	Number of Quarters Reported	Bias Motivation				
		Race	Religion	Sexual Orientation	Ethnicity	Disability
Area[2]	4	0	0	0	0	0

Note: (2) Figures cover Athens-Clarke County.
Source: Federal Bureau of Investigation, Hate Crime Statistics 2010

Identity Theft Consumer Complaints

Area	Complaints	Complaints per 100,000 Population	Rank[2]
MSA[1]	206	109.9	64
U.S.	279,156	90.4	-

Note: (1) Metropolitan Statistical Area—see Appendix B for areas included; (2) Rank ranges from 1 to 384 where 1 indicates greatest number of identity theft complaints per 100,000 population
Source: Federal Trade Commission, Consumer Sentinel Network Data Book for January–December 2011

Fraud and Other Consumer Complaints

Area	Complaints	Complaints per 100,000 Population	Rank[2]
MSA[1]	889	474.4	188
U.S.	1,533,924	496.8	-

Note: (1) Metropolitan Statistical Area—see Appendix B for areas included; (2) Rank ranges from 1 to 384 where 1 indicates greatest number of fraud and other complaints per 100,000 population
Source: Federal Trade Commission, Consumer Sentinel Network Data Book for January–December 2011

RECREATION

Culture

Dance[1]	Theatre[1]	Instrumental Music[1]	Vocal Music[1]	Series/ Festivals	Museums	Zoos and Aquariums[2]
2	2	0	0	1	5	0

Note: (1) Number of professional perfoming groups; (2) AZA-accredited
Source: The Grey House Performing Arts Directory, 2011-2012; Official Museum Directory, 2011; American Association of Museums, AAM Member Museums, April 2012; Association of Zoos & Aquariums, AZA Member Zoos & Aquariums, April 2012

Professional Sports Teams

Team Name	League

No teams are located in the metro area
Source: Original research

CLIMATE

Average and Extreme Temperatures

Temperature	Jan	Feb	Mar	Apr	May	Jun	Jul	Aug	Sep	Oct	Nov	Dec	Yr.
Extreme High (°F)	79	80	85	93	95	101	105	102	98	95	84	77	105
Average High (°F)	52	56	64	73	80	86	88	88	82	73	63	54	72
Average Temp. (°F)	43	46	53	62	70	77	79	79	73	63	53	45	62
Average Low (°F)	33	36	42	51	59	66	70	69	64	52	42	35	52
Extreme Low (°F)	-8	5	10	26	37	46	53	55	36	28	3	0	-8

Note: Figures cover the years 1945-1990
Source: National Climatic Data Center, International Station Meteorological Climate Summary, 9/96

Average Precipitation/Snowfall/Humidity

Precip./Humidity	Jan	Feb	Mar	Apr	May	Jun	Jul	Aug	Sep	Oct	Nov	Dec	Yr.
Avg. Precip. (in.)	4.7	4.6	5.7	4.3	4.0	3.5	5.1	3.6	3.4	2.8	3.8	4.2	49.8
Avg. Snowfall (in.)	1	1	Tr	Tr	0	0	0	0	0	0	Tr	Tr	2
Avg. Rel. Hum. 7am (%)	79	77	78	78	82	83	88	89	88	84	81	79	82
Avg. Rel. Hum. 4pm (%)	56	50	48	45	49	52	57	56	56	51	52	55	52

Note: Figures cover the years 1945-1990; Tr = Trace amounts (<0.05 in. of rain; <0.5 in. of snow)
Source: National Climatic Data Center, International Station Meteorological Climate Summary, 9/96

Weather Conditions

Temperature			Daytime Sky			Precipitation		
10°F & below	32°F & below	90°F & above	Clear	Partly cloudy	Cloudy	0.01 inch or more precip.	0.1 inch or more snow/ice	Thunder-storms
1	49	38	98	147	120	116	3	48

Note: Figures are average number of days per year and cover the years 1945-1990
Source: National Climatic Data Center, International Station Meteorological Climate Summary, 9/96

HAZARDOUS WASTE

Superfund Sites

Athens has no sites on the EPA's Superfund Final National Priorities List.
U.S. Environmental Protection Agency, Final National Priorities List, April 17, 2012

**AIR & WATER
QUALITY**

Air Quality Index

Area	Percent of Days when Air Quality was...[2]					AQI Statistics[2]	
	Good	Moderate	Unhealthy for Sensitive Groups	Unhealthy	Very Unhealthy	Maximum	Median
Area[1]	71.2	27.7	1.1	0.0	0.0	106	41

Note: Air Quality Index (AQI) is an index for reporting daily air quality. EPA calculates the AQI for five major air pollutants regulated by the Clean Air Act: ground-level ozone, particle pollution (aka particulate matter), carbon monoxide, sulfur dioxide, and nitrogen dioxide. The AQI runs from 0 to 500. The higher the AQI value, the greater the level of air pollution and the greater the health concern. There are six AQI categories: "Good" AQI is between 0 and 50. Air quality is considered satisfactory; "Moderate" AQI is between 51 and 100. Air quality is acceptable; "Unhealthy for Sensitive Groups" When AQI values are between 101 and 150, members of sensitive groups may experience health effects; "Unhealthy" When AQI values are between 151 and 200 everyone may begin to experience health effects; "Very Unhealthy" AQI values between 201 and 300 trigger a health alert; "Hazardous" AQI values over 300 trigger warnings of emergency conditions (not shown); (1) Data covers Clarke County; (2) Based on 365 days with AQI data in 2011.
Source: U.S. Environmental Protection Agency, AirData Report, 2011

Air Quality Index Pollutants

Area	Percent of Days when AQI Pollutant was...[2]					
	Carbon Monoxide	Nitrogen Dioxide	Ozone	Sulfur Dioxide	Particulate Matter 2.5	Particulate Matter 10
Area[1]	0.0	0.0	45.5	0.0	54.5	0.0

Note: The Air Quality Index (AQI) is an index for reporting daily air quality. EPA calculates the AQI for five major air pollutants regulated by the Clean Air Act: ground-level ozone, particle pollution (also known as particulate matter), carbon monoxide, sulfur dioxide, and nitrogen dioxide. The AQI runs from 0 to 500. The higher the AQI value, the greater the level of air pollution and the greater the health concern; (1) Data covers Clarke County; (2) Based on 365 days with AQI data in 2011.
Source: U.S. Environmental Protection Agency, AirData Report, 2011

Air Quality Index Trends

Area	Trend Sites (days)								All Sites (days)
	2003	2004	2005	2006	2007	2008	2009	2010	2010
MSA[1]	n/a	n/a	n/a	n/a	n/a	n/a	n/a	n/a	n/a

Note: Figures are the number of days the AQI value exceeded 100 in a given year. An AQI value greater than 100 indicates that air quality would have been in the unhealthful range on that day. Data from exceptional events are included. These counts are presented in two ways. First, the counts are based on sites having an adequate record of monitoring data during the trend period (trend sites). These counts represent the relative change in the number of days with AQI values greater than 100. In the last column, the counts are based on all sites with data in the most recent year (because it is possible for a site to have data in the most recent year but not enough data to be a trend site); (1) Data covers the Athens-Clarke County, GA—see Appendix B for areas included; n/a not available.
Source: U.S. Environmental Protection Agency, Air Quality Index Information, "Number of Days with Air Quality Index Values Greater than 100 at Trend Sites, 2000-2010, and at All Sites in 2010"

Maximum Air Pollutant Concentrations: Particulate Matter, Ozone, CO and Lead

	Particulate Matter 10 (ug/m³)	Particulate Matter 2.5 Wtd AM (ug/m³)	Particulate Matter 2.5 24-Hr (ug/m³)	Ozone (ppm)	Carbon Monoxide (ppm)	Lead (ug/m³)
MSA[1] Level	n/a	11.3	23	0.073	n/a	n/a
NAAQS[2]	150	15	35	0.075	9	0.15
Met NAAQS[2]	n/a	Yes	Yes	Yes	n/a	n/a

Note: Data from exceptional events are not included; (1) Data covers the Athens-Clarke County, GA—see Appendix B for areas included; (2) National Ambient Air Quality Standards; ppm = parts per million; ug/m³ = micrograms per cubic meter; n/a not available
Concentrations: Particulate Matter 10 (coarse particulate)—highest second maximum 24-hour concentration; Particulate Matter 2.5 Wtd AM (fine particulate)—highest weighted annual mean concentration; Particulate Matter 2.5 24-Hour (fine particulate)—highest 98th percentile 24-hour concentration; Ozone—highest fourth daily maximum 8-hour concentration; Carbon Monoxide—highest second maximum non-overlapping 8-hour concentration; Lead—maximum running 3-month average
Source: U.S. Environmental Protection Agency, CBSA Factbook 2010, Air Quality Statistics by City, 2010

Maximum Air Pollutant Concentrations: Nitrogen Dioxide and Sulfur Dioxide

	Nitrogen Dioxide AM (ppb)	Nitrogen Dioxide 1-Hr (ppb)	Sulfur Dioxide AM (ppb)	Sulfur Dioxide 1-Hr (ppb)	Sulfur Dioxide 24-Hr (ppb)
MSA[1] Level	n/a	n/a	n/a	n/a	n/a
NAAQS[2]	53	100	30	75	140
Met NAAQS[2]	n/a	n/a	n/a	n/a	n/a

Note: Data from exceptional events are not included; (1) Data covers the Athens-Clarke County, GA—see Appendix B for areas included; (2) National Ambient Air Quality Standards; ppb = parts per billion; n/a not available
Concentrations: Nitrogen Dioxide AM—highest arithmetic mean concentration; Nitrogen Dioxide 1-Hr—highest 98th percentile 1-hour daily maximum concentration; Sulfur Dioxide AM—highest annual mean concentration; Sulfur Dioxide 1-Hr—highest 99th percentile 1-hour daily maximum concentration; Sulfur Dioxide 24-Hr—highest second maximum 24-hour concentration
Source: U.S. Environmental Protection Agency, CBSA Factbook 2010, Air Quality Statistics by City, 2010

Drinking Water

Water System Name	Pop. Served	Primary Water Source Type	Violations[1]	
			Health Based	Monitoring/ Reporting
Athens-Clarke Co. Water System	102,811	Surface	0	0

Note: (1) Based on violation data from January 1, 2011 to December 31, 2011 (includes unresolved violations from earlier years)
Source: U.S. Environmental Protection Agency, Office of Ground Water and Drinking Water, Safe Drinking Water Information System (based on data extracted April 18, 2012)

Atlanta, Georgia

Background

Atlanta was born of a rough-and-tumble past, first as a natural outgrowth of a thriving railroad network in the 1840s, and second as a resilient go-getter that proudly rose again above the rubble of the Civil War.

Blanketed over the rolling hills of the Piedmont Plateau, at the foot of the Blue Ridge Mountains, Georgia's capital stands 1,000 feet above sea level. Atlanta is located in the northwest corner of Georgia where the terrain is rolling to hilly, and slopes downward to the east, west, and south.

Atlanta proper begins at the "terminus," or zero mile mark, of the now defunct Western and Atlantic Railroad Line. However its metropolitan area comprises 28 counties that include Fulton, DeKalb, Clayton and Gwinnet, among others. Population-wise, Atlanta is the largest city in the southeast United States, and has been growing at a steady rate for the last decade. In 2007, the census bureau declared Atlanta the fastest growing metropolitan area in the nation. Understandably, the city contributes to nearly two thirds of the state's economy.

Within the city itself, Atlanta's has a diversified economy that allows for employment in a variety of sectors such as manufacturing, retail, and government. The city hosts many of the nation's Fortune 500 company headquarters, including Home Depot, United Parcel Service, Coca-Cola, Delta Air Lines, AT&T Mobility, CNN headquarters, as well as the nation's Centers for Disease Control and Prevention (CDC).

These accomplishments are the result of an involved city government that seeks to work closely with its business community, due in part to a change in the city charter in 1974, when greater administrative powers were vested in the mayoral office, and the city inaugurated its first black mayor.

As middle class residents, both white and black, continue to move to the suburbs separating themselves from Atlanta's old downtown, the city faces the complex issue of where it plans to move as an urban center in light of the conflict between the city and its surroundings.

While schools in the city remain predominantly black and schools in its suburbs predominantly white, Atlanta boasts a racially progressive climate. The Martin Luther King, Jr. Historic Site and Preservation District is located in the Sweet Auburn neighborhood, which includes King's birth home and the Ebenezer Baptist Church, where both he and his father preached. The city's consortium of black colleges that includes Morehouse College and the Interdenominational Theological Center testifies to the city's appreciation for a people who have always been one-third of Atlanta's population. Atlanta has become a major regional center for film and television production in recent years, with Tyler Perry Studios, TurnerStudios and EVE/ScreenGems Studio in the city.

Indeed, King is one of Atlanta's two Nobel Peace Prize winners. The second, former President Jimmy Carter, famously of Plains, Georgia, also brings his name to Atlanta as namesake to the Carter Center. Devoted to human rights, the center is operated with neighboring Emory University, and sits adjacent to the Jimmy Carter Library and Museum on a hill overlooking the city. Habitat for Humanity, also founded by Carter, moved its international administrative headquarters to Atlanta in 2006.

Hartsfield-Jackson Atlanta International Airport, the world's busiest passenger airport, underwent significant expansion in recent years. MARTA, the city's public transport system, is the nation's 9th largest and transports on average 500,000 passengers daily on a 48-mile, 38-station rapid rail system with connections to hundreds of bus routes.

The Appalachian chain of mountains, the Gulf of Mexico, and the Atlantic Ocean influence Atlanta's climate. Temperatures are moderate to hot throughout the year, but extended periods of heat are unusual and 100-degree heat is rarely experienced. Atlanta winters are mild with a few, short-lived cold spells. Summers can be humid. A rare event occurred in March 2008, when a tornado caused considerable damage to the city.

Rankings

General Rankings

- *Men's Health Living* ranked 100 U.S. cities in terms of quality of life. Atlanta was ranked #64 and received a grade of C-. Criteria: number of fitness facilities; air quality; number of physicians; male/female ratio; education levels; household income; cost of living. *Men's Health Living, Spring 2008*

- Atlanta was selected as one of America's best cities by *Bloomberg Businessweek*. The city ranked #32 out of 50. Criteria: number of restaurants, bars and museums per capita; number of colleges, libraries, and professional sports teams; income, poverty, unemployment, crime, and foreclosure rates; percent of population with bachelor's degrees; public school performance; park acres per capita; air quality. *BusinessWeek, "America's 50 Best Cities," September 20, 2011*

- Atlanta was identified as one of the top places to live in the U.S. by Harris Interactive. The city ranked #15 out of 15. Criteria: 2,463 adults (age 18 and over) were polled and asked "if you could live in or near any city in the country except the one you live in or nearest to now, which city would you choose?" The poll was conducted online within the U.S. between September 14 and 20, 2010. *Harris Interactive, November 9, 2011*

Business/Finance Rankings

- Atlanta was identified as one of the 20 weakest-performing metro areas during the recession and recovery from trough quarter through the third quarter of 2011. Criteria: percent change in employment; percentage point change in unemployment rate; percent change in gross metropolitan product; percent change in House Price Index. *Brookings Institution, MetroMonitor: Tracking Economic Recession and Recovery in America's 100 Largest Metropolitan Areas, December 2011*

- The Atlanta metro area was identified as one of 10 places with the fastest-growing wages in America. The area ranked #9. Criteria: private-sector wage growth between the 4th quarter of 2010 and the 4th quarter of 2011. *PayScale, "The 10 Cities with the Fastest-Growing Wages in America," January 12, 2012*

- Experian ranked the top 20 major U.S. metropolitan areas by average debt per consumer. The Atlanta metro area was ranked #4. Criteria: average debt per consumer. Debt for this study includes credit cards, auto loans and personal loans. It does not include mortgages. *Experian, May 13, 2010*

- Atlanta was identified as one of America's most coupon-loving cities by *Coupons.com*. The city ranked #1 out of 25. Criteria: online coupon usage. *Coupons.com, "Top 25 Most Frugal Cities of 2011," February 23, 2012*

- Atlanta was identified as one of the top 25 U.S. cities with the most credit card debt by credit reporting bureau Experian. The city was ranked #3. *Experian, March 4, 2011*

- Atlanta was cited as one of America's top metros for new and expanded facility projects in 2011. The area ranked #9 in the large metro area category (population over 1 million). *Site Selection, "2011 Top Metros," March 2012*

- Atlanta was identified as one of the "Best Cities for Recent College Graduates." The city ranked #9. Criteria: concentration of young adults (age 20 to 24); inventory of jobs requiring less than one year of experience; average cost of rent for a one bedroom apartment. *CareerBuilder.com, "Top 10 Best Cities for Recent College Graduates," August 30, 2011*

- Atlanta was identified as one of the "Happiest Cities to Work in 2012" by *CareerBliss.com*, an online community for career advancement. The city ranked #16 out of 50. Criteria: independent company reviews from employees all over the country on: relationship with their boss and co-workers; work environment; job resources; growth opportunities; compensation; company culture; company reputation; daily tasks; job control over work performed on a daily basis. *CareerBliss.com, "Happiest and Unhappiest Cities to Work in 2012"*

- Atlanta was identified as one of the best cities for new college graduates. The city ranked #4. Criteria: cost of living; average annual salary; unemployment rate; number of employers looking to hire people at entry-level. *Business Week, "The Best Cities for New Grads," July 20, 2010*

- Atlanta was selected as one of the best metro areas for telecommuters in America. The area ranked #3 out of 11. Criteria: low cost of living; educational attainment; number of universities and libraries; literacy rates; personal fitness. *DailyFinance.com, "The 11 Best Cities for Telecommuters," December 2, 2010*

- Atlanta was selected as one of the best cities in the world for telecommuting. The city ranked #11. The editors at *Cartridge Save* (printer technology news, guides and reviews) identified the 20 best cities in which to be an at-home, tech-using employee. *Cartridge Save, "20 of the Best Cities in the World for Telecommuting," May 14, 2008*

- *American City Business Journals* ranked America's 261 largest cities in terms of their resident's wealth. Atlanta ranked #52. Criteria: per capita income; median household income; percentage of households with annual incomes of $200,000 or more; median home value. *American City Business Journals, "Where the Money Is: America's Wealth Centers," August 18, 2008*

- The Atlanta metro area appeared on the Milken Institute "2011 Best Performing Metros" list. Rank: #145 out of 200 large metro areas. Criteria: job growth; wage and salary growth; high-tech output growth. *Milken Institute, "2011 Best Performing Metros"*

- The Atlanta metro area was selected as one of the best cities for entrepreneurs in America by *Inc. Magazine*. Criteria: job-growth data for 335 metro areas was analyzed for: recent growth trend; mid-term growth; long-term trend; current year growth. The Atlanta metro area ranked #16 among large metro areas and #85 overall. *Inc. Magazine, "The Best Cities for Doing Business," July 2008*

- Atlanta was identified as one of the top 10 cities with the greatest number of *Inc. 500* companies per million residents. The city ranked #8. *Inc. Magazine, September 2008*

- Atlanta was ranked #95 out of 145 regions worldwide in terms of its "Knowledge Competitiveness Index." The index attempts to measure the knowledge-based development taking place throughout the world and is based on 19 measures of economic performance that indicate a region's ability to translate its knowledge capacity into economic value. *Centre for International Competitiveness, World Knowledge Competitiveness Index 2008*

- *Forbes* ranked the 200 most populous metro areas in the U.S. in terms of the "Best Places for Business and Careers." The Atlanta metro area was ranked #33. Criteria: costs (business and living); job growth (past and projected); income growth; educational attainment; projected economic growth; crime; cultural and recreational opportunities; net migration patterns; number of highly ranked colleges. *Forbes, "Best Places for Business and Careers," June 2011*

Children/Family Rankings

- The Atlanta metro area was selected as one of the "Best Cities for Relocating Families" by Worldwide ERC and Primacy Relocation. The 2008 study looked at nearly 50 factors important to relocating families including: recent job growth; nearby top-ranked colleges; in-state tuition for four-year public colleges; population growth since 2000; pediatricians per 100,000 population; and a Green Living index. *Worldwide ERC and Primacy Relocation, "2008 Best Cities for Relocating Families"*

- *Fit Pregnancy* magazine ranked the 50 best U.S. cities in which to have a baby. Atlanta was ranked #15. Criteria: access to hospitals and doctors; affordability; birthing options; breastfeeding; child care; fertility laws/resources; maternal and infant health risk; parks/stroller friendliness; safety. *Fit Pregnancy, "The Best Cities in America to Have a Baby 2008"*

Culture/Performing Arts Rankings

- Atlanta was selected as one of 10 best U.S. cities to be a moviemaker. The city was ranked #7. Criteria: cost of living; average salary; unemployment rate; job growth; median home price; crime rate; number of film schools, festivals, movie-related vendors and local movie theaters; current production scene (i.e. production days, size of talent pool); financial incentives for shooting in a particular area. *MovieMaker Magazine, "Top 10 Cities to be a Moviemaker: 2012," January 16, 2012*

- Atlanta was selected as one of "America's Top 25 Arts Destinations." The city ranked #9 in the big city (population 500,000 and over) category. Criteria: readers' top choices for arts travel destinations based on the richness and variety of visual arts sites, activities and events. *American Style, "America's Top 25 Arts Destinations," May 2010*

Dating/Romance Rankings

- Atlanta appeared on *Men's Health's* list of the most sex-happy cities in America. The city ranked #21 of 100. Criteria: condom sales; birth rates; sex toy sales; rates of chlamydia, gonorrhea, and syphilis. *Men's Health, "America's Most Sex-Happy Cities," October 2010*

- *Men's Health* ranked 100 U.S. cities in terms of best (and worst) marriages. Atlanta was ranked #66 (#1 = worst). Criteria: rate of failed marriages; stringency of divorce laws; percentage of population who've split; number of licensed marriage and family therapists. *Men's Health, "Splitsville, USA," May 2010*

- Eli Lily and Company, in partnership with Sperling's BestPlaces, ranked the nation's 50 largest metro areas in terms of the "Most Romantic Cities for Baby Boomers." The Atlanta metro area ranked #20. Criteria: marriage and divorce rates among baby boomers age 45 to 60; great restaurants; dance studios; chocolate, jewelry and flower sales. *Eli Lily and Company, "Most Romantic Cities for Baby Boomers," April 20, 2007*

- The Atlanta metro area was selected as one of the "Best Cities for Relocating Singles" by Worldwide ERC and Primacy Relocation. The area ranked #6 out of the 100 largest metro areas in the U.S. Criteria: recent job growth; recent singles population growth; overall population growth; affordable rental housing; cost-of-living index; expanded arts and recreation opportunities; ratio of single men and single women; affordability of quality higher education (including state residency requirements); diversity index; climate; population density. *Worldwide ERC and Primacy Relocation, "2008 Best Cities for Relocating Singles"*

- *Forbes* ranked the 40 most populous urbanized areas in the U.S. in terms of the "Best Cities for Singles." The Atlanta metro area ranked #6. Criteria: number of singles; cost of living alone; nightlife; culture; job growth; coolness; and online dating participation. *Forbes.com, "Best Cities for Singles," July 27, 2009*

Education Rankings

- *Men's Health* ranked 100 U.S. cities in terms of their education levels. Atlanta was ranked #25 (#1 = most educated city). Criteria: high school graduation rates; school enrollment; educational attainment; number of households who have outstanding student loans; number of households whose members have taken adult-education courses. *Men's Health, "Where School Is In: The Most and Least Educated Cities," September 12, 2011*

- Atlanta was selected as one of the most well-read cities in America by *Amazon.com*. The city ranked #20 of 20. Cities with populations greater than 100,000 were evaluated based on per capita sales of books, magazines and newspapers. *Amazon.com, "Top 20 Most Well-Read Cities in America," June 4, 2011*

- Atlanta was selected as one of "America's Most Literate Cities." The city ranked #4 out of the 75 largest U.S. cities. Criteria: number of booksellers; library resources; Internet resources; educational attainment; periodical publishing resources; newspaper circulation. *Central Connecticut State University, "America's Most Literate Cities 2011"*

- Atlanta was identified as one of the 100 "smartest" metro areas in the U.S. The area ranked #30. Criteria: the editors rated the collective brainpower of the 100 largest metro areas in the U.S. based on their residents' educational attainment. *American City Business Journals, April 14, 2008*

- Atlanta was identified as one of "America's Brainiest Bastions" by *Portfolio.com*. The metro area ranked #42 out of 200. *Portfolio.com* analyzed levels of educational attainment in the nation's 200 largest metropolitan areas. The editors established scores for five levels of educational attainment, based on relative earning power of adult workers age 25 or older. Scores were determined by comparing the median income for all workers with the median income for those workers at a specified educational level. *Portfolio.com, "America's Brainiest Bastions," December 1, 2010*

Environmental Rankings

- The Atlanta was identified as one of North America's greenest metropolitan areas. The area ranked #21. The Green City Index is comprised of 31 indicators, and scores cities across nine categories: carbon dioxide; energy; land use; buildings; transport; water; waste; air quality; environmental governance. The 27 largest metropolitan areas in the U.S. and Canada were considered. *Economist Intelligence Unit, sponsored by Siemens, "U.S. and Canada Green City Index, 2011"*

- The Atlanta was identified as one of America's cities with the most ENERGY STAR certified buildings. The area ranked #6 out of 25. Criteria: number of ENERGY STAR labeled buildings in 2010. *U.S. Environmental Protection Agency, "Top Cities With the Most ENERGY STAR Certified Buildings," March 15, 2011*

- The Atlanta metro area was identified as one of "The Ten Biggest American Cities that are Running Out of Water" by *24/7 Wall St.* The metro area ranked #9 out of 10. *24/7 Wall St.* did an analysis of the water supply and consumption in the 30 largest metropolitan areas in the U.S. Criteria include: projected water demand as a share of available precipitation; groundwater use as a share or projected available precipitation; susceptibility to drought; projected increase in freshwater withdrawals; projected increase in summer water deficit. *24/7 Wall St., "The Ten Biggest American Cities that are Running Out of Water," November 1, 2010*

- Atlanta was selected as one of 22 "Smarter Cities" for energy by the Natural Resources Defense Council. Criteria: investment in green power; energy efficiency measures; conservation. *Natural Resources Defense Council, "2010 Smarter Cities," July 19, 2010*

- *American City Business Journal* ranked 43 metropolitan areas in terms of their "greenness." The Atlanta metro area ranked #32. Criteria: Forty-one metros in which *ACBJ* has business weeklies, plus Indianapolis and Cleveland, were ranked based on 20 different indicators such as adoption of green technologies, utilization of environmentally sound practices, and air and water quality. *American City Business Journals, "Green City Index," March 11, 2010*

- 100 of the largest metro areas in the U.S. were analyzed in terms of their current drought severity. The Atlanta metro area ranked #12 (#1 = driest). The rankings were based on statistics such as long-term precipitation trends and patterns and the Palmer drought indices. *Sperling's BestPlaces, www.BestPlaces.net, "America's Drought-Riskiest Cities," November 2007*

- The Atlanta metro area appeared in *Country Home's* "Best Green Places" report. The area ranked #210 out of 379. Criteria: official energy policies; green power; green buildings; availability of fresh, locally grown food. *Country Home, "Best Green Places," 2008*

- Atlanta was highlighted as one of the 25 most ozone-polluted metro areas in the U.S. The area ranked #23. *American Lung Association, State of the Air 2011*

Food/Drink Rankings

- Turner Field (Atlanta Braves) was selected as one of PETA's "2011 Top 10 Vegetarian-Friendly Major League Ballparks." The park ranked #4. *People for the Ethical Treatment of Animals, "2011 Top 10 Vegetarian-Friendly Major League Ballparks"*

- Atlanta was selected as one of North America's most vegetarian- and vegan-friendly large cities (population 300,000 or more). The city was ranked #4. Criteria: number of vegetarian restaurants and vegetarian-friendly restaurants per capita; input from PETA supporters and staff members on the quality of the options. *People for the Ethical Treatment of Animals, "North America's Best Vegetarian- and Vegan-Friendly Cities," July 23, 2010*

Health/Fitness Rankings

- The Atlanta metro area was selected as one of the worst cities for bed bugs in America by Rollins corporation, the owner of seven pest control companies, including Orkin. The area ranked #21 based on the number of bed bug treatments from January to December 2011. *Rollins, "The Top 50 U.S. Cities for Bed Bugs," March 19, 2012*

- Atlanta was selected as one of the 25 fattest cities in America by *Men's Fitness Online*. It ranked #20 out of America's 50 largest cities. Criteria: fitness centers and sport stores; nutrition; sports participation; TV viewing; overweight/sedentary; junk food; air quality; geography; commute; parks and open space; city recreational facilities; access to healthcare; motivation; mayor and city initiatives; state obesity initiatives. *Men's Fitness, "The Fittest and Fattest Cities in America," March 5, 2012*

- Atlanta was identified as a "2011 Asthma Capital." The area ranked #13 out of the nation's 100 largest metropolitan areas. Twelve factors were used to identify the most challenging places to live for people with asthma: estimated prevalence; self-reported prevalence; crude death rate for asthma; annual pollen score; annual air quality; public smoking laws; number of board-certified asthma specialists; school inhaler access laws; rescue medication use; controller medication use; uninsured rate; poverty rate. *Asthma and Allergy Foundation of America, "2011 Asthma Capitals"*

- Atlanta was identified as a "2011 Fall Allergy Capital." The area ranked #59 out of 100. Three groups of factors were used to identify the most severe cities for people with allergies during the fall season: annual pollen levels; medicine utilization; access to board-certified allergists. *Asthma and Allergy Foundation of America, "2011 Fall Allergy Capitals"*

- Atlanta was identified as a "2012 Spring Allergy Capital." The area ranked #73 out of 100. Three groups of factors were used to identify the most severe cities for people with allergies during the spring season: annual pollen levels; medicine utilization; access to board-certified allergists. *Asthma and Allergy Foundation of America, "2012 Spring Allergy Capitals"*

- *Men's Health* examined 100 major U.S. cities and selected the best and worst cities for men. Atlanta ranked #36. Criteria: 35 statistical parameters of long life in the categories of health, quality of life, and fitness. *Men's Health, "The 10 Best and Worst Cities for Men 2012," January/February 2012*

- Atlanta was selected as one of America's noisiest cities by *Men's Health*. The city ranked #7 of 10. Criteria: laws limiting excessive noise; traffic congestion levels; airports' overnight flight curfews; percentage of people who report sleeping seven hours or less. *Men's Health, "Ranking America's Cities: America's Noisiest Cities," May 2009*

- The Atlanta metropolitan area was selected as one of the best metros for hospital care in America by *HealthGrades.com*. The rankings are based on a comprehensive study of patient death and complication rates in the nation's nearly 5,000 hospitals. Hospitals performing in the top 5% nationwide across 26 different medical procedures and diagnoses were identified. *HealthGrades.com* then ranked cities by the highest percentage of these Distinguished Hospitals for Clinical Excellence™. The Atlanta metro area ranked #50. *HealthGrades.com, "America's Top 50 Cities for Hospital Care," January 21, 2012*

- The American Academy of Dermatology ranked 26 U.S. metropolitan regions in terms of their residents knowledge, attitude and behaviors towards tanning, sun protection and skin cancer detection. The Atlanta metro area ranked #7. The results of the study are based on an online survey of over 7,000 adults nationwide. *American Academy of Dermatology, "Suntelligence: How Sun Smart is Your City," May 3, 2010*

- The Atlanta metro area appeared in the 2011 Gallup-Healthways Well-Being Index. The index, based on interviews with more than 350,000 Americans, measured jobs, finances, physical health, emotional state of mind and communities. The metro area ranked #54 out of 190. Criteria: life evaluation; emotional health; work environment; physical health; healthy behaviors; basic access (basic needs optimal for a healthy life, such as access to food and medicine, having health insurance and feeling safe while walking at night). *Gallup-Healthways, "State of Well-Being 2011"*

- The Atlanta metro area was identified as one of "America's Most Stressful Cities" by *Sperling's BestPlaces*. The metro area ranked #15 out of 50. Criteria: unemployment rate; suicide rate; commute time; mental health; poor rest; alcohol use; violent crime rate; property crime rate; cloudy days annually. *Sperling's BestPlaces, www.BestPlaces.net, "Stressful Cities 2012*

- *Men's Health* ranked 100 U.S. cities in terms of their activity levels. Atlanta was ranked #8 (#1 = most active city). Criteria: where and how often residents exercise; percentage of households that watch more than 15 hours of cable television a week and buy more than 11 video games a year; death rate from deep-vein thrombosis, a condition linked to sitting for extended periods of time. *Men's Health, "Where Sit Happens: The Most and Least Active Cities in America," June 20, 2011*

- *Men's Health* examined the nation's largest 100 cities and identified the 10 cities at lowest risk of erectile dysfunction. Atlanta ranked #4. Criteria: percentage of current male smokers; percentage of adults with a BMI of at least 30; percentage of adults with diabetes; percentage of men working out three or more times per week; percentage of urologists per 100,000 men; number of ED drug prescriptions filled in 2007. *Men's Health, "Ranking America's Cities: Cities that Need Viagara," April 2009*

- 50 of the largest metro areas in the U.S. were analyzed in terms of their health and fitness by the American College of Sports Medicine in their "American Fitness Index." The Atlanta metro area ranked #16 (#1 = healthiest). Criteria: preventative health behaviors; levels of chronic disease; health care access; community resources and policies that support physical activity. *American College of Sports Medicine, "Health and Community Fitness Status of the 50 Largest Metropolitan Areas," August 1, 2011*

- Atlanta was selected as one of the "20 Most Livable U.S. Cities for Wheelchair Users" by the Christopher & Dana Reeve Foundation. The city ranked #20. Criteria: Medicaid eligibility and spending; access to physicians and rehabilitation facilities; access to fitness facilities and recreation; access to paratransit; percentage of people living with disabilities who are employed; clean air; climate. *Christopher & Dana Reeve Foundation, "20 Most Livable U.S. Cities for Wheelchair Users," July 26, 2010*

Pet Rankings

- Atlanta was selected as one of the "Top 10 Cat-Friendly Cities" in the U.S. The area ranked #9. Criteria: cat ownership per capita; level of veterinary care; microchipping; cat-friendly local ordinances. *CATalyst Council, "Top 10 Cat-Friendly Cities," March 27, 2009*

Real Estate Rankings

- Atlanta was identified as one of 13 metro areas where home prices are falling dangerously. Criteria: home price change from October 2010 to September 2011; projected home price change through 2012. *Forbes.com, "Cities Where Home Prices are Falling Dangerously," January 10, 2012*

- Atlanta was identified as one of the best cities for home buyers in the U.S. The area ranked #1 out of 10. The affordability of home ownership was calculated by comparing the cost of renting vs. owning. Criteria: cost to rent as a percent of after-tax mortgage payment. *Fortune, "The 10 Best Cities for Buyers," April 11, 2011*

- *Fortune* ranked the 100 largest metro areas in the U.S. in terms of projected median home price change in 2010. The Atlanta metro area ranked #41. *Fortune, "The 2010 Housing Outlook," December 9, 2009*

- Atlanta was selected as one of the 10 best U.S. cities for real estate investment. The city ranked #9. *Association of Foreign Investors in Real Estate, "AFIRE News," January/February, 2011*

- The Atlanta was selected as one of the 10 U.S. metro areas that "Offer the Best Bang for Your Buck." The area ranked #6. Criteria: average home price per square foot. *CNBC, "Cities That Offer the Best Bang for Your Buck," December 15, 2011*

- The Atlanta metro area was identified as one of the 25 worst housing markets in the U.S. in 2011. The area ranked #4 out of 149 markets with a home price appreciation of -17.0%. Criteria: year-over-year change of median sales price of existing single-family homes between the 4th quarter of 2010 and the 4th quarter of 2011. *National Association of Realtors®, Median Sales Price of Existing Single-Family Homes for Metropolitan Areas, 4th Quarter 2011*

- Atlanta appeared on *ApartmentRatings.com* "Top Cities for Renters" list in 2009." The area ranked #52. Overall satisfaction ratings were ranked using thousands of user submitted scores for hundreds of apartment complexes located in the 100 most populated U.S. municipalities. *ApartmentRatings.com, "2009 Renter Satisfaction Rankings"*

- Atlanta appeared on *ApartmentRatings.com* "Top College Towns & Cities" for renters list in 2011." The area ranked #35 out of 87. Overall satisfaction ratings were ranked using thousands of user submitted scores for hundreds of apartment complexes located in cities and towns that are home to the 100 largest four-year institutions in the U.S. *ApartmentRatings.com, "2011 College Town Renter Satisfaction Rankings"*

- The nation's largest metro areas were analyzed in terms of the percentage of households entering some stage of foreclosure in 2011. The Atlanta metro area ranked #12 out of 20 (#1 = highest foreclosure rate). *RealtyTrac, 2011 Year-End Foreclosure Market Report, January 12, 2012*

- The nation's largest metro areas were analyzed in terms of the best places to buy bank-owned properties. The Atlanta metro area ranked #5 out of 10. Criteria: at least 500 REO sales during the fourth quarter and an REO sales increase of at least five percent from a year ago. The areas selected posted the biggest discounts on the sales of bank-owned properties. *RealtyTrac, "Fourth Quarter and Year-End 2011 U.S. Foreclosure Sales Report: Shifting Towards Short Sales," February 28, 2012*

- The nation's largest metro areas were analyzed in terms of the best places to buy pre-foreclosures (short sales). The Atlanta metro area ranked #4 out of 10. Criteria: at least 500 pre-foreclosure sales during the fourth quarter and a short sales increase of at least five percent from a year ago. The areas selected posted the biggest discounts on the sales of pre-foreclosure properties. *RealtyTrac, "Fourth Quarter and Year-End 2011 U.S. Foreclosure Sales Report: Shifting Towards Short Sales," February 28, 2012*

- The Atlanta metro area appeared in a *Wall Street Journal* article ranking cities by "housing stress." The metro area was ranked #18 (#1 = most stress). Criteria: fraction of mortgage-holding homeowners with a monthly housing payment in excess of 30 percent of income; percentage of people without health insurance; unemployment rate. *The Wall Street Journal, "Which Cities Face Biggest Housing Risk," October 5, 2010*

- The Center for Housing Policy ranked 210 U.S. metropolitan areas by the fair market rent for a two-bedroom unit. The Atlanta metro area was ranked #78. (#1 = most expensive) with a rent of $912. Criteria: Fair Market Rent (FMR) in effect during the fourth quarter of 2009 based on HUD's fiscal year 2010 FMRs. *The Center for Housing Policy, "Paycheck to Paycheck: Most to Least Expensive Rental Markets in 2009"*

- The Atlanta metro area was identified as one of the worst housing markets of the decade by *Forbes*. Criteria: decrease in housing values per square foot since January 2000. *Forbes, "America's 5 Best (and Worst) Housing Markets of the Decade," December 7, 2010*

- The Atlanta metro area was identified as one of the top 20 cities in terms of decreasing home equity. The metro area was ranked #15. Criteria: percentage of home equity relative to the home's current value. *Forbes.com, "Where Americans are Losing Home Equity Most," May 1, 2010*

- The Atlanta metro area was identified as one of the markets with the worst expected performance in home prices over the next 12 months. *Local Market Monitor, "First Quarter Home Price Forecast for Largest US Markets," March 2, 2011*

- The Atlanta metro area was identified as one of the best U.S. markets to invest in rental property" by HomeVestors and Local Market Monitor. The area ranked #9 out of 100. Criteria: risk-return premium relative to national average. *HomeVestors and Local Market Monitor, "Best 100 U.S. Markets to Invest in Rental Property," March 9, 2012*

Safety Rankings

- Symantec, the makers of Norton, in partnership with Sperling's BestPlaces, ranked the 50 largest cities in the U.S. in terms of their vulnerability to cybercrime. The city ranked #4. Criteria: number of cyberattacks and potential infections; level of Internet access; expenditures on smartphones and computer hardware/software; wireless hotspots; broadband connectivity; Internet usage; online purchases. *Symantec, "Riskiest Online Cities of 2012" February 15, 2012*

- Allstate ranked the 193 largest cities in America in terms of driver safety. Atlanta ranked #151. In addition, drivers were 26.4% more likely to have had an accident compared to the national average. Allstate researchers analyzed internal property damage reported claims over a two-year period (from January 2008 to December 2009) to protect findings from external influences such as weather or road construction. A weighted average of the two-year numbers determined the annual percentages. The report defines an auto crash as any collision resulting in a property damage claim. *Allstate, "2011 Allstate America's Best Drivers Report™"*

- Atlanta was identified as one of America's "11 Most Dangerous Cities" by *U.S. News & World Report*. The city ranked #2. Criteria: crime risk was calculated using the most recent seven years (2003-2009) of FBI crime reporting data. The data includes both property crimes and violent crimes. *U.S. News & World Report, "The 11 Most Dangerous Cities," February 16, 2011*

- Atlanta was identified as one of the most dangerous large cities in America by CQ Press. All 34 cities with populations of 500,000 or more that reported crime rates in 2010 for murder, rape, robbery, aggravated assault, burglary, and motor vehicle thefts were ranked. The city ranked #5 out of the top 10. *CQ Press, City Crime Rankings 2011-2012*

- The National Insurance Crime Bureau ranked 366 metro areas in the U.S. in terms of per capita rates of vehicle theft. The Atlanta metro area ranked #30 (#1 = highest rate). Criteria: number of vehicle theft offenses per 100,000 inhabitants in 2010. *National Insurance Crime Bureau, "Hot Spots," June 21, 2011*

- The Atlanta metro area was identified as one of the most dangerous metro areas for pedestrians by Transportation for America. The metro area ranked #11 out of 52 metro areas with over 1 million residents. Criteria: area's population divided by the number of pedestrian fatalities in that area. *Transportation for America, "Dangerous by Design 2011"*

Seniors/Retirement Rankings

- Bankers Life and Casualty Company, in partnership with Sperling's BestPlaces, ranked the nation's 50 largest metro areas in terms of the "Best U.S. Cities for Seniors." The Atlanta metro area ranked #39. Criteria: healthcare; transportation; housing; environment; economy; health and longevity; social and spiritual life; crime. *Bankers Life and Casualty Company, Center for a Secure Retirement, "Best U.S. Cities for Seniors 2011," September 2011*

- The Atlanta metro area was identified as one of "America's Most Affordable Places to Retire" by *Forbes*. The metro area ranked #9. Criteria: housing affordability; inflation; number of persons over 65 who are employed; net migration for persons over 65; percent of persons over 65 living below poverty level; doctors per capita; number of citizens tapping their Medicare benefits per thousand people. *Forbes.com, "America's Most Affordable Places to Retire," September 5, 2008*

- The Atlanta metro area was identified as one of the "Best Places for Bargain Retirement Homes" by *Forbes*. The metro area ranked #8 out of 10. Criteria: low cost of living; stable home prices; low taxes; reasonable average home prices. *Forbes.com, "Best Places for Bargain Retirement Homes," January 12, 2011*

- The Atlanta metro area was selected as one of "America's Best Places to Grow Old" by *Forbes*. The area was ranked #9 out of 10. Criteria: housing affordability; inflationary pressures; number of persons over 65 who are currently employed; net migration for persons over 65; percent of seniors living below poverty level; doctors per capita; number of citizens tapping their Medicare benefits per 1,000 people. *Forbes, "America's Best Places to Grow Old," December 12, 2008*

- The Atlanta metro area was selected as one of "The 10 Most Affordable Cities for Long-Term Care" by *U.S. News & World Report*. Criteria: costs at nursing homes, assisted living facilities, and adult day health care facilities; cost for licensed home health aides. *U.S. News & World Report, "The 10 Most Affordable Cities for Long-Term Care," May 17, 2010*

Sports/Recreation Rankings

- Atlanta was selected as one of "America's Most Miserable Sports Cities" by *Forbes*. The city was ranked #1. Criteria: postseason losses; years since last title; ratio of cumulative seasons to championships won. Contenders were limited to cities with at least 75 total seasons of NFL, NBA, NHL and MLB play. *Forbes, "America's Most Miserable Sports Cities," February 28, 2012*

- Atlanta appeared on the *Sporting News* list of the "Best Sports Cities" for 2011. The area ranked #7 out of 271 cities in the U.S. *Sporting News* takes a 12-month snapshot of each city's sports, putting a heavy premium on regular-season won-lost records (from the most recently completed season). Other criteria include: playoff berths, bowl appearances and tournament bids; championships; applicable power ratings; quality of competition; overall fan fervor (measured in part by attendance); abundance of teams (rewarding quality over quantity); stadium and arena quality; ticket availability and prices; franchise ownership; and marquee appeal of athletes. *Sporting News, "Best Sports Cities 2011," October 4, 2011*

- Atlanta was selected as one of the most playful cities in the U.S. by KaBOOM! The organization's Playful City USA initiative is a national recognition program that honors cities and towns across the nation for a vision, plan and commitment to creating an agenda for play. Cities were recognized based on a pledge to five specific commitments to play: creating a local play commission or task force; designing an annual action plan for play; conducting a play space audit; outlining a financial investment in play for the current fiscal year; and proclaiming and celebrating an annual "play day." *KaBOOM! National Campaign for Play, "2011 Playful City USA Communities"*

- *Golf.com* and the research arm of the National Golf Foundation analyzed the 50 largest metropolitan areas in the U.S. in terms of golf. The Atlanta metro area ranked #8. Criteria: weather; affordability; quality of courses; accessibility; number of courses designed by esteemed architects; availability; crowdedness. *Golf.com, November 15, 2007*

Technology Rankings

- The Atlanta metro area was selected as one of "America's Most Wired Cities" by *Forbes*. The metro area was ranked #2 out of 20. Criteria: percentage of Internet users with high-speed access; number of companies providing high-speed Internet; number of public wireless hot spots. *Forbes, "America's Most Wired Cities," March 2, 2010*

- Scarborough Research, a leading market research firm, identified the Atlanta DMA (Designated Market Area) as one of the top markets for text messaging with more than 50% of cell phone subscribers age 18+ utilizing the text messaging feature on their phone. *Scarborough Research, November 24, 2008*

Transportation Rankings

- Atlanta was selected as one of the "Least Courteous Cities (Worst Road Rage)" in the U.S. by AutoVantage. The city ranked #4. Criteria: 2,518 consumers were interviewed in 25 major metropolitan areas about their views on road rage. *AutoVantage, "2009 AutoVantage Road Rage Survey"*

- The Atlanta metro area appeared on *Forbes* list of the best and worst cities for commuters. The metro area ranked #58 out of 60 (#1 is best). Criteria: travel time; road congestion; travel delays. *Forbes.com, "Best and Worst Cities for Commuters," February 16, 2010*

Women/Minorities Rankings

- *Women's Health* examined U.S. cities and identified the 100 best cities for women. Atlanta was ranked #39. Criteria: 30 categories were examined from obesity and breast cancer rates to commuting times and hours spent working out. *Women's Health, "Best Cities for Women 2012"*

- Atlanta was ranked #33 out of 100 metro areas in *SELF Magazine's* ranking of America's healthiest places for women." A panel of experts came up with more than 50 criteria including death and disease rates, environmental indicators, community resources, and lifestyle habits. *SELF Magazine, "Secrets of America's Healthiest Women," December 2008*

- Atlanta was selected as one of the "Gayest Cities in America" by *The Advocate*. The city ranked #9 out of 15. *The Advocate* used several different measures to establish "per capita queerness"—including a city's number of teams entered in the Gay Softball World Series, gay bookstores, openly gay elected officials and semifinalists in the International Mr. Leather Contest. *The Advocate, "Gayest Cities in America, 2012" January 2012*

- Atlanta appeared on *Black Enterprise's* list of the "Ten Best Cities for African Americans." The top picks were culled from more than 2,000 interactive surveys completed on *BlackEnterprise.com* and by editorial staff evaluation. The editors weighed the following criteria as it pertained to African Americans in each city: median household income; percentage of households earning more than $100,000; percentage of businesses owned; percentage of college graduates; unemployment rates; home loan rejections; and homeownership rates. *Black Enterprise, May 2007*

- The Atlanta metro area appeared on *Forbes'* list of the "Best Cities for Minority Entrepreneurs." The area ranked #9 out of 10. Criteria: 52 metropolitan statistical areas were examined. For each ethnicity (African Americans, Asians and Hispanics), the editors measured housing affordability, population growth, income growth, and entrepreneurship (per capita self-employment). *Forbes, "Best Cities for Minority Entrepreneurs," March 23, 2011*

Miscellaneous Rankings

- *Men's Health* ranked 100 U.S. cities by their level of sadness. Atlanta was ranked #87 (#1 = saddest city). Criteria: suicide rates; unemployment rates; percentage of households that use antidepressants; percent of population who report feeling blue all or most of the time. *Men's Health, "Frown Towns," November 28, 2011*

- Energizer Holdings, the makers of Edge® shave gel, in partnership with Sperling's BestPlaces, ranked 50 major metro areas in terms of everyday irritations. The Atlanta metro area ranked #1. Criteria: humidity levels; weather conditions; incidence of traffic delays and congestion; average commute times; frequency of flight delays and cancellations; rates of sleeplessness; underemployment; pollens and allergens; pests; comedy clubs per capita. *Energizer Holdings, "Most Irritation Prone Cities," July 23, 2010*

- Mars Chocolate North America, the makers of COMBOS®, in partnership with Sperling's BestPlaces, ranked 50 major metro areas in terms of their "manliness." The Atlanta metro area ranked #23. Criteria: number of professional sports teams; number of nearby NASCAR tracks and racing events; manly lifestyle; concentration of manly retail stores; manly occupations per capita; salty snack sales; "Board of Manliness" rankings. *Mars Chocolate North America, "America's Manliest Cities 2011," September 1, 2011*

- The Atlanta metro area appeared in *AutoMD.com's* ranking of the "Best and Worst Cities for Auto Repair." The metro area ranked #35 (#1 is best). The 50 most-populated metro areas in the U.S. were ranked on three critical factors: repair affordability; price disparity range; shop integrity factor. *AutoMD.com, "Advocacy for Repair Shop Fairness Report," February 24, 2010*

- Atlanta was selected as one of America's "10 Meanest Cities" by the National Coalition for the Homeless and The National Law Center on Homelessness & Poverty. The city was ranked #4. Criteria: the number of anti-homeless laws; the enforcement of those laws and severity of penalties; the general political climate towards homeless people; local advocate support for the meanest designation; the city's history of criminalization measures; and the existence of pending or recently enacted criminalization legislation in the city. *National Coalition for the Homeless and The National Law Center on Homelessness & Poverty, "Homes Not Handcuffs: The Criminalization of Homelessness in U.S. Cities," July 2009*

Business Environment

CITY FINANCES

City Government Finances

Component	2009 ($000)	2009 ($ per capita)
Total Revenues	1,547,903	2,982
Total Expenditures	2,396,558	4,616
Debt Outstanding	7,245,557	13,957
Cash and Securities[1]	5,089,567	9,804

Note: (1) Cash and security holdings of a government at the close of its fiscal year, including those of its dependent agencies, utilities, and liquor stores.
Source: U.S Census Bureau, State & Local Government Finances 2009

City Government Revenue by Source

Source	2009 ($000)	2009 ($ per capita)
General Revenue		
From Federal Government	37,044	71
From State Government	14,959	29
From Local Governments	88,344	170
Taxes		
Property	266,495	513
Sales and Gross Receipts	129,917	250
Personal Income	0	0
Corporate Income	0	0
Motor Vehicle License	0	0
Other Taxes	71,424	138
Current Charges	824,898	1,589
Liquor Store	0	0
Utility	219,579	423
Employee Retirement	-204,803	-395

Source: U.S Census Bureau, State & Local Government Finances 2009

City Government Expenditures by Function

Function	2009 ($000)	2009 ($ per capita)	2009 (%)
General Direct Expenditures			
Air Transportation	758,053	1,460	31.6
Corrections	36,503	70	1.5
Education	0	0	0.0
Employment Security Administration	0	0	0.0
Financial Administration	32,891	63	1.4
Fire Protection	84,619	163	3.5
General Public Buildings	26,384	51	1.1
Governmental Administration, Other	110,361	213	4.6
Health	925	2	0.0
Highways	41,357	80	1.7
Hospitals	0	0	0.0
Housing and Community Development	17,624	34	0.7
Interest on General Debt	117,130	226	4.9
Judicial and Legal	13,559	26	0.6
Libraries	0	0	0.0
Parking	0	0	0.0
Parks and Recreation	80,758	156	3.4
Police Protection	172,900	333	7.2
Public Welfare	15,623	30	0.7
Sewerage	218,138	420	9.1
Solid Waste Management	43,616	84	1.8
Veterans' Services	0	0	0.0
Liquor Store	0	0	0.0
Utility	350,884	676	14.6
Employee Retirement	143,370	276	6.0

Source: U.S Census Bureau, State & Local Government Finances 2009

Municipal Bond Ratings

Area	Moody's	S&P	Fitch
City	A1	A	w/d

Rating Systems (shown in declining order of credit quality): Moody's– Aaa, Aa, A, Baa, Ba, B, Caa, Ca, C (numerical modifiers 1, 2, and 3 are added to letter-rating); S&P– AAA, AA, A, BBB, BB, B, CCC, CC, C; Fitch– AAA, AA, A, BBB, BB, B, CCC, CC, C. Ratings may be modified by the addition of a plus or minus sign to show relative standing within the major rating categories.

Notes: n/a Not Available; w/d Withdrawn (1) Not Reviewed; (2) Issuer Rating/No General Obligation; (3) Standard and Poor's Issue Credit Rating (ICR) is a current opinion of an obliger with respect to a specific financial obligation, a specific class of financial obligations, or a specific financial program.

Source: U.S. Census Bureau, 2012 Statistical Abstract, Bond Ratings for City Governments by Largest Cities: 2010

DEMOGRAPHICS

Population Growth

Area	1990 Census	2000 Census	2010 Census	Population Growth (%) 1990-2000	Population Growth (%) 2000-2010
City	394,092	416,474	420,003	5.7	0.8
MSA[1]	3,069,411	4,247,981	5,268,860	38.4	24.0
U.S.	248,709,873	281,421,906	308,745,538	13.2	9.7

Note: (1) Figures cover the Atlanta-Sandy Springs-Marietta, GA Metropolitan Statistical Area—see Appendix B for areas included
Source: U.S. Census Bureau, 2010 Census

Household Size

Area	Persons in Household (%) One	Two	Three	Four	Five	Six	Seven or More	Average Household Size
City	44.0	29.1	11.9	8.0	3.8	1.6	1.5	2.11
MSA[1]	25.3	30.2	17.3	15.1	7.2	2.9	2.1	2.68
U.S.	26.7	32.8	16.1	13.4	6.5	2.6	1.9	2.58

Note: (1) Figures cover the Atlanta-Sandy Springs-Marietta, GA Metropolitan Statistical Area—see Appendix B for areas included
Source: U.S. Census Bureau, 2010 Census

Race

Area	White Alone[2] (%)	Black Alone[2] (%)	Asian Alone[2] (%)	AIAN[3] Alone[2] (%)	NHOPI[4] Alone[2] (%)	Other Race Alone[2] (%)	Two or More Races (%)
City	38.4	54.0	3.1	0.2	0.0	2.2	2.0
MSA[1]	55.4	32.4	4.8	0.3	0.1	4.5	2.4
U.S.	72.4	12.6	4.8	0.9	0.2	6.2	2.9

Note: (1) Figures cover the Atlanta-Sandy Springs-Marietta, GA Metropolitan Statistical Area—see Appendix B for areas included; (2) Alone is defined as not being in combination with one or more other races; (3) American Indian and Alaska Native; (4) Native Hawaiian and Other Pacific Islander
Source: U.S. Census Bureau, 2010 Census

Hispanic or Latino Origin

Area	Hispanic or Latino (%)	Mexican (%)	Puerto Rican (%)	Cuban (%)	Other Hispanic or Latino (%)
City	5.2	2.8	0.5	0.3	1.5
MSA[1]	10.4	6.0	0.8	0.3	3.3
U.S.	16.3	10.3	1.5	0.6	4.0

Note: Persons of Hispanic or Latino origin can be of any race; (1) Figures cover the Atlanta-Sandy Springs-Marietta, GA Metropolitan Statistical Area—see Appendix B for areas included
Source: U.S. Census Bureau, 2010 Census

Segregation

Type	Segregation Indices[1]				Percent Change		
	1990	2000	2010	2010 Rank[2]	1990-2000	1990-2010	2000-2010
Black/White	66.3	64.3	59.0	41	-2.0	-7.2	-5.3
Asian/White	42.5	46.9	48.5	10	4.4	6.0	1.5
Hispanic/White	35.3	51.6	49.5	27	16.3	14.1	-2.1

Note: Figures are based on an analysis of 1990, 2000, and 2010 Census Decennial Census tract data by William H. Frey, Brookings Institution and the University of Michigan Social Science Data Analysis Network. In this analysis all racial groups (whites, blacks, and asians) are non-Hispanic members of those races. Hispanics are shown as a separate category; All figures cover the Metropolitan Statistical Area (see Appendix B for areas included); (1) Segregation Indices are Dissimilarity Indices that measure the degree to which the minority group is distributed differently than whites across census tracts. They range from 0 (complete integration) to 100 (complete segregation) where the value indicates the percentage of the minority group that needs to move to be distributed exactly like whites; (2) Ranges from 1 (most segregated) to 102 (least segregated); n/a not available.
Source: www.CensusScope.org

Ancestry

Area	German	Irish	English	American	Italian	Polish	French[2]	Scottish	Dutch
City	6.4	5.4	6.6	6.1	1.9	1.3	1.7	1.9	0.7
MSA[1]	8.1	8.2	8.1	8.9	2.7	1.3	1.6	1.9	0.9
U.S.	16.1	11.6	8.8	6.1	5.7	3.2	3.0	1.9	1.6

Note: Figures are the percentage of the total population reporting a particular ancestry. The nine most commonly reported ancestries in the U.S. are shown. Figures include multiple ancestries (e.g. if a person reported being Irish and Italian, they were included in both columns); (1) Figures cover the Atlanta-Sandy Springs-Marietta, GA Metropolitan Statistical Area—see Appendix B for areas included; (2) Excludes Basque
Source: U.S. Census Bureau, 2008-2010 American Community Survey 3-Year Estimates

Foreign-Born Population

Area	Percent of Population Born in								
	Any Foreign Country	Mexico	Asia	Europe	Carribean	South America	Central America[2]	Africa	Canada
City	7.8	1.9	2.4	1.2	0.6	0.5	0.3	0.5	0.2
MSA[1]	13.7	3.5	3.8	1.3	1.4	1.0	1.1	1.3	0.2
U.S.	12.8	3.8	3.6	1.6	1.2	0.9	1.0	0.5	0.3

Note: (1) Figures cover the Atlanta-Sandy Springs-Marietta, GA Metropolitan Statistical Area—see Appendix B for areas included; (2) Excludes Mexico.
Source: U.S. Census Bureau, 2008-2010 American Community Survey 3-Year Estimates

Marital Status

Area	Never Married	Now Married[2]	Separated	Widowed	Divorced
City	53.5	27.6	2.4	5.5	11.0
MSA[1]	32.7	49.6	2.3	4.6	10.9
U.S.	31.6	49.6	2.2	6.1	10.7

Note: Figures are percentages and cover the population 15 years of age and older; (1) Figures cover the Atlanta-Sandy Springs-Marietta, GA Metropolitan Statistical Area—see Appendix B for areas included; (2) Excludes separated
Source: U.S. Census Bureau, 2008-2010 American Community Survey 3-Year Estimates

Age

Area	Percent of Population							Median Age
	Under Age 5	Age 5 to 17	Age 18 to 34	Age 35 to 49	Age 50 to 64	Age 65 to 79	80 Years and Over	
City	6.4	13.0	34.1	21.2	15.5	7.2	2.6	32.9
MSA[1]	7.2	19.3	23.6	23.6	17.4	6.9	2.0	34.9
U.S.	6.5	17.5	23.2	20.7	19.0	9.4	3.6	37.2

Note: (1) Figures cover the Atlanta-Sandy Springs-Marietta, GA Metropolitan Statistical Area—see Appendix B for areas included
Source: U.S. Census Bureau, 2010 Census

Male/Female Ratio

Area	Males	Females	Males per 100 Females
City	208,968	211,035	99.0
MSA[1]	2,563,887	2,704,973	94.8
U.S.	151,781,326	156,964,212	96.7

Note: (1) Figures cover the Atlanta-Sandy Springs-Marietta, GA Metropolitan Statistical Area—see Appendix B for areas included
Source: U.S. Census Bureau, 2010 Census

Religious Groups

Area	Catholic	Baptist	Non-Den.	Methodist[2]	Lutheran	LDS[3]	Pentecostal	Presbyterian[4]	Muslim[5]	Judaism
MSA[1]	7.5	17.5	6.9	7.9	0.5	0.8	2.6	1.8	0.6	0.8
U.S.	19.1	9.3	4.0	4.0	2.3	2.0	1.9	1.6	0.8	0.7

Note: Figures are the number of adherents as a percentage of the total population; (1) Figures cover the Atlanta-Sandy Springs-Marietta, GA Metropolitan Statistical Area—see Appendix B for areas included; (2) Methodist/Pietist; (3) Latter Day Saints; (4) Reformed; (5) Figures are estimates
Source: Association of Statisticians of American Religious Bodies, 2010 U.S. Religion Census: Religious Congregations & Membership Study

ECONOMY

Gross Metropolitan Product

Area	2007	2008	2009	2010	2010 Rank[2]
MSA[1]	271.9	274.2	265.2	270.6	10

Note: Figures are in billions of dollars; (1) Figures cover the Atlanta-Sandy Springs-Marietta, GA Metropolitan Statistical Area—see Appendix B for areas included; (2) Rank ranges from 1 to 363
Source: The United States Conference of Mayors, "U.S. Metro Economies: GMP and Employment Forecasts," June 2011

Economic Growth

Area	2007-2009 (%)	2010 (%)	2011 (%)	Rank[2]
MSA[1]	-2.9	1.2	1.8	268
U.S.	-1.3	2.9	2.5	–

Note: Figures are real Gross Metropolitan Product growth rates and represent annual average percent change; (1) Figures cover the Atlanta-Sandy Springs-Marietta, GA Metropolitan Statistical Area—see Appendix B for areas included; (2) Rank ranges from 1 to 363
Source: The United States Conference of Mayors, "U.S. Metro Economies: GMP and Employment Forecasts," June 2011

Metropolitan Area Exports

Area	2005	2006	2007	2008	2009	2010	2010 Rank[2]
MSA[1]	11,063.0	11,393.6	12,551.0	14,432.9	13,405.9	15,009.7	18

Note: Figures are in millions of dollars; (1) Figures cover the Atlanta-Sandy Springs-Marietta, GA Metropolitan Statistical Area—see Appendix B for areas included; (2) Rank ranges from 1 to 369
Source: U.S. Department of Commerce, International Trade Administration, Office of Trade & Industry Information, Manufacturing & Services, data extracted April 2, 2012

INCOME

Income

Area	Per Capita ($)	Median Household ($)	Average Household ($)
City	34,475	44,771	77,979
MSA[1]	28,075	56,448	75,563
U.S.	26,942	51,222	70,116

Note: (1) Figures cover the Atlanta-Sandy Springs-Marietta, GA Metropolitan Statistical Area—see Appendix B for areas included
Source: U.S. Census Bureau, 2008-2010 American Community Survey 3-Year Estimates

Household Income Distribution

Area	Percent of Households Earning							
	Under $15,000	$15,000 -24,999	$25,000 -34,999	$35,000 -49,999	$50,000 -74,999	$75,000 -99,000	$100,000 -149,999	$150,000 and up
City	21.0	11.0	10.2	11.4	14.7	9.0	10.4	12.3
MSA[1]	11.1	9.2	10.1	13.8	19.3	12.9	13.6	10.2
U.S.	13.0	11.0	10.6	14.2	18.5	12.1	12.2	8.4

Note: (1) Figures cover the Atlanta-Sandy Springs-Marietta, GA Metropolitan Statistical Area—see Appendix B for areas included
Source: U.S. Census Bureau, 2008-2010 American Community Survey 3-Year Estimates

Poverty Rate

Area	All Ages	Under 18 Years Old	18 to 64 Years Old	65 Years and Over
City	23.8	35.3	20.9	20.8
MSA[1]	13.2	18.1	11.7	9.8
U.S.	14.4	20.1	13.1	9.4

Note: Figures are percentage of people whose income during the past 12 months was below the poverty level; (1) Figures cover the Atlanta-Sandy Springs-Marietta, GA Metropolitan Statistical Area—see Appendix B for areas included
Source: U.S. Census Bureau, 2008-2010 American Community Survey 3-Year Estimates

Personal Bankruptcy Filing Rate

Area	2006	2007	2008	2009	2010	2011
Fulton County	3.78	4.89	5.68	7.45	8.21	7.68
U.S.	2.00	2.73	3.53	4.61	4.97	4.37

Note: Numbers are per 1,000 population and include Chapter 7 and Chapter 13 filings
Source: Federal Deposit Insurance Corporation, Regional Economic Conditions, March 9, 2012

EMPLOYMENT

Labor Force and Employment

Area	Civilian Labor Force			Workers Employed		
	Dec. 2010	Dec. 2011	% Chg.	Dec. 2010	Dec. 2011	% Chg.
City	232,329	235,446	1.3	206,028	210,598	2.2
MSA[1]	2,661,869	2,697,848	1.4	2,391,846	2,444,914	2.2
U.S.	153,156,000	153,373,000	0.1	139,159,000	140,681,000	1.1

Note: Data is not seasonally adjusted and covers workers 16 years of age and older; (1) Metropolitan Statistical Area—see Appendix B for areas included
Source: Bureau of Labor Statistics, http://stats.bls.gov

Unemployment Rate

Area	2011											
	Jan.	Feb.	Mar.	Apr.	May	Jun.	Jul.	Aug.	Sep.	Oct.	Nov.	Dec.
City	11.5	11.2	10.7	10.5	10.6	11.7	11.5	11.7	11.5	11.0	10.3	10.6
MSA[1]	10.4	10.2	9.8	9.6	9.7	10.5	10.3	10.3	10.2	9.9	9.2	9.4
U.S.	9.8	9.5	9.2	8.7	8.7	9.3	9.3	9.1	8.8	8.5	8.2	8.3

Note: Data is not seasonally adjusted and covers workers 16 years of age and older; All figures are percentages; (1) Metropolitan Statistical Area—see Appendix B for areas included
Source: Bureau of Labor Statistics, http://stats.bls.gov

Projected Unemployment Rate

Area	2010 (%)	2011 (%)	2012 (%)	2013 (%)
MSA[1]	10.5	9.8	9.0	8.2

Note: (1) Metropolitan Statistical Area—see Appendix B for areas included
Source: The United States Conference of Mayors, "U.S. Metro Economies: GMP and Employment Forecasts," June 2011

Employment by Occupation

Occupation Classification	City (%)	MSA[1] (%)	U.S. (%)
Management, Business, Science, and Arts	48.1	38.7	35.6
Natural Resources, Construction, and Maintenance	5.2	8.8	9.5
Production, Transportation, and Material Moving	7.6	10.8	12.1
Sales and Office	23.5	26.7	25.2
Service	15.6	15.1	17.6

Note: Figures cover employed civilians 16 years of age and older; (1) Figures cover the Atlanta-Sandy Springs-Marietta, GA Metropolitan Statistical Area—see Appendix B for areas included
Source: U.S. Census Bureau, 2008-2010 American Community Survey 3-Year Estimates

Employment by Industry

Sector	MSA[1] Number of Employees	MSA[1] Percent of Total	U.S. Percent of Total
Construction	91,500	3.9	4.1
Education and Health Services	294,100	12.6	15.2
Financial Activities	138,800	5.9	5.8
Government	317,100	13.6	16.8
Information	79,000	3.4	2.0
Leisure and Hospitality	219,600	9.4	9.9
Manufacturing	148,100	6.3	8.9
Mining and Logging	1,300	0.1	0.6
Other Services	91,300	3.9	4.0
Professional and Business Services	411,700	17.6	13.3
Retail Trade	265,300	11.4	11.5
Transportation and Utilities	128,800	5.5	3.8
Wholesale Trade	147,500	6.3	4.2

Note: Figures cover non-farm employment as of December 2011 and are not seasonally adjusted; (1) Metropolitan Statistical Area—see Appendix B for areas included
Source: Bureau of Labor Statistics, http://stats.bls.gov

Occupations with Greatest Projected Employment Growth: 2008 – 2018

Occupation[1]	2008 Employment	2018 Projected Employment	Numeric Employment Change	Percent Employment Change
Combined Food Preparation and Serving Workers, Including Fast Food	102,970	134,890	31,920	31.0
Retail Salespersons	156,260	186,090	29,830	19.1
Registered Nurses	66,610	90,440	23,830	35.8
Customer Service Representatives	99,680	122,990	23,310	23.4
Janitors and Cleaners, Except Maids and Housekeeping Cleaners	78,880	95,000	16,120	20.4
Waiters and Waitresses	66,470	82,520	16,050	24.1
Elementary School Teachers, Except Special Education	46,730	61,680	14,950	32.0
Office Clerks, General	86,710	101,420	14,710	17.0
Postsecondary Teachers	36,460	49,930	13,470	36.9
Management Analysts	50,150	62,340	12,190	24.3

Note: Projections cover Georgia; (1) Sorted by numeric employment change
Source: www.projectionscentral.com, State Occupational Projections, 2008–2018 Long-Term Projections

Fastest Growing Occupations: 2008 – 2018

Occupation[1]	2008 Employment	2018 Projected Employment	Numeric Employment Change	Percent Employment Change
Marriage and Family Therapists	260	470	210	80.8
Home Health Aides	11,010	18,230	7,220	65.6
Shoe and Leather Workers and Repairers	290	470	180	62.1
Skin Care Specialists	1,740	2,780	1,040	59.8
Actors	1,150	1,760	610	53.0
Network Systems and Data Communications Analysts	7,800	11,850	4,050	51.9
Makeup Artists, Theatrical and Performance	270	410	140	51.9
Manicurists and Pedicurists	540	810	270	50.0
Mental Health Counselors	1,860	2,730	870	46.8
Physical Therapist Assistants	1,030	1,510	480	46.6

Note: Projections cover Georgia; (1) Sorted by percent employment change and excludes occupations with numeric employment change less than 100
Source: www.projectionscentral.com, State Occupational Projections, 2008–2018 Long-Term Projections

Average Wages

Occupation	$/Hr.	Occupation	$/Hr.
Accountants and Auditors	34.96	Maids and Housekeeping Cleaners	9.18
Automotive Mechanics	18.96	Maintenance and Repair Workers	17.74
Bookkeepers	17.81	Marketing Managers	58.21
Carpenters	19.36	Nuclear Medicine Technologists	32.61
Cashiers	9.39	Nurses, Licensed Practical	18.73
Clerks, General Office	12.78	Nurses, Registered	31.13
Clerks, Receptionists/Information	12.76	Nursing Aides/Orderlies/Attendants	11.18
Clerks, Shipping/Receiving	14.54	Packers and Packagers, Hand	10.67
Computer Programmers	37.52	Physical Therapists	36.50
Computer Support Specialists	24.14	Postal Service Mail Carriers	24.66
Computer Systems Analysts	38.12	Real Estate Brokers	36.66
Cooks, Restaurant	10.65	Retail Salespersons	11.33
Dentists	98.25	Sales Reps., Exc. Tech./Scientific	31.30
Electrical Engineers	39.01	Sales Reps., Tech./Scientific	38.03
Electricians	21.62	Secretaries, Exc. Legal/Med./Exec.	15.54
Financial Managers	60.72	Security Guards	11.44
First-Line Supervisors/Managers, Sales	19.34	Surgeons	111.35
Food Preparation Workers	10.24	Teacher Assistants	10.10
General and Operations Managers	55.36	Teachers, Elementary School	26.10
Hairdressers/Cosmetologists	10.88	Teachers, Secondary School	26.30
Internists	92.73	Telemarketers	14.02
Janitors and Cleaners	11.33	Truck Drivers, Heavy/Tractor-Trailer	19.76
Landscaping/Groundskeeping Workers	12.62	Truck Drivers, Light/Delivery Svcs.	16.52
Lawyers	68.30	Waiters and Waitresses	9.63

Note: Wage data covers the Atlanta-Sandy Springs-Marietta, GA Metropolitan Statistical Area—see Appendix B for areas included. Hourly wages for elementary/secondary school teachers and teacher assistants were calculated by the editors from annual wage data assuming a 40 hour work week; n/a not available.
Source: Bureau of Labor Statistics, Metro Area Occupational Employment and Wage Estimates, May 2011

RESIDENTIAL REAL ESTATE

Building Permits

Area	Single-Family			Multi-Family			Total		
	2010	2011	Pct. Chg.	2010	2011	Pct. Chg.	2010	2011	Pct. Chg.
City	83	227	173.5	196	510	160.2	279	737	164.2
MSA[1]	6,384	6,214	-2.7	1,191	2,420	103.2	7,575	8,634	14.0
U.S.	447,311	418,498	-6.4	157,299	205,563	30.7	604,610	624,061	3.2

Note: (1) Metropolitan Statistical Area—see Appendix B for areas included; figures represent new, privately-owned housing units authorized (unadjusted data); All permit data are based on estimates with imputation.
Source: U.S. Census Bureau, Manufacturing, Mining, and Construction Statistics, Building Permits, 2010, 2011

Homeownership Rate

Area	2005 (%)	2006 (%)	2007 (%)	2008 (%)	2009 (%)	2010 (%)	2011 (%)
MSA[1]	66.4	67.9	66.4	67.5	67.7	67.2	65.8
U.S.	68.9	68.8	68.1	67.8	67.4	66.9	66.1

Note: (1) Metropolitan Statistical Area—see Appendix B for areas included
Source: U.S. Census Bureau, Housing Vacancies and Homeownership Annual Statistics: 2011

Housing Vacancy Rates

Area	Gross Vacancy Rate[2] (%)			Year-Round Vacancy Rate[3] (%)			Rental Vacancy Rate[4] (%)			Homeowner Vacancy Rate[5] (%)		
	2009	2010	2011	2009	2010	2011	2009	2010	2011	2009	2010	2011
MSA[1]	13.0	11.7	12.8	12.8	11.4	12.4	16.6	13.8	11.6	4.1	3.0	4.3
U.S.	14.5	14.3	14.2	11.3	11.3	11.1	10.6	10.2	9.5	2.6	2.6	2.5

Note: (1) Metropolitan Statistical Area—see Appendix B for areas included; (2) The percentage of the total housing inventory that is vacant; (3) The percentage of the housing inventory (excluding seasonal units) that is year-round vacant; (4) The percentage of rental inventory that is vacant for rent; (5) The percentage of homeowner inventory that is vacant for sale
Source: U.S. Census Bureau, Housing Vacancies and Homeownership Annual Statistics: 2011

TAXES

State Corporate Income Tax Rates

State	Tax Rate (%)	Income Brackets ($)	Num. of Brackets	Financial Institution Tax Rate (%)[a]	Federal Income Tax Ded.
Georgia	6.0	Flat rate	1	6.0	No

Note: Tax rates as of January 1, 2012; (a) Rates listed are the corporate income tax rate applied to financial institutions or excise taxes based on income. Some states have other taxes based upon the value of deposits or shares.
Source: Federation of Tax Administrators, "State Corporate Income Tax Rates, 2012"

State Individual Income Tax Rates

State	Tax Rate (%)	Income Brackets ($)	Num. of Brackets	Personal Exempt. ($)[1] Single	Personal Exempt. ($)[1] Dependents	Fed. Inc. Tax Ded.
Georgia	1.0 - 6.0	750 (h) - 7,001 (h)	6	2,700	3,000	No

Note: Tax rates as of January 1, 2012; Local- and county-level taxes are not included; n/a not applicable; (1) Married joint filers generally receive double the single exemption; (h) The Georgia income brackets reported are for single individuals. For married couples filing jointly, the same tax rates apply to income brackets ranging from $1,000, to $10,000.
Source: Federation of Tax Administrators, "State Individual Income Tax Rates, 2012"

Various State and Local Tax Rates

State	State and Local Sales and Use (%)	State Sales and Use (%)	Gasoline[1] (¢/gal.)	Cigarette[2] ($/pack)	Spirits[3] ($/gal.)	Wine[4] ($/gal.)	Beer[5] ($/gal.)
Georgia	8.0	4.00	29.4	0.37	3.79	1.51	1.01 (n)

Note: All tax rates as of January 1, 2012 except beer, wine and spirits (September 1, 2011); (1) The American Petroleum Institute has developed a methodology for determining the average tax rate on a gallon of fuel. Rates may include any of the following: excise taxes, environmental fees, storage tank fees, other fees or taxes, general sales tax, and local taxes. In states where gasoline is subject to the general sales tax, or where the fuel tax is based on the average sale price, the average rate determined by API is sensitive to changes in the price of gasoline. States that fully or partially apply general sales taxes to gasoline: CA, CO, GA, IL, IN, MI, NY; (2) The federal excise tax of $1.0066 per pack and local taxes are not included; (3) Rates are those applicable to off-premise sales of 40% alcohol by volume (a.b.v.) distilled spirits in 750ml containers. Local excise taxes are excluded; (4) Rates are those applicable to off-premise sales of 11% a.b.v. non-carbonated wine in 750ml containers; (5) Rates are those applicable to off-premise sales of 4.7% a.b.v. beer in 12 ounce containers; (n) Includes statewide local rate in Alabama ($0.52) and Georgia ($0.53).
Source: Tax Foundation, 2012 Facts & Figures: How Does Your State Compare?

State-Local Tax Burdens

Area	Rate (%)	Rank[1]	Per Capita Taxes Paid to Home State ($)	Total State and Local Per Capita Taxes Paid ($)	Per Capita Income ($)
Georgia	9.1	32	2,411	3,350	36,738
U.S. Average	9.8	-	3,057	4,160	42,539

Note: Figures cover 2009; (1) Rank ranges from 1 to 50 where 1 is highest tax burden
Source: Tax Foundation, State-Local Tax Burdens, All States, 2009

State Business Tax Climate Index Rankings

State	Overall Rank	Corporate Tax Index Rank	Individual Income Tax Index Rank	Sales Tax Index Rank	Unemployment Insurance Tax Index Rank	Property Tax Index Rank
Georgia	34	9	40	12	22	39

Note: The index is a measure of how each state's tax laws affect economic performance. The lower the rank, the more favorable a state's tax system is for business. States without a given tax are given a ranking of 1.
Source: Tax Foundation, Major Components of the State Business Tax Climate Index, FY 2012

COMMERCIAL REAL ESTATE

Office Market

Market Area	Inventory (sq. ft.)	Vacant (sq. ft.)	Vac. Rate (%)	Under Constr. (sq. ft.)	Asking Rent ($/sf/yr) Class A	Asking Rent ($/sf/yr) Class B
Atlanta	144,422,808	33,281,077	23.0	450,000	22.57	17.47

Source: Grubb & Ellis, Office Markets Trends, 4th Quarter 2011

Industrial Market

Market Area	Inventory (sq. ft.)	Vacant (sq. ft.)	Vac. Rate (%)	Under Constr. (sq. ft.)	Asking Rent ($/sf/yr) WH/Dist	Asking Rent ($/sf/yr) R&D/Flex
Atlanta	590,428,350	79,783,880	13.5	0	3.44	6.41

Source: Grubb & Ellis, Industrial Markets Trends, 4th Quarter 2011

COMMERCIAL UTILITIES

Typical Monthly Electric Bills

Area	Commercial Service ($/month) 1,500 kWh	Commercial Service ($/month) 40 kW demand 14,000 kWh	Industrial Service ($/month) 1,000 kW demand 200,000 kWh	Industrial Service ($/month) 50,000 kW demand 15,000,000 kWh
City	252	1,660	31,345	1,601,449
Average[1]	189	1,616	25,197	1,470,813

Note: Based on total rates in effect July 1, 2011; (1) average based on 184 utilities surveyed
Source: Edison Electric Institute, Typical Bills and Average Rates Report, Summer 2011

TRANSPORTATION

Means of Transportation to Work

Area	Car/Truck/Van Drove Alone	Car/Truck/Van Car-pooled	Public Transportation Bus	Public Transportation Subway	Public Transportation Railroad	Bicycle	Walked	Other Means	Worked at Home
City	66.0	8.1	9.3	2.8	0.4	0.8	4.4	1.7	6.5
MSA[1]	77.2	10.8	2.5	0.7	0.1	0.2	1.3	1.6	5.6
U.S.	76.0	10.2	2.7	1.7	0.5	0.5	2.8	1.3	4.2

Note: Figures are percentages and cover workers 16 years of age and older; (1) Figures cover the Atlanta-Sandy Springs-Marietta, GA Metropolitan Statistical Area—see Appendix B for areas included
Source: U.S. Census Bureau, 2008-2010 American Community Survey 3-Year Estimates

Travel Time to Work

Area	Less Than 10 Minutes	10 to 19 Minutes	20 to 29 Minutes	30 to 44 Minutes	45 to 59 Minutes	60 to 89 Minutes	90 Minutes or More
City	9.4	31.8	24.9	20.7	5.6	4.4	3.2
MSA[1]	8.2	23.5	20.3	24.6	11.6	8.7	3.1
U.S.	13.9	30.1	20.8	19.8	7.5	5.5	2.5

Note: Figures are percentages and include workers 16 years old and over; (1) Figures cover the Atlanta-Sandy Springs-Marietta, GA Metropolitan Statistical Area—see Appendix B for areas included
Source: U.S. Census Bureau, 2008-2010 American Community Survey 3-Year Estimates

Travel Time Index

Area	1985	1990	1995	2000	2005	2010
Urban Area[1]	1.10	1.13	1.20	1.25	1.28	1.23
Average[2]	1.11	1.16	1.18	1.21	1.25	1.20

Note: Travel Time Index—the ratio of travel time in the peak period to the travel time at free-flow conditions. A value of 1.30 indicates a 20-minute free-flow trip takes 26 minutes in the peak. Free-flow speeds (60 mph on freeways and 35 mph on principal arterials) are used as the comparison threshold; (1) Covers the Atlanta GA urban area; (2) average of 439 urban areas
Source: Texas Transportation Institute, Urban Mobility Report 2011, September 2011

Public Transportation

Agency Name / Mode of Transportation	Vehicles Operated in Maximum Service	Annual Unlinked Passenger Trips ('000)	Annual Passenger Miles ('000)
Metropolitan Atlanta Rapid Transit Authority (MARTA)			
Bus (directly operated)	491	68,008.9	272,622.5
Demand Response (directly operated)	135	508.2	6,865.9
Heavy Rail (directly operated)	188	77,732.0	493,205.6

Source: Federal Transit Administration, National Transit Database, 2010

Air Transportation

Airport Name and Code / Type of Service	Passenger Airlines[1]	Passenger Enplanements	Freight Carriers[2]	Freight (lbs.)
Hartsfield-Jackson Atlanta International Airport (ATL)				
Domestic service (U.S. carriers - 2011)	35	39,592,445	31	287,144,645
International service (U.S. carriers - 2010)	16	4,034,292	11	138,870,208

Note: (1) Includes all U.S.-based major, minor and commuter airlines that carried at least one passenger during the year; (2) Includes all U.S.-based airlines and freight carriers that transported at least one pound of freight during the year
Source: Bureau of Transportation Statistics, The Intermodal Transportation Database, Air Carriers: T-100 Domestic Market (U.S. Carriers), 2011; Bureau of Transportation Statistics, The Intermodal Transportation Database, Air Carriers: T-100 International Market (U.S. Carriers), 2010

Other Transportation Statistics

Major Highways:	I-20; I-75; I-85
Amtrak Service:	Yes
Major Waterways/Ports:	None

Source: Amtrak.com; Google Maps

BUSINESSES

Major Business Headquarters

Company Name	Rankings	
	Fortune[1]	Forbes[2]
Coca-Cola	70	-
Coca-Cola Enterprises	347	-
Cox Enterprises	-	14
Delta Air Lines	88	-
First Data	236	24
Genuine Parts	215	-
Home Depot	30	-
Newell Rubbermaid	397	-
RaceTrac Petroleum	-	54
Southern	147	-
SunTrust Banks	244	-
United Parcel Service	48	-

Note: (1) Fortune 500—companies that produce a 10-K are ranked 1 to 500 based on 2010 revenue; (2) all private companies with at least $2 billion in annual revenue are ranked 1 to 212; companies listed are headquartered in the city; dashes indicate no ranking
Source: Fortune, "Fortune 500," May 23, 2011; Forbes, "America's Largest Private Companies," November 16, 2011

Fast-Growing Businesses

According to *Inc.*, Atlanta is home to seven of America's 500 fastest-growing private companies: **Sixthman** (#87); **UniqueSquared.com** (#110); **PalmerHouse Properties** (#172); **Capitol Media Solutions** (#239); **Vendormate** (#250); **LogFire** (#449); **M9 Solutions** (#456). Criteria: must be an independent, privately-held, for-profit, U.S. corporation, proprietorship or partnership; revenues must be at least $80,000 in 2007 and $2 million in 2010; must have four-year operating/sales history. Holding companies, regulated banks, and utilities were excluded. *Inc., "America's 500 Fastest-Growing Private Companies," September 2011*

According to *Fortune*, Atlanta is home to one of the 100 fastest-growing companies in the world: **Ebix** (#19). Companies were ranked by their revenue growth rate; their EPS growth rate; and their three-year annualized total return to investors for the period ending June 30, 2011. Criteria for inclusion: a company, foreign or domestic, must trade on a major U.S. stock exchange; must file quarterly reports with the SEC; must have a minimum market capitalization of $250 million; must have a stock price of at least $5 on June 30, 2011; must have been trading continuously since June 30, 2008; must have revenue and net income for the four quarters ended on or before April 30, 2011, of at least $50 million and $10 million, respectively; and must have posted a compound annual growth in revenue and earnings per share of at least 15% annually over the three years ending on or before April 30, 2011. REITs, limited-liability companies, limited partnerships, companies about to be acquired, and companies that lost money in the quarter ending April 30, 2011 were excluded. *Fortune, "100 Fastest-Growing Companies," September 26, 2011*

According to *Initiative for a Competitive Inner City (ICIC)*, Atlanta is home to one of America's 100 fastest-growing "inner city" companies: **Boulevard Group** (#73). Companies were ranked by their five-year compound annual growth rate. Criteria for inclusion: company must be headquartered in or have 51 percent or more of its physical operations in an economically distressed urban area; must be an independent, for-profit corporation, partnership or proprietorship; must have 10 or more employees and have a five-year sales history that includes sales of at least $200,000 in the base year and at least $1 million in the current year with no decrease in sales over the two most recent years. *Initiative for a Competitive Inner City (ICIC), "Inner City 100 Companies, 2011"*

According to Deloitte, Atlanta is home to four of North America's 500 fastest-growing high-technology companies: **Vocalocity** (#62); **Hughes Telematics** (#195); **Ebix** (#252); **Servigistics** (#491). Companies are ranked by percentage growth in revenue over a five-year period. Criteria for inclusion: company must be headquartered within North America; must own proprietary intellectual property or proprietary technology that contributes to a significant portion of the company's operating revenue, or devote a significant proportion of revenues to research and development of technology; must have been in business for a minumum of five years with 2006 operating revenues of at least $50,000 USD/CD and 2010 operating revenues of at least $5 million USD/CD. *Deloitte Touche Tohmatsu, 2011 Deloitte Technology Fast 500[TM]*

Minority Business Opportunity

Atlanta is home to five companies which are on the *Black Enterprise* Industrial/Service 100 list (100 largest companies based on gross sales): **H. J. Russell & Co.** (#15); **The Gourmet Companies** (#20); **B & S Electric Supply Co.** (#45); **Carter Brothers** (#61); **Jackmont Hospitality** (#72). Criteria: operational in previous calendar year; at least 51% black-owned and manufactures/owns the product it sells or provides industrial or consumer services. Brokerages, real estate firms and firms that provide professional services are not eligible. *Black Enterprise, B.E. 100s, 2011*

Atlanta is home to two companies which are on the *Black Enterprise* Auto Dealer 60 list (60 largest dealers based on gross sales): **Mercedes-Benz of Buckhead** (#14); **Malcolm Cunningham Automotive Group** (#32). Criteria: company must be operational in previous calendar year and be at least 51% black-owned. *Black Enterprise, B.E. 100s, 2011*

Atlanta is home to two companies which are on the *Black Enterprise* Bank 20 list (20 largest banks based on total assets, capital, deposits and loans, including mortgage-backed securities for the calendar year): **Citizens Bancshares Corporation** (#6); **Capitol City Bank & Trust Company** (#10). Only commercial banks or savings and loans that are classified by the Federal Reserve as black institutions and have been fully operational for the previous calendar year were considered. *Black Enterprise, B.E. 100s, 2011*

Atlanta is home to two companies which are on the *Black Enterprise* Asset Manager 15 list (15 largest asset management firms based on assets under management): **EARNEST Partners** (#3); **Herndon Capital Management** (#12). Criteria: company must have been operational in previous calendar year and be at least 51% black-owned. *Black Enterprise, B.E. 100s, 2011*

Atlanta is home to three companies which are on the *Hispanic Business* 500 list (500 largest U.S. Hispanic-owned companies based on 2010 revenue): **PS Energy Group** (#48); **CAPE** (#54); **Precision 2000** (#375). Companies included must show at least 51 percent ownership by Hispanic U.S. citizens, and must maintain headquarters in one of the 50 states or Washington, D.C. *Hispanic Business, "Hispanic Business 500," June 2011*

Minority- and Women-Owned Businesses

Group	All Firms		Firms with Paid Employees			
	Firms	Sales ($000)	Firms	Sales ($000)	Employees	Payroll ($000)
Asian	2,257	1,178,708	1,025	1,131,161	5,837	164,452
Black	15,738	1,256,723	981	895,035	7,367	230,657
Hispanic	1,240	415,116	200	356,231	2,051	78,188
Women	17,047	5,316,681	2,348	4,800,357	24,541	851,096
All Firms	50,966	105,935,888	12,824	103,541,309	347,658	19,829,323

Note: Figures cover firms located in the city; minority- and women-owned business are defined as firms in which the corresponding group own 51% or more of the stock or equity of the company
Source: U.S. Census Bureau, 2007 Economic Census, Survey of Business Owners

HOTELS

Hotels/Motels

Area	5 Star		4 Star		3 Star		2 Star		1 Star		Not Rated	
	Num.	Pct.[3]	Num.	Pct.[3]	Num.	Pct.[3]	Num.	Pct.[3]	Num.	Pct.[3]	Num.	Pct.[3]
City[1]	4	0.8	21	4.1	148	29.0	291	57.1	18	3.5	28	5.5
Total[2]	133	0.9	940	6.5	4,569	31.8	7,033	48.9	351	2.4	1,343	9.3

Note: (1) Figures cover Atlanta and vicinity; (2) Figures cover all 100 cities in this book; (3) Percentage of hotels which have a given star rating; Star ratings are determined by expedia.com and offer an indication of the general quality of a particular hotel.
Source: expedia.com, April 25, 2012

The Atlanta-Sandy Springs-Marietta, GA metro area is home to one of the best hotels in the U.S. according to *Travel & Leisure*: **Ritz-Carlton, Buckhead** (#188). Criteria: service; location; rooms; food; and value. *Travel & Leisure, "T+L 500, The World's Best Hotels 2012"*

The Atlanta-Sandy Springs-Marietta, GA metro area is home to two of the best hotels in the U.S. according to *Condé Nast Traveler*: **Ritz-Carlton Buckhead** (#66); **Mansion on Peachtree** (#80). The selections are based on over 25,000 responses to the magazine's annual Readers' Choice Survey. *Condé Nast Traveler, "2011 Readers' Choice Awards"*

EVENT SITES

Major Stadiums, Arenas, and Auditoriums

Name	Max. Capacity
Alexander Memorial Coliseum	9,191
B.T. Harvey Stadium	9,000
Bobby Dodd Stadium at Historic Grant Field	55,000
Boisfeuillet Jones Atlanta Civic Center	4,600
Forbes Arena	6,000
Georgia Dome	71,228
Philips Arena	21,000
Russ Chandler Stadium	4,157
Turner Field	50,096

Source: Original research

Convention Centers

Name	Overall Space (sq. ft.)	Exhibit Space (sq. ft.)	Meeting Space (sq. ft.)	Meeting Rooms
AmericasMart Atlanta	n/a	n/a	441,000	38
Cobb Galleria Centre	320,000	20,000	144,000	20
Georgia International Convention Center	n/a	16,000	150,000	n/a
Georgia World Congress Center	3,900,000	n/a	1,400,000	106

Note: n/a not available
Source: Original research

Living Environment

COST OF LIVING

Cost of Living Index

Composite Index	Groceries	Housing	Utilities	Trans-portation	Health Care	Misc. Goods/Services
97.4	101.7	89.4	93.4	102.1	101.0	101.8

Note: U.S. = 100; Figures cover the Atlanta GA urban area.
Source: The Council for Community and Economic Research, ACCRA Cost of Living Index, 2011

Grocery Prices

Area[1]	T-Bone Steak ($/pound)	Frying Chicken ($/pound)	Whole Milk ($/half gal.)	Eggs ($/dozen)	Orange Juice ($/64 oz.)	Coffee ($/11.5 oz.)
City[2]	9.79	1.16	2.12	1.65	3.35	4.30
Avg.	9.25	1.18	2.22	1.66	3.19	4.40
Min.	6.70	0.88	1.31	0.95	2.46	2.94
Max.	14.30	2.16	3.50	3.18	4.75	6.83

Note: (1) Values for the local area are compared with the average, minimum and maximum values for all 335 areas in the Cost of Living Index; (2) Figures cover the Atlanta GA urban area; **T-Bone Steak** *(price per pound);* **Frying Chicken** *(price per pound, whole fryer);* **Whole Milk** *(half gallon carton);* **Eggs** *(price per dozen, Grade A, large);* **Orange Juice** *(64 oz. Tropicana or Florida Natural);* **Coffee** *(11.5 oz. can, vacuum-packed, Maxwell House, Hills Bros, or Folgers).*
Source: The Council for Community and Economic Research, ACCRA Cost of Living Index, 2011

Housing and Utility Costs

Area[1]	New Home Price ($)	Apartment Rent ($/month)	All Electric ($/month)	Part Electric ($/month)	Other Energy ($/month)	Telephone ($/month)
City[2]	244,734	882	-	96.05	59.20	25.06
Avg.	285,990	839	163.23	89.00	77.52	26.92
Min.	188,005	460	125.58	45.39	33.89	17.98
Max.	1,197,028	3,244	339.16	181.97	348.69	40.01

Note: (1) Values for the local area are compared with the average, minimum and maximum values for all 335 areas in the Cost of Living Index; (2) Figures cover the Atlanta GA urban area; **New Home Price** *(2,400 sf living area, 8,000 sf lot, in urban area with full utilities);* **Apartment Rent** *(950 sf 2 bedroom/1.5 or 2 bath, unfurnished, excluding all utilities except water);* **All Electric** *(average monthly cost for an all-electric home);* **Part Electric** *(average monthly cost for a part-electric home);* **Other Energy** *(average monthly cost for natural gas, fuel oil, coal, wood, and any other forms of energy except electricity);* **Telephone** *(price includes basic monthly rate for a private residential line plus additional local usage charges incurred by a family of four).*
Source: The Council for Community and Economic Research, ACCRA Cost of Living Index, 2011

Health Care, Transportation, and Other Costs

Area[1]	Doctor ($/visit)	Dentist ($/visit)	Optometrist ($/visit)	Gasoline ($/gallon)	Beauty Salon ($/visit)	Men's Shirt ($)
City[2]	89.59	93.46	71.27	3.50	43.14	24.03
Avg.	93.88	81.72	90.54	3.48	32.65	25.06
Min.	60.00	55.33	53.66	3.18	19.78	13.44
Max.	154.98	145.97	183.72	4.31	63.21	46.00

Note: (1) Values for the local area are compared with the average, minimum and maximum values for all 335 areas in the Cost of Living Index; (2) Figures cover the Atlanta GA urban area; **Doctor** *(general practitioners routine exam of an established patient);* **Dentist** *(adult teeth cleaning and periodic oral examination);* **Optometrist** *(full vision eye exam for established adult patient);* **Gasoline** *(one gallon regular unleaded, national brand, including all taxes, cash price at self-service pump if available);* **Beauty Salon** *(woman's shampoo, trim, and blow-dry);* **Men's Shirt** *(cotton/polyester dress shirt, pinpoint weave, long sleeves).*
Source: The Council for Community and Economic Research, ACCRA Cost of Living Index, 2011

HOUSING

House Price Index (HPI)

Area	National Ranking[2]	Quarterly Change (%)	One-Year Change (%)	Five-Year Change (%)
MSA[1]	274	-0.43	-7.04	-19.74
U.S.[3]	-	-0.10	-2.43	-19.16

Note: The HPI is a weighted repeat sales index. It measures average price changes in repeat sales or refinancings on the same properties. This information is obtained by reviewing repeat mortgage transactions on single-family properties whose mortgages have been purchased or securitized by Fannie Mae or Freddie Mac in January 1975; (1) Metropolitan/Micropolitan Statistical Area—see Appendix B for areas included; (2) Rankings are based on annual percentage change for all metro areas containing at least 15,000 transactions over the last 10 years and ranges from 1 to 306; (3) figures based on a weighted average of Census Division estimates using a purchase only index; all figures are for the period ending December 31, 2011
Source: Federal Housing Finance Agency, House Price Index, February 23, 2012

House Price Valuations

Area	Q4 2005 Price ($000)	Over-valuation	Q4 2006 Price ($000)	Over-valuation	Q4 2007 Price ($000)	Over-valuation	Q4 2008 Price ($000)	Over-valuation	Q4 2009 Price ($000)	Over-valuation
MSA[1]	172.9	-3.4	177.0	-4.7	171.9	-10.7	153.2	-20.3	149.1	-21.9

Note: Figures show the percentage of over- or under-valuation of single family homes relative to statistically normal house values (e.g. a value of 23.6 indicates that house values are 23.6% overvalued). Statistically normal house values are based on house prices, interest rates, household incomes, population densities, and any historical premiums or discounts metropolitan areas have exhibited over time; (1) Figures cover the Atlanta-Sandy Springs-Marietta, GA - see Appendix B for areas included
Source: Global Insight/PNC Financial Services Group, House Prices in America: 4th Quarter 2009 Update

Median Single-Family Home Prices

Area	2009	2010	2011p	Percent Change 2010 to 2011
MSA[1]	123.5	114.8	98.6	-14.1
U.S. Average	172.1	173.1	166.2	-4.0

Note: Figures are median sales prices of existing single-family homes in thousands of dollars; (p) preliminary; n/a not available; (1) Metropolitan Statistical Area—see Appendix B for areas included
Source: National Association of Realtors, Median Sales Price of Existing Single-Family Homes for Metropolitan Areas, 4th Quarter 2011

Affordability Index of Existing Single-Family Homes

Area	2009	2010	2011p	Percent Change 2010 to 2011
MSA[1]	150.6	170.7	206.0	20.7

Note: The housing affordability index measures whether or not a typical family could qualify for a mortgage loan on a typical home. The higher the index, the greater the household purchasing power. An index of 100 is defined as the point where a median-income household has exactly enough income to qualify for the purchase of a median-priced existing single-family home, assuming a 20 percent downpayment and 25 percent of gross income devoted to mortgage principal and interest payments; (p) preliminary; n/a not available; (1) Metropolitan Statistical Area—see Appendix B for areas included
Source: National Association of Realtors, Affordability Index of Existing Single-Family Homes, 2011

Median Apartment Condo-Coop Home Prices

Area	2009	2010	2011p	Percent Change 2010 to 2011
MSA[1]	n/a	n/a	38.8	n/a
U.S. Average	175.6	171.7	165.1	-3.8

Note: Figures are median sales prices of existing apartment condo-coop homes in thousands of dollars; (p) preliminary; n/a not available; (1) Metropolitan Statistical Area—see Appendix B for areas included
Source: National Association of Realtors, Median Sales Price of Existing Apartment Condo-Coop Homes for Metropolitan Areas, 4th Quarter 2011

Year Housing Structure Built

Area	2005 or Later	2000 -2004	1990 -1999	1980 -1989	1970 -1979	1960 -1969	1950 -1959	Before 1950	Median Year
City	8.8	13.2	9.4	8.0	11.5	15.2	13.4	20.6	1971
MSA[1]	8.8	16.8	22.1	19.0	13.8	8.6	5.4	5.5	1989
U.S.	5.0	8.6	14.0	14.1	16.3	11.3	11.2	19.6	1975

Note: Figures are percentages except for Median Year; (1) Figures cover the Atlanta-Sandy Springs-Marietta, GA Metropolitan Statistical Area—see Appendix B for areas included
Source: U.S. Census Bureau, 2008-2010 American Community Survey 3-Year Estimates

HEALTH

Health Risk Data

Category	MSA[1] (%)	U.S. (%)
Adults who have been told they have high blood pressure[2]	27.4	28.7
Adults who have been told they have high blood cholesterol[2]	37.0	37.5
Adults who have been told they have diabetes[3]	8.7	8.7
Adults who have been told they have arthritis[2]	20.3	26.0
Adults who have been told they currently have asthma	8.9	9.1
Adults who are current smokers	14.9	17.3
Adults who are heavy drinkers[4]	4.1	5.0
Adults who are binge drinkers[5]	12.4	15.1
Adults who are overweight (BMI 25.0 - 29.9)	33.9	36.2
Adults who are obese (BMI 30.0 - 99.8)	28.7	27.5
Adults who participated in any physical activities in the past month	77.9	76.1
Adults 50+ who have ever had a sigmoidoscopy or colonoscopy	69.2	65.2
Women aged 40+ who have had a mammogram within the past two years	78.2	75.2
Men aged 40+ who have had a PSA test within the past two years	59.1	53.2
Adults aged 65+ who have had flu shot within the past year	58.3	67.5
Adults aged 18–64 who have any kind of health care coverage	82.8	82.2

Note: Data as of 2010 unless otherwise noted; (1) Figures cover the Atlanta-Sandy Springs-Marietta, GA Metropolitan Statistical Area—see Appendix B for areas included; (2) Data as of 2009; (3) Figures do not include pregnancy-related, borderline, or pre-diabetes; (4) Heavy drinkers are classified as males having more than two drinks per day or females having more than one drink per day; (5) Binge drinkers are classified as males having five or more drinks on one occasion or females having four or more drinks on one occasion
Source: Centers for Disease Control and Prevention, Behaviorial Risk Factor Surveillance System, SMART: Selected Metropolitan/Micropolitan Area Risk Trends, 2009, 2010

Mortality Rates for the Top 10 Causes of Death in the U.S.

ICD-10[a] Sub-Chapter	ICD-10[a] Code	Age-Adjusted Mortality Rate[1] per 100,000 population County[2]	U.S.
Malignant neoplasms	C00-C97	160.9	175.6
Ischaemic heart diseases	I20-I25	80.7	121.6
Other forms of heart disease	I30-I51	71.9	48.6
Chronic lower respiratory diseases	J40-J47	29.0	42.3
Cerebrovascular diseases	I60-I69	45.5	40.6
Organic, including symptomatic, mental disorders	F01-F09	49.3	26.7
Other degenerative diseases of the nervous system	G30-G31	19.5	24.7
Other external causes of accidental injury	W00-X59	24.4	24.4
Diabetes mellitus	E10-E14	16.9	21.7
Hypertensive diseases	I10-I15	40.1	18.2

Note: (a) ICD-10 = International Classification of Diseases 10th Revision; (1) Mortality rates are a three year average covering 2007-2009; (2) Figures cover Fulton County
Source: Centers for Disease Control and Prevention, National Center for Health Statistics. Underlying Cause of Death 1999-2009 on CDC WONDER Online Database, released 2012. Data for year 2009 are compiled from the Multiple Cause of Death File 2009, Series 20 No. 2O, 2012, Data for year 2008 are compiled from the Multiple Cause of Death File 2008, Series 20 No. 2N, 2011, Data for year 2007 are compiled from Multiple Cause of Death File 2007, Series 20 No. 2M, 2010.

Mortality Rates for Selected Causes of Death

ICD-10[a] Sub-Chapter	ICD-10[a] Code	Age-Adjusted Mortality Rate[1] per 100,000 population	
		County[2]	U.S.
Assault	X85-Y09	11.5	5.7
Human immunodeficiency virus (HIV) disease	B20-B24	15.2	3.3
Influenza and pneumonia	J09-J18	17.4	16.4
Intentional self-harm	X60-X84	7.8	11.5
Malnutrition	E40-E46	1.3	0.8
Obesity and other hyperalimentation	E65-E68	0.9	1.6
Transport accidents	V01-V99	11.4	13.7
Viral hepatitis	B15-B19	1.2	2.2

Note: (a) ICD-10 = International Classification of Diseases 10th Revision; (1) Mortality rates are a three year average covering 2007-2009; (2) Figures cover Fulton County
Source: Centers for Disease Control and Prevention, National Center for Health Statistics. Underlying Cause of Death 1999-2009 on CDC WONDER Online Database, released 2012. Data for year 2009 are compiled from the Multiple Cause of Death File 2009, Series 20 No. 2O, 2012, Data for year 2008 are compiled from the Multiple Cause of Death File 2008, Series 20 No. 2N, 2011, Data for year 2007 are compiled from Multiple Cause of Death File 2007, Series 20 No. 2M, 2010.

Distribution of Physicians and Dentists

Area[1]	Dentists[2]	D.O.[3]	M.D.[4]				
			Total	Family/ General Practice	Pediatrics	Medical Specialties	Surgical Specialties
Local (number)	563	80	3,160	185	226	1,163	862
Local (rate[5])	5.7	0.8	31.2	1.8	2.2	11.5	8.5
U.S. (rate[5])	4.5	1.9	18.3	2.5	1.4	6.8	4.1

Note: Data as of 2008 unless noted; (1) Local data covers Fulton County; (2) Data as of 2007; (3) Doctor of Osteopathic Medicine; (4) Includes active, non-federal, patient-care, office-based Doctors of Medicine; (5) rate per 10,000 population
Source: Area Resource File (ARF). 2009-2010 Release. U.S. Department of Health and Human Services, Health Resources and Services Administration, Bureau of Health Professions, Rockville, MD, August 2010

Best Hospitals

According to *U.S. News,* the Atlanta-Sandy Springs-Marietta, GA is home to four of the best hospitals in the U.S.: **Emory University Hospital** (9 specialties); **Piedmont Hospital** (1 specialty); **Shepherd Center** (1 specialty); **Wesley Woods Geriatric Hospital-Emory University Hospital** (1 specialty). The hospitals listed were highly ranked in at least one adult specialty. *U.S. News Online, "America's Best Hospitals 2011-12"*

According to *U.S. News,* the Atlanta-Sandy Springs-Marietta, GA is home to one of the best children's hospitals in the U.S.: **Children's Healthcare of Atlanta** (10 specialties). The hospital listed was highly ranked in at least one pediatric specialty. *U.S. News Online, "America's Best Children's Hospitals 2011-12"*

EDUCATION

Public School District Statistics

District Name	Schls	Pupils	Pupil/ Teacher Ratio	Minority Pupils[1] (%)	Free Lunch Eligible[2] (%)	IEP[3] (%)
Atlanta Public Schools	106	48,909	13.0	88.8	73.2	8.8
Fulton County	103	90,399	14.0	65.6	37.5	10.2

Note: Table includes school districts with 2,000 or more students; (1) Percentage of students that are not non-Hispanic white; (2) Percentage of students that are eligible for the free lunch program; (3) Percentage of students that have an Individualized Education Program.
Source: U.S. Department of Education, National Center for Education Statistics, Common Core of Data, Local Education Agency (School District) Universe Survey: School Year 2009-2010; U.S. Department of Education, National Center for Education Statistics, Common Core of Data, Public Elementary/Secondary School Universe Survey: School Year 2009-2010

Highest Level of Education

Area	Less than H.S.	H.S. Diploma	Some College, No Deg.	Associate Degree	Bachelors Degree	Masters Degree	Profess. School Degree	Doctorate Degree
City	13.4	21.0	16.3	3.8	27.5	11.5	4.4	2.1
MSA[1]	12.6	25.2	21.0	6.7	22.5	8.6	2.1	1.2
U.S.	14.7	28.4	21.3	7.6	17.6	7.2	1.9	1.2

Note: Figures cover persons age 25 and over; (1) Figures cover the Atlanta-Sandy Springs-Marietta, GA Metropolitan Statistical Area—see Appendix B for areas included
Source: U.S. Census Bureau, 2008-2010 American Community Survey 3-Year Estimates

Educational Attainment by Race

Area	High School Graduate or Higher (%)					Bachelor's Degree or Higher (%)				
	Total	White	Black	Asian	Hisp.[2]	Total	White	Black	Asian	Hisp.[2]
City	86.6	96.3	79.0	93.8	68.8	45.5	74.0	20.5	77.0	29.2
MSA[1]	87.4	89.0	88.1	87.4	59.0	34.5	38.4	26.3	52.9	15.7
U.S.	85.3	87.5	81.4	85.5	61.6	28.0	29.3	17.8	50.2	13.0

Note: Figures shown cover persons 25 years old and over; (1) Figures cover the Atlanta-Sandy Springs-Marietta, GA Metropolitan Statistical Area—see Appendix B for areas included; (2) People of Hispanic origin can be of any race
Source: U.S. Census Bureau, 2008-2010 American Community Survey 3-Year Estimates

School Enrollment by Grade and Control

Area	Preschool (%)		Kindergarten (%)		Grades 1 - 4 (%)		Grades 5 - 8 (%)		Grades 9 - 12 (%)	
	Public	Private	Public	Private	Public	Private	Public	Private	Public	Private
City	52.1	47.9	81.9	18.1	86.5	13.5	84.7	15.3	83.6	16.4
MSA[1]	48.3	51.7	86.0	14.0	89.7	10.3	89.1	10.9	90.2	9.8
U.S.	55.4	44.6	87.1	12.9	89.4	10.6	89.5	10.5	90.4	9.6

Note: Figures shown cover persons 3 years old and over; (1) Figures cover the Atlanta-Sandy Springs-Marietta, GA Metropolitan Statistical Area—see Appendix B for areas included
Source: U.S. Census Bureau, 2008-2010 American Community Survey 3-Year Estimates

Average Salaries of Public School Classroom Teachers

Area	2010-11		2011-12		Percent Change 2010-11 to 2011-12	Percent Change 2001-02 to 2011-12
	Dollars	Rank[1]	Dollars	Rank[1]		
Georgia	52,815	22	52,938	23	0.23	20.10
U.S. Average	55,623	-	56,643	-	1.83	26.8

Note: (1) State rank ranges from 1 to 51 where 1 indicates highest salary.
Source: National Education Association, Rankings & Estimates: Rankings of the States 2011 and Estimates of School Statistics 2012, December 2011

Higher Education

Four-Year Colleges			Two-Year Colleges			Medical Schools[1]	Law Schools[2]	Voc/ Tech[3]
Public	Private Non-profit	Private For-profit	Public	Private Non-profit	Private For-profit			
2	10	11	3	0	7	2	3	6

Note: Figures cover institutions located within the city limits and include main campuses only; (1) includes schools accredited by the Liaison Committee on Medical Education and the American Osteopathic Association's Commission on Osteopathic College Accreditation; (2) includes American Bar Association-accredited law schools; (3) includes all schools with programs that are less than 2 years.
Source: National Center for Education Statistics, Integrated Postsecondary Education System (IPEDS) Peer Analysis System, 2011-12; Association of American Medical Colleges, Member List, April 23, 2012; American Osteopathic Association, Member List, April 23, 2012; Law School Admission Council, Official Guide to ABA-Approved Law Schools Online, April 23, 2012

According to *U.S. News & World Report*, the Atlanta-Sandy Springs-Marietta, GA is home to two of the best national universities in the U.S.: **Emory University** (#20); **Georgia Institute of Technology** (#36). The indicators used to capture academic quality fall into a number of categories: assessment by administrators at peer institutions; retention of students; faculty resources; student selectivity; financial resources; alumni giving; high school counselor ratings of colleges; and graduation rate. *U.S. News & World Report, "America's Best Colleges 2012"*

According to *U.S. News & World Report,* the Atlanta-Sandy Springs-Marietta, GA is home to four of the best liberal arts colleges in the U.S.: **Spelman College** (#62); **Agnes Scott College** (#68); **Morehouse College** (#127); **Oglethorpe University** (#157). The indicators used to capture academic quality fall into a number of categories: assessment by administrators at peer institutions; retention of students; faculty resources; student selectivity; financial resources; alumni giving; high school counselor ratings of colleges; and graduation rate. *U.S. News & World Report, "America's Best Colleges 2012"*

According to *U.S. News & World Report,* the Atlanta-Sandy Springs-Marietta, GA is home to one of the best law schools in the U.S.: **Emory University** (#24). The rankings are based on a weighted average of 12 measures of quality: peer assessment score; assessment score by lawyers/judges; median LSAT scores; median undergrad GPA; acceptance rate; employment rates for graduates; placement success; bar passage rate; faculty resources; expenditures per student; student/faculty ratio; and library resources. *U.S. News & World Report, "America's Best Law Schools 2013"*

According to *Forbes,* the Atlanta-Sandy Springs-Marietta, GA is home to two of the best business schools in the U.S.: **Emory (Goizueta)** (#22); **Georgia Tech** (#43). The rankings are based on the return on investment that graduates of the Class of 2006 received (median salary five years after graduation). *Forbes, "Best Business Schools," August 3, 2011*

PRESIDENTIAL ELECTION

2008 Presidential Election Results

Area	Obama	McCain	Nader	Other
Fulton County	67.1	32.1	0.0	0.8
U.S.	52.9	45.6	0.6	0.9

Note: Results are percentages and may not add to 100% due to rounding
Source: Dave Leip's Atlas of U.S. Presidential Elections, www.uselectionatlas.org

EMPLOYERS

Major Employers

Company Name	Industry
Apartments.Com	Apartment locating service
Aquilex Holdings	Facilities support services
AT&T Corp.	Engineering services
Behavioral Health, Georgia Department of	Administration of public health programs
Clayton County Board of Education	Public elementary and secondary schools
County of Gwinnett	County commissioner
Delta Air Lines	Air transportation, scheduled
Georgia Department of Human Resoures	Administration of public health programs
Georgia Department of Transportation	Regulation, administration of transportation
Internal Revenue Service	Taxation department, government
Lockheed Martin Aeronautical Company	Aircraft
NCR Corporation	Calculating and accounting equipment
Progressive Logistics Services	Labor organizations
Robert Half International	Employment agencies
The Army, United States Department of	Army
The Coca-Cola Company	Bottled and canned soft drinks
The Fulton-Dekalb Hospital Authority	General medical and surgical hospitals
The Home Depot	Hardware stores
WellStar Kennestone Hospital	General medical and surgical hospitals
World Travel Partners Group	Travel agencies

Note: Companies shown are located within the Atlanta-Sandy Springs-Marietta, GA metropolitan area.
Source: Hoovers.com, data extracted April 25 2012

Best Companies to Work For

Alston & Bird; Children's Healthcare of Atlanta; Intercontinental Hotels Group, headquartered in Atlanta, are among "The 100 Best Companies to Work For." To pick the 100 Best Companies to Work For, *Fortune* partnered with the Great Place to Work Institute. Two hundred eighty firms participated in this year's survey. Two-thirds of a company's score is based on the results of the Institute's Trust Index survey, which is sent to a random sample of employees from each company. The questions related to attitudes about management's credibility, job satisfaction, and camaraderie. The other third of the scoring is based on the company's responses to the Institute's Culture Audit, which includes detailed questions about pay and benefit programs, and a series of open-ended questions about hiring practices, internal communication, training, recognition programs, and diversity efforts. Any company that is at least five years old with more than 1,000 U.S. employees is eligible. *Fortune, "The 100 Best Companies to Work For," February 6, 2012*

Children's Healthcare of Atlanta; Turner Broadcasting System, headquartered in Atlanta, are among the "100 Best Companies for Working Mothers." Criteria: workforce profile; benefits; child care; women's issues and advancement; flexible work; paid time off and leave; company culture; and work-life programs. This year *Working Mother* gave particular weight to workforce profile, paid time off and company culture. *Working Mother, "100 Best Companies 2011"*

Manheim, headquartered in Atlanta, is among the "50 Best Employers for Workers Over 50." Criteria: recruiting practices; opportunities for training, education, and career development; workplace accommodations; alternative work options, such as flexible scheduling, job sharing, and phased retirement; employee health and pension benefits; and retiree benefits. Employers with at least 50 employees based in the U.S. are eligible, including for-profit companies, not-for-profit organizations, and government employers. *AARP, "2011 AARP Best Employers for Workers Over 50"*

Coca-Cola Enterprises; Southern Co, headquartered in Atlanta, are among the "100 Best Places to Work in IT." To qualify, companies, both public and private, had to have a minimum of 50 IT employees and were selected based on average salary and bonus increases, the percentage of IT staffers promoted, IT staff turnover rates, training and development programs, and the percentage of women and minorities in IT staff and management positions. In addition, *Computerworld* looked at retention efforts, programs for recognizing and rewarding outstanding performances, and benefits such as flextime, elder care and child care, and reimbursement for college tuition and the cost of pursuing technology certifications. *Computerworld, "100 Best Places to Work in IT 2011"*

PUBLIC SAFETY

Crime Rate

Area	All Crimes	Violent Crimes				Property Crimes		
		Murder	Forcible Rape	Robbery	Aggrav. Assault	Burglary	Larceny -Theft	Motor Vehicle Theft
City	6,812.8	17.3	16.6	403.0	634.7	1,494.2	3,307.0	940.0
Suburbs[1]	3,554.7	4.9	21.3	122.0	193.5	898.1	2,007.3	307.5
Metro[2]	3,876.4	6.1	20.9	149.7	237.1	957.0	2,135.7	370.0
U.S.	3,345.5	4.8	27.5	119.1	252.3	699.6	2,003.5	238.8

Note: Figures are crimes per 100,000 population; (1) All areas within the metro area that are located outside the city limits; (2) Metropolitan Statistical Area—see Appendix B for areas included
Source: FBI Uniform Crime Reports, 2010

Hate Crimes

Area	Number of Quarters Reported	Bias Motivation				
		Race	Religion	Sexual Orientation	Ethnicity	Disability
City	4	3	0	1	0	0

Source: Federal Bureau of Investigation, Hate Crime Statistics 2010

Identity Theft Consumer Complaints

Area	Complaints	Complaints per 100,000 Population	Rank[2]
MSA[1]	7,787	147.5	11
U.S.	279,156	90.4	-

Note: (1) Metropolitan Statistical Area—see Appendix B for areas included; (2) Rank ranges from 1 to 384 where 1 indicates greatest number of identity theft complaints per 100,000 population
Source: Federal Trade Commission, Consumer Sentinel Network Data Book for January–December 2011

Fraud and Other Consumer Complaints

Area	Complaints	Complaints per 100,000 Population	Rank[2]
MSA[1]	24,636	466.7	201
U.S.	1,533,924	496.8	-

Note: (1) Metropolitan Statistical Area—see Appendix B for areas included; (2) Rank ranges from 1 to 384 where 1 indicates greatest number of fraud and other complaints per 100,000 population
Source: Federal Trade Commission, Consumer Sentinel Network Data Book for January–December 2011

RECREATION

Culture

Dance[1]	Theatre[1]	Instrumental Music[1]	Vocal Music[1]	Series/ Festivals	Museums	Zoos and Aquariums[2]
4	20	6	7	9	22	2

Note: (1) Number of professional performing groups; (2) AZA-accredited
Source: The Grey House Performing Arts Directory, 2011-2012; Official Museum Directory, 2011; American Association of Museums, AAM Member Museums, April 2012; Association of Zoos & Aquariums, AZA Member Zoos & Aquariums, April 2012

Professional Sports Teams

Team Name	League
Atlanta Braves	Major League Baseball (MLB)
Atlanta Falcons	National Football League (NFL)
Atlanta Hawks	National Basketball Association (NBA)

Note: Includes teams located in the Atlanta metro area.
Source: Original research

CLIMATE

Average and Extreme Temperatures

Temperature	Jan	Feb	Mar	Apr	May	Jun	Jul	Aug	Sep	Oct	Nov	Dec	Yr.
Extreme High (°F)	79	80	85	93	95	101	105	102	98	95	84	77	105
Average High (°F)	52	56	64	73	80	86	88	88	82	73	63	54	72
Average Temp. (°F)	43	46	53	62	70	77	79	79	73	63	53	45	62
Average Low (°F)	33	36	42	51	59	66	70	69	64	52	42	35	52
Extreme Low (°F)	-8	5	10	26	37	46	53	55	36	28	3	0	-8

Note: Figures cover the years 1945-1990
Source: National Climatic Data Center, International Station Meteorological Climate Summary, 9/96

Average Precipitation/Snowfall/Humidity

Precip./Humidity	Jan	Feb	Mar	Apr	May	Jun	Jul	Aug	Sep	Oct	Nov	Dec	Yr.
Avg. Precip. (in.)	4.7	4.6	5.7	4.3	4.0	3.5	5.1	3.6	3.4	2.8	3.8	4.2	49.8
Avg. Snowfall (in.)	1	1	Tr	Tr	0	0	0	0	0	0	Tr	Tr	2
Avg. Rel. Hum. 7am (%)	79	77	78	78	82	83	88	89	88	84	81	79	82
Avg. Rel. Hum. 4pm (%)	56	50	48	45	49	52	57	56	56	51	52	55	52

Note: Figures cover the years 1945-1990; Tr = Trace amounts (<0.05 in. of rain; <0.5 in. of snow)
Source: National Climatic Data Center, International Station Meteorological Climate Summary, 9/96

Weather Conditions

Temperature			Daytime Sky			Precipitation		
10°F & below	32°F & below	90°F & above	Clear	Partly cloudy	Cloudy	0.01 inch or more precip.	0.1 inch or more snow/ice	Thunder-storms
1	49	38	98	147	120	116	3	48

Note: Figures are average number of days per year and cover the years 1945-1990
Source: National Climatic Data Center, International Station Meteorological Climate Summary, 9/96

HAZARDOUS WASTE

Superfund Sites

Atlanta has no sites on the EPA's Superfund Final National Priorities List.
U.S. Environmental Protection Agency, Final National Priorities List, April 17, 2012

**AIR & WATER
QUALITY**

Air Quality Index

Area	Percent of Days when Air Quality was...[2]					AQI Statistics[2]	
	Good	Moderate	Unhealthy for Sensitive Groups	Unhealthy	Very Unhealthy	Maximum	Median
Area[1]	66.0	29.9	4.1	0.0	0.0	145	43

Note: Air Quality Index (AQI) is an index for reporting daily air quality. EPA calculates the AQI for five major air pollutants regulated by the Clean Air Act: ground-level ozone, particle pollution (aka particulate matter), carbon monoxide, sulfur dioxide, and nitrogen dioxide. The AQI runs from 0 to 500. The higher the AQI value, the greater the level of air pollution and the greater the health concern. There are six AQI categories: "Good" AQI is between 0 and 50. Air quality is considered satisfactory; "Moderate" AQI is between 51 and 100. Air quality is acceptable; "Unhealthy for Sensitive Groups" When AQI values are between 101 and 150, members of sensitive groups may experience health effects; "Unhealthy" When AQI values are between 151 and 200 everyone may begin to experience health effects; "Very Unhealthy" AQI values between 201 and 300 trigger a health alert; "Hazardous" AQI values over 300 trigger warnings of emergency conditions (not shown); (1) Data covers Fulton County; (2) Based on 365 days with AQI data in 2011.
Source: U.S. Environmental Protection Agency, AirData Report, 2011

Air Quality Index Pollutants

Area	Percent of Days when AQI Pollutant was...[2]					
	Carbon Monoxide	Nitrogen Dioxide	Ozone	Sulfur Dioxide	Particulate Matter 2.5	Particulate Matter 10
Area[1]	0.0	0.0	39.5	4.7	55.9	0.0

Note: The Air Quality Index (AQI) is an index for reporting daily air quality. EPA calculates the AQI for five major air pollutants regulated by the Clean Air Act: ground-level ozone, particle pollution (also known as particulate matter), carbon monoxide, sulfur dioxide, and nitrogen dioxide. The AQI runs from 0 to 500. The higher the AQI value, the greater the level of air pollution and the greater the health concern; (1) Data covers Fulton County; (2) Based on 365 days with AQI data in 2011.
Source: U.S. Environmental Protection Agency, AirData Report, 2011

Air Quality Index Trends

Area	Trend Sites (days)								All Sites (days)
	2003	2004	2005	2006	2007	2008	2009	2010	2010
MSA[1]	36	32	52	65	56	31	16	27	27

Note: Figures are the number of days the AQI value exceeded 100 in a given year. An AQI value greater than 100 indicates that air quality would have been in the unhealthful range on that day. Data from exceptional events are included. These counts are presented in two ways. First, the counts are based on sites having an adequate record of monitoring data during the trend period (trend sites). These counts represent the relative change in the number of days with AQI values greater than 100. In the last column, the counts are based on all sites with data in the most recent year (because it is possible for a site to have data in the most recent year but not enough data to be a trend site); (1) Data covers the Atlanta-Sandy Springs-Marietta, GA—see Appendix B for areas included
Source: U.S. Environmental Protection Agency, Air Quality Index Information, "Number of Days with Air Quality Index Values Greater than 100 at Trend Sites, 2000-2010, and at All Sites in 2010"

Maximum Air Pollutant Concentrations: Particulate Matter, Ozone, CO and Lead

	Particulate Matter 10 (ug/m³)	Particulate Matter 2.5 Wtd AM (ug/m³)	Particulate Matter 2.5 24-Hr (ug/m³)	Ozone (ppm)	Carbon Monoxide (ppm)	Lead (ug/m³)
MSA[1] Level	51	14.5	25	0.08	2	0.02
NAAQS[2]	150	15	35	0.075	9	0.15
Met NAAQS[2]	Yes	Yes	Yes	No	Yes	Yes

Note: Data from exceptional events are not included; (1) Data covers the Atlanta-Sandy Springs-Marietta, GA—see Appendix B for areas included; (2) National Ambient Air Quality Standards; ppm = parts per million; ug/m³ = micrograms per cubic meter; n/a not available
Concentrations: Particulate Matter 10 (coarse particulate)—highest second maximum 24-hour concentration; Particulate Matter 2.5 Wtd AM (fine particulate)—highest weighted annual mean concentration; Particulate Matter 2.5 24-Hour (fine particulate)—highest 98th percentile 24-hour concentration; Ozone—highest fourth daily maximum 8-hour concentration; Carbon Monoxide—highest second maximum non-overlapping 8-hour concentration; Lead—maximum running 3-month average
Source: U.S. Environmental Protection Agency, CBSA Factbook 2010, Air Quality Statistics by City, 2010

Maximum Air Pollutant Concentrations: Nitrogen Dioxide and Sulfur Dioxide

	Nitrogen Dioxide AM (ppb)	Nitrogen Dioxide 1-Hr (ppb)	Sulfur Dioxide AM (ppb)	Sulfur Dioxide 1-Hr (ppb)	Sulfur Dioxide 24-Hr (ppb)
MSA[1] Level	13.657	58	1.908	33	10
NAAQS[2]	53	100	30	75	140
Met NAAQS[2]	Yes	Yes	Yes	Yes	Yes

Note: Data from exceptional events are not included; (1) Data covers the Atlanta-Sandy Springs-Marietta, GA—see Appendix B for areas included; (2) National Ambient Air Quality Standards; ppb = parts per billion; n/a not available
Concentrations: Nitrogen Dioxide AM—highest arithmetic mean concentration; Nitrogen Dioxide 1-Hr—highest 98th percentile 1-hour daily maximum concentration; Sulfur Dioxide AM—highest annual mean concentration; Sulfur Dioxide 1-Hr—highest 99th percentile 1-hour daily maximum concentration; Sulfur Dioxide 24-Hr—highest second maximum 24-hour concentration
Source: U.S. Environmental Protection Agency, CBSA Factbook 2010, Air Quality Statistics by City, 2010

Drinking Water

Water System Name	Pop. Served	Primary Water Source Type	Violations[1] Health Based	Violations[1] Monitoring/ Reporting
Atlanta	650,000	Surface	0	1

Note: (1) Based on violation data from January 1, 2011 to December 31, 2011 (includes unresolved violations from earlier years)
Source: U.S. Environmental Protection Agency, Office of Ground Water and Drinking Water, Safe Drinking Water Information System (based on data extracted April 18, 2012)

Austin, Texas

Background

Starting out in 1730 as a peaceful Spanish mission on the north bank of the Colorado River in south-central Texas, Austin soon engaged in an imbroglio of territorial wars, beginning when the "Father of Texas," Stephen F. Austin, annexed the territory from Mexico in 1833 as his own. Later, the Republic of Texas named the territory Austin in honor of the colonizer, and conferred upon it state capital status. Challenges to this decision ensued, ranging from an invasion by the Mexican government to reclaim its land, to Sam Houston's call that the capital ought to move from Austin to Houston.

During peaceful times, however, Austin has been called the "City of the Violet Crown." Coined by the short story writer, William Sydney Porter, or O. Henry, the name refers to the purple mist that circles the surrounding hills of the Colorado River Valley.

This city of technological innovation is home to a strong computer and electronics industry. Austin offers more free wireless spots—including its city parks—per capita than any other city in the nation. Austin's technology focus has traditionally drawn numerous high-tech companies, including Dell, Inc., IBM Corp., Freescale Semiconductor, SolectronTexas LP, Advanced Micro Devices, and Silicon Laboratories. Samsung Electronics' major computer chip plant was built in Austin in the late 1990s with expansions and a new facility, nine football fields big, recently completed. It is the company's only semiconductor manufacturing plant located outside of Korea. Along with this technology growth has come the problem of increased traffic, especially on Interstate 35, the main highway linking the U.S. and Mexico. A recently developed 89-mile bypass has helped to relieve some of the traffic difficulties long associated with I-35. In May 2010, Facebook opened a sales and operations facility in the city.

In addition to its traditional business community, Austin is home to the main campus of the University of Texas. The university provides Austin with even further diverse lifestyles; today there is a solid mix of white-collar workers, students, professors, blue-collar workers, musicians and artists, and members of the booming tech industry who all call themselves Austinites.

The influx of young people centered on university life has contributed to the city's growth as a thriving live music scene. It is so important to the city that its local government maintains the Austin Music Commission to promote the local music industry.

Not only does the popular PBS music series Austin City Limits hail from the city, but also a notable industry conference takes place here each spring. The South by Southwest Conference (SXSW) showcases more than 2,000 performers at 90+ venues throughout the city. The growing film and interactive industries have been added to the conference in recent years.

The civic-minded city, whose mayor is working toward making Austin the nation's fittest city, is operating from a new city hall, which was completed in late 2004. The building, at about 115,000 square feet, is also home to a public plaza facing Town Lake. One of the town's cultural hubs, the Long Center for the Performing Arts, underwent renovation in 2006, and reopened in 2008.

It is most likely Austinites' pride in their creative and independent culture that has spawned a movement to keep the city from too much corporate development. The slogan "Keep Austin Weird" was adopted by the Austin Independent Business Alliance in 2003 as a way to promote local and alternative business.

The city sits at a desirable location along the Colorado River, and many recreational activities center on the water. For instance, Austin boasts three spring-fed swimming pools enjoyed by its residents, as well as the Lance Armstrong Crosstown Bikeway, named for the seven-time winner of the Tour de France. The city is working on a six-mile bike route through downtown Austin, which will add to the town's more than 100 miles of bike paths. There are dozens of projects currently either under construction or being planned for downtown Austin.

The climate of Austin is subtropical with hot summers. Winters are mild, with below-freezing temperatures occurring on an average of 25 days a year. Cold spells are short, seldom lasting more than two days. Daytime temperatures in summer are hot, while summer nights are usually pleasant.

Rankings

General Rankings

- The Austin metro area was selected as one of the best cities to relocate to in America by Sperling's BestPlaces. The metro area ranked #5 out of 10. Criteria: unemployment; cost of living; crime rates; population health; cultural events; economic stability. *Sperling's BestPlaces, www.BestPlaces.net, "The Best Cities to Relocate to in America," October 2010*

- The Austin metro area was selected one of America's "Best Cities to Live, Work and Play" by *Kiplinger's Personal Finance*. Criteria: population growth; percentage of workforce in the creative class (scientists, engineers, educators, writers, artists, entertainers, etc.); job quality; income growth; cost of living. *Kiplinger's Personal Finance, "Best Cities to Live, Work and Play," July 2008*

- The Austin metro area was selected one of America's "Best Cities" by *Kiplinger's Personal Finance*. Criteria: stable employment; income growth; cost of living; percentage of workforce in the creative class (scientists, engineers, educators, writers, artists, entertainers, etc.). *Kiplinger's Personal Finance, "Best Cities 2009: It's All About Jobs," July 2009*

- *Men's Health Living* ranked 100 U.S. cities in terms of quality of life. Austin was ranked #32 and received a grade of C+. Criteria: number of fitness facilities; air quality; number of physicians; male/female ratio; education levels; household income; cost of living. *Men's Health Living, Spring 2008*

- Austin was selected as one of America's best cities by *Bloomberg Businessweek*. The city ranked #12 out of 50. Criteria: number of restaurants, bars and museums per capita; number of colleges, libraries, and professional sports teams; income, poverty, unemployment, crime, and foreclosure rates; percent of population with bachelor's degrees; public school performance; park acres per capita; air quality. *BusinessWeek, "America's 50 Best Cities," September 20, 2011*

- Austin was selected as one of the "10 Best Cities for the Next Decade" by *Kiplinger's Personal Finance*. The city ranked #1. Criteria: innovation factor (smart people, great ideas, and collaboration between governments, universities, and businesses); economic growth and growth potential; creativity in music, arts and culture; neighborhoods and recreational facilities that rank high for "coolness." *Kiplinger's Personal Finance, "10 Best Cities for the Next Decade," July 2010*

- Austin appeared on RelocateAmerica's list of best places to live in America. The annual "Top 100 Places to Live" list recognizes the top communities as nominated by their residents & local businesses. RelocateAmerica's Research Group determines the list based on review of various data gathered for economic, employment, housing, education, industry, opportunity, environment and recreation along with feedback from area leaders and residents. *RelocateAmerica.com, "Top 100 Places to Live for 2011"*

- Austin was selected as one of "America's Top 10 Places to Live" by *RelocateAmerica.com*. The city ranked #1. Criteria: real estate and housing; economic health; recreation; safety; input from local residents, business and community leaders. *RelocateAmerica.com, "Top 10 Places to Live for 2011"*

- Austin was selected as one of "America's Favorite Cities." The city ranked #10 in the "Quality of Life and Visitor Experience" category. Respondents to an online survey were asked to rate 35 top urban destinations in the U.S. from a visitor's perspective. Criteria: noteworthy neighborhoods; skyline/views; public parks and outdoor access; cleanliness; public transportation and pedestrian friendliness; safety; weather; peace and quiet; people-watching; environmental friendliness. *Travelandleisure.com, "America's Favorite Cities 2010," November 2010*

- Austin was selected as one of "America's Favorite Cities." The city ranked #4 in the "People" category. Respondents to an online survey were asked to rate 35 top urban destinations in the U.S. from a visitor's perspective. Criteria: attractive; friendly; stylish; intelligent; athletic/active; diverse. *Travelandleisure.com, "America's Favorite Cities 2010," November 2010*

- Austin was selected as one of "America's Favorite Cities." The city ranked #2 in the "Nightlife" category. Respondents to an online survey were asked to rate 35 top urban destinations in the U.S. from a visitor's perspective. Criteria: cocktail hour; live music/concerts and bands; singles/bar scene. *Travelandleisure.com, "America's Favorite Cities 2010," November 2010*

Business/Finance Rankings

- *Forbes* ranked the largest metro areas in the U.S. in terms of the "Best Cities for Young Professionals." The Austin metro area ranked #11out of 15. Criteria: job growth; unemployment rate; median salary of college graduates age 24 to 34; cost of living; number of small businesses per capita; number of large companies; percentage of population 25 years of age and older with college degrees. *Forbes.com, "America's Best Cities for Young Professionals," July 12, 2011*

- The Austin metro area was identified as one of 10 "Cities Where the Recession is Easing." The metro area was ranked #1. Criteria: job growth; goods produced; home sale prices; unemployment rates. *Forbes.com, "Cities Where the Recession is Easing," March 3, 2010*

- Austin was identified as one of America's "10 Best Cities to Get a Job" by *U.S. News & World Report*. The city ranked #6. Criteria: number of available jobs; unemployment rate. *U.S. News & World Report, "10 Best Cities to Get a Job," February 1, 2011*

- Austin was identified as one of the top 25 U.S. cities with the most credit card debt by credit reporting bureau Experian. The city was ranked #8. *Experian, March 4, 2011*

- Austin was identified as one of the "Unhappiest Cities to Work in 2012" by *CareerBliss.com*, an online community for career advancement. The city ranked #9 out of 30. Criteria: independent company reviews from employees all over the country on: relationship with their boss and co-workers; work environment; job resources; growth opportunities; compensation; company culture; company reputation; daily tasks; job control over work performed on a daily basis. *CareerBliss.com, "Happiest and Unhappiest Cities to Work in 2012"*

- Austin was identified as one of the best cities for new college graduates. The city ranked #5. Criteria: cost of living; average annual salary; unemployment rate; number of employers looking to hire people at entry-level. *Business Week, "The Best Cities for New Grads," July 20, 2010*

- Austin was selected as one of the best metro areas for telecommuters in America. The area ranked #1 out of 11. Criteria: low cost of living; educational attainment; number of universities and libraries; literacy rates; personal fitness. *DailyFinance.com, "The 11 Best Cities for Telecommuters," December 2, 2010*

- Austin was selected as one of the best cities in the world for telecommuting. The city ranked #2. The editors at *Cartridge Save* (printer technology news, guides and reviews) identified the 20 best cities in which to be an at-home, tech-using employee. *Cartridge Save, "20 of the Best Cities in the World for Telecommuting," May 14, 2008*

- *American City Business Journals* ranked America's 261 largest cities in terms of their resident's wealth. Austin ranked #111. Criteria: per capita income; median household income; percentage of households with annual incomes of $200,000 or more; median home value. *American City Business Journals, "Where the Money Is: America's Wealth Centers," August 18, 2008*

- The Austin metro area appeared on the Milken Institute "2011 Best Performing Metros" list. Rank: #4 out of 200 large metro areas. Criteria: job growth; wage and salary growth; high-tech output growth. *Milken Institute, "2011 Best Performing Metros"*

- The Austin metro area was selected as one of the best cities for entrepreneurs in America by *Inc. Magazine*. Criteria: job-growth data for 335 metro areas was analyzed for: recent growth trend; mid-term growth; long-term trend; current year growth. The Austin metro area ranked #2 among large metro areas and #19 overall. *Inc. Magazine, "The Best Cities for Doing Business," July 2008*

- Austin was identified as one of the top 10 cities with the greatest number of *Inc. 500* companies per million residents. The city ranked #2. *Inc. Magazine, September 2008*

- Austin was ranked #42 out of 145 regions worldwide in terms of its "Knowledge Competitiveness Index." The index attempts to measure the knowledge-based development taking place throughout the world and is based on 19 measures of economic performance that indicate a region's ability to translate its knowledge capacity into economic value. *Centre for International Competitiveness, World Knowledge Competitiveness Index 2008*

- *Forbes* ranked the 200 most populous metro areas in the U.S. in terms of the "Best Places for Business and Careers." The Austin metro area was ranked #7. Criteria: costs (business and living); job growth (past and projected); income growth; educational attainment; projected economic growth; crime; cultural and recreational opportunities; net migration patterns; number of highly ranked colleges. *Forbes, "Best Places for Business and Careers," June 2011*

Children/Family Rankings

- Austin was selected as one of the 10 best cities to raise children in the U.S. by *KidFriendlyCities.org*. Criteria: education; environment; health; employment; crime; diversity; cost of living. *KidFriendlyCities.org, "Top Rated Kid/Family Friendly Cities 2009"*

- The Austin metro area was selected as one of the "Best Cities for Relocating Families" by Worldwide ERC and Primacy Relocation. The 2008 study looked at nearly 50 factors important to relocating families including: recent job growth; nearby top-ranked colleges; in-state tuition for four-year public colleges; population growth since 2000; pediatricians per 100,000 population; and a Green Living index. *Worldwide ERC and Primacy Relocation, "2008 Best Cities for Relocating Families"*

- *Fit Pregnancy* magazine ranked the 50 best U.S. cities in which to have a baby. Austin was ranked #9. Criteria: access to hospitals and doctors; affordability; birthing options; breastfeeding; child care; fertility laws/resources; maternal and infant health risk; parks/stroller friendliness; safety. *Fit Pregnancy, "The Best Cities in America to Have a Baby 2008"*

Culture/Performing Arts Rankings

- Austin was selected as one of 10 best U.S. cities to be a moviemaker. The city was ranked #2. Criteria: cost of living; average salary; unemployment rate; job growth; median home price; crime rate; number of film schools, festivals, movie-related vendors and local movie theaters; current production scene (i.e. production days, size of talent pool); financial incentives for shooting in a particular area. *MovieMaker Magazine, "Top 10 Cities to be a Moviemaker: 2012," January 16, 2012*

- Austin was selected as one of "America's Top 25 Arts Destinations." The city ranked #14 in the big city (population 500,000 and over) category. Criteria: readers' top choices for arts travel destinations based on the richness and variety of visual arts sites, activities and events. *American Style, "America's Top 25 Arts Destinations," May 2010*

Dating/Romance Rankings

- Austin was selected as one of the best cities for single women by *Rent.com*. The city ranked #3 of 10. Criteria: high single male-to-female ratio; lively nightlife; low divorce rate; low cost of living. *Rent.com, "Top 10 Cities for Single Women," August 19, 2011*

- Austin was selected as one of "America's Best Cities for Dating" by *Yahoo! Travel*. Criteria: high proportion of singles; excellent dating venues and/or stunning natural settings. *Yahoo! Travel, "America's Best Cities for Dating," February 7, 2012*

- Austin appeared on *Men's Health's* list of the most sex-happy cities in America. The city ranked #1 of 100. Criteria: condom sales; birth rates; sex toy sales; rates of chlamydia, gonorrhea, and syphilis. *Men's Health, "America's Most Sex-Happy Cities," October 2010*

- Austin was selected as one of the best cities for single women in America by *SingleMindedWomen.com*. The city ranked #10. Criteria: ratio of women to men; singles population; healthy lifestyle; employment opportunities; cost of living; access to travel; entertainment options; social opportunities. *SingleMindedWomen.com, "Top 10 Cities for Single Women," 2011*

- *Men's Health* ranked 100 U.S. cities in terms of best (and worst) marriages. Austin was ranked #84 (#1 = worst). Criteria: rate of failed marriages; stringency of divorce laws; percentage of population who've split; number of licensed marriage and family therapists. *Men's Health, "Splitsville, USA," May 2010*

- Eli Lily and Company, in partnership with Sperling's BestPlaces, ranked the nation's 50 largest metro areas in terms of the "Most Romantic Cities for Baby Boomers." The Austin metro area ranked #32. Criteria: marriage and divorce rates among baby boomers age 45 to 60; great restaurants; dance studios; chocolate, jewelry and flower sales. *Eli Lily and Company, "Most Romantic Cities for Baby Boomers," April 20, 2007*

- The Austin metro area was selected as one of the "Best Cities for Relocating Singles" by Worldwide ERC and Primacy Relocation. The area ranked #33 out of the 100 largest metro areas in the U.S. Criteria: recent job growth; recent singles population growth; overall population growth; affordable rental housing; cost-of-living index; expanded arts and recreation opportunities; ratio of single men and single women; affordability of quality higher education (including state residency requirements); diversity index; climate; population density. *Worldwide ERC and Primacy Relocation, "2008 Best Cities for Relocating Singles"*

- *Forbes* ranked the 40 most populous urbanized areas in the U.S. in terms of the "Best Cities for Singles." The Austin metro area ranked #11. Criteria: number of singles; cost of living alone; nightlife; culture; job growth; coolness; and online dating participation. *Forbes.com, "Best Cities for Singles," July 27, 2009*

Education Rankings

- *Men's Health* ranked 100 U.S. cities in terms of their education levels. Austin was ranked #31 (#1 = most educated city). Criteria: high school graduation rates; school enrollment; educational attainment; number of households who have outstanding student loans; number of households whose members have taken adult-education courses. *Men's Health, "Where School Is In: The Most and Least Educated Cities," September 12, 2011*

- Austin was selected as one of "America's Geekiest Cities" by *Forbes.com*. The city ranked #12 of 20. Criteria: percentage of workers with jobs in science, technology, engineering and mathematics. *Forbes.com, "America's Geekiest Cities," August 5, 2011*

- Austin was selected as one of "America's Most Literate Cities." The city ranked #22 out of the 75 largest U.S. cities. Criteria: number of booksellers; library resources; Internet resources; educational attainment; periodical publishing resources; newspaper circulation. *Central Connecticut State University, "America's Most Literate Cities 2011"*

- Austin was identified as one of the 100 "smartest" metro areas in the U.S. The area ranked #12. Criteria: the editors rated the collective brainpower of the 100 largest metro areas in the U.S. based on their residents' educational attainment. *American City Business Journals, April 14, 2008*

- Austin was identified as one of "America's Smartest Cities" by *The Daily Beast*. The metro area ranked #7 out of 55. The editors ranked metropolitan areas with one million or more residents on the following criteria: percentage of residents over age 25 with bachelor's or graduate degrees; non-fiction book sales; ratio of institutions of higher education; libraries per capita. *The Daily Beast, "America's Smartest Cities," October 24, 2010*

- Austin was identified as one of America's most inventive cities by *The Daily Beast*. The city ranked #14 out of 25. The 200 largest cities in the U.S. were ranked by the number of patents (applied and approved) per capita. *The Daily Beast, "The 25 Most Inventive Cities," October 2, 2011*

- Austin was identified as one of "America's Brainiest Bastions" by *Portfolio.com*. The metro area ranked #22 out of 200. *Portfolio.com* analyzed levels of educational attainment in the nation's 200 largest metropolitan areas. The editors established scores for five levels of educational attainment, based on relative earning power of adult workers age 25 or older. Scores were determined by comparing the median income for all workers with the median income for those workers at a specified educational level. *Portfolio.com, "America's Brainiest Bastions," December 1, 2010*

- Austin was identified as one of "America's Smartest Cities" by *CNNMoney.com*. The area ranked #6. Criteria: percentage of residents with bachelors or graduate degrees. *CNNMoney.com, "America's Smartest Cities," October 1, 2010*

- Austin was identified as one of America's smartest cities" by *Forbes*. The area ranked #24 out of 25. Criteria: percentage of the population age 25 and over with at least a bachelor's degree. *Forbes.com, "The Smartest Cities in America," February 8, 2008*

Environmental Rankings

- The Austin was identified as one of America's cities with the most ENERGY STAR certified buildings. The area ranked #18 out of 25. Criteria: number of ENERGY STAR labeled buildings in 2010. *U.S. Environmental Protection Agency, "Top Cities With the Most ENERGY STAR Certified Buildings," March 15, 2011*

- Austin was selected as one of 22 "Smarter Cities" for energy by the Natural Resources Defense Council. The city appeared as one of 12 cities in the large city (population 250,000 and over) category. Criteria: investment in green power; energy efficiency measures; conservation. *Natural Resources Defense Council, "2010 Smarter Cities," July 19, 2010*

- *American City Business Journal* ranked 43 metropolitan areas in terms of their "greenness." The Austin metro area ranked #4. Criteria: Forty-one metros in which *ACBJ* has business weeklies, plus Indianapolis and Cleveland, were ranked based on 20 different indicators such as adoption of green technologies, utilization of environmentally sound practices, and air and water quality. *American City Business Journals, "Green City Index," March 11, 2010*

- Austin was selected as one of "America's 50 Greenest Cities" by *Popular Science*. The city ranked #10. Criteria: electricity; transportation; green living; recycling and green perspective. *Popular Science, February 2008*

- 100 of the largest metro areas in the U.S. were analyzed in terms of their current drought severity. The Austin metro area ranked #98 (#1 = driest). The rankings were based on statistics such as long-term precipitation trends and patterns and the Palmer drought indices. *Sperling's BestPlaces, www.BestPlaces.net, "America's Drought-Riskiest Cities," November 2007*

- The Austin metro area appeared in *Country Home's* "Best Green Places" report. The area ranked #33 out of 379. Criteria: official energy policies; green power; green buildings; availability of fresh, locally grown food. *Country Home, "Best Green Places," 2008*

- Austin was highlighted as one of the top 25 cleanest metro areas for short-term particle pollution (24-hour PM 2.5) in the U.S. Monitors in these cities reported no days with unhealthful PM 2.5 levels. *American Lung Association, State of the Air 2011*

Food/Drink Rankings

- Austin was identified as one of "America's Drunkest Cities of 2011" by *The Daily Beast*. The city ranked #7 out of 25. Criteria: binge drinking; drinks consumed per month. *The Daily Beast, "Tipsy Towns: Where are America's Drunkest Cities?," December 31, 2011*

- Austin was selected as one of the seven best cities for barbeque by *U.S. News & World Report*. The city was ranked #5. *U.S. New & World Report, "America's Best BBQ Cities," February 29, 2012*

- Austin was selected as one of America's best cities for hamburgers by the readers of *Travel + Leisure* in their annual America's Favorite Cities survey. The city was ranked #5 out of 10. Criteria:. *Travel + Leisure, "America's Best Burger Cities," May 2011*

Health/Fitness Rankings

- The American Podiatric Medical Association and *Prevention* magazine ranked 100 American cities based on walkability. Nineteen walking criteria were evaluated including the percentage of adults who walk to work, number of parks per square mile, number of trails for walking and hiking, air pollution, use of mass transit, crime rate, pedestrian fatalities, and percentage of adults who walk for fitness. Austin ranked #23. *Prevention, "The Best Walking Cities of 2009," May 2009; American Podiatric Medical Association, "2009 Best Fitness-Walking Cities," April 7, 2009*

- Austin was selected as one of the 25 fittest cities in America by *Men's Fitness Online*. It ranked #12 out of America's 50 largest cities. Criteria: fitness centers and sport stores; nutrition; sports participation; TV viewing; overweight/sedentary; junk food; air quality; geography; commute; parks and open space; city recreational facilities; access to healthcare; motivation; mayor and city initiatives; state obesity initiatives. *Men's Fitness, "The Fittest and Fattest Cities in America," March 5, 2012*

- Austin was identified as a "2011 Asthma Capital." The area ranked #94 out of the nation's 100 largest metropolitan areas. Twelve factors were used to identify the most challenging places to live for people with asthma: estimated prevalence; self-reported prevalence; crude death rate for asthma; annual pollen score; annual air quality; public smoking laws; number of board-certified asthma specialists; school inhaler access laws; rescue medication use; controller medication use; uninsured rate; poverty rate. *Asthma and Allergy Foundation of America, "2011 Asthma Capitals"*

- Austin was identified as a "2011 Fall Allergy Capital." The area ranked #42 out of 100. Three groups of factors were used to identify the most severe cities for people with allergies during the fall season: annual pollen levels; medicine utilization; access to board-certified allergists. *Asthma and Allergy Foundation of America, "2011 Fall Allergy Capitals"*

- Austin was identified as a "2012 Spring Allergy Capital." The area ranked #26 out of 100. Three groups of factors were used to identify the most severe cities for people with allergies during the spring season: annual pollen levels; medicine utilization; access to board-certified allergists. *Asthma and Allergy Foundation of America, "2012 Spring Allergy Capitals"*

- *Men's Health* examined 100 major U.S. cities and selected the best and worst cities for men. Austin ranked #6. Criteria: 35 statistical parameters of long life in the categories of health, quality of life, and fitness. *Men's Health, "The 10 Best and Worst Cities for Men 2012," January/February 2012*

- *Men's Health* examined 100 U.S. cities and selected the best and worst cities for women. Austin was ranked among the ten best at #5. Criteria: dozens of statistical parameters of long life in the categories of health, quality of life, and fitness. *Men's Health, "The 10 Best and Worst Cities for Women 2011," January/February 2011*

- The makers of Breath Right Nasal Strips, in partnership with Sperling's BestPlaces, analyzed 50 metro areas and identified those U.S. cities most challenged by chronic nasal congestion. The Austin metro area ranked #14. Criteria: tree, grass and weed pollens; molds and spores; air pollution; climate; smoking; purchase habits of congestion products; prescriptions of drugs for congestion relief; incidence of influenza. *Breathe Right Nasal Strips, "Most Congested Cities," October 3, 2011*

- The Austin metropolitan area was selected as one of the best metros for hospital care in America by *HealthGrades.com*. The rankings are based on a comprehensive study of patient death and complication rates in the nation's nearly 5,000 hospitals. Hospitals performing in the top 5% nationwide across 26 different medical procedures and diagnoses were identified. *HealthGrades.com* then ranked cities by the highest percentage of these Distinguished Hospitals for Clinical Excellence™. The Austin metro area ranked #45. *HealthGrades.com, "America's Top 50 Cities for Hospital Care," January 21, 2012*

- The Austin metro area appeared in the 2011 Gallup-Healthways Well-Being Index. The index, based on interviews with more than 350,000 Americans, measured jobs, finances, physical health, emotional state of mind and communities. The metro area ranked #36 out of 190. Criteria: life evaluation; emotional health; work environment; physical health; healthy behaviors; basic access (basic needs optimal for a healthy life, such as access to food and medicine, having health insurance and feeling safe while walking at night). *Gallup-Healthways, "State of Well-Being 2011"*

- The Austin metro area was identified as one of "America's Most Stressful Cities" by *Sperling's BestPlaces*. The metro area ranked #38 out of 50. Criteria: unemployment rate; suicide rate; commute time; mental health; poor rest; alcohol use; violent crime rate; property crime rate; cloudy days annually. *Sperling's BestPlaces, www.BestPlaces.net, "Stressful Cities 2012*

- *Men's Health* ranked 100 U.S. cities in terms of their activity levels. Austin was ranked #14 (#1 = most active city). Criteria: where and how often residents exercise; percentage of households that watch more than 15 hours of cable television a week and buy more than 11 video games a year; death rate from deep-vein thrombosis, a condition linked to sitting for extended periods of time. *Men's Health, "Where Sit Happens: The Most and Least Active Cities in America," June 20, 2011*

- 50 of the largest metro areas in the U.S. were analyzed in terms of their health and fitness by the American College of Sports Medicine in their "American Fitness Index." The Austin metro area ranked #10 (#1 = healthiest). Criteria: preventative health behaviors; levels of chronic disease; health care access; community resources and policies that support physical activity. *American College of Sports Medicine, "Health and Community Fitness Status of the 50 Largest Metropolitan Areas," August 1, 2011*

Real Estate Rankings

- The Austin metro area was identified as one of ten places where real estate is ripe for a rebound by *Forbes*. Criteria: change in home price over the past 12 months and three years; unemployment rates; 12-month job-growth projections; population change from 2006 through 2009; new home construction rates for the third quarter of 2011 as compared to the same quarter in 2010. *Forbes.com, "Cities Where Real Estate is Ripe for a Rebound," January 12, 2012*

- *Fortune* ranked the 100 largest metro areas in the U.S. in terms of projected median home price change in 2010. The Austin metro area ranked #26. *Fortune, "The 2010 Housing Outlook," December 9, 2009*

- Austin was identified as one of the top 20 metro areas with the highest rate of house price appreciation in 2011. The area ranked #18 with a one-year price appreciation of 0.6% through the 4th quarter 2011. *Federal Housing Finance Agency, House Price Index, 4th Quarter 2011*

- The Austin metro area was identified as one of "The 15 Worst Housing Markets for the Next Five Years." Criteria: cities with home prices that are projected to appreciate at an annual rate of less than 1.5% rate between the second quarter 2011 and the second quarter 2016. *The Business Insider, "The 15 Worst Housing Markets for the Next Five Years," July 1, 2011*

- The Austin metro area was identified as one of the 10 best condo markets in the U.S. in 2011. The area ranked #5 out of 54 markets with a price appreciation of 5.0%. Criteria: year-over-year change of median sales price of existing apartment condo-coop homes between the 4th quarter of 2010 and the 4th quarter of 2011. *National Association of Realtors®, Median Sales Price of Existing Apartment Condo-Coop Homes for Metropolitan Areas, 4th Quarter 2011*

- Austin appeared on *ApartmentRatings.com* "Top Cities for Renters" list in 2009." The area ranked #57. Overall satisfaction ratings were ranked using thousands of user submitted scores for hundreds of apartment complexes located in the 100 most populated U.S. municipalities. *ApartmentRatings.com, "2009 Renter Satisfaction Rankings"*

- Austin appeared on *ApartmentRatings.com* "Top College Towns & Cities" for renters list in 2011." The area ranked #44 out of 87. Overall satisfaction ratings were ranked using thousands of user submitted scores for hundreds of apartment complexes located in cities and towns that are home to the 100 largest four-year institutions in the U.S. *ApartmentRatings.com, "2011 College Town Renter Satisfaction Rankings"*

- The Austin metro area was identified as one of "America's Best Housing Markets" by *Forbes*. The metro area ranked #10. Criteria: housing affordability; rising home prices; percentage of foreclosures. *Forbes.com, "America's Best Housing Markets," February 19, 2010*

- The Austin metro area appeared in a *Wall Street Journal* article ranking cities by "housing stress." The metro area was ranked #26 (#1 = most stress). Criteria: fraction of mortgage-holding homeowners with a monthly housing payment in excess of 30 percent of income; percentage of people without health insurance; unemployment rate. *The Wall Street Journal, "Which Cities Face Biggest Housing Risk," October 5, 2010*

- The Center for Housing Policy ranked 210 U.S. metropolitan areas by the fair market rent for a two-bedroom unit. The Austin metro area was ranked #65. (#1 = most expensive) with a rent of $954. Criteria: Fair Market Rent (FMR) in effect during the fourth quarter of 2009 based on HUD's fiscal year 2010 FMRs. *The Center for Housing Policy, "Paycheck to Paycheck: Most to Least Expensive Rental Markets in 2009"*

- The Austin metro area was identified as one of the best U.S. markets to invest in rental property" by HomeVestors and Local Market Monitor. The area ranked #25 out of 100. Criteria: risk-return premium relative to national average. *HomeVestors and Local Market Monitor, "Best 100 U.S. Markets to Invest in Rental Property," March 9, 2012*

Safety Rankings

- Symantec, the makers of Norton, in partnership with Sperling's BestPlaces, ranked the 50 largest cities in the U.S. in terms of their vulnerability to cybercrime. The city ranked #10. Criteria: number of cyberattacks and potential infections; level of Internet access; expenditures on smartphones and computer hardware/software; wireless hotspots; broadband connectivity; Internet usage; online purchases. *Symantec, "Riskiest Online Cities of 2012" February 15, 2012*

- Farmers Insurance Group of Companies, in partnership with Sperling's BestPlaces, ranked 379 metro areas and identified the "Most Secure U.S. Places to Live." The Austin metro area ranked #10 out of the top 20 in the large metro area category (500,000 or more residents). Criteria: crime statistics; extreme weather; risk of natural disasters; housing depreciation; foreclosures; environmental hazards; terrorist threats; air quality; life expectancy; mortality rates from cancer and motor vehicle accidents; job loss numbers. *Farmers Insurance Group, "Most Secure U.S. Places to Live 2011," December 15, 2011*

- Allstate ranked the 193 largest cities in America in terms of driver safety. Austin ranked #150. In addition, drivers were 26.0% more likely to have had an accident compared to the national average. Allstate researchers analyzed internal property damage reported claims over a two-year period (from January 2008 to December 2009) to protect findings from external influences such as weather or road construction. A weighted average of the two-year numbers determined the annual percentages. The report defines an auto crash as any collision resulting in a property damage claim. *Allstate, "2011 Allstate America's Best Drivers Report™"*

- Austin was identified as one of the safest large cities in America by CQ Press. All 34 cities with populations of 500,000 or more that reported crime rates in 2010 for murder, rape, robbery, aggravated assault, burglary, and motor vehicle thefts were ranked. The city ranked #6 out of the top 10. *CQ Press, City Crime Rankings 2011-2012*

- The National Insurance Crime Bureau ranked 366 metro areas in the U.S. in terms of per capita rates of vehicle theft. The Austin metro area ranked #122 (#1 = highest rate). Criteria: number of vehicle theft offenses per 100,000 inhabitants in 2010. *National Insurance Crime Bureau, "Hot Spots," June 21, 2011*

- The Austin metro area was identified as one of the most dangerous metro areas for pedestrians by Transportation for America. The metro area ranked #18 out of 52 metro areas with over 1 million residents. Criteria: area's population divided by the number of pedestrian fatalities in that area. *Transportation for America, "Dangerous by Design 2011"*

Seniors/Retirement Rankings

- Bankers Life and Casualty Company, in partnership with Sperling's BestPlaces, ranked the nation's 50 largest metro areas in terms of the "Best U.S. Cities for Seniors." The Austin metro area ranked #24. Criteria: healthcare; transportation; housing; environment; economy; health and longevity; social and spiritual life; crime. *Bankers Life and Casualty Company, Center for a Secure Retirement, "Best U.S. Cities for Seniors 2011," September 2011*

- USAA and *Military.com*, in partnership with Sperling's BestPlaces, ranked 379 metropolitan areas in terms of which are the best places for military retirees. The metro area ranked #4 out of 10. Criteria: military skill related jobs; unemployment rate; number of federal government jobs; volume of DoD contracts; number of small businesses; number of veteran-owned businesses; military installation proximity/amenities; Veteran's Affairs hospitals; affordability; military pension taxation; presence of colleges/universities; sales tax; climate; crime level. *USAA and Military.com, "2011 Best Places for Military Retirement: Second Careers*

- Austin was identified as one of the "100 Most Popular Retirement Towns" by *Topretirements.com* The list reflects the 100 cities (out of 815+ total cities reviewed) that visitors to the website are most interested in for retirement. *Topretirements.com, "100 Most Popular Retirement Towns," February 21, 2012*

- Austin was selected as one of the best places to retire by *CNNMoney.com*. Criteria: low cost of living; low violent-crime rate; good medical care; large population over age 50; abundant amenities for retirees. *CNNMoney.com, "Best Places to Retire 2011"*

- The Austin metro area was selected as one of the "Best Places for Military Retirees" by *U.S. News & World Report*. The area ranked #3 out of 10. Criteria: climate; health resources; health indicators; crime levels; local school performance; recreational resources; arts and culture; airport and mass transit resources; susceptibility to natural disasters; military facilities and base amenities; VA medical services; tax policies affecting military pensions, unemployment trends; higher education resources; overall affordability; housing costs; home price trends; economic stability. *U.S. News & World Report, "Best Places for Military Retirees," December 8, 2010*

Sports/Recreation Rankings

- Austin appeared on the *Sporting News* list of the "Best Sports Cities" for 2011. The area ranked #76 out of 271 cities in the U.S. *Sporting News* takes a 12-month snapshot of each city's sports, putting a heavy premium on regular-season won-lost records (from the most recently completed season). Other criteria include: playoff berths, bowl appearances and tournament bids; championships; applicable power ratings; quality of competition; overall fan fervor (measured in part by attendance); abundance of teams (rewarding quality over quantity); stadium and arena quality; ticket availability and prices; franchise ownership; and marquee appeal of athletes. *Sporting News, "Best Sports Cities 2011," October 4, 2011*

- Austin was selected as one of the five best boat cities in the U.S. The city ranked #5. Criteria: climate; scenery; fishing; boat communities with water access. *Best Boat News, "The 5 Best Boat Cities to Live In (in the U.S.)," April 16, 2010*

- Austin was chosen as a bicycle friendly community by the League of American Bicyclists. A Bicycle Friendly Community welcomes cyclists by providing safe accommodation for cycling and encouraging people to bike for transportation and recreation. There are four award levels: Platinum; Gold; Silver; and Bronze. The community achieved an award level of Silver. *League of American Bicyclists, "Bicycle Friendly Community Master List 2011"*

- Austin was chosen as one of America's 10 best places to live and boat. Criteria: boating opportunities; boat-friendly regulations; water access; availability of waterfront homes; health of the local economy; and overall lifestyle for boaters. *Boating Magazine, "10 Best Places to Live and Boat," June 2010*

- Austin was chosen as one of America's best cities for bicycling. The city ranked #11 out of 50. Criteria: number of segregated bike lanes, municipal bike racks, and bike boulevards; vibrant and diverse bike culture; smart, savvy bike shops; interviews with national and local advocates, bike shops and other experts. The editors only considered cities with populations of 100,000 or more. *Bicycling, "America's Best Bike Cities," April 2010*

- *Golf.com* and the research arm of the National Golf Foundation analyzed the 50 largest metropolitan areas in the U.S. in terms of golf. The Austin metro area ranked #1. Criteria: weather; affordability; quality of courses; accessibility; number of courses designed by esteemed architects; availability; crowdedness. *Golf.com, November 15, 2007*

Technology Rankings

- The Austin metro area was selected as one of "America's Most Wired Cities" by *Forbes*. The metro area was ranked #20 out of 20. Criteria: percentage of Internet users with high-speed access; number of companies providing high-speed Internet; number of public wireless hot spots. *Forbes, "America's Most Wired Cities," March 2, 2010*

- The Austin metro area was selected as one of "America's Most Innovative Cities" by *Forbes*. The metro area was ranked #2 out of 20. Criteria: patents per capita; venture capital investment per capita; ratio of high-tech, science and "creative" jobs. *Forbes, "America's Most Innovative Cities," May 24, 2010*

- The Austin metro area was identified as one of the "Top 14 Nano Metros" in the U.S. by the Project on Emerging Nanotechnologies. The metro area is home to 24 companies, universities, government laboratories and/or organizations working in nanotechnology. *Project on Emerging Nanotechnologies, "Nano Metros 2009"*

Transportation Rankings

- Austin appeared on *Trapster.com's* list of the 10 most-active U.S. cities for speed traps. The city ranked #10 of 10. *Trapster.com* is a community platform accessed online and via smartphone app that alerts drivers to traps, hazards and other traffic issues nearby. *Trapster.com, "Speeders Beware: Cities With the Most Speed Traps," February 10, 2012*

- Austin was identified as one of America's "10 Best Cities for Public Transportation" by *U.S. News & World Report*. The city ranked #9. The ten cities selected had the best combination of public transportation investment, ridership, and safety. *U.S. News & World Report, "10 Best Cities for Public Transportation," February 8, 2011*

- Austin was identified as one of America's worst cities for speed traps by the National Motorists Association. The city ranked #9 out of 25. Criteria: speed trap locations per 100,000 residents. *National Motorists Association, September 2011*

- The Austin metro area appeared on *Forbes* list of the best and worst cities for commuters. The metro area ranked #27 out of 60 (#1 is best). Criteria: travel time; road congestion; travel delays. *Forbes.com, "Best and Worst Cities for Commuters," February 16, 2010*

Women/Minorities Rankings

- *Women's Health* examined U.S. cities and identified the 100 best cities for women. Austin was ranked #9. Criteria: 30 categories were examined from obesity and breast cancer rates to commuting times and hours spent working out. *Women's Health, "Best Cities for Women 2012"*

- Austin was ranked #36 out of 100 metro areas in *SELF Magazine's* ranking of America's healthiest places for women." A panel of experts came up with more than 50 criteria including death and disease rates, environmental indicators, community resources, and lifestyle habits. *SELF Magazine, "Secrets of America's Healthiest Women," December 2008*

- Austin was selected as one of the "Gayest Cities in America" by *The Advocate*. The city ranked #13 out of 15. *The Advocate* used several different measures to establish "per capita queerness"—including a city's number of teams entered in the Gay Softball World Series, gay bookstores, openly gay elected officials and semifinalists in the International Mr. Leather Contest. *The Advocate, "Gayest Cities in America, 2012" January 2012*

- Austin was selected as one of the 25 healthiest cities for Latinas by *Latina Magazine*. The city ranked #2. Criteria: U.S. cities with populations over 500,000 residents were evaluated on the following criteria: percentage of 18-34 year-olds per city; Latino college graduation rates; number of colleges and universities; affordability; housing costs; income growth over time; average salary; percentage of singles; climate; safety; how the city's diversity compares to the national average; opportunities for minority entrepreneurs. *Latina Magazine, "Top 15 U.S. Cities for Young Latinos to Live In," August 19, 2011*

- The Austin metro area appeared on *Forbes'* list of the "Best Cities for Minority Entrepreneurs." The area ranked #2 out of 10. Criteria: 52 metropolitan statistical areas were examined. For each ethnicity (African Americans, Asians and Hispanics), the editors measured housing affordability, population growth, income growth, and entrepreneurship (per capita self-employment). *Forbes, "Best Cities for Minority Entrepreneurs," March 23, 2011*

- Austin was selected as one of the "Top 10 Cities for Hispanics." Criteria: the prospect of a good job; a safe place to raise a family; a manageable cost of living; the ability to buy and keep a home; a culture of inclusion where Hispanics are highly represented; resources to help start a business; the presence of Hispanic or Spanish-language media; representation of Hispanic needs on local government; a thriving arts and culture community; air quality; energy costs; city's state of health and rates of obesity. *Hispanic Magazine, August 2008*

Miscellaneous Rankings

- *Men's Health* ranked 100 U.S. cities by their level of sadness. Austin was ranked #19 (#1 = saddest city). Criteria: suicide rates; unemployment rates; percentage of households that use antidepressants; percent of population who report feeling blue all or most of the time. *Men's Health, "Frown Towns," November 28, 2011*

- The Austin metro area was selected as one of "The Best U.S. Cities for Bargain Shopping" by *Forbes*. The area ranked #2 out of 10. Criteria: number of outlet stores; gross leasable retail space in major malls; low consumer price index; low sales tax rate. Indicators were examined in the nation's 50 largest metropolitan areas. *Forbes, "The Best U.S. Cities for Bargain Shopping," January 20, 2012*

- Energizer Holdings, the makers of Edge® shave gel, in partnership with Sperling's BestPlaces, ranked 50 major metro areas in terms of everyday irritations. The Austin metro area ranked #32. Criteria: humidity levels; weather conditions; incidence of traffic delays and congestion; average commute times; frequency of flight delays and cancellations; rates of sleeplessness; underemployment; pollens and allergens; pests; comedy clubs per capita. *Energizer Holdings, "Most Irritation Prone Cities," July 23, 2010*

- Austin was selected as one of the most tattooed cities in America by *TotalBeauty.com*. The city was ranked #6. Criteria: number of tattoo and permanent makeup shops per capita; number of tattoo conventions hosted. *TotalBeauty.com, "Top 10 Most Tattooed Cities in America," August 2010*

- Austin was selected as one of "America's Best Cities for Hipsters" by *Travel + Leisure*. The city was ranked #7 out of 10. Criteria: live music; coffee bars; independent boutiques; best microbrews; offbeat and tech-savvy locals. *Travel + Leisure, "America's Best Cities for Hipsters," April 11, 2012*

- The Austin metro area appeared in *AutoMD.com's* ranking of the "Best and Worst Cities for Auto Repair." The metro area ranked #5 (#1 is best). The 50 most-populated metro areas in the U.S. were ranked on three critical factors: repair affordability; price disparity range; shop integrity factor. *AutoMD.com, "Advocacy for Repair Shop Fairness Report," February 24, 2010*

- Austin appeared on Procter & Gamble's list of the "Top-20 All-Time Sweatiest Cities." The city was ranked #16. The rankings are based on computer simulations of the amount of sweat a person of average height and weight would produce walking around for an hour in the average temperatures during the summer months, based on historical weather data during June, July and August from 2001-2008 for each city. *Procter & Gamble, Old Spice Press Release, "Top-20 All-Time Sweatiest Cities," July 1, 2009*

Business Environment

CITY FINANCES

City Government Finances

Component	2009 ($000)	2009 ($ per capita)
Total Revenues	2,015,860	2,713
Total Expenditures	3,095,637	4,166
Debt Outstanding	5,043,226	6,787
Cash and Securities[1]	3,898,091	5,246

Note: (1) Cash and security holdings of a government at the close of its fiscal year, including those of its dependent agencies, utilities, and liquor stores.
Source: U.S Census Bureau, State & Local Government Finances 2009

City Government Revenue by Source

Source	2009 ($000)	2009 ($ per capita)
General Revenue		
From Federal Government	71,418	96
From State Government	31,646	43
From Local Governments	54,805	74
Taxes		
Property	277,886	374
Sales and Gross Receipts	242,140	326
Personal Income	0	0
Corporate Income	0	0
Motor Vehicle License	0	0
Other Taxes	24,268	33
Current Charges	502,128	676
Liquor Store	0	0
Utility	1,399,250	1,883
Employee Retirement	-760,962	-1,024

Source: U.S Census Bureau, State & Local Government Finances 2009

City Government Expenditures by Function

Function	2009 ($000)	2009 ($ per capita)	2009 (%)
General Direct Expenditures			
Air Transportation	67,193	90	2.2
Corrections	0	0	0.0
Education	0	0	0.0
Employment Security Administration	0	0	0.0
Financial Administration	26,321	35	0.9
Fire Protection	120,599	162	3.9
General Public Buildings	0	0	0.0
Governmental Administration, Other	30,198	41	1.0
Health	140,009	188	4.5
Highways	82,271	111	2.7
Hospitals	901	1	0.0
Housing and Community Development	44,093	59	1.4
Interest on General Debt	96,514	130	3.1
Judicial and Legal	21,283	29	0.7
Libraries	26,659	36	0.9
Parking	89	< 1	< 0.1
Parks and Recreation	117,908	159	3.8
Police Protection	222,656	300	7.2
Public Welfare	0	0	0.0
Sewerage	187,214	252	6.0
Solid Waste Management	71,782	97	2.3
Veterans' Services	0	0	0.0
Liquor Store	0	0	0.0
Utility	1,505,391	2,026	48.6
Employee Retirement	157,837	212	5.1

Source: U.S Census Bureau, State & Local Government Finances 2009

Municipal Bond Ratings

Area	Moody's	S&P	Fitch
City	Aa1	AAA	n/a

Rating Systems (shown in declining order of credit quality): Moody's– Aaa, Aa, A, Baa, Ba, B, Caa, Ca, C (numerical modifiers 1, 2, and 3 are added to letter-rating); S&P– AAA, AA, A, BBB, BB, B, CCC, CC, C; Fitch– AAA, AA, A, BBB, BB, B, CCC, CC, C. Ratings may be modified by the addition of a plus or minus sign to show relative standing within the major rating categories.
Notes: n/a Not Available; w/d Withdrawn (1) Not Reviewed; (2) Issuer Rating/No General Obligation; (3) Standard and Poor's Issue Credit Rating (ICR) is a current opinion of an obliger with respect to a specific financial obligation, a specific class of financial obligations, or a specific financial program.
Source: U.S. Census Bureau, 2012 Statistical Abstract, Bond Ratings for City Governments by Largest Cities: 2010

DEMOGRAPHICS

Population Growth

Area	1990 Census	2000 Census	2010 Census	Population Growth (%) 1990-2000	Population Growth (%) 2000-2010
City	499,053	656,562	790,390	31.6	20.4
MSA[1]	846,217	1,249,763	1,716,289	47.7	37.3
U.S.	248,709,873	281,421,906	308,745,538	13.2	9.7

Note: (1) Figures cover the Austin-Round Rock-San Marcos, TX Metropolitan Statistical Area—see Appendix B for areas included
Source: U.S. Census Bureau, 2010 Census

Household Size

Area	Persons in Household (%) One	Two	Three	Four	Five	Six	Seven or More	Average Household Size
City	34.0	31.4	14.4	11.2	5.0	2.2	1.8	2.37
MSA[1]	27.3	32.0	16.0	13.7	6.4	2.6	2.0	2.58
U.S.	26.7	32.8	16.1	13.4	6.5	2.6	1.9	2.58

Note: (1) Figures cover the Austin-Round Rock-San Marcos, TX Metropolitan Statistical Area—see Appendix B for areas included
Source: U.S. Census Bureau, 2010 Census

Race

Area	White Alone[2] (%)	Black Alone[2] (%)	Asian Alone[2] (%)	AIAN[3] Alone[2] (%)	NHOPI[4] Alone[2] (%)	Other Race Alone[2] (%)	Two or More Races (%)
City	68.3	8.1	6.3	0.9	0.1	12.9	3.4
MSA[1]	72.9	7.4	4.8	0.8	0.1	10.9	3.2
U.S.	72.4	12.6	4.8	0.9	0.2	6.2	2.9

Note: (1) Figures cover the Austin-Round Rock-San Marcos, TX Metropolitan Statistical Area—see Appendix B for areas included; (2) Alone is defined as not being in combination with one or more other races; (3) American Indian and Alaska Native; (4) Native Hawaiian and Other Pacific Islander
Source: U.S. Census Bureau, 2010 Census

Hispanic or Latino Origin

Area	Hispanic or Latino (%)	Mexican (%)	Puerto Rican (%)	Cuban (%)	Other Hispanic or Latino (%)
City	35.1	29.1	0.5	0.4	5.1
MSA[1]	31.4	26.2	0.6	0.3	4.3
U.S.	16.3	10.3	1.5	0.6	4.0

Note: Persons of Hispanic or Latino origin can be of any race; (1) Figures cover the Austin-Round Rock-San Marcos, TX Metropolitan Statistical Area—see Appendix B for areas included
Source: U.S. Census Bureau, 2010 Census

Segregation

Type	Segregation Indices[1]				Percent Change		
	1990	2000	2010	2010 Rank[2]	1990-2000	1990-2010	2000-2010
Black/White	54.1	52.1	50.1	70	-1.9	-4.0	-2.1
Asian/White	39.4	42.3	41.2	49	2.9	1.8	-1.2
Hispanic/White	41.7	45.6	43.2	51	3.9	1.5	-2.4

Note: Figures are based on an analysis of 1990, 2000, and 2010 Census Decennial Census tract data by William H. Frey, Brookings Institution and the University of Michigan Social Science Data Analysis Network. In this analysis all racial groups (whites, blacks, and asians) are non-Hispanic members of those races. Hispanics are shown as a separate category; All figures cover the Metropolitan Statistical Area (see Appendix B for areas included); (1) Segregation Indices are Dissimilarity Indices that measure the degree to which the minority group is distributed differently than whites across census tracts. They range from 0 (complete integration) to 100 (complete segregation) where the value indicates the percentage of the minority group that needs to move to be distributed exactly like whites; (2) Ranges from 1 (most segregated) to 102 (least segregated); n/a not available.
Source: www.CensusScope.org

Ancestry

Area	German	Irish	English	American	Italian	Polish	French[2]	Scottish	Dutch
City	12.5	8.6	9.4	2.8	2.7	1.6	2.9	2.6	1.0
MSA[1]	15.6	9.5	9.5	3.6	2.7	1.6	2.9	2.5	1.1
U.S.	16.1	11.6	8.8	6.1	5.7	3.2	3.0	1.9	1.6

Note: Figures are the percentage of the total population reporting a particular ancestry. The nine most commonly reported ancestries in the U.S. are shown. Figures include multiple ancestries (e.g. if a person reported being Irish and Italian, they were included in both columns); (1) Figures cover the Austin-Round Rock-San Marcos, TX Metropolitan Statistical Area—see Appendix B for areas included; (2) Excludes Basque
Source: U.S. Census Bureau, 2008-2010 American Community Survey 3-Year Estimates

Foreign-Born Population

Area	Percent of Population Born in								
	Any Foreign Country	Mexico	Asia	Europe	Carribean	South America	Central America[2]	Africa	Canada
City	19.7	10.5	4.7	1.1	0.3	0.5	1.8	0.5	0.3
MSA[1]	14.6	7.6	3.6	1.0	0.2	0.4	1.1	0.4	0.3
U.S.	12.8	3.8	3.6	1.6	1.2	0.9	1.0	0.5	0.3

Note: (1) Figures cover the Austin-Round Rock-San Marcos, TX Metropolitan Statistical Area—see Appendix B for areas included; (2) Excludes Mexico.
Source: U.S. Census Bureau, 2008-2010 American Community Survey 3-Year Estimates

Marital Status

Area	Never Married	Now Married[2]	Separated	Widowed	Divorced
City	43.0	41.1	2.1	3.2	10.6
MSA[1]	34.8	49.2	1.9	3.6	10.4
U.S.	31.6	49.6	2.2	6.1	10.7

Note: Figures are percentages and cover the population 15 years of age and older; (1) Figures cover the Austin-Round Rock-San Marcos, TX Metropolitan Statistical Area—see Appendix B for areas included; (2) Excludes separated
Source: U.S. Census Bureau, 2008-2010 American Community Survey 3-Year Estimates

Age

Area	Percent of Population							Median Age
	Under Age 5	Age 5 to 17	Age 18 to 34	Age 35 to 49	Age 50 to 64	Age 65 to 79	80 Years and Over	
City	7.3	14.9	35.2	21.0	14.5	5.1	1.9	31.0
MSA[1]	7.4	17.9	28.6	22.1	15.9	6.1	2.0	32.6
U.S.	6.5	17.5	23.2	20.7	19.0	9.4	3.6	37.2

Note: (1) Figures cover the Austin-Round Rock-San Marcos, TX Metropolitan Statistical Area—see Appendix B for areas included
Source: U.S. Census Bureau, 2010 Census

Male/Female Ratio

Area	Males	Females	Males per 100 Females
City	399,738	390,652	102.3
MSA[1]	860,101	856,188	100.5
U.S.	151,781,326	156,964,212	96.7

Note: (1) Figures cover the Austin-Round Rock-San Marcos, TX Metropolitan Statistical Area—see Appendix B for areas included
Source: U.S. Census Bureau, 2010 Census

Religious Groups

Area	Catholic	Baptist	Non-Den.	Methodist[2]	Lutheran	LDS[3]	Pentecostal	Presbyterian[4]	Muslim[5]	Judaism
MSA[1]	16.0	10.3	4.5	3.6	2.0	1.2	0.8	1.1	0.3	1.2
U.S.	19.1	9.3	4.0	4.0	2.3	2.0	1.9	1.6	0.8	0.7

Note: Figures are the number of adherents as a percentage of the total population; (1) Figures cover the Austin-Round Rock-San Marcos, TX Metropolitan Statistical Area—see Appendix B for areas included; (2) Methodist/Pietist; (3) Latter Day Saints; (4) Reformed; (5) Figures are estimates
Source: Association of Statisticians of American Religious Bodies, 2010 U.S. Religion Census: Religious Congregations & Membership Study

ECONOMY

Gross Metropolitan Product

Area	2007	2008	2009	2010	2010 Rank[2]
MSA[1]	76.4	79.8	78.8	84.2	37

Note: Figures are in billions of dollars; (1) Figures cover the Austin-Round Rock-San Marcos, TX Metropolitan Statistical Area—see Appendix B for areas included; (2) Rank ranges from 1 to 363
Source: The United States Conference of Mayors, "U.S. Metro Economies: GMP and Employment Forecasts," June 2011

Economic Growth

Area	2007-2009 (%)	2010 (%)	2011 (%)	Rank[2]
MSA[1]	1.7	6.7	3.0	41
U.S.	-1.3	2.9	2.5	–

Note: Figures are real Gross Metropolitan Product growth rates and represent annual average percent change; (1) Figures cover the Austin-Round Rock-San Marcos, TX Metropolitan Statistical Area—see Appendix B for areas included; (2) Rank ranges from 1 to 363
Source: The United States Conference of Mayors, "U.S. Metro Economies: GMP and Employment Forecasts," June 2011

Metropolitan Area Exports

Area	2005	2006	2007	2008	2009	2010	2010 Rank[2]
MSA[1]	7,687.0	8,204.6	8,428.6	7,405.5	5,963.7	8,867.8	31

Note: Figures are in millions of dollars; (1) Figures cover the Austin-Round Rock-San Marcos, TX Metropolitan Statistical Area—see Appendix B for areas included; (2) Rank ranges from 1 to 369
Source: U.S. Department of Commerce, International Trade Administration, Office of Trade & Industry Information, Manufacturing & Services, data extracted April 2, 2012

INCOME

Income

Area	Per Capita ($)	Median Household ($)	Average Household ($)
City	29,655	50,147	71,045
MSA[1]	29,482	56,732	76,321
U.S.	26,942	51,222	70,116

Note: (1) Figures cover the Austin-Round Rock-San Marcos, TX Metropolitan Statistical Area—see Appendix B for areas included
Source: U.S. Census Bureau, 2008-2010 American Community Survey 3-Year Estimates

Household Income Distribution

Area	Percent of Households Earning							
	Under $15,000	$15,000 -24,999	$25,000 -34,999	$35,000 -49,999	$50,000 -74,999	$75,000 -99,000	$100,000 -149,999	$150,000 and up
City	13.8	10.2	11.0	15.0	17.7	11.2	11.6	9.5
MSA[1]	11.0	9.0	9.7	14.2	18.9	12.9	14.0	10.2
U.S.	13.0	11.0	10.6	14.2	18.5	12.1	12.2	8.4

Note: (1) Figures cover the Austin-Round Rock-San Marcos, TX Metropolitan Statistical Area—see Appendix B for areas included
Source: U.S. Census Bureau, 2008-2010 American Community Survey 3-Year Estimates

Poverty Rate

Area	All Ages	Under 18 Years Old	18 to 64 Years Old	65 Years and Over
City	19.2	26.1	18.0	8.7
MSA[1]	14.5	18.5	13.9	7.1
U.S.	14.4	20.1	13.1	9.4

Note: Figures are percentage of people whose income during the past 12 months was below the poverty level; (1) Figures cover the Austin-Round Rock-San Marcos, TX Metropolitan Statistical Area—see Appendix B for areas included
Source: U.S. Census Bureau, 2008-2010 American Community Survey 3-Year Estimates

Personal Bankruptcy Filing Rate

Area	2006	2007	2008	2009	2010	2011
Travis County	1.26	1.34	1.35	1.81	1.86	1.54
U.S.	2.00	2.73	3.53	4.61	4.97	4.37

Note: Numbers are per 1,000 population and include Chapter 7 and Chapter 13 filings
Source: Federal Deposit Insurance Corporation, Regional Economic Conditions, March 9, 2012

EMPLOYMENT

Labor Force and Employment

Area	Civilian Labor Force			Workers Employed		
	Dec. 2010	Dec. 2011	% Chg.	Dec. 2010	Dec. 2011	% Chg.
City	429,920	437,604	1.8	402,844	412,519	2.4
MSA[1]	902,646	918,215	1.7	840,510	860,696	2.4
U.S.	153,156,000	153,373,000	0.1	139,159,000	140,681,000	1.1

Note: Data is not seasonally adjusted and covers workers 16 years of age and older; (1) Metropolitan Statistical Area—see Appendix B for areas included
Source: Bureau of Labor Statistics, http://stats.bls.gov

Unemployment Rate

Area	2011											
	Jan.	Feb.	Mar.	Apr.	May	Jun.	Jul.	Aug.	Sep.	Oct.	Nov.	Dec.
City	6.7	6.4	6.3	6.1	6.3	7.0	7.0	6.8	6.9	6.5	6.0	5.7
MSA[1]	7.3	6.9	6.8	6.5	6.8	7.6	7.6	7.4	7.5	7.1	6.6	6.3
U.S.	9.8	9.5	9.2	8.7	8.7	9.3	9.3	9.1	8.8	8.5	8.2	8.3

Note: Data is not seasonally adjusted and covers workers 16 years of age and older; All figures are percentages; (1) Metropolitan Statistical Area—see Appendix B for areas included
Source: Bureau of Labor Statistics, http://stats.bls.gov

Projected Unemployment Rate

Area	2010 (%)	2011 (%)	2012 (%)	2013 (%)
MSA[1]	7.3	6.9	6.6	6.3

Note: (1) Metropolitan Statistical Area—see Appendix B for areas included
Source: The United States Conference of Mayors, "U.S. Metro Economies: GMP and Employment Forecasts," June 2011

Employment by Occupation

Occupation Classification	City (%)	MSA[1] (%)	U.S. (%)
Management, Business, Science, and Arts	43.7	42.8	35.6
Natural Resources, Construction, and Maintenance	9.6	9.5	9.5
Production, Transportation, and Material Moving	6.1	7.1	12.1
Sales and Office	22.9	24.8	25.2
Service	17.7	15.8	17.6

Note: Figures cover employed civilians 16 years of age and older; (1) Figures cover the Austin-Round Rock-San Marcos, TX Metropolitan Statistical Area—see Appendix B for areas included
Source: U.S. Census Bureau, 2008-2010 American Community Survey 3-Year Estimates

Employment by Industry

Sector	MSA[1] Number of Employees	MSA[1] Percent of Total	U.S. Percent of Total
Construction	n/a	n/a	4.1
Education and Health Services	92,400	11.6	15.2
Financial Activities	45,300	5.7	5.8
Government	167,400	20.9	16.8
Information	20,300	2.5	2.0
Leisure and Hospitality	91,600	11.5	9.9
Manufacturing	50,900	6.4	8.9
Mining and Logging	n/a	n/a	0.6
Other Services	33,700	4.2	4.0
Professional and Business Services	116,500	14.6	13.3
Retail Trade	86,400	10.8	11.5
Transportation and Utilities	13,700	1.7	3.8
Wholesale Trade	42,500	5.3	4.2

Note: Figures cover non-farm employment as of December 2011 and are not seasonally adjusted; (1) Metropolitan Statistical Area—see Appendix B for areas included; n/a not available
Source: Bureau of Labor Statistics, http://stats.bls.gov

Occupations with Greatest Projected Employment Growth: 2008 – 2018

Occupation[1]	2008 Employment	2018 Projected Employment	Numeric Employment Change	Percent Employment Change
Combined Food Preparation and Serving Workers, Including Fast Food	247,750	326,190	78,440	31.7
Elementary School Teachers, Except Special Education	156,930	218,030	61,100	38.9
Retail Salespersons	361,780	416,090	54,310	15.0
Registered Nurses	166,240	219,880	53,640	32.3
Home Health Aides	92,660	143,720	51,060	55.1
Customer Service Representatives	217,250	267,290	50,040	23.0
Waiters and Waitresses	192,340	237,660	45,320	23.6
Personal and Home Care Aides	94,530	138,530	44,000	46.5
Office Clerks, General	239,400	279,000	39,600	16.5
Cashiers	276,070	312,940	36,870	13.4

Note: Projections cover Texas; (1) Sorted by numeric employment change
Source: www.projectionscentral.com, State Occupational Projections, 2008–2018 Long-Term Projections

Fastest Growing Occupations: 2008 – 2018

Occupation[1]	2008 Employment	2018 Projected Employment	Numeric Employment Change	Percent Employment Change
Biomedical Engineers	650	1,150	500	76.9
Home Health Aides	92,660	143,720	51,060	55.1
Network Systems and Data Communications Analysts	19,160	29,490	10,330	53.9
Petroleum Engineers	13,440	20,140	6,700	49.9
Athletic Trainers	1,560	2,300	740	47.4
Personal and Home Care Aides	94,530	138,530	44,000	46.5
Electrical and Electronics Repairers, Powerhouse, Substation, and Relay	1,550	2,260	710	45.8
Financial Examiners	2,150	3,130	980	45.6
Medical Scientists, Except Epidemiologists	3,670	5,320	1,650	45.0
Biochemists and Biophysicists	740	1,060	320	43.2

Note: Projections cover Texas; (1) Sorted by percent employment change and excludes occupations with numeric employment change less than 100
Source: www.projectionscentral.com, State Occupational Projections, 2008–2018 Long-Term Projections

Average Wages

Occupation	$/Hr.	Occupation	$/Hr.
Accountants and Auditors	33.31	Maids and Housekeeping Cleaners	9.22
Automotive Mechanics	22.03	Maintenance and Repair Workers	16.02
Bookkeepers	18.23	Marketing Managers	65.36
Carpenters	15.60	Nuclear Medicine Technologists	32.42
Cashiers	9.71	Nurses, Licensed Practical	21.93
Clerks, General Office	15.47	Nurses, Registered	33.09
Clerks, Receptionists/Information	12.65	Nursing Aides/Orderlies/Attendants	11.00
Clerks, Shipping/Receiving	14.00	Packers and Packagers, Hand	11.36
Computer Programmers	38.53	Physical Therapists	38.51
Computer Support Specialists	26.47	Postal Service Mail Carriers	25.00
Computer Systems Analysts	40.99	Real Estate Brokers	45.04
Cooks, Restaurant	10.93	Retail Salespersons	12.19
Dentists	90.89	Sales Reps., Exc. Tech./Scientific	33.93
Electrical Engineers	45.14	Sales Reps., Tech./Scientific	39.52
Electricians	19.31	Secretaries, Exc. Legal/Med./Exec.	15.34
Financial Managers	57.82	Security Guards	11.96
First-Line Supervisors/Managers, Sales	19.65	Surgeons	n/a
Food Preparation Workers	9.75	Teacher Assistants	12.00
General and Operations Managers	54.61	Teachers, Elementary School	24.40
Hairdressers/Cosmetologists	10.68	Teachers, Secondary School	25.10
Internists	100.65	Telemarketers	15.46
Janitors and Cleaners	10.51	Truck Drivers, Heavy/Tractor-Trailer	16.34
Landscaping/Groundskeeping Workers	11.79	Truck Drivers, Light/Delivery Svcs.	16.12
Lawyers	47.69	Waiters and Waitresses	8.82

Note: Wage data covers the Austin-Round Rock-San Marcos, TX Metropolitan Statistical Area—see Appendix B for areas included. Hourly wages for elementary/secondary school teachers and teacher assistants were calculated by the editors from annual wage data assuming a 40 hour work week; n/a not available.
Source: Bureau of Labor Statistics, Metro Area Occupational Employment and Wage Estimates, May 2011

RESIDENTIAL REAL ESTATE

Building Permits

Area	Single-Family			Multi-Family			Total		
	2010	2011	Pct. Chg.	2010	2011	Pct. Chg.	2010	2011	Pct. Chg.
City	1,664	1,713	2.9	1,110	2,465	122.1	2,774	4,178	50.6
MSA[1]	6,200	6,231	0.5	2,586	4,008	55.0	8,786	10,239	16.5
U.S.	447,311	418,498	-6.4	157,299	205,563	30.7	604,610	624,061	3.2

Note: (1) Metropolitan Statistical Area—see Appendix B for areas included; figures represent new, privately-owned housing units authorized (unadjusted data); All permit data are based on estimates with imputation.
Source: U.S. Census Bureau, Manufacturing, Mining, and Construction Statistics, Building Permits, 2010, 2011

Homeownership Rate

Area	2005 (%)	2006 (%)	2007 (%)	2008 (%)	2009 (%)	2010 (%)	2011 (%)
MSA[1]	63.9	66.7	66.4	65.5	64.0	65.8	58.4
U.S.	68.9	68.8	68.1	67.8	67.4	66.9	66.1

Note: (1) Metropolitan Statistical Area—see Appendix B for areas included
Source: U.S. Census Bureau, Housing Vacancies and Homeownership Annual Statistics: 2011

Housing Vacancy Rates

Area	Gross Vacancy Rate[2] (%)			Year-Round Vacancy Rate[3] (%)			Rental Vacancy Rate[4] (%)			Homeowner Vacancy Rate[5] (%)		
	2009	2010	2011	2009	2010	2011	2009	2010	2011	2009	2010	2011
MSA[1]	12.8	15.8	12.6	12.7	15.7	11.7	12.2	11.8	6.4	1.6	1.9	0.6
U.S.	14.5	14.3	14.2	11.3	11.3	11.1	10.6	10.2	9.5	2.6	2.6	2.5

Note: (1) Metropolitan Statistical Area—see Appendix B for areas included; (2) The percentage of the total housing inventory that is vacant; (3) The percentage of the housing inventory (excluding seasonal units) that is year-round vacant; (4) The percentage of rental inventory that is vacant for rent; (5) The percentage of homeowner inventory that is vacant for sale
Source: U.S. Census Bureau, Housing Vacancies and Homeownership Annual Statistics: 2011

TAXES

State Corporate Income Tax Rates

State	Tax Rate (%)	Income Brackets ($)	Num. of Brackets	Financial Institution Tax Rate (%)[a]	Federal Income Tax Ded.
Texas	(x)	—	-	(x)	No

Note: Tax rates as of January 1, 2012; (a) Rates listed are the corporate income tax rate applied to financial institutions or excise taxes based on income. Some states have other taxes based upon the value of deposits or shares; (x) Texas imposes a Franchise Tax, otherwise known as margin tax, imposed on entities with more than $1,000,000 total revenues at rate of 1%, or 0.5% for entities primarily engaged in retail or wholesale trade, on lesser of 70% of total revenues or 100% of gross receipts after deductions for either compensation or cost of goods sold.
Source: Federation of Tax Administrators, "State Corporate Income Tax Rates, 2012"

State Individual Income Tax Rates

State	Tax Rate (%)	Income Brackets ($)	Num. of Brackets	Personal Exempt. ($)[1] Single	Dependents	Fed. Inc. Tax Ded.

Texas – No State Income Tax

Note: Tax rates as of January 1, 2012; Local- and county-level taxes are not included; n/a not applicable; (1) Married joint filers generally receive double the single exemption
Source: Federation of Tax Administrators, "State Individual Income Tax Rates, 2012"

Various State and Local Tax Rates

State	State and Local Sales and Use (%)	State Sales and Use (%)	Gasoline[1] (¢/gal.)	Cigarette[2] ($/pack)	Spirits[3] ($/gal.)	Wine[4] ($/gal.)	Beer[5] ($/gal.)
Texas	8.25	6.25	20.0	1.41	2.40	0.20	0.20

Note: All tax rates as of January 1, 2012 except beer, wine and spirits (September 1, 2011); (1) The American Petroleum Institute has developed a methodology for determining the average tax rate on a gallon of fuel. Rates may include any of the following: excise taxes, environmental fees, storage tank fees, other fees or taxes, general sales tax, and local taxes. In states where gasoline is subject to the general sales tax, or where the fuel tax is based on the average sale price, the average rate determined by API is sensitive to changes in the price of gasoline. States that fully or partially apply general sales taxes to gasoline: CA, CO, GA, IL, IN, MI, NY; (2) The federal excise tax of $1.0066 per pack and local taxes are not included; (3) Rates are those applicable to off-premise sales of 40% alcohol by volume (a.b.v.) distilled spirits in 750ml containers. Local excise taxes are excluded; (4) Rates are those applicable to off-premise sales of 11% a.b.v. non-carbonated wine in 750ml containers; (5) Rates are those applicable to off-premise sales of 4.7% a.b.v. beer in 12 ounce containers.
Source: Tax Foundation, 2012 Facts & Figures: How Does Your State Compare?

State-Local Tax Burdens

Area	Rate (%)	Rank[1]	Per Capita Taxes Paid to Home State ($)	Total State and Local Per Capita Taxes Paid ($)	Per Capita Income ($)
Texas	7.9	45	2,248	3,197	40,498
U.S. Average	9.8	-	3,057	4,160	42,539

Note: Figures cover 2009; (1) Rank ranges from 1 to 50 where 1 is highest tax burden
Source: Tax Foundation, State-Local Tax Burdens, All States, 2009

State Business Tax Climate Index Rankings

State	Overall Rank	Corporate Tax Index Rank	Individual Income Tax Index Rank	Sales Tax Index Rank	Unemployment Insurance Tax Index Rank	Property Tax Index Rank
Texas	9	37	7	35	15	31

Note: The index is a measure of how each state's tax laws affect economic performance. The lower the rank, the more favorable a state's tax system is for business. States without a given tax are given a ranking of 1.
Source: Tax Foundation, Major Components of the State Business Tax Climate Index, FY 2012

COMMERCIAL REAL ESTATE

Office Market

Market Area	Inventory (sq. ft.)	Vacant (sq. ft.)	Vac. Rate (%)	Under Constr. (sq. ft.)	Asking Rent ($/sf/yr) Class A	Class B
Austin	43,215,201	6,639,265	15.4	23,000	28.85	21.15

Source: Grubb & Ellis, Office Markets Trends, 4th Quarter 2011

Industrial Market

Market Area	Inventory (sq. ft.)	Vacant (sq. ft.)	Vac. Rate (%)	Under Constr. (sq. ft.)	Asking Rent ($/sf/yr) WH/Dist	R&D/Flex
Austin	77,110,746	9,620,024	12.5	72,000	5.57	9.43

Source: Grubb & Ellis, Industrial Markets Trends, 4th Quarter 2011

COMMERCIAL UTILITIES

Typical Monthly Electric Bills

Area	Commercial Service ($/month) 1,500 kWh	40 kW demand 14,000 kWh	Industrial Service ($/month) 1,000 kW demand 200,000 kWh	50,000 kW demand 15,000,000 kWh
City	n/a	n/a	n/a	n/a
Average[1]	189	1,616	25,197	1,470,813

Note: Based on total rates in effect July 1, 2011; (1) average based on 184 utilities surveyed; n/a not available
Source: Edison Electric Institute, Typical Bills and Average Rates Report, Summer 2011

TRANSPORTATION

Means of Transportation to Work

Area	Car/Truck/Van Drove Alone	Car-pooled	Public Transportation Bus	Subway	Railroad	Bicycle	Walked	Other Means	Worked at Home
City	71.0	11.1	4.9	0.0	0.0	1.2	2.4	3.1	6.2
MSA[1]	74.9	11.4	2.6	0.0	0.0	0.7	1.8	2.2	6.5
U.S.	76.0	10.2	2.7	1.7	0.5	0.5	2.8	1.3	4.2

Note: Figures are percentages and cover workers 16 years of age and older; (1) Figures cover the Austin-Round Rock-San Marcos, TX Metropolitan Statistical Area—see Appendix B for areas included
Source: U.S. Census Bureau, 2008-2010 American Community Survey 3-Year Estimates

Travel Time to Work

Area	Less Than 10 Minutes	10 to 19 Minutes	20 to 29 Minutes	30 to 44 Minutes	45 to 59 Minutes	60 to 89 Minutes	90 Minutes or More
City	11.1	35.5	24.8	19.2	4.6	3.1	1.6
MSA[1]	10.9	30.1	22.9	22.0	7.9	4.4	1.7
U.S.	13.9	30.1	20.8	19.8	7.5	5.5	2.5

Note: Figures are percentages and include workers 16 years old and over; (1) Figures cover the Austin-Round Rock-San Marcos, TX Metropolitan Statistical Area—see Appendix B for areas included
Source: U.S. Census Bureau, 2008-2010 American Community Survey 3-Year Estimates

Travel Time Index

Area	1985	1990	1995	2000	2005	2010
Urban Area[1]	1.11	1.14	1.20	1.23	1.32	1.28
Average[2]	1.11	1.16	1.18	1.21	1.25	1.20

Note: Travel Time Index—the ratio of travel time in the peak period to the travel time at free-flow conditions. A value of 1.30 indicates a 20-minute free-flow trip takes 26 minutes in the peak. Free-flow speeds (60 mph on freeways and 35 mph on principal arterials) are used as the comparison threshold; (1) Covers the Austin TX urban area; (2) average of 439 urban areas
Source: Texas Transportation Institute, Urban Mobility Report 2011, September 2011

Public Transportation

Agency Name / Mode of Transportation	Vehicles Operated in Maximum Service	Annual Unlinked Passenger Trips ('000)	Annual Passenger Miles ('000)
Capital Metropolitan Transportation Authority (CMTA)			
Bus (directly operated)	200	22,655.4	99,719.1
Bus (purchased transportation)	141	12,158.9	41,987.9
Commuter Rail (purchased transportation)	4	120.8	2,145.3
Demand Response (directly operated)	94	471.8	3,473.7
Demand Response (purchased transportation)	13	4.7	42.8
Demand Response Taxi (purchased transportation)	445	189.6	1,234.5
Vanpool (directly operated)	133	258.3	6,117.8

Source: Federal Transit Administration, National Transit Database, 2010

Air Transportation

Airport Name and Code / Type of Service	Passenger Airlines[1]	Passenger Enplanements	Freight Carriers[2]	Freight (lbs.)
Austin-Bergstrom International (AUS)				
Domestic service (U.S. carriers - 2011)	33	4,412,298	18	74,894,957
International service (U.S. carriers - 2010)	9	5,376	3	7,763,158

Note: (1) Includes all U.S.-based major, minor and commuter airlines that carried at least one passenger during the year; (2) Includes all U.S.-based airlines and freight carriers that transported at least one pound of freight during the year
Source: Bureau of Transportation Statistics, The Intermodal Transportation Database, Air Carriers: T-100 Domestic Market (U.S. Carriers), 2011; Bureau of Transportation Statistics, The Intermodal Transportation Database, Air Carriers: T-100 International Market (U.S. Carriers), 2010

Other Transportation Statistics

Major Highways:	I-35
Amtrak Service:	Yes
Major Waterways/Ports:	None

Source: Amtrak.com; Google Maps

BUSINESSES

Major Business Headquarters

Company Name	Rankings	
	Fortune[1]	Forbes[2]
Whole Foods Market	273	-

Note: (1) Fortune 500—companies that produce a 10-K are ranked 1 to 500 based on 2010 revenue; (2) all private companies with at least $2 billion in annual revenue are ranked 1 to 212; companies listed are headquartered in the city; dashes indicate no ranking
Source: Fortune, "Fortune 500," May 23, 2011; Forbes, "America's Largest Private Companies," November 16, 2011

Fast-Growing Businesses

According to *Inc.*, Austin is home to 10 of America's 500 fastest-growing private companies: **Charfen Institute** (#21); **Software Advice** (#134); **Cloud 8 Sixteen** (#167); **SPIbelt** (#175); **Medigap360** (#190); **Kinnser Software** (#334); **Vintage IT Services** (#348); **Q2ebanking** (#377); **CLEAResult Consulting** (#422); **Trade the Markets** (#452). Criteria: must be an independent, privately-held, for-profit, U.S. corporation, proprietorship or partnership; revenues must be at least $80,000 in 2007 and $2 million in 2010; must have four-year operating/sales history. Holding companies, regulated banks, and utilities were excluded. *Inc., "America's 500 Fastest-Growing Private Companies," September 2011*

According to *Fortune*, Austin is home to two of the 100 fastest-growing companies in the world: **Cirrus Logic** (#11); **EZCORP** (#66). Companies were ranked by their revenue growth rate; their EPS growth rate; and their three-year annualized total return to investors for the period ending June 30, 2011. Criteria for inclusion: a company, foreign or domestic, must trade on a major U.S. stock exchange; must file quarterly reports with the SEC; must have a minimum market capitalization of $250 million; must have a stock price of at least $5 on June 30, 2011; must have been trading continuously since June 30, 2008; must have revenue and net income for the four quarters ended on or before April 30, 2011, of at least $50 million and $10 million, respectively; and must have posted a compound annual growth in revenue and earnings per share of at least 15% annually over the three years ending on or before April 30, 2011. REITs, limited-liability companies, limited parterships, companies about to be acquired, and companies that lost money in the quarter ending April 30, 2011 were excluded. *Fortune, "100 Fastest-Growing Companies," September 26, 2011*

According to *Initiative for a Competitive Inner City (ICIC)*, Austin is home to three of America's 100 fastest-growing "inner city" companies: **Aztec Promotional Group** (#40); **OriGen Biomedical** (#52); **PrintGlobe** (#75). Companies were ranked by their five-year compound annual growth rate. Criteria for inclusion: company must be headquartered in or have 51 percent or more of its physical operations in an economically distressed urban area; must be an independent, for-profit corporation, partnership or proprietorship; must have 10 or more employees and have a five-year sales history that includes sales of at least $200,000 in the base year and at least $1 million in the current year with no decrease in sales over the two most recent years. *Initiative for a Competitive Inner City (ICIC), "Inner City 100 Companies, 2011"*

According to Deloitte, Austin is home to six of North America's 500 fastest-growing high-technology companies: **HomeAway.com** (#126); **Applied Nanotech Holdings** (#163); **SolarWinds** (#285); **Convio** (#359); **Luminex Corp.** (#436); **Active Power** (#455). Companies are ranked by percentage growth in revenue over a five-year period. Criteria for inclusion: company must be headquartered within North America; must own proprietary intellectual property or proprietary technology that contributes to a significant portion of the company's operating revenue, or devote a significant proportion of revenues to research and development of technology; must have been in business for a minumum of five years with 2006 operating revenues of at least $50,000 USD/CD and 2010 operating revenues of at least $5 million USD/CD. *Deloitte Touche Tohmatsu, 2011 Deloitte Technology Fast 500[TM]*

Minority Business Opportunity

Austin is home to two companies which are on the *Black Enterprise* Auto Dealer 60 list (60 largest dealers based on gross sales): **JMC Auto Group** (#16); **Davis Automotive** (#26). Criteria: company must be operational in previous calendar year and be at least 51% black-owned. *Black Enterprise, B.E. 100s, 2011*

Austin is home to two companies which are on the *Hispanic Business* 500 list (500 largest U.S. Hispanic-owned companies based on 2010 revenue): **Tramex Travel** (#269); **Realty Marketing Assoc.** (#331). Companies included must show at least 51 percent ownership by Hispanic U.S. citizens, and must maintain headquarters in one of the 50 states or Washington, D.C. *Hispanic Business, "Hispanic Business 500," June 2011*

Minority- and Women-Owned Businesses

Group	All Firms		Firms with Paid Employees			
	Firms	Sales ($000)	Firms	Sales ($000)	Employees	Payroll ($000)
Asian	n/a	n/a	n/a	n/a	n/a	n/a
Black	n/a	n/a	n/a	n/a	n/a	n/a
Hispanic	n/a	n/a	n/a	n/a	n/a	n/a
Women	n/a	n/a	n/a	n/a	n/a	n/a
All Firms	926	302,823	151	235,751	3,366	69,442

Note: Figures cover firms located in the city; minority- and women-owned business are defined as firms in which the corresponding group own 51% or more of the stock or equity of the company; n/a not available
Source: U.S. Census Bureau, 2007 Economic Census, Survey of Business Owners

HOTELS

Hotels/Motels

Area	5 Star		4 Star		3 Star		2 Star		1 Star		Not Rated	
	Num.	Pct.[3]	Num.	Pct.[3]	Num.	Pct.[3]	Num.	Pct.[3]	Num.	Pct.[3]	Num.	Pct.[3]
City[1]	0	0.0	16	7.3	59	26.9	117	53.4	6	2.7	21	9.6
Total[2]	133	0.9	940	6.5	4,569	31.8	7,033	48.9	351	2.4	1,343	9.3

Note: (1) Figures cover Austin and vicinity; (2) Figures cover all 100 cities in this book; (3) Percentage of hotels which have a given star rating; Star ratings are determined by expedia.com and offer an indication of the general quality of a particular hotel.
Source: expedia.com, April 25, 2012

The Austin-Round Rock-San Marcos, TX metro area is home to one of the best hotels in the U.S. according to *Travel & Leisure*: **Four Seasons Hotel, Austin** (#181). Criteria: service; location; rooms; food; and value. *Travel & Leisure, "T+L 500, The World's Best Hotels 2012"*

EVENT SITES

Major Stadiums, Arenas, and Auditoriums

Name	Max. Capacity
Darrell K. Royal-Texas Memorial Stadium	100,119
Frank Erwin Center	17,829

Source: Original research

Convention Centers

Name	Overall Space (sq. ft.)	Exhibit Space (sq. ft.)	Meeting Space (sq. ft.)	Meeting Rooms
Austin Convention Center	881,400	37,170	246,097	54

Source: Original research

Living Environment

COST OF LIVING

Cost of Living Index

Composite Index	Groceries	Housing	Utilities	Trans-portation	Health Care	Misc. Goods/ Services
92.8	85.0	82.3	99.1	101.1	102.1	99.3

Note: U.S. = 100; Figures cover the Austin TX urban area.
Source: The Council for Community and Economic Research, ACCRA Cost of Living Index, 2011

Grocery Prices

Area[1]	T-Bone Steak ($/pound)	Frying Chicken ($/pound)	Whole Milk ($/half gal.)	Eggs ($/dozen)	Orange Juice ($/64 oz.)	Coffee ($/11.5 oz.)
City[2]	9.08	1.17	2.05	1.45	3.43	3.64
Avg.	9.25	1.18	2.22	1.66	3.19	4.40
Min.	6.70	0.88	1.31	0.95	2.46	2.94
Max.	14.30	2.16	3.50	3.18	4.75	6.83

*Note: (1) Values for the local area are compared with the average, minimum and maximum values for all 335 areas in the Cost of Living Index; (2) Figures cover the Austin TX urban area; **T-Bone Steak** (price per pound); **Frying Chicken** (price per pound, whole fryer); **Whole Milk** (half gallon carton); **Eggs** (price per dozen, Grade A, large); **Orange Juice** (64 oz. Tropicana or Florida Natural); **Coffee** (11.5 oz. can, vacuum-packed, Maxwell House, Hills Bros, or Folgers).*
Source: The Council for Community and Economic Research, ACCRA Cost of Living Index, 2011

Housing and Utility Costs

Area[1]	New Home Price ($)	Apartment Rent ($/month)	All Electric ($/month)	Part Electric ($/month)	Other Energy ($/month)	Telephone ($/month)
City[2]	222,483	878	-	92.80	79.38	24.67
Avg.	285,990	839	163.23	89.00	77.52	26.92
Min.	188,005	460	125.58	45.39	33.89	17.98
Max.	1,197,028	3,244	339.16	181.97	348.69	40.01

*Note: (1) Values for the local area are compared with the average, minimum and maximum values for all 335 areas in the Cost of Living Index; (2) Figures cover the Austin TX urban area; **New Home Price** (2,400 sf living area, 8,000 sf lot, in urban area with full utilities); **Apartment Rent** (950 sf 2 bedroom/1.5 or 2 bath, unfurnished, excluding all utilities except water); **All Electric** (average monthly cost for an all-electric home); **Part Electric** (average monthly cost for a part-electric home); **Other Energy** (average monthly cost for natural gas, fuel oil, coal, wood, and any other forms of energy except electricity); **Telephone** (price includes basic monthly rate for a private residential line plus additional local usage charges incurred by a family of four).*
Source: The Council for Community and Economic Research, ACCRA Cost of Living Index, 2011

Health Care, Transportation, and Other Costs

Area[1]	Doctor ($/visit)	Dentist ($/visit)	Optometrist ($/visit)	Gasoline ($/gallon)	Beauty Salon ($/visit)	Men's Shirt ($)
City[2]	80.31	94.25	91.08	3.38	46.67	17.99
Avg.	93.88	81.72	90.54	3.48	32.65	25.06
Min.	60.00	55.33	53.66	3.18	19.78	13.44
Max.	154.98	145.97	183.72	4.31	63.21	46.00

*Note: (1) Values for the local area are compared with the average, minimum and maximum values for all 335 areas in the Cost of Living Index; (2) Figures cover the Austin TX urban area; **Doctor** (general practitioners routine exam of an established patient); **Dentist** (adult teeth cleaning and periodic oral examination); **Optometrist** (full vision eye exam for established adult patient); **Gasoline** (one gallon regular unleaded, national brand, including all taxes, cash price at self-service pump if available); **Beauty Salon** (woman's shampoo, trim, and blow-dry); **Men's Shirt** (cotton/polyester dress shirt, pinpoint weave, long sleeves).*
Source: The Council for Community and Economic Research, ACCRA Cost of Living Index, 2011

HOUSING

House Price Index (HPI)

Area	National Ranking[2]	Quarterly Change (%)	One-Year Change (%)	Five-Year Change (%)
MSA[1]	18	0.87	0.60	9.27
U.S.[3]	-	-0.10	-2.43	-19.16

Note: The HPI is a weighted repeat sales index. It measures average price changes in repeat sales or refinancings on the same properties. This information is obtained by reviewing repeat mortgage transactions on single-family properties whose mortgages have been purchased or securitized by Fannie Mae or Freddie Mac in January 1975; (1) Metropolitan/Micropolitan Statistical Area—see Appendix B for areas included; (2) Rankings are based on annual percentage change for all metro areas containing at least 15,000 transactions over the last 10 years and ranges from 1 to 306; (3) figures based on a weighted average of Census Division estimates using a purchase only index; all figures are for the period ending December 31, 2011
Source: Federal Housing Finance Agency, House Price Index, February 23, 2012

House Price Valuations

Area	Q4 2005 Price ($000)	Over-valuation	Q4 2006 Price ($000)	Over-valuation	Q4 2007 Price ($000)	Over-valuation	Q4 2008 Price ($000)	Over-valuation	Q4 2009 Price ($000)	Over-valuation
MSA[1]	148.8	-10.8	163.3	-7.1	174.1	-4.4	177.4	-2.9	177.0	-2.2

Note: Figures show the percentage of over- or under-valuation of single family homes relative to statistically normal house values (e.g. a value of 23.6 indicates that house values are 23.6% overvalued). Statistically normal house values are based on house prices, interest rates, household incomes, population densities, and any historical premiums or discounts metropolitan areas have exhibited over time; (1) Figures cover the Austin-Round Rock-San Marcos, TX - see Appendix B for areas included
Source: Global Insight/PNC Financial Services Group, House Prices in America: 4th Quarter 2009 Update

Median Single-Family Home Prices

Area	2009	2010	2011p	Percent Change 2010 to 2011
MSA[1]	187.4	193.6	193.1	-0.3
U.S. Average	172.1	173.1	166.2	-4.0

Note: Figures are median sales prices of existing single-family homes in thousands of dollars; (p) preliminary; n/a not available; (1) Metropolitan Statistical Area—see Appendix B for areas included
Source: National Association of Realtors, Median Sales Price of Existing Single-Family Homes for Metropolitan Areas, 4th Quarter 2011

Affordability Index of Existing Single-Family Homes

Area	2009	2010	2011p	Percent Change 2010 to 2011
MSA[1]	97.1	99.6	104.6	5.0

Note: The housing affordability index measures whether or not a typical family could qualify for a mortgage loan on a typical home. The higher the index, the greater the household purchasing power. An index of 100 is defined as the point where a median-income household has exactly enough income to qualify for the purchase of a median-priced existing single-family home, assuming a 20 percent downpayment and 25 percent of gross income devoted to mortgage principal and interest payments; (p) preliminary; n/a not available; (1) Metropolitan Statistical Area—see Appendix B for areas included
Source: National Association of Realtors, Affordability Index of Existing Single-Family Homes, 2011

Median Apartment Condo-Coop Home Prices

Area	2009	2010	2011p	Percent Change 2010 to 2011
MSA[1]	150.9	155.5	168.8	8.6
U.S. Average	175.6	171.7	165.1	-3.8

Note: Figures are median sales prices of existing apartment condo-coop homes in thousands of dollars; (p) preliminary; n/a not available; (1) Metropolitan Statistical Area—see Appendix B for areas included
Source: National Association of Realtors, Median Sales Price of Existing Apartment Condo-Coop Homes for Metropolitan Areas, 4th Quarter 2011

Year Housing Structure Built

Area	2005 or Later	2000 -2004	1990 -1999	1980 -1989	1970 -1979	1960 -1969	1950 -1959	Before 1950	Median Year
City	8.6	11.4	16.2	21.6	20.6	8.9	6.3	6.5	1984
MSA[1]	12.1	16.6	20.5	19.9	15.5	5.9	4.5	5.1	1990
U.S.	5.0	8.6	14.0	14.1	16.3	11.3	11.2	19.6	1975

Note: Figures are percentages except for Median Year; (1) Figures cover the Austin-Round Rock-San Marcos, TX Metropolitan Statistical Area—see Appendix B for areas included
Source: U.S. Census Bureau, 2008-2010 American Community Survey 3-Year Estimates

HEALTH

Health Risk Data

Category	MSA[1] (%)	U.S. (%)
Adults who have been told they have high blood pressure[2]	27.8	28.7
Adults who have been told they have high blood cholesterol[2]	37.9	37.5
Adults who have been told they have diabetes[3]	5.7	8.7
Adults who have been told they have arthritis[2]	18.6	26.0
Adults who have been told they currently have asthma	7.0	9.1
Adults who are current smokers	10.4	17.3
Adults who are heavy drinkers[4]	5.0	5.0
Adults who are binge drinkers[5]	18.4	15.1
Adults who are overweight (BMI 25.0 - 29.9)	37.1	36.2
Adults who are obese (BMI 30.0 - 99.8)	27.0	27.5
Adults who participated in any physical activities in the past month	80.7	76.1
Adults 50+ who have ever had a sigmoidoscopy or colonoscopy	71.4	65.2
Women aged 40+ who have had a mammogram within the past two years	75.0	75.2
Men aged 40+ who have had a PSA test within the past two years	n/a	53.2
Adults aged 65+ who have had flu shot within the past year	71.1	67.5
Adults aged 18–64 who have any kind of health care coverage	86.5	82.2

Note: Data as of 2010 unless otherwise noted; n/a not available; (1) Figures cover the Austin-Round Rock, TX Metropolitan Statistical Area—see Appendix B for areas included; (2) Data as of 2009; (3) Figures do not include pregnancy-related, borderline, or pre-diabetes; (4) Heavy drinkers are classified as males having more than two drinks per day or females having more than one drink per day; (5) Binge drinkers are classified as males having five or more drinks on one occasion or females having four or more drinks on one occasion
Source: Centers for Disease Control and Prevention, Behaviorial Risk Factor Surveillance System, SMART: Selected Metropolitan/Micropolitan Area Risk Trends, 2009, 2010

Mortality Rates for the Top 10 Causes of Death in the U.S.

ICD-10[a] Sub-Chapter	ICD-10[a] Code	County[2]	U.S.
Malignant neoplasms	C00-C97	155.2	175.6
Ischaemic heart diseases	I20-I25	88.9	121.6
Other forms of heart disease	I30-I51	40.4	48.6
Chronic lower respiratory diseases	J40-J47	34.6	42.3
Cerebrovascular diseases	I60-I69	42.3	40.6
Organic, including symptomatic, mental disorders	F01-F09	46.1	26.7
Other degenerative diseases of the nervous system	G30-G31	25.7	24.7
Other external causes of accidental injury	W00-X59	29.4	24.4
Diabetes mellitus	E10-E14	17.5	21.7
Hypertensive diseases	I10-I15	20.2	18.2

Age-Adjusted Mortality Rate[1] per 100,000 population

Note: (a) ICD-10 = International Classification of Diseases 10th Revision; (1) Mortality rates are a three year average covering 2007-2009; (2) Figures cover Travis County
Source: Centers for Disease Control and Prevention, National Center for Health Statistics. Underlying Cause of Death 1999-2009 on CDC WONDER Online Database, released 2012. Data for year 2009 are compiled from the Multiple Cause of Death File 2009, Series 20 No. 2O, 2012, Data for year 2008 are compiled from the Multiple Cause of Death File 2008, Series 20 No. 2N, 2011, Data for year 2007 are compiled from Multiple Cause of Death File 2007, Series 20 No. 2M, 2010.

Mortality Rates for Selected Causes of Death

ICD-10[a] Sub-Chapter	ICD-10[a] Code	Age-Adjusted Mortality Rate[1] per 100,000 population	
		County[2]	U.S.
Assault	X85-Y09	2.5	5.7
Human immunodeficiency virus (HIV) disease	B20-B24	3.6	3.3
Influenza and pneumonia	J09-J18	11.1	16.4
Intentional self-harm	X60-X84	11.1	11.5
Malnutrition	E40-E46	*Unreliable	0.8
Obesity and other hyperalimentation	E65-E68	1.5	1.6
Transport accidents	V01-V99	11.2	13.7
Viral hepatitis	B15-B19	2.7	2.2

Note: (a) ICD-10 = International Classification of Diseases 10th Revision; (1) Mortality rates are a three year average covering 2007-2009; (2) Figures cover Travis County; (*) Unreliable data as per CDC
Source: Centers for Disease Control and Prevention, National Center for Health Statistics. Underlying Cause of Death 1999-2009 on CDC WONDER Online Database, released 2012. Data for year 2009 are compiled from the Multiple Cause of Death File 2009, Series 20 No. 2O, 2012, Data for year 2008 are compiled from the Multiple Cause of Death File 2008, Series 20 No. 2N, 2011, Data for year 2007 are compiled from Multiple Cause of Death File 2007, Series 20 No. 2M, 2010.

Distribution of Physicians and Dentists

Area[1]	Dentists[2]	D.O.[3]	M.D.[4]				
			Total	Family/ General Practice	Pediatrics	Medical Specialties	Surgical Specialties
Local (number)	440	124	2,261	286	174	769	516
Local (rate[5])	4.5	1.2	22.6	2.9	1.7	7.7	5.2
U.S. (rate[5])	4.5	1.9	18.3	2.5	1.4	6.8	4.1

Note: Data as of 2008 unless noted; (1) Local data covers Travis County; (2) Data as of 2007; (3) Doctor of Osteopathic Medicine; (4) Includes active, non-federal, patient-care, office-based Doctors of Medicine; (5) rate per 10,000 population
Source: Area Resource File (ARF). 2009-2010 Release. U.S. Department of Health and Human Services, Health Resources and Services Administration, Bureau of Health Professions, Rockville, MD, August 2010

EDUCATION

Public School District Statistics

District Name	Schls	Pupils	Pupil/ Teacher Ratio	Minority Pupils[1] (%)	Free Lunch Eligible[2] (%)	IEP[3] (%)
Austin ISD	122	84,676	14.2	74.2	56.6	9.5
Eanes ISD	9	7,498	13.4	19.8	2.0	7.8
Lake Travis ISD	9	6,577	15.1	22.9	11.3	7.5

Note: Table includes school districts with 2,000 or more students; (1) Percentage of students that are not non-Hispanic white; (2) Percentage of students that are eligible for the free lunch program; (3) Percentage of students that have an Individualized Education Program.
Source: U.S. Department of Education, National Center for Education Statistics, Common Core of Data, Local Education Agency (School District) Universe Survey: School Year 2009-2010; U.S. Department of Education, National Center for Education Statistics, Common Core of Data, Public Elementary/Secondary School Universe Survey: School Year 2009-2010

Top Public High Schools

High School Name	Rank[1]	Score[1]	Grad. Rate[2] (%)	College[3] (%)	AP/IB/ AICE[4] (%)	SAT/ ACT[5] (%)
L C Anderson	474	0.122	93	77	2.6	1721
Lake Travis	488	0.102	94	79	1.8	1674
Liberal Arts and Science Academy	21	1.416	100	96	6.7	1877
Westlake	72	0.858	98	87	5.3	1795
Westwood	47	1.036	98	93	4.6	1801

Note: (1) Public schools are ranked from 1 to 500 based on the following self-reported statistics (with their corresponding weight in the final score). Schools that had fewer than 10 graduates, as well as those that were newly founded and did not have a graduating senior class in 2010 were excluded; (2) Four-year, on-time graduation rate (25%); (3) Percent of 2010 graduates who enrolled immediately in college (25%); (4) AP/IB/AICE tests per graduate (25%); (5) Average SAT and/or ACT score (10%); Average AP/IB/AICE exam score (10%); AP/IB/AICE courses offered per graduate (5%); (6) School is unranked, but has been identified by Newsweek as one of the nation's most elite public high schools.
Source: Newsweek Online, "Top High Schools 2011"

Highest Level of Education

Area	Less than H.S.	H.S. Diploma	Some College, No Deg.	Associate Degree	Bachelors Degree	Masters Degree	Profess. School Degree	Doctorate Degree
City	14.9	16.8	19.1	5.4	27.5	11.2	2.9	2.3
MSA[1]	12.7	19.7	22.0	6.4	25.5	9.7	2.3	1.7
U.S.	14.7	28.4	21.3	7.6	17.6	7.2	1.9	1.2

Note: Figures cover persons age 25 and over; (1) Figures cover the Austin-Round Rock-San Marcos, TX Metropolitan Statistical Area—see Appendix B for areas included
Source: U.S. Census Bureau, 2008-2010 American Community Survey 3-Year Estimates

Educational Attainment by Race

Area	High School Graduate or Higher (%)					Bachelor's Degree or Higher (%)				
	Total	White	Black	Asian	Hisp.[2]	Total	White	Black	Asian	Hisp.[2]
City	85.1	89.8	85.9	92.6	60.6	43.9	49.8	20.8	70.0	17.6
MSA[1]	87.3	90.5	87.9	91.6	64.5	39.2	42.5	21.8	66.4	16.9
U.S.	85.3	87.5	81.4	85.5	61.6	28.0	29.3	17.8	50.2	13.0

Note: Figures shown cover persons 25 years old and over; (1) Figures cover the Austin-Round Rock-San Marcos, TX Metropolitan Statistical Area—see Appendix B for areas included; (2) People of Hispanic origin can be of any race
Source: U.S. Census Bureau, 2008-2010 American Community Survey 3-Year Estimates

School Enrollment by Grade and Control

Area	Preschool (%)		Kindergarten (%)		Grades 1 - 4 (%)		Grades 5 - 8 (%)		Grades 9 - 12 (%)	
	Public	Private	Public	Private	Public	Private	Public	Private	Public	Private
City	53.7	46.3	92.7	7.3	91.4	8.6	92.5	7.5	93.2	6.8
MSA[1]	50.0	50.0	90.8	9.2	92.4	7.6	93.0	7.0	93.2	6.8
U.S.	55.4	44.6	87.1	12.9	89.4	10.6	89.5	10.5	90.4	9.6

Note: Figures shown cover persons 3 years old and over; (1) Figures cover the Austin-Round Rock-San Marcos, TX Metropolitan Statistical Area—see Appendix B for areas included
Source: U.S. Census Bureau, 2008-2010 American Community Survey 3-Year Estimates

Average Salaries of Public School Classroom Teachers

Area	2010-11		2011-12		Percent Change 2010-11 to 2011-12	Percent Change 2001-02 to 2011-12
	Dollars	Rank[1]	Dollars	Rank[1]		
Texas	48,638	31	49,017	31	0.78	24.90
U.S. Average	55,623	-	56,643	-	1.83	26.8

Note: (1) State rank ranges from 1 to 51 where 1 indicates highest salary.
Source: National Education Association, Rankings & Estimates: Rankings of the States 2011 and Estimates of School Statistics 2012, December 2011

Higher Education

Four-Year Colleges			Two-Year Colleges			Medical Schools[1]	Law Schools[2]	Voc/ Tech[3]
Public	Private Non-profit	Private For-profit	Public	Private Non-profit	Private For-profit			
1	6	7	1	0	7	0	1	10

Note: Figures cover institutions located within the city limits and include main campuses only; (1) includes schools accredited by the Liaison Committee on Medical Education and the American Osteopathic Association's Commission on Osteopathic College Accreditation; (2) includes American Bar Association-accredited law schools; (3) includes all schools with programs that are less than 2 years.
Source: National Center for Education Statistics, Integrated Postsecondary Education System (IPEDS) Peer Analysis System, 2011-12; Association of American Medical Colleges, Member List, April 23, 2012; American Osteopathic Association, Member List, April 23, 2012; Law School Admission Council, Official Guide to ABA-Approved Law Schools Online, April 23, 2012

According to *U.S. News & World Report,* the Austin-Round Rock-San Marcos, TX is home to one of the best national universities in the U.S.: **University of Texas–Austin** (#45). The indicators used to capture academic quality fall into a number of categories: assessment by administrators at peer institutions; retention of students; faculty resources; student selectivity; financial resources; alumni giving; high school counselor ratings of colleges; and graduation rate.*U.S. News & World Report, "America's Best Colleges 2012"*

According to *U.S. News & World Report,* the Austin-Round Rock-San Marcos, TX is home to one of the best liberal arts colleges in the U.S.: **Southwestern University** (#71). The indicators used to capture academic quality fall into a number of categories: assessment by administrators at peer institutions; retention of students; faculty resources; student selectivity; financial resources; alumni giving; high school counselor ratings of colleges; and graduation rate.*U.S. News & World Report, "America's Best Colleges 2012"*

According to *U.S. News & World Report,* the Austin-Round Rock-San Marcos, TX is home to one of the best law schools in the U.S.: **University of Texas–Austin** (#16). The rankings are based on a weighted average of 12 measures of quality: peer assessment score; assessment score by lawyers/judges; median LSAT scores; median undergrad GPA; acceptance rate; employment rates for graduates; placement success; bar passage rate; faculty resources; expenditures per student; student/faculty ratio; and library resources. *U.S. News & World Report, "America's Best Law Schools 2013"*

According to *Forbes,* the Austin-Round Rock-San Marcos, TX is home to one of the best business schools in the U.S.: **Texas-Austin (McCombs)** (#17). The rankings are based on the return on investment that graduates of the Class of 2006 received (median salary five years after graduation). *Forbes, "Best Business Schools," August 3, 2011*

PRESIDENTIAL ELECTION

2008 Presidential Election Results

Area	Obama	McCain	Nader	Other
Travis County	63.5	34.3	0.2	2.0
U.S.	52.9	45.6	0.6	0.9

Note: Results are percentages and may not add to 100% due to rounding
Source: Dave Leip's Atlas of U.S. Presidential Elections, www.uselectionatlas.org

EMPLOYERS

Major Employers

Company Name	Industry
3M Company	Tape, pressure sensitive: made from purchased materials
Attorney General, Texas	Attorney general's office
Dell	Electronic computers
Dell USA Corporation	Business management
Environmental Quality, Texas Comm On	Air, water, & solid waste management
Environmental Quality, Texas Comm On	Air, water, and solid waste management
Freescale Semiconductor	Semiconductors and related devices
Freescale Semiconductor	Electronic research
Hospital Housekeeping Systems GP	Cleaning service, industrial or commercial
Internal Revenue Service	Taxation department, government
Legislative Office, Texas	Legislative bodies
Nextel of Texas	Radiotelephone communication
Pleasant Hill Preservation LP	Apartment building operators
State Farm	Automobile insurance
Texas Department of Public Safety	Public order and safety statistics centers
Texas Department of State Health Services	Administration of public health programs
Texas State University-San Marcos	Colleges and universities
Texas Workforce Commission	Administration of social and manpower programs
Univ of Texas System	Academy
Univ of Texas System	Generation, electric power
University of Texas at Austin	University

Note: Companies shown are located within the Austin-Round Rock-San Marcos, TX metropolitan area.
Source: Hoovers.com, data extracted April 25 2012

Best Companies to Work For

National Instruments; Whole Foods Market, headquartered in Austin, are among "The 100 Best Companies to Work For." To pick the 100 Best Companies to Work For, *Fortune* partnered with the Great Place to Work Institute. Two hundred eighty firms participated in this year's survey. Two-thirds of a company's score is based on the results of the Institute's Trust Index survey, which is sent to a random sample of employees from each company. The questions related to attitudes about management's credibility, job satisfaction, and camaraderie. The other third of the scoring is based on the company's responses to the Institute's Culture Audit, which includes detailed questions about pay and benefit programs, and a series of open-ended questions about hiring practices, internal communication, training, recognition programs, and diversity efforts. Any company that is at least five years old with more than 1,000 U.S. employees is eligible. *Fortune, "The 100 Best Companies to Work For," February 6, 2012*

PUBLIC SAFETY

Crime Rate

Area	All Crimes	Violent Crimes				Property Crimes		
		Murder	Forcible Rape	Robbery	Aggrav. Assault	Burglary	Larceny -Theft	Motor Vehicle Theft
City	6,230.7	4.8	33.3	154.6	283.3	1,098.7	4,373.5	282.6
Suburbs[1]	2,362.0	2.3	17.5	25.2	159.6	467.5	1,612.2	77.8
Metro[2]	4,119.9	3.4	24.7	84.0	215.8	754.3	2,866.9	170.8
U.S.	3,345.5	4.8	27.5	119.1	252.3	699.6	2,003.5	238.8

Note: Figures are crimes per 100,000 population; (1) All areas within the metro area that are located outside the city limits; (2) Metropolitan Statistical Area—see Appendix B for areas included
Source: FBI Uniform Crime Reports, 2010

Hate Crimes

Area	Number of Quarters Reported	Bias Motivation				
		Race	Religion	Sexual Orientation	Ethnicity	Disability
City	4	0	1	3	1	0

Source: Federal Bureau of Investigation, Hate Crime Statistics 2010

Identity Theft Consumer Complaints

Area	Complaints	Complaints per 100,000 Population	Rank[2]
MSA[1]	1,367	85.5	143
U.S.	279,156	90.4	-

Note: (1) Metropolitan Statistical Area—see Appendix B for areas included; (2) Rank ranges from 1 to 384
where 1 indicates greatest number of identity theft complaints per 100,000 population
Source: Federal Trade Commission, Consumer Sentinel Network Data Book for January–December 2011

Fraud and Other Consumer Complaints

Area	Complaints	Complaints per 100,000 Population	Rank[2]
MSA[1]	8,347	522.3	122
U.S.	1,533,924	496.8	-

Note: (1) Metropolitan Statistical Area—see Appendix B for areas included; (2) Rank ranges from 1 to 384
where 1 indicates greatest number of fraud and other complaints per 100,000 population
Source: Federal Trade Commission, Consumer Sentinel Network Data Book for January–December 2011

RECREATION

Culture

Dance[1]	Theatre[1]	Instrumental Music[1]	Vocal Music[1]	Series/ Festivals	Museums	Zoos and Aquariums[2]
3	7	3	2	5	17	0

Note: (1) Number of professional performing groups; (2) AZA-accredited
Source: The Grey House Performing Arts Directory, 2011-2012; Official Museum Directory, 2011; American
Association of Museums, AAM Member Museums, April 2012; Association of Zoos & Aquariums, AZA Member
Zoos & Aquariums, April 2012

Professional Sports Teams

Team Name	League
No teams are located in the metro area	

Source: Original research

CLIMATE

Average and Extreme Temperatures

Temperature	Jan	Feb	Mar	Apr	May	Jun	Jul	Aug	Sep	Oct	Nov	Dec	Yr.
Extreme High (°F)	90	97	98	98	100	105	109	106	104	98	91	90	109
Average High (°F)	60	64	72	79	85	91	95	96	90	81	70	63	79
Average Temp. (°F)	50	53	61	69	75	82	85	85	80	70	60	52	69
Average Low (°F)	39	43	50	58	65	72	74	74	69	59	49	41	58
Extreme Low (°F)	-2	7	18	35	43	53	64	61	47	32	20	4	-2

Note: Figures cover the years 1948-1990
Source: National Climatic Data Center, International Station Meteorological Climate Summary, 9/96

Average Precipitation/Snowfall/Humidity

Precip./Humidity	Jan	Feb	Mar	Apr	May	Jun	Jul	Aug	Sep	Oct	Nov	Dec	Yr.
Avg. Precip. (in.)	1.6	2.3	1.8	2.9	4.3	3.5	1.9	1.9	3.3	3.5	2.1	1.9	31.1
Avg. Snowfall (in.)	1	Tr	Tr	0	0	0	0	0	0	0	Tr	Tr	1
Avg. Rel. Hum. 6am (%)	79	80	79	83	88	89	88	87	86	84	81	79	84
Avg. Rel. Hum. 3pm (%)	53	51	47	50	53	49	43	42	47	47	49	51	48

Note: Figures cover the years 1948-1990; Tr = Trace amounts (<0.05 in. of rain; <0.5 in. of snow)
Source: National Climatic Data Center, International Station Meteorological Climate Summary, 9/96

Weather Conditions

Temperature			Daytime Sky			Precipitation		
10°F & below	32°F & below	90°F & above	Clear	Partly cloudy	Cloudy	0.01 inch or more precip.	0.1 inch or more snow/ice	Thunder-storms
<1	20	111	105	148	112	83	1	41

Note: Figures are average number of days per year and cover the years 1948-1990
Source: National Climatic Data Center, International Station Meteorological Climate Summary, 9/96

HAZARDOUS WASTE

Superfund Sites

Austin has no sites on the EPA's Superfund Final National Priorities List.
U.S. Environmental Protection Agency, Final National Priorities List, April 17, 2012

AIR & WATER QUALITY

Air Quality Index

Area	Percent of Days when Air Quality was...[2]					AQI Statistics[2]	
	Good	Moderate	Unhealthy for Sensitive Groups	Unhealthy	Very Unhealthy	Maximum	Median
Area[1]	74.0	25.2	0.8	0.0	0.0	116	40

Note: Air Quality Index (AQI) is an index for reporting daily air quality. EPA calculates the AQI for five major air pollutants regulated by the Clean Air Act: ground-level ozone, particle pollution (aka particulate matter), carbon monoxide, sulfur dioxide, and nitrogen dioxide. The AQI runs from 0 to 500. The higher the AQI value, the greater the level of air pollution and the greater the health concern. There are six AQI categories: "Good" AQI is between 0 and 50. Air quality is considered satisfactory; "Moderate" AQI is between 51 and 100. Air quality is acceptable; "Unhealthy for Sensitive Groups" When AQI values are between 101 and 150, members of sensitive groups may experience health effects; "Unhealthy" When AQI values are between 151 and 200 everyone may begin to experience health effects; "Very Unhealthy" AQI values between 201 and 300 trigger a health alert; "Hazardous" AQI values over 300 trigger warnings of emergency conditions (not shown); (1) Data covers Travis County; (2) Based on 365 days with AQI data in 2011.
Source: U.S. Environmental Protection Agency, AirData Report, 2011

Air Quality Index Pollutants

Area	Percent of Days when AQI Pollutant was...[2]					
	Carbon Monoxide	Nitrogen Dioxide	Ozone	Sulfur Dioxide	Particulate Matter 2.5	Particulate Matter 10
Area[1]	0.0	0.5	69.9	0.0	29.6	0.0

Note: The Air Quality Index (AQI) is an index for reporting daily air quality. EPA calculates the AQI for five major air pollutants regulated by the Clean Air Act: ground-level ozone, particle pollution (also known as particulate matter), carbon monoxide, sulfur dioxide, and nitrogen dioxide. The AQI runs from 0 to 500. The higher the AQI value, the greater the level of air pollution and the greater the health concern; (1) Data covers Travis County; (2) Based on 365 days with AQI data in 2011.
Source: U.S. Environmental Protection Agency, AirData Report, 2011

Air Quality Index Trends

Area	Trend Sites (days)								All Sites (days)
	2003	2004	2005	2006	2007	2008	2009	2010	2010
MSA[1]	10	10	11	14	4	2	4	2	3

Note: Figures are the number of days the AQI value exceeded 100 in a given year. An AQI value greater than 100 indicates that air quality would have been in the unhealthful range on that day. Data from exceptional events are included. These counts are presented in two ways. First, the counts are based on sites having an adequate record of monitoring data during the trend period (trend sites). These counts represent the relative change in the number of days with AQI values greater than 100. In the last column, the counts are based on all sites with data in the most recent year (because it is possible for a site to have data in the most recent year but not enough data to be a trend site); (1) Data covers the Austin-Round Rock-San Marcos, TX—see Appendix B for areas included
Source: U.S. Environmental Protection Agency, Air Quality Index Information, "Number of Days with Air Quality Index Values Greater than 100 at Trend Sites, 2000-2010, and at All Sites in 2010"

Maximum Air Pollutant Concentrations: Particulate Matter, Ozone, CO and Lead

	Particulate Matter 10 (ug/m³)	Particulate Matter 2.5 Wtd AM (ug/m³)	Particulate Matter 2.5 24-Hr (ug/m³)	Ozone (ppm)	Carbon Monoxide (ppm)	Lead (ug/m³)
MSA[1] Level	34	10	19	0.074	0	n/a
NAAQS[2]	150	15	35	0.075	9	0.15
Met NAAQS[2]	Yes	Yes	Yes	Yes	Yes	n/a

Note: Data from exceptional events are not included; (1) Data covers the Austin-Round Rock-San Marcos, TX—see Appendix B for areas included; (2) National Ambient Air Quality Standards; ppm = parts per million; ug/m³ = micrograms per cubic meter; n/a not available
Concentrations: Particulate Matter 10 (coarse particulate)—highest second maximum 24-hour concentration; Particulate Matter 2.5 Wtd AM (fine particulate)—highest weighted annual mean concentration; Particulate Matter 2.5 24-Hour (fine particulate)—highest 98th percentile 24-hour concentration; Ozone—highest fourth daily maximum 8-hour concentration; Carbon Monoxide—highest second maximum non-overlapping 8-hour concentration; Lead—maximum running 3-month average
Source: U.S. Environmental Protection Agency, CBSA Factbook 2010, Air Quality Statistics by City, 2010

Maximum Air Pollutant Concentrations: Nitrogen Dioxide and Sulfur Dioxide

	Nitrogen Dioxide AM (ppb)	Nitrogen Dioxide 1-Hr (ppb)	Sulfur Dioxide AM (ppb)	Sulfur Dioxide 1-Hr (ppb)	Sulfur Dioxide 24-Hr (ppb)
MSA[1] Level	3.314	21.1	n/a	n/a	n/a
NAAQS[2]	53	100	30	75	140
Met NAAQS[2]	Yes	Yes	n/a	n/a	n/a

Note: Data from exceptional events are not included; (1) Data covers the Austin-Round Rock-San Marcos, TX—see Appendix B for areas included; (2) National Ambient Air Quality Standards; ppb = parts per billion; n/a not available
Concentrations: Nitrogen Dioxide AM—highest arithmetic mean concentration; Nitrogen Dioxide 1-Hr—highest 98th percentile 1-hour daily maximum concentration; Sulfur Dioxide AM—highest annual mean concentration; Sulfur Dioxide 1-Hr—highest 99th percentile 1-hour daily maximum concentration; Sulfur Dioxide 24-Hr—highest second maximum 24-hour concentration
Source: U.S. Environmental Protection Agency, CBSA Factbook 2010, Air Quality Statistics by City, 2010

Drinking Water

Water System Name	Pop. Served	Primary Water Source Type	Violations[1] Health Based	Violations[1] Monitoring/ Reporting
Austin Water & Wastewater	780,647	Surface	0	0

Note: (1) Based on violation data from January 1, 2011 to December 31, 2011 (includes unresolved violations from earlier years)
Source: U.S. Environmental Protection Agency, Office of Ground Water and Drinking Water, Safe Drinking Water Information System (based on data extracted April 18, 2012)

Cape Coral, Florida

Background

Tucked along Florida's Gulf Coast 71 miles south of Sarasota, Cape Coral is a mid-twentieth century community grown from a development launched in 1957. Today, at 115 square miles, it is Florida's third-largest city by land mass and the most populous city between Tampa and Miami. To the east across the Caloosahatchie River lies Fort Myers, and to the west across Pine Island and Pine Island sound lie the fabled barrier islands of Captiva and Sanibel by Pine Island and Pine Island Sound.

Baltimore brothers Leonard and Jack Rosen purchased the former Redfish Point for $678,000 and renamed the property Cape Coral. By June of the following year "the Cape," as it is known, was receiving its first residents. The city incorporated in 1970 when its population reached 11,470.

Despite the city's relative youth, this self-named "Waterfront Wonderland" has developed an interest in its roots. It fosters a Cape Coral Historical Museum that is housed in the original snack bar from the local country club, and one of its oldest historical documents is the Cape's 1961 phone book.

Four hundred precious miles of salt water and fresh water canals slice through the city, providing water access to abundant recreational boaters and numerous opportunities for waterfront living.

Following the economic downturn, Cape Coral in 2012 is rebounding nicely. It was named a "most improved" housing market in a National Association of Builders report, and Realty Trac showed improvement in the area's foreclosures at the same time. The Army Reserve finalized purchase of a 15-acre Cape Coral site where it will open an Army Reserve Training Center for local reservists.

In April, the city won an auction by bidding just over $13 million for 491 parcels of foreclosed property—a total of 652 acres mostly north of Pine Island Road—that will be most likely be used for retention ponds and related efforts to upgrade storm-water utilities.

Industry-wise, Cape Coral has Foreign Trade Zones in two of its three industrial parks, the 92.5 acre North Cape Industrial Park—home to light manufacturers, service industry and warehouses—and the Mid Cape Commerce Park which, at 143.37 acres, is comprised of service industries and warehouses. In addition, the city has several other development districts for purposes ranging from housing to a proposed VA Clinic to be built by the U.S. Dept. of Veteran's Affairs at the Hancock Creek Commerce Park and Indian Oaks Trade Centre.

The VA Clinic will provide a full range of services ranging from mental health and diagnostic radiology to urology and a full complement of imaging services such as CT scans and nuclear medicine. It is the centerpiece of a Veterans Investment Zone initiative that is proposed to draw office, medical parks, assisted living facilities and the like.

Today the U.S. Bureau of Labor Statistics tracks Cape Coral's success in conjunction with that of nearby Fort Myers, and the region boasts trade, transportation and utilities as its largest economic sector. Essentially, this is a retirement and tourism destination.

Significant recreational opportunities are available in the area, and include the Four Mile Cove Ecological Preserve with its nature trail, picnic area, and warm weather kayak rentals. The Cape Coral Yacht Club, located where the city first began, includes a fishing pier, beach, and community pool. The 18-hole public Coral Oaks Golf Course (replete with pro shop and pub), the Northwest Softball Complex, the William Bill Austen Youth Center Eagle Skate Park, the Strausser BMX Sports Complex, and even the Pelican Sport Soccer Complex show the city's diverse recreational opportunities.

To the east of Cape Coral—on the other side of Fort Myers—is both the Florida Gulf Coast University and Southwest Florida International Airport.

Cape Coral's climate borders on perfect, with an average 335 days per year of sunshine (albeit hot and humid ones in summer time). Annual rainfall is 53.37 inches, with the most rain coming in summer. The city dries out from October into May.

Rankings

Business/Finance Rankings

- *American City Business Journals* ranked America's 261 largest cities in terms of their resident's wealth. Cape Coral ranked #115. Criteria: per capita income; median household income; percentage of households with annual incomes of $200,000 or more; median home value. *American City Business Journals, "Where the Money Is: America's Wealth Centers," August 18, 2008*

- The Cape Coral metro area appeared on the Milken Institute "2011 Best Performing Metros" list. Rank: #200 out of 200 large metro areas. Criteria: job growth; wage and salary growth; high-tech output growth. *Milken Institute, "2011 Best Performing Metros"*

- *Forbes* ranked the 200 most populous metro areas in the U.S. in terms of the "Best Places for Business and Careers." The Cape Coral metro area was ranked #158. Criteria: costs (business and living); job growth (past and projected); income growth; educational attainment; projected economic growth; crime; cultural and recreational opportunities; net migration patterns; number of highly ranked colleges. *Forbes, "Best Places for Business and Careers," June 2011*

Children/Family Rankings

- The Cape Coral metro area was selected as one of the "Best Cities for Relocating Families" by Worldwide ERC and Primacy Relocation. The 2008 study looked at nearly 50 factors important to relocating families including: recent job growth; nearby top-ranked colleges; in-state tuition for four-year public colleges; population growth since 2000; pediatricians per 100,000 population; and a Green Living index. *Worldwide ERC and Primacy Relocation, "2008 Best Cities for Relocating Families"*

Education Rankings

- Cape Coral was identified as one of the 100 "smartest" metro areas in the U.S. The area ranked #80. Criteria: the editors rated the collective brainpower of the 100 largest metro areas in the U.S. based on their residents' educational attainment. *American City Business Journals, April 14, 2008*

- Cape Coral was identified as one of "America's Brainiest Bastions" by *Portfolio.com*. The metro area ranked #125 out of 200. *Portfolio.com* analyzed levels of educational attainment in the nation's 200 largest metropolitan areas. The editors established scores for five levels of educational attainment, based on relative earning power of adult workers age 25 or older. Scores were determined by comparing the median income for all workers with the median income for those workers at a specified educational level. *Portfolio.com, "America's Brainiest Bastions," December 1, 2010*

Environmental Rankings

- Cape Coral was selected as one of 22 "Smarter Cities" for energy by the Natural Resources Defense Council. Criteria: investment in green power; energy efficiency measures; conservation. *Natural Resources Defense Council, "2010 Smarter Cities," July 19, 2010*

- 100 of the largest metro areas in the U.S. were analyzed in terms of their current drought severity. The Cape Coral metro area ranked #20 (#1 = driest). The rankings were based on statistics such as long-term precipitation trends and patterns and the Palmer drought indices. *Sperling's BestPlaces, www.BestPlaces.net, "America's Drought-Riskiest Cities," November 2007*

- The Cape Coral metro area appeared in *Country Home's* "Best Green Places" report. The area ranked #275 out of 379. Criteria: official energy policies; green power; green buildings; availability of fresh, locally grown food. *Country Home, "Best Green Places," 2008*

- Cape Coral was highlighted as one of the top 25 cleanest metro areas for year-round particle pollution (Annual PM 2.5) in the U.S. The area ranked #14. *American Lung Association, State of the Air 2011*

- Cape Coral was highlighted as one of the top 25 cleanest metro areas for short-term particle pollution (24-hour PM 2.5) in the U.S. Monitors in these cities reported no days with unhealthful PM 2.5 levels. *American Lung Association, State of the Air 2011*

Health/Fitness Rankings

- Cape Coral was identified as a "2011 Asthma Capital." The area ranked #93 out of the nation's 100 largest metropolitan areas. Twelve factors were used to identify the most challenging places to live for people with asthma: estimated prevalence; self-reported prevalence; crude death rate for asthma; annual pollen score; annual air quality; public smoking laws; number of board-certified asthma specialists; school inhaler access laws; rescue medication use; controller medication use; uninsured rate; poverty rate. *Asthma and Allergy Foundation of America, "2011 Asthma Capitals"*

- Cape Coral was identified as a "2011 Fall Allergy Capital." The area ranked #74 out of 100. Three groups of factors were used to identify the most severe cities for people with allergies during the fall season: annual pollen levels; medicine utilization; access to board-certified allergists. *Asthma and Allergy Foundation of America, "2011 Fall Allergy Capitals"*

- Cape Coral was identified as a "2012 Spring Allergy Capital." The area ranked #58 out of 100. Three groups of factors were used to identify the most severe cities for people with allergies during the spring season: annual pollen levels; medicine utilization; access to board-certified allergists. *Asthma and Allergy Foundation of America, "2012 Spring Allergy Capitals"*

- The Cape Coral metropolitan area was selected as one of the best metros for hospital care in America by *HealthGrades.com.* The rankings are based on a comprehensive study of patient death and complication rates in the nation's nearly 5,000 hospitals. Hospitals performing in the top 5% nationwide across 26 different medical procedures and diagnoses were identified. *HealthGrades.com* then ranked cities by the highest percentage of these Distinguished Hospitals for Clinical Excellence™. The Cape Coral metro area ranked #11. *HealthGrades.com, "America's Top 50 Cities for Hospital Care," January 21, 2012*

- The Cape Coral metro area appeared in the 2011 Gallup-Healthways Well-Being Index. The index, based on interviews with more than 350,000 Americans, measured jobs, finances, physical health, emotional state of mind and communities. The metro area ranked #86 out of 190. Criteria: life evaluation; emotional health; work environment; physical health; healthy behaviors; basic access (basic needs optimal for a healthy life, such as access to food and medicine, having health insurance and feeling safe while walking at night). *Gallup-Healthways, "State of Well-Being 2011"*

Real Estate Rankings

- Cape Coral was identified as one of the "Top Turnaround Housing Markets for 2012." The area ranked #4 out of 10. Criteria: year-over-year median home price appreciation; year-over-year median inventory age; year-over-year inventory reduction. *AOL Real Estate, "Top Turnaround Housing Markets for 2012," February 4, 2012*

- The Cape Coral metro area was identified as one of the 25 best housing markets in the U.S. in 2011. The area ranked #1 out of 149 markets with a home price appreciation of 25.6%. Criteria: year-over-year change of median sales price of existing single-family homes between the 4th quarter of 2010 and the 4th quarter of 2011. *National Association of Realtors®, Median Sales Price of Existing Single-Family Homes for Metropolitan Areas, 4th Quarter 2011*

- The Cape Coral metro area was identified as one of "America's 25 Weakest Housing Markets" by *Forbes.* The metro area ranked #24. Criteria: metro areas with populations over 500,000 were ranked based on projected home values through 2011. *Forbes.com, "America's 25 Weakest Housing Markets," January 7, 2009*

- The nation's largest metro areas were analyzed in terms of the percentage of households entering some stage of foreclosure in 2011. The Cape Coral metro area ranked #15 out of 20 (#1 = highest foreclosure rate). *RealtyTrac, 2011 Year-End Foreclosure Market Report, January 12, 2012*

- The Center for Housing Policy ranked 210 U.S. metropolitan areas by the fair market rent for a two-bedroom unit. The Cape Coral metro area was ranked #52. (#1 = most expensive) with a rent of $1,029. Criteria: Fair Market Rent (FMR) in effect during the fourth quarter of 2009 based on HUD's fiscal year 2010 FMRs. *The Center for Housing Policy, "Paycheck to Paycheck: Most to Least Expensive Rental Markets in 2009"*

- The Cape Coral metro area was identified as one of the top 20 cities in terms of decreasing home equity. The metro area was ranked #2. Criteria: percentage of home equity relative to the home's current value. *Forbes.com, "Where Americans are Losing Home Equity Most," May 1, 2010*

- The Cape Coral metro area was identified as one of the best U.S. markets to invest in rental property" by HomeVestors and Local Market Monitor. The area ranked #6 out of 100. Criteria: risk-return premium relative to national average. *HomeVestors and Local Market Monitor, "Best 100 U.S. Markets to Invest in Rental Property," March 9, 2012*

Safety Rankings

- Allstate ranked the 193 largest cities in America in terms of driver safety. Cape Coral ranked #42. In addition, drivers were 4.8% less likely to have had an accident compared to the national average. Allstate researchers analyzed internal property damage reported claims over a two-year period (from January 2008 to December 2009) to protect findings from external influences such as weather or road construction. A weighted average of the two-year numbers determined the annual percentages. The report defines an auto crash as any collision resulting in a property damage claim. *Allstate, "2011 Allstate America's Best Drivers Report™"*

- Sperling's BestPlaces analyzed the tracks of tropical storms for the past 100 years and ranked which areas are most likely to be hit by a major hurricane. The Cape Coral metro area ranked #3 out of 10. *Sperling's BestPlaces, www.bestplaces.net, February 2, 2006*

- The National Insurance Crime Bureau ranked 366 metro areas in the U.S. in terms of per capita rates of vehicle theft. The Cape Coral metro area ranked #204 (#1 = highest rate). Criteria: number of vehicle theft offenses per 100,000 inhabitants in 2010. *National Insurance Crime Bureau, "Hot Spots," June 21, 2011*

Seniors/Retirement Rankings

- Cape Coral was identified as one of the "100 Most Popular Retirement Towns" by *Topretirements.com* The list reflects the 100 cities (out of 815+ total cities reviewed) that visitors to the website are most interested in for retirement. *Topretirements.com, "100 Most Popular Retirement Towns," February 21, 2012*

- Cape Coral was selected as one of the best places to retire by *CNNMoney.com*. Criteria: low cost of living; low violent-crime rate; good medical care; large population over age 50; abundant amenities for retirees. *CNNMoney.com, "Best Places to Retire 2011"*

Business Environment

CITY FINANCES

City Government Finances

Component	2009 ($000)	2009 ($ per capita)
Total Revenues	263,651	1,680
Total Expenditures	459,935	2,930
Debt Outstanding	769,688	4,903
Cash and Securities[1]	475,876	3,031

Note: (1) Cash and security holdings of a government at the close of its fiscal year, including those of its dependent agencies, utilities, and liquor stores.
Source: U.S Census Bureau, State & Local Government Finances 2009

City Government Revenue by Source

Source	2009 ($000)	2009 ($ per capita)
General Revenue		
From Federal Government	1,556	10
From State Government	17,876	114
From Local Governments	1,670	11
Taxes		
Property	100,955	643
Sales and Gross Receipts	18,824	120
Personal Income	0	0
Corporate Income	0	0
Motor Vehicle License	0	0
Other Taxes	2,641	17
Current Charges	50,699	323
Liquor Store	0	0
Utility	21,893	139
Employee Retirement	-24,898	-159

Source: U.S Census Bureau, State & Local Government Finances 2009

City Government Expenditures by Function

Function	2009 ($000)	2009 ($ per capita)	2009 (%)
General Direct Expenditures			
Air Transportation	0	0	0.0
Corrections	0	0	0.0
Education	10,792	69	2.3
Employment Security Administration	0	0	0.0
Financial Administration	11,260	72	2.4
Fire Protection	29,507	188	6.4
General Public Buildings	0	0	0.0
Governmental Administration, Other	5,664	36	1.2
Health	0	0	0.0
Highways	59,414	378	12.9
Hospitals	0	0	0.0
Housing and Community Development	6,636	42	1.4
Interest on General Debt	10,348	66	2.2
Judicial and Legal	992	6	0.2
Libraries	0	0	0.0
Parking	0	0	0.0
Parks and Recreation	27,249	174	5.9
Police Protection	43,365	276	9.4
Public Welfare	0	0	0.0
Sewerage	18,307	117	4.0
Solid Waste Management	0	0	0.0
Veterans' Services	0	0	0.0
Liquor Store	0	0	0.0
Utility	192,612	1,227	41.9
Employee Retirement	9,942	63	2.2

Source: U.S Census Bureau, State & Local Government Finances 2009

Municipal Bond Ratings

Area	Moody's	S&P	Fitch
City	n/a	n/a	n/a

Rating Systems (shown in declining order of credit quality): Moody's– Aaa, Aa, A, Baa, Ba, B, Caa, Ca, C (numerical modifiers 1, 2, and 3 are added to letter-rating); S&P– AAA, AA, A, BBB, BB, B, CCC, CC, C; Fitch– AAA, AA, A, BBB, BB, B, CCC, CC, C. Ratings may be modified by the addition of a plus or minus sign to show relative standing within the major rating categories.
Notes: n/a Not Available; w/d Withdrawn (1) Not Reviewed; (2) Issuer Rating/No General Obligation; (3) Standard and Poor's Issue Credit Rating (ICR) is a current opinion of an obliger with respect to a specific financial obligation, a specific class of financial obligations, or a specific financial program.
Source: U.S. Census Bureau, 2012 Statistical Abstract, Bond Ratings for City Governments by Largest Cities: 2010

DEMOGRAPHICS

Population Growth

Area	1990 Census	2000 Census	2010 Census	Population Growth (%) 1990-2000	2000-2010
City	75,507	102,286	154,305	35.5	50.9
MSA[1]	335,113	440,888	618,754	31.6	40.3
U.S.	248,709,873	281,421,906	308,745,538	13.2	9.7

Note: (1) Figures cover the Cape Coral-Fort Myers, FL Metropolitan Statistical Area—see Appendix B for areas included
Source: U.S. Census Bureau, 2010 Census

Household Size

Area	One	Two	Three	Four	Five	Six	Seven or More	Average Household Size
City	21.4	39.8	16.7	13.2	5.8	2.1	1.0	2.53
MSA[1]	26.7	42.7	12.9	9.8	4.7	1.9	1.2	2.35
U.S.	26.7	32.8	16.1	13.4	6.5	2.6	1.9	2.58

Note: (1) Figures cover the Cape Coral-Fort Myers, FL Metropolitan Statistical Area—see Appendix B for areas included
Source: U.S. Census Bureau, 2010 Census

Race

Area	White Alone[2] (%)	Black Alone[2] (%)	Asian Alone[2] (%)	AIAN[3] Alone[2] (%)	NHOPI[4] Alone[2] (%)	Other Race Alone[2] (%)	Two or More Races (%)
City	88.2	4.3	1.5	0.3	0.1	3.3	2.3
MSA[1]	83.0	8.3	1.4	0.4	0.1	4.9	2.1
U.S.	72.4	12.6	4.8	0.9	0.2	6.2	2.9

Note: (1) Figures cover the Cape Coral-Fort Myers, FL Metropolitan Statistical Area—see Appendix B for areas included; (2) Alone is defined as not being in combination with one or more other races; (3) American Indian and Alaska Native; (4) Native Hawaiian and Other Pacific Islander
Source: U.S. Census Bureau, 2010 Census

Hispanic or Latino Origin

Area	Hispanic or Latino (%)	Mexican (%)	Puerto Rican (%)	Cuban (%)	Other Hispanic or Latino (%)
City	19.5	1.8	4.7	6.4	6.6
MSA[1]	18.3	5.5	4.0	3.3	5.5
U.S.	16.3	10.3	1.5	0.6	4.0

Note: Persons of Hispanic or Latino origin can be of any race; (1) Figures cover the Cape Coral-Fort Myers, FL Metropolitan Statistical Area—see Appendix B for areas included
Source: U.S. Census Bureau, 2010 Census

Segregation

Type	Segregation Indices[1]				Percent Change		
	1990	2000	2010	2010 Rank[2]	1990-2000	1990-2010	2000-2010
Black/White	76.8	69.4	61.6	35	-7.5	-15.3	-7.8
Asian/White	23.3	28.5	25.3	96	5.3	2.0	-3.3
Hispanic/White	36.1	40.8	40.2	63	4.7	4.1	-0.6

Note: Figures are based on an analysis of 1990, 2000, and 2010 Census Decennial Census tract data by William H. Frey, Brookings Institution and the University of Michigan Social Science Data Analysis Network. In this analysis all racial groups (whites, blacks, and asians) are non-Hispanic members of those races. Hispanics are shown as a separate category; All figures cover the Metropolitan Statistical Area (see Appendix B for areas included); (1) Segregation Indices are Dissimilarity Indices that measure the degree to which the minority group is distributed differently than whites across census tracts. They range from 0 (complete integration) to 100 (complete segregation) where the value indicates the percentage of the minority group that needs to move to be distributed exactly like whites; (2) Ranges from 1 (most segregated) to 102 (least segregated); n/a not available.
Source: www.CensusScope.org

Ancestry

Area	German	Irish	English	American	Italian	Polish	French[2]	Scottish	Dutch
City	17.0	14.0	8.9	12.3	10.9	4.3	3.4	1.8	1.6
MSA[1]	16.0	12.5	10.7	12.0	8.0	3.7	3.1	2.2	1.4
U.S.	16.1	11.6	8.8	6.1	5.7	3.2	3.0	1.9	1.6

Note: Figures are the percentage of the total population reporting a particular ancestry. The nine most commonly reported ancestries in the U.S. are shown. Figures include multiple ancestries (e.g. if a person reported being Irish and Italian, they were included in both columns); (1) Figures cover the Cape Coral-Fort Myers, FL Metropolitan Statistical Area—see Appendix B for areas included; (2) Excludes Basque
Source: U.S. Census Bureau, 2008-2010 American Community Survey 3-Year Estimates

Foreign-Born Population

Area	Percent of Population Born in								
	Any Foreign Country	Mexico	Asia	Europe	Carribean	South America	Central America[2]	Africa	Canada
City	n/a	n/a	n/a	n/a	n/a	n/a	n/a	n/a	n/a
MSA[1]	15.4	2.4	1.3	2.2	4.5	2.3	1.7	0.1	0.8
U.S.	12.8	3.8	3.6	1.6	1.2	0.9	1.0	0.5	0.3

Note: (1) Figures cover the Cape Coral-Fort Myers, FL Metropolitan Statistical Area—see Appendix B for areas included; (2) Excludes Mexico.
Source: U.S. Census Bureau, 2008-2010 American Community Survey 3-Year Estimates

Marital Status

Area	Never Married	Now Married[2]	Separated	Widowed	Divorced
City	25.2	55.0	1.3	6.4	12.1
MSA[1]	24.3	53.8	1.8	7.6	12.4
U.S.	31.6	49.6	2.2	6.1	10.7

Note: Figures are percentages and cover the population 15 years of age and older; (1) Figures cover the Cape Coral-Fort Myers, FL Metropolitan Statistical Area—see Appendix B for areas included; (2) Excludes separated
Source: U.S. Census Bureau, 2008-2010 American Community Survey 3-Year Estimates

Age

Area	Percent of Population							Median Age
	Under Age 5	Age 5 to 17	Age 18 to 34	Age 35 to 49	Age 50 to 64	Age 65 to 79	80 Years and Over	
City	5.4	17.1	17.8	21.3	21.5	12.9	4.1	42.4
MSA[1]	5.3	14.2	18.3	18.0	20.7	17.5	6.0	45.6
U.S.	6.5	17.5	23.2	20.7	19.0	9.4	3.6	37.2

Note: (1) Figures cover the Cape Coral-Fort Myers, FL Metropolitan Statistical Area—see Appendix B for areas included
Source: U.S. Census Bureau, 2010 Census

Male/Female Ratio

Area	Males	Females	Males per 100 Females
City	75,364	78,941	95.5
MSA[1]	303,600	315,154	96.3
U.S.	151,781,326	156,964,212	96.7

Note: (1) Figures cover the Cape Coral-Fort Myers, FL
Metropolitan Statistical Area—see Appendix B for areas included
Source: U.S. Census Bureau, 2010 Census

Religious Groups

Area	Catholic	Baptist	Non-Den.	Methodist[2]	Lutheran	LDS[3]	Pentecostal	Presbyterian[4]	Muslim[5]	Judaism
MSA[1]	16.2	5.0	3.0	2.5	1.2	0.5	4.4	1.4	0.2	0.9
U.S.	19.1	9.3	4.0	4.0	2.3	2.0	1.9	1.6	0.8	0.7

Note: Figures are the number of adherents as a percentage of the total population; (1) Figures cover the Cape Coral-Fort Myers, FL Metropolitan Statistical Area—see Appendix B for areas included; (2) Methodist/Pietist; (3) Latter Day Saints; (4) Reformed; (5) Figures are estimates
Source: Association of Statisticians of American Religious Bodies, 2010 U.S. Religion Census: Religious Congregations & Membership Study

ECONOMY

Gross Metropolitan Product

Area	2007	2008	2009	2010	2010 Rank[2]
MSA[1]	22.2	20.9	20.0	20.2	98

Note: Figures are in billions of dollars; (1) Figures cover the Cape Coral-Fort Myers, FL Metropolitan Statistical Area—see Appendix B for areas included; (2) Rank ranges from 1 to 363
Source: The United States Conference of Mayors, "U.S. Metro Economies: GMP and Employment Forecasts," June 2011

Economic Growth

Area	2007-2009 (%)	2010 (%)	2011 (%)	Rank[2]
MSA[1]	-6.8	0.1	1.0	355
U.S.	-1.3	2.9	2.5	–

Note: Figures are real Gross Metropolitan Product growth rates and represent annual average percent change; (1) Figures cover the Cape Coral-Fort Myers, FL Metropolitan Statistical Area—see Appendix B for areas included; (2) Rank ranges from 1 to 363
Source: The United States Conference of Mayors, "U.S. Metro Economies: GMP and Employment Forecasts," June 2011

Metropolitan Area Exports

Area	2005	2006	2007	2008	2009	2010	2010 Rank[2]
MSA[1]	178.4	170.1	198.3	282.8	237.5	298.0	236

Note: Figures are in millions of dollars; (1) Figures cover the Cape Coral-Fort Myers, FL Metropolitan Statistical Area—see Appendix B for areas included; (2) Rank ranges from 1 to 369
Source: U.S. Department of Commerce, International Trade Administration, Office of Trade & Industry Information, Manufacturing & Services, data extracted April 2, 2012

INCOME

Income

Area	Per Capita ($)	Median Household ($)	Average Household ($)
City	23,541	49,111	61,493
MSA[1]	27,392	47,232	66,948
U.S.	26,942	51,222	70,116

Note: (1) Figures cover the Cape Coral-Fort Myers, FL Metropolitan Statistical Area—see Appendix B for areas included
Source: U.S. Census Bureau, 2008-2010 American Community Survey 3-Year Estimates

Household Income Distribution

Area	Percent of Households Earning							
	Under $15,000	$15,000 -24,999	$25,000 -34,999	$35,000 -49,999	$50,000 -74,999	$75,000 -99,000	$100,000 -149,999	$150,000 and up
City	9.5	11.3	12.9	17.0	22.0	12.5	10.2	4.5
MSA[1]	11.6	12.0	11.9	17.2	18.9	11.6	10.0	6.8
U.S.	13.0	11.0	10.6	14.2	18.5	12.1	12.2	8.4

Note: (1) Figures cover the Cape Coral-Fort Myers, FL Metropolitan Statistical Area—see Appendix B for areas included
Source: U.S. Census Bureau, 2008-2010 American Community Survey 3-Year Estimates

Poverty Rate

Area	All Ages	Under 18 Years Old	18 to 64 Years Old	65 Years and Over
City	12.1	18.0	10.8	8.9
MSA[1]	13.7	20.7	13.8	7.3
U.S.	14.4	20.1	13.1	9.4

Note: Figures are percentage of people whose income during the past 12 months was below the poverty level; (1) Figures cover the Cape Coral-Fort Myers, FL Metropolitan Statistical Area—see Appendix B for areas included
Source: U.S. Census Bureau, 2008-2010 American Community Survey 3-Year Estimates

Personal Bankruptcy Filing Rate

Area	2006	2007	2008	2009	2010	2011
Lee County	0.89	2.27	4.92	7.38	7.32	5.33
U.S.	2.00	2.73	3.53	4.61	4.97	4.37

Note: Numbers are per 1,000 population and include Chapter 7 and Chapter 13 filings
Source: Federal Deposit Insurance Corporation, Regional Economic Conditions, March 9, 2012

EMPLOYMENT

Labor Force and Employment

Area	Civilian Labor Force			Workers Employed		
	Dec. 2010	Dec. 2011	% Chg.	Dec. 2010	Dec. 2011	% Chg.
City	79,492	77,945	-1.9	69,476	70,234	1.1
MSA[1]	275,835	271,425	-1.6	241,175	243,805	1.1
U.S.	153,156,000	153,373,000	0.1	139,159,000	140,681,000	1.1

Note: Data is not seasonally adjusted and covers workers 16 years of age and older; (1) Metropolitan Statistical Area—see Appendix B for areas included
Source: Bureau of Labor Statistics, http://stats.bls.gov

Unemployment Rate

Area	2011											
	Jan.	Feb.	Mar.	Apr.	May	Jun.	Jul.	Aug.	Sep.	Oct.	Nov.	Dec.
City	12.6	11.8	11.2	10.6	10.7	11.3	11.1	11.1	10.8	10.4	10.3	9.9
MSA[1]	12.7	11.7	11.2	10.8	10.9	11.7	11.6	11.5	11.3	10.7	10.5	10.2
U.S.	9.8	9.5	9.2	8.7	8.7	9.3	9.3	9.1	8.8	8.5	8.2	8.3

Note: Data is not seasonally adjusted and covers workers 16 years of age and older; All figures are percentages; (1) Metropolitan Statistical Area—see Appendix B for areas included
Source: Bureau of Labor Statistics, http://stats.bls.gov

Projected Unemployment Rate

Area	2010 (%)	2011 (%)	2012 (%)	2013 (%)
MSA[1]	13.1	11.7	12.0	11.4

Note: (1) Metropolitan Statistical Area—see Appendix B for areas included
Source: The United States Conference of Mayors, "U.S. Metro Economies: GMP and Employment Forecasts," June 2011

Employment by Occupation

Occupation Classification	City (%)	MSA[1] (%)	U.S. (%)
Management, Business, Science, and Arts	27.4	29.2	35.6
Natural Resources, Construction, and Maintenance	12.3	11.8	9.5
Production, Transportation, and Material Moving	7.7	8.0	12.1
Sales and Office	31.3	29.2	25.2
Service	21.3	21.7	17.6

Note: Figures cover employed civilians 16 years of age and older; (1) Figures cover the Cape Coral-Fort Myers, FL Metropolitan Statistical Area—see Appendix B for areas included
Source: U.S. Census Bureau, 2008-2010 American Community Survey 3-Year Estimates

Employment by Industry

Sector	MSA[1] Number of Employees	MSA[1] Percent of Total	U.S. Percent of Total
Construction	n/a	n/a	4.1
Education and Health Services	24,400	11.8	15.2
Financial Activities	10,400	5.0	5.8
Government	37,100	18.0	16.8
Information	2,900	1.4	2.0
Leisure and Hospitality	30,100	14.6	9.9
Manufacturing	4,700	2.3	8.9
Mining and Logging	n/a	n/a	0.6
Other Services	8,700	4.2	4.0
Professional and Business Services	27,800	13.5	13.3
Retail Trade	34,200	16.6	11.5
Transportation and Utilities	3,600	1.7	3.8
Wholesale Trade	5,900	2.9	4.2

Note: Figures cover non-farm employment as of December 2011 and are not seasonally adjusted; (1) Metropolitan Statistical Area—see Appendix B for areas included; n/a not available
Source: Bureau of Labor Statistics, http://stats.bls.gov

Occupations with Greatest Projected Employment Growth: 2008 – 2018

Occupation[1]	2008 Employment	2018 Projected Employment	Numeric Employment Change	Percent Employment Change
Registered Nurses	151,100	187,380	36,280	24.0
Combined Food Preparation and Serving Workers, Including Fast Food	162,570	186,400	23,830	14.7
Customer Service Representatives	169,080	190,780	21,700	12.8
Nursing Aides, Orderlies, and Attendants	88,630	106,860	18,230	20.6
Home Health Aides	30,480	47,860	17,380	57.0
Postsecondary Teachers	70,790	85,380	14,590	20.6
Retail Salespersons	274,490	288,660	14,170	5.2
Elementary School Teachers, Except Special Education	74,130	86,390	12,260	16.5
Stock Clerks and Order Fillers	167,450	179,420	11,970	7.1
Accountants and Auditors	86,390	97,670	11,280	13.1

Note: Projections cover Florida; (1) Sorted by numeric employment change
Source: www.projectionscentral.com, State Occupational Projections, 2008–2018 Long-Term Projections

Fastest Growing Occupations: 2008 – 2018

Occupation[1]	2008 Employment	2018 Projected Employment	Numeric Employment Change	Percent Employment Change
Biomedical Engineers	520	840	320	61.5
Home Health Aides	30,480	47,860	17,380	57.0
Medical Scientists, Except Epidemiologists	2,640	3,870	1,230	46.6
Physician Assistants	3,900	5,490	1,590	40.8
Personal and Home Care Aides	13,890	19,430	5,540	39.9
Network Systems and Data Communications Analysts	21,550	30,110	8,560	39.7
Radiation Therapists	1,270	1,730	460	36.2
Dental Hygienists	9,030	11,890	2,860	31.7
Physical Therapist Assistants	3,550	4,660	1,110	31.3
Financial Examiners	610	800	190	31.1

Note: Projections cover Florida; (1) Sorted by percent employment change and excludes occupations with numeric employment change less than 100
Source: www.projectionscentral.com, State Occupational Projections, 2008–2018 Long-Term Projections

Average Wages

Occupation	$/Hr.	Occupation	$/Hr.
Accountants and Auditors	31.82	Maids and Housekeeping Cleaners	9.60
Automotive Mechanics	18.95	Maintenance and Repair Workers	15.87
Bookkeepers	16.69	Marketing Managers	43.92
Carpenters	19.21	Nuclear Medicine Technologists	35.94
Cashiers	9.82	Nurses, Licensed Practical	20.26
Clerks, General Office	12.63	Nurses, Registered	31.16
Clerks, Receptionists/Information	12.90	Nursing Aides/Orderlies/Attendants	12.32
Clerks, Shipping/Receiving	11.94	Packers and Packagers, Hand	9.89
Computer Programmers	32.56	Physical Therapists	39.19
Computer Support Specialists	22.02	Postal Service Mail Carriers	24.14
Computer Systems Analysts	36.58	Real Estate Brokers	n/a
Cooks, Restaurant	11.46	Retail Salespersons	12.20
Dentists	42.76	Sales Reps., Exc. Tech./Scientific	27.71
Electrical Engineers	36.16	Sales Reps., Tech./Scientific	41.79
Electricians	16.37	Secretaries, Exc. Legal/Med./Exec.	14.85
Financial Managers	61.00	Security Guards	11.15
First-Line Supervisors/Managers, Sales	21.14	Surgeons	120.15
Food Preparation Workers	10.01	Teacher Assistants	9.40
General and Operations Managers	46.02	Teachers, Elementary School	16.60
Hairdressers/Cosmetologists	12.59	Teachers, Secondary School	23.50
Internists	113.39	Telemarketers	18.47
Janitors and Cleaners	10.47	Truck Drivers, Heavy/Tractor-Trailer	16.80
Landscaping/Groundskeeping Workers	10.92	Truck Drivers, Light/Delivery Svcs.	15.29
Lawyers	46.78	Waiters and Waitresses	10.07

Note: Wage data covers the Cape Coral-Fort Myers, FL Metropolitan Statistical Area—see Appendix B for areas included. Hourly wages for elementary/secondary school teachers and teacher assistants were calculated by the editors from annual wage data assuming a 40 hour work week; n/a not available.
Source: Bureau of Labor Statistics, Metro Area Occupational Employment and Wage Estimates, May 2011

RESIDENTIAL REAL ESTATE

Building Permits

Area	Single-Family			Multi-Family			Total		
	2010	2011	Pct. Chg.	2010	2011	Pct. Chg.	2010	2011	Pct. Chg.
City	216	269	24.5	0	8	-	216	277	28.2
MSA[1]	1,175	1,262	7.4	101	325	221.8	1,276	1,587	24.4
U.S.	447,311	418,498	-6.4	157,299	205,563	30.7	604,610	624,061	3.2

Note: (1) Metropolitan Statistical Area—see Appendix B for areas included; figures represent new, privately-owned housing units authorized (unadjusted data); All permit data are based on estimates with imputation.
Source: U.S. Census Bureau, Manufacturing, Mining, and Construction Statistics, Building Permits, 2010, 2011

Homeownership Rate

Area	2005 (%)	2006 (%)	2007 (%)	2008 (%)	2009 (%)	2010 (%)	2011 (%)
MSA[1]	n/a	n/a	n/a	n/a	n/a	n/a	n/a
U.S.	68.9	68.8	68.1	67.8	67.4	66.9	66.1

Note: (1) Metropolitan Statistical Area—see Appendix B for areas included; n/a not available
Source: U.S. Census Bureau, Housing Vacancies and Homeownership Annual Statistics: 2011

Housing Vacancy Rates

Area	Gross Vacancy Rate[2] (%)			Year-Round Vacancy Rate[3] (%)			Rental Vacancy Rate[4] (%)			Homeowner Vacancy Rate[5] (%)		
	2009	2010	2011	2009	2010	2011	2009	2010	2011	2009	2010	2011
MSA[1]	n/a	n/a	n/a	n/a	n/a	n/a	n/a	n/a	n/a	n/a	n/a	n/a
U.S.	14.5	14.3	14.2	11.3	11.3	11.1	10.6	10.2	9.5	2.6	2.6	2.5

Note: (1) Metropolitan Statistical Area—see Appendix B for areas included; (2) The percentage of the total housing inventory that is vacant; (3) The percentage of the housing inventory (excluding seasonal units) that is year-round vacant; (4) The percentage of rental inventory that is vacant for rent; (5) The percentage of homeowner inventory that is vacant for sale; n/a not available
Source: U.S. Census Bureau, Housing Vacancies and Homeownership Annual Statistics: 2011

TAXES

State Corporate Income Tax Rates

State	Tax Rate (%)	Income Brackets ($)	Num. of Brackets	Financial Institution Tax Rate (%)[a]	Federal Income Tax Ded.
Florida	5.5 (f)	Flat rate	1	5.5 (f)	No

Note: Tax rates as of January 1, 2012; (a) Rates listed are the corporate income tax rate applied to financial institutions or excise taxes based on income. Some states have other taxes based upon the value of deposits or shares; (f) An exemption of $5,000 is allowed. Florida's Alternative Minimum Tax rate is 3.3%.
Source: Federation of Tax Administrators, "State Corporate Income Tax Rates, 2012"

State Individual Income Tax Rates

State	Tax Rate (%)	Income Brackets ($)	Num. of Brackets	Personal Exempt. ($)[1] Single	Dependents	Fed. Inc. Tax Ded.

Florida – No State Income Tax

Note: Tax rates as of January 1, 2012; Local- and county-level taxes are not included; n/a not applicable; (1) Married joint filers generally receive double the single exemption
Source: Federation of Tax Administrators, "State Individual Income Tax Rates, 2012"

Various State and Local Tax Rates

State	State and Local Sales and Use (%)	State Sales and Use (%)	Gasoline[1] (¢/gal.)	Cigarette[2] ($/pack)	Spirits[3] ($/gal.)	Wine[4] ($/gal.)	Beer[5] ($/gal.)
Florida	6.0	6.00	35.0	1.34	6.50	2.25	0.48

Note: All tax rates as of January 1, 2012 except beer, wine and spirits (September 1, 2011); (1) The American Petroleum Institute has developed a methodology for determining the average tax rate on a gallon of fuel. Rates may include any of the following: excise taxes, environmental fees, storage tank fees, other fees or taxes, general sales tax, and local taxes. In states where gasoline is subject to the general sales tax, or where the fuel tax is based on the average sale price, the average rate determined by API is sensitive to changes in the price of gasoline. States that fully or partially apply general sales taxes to gasoline: CA, CO, GA, IL, IN, MI, NY; (2) The federal excise tax of $1.0066 per pack and local taxes are not included; (3) Rates are those applicable to off-premise sales of 40% alcohol by volume (a.b.v.) distilled spirits in 750ml containers. Local excise taxes are excluded; (4) Rates are those applicable to off-premise sales of 11% a.b.v. non-carbonated wine in 750ml containers; (5) Rates are those applicable to off-premise sales of 4.7% a.b.v. beer in 12 ounce containers.
Source: Tax Foundation, 2012 Facts & Figures: How Does Your State Compare?

State-Local Tax Burdens

Area	Rate (%)	Rank[1]	Per Capita Taxes Paid to Home State ($)	Total State and Local Per Capita Taxes Paid ($)	Per Capita Income ($)
Florida	9.2	31	2,713	3,897	42,146
U.S. Average	9.8	-	3,057	4,160	42,539

Note: Figures cover 2009; (1) Rank ranges from 1 to 50 where 1 is highest tax burden
Source: Tax Foundation, State-Local Tax Burdens, All States, 2009

State Business Tax Climate Index Rankings

State	Overall Rank	Corporate Tax Index Rank	Individual Income Tax Index Rank	Sales Tax Index Rank	Unemployment Insurance Tax Index Rank	Property Tax Index Rank
Florida	5	12	1	19	5	24

Note: The index is a measure of how each state's tax laws affect economic performance. The lower the rank, the more favorable a state's tax system is for business. States without a given tax are given a ranking of 1.
Source: Tax Foundation, Major Components of the State Business Tax Climate Index, FY 2012

COMMERCIAL UTILITIES

Typical Monthly Electric Bills

Area	Commercial Service ($/month)		Industrial Service ($/month)	
	1,500 kWh	40 kW demand 14,000 kWh	1,000 kW demand 200,000 kWh	50,000 kW demand 15,000,000 kWh
City	n/a	n/a	n/a	n/a
Average[1]	189	1,616	25,197	1,470,813

Note: Based on total rates in effect July 1, 2011; (1) average based on 184 utilities surveyed; n/a not available
Source: Edison Electric Institute, Typical Bills and Average Rates Report, Summer 2011

TRANSPORTATION

Means of Transportation to Work

Area	Car/Truck/Van Drove Alone	Car-pooled	Bus	Subway	Railroad	Bicycle	Walked	Other Means	Worked at Home
City	81.6	10.1	0.4	0.0	0.0	0.3	0.7	1.6	5.4
MSA[1]	75.1	14.5	1.0	0.0	0.0	0.8	0.9	1.7	6.0
U.S.	76.0	10.2	2.7	1.7	0.5	0.5	2.8	1.3	4.2

Note: Figures are percentages and cover workers 16 years of age and older; (1) Figures cover the Cape Coral-Fort Myers, FL Metropolitan Statistical Area—see Appendix B for areas included
Source: U.S. Census Bureau, 2008-2010 American Community Survey 3-Year Estimates

Travel Time to Work

Area	Less Than 10 Minutes	10 to 19 Minutes	20 to 29 Minutes	30 to 44 Minutes	45 to 59 Minutes	60 to 89 Minutes	90 Minutes or More
City	7.4	29.0	25.4	26.0	6.5	3.4	2.3
MSA[1]	9.8	29.5	23.0	24.9	7.3	3.3	2.3
U.S.	13.9	30.1	20.8	19.8	7.5	5.5	2.5

Note: Figures are percentages and include workers 16 years old and over; (1) Figures cover the Cape Coral-Fort Myers, FL Metropolitan Statistical Area—see Appendix B for areas included
Source: U.S. Census Bureau, 2008-2010 American Community Survey 3-Year Estimates

Travel Time Index

Area	1985	1990	1995	2000	2005	2010
Urban Area[1]	1.07	1.09	1.14	1.10	1.12	1.10
Average[2]	1.11	1.16	1.18	1.21	1.25	1.20

Note: Travel Time Index—the ratio of travel time in the peak period to the travel time at free-flow conditions. A value of 1.30 indicates a 20-minute free-flow trip takes 26 minutes in the peak. Free-flow speeds (60 mph on freeways and 35 mph on principal arterials) are used as the comparison threshold; (1) Covers the Cape Coral FL urban area; (2) average of 439 urban areas
Source: Texas Transportation Institute, Urban Mobility Report 2011, September 2011

Public Transportation

Agency Name / Mode of Transportation	Vehicles Operated in Maximum Service	Annual Unlinked Passenger Trips ('000)	Annual Passenger Miles ('000)
Lee County Transit (LeeTran)			
Bus (directly operated)	47	3,016.5	15,534.8
Demand Response (directly operated)	39	104.3	1,195.8
Vanpool (purchased transportation)	6	18.8	767.9

Source: Federal Transit Administration, National Transit Database, 2010

Air Transportation

Airport Name and Code / Type of Service	Passenger Airlines[1]	Passenger Enplanements	Freight Carriers[2]	Freight (lbs.)
Southwest Florida International Airport (RSW)				
Domestic service (U.S. carriers - 2011)	31	3,631,785	12	9,447,498
International service (U.S. carriers - 2010)	3	1,338	0	0

Note: (1) Includes all U.S.-based major, minor and commuter airlines that carried at least one passenger during the year; (2) Includes all U.S.-based airlines and freight carriers that transported at least one pound of freight during the year
Source: Bureau of Transportation Statistics, The Intermodal Transportation Database, Air Carriers: T-100 Domestic Market (U.S. Carriers), 2011; Bureau of Transportation Statistics, The Intermodal Transportation Database, Air Carriers: T-100 International Market (U.S. Carriers), 2010

Other Transportation Statistics

Major Highways:	I-75
Amtrak Service:	Bus service only (station is in Ft. Myers)
Major Waterways/Ports:	Gulf of Mexico; Caloosahatchee River

Source: Amtrak.com; Google Maps

BUSINESSES

Major Business Headquarters

Company Name	Rankings	
	Fortune[1]	Forbes[2]
No companies listed	-	-

Note: (1) Fortune 500—companies that produce a 10-K are ranked 1 to 500 based on 2010 revenue; (2) all private companies with at least $2 billion in annual revenue are ranked 1 to 212; companies listed are headquartered in the city; dashes indicate no ranking
Source: Fortune, "Fortune 500," May 23, 2011; Forbes, "America's Largest Private Companies," November 16, 2011

Minority- and Women-Owned Businesses

Group	All Firms		Firms with Paid Employees			
	Firms	Sales ($000)	Firms	Sales ($000)	Employees	Payroll ($000)
Asian	374	46,704	(s)	(s)	(s)	(s)
Black	741	36,991	65	16,996	322	4,468
Hispanic	3,487	149,403	(s)	(s)	(s)	(s)
Women	5,213	365,051	505	252,724	2,110	58,541
All Firms	18,476	4,711,956	3,366	4,140,517	26,555	820,005

Note: Figures cover firms located in the city; minority- and women-owned business are defined as firms in which the corresponding group own 51% or more of the stock or equity of the company; (s) estimates are suppressed when publication standards are not met
Source: U.S. Census Bureau, 2007 Economic Census, Survey of Business Owners

HOTELS

Hotels/Motels

Area	5 Star		4 Star		3 Star		2 Star		1 Star		Not Rated	
	Num.	Pct.[3]	Num.	Pct.[3]	Num.	Pct.[3]	Num.	Pct.[3]	Num.	Pct.[3]	Num.	Pct.[3]
City[1]	0	0.0	2	5.1	11	28.2	24	61.5	1	2.6	1	2.6
Total[2]	133	0.9	940	6.5	4,569	31.8	7,033	48.9	351	2.4	1,343	9.3

Note: (1) Figures cover Cape Coral and vicinity; (2) Figures cover all 100 cities in this book; (3) Percentage of hotels which have a given star rating; Star ratings are determined by expedia.com and offer an indication of the general quality of a particular hotel.
Source: expedia.com, April 25, 2012

The Cape Coral-Fort Myers, FL metro area is home to one of the best hotels in the U.S. according to *Travel & Leisure*: **Hyatt Regency Coconut Point Resort & Spa** (#30). Criteria: service; location; rooms; food; and value. *Travel & Leisure, "T+L 500, The World's Best Hotels 2012"*

Living Environment

COST OF LIVING

Cost of Living Index

Composite Index	Groceries	Housing	Utilities	Trans-portation	Health Care	Misc. Goods/ Services
95.6	105.2	90.5	81.1	101.8	99.1	98.2

Note: U.S. = 100; Figures cover the Cape Coral-Fort Myers FL urban area.
Source: The Council for Community and Economic Research, ACCRA Cost of Living Index, 2011

Grocery Prices

Area[1]	T-Bone Steak ($/pound)	Frying Chicken ($/pound)	Whole Milk ($/half gal.)	Eggs ($/dozen)	Orange Juice ($/64 oz.)	Coffee ($/11.5 oz.)
City[2]	9.05	1.33	2.58	1.65	3.71	4.41
Avg.	9.25	1.18	2.22	1.66	3.19	4.40
Min.	6.70	0.88	1.31	0.95	2.46	2.94
Max.	14.30	2.16	3.50	3.18	4.75	6.83

Note: (1) Values for the local area are compared with the average, minimum and maximum values for all 335 areas in the Cost of Living Index; (2) Figures cover the Cape Coral-Fort Myers FL urban area; **T-Bone Steak** *(price per pound);* **Frying Chicken** *(price per pound, whole fryer);* **Whole Milk** *(half gallon carton);* **Eggs** *(price per dozen, Grade A, large);* **Orange Juice** *(64 oz. Tropicana or Florida Natural);* **Coffee** *(11.5 oz. can, vacuum-packed, Maxwell House, Hills Bros, or Folgers).*
Source: The Council for Community and Economic Research, ACCRA Cost of Living Index, 2011

Housing and Utility Costs

Area[1]	New Home Price ($)	Apartment Rent ($/month)	All Electric ($/month)	Part Electric ($/month)	Other Energy ($/month)	Telephone ($/month)
City[2]	250,980	817	149.19	-	-	17.98
Avg.	285,990	839	163.23	89.00	77.52	26.92
Min.	188,005	460	125.58	45.39	33.89	17.98
Max.	1,197,028	3,244	339.16	181.97	348.69	40.01

Note: (1) Values for the local area are compared with the average, minimum and maximum values for all 335 areas in the Cost of Living Index; (2) Figures cover the Cape Coral-Fort Myers FL urban area; **New Home Price** *(2,400 sf living area, 8,000 sf lot, in urban area with full utilities);* **Apartment Rent** *(950 sf 2 bedroom/1.5 or 2 bath, unfurnished, excluding all utilities except water);* **All Electric** *(average monthly cost for an all-electric home);* **Part Electric** *(average monthly cost for a part-electric home);* **Other Energy** *(average monthly cost for natural gas, fuel oil, coal, wood, and any other forms of energy except electricity);* **Telephone** *(price includes basic monthly rate for a private residential line plus additional local usage charges incurred by a family of four).*
Source: The Council for Community and Economic Research, ACCRA Cost of Living Index, 2011

Health Care, Transportation, and Other Costs

Area[1]	Doctor ($/visit)	Dentist ($/visit)	Optometrist ($/visit)	Gasoline ($/gallon)	Beauty Salon ($/visit)	Men's Shirt ($)
City[2]	86.37	77.36	77.14	3.58	35.30	21.93
Avg.	93.88	81.72	90.54	3.48	32.65	25.06
Min.	60.00	55.33	53.66	3.18	19.78	13.44
Max.	154.98	145.97	183.72	4.31	63.21	46.00

Note: (1) Values for the local area are compared with the average, minimum and maximum values for all 335 areas in the Cost of Living Index; (2) Figures cover the Cape Coral-Fort Myers FL urban area; **Doctor** *(general practitioners routine exam of an established patient);* **Dentist** *(adult teeth cleaning and periodic oral examination);* **Optometrist** *(full vision eye exam for established adult patient);* **Gasoline** *(one gallon regular unleaded, national brand, including all taxes, cash price at self-service pump if available);* **Beauty Salon** *(woman's shampoo, trim, and blow-dry);* **Men's Shirt** *(cotton/polyester dress shirt, pinpoint weave, long sleeves).*
Source: The Council for Community and Economic Research, ACCRA Cost of Living Index, 2011

HOUSING

House Price Index (HPI)

Area	National Ranking[2]	Quarterly Change (%)	One-Year Change (%)	Five-Year Change (%)
MSA[1]	187	4.51	-3.44	-51.23
U.S.[3]	-	-0.10	-2.43	-19.16

Note: The HPI is a weighted repeat sales index. It measures average price changes in repeat sales or refinancings on the same properties. This information is obtained by reviewing repeat mortgage transactions on single-family properties whose mortgages have been purchased or securitized by Fannie Mae or Freddie Mac in January 1975; (1) Metropolitan/Micropolitan Statistical Area—see Appendix B for areas included; (2) Rankings are based on annual percentage change for all metro areas containing at least 15,000 transactions over the last 10 years and ranges from 1 to 306; (3) figures based on a weighted average of Census Division estimates using a purchase only index; all figures are for the period ending December 31, 2011
Source: Federal Housing Finance Agency, House Price Index, February 23, 2012

House Price Valuations

Area	Q4 2005 Price ($000)	Q4 2005 Over-valuation	Q4 2006 Price ($000)	Q4 2006 Over-valuation	Q4 2007 Price ($000)	Q4 2007 Over-valuation	Q4 2008 Price ($000)	Q4 2008 Over-valuation	Q4 2009 Price ($000)	Q4 2009 Over-valuation
MSA[1]	236.2	31.5	236.2	21.0	193.0	-1.2	121.0	-36.7	112.8	-40.5

Note: Figures show the percentage of over- or under-valuation of single family homes relative to statistically normal house values (e.g. a value of 23.6 indicates that house values are 23.6% overvalued). Statistically normal house values are based on house prices, interest rates, household incomes, population densities, and any historical premiums or discounts metropolitan areas have exhibited over time; (1) Figures cover the Cape Coral-Fort Myers, FL MSA - see Appendix B for areas included
Source: Global Insight/PNC Financial Services Group, House Prices in America: 4th Quarter 2009 Update

Median Single-Family Home Prices

Area	2009	2010	2011p	Percent Change 2010 to 2011
MSA[1]	87.6	88.9	102.9	15.7
U.S. Average	172.1	173.1	166.2	-4.0

Note: Figures are median sales prices of existing single-family homes in thousands of dollars; (p) preliminary; n/a not available; (1) Metropolitan Statistical Area—see Appendix B for areas included
Source: National Association of Realtors, Median Sales Price of Existing Single-Family Homes for Metropolitan Areas, 4th Quarter 2011

Affordability Index of Existing Single-Family Homes

Area	2009	2010	2011p	Percent Change 2010 to 2011
MSA[1]	213.2	219.1	195.6	-10.7

Note: The housing affordability index measures whether or not a typical family could qualify for a mortgage loan on a typical home. The higher the index, the greater the household purchasing power. An index of 100 is defined as the point where a median-income household has exactly enough income to qualify for the purchase of a median-priced existing single-family home, assuming a 20 percent downpayment and 25 percent of gross income devoted to mortgage principal and interest payments; (p) preliminary; n/a not available; (1) Metropolitan Statistical Area—see Appendix B for areas included
Source: National Association of Realtors, Affordability Index of Existing Single-Family Homes, 2011

Median Apartment Condo-Coop Home Prices

Area	2009	2010	2011p	Percent Change 2010 to 2011
MSA[1]	119.5	117.1	n/a	n/a
U.S. Average	175.6	171.7	165.1	-3.8

Note: Figures are median sales prices of existing apartment condo-coop homes in thousands of dollars; (p) preliminary; n/a not available; (1) Metropolitan Statistical Area—see Appendix B for areas included
Source: National Association of Realtors, Median Sales Price of Existing Apartment Condo-Coop Homes for Metropolitan Areas, 4th Quarter 2011

Year Housing Structure Built

Area	2005 or Later	2000 -2004	1990 -1999	1980 -1989	1970 -1979	1960 -1969	1950 -1959	Before 1950	Median Year
City	12.6	28.3	17.1	23.1	12.4	5.3	0.6	0.6	1995
MSA[1]	8.9	22.6	18.5	23.1	16.7	6.1	2.6	1.4	1990
U.S.	5.0	8.6	14.0	14.1	16.3	11.3	11.2	19.6	1975

Note: Figures are percentages except for Median Year; (1) Figures cover the Cape Coral-Fort Myers, FL Metropolitan Statistical Area—see Appendix B for areas included
Source: U.S. Census Bureau, 2008-2010 American Community Survey 3-Year Estimates

HEALTH

Health Risk Data

Category	MSA[1] (%)	U.S. (%)
Adults who have been told they have high blood pressure[2]	n/a	28.7
Adults who have been told they have high blood cholesterol[2]	n/a	37.5
Adults who have been told they have diabetes[3]	8.4	8.7
Adults who have been told they have arthritis[2]	n/a	26.0
Adults who have been told they currently have asthma	13.9	9.1
Adults who are current smokers	27.1	17.3
Adults who are heavy drinkers[4]	6.0	5.0
Adults who are binge drinkers[5]	19.1	15.1
Adults who are overweight (BMI 25.0 - 29.9)	34.2	36.2
Adults who are obese (BMI 30.0 - 99.8)	25.8	27.5
Adults who participated in any physical activities in the past month	72.1	76.1
Adults 50+ who have ever had a sigmoidoscopy or colonoscopy	73.0	65.2
Women aged 40+ who have had a mammogram within the past two years	73.7	75.2
Men aged 40+ who have had a PSA test within the past two years	68.4	53.2
Adults aged 65+ who have had flu shot within the past year	72.7	67.5
Adults aged 18–64 who have any kind of health care coverage	n/a	82.2

Note: Data as of 2010 unless otherwise noted; n/a not available; (1) Figures cover the Cape Coral-Fort Myers, FL Metropolitan Statistical Area—see Appendix B for areas included; (2) Data as of 2009; (3) Figures do not include pregnancy-related, borderline, or pre-diabetes; (4) Heavy drinkers are classified as males having more than two drinks per day or females having more than one drink per day; (5) Binge drinkers are classified as males having five or more drinks on one occasion or females having four or more drinks on one occasion
Source: Centers for Disease Control and Prevention, Behaviorial Risk Factor Surveillance System, SMART: Selected Metropolitan/Micropolitan Area Risk Trends, 2009, 2010

Mortality Rates for the Top 10 Causes of Death in the U.S.

ICD-10[a] Sub-Chapter	ICD-10[a] Code	Age-Adjusted Mortality Rate[1] per 100,000 population	
		County[2]	U.S.
Malignant neoplasms	C00-C97	152.1	175.6
Ischaemic heart diseases	I20-I25	101.2	121.6
Other forms of heart disease	I30-I51	23.1	48.6
Chronic lower respiratory diseases	J40-J47	32.3	42.3
Cerebrovascular diseases	I60-I69	26.5	40.6
Organic, including symptomatic, mental disorders	F01-F09	22.1	26.7
Other degenerative diseases of the nervous system	G30-G31	15.5	24.7
Other external causes of accidental injury	W00-X59	32.5	24.4
Diabetes mellitus	E10-E14	18.1	21.7
Hypertensive diseases	I10-I15	18.1	18.2

Note: (a) ICD-10 = International Classification of Diseases 10th Revision; (1) Mortality rates are a three year average covering 2007-2009; (2) Figures cover Lee County
Source: Centers for Disease Control and Prevention, National Center for Health Statistics. Underlying Cause of Death 1999-2009 on CDC WONDER Online Database, released 2012. Data for year 2009 are compiled from the Multiple Cause of Death File 2009, Series 20 No. 2O, 2012, Data for year 2008 are compiled from the Multiple Cause of Death File 2008, Series 20 No. 2N, 2011, Data for year 2007 are compiled from Multiple Cause of Death File 2007, Series 20 No. 2M, 2010.

Mortality Rates for Selected Causes of Death

ICD-10[a] Sub-Chapter	ICD-10[a] Code	Age-Adjusted Mortality Rate[1] per 100,000 population	
		County[2]	U.S.
Assault	X85-Y09	9.0	5.7
Human immunodeficiency virus (HIV) disease	B20-B24	3.6	3.3
Influenza and pneumonia	J09-J18	6.8	16.4
Intentional self-harm	X60-X84	15.7	11.5
Malnutrition	E40-E46	*Unreliable	0.8
Obesity and other hyperalimentation	E65-E68	1.2	1.6
Transport accidents	V01-V99	18.2	13.7
Viral hepatitis	B15-B19	1.6	2.2

Note: (a) ICD-10 = International Classification of Diseases 10th Revision; (1) Mortality rates are a three year average covering 2007-2009; (2) Figures cover Lee County; (*) Unreliable data as per CDC
Source: Centers for Disease Control and Prevention, National Center for Health Statistics. Underlying Cause of Death 1999-2009 on CDC WONDER Online Database, released 2012. Data for year 2009 are compiled from the Multiple Cause of Death File 2009, Series 20 No. 2O, 2012, Data for year 2008 are compiled from the Multiple Cause of Death File 2008, Series 20 No. 2N, 2011, Data for year 2007 are compiled from Multiple Cause of Death File 2007, Series 20 No. 2M, 2010.

Distribution of Physicians and Dentists

Area[1]	Dentists[2]	D.O.[3]	M.D.[4] Total	Family/General Practice	Pediatrics	Medical Specialties	Surgical Specialties
Local (number)	187	167	922	79	62	347	252
Local (rate[5])	3.2	2.8	15.7	1.3	1.1	5.9	4.3
U.S. (rate[5])	4.5	1.9	18.3	2.5	1.4	6.8	4.1

Note: Data as of 2008 unless noted; (1) Local data covers Lee County; (2) Data as of 2007; (3) Doctor of Osteopathic Medicine; (4) Includes active, non-federal, patient-care, office-based Doctors of Medicine; (5) rate per 10,000 population
Source: Area Resource File (ARF). 2009-2010 Release. U.S. Department of Health and Human Services, Health Resources and Services Administration, Bureau of Health Professions, Rockville, MD, August 2010

EDUCATION

Public School District Statistics

District Name	Schls	Pupils	Pupil/Teacher Ratio	Minority Pupils[1] (%)	Free Lunch Eligible[2] (%)	IEP[3] (%)
Lee	118	80,484	15.3	49.9	50.9	14.7

Note: Table includes school districts with 2,000 or more students; (1) Percentage of students that are not non-Hispanic white; (2) Percentage of students that are eligible for the free lunch program; (3) Percentage of students that have an Individualized Education Program.
Source: U.S. Department of Education, National Center for Education Statistics, Common Core of Data, Local Education Agency (School District) Universe Survey: School Year 2009-2010; U.S. Department of Education, National Center for Education Statistics, Common Core of Data, Public Elementary/Secondary School Universe Survey: School Year 2009-2010

Highest Level of Education

Area	Less than H.S.	H.S. Diploma	Some College, No Deg.	Associate Degree	Bachelors Degree	Masters Degree	Profess. School Degree	Doctorate Degree
City	11.7	34.8	24.6	8.3	14.6	4.0	1.4	0.6
MSA[1]	13.2	32.1	22.8	7.4	15.5	6.1	1.9	0.9
U.S.	14.7	28.4	21.3	7.6	17.6	7.2	1.9	1.2

Note: Figures cover persons age 25 and over; (1) Figures cover the Cape Coral-Fort Myers, FL Metropolitan Statistical Area—see Appendix B for areas included
Source: U.S. Census Bureau, 2008-2010 American Community Survey 3-Year Estimates

Educational Attainment by Race

Area	High School Graduate or Higher (%)					Bachelor's Degree or Higher (%)				
	Total	White	Black	Asian	Hisp.[2]	Total	White	Black	Asian	Hisp.[2]
City	88.3	88.6	82.5	87.7	78.6	20.6	20.5	18.1	36.3	19.6
MSA[1]	86.8	89.0	73.3	86.7	65.3	24.4	25.5	13.1	41.6	13.8
U.S.	85.3	87.5	81.4	85.5	61.6	28.0	29.3	17.8	50.2	13.0

Note: Figures shown cover persons 25 years old and over; (1) Figures cover the Cape Coral-Fort Myers, FL Metropolitan Statistical Area—see Appendix B for areas included; (2) People of Hispanic origin can be of any race
Source: U.S. Census Bureau, 2008-2010 American Community Survey 3-Year Estimates

School Enrollment by Grade and Control

Area	Preschool (%)		Kindergarten (%)		Grades 1 - 4 (%)		Grades 5 - 8 (%)		Grades 9 - 12 (%)	
	Public	Private	Public	Private	Public	Private	Public	Private	Public	Private
City	72.9	27.1	90.8	9.2	92.7	7.3	92.9	7.1	94.3	5.7
MSA[1]	62.7	37.3	90.2	9.8	91.4	8.6	90.4	9.6	91.8	8.2
U.S.	55.4	44.6	87.1	12.9	89.4	10.6	89.5	10.5	90.4	9.6

Note: Figures shown cover persons 3 years old and over; (1) Figures cover the Cape Coral-Fort Myers, FL Metropolitan Statistical Area—see Appendix B for areas included
Source: U.S. Census Bureau, 2008-2010 American Community Survey 3-Year Estimates

Average Salaries of Public School Classroom Teachers

Area	2010-11		2011-12		Percent Change 2010-11 to 2011-12	Percent Change 2001-02 to 2011-12
	Dollars	Rank[1]	Dollars	Rank[1]		
Florida	45,732	45	46,232	46	1.09	17.70
U.S. Average	55,623	-	56,643	-	1.83	26.8

Note: (1) State rank ranges from 1 to 51 where 1 indicates highest salary.
Source: National Education Association, Rankings & Estimates: Rankings of the States 2011 and Estimates of School Statistics 2012, December 2011

Higher Education

Four-Year Colleges			Two-Year Colleges			Medical Schools[1]	Law Schools[2]	Voc/ Tech[3]
Public	Private Non-profit	Private For-profit	Public	Private Non-profit	Private For-profit			
0	0	0	0	0	0	0	0	1

Note: Figures cover institutions located within the city limits and include main campuses only; (1) includes schools accredited by the Liaison Committee on Medical Education and the American Osteopathic Association's Commission on Osteopathic College Accreditation; (2) includes American Bar Association-accredited law schools; (3) includes all schools with programs that are less than 2 years.
Source: National Center for Education Statistics, Integrated Postsecondary Education System (IPEDS) Peer Analysis System, 2011-12; Association of American Medical Colleges, Member List, April 23, 2012; American Osteopathic Association, Member List, April 23, 2012; Law School Admission Council, Official Guide to ABA-Approved Law Schools Online, April 23, 2012

PRESIDENTIAL ELECTION

2008 Presidential Election Results

Area	Obama	McCain	Nader	Other
Lee County	44.3	54.7	0.4	0.6
U.S.	52.9	45.6	0.6	0.9

Note: Results are percentages and may not add to 100% due to rounding
Source: Dave Leip's Atlas of U.S. Presidential Elections, www.uselectionatlas.org

EMPLOYERS

Major Employers

Company Name	Industry
Aris Horticulture	Flowers: grown under cover (e.g., greenhouse production)
Chico's FAS	Women's clothing stores
Christian & Missionary Alliance Fndn	Retirement hotel operation
City of Cape Coral	City and town managers' office
County of Lee	Sheriffs' office
Crowther Roofing & Sheet Metal of FL	Roofing contractor
Doctors Osteopathic Medical Center	General medical and surgical hospitals
Edison State College	Community college
Florida Department of Military	National guard
General Electric Company	Aircraft engines and engine parts
K Corp Lee	Restaurant management
Lee Memorial Health System	General medical and surgical hospitals
Lee Memorial Health System Foundation	Health systems agency
MCI Communications Services	Telephone communication, except radio
Raymond Building Supply Corporation	Lumber plywood, and millwork
Robby & Stucky Limited	Furniture stores
Schear, Corp.	Multi-family dwellings, new construction
Sunshine Masonry	Concrete block masonry laying
United States Postal Service	U.s. postal service
Wal-Mart Stores	Department stores, discount

Note: Companies shown are located within the Cape Coral-Fort Myers, FL metropolitan area.
Source: Hoovers.com, data extracted April 25 2012

PUBLIC SAFETY

Crime Rate

Area	All Crimes	Murder	Forcible Rape	Robbery	Aggrav. Assault	Burglary	Larceny -Theft	Motor Vehicle Theft
City	2,532.5	1.9	14.3	39.9	115.9	675.1	1,617.5	67.9
Suburbs[1]	3,269.3	5.4	25.5	122.0	310.4	873.4	1,751.5	181.2
Metro[2]	3,073.3	4.5	22.6	100.2	258.7	820.6	1,715.8	151.1
U.S.	3,345.5	4.8	27.5	119.1	252.3	699.6	2,003.5	238.8

Note: Figures are crimes per 100,000 population; (1) All areas within the metro area that are located outside the city limits; (2) Metropolitan Statistical Area—see Appendix B for areas included
Source: FBI Uniform Crime Reports, 2010

Hate Crimes

Area	Number of Quarters Reported	Race	Religion	Sexual Orientation	Ethnicity	Disability
City	4	0	0	1	0	0

Source: Federal Bureau of Investigation, Hate Crime Statistics 2010

Identity Theft Consumer Complaints

Area	Complaints	Complaints per 100,000 Population	Rank[2]
MSA[1]	678	114.8	49
U.S.	279,156	90.4	-

Note: (1) Metropolitan Statistical Area—see Appendix B for areas included; (2) Rank ranges from 1 to 384 where 1 indicates greatest number of identity theft complaints per 100,000 population
Source: Federal Trade Commission, Consumer Sentinel Network Data Book for January–December 2011

Fraud and Other Consumer Complaints

Area	Complaints	Complaints per 100,000 Population	Rank[2]
MSA[1]	2,931	496.3	156
U.S.	1,533,924	496.8	-

Note: (1) Metropolitan Statistical Area—see Appendix B for areas included; (2) Rank ranges from 1 to 384 where 1 indicates greatest number of fraud and other complaints per 100,000 population
Source: Federal Trade Commission, Consumer Sentinel Network Data Book for January–December 2011

RECREATION

Culture

Dance[1]	Theatre[1]	Instrumental Music[1]	Vocal Music[1]	Series/ Festivals	Museums	Zoos and Aquariums[2]
0	0	0	0	0	n/a	0

Note: (1) Number of professional performing groups; (2) AZA-accredited; n/a not available
Source: The Grey House Performing Arts Directory, 2011-2012; Official Museum Directory, 2011; American Association of Museums, AAM Member Museums, April 2012; Association of Zoos & Aquariums, AZA Member Zoos & Aquariums, April 2012

Professional Sports Teams

Team Name	League

No teams are located in the metro area
Source: Original research

CLIMATE

Average and Extreme Temperatures

Temperature	Jan	Feb	Mar	Apr	May	Jun	Jul	Aug	Sep	Oct	Nov	Dec	Yr.
Extreme High (°F)	88	91	93	96	99	103	98	98	96	95	95	90	103
Average High (°F)	75	76	80	85	89	91	91	92	90	86	80	76	84
Average Temp. (°F)	65	65	70	74	79	82	83	83	82	77	71	66	75
Average Low (°F)	54	54	59	62	68	73	74	75	74	68	61	55	65
Extreme Low (°F)	28	32	33	39	52	60	66	67	64	48	34	26	26

Note: Figures cover the years 1948-1995
Source: National Climatic Data Center, International Station Meteorological Climate Summary, 9/96

Average Precipitation/Snowfall/Humidity

Precip./Humidity	Jan	Feb	Mar	Apr	May	Jun	Jul	Aug	Sep	Oct	Nov	Dec	Yr.
Avg. Precip. (in.)	2.0	2.2	2.6	1.7	3.6	9.3	8.9	8.9	8.2	3.5	1.4	1.5	53.9
Avg. Snowfall (in.)	0	0	0	0	0	0	0	0	0	0	0	0	0
Avg. Rel. Hum. 7am (%)	90	89	89	88	87	89	90	91	92	90	90	90	90
Avg. Rel. Hum. 4pm (%)	56	54	52	50	53	64	68	67	66	59	58	57	59

Note: Figures cover the years 1948-1995; Tr = Trace amounts (<0.05 in. of rain; <0.5 in. of snow)
Source: National Climatic Data Center, International Station Meteorological Climate Summary, 9/96

Weather Conditions

Temperature			Daytime Sky			Precipitation		
32°F & below	45°F & below	90°F & above	Clear	Partly cloudy	Cloudy	0.01 inch or more precip.	0.1 inch or more snow/ice	Thunder-storms
1	18	115	93	220	52	110	0	92

Note: Figures are average number of days per year and cover the years 1948-1995
Source: National Climatic Data Center, International Station Meteorological Climate Summary, 9/96

HAZARDOUS WASTE

Superfund Sites

Cape Coral has no sites on the EPA's Superfund Final National Priorities List.
U.S. Environmental Protection Agency, Final National Priorities List, April 17, 2012

**AIR & WATER
QUALITY**

Air Quality Index

Area	Percent of Days when Air Quality was...[2]					AQI Statistics[2]	
	Good	Moderate	Unhealthy for Sensitive Groups	Unhealthy	Very Unhealthy	Maximum	Median
Area[1]	95.1	4.9	0.0	0.0	0.0	74	34

Note: Air Quality Index (AQI) is an index for reporting daily air quality. EPA calculates the AQI for five major air pollutants regulated by the Clean Air Act: ground-level ozone, particle pollution (aka particulate matter), carbon monoxide, sulfur dioxide, and nitrogen dioxide. The AQI runs from 0 to 500. The higher the AQI value, the greater the level of air pollution and the greater the health concern. There are six AQI categories: "Good" AQI is between 0 and 50. Air quality is considered satisfactory; "Moderate" AQI is between 51 and 100. Air quality is acceptable; "Unhealthy for Sensitive Groups" When AQI values are between 101 and 150, members of sensitive groups may experience health effects; "Unhealthy" When AQI values are between 151 and 200 everyone may begin to experience health effects; "Very Unhealthy" AQI values between 201 and 300 trigger a health alert; "Hazardous" AQI values over 300 trigger warnings of emergency conditions (not shown); (1) Data covers Lee County; (2) Based on 365 days with AQI data in 2011.
Source: U.S. Environmental Protection Agency, AirData Report, 2011

Air Quality Index Pollutants

Area	Percent of Days when AQI Pollutant was...[2]					
	Carbon Monoxide	Nitrogen Dioxide	Ozone	Sulfur Dioxide	Particulate Matter 2.5	Particulate Matter 10
Area[1]	0.0	0.0	73.2	0.0	26.6	0.3

Note: The Air Quality Index (AQI) is an index for reporting daily air quality. EPA calculates the AQI for five major air pollutants regulated by the Clean Air Act: ground-level ozone, particle pollution (also known as particulate matter), carbon monoxide, sulfur dioxide, and nitrogen dioxide. The AQI runs from 0 to 500. The higher the AQI value, the greater the level of air pollution and the greater the health concern; (1) Data covers Lee County; (2) Based on 365 days with AQI data in 2011.
Source: U.S. Environmental Protection Agency, AirData Report, 2011

Air Quality Index Trends

Area	Trend Sites (days)								All Sites (days)
	2003	2004	2005	2006	2007	2008	2009	2010	2010
MSA[1]	n/a	n/a	n/a	n/a	n/a	n/a	n/a	n/a	n/a

Note: Figures are the number of days the AQI value exceeded 100 in a given year. An AQI value greater than 100 indicates that air quality would have been in the unhealthful range on that day. Data from exceptional events are included. These counts are presented in two ways. First, the counts are based on sites having an adequate record of monitoring data during the trend period (trend sites). These counts represent the relative change in the number of days with AQI values greater than 100. In the last column, the counts are based on all sites with data in the most recent year (because it is possible for a site to have data in the most recent year but not enough data to be a trend site); (1) Data covers the Cape Coral-Fort Myers, FL—see Appendix B for areas included; n/a not available.
Source: U.S. Environmental Protection Agency, Air Quality Index Information, "Number of Days with Air Quality Index Values Greater than 100 at Trend Sites, 2000-2010, and at All Sites in 2010"

Maximum Air Pollutant Concentrations: Particulate Matter, Ozone, CO and Lead

	Particulate Matter 10 (ug/m^3)	Particulate Matter 2.5 Wtd AM (ug/m^3)	Particulate Matter 2.5 24-Hr (ug/m^3)	Ozone (ppm)	Carbon Monoxide (ppm)	Lead (ug/m^3)
MSA[1] Level	67	7	13	0.065	n/a	n/a
NAAQS[2]	150	15	35	0.075	9	0.15
Met NAAQS[2]	Yes	Yes	Yes	Yes	n/a	n/a

Note: Data from exceptional events are not included; (1) Data covers the Cape Coral-Fort Myers, FL—see Appendix B for areas included; (2) National Ambient Air Quality Standards; ppm = parts per million; ug/m^3 = micrograms per cubic meter; n/a not available
Concentrations: Particulate Matter 10 (coarse particulate)—highest second maximum 24-hour concentration; Particulate Matter 2.5 Wtd AM (fine particulate)—highest weighted annual mean concentration; Particulate Matter 2.5 24-Hour (fine particulate)—highest 98th percentile 24-hour concentration; Ozone—highest fourth daily maximum 8-hour concentration; Carbon Monoxide—highest second maximum non-overlapping 8-hour concentration; Lead—maximum running 3-month average
Source: U.S. Environmental Protection Agency, CBSA Factbook 2010, Air Quality Statistics by City, 2010

Maximum Air Pollutant Concentrations: Nitrogen Dioxide and Sulfur Dioxide

	Nitrogen Dioxide AM (ppb)	Nitrogen Dioxide 1-Hr (ppb)	Sulfur Dioxide AM (ppb)	Sulfur Dioxide 1-Hr (ppb)	Sulfur Dioxide 24-Hr (ppb)
MSA[1] Level	n/a	n/a	n/a	n/a	n/a
NAAQS[2]	53	100	30	75	140
Met NAAQS[2]	n/a	n/a	n/a	n/a	n/a

Note: Data from exceptional events are not included; (1) Data covers the Cape Coral-Fort Myers, FL—see Appendix B for areas included; (2) National Ambient Air Quality Standards; ppb = parts per billion; n/a not available
Concentrations: Nitrogen Dioxide AM—highest arithmetic mean concentration; Nitrogen Dioxide 1-Hr—highest 98th percentile 1-hour daily maximum concentration; Sulfur Dioxide AM—highest annual mean concentration; Sulfur Dioxide 1-Hr—highest 99th percentile 1-hour daily maximum concentration; Sulfur Dioxide 24-Hr—highest second maximum 24-hour concentration
Source: U.S. Environmental Protection Agency, CBSA Factbook 2010, Air Quality Statistics by City, 2010

Drinking Water

Water System Name	Pop. Served	Primary Water Source Type	Violations[1] Health Based	Violations[1] Monitoring/ Reporting
City of Cape Coral	120,262	Ground	0	1

Note: (1) Based on violation data from January 1, 2011 to December 31, 2011 (includes unresolved violations from earlier years)
Source: U.S. Environmental Protection Agency, Office of Ground Water and Drinking Water, Safe Drinking Water Information System (based on data extracted April 18, 2012)

Charleston, South Carolina

Background

Charleston, South Carolina is located on the state's Atlantic coastline, 110 miles southeast of Columbia and 100 miles north of Savannah, Georgia. The city, named for King Charles II of England, is the county seat of Charleston County. Charleston is located on a bay at the end of a peninsula between the Ashley and Cooper rivers. The terrain is low-lying and coastal with nearby islands and inlets.

In 1670, English colonists established a nearby settlement, and subsequently moved to Charleston's present site. Charleston became an early trading center for rice, indigo, cotton and other goods. As the plantation economy grew, Charleston became a slave-trading center. In 1861, the Confederacy fired the cannon shot that launched the Civil War from the city's Battery, aimed at the Union's Fort Sumter in Charleston Harbor. Charleston was under siege during the Civil War, and experienced many difficulties during Reconstruction. Manufacturing industries including textiles and ironwork became important in the nineteenth century.

Charleston is part of a larger metropolitan area that includes North Charleston and Mount Pleasant and covers Charleston, Berkley and Dorchester counties. This area is a regional commercial and cultural center and a southern transportation hub whose port is among the nation's busiest shipping facilities. Charleston's other contemporary economic sectors include manufacturing, health care, business and professional services, defense activity, retail and wholesale trade, tourism, education and construction.

Charleston is a popular tourist area, based on its scenery, history and recreation. The city's center is well known for its historic neighborhoods with distinctive early southern architecture and ambiance. As one of the first American cities in the early twentieth century to actively encourage historic restoration and preservation, Charleston has more recently undertaken numerous revitalization initiatives, including the Charleston Place Hotel and retail complex, and Waterfront Park. North Charleston and other communities are also growing with industry and suburban development.

The founding of the Charleston Naval Shipyard stimulated a military-based economy after 1901. Numerous other defense facilities were later established, including the Charleston Air Force Base, located in North Charleston. Several military facilities were closed in the 1990s, including the shipyard, although other defense-related operations have remained.

In 2000, the Confederate submarine the *HL Hunley,* which sank in 1864, was raised, and brought to a conservation laboratory at the old Charleston Naval Base. Author Patricia Cornwell has taken a great interest in the project, and is involved in the current planning of a museum to house the submarine. Also in development is an International Museum of African American History, proposed to sit across from Liberty Square.

Charleston is a center for health care and medical research. SPAWAR (US Navy Space and Naval Warfare Systems Command) is the area's largest single employer followed by the Medical University of South Carolina, founded in 1824, with approximately 8,000 employees. Other area educational institutions include The College of Charleston, The Citadel Military College, Trident Technical College, Charleston Southern University, and a campus of Johnson and Wales University offering culinary and hospitality education.

The Charleston area has numerous parks, including one with a skateboard center, and public waterfront areas. Coastal recreation activities such as boating, swimming, fishing and beaches are popular, as are golf and other land sports.

The Charleston Museum is the nation's oldest, founded in 1773. There are also several former plantations in the area, including Boone Hall Plantation, Drayton Hall, Magnolia Plantation, and Middleton Place. Other attractions include the South Carolina Aquarium with its IMAX Theater, the American Military Museum, the Drayton Hall Plantation Museum, the Gibbes Museum of Art and the Karpeles Manuscript Museum. A North Charleston Convention Center and Performing Arts Center complex opened in 1999. Cultural organizations include the Spoleto Festival USA annual summer arts festival. The fifth annual Charleston International Film Festival, CIFF, was held in 2011.)

The Arthur Ravenel Jr. Bridge is the longest cable-stayed bridge in all of the Americas, running across Charleston's Cooper River.

The nearby Atlantic Ocean moderates the climate, especially in winter, and keeps summer a bit cooler than expected. Expect Indian summers in fall, and a possible hurricane, while spring sharply turns from the cold winds of March to lovely May. Severe storms are possible.

Rankings

General Rankings

- Charleston was chosen as one of America's best cities by *Outside Magazine* in the "Best for Surfing in the East" category. Criteria: educational attainment; cost of living; cultural vibrancy; economic resilience; housing market sanity; sport-specific facts such as the miles of trail within a hour's drive, frequency of group rides, and proximity to worthy ski areas. *Outside Magazine, "Best Towns 2010," August 2010*

- Charleston was selected as one the "finest places you'd ever want to call home" by *Outside Magazine*. Criteria: affordable homes; solid job prospects; vibrant nightlife. *Outside Magazine, "Life is Better Here," October 2011*

- Charleston was selected as one of "America's Favorite Cities." The city ranked #2 in the "Quality of Life and Visitor Experience" category. Respondents to an online survey were asked to rate 35 top urban destinations in the U.S. from a visitor's perspective. Criteria: noteworthy neighborhoods; skyline/views; public parks and outdoor access; cleanliness; public transportation and pedestrian friendliness; safety; weather; peace and quiet; people-watching; environmental friendliness. *Travelandleisure.com, "America's Favorite Cities 2010," November 2010*

- Charleston was selected as one of "America's Favorite Cities." The city ranked #2 in the "People" category. Respondents to an online survey were asked to rate 35 top urban destinations in the U.S. from a visitor's perspective. Criteria: attractive; friendly; stylish; intelligent; athletic/active; diverse. *Travelandleisure.com, "America's Favorite Cities 2010," November 2010*

- Charleston appeared on *Travel + Leisure's* list of the ten best cities in the continental U.S. and Canada. The city was ranked #2. Criteria: activities/attractions; culture/arts; restaurants/food; people; and value. *Travel + Leisure, "The World's Best Awards 2011"*

- *Condé Nast Traveler* polled thousands of readers for travel satisfaction. American cities were ranked based on the following criteria: friendliness; atmosphere/ambiance; culture/sites; restaurants; lodging; and shopping. Charleston appeared in the top 10, ranking #1. *Condé Nast Traveler, 2011 Readers' Choice Awards*

Business/Finance Rankings

- Charleston was selected as one of the "100 Best Places to Live and Launch" in the U.S. The city ranked #81. The editors at *Fortune Small Business* ranked 296 Census-designated metro areas by business friendliness (Launching Score, % New Businesses) and lifestyle offerings (Living Score). Then they picked the town within each of the top 100 metro areas that best blends business and pleasure. *Fortune Small Business, "100 Best Places to Live and Launch 2008," April 2008*

- The Charleston metro area appeared on the Milken Institute "2011 Best Performing Metros" list. Rank: #11 out of 200 large metro areas. Criteria: job growth; wage and salary growth; high-tech output growth. *Milken Institute, "2011 Best Performing Metros"*

- The Charleston metro area was selected as one of the best cities for entrepreneurs in America by *Inc. Magazine*. Criteria: job-growth data for 335 metro areas was analyzed for: recent growth trend; mid-term growth; long-term trend; current year growth. The Charleston metro area ranked #6 among mid-sized metro areas and #35 overall. *Inc. Magazine, "The Best Cities for Doing Business," July 2008*

- *Forbes* ranked the 200 most populous metro areas in the U.S. in terms of the "Best Places for Business and Careers." The Charleston metro area was ranked #40. Criteria: costs (business and living); job growth (past and projected); income growth; educational attainment; projected economic growth; crime; cultural and recreational opportunities; net migration patterns; number of highly ranked colleges. *Forbes, "Best Places for Business and Careers," June 2011*

Children/Family Rankings

- The Charleston metro area was selected as one of the "Best Cities for Relocating Families" by Worldwide ERC and Primacy Relocation. The 2008 study looked at nearly 50 factors important to relocating families including: recent job growth; nearby top-ranked colleges; in-state tuition for four-year public colleges; population growth since 2000; pediatricians per 100,000 population; and a Green Living index. *Worldwide ERC and Primacy Relocation, "2008 Best Cities for Relocating Families"*

Culture/Performing Arts Rankings

- Charleston was selected as one of "America's Favorite Cities." The city ranked #5 in the "Culture" category. Respondents to an online survey were asked to rate 35 top urban destinations in the U.S. from a visitor's perspective. Criteria: classical music; live music/bands; theater; museums/galleries; historical sites/monuments. *Travelandleisure.com, "America's Favorite Cities 2010," November 2010*

- Charleston was selected as one of "America's Top 25 Arts Destinations." The city ranked #7 in the mid-sized city (population 100,000 to 499,999) category. Criteria: readers' top choices for arts travel destinations based on the richness and variety of visual arts sites, activities and events. *American Style, "America's Top 25 Arts Destinations," May 2010*

Dating/Romance Rankings

- The Charleston metro area was selected as one of the "Best Cities for Relocating Singles" by Worldwide ERC and Primacy Relocation. The area ranked #16 out of the 100 largest metro areas in the U.S. Criteria: recent job growth; recent singles population growth; overall population growth; affordable rental housing; cost-of-living index; expanded arts and recreation opportunities; ratio of single men and single women; affordability of quality higher education (including state residency requirements); diversity index; climate; population density. *Worldwide ERC and Primacy Relocation, "2008 Best Cities for Relocating Singles"*

Education Rankings

- Charleston was identified as one of the 100 "smartest" metro areas in the U.S. The area ranked #51. Criteria: the editors rated the collective brainpower of the 100 largest metro areas in the U.S. based on their residents' educational attainment. *American City Business Journals, April 14, 2008*

- Charleston was identified as one of "America's Brainiest Bastions" by *Portfolio.com*. The metro area ranked #67 out of 200. *Portfolio.com* analyzed levels of educational attainment in the nation's 200 largest metropolitan areas. The editors established scores for five levels of educational attainment, based on relative earning power of adult workers age 25 or older. Scores were determined by comparing the median income for all workers with the median income for those workers at a specified educational level. *Portfolio.com, "America's Brainiest Bastions," December 1, 2010*

Environmental Rankings

- Charleston was selected as one of 22 "Smarter Cities" for energy by the Natural Resources Defense Council. Criteria: investment in green power; energy efficiency measures; conservation. *Natural Resources Defense Council, "2010 Smarter Cities," July 19, 2010*

- 100 of the largest metro areas in the U.S. were analyzed in terms of their current drought severity. The Charleston metro area ranked #36 (#1 = driest). The rankings were based on statistics such as long-term precipitation trends and patterns and the Palmer drought indices. *Sperling's BestPlaces, www.BestPlaces.net, "America's Drought-Riskiest Cities," November 2007*

- The U.S. Conference of Mayors and Wal-Mart Stores sponsor the Mayors' Climate Protection Awards Program. The awards recognize and honor mayors for outstanding and innovative practices that mayors are taking to increase energy efficiency in their cities, and to help curb global warming. Charleston was a Large City Best Practice Model. *U.S. Conference of Mayors, "2009 Mayors' Climate Protection Awards Program"*

- The Charleston metro area appeared in *Country Home's* "Best Green Places" report. The area ranked #146 out of 379. Criteria: official energy policies; green power; green buildings; availability of fresh, locally grown food. *Country Home, "Best Green Places," 2008*

Food/Drink Rankings

- Charleston was identified as one of "America's Drunkest Cities of 2011" by *The Daily Beast*. The city ranked #12 out of 25. Criteria: binge drinking; drinks consumed per month. *The Daily Beast, "Tipsy Towns: Where are America's Drunkest Cities?," December 31, 2011*

- Charleston was selected as one of "America's Favorite Cities." The city ranked #9 in the "Food/Dining" category. Respondents to an online survey were asked to rate 35 top urban destinations in the U.S. from a visitor's perspective. Criteria: big-name restaurants; ethnic food; farmers' markets; neighborhood joints and cafes. *Travelandleisure.com, "America's Favorite Cities 2010," November 2010*

Health/Fitness Rankings

- Charleston was identified as a "2011 Asthma Capital." The area ranked #66 out of the nation's 100 largest metropolitan areas. Twelve factors were used to identify the most challenging places to live for people with asthma: estimated prevalence; self-reported prevalence; crude death rate for asthma; annual pollen score; annual air quality; public smoking laws; number of board-certified asthma specialists; school inhaler access laws; rescue medication use; controller medication use; uninsured rate; poverty rate. *Asthma and Allergy Foundation of America, "2011 Asthma Capitals"*

- Charleston was identified as a "2011 Fall Allergy Capital." The area ranked #32 out of 100. Three groups of factors were used to identify the most severe cities for people with allergies during the fall season: annual pollen levels; medicine utilization; access to board-certified allergists. *Asthma and Allergy Foundation of America, "2011 Fall Allergy Capitals"*

- Charleston was identified as a "2012 Spring Allergy Capital." The area ranked #37 out of 100. Three groups of factors were used to identify the most severe cities for people with allergies during the spring season: annual pollen levels; medicine utilization; access to board-certified allergists. *Asthma and Allergy Foundation of America, "2012 Spring Allergy Capitals"*

- The Charleston metro area appeared in the 2011 Gallup-Healthways Well-Being Index. The index, based on interviews with more than 350,000 Americans, measured jobs, finances, physical health, emotional state of mind and communities. The metro area ranked #108 out of 190. Criteria: life evaluation; emotional health; work environment; physical health; healthy behaviors; basic access (basic needs optimal for a healthy life, such as access to food and medicine, having health insurance and feeling safe while walking at night). *Gallup-Healthways, "State of Well-Being 2011"*

Real Estate Rankings

- The Charleston metro area was identified as one of "10 Housing Markets for the Next Decade" by *U.S. News and World Report*. The metro area was ranked #7. Criteria: 10-year home price projections from 2009 to 2019. *U.S. News and World Report, "10 Housing Markets for the Next Decade," March 2010*

- The Center for Housing Policy ranked 210 U.S. metropolitan areas by the fair market rent for a two-bedroom unit. The Charleston metro area was ranked #88, (#1 = most expensive) with a rent of $863. Criteria: Fair Market Rent (FMR) in effect during the fourth quarter of 2009 based on HUD's fiscal year 2010 FMRs. *The Center for Housing Policy, "Paycheck to Paycheck: Most to Least Expensive Rental Markets in 2009"*

- The Charleston metro area was identified as one of the best U.S. markets to invest in rental property" by HomeVestors and Local Market Monitor. The area ranked #88 out of 100. Criteria: risk-return premium relative to national average. *HomeVestors and Local Market Monitor, "Best 100 U.S. Markets to Invest in Rental Property," March 9, 2012*

Safety Rankings

- The National Insurance Crime Bureau ranked 366 metro areas in the U.S. in terms of per capita rates of vehicle theft. The Charleston metro area ranked #55 (#1 = highest rate). Criteria: number of vehicle theft offenses per 100,000 inhabitants in 2010. *National Insurance Crime Bureau, "Hot Spots," June 21, 2011*

Seniors/Retirement Rankings

- Charleston was selected as one of "10 Historic Places to Retire" by *U.S. News & World Report*. The editors looked for places filled with museums, libraries, and national historic monuments that also offer a good quality of life and plenty of amenities for seniors. *U.S. News & World Report, "10 Historic Places to Retire," September 6, 2010*

- Charleston was identified as one of the "100 Most Popular Retirement Towns" by *Topretirements.com* The list reflects the 100 cities (out of 815+ total cities reviewed) that visitors to the website are most interested in for retirement. *Topretirements.com, "100 Most Popular Retirement Towns," February 21, 2012*

- Charleston was selected as one of "The Best Retirement Places" by *Forbes*. The magazine considered a wide range of factors such as climate, availability of doctors, driving environment, and crime rates, but focused especially on tax burden and cost of living. *Forbes, "The Best Retirement Places," March 27, 2011*

Sports/Recreation Rankings

- Charleston appeared on the *Sporting News* list of the "Best Sports Cities" for 2011. The area ranked #173 out of 271 cities in the U.S. *Sporting News* takes a 12-month snapshot of each city's sports, putting a heavy premium on regular-season won-lost records (from the most recently completed season). Other criteria include: playoff berths, bowl appearances and tournament bids; championships; applicable power ratings; quality of competition; overall fan fervor (measured in part by attendance); abundance of teams (rewarding quality over quantity); stadium and arena quality; ticket availability and prices; franchise ownership; and marquee appeal of athletes. *Sporting News, "Best Sports Cities 2011," October 4, 2011*

- Charleston was chosen as a bicycle friendly community by the League of American Bicyclists. A Bicycle Friendly Community welcomes cyclists by providing safe accommodation for cycling and encouraging people to bike for transportation and recreation. There are four award levels: Platinum; Gold; Silver; and Bronze. The community achieved an award level of Bronze. *League of American Bicyclists, "Bicycle Friendly Community Master List 2011"*

- Charleston was chosen as one of America's best cities for bicycling. The city ranked #29 out of 50. Criteria: number of segregated bike lanes, municipal bike racks, and bike boulevards; vibrant and diverse bike culture; smart, savvy bike shops; interviews with national and local advocates, bike shops and other experts. The editors only considered cities with populations of 100,000 or more. *Bicycling, "America's Best Bike Cities," April 2010*

Women/Minorities Rankings

- Charleston was ranked #62 out of 100 metro areas in *SELF Magazine's* ranking of America's healthiest places for women." A panel of experts came up with more than 50 criteria including death and disease rates, environmental indicators, community resources, and lifestyle habits. *SELF Magazine, "Secrets of America's Healthiest Women," December 2008*

Miscellaneous Rankings

- Charleston was selected as one of America's best-mannered cities. The area ranked #1. The general public determined the winners by casting votes online and by mail. *The Charleston School of Protocol and Etiquette, "2010 Most Mannerly City in America Contest," February 7, 2011*

Business Environment

CITY FINANCES

City Government Finances

Component	2009 ($000)	2009 ($ per capita)
Total Revenues	203,097	1,846
Total Expenditures	183,604	1,669
Debt Outstanding	1,180,068	10,726
Cash and Securities[1]	289,051	2,627

Note: (1) Cash and security holdings of a government at the close of its fiscal year, including those of its dependent agencies, utilities, and liquor stores.
Source: U.S Census Bureau, State & Local Government Finances 2009

City Government Revenue by Source

Source	2009 ($000)	2009 ($ per capita)
General Revenue		
From Federal Government	4,582	42
From State Government	22,560	205
From Local Governments	0	0
Taxes		
Property	56,074	510
Sales and Gross Receipts	36,820	335
Personal Income	0	0
Corporate Income	0	0
Motor Vehicle License	0	0
Other Taxes	36,826	335
Current Charges	29,589	269
Liquor Store	0	0
Utility	0	0
Employee Retirement	0	0

Source: U.S Census Bureau, State & Local Government Finances 2009

City Government Expenditures by Function

Function	2009 ($000)	2009 ($ per capita)	2009 (%)
General Direct Expenditures			
Air Transportation	0	0	0.0
Corrections	0	0	0.0
Education	0	0	0.0
Employment Security Administration	0	0	0.0
Financial Administration	9,508	86	5.2
Fire Protection	19,904	181	10.8
General Public Buildings	1,803	16	1.0
Governmental Administration, Other	6,937	63	3.8
Health	499	5	0.3
Highways	8,042	73	4.4
Hospitals	0	0	0.0
Housing and Community Development	9,000	82	4.9
Interest on General Debt	6,190	56	3.4
Judicial and Legal	5,694	52	3.1
Libraries	0	0	0.0
Parking	9,308	85	5.1
Parks and Recreation	24,908	226	13.6
Police Protection	37,815	344	20.6
Public Welfare	486	4	0.3
Sewerage	5,368	49	2.9
Solid Waste Management	5,862	53	3.2
Veterans' Services	0	0	0.0
Liquor Store	0	0	0.0
Utility	0	0	0.0
Employee Retirement	0	0	0.0

Source: U.S Census Bureau, State & Local Government Finances 2009

Municipal Bond Ratings

Area	Moody's	S&P	Fitch
City	Aa1	AAA	n/a

Rating Systems (shown in declining order of credit quality): Moody's– Aaa, Aa, A, Baa, Ba, B, Caa, Ca, C (numerical modifiers 1, 2, and 3 are added to letter-rating); S&P– AAA, AA, A, BBB, BB, B, CCC, CC, C; Fitch– AAA, AA, A, BBB, BB, B, CCC, CC, C. Ratings may be modified by the addition of a plus or minus sign to show relative standing within the major rating categories.
Notes: n/a Not Available; w/d Withdrawn (1) Not Reviewed; (2) Issuer Rating/No General Obligation; (3) Standard and Poor's Issue Credit Rating (ICR) is a current opinion of an obliger with respect to a specific financial obligation, a specific class of financial obligations, or a specific financial program.
Source: City of Charleston, South Carolina, Comprehensive Annual Financial Report, Fiscal Year Ended December 31, 2009

DEMOGRAPHICS

Population Growth

Area	1990 Census	2000 Census	2010 Census	Population Growth (%) 1990-2000	Population Growth (%) 2000-2010
City	96,102	96,650	120,083	0.6	24.2
MSA[1]	506,875	549,033	664,607	8.3	21.1
U.S.	248,709,873	281,421,906	308,745,538	13.2	9.7

Note: (1) Figures cover the Charleston-North Charleston-Summerville, SC Metropolitan Statistical Area—see Appendix B for areas included
Source: U.S. Census Bureau, 2010 Census

Household Size

Area	Persons in Household (%) One	Two	Three	Four	Five	Six	Seven or More	Average Household Size
City	34.6	35.5	14.9	9.5	3.6	1.1	0.7	2.18
MSA[1]	26.4	34.3	17.2	13.0	5.7	2.1	1.2	2.49
U.S.	26.7	32.8	16.1	13.4	6.5	2.6	1.9	2.58

Note: (1) Figures cover the Charleston-North Charleston-Summerville, SC Metropolitan Statistical Area—see Appendix B for areas included
Source: U.S. Census Bureau, 2010 Census

Race

Area	White Alone[2] (%)	Black Alone[2] (%)	Asian Alone[2] (%)	AIAN[3] Alone[2] (%)	NHOPI[4] Alone[2] (%)	Other Race Alone[2] (%)	Two or More Races (%)
City	70.2	25.4	1.6	0.2	0.1	1.0	1.5
MSA[1]	65.6	27.7	1.6	0.5	0.1	2.5	2.1
U.S.	72.4	12.6	4.8	0.9	0.2	6.2	2.9

Note: (1) Figures cover the Charleston-North Charleston-Summerville, SC Metropolitan Statistical Area—see Appendix B for areas included; (2) Alone is defined as not being in combination with one or more other races; (3) American Indian and Alaska Native; (4) Native Hawaiian and Other Pacific Islander
Source: U.S. Census Bureau, 2010 Census

Hispanic or Latino Origin

Area	Hispanic or Latino (%)	Mexican (%)	Puerto Rican (%)	Cuban (%)	Other Hispanic or Latino (%)
City	2.9	1.3	0.4	0.1	1.0
MSA[1]	5.4	3.1	0.7	0.1	1.5
U.S.	16.3	10.3	1.5	0.6	4.0

Note: Persons of Hispanic or Latino origin can be of any race; (1) Figures cover the Charleston-North Charleston-Summerville, SC Metropolitan Statistical Area—see Appendix B for areas included
Source: U.S. Census Bureau, 2010 Census

Segregation

Type	Segregation Indices[1]				Percent Change		
	1990	2000	2010	2010 Rank[2]	1990-2000	1990-2010	2000-2010
Black/White	47.4	44.2	41.5	88	-3.2	-5.9	-2.7
Asian/White	34.4	34.2	33.4	84	-0.3	-1.1	-0.8
Hispanic/White	26.6	32.2	39.8	66	5.6	13.2	7.6

Note: Figures are based on an analysis of 1990, 2000, and 2010 Census Decennial Census tract data by William H. Frey, Brookings Institution and the University of Michigan Social Science Data Analysis Network. In this analysis all racial groups (whites, blacks, and asians) are non-Hispanic members of those races. Hispanics are shown as a separate category; All figures cover the Metropolitan Statistical Area (see Appendix B for areas included); (1) Segregation Indices are Dissimilarity Indices that measure the degree to which the minority group is distributed differently than whites across census tracts. They range from 0 (complete integration) to 100 (complete segregation) where the value indicates the percentage of the minority group that needs to move to be distributed exactly like whites; (2) Ranges from 1 (most segregated) to 102 (least segregated); n/a not available.
Source: www.CensusScope.org

Ancestry

Area	German	Irish	English	American	Italian	Polish	French[2]	Scottish	Dutch
City	12.9	11.2	12.4	9.6	4.1	1.9	2.9	3.5	1.2
MSA[1]	12.0	10.4	9.6	11.7	3.5	1.8	2.7	2.6	1.0
U.S.	16.1	11.6	8.8	6.1	5.7	3.2	3.0	1.9	1.6

Note: Figures are the percentage of the total population reporting a particular ancestry. The nine most commonly reported ancestries in the U.S. are shown. Figures include multiple ancestries (e.g. if a person reported being Irish and Italian, they were included in both columns); (1) Figures cover the Charleston-North Charleston-Summerville, SC Metropolitan Statistical Area—see Appendix B for areas included; (2) Excludes Basque
Source: U.S. Census Bureau, 2008-2010 American Community Survey 3-Year Estimates

Foreign-Born Population

Area	Percent of Population Born in								
	Any Foreign Country	Mexico	Asia	Europe	Carribean	South America	Central America[2]	Africa	Canada
City	n/a	n/a	n/a	n/a	n/a	n/a	n/a	n/a	n/a
MSA[1]	5.5	1.7	1.2	1.1	0.2	0.5	0.5	0.1	0.2
U.S.	12.8	3.8	3.6	1.6	1.2	0.9	1.0	0.5	0.3

Note: (1) Figures cover the Charleston-North Charleston-Summerville, SC Metropolitan Statistical Area—see Appendix B for areas included; (2) Excludes Mexico.
Source: U.S. Census Bureau, 2008-2010 American Community Survey 3-Year Estimates

Marital Status

Area	Never Married	Now Married[2]	Separated	Widowed	Divorced
City	44.2	38.2	2.8	5.7	9.2
MSA[1]	33.9	47.1	3.0	5.5	10.5
U.S.	31.6	49.6	2.2	6.1	10.7

Note: Figures are percentages and cover the population 15 years of age and older; (1) Figures cover the Charleston-North Charleston-Summerville, SC Metropolitan Statistical Area—see Appendix B for areas included; (2) Excludes separated
Source: U.S. Census Bureau, 2008-2010 American Community Survey 3-Year Estimates

Age

Area	Percent of Population							Median Age
	Under Age 5	Age 5 to 17	Age 18 to 34	Age 35 to 49	Age 50 to 64	Age 65 to 79	80 Years and Over	
City	6.3	11.7	35.4	17.5	16.9	8.6	3.7	32.5
MSA[1]	6.9	16.4	26.2	20.3	18.7	8.8	2.7	35.4
U.S.	6.5	17.5	23.2	20.7	19.0	9.4	3.6	37.2

Note: (1) Figures cover the Charleston-North Charleston-Summerville, SC Metropolitan Statistical Area—see Appendix B for areas included
Source: U.S. Census Bureau, 2010 Census

Male/Female Ratio

Area	Males	Females	Males per 100 Females
City	56,741	63,342	89.6
MSA[1]	324,981	339,626	95.7
U.S.	151,781,326	156,964,212	96.7

Note: (1) Figures cover the Charleston-North Charleston-Summerville, SC Metropolitan Statistical Area—see Appendix B for areas included
Source: U.S. Census Bureau, 2010 Census

Religious Groups

Area	Catholic	Baptist	Non-Den.	Methodist[2]	Lutheran	LDS[3]	Pente-costal	Presby-terian[4]	Muslim[5]	Judaism
MSA[1]	6.2	12.4	7.1	10.0	1.1	1.0	2.0	2.4	0.3	0.2
U.S.	19.1	9.3	4.0	4.0	2.3	2.0	1.9	1.6	0.8	0.7

Note: Figures are the number of adherents as a percentage of the total population; (1) Figures cover the Charleston-North Charleston-Summerville, SC Metropolitan Statistical Area—see Appendix B for areas included; (2) Methodist/Pietist; (3) Latter Day Saints; (4) Reformed; (5) Figures are estimates
Source: Association of Statisticians of American Religious Bodies, 2010 U.S. Religion Census: Religious Congregations & Membership Study

ECONOMY

Gross Metropolitan Product

Area	2007	2008	2009	2010	2010 Rank[2]
MSA[1]	26.2	26.7	26.8	27.9	78

Note: Figures are in billions of dollars; (1) Figures cover the Charleston-North Charleston-Summerville, SC Metropolitan Statistical Area—see Appendix B for areas included; (2) Rank ranges from 1 to 363
Source: The United States Conference of Mayors, "U.S. Metro Economies: GMP and Employment Forecasts," June 2011

Economic Growth

Area	2007-2009 (%)	2010 (%)	2011 (%)	Rank[2]
MSA[1]	-0.8	2.8	3.0	150
U.S.	-1.3	2.9	2.5	–

Note: Figures are real Gross Metropolitan Product growth rates and represent annual average percent change; (1) Figures cover the Charleston-North Charleston-Summerville, SC Metropolitan Statistical Area—see Appendix B for areas included; (2) Rank ranges from 1 to 363
Source: The United States Conference of Mayors, "U.S. Metro Economies: GMP and Employment Forecasts," June 2011

Metropolitan Area Exports

Area	2005	2006	2007	2008	2009	2010	2010 Rank[2]
MSA[1]	1,414.5	1,615.3	1,842.9	2,005.5	1,455.7	2,120.0	81

Note: Figures are in millions of dollars; (1) Figures cover the Charleston-North Charleston-Summerville, SC Metropolitan Statistical Area—see Appendix B for areas included; (2) Rank ranges from 1 to 369
Source: U.S. Department of Commerce, International Trade Administration, Office of Trade & Industry Information, Manufacturing & Services, data extracted April 2, 2012

INCOME

Income

Area	Per Capita ($)	Median Household ($)	Average Household ($)
City	30,487	48,773	69,871
MSA[1]	26,132	49,606	66,540
U.S.	26,942	51,222	70,116

Note: (1) Figures cover the Charleston-North Charleston-Summerville, SC Metropolitan Statistical Area—see Appendix B for areas included
Source: U.S. Census Bureau, 2008-2010 American Community Survey 3-Year Estimates

Household Income Distribution

Area	Percent of Households Earning							
	Under $15,000	$15,000 -24,999	$25,000 -34,999	$35,000 -49,999	$50,000 -74,999	$75,000 -99,000	$100,000 -149,999	$150,000 and up
City	16.5	10.2	9.9	14.3	17.0	12.2	11.0	8.8
MSA[1]	13.4	11.3	10.5	15.2	18.3	12.9	11.2	7.3
U.S.	13.0	11.0	10.6	14.2	18.5	12.1	12.2	8.4

Note: (1) Figures cover the Charleston-North Charleston-Summerville, SC Metropolitan Statistical Area—see Appendix B for areas included
Source: U.S. Census Bureau, 2008-2010 American Community Survey 3-Year Estimates

Poverty Rate

Area	All Ages	Under 18 Years Old	18 to 64 Years Old	65 Years and Over
City	18.4	26.2	17.8	9.9
MSA[1]	15.4	22.5	13.7	10.2
U.S.	14.4	20.1	13.1	9.4

Note: Figures are percentage of people whose income during the past 12 months was below the poverty level;
(1) Figures cover the Charleston-North Charleston-Summerville, SC Metropolitan Statistical Area—see Appendix B for areas included
Source: U.S. Census Bureau, 2008-2010 American Community Survey 3-Year Estimates

Personal Bankruptcy Filing Rate

Area	2006	2007	2008	2009	2010	2011
Charleston County	0.91	1.24	1.45	1.71	1.88	1.52
U.S.	2.00	2.73	3.53	4.61	4.97	4.37

Note: Numbers are per 1,000 population and include Chapter 7 and Chapter 13 filings
Source: Federal Deposit Insurance Corporation, Regional Economic Conditions, March 9, 2012

EMPLOYMENT

Labor Force and Employment

Area	Civilian Labor Force			Workers Employed		
	Dec. 2010	Dec. 2011	% Chg.	Dec. 2010	Dec. 2011	% Chg.
City	58,080	58,384	0.5	53,354	54,387	1.9
MSA[1]	319,849	322,117	0.7	291,009	296,646	1.9
U.S.	153,156,000	153,373,000	0.1	139,159,000	140,681,000	1.1

Note: Data is not seasonally adjusted and covers workers 16 years of age and older;
(1) Metropolitan Statistical Area—see Appendix B for areas included
Source: Bureau of Labor Statistics, http://stats.bls.gov

Unemployment Rate

Area	2011											
	Jan.	Feb.	Mar.	Apr.	May	Jun.	Jul.	Aug.	Sep.	Oct.	Nov.	Dec.
City	7.5	7.8	7.0	7.1	7.9	9.1	8.8	8.7	7.9	7.2	6.9	6.8
MSA[1]	8.3	8.4	7.9	8.0	8.7	9.8	9.5	9.5	9.0	8.5	7.8	7.9
U.S.	9.8	9.5	9.2	8.7	8.7	9.3	9.3	9.1	8.8	8.5	8.2	8.3

Note: Data is not seasonally adjusted and covers workers 16 years of age and older; All figures are percentages; (1) Metropolitan Statistical Area—see Appendix B for areas included
Source: Bureau of Labor Statistics, http://stats.bls.gov

Projected Unemployment Rate

Area	2010 (%)	2011 (%)	2012 (%)	2013 (%)
MSA[1]	9.3	8.7	8.3	7.4

Note: (1) Metropolitan Statistical Area—see Appendix B for areas included
Source: The United States Conference of Mayors, "U.S. Metro Economies: GMP and Employment Forecasts," June 2011

Employment by Occupation

Occupation Classification	City (%)	MSA[1] (%)	U.S. (%)
Management, Business, Science, and Arts	43.8	35.1	35.6
Natural Resources, Construction, and Maintenance	5.5	10.2	9.5
Production, Transportation, and Material Moving	6.8	11.3	12.1
Sales and Office	24.3	25.6	25.2
Service	19.5	17.8	17.6

Note: Figures cover employed civilians 16 years of age and older; (1) Figures cover the Charleston-North Charleston-Summerville, SC Metropolitan Statistical Area—see Appendix B for areas included
Source: U.S. Census Bureau, 2008-2010 American Community Survey 3-Year Estimates

Employment by Industry

Sector	MSA[1] Number of Employees	MSA[1] Percent of Total	U.S. Percent of Total
Construction	n/a	n/a	4.1
Education and Health Services	35,800	12.0	15.2
Financial Activities	12,800	4.3	5.8
Government	58,700	19.7	16.8
Information	4,900	1.6	2.0
Leisure and Hospitality	35,000	11.8	9.9
Manufacturing	24,200	8.1	8.9
Mining and Logging	n/a	n/a	0.6
Other Services	10,500	3.5	4.0
Professional and Business Services	42,800	14.4	13.3
Retail Trade	38,000	12.8	11.5
Transportation and Utilities	11,900	4.0	3.8
Wholesale Trade	8,200	2.8	4.2

Note: Figures cover non-farm employment as of December 2011 and are not seasonally adjusted; (1) Metropolitan Statistical Area—see Appendix B for areas included; n/a not available
Source: Bureau of Labor Statistics, http://stats.bls.gov

Occupations with Greatest Projected Employment Growth: 2008 – 2018

Occupation[1]	2008 Employment	2018 Projected Employment	Numeric Employment Change	Percent Employment Change
Registered Nurses	38,400	48,020	9,620	25.1
Combined Food Preparation and Serving Workers, Including Fast Food	32,440	38,160	5,720	17.6
Retail Salespersons	65,260	69,880	4,620	7.1
Customer Service Representatives	28,910	33,430	4,520	15.6
Elementary School Teachers, Except Special Education	21,900	26,120	4,220	19.3
Office Clerks, General	42,130	46,010	3,880	9.2
Nursing Aides, Orderlies, and Attendants	20,090	23,400	3,310	16.5
Waiters and Waitresses	35,290	38,440	3,150	8.9
Cashiers	60,430	63,450	3,020	5.0
Postsecondary Teachers	15,490	18,420	2,930	18.9

Note: Projections cover South Carolina; (1) Sorted by numeric employment change
Source: www.projectionscentral.com, State Occupational Projections, 2008–2018 Long-Term Projections

Fastest Growing Occupations: 2008 – 2018

Occupation[1]	2008 Employment	2018 Projected Employment	Numeric Employment Change	Percent Employment Change
Network Systems and Data Communications Analysts	2,880	4,390	1,510	52.4
Self-Enrichment Education Teachers	2,220	3,190	970	43.7
Commercial Pilots	360	510	150	41.7
Pharmacy Technicians	5,490	7,630	2,140	39.0
Physician Assistants	600	830	230	38.3
Dental Hygienists	2,600	3,580	980	37.7
Dental Assistants	3,250	4,450	1,200	36.9
Computer Software Engineers, Systems Software	2,080	2,820	740	35.6
Medical Equipment Repairers	620	840	220	35.5
Personal and Home Care Aides	5,630	7,560	1,930	34.3

Note: Projections cover South Carolina; (1) Sorted by percent employment change and excludes occupations with numeric employment change less than 100
Source: www.projectionscentral.com, State Occupational Projections, 2008–2018 Long-Term Projections

Average Wages

Occupation	$/Hr.	Occupation	$/Hr.
Accountants and Auditors	29.13	Maids and Housekeeping Cleaners	9.27
Automotive Mechanics	19.27	Maintenance and Repair Workers	15.28
Bookkeepers	16.94	Marketing Managers	49.36
Carpenters	17.24	Nuclear Medicine Technologists	31.80
Cashiers	9.10	Nurses, Licensed Practical	20.09
Clerks, General Office	12.66	Nurses, Registered	32.68
Clerks, Receptionists/Information	12.68	Nursing Aides/Orderlies/Attendants	11.05
Clerks, Shipping/Receiving	16.03	Packers and Packagers, Hand	10.19
Computer Programmers	31.64	Physical Therapists	33.51
Computer Support Specialists	22.78	Postal Service Mail Carriers	23.97
Computer Systems Analysts	30.90	Real Estate Brokers	25.25
Cooks, Restaurant	10.38	Retail Salespersons	12.15
Dentists	69.44	Sales Reps., Exc. Tech./Scientific	25.40
Electrical Engineers	38.72	Sales Reps., Tech./Scientific	40.29
Electricians	19.10	Secretaries, Exc. Legal/Med./Exec.	15.43
Financial Managers	49.45	Security Guards	12.06
First-Line Supervisors/Managers, Sales	19.32	Surgeons	n/a
Food Preparation Workers	9.54	Teacher Assistants	11.10
General and Operations Managers	52.74	Teachers, Elementary School	22.70
Hairdressers/Cosmetologists	19.98	Teachers, Secondary School	n/a
Internists	n/a	Telemarketers	17.92
Janitors and Cleaners	10.02	Truck Drivers, Heavy/Tractor-Trailer	16.94
Landscaping/Groundskeeping Workers	10.84	Truck Drivers, Light/Delivery Svcs.	14.89
Lawyers	53.43	Waiters and Waitresses	9.24

Note: Wage data covers the Charleston-North Charleston-Summerville, SC Metropolitan Statistical Area—see Appendix B for areas included. Hourly wages for elementary/secondary school teachers and teacher assistants were calculated by the editors from annual wage data assuming a 40 hour work week; n/a not available.
Source: Bureau of Labor Statistics, Metro Area Occupational Employment and Wage Estimates, May 2011

RESIDENTIAL REAL ESTATE

Building Permits

Area	Single-Family			Multi-Family			Total		
	2010	2011	Pct. Chg.	2010	2011	Pct. Chg.	2010	2011	Pct. Chg.
City	400	392	-2.0	164	223	36.0	564	615	9.0
MSA[1]	2,787	2,597	-6.8	273	1,225	348.7	3,060	3,822	24.9
U.S.	447,311	418,498	-6.4	157,299	205,563	30.7	604,610	624,061	3.2

Note: (1) Metropolitan Statistical Area—see Appendix B for areas included; figures represent new, privately-owned housing units authorized (unadjusted data); All permit data are based on estimates with imputation.
Source: U.S. Census Bureau, Manufacturing, Mining, and Construction Statistics, Building Permits, 2010, 2011

Homeownership Rate

Area	2005 (%)	2006 (%)	2007 (%)	2008 (%)	2009 (%)	2010 (%)	2011 (%)
MSA[1]	n/a	n/a	n/a	n/a	n/a	n/a	n/a
U.S.	68.9	68.8	68.1	67.8	67.4	66.9	66.1

Note: (1) Metropolitan Statistical Area—see Appendix B for areas included; n/a not available
Source: U.S. Census Bureau, Housing Vacancies and Homeownership Annual Statistics: 2011

Housing Vacancy Rates

Area	Gross Vacancy Rate[2] (%)			Year-Round Vacancy Rate[3] (%)			Rental Vacancy Rate[4] (%)			Homeowner Vacancy Rate[5] (%)		
	2009	2010	2011	2009	2010	2011	2009	2010	2011	2009	2010	2011
MSA[1]	n/a	n/a	n/a	n/a	n/a	n/a	n/a	n/a	n/a	n/a	n/a	n/a
U.S.	14.5	14.3	14.2	11.3	11.3	11.1	10.6	10.2	9.5	2.6	2.6	2.5

Note: (1) Metropolitan Statistical Area—see Appendix B for areas included; (2) The percentage of the total housing inventory that is vacant; (3) The percentage of the housing inventory (excluding seasonal units) that is year-round vacant; (4) The percentage of rental inventory that is vacant for rent; (5) The percentage of homeowner inventory that is vacant for sale; n/a not available
Source: U.S. Census Bureau, Housing Vacancies and Homeownership Annual Statistics: 2011

TAXES

State Corporate Income Tax Rates

State	Tax Rate (%)	Income Brackets ($)	Num. of Brackets	Financial Institution Tax Rate (%)[a]	Federal Income Tax Ded.
South Carolina	5.0	Flat rate	1	4.5 (w)	No

Note: Tax rates as of January 1, 2012; (a) Rates listed are the corporate income tax rate applied to financial institutions or excise taxes based on income. Some states have other taxes based upon the value of deposits or shares; (w) South Carolina taxes savings and loans at a 6% rate.
Source: Federation of Tax Administrators, "State Corporate Income Tax Rates, 2012"

State Individual Income Tax Rates

State	Tax Rate (%)	Income Brackets ($)	Num. of Brackets	Personal Exempt. ($)[1] Single	Dependents	Fed. Inc. Tax Ded.
South Carolina (a)	0.0 - 7.0	2,800 - 14,000	6	3,700 (d)	3,700 (d)	No

Note: Tax rates as of January 1, 2012; Local- and county-level taxes are not included; n/a not applicable; (1) Married joint filers generally receive double the single exemption; (a) 17 states have statutory provision for automatically adjusting to the rate of inflation the dollar values of the income tax brackets, standard deductions, and/or personal exemptions. Massachusetts, Michigan, and Nebraska index the personal exemptiononly. Oregon does not index the income brackets for $125,000 and over. Because the inflation-adjustments for 2012 are not yet available in some cases, the table may report the 2011 amounts; (d) These states use the personal exemption amounts provided in the federal Internal Revenue Code.
Source: Federation of Tax Administrators, "State Individual Income Tax Rates, 2012"

Various State and Local Tax Rates

State	State and Local Sales and Use (%)	State Sales and Use (%)	Gasoline[1] (¢/gal.)	Cigarette[2] ($/pack)	Spirits[3] ($/gal.)	Wine[4] ($/gal.)	Beer[5] ($/gal.)
South Carolina	8.5	6.00	16.8	0.57	5.42 (h)(i)	1.08	0.77

Note: All tax rates as of January 1, 2012 except beer, wine and spirits (September 1, 2011); (1) The American Petroleum Institute has developed a methodology for determining the average tax rate on a gallon of fuel. Rates may include any of the following: excise taxes, environmental fees, storage tank fees, other fees or taxes, general sales tax, and local taxes. In states where gasoline is subject to the general sales tax, or where the fuel tax is based on the average sale price, the average rate determined by API is sensitive to changes in the price of gasoline. States that fully or partially apply general sales taxes to gasoline: CA, CO, GA, IL, IN, MI, NY; (2) The federal excise tax of $1.0066 per pack and local taxes are not included; (3) Rates are those applicable to off-premise sales of 40% alcohol by volume (a.b.v.) distilled spirits in 750ml containers. Local excise taxes are excluded; (4) Rates are those applicable to off-premise sales of 11% a.b.v. non-carbonated wine in 750ml containers; (5) Rates are those applicable to off-premise sales of 4.7% a.b.v. beer in 12 ounce containers; (h) Includes case fees and/or bottle fees which may vary with the size of the container; (i) Includes sales taxes specific to alcoholic beverages.
Source: Tax Foundation, 2012 Facts & Figures: How Does Your State Compare?

State-Local Tax Burdens

Area	Rate (%)	Rank[1]	Per Capita Taxes Paid to Home State ($)	Total State and Local Per Capita Taxes Paid ($)	Per Capita Income ($)
South Carolina	8.1	43	1,845	2,742	33,954
U.S. Average	9.8	-	3,057	4,160	42,539

Note: Figures cover 2009; (1) Rank ranges from 1 to 50 where 1 is highest tax burden
Source: Tax Foundation, State-Local Tax Burdens, All States, 2009

State Business Tax Climate Index Rankings

State	Overall Rank	Corporate Tax Index Rank	Individual Income Tax Index Rank	Sales Tax Index Rank	Unemployment Insurance Tax Index Rank	Property Tax Index Rank
South Carolina	36	10	39	20	38	21

Note: The index is a measure of how each state's tax laws affect economic performance. The lower the rank, the more favorable a state's tax system is for business. States without a given tax are given a ranking of 1.
Source: Tax Foundation, Major Components of the State Business Tax Climate Index, FY 2012

COMMERCIAL REAL ESTATE

Office Market

Market Area	Inventory (sq. ft.)	Vacant (sq. ft.)	Vac. Rate (%)	Under Constr. (sq. ft.)	Asking Rent ($/sf/yr) Class A	Asking Rent ($/sf/yr) Class B
Charleston	9,191,938	1,313,722	14.3	43,500	23.65	19.84

Source: Grubb & Ellis, Office Markets Trends, 4th Quarter 2011

Industrial Market

Market Area	Inventory (sq. ft.)	Vacant (sq. ft.)	Vac. Rate (%)	Under Constr. (sq. ft.)	Asking Rent ($/sf/yr) WH/Dist	Asking Rent ($/sf/yr) R&D/Flex
Charleston	42,877,673	5,180,987	12.1	1,018,000	4.03	6.64

Source: Grubb & Ellis, Industrial Markets Trends, 4th Quarter 2011

COMMERCIAL UTILITIES

Typical Monthly Electric Bills

Area	Commercial Service ($/month) 1,500 kWh	Commercial Service ($/month) 40 kW demand 14,000 kWh	Industrial Service ($/month) 1,000 kW demand 200,000 kWh	Industrial Service ($/month) 50,000 kW demand 15,000,000 kWh
City	190	1,701	24,729	1,381,575
Average[1]	189	1,616	25,197	1,470,813

Note: Based on total rates in effect July 1, 2011; (1) average based on 184 utilities surveyed
Source: Edison Electric Institute, Typical Bills and Average Rates Report, Summer 2011

TRANSPORTATION

Means of Transportation to Work

Area	Car/Truck/Van Drove Alone	Car/Truck/Van Car-pooled	Public Transportation Bus	Public Transportation Subway	Public Transportation Railroad	Bicycle	Walked	Other Means	Worked at Home
City	77.6	7.5	3.1	0.0	0.0	2.0	4.9	1.2	3.7
MSA[1]	80.9	9.7	1.2	0.0	0.0	0.7	2.7	1.1	3.7
U.S.	76.0	10.2	2.7	1.7	0.5	0.5	2.8	1.3	4.2

Note: Figures are percentages and cover workers 16 years of age and older; (1) Figures cover the Charleston-North Charleston-Summerville, SC Metropolitan Statistical Area—see Appendix B for areas included
Source: U.S. Census Bureau, 2008-2010 American Community Survey 3-Year Estimates

Travel Time to Work

Area	Less Than 10 Minutes	10 to 19 Minutes	20 to 29 Minutes	30 to 44 Minutes	45 to 59 Minutes	60 to 89 Minutes	90 Minutes or More
City	13.4	36.1	29.0	14.8	3.6	1.8	1.3
MSA[1]	11.2	29.1	24.9	22.1	7.4	3.7	1.6
U.S.	13.9	30.1	20.8	19.8	7.5	5.5	2.5

Note: Figures are percentages and include workers 16 years old and over; (1) Figures cover the Charleston-North Charleston-Summerville, SC Metropolitan Statistical Area—see Appendix B for areas included
Source: U.S. Census Bureau, 2008-2010 American Community Survey 3-Year Estimates

Travel Time Index

Area	1985	1990	1995	2000	2005	2010
Urban Area[1]	1.11	1.13	1.15	1.16	1.17	1.16
Average[2]	1.11	1.16	1.18	1.21	1.25	1.20

Note: Travel Time Index—the ratio of travel time in the peak period to the travel time at free-flow conditions. A value of 1.30 indicates a 20-minute free-flow trip takes 26 minutes in the peak. Free-flow speeds (60 mph on freeways and 35 mph on principal arterials) are used as the comparison threshold; (1) Covers the Charleston-North Charleston SC urban area; (2) average of 439 urban areas
Source: Texas Transportation Institute, Urban Mobility Report 2011, September 2011

Public Transportation

Agency Name / Mode of Transportation	Vehicles Operated in Maximum Service	Annual Unlinked Passenger Trips ('000)	Annual Passenger Miles ('000)
Charleston Area Regional Transportation (CARTA)			
Bus (purchased transportation)	81	4,203.7	15,478.4
Demand Response (purchased transportation)	18	77.3	801.5

Source: Federal Transit Administration, National Transit Database, 2010

Air Transportation

Airport Name and Code / Type of Service	Passenger Airlines[1]	Passenger Enplanements	Freight Carriers[2]	Freight (lbs.)
Charleston International Airport (CHS)				
Domestic service (U.S. carriers - 2011)	26	1,246,070	15	4,958,749
International service (U.S. carriers - 2010)	6	361	6	22,567,087

Note: (1) Includes all U.S.-based major, minor and commuter airlines that carried at least one passenger during the year; (2) Includes all U.S.-based airlines and freight carriers that transported at least one pound of freight during the year
Source: Bureau of Transportation Statistics, The Intermodal Transportation Database, Air Carriers: T-100 Domestic Market (U.S. Carriers), 2011; Bureau of Transportation Statistics, The Intermodal Transportation Database, Air Carriers: T-100 International Market (U.S. Carriers), 2010

Other Transportation Statistics

Major Highways:	I-26; I-95
Amtrak Service:	Yes (station is located in North Charleston)
Major Waterways/Ports:	Atlantic Ocean

Source: Amtrak.com; Google Maps

BUSINESSES

Major Business Headquarters

Company Name	Rankings	
	Fortune[1]	Forbes[2]
No companies listed	-	-

Note: (1) Fortune 500—companies that produce a 10-K are ranked 1 to 500 based on 2010 revenue; (2) all private companies with at least $2 billion in annual revenue are ranked 1 to 212; companies listed are headquartered in the city; dashes indicate no ranking
Source: Fortune, "Fortune 500," May 23, 2011; Forbes, "America's Largest Private Companies," November 16, 2011

Fast-Growing Businesses

According to *Inc.*, Charleston is home to two of America's 500 fastest-growing private companies: **BoomTown** (#174); **Levelwing** (#481). Criteria: must be an independent, privately-held, for-profit, U.S. corporation, proprietorship or partnership; revenues must be at least $80,000 in 2007 and $2 million in 2010; must have four-year operating/sales history. Holding companies, regulated banks, and utilities were excluded. *Inc., "America's 500 Fastest-Growing Private Companies," September 2011*

Minority- and Women-Owned Businesses

Group	All Firms		Firms with Paid Employees			
	Firms	Sales ($000)	Firms	Sales ($000)	Employees	Payroll ($000)
Asian	n/a	n/a	n/a	n/a	n/a	n/a
Black	n/a	n/a	n/a	n/a	n/a	n/a
Hispanic	n/a	n/a	n/a	n/a	n/a	n/a
Women	n/a	n/a	n/a	n/a	n/a	n/a
All Firms	697	230,181	174	219,350	1,409	31,384

Note: Figures cover firms located in the city; minority- and women-owned business are defined as firms in which the corresponding group own 51% or more of the stock or equity of the company; n/a not available
Source: U.S. Census Bureau, 2007 Economic Census, Survey of Business Owners

HOTELS

Hotels/Motels

Area	5 Star		4 Star		3 Star		2 Star		1 Star		Not Rated	
	Num.	Pct.[3]	Num.	Pct.[3]	Num.	Pct.[3]	Num.	Pct.[3]	Num.	Pct.[3]	Num.	Pct.[3]
City[1]	1	0.7	12	8.5	50	35.5	69	48.9	0	0.0	9	6.4
Total[2]	133	0.9	940	6.5	4,569	31.8	7,033	48.9	351	2.4	1,343	9.3

Note: (1) Figures cover Charleston and vicinity; (2) Figures cover all 100 cities in this book; (3) Percentage of hotels which have a given star rating; Star ratings are determined by expedia.com and offer an indication of the general quality of a particular hotel.
Source: expedia.com, April 25, 2012

The Charleston-North Charleston-Summerville, SC metro area is home to five of the best hotels in the U.S. according to *Travel & Leisure*: **Sanctuary at Kiawah Island Golf Resort** (#29); **Charleston Place** (#83); **Woodlands Inn, A Salamander Resort** (#94); **Planter's Inn** (#128); **Wentworth Mansion** (#172). Criteria: service; location; rooms; food; and value. *Travel & Leisure, "T+L 500, The World's Best Hotels 2012"*

The Charleston-North Charleston-Summerville, SC metro area is home to four of the best hotels in the U.S. according to *Condé Nast Traveler*: **French Quarter Inn** (#15); **Charleston Place** (#30); **Planters Inn** (#52); **Market Pavilion Hotel** (#62). The selections are based on over 25,000 responses to the magazine's annual Readers' Choice Survey. *Condé Nast Traveler, "2011 Readers' Choice Awards"*

EVENT SITES

Convention Centers

Name	Overall Space (sq. ft.)	Exhibit Space (sq. ft.)	Meeting Space (sq. ft.)	Meeting Rooms
Charleston Area Convention Center Complex	n/a	n/a	76,960	n/a

Note: n/a not available
Source: Original research

Living Environment

COST OF LIVING

Cost of Living Index

Composite Index	Groceries	Housing	Utilities	Trans-portation	Health Care	Misc. Goods/ Services
99.8	107.6	90.3	107.5	98.3	108.7	101.7

Note: U.S. = 100; Figures cover the Charleston-N Charleston SC urban area.
Source: The Council for Community and Economic Research, ACCRA Cost of Living Index, 2011

Grocery Prices

Area[1]	T-Bone Steak ($/pound)	Frying Chicken ($/pound)	Whole Milk ($/half gal.)	Eggs ($/dozen)	Orange Juice ($/64 oz.)	Coffee ($/11.5 oz.)
City[2]	9.33	1.32	2.59	1.71	3.26	4.49
Avg.	9.25	1.18	2.22	1.66	3.19	4.40
Min.	6.70	0.88	1.31	0.95	2.46	2.94
Max.	14.30	2.16	3.50	3.18	4.75	6.83

Note: (1) Values for the local area are compared with the average, minimum and maximum values for all 335 areas in the Cost of Living Index; (2) Figures cover the Charleston-N Charleston SC urban area; **T-Bone Steak** *(price per pound);* **Frying Chicken** *(price per pound, whole fryer);* **Whole Milk** *(half gallon carton);* **Eggs** *(price per dozen, Grade A, large);* **Orange Juice** *(64 oz. Tropicana or Florida Natural);* **Coffee** *(11.5 oz. can, vacuum-packed, Maxwell House, Hills Bros, or Folgers).*
Source: The Council for Community and Economic Research, ACCRA Cost of Living Index, 2011

Housing and Utility Costs

Area[1]	New Home Price ($)	Apartment Rent ($/month)	All Electric ($/month)	Part Electric ($/month)	Other Energy ($/month)	Telephone ($/month)
City[2]	240,230	977	185.13	-	-	27.15
Avg.	285,990	839	163.23	89.00	77.52	26.92
Min.	188,005	460	125.58	45.39	33.89	17.98
Max.	1,197,028	3,244	339.16	181.97	348.69	40.01

Note: (1) Values for the local area are compared with the average, minimum and maximum values for all 335 areas in the Cost of Living Index; (2) Figures cover the Charleston-N Charleston SC urban area; **New Home Price** *(2,400 sf living area, 8,000 sf lot, in urban area with full utilities);* **Apartment Rent** *(950 sf 2 bedroom/1.5 or 2 bath, unfurnished, excluding all utilities except water);* **All Electric** *(average monthly cost for an all-electric home);* **Part Electric** *(average monthly cost for a part-electric home);* **Other Energy** *(average monthly cost for natural gas, fuel oil, coal, wood, and any other forms of energy except electricity);* **Telephone** *(price includes basic monthly rate for a private residential line plus additional local usage charges incurred by a family of four).*
Source: The Council for Community and Economic Research, ACCRA Cost of Living Index, 2011

Health Care, Transportation, and Other Costs

Area[1]	Doctor ($/visit)	Dentist ($/visit)	Optometrist ($/visit)	Gasoline ($/gallon)	Beauty Salon ($/visit)	Men's Shirt ($)
City[2]	100.92	93.55	94.45	3.39	39.50	24.57
Avg.	93.88	81.72	90.54	3.48	32.65	25.06
Min.	60.00	55.33	53.66	3.18	19.78	13.44
Max.	154.98	145.97	183.72	4.31	63.21	46.00

Note: (1) Values for the local area are compared with the average, minimum and maximum values for all 335 areas in the Cost of Living Index; (2) Figures cover the Charleston-N Charleston SC urban area; **Doctor** *(general practitioners routine exam of an established patient);* **Dentist** *(adult teeth cleaning and periodic oral examination);* **Optometrist** *(full vision eye exam for established adult patient);* **Gasoline** *(one gallon regular unleaded, national brand, including all taxes, cash price at self-service pump if available);* **Beauty Salon** *(woman's shampoo, trim, and blow-dry);* **Men's Shirt** *(cotton/polyester dress shirt, pinpoint weave, long sleeves).*
Source: The Council for Community and Economic Research, ACCRA Cost of Living Index, 2011

HOUSING

House Price Index (HPI)

Area	National Ranking[2]	Quarterly Change (%)	One-Year Change (%)	Five-Year Change (%)
MSA[1]	182	1.68	-3.29	-15.04
U.S.[3]	-	-0.10	-2.43	-19.16

Note: The HPI is a weighted repeat sales index. It measures average price changes in repeat sales or refinancings on the same properties. This information is obtained by reviewing repeat mortgage transactions on single-family properties whose mortgages have been purchased or securitized by Fannie Mae or Freddie Mac in January 1975; (1) Metropolitan/Micropolitan Statistical Area—see Appendix B for areas included; (2) Rankings are based on annual percentage change for all metro areas containing at least 15,000 transactions over the last 10 years and ranges from 1 to 306; (3) figures based on a weighted average of Census Division estimates using a purchase only index; all figures are for the period ending December 31, 2011
Source: Federal Housing Finance Agency, House Price Index, February 23, 2012

House Price Valuations

Area	Q4 2005 Price ($000)	Over-valuation	Q4 2006 Price ($000)	Over-valuation	Q4 2007 Price ($000)	Over-valuation	Q4 2008 Price ($000)	Over-valuation	Q4 2009 Price ($000)	Over-valuation
MSA[1]	159.8	18.5	170.7	19.6	172.0	14.1	161.1	3.5	154.2	-2.0

Note: Figures show the percentage of over- or under-valuation of single family homes relative to statistically normal house values (e.g. a value of 23.6 indicates that house values are 23.6% overvalued). Statistically normal house values are based on house prices, interest rates, household incomes, population densities, and any historical premiums or discounts metropolitan areas have exhibited over time; (1) Figures cover the Charleston-North Charleston-Summerville, SC - see Appendix B for areas included
Source: Global Insight/PNC Financial Services Group, House Prices in America: 4th Quarter 2009 Update

Median Single-Family Home Prices

Area	2009	2010	2011[p]	Percent Change 2010 to 2011
MSA[1]	192.7	200.5	197.0	-1.7
U.S. Average	172.1	173.1	166.2	-4.0

Note: Figures are median sales prices of existing single-family homes in thousands of dollars; (p) preliminary; n/a not available; (1) Metropolitan Statistical Area—see Appendix B for areas included
Source: National Association of Realtors, Median Sales Price of Existing Single-Family Homes for Metropolitan Areas, 4th Quarter 2011

Affordability Index of Existing Single-Family Homes

Area	2009	2010	2011[p]	Percent Change 2010 to 2011
MSA[1]	88.2	89.9	96.5	7.3

Note: The housing affordability index measures whether or not a typical family could qualify for a mortgage loan on a typical home. The higher the index, the greater the household purchasing power. An index of 100 is defined as the point where a median-income household has exactly enough income to qualify for the purchase of a median-priced existing single-family home, assuming a 20 percent downpayment and 25 percent of gross income devoted to mortgage principal and interest payments; (p) preliminary; n/a not available; (1) Metropolitan Statistical Area—see Appendix B for areas included
Source: National Association of Realtors, Affordability Index of Existing Single-Family Homes, 2011

Median Apartment Condo-Coop Home Prices

Area	2009	2010	2011[p]	Percent Change 2010 to 2011
MSA[1]	n/a	n/a	n/a	n/a
U.S. Average	175.6	171.7	165.1	-3.8

Note: Figures are median sales prices of existing apartment condo-coop homes in thousands of dollars; (p) preliminary; n/a not available; (1) Metropolitan Statistical Area—see Appendix B for areas included
Source: National Association of Realtors, Median Sales Price of Existing Apartment Condo-Coop Homes for Metropolitan Areas, 4th Quarter 2011

Year Housing Structure Built

Area	2005 or Later	2000 -2004	1990 -1999	1980 -1989	1970 -1979	1960 -1969	1950 -1959	Before 1950	Median Year
City	9.3	15.3	13.6	13.2	11.8	9.5	7.9	19.4	1981
MSA[1]	10.2	13.4	17.5	19.0	16.2	9.2	6.5	8.2	1985
U.S.	5.0	8.6	14.0	14.1	16.3	11.3	11.2	19.6	1975

Note: Figures are percentages except for Median Year; (1) Figures cover the Charleston-North Charleston-Summerville, SC Metropolitan Statistical Area—see Appendix B for areas included
Source: U.S. Census Bureau, 2008-2010 American Community Survey 3-Year Estimates

HEALTH

Health Risk Data

Category	MSA[1] (%)	U.S. (%)
Adults who have been told they have high blood pressure[2]	30.8	28.7
Adults who have been told they have high blood cholesterol[2]	43.9	37.5
Adults who have been told they have diabetes[3]	11.6	8.7
Adults who have been told they have arthritis[2]	27.2	26.0
Adults who have been told they currently have asthma	5.5	9.1
Adults who are current smokers	21.8	17.3
Adults who are heavy drinkers[4]	8.7	5.0
Adults who are binge drinkers[5]	17.3	15.1
Adults who are overweight (BMI 25.0 - 29.9)	36.4	36.2
Adults who are obese (BMI 30.0 - 99.8)	29.0	27.5
Adults who participated in any physical activities in the past month	74.6	76.1
Adults 50+ who have ever had a sigmoidoscopy or colonoscopy	73.2	65.2
Women aged 40+ who have had a mammogram within the past two years	76.5	75.2
Men aged 40+ who have had a PSA test within the past two years	61.3	53.2
Adults aged 65+ who have had flu shot within the past year	68.9	67.5
Adults aged 18–64 who have any kind of health care coverage	81.3	82.2

Note: Data as of 2010 unless otherwise noted; (1) Figures cover the Charleston-North Charleston, SC Metropolitan Statistical Area—see Appendix B for areas included; (2) Data as of 2009; (3) Figures do not include pregnancy-related, borderline, or pre-diabetes; (4) Heavy drinkers are classified as males having more than two drinks per day or females having more than one drink per day; (5) Binge drinkers are classified as males having five or more drinks on one occasion or females having four or more drinks on one occasion
Source: Centers for Disease Control and Prevention, Behaviorial Risk Factor Surveillance System, SMART: Selected Metropolitan/Micropolitan Area Risk Trends, 2009, 2010

Mortality Rates for the Top 10 Causes of Death in the U.S.

ICD-10[a] Sub-Chapter	ICD-10[a] Code	Age-Adjusted Mortality Rate[1] per 100,000 population	
		County[2]	U.S.
Malignant neoplasms	C00-C97	185.3	175.6
Ischaemic heart diseases	I20-I25	87.6	121.6
Other forms of heart disease	I30-I51	50.0	48.6
Chronic lower respiratory diseases	J40-J47	37.4	42.3
Cerebrovascular diseases	I60-I69	51.0	40.6
Organic, including symptomatic, mental disorders	F01-F09	35.0	26.7
Other degenerative diseases of the nervous system	G30-G31	31.0	24.7
Other external causes of accidental injury	W00-X59	28.2	24.4
Diabetes mellitus	E10-E14	23.1	21.7
Hypertensive diseases	I10-I15	16.2	18.2

Note: (a) ICD-10 = International Classification of Diseases 10th Revision; (1) Mortality rates are a three year average covering 2007-2009; (2) Figures cover Charleston County
Source: Centers for Disease Control and Prevention, National Center for Health Statistics. Underlying Cause of Death 1999-2009 on CDC WONDER Online Database, released 2012. Data for year 2009 are compiled from the Multiple Cause of Death File 2009, Series 20 No. 2O, 2012, Data for year 2008 are compiled from the Multiple Cause of Death File 2008, Series 20 No. 2N, 2011, Data for year 2007 are compiled from Multiple Cause of Death File 2007, Series 20 No. 2M, 2010.

Mortality Rates for Selected Causes of Death

ICD-10[a] Sub-Chapter	ICD-10[a] Code	Age-Adjusted Mortality Rate[1] per 100,000 population	
		County[2]	U.S.
Assault	X85-Y09	9.7	5.7
Human immunodeficiency virus (HIV) disease	B20-B24	6.1	3.3
Influenza and pneumonia	J09-J18	9.8	16.4
Intentional self-harm	X60-X84	12.7	11.5
Malnutrition	E40-E46	*Unreliable	0.8
Obesity and other hyperalimentation	E65-E68	*Unreliable	1.6
Transport accidents	V01-V99	17.7	13.7
Viral hepatitis	B15-B19	2.0	2.2

Note: (a) ICD-10 = International Classification of Diseases 10th Revision; (1) Mortality rates are a three year average covering 2007-2009; (2) Figures cover Charleston County; (*) Unreliable data as per CDC
Source: Centers for Disease Control and Prevention, National Center for Health Statistics. Underlying Cause of Death 1999-2009 on CDC WONDER Online Database, released 2012. Data for year 2009 are compiled from the Multiple Cause of Death File 2009, Series 20 No. 2O, 2012, Data for year 2008 are compiled from the Multiple Cause of Death File 2008, Series 20 No. 2N, 2011, Data for year 2007 are compiled from Multiple Cause of Death File 2007, Series 20 No. 2M, 2010.

Distribution of Physicians and Dentists

Area[1]	Dentists[2]	D.O.[3]	M.D.[4]				
			Total	Family/ General Practice	Pediatrics	Medical Specialties	Surgical Specialties
Local (number)	244	73	1,424	117	93	474	353
Local (rate[5])	7.1	2.1	40.7	3.3	2.7	13.6	10.1
U.S. (rate[5])	4.5	1.9	18.3	2.5	1.4	6.8	4.1

Note: Data as of 2008 unless noted; (1) Local data covers Charleston County; (2) Data as of 2007; (3) Doctor of Osteopathic Medicine; (4) Includes active, non-federal, patient-care, office-based Doctors of Medicine; (5) rate per 10,000 population
Source: Area Resource File (ARF). 2009-2010 Release. U.S. Department of Health and Human Services, Health Resources and Services Administration, Bureau of Health Professions, Rockville, MD, August 2010

Best Hospitals

According to *U.S. News*, the Charleston-North Charleston-Summerville, SC is home to one of the best hospitals in the U.S.: **Medical University of South Carolina** (2 specialties). The hospital listed was highly ranked in at least one adult specialty. *U.S. News Online, "America's Best Hospitals 2011-12"*

According to *U.S. News*, the Charleston-North Charleston-Summerville, SC is home to one of the best children's hospitals in the U.S.: **Medical University of South Carolina Children's Hospital** (1 specialty). The hospital listed was highly ranked in at least one pediatric specialty. *U.S. News Online, "America's Best Children's Hospitals 2011-12"*

EDUCATION

Public School District Statistics

District Name	Schls	Pupils	Pupil/ Teacher Ratio	Minority Pupils[1] (%)	Free Lunch Eligible[2] (%)	IEP[3] (%)
Charleston 01	76	43,063	14.4	56.9	44.7	10.2

Note: Table includes school districts with 2,000 or more students; (1) Percentage of students that are not non-Hispanic white; (2) Percentage of students that are eligible for the free lunch program; (3) Percentage of students that have an Individualized Education Program.
Source: U.S. Department of Education, National Center for Education Statistics, Common Core of Data, Local Education Agency (School District) Universe Survey: School Year 2009-2010; U.S. Department of Education, National Center for Education Statistics, Common Core of Data, Public Elementary/Secondary School Universe Survey: School Year 2009-2010

Highest Level of Education

Area	Less than H.S.	H.S. Diploma	Some College, No Deg.	Associate Degree	Bachelors Degree	Masters Degree	Profess. School Degree	Doctorate Degree
City	9.2	17.7	19.7	6.5	29.4	11.3	3.9	2.2
MSA[1]	12.5	27.0	21.8	8.3	19.7	7.5	2.0	1.3
U.S.	14.7	28.4	21.3	7.6	17.6	7.2	1.9	1.2

Note: Figures cover persons age 25 and over; (1) Figures cover the Charleston-North Charleston-Summerville, SC Metropolitan Statistical Area—see Appendix B for areas included
Source: U.S. Census Bureau, 2008-2010 American Community Survey 3-Year Estimates

Educational Attainment by Race

Area	High School Graduate or Higher (%)					Bachelor's Degree or Higher (%)				
	Total	White	Black	Asian	Hisp.[2]	Total	White	Black	Asian	Hisp.[2]
City	90.8	95.1	78.1	91.9	72.8	46.8	55.8	19.0	60.9	20.7
MSA[1]	87.5	91.1	79.0	84.9	64.7	30.4	36.4	14.4	41.3	14.6
U.S.	85.3	87.5	81.4	85.5	61.6	28.0	29.3	17.8	50.2	13.0

Note: Figures shown cover persons 25 years old and over; (1) Figures cover the Charleston-North Charleston-Summerville, SC Metropolitan Statistical Area—see Appendix B for areas included; (2) People of Hispanic origin can be of any race
Source: U.S. Census Bureau, 2008-2010 American Community Survey 3-Year Estimates

School Enrollment by Grade and Control

Area	Preschool (%)		Kindergarten (%)		Grades 1 - 4 (%)		Grades 5 - 8 (%)		Grades 9 - 12 (%)	
	Public	Private	Public	Private	Public	Private	Public	Private	Public	Private
City	31.8	68.2	68.2	31.8	83.4	16.6	85.7	14.3	81.4	18.6
MSA[1]	47.9	52.1	81.9	18.1	87.7	12.3	87.3	12.7	86.3	13.7
U.S.	55.4	44.6	87.1	12.9	89.4	10.6	89.5	10.5	90.4	9.6

Note: Figures shown cover persons 3 years old and over; (1) Figures cover the Charleston-North Charleston-Summerville, SC Metropolitan Statistical Area—see Appendix B for areas included
Source: U.S. Census Bureau, 2008-2010 American Community Survey 3-Year Estimates

Average Salaries of Public School Classroom Teachers

Area	2010-11		2011-12		Percent Change 2010-11 to 2011-12	Percent Change 2001-02 to 2011-12
	Dollars	Rank[1]	Dollars	Rank[1]		
South Carolina	47,050	38	48,176	37	2.39	20.70
U.S. Average	55,623	-	56,643	-	1.83	26.8

Note: (1) State rank ranges from 1 to 51 where 1 indicates highest salary.
Source: National Education Association, Rankings & Estimates: Rankings of the States 2011 and Estimates of School Statistics 2012, December 2011

Higher Education

Four-Year Colleges			Two-Year Colleges			Medical Schools[1]	Law Schools[2]	Voc/ Tech[3]
Public	Private Non-profit	Private For-profit	Public	Private Non-profit	Private For-profit			
3	1	2	1	0	1	1	1	3

Note: Figures cover institutions located within the city limits and include main campuses only; (1) includes schools accredited by the Liaison Committee on Medical Education and the American Osteopathic Association's Commission on Osteopathic College Accreditation; (2) includes American Bar Association-accredited law schools; (3) includes all schools with programs that are less than 2 years.
Source: National Center for Education Statistics, Integrated Postsecondary Education System (IPEDS) Peer Analysis System, 2011-12; Association of American Medical Colleges, Member List, April 23, 2012; American Osteopathic Association, Member List, April 23, 2012; Law School Admission Council, Official Guide to ABA-Approved Law Schools Online, April 23, 2012

PRESIDENTIAL ELECTION

2008 Presidential Election Results

Area	Obama	McCain	Nader	Other
Charleston County	53.5	45.2	0.3	1.0
U.S.	52.9	45.6	0.6	0.9

Note: Results are percentages and may not add to 100% due to rounding
Source: Dave Leip's Atlas of U.S. Presidential Elections, www.uselectionatlas.org

EMPLOYERS

Major Employers

Company Name	Industry
Allergy Centers of America	Ears, nose, and throat specialist, physician/surgeon
Alternative Staffing	Help supply services
Behr Heat Transfer Systems	Radiators & radiator shells & cores, motor vehicle
Campground At James Island	Trailer parks and campsites
CELLCO Partnership	Cellular telephone services
College of Charleston	Colleges and universities
County of Charleston	Marshals' office, police
CUMMINS	Internal combustion engines
Kiawah Island Inn Company	Resort hotel
Medical University Hospital Authority	General medical and surgical hospitals
Medical University of South Carolina	General medical and surgical hospitals
Medical University of South Carolina	Special warehousing and storage
Medical University of South Carolina	Medical centers
Six Continents Hotels	Hotels and motels
The Boeing Company	Airplanes, fixed or rotary wing
Trident Medical Center	General medical and surgical hospitals
United States Department of the Navy	Navy
Veterans Health Administration	General medical and surgical hospitals

Note: Companies shown are located within the Charleston-North Charleston-Summerville, SC metropolitan area.
Source: Hoovers.com, data extracted April 25 2012

PUBLIC SAFETY

Crime Rate

Area	All Crimes	Violent Crimes				Property Crimes		
		Murder	Forcible Rape	Robbery	Aggrav. Assault	Burglary	Larceny -Theft	Motor Vehicle Theft
City	3,750.7	8.5	15.3	128.5	212.7	511.3	2,679.7	194.8
Suburbs[1]	4,165.2	5.4	28.1	121.8	390.0	803.8	2,522.8	293.1
Metro[2]	4,092.7	6.0	25.9	122.9	359.0	752.7	2,550.3	275.9
U.S.	3,345.5	4.8	27.5	119.1	252.3	699.6	2,003.5	238.8

Note: Figures are crimes per 100,000 population; (1) All areas within the metro area that are located outside the city limits; (2) Metropolitan Statistical Area—see Appendix B for areas included
Source: FBI Uniform Crime Reports, 2010

Hate Crimes

Area	Number of Quarters Reported	Bias Motivation				
		Race	Religion	Sexual Orientation	Ethnicity	Disability
City	4	0	1	0	0	0

Source: Federal Bureau of Investigation, Hate Crime Statistics 2010

Identity Theft Consumer Complaints

Area	Complaints	Complaints per 100,000 Population	Rank[2]
MSA[1]	470	74.6	201
U.S.	279,156	90.4	-

Note: (1) Metropolitan Statistical Area—see Appendix B for areas included; (2) Rank ranges from 1 to 384 where 1 indicates greatest number of identity theft complaints per 100,000 population
Source: Federal Trade Commission, Consumer Sentinel Network Data Book for January–December 2011

Fraud and Other Consumer Complaints

Area	Complaints	Complaints per 100,000 Population	Rank[2]
MSA[1]	2,995	475.3	185
U.S.	1,533,924	496.8	-

Note: (1) Metropolitan Statistical Area—see Appendix B for areas included; (2) Rank ranges from 1 to 384 where 1 indicates greatest number of fraud and other complaints per 100,000 population
Source: Federal Trade Commission, Consumer Sentinel Network Data Book for January–December 2011

RECREATION

Culture

Dance[1]	Theatre[1]	Instrumental Music[1]	Vocal Music[1]	Series/ Festivals	Museums	Zoos and Aquariums[2]
2	1	2	0	4	12	1

Note: (1) Number of professional perfoming groups; (2) AZA-accredited
Source: The Grey House Performing Arts Directory, 2011-2012; Official Museum Directory, 2011; American Association of Museums, AAM Member Museums, April 2012; Association of Zoos & Aquariums, AZA Member Zoos & Aquariums, April 2012

Professional Sports Teams

Team Name	League

No teams are located in the metro area
Source: Original research

CLIMATE

Average and Extreme Temperatures

Temperature	Jan	Feb	Mar	Apr	May	Jun	Jul	Aug	Sep	Oct	Nov	Dec	Yr.
Extreme High (°F)	83	87	90	94	98	101	104	102	97	94	88	83	104
Average High (°F)	59	62	68	76	83	88	90	89	85	77	69	61	76
Average Temp. (°F)	49	51	57	65	73	78	81	81	76	67	58	51	66
Average Low (°F)	38	40	46	53	62	69	72	72	67	56	46	39	55
Extreme Low (°F)	6	12	15	30	36	50	58	56	42	27	15	8	6

Note: Figures cover the years 1945-1995
Source: National Climatic Data Center, International Station Meteorological Climate Summary, 9/96

Average Precipitation/Snowfall/Humidity

Precip./Humidity	Jan	Feb	Mar	Apr	May	Jun	Jul	Aug	Sep	Oct	Nov	Dec	Yr.
Avg. Precip. (in.)	3.5	3.1	4.4	2.8	4.1	6.0	7.2	6.9	5.6	3.1	2.5	3.1	52.1
Avg. Snowfall (in.)	Tr	Tr	Tr	0	0	0	0	0	0	0	Tr	Tr	1
Avg. Rel. Hum. 7am (%)	83	81	83	84	85	86	88	90	91	89	86	83	86
Avg. Rel. Hum. 4pm (%)	55	52	51	51	56	62	66	66	65	58	56	55	58

Note: Figures cover the years 1945-1995; Tr = Trace amounts (<0.05 in. of rain; <0.5 in. of snow)
Source: National Climatic Data Center, International Station Meteorological Climate Summary, 9/96

Weather Conditions

Temperature			Daytime Sky			Precipitation		
10°F & below	32°F & below	90°F & above	Clear	Partly cloudy	Cloudy	0.01 inch or more precip.	0.1 inch or more snow/ice	Thunder-storms
<1	33	53	89	162	114	114	1	59

Note: Figures are average number of days per year and cover the years 1945-1995
Source: National Climatic Data Center, International Station Meteorological Climate Summary, 9/96

HAZARDOUS WASTE

Superfund Sites

Charleston has two hazardous waste sites on the EPA's Superfund Final National Priorities List: **Macalloy Corporation (North Charleston); Koppers Co., Inc. (Charleston Plant).**
U.S. Environmental Protection Agency, Final National Priorities List, April 17, 2012

AIR & WATER QUALITY

Air Quality Index

Area	Percent of Days when Air Quality was...[2]					AQI Statistics[2]	
	Good	Moderate	Unhealthy for Sensitive Groups	Unhealthy	Very Unhealthy	Maximum	Median
Area[1]	80.3	18.6	1.1	0.0	0.0	136	37

Note: Air Quality Index (AQI) is an index for reporting daily air quality. EPA calculates the AQI for five major air pollutants regulated by the Clean Air Act: ground-level ozone, particle pollution (aka particulate matter), carbon monoxide, sulfur dioxide, and nitrogen dioxide. The AQI runs from 0 to 500. The higher the AQI value, the greater the level of air pollution and the greater the health concern. There are six AQI categories: "Good" AQI is between 0 and 50. Air quality is considered satisfactory; "Moderate" AQI is between 51 and 100. Air quality is acceptable; "Unhealthy for Sensitive Groups" When AQI values are between 101 and 150, members of sensitive groups may experience health effects; "Unhealthy" When AQI values are between 151 and 200 everyone may begin to experience health effects; "Very Unhealthy" AQI values between 201 and 300 trigger a health alert; "Hazardous" AQI values over 300 trigger warnings of emergency conditions (not shown); (1) Data covers Charleston County; (2) Based on 365 days with AQI data in 2011.
Source: U.S. Environmental Protection Agency, AirData Report, 2011

Air Quality Index Pollutants

Area	Percent of Days when AQI Pollutant was...[2]					
	Carbon Monoxide	Nitrogen Dioxide	Ozone	Sulfur Dioxide	Particulate Matter 2.5	Particulate Matter 10
Area[1]	0.0	3.3	39.2	0.0	57.0	0.5

Note: The Air Quality Index (AQI) is an index for reporting daily air quality. EPA calculates the AQI for five major air pollutants regulated by the Clean Air Act: ground-level ozone, particle pollution (also known as particulate matter), carbon monoxide, sulfur dioxide, and nitrogen dioxide. The AQI runs from 0 to 500. The higher the AQI value, the greater the level of air pollution and the greater the health concern; (1) Data covers Charleston County; (2) Based on 365 days with AQI data in 2011.
Source: U.S. Environmental Protection Agency, AirData Report, 2011

Air Quality Index Trends

Area	Trend Sites (days)								All Sites (days)
	2003	2004	2005	2006	2007	2008	2009	2010	2010
MSA[1]	3	3	8	9	5	1	0	0	0

Note: Figures are the number of days the AQI value exceeded 100 in a given year. An AQI value greater than 100 indicates that air quality would have been in the unhealthful range on that day. Data from exceptional events are included. These counts are presented in two ways. First, the counts are based on sites having an adequate record of monitoring data during the trend period (trend sites). These counts represent the relative change in the number of days with AQI values greater than 100. In the last column, the counts are based on all sites with data in the most recent year (because it is possible for a site to have data in the most recent year but not enough data to be a trend site); (1) Data covers the Charleston-North Charleston-Summerville, SC—see Appendix B for areas included
Source: U.S. Environmental Protection Agency, Air Quality Index Information, "Number of Days with Air Quality Index Values Greater than 100 at Trend Sites, 2000-2010, and at All Sites in 2010"

Maximum Air Pollutant Concentrations: Particulate Matter, Ozone, CO and Lead

	Particulate Matter 10 (ug/m^3)	Particulate Matter 2.5 Wtd AM (ug/m^3)	Particulate Matter 2.5 24-Hr (ug/m^3)	Ozone (ppm)	Carbon Monoxide (ppm)	Lead (ug/m^3)
MSA[1] Level	49	9.9	23	0.068	0	n/a
NAAQS[2]	150	15	35	0.075	9	0.15
Met NAAQS[2]	Yes	Yes	Yes	Yes	Yes	n/a

Note: Data from exceptional events are not included; (1) Data covers the Charleston-North Charleston-Summerville, SC—see Appendix B for areas included; (2) National Ambient Air Quality Standards; ppm = parts per million; ug/m^3 = micrograms per cubic meter; n/a not available
Concentrations: Particulate Matter 10 (coarse particulate)—highest second maximum 24-hour concentration; Particulate Matter 2.5 Wtd AM (fine particulate)—highest weighted annual mean concentration; Particulate Matter 2.5 24-Hour (fine particulate)—highest 98th percentile 24-hour concentration; Ozone—highest fourth daily maximum 8-hour concentration; Carbon Monoxide—highest second maximum non-overlapping 8-hour concentration; Lead—maximum running 3-month average
Source: U.S. Environmental Protection Agency, CBSA Factbook 2010, Air Quality Statistics by City, 2010

Maximum Air Pollutant Concentrations: Nitrogen Dioxide and Sulfur Dioxide

	Nitrogen Dioxide AM (ppb)	Nitrogen Dioxide 1-Hr (ppb)	Sulfur Dioxide AM (ppb)	Sulfur Dioxide 1-Hr (ppb)	Sulfur Dioxide 24-Hr (ppb)
MSA[1] Level	7.573	n/a	1.07	21	9.5
NAAQS[2]	53	100	30	75	140
Met NAAQS[2]	Yes	n/a	Yes	Yes	Yes

Note: Data from exceptional events are not included; (1) Data covers the Charleston-North Charleston-Summerville, SC—see Appendix B for areas included; (2) National Ambient Air Quality Standards; ppb = parts per billion; n/a not available
Concentrations: Nitrogen Dioxide AM—highest arithmetic mean concentration; Nitrogen Dioxide 1-Hr—highest 98th percentile 1-hour daily maximum concentration; Sulfur Dioxide AM—highest annual mean concentration; Sulfur Dioxide 1-Hr—highest 99th percentile 1-hour daily maximum concentration; Sulfur Dioxide 24-Hr—highest second maximum 24-hour concentration
Source: U.S. Environmental Protection Agency, CBSA Factbook 2010, Air Quality Statistics by City, 2010

Drinking Water

Water System Name	Pop. Served	Primary Water Source Type	Violations[1] Health Based	Violations[1] Monitoring/ Reporting
Charleston Water System	213,127	Surface	0	0

Note: (1) Based on violation data from January 1, 2011 to December 31, 2011 (includes unresolved violations from earlier years)
Source: U.S. Environmental Protection Agency, Office of Ground Water and Drinking Water, Safe Drinking Water Information System (based on data extracted April 18, 2012)

Clarksville, Tennessee

Background

Located just south of the Kentucky border and 47 miles north of Nashville, Clarksville is Tennessee's fifth-largest town and has seen significant growth in recent years. Named for Gen. George Rogers Clark, a decorated veteran of the Indian and Revolutionary Wars, the city was found in 1784, and became incorporated by the state of Tennessee when it joined the union in 1796.

Located near the confluence of Red and Cumberland rivers, Clarksville was the site of three Confederate forts that the Union defeated in 1862. Fort Defiance transferred hands and became known as a place where fleeing or freed slaves could find refuge—and jobs. In the 1980s the well-preserved fort passed from the private hands of a local judge to the city itself, and in 2011 an interpretive center and walking trails were unveiled at what is now called Fort Defiance Civil War Park and Interpretive Center. The site features walking trails as well as the 1,500+ square foot center.

Clarksville is home to the 105,000-acre Fort Campbell, established as Camp Campbell in 1942, with nearly two-thirds of its land mass in Tennessee and the rest—including the post office—located in Kentucky. It is home to the world's only air assault division, known as the Screaming Eagles. Two special ops command units, a combat support hospital, and far more make this home to the U.S. Army's most-deployed contingency forces and the its fifth-largest military population. With more than 4,000 civilian jobs, it's the area's largest employer with services on the post ranging from bowling to the commissary to the Fort Campbell Credit Union, as well as medical services and child care.

Austin Peay State University's main campus is in Clarksville, another of the city's major employers, and named for a local son who became governor. The four-year public master's-level university saw its enrollment climb throughout the 2000's, crossing the 10,000 mark in 2009. Austin Peay also operates a center at Fort Campbell with fifteen associate, bachelor and master's level programs.

In 2012, Hemlock Semiconductor Corp, a subsidiary of Dow Corning, expects to open a $1.2 billion plant to generate polycrystalline silicon used in semiconductor chips and solar products that will generate hundreds of jobs. The state committed $6.4 million to create a new educational center at APSU to train workers, and also is spending $5 million to support Hemlock's worker training.

By the summer of 2012, the 146-acre Liberty Park and Marina redevelopment project is slated for completion, replete with pavilions, sports fields, picnic shelters, a dog park, and a ten-acre pond with a boardwalk and fishing piers. The Wilma Rudolph Pavilion and Great lawn is named for the great Olympic runner, Clarksville's native daughter. Another recent development came when the city created an Indoor Aquatic Center with an inflatable dome that allows for water sports in winter.

On the cultural side of Clarksville's quality of life, the popular Clarksville Downtown Market—with produce and arts and crafts—is enjoying significant popularity after opening in the summer of 2009.

Clarksville is also home to the state's second largest general museum, called the Customs House Museum and Cultural Center, which has seen a recent facelift. Model trains, a gallery devoted to sports champions, and even a bubble cave are all part of the experience.

The community is served by the Clarksville-Montgomery County School System, which is looking into a rezoning plan to change school zones due to growth in the community.

The climate in Clarksville means hot summers but relatively moderate winters with average lows reaching 25 degrees in January. Precipitation stays fairly steady year round, getting no higher than 5.39 in March and bottoming out at 3.27 inches in October.

Rankings

Business/Finance Rankings

- *American City Business Journals* ranked America's 261 largest cities in terms of their resident's wealth. Clarksville ranked #217. Criteria: per capita income; median household income; percentage of households with annual incomes of $200,000 or more; median home value. *American City Business Journals, "Where the Money Is: America's Wealth Centers," August 18, 2008*

- The Clarksville metro area appeared on the Milken Institute "2011 Best Performing Metros" list. Rank: #30 out of 200 large metro areas. Criteria: job growth; wage and salary growth; high-tech output growth. *Milken Institute, "2011 Best Performing Metros"*

- *Forbes* ranked the 200 most populous metro areas in the U.S. in terms of the "Best Places for Business and Careers." The Clarksville metro area was ranked #87. Criteria: costs (business and living); job growth (past and projected); income growth; educational attainment; projected economic growth; crime; cultural and recreational opportunities; net migration patterns; number of highly ranked colleges. *Forbes, "Best Places for Business and Careers," June 2011*

Dating/Romance Rankings

- Clarksville was selected as one of the most romantic cities in America by *Amazon.com*. The city ranked #15 of 20. Criteria: per capita sales of romance novels and relationship books, romantic comedy movies, Barry White albums, and sexual wellness products. *Amazon.com, "America's Most Romantic Cities Revealed," February 14, 2012*

Education Rankings

- Clarksville was identified as one of "America's Brainiest Bastions" by *Portfolio.com*. The metro area ranked #169 out of 200. *Portfolio.com* analyzed levels of educational attainment in the nation's 200 largest metropolitan areas. The editors established scores for five levels of educational attainment, based on relative earning power of adult workers age 25 or older. Scores were determined by comparing the median income for all workers with the median income for those workers at a specified educational level. *Portfolio.com, "America's Brainiest Bastions," December 1, 2010*

Environmental Rankings

- Clarksville was selected as one of 22 "Smarter Cities" for energy by the Natural Resources Defense Council. Criteria: investment in green power; energy efficiency measures; conservation. *Natural Resources Defense Council, "2010 Smarter Cities," July 19, 2010*

- The Clarksville metro area appeared in *Country Home's* "Best Green Places" report. The area ranked #242 out of 379. Criteria: official energy policies; green power; green buildings; availability of fresh, locally grown food. *Country Home, "Best Green Places," 2008*

Health/Fitness Rankings

- The Clarksville metro area appeared in the 2011 Gallup-Healthways Well-Being Index. The index, based on interviews with more than 350,000 Americans, measured jobs, finances, physical health, emotional state of mind and communities. The metro area ranked #172 out of 190. Criteria: life evaluation; emotional health; work environment; physical health; healthy behaviors; basic access (basic needs optimal for a healthy life, such as access to food and medicine, having health insurance and feeling safe while walking at night). *Gallup-Healthways, "State of Well-Being 2011"*

Safety Rankings

- Allstate ranked the 193 largest cities in America in terms of driver safety. Clarksville ranked #31. In addition, drivers were 8.1% less likely to have had an accident compared to the national average. Allstate researchers analyzed internal property damage reported claims over a two-year period (from January 2008 to December 2009) to protect findings from external influences such as weather or road construction. A weighted average of the two-year numbers determined the annual percentages. The report defines an auto crash as any collision resulting in a property damage claim. *Allstate, "2011 Allstate America's Best Drivers Report™"*

- The National Insurance Crime Bureau ranked 366 metro areas in the U.S. in terms of per capita rates of vehicle theft. The Clarksville metro area ranked #208 (#1 = highest rate). Criteria: number of vehicle theft offenses per 100,000 inhabitants in 2010. *National Insurance Crime Bureau, "Hot Spots," June 21, 2011*

Seniors/Retirement Rankings

- Clarksville was selected as one of the best places to retire by *CNNMoney.com*. Criteria: low cost of living; low violent-crime rate; good medical care; large population over age 50; abundant amenities for retirees. *CNNMoney.com, "Best Places to Retire 2011"*

Sports/Recreation Rankings

- Clarksville appeared on the *Sporting News* list of the "Best Sports Cities" for 2011. The area ranked #156 out of 271 cities in the U.S. *Sporting News* takes a 12-month snapshot of each city's sports, putting a heavy premium on regular-season won-lost records (from the most recently completed season). Other criteria include: playoff berths, bowl appearances and tournament bids; championships; applicable power ratings; quality of competition; overall fan fervor (measured in part by attendance); abundance of teams (rewarding quality over quantity); stadium and arena quality; ticket availability and prices; franchise ownership; and marquee appeal of athletes. *Sporting News, "Best Sports Cities 2011," October 4, 2011*

Business Environment

CITY FINANCES

City Government Finances

Component	2009 ($000)	2009 ($ per capita)
Total Revenues	313,634	2,629
Total Expenditures	320,162	2,684
Debt Outstanding	805,637	6,754
Cash and Securities[1]	373,351	3,130

Note: (1) Cash and security holdings of a government at the close of its fiscal year, including those of its dependent agencies, utilities, and liquor stores.
Source: U.S Census Bureau, State & Local Government Finances 2009

City Government Revenue by Source

Source	2009 ($000)	2009 ($ per capita)
General Revenue		
From Federal Government	3,314	28
From State Government	15,262	128
From Local Governments	12,001	101
Taxes		
Property	24,759	208
Sales and Gross Receipts	4,847	41
Personal Income	0	0
Corporate Income	0	0
Motor Vehicle License	0	0
Other Taxes	2,963	25
Current Charges	20,779	174
Liquor Store	0	0
Utility	205,095	1,719
Employee Retirement	0	0

Source: U.S Census Bureau, State & Local Government Finances 2009

City Government Expenditures by Function

Function	2009 ($000)	2009 ($ per capita)	2009 (%)
General Direct Expenditures			
Air Transportation	0	0	0.0
Corrections	0	0	0.0
Education	0	0	0.0
Employment Security Administration	0	0	0.0
Financial Administration	2,628	22	0.8
Fire Protection	12,319	103	3.8
General Public Buildings	647	5	0.2
Governmental Administration, Other	2,039	17	0.6
Health	0	0	0.0
Highways	9,567	80	3.0
Hospitals	0	0	0.0
Housing and Community Development	2,394	20	0.7
Interest on General Debt	7,217	61	2.3
Judicial and Legal	461	4	0.1
Libraries	0	0	0.0
Parking	276	2	0.1
Parks and Recreation	6,287	53	2.0
Police Protection	20,001	168	6.2
Public Welfare	0	0	0.0
Sewerage	16,945	142	5.3
Solid Waste Management	0	0	0.0
Veterans' Services	0	0	0.0
Liquor Store	0	0	0.0
Utility	214,794	1,801	67.1
Employee Retirement	0	0	0.0

Source: U.S Census Bureau, State & Local Government Finances 2009

Municipal Bond Ratings

Area	Moody's	S&P	Fitch
City	n/a	n/a	n/a

Rating Systems (shown in declining order of credit quality): Moody's– Aaa, Aa, A, Baa, Ba, B, Caa, Ca, C (numerical modifiers 1, 2, and 3 are added to letter-rating); S&P– AAA, AA, A, BBB, BB, B, CCC, CC, C; Fitch– AAA, AA, A, BBB, BB, B, CCC, CC, C. Ratings may be modified by the addition of a plus or minus sign to show relative standing within the major rating categories.
Notes: n/a Not Available; w/d Withdrawn (1) Not Reviewed; (2) Issuer Rating/No General Obligation; (3) Standard and Poor's Issue Credit Rating (ICR) is a current opinion of an obliger with respect to a specific financial obligation, a specific class of financial obligations, or a specific financial program.
Source: U.S. Census Bureau, 2012 Statistical Abstract, Bond Ratings for City Governments by Largest Cities: 2010

DEMOGRAPHICS

Population Growth

Area	1990 Census	2000 Census	2010 Census	Population Growth (%) 1990-2000	Population Growth (%) 2000-2010
City	78,569	103,455	132,929	31.7	28.5
MSA[1]	189,277	232,000	273,949	22.6	18.1
U.S.	248,709,873	281,421,906	308,745,538	13.2	9.7

Note: (1) Figures cover the Clarksville, TN-KY Metropolitan Statistical Area—see Appendix B for areas included
Source: U.S. Census Bureau, 2010 Census

Household Size

Area	One	Two	Three	Four	Five	Six	Seven or More	Average Household Size
City	23.7	31.4	19.6	14.6	6.8	2.5	1.3	2.63
MSA[1]	23.6	32.6	18.7	14.5	6.7	2.5	1.4	2.62
U.S.	26.7	32.8	16.1	13.4	6.5	2.6	1.9	2.58

Note: (1) Figures cover the Clarksville, TN-KY Metropolitan Statistical Area—see Appendix B for areas included
Source: U.S. Census Bureau, 2010 Census

Race

Area	White Alone[2] (%)	Black Alone[2] (%)	Asian Alone[2] (%)	AIAN[3] Alone[2] (%)	NHOPI[4] Alone[2] (%)	Other Race Alone[2] (%)	Two or More Races (%)
City	65.6	23.2	2.3	0.6	0.5	2.8	5.1
MSA[1]	73.2	18.3	1.6	0.6	0.4	2.1	3.8
U.S.	72.4	12.6	4.8	0.9	0.2	6.2	2.9

Note: (1) Figures cover the Clarksville, TN-KY Metropolitan Statistical Area—see Appendix B for areas included; (2) Alone is defined as not being in combination with one or more other races; (3) American Indian and Alaska Native; (4) Native Hawaiian and Other Pacific Islander
Source: U.S. Census Bureau, 2010 Census

Hispanic or Latino Origin

Area	Hispanic or Latino (%)	Mexican (%)	Puerto Rican (%)	Cuban (%)	Other Hispanic or Latino (%)
City	9.3	4.1	3.0	0.2	2.0
MSA[1]	6.8	3.2	2.0	0.2	1.4
U.S.	16.3	10.3	1.5	0.6	4.0

Note: Persons of Hispanic or Latino origin can be of any race; (1) Figures cover the Clarksville, TN-KY Metropolitan Statistical Area—see Appendix B for areas included
Source: U.S. Census Bureau, 2010 Census

Segregation

Type	Segregation Indices[1]				Percent Change		
	1990	2000	2010	2010 Rank[2]	1990-2000	1990-2010	2000-2010
Black/White	n/a	n/a	n/a	n/a	n/a	n/a	n/a
Asian/White	n/a	n/a	n/a	n/a	n/a	n/a	n/a
Hispanic/White	n/a	n/a	n/a	n/a	n/a	n/a	n/a

Note: Figures are based on an analysis of 1990, 2000, and 2010 Census Decennial Census tract data by William H. Frey, Brookings Institution and the University of Michigan Social Science Data Analysis Network. In this analysis all racial groups (whites, blacks, and asians) are non-Hispanic members of those races. Hispanics are shown as a separate category; All figures cover the Metropolitan Statistical Area (see Appendix B for areas included); (1) Segregation Indices are Dissimilarity Indices that measure the degree to which the minority group is distributed differently than whites across census tracts. They range from 0 (complete integration) to 100 (complete segregation) where the value indicates the percentage of the minority group that needs to move to be distributed exactly like whites; (2) Ranges from 1 (most segregated) to 102 (least segregated); n/a not available.
Source: www.CensusScope.org

Ancestry

Area	German	Irish	English	American	Italian	Polish	French[2]	Scottish	Dutch
City	13.2	10.6	6.9	12.4	2.9	1.3	2.3	1.6	1.0
MSA[1]	12.3	11.0	8.8	15.0	2.6	1.2	2.2	1.6	1.2
U.S.	16.1	11.6	8.8	6.1	5.7	3.2	3.0	1.9	1.6

Note: Figures are the percentage of the total population reporting a particular ancestry. The nine most commonly reported ancestries in the U.S. are shown. Figures include multiple ancestries (e.g. if a person reported being Irish and Italian, they were included in both columns); (1) Figures cover the Clarksville, TN-KY Metropolitan Statistical Area—see Appendix B for areas included; (2) Excludes Basque
Source: U.S. Census Bureau, 2008-2010 American Community Survey 3-Year Estimates

Foreign-Born Population

Area	Percent of Population Born in								
	Any Foreign Country	Mexico	Asia	Europe	Carribean	South America	Central America[2]	Africa	Canada
City	n/a	n/a	n/a	n/a	n/a	n/a	n/a	n/a	n/a
MSA[1]	n/a	n/a	n/a	n/a	n/a	n/a	n/a	n/a	n/a
U.S.	12.8	3.8	3.6	1.6	1.2	0.9	1.0	0.5	0.3

Note: (1) Figures cover the Clarksville, TN-KY Metropolitan Statistical Area—see Appendix B for areas included; (2) Excludes Mexico.
Source: U.S. Census Bureau, 2008-2010 American Community Survey 3-Year Estimates

Marital Status

Area	Never Married	Now Married[2]	Separated	Widowed	Divorced
City	29.0	50.7	3.2	4.8	12.2
MSA[1]	25.7	54.9	2.7	5.1	11.6
U.S.	31.6	49.6	2.2	6.1	10.7

Note: Figures are percentages and cover the population 15 years of age and older; (1) Figures cover the Clarksville, TN-KY Metropolitan Statistical Area—see Appendix B for areas included; (2) Excludes separated
Source: U.S. Census Bureau, 2008-2010 American Community Survey 3-Year Estimates

Age

Area	Percent of Population							Median Age
	Under Age 5	Age 5 to 17	Age 18 to 34	Age 35 to 49	Age 50 to 64	Age 65 to 79	80 Years and Over	
City	9.6	18.9	32.5	18.9	12.9	5.6	1.6	28.6
MSA[1]	8.8	18.8	28.5	19.2	15.1	7.4	2.2	30.7
U.S.	6.5	17.5	23.2	20.7	19.0	9.4	3.6	37.2

Note: (1) Figures cover the Clarksville, TN-KY Metropolitan Statistical Area—see Appendix B for areas included
Source: U.S. Census Bureau, 2010 Census

Male/Female Ratio

Area	Males	Females	Males per 100 Females
City	64,768	68,161	95.0
MSA[1]	135,630	138,319	98.1
U.S.	151,781,326	156,964,212	96.7

Note: (1) Figures cover the Clarksville, TN-KY
Metropolitan Statistical Area—see Appendix B for areas included
Source: U.S. Census Bureau, 2010 Census

Religious Groups

Area	Catholic	Baptist	Non-Den.	Methodist[2]	Lutheran	LDS[3]	Pente-costal	Presby-terian[4]	Muslim[5]	Judaism
MSA[1]	4.1	30.9	2.3	6.2	0.6	1.5	1.8	1.1	n/a	0.1
U.S.	19.1	9.3	4.0	4.0	2.3	2.0	1.9	1.6	0.8	0.7

Note: Figures are the number of adherents as a percentage of the total population; (1) Figures cover the
Clarksville, TN-KY Metropolitan Statistical Area—see Appendix B for areas included; (2) Methodist/Pietist;
(3) Latter Day Saints; (4) Reformed; (5) Figures are estimates
Source: Association of Statisticians of American Religious Bodies, 2010 U.S. Religion Census: Religious
Congregations & Membership Study

ECONOMY

Gross Metropolitan Product

Area	2007	2008	2009	2010	2010 Rank[2]
MSA[1]	9.1	9.6	10.0	10.9	163

Note: Figures are in billions of dollars; (1) Figures cover the Clarksville, TN-KY Metropolitan Statistical
Area—see Appendix B for areas included; (2) Rank ranges from 1 to 363
Source: The United States Conference of Mayors, "U.S. Metro Economies: GMP and Employment Forecasts,"
June 2011

Economic Growth

Area	2007-2009 (%)	2010 (%)	2011 (%)	Rank[2]
MSA[1]	3.3	7.7	4.0	20
U.S.	-1.3	2.9	2.5	–

Note: Figures are real Gross Metropolitan Product growth rates and represent annual average percent change;
(1) Figures cover the Clarksville, TN-KY Metropolitan Statistical Area—see Appendix B for areas included; (2)
Rank ranges from 1 to 363
Source: The United States Conference of Mayors, "U.S. Metro Economies: GMP and Employment Forecasts,"
June 2011

Metropolitan Area Exports

Area	2005	2006	2007	2008	2009	2010	2010 Rank[2]
MSA[1]	302.9	324.0	309.7	311.4	158.4	238.3	265

Note: Figures are in millions of dollars; (1) Figures cover the Clarksville, TN-KY Metropolitan Statistical
Area—see Appendix B for areas included; (2) Rank ranges from 1 to 369
Source: U.S. Department of Commerce, International Trade Administration, Office of Trade & Industry
Information, Manufacturing & Services, data extracted April 2, 2012

INCOME

Income

Area	Per Capita ($)	Median Household ($)	Average Household ($)
City	20,151	45,676	53,286
MSA[1]	20,524	43,491	53,321
U.S.	26,942	51,222	70,116

Note: (1) Figures cover the Clarksville, TN-KY Metropolitan Statistical Area—see Appendix B for areas included
Source: U.S. Census Bureau, 2008-2010 American Community Survey 3-Year Estimates

Household Income Distribution

Area	Percent of Households Earning							
	Under $15,000	$15,000 -24,999	$25,000 -34,999	$35,000 -49,999	$50,000 -74,999	$75,000 -99,000	$100,000 -149,999	$150,000 and up
City	14.9	10.4	11.8	18.1	22.3	11.8	8.1	2.7
MSA[1]	15.0	11.4	13.2	17.1	20.3	12.0	8.4	2.6
U.S.	13.0	11.0	10.6	14.2	18.5	12.1	12.2	8.4

Note: (1) Figures cover the Clarksville, TN-KY Metropolitan Statistical Area—see Appendix B for areas included
Source: U.S. Census Bureau, 2008-2010 American Community Survey 3-Year Estimates

Poverty Rate

Area	All Ages	Under 18 Years Old	18 to 64 Years Old	65 Years and Over
City	17.1	23.9	14.7	11.1
MSA[1]	16.5	23.3	14.2	11.3
U.S.	14.4	20.1	13.1	9.4

Note: Figures are percentage of people whose income during the past 12 months was below the poverty level;
(1) Figures cover the Clarksville, TN-KY Metropolitan Statistical Area—see Appendix B for areas included
Source: U.S. Census Bureau, 2008-2010 American Community Survey 3-Year Estimates

Personal Bankruptcy Filing Rate

Area	2006	2007	2008	2009	2010	2011
Montgomery County	2.84	3.29	4.14	4.65	5.03	4.53
U.S.	2.00	2.73	3.53	4.61	4.97	4.37

Note: Numbers are per 1,000 population and include Chapter 7 and Chapter 13 filings
Source: Federal Deposit Insurance Corporation, Regional Economic Conditions, March 9, 2012

EMPLOYMENT

Labor Force and Employment

Area	Civilian Labor Force			Workers Employed		
	Dec. 2010	Dec. 2011	% Chg.	Dec. 2010	Dec. 2011	% Chg.
City	53,642	55,136	2.8	48,676	50,390	3.5
MSA[1]	114,219	115,797	1.4	103,012	105,700	2.6
U.S.	153,156,000	153,373,000	0.1	139,159,000	140,681,000	1.1

Note: Data is not seasonally adjusted and covers workers 16 years of age and older;
(1) Metropolitan Statistical Area—see Appendix B for areas included
Source: Bureau of Labor Statistics, http://stats.bls.gov

Unemployment Rate

Area	2011											
	Jan.	Feb.	Mar.	Apr.	May	Jun.	Jul.	Aug.	Sep.	Oct.	Nov.	Dec.
City	10.3	10.2	9.7	9.4	9.5	10.3	9.8	9.9	9.9	9.6	9.3	8.6
MSA[1]	11.0	10.9	10.1	10.3	10.1	10.6	10.3	10.0	10.2	9.4	9.0	8.7
U.S.	9.8	9.5	9.2	8.7	8.7	9.3	9.3	9.1	8.8	8.5	8.2	8.3

Note: Data is not seasonally adjusted and covers workers 16 years of age and older; All figures are
percentages; (1) Metropolitan Statistical Area—see Appendix B for areas included
Source: Bureau of Labor Statistics, http://stats.bls.gov

Projected Unemployment Rate

Area	2010 (%)	2011 (%)	2012 (%)	2013 (%)
MSA[1]	10.3	9.9	9.4	8.5

Note: (1) Metropolitan Statistical Area—see Appendix B for areas included
Source: The United States Conference of Mayors, "U.S. Metro Economies: GMP and Employment Forecasts,"
June 2011

Employment by Occupation

Occupation Classification	City (%)	MSA[1] (%)	U.S. (%)
Management, Business, Science, and Arts	28.3	28.4	35.6
Natural Resources, Construction, and Maintenance	8.4	10.7	9.5
Production, Transportation, and Material Moving	15.8	17.0	12.1
Sales and Office	28.5	26.0	25.2
Service	19.0	17.9	17.6

Note: Figures cover employed civilians 16 years of age and older; (1) Figures cover the Clarksville, TN-KY Metropolitan Statistical Area—see Appendix B for areas included
Source: U.S. Census Bureau, 2008-2010 American Community Survey 3-Year Estimates

Employment by Industry

Sector	MSA[1]		U.S.
	Number of Employees	Percent of Total	Percent of Total
Construction	n/a	n/a	4.1
Education and Health Services	11,000	13.0	15.2
Financial Activities	2,700	3.2	5.8
Government	20,900	24.7	16.8
Information	900	1.1	2.0
Leisure and Hospitality	9,700	11.5	9.9
Manufacturing	9,900	11.7	8.9
Mining and Logging	n/a	n/a	0.6
Other Services	2,700	3.2	4.0
Professional and Business Services	8,100	9.6	13.3
Retail Trade	10,800	12.8	11.5
Transportation and Utilities	2,200	2.6	3.8
Wholesale Trade	n/a	n/a	4.2

Note: Figures cover non-farm employment as of December 2011 and are not seasonally adjusted; (1) Metropolitan Statistical Area—see Appendix B for areas included; n/a not available
Source: Bureau of Labor Statistics, http://stats.bls.gov

Occupations with Greatest Projected Employment Growth: 2008 – 2018

Occupation[1]	2008 Employment	2018 Projected Employment	Numeric Employment Change	Percent Employment Change
Registered Nurses	61,600	71,750	10,150	16.5
Customer Service Representatives	55,110	63,610	8,500	15.4
Home Health Aides	13,700	21,800	8,100	59.1
Truck Drivers, Heavy and Tractor-Trailer	64,760	72,460	7,700	11.9
Combined Food Preparation and Serving Workers, Including Fast Food	64,590	71,850	7,260	11.2
Retail Salespersons	84,220	91,130	6,910	8.2
Office Clerks, General	65,370	71,770	6,400	9.8
Elementary School Teachers, Except Special Education	33,140	39,390	6,250	18.9
Nursing Aides, Orderlies, and Attendants	30,710	35,800	5,090	16.6
Licensed Practical and Licensed Vocational Nurses	25,390	30,390	5,000	19.7

Note: Projections cover Tennessee; (1) Sorted by numeric employment change
Source: www.projectionscentral.com, State Occupational Projections, 2008–2018 Long-Term Projections

Fastest Growing Occupations: 2008 – 2018

Occupation[1]	2008 Employment	2018 Projected Employment	Numeric Employment Change	Percent Employment Change
Biomedical Engineers	250	410	160	64.0
Home Health Aides	13,700	21,800	8,100	59.1
Network Systems and Data Communications Analysts	3,000	4,500	1,500	50.0
Medical Scientists, Except Epidemiologists	820	1,140	320	39.0
Physician Assistants	1,370	1,880	510	37.2
Commercial Pilots	350	480	130	37.1
Self-Enrichment Education Teachers	2,890	3,960	1,070	37.0
Financial Examiners	790	1,080	290	36.7
Psychiatric Aides	980	1,330	350	35.7
Personal and Home Care Aides	14,070	18,950	4,880	34.7

Note: Projections cover Tennessee; (1) Sorted by percent employment change and excludes occupations with numeric employment change less than 100
Source: www.projectionscentral.com, State Occupational Projections, 2008–2018 Long-Term Projections

Average Wages

Occupation	$/Hr.	Occupation	$/Hr.
Accountants and Auditors	28.47	Maids and Housekeeping Cleaners	9.00
Automotive Mechanics	16.56	Maintenance and Repair Workers	16.97
Bookkeepers	15.66	Marketing Managers	37.70
Carpenters	19.68	Nuclear Medicine Technologists	n/a
Cashiers	8.87	Nurses, Licensed Practical	19.21
Clerks, General Office	12.72	Nurses, Registered	28.86
Clerks, Receptionists/Information	11.71	Nursing Aides/Orderlies/Attendants	10.69
Clerks, Shipping/Receiving	15.09	Packers and Packagers, Hand	11.48
Computer Programmers	32.29	Physical Therapists	34.68
Computer Support Specialists	20.71	Postal Service Mail Carriers	23.83
Computer Systems Analysts	26.81	Real Estate Brokers	n/a
Cooks, Restaurant	10.20	Retail Salespersons	10.60
Dentists	n/a	Sales Reps., Exc. Tech./Scientific	20.67
Electrical Engineers	32.34	Sales Reps., Tech./Scientific	44.24
Electricians	19.44	Secretaries, Exc. Legal/Med./Exec.	13.13
Financial Managers	37.77	Security Guards	11.99
First-Line Supervisors/Managers, Sales	16.11	Surgeons	n/a
Food Preparation Workers	9.27	Teacher Assistants	11.70
General and Operations Managers	37.50	Teachers, Elementary School	n/a
Hairdressers/Cosmetologists	12.11	Teachers, Secondary School	21.80
Internists	n/a	Telemarketers	10.69
Janitors and Cleaners	10.79	Truck Drivers, Heavy/Tractor-Trailer	14.70
Landscaping/Groundskeeping Workers	10.39	Truck Drivers, Light/Delivery Svcs.	12.94
Lawyers	45.21	Waiters and Waitresses	8.93

Note: Wage data covers the Clarksville, TN-KY Metropolitan Statistical Area—see Appendix B for areas included. Hourly wages for elementary/secondary school teachers and teacher assistants were calculated by the editors from annual wage data assuming a 40 hour work week; n/a not available.
Source: Bureau of Labor Statistics, Metro Area Occupational Employment and Wage Estimates, May 2011

RESIDENTIAL REAL ESTATE

Building Permits

Area	Single-Family 2010	2011	Pct. Chg.	Multi-Family 2010	2011	Pct. Chg.	Total 2010	2011	Pct. Chg.
City	675	996	47.6	760	510	-32.9	1,435	1,506	4.9
MSA[1]	1,092	1,427	30.7	829	574	-30.8	1,921	2,001	4.2
U.S.	447,311	418,498	-6.4	157,299	205,563	30.7	604,610	624,061	3.2

Note: (1) Metropolitan Statistical Area—see Appendix B for areas included; figures represent new, privately-owned housing units authorized (unadjusted data); All permit data are based on estimates with imputation.
Source: U.S. Census Bureau, Manufacturing, Mining, and Construction Statistics, Building Permits, 2010, 2011

Homeownership Rate

Area	2005 (%)	2006 (%)	2007 (%)	2008 (%)	2009 (%)	2010 (%)	2011 (%)
MSA[1]	n/a	n/a	n/a	n/a	n/a	n/a	n/a
U.S.	68.9	68.8	68.1	67.8	67.4	66.9	66.1

Note: (1) Metropolitan Statistical Area—see Appendix B for areas included; n/a not available
Source: U.S. Census Bureau, Housing Vacancies and Homeownership Annual Statistics: 2011

Housing Vacancy Rates

Area	Gross Vacancy Rate[2] (%)			Year-Round Vacancy Rate[3] (%)			Rental Vacancy Rate[4] (%)			Homeowner Vacancy Rate[5] (%)		
	2009	2010	2011	2009	2010	2011	2009	2010	2011	2009	2010	2011
MSA[1]	n/a	n/a	n/a	n/a	n/a	n/a	n/a	n/a	n/a	n/a	n/a	n/a
U.S.	14.5	14.3	14.2	11.3	11.3	11.1	10.6	10.2	9.5	2.6	2.6	2.5

Note: (1) Metropolitan Statistical Area—see Appendix B for areas included; (2) The percentage of the total housing inventory that is vacant; (3) The percentage of the housing inventory (excluding seasonal units) that is year-round vacant; (4) The percentage of rental inventory that is vacant for rent; (5) The percentage of homeowner inventory that is vacant for sale; n/a not available
Source: U.S. Census Bureau, Housing Vacancies and Homeownership Annual Statistics: 2011

TAXES

State Corporate Income Tax Rates

State	Tax Rate (%)	Income Brackets ($)	Num. of Brackets	Financial Institution Tax Rate (%)[a]	Federal Income Tax Ded.
Tennessee	6.5	Flat rate	1	6.5	No

Note: Tax rates as of January 1, 2012; (a) Rates listed are the corporate income tax rate applied to financial institutions or excise taxes based on income. Some states have other taxes based upon the value of deposits or shares.
Source: Federation of Tax Administrators, "State Corporate Income Tax Rates, 2012"

State Individual Income Tax Rates

State	Tax Rate (%)	Income Brackets ($)	Num. of Brackets	Personal Exempt. ($)[1] Single	Dependents	Fed. Inc. Tax Ded.
Tennessee – State Income Tax of 6% on Dividends and Interest Income Only						

Note: Tax rates as of January 1, 2012; Local- and county-level taxes are not included; n/a not applicable; (1) Married joint filers generally receive double the single exemption
Source: Federation of Tax Administrators, "State Individual Income Tax Rates, 2012"

Various State and Local Tax Rates

State	State and Local Sales and Use (%)	State Sales and Use (%)	Gasoline[1] (¢/gal.)	Cigarette[2] ($/pack)	Spirits[3] ($/gal.)	Wine[4] ($/gal.)	Beer[5] ($/gal.)
Tennessee	9.5	7.00	21.4	0.62	4.46 (h)	1.27	0.14

Note: All tax rates as of January 1, 2012 except beer, wine and spirits (September 1, 2011); (1) The American Petroleum Institute has developed a methodology for determining the average tax rate on a gallon of fuel. Rates may include any of the following: excise taxes, environmental fees, storage tank fees, other fees or taxes, general sales tax, and local taxes. In states where gasoline is subject to the general sales tax, or where the fuel tax is based on the average sale price, the average rate determined by API is sensitive to changes in the price of gasoline. States that fully or partially apply general sales taxes to gasoline: CA, CO, GA, IL, IN, MI, NY; (2) The federal excise tax of $1.0066 per pack and local taxes are not included; (3) Rates are those applicable to off-premise sales of 40% alcohol by volume (a.b.v.) distilled spirits in 750ml containers. Local excise taxes are excluded; (4) Rates are those applicable to off-premise sales of 11% a.b.v. non-carbonated wine in 750ml containers; (5) Rates are those applicable to off-premise sales of 4.7% a.b.v. beer in 12 ounce containers; (h) Includes case fees and/or bottle fees which may vary with the size of the container.
Source: Tax Foundation, 2012 Facts & Figures: How Does Your State Compare?

State-Local Tax Burdens

Area	Rate (%)	Rank[1]	Per Capita Taxes Paid to Home State ($)	Total State and Local Per Capita Taxes Paid ($)	Per Capita Income ($)
Tennessee	7.6	47	1,851	2,752	36,157
U.S. Average	9.8	-	3,057	4,160	42,539

Note: Figures cover 2009; (1) Rank ranges from 1 to 50 where 1 is highest tax burden
Source: Tax Foundation, State-Local Tax Burdens, All States, 2009

State Business Tax Climate Index Rankings

State	Overall Rank	Corporate Tax Index Rank	Individual Income Tax Index Rank	Sales Tax Index Rank	Unemployment Insurance Tax Index Rank	Property Tax Index Rank
Tennessee	14	13	8	43	27	48

Note: The index is a measure of how each state's tax laws affect economic performance. The lower the rank, the more favorable a state's tax system is for business. States without a given tax are given a ranking of 1.
Source: Tax Foundation, Major Components of the State Business Tax Climate Index, FY 2012

COMMERCIAL UTILITIES

Typical Monthly Electric Bills

Area	Commercial Service ($/month)		Industrial Service ($/month)	
	1,500 kWh	40 kW demand 14,000 kWh	1,000 kW demand 200,000 kWh	50,000 kW demand 15,000,000 kWh
City	n/a	n/a	n/a	n/a
Average[1]	189	1,616	25,197	1,470,813

Note: Based on total rates in effect July 1, 2011; (1) average based on 184 utilities surveyed; n/a not available
Source: Edison Electric Institute, Typical Bills and Average Rates Report, Summer 2011

TRANSPORTATION

Means of Transportation to Work

Area	Car/Truck/Van		Public Transportation			Bicycle	Walked	Other Means	Worked at Home
	Drove Alone	Car-pooled	Bus	Subway	Railroad				
City	84.5	10.6	0.6	0.1	0.0	0.1	1.1	0.8	2.2
MSA[1]	82.4	11.1	0.3	0.0	0.0	0.2	1.9	1.2	2.9
U.S.	76.0	10.2	2.7	1.7	0.5	0.5	2.8	1.3	4.2

Note: Figures are percentages and cover workers 16 years of age and older; (1) Figures cover the Clarksville, TN-KY Metropolitan Statistical Area—see Appendix B for areas included
Source: U.S. Census Bureau, 2008-2010 American Community Survey 3-Year Estimates

Travel Time to Work

Area	Less Than 10 Minutes	10 to 19 Minutes	20 to 29 Minutes	30 to 44 Minutes	45 to 59 Minutes	60 to 89 Minutes	90 Minutes or More
City	10.8	39.0	24.4	14.2	5.1	4.9	1.7
MSA[1]	13.2	36.3	21.8	16.2	6.1	4.4	1.9
U.S.	13.9	30.1	20.8	19.8	7.5	5.5	2.5

Note: Figures are percentages and include workers 16 years old and over; (1) Figures cover the Clarksville, TN-KY Metropolitan Statistical Area—see Appendix B for areas included
Source: U.S. Census Bureau, 2008-2010 American Community Survey 3-Year Estimates

Travel Time Index

Area	1985	1990	1995	2000	2005	2010
Urban Area[1]	n/a	n/a	n/a	n/a	n/a	n/a
Average[2]	1.11	1.16	1.18	1.21	1.25	1.20

Note: Travel Time Index—the ratio of travel time in the peak period to the travel time at free-flow conditions. A value of 1.30 indicates a 20-minute free-flow trip takes 26 minutes in the peak. Free-flow speeds (60 mph on freeways and 35 mph on principal arterials) are used as the comparison threshold; (1) Data for the Clarksville, TN-KY urban area was not available; (2) average of 439 urban areas
Source: Texas Transportation Institute, Urban Mobility Report 2011, September 2011

Public Transportation

Agency Name / Mode of Transportation	Vehicles Operated in Maximum Service	Annual Unlinked Passenger Trips ('000)	Annual Passenger Miles ('000)
Clarksville Transit System (CTS)			
Bus (directly operated)	16	703.5	3,904.2
Demand Response (directly operated)	8	30.3	200.3

Source: Federal Transit Administration, National Transit Database, 2010

Air Transportation

Airport Name and Code / Type of Service	Passenger Airlines[1]	Passenger Enplanements	Freight Carriers[2]	Freight (lbs.)
Outlaw Field (CKV)				
Domestic service (U.S. carriers - 2011)	0	0	1	13,824
International service (U.S. carriers - 2010)	0	0	0	0

Note: (1) Includes all U.S.-based major, minor and commuter airlines that carried at least one passenger during the year; (2) Includes all U.S.-based airlines and freight carriers that transported at least one pound of freight during the year
Source: Bureau of Transportation Statistics, The Intermodal Transportation Database, Air Carriers: T-100 Domestic Market (U.S. Carriers), 2011; Bureau of Transportation Statistics, The Intermodal Transportation Database, Air Carriers: T-100 International Market (U.S. Carriers), 2010

Other Transportation Statistics

Major Highways:	I-24; SR-79; SR-41A
Amtrak Service:	No
Major Waterways/Ports:	Cumberland River

Source: Amtrak.com; Google Maps

BUSINESSES

Major Business Headquarters

Company Name	Rankings	
	Fortune[1]	Forbes[2]
No companies listed	-	-

Note: (1) Fortune 500—companies that produce a 10-K are ranked 1 to 500 based on 2010 revenue; (2) all private companies with at least $2 billion in annual revenue are ranked 1 to 212; companies listed are headquartered in the city; dashes indicate no ranking
Source: Fortune, "Fortune 500," May 23, 2011; Forbes, "America's Largest Private Companies," November 16, 2011

Minority- and Women-Owned Businesses

Group	All Firms		Firms with Paid Employees			
	Firms	Sales ($000)	Firms	Sales ($000)	Employees	Payroll ($000)
Asian	n/a	n/a	n/a	n/a	n/a	n/a
Black	n/a	n/a	n/a	n/a	n/a	n/a
Hispanic	n/a	n/a	n/a	n/a	n/a	n/a
Women	n/a	n/a	n/a	n/a	n/a	n/a
All Firms	2,667	527,449	349	447,696	2,794	60,919

Note: Figures cover firms located in the city; minority- and women-owned business are defined as firms in which the corresponding group own 51% or more of the stock or equity of the company; n/a not available
Source: U.S. Census Bureau, 2007 Economic Census, Survey of Business Owners

HOTELS

Hotels/Motels

Area	5 Star		4 Star		3 Star		2 Star		1 Star		Not Rated	
	Num.	Pct.[3]	Num.	Pct.[3]	Num.	Pct.[3]	Num.	Pct.[3]	Num.	Pct.[3]	Num.	Pct.[3]
City[1]	0	0.0	0	0.0	3	9.7	22	71.0	0	0.0	6	19.4
Total[2]	133	0.9	940	6.5	4,569	31.8	7,033	48.9	351	2.4	1,343	9.3

Note: (1) Figures cover Clarksville and vicinity; (2) Figures cover all 100 cities in this book; (3) Percentage of hotels which have a given star rating; Star ratings are determined by expedia.com and offer an indication of the general quality of a particular hotel.
Source: expedia.com, April 25, 2012

Living Environment

COST OF LIVING

Cost of Living Index

Composite Index	Groceries	Housing	Utilities	Trans-portation	Health Care	Misc. Goods/ Services
97.6	90.9	89.5	93.5	93.0	99.8	110.0

Note: U.S. = 100; Figures cover the Clarksville TN urban area.
Source: The Council for Community and Economic Research, ACCRA Cost of Living Index, 2011

Grocery Prices

Area[1]	T-Bone Steak ($/pound)	Frying Chicken ($/pound)	Whole Milk ($/half gal.)	Eggs ($/dozen)	Orange Juice ($/64 oz.)	Coffee ($/11.5 oz.)
City[2]	8.53	0.97	2.36	1.98	3.08	3.91
Avg.	9.25	1.18	2.22	1.66	3.19	4.40
Min.	6.70	0.88	1.31	0.95	2.46	2.94
Max.	14.30	2.16	3.50	3.18	4.75	6.83

Note: (1) Values for the local area are compared with the average, minimum and maximum values for all 335 areas in the Cost of Living Index; (2) Figures cover the Clarksville TN urban area; **T-Bone Steak** (price per pound); **Frying Chicken** (price per pound, whole fryer); **Whole Milk** (half gallon carton); **Eggs** (price per dozen, Grade A, large); **Orange Juice** (64 oz. Tropicana or Florida Natural); **Coffee** (11.5 oz. can, vacuum-packed, Maxwell House, Hills Bros, or Folgers).
Source: The Council for Community and Economic Research, ACCRA Cost of Living Index, 2011

Housing and Utility Costs

Area[1]	New Home Price ($)	Apartment Rent ($/month)	All Electric ($/month)	Part Electric ($/month)	Other Energy ($/month)	Telephone ($/month)
City[2]	252,269	770	167.24	-	-	22.03
Avg.	285,990	839	163.23	89.00	77.52	26.92
Min.	188,005	460	125.58	45.39	33.89	17.98
Max.	1,197,028	3,244	339.16	181.97	348.69	40.01

Note: (1) Values for the local area are compared with the average, minimum and maximum values for all 335 areas in the Cost of Living Index; (2) Figures cover the Clarksville TN urban area; **New Home Price** (2,400 sf living area, 8,000 sf lot, in urban area with full utilities); **Apartment Rent** (950 sf 2 bedroom/1.5 or 2 bath, unfurnished, excluding all utilities except water); **All Electric** (average monthly cost for an all-electric home); **Part Electric** (average monthly cost for a part-electric home); **Other Energy** (average monthly cost for natural gas, fuel oil, coal, wood, and any other forms of energy except electricity); **Telephone** (price includes basic monthly rate for a private residential line plus additional local usage charges incurred by a family of four).
Source: The Council for Community and Economic Research, ACCRA Cost of Living Index, 2011

Health Care, Transportation, and Other Costs

Area[1]	Doctor ($/visit)	Dentist ($/visit)	Optometrist ($/visit)	Gasoline ($/gallon)	Beauty Salon ($/visit)	Men's Shirt ($)
City[2]	94.02	84.01	80.05	3.33	33.49	36.61
Avg.	93.88	81.72	90.54	3.48	32.65	25.06
Min.	60.00	55.33	53.66	3.18	19.78	13.44
Max.	154.98	145.97	183.72	4.31	63.21	46.00

Note: (1) Values for the local area are compared with the average, minimum and maximum values for all 335 areas in the Cost of Living Index; (2) Figures cover the Clarksville TN urban area; **Doctor** (general practitioners routine exam of an established patient); **Dentist** (adult teeth cleaning and periodic oral examination); **Optometrist** (full vision eye exam for established adult patient); **Gasoline** (one gallon regular unleaded, national brand, including all taxes, cash price at self-service pump if available); **Beauty Salon** (woman's shampoo, trim, and blow-dry); **Men's Shirt** (cotton/polyester dress shirt, pinpoint weave, long sleeves).
Source: The Council for Community and Economic Research, ACCRA Cost of Living Index, 2011

HOUSING

House Price Index (HPI)

Area	National Ranking[2]	Quarterly Change (%)	One-Year Change (%)	Five-Year Change (%)
MSA[1]	n/a	n/a	n/a	n/a
U.S.[3]	-	-0.10	-2.43	-19.16

Note: The HPI is a weighted repeat sales index. It measures average price changes in repeat sales or refinancings on the same properties. This information is obtained by reviewing repeat mortgage transactions on single-family properties whose mortgages have been purchased or securitized by Fannie Mae or Freddie Mac in January 1975; (1) Metropolitan/Micropolitan Statistical Area—see Appendix B for areas included; (2) Rankings are based on annual percentage change for all metro areas containing at least 15,000 transactions over the last 10 years and ranges from 1 to 306; (3) figures based on a weighted average of Census Division estimates using a purchase only index; all figures are for the period ending December 31, 2011; n/a not available
Source: Federal Housing Finance Agency, House Price Index, February 23, 2012

House Price Valuations

Area	Q4 2005 Price ($000)	Q4 2005 Over-valuation	Q4 2006 Price ($000)	Q4 2006 Over-valuation	Q4 2007 Price ($000)	Q4 2007 Over-valuation	Q4 2008 Price ($000)	Q4 2008 Over-valuation	Q4 2009 Price ($000)	Q4 2009 Over-valuation
MSA[1]	n/a	n/a	n/a	n/a	n/a	n/a	n/a	n/a	n/a	n/a

Note: Figures show the percentage of over- or under-valuation of single family homes relative to statistically normal house values (e.g. a value of 23.6 indicates that house values are 23.6% overvalued). Statistically normal house values are based on house prices, interest rates, household incomes, population densities, and any historical premiums or discounts metropolitan areas have exhibited over time; (1) Figures cover the Clarksville, TN-KY - see Appendix B for areas included; n/a not available
Source: Global Insight/PNC Financial Services Group, House Prices in America: 4th Quarter 2009 Update

Median Single-Family Home Prices

Area	2009	2010	2011p	Percent Change 2010 to 2011
MSA[1]	n/a	n/a	n/a	n/a
U.S. Average	172.1	173.1	166.2	-4.0

Note: Figures are median sales prices of existing single-family homes in thousands of dollars; (p) preliminary; n/a not available; (1) Metropolitan Statistical Area—see Appendix B for areas included
Source: National Association of Realtors, Median Sales Price of Existing Single-Family Homes for Metropolitan Areas, 4th Quarter 2011

Affordability Index of Existing Single-Family Homes

Area	2009	2010	2011p	Percent Change 2010 to 2011
MSA[1]	n/a	n/a	n/a	n/a

Note: The housing affordability index measures whether or not a typical family could qualify for a mortgage loan on a typical home. The higher the index, the greater the household purchasing power. An index of 100 is defined as the point where a median-income household has exactly enough income to qualify for the purchase of a median-priced existing single-family home, assuming a 20 percent downpayment and 25 percent of gross income devoted to mortgage principal and interest payments; (p) preliminary; n/a not available; (1) Metropolitan Statistical Area—see Appendix B for areas included
Source: National Association of Realtors, Affordability Index of Existing Single-Family Homes, 2011

Median Apartment Condo-Coop Home Prices

Area	2009	2010	2011p	Percent Change 2010 to 2011
MSA[1]	n/a	n/a	n/a	n/a
U.S. Average	175.6	171.7	165.1	-3.8

Note: Figures are median sales prices of existing apartment condo-coop homes in thousands of dollars; (p) preliminary; n/a not available; (1) Metropolitan Statistical Area—see Appendix B for areas included
Source: National Association of Realtors, Median Sales Price of Existing Apartment Condo-Coop Homes for Metropolitan Areas, 4th Quarter 2011

Year Housing Structure Built

Area	2005 or Later	2000 -2004	1990 -1999	1980 -1989	1970 -1979	1960 -1969	1950 -1959	Before 1950	Median Year
City	13.3	14.1	22.2	13.5	14.9	9.7	6.7	5.6	1990
MSA[1]	10.3	12.1	22.1	12.8	16.1	10.9	7.2	8.4	1986
U.S.	5.0	8.6	14.0	14.1	16.3	11.3	11.2	19.6	1975

Note: Figures are percentages except for Median Year; (1) Figures cover the Clarksville, TN-KY Metropolitan Statistical Area—see Appendix B for areas included
Source: U.S. Census Bureau, 2008-2010 American Community Survey 3-Year Estimates

HEALTH

Health Risk Data

Category	MSA[1] (%)	U.S. (%)
Adults who have been told they have high blood pressure[2]	n/a	28.7
Adults who have been told they have high blood cholesterol[2]	n/a	37.5
Adults who have been told they have diabetes[3]	n/a	8.7
Adults who have been told they have arthritis[2]	n/a	26.0
Adults who have been told they currently have asthma	n/a	9.1
Adults who are current smokers	n/a	17.3
Adults who are heavy drinkers[4]	n/a	5.0
Adults who are binge drinkers[5]	n/a	15.1
Adults who are overweight (BMI 25.0 - 29.9)	n/a	36.2
Adults who are obese (BMI 30.0 - 99.8)	n/a	27.5
Adults who participated in any physical activities in the past month	n/a	76.1
Adults 50+ who have ever had a sigmoidoscopy or colonoscopy	n/a	65.2
Women aged 40+ who have had a mammogram within the past two years	n/a	75.2
Men aged 40+ who have had a PSA test within the past two years	n/a	53.2
Adults aged 65+ who have had flu shot within the past year	n/a	67.5
Adults aged 18–64 who have any kind of health care coverage	n/a	82.2

Note: Data as of 2010 unless otherwise noted; n/a not available; (1) Figures cover the Clarksville, TN-KY—see Appendix B for areas included; (2) Data as of 2009; (3) Figures do not include pregnancy-related, borderline, or pre-diabetes; (4) Heavy drinkers are classified as males having more than two drinks per day or females having more than one drink per day; (5) Binge drinkers are classified as males having five or more drinks on one occasion or females having four or more drinks on one occasion
Source: Centers for Disease Control and Prevention, Behaviorial Risk Factor Surveillance System, SMART: Selected Metropolitan/Micropolitan Area Risk Trends, 2009, 2010

Mortality Rates for the Top 10 Causes of Death in the U.S.

ICD-10[a] Sub-Chapter	ICD-10[a] Code	Age-Adjusted Mortality Rate[1] per 100,000 population	
		County[2]	U.S.
Malignant neoplasms	C00-C97	192.4	175.6
Ischaemic heart diseases	I20-I25	137.3	121.6
Other forms of heart disease	I30-I51	39.5	48.6
Chronic lower respiratory diseases	J40-J47	66.1	42.3
Cerebrovascular diseases	I60-I69	67.4	40.6
Organic, including symptomatic, mental disorders	F01-F09	31.8	26.7
Other degenerative diseases of the nervous system	G30-G31	22.1	24.7
Other external causes of accidental injury	W00-X59	27.8	24.4
Diabetes mellitus	E10-E14	29.0	21.7
Hypertensive diseases	I10-I15	19.0	18.2

Note: (a) ICD-10 = International Classification of Diseases 10th Revision; (1) Mortality rates are a three year average covering 2007-2009; (2) Figures cover Montgomery County
Source: Centers for Disease Control and Prevention, National Center for Health Statistics. Underlying Cause of Death 1999-2009 on CDC WONDER Online Database, released 2012. Data for year 2009 are compiled from the Multiple Cause of Death File 2009, Series 20 No. 2O, 2012, Data for year 2008 are compiled from the Multiple Cause of Death File 2008, Series 20 No. 2N, 2011, Data for year 2007 are compiled from Multiple Cause of Death File 2007, Series 20 No. 2M, 2010.

Mortality Rates for Selected Causes of Death

ICD-10[a] Sub-Chapter	ICD-10[a] Code	Age-Adjusted Mortality Rate[1] per 100,000 population	
		County[2]	U.S.
Assault	X85-Y09	7.2	5.7
Human immunodeficiency virus (HIV) disease	B20-B24	*0.0	3.3
Influenza and pneumonia	J09-J18	19.9	16.4
Intentional self-harm	X60-X84	14.8	11.5
Malnutrition	E40-E46	*0.0	0.8
Obesity and other hyperalimentation	E65-E68	*Unreliable	1.6
Transport accidents	V01-V99	17.3	13.7
Viral hepatitis	B15-B19	*Unreliable	2.2

Note: (a) ICD-10 = International Classification of Diseases 10th Revision; (1) Mortality rates are a three year average covering 2007-2009; (2) Figures cover Montgomery County; (*) Unreliable data as per CDC
Source: Centers for Disease Control and Prevention, National Center for Health Statistics. Underlying Cause of Death 1999-2009 on CDC WONDER Online Database, released 2012. Data for year 2009 are compiled from the Multiple Cause of Death File 2009, Series 20 No. 2O, 2012, Data for year 2008 are compiled from the Multiple Cause of Death File 2008, Series 20 No. 2N, 2011, Data for year 2007 are compiled from Multiple Cause of Death File 2007, Series 20 No. 2M, 2010.

Distribution of Physicians and Dentists

Area[1]	Dentists[2]	D.O.[3]	M.D.[4]				
			Total	Family/ General Practice	Pediatrics	Medical Specialties	Surgical Specialties
Local (number)	53	23	159	22	18	57	45
Local (rate[5])	3.4	1.5	10.2	1.4	1.2	3.7	2.9
U.S. (rate[5])	4.5	1.9	18.3	2.5	1.4	6.8	4.1

Note: Data as of 2008 unless noted; (1) Local data covers Montgomery County; (2) Data as of 2007; (3) Doctor of Osteopathic Medicine; (4) Includes active, non-federal, patient-care, office-based Doctors of Medicine; (5) rate per 10,000 population
Source: Area Resource File (ARF). 2009-2010 Release. U.S. Department of Health and Human Services, Health Resources and Services Administration, Bureau of Health Professions, Rockville, MD, August 2010

EDUCATION

Public School District Statistics

District Name	Schls	Pupils	Pupil/ Teacher Ratio	Minority Pupils[1] (%)	Free Lunch Eligible[2] (%)	IEP[3] (%)
Montgomery County	36	29,138	14.8	39.2	33.1	10.9

Note: Table includes school districts with 2,000 or more students; (1) Percentage of students that are not non-Hispanic white; (2) Percentage of students that are eligible for the free lunch program; (3) Percentage of students that have an Individualized Education Program.
Source: U.S. Department of Education, National Center for Education Statistics, Common Core of Data, Local Education Agency (School District) Universe Survey: School Year 2009-2010; U.S. Department of Education, National Center for Education Statistics, Common Core of Data, Public Elementary/Secondary School Universe Survey: School Year 2009-2010

Highest Level of Education

Area	Less than H.S.	H.S. Diploma	Some College, No Deg.	Associate Degree	Bachelors Degree	Masters Degree	Profess. School Degree	Doctorate Degree
City	8.8	31.2	29.8	8.4	14.9	5.2	0.8	0.9
MSA[1]	12.2	34.0	27.2	8.1	12.0	5.1	0.9	0.6
U.S.	14.7	28.4	21.3	7.6	17.6	7.2	1.9	1.2

Note: Figures cover persons age 25 and over; (1) Figures cover the Clarksville, TN-KY Metropolitan Statistical Area—see Appendix B for areas included
Source: U.S. Census Bureau, 2008-2010 American Community Survey 3-Year Estimates

Educational Attainment by Race

Area	High School Graduate or Higher (%)					Bachelor's Degree or Higher (%)				
	Total	White	Black	Asian	Hisp.[2]	Total	White	Black	Asian	Hisp.[2]
City	91.2	91.5	91.7	89.5	84.4	21.7	23.4	16.5	30.5	18.8
MSA[1]	87.8	88.4	87.0	85.2	83.1	18.5	19.8	12.5	32.0	16.2
U.S.	85.3	87.5	81.4	85.5	61.6	28.0	29.3	17.8	50.2	13.0

Note: Figures shown cover persons 25 years old and over; (1) Figures cover the Clarksville, TN-KY
Metropolitan Statistical Area—see Appendix B for areas included; (2) People of Hispanic origin can be of any
race
Source: U.S. Census Bureau, 2008-2010 American Community Survey 3-Year Estimates

School Enrollment by Grade and Control

Area	Preschool (%)		Kindergarten (%)		Grades 1 - 4 (%)		Grades 5 - 8 (%)		Grades 9 - 12 (%)	
	Public	Private	Public	Private	Public	Private	Public	Private	Public	Private
City	57.4	42.6	84.9	15.1	90.0	10.0	93.6	6.4	92.5	7.5
MSA[1]	71.7	28.3	86.9	13.1	88.1	11.9	91.0	9.0	89.7	10.3
U.S.	55.4	44.6	87.1	12.9	89.4	10.6	89.5	10.5	90.4	9.6

Note: Figures shown cover persons 3 years old and over; (1) Figures cover the Clarksville, TN-KY Metropolitan
Statistical Area—see Appendix B for areas included
Source: U.S. Census Bureau, 2008-2010 American Community Survey 3-Year Estimates

Average Salaries of Public School Classroom Teachers

Area	2010-11		2011-12		Percent Change 2010-11 to 2011-12	Percent Change 2001-02 to 2011-12
	Dollars	Rank[1]	Dollars	Rank[1]		
Tennessee	45,891	44	46,613	43	1.57	21.00
U.S. Average	55,623	-	56,643	-	1.83	26.8

Note: (1) State rank ranges from 1 to 51 where 1 indicates highest salary.
Source: National Education Association, Rankings & Estimates: Rankings of the States 2011
and Estimates of School Statistics 2012, December 2011

Higher Education

Four-Year Colleges			Two-Year Colleges			Medical Schools[1]	Law Schools[2]	Voc/ Tech[3]
Public	Private Non-profit	Private For-profit	Public	Private Non-profit	Private For-profit			
1	0	1	0	0	2	0	0	1

Note: Figures cover institutions located within the city limits and include main campuses only; (1) includes
schools accredited by the Liaison Committee on Medical Education and the American Osteopathic Association's
Commission on Osteopathic College Accreditation; (2) includes American Bar Association-accredited law
schools; (3) includes all schools with programs that are less than 2 years.
Source: National Center for Education Statistics, Integrated Postsecondary Education System (IPEDS) Peer
Analysis System, 2011-12; Association of American Medical Colleges, Member List, April 23, 2012; American
Osteopathic Association, Member List, April 23, 2012; Law School Admission Council, Official Guide to
ABA-Approved Law Schools Online, April 23, 2012

**PRESIDENTIAL
ELECTION**

2008 Presidential Election Results

Area	Obama	McCain	Nader	Other
Montgomery County	45.5	53.4	0.4	0.7
U.S.	52.9	45.6	0.6	0.9

Note: Results are percentages and may not add to 100% due to rounding
Source: Dave Leip's Atlas of U.S. Presidential Elections, www.uselectionatlas.org

EMPLOYERS

Major Employers

Company Name	Industry
ABMA	Motor vehicle brake systems and parts
Army & Air Force Exchange Service	Army-navy goods stores
AT&T Corp.	Engineering services
Austin Peay State University	University
Bridgestone Metalpha U.S.A.	Steel tire cords and tire cord fabrics
Flynn Enterprises	Dungarees: men's, youths', and boys'
Gateway Health System	General medical and surgical hospitals
Jennie Stuart Medical Center	General medical and surgical hospitals
Jostens	Rings, finger: precious metal
Martinrea Industries	Body parts, automobile: stamped metal
Metalsa, S.A. De C.V.	Motor vehicle parts and accessories
Tg Automotive Sealing Kentucky	Automotive stampings
The Army, United States Department of	General medical and surgical hospitals
The Army, United States Department of	Army
Trigg County Board of Education	Elementary and secondary schools
Wal-Mart Stores	General warehousing and storage
Wal-Mart Stores	Department stores, discount

Note: Companies shown are located within the Clarksville, TN-KY metropolitan area.
Source: Hoovers.com, data extracted April 25 2012

PUBLIC SAFETY

Crime Rate

Area	All Crimes	Violent Crimes				Property Crimes		
		Murder	Forcible Rape	Robbery	Aggrav. Assault	Burglary	Larceny -Theft	Motor Vehicle Theft
City	3,875.2	7.1	43.5	95.6	487.6	1,085.0	1,995.3	161.2
Suburbs[1]	2,416.0	4.8	33.0	44.7	127.9	641.7	1,449.7	114.2
Metro[2]	3,095.0	5.9	37.9	68.4	295.3	847.9	1,703.6	136.1
U.S.	3,345.5	4.8	27.5	119.1	252.3	699.6	2,003.5	238.8

Note: Figures are crimes per 100,000 population; (1) All areas within the metro area that are located outside the city limits; (2) Metropolitan Statistical Area—see Appendix B for areas included
Source: FBI Uniform Crime Reports, 2010

Hate Crimes

Area	Number of Quarters Reported	Bias Motivation				
		Race	Religion	Sexual Orientation	Ethnicity	Disability
City	4	1	0	0	0	0

Source: Federal Bureau of Investigation, Hate Crime Statistics 2010

Identity Theft Consumer Complaints

Area	Complaints	Complaints per 100,000 Population	Rank[2]
MSA[1]	197	75.2	196
U.S.	279,156	90.4	-

Note: (1) Metropolitan Statistical Area—see Appendix B for areas included; (2) Rank ranges from 1 to 384 where 1 indicates greatest number of identity theft complaints per 100,000 population
Source: Federal Trade Commission, Consumer Sentinel Network Data Book for January–December 2011

Fraud and Other Consumer Complaints

Area	Complaints	Complaints per 100,000 Population	Rank[2]
MSA[1]	1,505	574.8	65
U.S.	1,533,924	496.8	-

Note: (1) Metropolitan Statistical Area—see Appendix B for areas included; (2) Rank ranges from 1 to 384 where 1 indicates greatest number of fraud and other complaints per 100,000 population
Source: Federal Trade Commission, Consumer Sentinel Network Data Book for January–December 2011

RECREATION

Culture

Dance[1]	Theatre[1]	Instrumental Music[1]	Vocal Music[1]	Series/ Festivals	Museums	Zoos and Aquariums[2]
0	1	0	0	1	n/a	0

Note: (1) Number of professional performing groups; (2) AZA-accredited; n/a not available
Source: The Grey House Performing Arts Directory, 2011-2012; Official Museum Directory, 2011; American Association of Museums, AAM Member Museums, April 2012; Association of Zoos & Aquariums, AZA Member Zoos & Aquariums, April 2012

Professional Sports Teams

Team Name	League
No teams are located in the metro area	

Source: Original research

CLIMATE

Average and Extreme Temperatures

Temperature	Jan	Feb	Mar	Apr	May	Jun	Jul	Aug	Sep	Oct	Nov	Dec	Yr.
Extreme High (°F)	78	84	86	91	95	106	107	104	105	94	84	79	107
Average High (°F)	47	51	60	71	79	87	90	89	83	72	60	50	70
Average Temp. (°F)	38	41	50	60	68	76	80	79	72	61	49	41	60
Average Low (°F)	28	31	39	48	57	65	69	68	61	48	39	31	49
Extreme Low (°F)	-17	-13	2	23	34	42	54	49	36	26	-1	-10	-17

Note: Figures cover the years 1948-1990
Source: National Climatic Data Center, International Station Meteorological Climate Summary, 9/96

Average Precipitation/Snowfall/Humidity

Precip./Humidity	Jan	Feb	Mar	Apr	May	Jun	Jul	Aug	Sep	Oct	Nov	Dec	Yr.
Avg. Precip. (in.)	4.4	4.2	5.0	4.1	4.6	3.7	3.8	3.3	3.2	2.6	3.9	4.6	47.4
Avg. Snowfall (in.)	4	3	1	Tr	0	0	0	0	0	Tr	1	1	11
Avg. Rel. Hum. 6am (%)	81	81	80	81	86	86	88	90	90	87	83	82	85
Avg. Rel. Hum. 3pm (%)	61	57	51	48	52	52	54	53	52	49	55	59	54

Note: Figures cover the years 1948-1990; Tr = Trace amounts (<0.05 in. of rain; <0.5 in. of snow)
Source: National Climatic Data Center, International Station Meteorological Climate Summary, 9/96

Weather Conditions

Temperature			Daytime Sky			Precipitation		
10°F & below	32°F & below	90°F & above	Clear	Partly cloudy	Cloudy	0.01 inch or more precip.	0.1 inch or more snow/ice	Thunder-storms
5	76	51	98	135	132	119	8	54

Note: Figures are average number of days per year and cover the years 1948-1990
Source: National Climatic Data Center, International Station Meteorological Climate Summary, 9/96

HAZARDOUS WASTE

Superfund Sites

Clarksville has no sites on the EPA's Superfund Final National Priorities List.
U.S. Environmental Protection Agency, Final National Priorities List, April 17, 2012

AIR & WATER QUALITY

Air Quality Index

Area	Percent of Days when Air Quality was...[2]					AQI Statistics[2]	
	Good	Moderate	Unhealthy for Sensitive Groups	Unhealthy	Very Unhealthy	Maximum	Median
Area[1]	76.2	23.6	0.3	0.0	0.0	141	35

Note: Air Quality Index (AQI) is an index for reporting daily air quality. EPA calculates the AQI for five major air pollutants regulated by the Clean Air Act: ground-level ozone, particle pollution (aka particulate matter), carbon monoxide, sulfur dioxide, and nitrogen dioxide. The AQI runs from 0 to 500. The higher the AQI value, the greater the level of air pollution and the greater the health concern. There are six AQI categories: "Good" AQI is between 0 and 50. Air quality is considered satisfactory; "Moderate" AQI is between 51 and 100. Air quality is acceptable; "Unhealthy for Sensitive Groups" When AQI values are between 101 and 150, members of sensitive groups may experience health effects; "Unhealthy" When AQI values are between 151 and 200 everyone may begin to experience health effects; "Very Unhealthy" AQI values between 201 and 300 trigger a health alert; "Hazardous" AQI values over 300 trigger warnings of emergency conditions (not shown); (1) Data covers Montgomery County; (2) Based on 365 days with AQI data in 2011.
Source: U.S. Environmental Protection Agency, AirData Report, 2011

Air Quality Index Pollutants

Area	Percent of Days when AQI Pollutant was...[2]					
	Carbon Monoxide	Nitrogen Dioxide	Ozone	Sulfur Dioxide	Particulate Matter 2.5	Particulate Matter 10
Area[1]	0.0	0.0	0.0	22.2	77.8	0.0

Note: The Air Quality Index (AQI) is an index for reporting daily air quality. EPA calculates the AQI for five major air pollutants regulated by the Clean Air Act: ground-level ozone, particle pollution (also known as particulate matter), carbon monoxide, sulfur dioxide, and nitrogen dioxide. The AQI runs from 0 to 500. The higher the AQI value, the greater the level of air pollution and the greater the health concern; (1) Data covers Montgomery County; (2) Based on 365 days with AQI data in 2011.
Source: U.S. Environmental Protection Agency, AirData Report, 2011

Air Quality Index Trends

Area	Trend Sites (days)								All Sites (days)
	2003	2004	2005	2006	2007	2008	2009	2010	2010
MSA[1]	n/a	n/a	n/a	n/a	n/a	n/a	n/a	n/a	n/a

Note: Figures are the number of days the AQI value exceeded 100 in a given year. An AQI value greater than 100 indicates that air quality would have been in the unhealthful range on that day. Data from exceptional events are included. These counts are presented in two ways. First, the counts are based on sites having an adequate record of monitoring data during the trend period (trend sites). These counts represent the relative change in the number of days with AQI values greater than 100. In the last column, the counts are based on all sites with data in the most recent year (because it is possible for a site to have data in the most recent year but not enough data to be a trend site); (1) Data covers the Clarksville, TN-KY—see Appendix B for areas included; n/a not available.
Source: U.S. Environmental Protection Agency, Air Quality Index Information, "Number of Days with Air Quality Index Values Greater than 100 at Trend Sites, 2000-2010, and at All Sites in 2010"

Maximum Air Pollutant Concentrations: Particulate Matter, Ozone, CO and Lead

	Particulate Matter 10 (ug/m^3)	Particulate Matter 2.5 Wtd AM (ug/m^3)	Particulate Matter 2.5 24-Hr (ug/m^3)	Ozone (ppm)	Carbon Monoxide (ppm)	Lead (ug/m^3)
MSA[1] Level	34	11.2	22	0.074	n/a	n/a
NAAQS[2]	150	15	35	0.075	9	0.15
Met NAAQS[2]	Yes	Yes	Yes	Yes	n/a	n/a

Note: Data from exceptional events are not included; (1) Data covers the Clarksville, TN-KY—see Appendix B for areas included; (2) National Ambient Air Quality Standards; ppm = parts per million; ug/m^3 = micrograms per cubic meter; n/a not available
Concentrations: Particulate Matter 10 (coarse particulate)—highest second maximum 24-hour concentration; Particulate Matter 2.5 Wtd AM (fine particulate)—highest weighted annual mean concentration; Particulate Matter 2.5 24-Hour (fine particulate)—highest 98th percentile 24-hour concentration; Ozone—highest fourth daily maximum 8-hour concentration; Carbon Monoxide—highest second maximum non-overlapping 8-hour concentration; Lead—maximum running 3-month average
Source: U.S. Environmental Protection Agency, CBSA Factbook 2010, Air Quality Statistics by City, 2010

Maximum Air Pollutant Concentrations: Nitrogen Dioxide and Sulfur Dioxide

	Nitrogen Dioxide AM (ppb)	Nitrogen Dioxide 1-Hr (ppb)	Sulfur Dioxide AM (ppb)	Sulfur Dioxide 1-Hr (ppb)	Sulfur Dioxide 24-Hr (ppb)
MSA[1] Level	n/a	n/a	3.654	51	12
NAAQS[2]	53	100	30	75	140
Met NAAQS[2]	n/a	n/a	Yes	Yes	Yes

Note: Data from exceptional events are not included; (1) Data covers the Clarksville, TN-KY—see Appendix B for areas included; (2) National Ambient Air Quality Standards; ppb = parts per billion; n/a not available
Concentrations: Nitrogen Dioxide AM—highest arithmetic mean concentration; Nitrogen Dioxide 1-Hr—highest 98th percentile 1-hour daily maximum concentration; Sulfur Dioxide AM—highest annual mean concentration; Sulfur Dioxide 1-Hr—highest 99th percentile 1-hour daily maximum concentration; Sulfur Dioxide 24-Hr—highest second maximum 24-hour concentration
Source: U.S. Environmental Protection Agency, CBSA Factbook 2010, Air Quality Statistics by City, 2010

Drinking Water

Water System Name	Pop. Served	Primary Water Source Type	Violations[1] Health Based	Violations[1] Monitoring/ Reporting
Clarksville Water Department	174,860	Surface	0	1

Note: (1) Based on violation data from January 1, 2011 to December 31, 2011 (includes unresolved violations from earlier years)
Source: U.S. Environmental Protection Agency, Office of Ground Water and Drinking Water, Safe Drinking Water Information System (based on data extracted April 18, 2012)

Columbia, South Carolina

Background

Columbia, on the Congaree River, is South Carolina's capital and largest city, and the seat of Richland County. It is a center for local and state government, and an important financial, insurance, and medical center.

The region has been a trade center from at least 1718, when a trading post opened just south of the present-day city. In 1754, a ferry was established to facilitate contact with the surrounding settlements, and in 1786, when the new state government introduced a bill to create a state capital, Columbia was chosen. Located at almost the dead center of the state, Columbia represented a compromise between South Carolinians on the coast and those in the interior.

The city was planned from the ground up and was originally designed to rest along the river in 400 blocks, which were then divided into half-acre lots. Buyers were required to build houses at least 30 feet long and 18 feet wide within three years, or face penalties. The main thoroughfares were 150 feet wide, and the other streets were also designed generously. Most of this spacious layout still survives, lending an expansive feel to the city as a whole. Columbia, only the second planned city in the United States, achieved a population of nearly 1,000 just after 1800. It was chartered as a town in 1805, and first governed by a mayor, or "intendent," John Taylor, who later served in the state general assembly, in the U.S. Congress, and, finally, as governor of the state.

By 1854, Columbia was a full-fledged chartered city with an elected mayor and six aldermen, a full-time police force, one schoolteacher who was also the city's attorney, and a waterworks, which pumped water via steam engine to a wooden tank and thence by iron and lead pipes to homes and businesses in the area.

Columbia was staunchly Confederate during the Civil War, and in 1865 it was attacked by General Sherman's troops and set ablaze by both Union attackers and Confederate evacuees. After the war and Reconstruction, Columbia saw a revitalization as the state's industrial and farm products hub.

Blue Cross and Blue Shield of S.C. and Palmetto Health, with its two hospitals, Palmetto Richland and Palmetto Baptist, are major employers. Other large employers include SCANA Corp., the area's electricity and natural gas utility; Fort Jackson, the U.S. Army's largest training installation; Humana/TriCare; and the United Parcel Service. Colonial Supplemental Insurance, the second-largest supplemental insurance company in the nation, is based here.

Columbia is the area's cultural center, hosting theaters, galleries, dance companies, and an orchestra. The Columbia Museum of Art is a major regional museum, and the Koger Center for the Arts at the University of South Carolina holds year-round theater, music, and dance productions. The city's Town Theatre is the country's oldest community theatre in continuous use. Annual music festivals include Main Street Jazz, which attracts world-renowned musicians to Columbia, and City Lights, a fall festival that focuses on local musical talent. The Columbia Festival of the Arts is an up-and-coming 11-day festival geared at promoting visual and performance art from the city and its surroundings.

The South Carolina State Museum offers exhibits in natural history, art, science, and technology. Nearing completion is a multi-million dollar observatory/planetarium and large-format OPT theater project including both a 55-foot domed theater in the planetarium and a 3-D theater.

Major historic architecture in Columbia includes the City Hall, designed by President Ulysses S. Grant's federal architect, Alfred Bult Mullet, and the Lutheran Survey Print Building. The city's 5-year (2012-2015) plan includes new housing and neighbood development. The region's economy will also benefit by the currently under-construction University of South Carolina's 200-acre Innovista research campus, which will focus on biomedical, environmental, nanotechnology sectors and future fuels. The city also offers 500 acres of parklands. The Charlie W. Johnson Stadium, home of Benedict College's soccer team, was completed and dedicated in 2006. The Carolina Stadium, USC's new baseball facility and the largest baseball stadium in the state, was completed in February 2009.

The city is home to the University of South Carolina, Lutheran Theological Seminary, Columbia College, Benedict College, Allen University, and Columbia International University.

Located about 150 miles southeast of the Appalachian Mountains, Columbia has a relatively temperate climate. Summers are long and often hot and humid with frequent thunderstorms, thanks to the Bermuda high-pressure force. Winters are mild with little snow, while spring is changeable and can include infrequent tornadoes or hail. Fall is considered the most pleasant season.

Rankings

General Rankings

- *Men's Health Living* ranked 100 U.S. cities in terms of quality of life. Columbia was ranked #39 and received a grade of C+. Criteria: number of fitness facilities; air quality; number of physicians; male/female ratio; education levels; household income; cost of living. *Men's Health Living, Spring 2008*

Business/Finance Rankings

- Columbia was identified as one of the 20 weakest-performing metro areas during the recession and recovery from trough quarter through the third quarter of 2011. Criteria: percent change in employment; percentage point change in unemployment rate; percent change in gross metropolitan product; percent change in House Price Index. *Brookings Institution, MetroMonitor: Tracking Economic Recession and Recovery in America's 100 Largest Metropolitan Areas, December 2011*

- *American City Business Journals* ranked America's 261 largest cities in terms of their resident's wealth. Columbia ranked #164. Criteria: per capita income; median household income; percentage of households with annual incomes of $200,000 or more; median home value. *American City Business Journals, "Where the Money Is: America's Wealth Centers," August 18, 2008*

- The Columbia metro area appeared on the Milken Institute "2011 Best Performing Metros" list. Rank: #115 out of 200 large metro areas. Criteria: job growth; wage and salary growth; high-tech output growth. *Milken Institute, "2011 Best Performing Metros"*

- The Columbia metro area was selected as one of the best cities for entrepreneurs in America by *Inc. Magazine*. Criteria: job-growth data for 335 metro areas was analyzed for: recent growth trend; mid-term growth; long-term trend; current year growth. The Columbia metro area ranked #19 among mid-sized metro areas and #79 overall. *Inc. Magazine, "The Best Cities for Doing Business," July 2008*

- *Forbes* ranked the 200 most populous metro areas in the U.S. in terms of the "Best Places for Business and Careers." The Columbia metro area was ranked #73. Criteria: costs (business and living); job growth (past and projected); income growth; educational attainment; projected economic growth; crime; cultural and recreational opportunities; net migration patterns; number of highly ranked colleges. *Forbes, "Best Places for Business and Careers," June 2011*

Children/Family Rankings

- The Columbia metro area was selected as one of the "Best Cities for Relocating Families" by Worldwide ERC and Primacy Relocation. The 2008 study looked at nearly 50 factors important to relocating families including: recent job growth; nearby top-ranked colleges; in-state tuition for four-year public colleges; population growth since 2000; pediatricians per 100,000 population; and a Green Living index. *Worldwide ERC and Primacy Relocation, "2008 Best Cities for Relocating Families"*

Dating/Romance Rankings

- Columbia was selected as one of the most romantic cities in America by *Amazon.com*. The city ranked #10 of 20. Criteria: per capita sales of romance novels and relationship books, romantic comedy movies, Barry White albums, and sexual wellness products. *Amazon.com, "America's Most Romantic Cities Revealed," February 14, 2012*

- Columbia appeared on *Men's Health's* list of the most sex-happy cities in America. The city ranked #32 of 100. Criteria: condom sales; birth rates; sex toy sales; rates of chlamydia, gonorrhea, and syphilis. *Men's Health, "America's Most Sex-Happy Cities," October 2010*

- *Men's Health* ranked 100 U.S. cities in terms of best (and worst) marriages. Columbia was ranked #99 (#1 = worst). Criteria: rate of failed marriages; stringency of divorce laws; percentage of population who've split; number of licensed marriage and family therapists. *Men's Health, "Splitsville, USA," May 2010*

- The Columbia metro area was selected as one of the "Best Cities for Relocating Singles" by Worldwide ERC and Primacy Relocation. The area ranked #50 out of the 100 largest metro areas in the U.S. Criteria: recent job growth; recent singles population growth; overall population growth; affordable rental housing; cost-of-living index; expanded arts and recreation opportunities; ratio of single men and single women; affordability of quality higher education (including state residency requirements); diversity index; climate; population density. *Worldwide ERC and Primacy Relocation, "2008 Best Cities for Relocating Singles"*

Education Rankings

- *Men's Health* ranked 100 U.S. cities in terms of their education levels. Columbia was ranked #12 (#1 = most educated city). Criteria: high school graduation rates; school enrollment; educational attainment; number of households who have outstanding student loans; number of households whose members have taken adult-education courses. *Men's Health, "Where School Is In: The Most and Least Educated Cities," September 12, 2011*

- Columbia was selected as one of the most well-read cities in America by *Amazon.com*. The city ranked #16 of 20. Cities with populations greater than 100,000 were evaluated based on per capita sales of books, magazines and newspapers. *Amazon.com, "Top 20 Most Well-Read Cities in America," June 4, 2011*

- Columbia was identified as one of the 100 "smartest" metro areas in the U.S. The area ranked #48. Criteria: the editors rated the collective brainpower of the 100 largest metro areas in the U.S. based on their residents' educational attainment. *American City Business Journals, April 14, 2008*

- Columbia was identified as one of "America's Brainiest Bastions" by *Portfolio.com*. The metro area ranked #54 out of 200. *Portfolio.com* analyzed levels of educational attainment in the nation's 200 largest metropolitan areas. The editors established scores for five levels of educational attainment, based on relative earning power of adult workers age 25 or older. Scores were determined by comparing the median income for all workers with the median income for those workers at a specified educational level. *Portfolio.com, "America's Brainiest Bastions," December 1, 2010*

Environmental Rankings

- Columbia was selected as one of 22 "Smarter Cities" for energy by the Natural Resources Defense Council. Criteria: investment in green power; energy efficiency measures; conservation. *Natural Resources Defense Council, "2010 Smarter Cities," July 19, 2010*

- 100 of the largest metro areas in the U.S. were analyzed in terms of their current drought severity. The Columbia metro area ranked #22 (#1 = driest). The rankings were based on statistics such as long-term precipitation trends and patterns and the Palmer drought indices. *Sperling's BestPlaces, www.BestPlaces.net, "America's Drought-Riskiest Cities," November 2007*

- The Columbia metro area appeared in *Country Home's* "Best Green Places" report. The area ranked #152 out of 379. Criteria: official energy policies; green power; green buildings; availability of fresh, locally grown food. *Country Home, "Best Green Places," 2008*

Health/Fitness Rankings

- Columbia was identified as a "2011 Asthma Capital." The area ranked #54 out of the nation's 100 largest metropolitan areas. Twelve factors were used to identify the most challenging places to live for people with asthma: estimated prevalence; self-reported prevalence; crude death rate for asthma; annual pollen score; annual air quality; public smoking laws; number of board-certified asthma specialists; school inhaler access laws; rescue medication use; controller medication use; uninsured rate; poverty rate. *Asthma and Allergy Foundation of America, "2011 Asthma Capitals"*

- Columbia was identified as a "2011 Fall Allergy Capital." The area ranked #18 out of 100. Three groups of factors were used to identify the most severe cities for people with allergies during the fall season: annual pollen levels; medicine utilization; access to board-certified allergists. *Asthma and Allergy Foundation of America, "2011 Fall Allergy Capitals"*

- Columbia was identified as a "2012 Spring Allergy Capital." The area ranked #27 out of 100. Three groups of factors were used to identify the most severe cities for people with allergies during the spring season: annual pollen levels; medicine utilization; access to board-certified allergists. *Asthma and Allergy Foundation of America, "2012 Spring Allergy Capitals"*

- *Men's Health* examined 100 major U.S. cities and selected the best and worst cities for men. Columbia ranked #86. Criteria: 35 statistical parameters of long life in the categories of health, quality of life, and fitness. *Men's Health, "The 10 Best and Worst Cities for Men 2012," January/February 2012*

- The makers of Breath Right Nasal Strips, in partnership with Sperling's BestPlaces, analyzed 50 metro areas and identified those U.S. cities most challenged by chronic nasal congestion. The Columbia metro area ranked #17. Criteria: tree, grass and weed pollens; molds and spores; air pollution; climate; smoking; purchase habits of congestion products; prescriptions of drugs for congestion relief; incidence of influenza. *Breathe Right Nasal Strips, "Most Congested Cities," October 3, 2011*

- The Columbia metro area appeared in the 2011 Gallup-Healthways Well-Being Index. The index, based on interviews with more than 350,000 Americans, measured jobs, finances, physical health, emotional state of mind and communities. The metro area ranked #94 out of 190. Criteria: life evaluation; emotional health; work environment; physical health; healthy behaviors; basic access (basic needs optimal for a healthy life, such as access to food and medicine, having health insurance and feeling safe while walking at night). *Gallup-Healthways, "State of Well-Being 2011"*

- *Men's Health* ranked 100 U.S. cities in terms of their activity levels. Columbia was ranked #69 (#1 = most active city). Criteria: where and how often residents exercise; percentage of households that watch more than 15 hours of cable television a week and buy more than 11 video games a year; death rate from deep-vein thrombosis, a condition linked to sitting for extended periods of time. *Men's Health, "Where Sit Happens: The Most and Least Active Cities in America," June 20, 2011*

Real Estate Rankings

- *Fortune* ranked the 100 largest metro areas in the U.S. in terms of projected median home price change in 2010. The Columbia metro area ranked #15. *Fortune, "The 2010 Housing Outlook," December 9, 2009*

- Columbia appeared on *ApartmentRatings.com* "Top College Towns & Cities" for renters list in 2011." The area ranked #51 out of 87. Overall satisfaction ratings were ranked using thousands of user submitted scores for hundreds of apartment complexes located in cities and towns that are home to the 100 largest four-year institutions in the U.S. *ApartmentRatings.com, "2011 College Town Renter Satisfaction Rankings"*

- The Center for Housing Policy ranked 210 U.S. metropolitan areas by the fair market rent for a two-bedroom unit. The Columbia metro area was ranked #130. (#1 = most expensive) with a rent of $767. Criteria: Fair Market Rent (FMR) in effect during the fourth quarter of 2009 based on HUD's fiscal year 2010 FMRs. *The Center for Housing Policy, "Paycheck to Paycheck: Most to Least Expensive Rental Markets in 2009"*

- The Columbia metro area was identified as one of the best U.S. markets to invest in rental property" by HomeVestors and Local Market Monitor. The area ranked #40 out of 100. Criteria: risk-return premium relative to national average. *HomeVestors and Local Market Monitor, "Best 100 U.S. Markets to Invest in Rental Property," March 9, 2012*

Safety Rankings

- Allstate ranked the 193 largest cities in America in terms of driver safety. Columbia ranked #108. In addition, drivers were 11.0% more likely to have had an accident compared to the national average. Allstate researchers analyzed internal property damage reported claims over a two-year period (from January 2008 to December 2009) to protect findings from external influences such as weather or road construction. A weighted average of the two-year numbers determined the annual percentages. The report defines an auto crash as any collision resulting in a property damage claim. *Allstate, "2011 Allstate America's Best Drivers Report™"*

- The National Insurance Crime Bureau ranked 366 metro areas in the U.S. in terms of per capita rates of vehicle theft. The Columbia metro area ranked #35 (#1 = highest rate). Criteria: number of vehicle theft offenses per 100,000 inhabitants in 2010. *National Insurance Crime Bureau, "Hot Spots," June 21, 2011*

Seniors/Retirement Rankings

- Columbia was selected as one of the best places to retire by *CNNMoney.com*. Criteria: low cost of living; low violent-crime rate; good medical care; large population over age 50; abundant amenities for retirees. *CNNMoney.com, "Best Places to Retire 2011"*

Sports/Recreation Rankings

- Columbia appeared on the *Sporting News* list of the "Best Sports Cities" for 2011. The area ranked #83 out of 271 cities in the U.S. *Sporting News* takes a 12-month snapshot of each city's sports, putting a heavy premium on regular-season won-lost records (from the most recently completed season). Other criteria include: playoff berths, bowl appearances and tournament bids; championships; applicable power ratings; quality of competition; overall fan fervor (measured in part by attendance); abundance of teams (rewarding quality over quantity); stadium and arena quality; ticket availability and prices; franchise ownership; and marquee appeal of athletes. *Sporting News, "Best Sports Cities 2011," October 4, 2011*

- Columbia was chosen as a bicycle friendly community by the League of American Bicyclists. A Bicycle Friendly Community welcomes cyclists by providing safe accommodation for cycling and encouraging people to bike for transportation and recreation. There are four award levels: Platinum; Gold; Silver; and Bronze. The community achieved an award level of Bronze. *League of American Bicyclists, "Bicycle Friendly Community Master List 2011"*

Women/Minorities Rankings

- *Women's Health* examined U.S. cities and identified the 100 best cities for women. Columbia was ranked #84. Criteria: 30 categories were examined from obesity and breast cancer rates to commuting times and hours spent working out. *Women's Health, "Best Cities for Women 2012"*

- Columbia was ranked #63 out of 100 metro areas in *SELF Magazine's* ranking of America's healthiest places for women." A panel of experts came up with more than 50 criteria including death and disease rates, environmental indicators, community resources, and lifestyle habits. *SELF Magazine, "Secrets of America's Healthiest Women," December 2008*

Miscellaneous Rankings

- *Men's Health* ranked 100 U.S. cities by their level of sadness. Columbia was ranked #77 (#1 = saddest city). Criteria: suicide rates; unemployment rates; percentage of households that use antidepressants; percent of population who report feeling blue all or most of the time. *Men's Health, "Frown Towns," November 28, 2011*

- Mars Chocolate North America, the makers of COMBOS®, in partnership with Sperling's BestPlaces, ranked 50 major metro areas in terms of their "manliness." The Columbia metro area ranked #5. Criteria: number of professional sports teams; number of nearby NASCAR tracks and racing events; manly lifestyle; concentration of manly retail stores; manly occupations per capita; salty snack sales; "Board of Manliness" rankings. *Mars Chocolate North America, "America's Manliest Cities 2011," September 1, 2011*

Business Environment

CITY FINANCES

City Government Finances

Component	2009 ($000)	2009 ($ per capita)
Total Revenues	278,218	2,229
Total Expenditures	227,260	1,821
Debt Outstanding	256,705	2,057
Cash and Securities[1]	203,078	1,627

Note: (1) Cash and security holdings of a government at the close of its fiscal year, including those of its dependent agencies, utilities, and liquor stores.
Source: U.S Census Bureau, State & Local Government Finances 2009

City Government Revenue by Source

Source	2009 ($000)	2009 ($ per capita)
General Revenue		
From Federal Government	13,987	112
From State Government	13,369	107
From Local Governments	0	0
Taxes		
Property	48,292	387
Sales and Gross Receipts	9,666	77
Personal Income	0	0
Corporate Income	0	0
Motor Vehicle License	0	0
Other Taxes	27,996	224
Current Charges	82,436	660
Liquor Store	0	0
Utility	57,871	464
Employee Retirement	0	0

Source: U.S Census Bureau, State & Local Government Finances 2009

City Government Expenditures by Function

Function	2009 ($000)	2009 ($ per capita)	2009 (%)
General Direct Expenditures			
Air Transportation	0	0	0.0
Corrections	0	0	0.0
Education	0	0	0.0
Employment Security Administration	0	0	0.0
Financial Administration	5,563	45	2.4
Fire Protection	23,744	190	10.4
General Public Buildings	1,341	11	0.6
Governmental Administration, Other	4,486	36	2.0
Health	1,224	10	0.5
Highways	5,617	45	2.5
Hospitals	0	0	0.0
Housing and Community Development	4,977	40	2.2
Interest on General Debt	11,513	92	5.1
Judicial and Legal	4,457	36	2.0
Libraries	0	0	0.0
Parking	3,103	25	1.4
Parks and Recreation	10,549	85	4.6
Police Protection	28,978	232	12.8
Public Welfare	843	7	0.4
Sewerage	32,102	257	14.1
Solid Waste Management	10,417	83	4.6
Veterans' Services	0	0	0.0
Liquor Store	0	0	0.0
Utility	34,859	279	15.3
Employee Retirement	0	0	0.0

Source: U.S Census Bureau, State & Local Government Finances 2009

Municipal Bond Ratings

Area	Moody's	S&P	Fitch
City	Aa2	AA	n/a

Rating Systems (shown in declining order of credit quality): Moody's– Aaa, Aa, A, Baa, Ba, B, Caa, Ca, C (numerical modifiers 1, 2, and 3 are added to letter-rating); S&P– AAA, AA, A, BBB, BB, B, CCC, CC, C; Fitch– AAA, AA, A, BBB, BB, B, CCC, CC, C. Ratings may be modified by the addition of a plus or minus sign to show relative standing within the major rating categories.
Notes: n/a Not Available; w/d Withdrawn (1) Not Reviewed; (2) Issuer Rating/No General Obligation; (3) Standard and Poor's Issue Credit Rating (ICR) is a current opinion of an obliger with respect to a specific financial obligation, a specific class of financial obligations, or a specific financial program.
Source: City of Columbia, South Carolina, Comprehensive Annual Financial Report, Fiscal Year Ended June 30, 2009

DEMOGRAPHICS

Population Growth

Area	1990 Census	2000 Census	2010 Census	Population Growth (%) 1990-2000	Population Growth (%) 2000-2010
City	115,475	116,278	129,272	0.7	11.2
MSA[1]	548,325	647,158	767,598	18.0	18.6
U.S.	248,709,873	281,421,906	308,745,538	13.2	9.7

Note: (1) Figures cover the Columbia, SC Metropolitan Statistical Area—see Appendix B for areas included
Source: U.S. Census Bureau, 2010 Census

Household Size

Area	Persons in Household (%) One	Two	Three	Four	Five	Six	Seven or More	Average Household Size
City	38.0	31.9	14.6	9.3	4.0	1.4	0.9	2.18
MSA[1]	27.5	33.3	17.1	13.1	5.7	2.1	1.2	2.48
U.S.	26.7	32.8	16.1	13.4	6.5	2.6	1.9	2.58

Note: (1) Figures cover the Columbia, SC Metropolitan Statistical Area—see Appendix B for areas included
Source: U.S. Census Bureau, 2010 Census

Race

Area	White Alone[2] (%)	Black Alone[2] (%)	Asian Alone[2] (%)	AIAN[3] Alone[2] (%)	NHOPI[4] Alone[2] (%)	Other Race Alone[2] (%)	Two or More Races (%)
City	51.7	42.2	2.2	0.3	0.1	1.5	2.0
MSA[1]	60.4	33.2	1.7	0.4	0.1	2.3	2.0
U.S.	72.4	12.6	4.8	0.9	0.2	6.2	2.9

Note: (1) Figures cover the Columbia, SC Metropolitan Statistical Area—see Appendix B for areas included; (2) Alone is defined as not being in combination with one or more other races; (3) American Indian and Alaska Native; (4) Native Hawaiian and Other Pacific Islander
Source: U.S. Census Bureau, 2010 Census

Hispanic or Latino Origin

Area	Hispanic or Latino (%)	Mexican (%)	Puerto Rican (%)	Cuban (%)	Other Hispanic or Latino (%)
City	4.3	1.9	1.0	0.2	1.3
MSA[1]	5.1	2.7	0.9	0.1	1.3
U.S.	16.3	10.3	1.5	0.6	4.0

Note: Persons of Hispanic or Latino origin can be of any race; (1) Figures cover the Columbia, SC Metropolitan Statistical Area—see Appendix B for areas included
Source: U.S. Census Bureau, 2010 Census

Segregation

Type	Segregation Indices[1]				Percent Change		
	1990	2000	2010	2010 Rank[2]	1990-2000	1990-2010	2000-2010
Black/White	50.4	48.1	48.8	74	-2.3	-1.6	0.7
Asian/White	43.9	43.8	41.9	46	-0.1	-2.0	-1.9
Hispanic/White	37.7	34.9	34.9	82	-2.8	-2.8	0.0

Note: Figures are based on an analysis of 1990, 2000, and 2010 Census Decennial Census tract data by William H. Frey, Brookings Institution and the University of Michigan Social Science Data Analysis Network. In this analysis all racial groups (whites, blacks, and asians) are non-Hispanic members of those races. Hispanics are shown as a separate category; All figures cover the Metropolitan Statistical Area (see Appendix B for areas included); (1) Segregation Indices are Dissimilarity Indices that measure the degree to which the minority group is distributed differently than whites across census tracts. They range from 0 (complete integration) to 100 (complete segregation) where the value indicates the percentage of the minority group that needs to move to be distributed exactly like whites; (2) Ranges from 1 (most segregated) to 102 (least segregated); n/a not available.
Source: www.CensusScope.org

Ancestry

Area	German	Irish	English	American	Italian	Polish	French[2]	Scottish	Dutch
City	8.4	8.4	9.3	7.0	2.4	1.2	2.1	2.6	0.8
MSA[1]	11.9	9.0	9.1	12.4	2.4	1.1	1.8	2.0	0.9
U.S.	16.1	11.6	8.8	6.1	5.7	3.2	3.0	1.9	1.6

Note: Figures are the percentage of the total population reporting a particular ancestry. The nine most commonly reported ancestries in the U.S. are shown. Figures include multiple ancestries (e.g. if a person reported being Irish and Italian, they were included in both columns); (1) Figures cover the Columbia, SC Metropolitan Statistical Area—see Appendix B for areas included; (2) Excludes Basque
Source: U.S. Census Bureau, 2008-2010 American Community Survey 3-Year Estimates

Foreign-Born Population

Area	Any Foreign Country	Mexico	Asia	Europe	Carribean	South America	Central America[2]	Africa	Canada
City	4.6	0.3	2.0	0.8	0.3	0.3	0.1	0.5	0.2
MSA[1]	4.8	1.5	1.4	0.7	0.3	0.2	0.5	0.2	0.1
U.S.	12.8	3.8	3.6	1.6	1.2	0.9	1.0	0.5	0.3

Note: (1) Figures cover the Columbia, SC Metropolitan Statistical Area—see Appendix B for areas included; (2) Excludes Mexico.
Source: U.S. Census Bureau, 2008-2010 American Community Survey 3-Year Estimates

Marital Status

Area	Never Married	Now Married[2]	Separated	Widowed	Divorced
City	54.5	28.2	3.3	5.2	8.8
MSA[1]	34.7	46.4	3.2	5.8	9.9
U.S.	31.6	49.6	2.2	6.1	10.7

Note: Figures are percentages and cover the population 15 years of age and older; (1) Figures cover the Columbia, SC Metropolitan Statistical Area—see Appendix B for areas included; (2) Excludes separated
Source: U.S. Census Bureau, 2008-2010 American Community Survey 3-Year Estimates

Age

Area	Percent of Population							Median Age
	Under Age 5	Age 5 to 17	Age 18 to 34	Age 35 to 49	Age 50 to 64	Age 65 to 79	80 Years and Over	
City	5.4	11.5	43.6	16.4	14.4	6.0	2.7	28.1
MSA[1]	6.5	17.0	25.7	20.5	18.9	8.6	2.8	35.7
U.S.	6.5	17.5	23.2	20.7	19.0	9.4	3.6	37.2

Note: (1) Figures cover the Columbia, SC Metropolitan Statistical Area—see Appendix B for areas included
Source: U.S. Census Bureau, 2010 Census

Male/Female Ratio

Area	Males	Females	Males per 100 Females
City	66,532	62,740	106.0
MSA[1]	374,340	393,258	95.2
U.S.	151,781,326	156,964,212	96.7

Note: (1) Figures cover the Columbia, SC
Metropolitan Statistical Area—see Appendix B for areas included
Source: U.S. Census Bureau, 2010 Census

Religious Groups

Area	Catholic	Baptist	Non-Den.	Methodist[2]	Lutheran	LDS[3]	Pente-costal	Presby-terian[4]	Muslim[5]	Judaism
MSA[1]	3.1	18.1	5.2	9.4	3.4	1.1	2.7	3.3	0.2	0.1
U.S.	19.1	9.3	4.0	4.0	2.3	2.0	1.9	1.6	0.8	0.7

Note: Figures are the number of adherents as a percentage of the total population; (1) Figures cover the
Columbia, SC Metropolitan Statistical Area—see Appendix B for areas included; (2) Methodist/Pietist;
(3) Latter Day Saints; (4) Reformed; (5) Figures are estimates
Source: Association of Statisticians of American Religious Bodies, 2010 U.S. Religion Census: Religious
Congregations & Membership Study

ECONOMY

Gross Metropolitan Product

Area	2007	2008	2009	2010	2010 Rank[2]
MSA[1]	30.4	30.8	31.3	32.2	69

Note: Figures are in billions of dollars; (1) Figures cover the Columbia, SC Metropolitan Statistical Area—see
Appendix B for areas included; (2) Rank ranges from 1 to 363
Source: The United States Conference of Mayors, "U.S. Metro Economies: GMP and Employment Forecasts,"
June 2011

Economic Growth

Area	2007-2009 (%)	2010 (%)	2011 (%)	Rank[2]
MSA[1]	-0.8	2.1	1.9	146
U.S.	-1.3	2.9	2.5	–

Note: Figures are real Gross Metropolitan Product growth rates and represent annual average percent change;
(1) Figures cover the Columbia, SC Metropolitan Statistical Area—see Appendix B for areas included; (2) Rank
ranges from 1 to 363
Source: The United States Conference of Mayors, "U.S. Metro Economies: GMP and Employment Forecasts,"
June 2011

Metropolitan Area Exports

Area	2005	2006	2007	2008	2009	2010	2010 Rank[2]
MSA[1]	1,456.0	1,143.5	1,048.0	1,483.5	1,362.5	1,511.3	108

Note: Figures are in millions of dollars; (1) Figures cover the Columbia, SC Metropolitan Statistical Area—see
Appendix B for areas included; (2) Rank ranges from 1 to 369
Source: U.S. Department of Commerce, International Trade Administration, Office of Trade & Industry
Information, Manufacturing & Services, data extracted April 2, 2012

INCOME

Income

Area	Per Capita ($)	Median Household ($)	Average Household ($)
City	23,958	36,546	58,642
MSA[1]	24,841	47,511	62,437
U.S.	26,942	51,222	70,116

Note: (1) Figures cover the Columbia, SC Metropolitan Statistical Area—see Appendix B for areas included
Source: U.S. Census Bureau, 2008-2010 American Community Survey 3-Year Estimates

Household Income Distribution

Area	Percent of Households Earning							
	Under $15,000	$15,000 -24,999	$25,000 -34,999	$35,000 -49,999	$50,000 -74,999	$75,000 -99,000	$100,000 -149,999	$150,000 and up
City	20.6	14.2	13.5	14.1	14.1	8.7	8.3	6.6
MSA[1]	13.7	11.8	11.5	15.2	19.2	12.2	11.0	5.5
U.S.	13.0	11.0	10.6	14.2	18.5	12.1	12.2	8.4

Note: (1) Figures cover the Columbia, SC Metropolitan Statistical Area—see Appendix B for areas included
Source: U.S. Census Bureau, 2008-2010 American Community Survey 3-Year Estimates

Poverty Rate

Area	All Ages	Under 18 Years Old	18 to 64 Years Old	65 Years and Over
City	23.6	31.2	23.1	13.4
MSA[1]	14.2	18.4	13.4	10.0
U.S.	14.4	20.1	13.1	9.4

Note: Figures are percentage of people whose income during the past 12 months was below the poverty level;
(1) Figures cover the Columbia, SC Metropolitan Statistical Area—see Appendix B for areas included
Source: U.S. Census Bureau, 2008-2010 American Community Survey 3-Year Estimates

Personal Bankruptcy Filing Rate

Area	2006	2007	2008	2009	2010	2011
Richland County	2.08	2.20	2.41	2.37	2.26	2.04
U.S.	2.00	2.73	3.53	4.61	4.97	4.37

Note: Numbers are per 1,000 population and include Chapter 7 and Chapter 13 filings
Source: Federal Deposit Insurance Corporation, Regional Economic Conditions, March 9, 2012

EMPLOYMENT

Labor Force and Employment

Area	Civilian Labor Force			Workers Employed		
	Dec. 2010	Dec. 2011	% Chg.	Dec. 2010	Dec. 2011	% Chg.
City	54,922	54,995	0.1	49,714	50,533	1.6
MSA[1]	366,913	368,534	0.4	333,605	339,100	1.6
U.S.	153,156,000	153,373,000	0.1	139,159,000	140,681,000	1.1

Note: Data is not seasonally adjusted and covers workers 16 years of age and older;
(1) Metropolitan Statistical Area—see Appendix B for areas included
Source: Bureau of Labor Statistics, http://stats.bls.gov

Unemployment Rate

Area	2011											
	Jan.	Feb.	Mar.	Apr.	May	Jun.	Jul.	Aug.	Sep.	Oct.	Nov.	Dec.
City	8.3	8.5	8.5	8.3	10.0	11.5	11.3	10.6	9.8	9.0	8.0	8.1
MSA[1]	8.3	8.5	8.0	8.1	8.9	10.0	9.9	9.7	9.1	8.5	7.8	8.0
U.S.	9.8	9.5	9.2	8.7	8.7	9.3	9.3	9.1	8.8	8.5	8.2	8.3

Note: Data is not seasonally adjusted and covers workers 16 years of age and older; All figures are
percentages; (1) Metropolitan Statistical Area—see Appendix B for areas included
Source: Bureau of Labor Statistics, http://stats.bls.gov

Projected Unemployment Rate

Area	2010 (%)	2011 (%)	2012 (%)	2013 (%)
MSA[1]	9.2	8.7	8.5	7.8

Note: (1) Metropolitan Statistical Area—see Appendix B for areas included
Source: The United States Conference of Mayors, "U.S. Metro Economies: GMP and Employment Forecasts,"
June 2011

Employment by Occupation

Occupation Classification	City (%)	MSA[1] (%)	U.S. (%)
Management, Business, Science, and Arts	41.7	36.6	35.6
Natural Resources, Construction, and Maintenance	5.6	9.5	9.5
Production, Transportation, and Material Moving	7.2	10.8	12.1
Sales and Office	24.7	25.8	25.2
Service	20.8	17.2	17.6

Note: Figures cover employed civilians 16 years of age and older; (1) Figures cover the Columbia, SC Metropolitan Statistical Area—see Appendix B for areas included
Source: U.S. Census Bureau, 2008-2010 American Community Survey 3-Year Estimates

Employment by Industry

Sector	MSA[1] Number of Employees	MSA[1] Percent of Total	U.S. Percent of Total
Construction	n/a	n/a	4.1
Education and Health Services	42,300	12.1	15.2
Financial Activities	27,300	7.8	5.8
Government	78,300	22.4	16.8
Information	5,600	1.6	2.0
Leisure and Hospitality	31,700	9.1	9.9
Manufacturing	28,900	8.3	8.9
Mining and Logging	n/a	n/a	0.6
Other Services	12,600	3.6	4.0
Professional and Business Services	43,300	12.4	13.3
Retail Trade	40,000	11.4	11.5
Transportation and Utilities	11,400	3.3	3.8
Wholesale Trade	13,700	3.9	4.2

Note: Figures cover non-farm employment as of December 2011 and are not seasonally adjusted; (1) Metropolitan Statistical Area—see Appendix B for areas included; n/a not available
Source: Bureau of Labor Statistics, http://stats.bls.gov

Occupations with Greatest Projected Employment Growth: 2008 – 2018

Occupation[1]	2008 Employment	2018 Projected Employment	Numeric Employment Change	Percent Employment Change
Registered Nurses	38,400	48,020	9,620	25.1
Combined Food Preparation and Serving Workers, Including Fast Food	32,440	38,160	5,720	17.6
Retail Salespersons	65,260	69,880	4,620	7.1
Customer Service Representatives	28,910	33,430	4,520	15.6
Elementary School Teachers, Except Special Education	21,900	26,120	4,220	19.3
Office Clerks, General	42,130	46,010	3,880	9.2
Nursing Aides, Orderlies, and Attendants	20,090	23,400	3,310	16.5
Waiters and Waitresses	35,290	38,440	3,150	8.9
Cashiers	60,430	63,450	3,020	5.0
Postsecondary Teachers	15,490	18,420	2,930	18.9

Note: Projections cover South Carolina; (1) Sorted by numeric employment change
Source: www.projectionscentral.com, State Occupational Projections, 2008–2018 Long-Term Projections

Fastest Growing Occupations: 2008 – 2018

Occupation[1]	2008 Employment	2018 Projected Employment	Numeric Employment Change	Percent Employment Change
Network Systems and Data Communications Analysts	2,880	4,390	1,510	52.4
Self-Enrichment Education Teachers	2,220	3,190	970	43.7
Commercial Pilots	360	510	150	41.7
Pharmacy Technicians	5,490	7,630	2,140	39.0
Physician Assistants	600	830	230	38.3
Dental Hygienists	2,600	3,580	980	37.7
Dental Assistants	3,250	4,450	1,200	36.9
Computer Software Engineers, Systems Software	2,080	2,820	740	35.6
Medical Equipment Repairers	620	840	220	35.5
Personal and Home Care Aides	5,630	7,560	1,930	34.3

Note: Projections cover South Carolina; (1) Sorted by percent employment change and excludes occupations with numeric employment change less than 100
Source: www.projectionscentral.com, State Occupational Projections, 2008–2018 Long-Term Projections

Average Wages

Occupation	$/Hr.	Occupation	$/Hr.
Accountants and Auditors	26.80	Maids and Housekeeping Cleaners	9.55
Automotive Mechanics	19.36	Maintenance and Repair Workers	16.95
Bookkeepers	16.97	Marketing Managers	45.82
Carpenters	16.13	Nuclear Medicine Technologists	29.31
Cashiers	8.61	Nurses, Licensed Practical	19.64
Clerks, General Office	13.51	Nurses, Registered	28.95
Clerks, Receptionists/Information	13.24	Nursing Aides/Orderlies/Attendants	11.39
Clerks, Shipping/Receiving	13.56	Packers and Packagers, Hand	11.67
Computer Programmers	30.43	Physical Therapists	37.01
Computer Support Specialists	23.42	Postal Service Mail Carriers	24.01
Computer Systems Analysts	32.61	Real Estate Brokers	26.83
Cooks, Restaurant	9.44	Retail Salespersons	11.77
Dentists	91.03	Sales Reps., Exc. Tech./Scientific	30.05
Electrical Engineers	39.73	Sales Reps., Tech./Scientific	32.46
Electricians	19.61	Secretaries, Exc. Legal/Med./Exec.	14.65
Financial Managers	49.15	Security Guards	11.16
First-Line Supervisors/Managers, Sales	19.28	Surgeons	102.05
Food Preparation Workers	9.10	Teacher Assistants	9.90
General and Operations Managers	49.52	Teachers, Elementary School	24.00
Hairdressers/Cosmetologists	13.54	Teachers, Secondary School	25.10
Internists	104.61	Telemarketers	10.60
Janitors and Cleaners	10.43	Truck Drivers, Heavy/Tractor-Trailer	18.38
Landscaping/Groundskeeping Workers	9.98	Truck Drivers, Light/Delivery Svcs.	14.34
Lawyers	53.98	Waiters and Waitresses	8.45

Note: Wage data covers the Columbia, SC Metropolitan Statistical Area—see Appendix B for areas included. Hourly wages for elementary/secondary school teachers and teacher assistants were calculated by the editors from annual wage data assuming a 40 hour work week; n/a not available.
Source: Bureau of Labor Statistics, Metro Area Occupational Employment and Wage Estimates, May 2011

RESIDENTIAL REAL ESTATE

Building Permits

Area	Single-Family			Multi-Family			Total		
	2010	2011	Pct. Chg.	2010	2011	Pct. Chg.	2010	2011	Pct. Chg.
City	203	199	-2.0	96	52	-45.8	299	251	-16.1
MSA[1]	2,527	2,390	-5.4	415	507	22.2	2,942	2,897	-1.5
U.S.	447,311	418,498	-6.4	157,299	205,563	30.7	604,610	624,061	3.2

Note: (1) Metropolitan Statistical Area—see Appendix B for areas included; figures represent new, privately-owned housing units authorized (unadjusted data); All permit data are based on estimates with imputation.
Source: U.S. Census Bureau, Manufacturing, Mining, and Construction Statistics, Building Permits, 2010, 2011

Homeownership Rate

Area	2005 (%)	2006 (%)	2007 (%)	2008 (%)	2009 (%)	2010 (%)	2011 (%)
MSA[1]	76.3	72.2	71.1	71.4	71.5	74.1	69.0
U.S.	68.9	68.8	68.1	67.8	67.4	66.9	66.1

Note: (1) Metropolitan Statistical Area—see Appendix B for areas included
Source: U.S. Census Bureau, Housing Vacancies and Homeownership Annual Statistics: 2011

Housing Vacancy Rates

Area	Gross Vacancy Rate[2] (%)			Year-Round Vacancy Rate[3] (%)			Rental Vacancy Rate[4] (%)			Homeowner Vacancy Rate[5] (%)		
	2009	2010	2011	2009	2010	2011	2009	2010	2011	2009	2010	2011
MSA[1]	13.3	11.1	12.4	13.0	10.9	12.4	8.4	9.4	8.7	3.1	2.5	5.1
U.S.	14.5	14.3	14.2	11.3	11.3	11.1	10.6	10.2	9.5	2.6	2.6	2.5

Note: (1) Metropolitan Statistical Area—see Appendix B for areas included; (2) The percentage of the total housing inventory that is vacant; (3) The percentage of the housing inventory (excluding seasonal units) that is year-round vacant; (4) The percentage of rental inventory that is vacant for rent; (5) The percentage of homeowner inventory that is vacant for sale
Source: U.S. Census Bureau, Housing Vacancies and Homeownership Annual Statistics: 2011

TAXES

State Corporate Income Tax Rates

State	Tax Rate (%)	Income Brackets ($)	Num. of Brackets	Financial Institution Tax Rate (%)[a]	Federal Income Tax Ded.
South Carolina	5.0	Flat rate	1	4.5 (w)	No

Note: Tax rates as of January 1, 2012; (a) Rates listed are the corporate income tax rate applied to financial institutions or excise taxes based on income. Some states have other taxes based upon the value of deposits or shares; (w) South Carolina taxes savings and loans at a 6% rate.
Source: Federation of Tax Administrators, "State Corporate Income Tax Rates, 2012"

State Individual Income Tax Rates

State	Tax Rate (%)	Income Brackets ($)	Num. of Brackets	Personal Exempt. ($)[1] Single	Dependents	Fed. Inc. Tax Ded.
South Carolina (a)	0.0 - 7.0	2,800 - 14,000	6	3,700 (d)	3,700 (d)	No

Note: Tax rates as of January 1, 2012; Local- and county-level taxes are not included; n/a not applicable; (1) Married joint filers generally receive double the single exemption; (a) 17 states have statutory provision for automatically adjusting to the rate of inflation the dollar values of the income tax brackets, standard deductions, and/or personal exemptions. Massachusetts, Michigan, and Nebraska index the personal exemption only. Oregon does not index the income brackets for $125,000 and over. Because the inflation-adjustments for 2012 are not yet available in some cases, the table may report the 2011 amounts; (d) These states use the personal exemption amounts provided in the federal Internal Revenue Code.
Source: Federation of Tax Administrators, "State Individual Income Tax Rates, 2012"

Various State and Local Tax Rates

State	State and Local Sales and Use (%)	State Sales and Use (%)	Gasoline[1] (¢/gal.)	Cigarette[2] ($/pack)	Spirits[3] ($/gal.)	Wine[4] ($/gal.)	Beer[5] ($/gal.)
South Carolina	7.0	6.00	16.8	0.57	5.42 (h)(i)	1.08	0.77

Note: All tax rates as of January 1, 2012 except beer, wine and spirits (September 1, 2011); (1) The American Petroleum Institute has developed a methodology for determining the average tax rate on a gallon of fuel. Rates may include any of the following: excise taxes, environmental fees, storage tank fees, other fees or taxes, general sales tax, and local taxes. In states where gasoline is subject to the general sales tax, or where the fuel tax is based on the average sale price, the average rate determined by API is sensitive to changes in the price of gasoline. States that fully or partially apply general sales taxes to gasoline: CA, CO, GA, IL, IN, MI, NY; (2) The federal excise tax of $1.0066 per pack and local taxes are not included; (3) Rates are those applicable to off-premise sales of 40% alcohol by volume (a.b.v.) distilled spirits in 750ml containers. Local excise taxes are excluded; (4) Rates are those applicable to off-premise sales of 11% a.b.v. non-carbonated wine in 750ml containers; (5) Rates are those applicable to off-premise sales of 4.7% a.b.v. beer in 12 ounce containers; (h) Includes case fees and/or bottle fees which may vary with the size of the container; (i) Includes sales taxes specific to alcoholic beverages.
Source: Tax Foundation, 2012 Facts & Figures: How Does Your State Compare?

State-Local Tax Burdens

Area	Rate (%)	Rank[1]	Per Capita Taxes Paid to Home State ($)	Total State and Local Per Capita Taxes Paid ($)	Per Capita Income ($)
South Carolina	8.1	43	1,845	2,742	33,954
U.S. Average	9.8	-	3,057	4,160	42,539

Note: Figures cover 2009; (1) Rank ranges from 1 to 50 where 1 is highest tax burden
Source: Tax Foundation, State-Local Tax Burdens, All States, 2009

State Business Tax Climate Index Rankings

State	Overall Rank	Corporate Tax Index Rank	Individual Income Tax Index Rank	Sales Tax Index Rank	Unemployment Insurance Tax Index Rank	Property Tax Index Rank
South Carolina	36	10	39	20	38	21

Note: The index is a measure of how each state's tax laws affect economic performance. The lower the rank, the more favorable a state's tax system is for business. States without a given tax are given a ranking of 1.
Source: Tax Foundation, Major Components of the State Business Tax Climate Index, FY 2012

COMMERCIAL UTILITIES

Typical Monthly Electric Bills

Area	Commercial Service ($/month)		Industrial Service ($/month)	
	1,500 kWh	40 kW demand 14,000 kWh	1,000 kW demand 200,000 kWh	50,000 kW demand 15,000,000 kWh
City	n/a	n/a	n/a	n/a
Average[1]	189	1,616	25,197	1,470,813

Note: Based on total rates in effect July 1, 2011; (1) average based on 184 utilities surveyed; n/a not available
Source: Edison Electric Institute, Typical Bills and Average Rates Report, Summer 2011

TRANSPORTATION

Means of Transportation to Work

Area	Car/Truck/Van		Public Transportation			Bicycle	Walked	Other Means	Worked at Home
	Drove Alone	Car-pooled	Bus	Subway	Railroad				
City	68.4	7.5	2.2	0.2	0.0	0.6	4.5	2.2	14.4
MSA[1]	80.8	8.9	0.7	0.1	0.0	0.2	1.5	2.5	5.3
U.S.	76.0	10.2	2.7	1.7	0.5	0.5	2.8	1.3	4.2

Note: Figures are percentages and cover workers 16 years of age and older; (1) Figures cover the Columbia, SC Metropolitan Statistical Area—see Appendix B for areas included
Source: U.S. Census Bureau, 2008-2010 American Community Survey 3-Year Estimates

Travel Time to Work

Area	Less Than 10 Minutes	10 to 19 Minutes	20 to 29 Minutes	30 to 44 Minutes	45 to 59 Minutes	60 to 89 Minutes	90 Minutes or More
City	19.9	45.7	19.7	9.4	2.5	1.4	1.5
MSA[1]	11.9	32.2	24.3	20.9	6.2	2.8	1.6
U.S.	13.9	30.1	20.8	19.8	7.5	5.5	2.5

Note: Figures are percentages and include workers 16 years old and over; (1) Figures cover the Columbia, SC Metropolitan Statistical Area—see Appendix B for areas included
Source: U.S. Census Bureau, 2008-2010 American Community Survey 3-Year Estimates

Travel Time Index

Area	1985	1990	1995	2000	2005	2010
Urban Area[1]	1.03	1.04	1.04	1.06	1.07	1.09
Average[2]	1.11	1.16	1.18	1.21	1.25	1.20

Note: Travel Time Index—the ratio of travel time in the peak period to the travel time at free-flow conditions. A value of 1.30 indicates a 20-minute free-flow trip takes 26 minutes in the peak. Free-flow speeds (60 mph on freeways and 35 mph on principal arterials) are used as the comparison threshold; (1) Covers the Columbia SC urban area; (2) average of 439 urban areas
Source: Texas Transportation Institute, Urban Mobility Report 2011, September 2011

Public Transportation

Agency Name / Mode of Transportation	Vehicles Operated in Maximum Service	Annual Unlinked Passenger Trips ('000)	Annual Passenger Miles ('000)
Central Midlands Regional Transit Authority			
Bus (purchased transportation)	36	1,886.0	9,467.5
Demand Response (purchased transportation)	19	73.3	777.6

Source: Federal Transit Administration, National Transit Database, 2010

Air Transportation

Airport Name and Code / Type of Service	Passenger Airlines[1]	Passenger Enplanements	Freight Carriers[2]	Freight (lbs.)
Columbia Metropolitan (CAE)				
Domestic service (U.S. carriers - 2011)	27	480,713	15	62,129,636
International service (U.S. carriers - 2010)	2	68	2	6,052

Note: (1) Includes all U.S.-based major, minor and commuter airlines that carried at least one passenger during the year; (2) Includes all U.S.-based airlines and freight carriers that transported at least one pound of freight during the year
Source: Bureau of Transportation Statistics, The Intermodal Transportation Database, Air Carriers: T-100 Domestic Market (U.S. Carriers), 2011; Bureau of Transportation Statistics, The Intermodal Transportation Database, Air Carriers: T-100 International Market (U.S. Carriers), 2010

Other Transportation Statistics

Major Highways:	I-20; I-26; I-77
Amtrak Service:	Yes
Major Waterways/Ports:	Congaree River

Source: Amtrak.com; Google Maps

BUSINESSES

Major Business Headquarters

Company Name	Rankings	
	Fortune[1]	Forbes[2]
No companies listed	-	-

Note: (1) Fortune 500—companies that produce a 10-K are ranked 1 to 500 based on 2010 revenue; (2) all private companies with at least $2 billion in annual revenue are ranked 1 to 212; companies listed are headquartered in the city; dashes indicate no ranking
Source: Fortune, "Fortune 500," May 23, 2011; Forbes, "America's Largest Private Companies," November 16, 2011

Minority Business Opportunity

Columbia is home to one company which is on the *Black Enterprise* Bank 20 list (20 largest banks based on total assets, capital, deposits and loans, including mortgage-backed securities for the calendar year): **South Carolina Community Bank** (#18). Only commercial banks or savings and loans that are classified by the Federal Reserve as black institutions and have been fully operational for the previous calendar year were considered. *Black Enterprise, B.E. 100s, 2011*

Minority- and Women-Owned Businesses

Group	All Firms		Firms with Paid Employees			
	Firms	Sales ($000)	Firms	Sales ($000)	Employees	Payroll ($000)
Asian	n/a	n/a	n/a	n/a	n/a	n/a
Black	n/a	n/a	n/a	n/a	n/a	n/a
Hispanic	n/a	n/a	n/a	n/a	n/a	n/a
Women	n/a	n/a	n/a	n/a	n/a	n/a
All Firms	923	265,389	166	239,994	2,543	40,740

Note: Figures cover firms located in the city; minority- and women-owned business are defined as firms in which the corresponding group own 51% or more of the stock or equity of the company; n/a not available
Source: U.S. Census Bureau, 2007 Economic Census, Survey of Business Owners

HOTELS

Hotels/Motels

Area	5 Star		4 Star		3 Star		2 Star		1 Star		Not Rated	
	Num.	Pct.[3]	Num.	Pct.[3]	Num.	Pct.[3]	Num.	Pct.[3]	Num.	Pct.[3]	Num.	Pct.[3]
City[1]	0	0.0	0	0.0	24	21.8	70	63.6	5	4.5	11	10.0
Total[2]	133	0.9	940	6.5	4,569	31.8	7,033	48.9	351	2.4	1,343	9.3

Note: (1) Figures cover Columbia and vicinity; (2) Figures cover all 100 cities in this book; (3) Percentage of hotels which have a given star rating; Star ratings are determined by expedia.com and offer an indication of the general quality of a particular hotel.
Source: expedia.com, April 25, 2012

EVENT SITES

Major Stadiums, Arenas, and Auditoriums

Name	Max. Capacity
Carolina Coliseum	12,803
Williams-Brice Stadium	80,250

Source: Original research

Convention Centers

Name	Overall Space (sq. ft.)	Exhibit Space (sq. ft.)	Meeting Space (sq. ft.)	Meeting Rooms
Columbia Metropolitan Convention Center	142,500	n/a	24,700	n/a

Note: n/a not available
Source: Original research

182 Columbia, South Carolina

Living Environment

COST OF LIVING

Cost of Living Index

Composite Index	Groceries	Housing	Utilities	Trans-portation	Health Care	Misc. Goods/ Services
95.6	104.7	78.7	106.6	104.0	101.2	99.7

Note: U.S. = 100; Figures cover the Columbia SC urban area.
Source: The Council for Community and Economic Research, ACCRA Cost of Living Index, 2011

Grocery Prices

Area[1]	T-Bone Steak ($/pound)	Frying Chicken ($/pound)	Whole Milk ($/half gal.)	Eggs ($/dozen)	Orange Juice ($/64 oz.)	Coffee ($/11.5 oz.)
City[2]	9.94	1.40	2.46	1.63	3.33	4.21
Avg.	9.25	1.18	2.22	1.66	3.19	4.40
Min.	6.70	0.88	1.31	0.95	2.46	2.94
Max.	14.30	2.16	3.50	3.18	4.75	6.83

Note: (1) Values for the local area are compared with the average, minimum and maximum values for all 335 areas in the Cost of Living Index; (2) Figures cover the Columbia SC urban area; **T-Bone Steak** (price per pound); **Frying Chicken** (price per pound, whole fryer); **Whole Milk** (half gallon carton); **Eggs** (price per dozen, Grade A, large); **Orange Juice** (64 oz. Tropicana or Florida Natural); **Coffee** (11.5 oz. can, vacuum-packed, Maxwell House, Hills Bros, or Folgers).
Source: The Council for Community and Economic Research, ACCRA Cost of Living Index, 2011

Housing and Utility Costs

Area[1]	New Home Price ($)	Apartment Rent ($/month)	All Electric ($/month)	Part Electric ($/month)	Other Energy ($/month)	Telephone ($/month)
City[2]	211,375	793	-	95.48	83.90	28.01
Avg.	285,990	839	163.23	89.00	77.52	26.92
Min.	188,005	460	125.58	45.39	33.89	17.98
Max.	1,197,028	3,244	339.16	181.97	348.69	40.01

Note: (1) Values for the local area are compared with the average, minimum and maximum values for all 335 areas in the Cost of Living Index; (2) Figures cover the Columbia SC urban area; **New Home Price** (2,400 sf living area, 8,000 sf lot, in urban area with full utilities); **Apartment Rent** (950 sf 2 bedroom/1.5 or 2 bath, unfurnished, excluding all utilities except water); **All Electric** (average monthly cost for an all-electric home); **Part Electric** (average monthly cost for a part-electric home); **Other Energy** (average monthly cost for natural gas, fuel oil, coal, wood, and any other forms of energy except electricity); **Telephone** (price includes basic monthly rate for a private residential line plus additional local usage charges incurred by a family of four).
Source: The Council for Community and Economic Research, ACCRA Cost of Living Index, 2011

Health Care, Transportation, and Other Costs

Area[1]	Doctor ($/visit)	Dentist ($/visit)	Optometrist ($/visit)	Gasoline ($/gallon)	Beauty Salon ($/visit)	Men's Shirt ($)
City[2]	104.50	83.33	93.94	3.32	29.53	24.13
Avg.	93.88	81.72	90.54	3.48	32.65	25.06
Min.	60.00	55.33	53.66	3.18	19.78	13.44
Max.	154.98	145.97	183.72	4.31	63.21	46.00

Note: (1) Values for the local area are compared with the average, minimum and maximum values for all 335 areas in the Cost of Living Index; (2) Figures cover the Columbia SC urban area; **Doctor** (general practitioners routine exam of an established patient); **Dentist** (adult teeth cleaning and periodic oral examination); **Optometrist** (full vision eye exam for established adult patient); **Gasoline** (one gallon regular unleaded, national brand, including all taxes, cash price at self-service pump if available); **Beauty Salon** (woman's shampoo, trim, and blow-dry); **Men's Shirt** (cotton/polyester dress shirt, pinpoint weave, long sleeves).
Source: The Council for Community and Economic Research, ACCRA Cost of Living Index, 2011

HOUSING

House Price Index (HPI)

Area	National Ranking[2]	Quarterly Change (%)	One-Year Change (%)	Five-Year Change (%)
MSA[1]	192	-0.60	-3.60	-3.40
U.S.[3]	-	-0.10	-2.43	-19.16

Note: The HPI is a weighted repeat sales index. It measures average price changes in repeat sales or refinancings on the same properties. This information is obtained by reviewing repeat mortgage transactions on single-family properties whose mortgages have been purchased or securitized by Fannie Mae or Freddie Mac in January 1975; (1) Metropolitan/Micropolitan Statistical Area—see Appendix B for areas included; (2) Rankings are based on annual percentage change for all metro areas containing at least 15,000 transactions over the last 10 years and ranges from 1 to 306; (3) figures based on a weighted average of Census Division estimates using a purchase only index; all figures are for the period ending December 31, 2011
Source: Federal Housing Finance Agency, House Price Index, February 23, 2012

House Price Valuations

Area	Q4 2005 Price ($000)	Q4 2005 Over-valuation	Q4 2006 Price ($000)	Q4 2006 Over-valuation	Q4 2007 Price ($000)	Q4 2007 Over-valuation	Q4 2008 Price ($000)	Q4 2008 Over-valuation	Q4 2009 Price ($000)	Q4 2009 Over-valuation
MSA[1]	112.3	-2.2	116.9	-3.3	118.7	-5.5	115.9	-9.9	119.0	-9.5

Note: Figures show the percentage of over- or under-valuation of single family homes relative to statistically normal house values (e.g. a value of 23.6 indicates that house values are 23.6% overvalued). Statistically normal house values are based on house prices, interest rates, household incomes, population densities, and any historical premiums or discounts metropolitan areas have exhibited over time; (1) Figures cover the Columbia, SC - see Appendix B for areas included
Source: Global Insight/PNC Financial Services Group, House Prices in America: 4th Quarter 2009 Update

Median Single-Family Home Prices

Area	2009	2010	2011p	Percent Change 2010 to 2011
MSA[1]	139.2	142.6	140.6	-1.4
U.S. Average	172.1	173.1	166.2	-4.0

Note: Figures are median sales prices of existing single-family homes in thousands of dollars; (p) preliminary; n/a not available; (1) Metropolitan Statistical Area—see Appendix B for areas included
Source: National Association of Realtors, Median Sales Price of Existing Single-Family Homes for Metropolitan Areas, 4th Quarter 2011

Affordability Index of Existing Single-Family Homes

Area	2009	2010	2011p	Percent Change 2010 to 2011
MSA[1]	119.5	122.5	130.5	6.5

Note: The housing affordability index measures whether or not a typical family could qualify for a mortgage loan on a typical home. The higher the index, the greater the household purchasing power. An index of 100 is defined as the point where a median-income household has exactly enough income to qualify for the purchase of a median-priced existing single-family home, assuming a 20 percent downpayment and 25 percent of gross income devoted to mortgage principal and interest payments; (p) preliminary; n/a not available; (1) Metropolitan Statistical Area—see Appendix B for areas included
Source: National Association of Realtors, Affordability Index of Existing Single-Family Homes, 2011

Median Apartment Condo-Coop Home Prices

Area	2009	2010	2011p	Percent Change 2010 to 2011
MSA[1]	n/a	n/a	n/a	n/a
U.S. Average	175.6	171.7	165.1	-3.8

Note: Figures are median sales prices of existing apartment condo-coop homes in thousands of dollars; (p) preliminary; n/a not available; (1) Metropolitan Statistical Area—see Appendix B for areas included
Source: National Association of Realtors, Median Sales Price of Existing Apartment Condo-Coop Homes for Metropolitan Areas, 4th Quarter 2011

Year Housing Structure Built

Area	2005 or Later	2000 -2004	1990 -1999	1980 -1989	1970 -1979	1960 -1969	1950 -1959	Before 1950	Median Year
City	5.9	8.7	10.2	11.4	11.6	14.2	17.1	21.0	1968
MSA[1]	8.1	11.8	19.5	15.4	17.6	11.1	8.4	8.1	1983
U.S.	5.0	8.6	14.0	14.1	16.3	11.3	11.2	19.6	1975

Note: Figures are percentages except for Median Year; (1) Figures cover the Columbia, SC Metropolitan Statistical Area—see Appendix B for areas included
Source: U.S. Census Bureau, 2008-2010 American Community Survey 3-Year Estimates

HEALTH

Health Risk Data

Category	MSA[1] (%)	U.S. (%)
Adults who have been told they have high blood pressure[2]	29.2	28.7
Adults who have been told they have high blood cholesterol[2]	38.5	37.5
Adults who have been told they have diabetes[3]	9.4	8.7
Adults who have been told they have arthritis[2]	28.8	26.0
Adults who have been told they currently have asthma	7.5	9.1
Adults who are current smokers	21.8	17.3
Adults who are heavy drinkers[4]	5.1	5.0
Adults who are binge drinkers[5]	14.4	15.1
Adults who are overweight (BMI 25.0 - 29.9)	36.1	36.2
Adults who are obese (BMI 30.0 - 99.8)	31.0	27.5
Adults who participated in any physical activities in the past month	72.3	76.1
Adults 50+ who have ever had a sigmoidoscopy or colonoscopy	66.0	65.2
Women aged 40+ who have had a mammogram within the past two years	77.3	75.2
Men aged 40+ who have had a PSA test within the past two years	64.9	53.2
Adults aged 65+ who have had flu shot within the past year	65.9	67.5
Adults aged 18–64 who have any kind of health care coverage	77.5	82.2

Note: Data as of 2010 unless otherwise noted; (1) Figures cover the Columbia, SC Metropolitan Statistical Area—see Appendix B for areas included; (2) Data as of 2009; (3) Figures do not include pregnancy-related, borderline, or pre-diabetes; (4) Heavy drinkers are classified as males having more than two drinks per day or females having more than one drink per day; (5) Binge drinkers are classified as males having five or more drinks on one occasion or females having four or more drinks on one occasion
Source: Centers for Disease Control and Prevention, Behaviorial Risk Factor Surveillance System, SMART: Selected Metropolitan/Micropolitan Area Risk Trends, 2009, 2010

Mortality Rates for the Top 10 Causes of Death in the U.S.

ICD-10[a] Sub-Chapter	ICD-10[a] Code	Age-Adjusted Mortality Rate[1] per 100,000 population County[2]	U.S.
Malignant neoplasms	C00-C97	187.6	175.6
Ischaemic heart diseases	I20-I25	133.4	121.6
Other forms of heart disease	I30-I51	55.2	48.6
Chronic lower respiratory diseases	J40-J47	31.0	42.3
Cerebrovascular diseases	I60-I69	44.9	40.6
Organic, including symptomatic, mental disorders	F01-F09	48.0	26.7
Other degenerative diseases of the nervous system	G30-G31	38.0	24.7
Other external causes of accidental injury	W00-X59	22.4	24.4
Diabetes mellitus	E10-E14	24.2	21.7
Hypertensive diseases	I10-I15	11.6	18.2

Note: (a) ICD-10 = International Classification of Diseases 10th Revision; (1) Mortality rates are a three year average covering 2007-2009; (2) Figures cover Richland County
Source: Centers for Disease Control and Prevention, National Center for Health Statistics. Underlying Cause of Death 1999-2009 on CDC WONDER Online Database, released 2012. Data for year 2009 are compiled from the Multiple Cause of Death File 2009, Series 20 No. 2O, 2012, Data for year 2008 are compiled from the Multiple Cause of Death File 2008, Series 20 No. 2N, 2011, Data for year 2007 are compiled from Multiple Cause of Death File 2007, Series 20 No. 2M, 2010.

Mortality Rates for Selected Causes of Death

ICD-10[a] Sub-Chapter	ICD-10[a] Code	Age-Adjusted Mortality Rate[1] per 100,000 population	
		County[2]	U.S.
Assault	X85-Y09	8.3	5.7
Human immunodeficiency virus (HIV) disease	B20-B24	9.7	3.3
Influenza and pneumonia	J09-J18	12.0	16.4
Intentional self-harm	X60-X84	10.2	11.5
Malnutrition	E40-E46	*Unreliable	0.8
Obesity and other hyperalimentation	E65-E68	*Unreliable	1.6
Transport accidents	V01-V99	15.0	13.7
Viral hepatitis	B15-B19	2.7	2.2

Note: (a) ICD-10 = International Classification of Diseases 10th Revision; (1) Mortality rates are a three year average covering 2007-2009; (2) Figures cover Richland County; (*) Unreliable data as per CDC
Source: Centers for Disease Control and Prevention, National Center for Health Statistics. Underlying Cause of Death 1999-2009 on CDC WONDER Online Database, released 2012. Data for year 2009 are compiled from the Multiple Cause of Death File 2009, Series 20 No. 2O, 2012, Data for year 2008 are compiled from the Multiple Cause of Death File 2008, Series 20 No. 2N, 2011, Data for year 2007 are compiled from Multiple Cause of Death File 2007, Series 20 No. 2M, 2010.

Distribution of Physicians and Dentists

Area[1]	Dentists[2]	D.O.[3]	M.D.[4]				
			Total	Family/ General Practice	Pediatrics	Medical Specialties	Surgical Specialties
Local (number)	178	21	958	106	73	361	231
Local (rate[5])	4.9	0.6	26.1	2.9	2.0	9.9	6.3
U.S. (rate[5])	4.5	1.9	18.3	2.5	1.4	6.8	4.1

Note: Data as of 2008 unless noted; (1) Local data covers Richland County; (2) Data as of 2007; (3) Doctor of Osteopathic Medicine; (4) Includes active, non-federal, patient-care, office-based Doctors of Medicine; (5) rate per 10,000 population
Source: Area Resource File (ARF). 2009-2010 Release. U.S. Department of Health and Human Services, Health Resources and Services Administration, Bureau of Health Professions, Rockville, MD, August 2010

EDUCATION

Public School District Statistics

District Name	Schls	Pupils	Pupil/ Teacher Ratio	Minority Pupils[1] (%)	Free Lunch Eligible[2] (%)	IEP[3] (%)
Richland 01	50	24,460	13.4	81.8	59.9	14.7
Richland 02	27	24,949	14.9	70.0	31.4	11.4
Sc Public Charter School District	8	6,245	48.4	28.5	32.5	7.8

Note: Table includes school districts with 2,000 or more students; (1) Percentage of students that are not non-Hispanic white; (2) Percentage of students that are eligible for the free lunch program; (3) Percentage of students that have an Individualized Education Program.
Source: U.S. Department of Education, National Center for Education Statistics, Common Core of Data, Local Education Agency (School District) Universe Survey: School Year 2009-2010; U.S. Department of Education, National Center for Education Statistics, Common Core of Data, Public Elementary/Secondary School Universe Survey: School Year 2009-2010

Highest Level of Education

Area	Less than H.S.	H.S. Diploma	Some College, No Deg.	Associate Degree	Bachelors Degree	Masters Degree	Profess. School Degree	Doctorate Degree
City	14.6	20.7	20.1	6.1	22.1	10.7	3.7	2.0
MSA[1]	12.3	26.8	22.4	8.5	18.8	8.0	1.8	1.3
U.S.	14.7	28.4	21.3	7.6	17.6	7.2	1.9	1.2

Note: Figures cover persons age 25 and over; (1) Figures cover the Columbia, SC Metropolitan Statistical Area—see Appendix B for areas included
Source: U.S. Census Bureau, 2008-2010 American Community Survey 3-Year Estimates

Educational Attainment by Race

Area	High School Graduate or Higher (%)					Bachelor's Degree or Higher (%)				
	Total	White	Black	Asian	Hisp.[2]	Total	White	Black	Asian	Hisp.[2]
City	85.4	94.9	74.1	n/a	90.1	38.5	57.7	14.9	n/a	23.2
MSA[1]	87.7	90.7	82.9	85.8	62.2	30.0	34.9	19.3	59.2	16.0
U.S.	85.3	87.5	81.4	85.5	61.6	28.0	29.3	17.8	50.2	13.0

Note: Figures shown cover persons 25 years old and over; (1) Figures cover the Columbia, SC Metropolitan
Statistical Area—see Appendix B for areas included; (2) People of Hispanic origin can be of any race
Source: U.S. Census Bureau, 2008-2010 American Community Survey 3-Year Estimates

School Enrollment by Grade and Control

Area	Preschool (%)		Kindergarten (%)		Grades 1 - 4 (%)		Grades 5 - 8 (%)		Grades 9 - 12 (%)	
	Public	Private	Public	Private	Public	Private	Public	Private	Public	Private
City	54.2	45.8	82.9	17.1	84.7	15.3	85.0	15.0	92.6	7.4
MSA[1]	52.7	47.3	86.9	13.1	90.4	9.6	91.5	8.5	92.7	7.3
U.S.	55.4	44.6	87.1	12.9	89.4	10.6	89.5	10.5	90.4	9.6

Note: Figures shown cover persons 3 years old and over; (1) Figures cover the Columbia, SC Metropolitan
Statistical Area—see Appendix B for areas included
Source: U.S. Census Bureau, 2008-2010 American Community Survey 3-Year Estimates

Average Salaries of Public School Classroom Teachers

Area	2010-11		2011-12		Percent Change 2010-11 to 2011-12	Percent Change 2001-02 to 2011-12
	Dollars	Rank[1]	Dollars	Rank[1]		
South Carolina	47,050	38	48,176	37	2.39	20.70
U.S. Average	55,623	-	56,643	-	1.83	26.8

Note: (1) State rank ranges from 1 to 51 where 1 indicates highest salary.
Source: National Education Association, Rankings & Estimates: Rankings of the States 2011
and Estimates of School Statistics 2012, December 2011

Higher Education

Four-Year Colleges			Two-Year Colleges			Medical Schools[1]	Law Schools[2]	Voc/ Tech[3]
Public	Private Non-profit	Private For-profit	Public	Private Non-profit	Private For-profit			
1	6	3	0	0	2	1	1	8

Note: Figures cover institutions located within the city limits and include main campuses only; (1) includes
schools accredited by the Liaison Committee on Medical Education and the American Osteopathic Association's
Commission on Osteopathic College Accreditation; (2) includes American Bar Association-accredited law
schools; (3) includes all schools with programs that are less than 2 years.
Source: National Center for Education Statistics, Integrated Postsecondary Education System (IPEDS) Peer
Analysis System, 2011-12; Association of American Medical Colleges, Member List, April 23, 2012; American
Osteopathic Association, Member List, April 23, 2012; Law School Admission Council, Official Guide to
ABA-Approved Law Schools Online, April 23, 2012

According to *U.S. News & World Report*, the Columbia, SC is home to one of the best
national universities in the U.S.: **University of South Carolina** (#111). The indicators used
to capture academic quality fall into a number of categories: assessment by administrators at
peer institutions; retention of students; faculty resources; student selectivity; financial
resources; alumni giving; high school counselor ratings of colleges; and graduation rate.*U.S.
News & World Report, "America's Best Colleges 2012"*

According to *Forbes,* the Columbia, SC is home to one of the best business schools in the
U.S.: **South Carolina (Moore)** (#70). The rankings are based on the return on investment
that graduates of the Class of 2006 received (median salary five years after graduation).
Forbes, "Best Business Schools," August 3, 2011

**PRESIDENTIAL
ELECTION**

2008 Presidential Election Results

Area	Obama	McCain	Nader	Other
Richland County	64.0	35.1	0.2	0.7
U.S.	52.9	45.6	0.6	0.9

Note: Results are percentages and may not add to 100% due to rounding
Source: Dave Leip's Atlas of U.S. Presidential Elections, www.uselectionatlas.org

EMPLOYERS

Major Employers

Company Name	Industry
Amfinity Business Solution	Employee leasing service
Blue Cross & Blue Shield of SC	Hospital and medical service plans
Colonial Life & Accident Insurance Company	Accident and health insurance
County of Richland	Executive offices
Johnson Food Services	Eating places
Lexington County Health Services District	General medical and surgical hospitals
Lexington Medical Center	General medical and surgical hospitals
Nelson Mullins Riley & Scarborough	Finance, taxation, and monetary policy
Palmetto GBA	Hospital and medical service plans
Palmetto Health Alliance	General medical and surgical hospitals
Palmetto-Richland Memorial Hospital	Hospital, med school affiliated with nursing & residency
Pgba	Individual and family services
SC Dept of Health & Env Control	Administration of public health programs
South Carolina Department of Mental Health	Mental health agency administration, government
South Carolina Dept of Trans	Regulation, administration of transportation
The Army, United States Department of	Army
United States Department of the Army	General medical and surgical hospitals
University of South Carolina	Colleges and universities
Veterans Health Administration	Administration of veterans' affairs

Note: Companies shown are located within the Columbia, SC metropolitan area.
Source: Hoovers.com, data extracted April 25 2012

Best Companies to Work For

Palmetto Health, headquartered in Columbia, is among the "100 Best Places to Work in IT." To qualify, companies, both public and private, had to have a minimum of 50 IT employees and were selected based on average salary and bonus increases, the percentage of IT staffers promoted, IT staff turnover rates, training and development programs, and the percentage of women and minorities in IT staff and management positions. In addition, *Computerworld* looked at retention efforts, programs for recognizing and rewarding outstanding performances, and benefits such as flextime, elder care and child care, and reimbursement for college tuition and the cost of pursuing technology certifications. *Computerworld, "100 Best Places to Work in IT 2011"*

PUBLIC SAFETY

Crime Rate

Area	All Crimes	Violent Crimes				Property Crimes		
		Murder	Forcible Rape	Robbery	Aggrav. Assault	Burglary	Larceny -Theft	Motor Vehicle Theft
City	7,053.0	12.3	56.7	264.4	667.4	1,301.9	4,236.1	514.2
Suburbs[1]	4,124.6	3.8	32.0	91.6	530.2	896.7	2,270.3	299.9
Metro[2]	4,630.2	5.3	36.3	121.5	553.9	966.7	2,609.8	336.9
U.S.	3,345.5	4.8	27.5	119.1	252.3	699.6	2,003.5	238.8

Note: Figures are crimes per 100,000 population; (1) All areas within the metro area that are located outside the city limits; (2) Metropolitan Statistical Area—see Appendix B for areas included
Source: FBI Uniform Crime Reports, 2010

Hate Crimes

Area	Number of Quarters Reported	Bias Motivation				
		Race	Religion	Sexual Orientation	Ethnicity	Disability
City	4	4	0	4	0	0

Source: Federal Bureau of Investigation, Hate Crime Statistics 2010

Identity Theft Consumer Complaints

Area	Complaints	Complaints per 100,000 Population	Rank[2]
MSA[1]	624	87.1	134
U.S.	279,156	90.4	-

Note: (1) Metropolitan Statistical Area—see Appendix B for areas included; (2) Rank ranges from 1 to 384 where 1 indicates greatest number of identity theft complaints per 100,000 population
Source: Federal Trade Commission, Consumer Sentinel Network Data Book for January–December 2011

Fraud and Other Consumer Complaints

Area	Complaints	Complaints per 100,000 Population	Rank[2]
MSA[1]	3,505	489.5	168
U.S.	1,533,924	496.8	-

Note: (1) Metropolitan Statistical Area—see Appendix B for areas included; (2) Rank ranges from 1 to 384 where 1 indicates greatest number of fraud and other complaints per 100,000 population
Source: Federal Trade Commission, Consumer Sentinel Network Data Book for January–December 2011

RECREATION

Culture

Dance[1]	Theatre[1]	Instrumental Music[1]	Vocal Music[1]	Series/ Festivals	Museums	Zoos and Aquariums[2]
8	2	0	0	3	11	1

Note: (1) Number of professional performing groups; (2) AZA-accredited
Source: The Grey House Performing Arts Directory, 2011-2012; Official Museum Directory, 2011; American Association of Museums, AAM Member Museums, April 2012; Association of Zoos & Aquariums, AZA Member Zoos & Aquariums, April 2012

Professional Sports Teams

Team Name	League
No teams are located in the metro area	

Source: Original research

CLIMATE

Average and Extreme Temperatures

Temperature	Jan	Feb	Mar	Apr	May	Jun	Jul	Aug	Sep	Oct	Nov	Dec	Yr.
Extreme High (°F)	84	84	91	94	101	107	107	107	101	101	90	83	107
Average High (°F)	56	60	67	77	84	90	92	91	85	77	67	59	75
Average Temp. (°F)	45	48	55	64	72	78	82	80	75	64	54	47	64
Average Low (°F)	33	35	42	50	59	66	70	69	64	51	41	35	51
Extreme Low (°F)	-1	5	4	26	34	44	54	53	40	23	12	4	-1

Note: Figures cover the years 1948-1990
Source: National Climatic Data Center, International Station Meteorological Climate Summary, 9/96

Average Precipitation/Snowfall/Humidity

Precip./Humidity	Jan	Feb	Mar	Apr	May	Jun	Jul	Aug	Sep	Oct	Nov	Dec	Yr.
Avg. Precip. (in.)	4.0	4.0	4.7	3.4	3.6	4.2	5.5	5.9	4.0	2.9	2.7	3.4	48.3
Avg. Snowfall (in.)	1	1	Tr	0	0	0	0	0	0	0	Tr	Tr	2
Avg. Rel. Hum. 7am (%)	83	83	84	82	84	85	88	91	91	90	88	84	86
Avg. Rel. Hum. 4pm (%)	51	47	44	41	46	50	54	56	54	49	48	51	49

Note: Figures cover the years 1948-1990; Tr = Trace amounts (<0.05 in. of rain; <0.5 in. of snow)
Source: National Climatic Data Center, International Station Meteorological Climate Summary, 9/96

Weather Conditions

Temperature			Daytime Sky			Precipitation		
10°F & below	32°F & below	90°F & above	Clear	Partly cloudy	Cloudy	0.01 inch or more precip.	0.1 inch or more snow/ice	Thunder-storms
<1	58	77	97	149	119	110	1	53

Note: Figures are average number of days per year and cover the years 1948-1990
Source: National Climatic Data Center, International Station Meteorological Climate Summary, 9/96

HAZARDOUS WASTE

Superfund Sites

Columbia has one hazardous waste site on the EPA's Superfund Final National Priorities List: **SCRDI Bluff Road**. *U.S. Environmental Protection Agency, Final National Priorities List, April 17, 2012*

AIR & WATER QUALITY

Air Quality Index

Area	Percent of Days when Air Quality was...[2]					AQI Statistics[2]	
	Good	Moderate	Unhealthy for Sensitive Groups	Unhealthy	Very Unhealthy	Maximum	Median
Area[1]	66.8	30.7	2.5	0.0	0.0	124	43

Note: Air Quality Index (AQI) is an index for reporting daily air quality. EPA calculates the AQI for five major air pollutants regulated by the Clean Air Act: ground-level ozone, particle pollution (aka particulate matter), carbon monoxide, sulfur dioxide, and nitrogen dioxide. The AQI runs from 0 to 500. The higher the AQI value, the greater the level of air pollution and the greater the health concern. There are six AQI categories: "Good" AQI is between 0 and 50. Air quality is considered satisfactory; "Moderate" AQI is between 51 and 100. Air quality is acceptable; "Unhealthy for Sensitive Groups" When AQI values are between 101 and 150, members of sensitive groups may experience health effects; "Unhealthy" When AQI values are between 151 and 200 everyone may begin to experience health effects; "Very Unhealthy" AQI values between 201 and 300 trigger a health alert; "Hazardous" AQI values over 300 trigger warnings of emergency conditions (not shown); (1) Data covers Richland County; (2) Based on 365 days with AQI data in 2011.
Source: U.S. Environmental Protection Agency, AirData Report, 2011

Air Quality Index Pollutants

Area	Percent of Days when AQI Pollutant was...[2]					
	Carbon Monoxide	Nitrogen Dioxide	Ozone	Sulfur Dioxide	Particulate Matter 2.5	Particulate Matter 10
Area[1]	0.0	3.3	56.4	0.0	40.3	0.0

Note: The Air Quality Index (AQI) is an index for reporting daily air quality. EPA calculates the AQI for five major air pollutants regulated by the Clean Air Act: ground-level ozone, particle pollution (also known as particulate matter), carbon monoxide, sulfur dioxide, and nitrogen dioxide. The AQI runs from 0 to 500. The higher the AQI value, the greater the level of air pollution and the greater the health concern; (1) Data covers Richland County; (2) Based on 365 days with AQI data in 2011.
Source: U.S. Environmental Protection Agency, AirData Report, 2011

Air Quality Index Trends

Area	Trend Sites (days)								All Sites (days)
	2003	2004	2005	2006	2007	2008	2009	2010	2010
MSA[1]	22	24	29	22	21	14	3	9	9

Note: Figures are the number of days the AQI value exceeded 100 in a given year. An AQI value greater than 100 indicates that air quality would have been in the unhealthful range on that day. Data from exceptional events are included. These counts are presented in two ways. First, the counts are based on sites having an adequate record of monitoring data during the trend period (trend sites). These counts represent the relative change in the number of days with AQI values greater than 100. In the last column, the counts are based on all sites with data in the most recent year (because it is possible for a site to have data in the most recent year but not enough data to be a trend site); (1) Data covers the Columbia, SC—see Appendix B for areas included
Source: U.S. Environmental Protection Agency, Air Quality Index Information, "Number of Days with Air Quality Index Values Greater than 100 at Trend Sites, 2000-2010, and at All Sites in 2010"

Maximum Air Pollutant Concentrations: Particulate Matter, Ozone, CO and Lead

	Particulate Matter 10 (ug/m³)	Particulate Matter 2.5 Wtd AM (ug/m³)	Particulate Matter 2.5 24-Hr (ug/m³)	Ozone (ppm)	Carbon Monoxide (ppm)	Lead (ug/m³)
MSA[1] Level	76	11.6	24	0.072	n/a	0
NAAQS[2]	150	15	35	0.075	9	0.15
Met NAAQS[2]	Yes	Yes	Yes	Yes	n/a	Yes

Note: Data from exceptional events are not included; (1) Data covers the Columbia, SC—see Appendix B for areas included; (2) National Ambient Air Quality Standards; ppm = parts per million; ug/m³ = micrograms per cubic meter; n/a not available
Concentrations: Particulate Matter 10 (coarse particulate)—highest second maximum 24-hour concentration; Particulate Matter 2.5 Wtd AM (fine particulate)—highest weighted annual mean concentration; Particulate Matter 2.5 24-Hour (fine particulate)—highest 98th percentile 24-hour concentration; Ozone—highest fourth daily maximum 8-hour concentration; Carbon Monoxide—highest second maximum non-overlapping 8-hour concentration; Lead—maximum running 3-month average
Source: U.S. Environmental Protection Agency, CBSA Factbook 2010, Air Quality Statistics by City, 2010

Maximum Air Pollutant Concentrations: Nitrogen Dioxide and Sulfur Dioxide

	Nitrogen Dioxide AM (ppb)	Nitrogen Dioxide 1-Hr (ppb)	Sulfur Dioxide AM (ppb)	Sulfur Dioxide 1-Hr (ppb)	Sulfur Dioxide 24-Hr (ppb)
MSA[1] Level	5.345	n/a	1.974	85	12
NAAQS[2]	53	100	30	75	140
Met NAAQS[2]	Yes	n/a	Yes	No	Yes

Note: Data from exceptional events are not included; (1) Data covers the Columbia, SC—see Appendix B for areas included; (2) National Ambient Air Quality Standards; ppb = parts per billion; n/a not available
Concentrations: Nitrogen Dioxide AM—highest arithmetic mean concentration; Nitrogen Dioxide 1-Hr—highest 98th percentile 1-hour daily maximum concentration; Sulfur Dioxide AM—highest annual mean concentration; Sulfur Dioxide 1-Hr—highest 99th percentile 1-hour daily maximum concentration; Sulfur Dioxide 24-Hr—highest second maximum 24-hour concentration
Source: U.S. Environmental Protection Agency, CBSA Factbook 2010, Air Quality Statistics by City, 2010

Drinking Water

Water System Name	Pop. Served	Primary Water Source Type	Violations[1] Health Based	Violations[1] Monitoring/ Reporting
City of Columbia	301,500	Surface	0	0

Note: (1) Based on violation data from January 1, 2011 to December 31, 2011 (includes unresolved violations from earlier years)
Source: U.S. Environmental Protection Agency, Office of Ground Water and Drinking Water, Safe Drinking Water Information System (based on data extracted April 18, 2012)

Dallas, Texas

Background

Dallas is one of those cities that offer everything. Founded in 1841 by Tennessee lawyer and trader, John Neely Bryan, Dallas has come to symbolize in modern times all that is big, exciting, and affluent. The city itself is home to 15 billionaires, placing it ninth worldwide among cities with the most billionaires. When combined with the eight billionaires who live in Dallas's neighboring city of Fort Worth, the area has one of the greatest concentrations of billionaires in the world.

Originally one of the largest markets for cotton in the U.S., Dallas moved on to become one of the largest markets for oil in the country. In the 1930s, oil was struck on the eastern fields of Texas. As a result, oil companies were founded and millionaires were made. The face we now associate with Dallas and the state of Texas had emerged.

Today, oil still plays a dominant role in the Dallas economy. Outside of Alaska, Texas holds most of the U.S. oil reserves. For that reason, many oil companies choose to headquarter in the silver skyscrapers of Dallas.

In addition to employment opportunities in the oil industry, the Dallas branch of the Federal Reserve Bank, and a host of other banks and investment firms clustering around the Federal Reserve hub employ thousands. Other opportunities are offered in the aircraft, advertising, motion picture, and publishing industries.

Major employers in the Dallas area include American Airlines (Dallas-Fort Worth Airport); Lockheed Martin (in nearby Fort Worth); University of North Texas in Denton; Parkland Memorial Hospital; and Baylor University Medical center. Vought Aircraft Industries, a major supplier of aircraft components to Boeing, Sikorsky and other aircraft manufacturers, continues to expand its local operations. The city is sometimes referred to as Texas's "Silicon Prairie" because of a high concentration of telecommunications companies including Texas Instruments and regional offices for Alcatel, Ericsson, Fujitsu, MCI, Nokia, Rockwell, Sprint, and Verizon, as well as the national offices of CompUSA and Canadian Nortel. AT&T relocated its headquarters from San Antonio Texas to downtown Dallas in 2008.

The Dallas Convention Center, with more than two million square feet of space, is the largest convention center in Texas with more than 1 million square feet of exhibit area, including nearly 800,000 square feet of same level, contiguous prime exhibit space with more than 3.8 million people attending more than 3,600 conventions and spending more than $4.2 billion annually.

Dallas also offers a busy cultural calendar. A host of independent theater groups is sponsored by Southern Methodist University. The Museum of Art houses an excellent collection of modern art, especially American paintings. The Winspear Opera House, along with 3 other venues that make up the AT&T Performing Arts Center was dedicated in 2009. The Dallas Opera has showcased Maria Callas, Joan Sutherland, and Monserrat Caballe. The city also contains many historical districts such as the Swiss Avenue District, and elegant buildings such as the City Hall Building designed by I.M. Pei. The most notable event held in Dallas is the State Fair of Texas, which has been held annually at Fair Park since 1886. The fair is a massive event for the state of Texas and brings an estimated $350 million to the city's economy annually.

The area's high concentration of wealth undoubtedly contributes to Dallas's wide array of shopping centers and high-end boutiques. Downtown Dallas is home to many cafes, restaurants and clubs. The city's centrally located "Arts District" is appropriately named for the independent theaters and art galleries located in the neighborhood. While northern districts of the city and the central downtown have seen much urban revival in the last 30 years, neighborhoods south of downtown have not experienced the same growth.

Colleges and universities in the Dallas area include Southern Methodist University, University of Dallas, and University of Texas at Dallas. In 2006, University of North Texas opened a branch in the southern part of the city, in part, to help accelerate development south of downtown Dallas.

The city maintains around 21,000 acres of park land, with over 400 parks.

The climate of Dallas is generally temperate. Occasional periods of extreme cold are short-lived, and extremely high temperatures that sometimes occur in summer usually do not last for extended periods.

Rankings

General Rankings

- *Men's Health Living* ranked 100 U.S. cities in terms of quality of life. Dallas was ranked #97 and received a grade of F. Criteria: number of fitness facilities; air quality; number of physicians; male/female ratio; education levels; household income; cost of living. *Men's Health Living, Spring 2008*

- Dallas was selected as one of America's best cities by *Bloomberg Businessweek*. The city ranked #42 out of 50. Criteria: number of restaurants, bars and museums per capita; number of colleges, libraries, and professional sports teams; income, poverty, unemployment, crime, and foreclosure rates; percent of population with bachelor's degrees; public school performance; park acres per capita; air quality. *BusinessWeek, "America's 50 Best Cities," September 20, 2011*

- Dallas appeared on RelocateAmerica's list of best places to live in America. The annual "Top 100 Places to Live" list recognizes the top communities as nominated by their residents & local businesses. RelocateAmerica's Research Group determines the list based on review of various data gathered for economic, employment, housing, education, industry, opportunity, environment and recreation along with feedback from area leaders and residents. *RelocateAmerica.com, "Top 100 Places to Live for 2011"*

- Dallas was selected as one of "America's Top 10 Places to Live" by *RelocateAmerica.com*. The city ranked #5. Criteria: real estate and housing; economic health; recreation; safety; input from local residents, business and community leaders. *RelocateAmerica.com, "Top 10 Places to Live for 2011"*

- Dallas was identified as one of the top places to live in the U.S. by Harris Interactive. The city ranked #4 out of 15. Criteria: 2,463 adults (age 18 and over) were polled and asked "if you could live in or near any city in the country except the one you live in or nearest to now, which city would you choose?" The poll was conducted online within the U.S. between September 14 and 20, 2010. *Harris Interactive, November 9, 2011*

Business/Finance Rankings

- Dallas was identified as one of the 20 strongest-performing metro areas during the recession and recovery from trough quarter through the third quarter of 2011. Criteria: percent change in employment; percentage point change in unemployment rate; percent change in gross metropolitan product; percent change in House Price Index. *Brookings Institution, MetroMonitor: Tracking Economic Recession and Recovery in America's 100 Largest Metropolitan Areas, December 2011*

- The Dallas metro area was identified as one of 10 "Cities Where the Recession is Easing." The metro area was ranked #3. Criteria: job growth; goods produced; home sale prices; unemployment rates. *Forbes.com, "Cities Where the Recession is Easing," March 3, 2010*

- The Dallas metro area was identified as one of five places with the worst wage growth in America. The area ranked #4. Criteria: private-sector wage growth between the 4th quarter of 2010 and the 4th quarter of 2011. *PayScale, "Five Worst Cities for Wage Growth," January 12, 2012*

- The Dallas metro area was identified as one of the most affordable major metropolitan areas in America by *Forbes*. The metro area was ranked #14 out of 15. Criteria: median asking price of homes for sale; median salaries of workers with bachelor's degrees or higher compared to a cost-of-living index; unemployment rates. *Forbes.com, "The Most Affordable Cities in America," January 7, 2011*

- Experian ranked the top 20 major U.S. metropolitan areas by average debt per consumer. The Dallas metro area was ranked #2. Criteria: average debt per consumer. Debt for this study includes credit cards, auto loans and personal loans. It does not include mortgages. *Experian, May 13, 2010*

- Dallas was identified as one of "America's Hardest-Working Towns." The city ranked #25 out of 25. Criteria: average hours worked per capita; willingness to work during personal time; number of dual income households; local employment rate. *Parade, "What is America's Hardest-Working Town?," April 15, 2012*

- Dallas was identified as one of America's most coupon-loving cities by *Coupons.com*. The city ranked #15 out of 25. Criteria: online coupon usage. *Coupons.com, "Top 25 Most Frugal Cities of 2011," February 23, 2012*

- Dallas was identified as one of the top 25 U.S. cities with the most credit card debt by credit reporting bureau Experian. The city was ranked #5. *Experian, March 4, 2011*

- The Dallas metro area was identified as one of the "Best U.S. Cities for Earning a Living" by *Forbes*. The metro area ranked #8. Criteria: median income; cost of living; job growth; number of companies on *Forbes* 400 best big company and 200 best small company lists. *Forbes.com, "Best U.S. Cities for Earning a Living," August 21, 2008*

- Dallas was cited as one of America's top metros for new and expanded facility projects in 2011. The area ranked #4 in the large metro area category (population over 1 million). *Site Selection, "2011 Top Metros," March 2012*

- Dallas was identified as one of the "Happiest Cities to Work in 2012" by *CareerBliss.com*, an online community for career advancement. The city ranked #41 out of 50. Criteria: independent company reviews from employees all over the country on: relationship with their boss and co-workers; work environment; job resources; growth opportunities; compensation; company culture; company reputation; daily tasks; job control over work performed on a daily basis. *CareerBliss.com, "Happiest and Unhappiest Cities to Work in 2012"*

- Dallas was identified as one of the best cities for new college graduates. The city ranked #3. Criteria: cost of living; average annual salary; unemployment rate; number of employers looking to hire people at entry-level. *Business Week, "The Best Cities for New Grads," July 20, 2010*

- *American City Business Journals* ranked America's 261 largest cities in terms of their resident's wealth. Dallas ranked #147. Criteria: per capita income; median household income; percentage of households with annual incomes of $200,000 or more; median home value. *American City Business Journals, "Where the Money Is: America's Wealth Centers," August 18, 2008*

- The Dallas metro area appeared on the Milken Institute "2011 Best Performing Metros" list. Rank: #20 out of 200 large metro areas. Criteria: job growth; wage and salary growth; high-tech output growth. *Milken Institute, "2011 Best Performing Metros"*

- The Dallas metro area was selected as one of the best cities for entrepreneurs in America by *Inc. Magazine*. Criteria: job-growth data for 335 metro areas was analyzed for: recent growth trend; mid-term growth; long-term trend; current year growth. The Dallas metro area ranked #12 among large metro areas and #57 overall. *Inc. Magazine, "The Best Cities for Doing Business," July 2008*

- Dallas was ranked #52 out of 145 regions worldwide in terms of its "Knowledge Competitiveness Index." The index attempts to measure the knowledge-based development taking place throughout the world and is based on 19 measures of economic performance that indicate a region's ability to translate its knowledge capacity into economic value. *Centre for International Competitiveness, World Knowledge Competitiveness Index 2008*

- *Forbes* ranked the 200 most populous metro areas in the U.S. in terms of the "Best Places for Business and Careers." The Dallas metro area was ranked #10. Criteria: costs (business and living); job growth (past and projected); income growth; educational attainment; projected economic growth; crime; cultural and recreational opportunities; net migration patterns; number of highly ranked colleges. *Forbes, "Best Places for Business and Careers," June 2011*

Children/Family Rankings

- The Dallas metro area was selected as one of the "Best Cities for Relocating Families" by Worldwide ERC and Primacy Relocation. The 2008 study looked at nearly 50 factors important to relocating families including: recent job growth; nearby top-ranked colleges; in-state tuition for four-year public colleges; population growth since 2000; pediatricians per 100,000 population; and a Green Living index. *Worldwide ERC and Primacy Relocation, "2008 Best Cities for Relocating Families"*

- *Fit Pregnancy* magazine ranked the 50 best U.S. cities in which to have a baby. Dallas was ranked #43. Criteria: access to hospitals and doctors; affordability; birthing options; breastfeeding; child care; fertility laws/resources; maternal and infant health risk; parks/stroller friendliness; safety. *Fit Pregnancy, "The Best Cities in America to Have a Baby 2008"*

Culture/Performing Arts Rankings

- Dallas was selected as one of "America's Top 25 Arts Destinations." The city ranked #24 in the big city (population 500,000 and over) category. Criteria: readers' top choices for arts travel destinations based on the richness and variety of visual arts sites, activities and events. *American Style, "America's Top 25 Arts Destinations," May 2010*

Dating/Romance Rankings

- Dallas appeared on *Men's Health's* list of the most sex-happy cities in America. The city ranked #2 of 100. Criteria: condom sales; birth rates; sex toy sales; rates of chlamydia, gonorrhea, and syphilis. *Men's Health, "America's Most Sex-Happy Cities," October 2010*

- Dallas was selected as one of the best cities for single women in America by *SingleMindedWomen.com.* The city ranked #9. Criteria: ratio of women to men; singles population; healthy lifestyle; employment opportunities; cost of living; access to travel; entertainment options; social opportunities. *SingleMindedWomen.com, "Top 10 Cities for Single Women," 2011*

- *Men's Health* ranked 100 U.S. cities in terms of best (and worst) marriages. Dallas was ranked #72 (#1 = worst). Criteria: rate of failed marriages; stringency of divorce laws; percentage of population who've split; number of licensed marriage and family therapists. *Men's Health, "Splitsville, USA," May 2010*

- Eli Lily and Company, in partnership with Sperling's BestPlaces, ranked the nation's 50 largest metro areas in terms of the "Most Romantic Cities for Baby Boomers." The Dallas metro area ranked #9. Criteria: marriage and divorce rates among baby boomers age 45 to 60; great restaurants; dance studios; chocolate, jewelry and flower sales. *Eli Lily and Company, "Most Romantic Cities for Baby Boomers," April 20, 2007*

- The Dallas metro area was selected as one of the "Best Cities for Relocating Singles" by Worldwide ERC and Primacy Relocation. The area ranked #37 out of the 100 largest metro areas in the U.S. Criteria: recent job growth; recent singles population growth; overall population growth; affordable rental housing; cost-of-living index; expanded arts and recreation opportunities; ratio of single men and single women; affordability of quality higher education (including state residency requirements); diversity index; climate; population density. *Worldwide ERC and Primacy Relocation, "2008 Best Cities for Relocating Singles"*

- *Forbes* ranked the 40 most populous urbanized areas in the U.S. in terms of the "Best Cities for Singles." The Dallas metro area ranked #17. Criteria: number of singles; cost of living alone; nightlife; culture; job growth; coolness; and online dating participation. *Forbes.com, "Best Cities for Singles," July 27, 2009*

Education Rankings

- *Men's Health* ranked 100 U.S. cities in terms of their education levels. Dallas was ranked #86 (#1 = most educated city). Criteria: high school graduation rates; school enrollment; educational attainment; number of households who have outstanding student loans; number of households whose members have taken adult-education courses. *Men's Health, "Where School Is In: The Most and Least Educated Cities," September 12, 2011*

- Dallas was selected as one of "America's Most Literate Cities." The city ranked #51 out of the 75 largest U.S. cities. Criteria: number of booksellers; library resources; Internet resources; educational attainment; periodical publishing resources; newspaper circulation. *Central Connecticut State University, "America's Most Literate Cities 2011"*

- Dallas was identified as one of the 100 "smartest" metro areas in the U.S. The area ranked #72. Criteria: the editors rated the collective brainpower of the 100 largest metro areas in the U.S. based on their residents' educational attainment. *American City Business Journals, April 14, 2008*

- Dallas was identified as one of "America's Brainiest Bastions" by *Portfolio.com*. The metro area ranked #96 out of 200. *Portfolio.com* analyzed levels of educational attainment in the nation's 200 largest metropolitan areas. The editors established scores for five levels of educational attainment, based on relative earning power of adult workers age 25 or older. Scores were determined by comparing the median income for all workers with the median income for those workers at a specified educational level. *Portfolio.com, "America's Brainiest Bastions," December 1, 2010*

Environmental Rankings

- The Dallas was identified as one of North America's greenest metropolitan areas. The area ranked #17. The Green City Index is comprised of 31 indicators, and scores cities across nine categories: carbon dioxide; energy; land use; buildings; transport; water; waste; air quality; environmental governance. The 27 largest metropolitan areas in the U.S. and Canada were considered. *Economist Intelligence Unit, sponsored by Siemens, "U.S. and Canada Green City Index, 2011"*

- The Dallas was identified as one of America's cities with the most ENERGY STAR certified buildings. The area ranked #10 out of 25. Criteria: number of ENERGY STAR labeled buildings in 2010. *U.S. Environmental Protection Agency, "Top Cities With the Most ENERGY STAR Certified Buildings," March 15, 2011*

- Dallas was selected as one of 22 "Smarter Cities" for energy by the Natural Resources Defense Council. The city appeared as one of 12 cities in the large city (population 250,000 and over) category. Criteria: investment in green power; energy efficiency measures; conservation. *Natural Resources Defense Council, "2010 Smarter Cities," July 19, 2010*

- Dallas was selected as one of worst summer weather cities in the U.S. by the *Farmers' Almanac*. The city ranked #3 out of 5. Criteria: average summer and winter temperatures; humidity; precipitation; number of overcast days. The editors only considered cities with populations of 50,000 or more. *Farmers' Almanac, "America's Ten Worst Weather Cities," September 7, 2010*

- *American City Business Journal* ranked 43 metropolitan areas in terms of their "greenness." The Dallas metro area ranked #37. Criteria: Forty-one metros in which *ACBJ* has business weeklies, plus Indianapolis and Cleveland, were ranked based on 20 different indicators such as adoption of green technologies, utilization of environmentally sound practices, and air and water quality. *American City Business Journals, "Green City Index," March 11, 2010*

- 100 of the largest metro areas in the U.S. were analyzed in terms of their current drought severity. The Dallas metro area ranked #97 (#1 = driest). The rankings were based on statistics such as long-term precipitation trends and patterns and the Palmer drought indices. *Sperling's BestPlaces, www.BestPlaces.net, "America's Drought-Riskiest Cities," November 2007*

- The Dallas metro area appeared in *Country Home's* "Best Green Places" report. The area ranked #94 out of 379. Criteria: official energy policies; green power; green buildings; availability of fresh, locally grown food. *Country Home, "Best Green Places," 2008*

- Dallas was highlighted as one of the 25 most ozone-polluted metro areas in the U.S. The area ranked #12. *American Lung Association, State of the Air 2011*

Health/Fitness Rankings

- The Dallas metro area was selected as one of the worst cities for bed bugs in America by Rollins corporation, the owner of seven pest control companies, including Orkin. The area ranked #7 based on the number of bed bug treatments from January to December 2011. *Rollins, "The Top 50 U.S. Cities for Bed Bugs," March 19, 2012*

- Dallas was identified as one of the most bed bug-infested cities in the U.S. by Terminix. Dallas ranked #15.Criteria: complaint calls from customers; confirmed cases by professionals. *Terminix, "2011 Most Bedbug-Infested Cities," May 24, 2011*

- Dallas was selected as one of the 25 fattest cities in America by *Men's Fitness Online*. It ranked #25 out of America's 50 largest cities. Criteria: fitness centers and sport stores; nutrition; sports participation; TV viewing; overweight/sedentary; junk food; air quality; geography; commute; parks and open space; city recreational facilities; access to healthcare; motivation; mayor and city initiatives; state obesity initiatives. *Men's Fitness, "The Fittest and Fattest Cities in America," March 5, 2012*

- Dallas was identified as one of "The 8 Most Artery-Clogging Cities in America." The metro area ranked #5. Criteria: obesity rates; heart disease rates. *Prevention, "The 8 Most Artery-Clogging Cities in America," December 2011*

- Dallas was identified as a "2011 Asthma Capital." The area ranked #34 out of the nation's 100 largest metropolitan areas. Twelve factors were used to identify the most challenging places to live for people with asthma: estimated prevalence; self-reported prevalence; crude death rate for asthma; annual pollen score; annual air quality; public smoking laws; number of board-certified asthma specialists; school inhaler access laws; rescue medication use; controller medication use; uninsured rate; poverty rate. *Asthma and Allergy Foundation of America, "2011 Asthma Capitals"*

- Dallas was identified as a "2011 Fall Allergy Capital." The area ranked #22 out of 100. Three groups of factors were used to identify the most severe cities for people with allergies during the fall season: annual pollen levels; medicine utilization; access to board-certified allergists. *Asthma and Allergy Foundation of America, "2011 Fall Allergy Capitals"*

- Dallas was identified as a "2012 Spring Allergy Capital." The area ranked #24 out of 100. Three groups of factors were used to identify the most severe cities for people with allergies during the spring season: annual pollen levels; medicine utilization; access to board-certified allergists. *Asthma and Allergy Foundation of America, "2012 Spring Allergy Capitals"*

- *Men's Health* examined 100 major U.S. cities and selected the best and worst cities for men. Dallas ranked #47. Criteria: 35 statistical parameters of long life in the categories of health, quality of life, and fitness. *Men's Health, "The 10 Best and Worst Cities for Men 2012," January/February 2012*

- The makers of Breath Right Nasal Strips, in partnership with Sperling's BestPlaces, analyzed 50 metro areas and identified those U.S. cities most challenged by chronic nasal congestion. The Dallas metro area ranked #7. Criteria: tree, grass and weed pollens; molds and spores; air pollution; climate; smoking; purchase habits of congestion products; prescriptions of drugs for congestion relief; incidence of influenza. *Breathe Right Nasal Strips, "Most Congested Cities," October 3, 2011*

- The American Academy of Dermatology ranked 26 U.S. metropolitan regions in terms of their residents knowledge, attitude and behaviors towards tanning, sun protection and skin cancer detection. The Dallas metro area ranked #11. The results of the study are based on an online survey of over 7,000 adults nationwide. *American Academy of Dermatology, "Suntelligence: How Sun Smart is Your City," May 3, 2010*

- The Dallas metro area appeared in the 2011 Gallup-Healthways Well-Being Index. The index, based on interviews with more than 350,000 Americans, measured jobs, finances, physical health, emotional state of mind and communities. The metro area ranked #64 out of 190. Criteria: life evaluation; emotional health; work environment; physical health; healthy behaviors; basic access (basic needs optimal for a healthy life, such as access to food and medicine, having health insurance and feeling safe while walking at night). *Gallup-Healthways, "State of Well-Being 2011"*

- The Dallas metro area was identified as one of "America's Most Stressful Cities" by *Sperling's BestPlaces*. The metro area ranked #43 out of 50. Criteria: unemployment rate; suicide rate; commute time; mental health; poor rest; alcohol use; violent crime rate; property crime rate; cloudy days annually. *Sperling's BestPlaces, www.BestPlaces.net, "Stressful Cities 2012*

- The Dallas metro area was identified as one of "America's Most Stressful Cities" by *Forbes*. The metro area ranked #9 out of 40. Criteria: housing affordability; unemployment rate; cost of living; air quality; traffic congestion; sunny days; population density. *Forbes.com, "America's Most Stressful Cities," September 23, 2011*

- *Men's Health* ranked 100 U.S. cities in terms of their activity levels. Dallas was ranked #56 (#1 = most active city). Criteria: where and how often residents exercise; percentage of households that watch more than 15 hours of cable television a week and buy more than 11 video games a year; death rate from deep-vein thrombosis, a condition linked to sitting for extended periods of time. *Men's Health, "Where Sit Happens: The Most and Least Active Cities in America," June 20, 2011*

- 50 of the largest metro areas in the U.S. were analyzed in terms of their health and fitness by the American College of Sports Medicine in their "American Fitness Index." The Dallas metro area ranked #40 (#1 = healthiest). Criteria: preventative health behaviors; levels of chronic disease; health care access; community resources and policies that support physical activity. *American College of Sports Medicine, "Health and Community Fitness Status of the 50 Largest Metropolitan Areas," August 1, 2011*

Real Estate Rankings

- *Fortune* ranked the 100 largest metro areas in the U.S. in terms of projected median home price change in 2010. The Dallas metro area ranked #13. *Fortune, "The 2010 Housing Outlook," December 9, 2009*

- Dallas appeared on *ApartmentRatings.com* "Top Cities for Renters" list in 2009." The area ranked #73. Overall satisfaction ratings were ranked using thousands of user submitted scores for hundreds of apartment complexes located in the 100 most populated U.S. municipalities. *ApartmentRatings.com, "2009 Renter Satisfaction Rankings"*

- The Dallas metro area was identified as one of the "Top 25 Real Estate Investment Markets" by *FinestExperts.com*. The metro area ranked #1. Over 10,000 real estate markets were analyzed to identify the most suitable places for real estate investors to seek stability and growth. Criteria: employment; rental markets; growth levels as offset by foreclosures. *FinestExperts.com, "Top 25 Real Estate Investment Markets," January 7, 2010*

- The Dallas metro area was identified as one of "America's Best Housing Markets" by *Forbes*. The metro area ranked #9. Criteria: housing affordability; rising home prices; percentage of foreclosures. *Forbes.com, "America's Best Housing Markets," February 19, 2010*

- The Dallas metro area appeared in a *Wall Street Journal* article ranking cities by "housing stress." The metro area was ranked #22 (#1 = most stress). Criteria: fraction of mortgage-holding homeowners with a monthly housing payment in excess of 30 percent of income; percentage of people without health insurance; unemployment rate. *The Wall Street Journal, "Which Cities Face Biggest Housing Risk," October 5, 2010*

- The Center for Housing Policy ranked 210 U.S. metropolitan areas by the fair market rent for a two-bedroom unit. The Dallas metro area was ranked #82. (#1 = most expensive) with a rent of $894. Criteria: Fair Market Rent (FMR) in effect during the fourth quarter of 2009 based on HUD's fiscal year 2010 FMRs. *The Center for Housing Policy, "Paycheck to Paycheck: Most to Least Expensive Rental Markets in 2009"*

- The Dallas metro area was identified as one of the markets with the best expected performance in home prices over the next 12 months. *Local Market Monitor, "First Quarter Home Price Forecast for Largest US Markets," March 2, 2011*

- The Dallas metro area was identified as one of the best U.S. markets to invest in rental property" by HomeVestors and Local Market Monitor. The area ranked #14 out of 100. Criteria: risk-return premium relative to national average. *HomeVestors and Local Market Monitor, "Best 100 U.S. Markets to Invest in Rental Property," March 9, 2012*

Safety Rankings

- Symantec, the makers of Norton, in partnership with Sperling's BestPlaces, ranked the 50 largest cities in the U.S. in terms of their vulnerability to cybercrime. The city ranked #15. Criteria: number of cyberattacks and potential infections; level of Internet access; expenditures on smartphones and computer hardware/software; wireless hotspots; broadband connectivity; Internet usage; online purchases. *Symantec, "Riskiest Online Cities of 2012" February 15, 2012*

- Allstate ranked the 193 largest cities in America in terms of driver safety. Dallas ranked #167. In addition, drivers were 32.9% more likely to have had an accident compared to the national average. Allstate researchers analyzed internal property damage reported claims over a two-year period (from January 2008 to December 2009) to protect findings from external influences such as weather or road construction. A weighted average of the two-year numbers determined the annual percentages. The report defines an auto crash as any collision resulting in a property damage claim. *Allstate, "2011 Allstate America's Best Drivers Report™"*

- Dallas was identified as one of the least safe places in the U.S. in terms of its vulnerability to natural disasters and weather extremes. The city ranked #2 out of 10. Data was analyzed to show a metro areas' relative tendency to experience natural disasters (hail, tornadoes, high winds, hurricanes, earthquakes, and brush fires) or extreme weather (abundant rain or snowfall or days that are below freezing or above 90 degrees Fahrenheit). *Forbes, "Safest and Least Safe Places in the U.S.," August 30, 2005*

- The National Insurance Crime Bureau ranked 366 metro areas in the U.S. in terms of per capita rates of vehicle theft. The Dallas metro area ranked #47 (#1 = highest rate). Criteria: number of vehicle theft offenses per 100,000 inhabitants in 2010. *National Insurance Crime Bureau, "Hot Spots," June 21, 2011*

- The Dallas metro area was identified as one of the most dangerous metro areas for pedestrians by Transportation for America. The metro area ranked #10 out of 52 metro areas with over 1 million residents. Criteria: area's population divided by the number of pedestrian fatalities in that area. *Transportation for America, "Dangerous by Design 2011"*

Seniors/Retirement Rankings

- Bankers Life and Casualty Company, in partnership with Sperling's BestPlaces, ranked the nation's 50 largest metro areas in terms of the "Best U.S. Cities for Seniors." The Dallas metro area ranked #29. Criteria: healthcare; transportation; housing; environment; economy; health and longevity; social and spiritual life; crime. *Bankers Life and Casualty Company, Center for a Secure Retirement, "Best U.S. Cities for Seniors 2011," September 2011*

- The Dallas metro area was identified as one of "America's Most Affordable Places to Retire" by *Forbes*. The metro area ranked #2. Criteria: housing affordability; inflation; number of persons over 65 who are employed; net migration for persons over 65; percent of persons over 65 living below poverty level; doctors per capita; number of citizens tapping their Medicare benefits per thousand people. *Forbes.com, "America's Most Affordable Places to Retire," September 5, 2008*

- The Dallas metro area was selected as one of "America's Best Places to Grow Old" by *Forbes*. The area was ranked #2 out of 10. Criteria: housing affordability; inflationary pressures; number of persons over 65 who are currently employed; net migration for persons over 65; percent of seniors living below poverty level; doctors per capita; number of citizens tapping their Medicare benefits per 1,000 people. *Forbes, "America's Best Places to Grow Old," December 12, 2008*

- The Dallas metro area was selected as one of "The 10 Most Affordable Cities for Long-Term Care" by *U.S. News & World Report*. Criteria: costs at nursing homes, assisted living facilities, and adult day health care facilities; cost for licensed home health aides. *U.S. News & World Report, "The 10 Most Affordable Cities for Long-Term Care," May 17, 2010*

Sports/Recreation Rankings

- Dallas appeared on the *Sporting News* list of the "Best Sports Cities" for 2011. The area ranked #1 out of 271 cities in the U.S. *Sporting News* takes a 12-month snapshot of each city's sports, putting a heavy premium on regular-season won-lost records (from the most recently completed season). Other criteria include: playoff berths, bowl appearances and tournament bids; championships; applicable power ratings; quality of competition; overall fan fervor (measured in part by attendance); abundance of teams (rewarding quality over quantity); stadium and arena quality; ticket availability and prices; franchise ownership; and marquee appeal of athletes. *Sporting News, "Best Sports Cities 2011," October 4, 2011*

- The Dallas was selected as one of the best metro areas for golf in America by *Golf Digest*. The Dallas area was ranked #1 out of 20. Criteria: climate; cost of public golf; quality of public golf; accessibility. *Golf Digest, "The Top 20 Cities for Golf," October 2011*

- *Golf.com* and the research arm of the National Golf Foundation analyzed the 50 largest metropolitan areas in the U.S. in terms of golf. The Dallas metro area ranked #4. Criteria: weather; affordability; quality of courses; accessibility; number of courses designed by esteemed architects; availability; crowdedness. *Golf.com, November 15, 2007*

Technology Rankings

- Scarborough Research, a leading market research firm, identified the Dallas DMA (Designated Market Area) as one of the top markets for text messaging with more than 50% of cell phone subscribers age 18+ utilizing the text messaging feature on their phone. *Scarborough Research, November 24, 2008*

Transportation Rankings

- Dallas was selected as one of the "Least Courteous Cities (Worst Road Rage)" in the U.S. by AutoVantage. The city ranked #2. Criteria: 2,518 consumers were interviewed in 25 major metropolitan areas about their views on road rage. *AutoVantage, "2009 AutoVantage Road Rage Survey"*

- The Dallas metro area appeared on *Forbes* list of the best and worst cities for commuters. The metro area ranked #56 out of 60 (#1 is best). Criteria: travel time; road congestion; travel delays. *Forbes.com, "Best and Worst Cities for Commuters," February 16, 2010*

Women/Minorities Rankings

- *Women's Health* examined U.S. cities and identified the 100 best cities for women. Dallas was ranked #53. Criteria: 30 categories were examined from obesity and breast cancer rates to commuting times and hours spent working out. *Women's Health, "Best Cities for Women 2012"*

- Dallas was ranked #68 out of 100 metro areas in *SELF Magazine's* ranking of America's healthiest places for women." A panel of experts came up with more than 50 criteria including death and disease rates, environmental indicators, community resources, and lifestyle habits. *SELF Magazine, "Secrets of America's Healthiest Women," December 2008*

- Dallas was selected as one of the 25 healthiest cities for Latinas by *Latina Magazine*. The city ranked #7. Criteria: U.S. cities with populations over 500,000 residents were evaluated on the following criteria: percentage of 18-34 year-olds per city; Latino college graduation rates; number of colleges and universities; affordability; housing costs; income growth over time; average salary; percentage of singles; climate; safety; how the city's diversity compares to the national average; opportunities for minority entrepreneurs. *Latina Magazine, "Top 15 U.S. Cities for Young Latinos to Live In," August 19, 2011*

- Dallas appeared on *Black Enterprise's* list of the "Ten Best Cities for African Americans." The top picks were culled from more than 2,000 interactive surveys completed on *BlackEnterprise.com* and by editorial staff evaluation. The editors weighed the following criteria as it pertained to African Americans in each city: median household income; percentage of households earning more than $100,000; percentage of businesses owned; percentage of college graduates; unemployment rates; home loan rejections; and homeownership rates. *Black Enterprise, May 2007*

- The Dallas metro area appeared on *Forbes'* list of the "Best Cities for Minority Entrepreneurs." The area ranked #7 out of 10. Criteria: 52 metropolitan statistical areas were examined. For each ethnicity (African Americans, Asians and Hispanics), the editors measured housing affordability, population growth, income growth, and entrepreneurship (per capita self-employment). *Forbes, "Best Cities for Minority Entrepreneurs," March 23, 2011*

- Dallas was selected as one of the "Top 10 Cities for Hispanics." Criteria: the prospect of a good job; a safe place to raise a family; a manageable cost of living; the ability to buy and keep a home; a culture of inclusion where Hispanics are highly represented; resources to help start a business; the presence of Hispanic or Spanish-language media; representation of Hispanic needs on local government; a thriving arts and culture community; air quality; energy costs; city's state of health and rates of obesity. *Hispanic Magazine, August 2008*

Miscellaneous Rankings

- *Men's Health* ranked 100 U.S. cities by their level of sadness. Dallas was ranked #48 (#1 = saddest city). Criteria: suicide rates; unemployment rates; percentage of households that use antidepressants; percent of population who report feeling blue all or most of the time. *Men's Health, "Frown Towns," November 28, 2011*

- Energizer Holdings, the makers of Edge® shave gel, in partnership with Sperling's BestPlaces, ranked 50 major metro areas in terms of everyday irritations. The Dallas metro area ranked #13. Criteria: humidity levels; weather conditions; incidence of traffic delays and congestion; average commute times; frequency of flight delays and cancellations; rates of sleeplessness; underemployment; pollens and allergens; pests; comedy clubs per capita. *Energizer Holdings, "Most Irritation Prone Cities," July 23, 2010*

- Mars Chocolate North America, the makers of COMBOS®, in partnership with Sperling's BestPlaces, ranked 50 major metro areas in terms of their "manliness." The Dallas metro area ranked #21. Criteria: number of professional sports teams; number of nearby NASCAR tracks and racing events; manly lifestyle; concentration of manly retail stores; manly occupations per capita; salty snack sales; "Board of Manliness" rankings. *Mars Chocolate North America, "America's Manliest Cities 2011," September 1, 2011*

- The Dallas metro area was selected as one of "America's Greediest Cities" by *Forbes*. The area was ranked #7 out of 10. Criteria: number of Forbes 400 (*Forbes* annual list of the richest Americans) members per capita. *Forbes, "America's Greediest Cities," December 7, 2007*

- Dallas was selected as one of the best cities for shopping in the U.S. by *Forbes*. The city was ranked #3. Criteria: number of major shopping centers; retail locations; Consumer Price Index (CPI); combined state and local sales tax. *Forbes, "America's 25 Best Cities for Shopping," December 13, 2010*

- The Dallas metro area appeared in *AutoMD.com's* ranking of the "Best and Worst Cities for Auto Repair." The metro area ranked #25 (#1 is best). The 50 most-populated metro areas in the U.S. were ranked on three critical factors: repair affordability; price disparity range; shop integrity factor. *AutoMD.com, "Advocacy for Repair Shop Fairness Report," February 24, 2010*

- Dallas appeared on Procter & Gamble's list of the "Top-20 All-Time Sweatiest Cities." The city was ranked #4. The rankings are based on computer simulations of the amount of sweat a person of average height and weight would produce walking around for an hour in the average temperatures during the summer months, based on historical weather data during June, July and August from 2001-2008 for each city. *Procter & Gamble, Old Spice Press Release, "Top-20 All-Time Sweatiest Cities," July 1, 2009*

Business Environment

CITY FINANCES

City Government Finances

Component	2009 ($000)	2009 ($ per capita)
Total Revenues	1,225,840	988
Total Expenditures	3,272,709	2,638
Debt Outstanding	9,117,646	7,350
Cash and Securities[1]	8,006,812	6,455

Note: (1) Cash and security holdings of a government at the close of its fiscal year, including those of its dependent agencies, utilities, and liquor stores.
Source: U.S Census Bureau, State & Local Government Finances 2009

City Government Revenue by Source

Source	2009 ($000)	2009 ($ per capita)
General Revenue		
From Federal Government	64,924	52
From State Government	56,540	46
From Local Governments	5,685	5
Taxes		
Property	632,597	510
Sales and Gross Receipts	390,499	315
Personal Income	0	0
Corporate Income	0	0
Motor Vehicle License	0	0
Other Taxes	31,993	26
Current Charges	1,157,151	933
Liquor Store	0	0
Utility	265,028	214
Employee Retirement	-1,711,963	-1,380

Source: U.S Census Bureau, State & Local Government Finances 2009

City Government Expenditures by Function

Function	2009 ($000)	2009 ($ per capita)	2009 (%)
General Direct Expenditures			
Air Transportation	504,291	407	15.4
Corrections	2,560	2	0.1
Education	0	0	0.0
Employment Security Administration	0	0	0.0
Financial Administration	35,323	28	1.1
Fire Protection	190,230	153	5.8
General Public Buildings	50,339	41	1.5
Governmental Administration, Other	21,648	17	0.7
Health	39,036	31	1.2
Highways	193,833	156	5.9
Hospitals	0	0	0.0
Housing and Community Development	35,968	29	1.1
Interest on General Debt	392,887	317	12.0
Judicial and Legal	25,943	21	0.8
Libraries	46,008	37	1.4
Parking	2,010	2	0.1
Parks and Recreation	242,913	196	7.4
Police Protection	345,165	278	10.5
Public Welfare	21,969	18	0.7
Sewerage	235,379	190	7.2
Solid Waste Management	64,332	52	2.0
Veterans' Services	0	0	0.0
Liquor Store	0	0	0.0
Utility	349,348	282	10.7
Employee Retirement	315,774	255	9.6

Source: U.S Census Bureau, State & Local Government Finances 2009

Municipal Bond Ratings

Area	Moody's	S&P	Fitch
City	Aa1	AA+	n/a

Rating Systems (shown in declining order of credit quality): Moody's– Aaa, Aa, A, Baa, Ba, B, Caa, Ca, C (numerical modifiers 1, 2, and 3 are added to letter-rating); S&P– AAA, AA, A, BBB, BB, B, CCC, CC, C; Fitch– AAA, AA, A, BBB, BB, B, CCC, CC, C. Ratings may be modified by the addition of a plus or minus sign to show relative standing within the major rating categories.
Notes: n/a Not Available; w/d Withdrawn (1) Not Reviewed; (2) Issuer Rating/No General Obligation; (3) Standard and Poor's Issue Credit Rating (ICR) is a current opinion of an obliger with respect to a specific financial obligation, a specific class of financial obligations, or a specific financial program.
Source: U.S. Census Bureau, 2012 Statistical Abstract, Bond Ratings for City Governments by Largest Cities: 2010

DEMOGRAPHICS

Population Growth

Area	1990 Census	2000 Census	2010 Census	Population Growth (%) 1990-2000	Population Growth (%) 2000-2010
City	1,006,971	1,188,580	1,197,816	18.0	0.8
MSA[1]	3,989,294	5,161,544	6,371,773	29.4	23.4
U.S.	248,709,873	281,421,906	308,745,538	13.2	9.7

Note: (1) Figures cover the Dallas-Fort Worth-Arlington, TX Metropolitan Statistical Area—see Appendix B for areas included
Source: U.S. Census Bureau, 2010 Census

Household Size

Area	Persons in Household (%) One	Two	Three	Four	Five	Six	Seven or More	Average Household Size
City	33.9	27.2	13.8	11.4	7.0	3.5	3.3	2.57
MSA[1]	24.8	29.6	16.7	15.2	7.9	3.3	2.5	2.74
U.S.	26.7	32.8	16.1	13.4	6.5	2.6	1.9	2.58

Note: (1) Figures cover the Dallas-Fort Worth-Arlington, TX Metropolitan Statistical Area—see Appendix B for areas included
Source: U.S. Census Bureau, 2010 Census

Race

Area	White Alone[2] (%)	Black Alone[2] (%)	Asian Alone[2] (%)	AIAN[3] Alone[2] (%)	NHOPI[4] Alone[2] (%)	Other Race Alone[2] (%)	Two or More Races (%)
City	50.7	25.0	2.9	0.7	0.0	18.1	2.6
MSA[1]	65.3	15.1	5.4	0.7	0.1	10.6	2.8
U.S.	72.4	12.6	4.8	0.9	0.2	6.2	2.9

Note: (1) Figures cover the Dallas-Fort Worth-Arlington, TX Metropolitan Statistical Area—see Appendix B for areas included; (2) Alone is defined as not being in combination with one or more other races; (3) American Indian and Alaska Native; (4) Native Hawaiian and Other Pacific Islander
Source: U.S. Census Bureau, 2010 Census

Hispanic or Latino Origin

Area	Hispanic or Latino (%)	Mexican (%)	Puerto Rican (%)	Cuban (%)	Other Hispanic or Latino (%)
City	42.4	36.7	0.3	0.2	5.2
MSA[1]	27.5	22.9	0.5	0.2	3.9
U.S.	16.3	10.3	1.5	0.6	4.0

Note: Persons of Hispanic or Latino origin can be of any race; (1) Figures cover the Dallas-Fort Worth-Arlington, TX Metropolitan Statistical Area—see Appendix B for areas included
Source: U.S. Census Bureau, 2010 Census

Segregation

Type	Segregation Indices[1]				Percent Change		
	1990	2000	2010	2010 Rank[2]	1990-2000	1990-2010	2000-2010
Black/White	62.8	59.8	56.6	48	-3.1	-6.2	-3.2
Asian/White	41.8	45.6	46.6	19	3.8	4.8	1.0
Hispanic/White	48.8	52.3	50.3	24	3.5	1.5	-2.0

Note: Figures are based on an analysis of 1990, 2000, and 2010 Census Decennial Census tract data by William H. Frey, Brookings Institution and the University of Michigan Social Science Data Analysis Network. In this analysis all racial groups (whites, blacks, and asians) are non-Hispanic members of those races. Hispanics are shown as a separate category; All figures cover the Metropolitan Statistical Area (see Appendix B for areas included); (1) Segregation Indices are Dissimilarity Indices that measure the degree to which the minority group is distributed differently than whites across census tracts. They range from 0 (complete integration) to 100 (complete segregation) where the value indicates the percentage of the minority group that needs to move to be distributed exactly like whites; (2) Ranges from 1 (most segregated) to 102 (least segregated); n/a not available.
Source: www.CensusScope.org

Ancestry

Area	German	Irish	English	American	Italian	Polish	French[2]	Scottish	Dutch
City	6.1	4.8	5.3	2.7	1.4	0.8	1.4	1.2	0.6
MSA[1]	11.1	8.6	8.2	6.0	2.3	1.1	2.2	1.8	1.1
U.S.	16.1	11.6	8.8	6.1	5.7	3.2	3.0	1.9	1.6

Note: Figures are the percentage of the total population reporting a particular ancestry. The nine most commonly reported ancestries in the U.S. are shown. Figures include multiple ancestries (e.g. if a person reported being Irish and Italian, they were included in both columns); (1) Figures cover the Dallas-Fort Worth-Arlington, TX Metropolitan Statistical Area—see Appendix B for areas included; (2) Excludes Basque
Source: U.S. Census Bureau, 2008-2010 American Community Survey 3-Year Estimates

Foreign-Born Population

Area	Percent of Population Born in								
	Any Foreign Country	Mexico	Asia	Europe	Carribean	South America	Central America[2]	Africa	Canada
City	24.7	17.1	2.6	0.7	0.2	0.4	2.4	1.1	0.1
MSA[1]	17.5	9.3	4.2	0.8	0.2	0.5	1.3	0.9	0.2
U.S.	12.8	3.8	3.6	1.6	1.2	0.9	1.0	0.5	0.3

Note: (1) Figures cover the Dallas-Fort Worth-Arlington, TX Metropolitan Statistical Area—see Appendix B for areas included; (2) Excludes Mexico.
Source: U.S. Census Bureau, 2008-2010 American Community Survey 3-Year Estimates

Marital Status

Area	Never Married	Now Married[2]	Separated	Widowed	Divorced
City	39.6	40.5	3.7	5.1	11.2
MSA[1]	30.4	51.6	2.6	4.5	10.9
U.S.	31.6	49.6	2.2	6.1	10.7

Note: Figures are percentages and cover the population 15 years of age and older; (1) Figures cover the Dallas-Fort Worth-Arlington, TX Metropolitan Statistical Area—see Appendix B for areas included; (2) Excludes separated
Source: U.S. Census Bureau, 2008-2010 American Community Survey 3-Year Estimates

Age

Area	Percent of Population							Median Age
	Under Age 5	Age 5 to 17	Age 18 to 34	Age 35 to 49	Age 50 to 64	Age 65 to 79	80 Years and Over	
City	8.6	17.9	28.8	20.7	15.1	6.4	2.5	31.8
MSA[1]	7.8	20.0	24.3	22.5	16.6	6.7	2.1	33.5
U.S.	6.5	17.5	23.2	20.7	19.0	9.4	3.6	37.2

Note: (1) Figures cover the Dallas-Fort Worth-Arlington, TX Metropolitan Statistical Area—see Appendix B for areas included
Source: U.S. Census Bureau, 2010 Census

Male/Female Ratio

Area	Males	Females	Males per 100 Females
City	598,962	598,854	100.0
MSA[1]	3,141,634	3,230,139	97.3
U.S.	151,781,326	156,964,212	96.7

Note: (1) Figures cover the Dallas-Fort Worth-Arlington, TX Metropolitan Statistical Area—see Appendix B for areas included
Source: U.S. Census Bureau, 2010 Census

Religious Groups

Area	Catholic	Baptist	Non-Den.	Methodist[2]	Lutheran	LDS[3]	Pente-costal	Presby-terian[4]	Muslim[5]	Judaism
MSA[1]	13.3	18.7	7.8	5.3	0.8	1.2	2.2	1.0	0.4	2.4
U.S.	19.1	9.3	4.0	4.0	2.3	2.0	1.9	1.6	0.8	0.7

Note: Figures are the number of adherents as a percentage of the total population; (1) Figures cover the Dallas-Fort Worth-Arlington, TX Metropolitan Statistical Area—see Appendix B for areas included; (2) Methodist/Pietist; (3) Latter Day Saints; (4) Reformed; (5) Figures are estimates
Source: Association of Statisticians of American Religious Bodies, 2010 U.S. Religion Census: Religious Congregations & Membership Study

ECONOMY

Gross Metropolitan Product

Area	2007	2008	2009	2010	2010 Rank[2]
MSA[1]	358.1	370.8	358.3	376.8	6

Note: Figures are in billions of dollars; (1) Figures cover the Dallas-Fort Worth-Arlington, TX Metropolitan Statistical Area—see Appendix B for areas included; (2) Rank ranges from 1 to 363
Source: The United States Conference of Mayors, "U.S. Metro Economies: GMP and Employment Forecasts," June 2011

Economic Growth

Area	2007-2009 (%)	2010 (%)	2011 (%)	Rank[2]
MSA[1]	-0.3	5.0	4.1	114
U.S.	-1.3	2.9	2.5	–

Note: Figures are real Gross Metropolitan Product growth rates and represent annual average percent change; (1) Figures cover the Dallas-Fort Worth-Arlington, TX Metropolitan Statistical Area—see Appendix B for areas included; (2) Rank ranges from 1 to 363
Source: The United States Conference of Mayors, "U.S. Metro Economies: GMP and Employment Forecasts," June 2011

Metropolitan Area Exports

Area	2005	2006	2007	2008	2009	2010	2010 Rank[2]
MSA[1]	20,541.2	22,461.6	22,079.1	22,503.7	19,881.8	22,500.4	11

Note: Figures are in millions of dollars; (1) Figures cover the Dallas-Fort Worth-Arlington, TX Metropolitan Statistical Area—see Appendix B for areas included; (2) Rank ranges from 1 to 369
Source: U.S. Department of Commerce, International Trade Administration, Office of Trade & Industry Information, Manufacturing & Services, data extracted April 2, 2012

INCOME

Income

Area	Per Capita ($)	Median Household ($)	Average Household ($)
City	26,032	41,011	66,620
MSA[1]	28,035	55,740	76,630
U.S.	26,942	51,222	70,116

Note: (1) Figures cover the Dallas-Fort Worth-Arlington, TX Metropolitan Statistical Area—see Appendix B for areas included
Source: U.S. Census Bureau, 2008-2010 American Community Survey 3-Year Estimates

Household Income Distribution

Area	Percent of Households Earning							
	Under $15,000	$15,000 -24,999	$25,000 -34,999	$35,000 -49,999	$50,000 -74,999	$75,000 -99,000	$100,000 -149,999	$150,000 and up
City	16.3	13.6	13.0	15.1	16.4	8.5	8.3	8.7
MSA[1]	10.3	10.1	10.2	14.0	18.7	12.5	13.8	10.2
U.S.	13.0	11.0	10.6	14.2	18.5	12.1	12.2	8.4

Note: (1) Figures cover the Dallas-Fort Worth-Arlington, TX Metropolitan Statistical Area—see Appendix B for areas included
Source: U.S. Census Bureau, 2008-2010 American Community Survey 3-Year Estimates

Poverty Rate

Area	All Ages	Under 18 Years Old	18 to 64 Years Old	65 Years and Over
City	23.2	36.1	19.2	13.0
MSA[1]	14.0	20.1	12.0	8.7
U.S.	14.4	20.1	13.1	9.4

Note: Figures are percentage of people whose income during the past 12 months was below the poverty level;
(1) Figures cover the Dallas-Fort Worth-Arlington, TX Metropolitan Statistical Area—see Appendix B for areas included
Source: U.S. Census Bureau, 2008-2010 American Community Survey 3-Year Estimates

Personal Bankruptcy Filing Rate

Area	2006	2007	2008	2009	2010	2011
Dallas County	2.20	2.39	2.39	2.90	2.86	2.63
U.S.	2.00	2.73	3.53	4.61	4.97	4.37

Note: Numbers are per 1,000 population and include Chapter 7 and Chapter 13 filings
Source: Federal Deposit Insurance Corporation, Regional Economic Conditions, March 9, 2012

EMPLOYMENT

Labor Force and Employment

Area	Civilian Labor Force			Workers Employed		
	Dec. 2010	Dec. 2011	% Chg.	Dec. 2010	Dec. 2011	% Chg.
City	602,997	609,820	1.1	551,590	562,113	1.9
MD[1]	2,158,513	2,180,878	1.0	1,985,464	2,023,344	1.9
U.S.	153,156,000	153,373,000	0.1	139,159,000	140,681,000	1.1

Note: Data is not seasonally adjusted and covers workers 16 years of age and older;
(1) Metropolitan Division—see Appendix B for areas included
Source: Bureau of Labor Statistics, http://stats.bls.gov

Unemployment Rate

Area	2011											
	Jan.	Feb.	Mar.	Apr.	May	Jun.	Jul.	Aug.	Sep.	Oct.	Nov.	Dec.
City	9.0	8.6	8.5	8.2	8.4	9.2	9.1	8.8	8.9	8.7	8.1	7.8
MD[1]	8.5	8.2	8.1	7.7	7.9	8.7	8.7	8.4	8.4	8.1	7.5	7.2
U.S.	9.8	9.5	9.2	8.7	8.7	9.3	9.3	9.1	8.8	8.5	8.2	8.3

Note: Data is not seasonally adjusted and covers workers 16 years of age and older; All figures are percentages; (1) Metropolitan Division—see Appendix B for areas included
Source: Bureau of Labor Statistics, http://stats.bls.gov

Projected Unemployment Rate

Area	2010 (%)	2011 (%)	2012 (%)	2013 (%)
MSA[1]	8.4	8.1	7.7	7.2

Note: (1) Metropolitan Statistical Area—see Appendix B for areas included
Source: The United States Conference of Mayors, "U.S. Metro Economies: GMP and Employment Forecasts," June 2011

Employment by Occupation

Occupation Classification	City (%)	MSA[1] (%)	U.S. (%)
Management, Business, Science, and Arts	31.5	36.4	35.6
Natural Resources, Construction, and Maintenance	13.1	10.1	9.5
Production, Transportation, and Material Moving	12.3	11.6	12.1
Sales and Office	24.8	26.8	25.2
Service	18.4	15.2	17.6

Note: Figures cover employed civilians 16 years of age and older; (1) Figures cover the Dallas-Fort Worth-Arlington, TX Metropolitan Statistical Area—see Appendix B for areas included
Source: U.S. Census Bureau, 2008-2010 American Community Survey 3-Year Estimates

Employment by Industry

Sector	MD[1] Number of Employees	MD[1] Percent of Total	U.S. Percent of Total
Construction	n/a	n/a	4.1
Education and Health Services	254,000	12.2	15.2
Financial Activities	184,600	8.9	5.8
Government	275,100	13.2	16.8
Information	65,100	3.1	2.0
Leisure and Hospitality	200,700	9.6	9.9
Manufacturing	167,000	8.0	8.9
Mining and Logging	n/a	n/a	0.6
Other Services	71,300	3.4	4.0
Professional and Business Services	352,400	16.9	13.3
Retail Trade	216,400	10.4	11.5
Transportation and Utilities	78,800	3.8	3.8
Wholesale Trade	121,700	5.8	4.2

Note: Figures cover non-farm employment as of December 2011 and are not seasonally adjusted; (1) Metropolitan Division—see Appendix B for areas included; n/a not available
Source: Bureau of Labor Statistics, http://stats.bls.gov

Occupations with Greatest Projected Employment Growth: 2008 – 2018

Occupation[1]	2008 Employment	2018 Projected Employment	Numeric Employment Change	Percent Employment Change
Combined Food Preparation and Serving Workers, Including Fast Food	247,750	326,190	78,440	31.7
Elementary School Teachers, Except Special Education	156,930	218,030	61,100	38.9
Retail Salespersons	361,780	416,090	54,310	15.0
Registered Nurses	166,240	219,880	53,640	32.3
Home Health Aides	92,660	143,720	51,060	55.1
Customer Service Representatives	217,250	267,290	50,040	23.0
Waiters and Waitresses	192,340	237,660	45,320	23.6
Personal and Home Care Aides	94,530	138,530	44,000	46.5
Office Clerks, General	239,400	279,000	39,600	16.5
Cashiers	276,070	312,940	36,870	13.4

Note: Projections cover Texas; (1) Sorted by numeric employment change
Source: www.projectionscentral.com, State Occupational Projections, 2008–2018 Long-Term Projections

Fastest Growing Occupations: 2008 – 2018

Occupation[1]	2008 Employment	2018 Projected Employment	Numeric Employment Change	Percent Employment Change
Biomedical Engineers	650	1,150	500	76.9
Home Health Aides	92,660	143,720	51,060	55.1
Network Systems and Data Communications Analysts	19,160	29,490	10,330	53.9
Petroleum Engineers	13,440	20,140	6,700	49.9
Athletic Trainers	1,560	2,300	740	47.4
Personal and Home Care Aides	94,530	138,530	44,000	46.5
Electrical and Electronics Repairers, Powerhouse, Substation, and Relay	1,550	2,260	710	45.8
Financial Examiners	2,150	3,130	980	45.6
Medical Scientists, Except Epidemiologists	3,670	5,320	1,650	45.0
Biochemists and Biophysicists	740	1,060	320	43.2

Note: Projections cover Texas; (1) Sorted by percent employment change and excludes occupations with numeric employment change less than 100
Source: www.projectionscentral.com, State Occupational Projections, 2008–2018 Long-Term Projections

Average Wages

Occupation	$/Hr.	Occupation	$/Hr.
Accountants and Auditors	35.62	Maids and Housekeeping Cleaners	9.01
Automotive Mechanics	17.75	Maintenance and Repair Workers	16.80
Bookkeepers	18.20	Marketing Managers	62.63
Carpenters	15.57	Nuclear Medicine Technologists	31.31
Cashiers	9.39	Nurses, Licensed Practical	21.67
Clerks, General Office	14.88	Nurses, Registered	32.86
Clerks, Receptionists/Information	12.90	Nursing Aides/Orderlies/Attendants	11.46
Clerks, Shipping/Receiving	14.09	Packers and Packagers, Hand	10.61
Computer Programmers	41.54	Physical Therapists	45.67
Computer Support Specialists	28.05	Postal Service Mail Carriers	25.10
Computer Systems Analysts	41.07	Real Estate Brokers	49.69
Cooks, Restaurant	10.09	Retail Salespersons	12.80
Dentists	98.53	Sales Reps., Exc. Tech./Scientific	32.42
Electrical Engineers	46.14	Sales Reps., Tech./Scientific	50.79
Electricians	21.29	Secretaries, Exc. Legal/Med./Exec.	15.88
Financial Managers	59.28	Security Guards	12.77
First-Line Supervisors/Managers, Sales	20.33	Surgeons	n/a
Food Preparation Workers	9.15	Teacher Assistants	11.30
General and Operations Managers	59.82	Teachers, Elementary School	26.40
Hairdressers/Cosmetologists	14.08	Teachers, Secondary School	27.90
Internists	79.49	Telemarketers	12.69
Janitors and Cleaners	10.27	Truck Drivers, Heavy/Tractor-Trailer	19.42
Landscaping/Groundskeeping Workers	10.86	Truck Drivers, Light/Delivery Svcs.	16.73
Lawyers	68.66	Waiters and Waitresses	9.75

Note: Wage data covers the Dallas-Plano-Irving, TX Metropolitan Division—see Appendix B for areas included.
Hourly wages for elementary/secondary school teachers and teacher assistants were calculated by the editors
from annual wage data assuming a 40 hour work week; n/a not available.
Source: Bureau of Labor Statistics, Metro Area Occupational Employment and Wage Estimates, May 2011

RESIDENTIAL REAL ESTATE

Building Permits

Area	Single-Family			Multi-Family			Total		
	2010	2011	Pct. Chg.	2010	2011	Pct. Chg.	2010	2011	Pct. Chg.
City	865	809	-6.5	1,744	3,441	97.3	2,609	4,250	62.9
MSA[1]	14,420	14,039	-2.6	5,138	10,788	110.0	19,558	24,827	26.9
U.S.	447,311	418,498	-6.4	157,299	205,563	30.7	604,610	624,061	3.2

Note: (1) Metropolitan Statistical Area—see Appendix B for areas included; figures represent new, privately-
owned housing units authorized (unadjusted data); All permit data are based on estimates with imputation.
Source: U.S. Census Bureau, Manufacturing, Mining, and Construction Statistics, Building Permits, 2010, 2011

Homeownership Rate

Area	2005 (%)	2006 (%)	2007 (%)	2008 (%)	2009 (%)	2010 (%)	2011 (%)
MSA[1]	62.3	60.7	60.9	60.9	61.6	63.8	62.6
U.S.	68.9	68.8	68.1	67.8	67.4	66.9	66.1

Note: (1) Metropolitan Statistical Area—see Appendix B for areas included
Source: U.S. Census Bureau, Housing Vacancies and Homeownership Annual Statistics: 2011

Housing Vacancy Rates

Area	Gross Vacancy Rate[2] (%)			Year-Round Vacancy Rate[3] (%)			Rental Vacancy Rate[4] (%)			Homeowner Vacancy Rate[5] (%)		
	2009	2010	2011	2009	2010	2011	2009	2010	2011	2009	2010	2011
MSA[1]	9.4	10.5	9.8	9.3	10.4	9.6	11.7	13.5	11.8	2.1	2.3	2.0
U.S.	14.5	14.3	14.2	11.3	11.3	11.1	10.6	10.2	9.5	2.6	2.6	2.5

Note: (1) Metropolitan Statistical Area—see Appendix B for areas included; (2) The percentage of the total housing inventory that is vacant; (3) The percentage of the housing inventory (excluding seasonal units) that is year-round vacant; (4) The percentage of rental inventory that is vacant for rent; (5) The percentage of homeowner inventory that is vacant for sale
Source: U.S. Census Bureau, Housing Vacancies and Homeownership Annual Statistics: 2011

TAXES

State Corporate Income Tax Rates

State	Tax Rate (%)	Income Brackets ($)	Num. of Brackets	Financial Institution Tax Rate (%)[a]	Federal Income Tax Ded.
Texas	(x)	–	–	(x)	No

Note: Tax rates as of January 1, 2012; (a) Rates listed are the corporate income tax rate applied to financial institutions or excise taxes based on income. Some states have other taxes based upon the value of deposits or shares; (x) Texas imposes a Franchise Tax, otherwise known as margin tax, imposed on entities with more than $1,000,000 total revenues at rate of 1%, or 0.5% for entities primarily engaged in retail or wholesale trade, on lesser of 70% of total revenues or 100%of gross receipts after deductions for either compensation or cost of goods sold.
Source: Federation of Tax Administrators, "State Corporate Income Tax Rates, 2012"

State Individual Income Tax Rates

State	Tax Rate (%)	Income Brackets ($)	Num. of Brackets	Personal Exempt. ($)[1] Single	Dependents	Fed. Inc. Tax Ded.

Texas – No State Income Tax

Note: Tax rates as of January 1, 2012; Local- and county-level taxes are not included; n/a not applicable; (1) Married joint filers generally receive double the single exemption
Source: Federation of Tax Administrators, "State Individual Income Tax Rates, 2012"

Various State and Local Tax Rates

State	State and Local Sales and Use (%)	State Sales and Use (%)	Gasoline[1] (¢/gal.)	Cigarette[2] ($/pack)	Spirits[3] ($/gal.)	Wine[4] ($/gal.)	Beer[5] ($/gal.)
Texas	8.25	6.25	20.0	1.41	2.40	0.20	0.20

Note: All tax rates as of January 1, 2012 except beer, wine and spirits (September 1, 2011); (1) The American Petroleum Institute has developed a methodology for determining the average tax rate on a gallon of fuel. Rates may include any of the following: excise taxes, environmental fees, storage tank fees, other fees or taxes, general sales tax, and local taxes. In states where gasoline is subject to the general sales tax, or where the fuel tax is based on the average sale price, the average rate determined by API is sensitive to changes in the price of gasoline. States that fully or partially apply general sales taxes to gasoline: CA, CO, GA, IL, IN, MI, NY; (2) The federal excise tax of $1.0066 per pack and local taxes are not included; (3) Rates are those applicable to off-premise sales of 40% alcohol by volume (a.b.v.) distilled spirits in 750ml containers. Local excise taxes are excluded; (4) Rates are those applicable to off-premise sales of 11% a.b.v. non-carbonated wine in 750ml containers; (5) Rates are those applicable to off-premise sales of 4.7% a.b.v. beer in 12 ounce containers.
Source: Tax Foundation, 2012 Facts & Figures: How Does Your State Compare?

State-Local Tax Burdens

Area	Rate (%)	Rank[1]	Per Capita Taxes Paid to Home State ($)	Total State and Local Per Capita Taxes Paid ($)	Per Capita Income ($)
Texas	7.9	45	2,248	3,197	40,498
U.S. Average	9.8	-	3,057	4,160	42,539

Note: Figures cover 2009; (1) Rank ranges from 1 to 50 where 1 is highest tax burden
Source: Tax Foundation, State-Local Tax Burdens, All States, 2009

State Business Tax Climate Index Rankings

State	Overall Rank	Corporate Tax Index Rank	Individual Income Tax Index Rank	Sales Tax Index Rank	Unemployment Insurance Tax Index Rank	Property Tax Index Rank
Texas	9	37	7	35	15	31

Note: The index is a measure of how each state's tax laws affect economic performance. The lower the rank, the more favorable a state's tax system is for business. States without a given tax are given a ranking of 1.
Source: Tax Foundation, Major Components of the State Business Tax Climate Index, FY 2012

COMMERCIAL REAL ESTATE

Office Market

Market Area	Inventory (sq. ft.)	Vacant (sq. ft.)	Vac. Rate (%)	Under Constr. (sq. ft.)	Asking Rent ($/sf/yr) Class A	Asking Rent ($/sf/yr) Class B
Dallas-Fort Worth	190,863,123	41,477,914	21.7	615,600	22.92	17.72

Source: Grubb & Ellis, Office Markets Trends, 4th Quarter 2011

Industrial Market

Market Area	Inventory (sq. ft.)	Vacant (sq. ft.)	Vac. Rate (%)	Under Constr. (sq. ft.)	Asking Rent ($/sf/yr) WH/Dist	Asking Rent ($/sf/yr) R&D/Flex
Dallas-Fort Worth	663,801,566	69,153,380	10.4	725,976	3.50	6.47

Source: Grubb & Ellis, Industrial Markets Trends, 4th Quarter 2011

COMMERCIAL UTILITIES

Typical Monthly Electric Bills

Area	Commercial Service ($/month) 1,500 kWh	Commercial Service ($/month) 40 kW demand 14,000 kWh	Industrial Service ($/month) 1,000 kW demand 200,000 kWh	Industrial Service ($/month) 50,000 kW demand 15,000,000 kWh
City	n/a	n/a	n/a	n/a
Average[1]	189	1,616	25,197	1,470,813

Note: Based on total rates in effect July 1, 2011; (1) average based on 184 utilities surveyed; n/a not available
Source: Edison Electric Institute, Typical Bills and Average Rates Report, Summer 2011

TRANSPORTATION

Means of Transportation to Work

Area	Car/Truck/Van Drove Alone	Car/Truck/Van Car-pooled	Bus	Subway	Railroad	Bicycle	Walked	Other Means	Worked at Home
City	77.6	11.1	3.5	0.3	0.3	0.1	1.9	1.4	3.8
MSA[1]	80.8	10.6	1.1	0.1	0.2	0.2	1.3	1.4	4.3
U.S.	76.0	10.2	2.7	1.7	0.5	0.5	2.8	1.3	4.2

Note: Figures are percentages and cover workers 16 years of age and older; (1) Figures cover the Dallas-Fort Worth-Arlington, TX Metropolitan Statistical Area—see Appendix B for areas included
Source: U.S. Census Bureau, 2008-2010 American Community Survey 3-Year Estimates

Travel Time to Work

Area	Less Than 10 Minutes	10 to 19 Minutes	20 to 29 Minutes	30 to 44 Minutes	45 to 59 Minutes	60 to 89 Minutes	90 Minutes or More
City	9.3	30.4	23.6	23.9	6.8	4.3	1.6
MSA[1]	10.2	27.1	21.4	24.5	9.5	5.6	1.7
U.S.	13.9	30.1	20.8	19.8	7.5	5.5	2.5

Note: Figures are percentages and include workers 16 years old and over; (1) Figures cover the Dallas-Fort Worth-Arlington, TX Metropolitan Statistical Area—see Appendix B for areas included
Source: U.S. Census Bureau, 2008-2010 American Community Survey 3-Year Estimates

Travel Time Index

Area	1985	1990	1995	2000	2005	2010
Urban Area[1]	1.07	1.11	1.14	1.20	1.27	1.23
Average[2]	1.11	1.16	1.18	1.21	1.25	1.20

Note: Travel Time Index—the ratio of travel time in the peak period to the travel time at free-flow conditions. A value of 1.30 indicates a 20-minute free-flow trip takes 26 minutes in the peak. Free-flow speeds (60 mph on freeways and 35 mph on principal arterials) are used as the comparison threshold; (1) Covers the Dallas-Fort Worth-Arlington TX urban area; (2) average of 439 urban areas
Source: Texas Transportation Institute, Urban Mobility Report 2011, September 2011

Public Transportation

Agency Name / Mode of Transportation	Vehicles Operated in Maximum Service	Annual Unlinked Passenger Trips ('000)	Annual Passenger Miles ('000)
Dallas Area Rapid Transit Authority (DART)			
Bus (directly operated)	556	37,693.4	164,323.6
Commuter Rail (purchased transportation)	36	2,432.2	43,689.3
Demand Response (purchased transportation)	197	1,136.0	13,896.9
Light Rail (directly operated)	76	17,799.2	125,403.0
Vanpool (directly operated)	177	924.6	36,784.7

Source: Federal Transit Administration, National Transit Database, 2010

Air Transportation

Airport Name and Code / Type of Service	Passenger Airlines[1]	Passenger Enplanements	Freight Carriers[2]	Freight (lbs.)
Dallas-Fort Worth International (DFW)				
Domestic service (U.S. carriers - 2011)	35	24,839,278	22	310,694,455
International service (U.S. carriers - 2010)	12	2,209,457	7	72,348,682
Dallas Love Field (DAL)				
Domestic service (U.S. carriers - 2011)	25	3,849,150	6	9,050,237
International service (U.S. carriers - 2010)	6	677	1	14,019

Note: (1) Includes all U.S.-based major, minor and commuter airlines that carried at least one passenger during the year; (2) Includes all U.S.-based airlines and freight carriers that transported at least one pound of freight during the year
Source: Bureau of Transportation Statistics, The Intermodal Transportation Database, Air Carriers: T-100 Domestic Market (U.S. Carriers), 2011; Bureau of Transportation Statistics, The Intermodal Transportation Database, Air Carriers: T-100 International Market (U.S. Carriers), 2010

Other Transportation Statistics

Major Highways:	I-20; I-30; I-35E; I-45
Amtrak Service:	Yes
Major Waterways/Ports:	None

Source: Amtrak.com; Google Maps

BUSINESSES

Major Business Headquarters

Company Name	Rankings	
	Fortune[1]	Forbes[2]
AT&T	12	-
Atmos Energy	473	-
Celanese	388	-
Dean Foods	203	-
Energy Future Holdings	292	35
Energy Transfer Equity	351	-
Glazer's	-	126
Holly	289	-
Hunt Consolidated/Hunt Oil	-	90
Neiman Marcus Group	-	89
Sammons Enterprises	-	121
Southwest Airlines	205	-
Tenet Healthcare	266	-
Texas Instruments	175	-

Note: (1) Fortune 500—companies that produce a 10-K are ranked 1 to 500 based on 2010 revenue; (2) all private companies with at least $2 billion in annual revenue are ranked 1 to 212; companies listed are headquartered in the city; dashes indicate no ranking
Source: Fortune, "Fortune 500," May 23, 2011; Forbes, "America's Largest Private Companies," November 16, 2011

Fast-Growing Businesses

According to *Inc.*, Dallas is home to three of America's 500 fastest-growing private companies: **SoftLayer Technologies** (#277); **Ambit Energy** (#390); **Group Excellence** (#450). Criteria: must be an independent, privately-held, for-profit, U.S. corporation, proprietorship or partnership; revenues must be at least $80,000 in 2007 and $2 million in 2010; must have four-year operating/sales history. Holding companies, regulated banks, and utilities were excluded. *Inc., "America's 500 Fastest-Growing Private Companies," September 2011*

According to Deloitte, Dallas is home to six of North America's 500 fastest-growing high-technology companies: **SoftLayer** (#32); **Archipelago Learning** (#196); **One Technologies, LP** (#207); **SPEED FC** (#258); **XT GLOBAL** (#365); **ZixCorp** (#499). Companies are ranked by percentage growth in revenue over a five-year period. Criteria for inclusion: company must be headquartered within North America; must own proprietary intellectual property or proprietary technology that contributes to a significant portion of the company's operating revenue, or devote a significant proportion of revenues to research and development of technology; must have been in business for a minumum of five years with 2006 operating revenues of at least $50,000 USD/CD and 2010 operating revenues of at least $5 million USD/CD. *Deloitte Touche Tohmatsu, 2011 Deloitte Technology Fast 500*[TM]

Minority Business Opportunity

Dallas is home to three companies which are on the *Black Enterprise* Industrial/Service 100 list (100 largest companies based on gross sales): **PrimeSource FoodService Equipment** (#55); **Facility Interiors** (#56); **Parrish McDonald's Restaurants Ltd** (#64). Criteria: operational in previous calendar year; at least 51% black-owned and manufactures/owns the product it sells or provides industrial or consumer services. Brokerages, real estate firms and firms that provide professional services are not eligible. *Black Enterprise, B.E. 100s, 2011*

Dallas is home to two companies which are on the *Black Enterprise* Private Equity 15 list (15 largest private equity firms based on capital under management): **Pharos Capital Group** (#4); **21st Century Group** (#11). Criteria: company must be operational in previous calendar year and be at least 51% black-owned. *Black Enterprise, B.E. 100s, 2011*

Dallas is home to 11 companies which are on the *Hispanic Business* 500 list (500 largest U.S. Hispanic-owned companies based on 2010 revenue): **Pinnacle Technical Resources** (#34); **Azteca-Omega Group** (#60); **Gilbert May** (#112); **Puente Enterprises** (#140); **Aguirre Roden** (#182); **Alman Electric** (#230); **Estrada Hinojosa & Company** (#267); **Southwest Office Systems** (#289); **Pursuit of Excellence HR** (#363); **Carrco Painting Contractor** (#393); **ROC Construction** (#396). Companies included must show at least 51 percent ownership by Hispanic U.S. citizens, and must maintain headquarters in one of the 50 states or Washington, D.C. *Hispanic Business, "Hispanic Business 500," June 2011*

Dallas is home to two companies which are on the *Hispanic Business* Fastest-Growing 100 list (greatest sales growth from 2006 to 2010): **Pinnacle Technical Resources** (#13); **Azteca-Omega Group** (#91). Companies included must show at least 51 percent ownership by Hispanic U.S. citizens, and must maintain headquarters in one of the 50 states or Washington, D.C. In addition, companies must have minimum revenues of $200,000 for calendar year 2005. *Hispanic Business, July/August 2011*

Minority- and Women-Owned Businesses

Group	All Firms		Firms with Paid Employees			
	Firms	Sales ($000)	Firms	Sales ($000)	Employees	Payroll ($000)
Asian	n/a	n/a	n/a	n/a	n/a	n/a
Black	n/a	n/a	n/a	n/a	n/a	n/a
Hispanic	n/a	n/a	n/a	n/a	n/a	n/a
Women	n/a	n/a	n/a	n/a	n/a	n/a
All Firms	268	73,943	91	55,262	533	8,953

Note: Figures cover firms located in the city; minority- and women-owned business are defined as firms in which the corresponding group own 51% or more of the stock or equity of the company; n/a not available
Source: U.S. Census Bureau, 2007 Economic Census, Survey of Business Owners

HOTELS

Hotels/Motels

Area	5 Star		4 Star		3 Star		2 Star		1 Star		Not Rated	
	Num.	Pct.[3]	Num.	Pct.[3]	Num.	Pct.[3]	Num.	Pct.[3]	Num.	Pct.[3]	Num.	Pct.[3]
City[1]	3	0.6	32	6.3	158	31.3	284	56.2	6	1.2	22	4.4
Total[2]	133	0.9	940	6.5	4,569	31.8	7,033	48.9	351	2.4	1,343	9.3

Note: (1) Figures cover Dallas and vicinity; (2) Figures cover all 100 cities in this book; (3) Percentage of hotels which have a given star rating; Star ratings are determined by expedia.com and offer an indication of the general quality of a particular hotel.
Source: expedia.com, April 25, 2012

The Dallas-Plano-Irving, TX metro area is home to two of the best hotels in the U.S. according to *Travel & Leisure*: **Rosewood Mansion on Turtle Creek** (#30); **Rosewood Crescent Hotel** (#152). Criteria: service; location; rooms; food; and value. *Travel & Leisure, "T+L 500, The World's Best Hotels 2012"*

The Dallas-Plano-Irving, TX metro area is home to two of the best hotels in the U.S. according to *Condé Nast Traveler*: **Rosewood Crescent Hotel** (#9); **Rosewood Mansion on Turtle Creek** (#13). The selections are based on over 25,000 responses to the magazine's annual Readers' Choice Survey. *Condé Nast Traveler, "2011 Readers' Choice Awards"*

EVENT SITES

Major Stadiums, Arenas, and Auditoriums

Name	Max. Capacity
American Airlines Center	20,000
Cotton Bowl	92,100
Superpages.com Center	20,111

Source: Original research

Convention Centers

Name	Overall Space (sq. ft.)	Exhibit Space (sq. ft.)	Meeting Space (sq. ft.)	Meeting Rooms
Dallas Convention Center	2,000,000	n/a	929,726	96

Note: n/a not available
Source: Original research

Living Environment

COST OF LIVING

Cost of Living Index

Composite Index	Groceries	Housing	Utilities	Trans-portation	Health Care	Misc. Goods/ Services
96.3	100.7	75.4	108.1	105.0	104.5	105.0

Note: U.S. = 100; Figures cover the Dallas TX urban area.
Source: The Council for Community and Economic Research, ACCRA Cost of Living Index, 2011

Grocery Prices

Area[1]	T-Bone Steak ($/pound)	Frying Chicken ($/pound)	Whole Milk ($/half gal.)	Eggs ($/dozen)	Orange Juice ($/64 oz.)	Coffee ($/11.5 oz.)
City[2]	8.98	1.07	2.05	1.63	3.32	4.87
Avg.	9.25	1.18	2.22	1.66	3.19	4.40
Min.	6.70	0.88	1.31	0.95	2.46	2.94
Max.	14.30	2.16	3.50	3.18	4.75	6.83

Note: (1) Values for the local area are compared with the average, minimum and maximum values for all 335 areas in the Cost of Living Index; (2) Figures cover the Dallas TX urban area; **T-Bone Steak** *(price per pound);* **Frying Chicken** *(price per pound, whole fryer);* **Whole Milk** *(half gallon carton);* **Eggs** *(price per dozen, Grade A, large);* **Orange Juice** *(64 oz. Tropicana or Florida Natural);* **Coffee** *(11.5 oz. can, vacuum-packed, Maxwell House, Hills Bros, or Folgers).*
Source: The Council for Community and Economic Research, ACCRA Cost of Living Index, 2011

Housing and Utility Costs

Area[1]	New Home Price ($)	Apartment Rent ($/month)	All Electric ($/month)	Part Electric ($/month)	Other Energy ($/month)	Telephone ($/month)
City[2]	207,192	738	-	131.03	51.86	28.15
Avg.	285,990	839	163.23	89.00	77.52	26.92
Min.	188,005	460	125.58	45.39	33.89	17.98
Max.	1,197,028	3,244	339.16	181.97	348.69	40.01

Note: (1) Values for the local area are compared with the average, minimum and maximum values for all 335 areas in the Cost of Living Index; (2) Figures cover the Dallas TX urban area; **New Home Price** *(2,400 sf living area, 8,000 sf lot, in urban area with full utilities);* **Apartment Rent** *(950 sf 2 bedroom/1.5 or 2 bath, unfurnished, excluding all utilities except water);* **All Electric** *(average monthly cost for an all-electric home);* **Part Electric** *(average monthly cost for a part-electric home);* **Other Energy** *(average monthly cost for natural gas, fuel oil, coal, wood, and any other forms of energy except electricity);* **Telephone** *(price includes basic monthly rate for a private residential line plus additional local usage charges incurred by a family of four).*
Source: The Council for Community and Economic Research, ACCRA Cost of Living Index, 2011

Health Care, Transportation, and Other Costs

Area[1]	Doctor ($/visit)	Dentist ($/visit)	Optometrist ($/visit)	Gasoline ($/gallon)	Beauty Salon ($/visit)	Men's Shirt ($)
City[2]	100.25	85.21	89.17	3.46	27.60	29.72
Avg.	93.88	81.72	90.54	3.48	32.65	25.06
Min.	60.00	55.33	53.66	3.18	19.78	13.44
Max.	154.98	145.97	183.72	4.31	63.21	46.00

Note: (1) Values for the local area are compared with the average, minimum and maximum values for all 335 areas in the Cost of Living Index; (2) Figures cover the Dallas TX urban area; **Doctor** *(general practitioners routine exam of an established patient);* **Dentist** *(adult teeth cleaning and periodic oral examination);* **Optometrist** *(full vision eye exam for established adult patient);* **Gasoline** *(one gallon regular unleaded, national brand, including all taxes, cash price at self-service pump if available);* **Beauty Salon** *(woman's shampoo, trim, and blow-dry);* **Men's Shirt** *(cotton/polyester dress shirt, pinpoint weave, long sleeves).*
Source: The Council for Community and Economic Research, ACCRA Cost of Living Index, 2011

HOUSING

House Price Index (HPI)

Area	National Ranking[2]	Quarterly Change (%)	One-Year Change (%)	Five-Year Change (%)
MD[1]	91	-0.11	-1.44	1.58
U.S.[3]	-	-0.10	-2.43	-19.16

Note: The HPI is a weighted repeat sales index. It measures average price changes in repeat sales or refinancings on the same properties. This information is obtained by reviewing repeat mortgage transactions on single-family properties whose mortgages have been purchased or securitized by Fannie Mae or Freddie Mac in January 1975; (1) Metropolitan Division - see Appendix B for areas included; (2) Rankings are based on annual percentage change for all metro areas containing at least 15,000 transactions over the last 10 years and ranges from 1 to 306; (3) figures based on a weighted average of Census Division estimates using a purchase only index; all figures are for the period ending December 31, 2011
Source: Federal Housing Finance Agency, House Price Index, February 23, 2012

House Price Valuations

Area	Q4 2005 Price ($000)	Q4 2005 Over-valuation	Q4 2006 Price ($000)	Q4 2006 Over-valuation	Q4 2007 Price ($000)	Q4 2007 Over-valuation	Q4 2008 Price ($000)	Q4 2008 Over-valuation	Q4 2009 Price ($000)	Q4 2009 Over-valuation
MD[1]	127.1	-20.5	131.9	-22.2	134.1	-24.6	136.4	-24.0	137.1	-23.1

Note: Figures show the percentage of over- or under-valuation of single family homes relative to statistically normal house values (e.g. a value of 23.6 indicates that house values are 23.6% overvalued). Statistically normal house values are based on house prices, interest rates, household incomes, population densities, and any historical premiums or discounts metropolitan areas have exhibited over time; (1) Figures cover the Dallas-Plano-Irving, TX - see Appendix B for areas included
Source: Global Insight/PNC Financial Services Group, House Prices in America: 4th Quarter 2009 Update

Median Single-Family Home Prices

Area	2009	2010	2011p	Percent Change 2010 to 2011
MSA[1]	140.5	143.8	148.9	3.5
U.S. Average	172.1	173.1	166.2	-4.0

Note: Figures are median sales prices of existing single-family homes in thousands of dollars; (p) preliminary; n/a not available; (1) Metropolitan Statistical Area—see Appendix B for areas included
Source: National Association of Realtors, Median Sales Price of Existing Single-Family Homes for Metropolitan Areas, 4th Quarter 2011

Affordability Index of Existing Single-Family Homes

Area	2009	2010	2011p	Percent Change 2010 to 2011
MSA[1]	145.7	150.0	152.5	1.7

Note: The housing affordability index measures whether or not a typical family could qualify for a mortgage loan on a typical home. The higher the index, the greater the household purchasing power. An index of 100 is defined as the point where a median-income household has exactly enough income to qualify for the purchase of a median-priced existing single-family home, assuming a 20 percent downpayment and 25 percent of gross income devoted to mortgage principal and interest payments; (p) preliminary; n/a not available; (1) Metropolitan Statistical Area—see Appendix B for areas included
Source: National Association of Realtors, Affordability Index of Existing Single-Family Homes, 2011

Median Apartment Condo-Coop Home Prices

Area	2009	2010	2011p	Percent Change 2010 to 2011
MSA[1]	130.5	132.6	126.0	-5.0
U.S. Average	175.6	171.7	165.1	-3.8

Note: Figures are median sales prices of existing apartment condo-coop homes in thousands of dollars; (p) preliminary; n/a not available; (1) Metropolitan Statistical Area—see Appendix B for areas included
Source: National Association of Realtors, Median Sales Price of Existing Apartment Condo-Coop Homes for Metropolitan Areas, 4th Quarter 2011

Year Housing Structure Built

Area	2005 or Later	2000 -2004	1990 -1999	1980 -1989	1970 -1979	1960 -1969	1950 -1959	Before 1950	Median Year
City	4.4	7.3	9.5	17.7	18.6	15.4	15.2	12.0	1974
MSA[1]	8.6	13.9	16.9	20.1	15.5	10.1	8.4	6.5	1985
U.S.	5.0	8.6	14.0	14.1	16.3	11.3	11.2	19.6	1975

Note: Figures are percentages except for Median Year; (1) Figures cover the Dallas-Fort Worth-Arlington, TX Metropolitan Statistical Area—see Appendix B for areas included
Source: U.S. Census Bureau, 2008-2010 American Community Survey 3-Year Estimates

HEALTH

Health Risk Data

Category	MSA[1] (%)	U.S. (%)
Adults who have been told they have high blood pressure[2]	25.4	28.7
Adults who have been told they have high blood cholesterol[2]	41.8	37.5
Adults who have been told they have diabetes[3]	8.1	8.7
Adults who have been told they have arthritis[2]	18.5	26.0
Adults who have been told they currently have asthma	8.4	9.1
Adults who are current smokers	14.6	17.3
Adults who are heavy drinkers[4]	4.5	5.0
Adults who are binge drinkers[5]	13.2	15.1
Adults who are overweight (BMI 25.0 - 29.9)	29.8	36.2
Adults who are obese (BMI 30.0 - 99.8)	33.8	27.5
Adults who participated in any physical activities in the past month	73.6	76.1
Adults 50+ who have ever had a sigmoidoscopy or colonoscopy	60.5	65.2
Women aged 40+ who have had a mammogram within the past two years	77.2	75.2
Men aged 40+ who have had a PSA test within the past two years	65.2	53.2
Adults aged 65+ who have had flu shot within the past year	68.3	67.5
Adults aged 18–64 who have any kind of health care coverage	75.6	82.2

Note: Data as of 2010 unless otherwise noted; (1) Figures cover the Dallas-Plano-Irving, TX Metropolitan Division—see Appendix B for areas included; (2) Data as of 2009; (3) Figures do not include pregnancy-related, borderline, or pre-diabetes; (4) Heavy drinkers are classified as males having more than two drinks per day or females having more than one drink per day; (5) Binge drinkers are classified as males having five or more drinks on one occasion or females having four or more drinks on one occasion
Source: Centers for Disease Control and Prevention, Behaviorial Risk Factor Surveillance System, SMART: Selected Metropolitan/Micropolitan Area Risk Trends, 2009, 2010

Mortality Rates for the Top 10 Causes of Death in the U.S.

ICD-10[a] Sub-Chapter	ICD-10[a] Code	Age-Adjusted Mortality Rate[1] per 100,000 population County[2]	U.S.
Malignant neoplasms	C00-C97	164.5	175.6
Ischaemic heart diseases	I20-I25	109.4	121.6
Other forms of heart disease	I30-I51	46.1	48.6
Chronic lower respiratory diseases	J40-J47	37.6	42.3
Cerebrovascular diseases	I60-I69	46.6	40.6
Organic, including symptomatic, mental disorders	F01-F09	32.2	26.7
Other degenerative diseases of the nervous system	G30-G31	29.7	24.7
Other external causes of accidental injury	W00-X59	21.8	24.4
Diabetes mellitus	E10-E14	21.6	21.7
Hypertensive diseases	I10-I15	26.5	18.2

Note: (a) ICD-10 = International Classification of Diseases 10th Revision; (1) Mortality rates are a three year average covering 2007-2009; (2) Figures cover Dallas County
Source: Centers for Disease Control and Prevention, National Center for Health Statistics. Underlying Cause of Death 1999-2009 on CDC WONDER Online Database, released 2012. Data for year 2009 are compiled from the Multiple Cause of Death File 2009, Series 20 No. 2O, 2012, Data for year 2008 are compiled from the Multiple Cause of Death File 2008, Series 20 No. 2N, 2011, Data for year 2007 are compiled from Multiple Cause of Death File 2007, Series 20 No. 2M, 2010.

Mortality Rates for Selected Causes of Death

ICD-10[a] Sub-Chapter	ICD-10[a] Code	Age-Adjusted Mortality Rate[1] per 100,000 population	
		County[2]	U.S.
Assault	X85-Y09	9.2	5.7
Human immunodeficiency virus (HIV) disease	B20-B24	7.1	3.3
Influenza and pneumonia	J09-J18	15.4	16.4
Intentional self-harm	X60-X84	9.7	11.5
Malnutrition	E40-E46	0.9	0.8
Obesity and other hyperalimentation	E65-E68	2.0	1.6
Transport accidents	V01-V99	11.1	13.7
Viral hepatitis	B15-B19	2.1	2.2

Note: (a) ICD-10 = International Classification of Diseases 10th Revision; (1) Mortality rates are a three year average covering 2007-2009; (2) Figures cover Dallas County
Source: Centers for Disease Control and Prevention, National Center for Health Statistics. Underlying Cause of Death 1999-2009 on CDC WONDER Online Database, released 2012. Data for year 2009 are compiled from the Multiple Cause of Death File 2009, Series 20 No. 2O, 2012, Data for year 2008 are compiled from the Multiple Cause of Death File 2008, Series 20 No. 2N, 2011, Data for year 2007 are compiled from Multiple Cause of Death File 2007, Series 20 No. 2M, 2010.

Distribution of Physicians and Dentists

Area[1]	Dentists[2]	D.O.[3]	M.D.[4]				
			Total	Family/ General Practice	Pediatrics	Medical Specialties	Surgical Specialties
Local (number)	1,068	425	4,513	371	298	1,651	1,114
Local (rate[5])	4.5	1.8	18.7	1.5	1.2	6.8	4.6
U.S. (rate[5])	4.5	1.9	18.3	2.5	1.4	6.8	4.1

Note: Data as of 2008 unless noted; (1) Local data covers Dallas County; (2) Data as of 2007; (3) Doctor of Osteopathic Medicine; (4) Includes active, non-federal, patient-care, office-based Doctors of Medicine; (5) rate per 10,000 population
Source: Area Resource File (ARF). 2009-2010 Release. U.S. Department of Health and Human Services, Health Resources and Services Administration, Bureau of Health Professions, Rockville, MD, August 2010

Best Hospitals

According to *U.S. News,* the Dallas-Plano-Irving, TX is home to three of the best hospitals in the U.S.: **Baylor University Medical Center** (4 specialties); **Parkland Memorial Hospital** (2 specialties); **University of Texas Southwestern Medical Center** (6 specialties). The hospitals listed were highly ranked in at least one adult specialty. *U.S. News Online, "America's Best Hospitals 2011-12"*

According to *U.S. News,* the Dallas-Plano-Irving, TX is home to two of the best children's hospitals in the U.S.: **Children's Medical Center Dallas** (9 specialties); **Children's Medical Center-Texas Scottish Rite Hospital for Children** (1 specialty). The hospitals listed were highly ranked in at least one pediatric specialty. *U.S. News Online, "America's Best Children's Hospitals 2011-12"*

EDUCATION

Public School District Statistics

District Name	Schls	Pupils	Pupil/ Teacher Ratio	Minority Pupils[1] (%)	Free Lunch Eligible[2] (%)	IEP[3] (%)
Dallas Can Academy Charter	4	2,137	21.9	97.0	80.4	13.6
Dallas ISD	231	157,111	14.7	95.4	80.3	7.7
Highland Park ISD	7	6,448	15.4	7.6	n/a	7.9

Note: Table includes school districts with 2,000 or more students; (1) Percentage of students that are not non-Hispanic white; (2) Percentage of students that are eligible for the free lunch program; (3) Percentage of students that have an Individualized Education Program.
Source: U.S. Department of Education, National Center for Education Statistics, Common Core of Data, Local Education Agency (School District) Universe Survey: School Year 2009-2010; U.S. Department of Education, National Center for Education Statistics, Common Core of Data, Public Elementary/Secondary School Universe Survey: School Year 2009-2010

Top Public High Schools

High School Name	Rank[1]	Score[1]	Grad. Rate[2] (%)	College[3] (%)	AP/IB/ AICE[4] (%)	SAT/ ACT[5] (%)
Booker T. Washington High School for the Performing and Visual Arts	150	0.583	98	94	4.1	1556
Harmony Science Academy-Dallas	165	0.564	100	96	3.8	1502
Highland Park	31	1.210	100	97	6.5	1762
Judge Barefoot Sanders Magnet Center for Public Service	135	0.626	98	96	5.0	1488
School for the Talented and Gifted Magnet	2	2.807	100	93	16.7	1885
School of Business and Management	65	0.932	100	100	5.0	1448
School of Health Professions	261	0.431	100	80	5.0	1200
School of Science and Engineering Magnet	1	2.874	100	100	17.2	1786

Note: (1) Public schools are ranked from 1 to 500 based on the following self-reported statistics (with their corresponding weight in the final score). Schools that had fewer than 10 graduates, as well as those that were newly founded and did not have a graduating senior class in 2010 were excluded; (2) Four-year, on-time graduation rate (25%); (3) Percent of 2010 graduates who enrolled immediately in college (25%); (4) AP/IB/AICE tests per graduate (25%); (5) Average SAT and/or ACT score (10%); Average AP/IB/AICE exam score (10%); AP/IB/AICE courses offered per graduate (5%); (6) School is unranked, but has been identified by Newsweek as one of the nation's most elite public high schools.
Source: Newsweek Online, "Top High Schools 2011"

Highest Level of Education

Area	Less than H.S.	H.S. Diploma	Some College, No Deg.	Associate Degree	Bachelors Degree	Masters Degree	Profess. School Degree	Doctorate Degree
City	26.9	21.6	18.3	4.4	18.5	6.8	2.5	1.0
MSA[1]	17.1	23.0	22.7	6.4	20.9	7.4	1.6	1.0
U.S.	14.7	28.4	21.3	7.6	17.6	7.2	1.9	1.2

Note: Figures cover persons age 25 and over; (1) Figures cover the Dallas-Fort Worth-Arlington, TX Metropolitan Statistical Area—see Appendix B for areas included
Source: U.S. Census Bureau, 2008-2010 American Community Survey 3-Year Estimates

Educational Attainment by Race

Area	High School Graduate or Higher (%)					Bachelor's Degree or Higher (%)				
	Total	White	Black	Asian	Hisp.[2]	Total	White	Black	Asian	Hisp.[2]
City	73.1	76.1	81.3	85.5	42.2	28.8	38.8	13.7	58.5	7.6
MSA[1]	82.9	85.4	87.2	87.8	51.7	30.9	33.2	22.2	55.8	10.5
U.S.	85.3	87.5	81.4	85.5	61.6	28.0	29.3	17.8	50.2	13.0

Note: Figures shown cover persons 25 years old and over; (1) Figures cover the Dallas-Fort Worth-Arlington, TX Metropolitan Statistical Area—see Appendix B for areas included; (2) People of Hispanic origin can be of any race
Source: U.S. Census Bureau, 2008-2010 American Community Survey 3-Year Estimates

School Enrollment by Grade and Control

Area	Preschool (%)		Kindergarten (%)		Grades 1 - 4 (%)		Grades 5 - 8 (%)		Grades 9 - 12 (%)	
	Public	Private	Public	Private	Public	Private	Public	Private	Public	Private
City	67.4	32.6	89.1	10.9	90.4	9.6	90.7	9.3	91.1	8.9
MSA[1]	51.9	48.1	89.1	10.9	91.6	8.4	92.4	7.6	92.6	7.4
U.S.	55.4	44.6	87.1	12.9	89.4	10.6	89.5	10.5	90.4	9.6

Note: Figures shown cover persons 3 years old and over; (1) Figures cover the Dallas-Fort Worth-Arlington, TX Metropolitan Statistical Area—see Appendix B for areas included
Source: U.S. Census Bureau, 2008-2010 American Community Survey 3-Year Estimates

Average Salaries of Public School Classroom Teachers

Area	2010-11		2011-12		Percent Change 2010-11 to 2011-12	Percent Change 2001-02 to 2011-12
	Dollars	Rank[1]	Dollars	Rank[1]		
Texas	48,638	31	49,017	31	0.78	24.90
U.S. Average	55,623	-	56,643	-	1.83	26.8

Note: (1) State rank ranges from 1 to 51 where 1 indicates highest salary.
Source: National Education Association, Rankings & Estimates: Rankings of the States 2011 and Estimates of School Statistics 2012, December 2011

Higher Education

Four-Year Colleges			Two-Year Colleges			Medical Schools[1]	Law Schools[2]	Voc/ Tech[3]
Public	Private Non-profit	Private For-profit	Public	Private Non-profit	Private For-profit			
1	6	4	3	1	9	1	1	15

Note: Figures cover institutions located within the city limits and include main campuses only; (1) includes schools accredited by the Liaison Committee on Medical Education and the American Osteopathic Association's Commission on Osteopathic College Accreditation; (2) includes American Bar Association-accredited law schools; (3) includes all schools with programs that are less than 2 years.
Source: National Center for Education Statistics, Integrated Postsecondary Education System (IPEDS) Peer Analysis System, 2011-12; Association of American Medical Colleges, Member List, April 23, 2012; American Osteopathic Association, Member List, April 23, 2012; Law School Admission Council, Official Guide to ABA-Approved Law Schools Online, April 23, 2012

According to *U.S. News & World Report*, the Dallas-Plano-Irving, TX is home to two of the best national universities in the U.S.: **Southern Methodist University** (#62); **University of Texas–Dallas** (#143). The indicators used to capture academic quality fall into a number of categories: assessment by administrators at peer institutions; retention of students; faculty resources; student selectivity; financial resources; alumni giving; high school counselor ratings of colleges; and graduation rate.*U.S. News & World Report, "America's Best Colleges 2012"*

According to *Forbes,* the Dallas-Plano-Irving, TX is home to one of the best business schools in the U.S.: **SMU (Cox)** (#25). The rankings are based on the return on investment that graduates of the Class of 2006 received (median salary five years after graduation). *Forbes, "Best Business Schools," August 3, 2011*

PRESIDENTIAL ELECTION

2008 Presidential Election Results

Area	Obama	McCain	Nader	Other
Dallas County	57.2	41.9	0.1	0.9
U.S.	52.9	45.6	0.6	0.9

Note: Results are percentages and may not add to 100% due to rounding
Source: Dave Leip's Atlas of U.S. Presidential Elections, www.uselectionatlas.org

EMPLOYERS

Major Employers

Company Name	Industry
AMR Corporation	Air transportation, scheduled
Associates First Capital Corporation	Mortgage bankers
Baylor University Medical Center	General medical and surgical hospitals
Children's Medical Center Dallas	Specialty hospitals, except psychiatric
Combat Support Associates	Engineering services
County of Dallas	County supervisors' and executives' office
Dallas County Hospital District	General medical and surgical hospitals
Fort Worth Independent School District	Public elementary and secondary schools
Housewares Holding Company	Toasters, electric: household
HP Enterprise Services	Computer integrated systems design
J.C. Penney Company	Department stores
JCP Publications Corp.	Department stores
L-3 Communications Corporation	Business economic service
Odyssey HealthCare	Home health care services
Romano's Macaroni Grill	Italian restaurant
SFG Management Limited Liability	Milk processing (pasteurizing, homogenizing, bottling)
Texas Instruments Incorporated	Semiconductors and related devices
University of North Texas	Colleges and universities
University of Texas SW Medical Center	Accident and health insurance
Verizon Business Global	Telephone communication, except radio

Note: Companies shown are located within the Dallas-Fort Worth-Arlington, TX metropolitan area.
Source: Hoovers.com, data extracted April 25 2012

Best Companies to Work For

Balfour Beatty Construction; TDIndustries, headquartered in Dallas, are among "The 100 Best Companies to Work For." To pick the 100 Best Companies to Work For, *Fortune* partnered with the Great Place to Work Institute. Two hundred eighty firms participated in this year's survey. Two-thirds of a company's score is based on the results of the Institute's Trust Index survey, which is sent to a random sample of employees from each company. The questions related to attitudes about management's credibility, job satisfaction, and camaraderie. The other third of the scoring is based on the company's responses to the Institute's Culture Audit, which includes detailed questions about pay and benefit programs, and a series of open-ended questions about hiring practices, internal communication, training, recognition programs, and diversity efforts. Any company that is at least five years old with more than 1,000 U.S. employees is eligible. *Fortune, "The 100 Best Companies to Work For," February 6, 2012*

Texas Instruments, headquartered in Dallas, is among the "100 Best Companies for Working Mothers." Criteria: workforce profile; benefits; child care; women's issues and advancement; flexible work; paid time off and leave; company culture; and work-life programs. This year *Working Mother* gave particular weight to workforce profile, paid time off and company culture. *Working Mother, "100 Best Companies 2011"*

Comerica Bank, headquartered in Dallas, is among the "100 Best Places to Work in IT." To qualify, companies, both public and private, had to have a minimum of 50 IT employees and were selected based on average salary and bonus increases, the percentage of IT staffers promoted, IT staff turnover rates, training and development programs, and the percentage of women and minorities in IT staff and management positions. In addition, *Computerworld* looked at retention efforts, programs for recognizing and rewarding outstanding performances, and benefits such as flextime, elder care and child care, and reimbursement for college tuition and the cost of pursuing technology certifications. *Computerworld, "100 Best Places to Work in IT 2011"*

AT&T; Texas Instruments, located in Dallas, are among the "Top Companies for Executive Women." To be named to the list, companies with a minimum of two women on the board complete a comprehensive application that focuses on the number of women in senior ranks. In addition to assessing corporate programs and policies dedicated to advancing women, NAFE examined the number of women in each company overall, in senior management, and on its board of directors, paying particular attention to the number of women with profit-and-loss responsibility. *National Association for Female Executives, "2012 NAFE Top 50 Companies for Executive Women"*

PUBLIC SAFETY

Crime Rate

Area	All Crimes	Violent Crimes				Property Crimes		
		Murder	Forcible Rape	Robbery	Aggrav. Assault	Burglary	Larceny -Theft	Motor Vehicle Theft
City	5,608.2	11.3	38.6	343.4	307.7	1,499.4	2,766.1	641.6
Suburbs[1]	3,066.5	1.9	21.1	57.2	132.2	658.3	1,979.6	216.3
Metro[2]	3,818.8	4.7	26.3	141.9	184.1	907.2	2,212.4	342.2
U.S.	3,345.5	4.8	27.5	119.1	252.3	699.6	2,003.5	238.8

Note: Figures are crimes per 100,000 population; (1) All areas within the metro area that are located outside the city limits; (2) Metropolitan Division—see Appendix B for areas included
Source: FBI Uniform Crime Reports, 2010

Hate Crimes

Area	Number of Quarters Reported	Bias Motivation				
		Race	Religion	Sexual Orientation	Ethnicity	Disability
City	4	2	3	5	2	0

Source: Federal Bureau of Investigation, Hate Crime Statistics 2010

Identity Theft Consumer Complaints

Area	Complaints	Complaints per 100,000 Population	Rank[2]
MSA[1]	7,171	116.7	47
U.S.	279,156	90.4	-

Note: (1) Metropolitan Statistical Area—see Appendix B for areas included; (2) Rank ranges from 1 to 384 where 1 indicates greatest number of identity theft complaints per 100,000 population
Source: Federal Trade Commission, Consumer Sentinel Network Data Book for January–December 2011

Fraud and Other Consumer Complaints

Area	Complaints	Complaints per 100,000 Population	Rank[2]
MSA[1]	30,244	492.2	163
U.S.	1,533,924	496.8	-

Note: (1) Metropolitan Statistical Area—see Appendix B for areas included; (2) Rank ranges from 1 to 384 where 1 indicates greatest number of fraud and other complaints per 100,000 population
Source: Federal Trade Commission, Consumer Sentinel Network Data Book for January–December 2011

RECREATION

Culture

Dance[1]	Theatre[1]	Instrumental Music[1]	Vocal Music[1]	Series/ Festivals	Museums	Zoos and Aquariums[2]
2	16	7	3	6	18	2

Note: (1) Number of professional perfoming groups; (2) AZA-accredited
Source: The Grey House Performing Arts Directory, 2011-2012; Official Museum Directory, 2011; American Association of Museums, AAM Member Museums, April 2012; Association of Zoos & Aquariums, AZA Member Zoos & Aquariums, April 2012

Professional Sports Teams

Team Name	League
Dallas Cowboys	National Football League (NFL)
Dallas Mavericks	National Basketball Association (NBA)
Dallas Stars	National Hockey League (NHL)
FC Dallas	Major League Soccer (MLS)
Texas Rangers	Major League Baseball (MLB)

Note: Includes teams located in the Dallas-Fort Worth metro area.
Source: Original research

CLIMATE

Average and Extreme Temperatures

Temperature	Jan	Feb	Mar	Apr	May	Jun	Jul	Aug	Sep	Oct	Nov	Dec	Yr.
Extreme High (°F)	85	90	100	100	101	112	111	109	107	101	91	87	112
Average High (°F)	55	60	68	76	84	92	96	96	89	79	67	58	77
Average Temp. (°F)	45	50	57	66	74	82	86	86	79	68	56	48	67
Average Low (°F)	35	39	47	56	64	72	76	75	68	57	46	38	56
Extreme Low (°F)	-2	9	12	30	39	53	58	58	42	24	16	0	-2

Note: Figures cover the years 1945-1993
Source: National Climatic Data Center, International Station Meteorological Climate Summary, 9/96

Average Precipitation/Snowfall/Humidity

Precip./Humidity	Jan	Feb	Mar	Apr	May	Jun	Jul	Aug	Sep	Oct	Nov	Dec	Yr.
Avg. Precip. (in.)	1.9	2.3	2.6	3.8	4.9	3.4	2.1	2.3	2.9	3.3	2.3	2.1	33.9
Avg. Snowfall (in.)	1	1	Tr	Tr	0	0	0	0	0	Tr	Tr	Tr	3
Avg. Rel. Hum. 6am (%)	78	77	75	77	82	81	77	76	80	79	78	77	78
Avg. Rel. Hum. 3pm (%)	53	51	47	49	51	48	43	41	46	46	48	51	48

Note: Figures cover the years 1945-1993; Tr = Trace amounts (<0.05 in. of rain; <0.5 in. of snow)
Source: National Climatic Data Center, International Station Meteorological Climate Summary, 9/96

Weather Conditions

Temperature			Daytime Sky			Precipitation		
10°F & below	32°F & below	90°F & above	Clear	Partly cloudy	Cloudy	0.01 inch or more precip.	0.1 inch or more snow/ice	Thunder-storms
1	34	102	108	160	97	78	2	49

Note: Figures are average number of days per year and cover the years 1945-1993
Source: National Climatic Data Center, International Station Meteorological Climate Summary, 9/96

HAZARDOUS WASTE

Superfund Sites

Dallas has one hazardous waste site on the EPA's Superfund Final National Priorities List: **RSR Corp.** *U.S. Environmental Protection Agency, Final National Priorities List, April 17, 2012*

AIR & WATER QUALITY

Air Quality Index

Area	Percent of Days when Air Quality was...[2]					AQI Statistics[2]	
	Good	Moderate	Unhealthy for Sensitive Groups	Unhealthy	Very Unhealthy	Maximum	Median
Area[1]	66.0	28.2	4.9	0.8	0.0	156	44

Note: Air Quality Index (AQI) is an index for reporting daily air quality. EPA calculates the AQI for five major air pollutants regulated by the Clean Air Act: ground-level ozone, particle pollution (aka particulate matter), carbon monoxide, sulfur dioxide, and nitrogen dioxide. The AQI runs from 0 to 500. The higher the AQI value, the greater the level of air pollution and the greater the health concern. There are six AQI categories: "Good" AQI is between 0 and 50. Air quality is considered satisfactory; "Moderate" AQI is between 51 and 100. Air quality is acceptable; "Unhealthy for Sensitive Groups" When AQI values are between 101 and 150, members of sensitive groups may experience health effects; "Unhealthy" When AQI values are between 151 and 200 everyone may begin to experience health effects; "Very Unhealthy" AQI values between 201 and 300 trigger a health alert; "Hazardous" AQI values over 300 trigger warnings of emergency conditions (not shown); (1) Data covers Dallas County; (2) Based on 365 days with AQI data in 2011.
Source: U.S. Environmental Protection Agency, AirData Report, 2011

Air Quality Index Pollutants

Area	Percent of Days when AQI Pollutant was...[2]					
	Carbon Monoxide	Nitrogen Dioxide	Ozone	Sulfur Dioxide	Particulate Matter 2.5	Particulate Matter 10
Area[1]	0.0	13.2	49.0	0.0	35.3	2.5

Note: The Air Quality Index (AQI) is an index for reporting daily air quality. EPA calculates the AQI for five major air pollutants regulated by the Clean Air Act: ground-level ozone, particle pollution (also known as particulate matter), carbon monoxide, sulfur dioxide, and nitrogen dioxide. The AQI runs from 0 to 500. The higher the AQI value, the greater the level of air pollution and the greater the health concern; (1) Data covers Dallas County; (2) Based on 365 days with AQI data in 2011.
Source: U.S. Environmental Protection Agency, AirData Report, 2011

Air Quality Index Trends

Area	Trend Sites (days)								All Sites (days)
	2003	2004	2005	2006	2007	2008	2009	2010	2010
MSA[1]	49	50	80	54	34	30	32	15	18

Note: Figures are the number of days the AQI value exceeded 100 in a given year. An AQI value greater than 100 indicates that air quality would have been in the unhealthful range on that day. Data from exceptional events are included. These counts are presented in two ways. First, the counts are based on sites having an adequate record of monitoring data during the trend period (trend sites). These counts represent the relative change in the number of days with AQI values greater than 100. In the last column, the counts are based on all sites with data in the most recent year (because it is possible for a site to have data in the most recent year but not enough data to be a trend site); (1) Data covers the Dallas-Fort Worth-Arlington, TX—see Appendix B for areas included
Source: U.S. Environmental Protection Agency, Air Quality Index Information, "Number of Days with Air Quality Index Values Greater than 100 at Trend Sites, 2000-2010, and at All Sites in 2010"

Maximum Air Pollutant Concentrations: Particulate Matter, Ozone, CO and Lead

	Particulate Matter 10 (ug/m³)	Particulate Matter 2.5 Wtd AM (ug/m³)	Particulate Matter 2.5 24-Hr (ug/m³)	Ozone (ppm)	Carbon Monoxide (ppm)	Lead (ug/m³)
MSA[1] Level	62	10.8	25	0.085	2	0.77
NAAQS[2]	150	15	35	0.075	9	0.15
Met NAAQS[2]	Yes	Yes	Yes	No	Yes	No

Note: Data from exceptional events are not included; (1) Data covers the Dallas-Fort Worth-Arlington, TX—see Appendix B for areas included; (2) National Ambient Air Quality Standards; ppm = parts per million; ug/m³ = micrograms per cubic meter; n/a not available
Concentrations: Particulate Matter 10 (coarse particulate)—highest second maximum 24-hour concentration; Particulate Matter 2.5 Wtd AM (fine particulate)—highest weighted annual mean concentration; Particulate Matter 2.5 24-Hour (fine particulate)—highest 98th percentile 24-hour concentration; Ozone—highest fourth daily maximum 8-hour concentration; Carbon Monoxide—highest second maximum non-overlapping 8-hour concentration; Lead—maximum running 3-month average
Source: U.S. Environmental Protection Agency, CBSA Factbook 2010, Air Quality Statistics by City, 2010

Maximum Air Pollutant Concentrations: Nitrogen Dioxide and Sulfur Dioxide

	Nitrogen Dioxide AM (ppb)	Nitrogen Dioxide 1-Hr (ppb)	Sulfur Dioxide AM (ppb)	Sulfur Dioxide 1-Hr (ppb)	Sulfur Dioxide 24-Hr (ppb)
MSA[1] Level	13.186	56.9	0.808	17.3	4.5
NAAQS[2]	53	100	30	75	140
Met NAAQS[2]	Yes	Yes	Yes	Yes	Yes

Note: Data from exceptional events are not included; (1) Data covers the Dallas-Fort Worth-Arlington, TX—see Appendix B for areas included; (2) National Ambient Air Quality Standards; ppb = parts per billion; n/a not available
Concentrations: Nitrogen Dioxide AM—highest arithmetic mean concentration; Nitrogen Dioxide 1-Hr—highest 98th percentile 1-hour daily maximum concentration; Sulfur Dioxide AM—highest annual mean concentration; Sulfur Dioxide 1-Hr—highest 99th percentile 1-hour daily maximum concentration; Sulfur Dioxide 24-Hr—highest second maximum 24-hour concentration
Source: U.S. Environmental Protection Agency, CBSA Factbook 2010, Air Quality Statistics by City, 2010

Drinking Water

Water System Name	Pop. Served	Primary Water Source Type	Violations[1] Health Based	Violations[1] Monitoring/ Reporting
Dallas Water Utility	1,280,500	Surface	0	0

Note: (1) Based on violation data from January 1, 2011 to December 31, 2011 (includes unresolved violations from earlier years)
Source: U.S. Environmental Protection Agency, Office of Ground Water and Drinking Water, Safe Drinking Water Information System (based on data extracted April 18, 2012)

El Paso, Texas

Background

El Paso is so named because it sits in a spectacular pass through the Franklin Mountains, at an average elevation of 3,700 feet and in direct view of peaks that rise to 7,200 feet. El Paso is the fourth-largest city in Texas. It lies just south of New Mexico on the Rio Grande and just north of Juarez, Mexico.

The early Spanish explorer Alvar Nunez Cabeza de Vaca (circa 1530) probably passed through this area, but the city was named in 1598 by Juan de Onante, who dubbed it El Paso del Rio del Norte, or The Pass at the River of the North. It was also Onante who declared the area Spanish, on the authority of King Philip II, but a mission was not established until 1649. For some time, El Paso del Norte was the seat of government for northern Mexico, but settlement in and around the present-day city was sparse for many years.

This had changed considerably by 1807, when Zebulon A. Pike, a United States Army officer, was interned in El Paso after being convicted of trespassing on Spanish territory. He found the area pleasant and well tended, with many irrigated fields and vineyards and a thriving trade in brandy and wine. In spite of Pike's stay there, though, El Paso remained for many years a largely Mexican region, escaping most of the military action connected to the Texas Revolution.

In the wake of the Mexican War (1846-1848) and in response to the California gold rush in 1849, El Paso emerged as a significant way station on the road West. A federal garrison, Fort Bliss, was established there in 1849, and was briefly occupied by Confederate sympathizers in 1862. Federal forces quickly reoccupied the fort, however, and the area was firmly controlled by Union armies. El Paso was incorporated in 1873, and after 1881, growth accelerated considerably with the building of rail links through the city, giving rise to ironworks, mills, and breweries.

During the Mexican Revolution (1911), El Paso was an important and disputed city, with Pancho Villa himself a frequent visitor, and many of his followers residents of the town. Mexico's national history, in fact, continued to affect El Paso until 1967 when, by way of settling a historic border dispute, 437 acres of the city was ceded to Mexico. Much of the disputed area on both sides of the border was made into parkland. The U.S. National Parks Service maintains the Chamizal Park on the U.S. side and it plays host to a variety of community events during the year including the Chamizal Film Festival and the summer concert series, Music Under the Stars.

One of the major points of entry to the U.S. from Mexico, El Paso is a vitally important international city and a burgeoning center of rail, road, and air transportation. During the 1990s, the city's economy shifted more toward a service-oriented economy and away from a manufacturing base.

Transportation services and motor freight transportation and warehousing has been increasing, and tourism is becoming a growing segment of the economy. Government and military are also sources of employment, with Ft. Bliss being the largest Air Defense Artillery Training Center in the world. The city hosts the University of Texas at El Paso, and a community college. Cultural amenities include the Tigua Indian Cultural Center, a Wilderness Park Museum, the El Paso Zoo, museums, a symphony orchestra, a ballet company, and many theaters. The city's "Wild West" qualities have long made it a popular destination for musicians-many of whom have recorded albums at El Paso's Sonic Ranch recording studio.

El Paso 2015 downtown renovation project began in 2006, with the goal of increasing El Paso's aesthetic appeal. The first stages of this project are complete, and have included an open-air mall and "lifestyle center" in the city's central area, a new Doubletree by Hilton Hotel, and renovations of several historic downtown buildings.

In August 2007, El Paso became the site of the world's largest inland desalination plant, designed to produce 27.5 million gallons of fresh water daily making it a critical component of the region's water portfolio.

The weather in El Paso is of the mountain-desert type, with very little precipitation. Summers are hot, humidity is low and winters are mild. However, temperatures in the flat Rio Grande Valley nearby are notably cooler at night year-round. There is plenty of sunshine and clear skies 202 days of the year.

Rankings

General Rankings

- *Men's Health Living* ranked 100 U.S. cities in terms of quality of life. El Paso was ranked #63 and received a grade of C-. Criteria: number of fitness facilities; air quality; number of physicians; male/female ratio; education levels; household income; cost of living. *Men's Health Living, Spring 2008*

- El Paso appeared on RelocateAmerica's list of best places to live in America. The annual "Top 100 Places to Live" list recognizes the top communities as nominated by their residents & local businesses. RelocateAmerica's Research Group determines the list based on review of various data gathered for economic, employment, housing, education, industry, opportunity, environment and recreation along with feedback from area leaders and residents. *RelocateAmerica.com, "Top 100 Places to Live for 2011"*

Business/Finance Rankings

- El Paso was identified as one of the 20 weakest-performing metro areas during the recession and recovery from trough quarter through the third quarter of 2011. Criteria: percent change in employment; percentage point change in unemployment rate; percent change in gross metropolitan product; percent change in House Price Index. *Brookings Institution, MetroMonitor: Tracking Economic Recession and Recovery in America's 100 Largest Metropolitan Areas, December 2011*

- The El Paso metro area was identified as one of the most debt-ridden places in America by credit reporting agency Equifax. The metro area was ranked #2. Criteria: proportion of average yearly income owed to credit card companies. *Equifax, "The Most Debt-Ridden Cities in America," February 23, 2012*

- *American City Business Journals* ranked America's 261 largest cities in terms of their resident's wealth. El Paso ranked #244. Criteria: per capita income; median household income; percentage of households with annual incomes of $200,000 or more; median home value. *American City Business Journals, "Where the Money Is: America's Wealth Centers," August 18, 2008*

- The El Paso metro area appeared on the Milken Institute "2011 Best Performing Metros" list. Rank: #2 out of 200 large metro areas. Criteria: job growth; wage and salary growth; high-tech output growth. *Milken Institute, "2011 Best Performing Metros"*

- The El Paso metro area was selected as one of the best cities for entrepreneurs in America by *Inc. Magazine*. Criteria: job-growth data for 335 metro areas was analyzed for: recent growth trend; mid-term growth; long-term trend; current year growth. The El Paso metro area ranked #26 among mid-sized metro areas and #96 overall. *Inc. Magazine, "The Best Cities for Doing Business," July 2008*

- *Forbes* ranked the 200 most populous metro areas in the U.S. in terms of the "Best Places for Business and Careers." The El Paso metro area was ranked #36. Criteria: costs (business and living); job growth (past and projected); income growth; educational attainment; projected economic growth; crime; cultural and recreational opportunities; net migration patterns; number of highly ranked colleges. *Forbes, "Best Places for Business and Careers," June 2011*

Children/Family Rankings

- The El Paso metro area was selected as one of the "Best Cities for Relocating Families" by Worldwide ERC and Primacy Relocation. The 2008 study looked at nearly 50 factors important to relocating families including: recent job growth; nearby top-ranked colleges; in-state tuition for four-year public colleges; population growth since 2000; pediatricians per 100,000 population; and a Green Living index. *Worldwide ERC and Primacy Relocation, "2008 Best Cities for Relocating Families"*

- *Fit Pregnancy* magazine ranked the 50 best U.S. cities in which to have a baby. El Paso was ranked #34. Criteria: access to hospitals and doctors; affordability; birthing options; breastfeeding; child care; fertility laws/resources; maternal and infant health risk; parks/stroller friendliness; safety. *Fit Pregnancy, "The Best Cities in America to Have a Baby 2008"*

Dating/Romance Rankings

- El Paso appeared on *Men's Health's* list of the most sex-happy cities in America. The city ranked #27 of 100. Criteria: condom sales; birth rates; sex toy sales; rates of chlamydia, gonorrhea, and syphilis. *Men's Health, "America's Most Sex-Happy Cities," October 2010*

- *Men's Health* ranked 100 U.S. cities in terms of best (and worst) marriages. El Paso was ranked #98 (#1 = worst). Criteria: rate of failed marriages; stringency of divorce laws; percentage of population who've split; number of licensed marriage and family therapists. *Men's Health, "Splitsville, USA," May 2010*

- The El Paso metro area was selected as one of the "Best Cities for Relocating Singles" by Worldwide ERC and Primacy Relocation. The area ranked #79 out of the 100 largest metro areas in the U.S. Criteria: recent job growth; recent singles population growth; overall population growth; affordable rental housing; cost-of-living index; expanded arts and recreation opportunities; ratio of single men and single women; affordability of quality higher education (including state residency requirements); diversity index; climate; population density. *Worldwide ERC and Primacy Relocation, "2008 Best Cities for Relocating Singles"*

Education Rankings

- *Men's Health* ranked 100 U.S. cities in terms of their education levels. El Paso was ranked #77 (#1 = most educated city). Criteria: high school graduation rates; school enrollment; educational attainment; number of households who have outstanding student loans; number of households whose members have taken adult-education courses. *Men's Health, "Where School Is In: The Most and Least Educated Cities," September 12, 2011*

- El Paso was selected as one of "America's Most Literate Cities." The city ranked #73 out of the 75 largest U.S. cities. Criteria: number of booksellers; library resources; Internet resources; educational attainment; periodical publishing resources; newspaper circulation. *Central Connecticut State University, "America's Most Literate Cities 2011"*

- El Paso was identified as one of the 100 "smartest" metro areas in the U.S. The area ranked #96. Criteria: the editors rated the collective brainpower of the 100 largest metro areas in the U.S. based on their residents' educational attainment. *American City Business Journals, April 14, 2008*

- El Paso was identified as one of "America's Brainiest Bastions" by *Portfolio.com*. The metro area ranked #186 out of 200. *Portfolio.com* analyzed levels of educational attainment in the nation's 200 largest metropolitan areas. The editors established scores for five levels of educational attainment, based on relative earning power of adult workers age 25 or older. Scores were determined by comparing the median income for all workers with the median income for those workers at a specified educational level. *Portfolio.com, "America's Brainiest Bastions," December 1, 2010*

Environmental Rankings

- El Paso was selected as one of 22 "Smarter Cities" for energy by the Natural Resources Defense Council. The city appeared as one of 12 cities in the large city (population 250,000 and over) category. Criteria: investment in green power; energy efficiency measures; conservation. *Natural Resources Defense Council, "2010 Smarter Cities," July 19, 2010*

- 100 of the largest metro areas in the U.S. were analyzed in terms of their current drought severity. The El Paso metro area ranked #95 (#1 = driest). The rankings were based on statistics such as long-term precipitation trends and patterns and the Palmer drought indices. *Sperling's BestPlaces, www.BestPlaces.net, "America's Drought-Riskiest Cities," November 2007*

- The El Paso metro area appeared in *Country Home's* "Best Green Places" report. The area ranked #156 out of 379. Criteria: official energy policies; green power; green buildings; availability of fresh, locally grown food. *Country Home, "Best Green Places," 2008*

Health/Fitness Rankings

- El Paso was selected as one of the 25 fattest cities in America by *Men's Fitness Online*. It ranked #7 out of America's 50 largest cities. Criteria: fitness centers and sport stores; nutrition; sports participation; TV viewing; overweight/sedentary; junk food; air quality; geography; commute; parks and open space; city recreational facilities; access to healthcare; motivation; mayor and city initiatives; state obesity initiatives. *Men's Fitness, "The Fittest and Fattest Cities in America," March 5, 2012*

- El Paso was identified as a "2011 Asthma Capital." The area ranked #50 out of the nation's 100 largest metropolitan areas. Twelve factors were used to identify the most challenging places to live for people with asthma: estimated prevalence; self-reported prevalence; crude death rate for asthma; annual pollen score; annual air quality; public smoking laws; number of board-certified asthma specialists; school inhaler access laws; rescue medication use; controller medication use; uninsured rate; poverty rate. *Asthma and Allergy Foundation of America, "2011 Asthma Capitals"*

- El Paso was identified as a "2011 Fall Allergy Capital." The area ranked #33 out of 100. Three groups of factors were used to identify the most severe cities for people with allergies during the fall season: annual pollen levels; medicine utilization; access to board-certified allergists. *Asthma and Allergy Foundation of America, "2011 Fall Allergy Capitals"*

- El Paso was identified as a "2012 Spring Allergy Capital." The area ranked #34 out of 100. Three groups of factors were used to identify the most severe cities for people with allergies during the spring season: annual pollen levels; medicine utilization; access to board-certified allergists. *Asthma and Allergy Foundation of America, "2012 Spring Allergy Capitals"*

- *Men's Health* examined 100 major U.S. cities and selected the best and worst cities for men. El Paso ranked #52. Criteria: 35 statistical parameters of long life in the categories of health, quality of life, and fitness. *Men's Health, "The 10 Best and Worst Cities for Men 2012," January/February 2012*

- *Men's Health* examined the nation's largest 100 cities and identified the cities with the best and worst teeth. El Paso was ranked among the ten worst at #6. Criteria: annual dentist visits; canceled appointments; regular flossers; fluoride usage; dental extractions. *Men's Health, April 2008*

- The El Paso metro area appeared in the 2011 Gallup-Healthways Well-Being Index. The index, based on interviews with more than 350,000 Americans, measured jobs, finances, physical health, emotional state of mind and communities. The metro area ranked #163 out of 190. Criteria: life evaluation; emotional health; work environment; physical health; healthy behaviors; basic access (basic needs optimal for a healthy life, such as access to food and medicine, having health insurance and feeling safe while walking at night). *Gallup-Healthways, "State of Well-Being 2011"*

- *Men's Health* ranked 100 U.S. cities in terms of their activity levels. El Paso was ranked #73 (#1 = most active city). Criteria: where and how often residents exercise; percentage of households that watch more than 15 hours of cable television a week and buy more than 11 video games a year; death rate from deep-vein thrombosis, a condition linked to sitting for extended periods of time. *Men's Health, "Where Sit Happens: The Most and Least Active Cities in America," June 20, 2011*

Real Estate Rankings

- *Fortune* ranked the 100 largest metro areas in the U.S. in terms of projected median home price change in 2010. The El Paso metro area ranked #33. *Fortune, "The 2010 Housing Outlook," December 9, 2009*

- The El Paso metro area was identified as one of the 25 best housing markets in the U.S. in 2011. The area ranked #20 out of 149 markets with a home price appreciation of 1.3%. Criteria: year-over-year change of median sales price of existing single-family homes between the 4th quarter of 2010 and the 4th quarter of 2011. *National Association of Realtors®, Median Sales Price of Existing Single-Family Homes for Metropolitan Areas, 4th Quarter 2011*

- El Paso appeared on *ApartmentRatings.com* "Top Cities for Renters" list in 2009." The area ranked #75. Overall satisfaction ratings were ranked using thousands of user submitted scores for hundreds of apartment complexes located in the 100 most populated U.S. municipalities. *ApartmentRatings.com, "2009 Renter Satisfaction Rankings"*

- The Center for Housing Policy ranked 210 U.S. metropolitan areas by the fair market rent for a two-bedroom unit. The El Paso metro area was ranked #208. (#1 = most expensive) with a rent of $598. Criteria: Fair Market Rent (FMR) in effect during the fourth quarter of 2009 based on HUD's fiscal year 2010 FMRs. *The Center for Housing Policy, "Paycheck to Paycheck: Most to Least Expensive Rental Markets in 2009"*

- The El Paso metro area was identified as one of the markets with the best expected performance in home prices over the next 12 months. *Local Market Monitor, "First Quarter Home Price Forecast for Largest US Markets," March 2, 2011*

- The El Paso metro area was identified as one of the best U.S. markets to invest in rental property" by HomeVestors and Local Market Monitor. The area ranked #32 out of 100. Criteria: risk-return premium relative to national average. *HomeVestors and Local Market Monitor, "Best 100 U.S. Markets to Invest in Rental Property," March 9, 2012*

Safety Rankings

- Symantec, the makers of Norton, in partnership with Sperling's BestPlaces, ranked the 50 largest cities in the U.S. in terms of their vulnerability to cybercrime. The city ranked #49. Criteria: number of cyberattacks and potential infections; level of Internet access; expenditures on smartphones and computer hardware/software; wireless hotspots; broadband connectivity; Internet usage; online purchases. *Symantec, "Riskiest Online Cities of 2012" February 15, 2012*

- Farmers Insurance Group of Companies, in partnership with Sperling's BestPlaces, ranked 379 metro areas and identified the "Most Secure U.S. Places to Live." The El Paso metro area ranked #3 out of the top 20 in the large metro area category (500,000 or more residents). Criteria: crime statistics; extreme weather; risk of natural disasters; housing depreciation; foreclosures; environmental hazards; terrorist threats; air quality; life expectancy; mortality rates from cancer and motor vehicle accidents; job loss numbers. *Farmers Insurance Group, "Most Secure U.S. Places to Live 2011," December 15, 2011*

- Allstate ranked the 193 largest cities in America in terms of driver safety. El Paso ranked #78. In addition, drivers were 3.9% more likely to have had an accident compared to the national average. Allstate researchers analyzed internal property damage reported claims over a two-year period (from January 2008 to December 2009) to protect findings from external influences such as weather or road construction. A weighted average of the two-year numbers determined the annual percentages. The report defines an auto crash as any collision resulting in a property damage claim. *Allstate, "2011 Allstate America's Best Drivers Report™"*

- El Paso was identified as one of the safest large cities in America by CQ Press. All 34 cities with populations of 500,000 or more that reported crime rates in 2010 for murder, rape, robbery, aggravated assault, burglary, and motor vehicle thefts were ranked. The city ranked #1 out of the top 10. *CQ Press, City Crime Rankings 2011-2012*

- The National Insurance Crime Bureau ranked 366 metro areas in the U.S. in terms of per capita rates of vehicle theft. The El Paso metro area ranked #34 (#1 = highest rate). Criteria: number of vehicle theft offenses per 100,000 inhabitants in 2010. *National Insurance Crime Bureau, "Hot Spots," June 21, 2011*

Sports/Recreation Rankings

- El Paso appeared on the *Sporting News* list of the "Best Sports Cities" for 2011. The area ranked #105 out of 271 cities in the U.S. *Sporting News* takes a 12-month snapshot of each city's sports, putting a heavy premium on regular-season won-lost records (from the most recently completed season). Other criteria include: playoff berths, bowl appearances and tournament bids; championships; applicable power ratings; quality of competition; overall fan fervor (measured in part by attendance); abundance of teams (rewarding quality over quantity); stadium and arena quality; ticket availability and prices; franchise ownership; and marquee appeal of athletes. *Sporting News, "Best Sports Cities 2011," October 4, 2011*

Technology Rankings

- El Paso was selected as a 2011 Digital Cities Survey winner. The city ranked #6 in the large city (250,000 or more population) category. The survey examined and assessed how city governments are utilizing information technology to operate and deliver quality service to their customers and citizens. Survey questions focused on implementation and adoption of online service delivery; planning and governance; and the infrastructure and architecture that make the transformation to digital government possible. *Center for Digital Government, "2011 Digital Cities Survey"*

- Scarborough Research, a leading market research firm, identified the El Paso DMA (Designated Market Area) as one of the top markets for text messaging with more than 50% of cell phone subscribers age 18+ utilizing the text messaging feature on their phone. *Scarborough Research, November 24, 2008*

Women/Minorities Rankings

- *Women's Health* examined U.S. cities and identified the 100 best cities for women. El Paso was ranked #42. Criteria: 30 categories were examined from obesity and breast cancer rates to commuting times and hours spent working out. *Women's Health, "Best Cities for Women 2012"*

- El Paso was ranked #75 out of 100 metro areas in *SELF Magazine's* ranking of America's healthiest places for women." A panel of experts came up with more than 50 criteria including death and disease rates, environmental indicators, community resources, and lifestyle habits. *SELF Magazine, "Secrets of America's Healthiest Women," December 2008*

- El Paso was selected as one of the 25 healthiest cities for Latinas by *Latina Magazine*. The city ranked #14. Criteria: U.S. cities with populations over 500,000 residents were evaluated on the following criteria: percentage of 18-34 year-olds per city; Latino college graduation rates; number of colleges and universities; affordability; housing costs; income growth over time; average salary; percentage of singles; climate; safety; how the city's diversity compares to the national average; opportunities for minority entrepreneurs. *Latina Magazine, "Top 15 U.S. Cities for Young Latinos to Live In," August 19, 2011*

Miscellaneous Rankings

- *Men's Health* ranked 100 U.S. cities by their level of sadness. El Paso was ranked #58 (#1 = saddest city). Criteria: suicide rates; unemployment rates; percentage of households that use antidepressants; percent of population who report feeling blue all or most of the time. *Men's Health, "Frown Towns," November 28, 2011*

- The El Paso metro area appeared in *AutoMD.com's* ranking of the "Best and Worst Cities for Auto Repair." The metro area ranked #13 (#1 is best). The 50 most-populated metro areas in the U.S. were ranked on three critical factors: repair affordability; price disparity range; shop integrity factor. *AutoMD.com, "Advocacy for Repair Shop Fairness Report," February 24, 2010*

- *Men's Health* examined the nation's largest 100 cities and identified "America's Most Political Cities." El Paso was ranked among the ten least political at #3. Criteria: percentage of active registered voters; percentage of ballots counted of active registration; percentage of income donated to 2008 presidential election; campaign spending; percentage of registrants who voted in the 2008 primaries; percentage of voters in the 2004/2006 Senate election; percentage of voters in the 2004-2007 gubernatorial election. *Men's Health, "Ranking America's Cities: America's Most Political Cities," October 2008*

- El Paso appeared on Procter & Gamble's list of the "Top-20 All-Time Sweatiest Cities." The city was ranked #13. The rankings are based on computer simulations of the amount of sweat a person of average height and weight would produce walking around for an hour in the average temperatures during the summer months, based on historical weather data during June, July and August from 2001-2008 for each city. *Procter & Gamble, Old Spice Press Release, "Top-20 All-Time Sweatiest Cities," July 1, 2009*

Business Environment

CITY FINANCES

City Government Finances

Component	2009 ($000)	2009 ($ per capita)
Total Revenues	425,836	702
Total Expenditures	888,825	1,465
Debt Outstanding	1,355,378	2,233
Cash and Securities[1]	1,384,675	2,282

Note: (1) Cash and security holdings of a government at the close of its fiscal year, including those of its dependent agencies, utilities, and liquor stores.
Source: U.S Census Bureau, State & Local Government Finances 2009

City Government Revenue by Source

Source	2009 ($000)	2009 ($ per capita)
General Revenue		
From Federal Government	46,565	77
From State Government	14,123	23
From Local Governments	3,363	6
Taxes		
Property	179,215	295
Sales and Gross Receipts	153,491	253
Personal Income	0	0
Corporate Income	0	0
Motor Vehicle License	0	0
Other Taxes	12,692	21
Current Charges	169,647	280
Liquor Store	0	0
Utility	87,651	144
Employee Retirement	-308,765	-509

Source: U.S Census Bureau, State & Local Government Finances 2009

City Government Expenditures by Function

Function	2009 ($000)	2009 ($ per capita)	2009 (%)
General Direct Expenditures			
Air Transportation	52,558	87	5.9
Corrections	0	0	0.0
Education	91	< 1	< 0.1
Employment Security Administration	0	0	0.0
Financial Administration	9,342	15	1.1
Fire Protection	64,772	107	7.3
General Public Buildings	16,883	28	1.9
Governmental Administration, Other	12,565	21	1.4
Health	22,332	37	2.5
Highways	43,916	72	4.9
Hospitals	0	0	0.0
Housing and Community Development	10,079	17	1.1
Interest on General Debt	44,656	74	5.0
Judicial and Legal	9,658	16	1.1
Libraries	8,871	15	1.0
Parking	0	0	0.0
Parks and Recreation	41,456	68	4.7
Police Protection	104,178	172	11.7
Public Welfare	1,665	3	0.2
Sewerage	104,083	171	11.7
Solid Waste Management	31,381	52	3.5
Veterans' Services	0	0	0.0
Liquor Store	0	0	0.0
Utility	196,411	324	22.1
Employee Retirement	74,734	123	8.4

Source: U.S Census Bureau, State & Local Government Finances 2009

Municipal Bond Ratings

Area	Moody's	S&P	Fitch
City	Aa3	AA	AA

Rating Systems (shown in declining order of credit quality): Moody's– Aaa, Aa, A, Baa, Ba, B, Caa, Ca, C (numerical modifiers 1, 2, and 3 are added to letter-rating); S&P– AAA, AA, A, BBB, BB, B, CCC, CC, C; Fitch– AAA, AA, A, BBB, BB, B, CCC, CC, C. Ratings may be modified by the addition of a plus or minus sign to show relative standing within the major rating categories.
Notes: n/a Not Available; w/d Withdrawn (1) Not Reviewed; (2) Issuer Rating/No General Obligation; (3) Standard and Poor's Issue Credit Rating (ICR) is a current opinion of an obliger with respect to a specific financial obligation, a specific class of financial obligations, or a specific financial program.
Source: U.S. Census Bureau, 2012 Statistical Abstract, Bond Ratings for City Governments by Largest Cities: 2010

DEMOGRAPHICS

Population Growth

Area	1990 Census	2000 Census	2010 Census	Population Growth (%) 1990-2000	2000-2010
City	515,541	563,662	649,121	9.3	15.2
MSA[1]	591,610	679,622	800,647	14.9	17.8
U.S.	248,709,873	281,421,906	308,745,538	13.2	9.7

Note: (1) Figures cover the El Paso, TX Metropolitan Statistical Area—see Appendix B for areas included
Source: U.S. Census Bureau, 2010 Census

Household Size

Area	Persons in Household (%) One	Two	Three	Four	Five	Six	Seven or More	Average Household Size
City	21.5	26.0	18.5	16.8	10.0	4.3	3.0	2.95
MSA[1]	19.8	24.9	18.5	17.5	11.0	4.8	3.5	3.06
U.S.	26.7	32.8	16.1	13.4	6.5	2.6	1.9	2.58

Note: (1) Figures cover the El Paso, TX Metropolitan Statistical Area—see Appendix B for areas included
Source: U.S. Census Bureau, 2010 Census

Race

Area	White Alone[2] (%)	Black Alone[2] (%)	Asian Alone[2] (%)	AIAN[3] Alone[2] (%)	NHOPI[4] Alone[2] (%)	Other Race Alone[2] (%)	Two or More Races (%)
City	80.8	3.4	1.2	0.7	0.1	11.0	2.7
MSA[1]	82.1	3.1	1.0	0.8	0.1	10.5	2.5
U.S.	72.4	12.6	4.8	0.9	0.2	6.2	2.9

Note: (1) Figures cover the El Paso, TX Metropolitan Statistical Area—see Appendix B for areas included; (2) Alone is defined as not being in combination with one or more other races; (3) American Indian and Alaska Native; (4) Native Hawaiian and Other Pacific Islander
Source: U.S. Census Bureau, 2010 Census

Hispanic or Latino Origin

Area	Hispanic or Latino (%)	Mexican (%)	Puerto Rican (%)	Cuban (%)	Other Hispanic or Latino (%)
City	80.7	74.9	0.9	0.1	4.8
MSA[1]	82.2	76.6	0.8	0.1	4.7
U.S.	16.3	10.3	1.5	0.6	4.0

Note: Persons of Hispanic or Latino origin can be of any race; (1) Figures cover the El Paso, TX Metropolitan Statistical Area—see Appendix B for areas included
Source: U.S. Census Bureau, 2010 Census

Segregation

Type	Segregation Indices[1]				Percent Change		
	1990	2000	2010	2010 Rank[2]	1990-2000	1990-2010	2000-2010
Black/White	37.5	36.2	30.7	100	-1.3	-6.8	-5.5
Asian/White	23.8	21.9	22.2	100	-1.9	-1.7	0.2
Hispanic/White	49.7	45.2	43.3	50	-4.5	-6.5	-1.9

Note: Figures are based on an analysis of 1990, 2000, and 2010 Census Decennial Census tract data by William H. Frey, Brookings Institution and the University of Michigan Social Science Data Analysis Network. In this analysis all racial groups (whites, blacks, and asians) are non-Hispanic members of those races. Hispanics are shown as a separate category; All figures cover the Metropolitan Statistical Area (see Appendix B for areas included); (1) Segregation Indices are Dissimilarity Indices that measure the degree to which the minority group is distributed differently than whites across census tracts. They range from 0 (complete integration) to 100 (complete segregation) where the value indicates the percentage of the minority group that needs to move to be distributed exactly like whites; (2) Ranges from 1 (most segregated) to 102 (least segregated); n/a not available.
Source: www.CensusScope.org

Ancestry

Area	German	Irish	English	American	Italian	Polish	French[2]	Scottish	Dutch
City	3.9	2.5	2.2	3.7	1.2	0.5	0.7	0.5	0.3
MSA[1]	3.6	2.4	1.9	3.5	1.1	0.5	0.6	0.4	0.2
U.S.	16.1	11.6	8.8	6.1	5.7	3.2	3.0	1.9	1.6

Note: Figures are the percentage of the total population reporting a particular ancestry. The nine most commonly reported ancestries in the U.S. are shown. Figures include multiple ancestries (e.g. if a person reported being Irish and Italian, they were included in both columns); (1) Figures cover the El Paso, TX Metropolitan Statistical Area—see Appendix B for areas included; (2) Excludes Basque
Source: U.S. Census Bureau, 2008-2010 American Community Survey 3-Year Estimates

Foreign-Born Population

Area	Percent of Population Born in								
	Any Foreign Country	Mexico	Asia	Europe	Carribean	South America	Central America[2]	Africa	Canada
City	25.4	22.9	1.1	0.6	0.2	0.2	0.2	0.1	0.1
MSA[1]	26.5	24.4	0.9	0.5	0.2	0.2	0.2	0.1	0.1
U.S.	12.8	3.8	3.6	1.6	1.2	0.9	1.0	0.5	0.3

Note: (1) Figures cover the El Paso, TX Metropolitan Statistical Area—see Appendix B for areas included; (2) Excludes Mexico.
Source: U.S. Census Bureau, 2008-2010 American Community Survey 3-Year Estimates

Marital Status

Area	Never Married	Now Married[2]	Separated	Widowed	Divorced
City	31.9	47.7	3.6	5.7	11.0
MSA[1]	32.1	48.3	3.7	5.5	10.3
U.S.	31.6	49.6	2.2	6.1	10.7

Note: Figures are percentages and cover the population 15 years of age and older; (1) Figures cover the El Paso, TX Metropolitan Statistical Area—see Appendix B for areas included; (2) Excludes separated
Source: U.S. Census Bureau, 2008-2010 American Community Survey 3-Year Estimates

Age

Area	Percent of Population							Median Age
	Under Age 5	Age 5 to 17	Age 18 to 34	Age 35 to 49	Age 50 to 64	Age 65 to 79	80 Years and Over	
City	7.9	21.3	24.0	19.6	16.1	8.1	3.1	32.5
MSA[1]	8.1	22.0	24.5	19.6	15.6	7.5	2.7	31.3
U.S.	6.5	17.5	23.2	20.7	19.0	9.4	3.6	37.2

Note: (1) Figures cover the El Paso, TX Metropolitan Statistical Area—see Appendix B for areas included
Source: U.S. Census Bureau, 2010 Census

Male/Female Ratio

Area	Males	Females	Males per 100 Females
City	311,280	337,841	92.1
MSA[1]	387,876	412,771	94.0
U.S.	151,781,326	156,964,212	96.7

Note: (1) Figures cover the El Paso, TX
Metropolitan Statistical Area—see Appendix B for areas included
Source: U.S. Census Bureau, 2010 Census

Religious Groups

Area	Catholic	Baptist	Non-Den.	Methodist[2]	Lutheran	LDS[3]	Pente-costal	Presby-terian[4]	Muslim[5]	Judaism
MSA[1]	43.2	3.8	5.0	0.9	0.3	1.6	1.4	0.2	0.2	0.1
U.S.	19.1	9.3	4.0	4.0	2.3	2.0	1.9	1.6	0.8	0.7

Note: Figures are the number of adherents as a percentage of the total population; (1) Figures cover the El Paso, TX Metropolitan Statistical Area—see Appendix B for areas included; (2) Methodist/Pietist; (3) Latter Day Saints; (4) Reformed; (5) Figures are estimates
Source: Association of Statisticians of American Religious Bodies, 2010 U.S. Religion Census: Religious Congregations & Membership Study

ECONOMY

Gross Metropolitan Product

Area	2007	2008	2009	2010	2010 Rank[2]
MSA[1]	25.3	25.7	26.5	28.7	75

Note: Figures are in billions of dollars; (1) Figures cover the El Paso, TX Metropolitan Statistical Area—see Appendix B for areas included; (2) Rank ranges from 1 to 363
Source: The United States Conference of Mayors, "U.S. Metro Economies: GMP and Employment Forecasts," June 2011

Economic Growth

Area	2007-2009 (%)	2010 (%)	2011 (%)	Rank[2]
MSA[1]	0.4	7.2	4.4	85
U.S.	-1.3	2.9	2.5	–

Note: Figures are real Gross Metropolitan Product growth rates and represent annual average percent change; (1) Figures cover the El Paso, TX Metropolitan Statistical Area—see Appendix B for areas included; (2) Rank ranges from 1 to 363
Source: The United States Conference of Mayors, "U.S. Metro Economies: GMP and Employment Forecasts," June 2011

Metropolitan Area Exports

Area	2005	2006	2007	2008	2009	2010	2010 Rank[2]
MSA[1]	9,654.6	10,105.8	9,608.0	9,390.5	7,748.0	10,315.9	26

Note: Figures are in millions of dollars; (1) Figures cover the El Paso, TX Metropolitan Statistical Area—see Appendix B for areas included; (2) Rank ranges from 1 to 369
Source: U.S. Department of Commerce, International Trade Administration, Office of Trade & Industry Information, Manufacturing & Services, data extracted April 2, 2012

INCOME

Income

Area	Per Capita ($)	Median Household ($)	Average Household ($)
City	18,119	37,836	52,689
MSA[1]	16,991	36,647	51,077
U.S.	26,942	51,222	70,116

Note: (1) Figures cover the El Paso, TX Metropolitan Statistical Area—see Appendix B for areas included
Source: U.S. Census Bureau, 2008-2010 American Community Survey 3-Year Estimates

Household Income Distribution

Area	Percent of Households Earning							
	Under $15,000	$15,000 -24,999	$25,000 -34,999	$35,000 -49,999	$50,000 -74,999	$75,000 -99,000	$100,000 -149,999	$150,000 and up
City	19.0	15.0	12.6	15.3	16.6	8.9	8.5	4.1
MSA[1]	19.2	15.7	13.0	15.5	16.3	8.5	8.0	3.8
U.S.	13.0	11.0	10.6	14.2	18.5	12.1	12.2	8.4

Note: (1) Figures cover the El Paso, TX Metropolitan Statistical Area—see Appendix B for areas included
Source: U.S. Census Bureau, 2008-2010 American Community Survey 3-Year Estimates

Poverty Rate

Area	All Ages	Under 18 Years Old	18 to 64 Years Old	65 Years and Over
City	22.6	32.2	18.4	19.5
MSA[1]	24.3	34.1	19.9	20.2
U.S.	14.4	20.1	13.1	9.4

Note: Figures are percentage of people whose income during the past 12 months was below the poverty level;
(1) Figures cover the El Paso, TX Metropolitan Statistical Area—see Appendix B for areas included
Source: U.S. Census Bureau, 2008-2010 American Community Survey 3-Year Estimates

Personal Bankruptcy Filing Rate

Area	2006	2007	2008	2009	2010	2011
El Paso County	2.04	2.19	2.87	3.71	3.41	3.14
U.S.	2.00	2.73	3.53	4.61	4.97	4.37

Note: Numbers are per 1,000 population and include Chapter 7 and Chapter 13 filings
Source: Federal Deposit Insurance Corporation, Regional Economic Conditions, March 9, 2012

EMPLOYMENT

Labor Force and Employment

Area	Civilian Labor Force			Workers Employed		
	Dec. 2010	Dec. 2011	% Chg.	Dec. 2010	Dec. 2011	% Chg.
City	274,211	276,634	0.9	249,990	253,316	1.3
MSA[1]	322,362	325,199	0.9	291,214	295,088	1.3
U.S.	153,156,000	153,373,000	0.1	139,159,000	140,681,000	1.1

Note: Data is not seasonally adjusted and covers workers 16 years of age and older;
(1) Metropolitan Statistical Area—see Appendix B for areas included
Source: Bureau of Labor Statistics, http://stats.bls.gov

Unemployment Rate

Area	2011											
	Jan.	Feb.	Mar.	Apr.	May	Jun.	Jul.	Aug.	Sep.	Oct.	Nov.	Dec.
City	9.5	9.2	9.2	8.9	9.1	10.0	10.1	9.8	9.7	9.4	8.7	8.4
MSA[1]	10.4	10.1	10.0	9.7	10.0	10.9	10.9	10.6	10.5	10.2	9.5	9.3
U.S.	9.8	9.5	9.2	8.7	8.7	9.3	9.3	9.1	8.8	8.5	8.2	8.3

Note: Data is not seasonally adjusted and covers workers 16 years of age and older; All figures are
percentages; (1) Metropolitan Statistical Area—see Appendix B for areas included
Source: Bureau of Labor Statistics, http://stats.bls.gov

Projected Unemployment Rate

Area	2010 (%)	2011 (%)	2012 (%)	2013 (%)
MSA[1]	10.2	10.3	10.3	9.9

Note: (1) Metropolitan Statistical Area—see Appendix B for areas included
Source: The United States Conference of Mayors, "U.S. Metro Economies: GMP and Employment Forecasts,"
June 2011

Employment by Occupation

Occupation Classification	City (%)	MSA[1] (%)	U.S. (%)
Management, Business, Science, and Arts	30.9	28.8	35.6
Natural Resources, Construction, and Maintenance	8.6	10.3	9.5
Production, Transportation, and Material Moving	12.2	13.3	12.1
Sales and Office	27.8	27.2	25.2
Service	20.4	20.5	17.6

Note: Figures cover employed civilians 16 years of age and older; (1) Figures cover the El Paso, TX Metropolitan Statistical Area—see Appendix B for areas included
Source: U.S. Census Bureau, 2008-2010 American Community Survey 3-Year Estimates

Employment by Industry

Sector	MSA[1] Number of Employees	MSA[1] Percent of Total	U.S. Percent of Total
Construction	n/a	n/a	4.1
Education and Health Services	38,900	13.7	15.2
Financial Activities	12,600	4.4	5.8
Government	66,200	23.3	16.8
Information	4,900	1.7	2.0
Leisure and Hospitality	29,600	10.4	9.9
Manufacturing	17,500	6.2	8.9
Mining and Logging	n/a	n/a	0.6
Other Services	9,700	3.4	4.0
Professional and Business Services	31,400	11.0	13.3
Retail Trade	36,900	13.0	11.5
Transportation and Utilities	13,000	4.6	3.8
Wholesale Trade	10,000	3.5	4.2

Note: Figures cover non-farm employment as of December 2011 and are not seasonally adjusted; (1) Metropolitan Statistical Area—see Appendix B for areas included; n/a not available
Source: Bureau of Labor Statistics, http://stats.bls.gov

Occupations with Greatest Projected Employment Growth: 2008 – 2018

Occupation[1]	2008 Employment	2018 Projected Employment	Numeric Employment Change	Percent Employment Change
Combined Food Preparation and Serving Workers, Including Fast Food	247,750	326,190	78,440	31.7
Elementary School Teachers, Except Special Education	156,930	218,030	61,100	38.9
Retail Salespersons	361,780	416,090	54,310	15.0
Registered Nurses	166,240	219,880	53,640	32.3
Home Health Aides	92,660	143,720	51,060	55.1
Customer Service Representatives	217,250	267,290	50,040	23.0
Waiters and Waitresses	192,340	237,660	45,320	23.6
Personal and Home Care Aides	94,530	138,530	44,000	46.5
Office Clerks, General	239,400	279,000	39,600	16.5
Cashiers	276,070	312,940	36,870	13.4

Note: Projections cover Texas; (1) Sorted by numeric employment change
Source: www.projectionscentral.com, State Occupational Projections, 2008–2018 Long-Term Projections

Fastest Growing Occupations: 2008 – 2018

Occupation[1]	2008 Employment	2018 Projected Employment	Numeric Employment Change	Percent Employment Change
Biomedical Engineers	650	1,150	500	76.9
Home Health Aides	92,660	143,720	51,060	55.1
Network Systems and Data Communications Analysts	19,160	29,490	10,330	53.9
Petroleum Engineers	13,440	20,140	6,700	49.9
Athletic Trainers	1,560	2,300	740	47.4
Personal and Home Care Aides	94,530	138,530	44,000	46.5
Electrical and Electronics Repairers, Powerhouse, Substation, and Relay	1,550	2,260	710	45.8
Financial Examiners	2,150	3,130	980	45.6
Medical Scientists, Except Epidemiologists	3,670	5,320	1,650	45.0
Biochemists and Biophysicists	740	1,060	320	43.2

Note: Projections cover Texas; (1) Sorted by percent employment change and excludes occupations with numeric employment change less than 100
Source: www.projectionscentral.com, State Occupational Projections, 2008–2018 Long-Term Projections

Average Wages

Occupation	$/Hr.	Occupation	$/Hr.
Accountants and Auditors	24.24	Maids and Housekeeping Cleaners	8.92
Automotive Mechanics	14.67	Maintenance and Repair Workers	12.47
Bookkeepers	14.00	Marketing Managers	52.13
Carpenters	12.20	Nuclear Medicine Technologists	30.81
Cashiers	8.69	Nurses, Licensed Practical	19.64
Clerks, General Office	11.60	Nurses, Registered	30.75
Clerks, Receptionists/Information	10.11	Nursing Aides/Orderlies/Attendants	10.19
Clerks, Shipping/Receiving	11.02	Packers and Packagers, Hand	8.82
Computer Programmers	25.66	Physical Therapists	50.67
Computer Support Specialists	20.42	Postal Service Mail Carriers	25.05
Computer Systems Analysts	35.74	Real Estate Brokers	n/a
Cooks, Restaurant	9.09	Retail Salespersons	10.68
Dentists	95.21	Sales Reps., Exc. Tech./Scientific	22.03
Electrical Engineers	40.18	Sales Reps., Tech./Scientific	32.45
Electricians	18.17	Secretaries, Exc. Legal/Med./Exec.	12.63
Financial Managers	47.49	Security Guards	11.86
First-Line Supervisors/Managers, Sales	19.16	Surgeons	n/a
Food Preparation Workers	8.46	Teacher Assistants	10.40
General and Operations Managers	45.95	Teachers, Elementary School	25.10
Hairdressers/Cosmetologists	10.47	Teachers, Secondary School	25.90
Internists	106.28	Telemarketers	8.77
Janitors and Cleaners	9.87	Truck Drivers, Heavy/Tractor-Trailer	16.91
Landscaping/Groundskeeping Workers	10.09	Truck Drivers, Light/Delivery Svcs.	15.38
Lawyers	51.70	Waiters and Waitresses	8.52

Note: Wage data covers the El Paso, TX Metropolitan Statistical Area—see Appendix B for areas included. Hourly wages for elementary/secondary school teachers and teacher assistants were calculated by the editors from annual wage data assuming a 40 hour work week; n/a not available.
Source: Bureau of Labor Statistics, Metro Area Occupational Employment and Wage Estimates, May 2011

RESIDENTIAL REAL ESTATE

Building Permits

Area	Single-Family			Multi-Family			Total		
	2010	2011	Pct. Chg.	2010	2011	Pct. Chg.	2010	2011	Pct. Chg.
City	2,478	2,966	19.7	1,584	871	-45.0	4,062	3,837	-5.5
MSA[1]	2,961	3,280	10.8	1,588	873	-45.0	4,549	4,153	-8.7
U.S.	447,311	418,498	-6.4	157,299	205,563	30.7	604,610	624,061	3.2

Note: (1) Metropolitan Statistical Area—see Appendix B for areas included; figures represent new, privately-owned housing units authorized (unadjusted data); All permit data are based on estimates with imputation.
Source: U.S. Census Bureau, Manufacturing, Mining, and Construction Statistics, Building Permits, 2010, 2011

Homeownership Rate

Area	2005 (%)	2006 (%)	2007 (%)	2008 (%)	2009 (%)	2010 (%)	2011 (%)
MSA[1]	72.6	65.0	68.2	64.8	63.8	70.1	72.0
U.S.	68.9	68.8	68.1	67.8	67.4	66.9	66.1

Note: (1) Metropolitan Statistical Area—see Appendix B for areas included
Source: U.S. Census Bureau, Housing Vacancies and Homeownership Annual Statistics: 2011

Housing Vacancy Rates

Area	Gross Vacancy Rate[2] (%)			Year-Round Vacancy Rate[3] (%)			Rental Vacancy Rate[4] (%)			Homeowner Vacancy Rate[5] (%)		
	2009	2010	2011	2009	2010	2011	2009	2010	2011	2009	2010	2011
MSA[1]	8.6	7.0	6.5	8.4	6.9	5.9	9.6	5.8	9.2	2.5	1.4	1.3
U.S.	14.5	14.3	14.2	11.3	11.3	11.1	10.6	10.2	9.5	2.6	2.6	2.5

Note: (1) Metropolitan Statistical Area—see Appendix B for areas included; (2) The percentage of the total housing inventory that is vacant; (3) The percentage of the housing inventory (excluding seasonal units) that is year-round vacant; (4) The percentage of rental inventory that is vacant for rent; (5) The percentage of homeowner inventory that is vacant for sale
Source: U.S. Census Bureau, Housing Vacancies and Homeownership Annual Statistics: 2011

TAXES

State Corporate Income Tax Rates

State	Tax Rate (%)	Income Brackets ($)	Num. of Brackets	Financial Institution Tax Rate (%)[a]	Federal Income Tax Ded.
Texas	(x)	–	–	(x)	No

Note: Tax rates as of January 1, 2012; (a) Rates listed are the corporate income tax rate applied to financial institutions or excise taxes based on income. Some states have other taxes based upon the value of deposits or shares; (x) Texas imposes a Franchise Tax, otherwise known as margin tax, imposed on entities with more than $1,000,000 total revenues at rate of 1%, or 0.5% for entities primarily engaged in retail or wholesale trade, on lesser of 70% of total revenues or 100%of gross receipts after deductions for either compensation or cost of goods sold.
Source: Federation of Tax Administrators, "State Corporate Income Tax Rates, 2012"

State Individual Income Tax Rates

State	Tax Rate (%)	Income Brackets ($)	Num. of Brackets	Personal Exempt. ($)[1] Single	Dependents	Fed. Inc. Tax Ded.

Texas – No State Income Tax

Note: Tax rates as of January 1, 2012; Local- and county-level taxes are not included; n/a not applicable; (1) Married joint filers generally receive double the single exemption
Source: Federation of Tax Administrators, "State Individual Income Tax Rates, 2012"

Various State and Local Tax Rates

State	State and Local Sales and Use (%)	State Sales and Use (%)	Gasoline[1] (¢/gal.)	Cigarette[2] ($/pack)	Spirits[3] ($/gal.)	Wine[4] ($/gal.)	Beer[5] ($/gal.)
Texas	8.25	6.25	20.0	1.41	2.40	0.20	0.20

Note: All tax rates as of January 1, 2012 except beer, wine and spirits (September 1, 2011); (1) The American Petroleum Institute has developed a methodology for determining the average tax rate on a gallon of fuel. Rates may include any of the following: excise taxes, environmental fees, storage tank fees, other fees or taxes, general sales tax, and local taxes. In states where gasoline is subject to the general sales tax, or where the fuel tax is based on the average sale price, the average rate determined by API is sensitive to changes in the price of gasoline. States that fully or partially apply general sales taxes to gasoline: CA, CO, GA, IL, IN, MI, NY; (2) The federal excise tax of $1.0066 per pack and local taxes are not included; (3) Rates are those applicable to off-premise sales of 40% alcohol by volume (a.b.v.) distilled spirits in 750ml containers. Local excise taxes are excluded; (4) Rates are those applicable to off-premise sales of 11% a.b.v. non-carbonated wine in 750ml containers; (5) Rates are those applicable to off-premise sales of 4.7% a.b.v. beer in 12 ounce containers.
Source: Tax Foundation, 2012 Facts & Figures: How Does Your State Compare?

State-Local Tax Burdens

Area	Rate (%)	Rank[1]	Per Capita Taxes Paid to Home State ($)	Total State and Local Per Capita Taxes Paid ($)	Per Capita Income ($)
Texas	7.9	45	2,248	3,197	40,498
U.S. Average	9.8	-	3,057	4,160	42,539

Note: Figures cover 2009; (1) Rank ranges from 1 to 50 where 1 is highest tax burden
Source: Tax Foundation, State-Local Tax Burdens, All States, 2009

State Business Tax Climate Index Rankings

State	Overall Rank	Corporate Tax Index Rank	Individual Income Tax Index Rank	Sales Tax Index Rank	Unemployment Insurance Tax Index Rank	Property Tax Index Rank
Texas	9	37	7	35	15	31

Note: The index is a measure of how each state's tax laws affect economic performance. The lower the rank, the more favorable a state's tax system is for business. States without a given tax are given a ranking of 1.
Source: Tax Foundation, Major Components of the State Business Tax Climate Index, FY 2012

COMMERCIAL UTILITIES

Typical Monthly Electric Bills

Area	Commercial Service ($/month)		Industrial Service ($/month)	
	1,500 kWh	40 kW demand 14,000 kWh	1,000 kW demand 200,000 kWh	50,000 kW demand 15,000,000 kWh
City	229	1,773	34,442	1,887,390
Average[1]	189	1,616	25,197	1,470,813

Note: Based on total rates in effect July 1, 2011; (1) average based on 184 utilities surveyed
Source: Edison Electric Institute, Typical Bills and Average Rates Report, Summer 2011

TRANSPORTATION

Means of Transportation to Work

Area	Drove Alone	Car-pooled	Bus	Subway	Railroad	Bicycle	Walked	Other Means	Worked at Home
City	80.1	10.4	2.1	0.0	0.0	0.2	2.0	2.7	2.5
MSA[1]	79.3	10.8	1.9	0.0	0.0	0.2	2.1	2.9	2.8
U.S.	76.0	10.2	2.7	1.7	0.5	0.5	2.8	1.3	4.2

Note: Figures are percentages and cover workers 16 years of age and older; (1) Figures cover the El Paso, TX Metropolitan Statistical Area—see Appendix B for areas included
Source: U.S. Census Bureau, 2008-2010 American Community Survey 3-Year Estimates

Travel Time to Work

Area	Less Than 10 Minutes	10 to 19 Minutes	20 to 29 Minutes	30 to 44 Minutes	45 to 59 Minutes	60 to 89 Minutes	90 Minutes or More
City	10.4	31.0	30.3	21.3	4.0	2.0	1.1
MSA[1]	10.2	29.8	29.2	22.8	4.8	2.3	1.0
U.S.	13.9	30.1	20.8	19.8	7.5	5.5	2.5

Note: Figures are percentages and include workers 16 years old and over; (1) Figures cover the El Paso, TX Metropolitan Statistical Area—see Appendix B for areas included
Source: U.S. Census Bureau, 2008-2010 American Community Survey 3-Year Estimates

Travel Time Index

Area	1985	1990	1995	2000	2005	2010
Urban Area[1]	1.04	1.06	1.09	1.16	1.18	1.16
Average[2]	1.11	1.16	1.18	1.21	1.25	1.20

Note: Travel Time Index—the ratio of travel time in the peak period to the travel time at free-flow conditions. A value of 1.30 indicates a 20-minute free-flow trip takes 26 minutes in the peak. Free-flow speeds (60 mph on freeways and 35 mph on principal arterials) are used as the comparison threshold; (1) Covers the El Paso TX-NM urban area; (2) average of 439 urban areas
Source: Texas Transportation Institute, Urban Mobility Report 2011, September 2011

Public Transportation

Agency Name / Mode of Transportation	Vehicles Operated in Maximum Service	Annual Unlinked Passenger Trips ('000)	Annual Passenger Miles ('000)
Mass Transit Department-City of El Paso (Sun Metro)			
Bus (directly operated)	119	14,733.2	76,334.0
Demand Response (directly operated)	47	224.2	2,040.2
Demand Response Taxi (purchased transportation)	20	17.7	193.4

Source: Federal Transit Administration, National Transit Database, 2010

Air Transportation

Airport Name and Code / Type of Service	Passenger Airlines[1]	Passenger Enplanements	Freight Carriers[2]	Freight (lbs.)
El Paso International (ELP)				
Domestic service (U.S. carriers - 2011)	24	1,445,239	19	90,898,187
International service (U.S. carriers - 2010)	6	4,346	4	839,371

Note: (1) Includes all U.S.-based major, minor and commuter airlines that carried at least one passenger during the year; (2) Includes all U.S.-based airlines and freight carriers that transported at least one pound of freight during the year
Source: Bureau of Transportation Statistics, The Intermodal Transportation Database, Air Carriers: T-100 Domestic Market (U.S. Carriers), 2011; Bureau of Transportation Statistics, The Intermodal Transportation Database, Air Carriers: T-100 International Market (U.S. Carriers), 2010

Other Transportation Statistics

Major Highways:	I-10
Amtrak Service:	Yes
Major Waterways/Ports:	Rio Grande

Source: Amtrak.com; Google Maps

BUSINESSES

Major Business Headquarters

Company Name	Rankings	
	Fortune[1]	Forbes[2]
Western Refining	298	-

Note: (1) Fortune 500—companies that produce a 10-K are ranked 1 to 500 based on 2010 revenue; (2) all private companies with at least $2 billion in annual revenue are ranked 1 to 212; companies listed are headquartered in the city; dashes indicate no ranking
Source: Fortune, "Fortune 500," May 23, 2011; Forbes, "America's Largest Private Companies," November 16, 2011

Fast-Growing Businesses

According to *Initiative for a Competitive Inner City (ICIC)*, El Paso is home to one of America's 100 fastest-growing "inner city" companies: **Facilities Connection (#20)**. Companies were ranked by their five-year compound annual growth rate. Criteria for inclusion: company must be headquartered in or have 51 percent or more of its physical operations in an economically distressed urban area; must be an independent, for-profit corporation, partnership or proprietorship; must have 10 or more employees and have a five-year sales history that includes sales of at least $200,000 in the base year and at least $1 million in the current year with no decrease in sales over the two most recent years. *Initiative for a Competitive Inner City (ICIC), "Inner City 100 Companies, 2011"*

Minority Business Opportunity

El Paso is home to seven companies which are on the *Hispanic Business* 500 list (500 largest U.S. Hispanic-owned companies based on 2010 revenue): **Fred Loya Insurance (#13); Bravo Southwest (#131); RMPersonnel (#170); Pro Auto Dealers (#185); Integrated Human Capital-Santana Group of Companie (#189); dmDickason Personnel Services (#240); Miratek Corp. (#253).** Companies included must show at least 51 percent ownership by Hispanic U.S. citizens, and must maintain headquarters in one of the 50 states or Washington, D.C. *Hispanic Business, "Hispanic Business 500," June 2011*

El Paso is home to one company which is on the *Hispanic Business* Fastest-Growing 100 list (greatest sales growth from 2006 to 2010): **Pro Auto Dealers** (#52). Companies included must show at least 51 percent ownership by Hispanic U.S. citizens, and must maintain headquarters in one of the 50 states or Washington, D.C. In addition, companies must have minimum revenues of $200,000 for calendar year 2005. *Hispanic Business, July/August 2011*

Minority- and Women-Owned Businesses

Group	All Firms		Firms with Paid Employees			
	Firms	Sales ($000)	Firms	Sales ($000)	Employees	Payroll ($000)
Asian	n/a	n/a	n/a	n/a	n/a	n/a
Black	n/a	n/a	n/a	n/a	n/a	n/a
Hispanic	n/a	n/a	n/a	n/a	n/a	n/a
Women	n/a	n/a	n/a	n/a	n/a	n/a
All Firms						

Note: Figures cover firms located in the city; minority- and women-owned business are defined as firms in which the corresponding group own 51% or more of the stock or equity of the company; n/a not available
Source: U.S. Census Bureau, 2007 Economic Census, Survey of Business Owners

HOTELS

Hotels/Motels

Area	5 Star		4 Star		3 Star		2 Star		1 Star		Not Rated	
	Num.	Pct.[3]	Num.	Pct.[3]	Num.	Pct.[3]	Num.	Pct.[3]	Num.	Pct.[3]	Num.	Pct.[3]
City[1]	0	0.0	0	0.0	17	26.6	39	60.9	1	1.6	7	10.9
Total[2]	133	0.9	940	6.5	4,569	31.8	7,033	48.9	351	2.4	1,343	9.3

Note: (1) Figures cover El Paso and vicinity; (2) Figures cover all 100 cities in this book; (3) Percentage of hotels which have a given star rating; Star ratings are determined by expedia.com and offer an indication of the general quality of a particular hotel.
Source: expedia.com, April 25, 2012

EVENT SITES

Major Stadiums, Arenas, and Auditoriums

Name	Max. Capacity
Cohen Stadium	10,000
El Paso County Coliseum	7,000
Magoffin Auditorium	1,200
Sun Bowl Stadium	52,000

Source: Original research

Convention Centers

Name	Overall Space (sq. ft.)	Exhibit Space (sq. ft.)	Meeting Space (sq. ft.)	Meeting Rooms
Judson F. Williams Convention Center	n/a	14,900	80,000	17

Note: n/a not available
Source: Original research

Living Environment

COST OF LIVING

Cost of Living Index

Composite Index	Groceries	Housing	Utilities	Trans-portation	Health Care	Misc. Goods/ Services
91.0	100.8	90.9	81.8	94.0	92.5	88.8

Note: U.S. = 100; Figures cover the El Paso TX urban area.
Source: The Council for Community and Economic Research, ACCRA Cost of Living Index, 2011

Grocery Prices

Area[1]	T-Bone Steak ($/pound)	Frying Chicken ($/pound)	Whole Milk ($/half gal.)	Eggs ($/dozen)	Orange Juice ($/64 oz.)	Coffee ($/11.5 oz.)
City[2]	8.61	1.10	2.01	1.65	3.31	5.04
Avg.	9.25	1.18	2.22	1.66	3.19	4.40
Min.	6.70	0.88	1.31	0.95	2.46	2.94
Max.	14.30	2.16	3.50	3.18	4.75	6.83

Note: (1) Values for the local area are compared with the average, minimum and maximum values for all 335 areas in the Cost of Living Index; (2) Figures cover the El Paso TX urban area; T-Bone Steak (price per pound); Frying Chicken (price per pound, whole fryer); Whole Milk (half gallon carton); Eggs (price per dozen, Grade A, large); Orange Juice (64 oz. Tropicana or Florida Natural); Coffee (11.5 oz. can, vacuum-packed, Maxwell House, Hills Bros, or Folgers).
Source: The Council for Community and Economic Research, ACCRA Cost of Living Index, 2011

Housing and Utility Costs

Area[1]	New Home Price ($)	Apartment Rent ($/month)	All Electric ($/month)	Part Electric ($/month)	Other Energy ($/month)	Telephone ($/month)
City[2]	239,227	942	-	83.02	33.89	26.95
Avg.	285,990	839	163.23	89.00	77.52	26.92
Min.	188,005	460	125.58	45.39	33.89	17.98
Max.	1,197,028	3,244	339.16	181.97	348.69	40.01

Note: (1) Values for the local area are compared with the average, minimum and maximum values for all 335 areas in the Cost of Living Index; (2) Figures cover the El Paso TX urban area; New Home Price (2,400 sf living area, 8,000 sf lot, in urban area with full utilities); Apartment Rent (950 sf 2 bedroom/1.5 or 2 bath, unfurnished, excluding all utilities except water); All Electric (average monthly cost for an all-electric home); Part Electric (average monthly cost for a part-electric home); Other Energy (average monthly cost for natural gas, fuel oil, coal, wood, and any other forms of energy except electricity); Telephone (price includes basic monthly rate for a private residential line plus additional local usage charges incurred by a family of four).
Source: The Council for Community and Economic Research, ACCRA Cost of Living Index, 2011

Health Care, Transportation, and Other Costs

Area[1]	Doctor ($/visit)	Dentist ($/visit)	Optometrist ($/visit)	Gasoline ($/gallon)	Beauty Salon ($/visit)	Men's Shirt ($)
City[2]	84.25	78.17	67.17	3.36	24.15	21.49
Avg.	93.88	81.72	90.54	3.48	32.65	25.06
Min.	60.00	55.33	53.66	3.18	19.78	13.44
Max.	154.98	145.97	183.72	4.31	63.21	46.00

Note: (1) Values for the local area are compared with the average, minimum and maximum values for all 335 areas in the Cost of Living Index; (2) Figures cover the El Paso TX urban area; Doctor (general practitioners routine exam of an established patient); Dentist (adult teeth cleaning and periodic oral examination); Optometrist (full vision eye exam for established adult patient); Gasoline (one gallon regular unleaded, national brand, including all taxes, cash price at self-service pump if available); Beauty Salon (woman's shampoo, trim, and blow-dry); Men's Shirt (cotton/polyester dress shirt, pinpoint weave, long sleeves).
Source: The Council for Community and Economic Research, ACCRA Cost of Living Index, 2011

HOUSING

House Price Index (HPI)

Area	National Ranking[2]	Quarterly Change (%)	One-Year Change (%)	Five-Year Change (%)
MSA[1]	118	0.64	-1.94	-0.07
U.S.[3]	-	-0.10	-2.43	-19.16

Note: The HPI is a weighted repeat sales index. It measures average price changes in repeat sales or refinancings on the same properties. This information is obtained by reviewing repeat mortgage transactions on single-family properties whose mortgages have been purchased or securitized by Fannie Mae or Freddie Mac in January 1975; (1) Metropolitan/Micropolitan Statistical Area—see Appendix B for areas included; (2) Rankings are based on annual percentage change for all metro areas containing at least 15,000 transactions over the last 10 years and ranges from 1 to 306; (3) figures based on a weighted average of Census Division estimates using a purchase only index; all figures are for the period ending December 31, 2011
Source: Federal Housing Finance Agency, House Price Index, February 23, 2012

House Price Valuations

Area	Q4 2005 Price ($000)	Q4 2005 Over-valuation	Q4 2006 Price ($000)	Q4 2006 Over-valuation	Q4 2007 Price ($000)	Q4 2007 Over-valuation	Q4 2008 Price ($000)	Q4 2008 Over-valuation	Q4 2009 Price ($000)	Q4 2009 Over-valuation
MSA[1]	89.6	-17.8	104.6	-9.0	109.4	-8.5	106.0	-11.3	104.6	-13.2

Note: Figures show the percentage of over- or under-valuation of single family homes relative to statistically normal house values (e.g. a value of 23.6 indicates that house values are 23.6% overvalued). Statistically normal house values are based on house prices, interest rates, household incomes, population densities, and any historical premiums or discounts metropolitan areas have exhibited over time; (1) Figures cover the El Paso, TX - see Appendix B for areas included
Source: Global Insight/PNC Financial Services Group, House Prices in America: 4th Quarter 2009 Update

Median Single-Family Home Prices

Area	2009	2010	2011p	Percent Change 2010 to 2011
MSA[1]	132.6	134.3	134.3	0.0
U.S. Average	172.1	173.1	166.2	-4.0

Note: Figures are median sales prices of existing single-family homes in thousands of dollars; (p) preliminary; n/a not available; (1) Metropolitan Statistical Area—see Appendix B for areas included
Source: National Association of Realtors, Median Sales Price of Existing Single-Family Homes for Metropolitan Areas, 4th Quarter 2011

Affordability Index of Existing Single-Family Homes

Area	2009	2010	2011p	Percent Change 2010 to 2011
MSA[1]	101.2	107.9	115.8	7.3

Note: The housing affordability index measures whether or not a typical family could qualify for a mortgage loan on a typical home. The higher the index, the greater the household purchasing power. An index of 100 is defined as the point where a median-income household has exactly enough income to qualify for the purchase of a median-priced existing single-family home, assuming a 20 percent downpayment and 25 percent of gross income devoted to mortgage principal and interest payments; (p) preliminary; n/a not available; (1) Metropolitan Statistical Area—see Appendix B for areas included
Source: National Association of Realtors, Affordability Index of Existing Single-Family Homes, 2011

Median Apartment Condo-Coop Home Prices

Area	2009	2010	2011p	Percent Change 2010 to 2011
MSA[1]	n/a	n/a	n/a	n/a
U.S. Average	175.6	171.7	165.1	-3.8

Note: Figures are median sales prices of existing apartment condo-coop homes in thousands of dollars; (p) preliminary; n/a not available; (1) Metropolitan Statistical Area—see Appendix B for areas included
Source: National Association of Realtors, Median Sales Price of Existing Apartment Condo-Coop Homes for Metropolitan Areas, 4th Quarter 2011

Year Housing Structure Built

Area	2005 or Later	2000 -2004	1990 -1999	1980 -1989	1970 -1979	1960 -1969	1950 -1959	Before 1950	Median Year
City	6.3	9.0	13.5	15.1	19.9	13.1	12.5	10.6	1977
MSA[1]	7.5	10.1	15.0	15.8	18.9	11.9	11.2	9.7	1979
U.S.	5.0	8.6	14.0	14.1	16.3	11.3	11.2	19.6	1975

Note: Figures are percentages except for Median Year; (1) Figures cover the El Paso, TX Metropolitan Statistical Area—see Appendix B for areas included
Source: U.S. Census Bureau, 2008-2010 American Community Survey 3-Year Estimates

HEALTH

Health Risk Data

Category	MSA[1] (%)	U.S. (%)
Adults who have been told they have high blood pressure[2]	29.1	28.7
Adults who have been told they have high blood cholesterol[2]	40.4	37.5
Adults who have been told they have diabetes[3]	12.2	8.7
Adults who have been told they have arthritis[2]	20.5	26.0
Adults who have been told they currently have asthma	5.8	9.1
Adults who are current smokers	14.4	17.3
Adults who are heavy drinkers[4]	4.3	5.0
Adults who are binge drinkers[5]	14.3	15.1
Adults who are overweight (BMI 25.0 - 29.9)	41.1	36.2
Adults who are obese (BMI 30.0 - 99.8)	28.6	27.5
Adults who participated in any physical activities in the past month	71.5	76.1
Adults 50+ who have ever had a sigmoidoscopy or colonoscopy	51.5	65.2
Women aged 40+ who have had a mammogram within the past two years	71.4	75.2
Men aged 40+ who have had a PSA test within the past two years	48.3	53.2
Adults aged 65+ who have had flu shot within the past year	64.8	67.5
Adults aged 18–64 who have any kind of health care coverage	55.9	82.2

Note: Data as of 2010 unless otherwise noted; (1) Figures cover the El Paso, TX Metropolitan Statistical Area—see Appendix B for areas included; (2) Data as of 2009; (3) Figures do not include pregnancy-related, borderline, or pre-diabetes; (4) Heavy drinkers are classified as males having more than two drinks per day or females having more than one drink per day; (5) Binge drinkers are classified as males having five or more drinks on one occasion or females having four or more drinks on one occasion
Source: Centers for Disease Control and Prevention, Behaviorial Risk Factor Surveillance System, SMART: Selected Metropolitan/Micropolitan Area Risk Trends, 2009, 2010

Mortality Rates for the Top 10 Causes of Death in the U.S.

ICD-10[a] Sub-Chapter	ICD-10[a] Code	Age-Adjusted Mortality Rate[1] per 100,000 population	
		County[2]	U.S.
Malignant neoplasms	C00-C97	146.4	175.6
Ischaemic heart diseases	I20-I25	80.8	121.6
Other forms of heart disease	I30-I51	36.8	48.6
Chronic lower respiratory diseases	J40-J47	34.1	42.3
Cerebrovascular diseases	I60-I69	44.0	40.6
Organic, including symptomatic, mental disorders	F01-F09	18.2	26.7
Other degenerative diseases of the nervous system	G30-G31	24.2	24.7
Other external causes of accidental injury	W00-X59	19.9	24.4
Diabetes mellitus	E10-E14	30.3	21.7
Hypertensive diseases	I10-I15	32.3	18.2

Note: (a) ICD-10 = International Classification of Diseases 10th Revision; (1) Mortality rates are a three year average covering 2007-2009; (2) Figures cover El Paso County
Source: Centers for Disease Control and Prevention, National Center for Health Statistics. Underlying Cause of Death 1999-2009 on CDC WONDER Online Database, released 2012. Data for year 2009 are compiled from the Multiple Cause of Death File 2009, Series 20 No. 2O, 2012, Data for year 2008 are compiled from the Multiple Cause of Death File 2008, Series 20 No. 2N, 2011, Data for year 2007 are compiled from Multiple Cause of Death File 2007, Series 20 No. 2M, 2010.

Mortality Rates for Selected Causes of Death

ICD-10[a] Sub-Chapter	ICD-10[a] Code	Age-Adjusted Mortality Rate[1] per 100,000 population	
		County[2]	U.S.
Assault	X85-Y09	3.1	5.7
Human immunodeficiency virus (HIV) disease	B20-B24	2.9	3.3
Influenza and pneumonia	J09-J18	8.7	16.4
Intentional self-harm	X60-X84	9.0	11.5
Malnutrition	E40-E46	1.4	0.8
Obesity and other hyperalimentation	E65-E68	1.8	1.6
Transport accidents	V01-V99	13.5	13.7
Viral hepatitis	B15-B19	3.9	2.2

Note: (a) ICD-10 = International Classification of Diseases 10th Revision; (1) Mortality rates are a three year average covering 2007-2009; (2) Figures cover El Paso County
Source: Centers for Disease Control and Prevention, National Center for Health Statistics. Underlying Cause of Death 1999-2009 on CDC WONDER Online Database, released 2012. Data for year 2009 are compiled from the Multiple Cause of Death File 2009, Series 20 No. 2O, 2012, Data for year 2008 are compiled from the Multiple Cause of Death File 2008, Series 20 No. 2N, 2011, Data for year 2007 are compiled from Multiple Cause of Death File 2007, Series 20 No. 2M, 2010.

Distribution of Physicians and Dentists

Area[1]	Dentists[2]	D.O.[3]	M.D.[4]				
			Total	Family/ General Practice	Pediatrics	Medical Specialties	Surgical Specialties
Local (number)	121	99	851	95	78	324	231
Local (rate[5])	1.7	1.3	11.5	1.3	1.1	4.4	3.1
U.S. (rate[5])	4.5	1.9	18.3	2.5	1.4	6.8	4.1

Note: Data as of 2008 unless noted; (1) Local data covers El Paso County; (2) Data as of 2007; (3) Doctor of Osteopathic Medicine; (4) Includes active, non-federal, patient-care, office-based Doctors of Medicine; (5) rate per 10,000 population
Source: Area Resource File (ARF). 2009-2010 Release. U.S. Department of Health and Human Services, Health Resources and Services Administration, Bureau of Health Professions, Rockville, MD, August 2010

EDUCATION

Public School District Statistics

District Name	Schls	Pupils	Pupil/ Teacher Ratio	Minority Pupils[1] (%)	Free Lunch Eligible[2] (%)	IEP[3] (%)
Canutillo ISD	9	5,867	14.5	95.0	64.3	8.3
Clint ISD	12	11,295	17.2	96.7	50.2	7.1
El Paso ISD	97	63,378	14.4	88.0	59.6	8.4
Socorro ISD	42	41,357	16.6	96.0	61.0	7.7
Ysleta ISD	61	44,620	14.7	94.8	48.2	10.1

Note: Table includes school districts with 2,000 or more students; (1) Percentage of students that are not non-Hispanic white; (2) Percentage of students that are eligible for the free lunch program; (3) Percentage of students that have an Individualized Education Program.
Source: U.S. Department of Education, National Center for Education Statistics, Common Core of Data, Local Education Agency (School District) Universe Survey: School Year 2009-2010; U.S. Department of Education, National Center for Education Statistics, Common Core of Data, Public Elementary/Secondary School Universe Survey: School Year 2009-2010

Highest Level of Education

Area	Less than H.S.	H.S. Diploma	Some College, No Deg.	Associate Degree	Bachelors Degree	Masters Degree	Profess. School Degree	Doctorate Degree
City	25.3	23.8	22.7	6.3	14.5	5.3	1.5	0.7
MSA[1]	28.1	24.1	22.1	6.0	13.1	4.7	1.3	0.6
U.S.	14.7	28.4	21.3	7.6	17.6	7.2	1.9	1.2

Note: Figures cover persons age 25 and over; (1) Figures cover the El Paso, TX Metropolitan Statistical Area—see Appendix B for areas included
Source: U.S. Census Bureau, 2008-2010 American Community Survey 3-Year Estimates

Educational Attainment by Race

Area	High School Graduate or Higher (%)					Bachelor's Degree or Higher (%)				
	Total	White	Black	Asian	Hisp.[2]	Total	White	Black	Asian	Hisp.[2]
City	74.7	75.2	93.7	88.2	69.1	21.9	22.3	27.0	55.5	17.3
MSA[1]	71.9	72.5	92.1	86.8	66.3	19.8	20.2	25.7	54.0	15.3
U.S.	85.3	87.5	81.4	85.5	61.6	28.0	29.3	17.8	50.2	13.0

Note: Figures shown cover persons 25 years old and over; (1) Figures cover the El Paso, TX Metropolitan Statistical Area—see Appendix B for areas included; (2) People of Hispanic origin can be of any race
Source: U.S. Census Bureau, 2008-2010 American Community Survey 3-Year Estimates

School Enrollment by Grade and Control

Area	Preschool (%)		Kindergarten (%)		Grades 1 - 4 (%)		Grades 5 - 8 (%)		Grades 9 - 12 (%)	
	Public	Private	Public	Private	Public	Private	Public	Private	Public	Private
City	80.0	20.0	91.9	8.1	94.8	5.2	94.8	5.2	95.6	4.4
MSA[1]	82.5	17.5	93.0	7.0	95.7	4.3	95.5	4.5	96.2	3.8
U.S.	55.4	44.6	87.1	12.9	89.4	10.6	89.5	10.5	90.4	9.6

Note: Figures shown cover persons 3 years old and over; (1) Figures cover the El Paso, TX Metropolitan Statistical Area—see Appendix B for areas included
Source: U.S. Census Bureau, 2008-2010 American Community Survey 3-Year Estimates

Average Salaries of Public School Classroom Teachers

Area	2010-11		2011-12		Percent Change 2010-11 to 2011-12	Percent Change 2001-02 to 2011-12
	Dollars	Rank[1]	Dollars	Rank[1]		
Texas	48,638	31	49,017	31	0.78	24.90
U.S. Average	55,623	-	56,643	-	1.83	26.8

Note: (1) State rank ranges from 1 to 51 where 1 indicates highest salary.
Source: National Education Association, Rankings & Estimates: Rankings of the States 2011 and Estimates of School Statistics 2012, December 2011

Higher Education

Four-Year Colleges			Two-Year Colleges			Medical Schools[1]	Law Schools[2]	Voc/Tech[3]
Public	Private Non-profit	Private For-profit	Public	Private Non-profit	Private For-profit			
1	0	0	1	0	8	1	0	5

Note: Figures cover institutions located within the city limits and include main campuses only; (1) includes schools accredited by the Liaison Committee on Medical Education and the American Osteopathic Association's Commission on Osteopathic College Accreditation; (2) includes American Bar Association-accredited law schools; (3) includes all schools with programs that are less than 2 years.
Source: National Center for Education Statistics, Integrated Postsecondary Education System (IPEDS) Peer Analysis System, 2011-12; Association of American Medical Colleges, Member List, April 23, 2012; American Osteopathic Association, Member List, April 23, 2012; Law School Admission Council, Official Guide to ABA-Approved Law Schools Online, April 23, 2012

PRESIDENTIAL ELECTION

2008 Presidential Election Results

Area	Obama	McCain	Nader	Other
El Paso County	65.7	33.3	0.1	0.9
U.S.	52.9	45.6	0.6	0.9

Note: Results are percentages and may not add to 100% due to rounding
Source: Dave Leip's Atlas of U.S. Presidential Elections, www.uselectionatlas.org

EMPLOYERS

Major Employers

Company Name	Industry
AHAC	Employmant agencies
Automatic Data Processing	Data processing service
Bureau of Customs and Border Protection	Customs
City of El Paso	Executive/legislative combined
Delphi Automotive Systems	Motor vehicle parts/accessories
Delphi Automotive Systems Corporation	Automotive, electrical equipment
El paso County Hospital Direct	General medical/surgical hospitals
El Paso Electric Company	Electric services
Elcom	Electrical circuits
Furukawa Wiring Systems America	Public building /related furniture
Genpact	Data processing/preparation
Justin Brands	Boots/dress or casual mens
Philips Consumer Electronic Company	Cameras/televisions
Redcats USA, LP	Catalog/mail order house
Tenet Hospitals Limited	General medical/surgical hospitals
Texas Tech University	University
Time Warner,, Advance Newhouse Prtnrshp	Cable television services
United States Postal Service	Postal service
University of Texas at El Paso	Colleges/universities
University of Texas System	University

Note: Companies shown are located within the El Paso, TX metropolitan area.
Source: Hoovers.com, data extracted April 25 2012

PUBLIC SAFETY

Crime Rate

Area	All Crimes	Violent Crimes				Property Crimes		
		Murder	Forcible Rape	Robbery	Aggrav. Assault	Burglary	Larceny -Theft	Motor Vehicle Theft
City	3,245.9	0.8	28.7	76.7	352.1	312.8	2,226.3	248.6
Suburbs[1]	2,980.0	1.5	32.6	38.6	350.0	566.7	1,801.8	188.7
Metro[2]	3,199.5	0.9	29.4	70.1	351.7	357.1	2,152.2	238.1
U.S.	3,345.5	4.8	27.5	119.1	252.3	699.6	2,003.5	238.8

Note: Figures are crimes per 100,000 population; (1) All areas within the metro area that are located outside the city limits; (2) Metropolitan Statistical Area—see Appendix B for areas included
Source: FBI Uniform Crime Reports, 2010

Hate Crimes

Area	Number of Quarters Reported	Bias Motivation				
		Race	Religion	Sexual Orientation	Ethnicity	Disability
City	4	3	0	2	0	0

Source: Federal Bureau of Investigation, Hate Crime Statistics 2010

Identity Theft Consumer Complaints

Area	Complaints	Complaints per 100,000 Population	Rank[2]
MSA[1]	1,009	137.3	18
U.S.	279,156	90.4	-

Note: (1) Metropolitan Statistical Area—see Appendix B for areas included; (2) Rank ranges from 1 to 384 where 1 indicates greatest number of identity theft complaints per 100,000 population
Source: Federal Trade Commission, Consumer Sentinel Network Data Book for January–December 2011

Fraud and Other Consumer Complaints

Area	Complaints	Complaints per 100,000 Population	Rank[2]
MSA[1]	2,613	355.7	354
U.S.	1,533,924	496.8	-

Note: (1) Metropolitan Statistical Area—see Appendix B for areas included; (2) Rank ranges from 1 to 384 where 1 indicates greatest number of fraud and other complaints per 100,000 population
Source: Federal Trade Commission, Consumer Sentinel Network Data Book for January–December 2011

RECREATION

Culture

Dance[1]	Theatre[1]	Instrumental Music[1]	Vocal Music[1]	Series/ Festivals	Museums	Zoos and Aquariums[2]
0	2	2	0	5	9	1

Note: (1) Number of professional perfoming groups; (2) AZA-accredited
Source: The Grey House Performing Arts Directory, 2011-2012; Official Museum Directory, 2011; American Association of Museums, AAM Member Museums, April 2012; Association of Zoos & Aquariums, AZA Member Zoos & Aquariums, April 2012

Professional Sports Teams

Team Name	League
No teams are located in the metro area	

Source: Original research

CLIMATE

Average and Extreme Temperatures

Temperature	Jan	Feb	Mar	Apr	May	Jun	Jul	Aug	Sep	Oct	Nov	Dec	Yr.
Extreme High (°F)	80	83	89	98	104	114	112	108	104	96	87	80	114
Average High (°F)	57	63	70	79	87	96	95	93	88	79	66	58	78
Average Temp. (°F)	44	49	56	64	73	81	83	81	75	65	52	45	64
Average Low (°F)	31	35	41	49	58	66	70	68	62	50	38	32	50
Extreme Low (°F)	-8	8	14	23	31	46	57	56	42	25	1	5	-8

Note: Figures cover the years 1948-1995
Source: National Climatic Data Center, International Station Meteorological Climate Summary, 9/96

Average Precipitation/Snowfall/Humidity

Precip./Humidity	Jan	Feb	Mar	Apr	May	Jun	Jul	Aug	Sep	Oct	Nov	Dec	Yr.
Avg. Precip. (in.)	0.4	0.4	0.3	0.2	0.3	0.7	1.6	1.5	1.4	0.7	0.3	0.6	8.6
Avg. Snowfall (in.)	1	1	Tr	Tr	0	0	0	0	0	Tr	1	2	6
Avg. Rel. Hum. 6am (%)	68	60	50	43	44	46	63	69	72	66	63	68	59
Avg. Rel. Hum. 3pm (%)	34	27	21	17	17	17	28	30	32	29	30	36	26

Note: Figures cover the years 1948-1995; Tr = Trace amounts (<0.05 in. of rain; <0.5 in. of snow)
Source: National Climatic Data Center, International Station Meteorological Climate Summary, 9/96

Weather Conditions

Temperature			Daytime Sky			Precipitation		
10°F & below	32°F & below	90°F & above	Clear	Partly cloudy	Cloudy	0.01 inch or more precip.	0.1 inch or more snow/ice	Thunder-storms
1	59	106	147	164	54	49	3	35

Note: Figures are average number of days per year and cover the years 1948-1995
Source: National Climatic Data Center, International Station Meteorological Climate Summary, 9/96

HAZARDOUS WASTE

Superfund Sites

El Paso has no sites on the EPA's Superfund Final National Priorities List.
U.S. Environmental Protection Agency, Final National Priorities List, April 17, 2012

**AIR & WATER
QUALITY**

Air Quality Index

Area	Percent of Days when Air Quality was...[2]					AQI Statistics[2]	
	Good	Moderate	Unhealthy for Sensitive Groups	Unhealthy	Very Unhealthy	Maximum	Median
Area[1]	46.3	50.4	2.7	0.5	0.0	186	52

Note: Air Quality Index (AQI) is an index for reporting daily air quality. EPA calculates the AQI for five major air pollutants regulated by the Clean Air Act: ground-level ozone, particle pollution (aka particulate matter), carbon monoxide, sulfur dioxide, and nitrogen dioxide. The AQI runs from 0 to 500. The higher the AQI value, the greater the level of air pollution and the greater the health concern. There are six AQI categories: "Good" AQI is between 0 and 50. Air quality is considered satisfactory; "Moderate" AQI is between 51 and 100. Air quality is acceptable; "Unhealthy for Sensitive Groups" When AQI values are between 101 and 150, members of sensitive groups may experience health effects; "Unhealthy" When AQI values are between 151 and 200 everyone may begin to experience health effects; "Very Unhealthy" AQI values between 201 and 300 trigger a health alert; "Hazardous" AQI values over 300 trigger warnings of emergency conditions (not shown); (1) Data covers El Paso County; (2) Based on 365 days with AQI data in 2011.
Source: U.S. Environmental Protection Agency, AirData Report, 2011

Air Quality Index Pollutants

Area	Percent of Days when AQI Pollutant was...[2]					
	Carbon Monoxide	Nitrogen Dioxide	Ozone	Sulfur Dioxide	Particulate Matter 2.5	Particulate Matter 10
Area[1]	0.0	16.4	38.4	0.0	36.2	9.0

Note: The Air Quality Index (AQI) is an index for reporting daily air quality. EPA calculates the AQI for five major air pollutants regulated by the Clean Air Act: ground-level ozone, particle pollution (also known as particulate matter), carbon monoxide, sulfur dioxide, and nitrogen dioxide. The AQI runs from 0 to 500. The higher the AQI value, the greater the level of air pollution and the greater the health concern; (1) Data covers El Paso County; (2) Based on 365 days with AQI data in 2011.
Source: U.S. Environmental Protection Agency, AirData Report, 2011

Air Quality Index Trends

Area	Trend Sites (days)								All Sites (days)
	2003	2004	2005	2006	2007	2008	2009	2010	2010
MSA[1]	18	10	18	12	15	10	3	5	9

Note: Figures are the number of days the AQI value exceeded 100 in a given year. An AQI value greater than 100 indicates that air quality would have been in the unhealthful range on that day. Data from exceptional events are included. These counts are presented in two ways. First, the counts are based on sites having an adequate record of monitoring data during the trend period (trend sites). These counts represent the relative change in the number of days with AQI values greater than 100. In the last column, the counts are based on all sites with data in the most recent year (because it is possible for a site to have data in the most recent year but not enough data to be a trend site); (1) Data covers the El Paso, TX—see Appendix B for areas included
Source: U.S. Environmental Protection Agency, Air Quality Index Information, "Number of Days with Air Quality Index Values Greater than 100 at Trend Sites, 2000-2010, and at All Sites in 2010"

Maximum Air Pollutant Concentrations: Particulate Matter, Ozone, CO and Lead

	Particulate Matter 10 (ug/m³)	Particulate Matter 2.5 Wtd AM (ug/m³)	Particulate Matter 2.5 24-Hr (ug/m³)	Ozone (ppm)	Carbon Monoxide (ppm)	Lead (ug/m³)
MSA[1] Level	249	8.4	61	0.073	3	0.04
NAAQS[2]	150	15	35	0.075	9	0.15
Met NAAQS[2]	No	Yes	No	Yes	Yes	Yes

Note: Data from exceptional events are not included; (1) Data covers the El Paso, TX—see Appendix B for areas included; (2) National Ambient Air Quality Standards; ppm = parts per million; ug/m³ = micrograms per cubic meter; n/a not available
Concentrations: Particulate Matter 10 (coarse particulate)—highest second maximum 24-hour concentration; Particulate Matter 2.5 Wtd AM (fine particulate)—highest weighted annual mean concentration; Particulate Matter 2.5 24-Hour (fine particulate)—highest 98th percentile 24-hour concentration; Ozone—highest fourth daily maximum 8-hour concentration; Carbon Monoxide—highest second maximum non-overlapping 8-hour concentration; Lead—maximum running 3-month average
Source: U.S. Environmental Protection Agency, CBSA Factbook 2010, Air Quality Statistics by City, 2010

Maximum Air Pollutant Concentrations: Nitrogen Dioxide and Sulfur Dioxide

	Nitrogen Dioxide AM (ppb)	Nitrogen Dioxide 1-Hr (ppb)	Sulfur Dioxide AM (ppb)	Sulfur Dioxide 1-Hr (ppb)	Sulfur Dioxide 24-Hr (ppb)
MSA[1] Level	17.067	62.7	0.756	10.3	3
NAAQS[2]	53	100	30	75	140
Met NAAQS[2]	Yes	Yes	Yes	Yes	Yes

Note: Data from exceptional events are not included; (1) Data covers the El Paso, TX—see Appendix B for areas included; (2) National Ambient Air Quality Standards; ppb = parts per billion; n/a not available Concentrations: Nitrogen Dioxide AM—highest arithmetic mean concentration; Nitrogen Dioxide 1-Hr—highest 98th percentile 1-hour daily maximum concentration; Sulfur Dioxide AM—highest annual mean concentration; Sulfur Dioxide 1-Hr—highest 99th percentile 1-hour daily maximum concentration; Sulfur Dioxide 24-Hr—highest second maximum 24-hour concentration
Source: U.S. Environmental Protection Agency, CBSA Factbook 2010, Air Quality Statistics by City, 2010

Drinking Water

Water System Name	Pop. Served	Primary Water Source Type	Violations[1] Health Based	Violations[1] Monitoring/ Reporting
El Paso Water Utilities	631,253	Surface	1	0

Note: (1) Based on violation data from January 1, 2011 to December 31, 2011 (includes unresolved violations from earlier years)
Source: U.S. Environmental Protection Agency, Office of Ground Water and Drinking Water, Safe Drinking Water Information System (based on data extracted April 18, 2012)

Fort Worth, Texas

Background

Fort Worth lies in north central Texas near the headwaters of the Trinity River. Despite its modern skyscrapers, multiple freeways, shopping malls, and extensive industry, the city is known for its easygoing, Western atmosphere.

The area has seen many travelers. Nomadic Native Americans of the plains rode through on horses bred from those brought by Spanish explorers. The 1840s saw American-Anglos settle in the region. On June 6, 1849, Major Ripley A. Arnold and his U.S. Cavalry troop established an outpost on the Trinity River to protect settlers moving westward. The fort was named for General William J. Worth, Commander of the U.S. Army's Texas department. When the fort was abandoned in 1853, settlers moved in and converted the vacant barracks into trading establishments and homes, stealing the county seat from Birdville (an act made legal in the 1860 election).

In the 1860s, Fort Worth, which was close to the Chisholm Trail, became an oasis for cowboys traveling to and from Kansas. Although the town's growth virtually stopped during the Civil War, Fort Worth was incorporated as a city in 1873. In a race against time, the final 26 miles of the Texas & Pacific Line were completed and Fort Worth survived to be a part of the West Texas oil boom in 1917.

Real prosperity followed at the end of World War II, when the city became a center for a number of military installations. Aviation has been the city's principal source of economic growth. The city's leading industries include the manufacture of aircraft, automobiles, machinery, and containers, as well as food processing and brewing. Emerging economic sectors in the new century include semiconductor manufacturing, communications equipment manufacturing, corporate offices, and distribution.

Major corporations here include American Airlines, RadioShack, Lockheed Martin, and Gallus Cycles.

Since it first began testing DNA samples in 2003, the DNA Identity Laboratory at the University of North Texas Health Science Center has made nearly 100 matches, helping to solve missing-persons cases and closing criminal cases. The university is also home to the national Osteopathic Research Center, the only academic DNA Lab qualified to work with the FBI, the Texas Center for Health Disparities and the Health Institutes of Texas. Other colleges in Fort Worth include Texas Christian University, Southwestern Baptist Seminary, and Texas Wesleyan University.

After a long period of planning, Fort Worth's most comprehensive mixed-use project at Walsh Ranch, is nearing completion. With designs for residential, commercial, office and retail development, the 7,275-acre planned communicy is named after the original owners of the property, F. Howard and Mary D. Walsh, who were well-known ranchers, philanthropists and civic leaders.

The Omni Fort Worth Hotel opened in January of 2009, and is the first new hotel in the city in over 20 years. It was host to the 2011 AFC champion Pittsburgh Steelers during Super Bowl XLV.

The city also boasts the 3,600-acre Greer Island Nature Center and Refuge, which will celebrate its 50th anniversary in 2014.

Winter temperatures and rainfall are both modified by the northeast-northwest mountain barrier, which prevents shallow cold air masses from crossing over from the west. Summer temperatures vary with cloud and shower activity, but are generally mild. Summer precipitation is largely from local thunderstorms and varies from year to year. Damaging rains are infrequent. Hurricanes have produced heavy rainfall, but are usually not accompanied by destructive winds.

Rankings

General Rankings

- The Fort Worth metro area was selected as one of the best cities to relocate to in America by Sperling's BestPlaces. The metro area ranked #4 out of 10. Criteria: unemployment; cost of living; crime rates; population health; cultural events; economic stability. *Sperling's BestPlaces, www.BestPlaces.net, "The Best Cities to Relocate to in America," October 2010*

- *Men's Health Living* ranked 100 U.S. cities in terms of quality of life. Fort Worth was ranked #85 and received a grade of D. Criteria: number of fitness facilities; air quality; number of physicians; male/female ratio; education levels; household income; cost of living. *Men's Health Living, Spring 2008*

- Fort Worth was selected as an "All-America City" by the National Civic League. The All-America City Award recognizes civic excellence and annually honors 10 communities that best exemplify the spirit of grassroots citizen involvement and cross-sector collaborative problem solving. *National Civic League, 2011 All-America City Awards*

Business/Finance Rankings

- Dallas was identified as one of the 20 strongest-performing metro areas during the recession and recovery from trough quarter through the third quarter of 2011. Criteria: percent change in employment; percentage point change in unemployment rate; percent change in gross metropolitan product; percent change in House Price Index. *Brookings Institution, MetroMonitor: Tracking Economic Recession and Recovery in America's 100 Largest Metropolitan Areas, December 2011*

- The Fort Worth metro area was identified as one of 10 "Cities Where the Recession is Easing." The metro area was ranked #3. Criteria: job growth; goods produced; home sale prices; unemployment rates. *Forbes.com, "Cities Where the Recession is Easing," March 3, 2010*

- The Dallas metro area was identified as one of five places with the worst wage growth in America. The area ranked #4. Criteria: private-sector wage growth between the 4th quarter of 2010 and the 4th quarter of 2011. *PayScale, "Five Worst Cities for Wage Growth," January 12, 2012*

- The Fort Worth metro area was identified as one of the most affordable major metropolitan areas in America by *Forbes*. The metro area was ranked #14 out of 15. Criteria: median asking price of homes for sale; median salaries of workers with bachelor's degrees or higher compared to a cost-of-living index; unemployment rates. *Forbes.com, "The Most Affordable Cities in America," January 7, 2011*

- Experian ranked the top 20 major U.S. metropolitan areas by average debt per consumer. The Dallas metro area was ranked #2. Criteria: average debt per consumer. Debt for this study includes credit cards, auto loans and personal loans. It does not include mortgages. *Experian, May 13, 2010*

- The Dallas metro area was identified as one of the "Best U.S. Cities for Earning a Living" by *Forbes*. The metro area ranked #8. Criteria: median income; cost of living; job growth; number of companies on *Forbes* 400 best big company and 200 best small company lists. *Forbes.com, "Best U.S. Cities for Earning a Living," August 21, 2008*

- Fort Worth was cited as one of America's top metros for new and expanded facility projects in 2011. The area ranked #4 in the large metro area category (population over 1 million). *Site Selection, "2011 Top Metros," March 2012*

- Fort Worth was identified as one of the best cities for new college graduates. The city ranked #10. Criteria: cost of living; average annual salary; unemployment rate; number of employers looking to hire people at entry-level. *Business Week, "The Best Cities for New Grads," July 20, 2010*

- Fort Worth was selected as one of the "100 Best Places to Live and Launch" in the U.S. The city ranked #9. The editors at *Fortune Small Business* ranked 296 Census-designated metro areas by business friendliness (Launching Score, % New Businesses) and lifestyle offerings (Living Score). Then they picked the town within each of the top 100 metro areas that best blends business and pleasure. *Fortune Small Business, "100 Best Places to Live and Launch 2008," April 2008*

- *American City Business Journals* ranked America's 261 largest cities in terms of their resident's wealth. Fort Worth ranked #178. Criteria: per capita income; median household income; percentage of households with annual incomes of $200,000 or more; median home value. *American City Business Journals, "Where the Money Is: America's Wealth Centers," August 18, 2008*

- The Fort Worth metro area appeared on the Milken Institute "2011 Best Performing Metros" list. Rank: #24 out of 200 large metro areas. Criteria: job growth; wage and salary growth; high-tech output growth. *Milken Institute, "2011 Best Performing Metros"*

- The Fort Worth metro area was selected as one of the best cities for entrepreneurs in America by *Inc. Magazine.* Criteria: job-growth data for 335 metro areas was analyzed for: recent growth trend; mid-term growth; long-term trend; current year growth. The Fort Worth metro area ranked #9 among large metro areas and #50 overall. *Inc. Magazine, "The Best Cities for Doing Business," July 2008*

- Fort Worth was ranked #52 out of 145 regions worldwide in terms of its "Knowledge Competitiveness Index." The index attempts to measure the knowledge-based development taking place throughout the world and is based on 19 measures of economic performance that indicate a region's ability to translate its knowledge capacity into economic value. *Centre for International Competitiveness, World Knowledge Competitiveness Index 2008*

- *Forbes* ranked the 200 most populous metro areas in the U.S. in terms of the "Best Places for Business and Careers." The Fort Worth metro area was ranked #16. Criteria: costs (business and living); job growth (past and projected); income growth; educational attainment; projected economic growth; crime; cultural and recreational opportunities; net migration patterns; number of highly ranked colleges. *Forbes, "Best Places for Business and Careers," June 2011*

Children/Family Rankings

- The Fort Worth metro area was selected as one of the "Best Cities for Relocating Families" by Worldwide ERC and Primacy Relocation. The 2008 study looked at nearly 50 factors important to relocating families including: recent job growth; nearby top-ranked colleges; in-state tuition for four-year public colleges; population growth since 2000; pediatricians per 100,000 population; and a Green Living index. *Worldwide ERC and Primacy Relocation, "2008 Best Cities for Relocating Families"*

- *Fit Pregnancy* magazine ranked the 50 best U.S. cities in which to have a baby. Fort Worth was ranked #45. Criteria: access to hospitals and doctors; affordability; birthing options; breastfeeding; child care; fertility laws/resources; maternal and infant health risk; parks/stroller friendliness; safety. *Fit Pregnancy, "The Best Cities in America to Have a Baby 2008"*

- Fort Worth was chosen as one of America's "100 Best Communities for Young People." The winners were selected based upon detailed information provided about each community's efforts to fulfill five essential promises critical to the well-being of young people: caring adults who are actively involved in their lives; safe places in which to learn and grow; a healthy start toward adulthood; an effective education that builds marketable skills; and opportunities to help others. *America's Promise Alliance, "100 Best Communities for Young People, 2010"*

Dating/Romance Rankings

- Fort Worth appeared on *Men's Health's* list of the most sex-happy cities in America. The city ranked #12 of 100. Criteria: condom sales; birth rates; sex toy sales; rates of chlamydia, gonorrhea, and syphilis. *Men's Health, "America's Most Sex-Happy Cities," October 2010*

- *Men's Health* ranked 100 U.S. cities in terms of best (and worst) marriages. Fort Worth was ranked #45 (#1 = worst). Criteria: rate of failed marriages; stringency of divorce laws; percentage of population who've split; number of licensed marriage and family therapists. *Men's Health, "Splitsville, USA," May 2010*

- Eli Lily and Company, in partnership with Sperling's BestPlaces, ranked the nation's 50 largest metro areas in terms of the "Most Romantic Cities for Baby Boomers." The Dallas metro area ranked #9. Criteria: marriage and divorce rates among baby boomers age 45 to 60; great restaurants; dance studios; chocolate, jewelry and flower sales. *Eli Lily and Company, "Most Romantic Cities for Baby Boomers," April 20, 2007*

- The Fort Worth metro area was selected as one of the "Best Cities for Relocating Singles" by Worldwide ERC and Primacy Relocation. The area ranked #46 out of the 100 largest metro areas in the U.S. Criteria: recent job growth; recent singles population growth; overall population growth; affordable rental housing; cost-of-living index; expanded arts and recreation opportunities; ratio of single men and single women; affordability of quality higher education (including state residency requirements); diversity index; climate; population density. *Worldwide ERC and Primacy Relocation, "2008 Best Cities for Relocating Singles"*

- *Forbes* ranked the 40 most populous urbanized areas in the U.S. in terms of the "Best Cities for Singles." The Dallas metro area ranked #17. Criteria: number of singles; cost of living alone; nightlife; culture; job growth; coolness; and online dating participation. *Forbes.com, "Best Cities for Singles," July 27, 2009*

Education Rankings

- *Men's Health* ranked 100 U.S. cities in terms of their education levels. Fort Worth was ranked #87 (#1 = most educated city). Criteria: high school graduation rates; school enrollment; educational attainment; number of households who have outstanding student loans; number of households whose members have taken adult-education courses. *Men's Health, "Where School Is In: The Most and Least Educated Cities," September 12, 2011*

- Fort Worth was selected as one of "America's Most Literate Cities." The city ranked #54 out of the 75 largest U.S. cities. Criteria: number of booksellers; library resources; Internet resources; educational attainment; periodical publishing resources; newspaper circulation. *Central Connecticut State University, "America's Most Literate Cities 2011"*

- Fort Worth was identified as one of the 100 "smartest" metro areas in the U.S. The area ranked #72. Criteria: the editors rated the collective brainpower of the 100 largest metro areas in the U.S. based on their residents' educational attainment. *American City Business Journals, April 14, 2008*

- Fort Worth was identified as one of "America's Brainiest Bastions" by *Portfolio.com*. The metro area ranked #96 out of 200. *Portfolio.com* analyzed levels of educational attainment in the nation's 200 largest metropolitan areas. The editors established scores for five levels of educational attainment, based on relative earning power of adult workers age 25 or older. Scores were determined by comparing the median income for all workers with the median income for those workers at a specified educational level. *Portfolio.com, "America's Brainiest Bastions," December 1, 2010*

Environmental Rankings

- The Dallas was identified as one of North America's greenest metropolitan areas. The area ranked #17. The Green City Index is comprised of 31 indicators, and scores cities across nine categories: carbon dioxide; energy; land use; buildings; transport; water; waste; air quality; environmental governance. The 27 largest metropolitan areas in the U.S. and Canada were considered. *Economist Intelligence Unit, sponsored by Siemens, "U.S. and Canada Green City Index, 2011"*

- The Fort Worth was identified as one of America's cities with the most ENERGY STAR certified buildings. The area ranked #10 out of 25. Criteria: number of ENERGY STAR labeled buildings in 2010. *U.S. Environmental Protection Agency, "Top Cities With the Most ENERGY STAR Certified Buildings," March 15, 2011*

- The Fort Worth metro area was identified as one of "The Ten Biggest American Cities that are Running Out of Water" by *24/7 Wall St.* The metro area ranked #6 out of 10. *24/7 Wall St.* did an analysis of the water supply and consumption in the 30 largest metropolitan areas in the U.S. Criteria include: projected water demand as a share of available precipitation; groundwater use as a share or projected available precipitation; susceptibility to drought; projected increase in freshwater withdrawals; projected increase in summer water deficit. *24/7 Wall St., "The Ten Biggest American Cities that are Running Out of Water," November 1, 2010*

- Fort Worth was selected as one of 22 "Smarter Cities" for energy by the Natural Resources Defense Council. Criteria: investment in green power; energy efficiency measures; conservation. *Natural Resources Defense Council, "2010 Smarter Cities," July 19, 2010*

- *American City Business Journal* ranked 43 metropolitan areas in terms of their "greenness." The Fort Worth metro area ranked #37. Criteria: Forty-one metros in which *ACBJ* has business weeklies, plus Indianapolis and Cleveland, were ranked based on 20 different indicators such as adoption of green technologies, utilization of environmentally sound practices, and air and water quality. *American City Business Journals, "Green City Index," March 11, 2010*

- Fort Worth was selected as one of "America's 50 Greenest Cities" by *Popular Science*. The city ranked #15. Criteria: electricity; transportation; green living; recycling and green perspective. *Popular Science, February 2008*

- 100 of the largest metro areas in the U.S. were analyzed in terms of their current drought severity. The Fort Worth metro area ranked #97 (#1 = driest). The rankings were based on statistics such as long-term precipitation trends and patterns and the Palmer drought indices. *Sperling's BestPlaces, www.BestPlaces.net, "America's Drought-Riskiest Cities," November 2007*

- The Fort Worth metro area appeared in *Country Home's* "Best Green Places" report. The area ranked #171 out of 379. Criteria: official energy policies; green power; green buildings; availability of fresh, locally grown food. *Country Home, "Best Green Places," 2008*

- Fort Worth was highlighted as one of the 25 most ozone-polluted metro areas in the U.S. The area ranked #12. *American Lung Association, State of the Air 2011*

Health/Fitness Rankings

- The Fort Worth metro area was selected as one of the worst cities for bed bugs in America by Rollins corporation, the owner of seven pest control companies, including Orkin. The area ranked #7 based on the number of bed bug treatments from January to December 2011. *Rollins, "The Top 50 U.S. Cities for Bed Bugs," March 19, 2012*

- Dallas was identified as one of "The 8 Most Artery-Clogging Cities in America." The metro area ranked #5. Criteria: obesity rates; heart disease rates. *Prevention, "The 8 Most Artery-Clogging Cities in America," December 2011*

- Dallas was identified as a "2011 Asthma Capital." The area ranked #34 out of the nation's 100 largest metropolitan areas. Twelve factors were used to identify the most challenging places to live for people with asthma: estimated prevalence; self-reported prevalence; crude death rate for asthma; annual pollen score; annual air quality; public smoking laws; number of board-certified asthma specialists; school inhaler access laws; rescue medication use; controller medication use; uninsured rate; poverty rate. *Asthma and Allergy Foundation of America, "2011 Asthma Capitals"*

- Dallas was identified as a "2011 Fall Allergy Capital." The area ranked #22 out of 100. Three groups of factors were used to identify the most severe cities for people with allergies during the fall season: annual pollen levels; medicine utilization; access to board-certified allergists. *Asthma and Allergy Foundation of America, "2011 Fall Allergy Capitals"*

- Dallas was identified as a "2012 Spring Allergy Capital." The area ranked #24 out of 100. Three groups of factors were used to identify the most severe cities for people with allergies during the spring season: annual pollen levels; medicine utilization; access to board-certified allergists. *Asthma and Allergy Foundation of America, "2012 Spring Allergy Capitals"*

- *Men's Health* examined 100 major U.S. cities and selected the best and worst cities for men. Fort Worth ranked #38. Criteria: 35 statistical parameters of long life in the categories of health, quality of life, and fitness. *Men's Health, "The 10 Best and Worst Cities for Men 2012," January/February 2012*

- The makers of Breath Right Nasal Strips, in partnership with Sperling's BestPlaces, analyzed 50 metro areas and identified those U.S. cities most challenged by chronic nasal congestion. The Dallas metro area ranked #7. Criteria: tree, grass and weed pollens; molds and spores; air pollution; climate; smoking; purchase habits of congestion products; prescriptions of drugs for congestion relief; incidence of influenza. *Breathe Right Nasal Strips, "Most Congested Cities," October 3, 2011*

- The American Academy of Dermatology ranked 26 U.S. metropolitan regions in terms of their residents knowledge, attitude and behaviors towards tanning, sun protection and skin cancer detection. The Dallas metro area ranked #11. The results of the study are based on an online survey of over 7,000 adults nationwide. *American Academy of Dermatology, "Suntelligence: How Sun Smart is Your City," May 3, 2010*

- The Dallas metro area appeared in the 2011 Gallup-Healthways Well-Being Index. The index, based on interviews with more than 350,000 Americans, measured jobs, finances, physical health, emotional state of mind and communities. The metro area ranked #64 out of 190. Criteria: life evaluation; emotional health; work environment; physical health; healthy behaviors; basic access (basic needs optimal for a healthy life, such as access to food and medicine, having health insurance and feeling safe while walking at night). *Gallup-Healthways, "State of Well-Being 2011"*

- The Fort Worth metro area was identified as one of "America's Most Stressful Cities" by *Sperling's BestPlaces*. The metro area ranked #33 out of 50. Criteria: unemployment rate; suicide rate; commute time; mental health; poor rest; alcohol use; violent crime rate; property crime rate; cloudy days annually. *Sperling's BestPlaces, www.BestPlaces.net, "Stressful Cities 2012*

- The Dallas metro area was identified as one of "America's Most Stressful Cities" by *Forbes*. The metro area ranked #9 out of 40. Criteria: housing affordability; unemployment rate; cost of living; air quality; traffic congestion; sunny days; population density. *Forbes.com, "America's Most Stressful Cities," September 23, 2011*

- *Men's Health* ranked 100 U.S. cities in terms of their activity levels. Fort Worth was ranked #50 (#1 = most active city). Criteria: where and how often residents exercise; percentage of households that watch more than 15 hours of cable television a week and buy more than 11 video games a year; death rate from deep-vein thrombosis, a condition linked to sitting for extended periods of time. *Men's Health, "Where Sit Happens: The Most and Least Active Cities in America," June 20, 2011*

- *Men's Health* examined the nation's largest 100 cities and identified the 10 cities at highest risk of erectile dysfunction. Fort Worth ranked #5. Criteria: percentage of current male smokers; percentage of adults with a BMI of at least 30; percentage of adults with diabetes; percentage of men working out three or more times per week; percentage of urologists per 100,000 men; number of ED drug prescriptions filled in 2007. *Men's Health, "Ranking America's Cities: Cities that Need Viagara," April 2009*

- 50 of the largest metro areas in the U.S. were analyzed in terms of their health and fitness by the American College of Sports Medicine in their "American Fitness Index." The Dallas metro area ranked #40 (#1 = healthiest). Criteria: preventative health behaviors; levels of chronic disease; health care access; community resources and policies that support physical activity. *American College of Sports Medicine, "Health and Community Fitness Status of the 50 Largest Metropolitan Areas," August 1, 2011*

- Fort Worth was selected as one of the "20 Most Livable U.S. Cities for Wheelchair Users" by the Christopher & Dana Reeve Foundation. The city ranked #14. Criteria: Medicaid eligibility and spending; access to physicians and rehabilitation facilities; access to fitness facilities and recreation; access to paratransit; percentage of people living with disabilities who are employed; clean air; climate. *Christopher & Dana Reeve Foundation, "20 Most Livable U.S. Cities for Wheelchair Users," July 26, 2010*

Real Estate Rankings

- The Fort Worth metro area was identified as one of ten places where real estate is ripe for a rebound by *Forbes*. Criteria: change in home price over the past 12 months and three years; unemployment rates; 12-month job-growth projections; population change from 2006 through 2009; new home construction rates for the third quarter of 2011 as compared to the same quarter in 2010. *Forbes.com, "Cities Where Real Estate is Ripe for a Rebound," January 12, 2012*

- *Fortune* ranked the 100 largest metro areas in the U.S. in terms of projected median home price change in 2010. The Fort Worth metro area ranked #14. *Fortune, "The 2010 Housing Outlook," December 9, 2009*

- Fort Worth appeared on *ApartmentRatings.com* "Top Cities for Renters" list in 2009." The area ranked #28. Overall satisfaction ratings were ranked using thousands of user submitted scores for hundreds of apartment complexes located in the 100 most populated U.S. municipalities. *ApartmentRatings.com, "2009 Renter Satisfaction Rankings"*

- The Fort Worth metro area was identified as one of the "Top 25 Real Estate Investment Markets" by *FinestExperts.com*. The metro area ranked #1. Over 10,000 real estate markets were analyzed to identify the most suitable places for real estate investors to seek stability and growth. Criteria: employment; rental markets; growth levels as offset by foreclosures. *FinestExperts.com, "Top 25 Real Estate Investment Markets," January 7, 2010*

- The Fort Worth metro area was identified as one of "America's Best Housing Markets" by *Forbes*. The metro area ranked #9. Criteria: housing affordability; rising home prices; percentage of foreclosures. *Forbes.com, "America's Best Housing Markets," February 19, 2010*

- The Fort Worth metro area was identified as one of the 10 best cities for "Real Estate Steals" in the U.S. by *U.S. News and World Report*. The metro area was ranked #9. Criteria: average and quarterly price-to-income ratios. *U.S. News and World Report, "10 Cities for Real Estate Steals," February 18, 2010*

- The Fort Worth metro area appeared in a *Wall Street Journal* article ranking cities by "housing stress." The metro area was ranked #22 (#1 = most stress). Criteria: fraction of mortgage-holding homeowners with a monthly housing payment in excess of 30 percent of income; percentage of people without health insurance; unemployment rate. *The Wall Street Journal, "Which Cities Face Biggest Housing Risk," October 5, 2010*

- The Center for Housing Policy ranked 210 U.S. metropolitan areas by the fair market rent for a two-bedroom unit. The Fort Worth metro area was ranked #90. (#1 = most expensive) with a rent of $861. Criteria: Fair Market Rent (FMR) in effect during the fourth quarter of 2009 based on HUD's fiscal year 2010 FMRs. *The Center for Housing Policy, "Paycheck to Paycheck: Most to Least Expensive Rental Markets in 2009"*

- The Dallas metro area was identified as one of the markets with the best expected performance in home prices over the next 12 months. *Local Market Monitor, "First Quarter Home Price Forecast for Largest US Markets," March 2, 2011*

- The Fort Worth metro area was identified as one of the best U.S. markets to invest in rental property" by HomeVestors and Local Market Monitor. The area ranked #15 out of 100. Criteria: risk-return premium relative to national average. *HomeVestors and Local Market Monitor, "Best 100 U.S. Markets to Invest in Rental Property," March 9, 2012*

Safety Rankings

- Symantec, the makers of Norton, in partnership with Sperling's BestPlaces, ranked the 50 largest cities in the U.S. in terms of their vulnerability to cybercrime. The city ranked #32. Criteria: number of cyberattacks and potential infections; level of Internet access; expenditures on smartphones and computer hardware/software; wireless hotspots; broadband connectivity; Internet usage; online purchases. *Symantec, "Riskiest Online Cities of 2012" February 15, 2012*

- Allstate ranked the 193 largest cities in America in terms of driver safety. Fort Worth ranked #130. In addition, drivers were 18.8% more likely to have had an accident compared to the national average. Allstate researchers analyzed internal property damage reported claims over a two-year period (from January 2008 to December 2009) to protect findings from external influences such as weather or road construction. A weighted average of the two-year numbers determined the annual percentages. The report defines an auto crash as any collision resulting in a property damage claim. *Allstate, "2011 Allstate America's Best Drivers Report™"*

- Dallas was identified as one of the least safe places in the U.S. in terms of its vulnerability to natural disasters and weather extremes. The city ranked #2 out of 10. Data was analyzed to show a metro areas' relative tendency to experience natural disasters (hail, tornadoes, high winds, hurricanes, earthquakes, and brush fires) or extreme weather (abundant rain or snowfall or days that are below freezing or above 90 degrees Fahrenheit). *Forbes, "Safest and Least Safe Places in the U.S.," August 30, 2005*

- The National Insurance Crime Bureau ranked 366 metro areas in the U.S. in terms of per capita rates of vehicle theft. The Fort Worth metro area ranked #47 (#1 = highest rate). Criteria: number of vehicle theft offenses per 100,000 inhabitants in 2010. *National Insurance Crime Bureau, "Hot Spots," June 21, 2011*

- The Dallas metro area was identified as one of the most dangerous metro areas for pedestrians by Transportation for America. The metro area ranked #10 out of 52 metro areas with over 1 million residents. Criteria: area's population divided by the number of pedestrian fatalities in that area. *Transportation for America, "Dangerous by Design 2011"*

Seniors/Retirement Rankings

- Bankers Life and Casualty Company, in partnership with Sperling's BestPlaces, ranked the nation's 50 largest metro areas in terms of the "Best U.S. Cities for Seniors." The Fort Worth metro area ranked #33. Criteria: healthcare; transportation; housing; environment; economy; health and longevity; social and spiritual life; crime. *Bankers Life and Casualty Company, Center for a Secure Retirement, "Best U.S. Cities for Seniors 2011," September 2011*

- The Dallas metro area was identified as one of "America's Most Affordable Places to Retire" by *Forbes*. The metro area ranked #2. Criteria: housing affordability; inflation; number of persons over 65 who are employed; net migration for persons over 65; percent of persons over 65 living below poverty level; doctors per capita; number of citizens tapping their Medicare benefits per thousand people. *Forbes.com, "America's Most Affordable Places to Retire," September 5, 2008*

- The Dallas metro area was selected as one of "America's Best Places to Grow Old" by *Forbes*. The area was ranked #2 out of 10. Criteria: housing affordability; inflationary pressures; number of persons over 65 who are currently employed; net migration for persons over 65; percent of seniors living below poverty level; doctors per capita; number of citizens tapping their Medicare benefits per 1,000 people. *Forbes, "America's Best Places to Grow Old," December 12, 2008*

- The Fort Worth metro area was selected as one of "The 10 Most Affordable Cities for Long-Term Care" by *U.S. News & World Report*. Criteria: costs at nursing homes, assisted living facilities, and adult day health care facilities; cost for licensed home health aides. *U.S. News & World Report, "The 10 Most Affordable Cities for Long-Term Care," May 17, 2010*

Sports/Recreation Rankings

- Fort Worth appeared on the *Sporting News* list of the "Best Sports Cities" for 2011. The area ranked #1 out of 271 cities in the U.S. *Sporting News* takes a 12-month snapshot of each city's sports, putting a heavy premium on regular-season won-lost records (from the most recently completed season). Other criteria include: playoff berths, bowl appearances and tournament bids; championships; applicable power ratings; quality of competition; overall fan fervor (measured in part by attendance); abundance of teams (rewarding quality over quantity); stadium and arena quality; ticket availability and prices; franchise ownership; and marquee appeal of athletes. *Sporting News, "Best Sports Cities 2011," October 4, 2011*

- The Fort Worth was selected as one of the best metro areas for golf in America by *Golf Digest*. The Fort Worth area was ranked #1 out of 20. Criteria: climate; cost of public golf; quality of public golf; accessibility. *Golf Digest, "The Top 20 Cities for Golf," October 2011*

- *Golf.com* and the research arm of the National Golf Foundation analyzed the 50 largest metropolitan areas in the U.S. in terms of golf. The Dallas metro area ranked #4. Criteria: weather; affordability; quality of courses; accessibility; number of courses designed by esteemed architects; availability; crowdedness. *Golf.com, November 15, 2007*

Technology Rankings

- Fort Worth was selected as a 2011 Digital Cities Survey winner. The city ranked #10 in the large city (250,000 or more population) category. The survey examined and assessed how city governments are utilizing information technology to operate and deliver quality service to their customers and citizens. Survey questions focused on implementation and adoption of online service delivery; planning and governance; and the infrastructure and architecture that make the transformation to digital government possible. *Center for Digital Government, "2011 Digital Cities Survey"*

- Scarborough Research, a leading market research firm, identified the Fort Worth DMA (Designated Market Area) as one of the top markets for text messaging with more than 50% of cell phone subscribers age 18+ utilizing the text messaging feature on their phone. *Scarborough Research, November 24, 2008*

Transportation Rankings

- Fort Worth was selected as one of the "Least Courteous Cities (Worst Road Rage)" in the U.S. by AutoVantage. The city ranked #2. Criteria: 2,518 consumers were interviewed in 25 major metropolitan areas about their views on road rage. *AutoVantage, "2009 AutoVantage Road Rage Survey"*

- The Fort Worth metro area appeared on *Forbes* list of the best and worst cities for commuters. The metro area ranked #56 out of 60 (#1 is best). Criteria: travel time; road congestion; travel delays. *Forbes.com, "Best and Worst Cities for Commuters," February 16, 2010*

Women/Minorities Rankings

- *Women's Health* examined U.S. cities and identified the 100 best cities for women. Fort Worth was ranked #43. Criteria: 30 categories were examined from obesity and breast cancer rates to commuting times and hours spent working out. *Women's Health, "Best Cities for Women 2012"*

- Fort Worth was ranked #88 out of 100 metro areas in *SELF Magazine's* ranking of America's healthiest places for women." A panel of experts came up with more than 50 criteria including death and disease rates, environmental indicators, community resources, and lifestyle habits. *SELF Magazine, "Secrets of America's Healthiest Women," December 2008*

- Dallas appeared on *Black Enterprise's* list of the "Ten Best Cities for African Americans." The top picks were culled from more than 2,000 interactive surveys completed on BlackEnterprise.com and by editorial staff evaluation. The editors weighed the following criteria as it pertained to African Americans in each city: median household income; percentage of households earning more than $100,000; percentage of businesses owned; percentage of college graduates; unemployment rates; home loan rejections; and homeownership rates. *Black Enterprise, May 2007*

- The Dallas metro area appeared on *Forbes'* list of the "Best Cities for Minority Entrepreneurs." The area ranked #88 out of 10. Criteria: 52 metropolitan statistical areas were examined. For each ethnicity (African Americans, Asians and Hispanics), the editors measured housing affordability, population growth, income growth, and entrepreneurship (per capita self-employment). *Forbes, "Best Cities for Minority Entrepreneurs," March 23, 2011*

Miscellaneous Rankings

- *Men's Health* ranked 100 U.S. cities by their level of sadness. Fort Worth was ranked #43 (#1 = saddest city). Criteria: suicide rates; unemployment rates; percentage of households that use antidepressants; percent of population who report feeling blue all or most of the time. *Men's Health, "Frown Towns," November 28, 2011*

- Proctor & Gamble, the makers of Pepto-Bismol, in partnership with Sperling's BestPlaces, ranked the nation's 100 most populated metro areas in terms of the "Best Places for Thanksgiving Celebrations." The Fort Worth metro area ranked #4. Criteria: turkey consumption per capita; increase in inbound air traffic during Thanksgiving; Pepto-Bismol sales; results from a consumer poll of 4,800 Americans recording the number of people attending Thanksgiving, the number of dishes served, and ways people intended to celebrate. *Proctor & Gamble, "Top 10 Best Places for Thanksgiving Celebrations," November 18, 2010*

- Energizer Holdings, the makers of Edge® shave gel, in partnership with Sperling's BestPlaces, ranked 50 major metro areas in terms of everyday irritations. The Dallas metro area ranked #13. Criteria: humidity levels; weather conditions; incidence of traffic delays and congestion; average commute times; frequency of flight delays and cancellations; rates of sleeplessness; underemployment; pollens and allergens; pests; comedy clubs per capita. *Energizer Holdings, "Most Irritation Prone Cities," July 23, 2010*

- Mars Chocolate North America, the makers of COMBOS®, in partnership with Sperling's BestPlaces, ranked 50 major metro areas in terms of their "manliness." The Dallas metro area ranked #21. Criteria: number of professional sports teams; number of nearby NASCAR tracks and racing events; manly lifestyle; concentration of manly retail stores; manly occupations per capita; salty snack sales; "Board of Manliness" rankings. *Mars Chocolate North America, "America's Manliest Cities 2011," September 1, 2011*

- The Dallas metro area was selected as one of "America's Greediest Cities" by *Forbes*. The area was ranked #7 out of 10. Criteria: number of Forbes 400 (*Forbes* annual list of the richest Americans) members per capita. *Forbes, "America's Greediest Cities," December 7, 2007*

- The Dallas metro area appeared in *AutoMD.com's* ranking of the "Best and Worst Cities for Auto Repair." The metro area ranked #34 (#1 is best). The 50 most-populated metro areas in the U.S. were ranked on three critical factors: repair affordability; price disparity range; shop integrity factor. *AutoMD.com, "Advocacy for Repair Shop Fairness Report," February 24, 2010*

Business Environment

CITY FINANCES

City Government Finances

Component	2009 ($000)	2009 ($ per capita)
Total Revenues	836,281	1,227
Total Expenditures	1,178,899	1,729
Debt Outstanding	2,028,544	2,975
Cash and Securities[1]	3,064,655	4,495

Note: (1) Cash and security holdings of a government at the close of its fiscal year, including those of its dependent agencies, utilities, and liquor stores.
Source: U.S Census Bureau, State & Local Government Finances 2009

City Government Revenue by Source

Source	2009 ($000)	2009 ($ per capita)
General Revenue		
From Federal Government	10,892	16
From State Government	23,606	35
From Local Governments	174	0
Taxes		
Property	333,962	490
Sales and Gross Receipts	211,528	310
Personal Income	0	0
Corporate Income	0	0
Motor Vehicle License	0	0
Other Taxes	36,399	53
Current Charges	211,933	311
Liquor Store	0	0
Utility	185,040	271
Employee Retirement	-347,359	-509

Source: U.S Census Bureau, State & Local Government Finances 2009

City Government Expenditures by Function

Function	2009 ($000)	2009 ($ per capita)	2009 (%)
General Direct Expenditures			
Air Transportation	4,018	6	0.3
Corrections	0	0	0.0
Education	0	0	0.0
Employment Security Administration	0	0	0.0
Financial Administration	9,243	14	0.8
Fire Protection	104,158	153	8.8
General Public Buildings	7,097	10	0.6
Governmental Administration, Other	13,694	20	1.2
Health	14,567	21	1.2
Highways	89,459	131	7.6
Hospitals	0	0	0.0
Housing and Community Development	14,973	22	1.3
Interest on General Debt	55,676	82	4.7
Judicial and Legal	18,568	27	1.6
Libraries	17,952	26	1.5
Parking	12,835	19	1.1
Parks and Recreation	48,282	71	4.1
Police Protection	197,050	289	16.7
Public Welfare	0	0	0.0
Sewerage	170,839	251	14.5
Solid Waste Management	40,544	59	3.4
Veterans' Services	0	0	0.0
Liquor Store	0	0	0.0
Utility	155,778	228	13.2
Employee Retirement	101,274	149	8.6

Source: U.S Census Bureau, State & Local Government Finances 2009

Municipal Bond Ratings

Area	Moody's	S&P	Fitch
City	Aa2	AA+	AA+

Rating Systems (shown in declining order of credit quality): Moody's– Aaa, Aa, A, Baa, Ba, B, Caa, Ca, C (numerical modifiers 1, 2, and 3 are added to letter-rating); S&P– AAA, AA, A, BBB, BB, B, CCC, CC, C; Fitch– AAA, AA, A, BBB, BB, B, CCC, CC, C. Ratings may be modified by the addition of a plus or minus sign to show relative standing within the major rating categories.

Notes: n/a Not Available; w/d Withdrawn (1) Not Reviewed; (2) Issuer Rating/No General Obligation; (3) Standard and Poor's Issue Credit Rating (ICR) is a current opinion of an obliger with respect to a specific financial obligation, a specific class of financial obligations, or a specific financial program.

Source: U.S. Census Bureau, 2012 Statistical Abstract, Bond Ratings for City Governments by Largest Cities: 2010

DEMOGRAPHICS

Population Growth

Area	1990 Census	2000 Census	2010 Census	Population Growth (%) 1990-2000	Population Growth (%) 2000-2010
City	448,311	534,694	741,206	19.3	38.6
MSA[1]	3,989,294	5,161,544	6,371,773	29.4	23.4
U.S.	248,709,873	281,421,906	308,745,538	13.2	9.7

Note: (1) Figures cover the Dallas-Fort Worth-Arlington, TX Metropolitan Statistical Area—see Appendix B for areas included
Source: U.S. Census Bureau, 2010 Census

Household Size

Area	Persons in Household (%) One	Two	Three	Four	Five	Six	Seven or More	Average Household Size
City	26.5	27.4	16.3	14.6	8.3	3.8	3.0	2.77
MSA[1]	24.8	29.6	16.7	15.2	7.9	3.3	2.5	2.74
U.S.	26.7	32.8	16.1	13.4	6.5	2.6	1.9	2.58

Note: (1) Figures cover the Dallas-Fort Worth-Arlington, TX Metropolitan Statistical Area—see Appendix B for areas included
Source: U.S. Census Bureau, 2010 Census

Race

Area	White Alone[2] (%)	Black Alone[2] (%)	Asian Alone[2] (%)	AIAN[3] Alone[2] (%)	NHOPI[4] Alone[2] (%)	Other Race Alone[2] (%)	Two or More Races (%)
City	61.1	18.9	3.7	0.6	0.1	12.4	3.1
MSA[1]	65.3	15.1	5.4	0.7	0.1	10.6	2.8
U.S.	72.4	12.6	4.8	0.9	0.2	6.2	2.9

Note: (1) Figures cover the Dallas-Fort Worth-Arlington, TX Metropolitan Statistical Area—see Appendix B for areas included; (2) Alone is defined as not being in combination with one or more other races; (3) American Indian and Alaska Native; (4) Native Hawaiian and Other Pacific Islander
Source: U.S. Census Bureau, 2010 Census

Hispanic or Latino Origin

Area	Hispanic or Latino (%)	Mexican (%)	Puerto Rican (%)	Cuban (%)	Other Hispanic or Latino (%)
City	34.1	29.6	0.8	0.2	3.5
MSA[1]	27.5	22.9	0.5	0.2	3.9
U.S.	16.3	10.3	1.5	0.6	4.0

Note: Persons of Hispanic or Latino origin can be of any race; (1) Figures cover the Dallas-Fort Worth-Arlington, TX Metropolitan Statistical Area—see Appendix B for areas included
Source: U.S. Census Bureau, 2010 Census

Segregation

Type	Segregation Indices[1]				Percent Change		
	1990	2000	2010	2010 Rank[2]	1990-2000	1990-2010	2000-2010
Black/White	62.8	59.8	56.6	48	-3.1	-6.2	-3.2
Asian/White	41.8	45.6	46.6	19	3.8	4.8	1.0
Hispanic/White	48.8	52.3	50.3	24	3.5	1.5	-2.0

Note: Figures are based on an analysis of 1990, 2000, and 2010 Census Decennial Census tract data by William H. Frey, Brookings Institution and the University of Michigan Social Science Data Analysis Network. In this analysis all racial groups (whites, blacks, and asians) are non-Hispanic members of those races. Hispanics are shown as a separate category; All figures cover the Metropolitan Statistical Area (see Appendix B for areas included); (1) Segregation Indices are Dissimilarity Indices that measure the degree to which the minority group is distributed differently than whites across census tracts. They range from 0 (complete integration) to 100 (complete segregation) where the value indicates the percentage of the minority group that needs to move to be distributed exactly like whites; (2) Ranges from 1 (most segregated) to 102 (least segregated); n/a not available.
Source: www.CensusScope.org

Ancestry

Area	German	Irish	English	American	Italian	Polish	French[2]	Scottish	Dutch
City	9.4	7.3	6.7	6.6	1.8	0.9	1.6	1.6	0.8
MSA[1]	11.1	8.6	8.2	6.0	2.3	1.1	2.2	1.8	1.1
U.S.	16.1	11.6	8.8	6.1	5.7	3.2	3.0	1.9	1.6

Note: Figures are the percentage of the total population reporting a particular ancestry. The nine most commonly reported ancestries in the U.S. are shown. Figures include multiple ancestries (e.g. if a person reported being Irish and Italian, they were included in both columns); (1) Figures cover the Dallas-Fort Worth-Arlington, TX Metropolitan Statistical Area—see Appendix B for areas included; (2) Excludes Basque
Source: U.S. Census Bureau, 2008-2010 American Community Survey 3-Year Estimates

Foreign-Born Population

Area	Percent of Population Born in								
	Any Foreign Country	Mexico	Asia	Europe	Carribean	South America	Central America[2]	Africa	Canada
City	17.8	11.9	2.9	0.8	0.2	0.4	0.8	0.6	0.1
MSA[1]	17.5	9.3	4.2	0.8	0.2	0.5	1.3	0.9	0.2
U.S.	12.8	3.8	3.6	1.6	1.2	0.9	1.0	0.5	0.3

Note: (1) Figures cover the Dallas-Fort Worth-Arlington, TX Metropolitan Statistical Area—see Appendix B for areas included; (2) Excludes Mexico.
Source: U.S. Census Bureau, 2008-2010 American Community Survey 3-Year Estimates

Marital Status

Area	Never Married	Now Married[2]	Separated	Widowed	Divorced
City	32.0	48.0	3.1	4.8	12.1
MSA[1]	30.4	51.6	2.6	4.5	10.9
U.S.	31.6	49.6	2.2	6.1	10.7

Note: Figures are percentages and cover the population 15 years of age and older; (1) Figures cover the Dallas-Fort Worth-Arlington, TX Metropolitan Statistical Area—see Appendix B for areas included; (2) Excludes separated
Source: U.S. Census Bureau, 2008-2010 American Community Survey 3-Year Estimates

Age

Area	Percent of Population							Median Age
	Under Age 5	Age 5 to 17	Age 18 to 34	Age 35 to 49	Age 50 to 64	Age 65 to 79	80 Years and Over	
City	9.0	20.3	26.6	21.2	14.7	6.0	2.2	31.2
MSA[1]	7.8	20.0	24.3	22.5	16.6	6.7	2.1	33.5
U.S.	6.5	17.5	23.2	20.7	19.0	9.4	3.6	37.2

Note: (1) Figures cover the Dallas-Fort Worth-Arlington, TX Metropolitan Statistical Area—see Appendix B for areas included
Source: U.S. Census Bureau, 2010 Census

Male/Female Ratio

Area	Males	Females	Males per 100 Females
City	363,896	377,310	96.4
MSA[1]	3,141,634	3,230,139	97.3
U.S.	151,781,326	156,964,212	96.7

Note: (1) Figures cover the Dallas-Fort Worth-Arlington, TX
Metropolitan Statistical Area—see Appendix B for areas included
Source: U.S. Census Bureau, 2010 Census

Religious Groups

Area	Catholic	Baptist	Non-Den.	Methodist[2]	Lutheran	LDS[3]	Pente-costal	Presby-terian[4]	Muslim[5]	Judaism
MSA[1]	13.3	18.7	7.8	5.3	0.8	1.2	2.2	1.0	0.4	2.4
U.S.	19.1	9.3	4.0	4.0	2.3	2.0	1.9	1.6	0.8	0.7

Note: Figures are the number of adherents as a percentage of the total population; (1) Figures cover the
Dallas-Fort Worth-Arlington, TX Metropolitan Statistical Area—see Appendix B for areas included;
(2) Methodist/Pietist; (3) Latter Day Saints; (4) Reformed; (5) Figures are estimates
Source: Association of Statisticians of American Religious Bodies, 2010 U.S. Religion Census: Religious
Congregations & Membership Study

ECONOMY

Gross Metropolitan Product

Area	2007	2008	2009	2010	2010 Rank[2]
MSA[1]	358.1	370.8	358.3	376.8	6

Note: Figures are in billions of dollars; (1) Figures cover the Dallas-Fort Worth-Arlington, TX Metropolitan
Statistical Area—see Appendix B for areas included; (2) Rank ranges from 1 to 363
Source: The United States Conference of Mayors, "U.S. Metro Economies: GMP and Employment Forecasts,"
June 2011

Economic Growth

Area	2007-2009 (%)	2010 (%)	2011 (%)	Rank[2]
MSA[1]	-0.3	5.0	4.1	114
U.S.	-1.3	2.9	2.5	–

Note: Figures are real Gross Metropolitan Product growth rates and represent annual average percent change;
(1) Figures cover the Dallas-Fort Worth-Arlington, TX Metropolitan Statistical Area—see Appendix B for areas
included; (2) Rank ranges from 1 to 363
Source: The United States Conference of Mayors, "U.S. Metro Economies: GMP and Employment Forecasts,"
June 2011

Metropolitan Area Exports

Area	2005	2006	2007	2008	2009	2010	2010 Rank[2]
MSA[1]	20,541.2	22,461.6	22,079.1	22,503.7	19,881.8	22,500.4	11

Note: Figures are in millions of dollars; (1) Figures cover the Dallas-Fort Worth-Arlington, TX Metropolitan
Statistical Area—see Appendix B for areas included; (2) Rank ranges from 1 to 369
Source: U.S. Department of Commerce, International Trade Administration, Office of Trade & Industry
Information, Manufacturing & Services, data extracted April 2, 2012

INCOME

Income

Area	Per Capita ($)	Median Household ($)	Average Household ($)
City	23,482	48,970	64,403
MSA[1]	28,035	55,740	76,630
U.S.	26,942	51,222	70,116

Note: (1) Figures cover the Dallas-Fort Worth-Arlington, TX Metropolitan Statistical Area—see Appendix B for
areas included
Source: U.S. Census Bureau, 2008-2010 American Community Survey 3-Year Estimates

Household Income Distribution

Area	Percent of Households Earning							
	Under $15,000	$15,000 -24,999	$25,000 -34,999	$35,000 -49,999	$50,000 -74,999	$75,000 -99,000	$100,000 -149,999	$150,000 and up
City	13.5	12.0	11.1	14.2	19.5	12.1	11.1	6.4
MSA[1]	10.3	10.1	10.2	14.0	18.7	12.5	13.8	10.2
U.S.	13.0	11.0	10.6	14.2	18.5	12.1	12.2	8.4

Note: (1) Figures cover the Dallas-Fort Worth-Arlington, TX Metropolitan Statistical Area—see Appendix B for areas included
Source: U.S. Census Bureau, 2008-2010 American Community Survey 3-Year Estimates

Poverty Rate

Area	All Ages	Under 18 Years Old	18 to 64 Years Old	65 Years and Over
City	17.9	25.8	15.0	11.4
MSA[1]	14.0	20.1	12.0	8.7
U.S.	14.4	20.1	13.1	9.4

Note: Figures are percentage of people whose income during the past 12 months was below the poverty level;
(1) Figures cover the Dallas-Fort Worth-Arlington, TX Metropolitan Statistical Area—see Appendix B for areas included
Source: U.S. Census Bureau, 2008-2010 American Community Survey 3-Year Estimates

Personal Bankruptcy Filing Rate

Area	2006	2007	2008	2009	2010	2011
Tarrant County	2.44	2.91	3.02	3.74	3.76	3.20
U.S.	2.00	2.73	3.53	4.61	4.97	4.37

Note: Numbers are per 1,000 population and include Chapter 7 and Chapter 13 filings
Source: Federal Deposit Insurance Corporation, Regional Economic Conditions, March 9, 2012

EMPLOYMENT

Labor Force and Employment

Area	Civilian Labor Force			Workers Employed		
	Dec. 2010	Dec. 2011	% Chg.	Dec. 2010	Dec. 2011	% Chg.
City	338,904	342,699	1.1	311,270	317,744	2.1
MD[1]	1,072,202	1,083,608	1.1	987,399	1,007,942	2.1
U.S.	153,156,000	153,373,000	0.1	139,159,000	140,681,000	1.1

Note: Data is not seasonally adjusted and covers workers 16 years of age and older;
(1) Metropolitan Division—see Appendix B for areas included
Source: Bureau of Labor Statistics, http://stats.bls.gov

Unemployment Rate

Area	2011											
	Jan.	Feb.	Mar.	Apr.	May	Jun.	Jul.	Aug.	Sep.	Oct.	Nov.	Dec.
City	8.7	8.3	8.4	8.0	8.3	9.1	9.1	8.7	8.7	8.2	7.6	7.3
MD[1]	8.4	8.1	8.0	7.6	7.8	8.6	8.5	8.3	8.2	7.8	7.3	7.0
U.S.	9.8	9.5	9.2	8.7	8.7	9.3	9.3	9.1	8.8	8.5	8.2	8.3

Note: Data is not seasonally adjusted and covers workers 16 years of age and older; All figures are percentages; (1) Metropolitan Division—see Appendix B for areas included
Source: Bureau of Labor Statistics, http://stats.bls.gov

Projected Unemployment Rate

Area	2010 (%)	2011 (%)	2012 (%)	2013 (%)
MSA[1]	8.4	8.1	7.7	7.2

Note: (1) Metropolitan Statistical Area—see Appendix B for areas included
Source: The United States Conference of Mayors, "U.S. Metro Economies: GMP and Employment Forecasts," June 2011

Employment by Occupation

Occupation Classification	City (%)	MSA[1] (%)	U.S. (%)
Management, Business, Science, and Arts	32.2	36.4	35.6
Natural Resources, Construction, and Maintenance	10.7	10.1	9.5
Production, Transportation, and Material Moving	14.4	11.6	12.1
Sales and Office	26.3	26.8	25.2
Service	16.3	15.2	17.6

Note: Figures cover employed civilians 16 years of age and older; (1) Figures cover the Dallas-Fort Worth-Arlington, TX Metropolitan Statistical Area—see Appendix B for areas included
Source: U.S. Census Bureau, 2008-2010 American Community Survey 3-Year Estimates

Employment by Industry

Sector	MD[1] Number of Employees	MD[1] Percent of Total	U.S. Percent of Total
Construction	n/a	n/a	4.1
Education and Health Services	108,700	12.4	15.2
Financial Activities	55,400	6.3	5.8
Government	119,300	13.6	16.8
Information	13,800	1.6	2.0
Leisure and Hospitality	97,100	11.1	9.9
Manufacturing	89,500	10.2	8.9
Mining and Logging	n/a	n/a	0.6
Other Services	31,500	3.6	4.0
Professional and Business Services	98,200	11.2	13.3
Retail Trade	104,700	12.0	11.5
Transportation and Utilities	62,700	7.2	3.8
Wholesale Trade	40,700	4.6	4.2

Note: Figures cover non-farm employment as of December 2011 and are not seasonally adjusted; (1) Metropolitan Division—see Appendix B for areas included; n/a not available
Source: Bureau of Labor Statistics, http://stats.bls.gov

Occupations with Greatest Projected Employment Growth: 2008 – 2018

Occupation[1]	2008 Employment	2018 Projected Employment	Numeric Employment Change	Percent Employment Change
Combined Food Preparation and Serving Workers, Including Fast Food	247,750	326,190	78,440	31.7
Elementary School Teachers, Except Special Education	156,930	218,030	61,100	38.9
Retail Salespersons	361,780	416,090	54,310	15.0
Registered Nurses	166,240	219,880	53,640	32.3
Home Health Aides	92,660	143,720	51,060	55.1
Customer Service Representatives	217,250	267,290	50,040	23.0
Waiters and Waitresses	192,340	237,660	45,320	23.6
Personal and Home Care Aides	94,530	138,530	44,000	46.5
Office Clerks, General	239,400	279,000	39,600	16.5
Cashiers	276,070	312,940	36,870	13.4

Note: Projections cover Texas; (1) Sorted by numeric employment change
Source: www.projectionscentral.com, State Occupational Projections, 2008–2018 Long-Term Projections

Fastest Growing Occupations: 2008 – 2018

Occupation[1]	2008 Employment	2018 Projected Employment	Numeric Employment Change	Percent Employment Change
Biomedical Engineers	650	1,150	500	76.9
Home Health Aides	92,660	143,720	51,060	55.1
Network Systems and Data Communications Analysts	19,160	29,490	10,330	53.9
Petroleum Engineers	13,440	20,140	6,700	49.9
Athletic Trainers	1,560	2,300	740	47.4
Personal and Home Care Aides	94,530	138,530	44,000	46.5
Electrical and Electronics Repairers, Powerhouse, Substation, and Relay	1,550	2,260	710	45.8
Financial Examiners	2,150	3,130	980	45.6
Medical Scientists, Except Epidemiologists	3,670	5,320	1,650	45.0
Biochemists and Biophysicists	740	1,060	320	43.2

Note: Projections cover Texas; (1) Sorted by percent employment change and excludes occupations with numeric employment change less than 100
Source: www.projectionscentral.com, State Occupational Projections, 2008–2018 Long-Term Projections

Average Wages

Occupation	$/Hr.	Occupation	$/Hr.
Accountants and Auditors	34.28	Maids and Housekeeping Cleaners	9.18
Automotive Mechanics	18.26	Maintenance and Repair Workers	16.59
Bookkeepers	17.07	Marketing Managers	54.92
Carpenters	14.74	Nuclear Medicine Technologists	34.77
Cashiers	9.34	Nurses, Licensed Practical	20.86
Clerks, General Office	14.34	Nurses, Registered	31.74
Clerks, Receptionists/Information	12.95	Nursing Aides/Orderlies/Attendants	11.16
Clerks, Shipping/Receiving	14.29	Packers and Packagers, Hand	9.53
Computer Programmers	35.64	Physical Therapists	41.00
Computer Support Specialists	25.12	Postal Service Mail Carriers	25.02
Computer Systems Analysts	37.32	Real Estate Brokers	n/a
Cooks, Restaurant	9.75	Retail Salespersons	11.79
Dentists	69.33	Sales Reps., Exc. Tech./Scientific	28.96
Electrical Engineers	39.08	Sales Reps., Tech./Scientific	48.18
Electricians	20.66	Secretaries, Exc. Legal/Med./Exec.	15.65
Financial Managers	52.01	Security Guards	12.08
First-Line Supervisors/Managers, Sales	19.25	Surgeons	77.40
Food Preparation Workers	9.54	Teacher Assistants	9.90
General and Operations Managers	52.48	Teachers, Elementary School	26.40
Hairdressers/Cosmetologists	12.21	Teachers, Secondary School	27.40
Internists	89.32	Telemarketers	12.61
Janitors and Cleaners	11.14	Truck Drivers, Heavy/Tractor-Trailer	19.77
Landscaping/Groundskeeping Workers	11.15	Truck Drivers, Light/Delivery Svcs.	15.76
Lawyers	56.38	Waiters and Waitresses	10.08

Note: Wage data covers the Fort Worth-Arlington, TX Metropolitan Division—see Appendix B for areas included. Hourly wages for elementary/secondary school teachers and teacher assistants were calculated by the editors from annual wage data assuming a 40 hour work week; n/a not available.
Source: Bureau of Labor Statistics, Metro Area Occupational Employment and Wage Estimates, May 2011

RESIDENTIAL REAL ESTATE

Building Permits

Area	Single-Family 2010	2011	Pct. Chg.	Multi-Family 2010	2011	Pct. Chg.	Total 2010	2011	Pct. Chg.
City	2,759	2,426	-12.1	818	1,144	39.9	3,577	3,570	-0.2
MSA[1]	14,420	14,039	-2.6	5,138	10,788	110.0	19,558	24,827	26.9
U.S.	447,311	418,498	-6.4	157,299	205,563	30.7	604,610	624,061	3.2

Note: (1) Metropolitan Statistical Area—see Appendix B for areas included; figures represent new, privately-owned housing units authorized (unadjusted data); All permit data are based on estimates with imputation.
Source: U.S. Census Bureau, Manufacturing, Mining, and Construction Statistics, Building Permits, 2010, 2011

Homeownership Rate

Area	2005 (%)	2006 (%)	2007 (%)	2008 (%)	2009 (%)	2010 (%)	2011 (%)
MSA[1]	62.3	60.7	60.9	60.9	61.6	63.8	62.6
U.S.	68.9	68.8	68.1	67.8	67.4	66.9	66.1

Note: (1) Metropolitan Statistical Area—see Appendix B for areas included
Source: U.S. Census Bureau, Housing Vacancies and Homeownership Annual Statistics: 2011

Housing Vacancy Rates

Area	Gross Vacancy Rate[2] (%)			Year-Round Vacancy Rate[3] (%)			Rental Vacancy Rate[4] (%)			Homeowner Vacancy Rate[5] (%)		
	2009	2010	2011	2009	2010	2011	2009	2010	2011	2009	2010	2011
MSA[1]	9.4	10.5	9.8	9.3	10.4	9.6	11.7	13.5	11.8	2.1	2.3	2.0
U.S.	14.5	14.3	14.2	11.3	11.3	11.1	10.6	10.2	9.5	2.6	2.6	2.5

Note: (1) Metropolitan Statistical Area—see Appendix B for areas included; (2) The percentage of the total housing inventory that is vacant; (3) The percentage of the housing inventory (excluding seasonal units) that is year-round vacant; (4) The percentage of rental inventory that is vacant for rent; (5) The percentage of homeowner inventory that is vacant for sale
Source: U.S. Census Bureau, Housing Vacancies and Homeownership Annual Statistics: 2011

TAXES

State Corporate Income Tax Rates

State	Tax Rate (%)	Income Brackets ($)	Num. of Brackets	Financial Institution Tax Rate (%)[a]	Federal Income Tax Ded.
Texas	(x)	–	-	(x)	No

Note: Tax rates as of January 1, 2012; (a) Rates listed are the corporate income tax rate applied to financial institutions or excise taxes based on income. Some states have other taxes based upon the value of deposits or shares; (x) Texas imposes a Franchise Tax, otherwise known as margin tax, imposed on entities with more than $1,000,000 total revenues at rate of 1%, or 0.5% for entities primarily engaged in retail or wholesale trade, on lesser of 70% of total revenues or 100%of gross receipts after deductions for either compensation or cost of goods sold.
Source: Federation of Tax Administrators, "State Corporate Income Tax Rates, 2012"

State Individual Income Tax Rates

State	Tax Rate (%)	Income Brackets ($)	Num. of Brackets	Personal Exempt. ($)[1] Single	Dependents	Fed. Inc. Tax Ded.

Texas – No State Income Tax

Note: Tax rates as of January 1, 2012; Local- and county-level taxes are not included; n/a not applicable; (1) Married joint filers generally receive double the single exemption
Source: Federation of Tax Administrators, "State Individual Income Tax Rates, 2012"

Various State and Local Tax Rates

State	State and Local Sales and Use (%)	State Sales and Use (%)	Gasoline[1] (¢/gal.)	Cigarette[2] ($/pack)	Spirits[3] ($/gal.)	Wine[4] ($/gal.)	Beer[5] ($/gal.)
Texas	8.25	6.25	20.0	1.41	2.40	0.20	0.20

Note: All tax rates as of January 1, 2012 except beer, wine and spirits (September 1, 2011); (1) The American Petroleum Institute has developed a methodology for determining the average tax rate on a gallon of fuel. Rates may include any of the following: excise taxes, environmental fees, storage tank fees, other fees or taxes, general sales tax, and local taxes. In states where gasoline is subject to the general sales tax, or where the fuel tax is based on the average sale price, the average rate determined by API is sensitive to changes in the price of gasoline. States that fully or partially apply general sales taxes to gasoline: CA, CO, GA, IL, IN, MI, NY; (2) The federal excise tax of $1.0066 per pack and local taxes are not included; (3) Rates are those applicable to off-premise sales of 40% alcohol by volume (a.b.v.) distilled spirits in 750ml containers. Local excise taxes are excluded; (4) Rates are those applicable to off-premise sales of 11% a.b.v. non-carbonated wine in 750ml containers; (5) Rates are those applicable to off-premise sales of 4.7% a.b.v. beer in 12 ounce containers.
Source: Tax Foundation, 2012 Facts & Figures: How Does Your State Compare?

State-Local Tax Burdens

Area	Rate (%)	Rank[1]	Per Capita Taxes Paid to Home State ($)	Total State and Local Per Capita Taxes Paid ($)	Per Capita Income ($)
Texas	7.9	45	2,248	3,197	40,498
U.S. Average	9.8	-	3,057	4,160	42,539

Note: Figures cover 2009; (1) Rank ranges from 1 to 50 where 1 is highest tax burden
Source: Tax Foundation, State-Local Tax Burdens, All States, 2009

State Business Tax Climate Index Rankings

State	Overall Rank	Corporate Tax Index Rank	Individual Income Tax Index Rank	Sales Tax Index Rank	Unemployment Insurance Tax Index Rank	Property Tax Index Rank
Texas	9	37	7	35	15	31

Note: The index is a measure of how each state's tax laws affect economic performance. The lower the rank, the more favorable a state's tax system is for business. States without a given tax are given a ranking of 1.
Source: Tax Foundation, Major Components of the State Business Tax Climate Index, FY 2012

COMMERCIAL REAL ESTATE

Office Market

Market Area	Inventory (sq. ft.)	Vacant (sq. ft.)	Vac. Rate (%)	Under Constr. (sq. ft.)	Asking Rent ($/sf/yr) Class A	Asking Rent ($/sf/yr) Class B
Dallas-Fort Worth	190,863,123	41,477,914	21.7	615,600	22.92	17.72

Source: Grubb & Ellis, Office Markets Trends, 4th Quarter 2011

Industrial Market

Market Area	Inventory (sq. ft.)	Vacant (sq. ft.)	Vac. Rate (%)	Under Constr. (sq. ft.)	Asking Rent ($/sf/yr) WH/Dist	Asking Rent ($/sf/yr) R&D/Flex
Dallas-Fort Worth	663,801,566	69,153,380	10.4	725,976	3.50	6.47

Source: Grubb & Ellis, Industrial Markets Trends, 4th Quarter 2011

COMMERCIAL UTILITIES

Typical Monthly Electric Bills

Area	Commercial Service ($/month) 1,500 kWh	Commercial Service ($/month) 40 kW demand 14,000 kWh	Industrial Service ($/month) 1,000 kW demand 200,000 kWh	Industrial Service ($/month) 50,000 kW demand 15,000,000 kWh
City	n/a	n/a	n/a	n/a
Average[1]	189	1,616	25,197	1,470,813

Note: Based on total rates in effect July 1, 2011; (1) average based on 184 utilities surveyed; n/a not available
Source: Edison Electric Institute, Typical Bills and Average Rates Report, Summer 2011

TRANSPORTATION

Means of Transportation to Work

Area	Car/Truck/Van Drove Alone	Car/Truck/Van Car-pooled	Public Transportation Bus	Public Transportation Subway	Public Transportation Railroad	Bicycle	Walked	Other Means	Worked at Home
City	80.6	11.6	1.0	0.0	0.2	0.1	1.2	1.9	3.3
MSA[1]	80.8	10.6	1.1	0.1	0.2	0.2	1.3	1.4	4.3
U.S.	76.0	10.2	2.7	1.7	0.5	0.5	2.8	1.3	4.2

Note: Figures are percentages and cover workers 16 years of age and older; (1) Figures cover the Dallas-Fort Worth-Arlington, TX Metropolitan Statistical Area—see Appendix B for areas included
Source: U.S. Census Bureau, 2008-2010 American Community Survey 3-Year Estimates

Travel Time to Work

Area	Less Than 10 Minutes	10 to 19 Minutes	20 to 29 Minutes	30 to 44 Minutes	45 to 59 Minutes	60 to 89 Minutes	90 Minutes or More
City	9.4	29.4	23.5	22.6	8.0	5.4	1.8
MSA[1]	10.2	27.1	21.4	24.5	9.5	5.6	1.7
U.S.	13.9	30.1	20.8	19.8	7.5	5.5	2.5

Note: Figures are percentages and include workers 16 years old and over; (1) Figures cover the Dallas-Fort Worth-Arlington, TX Metropolitan Statistical Area—see Appendix B for areas included
Source: U.S. Census Bureau, 2008-2010 American Community Survey 3-Year Estimates

Travel Time Index

Area	1985	1990	1995	2000	2005	2010
Urban Area[1]	1.07	1.11	1.14	1.20	1.27	1.23
Average[2]	1.11	1.16	1.18	1.21	1.25	1.20

Note: Travel Time Index—the ratio of travel time in the peak period to the travel time at free-flow conditions. A value of 1.30 indicates a 20-minute free-flow trip takes 26 minutes in the peak. Free-flow speeds (60 mph on freeways and 35 mph on principal arterials) are used as the comparison threshold; (1) Covers the Dallas-Fort Worth-Arlington TX urban area; (2) average of 439 urban areas
Source: Texas Transportation Institute, Urban Mobility Report 2011, September 2011

Public Transportation

Agency Name / Mode of Transportation	Vehicles Operated in Maximum Service	Annual Unlinked Passenger Trips ('000)	Annual Passenger Miles ('000)
Fort Worth Transportation Authority (The T)			
Bus (directly operated)	125	6,474.0	38,830.9
Bus (purchased transportation)	4	72.9	339.3
Demand Response (directly operated)	35	155.4	1,872.2
Demand Response (purchased transportation)	53	234.4	1,856.3

Source: Federal Transit Administration, National Transit Database, 2010

Air Transportation

Airport Name and Code / Type of Service	Passenger Airlines[1]	Passenger Enplanements	Freight Carriers[2]	Freight (lbs.)
Dallas-Fort Worth International (DFW)				
Domestic service (U.S. carriers - 2011)	35	24,839,278	22	310,694,455
International service (U.S. carriers - 2010)	12	2,209,457	7	72,348,682
Dallas Love Field (DAL)				
Domestic service (U.S. carriers - 2011)	25	3,849,150	6	9,050,237
International service (U.S. carriers - 2010)	6	677	1	14,019

Note: (1) Includes all U.S.-based major, minor and commuter airlines that carried at least one passenger during the year; (2) Includes all U.S.-based airlines and freight carriers that transported at least one pound of freight during the year
Source: Bureau of Transportation Statistics, The Intermodal Transportation Database, Air Carriers: T-100 Domestic Market (U.S. Carriers), 2011; Bureau of Transportation Statistics, The Intermodal Transportation Database, Air Carriers: T-100 International Market (U.S. Carriers), 2010

Other Transportation Statistics

Major Highways:	I-20; I-35W; I-30
Amtrak Service:	Yes
Major Waterways/Ports:	None

Source: Amtrak.com; Google Maps

BUSINESSES

Major Business Headquarters

Company Name	Rankings	
	Fortune[1]	Forbes[2]
AMR	118	-
Ben E Keith	-	144
D.R. Horton	499	-
RadioShack	492	-

Note: (1) Fortune 500—companies that produce a 10-K are ranked 1 to 500 based on 2010 revenue; (2) all private companies with at least $2 billion in annual revenue are ranked 1 to 212; companies listed are headquartered in the city; dashes indicate no ranking
Source: Fortune, "Fortune 500," May 23, 2011; Forbes, "America's Largest Private Companies," November 16, 2011

Minority Business Opportunity

Fort Worth is home to one company which is on the *Black Enterprise* Asset Manager 15 list (15 largest asset management firms based on assets under management): **American Beacon Advisors** (#1). Criteria: company must have been operational in previous calendar year and be at least 51% black-owned. *Black Enterprise, B.E. 100s, 2011*

Fort Worth is home to three companies which are on the *Hispanic Business* 500 list (500 largest U.S. Hispanic-owned companies based on 2010 revenue): **Thos. S. Byrne Ltd.** (#42); **Puente Enterprises** (#140); **Southwest Office Systems** (#289). Companies included must show at least 51 percent ownership by Hispanic U.S. citizens, and must maintain headquarters in one of the 50 states or Washington, D.C. *Hispanic Business, "Hispanic Business 500," June 2011*

Minority- and Women-Owned Businesses

Group	All Firms		Firms with Paid Employees			
	Firms	Sales ($000)	Firms	Sales ($000)	Employees	Payroll ($000)
Asian	n/a	n/a	n/a	n/a	n/a	n/a
Black	n/a	n/a	n/a	n/a	n/a	n/a
Hispanic	n/a	n/a	n/a	n/a	n/a	n/a
Women	n/a	n/a	n/a	n/a	n/a	n/a
All Firms	259	35,895	10	34,910	281	17,807

Note: Figures cover firms located in the city; minority- and women-owned business are defined as firms in which the corresponding group own 51% or more of the stock or equity of the company; n/a not available
Source: U.S. Census Bureau, 2007 Economic Census, Survey of Business Owners

HOTELS

Hotels/Motels

Area	5 Star		4 Star		3 Star		2 Star		1 Star		Not Rated	
	Num.	Pct.[3]	Num.	Pct.[3]	Num.	Pct.[3]	Num.	Pct.[3]	Num.	Pct.[3]	Num.	Pct.[3]
City[1]	0	0.0	3	2.3	29	22.7	73	57.0	4	3.1	19	14.8
Total[2]	133	0.9	940	6.5	4,569	31.8	7,033	48.9	351	2.4	1,343	9.3

Note: (1) Figures cover Fort Worth and vicinity; (2) Figures cover all 100 cities in this book; (3) Percentage of hotels which have a given star rating; Star ratings are determined by expedia.com and offer an indication of the general quality of a particular hotel.
Source: expedia.com, April 25, 2012

EVENT SITES

Major Stadiums, Arenas, and Auditoriums

Name	Max. Capacity
Amon G. Carter Stadium	44,008
LaGrave Field	4,100

Source: Original research

Convention Centers

Name	Overall Space (sq. ft.)	Exhibit Space (sq. ft.)	Meeting Space (sq. ft.)	Meeting Rooms
Fort Worth Convention Center	n/a	58,849	253,226	41

Note: n/a not available
Source: Original research

Living Environment

COST OF LIVING

Cost of Living Index

Composite Index	Groceries	Housing	Utilities	Trans-portation	Health Care	Misc. Goods/ Services
93.2	92.1	79.2	110.8	102.1	96.3	96.9

Note: U.S. = 100; Figures cover the Fort Worth TX urban area.
Source: The Council for Community and Economic Research, ACCRA Cost of Living Index, 2011

Grocery Prices

Area[1]	T-Bone Steak ($/pound)	Frying Chicken ($/pound)	Whole Milk ($/half gal.)	Eggs ($/dozen)	Orange Juice ($/64 oz.)	Coffee ($/11.5 oz.)
City[2]	8.97	0.98	2.01	1.66	2.90	4.55
Avg.	9.25	1.18	2.22	1.66	3.19	4.40
Min.	6.70	0.88	1.31	0.95	2.46	2.94
Max.	14.30	2.16	3.50	3.18	4.75	6.83

Note: (1) Values for the local area are compared with the average, minimum and maximum values for all 335 areas in the Cost of Living Index; (2) Figures cover the Fort Worth TX urban area; **T-Bone Steak** *(price per pound);* **Frying Chicken** *(price per pound, whole fryer);* **Whole Milk** *(half gallon carton);* **Eggs** *(price per dozen, Grade A, large);* **Orange Juice** *(64 oz. Tropicana or Florida Natural);* **Coffee** *(11.5 oz. can, vacuum-packed, Maxwell House, Hills Bros, or Folgers).*
Source: The Council for Community and Economic Research, ACCRA Cost of Living Index, 2011

Housing and Utility Costs

Area[1]	New Home Price ($)	Apartment Rent ($/month)	All Electric ($/month)	Part Electric ($/month)	Other Energy ($/month)	Telephone ($/month)
City[2]	199,901	952	-	131.65	51.86	29.95
Avg.	285,990	839	163.23	89.00	77.52	26.92
Min.	188,005	460	125.58	45.39	33.89	17.98
Max.	1,197,028	3,244	339.16	181.97	348.69	40.01

Note: (1) Values for the local area are compared with the average, minimum and maximum values for all 335 areas in the Cost of Living Index; (2) Figures cover the Fort Worth TX urban area; **New Home Price** *(2,400 sf living area, 8,000 sf lot, in urban area with full utilities);* **Apartment Rent** *(950 sf 2 bedroom/1.5 or 2 bath, unfurnished, excluding all utilities except water);* **All Electric** *(average monthly cost for an all-electric home);* **Part Electric** *(average monthly cost for a part-electric home);* **Other Energy** *(average monthly cost for natural gas, fuel oil, coal, wood, and any other forms of energy except electricity);* **Telephone** *(price includes basic monthly rate for a private residential line plus additional local usage charges incurred by a family of four).*
Source: The Council for Community and Economic Research, ACCRA Cost of Living Index, 2011

Health Care, Transportation, and Other Costs

Area[1]	Doctor ($/visit)	Dentist ($/visit)	Optometrist ($/visit)	Gasoline ($/gallon)	Beauty Salon ($/visit)	Men's Shirt ($)
City[2]	86.80	79.10	64.56	3.46	31.61	24.89
Avg.	93.88	81.72	90.54	3.48	32.65	25.06
Min.	60.00	55.33	53.66	3.18	19.78	13.44
Max.	154.98	145.97	183.72	4.31	63.21	46.00

Note: (1) Values for the local area are compared with the average, minimum and maximum values for all 335 areas in the Cost of Living Index; (2) Figures cover the Fort Worth TX urban area; **Doctor** *(general practitioners routine exam of an established patient);* **Dentist** *(adult teeth cleaning and periodic oral examination);* **Optometrist** *(full vision eye exam for established adult patient);* **Gasoline** *(one gallon regular unleaded, national brand, including all taxes, cash price at self-service pump if available);* **Beauty Salon** *(woman's shampoo, trim, and blow-dry);* **Men's Shirt** *(cotton/polyester dress shirt, pinpoint weave, long sleeves).*
Source: The Council for Community and Economic Research, ACCRA Cost of Living Index, 2011

HOUSING

House Price Index (HPI)

Area	National Ranking[2]	Quarterly Change (%)	One-Year Change (%)	Five-Year Change (%)
MD[1]	70	0.23	-1.02	0.65
U.S.[3]	-	-0.10	-2.43	-19.16

Note: The HPI is a weighted repeat sales index. It measures average price changes in repeat sales or refinancings on the same properties. This information is obtained by reviewing repeat mortgage transactions on single-family properties whose mortgages have been purchased or securitized by Fannie Mae or Freddie Mac in January 1975; (1) Metropolitan Division - see Appendix B for areas included; (2) Rankings are based on annual percentage change for all metro areas containing at least 15,000 transactions over the last 10 years and ranges from 1 to 306; (3) figures based on a weighted average of Census Division estimates using a purchase only index; all figures are for the period ending December 31, 2011
Source: Federal Housing Finance Agency, House Price Index, February 23, 2012

House Price Valuations

Area	Q4 2005		Q4 2006		Q4 2007		Q4 2008		Q4 2009	
	Price ($000)	Over-valuation	Price ($000)	Over-valuation	Price ($000)	Over-valuation	Price ($000)	Over-valuation	Price ($000)	Over-valuation
MD[1]	105.1	-19.5	110.2	-20.5	112.5	-22.3	112.0	-23.2	112.5	-23.2

Note: Figures show the percentage of over- or under-valuation of single family homes relative to statistically normal house values (e.g. a value of 23.6 indicates that house values are 23.6% overvalued). Statistically normal house values are based on house prices, interest rates, household incomes, population densities, and any historical premiums or discounts metropolitan areas have exhibited over time; (1) Figures cover the Fort Worth-Arlington, TX - see Appendix B for areas included
Source: Global Insight/PNC Financial Services Group, House Prices in America: 4th Quarter 2009 Update

Median Single-Family Home Prices

Area	2009	2010	2011p	Percent Change 2010 to 2011
MSA[1]	140.5	143.8	148.9	3.5
U.S. Average	172.1	173.1	166.2	-4.0

Note: Figures are median sales prices of existing single-family homes in thousands of dollars; (p) preliminary; n/a not available; (1) Metropolitan Statistical Area—see Appendix B for areas included
Source: National Association of Realtors, Median Sales Price of Existing Single-Family Homes for Metropolitan Areas, 4th Quarter 2011

Affordability Index of Existing Single-Family Homes

Area	2009	2010	2011p	Percent Change 2010 to 2011
MSA[1]	145.7	150.0	152.5	1.7

Note: The housing affordability index measures whether or not a typical family could qualify for a mortgage loan on a typical home. The higher the index, the greater the household purchasing power. An index of 100 is defined as the point where a median-income household has exactly enough income to qualify for the purchase of a median-priced existing single-family home, assuming a 20 percent downpayment and 25 percent of gross income devoted to mortgage principal and interest payments; (p) preliminary; n/a not available; (1) Metropolitan Statistical Area—see Appendix B for areas included
Source: National Association of Realtors, Affordability Index of Existing Single-Family Homes, 2011

Median Apartment Condo-Coop Home Prices

Area	2009	2010	2011p	Percent Change 2010 to 2011
MSA[1]	130.5	132.6	126.0	-5.0
U.S. Average	175.6	171.7	165.1	-3.8

Note: Figures are median sales prices of existing apartment condo-coop homes in thousands of dollars; (p) preliminary; n/a not available; (1) Metropolitan Statistical Area—see Appendix B for areas included
Source: National Association of Realtors, Median Sales Price of Existing Apartment Condo-Coop Homes for Metropolitan Areas, 4th Quarter 2011

Year Housing Structure Built

Area	2005 or Later	2000 -2004	1990 -1999	1980 -1989	1970 -1979	1960 -1969	1950 -1959	Before 1950	Median Year
City	12.6	15.0	11.0	14.1	10.9	9.3	12.1	15.0	1982
MSA[1]	8.6	13.9	16.9	20.1	15.5	10.1	8.4	6.5	1985
U.S.	5.0	8.6	14.0	14.1	16.3	11.3	11.2	19.6	1975

Note: Figures are percentages except for Median Year; (1) Figures cover the Dallas-Fort Worth-Arlington, TX Metropolitan Statistical Area—see Appendix B for areas included
Source: U.S. Census Bureau, 2008-2010 American Community Survey 3-Year Estimates

HEALTH

Health Risk Data

Category	MSA[1] (%)	U.S. (%)
Adults who have been told they have high blood pressure[2]	26.6	28.7
Adults who have been told they have high blood cholesterol[2]	41.0	37.5
Adults who have been told they have diabetes[3]	11.7	8.7
Adults who have been told they have arthritis[2]	27.2	26.0
Adults who have been told they currently have asthma	10.2	9.1
Adults who are current smokers	14.6	17.3
Adults who are heavy drinkers[4]	3.3	5.0
Adults who are binge drinkers[5]	13.8	15.1
Adults who are overweight (BMI 25.0 - 29.9)	34.4	36.2
Adults who are obese (BMI 30.0 - 99.8)	35.3	27.5
Adults who participated in any physical activities in the past month	76.0	76.1
Adults 50+ who have ever had a sigmoidoscopy or colonoscopy	67.4	65.2
Women aged 40+ who have had a mammogram within the past two years	78.7	75.2
Men aged 40+ who have had a PSA test within the past two years	52.3	53.2
Adults aged 65+ who have had flu shot within the past year	72.9	67.5
Adults aged 18–64 who have any kind of health care coverage	78.1	82.2

Note: Data as of 2010 unless otherwise noted; (1) Figures cover the Fort Worth-Arlington, TX Metropolitan Division—see Appendix B for areas included; (2) Data as of 2009; (3) Figures do not include pregnancy-related, borderline, or pre-diabetes; (4) Heavy drinkers are classified as males having more than two drinks per day or females having more than one drink per day; (5) Binge drinkers are classified as males having five or more drinks on one occasion or females having four or more drinks on one occasion
Source: Centers for Disease Control and Prevention, Behaviorial Risk Factor Surveillance System, SMART: Selected Metropolitan/Micropolitan Area Risk Trends, 2009, 2010

Mortality Rates for the Top 10 Causes of Death in the U.S.

ICD-10[a] Sub-Chapter	ICD-10[a] Code	Age-Adjusted Mortality Rate[1] per 100,000 population	
		County[2]	U.S.
Malignant neoplasms	C00-C97	173.7	175.6
Ischaemic heart diseases	I20-I25	122.8	121.6
Other forms of heart disease	I30-I51	49.7	48.6
Chronic lower respiratory diseases	J40-J47	48.2	42.3
Cerebrovascular diseases	I60-I69	53.5	40.6
Organic, including symptomatic, mental disorders	F01-F09	45.1	26.7
Other degenerative diseases of the nervous system	G30-G31	26.2	24.7
Other external causes of accidental injury	W00-X59	20.1	24.4
Diabetes mellitus	E10-E14	21.6	21.7
Hypertensive diseases	I10-I15	22.7	18.2

Note: (a) ICD-10 = International Classification of Diseases 10th Revision; (1) Mortality rates are a three year average covering 2007-2009; (2) Figures cover Tarrant County
Source: Centers for Disease Control and Prevention, National Center for Health Statistics. Underlying Cause of Death 1999-2009 on CDC WONDER Online Database, released 2012. Data for year 2009 are compiled from the Multiple Cause of Death File 2009, Series 20 No. 2O, 2012, Data for year 2008 are compiled from the Multiple Cause of Death File 2008, Series 20 No. 2N, 2011, Data for year 2007 are compiled from Multiple Cause of Death File 2007, Series 20 No. 2M, 2010.

Mortality Rates for Selected Causes of Death

ICD-10[a] Sub-Chapter	ICD-10[a] Code	Age-Adjusted Mortality Rate[1] per 100,000 population	
		County[2]	U.S.
Assault	X85-Y09	4.9	5.7
Human immunodeficiency virus (HIV) disease	B20-B24	3.5	3.3
Influenza and pneumonia	J09-J18	14.0	16.4
Intentional self-harm	X60-X84	10.3	11.5
Malnutrition	E40-E46	1.6	0.8
Obesity and other hyperalimentation	E65-E68	1.5	1.6
Transport accidents	V01-V99	11.9	13.7
Viral hepatitis	B15-B19	2.5	2.2

Note: (a) ICD-10 = International Classification of Diseases 10th Revision; (1) Mortality rates are a three year average covering 2007-2009; (2) Figures cover Tarrant County
Source: Centers for Disease Control and Prevention, National Center for Health Statistics. Underlying Cause of Death 1999-2009 on CDC WONDER Online Database, released 2012. Data for year 2009 are compiled from the Multiple Cause of Death File 2009, Series 20 No. 2O, 2012, Data for year 2008 are compiled from the Multiple Cause of Death File 2008, Series 20 No. 2N, 2011, Data for year 2007 are compiled from Multiple Cause of Death File 2007, Series 20 No. 2M, 2010.

Distribution of Physicians and Dentists

Area[1]	Dentists[2]	D.O.[3]	M.D.[4]				
			Total	Family/General Practice	Pediatrics	Medical Specialties	Surgical Specialties
Local (number)	637	632	2,390	306	166	825	628
Local (rate[5])	3.7	3.6	13.7	1.7	0.9	4.7	3.6
U.S. (rate[5])	4.5	1.9	18.3	2.5	1.4	6.8	4.1

Note: Data as of 2008 unless noted; (1) Local data covers Tarrant County; (2) Data as of 2007; (3) Doctor of Osteopathic Medicine; (4) Includes active, non-federal, patient-care, office-based Doctors of Medicine; (5) rate per 10,000 population
Source: Area Resource File (ARF). 2009-2010 Release. U.S. Department of Health and Human Services, Health Resources and Services Administration, Bureau of Health Professions, Rockville, MD, August 2010

Best Hospitals

According to *U.S. News,* the Fort Worth-Arlington, TX is home to one of the best children's hospitals in the U.S.: **Cook Children's Medical Center** (6 specialties). The hospital listed was highly ranked in at least one pediatric specialty. *U.S. News Online, "America's Best Children's Hospitals 2011-12"*

EDUCATION

Public School District Statistics

District Name	Schls	Pupils	Pupil/Teacher Ratio	Minority Pupils[1] (%)	Free Lunch Eligible[2] (%)	IEP[3] (%)
Castleberry ISD	7	3,641	16.7	72.3	62.6	6.9
Eagle Mt-Saginaw ISD	24	16,126	15.8	48.0	28.6	8.4
Fort Worth ISD	140	80,209	15.8	87.0	68.0	7.4

Note: Table includes school districts with 2,000 or more students; (1) Percentage of students that are not non-Hispanic white; (2) Percentage of students that are eligible for the free lunch program; (3) Percentage of students that have an Individualized Education Program.
Source: U.S. Department of Education, National Center for Education Statistics, Common Core of Data, Local Education Agency (School District) Universe Survey: School Year 2009-2010; U.S. Department of Education, National Center for Education Statistics, Common Core of Data, Public Elementary/Secondary School Universe Survey: School Year 2009-2010

Highest Level of Education

Area	Less than H.S.	H.S. Diploma	Some College, No Deg.	Associate Degree	Bachelors Degree	Masters Degree	Profess. School Degree	Doctorate Degree
City	21.7	24.3	22.4	6.0	17.7	5.6	1.4	0.9
MSA[1]	17.1	23.0	22.7	6.4	20.9	7.4	1.6	1.0
U.S.	14.7	28.4	21.3	7.6	17.6	7.2	1.9	1.2

Note: Figures cover persons age 25 and over; (1) Figures cover the Dallas-Fort Worth-Arlington, TX Metropolitan Statistical Area—see Appendix B for areas included
Source: U.S. Census Bureau, 2008-2010 American Community Survey 3-Year Estimates

Educational Attainment by Race

Area	High School Graduate or Higher (%)					Bachelor's Degree or Higher (%)				
	Total	White	Black	Asian	Hisp.[2]	Total	White	Black	Asian	Hisp.[2]
City	78.3	82.1	83.3	84.8	47.9	25.6	30.4	16.0	41.5	8.2
MSA[1]	82.9	85.4	87.2	87.8	51.7	30.9	33.2	22.2	55.8	10.5
U.S.	85.3	87.5	81.4	85.5	61.6	28.0	29.3	17.8	50.2	13.0

Note: Figures shown cover persons 25 years old and over; (1) Figures cover the Dallas-Fort Worth-Arlington, TX Metropolitan Statistical Area—see Appendix B for areas included; (2) People of Hispanic origin can be of any race
Source: U.S. Census Bureau, 2008-2010 American Community Survey 3-Year Estimates

School Enrollment by Grade and Control

Area	Preschool (%)		Kindergarten (%)		Grades 1 - 4 (%)		Grades 5 - 8 (%)		Grades 9 - 12 (%)	
	Public	Private	Public	Private	Public	Private	Public	Private	Public	Private
City	61.3	38.7	89.2	10.8	91.1	8.9	92.4	7.6	91.4	8.6
MSA[1]	51.9	48.1	89.1	10.9	91.6	8.4	92.4	7.6	92.6	7.4
U.S.	55.4	44.6	87.1	12.9	89.4	10.6	89.5	10.5	90.4	9.6

Note: Figures shown cover persons 3 years old and over; (1) Figures cover the Dallas-Fort Worth-Arlington, TX Metropolitan Statistical Area—see Appendix B for areas included
Source: U.S. Census Bureau, 2008-2010 American Community Survey 3-Year Estimates

Average Salaries of Public School Classroom Teachers

Area	2010-11		2011-12		Percent Change 2010-11 to 2011-12	Percent Change 2001-02 to 2011-12
	Dollars	Rank[1]	Dollars	Rank[1]		
Texas	48,638	31	49,017	31	0.78	24.90
U.S. Average	55,623	-	56,643	-	1.83	26.8

Note: (1) State rank ranges from 1 to 51 where 1 indicates highest salary.
Source: National Education Association, Rankings & Estimates: Rankings of the States 2011 and Estimates of School Statistics 2012, December 2011

Higher Education

Four-Year Colleges			Two-Year Colleges			Medical Schools[1]	Law Schools[2]	Voc/ Tech[3]
Public	Private Non-profit	Private For-profit	Public	Private Non-profit	Private For-profit			
1	4	2	1	1	2	1	1	3

Note: Figures cover institutions located within the city limits and include main campuses only; (1) includes schools accredited by the Liaison Committee on Medical Education and the American Osteopathic Association's Commission on Osteopathic College Accreditation; (2) includes American Bar Association-accredited law schools; (3) includes all schools with programs that are less than 2 years.
Source: National Center for Education Statistics, Integrated Postsecondary Education System (IPEDS) Peer Analysis System, 2011-12; Association of American Medical Colleges, Member List, April 23, 2012; American Osteopathic Association, Member List, April 23, 2012; Law School Admission Council, Official Guide to ABA-Approved Law Schools Online, April 23, 2012

According to *U.S. News & World Report,* the Fort Worth-Arlington, TX is home to one of the best national universities in the U.S.: **Texas Christian University** (#97). The indicators used to capture academic quality fall into a number of categories: assessment by administrators at peer institutions; retention of students; faculty resources; student selectivity; financial resources; alumni giving; high school counselor ratings of colleges; and graduation rate. *U.S. News & World Report, "America's Best Colleges 2012"*

**PRESIDENTIAL
ELECTION**

2008 Presidential Election Results

Area	Obama	McCain	Nader	Other
Tarrant County	43.7	55.4	0.1	0.8
U.S.	52.9	45.6	0.6	0.9

Note: Results are percentages and may not add to 100% due to rounding
Source: Dave Leip's Atlas of U.S. Presidential Elections, www.uselectionatlas.org

EMPLOYERS

Major Employers

Company Name	Industry
AMR Corporation	Air transportation, scheduled
Associates First Capital Corporation	Mortgage bankers
Baylor University Medical Center	General medical and surgical hospitals
Children's Medical Center Dallas	Specialty hospitals, except psychiatric
Combat Support Associates	Engineering services
County of Dallas	County supervisors' and executives' office
Dallas County Hospital District	General medical and surgical hospitals
Fort Worth Independent School District	Public elementary and secondary schools
Housewares Holding Company	Toasters, electric: household
HP Enterprise Services	Computer integrated systems design
J.C. Penney Company	Department stores
JCP Publications Corp.	Department stores
L-3 Communications Corporation	Business economic service
Odyssey HealthCare	Home health care services
Romano's Macaroni Grill	Italian restaurant
SFG Management Limited Liability	Milk processing (pasteurizing, homogenizing, bottling)
Texas Instruments Incorporated	Semiconductors and related devices
University of North Texas	Colleges and universities
University of Texas SW Medical Center	Accident and health insurance
Verizon Business Global	Telephone communication, except radio

Note: Companies shown are located within the Dallas-Fort Worth-Arlington, TX metropolitan area.
Source: Hoovers.com, data extracted April 25 2012

Best Companies to Work For

BNSF Railway Co, headquartered in Fort Worth, is among the "100 Best Places to Work in IT." To qualify, companies, both public and private, had to have a minimum of 50 IT employees and were selected based on average salary and bonus increases, the percentage of IT staffers promoted, IT staff turnover rates, training and development programs, and the percentage of women and minorities in IT staff and management positions. In addition, *Computerworld* looked at retention efforts, programs for recognizing and rewarding outstanding performances, and benefits such as flextime, elder care and child care, and reimbursement for college tuition and the cost of pursuing technology certifications. *Computerworld, "100 Best Places to Work in IT 2011"*

PUBLIC SAFETY

Crime Rate

Area	All Crimes	Violent Crimes				Property Crimes		
		Murder	Forcible Rape	Robbery	Aggrav. Assault	Burglary	Larceny -Theft	Motor Vehicle Theft
City	5,276.2	8.4	42.6	178.2	345.9	1,252.9	3,118.0	330.1
Suburbs[1]	3,798.3	2.9	26.4	72.1	212.7	814.2	2,462.5	207.5
Metro[2]	4,309.2	4.8	32.0	108.8	258.8	965.9	2,689.1	249.9
U.S.	3,345.5	4.8	27.5	119.1	252.3	699.6	2,003.5	238.8

Note: Figures are crimes per 100,000 population; (1) All areas within the metro area that are located outside the city limits; (2) Metropolitan Division—see Appendix B for areas included
Source: FBI Uniform Crime Reports, 2010

Hate Crimes

Area	Number of Quarters Reported	Bias Motivation				
		Race	Religion	Sexual Orientation	Ethnicity	Disability
City	4	5	1	5	3	0

Source: Federal Bureau of Investigation, Hate Crime Statistics 2010

Identity Theft Consumer Complaints

Area	Complaints	Complaints per 100,000 Population	Rank[2]
MSA[1]	7,171	116.7	47
U.S.	279,156	90.4	-

Note: (1) Metropolitan Statistical Area—see Appendix B for areas included; (2) Rank ranges from 1 to 384 where 1 indicates greatest number of identity theft complaints per 100,000 population
Source: Federal Trade Commission, Consumer Sentinel Network Data Book for January–December 2011

Fraud and Other Consumer Complaints

Area	Complaints	Complaints per 100,000 Population	Rank[2]
MSA[1]	30,244	492.2	163
U.S.	1,533,924	496.8	-

Note: (1) Metropolitan Statistical Area—see Appendix B for areas included; (2) Rank ranges from 1 to 384 where 1 indicates greatest number of fraud and other complaints per 100,000 population
Source: Federal Trade Commission, Consumer Sentinel Network Data Book for January–December 2011

RECREATION

Culture

Dance[1]	Theatre[1]	Instrumental Music[1]	Vocal Music[1]	Series/ Festivals	Museums	Zoos and Aquariums[2]
3	8	3	3	3	12	1

Note: (1) Number of professional performing groups; (2) AZA-accredited
Source: The Grey House Performing Arts Directory, 2011-2012; Official Museum Directory, 2011; American Association of Museums, AAM Member Museums, April 2012; Association of Zoos & Aquariums, AZA Member Zoos & Aquariums, April 2012

Professional Sports Teams

Team Name	League
Dallas Cowboys	National Football League (NFL)
Dallas Mavericks	National Basketball Association (NBA)
Dallas Stars	National Hockey League (NHL)
FC Dallas	Major League Soccer (MLS)
Texas Rangers	Major League Baseball (MLB)

Note: Includes teams located in the Dallas-Fort Worth metro area.
Source: Original research

CLIMATE

Average and Extreme Temperatures

Temperature	Jan	Feb	Mar	Apr	May	Jun	Jul	Aug	Sep	Oct	Nov	Dec	Yr.
Extreme High (°F)	88	88	96	98	103	113	110	108	107	106	89	90	113
Average High (°F)	54	59	67	76	83	92	96	96	88	79	67	58	76
Average Temp. (°F)	44	49	57	66	73	81	85	85	78	68	56	47	66
Average Low (°F)	33	38	45	54	63	71	75	74	67	56	45	37	55
Extreme Low (°F)	4	6	11	29	41	51	59	56	43	29	19	-1	-1

Note: Figures cover the years 1953-1990
Source: National Climatic Data Center, International Station Meteorological Climate Summary, 9/96

Average Precipitation/Snowfall/Humidity

Precip./Humidity	Jan	Feb	Mar	Apr	May	Jun	Jul	Aug	Sep	Oct	Nov	Dec	Yr.
Avg. Precip. (in.)	1.8	2.2	2.6	3.7	4.9	2.8	2.1	1.9	3.0	3.3	2.1	1.7	32.3
Avg. Snowfall (in.)	1	1	Tr	0	0	0	0	0	0	0	Tr	Tr	3
Avg. Rel. Hum. 6am (%)	79	79	79	81	86	85	80	79	83	82	80	79	81
Avg. Rel. Hum. 3pm (%)	52	51	48	50	53	47	42	41	46	47	49	51	48

Note: Figures cover the years 1953-1990; Tr = Trace amounts (<0.05 in. of rain; <0.5 in. of snow)
Source: National Climatic Data Center, International Station Meteorological Climate Summary, 9/96

Weather Conditions

Temperature			Daytime Sky			Precipitation		
10°F & below	32°F & below	90°F & above	Clear	Partly cloudy	Cloudy	0.01 inch or more precip.	0.1 inch or more snow/ice	Thunder-storms
1	40	100	123	136	106	79	3	47

Note: Figures are average number of days per year and cover the years 1953-1990
Source: National Climatic Data Center, International Station Meteorological Climate Summary, 9/96

HAZARDOUS WASTE

Superfund Sites

Fort Worth has one hazardous waste site on the EPA's Superfund Final National Priorities List: **Air Force Plant #4 (General Dynamics)**. *U.S. Environmental Protection Agency, Final National Priorities List, April 17, 2012*

AIR & WATER QUALITY

Air Quality Index

Area	Percent of Days when Air Quality was...[2]					AQI Statistics[2]	
	Good	Moderate	Unhealthy for Sensitive Groups	Unhealthy	Very Unhealthy	Maximum	Median
Area[1]	63.3	29.0	6.6	1.1	0.0	169	45

Note: Air Quality Index (AQI) is an index for reporting daily air quality. EPA calculates the AQI for five major air pollutants regulated by the Clean Air Act: ground-level ozone, particle pollution (aka particulate matter), carbon monoxide, sulfur dioxide, and nitrogen dioxide. The AQI runs from 0 to 500. The higher the AQI value, the greater the level of air pollution and the greater the health concern. There are six AQI categories: "Good" AQI is between 0 and 50. Air quality is considered satisfactory; "Moderate" AQI is between 51 and 100. Air quality is acceptable; "Unhealthy for Sensitive Groups" When AQI values are between 101 and 150, members of sensitive groups may experience health effects; "Unhealthy" When AQI values are between 151 and 200 everyone may begin to experience health effects; "Very Unhealthy" AQI values between 201 and 300 trigger a health alert; "Hazardous" AQI values over 300 trigger warnings of emergency conditions (not shown); (1) Data covers Tarrant County; (2) Based on 365 days with AQI data in 2011.
Source: U.S. Environmental Protection Agency, AirData Report, 2011

Air Quality Index Pollutants

Area	Percent of Days when AQI Pollutant was...[2]					
	Carbon Monoxide	Nitrogen Dioxide	Ozone	Sulfur Dioxide	Particulate Matter 2.5	Particulate Matter 10
Area[1]	0.0	12.6	59.5	0.0	27.7	0.3

Note: The Air Quality Index (AQI) is an index for reporting daily air quality. EPA calculates the AQI for five major air pollutants regulated by the Clean Air Act: ground-level ozone, particle pollution (also known as particulate matter), carbon monoxide, sulfur dioxide, and nitrogen dioxide. The AQI runs from 0 to 500. The higher the AQI value, the greater the level of air pollution and the greater the health concern; (1) Data covers Tarrant County; (2) Based on 365 days with AQI data in 2011.
Source: U.S. Environmental Protection Agency, AirData Report, 2011

Air Quality Index Trends

Area	Trend Sites (days)								All Sites (days)
	2003	2004	2005	2006	2007	2008	2009	2010	2010
MSA[1]	49	50	80	54	34	30	32	15	18

Note: Figures are the number of days the AQI value exceeded 100 in a given year. An AQI value greater than 100 indicates that air quality would have been in the unhealthful range on that day. Data from exceptional events are included. These counts are presented in two ways. First, the counts are based on sites having an adequate record of monitoring data during the trend period (trend sites). These counts represent the relative change in the number of days with AQI values greater than 100. In the last column, the counts are based on all sites with data in the most recent year (because it is possible for a site to have data in the most recent year but not enough data to be a trend site); (1) Data covers the Dallas-Fort Worth-Arlington, TX—see Appendix B for areas included
Source: U.S. Environmental Protection Agency, Air Quality Index Information, "Number of Days with Air Quality Index Values Greater than 100 at Trend Sites, 2000-2010, and at All Sites in 2010"

Maximum Air Pollutant Concentrations: Particulate Matter, Ozone, CO and Lead

	Particulate Matter 10 (ug/m^3)	Particulate Matter 2.5 Wtd AM (ug/m^3)	Particulate Matter 2.5 24-Hr (ug/m^3)	Ozone (ppm)	Carbon Monoxide (ppm)	Lead (ug/m^3)
MSA[1] Level	62	10.8	25	0.085	2	0.77
NAAQS[2]	150	15	35	0.075	9	0.15
Met NAAQS[2]	Yes	Yes	Yes	No	Yes	No

Note: Data from exceptional events are not included; (1) Data covers the Dallas-Fort Worth-Arlington, TX—see Appendix B for areas included; (2) National Ambient Air Quality Standards; ppm = parts per million; ug/m^3 = micrograms per cubic meter; n/a not available
Concentrations: Particulate Matter 10 (coarse particulate)—highest second maximum 24-hour concentration; Particulate Matter 2.5 Wtd AM (fine particulate)—highest weighted annual mean concentration; Particulate Matter 2.5 24-Hour (fine particulate)—highest 98th percentile 24-hour concentration; Ozone—highest fourth daily maximum 8-hour concentration; Carbon Monoxide—highest second maximum non-overlapping 8-hour concentration; Lead—maximum running 3-month average
Source: U.S. Environmental Protection Agency, CBSA Factbook 2010, Air Quality Statistics by City, 2010

Maximum Air Pollutant Concentrations: Nitrogen Dioxide and Sulfur Dioxide

	Nitrogen Dioxide AM (ppb)	Nitrogen Dioxide 1-Hr (ppb)	Sulfur Dioxide AM (ppb)	Sulfur Dioxide 1-Hr (ppb)	Sulfur Dioxide 24-Hr (ppb)
MSA[1] Level	13.186	56.9	0.808	17.3	4.5
NAAQS[2]	53	100	30	75	140
Met NAAQS[2]	Yes	Yes	Yes	Yes	Yes

Note: Data from exceptional events are not included; (1) Data covers the Dallas-Fort Worth-Arlington, TX—see Appendix B for areas included; (2) National Ambient Air Quality Standards; ppb = parts per billion; n/a not available
Concentrations: Nitrogen Dioxide AM—highest arithmetic mean concentration; Nitrogen Dioxide 1-Hr—highest 98th percentile 1-hour daily maximum concentration; Sulfur Dioxide AM—highest annual mean concentration; Sulfur Dioxide 1-Hr—highest 99th percentile 1-hour daily maximum concentration; Sulfur Dioxide 24-Hr—highest second maximum 24-hour concentration
Source: U.S. Environmental Protection Agency, CBSA Factbook 2010, Air Quality Statistics by City, 2010

Drinking Water

Water System Name	Pop. Served	Primary Water Source Type	Violations[1]	
			Health Based	Monitoring/ Reporting
City of Fort Worth	727,575	Surface	0	0

Note: (1) Based on violation data from January 1, 2011 to December 31, 2011 (includes unresolved violations from earlier years)
Source: U.S. Environmental Protection Agency, Office of Ground Water and Drinking Water, Safe Drinking Water Information System (based on data extracted April 18, 2012)

Houston, Texas

Background

Back in 1836, brothers John K. and Augustus C. Allen bought a 6,642-acre tract of marshy, mosquito-infested land 56 miles north of the Gulf of Mexico and named it Houston, after the hero of San Jacinto. From that moment on, Houston has experienced continued growth.

By the end of its first year in the Republic of Texas, Houston claimed 1,500 residents, one theater, and interestingly, no churches. The first churches came three years later. By the end of its second year, Houston saw its first steamship, establishing its position as one of the top-ranking ports in the country.

Certainly, Houston owes much to the Houston ship channel, the "golden strip" on which oil refineries, chemical plants, cement factories, and grain elevators conduct their bustling economic activity. The diversity of these industries is a testament to Houston's economy in general.

Tonnage through the Port of Houston has grown to the point of its claim of being number one in the nation for foreign tonnage. The port is important to the cruise industry as well, and the Norwegian Cruise Line has sailed from Houston since 2003.

As Texas' biggest city, Houston has also enjoyed manufacturing expansion in its diversified economy. The city is home to the second largest number of Fortune 500 companies, second only to New York City. Top employers in Houston include ConocoPhillips, Marathon Oil, Sysco and Halliburton.

Houston is also one of the major scientific research areas in the world. The presence of the Johnson Space Center has spawned a number of related industries in medical and technological research. The Texas Medical Center oversees a network of 45 medical institutions, including St. Luke's Episcopal Hospital, the Texas Children's Hospital, and the Methodist Hospital. As a city whose reputation rests upon advanced research, Houston is also devoted to education and the arts. Rice University, for example, whose admission standards rank as one of the highest in the nation, is located in Houston, as are Dominican College and the University of St. Thomas.

Today, this relatively young city is home to a diverse range of ethnicities, including Mexican-American, Nigerian, American-Indian and Pakistani.

Houston also is patron to the Museum of Fine Arts, the Contemporary Arts Museum, and the Houston Ballet and Grand Opera. A host of smaller cultural institutions, such as the Gilbert and Sullivan Society, the Virtuoso Quartet, and the Houston Harpsichord Society enliven the scene. Two privately funded museums, the Holocaust Museum Houston and the Houston Museum of Natural Science, are historical and educational attractions, and a new baseball stadium, Minute Maid Park, was completed in 2000 in the city's downtown.

Houstonians are eagerly embracing continued revitalization. This urban comeback has resulted in a virtual explosion of dining and entertainment options in the heart of the city. The opening of the Bayou Place, Huston's largest entertainment complex, has especially generated excitement, providing a variety of restaurants and entertainment options in one facility. A new highly active urban park opened in 2007 on 12 acres in front of the George R. Brown Convention Center. Reliant Stadium, located in downtown Houston, is home to the NFL's Houston Texans. The stadium hosted Superbowl XXXVIII in 2004 and WrestleMania XXV in the spring of 2009. In fact, the city has sports teams for every major professional league except the National Hockey League.

Located in the flat coastal plains, Houston's climate is predominantly marine. The terrain includes many small streams and bayous, which, together with the nearness to Galveston Bay, favor the development of fog. Temperatures are moderated by the influence of winds from the Gulf of Mexico, which is 50 miles away. Mild winters are the norm, as is abundant rainfall. Polar air penetrates the area frequently enough to provide variability in the weather.

Rankings

General Rankings

- The Houston metro area was selected one of America's "Best Cities to Live, Work and Play" by *Kiplinger's Personal Finance*. Criteria: population growth; percentage of workforce in the creative class (scientists, engineers, educators, writers, artists, entertainers, etc.); job quality; income growth; cost of living. *Kiplinger's Personal Finance, "Best Cities to Live, Work and Play," July 2008*

- *Men's Health Living* ranked 100 U.S. cities in terms of quality of life. Houston was ranked #93 and received a grade of F. Criteria: number of fitness facilities; air quality; number of physicians; male/female ratio; education levels; household income; cost of living. *Men's Health Living, Spring 2008*

- Houston was selected as one of America's best cities by *Bloomberg Businessweek*. The city ranked #35 out of 50. Criteria: number of restaurants, bars and museums per capita; number of colleges, libraries, and professional sports teams; income, poverty, unemployment, crime, and foreclosure rates; percent of population with bachelor's degrees; public school performance; park acres per capita; air quality. *BusinessWeek, "America's 50 Best Cities," September 20, 2011*

- The U.S. Conference of Mayors and Waste Management sponsor the City Livability Awards Program. The awards recognize and honor mayors for exemplary leadership in developing and implementing programs that improve the quality of life in America's cities. Houston received an Outstanding Achievement Award in the large cities category. *U.S. Conference of Mayors, "2011 City Livability Awards"*

Business/Finance Rankings

- Houston was identified as one of the 20 strongest-performing metro areas during the recession and recovery from trough quarter through the third quarter of 2011. Criteria: percent change in employment; percentage point change in unemployment rate; percent change in gross metropolitan product; percent change in House Price Index. *Brookings Institution, MetroMonitor: Tracking Economic Recession and Recovery in America's 100 Largest Metropolitan Areas, December 2011*

- The Houston metro area was identified as one of 10 "Cities Where the Recession is Easing." The metro area was ranked #4. Criteria: job growth; goods produced; home sale prices; unemployment rates. *Forbes.com, "Cities Where the Recession is Easing," March 3, 2010*

- The Houston metro area was identified as one of 10 places with the fastest-growing wages in America. The area ranked #1. Criteria: private-sector wage growth between the 4th quarter of 2010 and the 4th quarter of 2011. *PayScale, "The 10 Cities with the Fastest-Growing Wages in America," January 12, 2012*

- The Houston metro area was identified as one of the most affordable major metropolitan areas in America by *Forbes*. The metro area was ranked #10 out of 15. Criteria: median asking price of homes for sale; median salaries of workers with bachelor's degrees or higher compared to a cost-of-living index; unemployment rates. *Forbes.com, "The Most Affordable Cities in America," January 7, 2011*

- Experian ranked the top 20 major U.S. metropolitan areas by average debt per consumer. The Houston metro area was ranked #6. Criteria: average debt per consumer. Debt for this study includes credit cards, auto loans and personal loans. It does not include mortgages. *Experian, May 13, 2010*

- The Houston metro area was identified as one of the "Best U.S. Cities for Earning a Living" by *Forbes*. The metro area ranked #1. Criteria: median income; cost of living; job growth; number of companies on *Forbes* 400 best big company and 200 best small company lists. *Forbes.com, "Best U.S. Cities for Earning a Living," August 21, 2008*

- Houston was cited as one of America's top metros for new and expanded facility projects in 2011. The area ranked #1 in the large metro area category (population over 1 million). *Site Selection, "2011 Top Metros," March 2012*

- Houston was identified as one of the "Happiest Cities to Work in 2012" by *CareerBliss.com*, an online community for career advancement. The city ranked #17 out of 50. Criteria: independent company reviews from employees all over the country on: relationship with their boss and co-workers; work environment; job resources; growth opportunities; compensation; company culture; company reputation; daily tasks; job control over work performed on a daily basis. *CareerBliss.com, "Happiest and Unhappiest Cities to Work in 2012"*

- Houston was identified as one of the best cities for new college graduates. The city ranked #1. Criteria: cost of living; average annual salary; unemployment rate; number of employers looking to hire people at entry-level. *Business Week, "The Best Cities for New Grads," July 20, 2010*

- *American City Business Journals* ranked America's 261 largest cities in terms of their resident's wealth. Houston ranked #170. Criteria: per capita income; median household income; percentage of households with annual incomes of $200,000 or more; median home value. *American City Business Journals, "Where the Money Is: America's Wealth Centers," August 18, 2008*

- The Houston metro area appeared on the Milken Institute "2011 Best Performing Metros" list. Rank: #16 out of 200 large metro areas. Criteria: job growth; wage and salary growth; high-tech output growth. *Milken Institute, "2011 Best Performing Metros"*

- The Houston metro area was selected as one of the best cities for entrepreneurs in America by *Inc. Magazine*. Criteria: job-growth data for 335 metro areas was analyzed for: recent growth trend; mid-term growth; long-term trend; current year growth. The Houston metro area ranked #4 among large metro areas and #28 overall. *Inc. Magazine, "The Best Cities for Doing Business," July 2008*

- Houston was ranked #70 out of 145 regions worldwide in terms of its "Knowledge Competitiveness Index." The index attempts to measure the knowledge-based development taking place throughout the world and is based on 19 measures of economic performance that indicate a region's ability to translate its knowledge capacity into economic value. *Centre for International Competitiveness, World Knowledge Competitiveness Index 2008*

- *Forbes* ranked the 200 most populous metro areas in the U.S. in terms of the "Best Places for Business and Careers." The Houston metro area was ranked #19. Criteria: costs (business and living); job growth (past and projected); income growth; educational attainment; projected economic growth; crime; cultural and recreational opportunities; net migration patterns; number of highly ranked colleges. *Forbes, "Best Places for Business and Careers," June 2011*

Children/Family Rankings

- The Houston metro area was selected as one of the "Best Cities for Relocating Families" by Worldwide ERC and Primacy Relocation. The 2008 study looked at nearly 50 factors important to relocating families including: recent job growth; nearby top-ranked colleges; in-state tuition for four-year public colleges; population growth since 2000; pediatricians per 100,000 population; and a Green Living index. *Worldwide ERC and Primacy Relocation, "2008 Best Cities for Relocating Families"*

- *Fit Pregnancy* magazine ranked the 50 best U.S. cities in which to have a baby. Houston was ranked #35. Criteria: access to hospitals and doctors; affordability; birthing options; breastfeeding; child care; fertility laws/resources; maternal and infant health risk; parks/stroller friendliness; safety. *Fit Pregnancy, "The Best Cities in America to Have a Baby 2008"*

- Houston was chosen as one of America's "100 Best Communities for Young People." The winners were selected based upon detailed information provided about each community's efforts to fulfill five essential promises critical to the well-being of young people: caring adults who are actively involved in their lives; safe places in which to learn and grow; a healthy start toward adulthood; an effective education that builds marketable skills; and opportunities to help others. *America's Promise Alliance, "100 Best Communities for Young People, 2010"*

Dating/Romance Rankings

- Houston was selected as one of the best cities for single men by *Rent.com*. The city ranked #1 of 10. Criteria: high single female-to-male ratio; lively nightlife; low divorce rate; low cost of living. *Rent.com, "Top 10 Cities for Single Men," May 2, 2011*

- Houston appeared on *Men's Health's* list of the most sex-happy cities in America. The city ranked #10 of 100. Criteria: condom sales; birth rates; sex toy sales; rates of chlamydia, gonorrhea, and syphilis. *Men's Health, "America's Most Sex-Happy Cities," October 2010*

- *Men's Health* ranked 100 U.S. cities in terms of best (and worst) marriages. Houston was ranked #78 (#1 = worst). Criteria: rate of failed marriages; stringency of divorce laws; percentage of population who've split; number of licensed marriage and family therapists. *Men's Health, "Splitsville, USA," May 2010*

- Eli Lily and Company, in partnership with Sperling's BestPlaces, ranked the nation's 50 largest metro areas in terms of the "Most Romantic Cities for Baby Boomers." The Houston metro area ranked #10. Criteria: marriage and divorce rates among baby boomers age 45 to 60; great restaurants; dance studios; chocolate, jewelry and flower sales. *Eli Lily and Company, "Most Romantic Cities for Baby Boomers," April 20, 2007*

- The Houston metro area was selected as one of the "Best Cities for Relocating Singles" by Worldwide ERC and Primacy Relocation. The area ranked #23 out of the 100 largest metro areas in the U.S. Criteria: recent job growth; recent singles population growth; overall population growth; affordable rental housing; cost-of-living index; expanded arts and recreation opportunities; ratio of single men and single women; affordability of quality higher education (including state residency requirements); diversity index; climate; population density. *Worldwide ERC and Primacy Relocation, "2008 Best Cities for Relocating Singles"*

- *Forbes* ranked the 40 most populous urbanized areas in the U.S. in terms of the "Best Cities for Singles." The Houston metro area ranked #25. Criteria: number of singles; cost of living alone; nightlife; culture; job growth; coolness; and online dating participation. *Forbes.com, "Best Cities for Singles," July 27, 2009*

Education Rankings

- *Men's Health* ranked 100 U.S. cities in terms of their education levels. Houston was ranked #82 (#1 = most educated city). Criteria: high school graduation rates; school enrollment; educational attainment; number of households who have outstanding student loans; number of households whose members have taken adult-education courses. *Men's Health, "Where School Is In: The Most and Least Educated Cities," September 12, 2011*

- Houston was selected as one of "America's Most Literate Cities." The city ranked #60 out of the 75 largest U.S. cities. Criteria: number of booksellers; library resources; Internet resources; educational attainment; periodical publishing resources; newspaper circulation. *Central Connecticut State University, "America's Most Literate Cities 2011"*

- Houston was identified as one of the 100 "smartest" metro areas in the U.S. The area ranked #83. Criteria: the editors rated the collective brainpower of the 100 largest metro areas in the U.S. based on their residents' educational attainment. *American City Business Journals, April 14, 2008*

- Houston was identified as one of "America's Brainiest Bastions" by *Portfolio.com*. The metro area ranked #121 out of 200. *Portfolio.com* analyzed levels of educational attainment in the nation's 200 largest metropolitan areas. The editors established scores for five levels of educational attainment, based on relative earning power of adult workers age 25 or older. Scores were determined by comparing the median income for all workers with the median income for those workers at a specified educational level. *Portfolio.com, "America's Brainiest Bastions," December 1, 2010*

Environmental Rankings

- The Houston was identified as one of North America's greenest metropolitan areas. The area ranked #16. The Green City Index is comprised of 31 indicators, and scores cities across nine categories: carbon dioxide; energy; land use; buildings; transport; water; waste; air quality; environmental governance. The 27 largest metropolitan areas in the U.S. and Canada were considered. *Economist Intelligence Unit, sponsored by Siemens, "U.S. and Canada Green City Index, 2011"*

- The Houston was identified as one of America's cities with the most ENERGY STAR certified buildings. The area ranked #7 out of 25. Criteria: number of ENERGY STAR labeled buildings in 2010. *U.S. Environmental Protection Agency, "Top Cities With the Most ENERGY STAR Certified Buildings," March 15, 2011*

- The Houston metro area was identified as one of "The Ten Biggest American Cities that are Running Out of Water" by *24/7 Wall St.* The metro area ranked #2 out of 10. *24/7 Wall St.* did an analysis of the water supply and consumption in the 30 largest metropolitan areas in the U.S. Criteria include: projected water demand as a share of available precipitation; groundwater use as a share or projected available precipitation; susceptibility to drought; projected increase in freshwater withdrawals; projected increase in summer water deficit. *24/7 Wall St., "The Ten Biggest American Cities that are Running Out of Water," November 1, 2010*

- Houston was selected as one of 22 "Smarter Cities" for energy by the Natural Resources Defense Council. Criteria: investment in green power; energy efficiency measures; conservation. *Natural Resources Defense Council, "2010 Smarter Cities," July 19, 2010*

- The Houston metro area was selected as one of "America's Most Toxic Cities" by *Forbes*. The metro area ranked #7 out of 10. The 80 largest metropolitan areas were ranked on the following criteria: air quality; water quality; Superfund sites; toxic releases. *Forbes, "America's Most Toxic Cities, 2011," February 28, 2011*

- *American City Business Journal* ranked 43 metropolitan areas in terms of their "greenness." The Houston metro area ranked #26. Criteria: Forty-one metros in which *ACBJ* has business weeklies, plus Indianapolis and Cleveland, were ranked based on 20 different indicators such as adoption of green technologies, utilization of environmentally sound practices, and air and water quality. *American City Business Journals, "Green City Index," March 11, 2010*

- 100 of the largest metro areas in the U.S. were analyzed in terms of their current drought severity. The Houston metro area ranked #96 (#1 = driest). The rankings were based on statistics such as long-term precipitation trends and patterns and the Palmer drought indices. *Sperling's BestPlaces, www.BestPlaces.net, "America's Drought-Riskiest Cities," November 2007*

- The U.S. Conference of Mayors and Wal-Mart Stores sponsor the Mayors' Climate Protection Awards Program. The awards recognize and honor mayors for outstanding and innovative practices that mayors are taking to increase energy efficiency in their cities, and to help curb global warming. Houston was a Large City Best Practice Model. *U.S. Conference of Mayors, "2009 Mayors' Climate Protection Awards Program"*

- The Houston metro area appeared in *Country Home's* "Best Green Places" report. The area ranked #122 out of 379. Criteria: official energy policies; green power; green buildings; availability of fresh, locally grown food. *Country Home, "Best Green Places," 2008*

- Houston was highlighted as one of the 25 metro areas most polluted by year-round particle pollution (Annual PM 2.5) in the U.S. The area ranked #17. *American Lung Association, State of the Air 2011*

- Houston was highlighted as one of the 25 most ozone-polluted metro areas in the U.S. The area ranked #8. *American Lung Association, State of the Air 2011*

Food/Drink Rankings

- Houston was identified as one of "America's Drunkest Cities of 2011" by *The Daily Beast*. The city ranked #25 out of 25. Criteria: binge drinking; drinks consumed per month. *The Daily Beast, "Tipsy Towns: Where are America's Drunkest Cities?," December 31, 2011*

- Houston was selected as one of America's best cities for hamburgers by the readers of *Travel + Leisure* in their annual America's Favorite Cities survey. The city was ranked #1 out of 10. Criteria:. *Travel + Leisure, "America's Best Burger Cities," May 2011*

- Minute Maid Park (Houston Astros) was selected as one of PETA's "2011 Top 10 Vegetarian-Friendly Major League Ballparks." The park ranked #9. *People for the Ethical Treatment of Animals, "2011 Top 10 Vegetarian-Friendly Major League Ballparks"*

Health/Fitness Rankings

- The Houston metro area was selected as one of the worst cities for bed bugs in America by Rollins corporation, the owner of seven pest control companies, including Orkin. The area ranked #11 based on the number of bed bug treatments from January to December 2011. *Rollins, "The Top 50 U.S. Cities for Bed Bugs," March 19, 2012*

- Houston was selected as one of the 25 fattest cities in America by *Men's Fitness Online*. It ranked #1 out of America's 50 largest cities. Criteria: fitness centers and sport stores; nutrition; sports participation; TV viewing; overweight/sedentary; junk food; air quality; geography; commute; parks and open space; city recreational facilities; access to healthcare; motivation; mayor and city initiatives; state obesity initiatives. *Men's Fitness, "The Fittest and Fattest Cities in America," March 5, 2012*

- Houston was identified as a "2011 Asthma Capital." The area ranked #64 out of the nation's 100 largest metropolitan areas. Twelve factors were used to identify the most challenging places to live for people with asthma: estimated prevalence; self-reported prevalence; crude death rate for asthma; annual pollen score; annual air quality; public smoking laws; number of board-certified asthma specialists; school inhaler access laws; rescue medication use; controller medication use; uninsured rate; poverty rate. *Asthma and Allergy Foundation of America, "2011 Asthma Capitals"*

- Houston was identified as a "2011 Fall Allergy Capital." The area ranked #51 out of 100. Three groups of factors were used to identify the most severe cities for people with allergies during the fall season: annual pollen levels; medicine utilization; access to board-certified allergists. *Asthma and Allergy Foundation of America, "2011 Fall Allergy Capitals"*

- Houston was identified as a "2012 Spring Allergy Capital." The area ranked #47 out of 100. Three groups of factors were used to identify the most severe cities for people with allergies during the spring season: annual pollen levels; medicine utilization; access to board-certified allergists. *Asthma and Allergy Foundation of America, "2012 Spring Allergy Capitals"*

- *Men's Health* examined 100 major U.S. cities and selected the best and worst cities for men. Houston ranked #49. Criteria: 35 statistical parameters of long life in the categories of health, quality of life, and fitness. *Men's Health, "The 10 Best and Worst Cities for Men 2012," January/February 2012*

- Houston was selected as one of America's noisiest cities by *Men's Health*. The city ranked #9 of 10. Criteria: laws limiting excessive noise; traffic congestion levels; airports' overnight flight curfews; percentage of people who report sleeping seven hours or less. *Men's Health, "Ranking America's Cities: America's Noisiest Cities," May 2009*

- The makers of Breath Right Nasal Strips, in partnership with Sperling's BestPlaces, analyzed 50 metro areas and identified those U.S. cities most challenged by chronic nasal congestion. The Houston metro area ranked #9. Criteria: tree, grass and weed pollens; molds and spores; air pollution; climate; smoking; purchase habits of congestion products; prescriptions of drugs for congestion relief; incidence of influenza. *Breathe Right Nasal Strips, "Most Congested Cities," October 3, 2011*

- The Houston metropolitan area was selected as one of the best metros for hospital care in America by *HealthGrades.com*. The rankings are based on a comprehensive study of patient death and complication rates in the nation's nearly 5,000 hospitals. Hospitals performing in the top 5% nationwide across 26 different medical procedures and diagnoses were identified. *HealthGrades.com* then ranked cities by the highest percentage of these Distinguished Hospitals for Clinical Excellence™. The Houston metro area ranked #37. *HealthGrades.com, "America's Top 50 Cities for Hospital Care," January 21, 2012*

- The American Academy of Dermatology ranked 26 U.S. metropolitan regions in terms of their residents knowledge, attitude and behaviors towards tanning, sun protection and skin cancer detection. The Houston metro area ranked #12. The results of the study are based on an online survey of over 7,000 adults nationwide. *American Academy of Dermatology, "Suntelligence: How Sun Smart is Your City," May 3, 2010*

- The Houston metro area appeared in the 2011 Gallup-Healthways Well-Being Index. The index, based on interviews with more than 350,000 Americans, measured jobs, finances, physical health, emotional state of mind and communities. The metro area ranked #68 out of 190. Criteria: life evaluation; emotional health; work environment; physical health; healthy behaviors; basic access (basic needs optimal for a healthy life, such as access to food and medicine, having health insurance and feeling safe while walking at night). *Gallup-Healthways, "State of Well-Being 2011"*

- The Houston metro area was identified as one of "America's Most Stressful Cities" by *Sperling's BestPlaces*. The metro area ranked #26 out of 50. Criteria: unemployment rate; suicide rate; commute time; mental health; poor rest; alcohol use; violent crime rate; property crime rate; cloudy days annually. *Sperling's BestPlaces, www.BestPlaces.net, "Stressful Cities 2012*

- The Houston metro area was identified as one of "America's Most Stressful Cities" by *Forbes*. The metro area ranked #11 out of 40. Criteria: housing affordability; unemployment rate; cost of living; air quality; traffic congestion; sunny days; population density. *Forbes.com, "America's Most Stressful Cities," September 23, 2011*

- *Men's Health* ranked 100 U.S. cities in terms of their activity levels. Houston was ranked #70 (#1 = most active city). Criteria: where and how often residents exercise; percentage of households that watch more than 15 hours of cable television a week and buy more than 11 video games a year; death rate from deep-vein thrombosis, a condition linked to sitting for extended periods of time. *Men's Health, "Where Sit Happens: The Most and Least Active Cities in America," June 20, 2011*

- 50 of the largest metro areas in the U.S. were analyzed in terms of their health and fitness by the American College of Sports Medicine in their "American Fitness Index." The Houston metro area ranked #42 (#1 = healthiest). Criteria: preventative health behaviors; levels of chronic disease; health care access; community resources and policies that support physical activity. *American College of Sports Medicine, "Health and Community Fitness Status of the 50 Largest Metropolitan Areas," August 1, 2011*

Real Estate Rankings

- The Houston metro area was identified as one of ten places where real estate is ripe for a rebound by *Forbes*. Criteria: change in home price over the past 12 months and three years; unemployment rates; 12-month job-growth projections; population change from 2006 through 2009; new home construction rates for the third quarter of 2011 as compared to the same quarter in 2010. *Forbes.com, "Cities Where Real Estate is Ripe for a Rebound," January 12, 2012*

- *Fortune* ranked the 100 largest metro areas in the U.S. in terms of projected median home price change in 2010. The Houston metro area ranked #6. *Fortune, "The 2010 Housing Outlook," December 9, 2009*

- Houston was selected as one of the 10 best U.S. cities for real estate investment. The city ranked #7. *Association of Foreign Investors in Real Estate, "AFIRE News," January/February, 2011*

- The Houston metro area was identified as one of the 25 best housing markets in the U.S. in 2011. The area ranked #21 out of 149 markets with a home price appreciation of 1.2%. Criteria: year-over-year change of median sales price of existing single-family homes between the 4th quarter of 2010 and the 4th quarter of 2011. *National Association of Realtors®, Median Sales Price of Existing Single-Family Homes for Metropolitan Areas, 4th Quarter 2011*

- The Houston metro area was identified as one of the 10 best condo markets in the U.S. in 2011. The area ranked #2 out of 54 markets with a price appreciation of 8.6%. Criteria: year-over-year change of median sales price of existing apartment condo-coop homes between the 4th quarter of 2010 and the 4th quarter of 2011. *National Association of Realtors®, Median Sales Price of Existing Apartment Condo-Coop Homes for Metropolitan Areas, 4th Quarter 2011*

- Houston appeared on *ApartmentRatings.com* "Top Cities for Renters" list in 2009." The area ranked #71. Overall satisfaction ratings were ranked using thousands of user submitted scores for hundreds of apartment complexes located in the 100 most populated U.S. municipalities. *ApartmentRatings.com, "2009 Renter Satisfaction Rankings"*

- Houston appeared on *ApartmentRatings.com* "Top College Towns & Cities" for renters list in 2011." The area ranked #58 out of 87. Overall satisfaction ratings were ranked using thousands of user submitted scores for hundreds of apartment complexes located in cities and towns that are home to the 100 largest four-year institutions in the U.S. *ApartmentRatings.com, "2011 College Town Renter Satisfaction Rankings"*

- The Houston metro area was identified as one of the "Top 25 Real Estate Investment Markets" by *FinestExperts.com*. The metro area ranked #4. Over 10,000 real estate markets were analyzed to identify the most suitable places for real estate investors to seek stability and growth. Criteria: employment; rental markets; growth levels as offset by foreclosures. *FinestExperts.com, "Top 25 Real Estate Investment Markets," January 7, 2010*

- The Houston metro area was identified as one of "America's Best Housing Markets" by *Forbes*. The metro area ranked #3. Criteria: housing affordability; rising home prices; percentage of foreclosures. *Forbes.com, "America's Best Housing Markets," February 19, 2010*

- The Houston metro area appeared in a *Wall Street Journal* article ranking cities by "housing stress." The metro area was ranked #19 (#1 = most stress). Criteria: fraction of mortgage-holding homeowners with a monthly housing payment in excess of 30 percent of income; percentage of people without health insurance; unemployment rate. *The Wall Street Journal, "Which Cities Face Biggest Housing Risk," October 5, 2010*

- The Center for Housing Policy ranked 210 U.S. metropolitan areas by the fair market rent for a two-bedroom unit. The Houston metro area was ranked #84. (#1 = most expensive) with a rent of $892. Criteria: Fair Market Rent (FMR) in effect during the fourth quarter of 2009 based on HUD's fiscal year 2010 FMRs. *The Center for Housing Policy, "Paycheck to Paycheck: Most to Least Expensive Rental Markets in 2009"*

- The Houston metro area was identified as one of the best U.S. markets to invest in rental property" by HomeVestors and Local Market Monitor. The area ranked #31 out of 100. Criteria: risk-return premium relative to national average. *HomeVestors and Local Market Monitor, "Best 100 U.S. Markets to Invest in Rental Property," March 9, 2012*

Safety Rankings

- Symantec, the makers of Norton, in partnership with Sperling's BestPlaces, ranked the 50 largest cities in the U.S. in terms of their vulnerability to cybercrime. The city ranked #24. Criteria: number of cyberattacks and potential infections; level of Internet access; expenditures on smartphones and computer hardware/software; wireless hotspots; broadband connectivity; Internet usage; online purchases. *Symantec, "Riskiest Online Cities of 2012" February 15, 2012*

- Allstate ranked the 193 largest cities in America in terms of driver safety. Houston ranked #155. In addition, drivers were 28.7% more likely to have had an accident compared to the national average. Allstate researchers analyzed internal property damage reported claims over a two-year period (from January 2008 to December 2009) to protect findings from external influences such as weather or road construction. A weighted average of the two-year numbers determined the annual percentages. The report defines an auto crash as any collision resulting in a property damage claim. *Allstate, "2011 Allstate America's Best Drivers Report™"*

- Houston was identified as one of the most dangerous large cities in America by CQ Press. All 34 cities with populations of 500,000 or more that reported crime rates in 2010 for murder, rape, robbery, aggravated assault, burglary, and motor vehicle thefts were ranked. The city ranked #10 out of the top 10. *CQ Press, City Crime Rankings 2011-2012*

- The National Insurance Crime Bureau ranked 366 metro areas in the U.S. in terms of per capita rates of vehicle theft. The Houston metro area ranked #28 (#1 = highest rate). Criteria: number of vehicle theft offenses per 100,000 inhabitants in 2010. *National Insurance Crime Bureau, "Hot Spots," June 21, 2011*

- The Houston metro area was identified as one of the most dangerous metro areas for pedestrians by Transportation for America. The metro area ranked #9 out of 52 metro areas with over 1 million residents. Criteria: area's population divided by the number of pedestrian fatalities in that area. *Transportation for America, "Dangerous by Design 2011"*

Seniors/Retirement Rankings

- Bankers Life and Casualty Company, in partnership with Sperling's BestPlaces, ranked the nation's 50 largest metro areas in terms of the "Best U.S. Cities for Seniors." The Houston metro area ranked #45. Criteria: healthcare; transportation; housing; environment; economy; health and longevity; social and spiritual life; crime. *Bankers Life and Casualty Company, Center for a Secure Retirement, "Best U.S. Cities for Seniors 2011," September 2011*

- The Houston metro area was identified as one of "America's Most Affordable Places to Retire" by *Forbes*. The metro area ranked #4. Criteria: housing affordability; inflation; number of persons over 65 who are employed; net migration for persons over 65; percent of persons over 65 living below poverty level; doctors per capita; number of citizens tapping their Medicare benefits per thousand people. *Forbes.com, "America's Most Affordable Places to Retire," September 5, 2008*

- The Houston metro area was selected as one of "America's Best Places to Grow Old" by *Forbes*. The area was ranked #4 out of 10. Criteria: housing affordability; inflationary pressures; number of persons over 65 who are currently employed; net migration for persons over 65; percent of seniors living below poverty level; doctors per capita; number of citizens tapping their Medicare benefits per 1,000 people. *Forbes, "America's Best Places to Grow Old," December 12, 2008*

- The Houston metro area was selected as one of "The 10 Most Affordable Cities for Long-Term Care" by *U.S. News & World Report*. Criteria: costs at nursing homes, assisted living facilities, and adult day health care facilities; cost for licensed home health aides. *U.S. News & World Report, "The 10 Most Affordable Cities for Long-Term Care," May 17, 2010*

Sports/Recreation Rankings

- Houston was selected as one of "America's Most Miserable Sports Cities" by *Forbes*. The city was ranked #6. Criteria: postseason losses; years since last title; ratio of cumulative seasons to championships won. Contenders were limited to cities with at least 75 total seasons of NFL, NBA, NHL and MLB play. *Forbes, "America's Most Miserable Sports Cities," February 28, 2012*

- Houston appeared on the *Sporting News* list of the "Best Sports Cities" for 2011. The area ranked #24 out of 271 cities in the U.S. *Sporting News* takes a 12-month snapshot of each city's sports, putting a heavy premium on regular-season won-lost records (from the most recently completed season). Other criteria include: playoff berths, bowl appearances and tournament bids; championships; applicable power ratings; quality of competition; overall fan fervor (measured in part by attendance); abundance of teams (rewarding quality over quantity); stadium and arena quality; ticket availability and prices; franchise ownership; and marquee appeal of athletes. *Sporting News, "Best Sports Cities 2011," October 4, 2011*

- The Houston was selected as one of the best metro areas for golf in America by *Golf Digest*. The Houston area was ranked #8 out of 20. Criteria: climate; cost of public golf; quality of public golf; accessibility. *Golf Digest, "The Top 20 Cities for Golf," October 2011*

Technology Rankings

- The Houston metro area was identified as one of 10 "Top Up-and-Coming Tech Cities" by *Forbes*. The metro area ranked #4. Criteria: regional innovation trends; important patents. *Forbes.com, "Top Up-and-Coming Tech Cities," March 11, 2008*

- The Houston metro area was identified as one of the "Top 14 Nano Metros" in the U.S. by the Project on Emerging Nanotechnologies. The metro area is home to 24 companies, universities, government laboratories and/or organizations working in nanotechnology. *Project on Emerging Nanotechnologies, "Nano Metros 2009"*

Transportation Rankings

- Houston appeared on *Trapster.com's* list of the 10 most-active U.S. cities for speed traps. The city ranked #3 of 10. *Trapster.com* is a community platform accessed online and via smartphone app that alerts drivers to traps, hazards and other traffic issues nearby. *Trapster.com, "Speeders Beware: Cities With the Most Speed Traps," February 10, 2012*

- Houston was identified as one of America's worst cities for speed traps by the National Motorists Association. The city ranked #18 out of 25. Criteria: speed trap locations per 100,000 residents. *National Motorists Association, September 2011*

- The Houston metro area appeared on *Forbes* list of the best and worst cities for commuters. The metro area ranked #53 out of 60 (#1 is best). Criteria: travel time; road congestion; travel delays. *Forbes.com, "Best and Worst Cities for Commuters," February 16, 2010*

Women/Minorities Rankings

- *Women's Health* examined U.S. cities and identified the 100 best cities for women. Houston was ranked #46. Criteria: 30 categories were examined from obesity and breast cancer rates to commuting times and hours spent working out. *Women's Health, "Best Cities for Women 2012"*

- Houston was ranked #86 out of 100 metro areas in *SELF Magazine's* ranking of America's healthiest places for women." A panel of experts came up with more than 50 criteria including death and disease rates, environmental indicators, community resources, and lifestyle habits. *SELF Magazine, "Secrets of America's Healthiest Women," December 2008*

- Houston was selected as one of the 25 healthiest cities for Latinas by *Latina Magazine*. The city ranked #11. Criteria: U.S. cities with populations over 500,000 residents were evaluated on the following criteria: percentage of 18-34 year-olds per city; Latino college graduation rates; number of colleges and universities; affordability; housing costs; income growth over time; average salary; percentage of singles; climate; safety; how the city's diversity compares to the national average; opportunities for minority entrepreneurs. *Latina Magazine, "Top 15 U.S. Cities for Young Latinos to Live In," August 19, 2011*

- Houston appeared on *Black Enterprise's* list of the "Ten Best Cities for African Americans." The top picks were culled from more than 2,000 interactive surveys completed on *BlackEnterprise.com* and by editorial staff evaluation. The editors weighed the following criteria as it pertained to African Americans in each city: median household income; percentage of households earning more than $100,000; percentage of businesses owned; percentage of college graduates; unemployment rates; home loan rejections; and homeownership rates. *Black Enterprise, May 2007*

- The Houston metro area appeared on *Forbes'* list of the "Best Cities for Minority Entrepreneurs." The area ranked #11 out of 10. Criteria: 52 metropolitan statistical areas were examined. For each ethnicity (African Americans, Asians and Hispanics), the editors measured housing affordability, population growth, income growth, and entrepreneurship (per capita self-employment). *Forbes, "Best Cities for Minority Entrepreneurs," March 23, 2011*

- Houston was selected as one of the "Top 10 Cities for Hispanics." Criteria: the prospect of a good job; a safe place to raise a family; a manageable cost of living; the ability to buy and keep a home; a culture of inclusion where Hispanics are highly represented; resources to help start a business; the presence of Hispanic or Spanish-language media; representation of Hispanic needs on local government; a thriving arts and culture community; air quality; energy costs; city's state of health and rates of obesity. *Hispanic Magazine, August 2008*

Miscellaneous Rankings

- *Men's Health* ranked 100 U.S. cities by their level of sadness. Houston was ranked #49 (#1 = saddest city). Criteria: suicide rates; unemployment rates; percentage of households that use antidepressants; percent of population who report feeling blue all or most of the time. *Men's Health, "Frown Towns," November 28, 2011*

- Energizer Holdings, the makers of Edge® shave gel, in partnership with Sperling's BestPlaces, ranked 50 major metro areas in terms of everyday irritations. The Houston metro area ranked #2. Criteria: humidity levels; weather conditions; incidence of traffic delays and congestion; average commute times; frequency of flight delays and cancellations; rates of sleeplessness; underemployment; pollens and allergens; pests; comedy clubs per capita. *Energizer Holdings, "Most Irritation Prone Cities," July 23, 2010*

- Mars Chocolate North America, the makers of COMBOS®, in partnership with Sperling's BestPlaces, ranked 50 major metro areas in terms of their "manliness." The Houston metro area ranked #9. Criteria: number of professional sports teams; number of nearby NASCAR tracks and racing events; manly lifestyle; concentration of manly retail stores; manly occupations per capita; salty snack sales; "Board of Manliness" rankings. *Mars Chocolate North America, "America's Manliest Cities 2011," September 1, 2011*

- Houston was selected as one of the "Worst Hair Cities" by *NaturallyCurly.com*. The city was ranked #8. Criteria: humidity levels; pollution; rainfall; average wind speeds; water hardness; beauty salons per capita. *NaturallyCurly.com, "Best/Worst Hair Cities," April 29, 2009*

- Houston was selected as one of the best cities for shopping in the U.S. by *Forbes*. The city was ranked #1. Criteria: number of major shopping centers; retail locations; Consumer Price Index (CPI); combined state and local sales tax. *Forbes, "America's 25 Best Cities for Shopping," December 13, 2010*

- The Houston metro area appeared in *AutoMD.com's* ranking of the "Best and Worst Cities for Auto Repair." The metro area ranked #27 (#1 is best). The 50 most-populated metro areas in the U.S. were ranked on three critical factors: repair affordability; price disparity range; shop integrity factor. *AutoMD.com, "Advocacy for Repair Shop Fairness Report," February 24, 2010*

- *Men's Health* examined the nation's largest 100 cities and identified "America's Most Political Cities." Houston was ranked among the ten least political at #9. Criteria: percentage of active registered voters; percentage of ballots counted of active registration; percentage of income donated to 2008 presidential election; campaign spending; percentage of registrants who voted in the 2008 primaries; percentage of voters in the 2004/2006 Senate election; percentage of voters in the 2004-2007 gubernatorial election. *Men's Health, "Ranking America's Cities: America's Most Political Cities," October 2008*

- Houston appeared on Procter & Gamble's list of the "Top-20 All-Time Sweatiest Cities." The city was ranked #5. The rankings are based on computer simulations of the amount of sweat a person of average height and weight would produce walking around for an hour in the average temperatures during the summer months, based on historical weather data during June, July and August from 2001-2008 for each city. *Procter & Gamble, Old Spice Press Release, "Top-20 All-Time Sweatiest Cities," July 1, 2009*

Business Environment

CITY FINANCES

City Government Finances

Component	2009 ($000)	2009 ($ per capita)
Total Revenues	2,290,171	1,037
Total Expenditures	4,887,152	2,213
Debt Outstanding	13,106,077	5,935
Cash and Securities[1]	9,911,502	4,489

Note: (1) Cash and security holdings of a government at the close of its fiscal year, including those of its dependent agencies, utilities, and liquor stores.
Source: U.S Census Bureau, State & Local Government Finances 2009

City Government Revenue by Source

Source	2009 ($000)	2009 ($ per capita)
General Revenue		
From Federal Government	348,696	158
From State Government	59,383	27
From Local Governments	27,904	13
Taxes		
Property	1,018,686	461
Sales and Gross Receipts	760,740	345
Personal Income	0	0
Corporate Income	0	0
Motor Vehicle License	0	0
Other Taxes	61,778	28
Current Charges	862,594	391
Liquor Store	0	0
Utility	347,672	157
Employee Retirement	-1,574,335	-713

Source: U.S Census Bureau, State & Local Government Finances 2009

City Government Expenditures by Function

Function	2009 ($000)	2009 ($ per capita)	2009 (%)
General Direct Expenditures			
Air Transportation	640,280	290	13.1
Corrections	22,422	10	0.5
Education	0	0	0.0
Employment Security Administration	0	0	0.0
Financial Administration	51,617	23	1.1
Fire Protection	354,379	160	7.3
General Public Buildings	46,558	21	1.0
Governmental Administration, Other	49,726	23	1.0
Health	122,062	55	2.5
Highways	174,410	79	3.6
Hospitals	0	0	0.0
Housing and Community Development	100,893	46	2.1
Interest on General Debt	527,521	239	10.8
Judicial and Legal	49,555	22	1.0
Libraries	66,392	30	1.4
Parking	3,731	2	0.1
Parks and Recreation	283,296	128	5.8
Police Protection	676,255	306	13.8
Public Welfare	0	0	0.0
Sewerage	278,048	126	5.7
Solid Waste Management	180,207	82	3.7
Veterans' Services	0	0	0.0
Liquor Store	0	0	0.0
Utility	303,124	137	6.2
Employee Retirement	449,514	204	9.2

Source: U.S Census Bureau, State & Local Government Finances 2009

Municipal Bond Ratings

Area	Moody's	S&P	Fitch
City	Aa3	AA	AA

Rating Systems (shown in declining order of credit quality): Moody's– Aaa, Aa, A, Baa, Ba, B, Caa, Ca, C (numerical modifiers 1, 2, and 3 are added to letter-rating); S&P– AAA, AA, A, BBB, BB, B, CCC, CC, C; Fitch– AAA, AA, A, BBB, BB, B, CCC, CC, C. Ratings may be modified by the addition of a plus or minus sign to show relative standing within the major rating categories.
Notes: n/a Not Available; w/d Withdrawn (1) Not Reviewed; (2) Issuer Rating/No General Obligation; (3) Standard and Poor's Issue Credit Rating (ICR) is a current opinion of an obliger with respect to a specific financial obligation, a specific class of financial obligations, or a specific financial program.
Source: U.S. Census Bureau, 2012 Statistical Abstract, Bond Ratings for City Governments by Largest Cities: 2010

DEMOGRAPHICS

Population Growth

Area	1990 Census	2000 Census	2010 Census	Population Growth (%) 1990-2000	2000-2010
City	1,697,610	1,953,631	2,099,451	15.1	7.5
MSA[1]	3,767,335	4,715,407	5,946,800	25.2	26.1
U.S.	248,709,873	281,421,906	308,745,538	13.2	9.7

Note: (1) Figures cover the Houston-Sugar Land-Baytown, TX Metropolitan Statistical Area—see Appendix B for areas included
Source: U.S. Census Bureau, 2010 Census

Household Size

Area	One	Two	Three	Four	Five	Six	Seven or More	Average Household Size
City	31.0	27.6	15.1	12.3	7.3	3.6	3.1	2.64
MSA[1]	23.5	28.6	17.0	15.6	8.6	3.8	2.9	2.83
U.S.	26.7	32.8	16.1	13.4	6.5	2.6	1.9	2.58

Note: (1) Figures cover the Houston-Sugar Land-Baytown, TX Metropolitan Statistical Area—see Appendix B for areas included
Source: U.S. Census Bureau, 2010 Census

Race

Area	White Alone[2] (%)	Black Alone[2] (%)	Asian Alone[2] (%)	AIAN[3] Alone[2] (%)	NHOPI[4] Alone[2] (%)	Other Race Alone[2] (%)	Two or More Races (%)
City	50.5	23.7	6.0	0.7	0.1	15.7	3.3
MSA[1]	60.2	17.2	6.5	0.6	0.1	12.3	3.0
U.S.	72.4	12.6	4.8	0.9	0.2	6.2	2.9

Note: (1) Figures cover the Houston-Sugar Land-Baytown, TX Metropolitan Statistical Area—see Appendix B for areas included; (2) Alone is defined as not being in combination with one or more other races; (3) American Indian and Alaska Native; (4) Native Hawaiian and Other Pacific Islander
Source: U.S. Census Bureau, 2010 Census

Hispanic or Latino Origin

Area	Hispanic or Latino (%)	Mexican (%)	Puerto Rican (%)	Cuban (%)	Other Hispanic or Latino (%)
City	43.8	32.1	0.4	0.4	10.9
MSA[1]	35.3	26.6	0.5	0.3	7.9
U.S.	16.3	10.3	1.5	0.6	4.0

Note: Persons of Hispanic or Latino origin can be of any race; (1) Figures cover the Houston-Sugar Land-Baytown, TX Metropolitan Statistical Area—see Appendix B for areas included
Source: U.S. Census Bureau, 2010 Census

Segregation

Type	Segregation Indices[1]				Percent Change		
	1990	2000	2010	2010 Rank[2]	1990-2000	1990-2010	2000-2010
Black/White	65.5	65.7	61.4	36	0.1	-4.1	-4.2
Asian/White	48.0	51.4	50.4	7	3.4	2.4	-1.0
Hispanic/White	47.8	53.4	52.5	18	5.6	4.7	-0.9

Note: Figures are based on an analysis of 1990, 2000, and 2010 Census Decennial Census tract data by William H. Frey, Brookings Institution and the University of Michigan Social Science Data Analysis Network. In this analysis all racial groups (whites, blacks, and asians) are non-Hispanic members of those races. Hispanics are shown as a separate category; All figures cover the Metropolitan Statistical Area (see Appendix B for areas included); (1) Segregation Indices are Dissimilarity Indices that measure the degree to which the minority group is distributed differently than whites across census tracts. They range from 0 (complete integration) to 100 (complete segregation) where the value indicates the percentage of the minority group that needs to move to be distributed exactly like whites; (2) Ranges from 1 (most segregated) to 102 (least segregated); n/a not available.
Source: www.CensusScope.org

Ancestry

Area	German	Irish	English	American	Italian	Polish	French[2]	Scottish	Dutch
City	5.7	4.0	4.3	2.3	1.5	0.9	1.6	1.0	0.5
MSA[1]	9.5	6.5	6.1	4.3	2.2	1.2	2.6	1.3	0.8
U.S.	16.1	11.6	8.8	6.1	5.7	3.2	3.0	1.9	1.6

Note: Figures are the percentage of the total population reporting a particular ancestry. The nine most commonly reported ancestries in the U.S. are shown. Figures include multiple ancestries (e.g. if a person reported being Irish and Italian, they were included in both columns); (1) Figures cover the Houston-Sugar Land-Baytown, TX Metropolitan Statistical Area—see Appendix B for areas included; (2) Excludes Basque
Source: U.S. Census Bureau, 2008-2010 American Community Survey 3-Year Estimates

Foreign-Born Population

Area	Percent of Population Born in								
	Any Foreign Country	Mexico	Asia	Europe	Carribean	South America	Central America[2]	Africa	Canada
City	28.9	13.9	5.3	1.1	0.6	1.0	5.5	1.1	0.2
MSA[1]	22.2	10.2	5.2	1.0	0.5	1.0	3.3	0.8	0.2
U.S.	12.8	3.8	3.6	1.6	1.2	0.9	1.0	0.5	0.3

Note: (1) Figures cover the Houston-Sugar Land-Baytown, TX Metropolitan Statistical Area—see Appendix B for areas included; (2) Excludes Mexico.
Source: U.S. Census Bureau, 2008-2010 American Community Survey 3-Year Estimates

Marital Status

Area	Never Married	Now Married[2]	Separated	Widowed	Divorced
City	38.1	42.8	3.5	5.1	10.4
MSA[1]	31.5	51.0	2.8	4.7	10.0
U.S.	31.6	49.6	2.2	6.1	10.7

Note: Figures are percentages and cover the population 15 years of age and older; (1) Figures cover the Houston-Sugar Land-Baytown, TX Metropolitan Statistical Area—see Appendix B for areas included; (2) Excludes separated
Source: U.S. Census Bureau, 2008-2010 American Community Survey 3-Year Estimates

Age

Area	Percent of Population							Median Age
	Under Age 5	Age 5 to 17	Age 18 to 34	Age 35 to 49	Age 50 to 64	Age 65 to 79	80 Years and Over	
City	8.1	17.7	28.8	20.4	16.0	6.7	2.4	32.1
MSA[1]	7.9	20.0	24.7	21.6	17.2	6.6	2.0	33.2
U.S.	6.5	17.5	23.2	20.7	19.0	9.4	3.6	37.2

Note: (1) Figures cover the Houston-Sugar Land-Baytown, TX Metropolitan Statistical Area—see Appendix B for areas included
Source: U.S. Census Bureau, 2010 Census

Male/Female Ratio

Area	Males	Females	Males per 100 Females
City	1,053,517	1,045,934	100.7
MSA[1]	2,957,442	2,989,358	98.9
U.S.	151,781,326	156,964,212	96.7

Note: (1) Figures cover the Houston-Sugar Land-Baytown, TX Metropolitan Statistical Area—see Appendix B for areas included
Source: U.S. Census Bureau, 2010 Census

Religious Groups

Area	Catholic	Baptist	Non-Den.	Methodist[2]	Lutheran	LDS[3]	Pentecostal	Presbyterian[4]	Muslim[5]	Judaism
MSA[1]	17.1	16.0	7.3	4.9	1.1	1.1	1.5	0.9	0.4	2.7
U.S.	19.1	9.3	4.0	4.0	2.3	2.0	1.9	1.6	0.8	0.7

Note: Figures are the number of adherents as a percentage of the total population; (1) Figures cover the Houston-Sugar Land-Baytown, TX Metropolitan Statistical Area—see Appendix B for areas included; (2) Methodist/Pietist; (3) Latter Day Saints; (4) Reformed; (5) Figures are estimates
Source: Association of Statisticians of American Religious Bodies, 2010 U.S. Religion Census: Religious Congregations & Membership Study

ECONOMY

Gross Metropolitan Product

Area	2007	2008	2009	2010	2010 Rank[2]
MSA[1]	373.3	396.5	364.9	378.9	5

Note: Figures are in billions of dollars; (1) Figures cover the Houston-Sugar Land-Baytown, TX Metropolitan Statistical Area—see Appendix B for areas included; (2) Rank ranges from 1 to 363
Source: The United States Conference of Mayors, "U.S. Metro Economies: GMP and Employment Forecasts," June 2011

Economic Growth

Area	2007-2009 (%)	2010 (%)	2011 (%)	Rank[2]
MSA[1]	0.4	7.6	2.9	83
U.S.	-1.3	2.9	2.5	–

Note: Figures are real Gross Metropolitan Product growth rates and represent annual average percent change; (1) Figures cover the Houston-Sugar Land-Baytown, TX Metropolitan Statistical Area—see Appendix B for areas included; (2) Rank ranges from 1 to 363
Source: The United States Conference of Mayors, "U.S. Metro Economies: GMP and Employment Forecasts," June 2011

Metropolitan Area Exports

Area	2005	2006	2007	2008	2009	2010	2010 Rank[2]
MSA[1]	41,747.9	53,281.0	62,814.7	80,015.1	65,820.9	80,569.7	2

Note: Figures are in millions of dollars; (1) Figures cover the Houston-Sugar Land-Baytown, TX Metropolitan Statistical Area—see Appendix B for areas included; (2) Rank ranges from 1 to 369
Source: U.S. Department of Commerce, International Trade Administration, Office of Trade & Industry Information, Manufacturing & Services, data extracted April 2, 2012

INCOME

Income

Area	Per Capita ($)	Median Household ($)	Average Household ($)
City	25,700	43,349	67,252
MSA[1]	27,447	55,408	77,596
U.S.	26,942	51,222	70,116

Note: (1) Figures cover the Houston-Sugar Land-Baytown, TX Metropolitan Statistical Area—see Appendix B for areas included
Source: U.S. Census Bureau, 2008-2010 American Community Survey 3-Year Estimates

Household Income Distribution

Area	Percent of Households Earning							
	Under $15,000	$15,000 -24,999	$25,000 -34,999	$35,000 -49,999	$50,000 -74,999	$75,000 -99,000	$100,000 -149,999	$150,000 and up
City	15.4	13.4	12.3	14.3	17.0	9.6	9.4	8.6
MSA[1]	11.1	10.5	10.3	13.4	17.8	12.2	13.5	11.1
U.S.	13.0	11.0	10.6	14.2	18.5	12.1	12.2	8.4

Note: (1) Figures cover the Houston-Sugar Land-Baytown, TX Metropolitan Statistical Area—see Appendix B for areas included
Source: U.S. Census Bureau, 2008-2010 American Community Survey 3-Year Estimates

Poverty Rate

Area	All Ages	Under 18 Years Old	18 to 64 Years Old	65 Years and Over
City	21.1	32.6	17.5	13.8
MSA[1]	15.3	22.2	12.8	10.9
U.S.	14.4	20.1	13.1	9.4

Note: Figures are percentage of people whose income during the past 12 months was below the poverty level;
(1) Figures cover the Houston-Sugar Land-Baytown, TX Metropolitan Statistical Area—see Appendix B for areas included
Source: U.S. Census Bureau, 2008-2010 American Community Survey 3-Year Estimates

Personal Bankruptcy Filing Rate

Area	2006	2007	2008	2009	2010	2011
Harris County	1.50	1.74	1.52	1.78	2.08	1.95
U.S.	2.00	2.73	3.53	4.61	4.97	4.37

Note: Numbers are per 1,000 population and include Chapter 7 and Chapter 13 filings
Source: Federal Deposit Insurance Corporation, Regional Economic Conditions, March 9, 2012

EMPLOYMENT

Labor Force and Employment

Area	Civilian Labor Force			Workers Employed		
	Dec. 2010	Dec. 2011	% Chg.	Dec. 2010	Dec. 2011	% Chg.
City	1,080,233	1,106,150	2.4	994,389	1,028,242	3.4
MSA[1]	2,917,366	2,986,579	2.4	2,676,277	2,767,389	3.4
U.S.	153,156,000	153,373,000	0.1	139,159,000	140,681,000	1.1

Note: Data is not seasonally adjusted and covers workers 16 years of age and older;
(1) Metropolitan Statistical Area—see Appendix B for areas included
Source: Bureau of Labor Statistics, http://stats.bls.gov

Unemployment Rate

Area	2011											
	Jan.	Feb.	Mar.	Apr.	May	Jun.	Jul.	Aug.	Sep.	Oct.	Nov.	Dec.
City	8.4	8.1	8.0	7.7	7.9	8.8	8.7	8.4	8.5	7.9	7.3	7.0
MSA[1]	8.8	8.4	8.3	8.0	8.2	9.0	8.9	8.6	8.6	8.1	7.5	7.3
U.S.	9.8	9.5	9.2	8.7	8.7	9.3	9.3	9.1	8.8	8.5	8.2	8.3

Note: Data is not seasonally adjusted and covers workers 16 years of age and older; All figures are percentages; (1) Metropolitan Statistical Area—see Appendix B for areas included
Source: Bureau of Labor Statistics, http://stats.bls.gov

Projected Unemployment Rate

Area	2010 (%)	2011 (%)	2012 (%)	2013 (%)
MSA[1]	8.6	8.2	7.7	7.2

Note: (1) Metropolitan Statistical Area—see Appendix B for areas included
Source: The United States Conference of Mayors, "U.S. Metro Economies: GMP and Employment Forecasts," June 2011

Employment by Occupation

Occupation Classification	City (%)	MSA[1] (%)	U.S. (%)
Management, Business, Science, and Arts	31.6	35.3	35.6
Natural Resources, Construction, and Maintenance	13.0	11.7	9.5
Production, Transportation, and Material Moving	12.9	12.4	12.1
Sales and Office	23.4	24.4	25.2
Service	19.0	16.2	17.6

Note: Figures cover employed civilians 16 years of age and older; (1) Figures cover the Houston-Sugar Land-Baytown, TX Metropolitan Statistical Area—see Appendix B for areas included
Source: U.S. Census Bureau, 2008-2010 American Community Survey 3-Year Estimates

Employment by Industry

Sector	MSA[1] Number of Employees	MSA[1] Percent of Total	U.S. Percent of Total
Construction	168,900	6.4	4.1
Education and Health Services	331,000	12.5	15.2
Financial Activities	140,300	5.3	5.8
Government	375,900	14.2	16.8
Information	31,500	1.2	2.0
Leisure and Hospitality	245,900	9.3	9.9
Manufacturing	230,800	8.7	8.9
Mining and Logging	92,800	3.5	0.6
Other Services	95,700	3.6	4.0
Professional and Business Services	390,200	14.7	13.3
Retail Trade	281,700	10.6	11.5
Transportation and Utilities	124,800	4.7	3.8
Wholesale Trade	137,000	5.2	4.2

Note: Figures cover non-farm employment as of December 2011 and are not seasonally adjusted; (1) Metropolitan Statistical Area—see Appendix B for areas included
Source: Bureau of Labor Statistics, http://stats.bls.gov

Occupations with Greatest Projected Employment Growth: 2008 – 2018

Occupation[1]	2008 Employment	2018 Projected Employment	Numeric Employment Change	Percent Employment Change
Combined Food Preparation and Serving Workers, Including Fast Food	247,750	326,190	78,440	31.7
Elementary School Teachers, Except Special Education	156,930	218,030	61,100	38.9
Retail Salespersons	361,780	416,090	54,310	15.0
Registered Nurses	166,240	219,880	53,640	32.3
Home Health Aides	92,660	143,720	51,060	55.1
Customer Service Representatives	217,250	267,290	50,040	23.0
Waiters and Waitresses	192,340	237,660	45,320	23.6
Personal and Home Care Aides	94,530	138,530	44,000	46.5
Office Clerks, General	239,400	279,000	39,600	16.5
Cashiers	276,070	312,940	36,870	13.4

Note: Projections cover Texas; (1) Sorted by numeric employment change
Source: www.projectionscentral.com, State Occupational Projections, 2008–2018 Long-Term Projections

Fastest Growing Occupations: 2008 – 2018

Occupation[1]	2008 Employment	2018 Projected Employment	Numeric Employment Change	Percent Employment Change
Biomedical Engineers	650	1,150	500	76.9
Home Health Aides	92,660	143,720	51,060	55.1
Network Systems and Data Communications Analysts	19,160	29,490	10,330	53.9
Petroleum Engineers	13,440	20,140	6,700	49.9
Athletic Trainers	1,560	2,300	740	47.4
Personal and Home Care Aides	94,530	138,530	44,000	46.5
Electrical and Electronics Repairers, Powerhouse, Substation, and Relay	1,550	2,260	710	45.8
Financial Examiners	2,150	3,130	980	45.6
Medical Scientists, Except Epidemiologists	3,670	5,320	1,650	45.0
Biochemists and Biophysicists	740	1,060	320	43.2

Note: Projections cover Texas; (1) Sorted by percent employment change and excludes occupations with numeric employment change less than 100
Source: www.projectionscentral.com, State Occupational Projections, 2008–2018 Long-Term Projections

Average Wages

Occupation	$/Hr.	Occupation	$/Hr.
Accountants and Auditors	35.72	Maids and Housekeeping Cleaners	8.73
Automotive Mechanics	18.16	Maintenance and Repair Workers	16.98
Bookkeepers	18.56	Marketing Managers	64.43
Carpenters	17.02	Nuclear Medicine Technologists	30.60
Cashiers	9.44	Nurses, Licensed Practical	21.93
Clerks, General Office	14.59	Nurses, Registered	35.63
Clerks, Receptionists/Information	12.71	Nursing Aides/Orderlies/Attendants	11.44
Clerks, Shipping/Receiving	14.33	Packers and Packagers, Hand	11.31
Computer Programmers	37.32	Physical Therapists	40.26
Computer Support Specialists	26.49	Postal Service Mail Carriers	25.24
Computer Systems Analysts	43.60	Real Estate Brokers	48.78
Cooks, Restaurant	9.25	Retail Salespersons	11.33
Dentists	70.87	Sales Reps., Exc. Tech./Scientific	31.84
Electrical Engineers	43.82	Sales Reps., Tech./Scientific	41.40
Electricians	22.37	Secretaries, Exc. Legal/Med./Exec.	15.79
Financial Managers	63.28	Security Guards	10.52
First-Line Supervisors/Managers, Sales	20.04	Surgeons	66.07
Food Preparation Workers	9.73	Teacher Assistants	10.50
General and Operations Managers	58.09	Teachers, Elementary School	25.60
Hairdressers/Cosmetologists	12.77	Teachers, Secondary School	27.00
Internists	98.23	Telemarketers	16.77
Janitors and Cleaners	10.09	Truck Drivers, Heavy/Tractor-Trailer	18.15
Landscaping/Groundskeeping Workers	10.78	Truck Drivers, Light/Delivery Svcs.	15.95
Lawyers	78.76	Waiters and Waitresses	9.04

Note: Wage data covers the Houston-Sugar Land-Baytown, TX Metropolitan Statistical Area—see Appendix B for areas included. Hourly wages for elementary/secondary school teachers and teacher assistants were calculated by the editors from annual wage data assuming a 40 hour work week; n/a not available.
Source: Bureau of Labor Statistics, Metro Area Occupational Employment and Wage Estimates, May 2011

RESIDENTIAL REAL ESTATE

Building Permits

Area	Single-Family			Multi-Family			Total		
	2010	2011	Pct. Chg.	2010	2011	Pct. Chg.	2010	2011	Pct. Chg.
City	2,452	2,575	5.0	2,139	5,160	141.2	4,591	7,735	68.5
MSA[1]	22,330	22,889	2.5	5,122	8,382	63.6	27,452	31,271	13.9
U.S.	447,311	418,498	-6.4	157,299	205,563	30.7	604,610	624,061	3.2

Note: (1) Metropolitan Statistical Area—see Appendix B for areas included; figures represent new, privately-owned housing units authorized (unadjusted data); All permit data are based on estimates with imputation.
Source: U.S. Census Bureau, Manufacturing, Mining, and Construction Statistics, Building Permits, 2010, 2011

Homeownership Rate

Area	2005 (%)	2006 (%)	2007 (%)	2008 (%)	2009 (%)	2010 (%)	2011 (%)
MSA[1]	61.7	63.5	64.5	64.8	63.6	61.4	61.3
U.S.	68.9	68.8	68.1	67.8	67.4	66.9	66.1

Note: (1) Metropolitan Statistical Area—see Appendix B for areas included
Source: U.S. Census Bureau, Housing Vacancies and Homeownership Annual Statistics: 2011

Housing Vacancy Rates

Area	Gross Vacancy Rate[2] (%)			Year-Round Vacancy Rate[3] (%)			Rental Vacancy Rate[4] (%)			Homeowner Vacancy Rate[5] (%)		
	2009	2010	2011	2009	2010	2011	2009	2010	2011	2009	2010	2011
MSA[1]	12.5	12.2	11.8	12.3	11.9	11.4	15.6	16.2	16.5	1.9	2.8	2.0
U.S.	14.5	14.3	14.2	11.3	11.3	11.1	10.6	10.2	9.5	2.6	2.6	2.5

Note: (1) Metropolitan Statistical Area—see Appendix B for areas included; (2) The percentage of the total housing inventory that is vacant; (3) The percentage of the housing inventory (excluding seasonal units) that is year-round vacant; (4) The percentage of rental inventory that is vacant for rent; (5) The percentage of homeowner inventory that is vacant for sale
Source: U.S. Census Bureau, Housing Vacancies and Homeownership Annual Statistics: 2011

TAXES

State Corporate Income Tax Rates

State	Tax Rate (%)	Income Brackets ($)	Num. of Brackets	Financial Institution Tax Rate (%)[a]	Federal Income Tax Ded.
Texas	(x)	–	-	(x)	No

Note: Tax rates as of January 1, 2012; (a) Rates listed are the corporate income tax rate applied to financial institutions or excise taxes based on income. Some states have other taxes based upon the value of deposits or shares; (x) Texas imposes a Franchise Tax, otherwise known as margin tax, imposed on entities with more than $1,000,000 total revenues at rate of 1%, or 0.5% for entities primarily engaged in retail or wholesale trade, on lesser of 70% of total revenues or 100% of gross receipts after deductions for either compensation or cost of goods sold.
Source: Federation of Tax Administrators, "State Corporate Income Tax Rates, 2012"

State Individual Income Tax Rates

State	Tax Rate (%)	Income Brackets ($)	Num. of Brackets	Personal Exempt. ($)[1] Single	Dependents	Fed. Inc. Tax Ded.
Texas – No State Income Tax						

Note: Tax rates as of January 1, 2012; Local- and county-level taxes are not included; n/a not applicable; (1) Married joint filers generally receive double the single exemption
Source: Federation of Tax Administrators, "State Individual Income Tax Rates, 2012"

Various State and Local Tax Rates

State	State and Local Sales and Use (%)	State Sales and Use (%)	Gasoline[1] (¢/gal.)	Cigarette[2] ($/pack)	Spirits[3] ($/gal.)	Wine[4] ($/gal.)	Beer[5] ($/gal.)
Texas	8.25	6.25	20.0	1.41	2.40	0.20	0.20

Note: All tax rates as of January 1, 2012 except beer, wine and spirits (September 1, 2011); (1) The American Petroleum Institute has developed a methodology for determining the average tax rate on a gallon of fuel. Rates may include any of the following: excise taxes, environmental fees, storage tank fees, other fees or taxes, general sales tax, and local taxes. In states where gasoline is subject to the general sales tax, or where the fuel tax is based on the average sale price, the average rate determined by API is sensitive to changes in the price of gasoline. States that fully or partially apply general sales taxes to gasoline: CA, CO, GA, IL, IN, MI, NY; (2) The federal excise tax of $1.0066 per pack and local taxes are not included; (3) Rates are those applicable to off-premise sales of 40% alcohol by volume (a.b.v.) distilled spirits in 750ml containers. Local excise taxes are excluded; (4) Rates are those applicable to off-premise sales of 11% a.b.v. non-carbonated wine in 750ml containers; (5) Rates are those applicable to off-premise sales of 4.7% a.b.v. beer in 12 ounce containers.
Source: Tax Foundation, 2012 Facts & Figures: How Does Your State Compare?

State-Local Tax Burdens

Area	Rate (%)	Rank[1]	Per Capita Taxes Paid to Home State ($)	Total State and Local Per Capita Taxes Paid ($)	Per Capita Income ($)
Texas	7.9	45	2,248	3,197	40,498
U.S. Average	9.8	-	3,057	4,160	42,539

Note: Figures cover 2009; (1) Rank ranges from 1 to 50 where 1 is highest tax burden
Source: Tax Foundation, State-Local Tax Burdens, All States, 2009

State Business Tax Climate Index Rankings

State	Overall Rank	Corporate Tax Index Rank	Individual Income Tax Index Rank	Sales Tax Index Rank	Unemployment Insurance Tax Index Rank	Property Tax Index Rank
Texas	9	37	7	35	15	31

Note: The index is a measure of how each state's tax laws affect economic performance. The lower the rank, the more favorable a state's tax system is for business. States without a given tax are given a ranking of 1.
Source: Tax Foundation, Major Components of the State Business Tax Climate Index, FY 2012

COMMERCIAL REAL ESTATE

Office Market

Market Area	Inventory (sq. ft.)	Vacant (sq. ft.)	Vac. Rate (%)	Under Constr. (sq. ft.)	Asking Rent ($/sf/yr) Class A	Class B
Houston	170,420,371	27,284,281	16.0	1,080,279	29.40	19.15

Source: Grubb & Ellis, Office Markets Trends, 4th Quarter 2011

Industrial Market

Market Area	Inventory (sq. ft.)	Vacant (sq. ft.)	Vac. Rate (%)	Under Constr. (sq. ft.)	Asking Rent ($/sf/yr) WH/Dist	R&D/Flex
Houston	431,667,725	24,457,376	5.7	2,376,669	4.59	7.59

Source: Grubb & Ellis, Industrial Markets Trends, 4th Quarter 2011

COMMERCIAL UTILITIES

Typical Monthly Electric Bills

Area	Commercial Service ($/month) 1,500 kWh	40 kW demand 14,000 kWh	Industrial Service ($/month) 1,000 kW demand 200,000 kWh	50,000 kW demand 15,000,000 kWh
City	n/a	n/a	n/a	n/a
Average[1]	189	1,616	25,197	1,470,813

Note: Based on total rates in effect July 1, 2011; (1) average based on 184 utilities surveyed; n/a not available
Source: Edison Electric Institute, Typical Bills and Average Rates Report, Summer 2011

TRANSPORTATION

Means of Transportation to Work

Area	Car/Truck/Van Drove Alone	Car-pooled	Public Transportation Bus	Subway	Railroad	Bicycle	Walked	Other Means	Worked at Home
City	75.0	13.1	4.3	0.1	0.1	0.4	2.2	1.9	3.1
MSA[1]	78.7	12.1	2.3	0.0	0.0	0.3	1.4	1.7	3.4
U.S.	76.0	10.2	2.7	1.7	0.5	0.5	2.8	1.3	4.2

Note: Figures are percentages and cover workers 16 years of age and older; (1) Figures cover the Houston-Sugar Land-Baytown, TX Metropolitan Statistical Area—see Appendix B for areas included
Source: U.S. Census Bureau, 2008-2010 American Community Survey 3-Year Estimates

Travel Time to Work

Area	Less Than 10 Minutes	10 to 19 Minutes	20 to 29 Minutes	30 to 44 Minutes	45 to 59 Minutes	60 to 89 Minutes	90 Minutes or More
City	8.6	28.0	24.6	24.8	7.2	4.9	1.9
MSA[1]	8.9	25.5	20.9	25.2	10.2	7.1	2.2
U.S.	13.9	30.1	20.8	19.8	7.5	5.5	2.5

Note: Figures are percentages and include workers 16 years old and over; (1) Figures cover the Houston-Sugar Land-Baytown, TX Metropolitan Statistical Area—see Appendix B for areas included
Source: U.S. Census Bureau, 2008-2010 American Community Survey 3-Year Estimates

Travel Time Index

Area	1985	1990	1995	2000	2005	2010
Urban Area[1]	1.24	1.23	1.20	1.26	1.33	1.27
Average[2]	1.11	1.16	1.18	1.21	1.25	1.20

Note: Travel Time Index—the ratio of travel time in the peak period to the travel time at free-flow conditions. A value of 1.30 indicates a 20-minute free-flow trip takes 26 minutes in the peak. Free-flow speeds (60 mph on freeways and 35 mph on principal arterials) are used as the comparison threshold; (1) Covers the Houston TX urban area; (2) average of 439 urban areas
Source: Texas Transportation Institute, Urban Mobility Report 2011, September 2011

Public Transportation

Agency Name / Mode of Transportation	Vehicles Operated in Maximum Service	Annual Unlinked Passenger Trips ('000)	Annual Passenger Miles ('000)
Metropolitan Transit Authority of Harris County (METRO)			
Bus (directly operated)	862	54,320.9	358,730.9
Bus (purchased transportation)	185	12,218.0	84,342.8
Demand Response (purchased transportation)	249	1,373.6	16,346.8
Demand Response Taxi (purchased transportation)	183	199.4	883.3
Light Rail (directly operated)	17	10,616.3	24,167.5
Vanpool (purchased transportation)	738	2,423.0	67,337.1

Source: Federal Transit Administration, National Transit Database, 2010

Air Transportation

Airport Name and Code / Type of Service	Passenger Airlines[1]	Passenger Enplanements	Freight Carriers[2]	Freight (lbs.)
George Bush Intercontinental (IAH)				
Domestic service (U.S. carriers - 2011)	28	15,073,125	31	192,046,449
International service (U.S. carriers - 2010)	20	3,383,261	17	63,160,024
William P. Hobby (HOU)				
Domestic service (U.S. carriers - 2011)	25	4,752,274	8	12,795,012
International service (U.S. carriers - 2010)	2	8	0	0

Note: (1) Includes all U.S.-based major, minor and commuter airlines that carried at least one passenger during the year; (2) Includes all U.S.-based airlines and freight carriers that transported at least one pound of freight during the year
Source: Bureau of Transportation Statistics, The Intermodal Transportation Database, Air Carriers: T-100 Domestic Market (U.S. Carriers), 2011; Bureau of Transportation Statistics, The Intermodal Transportation Database, Air Carriers: T-100 International Market (U.S. Carriers), 2010

Other Transportation Statistics

Major Highways:	I-10; I-45
Amtrak Service:	Yes
Major Waterways/Ports:	Gulf of Mexico; Port of Houston

Source: Amtrak.com; Google Maps

BUSINESSES

Major Business Headquarters

Company Name	Rankings	
	Fortune[1]	Forbes[2]
Apache	206	-
Baker Hughes	170	-

Calpine	349	-
Cameron International	375	-
CenterPoint Energy	279	-
ConocoPhillips	4	-
EOG Resources	377	-
El Paso	481	-
Enbridge Energy Partners	309	-
Enterprise Products Partners	80	-
Frontier Oil	389	-
Grocers Supply	-	120
Group 1 Automotive	413	-
Gulf States Toyota	-	60
Halliburton	144	-
KBR	242	-
Kinder Morgan	294	-
Marathon Oil	29	-
McJunkin Red Man	-	92
National Oilwell Varco	202	-
Plains All American Pipeline	99	-
Republic National Distributing Company	-	74
Spectra Energy	441	-
Sysco	67	-
Targa Resources	416	-
Waste Management	196	-

Note: (1) Fortune 500—companies that produce a 10-K are ranked 1 to 500 based on 2010 revenue; (2) all private companies with at least $2 billion in annual revenue are ranked 1 to 212; companies listed are headquartered in the city; dashes indicate no ranking
Source: Fortune, "Fortune 500," May 23, 2011; Forbes, "America's Largest Private Companies," November 16, 2011

Fast-Growing Businesses

According to *Inc.*, Houston is home to six of America's 500 fastest-growing private companies: **ClearCorrect** (#17); **WBPromotions** (#31); **SightLine Health** (#86); **Bright Box** (#230); **The Ticket Experience** (#321); **Paradigm Partners** (#500). Criteria: must be an independent, privately-held, for-profit, U.S. corporation, proprietorship or partnership; revenues must be at least $80,000 in 2007 and $2 million in 2010; must have four-year operating/sales history. Holding companies, regulated banks, and utilities were excluded. *Inc., "America's 500 Fastest-Growing Private Companies," September 2011*

According to *Fortune*, Houston is home to one of the 100 fastest-growing companies in the world: **Cyberonics** (#73). Companies were ranked by their revenue growth rate; their EPS growth rate; and their three-year annualized total return to investors for the period ending June 30, 2011. Criteria for inclusion: a company, foreign or domestic, must trade on a major U.S. stock exchange; must file quarterly reports with the SEC; must have a minimum market capitalization of $250 million; must have a stock price of at least $5 on June 30, 2011; must have been trading continuously since June 30, 2008; must have revenue and net income for the four quarters ended on or before April 30, 2011, of at least $50 million and $10 million, respectively; and must have posted a compound annual growth in revenue and earnings per share of at least 15% annually over the three years ending on or before April 30, 2011. REITs, limited-liability companies, limited parterships, companies about to be acquired, and companies that lost money in the quarter ending April 30, 2011 were excluded. *Fortune, "100 Fastest-Growing Companies," September 26, 2011*

According to Deloitte, Houston is home to three of North America's 500 fastest-growing high-technology companies: **BBS Technologies** (#336); **RigNet** (#366); **Additech** (#371). Companies are ranked by percentage growth in revenue over a five-year period. Criteria for inclusion: company must be headquartered within North America; must own proprietary intellectual property or proprietary technology that contributes to a significant portion of the company's operating revenue, or devote a significant proportion of revenues to research and development of technology; must have been in business for a minumum of five years with 2006 operating revenues of at least $50,000 USD/CD and 2010 operating revenues of at least $5 million USD/CD. *Deloitte Touche Tohmatsu, 2011 Deloitte Technology Fast 500*[TM]

Minority Business Opportunity

Houston is home to two companies which are on the *Black Enterprise* Industrial/Service 100 list (100 largest companies based on gross sales): **CAMAC International Corporation** (#3); **The Lewis Group L.L.P.** (#34). Criteria: operational in previous calendar year; at least 51% black-owned and manufactures/owns the product it sells or provides industrial or consumer services. Brokerages, real estate firms and firms that provide professional services are not eligible. *Black Enterprise, B.E. 100s, 2011*

Houston is home to two companies which are on the *Black Enterprise* Auto Dealer 60 list (60 largest dealers based on gross sales): **Barnett Auto Group** (#23); **Gulfgate Dodge Chrysler Jeep** (#37). Criteria: company must be operational in previous calendar year and be at least 51% black-owned. *Black Enterprise, B.E. 100s, 2011*

Houston is home to one company which is on the *Black Enterprise* Private Equity 15 list (15 largest private equity firms based on capital under management): **Capital Point Partners** (#13). Criteria: company must be operational in previous calendar year and be at least 51% black-owned. *Black Enterprise, B.E. 100s, 2011*

Houston is home to one company which is on the *Black Enterprise* Asset Manager 15 list (15 largest asset management firms based on assets under management): **Smith, Graham & Co. Investment Advisors** (#7). Criteria: company must have been operational in previous calendar year and be at least 51% black-owned. *Black Enterprise, B.E. 100s, 2011*

Houston is home to 16 companies which are on the *Hispanic Business* 500 list (500 largest U.S. Hispanic-owned companies based on 2010 revenue): **G&A Partners** (#15); **Petro Amigos Supply** (#22); **The Plaza Group** (#31); **MEI Technologies** (#40); **Reytec Construction Resources** (#166); **Sweetlake Chemicals Ltd.** (#172); **Tejas Office Products** (#181); **Lopez Negrete Communications** (#186); **Today's Business Solutions** (#250); **MCA Communications** (#255); **Traf-Tex** (#309); **Milam & Co. Painting** (#358); **Nino Corp. Lodging** (#400); **Aviles Engineering Corp.** (#419); **Tube America** (#431); **Aztec Communications Ltd.** (#476). Companies included must show at least 51 percent ownership by Hispanic U.S. citizens, and must maintain headquarters in one of the 50 states or Washington, D.C. *Hispanic Business, "Hispanic Business 500," June 2011*

Houston is home to five companies which are on the *Hispanic Business* Fastest-Growing 100 list (greatest sales growth from 2006 to 2010): **Today's Business Solutions** (#38); **G&A Partners** (#50); **Tejas Office Products** (#80); **MEI Technologies** (#85); **Traf-Tex** (#98). Companies included must show at least 51 percent ownership by Hispanic U.S. citizens, and must maintain headquarters in one of the 50 states or Washington, D.C. In addition, companies must have minimum revenues of $200,000 for calendar year 2005. *Hispanic Business, July/August 2011*

Minority- and Women-Owned Businesses

Group	All Firms		Firms with Paid Employees			
	Firms	Sales ($000)	Firms	Sales ($000)	Employees	Payroll ($000)
Asian	n/a	n/a	n/a	n/a	n/a	n/a
Black	n/a	n/a	n/a	n/a	n/a	n/a
Hispanic	n/a	n/a	n/a	n/a	n/a	n/a
Women	n/a	n/a	n/a	n/a	n/a	n/a
All Firms						

Note: Figures cover firms located in the city; minority- and women-owned business are defined as firms in which the corresponding group own 51% or more of the stock or equity of the company; n/a not available
Source: U.S. Census Bureau, 2007 Economic Census, Survey of Business Owners

HOTELS

Hotels/Motels

Area	5 Star		4 Star		3 Star		2 Star		1 Star		Not Rated	
	Num.	Pct.[3]	Num.	Pct.[3]	Num.	Pct.[3]	Num.	Pct.[3]	Num.	Pct.[3]	Num.	Pct.[3]
City[1]	3	0.6	21	4.1	127	24.8	295	57.5	7	1.4	60	11.7
Total[2]	133	0.9	940	6.5	4,569	31.8	7,033	48.9	351	2.4	1,343	9.3

Note: (1) Figures cover Houston and vicinity; (2) Figures cover all 100 cities in this book; (3) Percentage of hotels which have a given star rating; Star ratings are determined by expedia.com and offer an indication of the general quality of a particular hotel.
Source: expedia.com, April 25, 2012

The Houston-Sugar Land-Baytown, TX metro area is home to three of the best hotels in the U.S. according to *Travel & Leisure*: **St. Regis, Houston** (#126); **Hotel ZaZa, Houston** (#153); **Omni Houston Hotel** (#188). Criteria: service; location; rooms; food; and value. *Travel & Leisure, "T+L 500, The World's Best Hotels 2012"*

The Houston-Sugar Land-Baytown, TX metro area is home to two of the best hotels in the U.S. according to *Condé Nast Traveler*: **Hotel Sorella** (#12); **Inn at the Ballpark** (#80). The selections are based on over 25,000 responses to the magazine's annual Readers' Choice Survey. *Condé Nast Traveler, "2011 Readers' Choice Awards"*

EVENT SITES

Major Stadiums, Arenas, and Auditoriums

Name	Max. Capacity
Berry Center	11,000
Hobby Center for the Performing Arts	3,150
Houston Livestock Show & Rodeo Inc.	74,000
John O'Quinn Field at Corbin J. Robertson Stadium	32,000
Majestic Theatre	2,311
Minute Maid Park	40,950
Reliant Arena	5,800
Reliant Astrodome	67,925
Reliant Stadium	72,000
Rice Stadium	70,000
Toyota Center	19,300

Source: Original research

Convention Centers

Name	Overall Space (sq. ft.)	Exhibit Space (sq. ft.)	Meeting Space (sq. ft.)	Meeting Rooms
George R. Brown Convention Center	1,200,000	185,000	862,000	100

Source: Original research

Living Environment

COST OF LIVING

Cost of Living Index

Composite Index	Groceries	Housing	Utilities	Trans-portation	Health Care	Misc. Goods/ Services
89.9	80.8	83.3	89.3	95.3	98.1	96.8

Note: U.S. = 100; Figures cover the Houston TX urban area.
Source: The Council for Community and Economic Research, ACCRA Cost of Living Index, 2011

Grocery Prices

Area[1]	T-Bone Steak ($/pound)	Frying Chicken ($/pound)	Whole Milk ($/half gal.)	Eggs ($/dozen)	Orange Juice ($/64 oz.)	Coffee ($/11.5 oz.)
City[2]	7.45	0.94	2.02	1.43	2.68	4.04
Avg.	9.25	1.18	2.22	1.66	3.19	4.40
Min.	6.70	0.88	1.31	0.95	2.46	2.94
Max.	14.30	2.16	3.50	3.18	4.75	6.83

*Note: (1) Values for the local area are compared with the average, minimum and maximum values for all 335 areas in the Cost of Living Index; (2) Figures cover the Houston TX urban area; **T-Bone Steak** (price per pound); **Frying Chicken** (price per pound, whole fryer); **Whole Milk** (half gallon carton); **Eggs** (price per dozen, Grade A, large); **Orange Juice** (64 oz. Tropicana or Florida Natural); **Coffee** (11.5 oz. can, vacuum-packed, Maxwell House, Hills Bros, or Folgers).*
Source: The Council for Community and Economic Research, ACCRA Cost of Living Index, 2011

Housing and Utility Costs

Area[1]	New Home Price ($)	Apartment Rent ($/month)	All Electric ($/month)	Part Electric ($/month)	Other Energy ($/month)	Telephone ($/month)
City[2]	224,736	892	-	88.47	42.02	28.69
Avg.	285,990	839	163.23	89.00	77.52	26.92
Min.	188,005	460	125.58	45.39	33.89	17.98
Max.	1,197,028	3,244	339.16	181.97	348.69	40.01

*Note: (1) Values for the local area are compared with the average, minimum and maximum values for all 335 areas in the Cost of Living Index; (2) Figures cover the Houston TX urban area; **New Home Price** (2,400 sf living area, 8,000 sf lot, in urban area with full utilities); **Apartment Rent** (950 sf 2 bedroom/1.5 or 2 bath, unfurnished, excluding all utilities except water); **All Electric** (average monthly cost for an all-electric home); **Part Electric** (average monthly cost for a part-electric home); **Other Energy** (average monthly cost for natural gas, fuel oil, coal, wood, and any other forms of energy except electricity); **Telephone** (price includes basic monthly rate for a private residential line plus additional local usage charges incurred by a family of four).*
Source: The Council for Community and Economic Research, ACCRA Cost of Living Index, 2011

Health Care, Transportation, and Other Costs

Area[1]	Doctor ($/visit)	Dentist ($/visit)	Optometrist ($/visit)	Gasoline ($/gallon)	Beauty Salon ($/visit)	Men's Shirt ($)
City[2]	92.50	79.30	88.50	3.30	41.27	20.39
Avg.	93.88	81.72	90.54	3.48	32.65	25.06
Min.	60.00	55.33	53.66	3.18	19.78	13.44
Max.	154.98	145.97	183.72	4.31	63.21	46.00

*Note: (1) Values for the local area are compared with the average, minimum and maximum values for all 335 areas in the Cost of Living Index; (2) Figures cover the Houston TX urban area; **Doctor** (general practitioners routine exam of an established patient); **Dentist** (adult teeth cleaning and periodic oral examination); **Optometrist** (full vision eye exam for established adult patient); **Gasoline** (one gallon regular unleaded, national brand, including all taxes, cash price at self-service pump if available); **Beauty Salon** (woman's shampoo, trim, and blow-dry); **Men's Shirt** (cotton/polyester dress shirt, pinpoint weave, long sleeves).*
Source: The Council for Community and Economic Research, ACCRA Cost of Living Index, 2011

HOUSING

House Price Index (HPI)

Area	National Ranking[2]	Quarterly Change (%)	One-Year Change (%)	Five-Year Change (%)
MSA[1]	53	0.67	-0.67	7.03
U.S.[3]	-	-0.10	-2.43	-19.16

Note: The HPI is a weighted repeat sales index. It measures average price changes in repeat sales or refinancings on the same properties. This information is obtained by reviewing repeat mortgage transactions on single-family properties whose mortgages have been purchased or securitized by Fannie Mae or Freddie Mac in January 1975; (1) Metropolitan/Micropolitan Statistical Area—see Appendix B for areas included; (2) Rankings are based on annual percentage change for all metro areas containing at least 15,000 transactions over the last 10 years and ranges from 1 to 306; (3) figures based on a weighted average of Census Division estimates using a purchase only index; all figures are for the period ending December 31, 2011
Source: Federal Housing Finance Agency, House Price Index, February 23, 2012

House Price Valuations

Area	Q4 2005 Price ($000)	Q4 2005 Over-valuation	Q4 2006 Price ($000)	Q4 2006 Over-valuation	Q4 2007 Price ($000)	Q4 2007 Over-valuation	Q4 2008 Price ($000)	Q4 2008 Over-valuation	Q4 2009 Price ($000)	Q4 2009 Over-valuation
MSA[1]	110.1	-20.4	116.8	-23.4	122.0	-25.0	122.7	-26.3	127.4	-22.7

Note: Figures show the percentage of over- or under-valuation of single family homes relative to statistically normal house values (e.g. a value of 23.6 indicates that house values are 23.6% overvalued). Statistically normal house values are based on house prices, interest rates, household incomes, population densities, and any historical premiums or discounts metropolitan areas have exhibited over time; (1) Figures cover the Houston-Sugar Land-Baytown, TX - see Appendix B for areas included
Source: Global Insight/PNC Financial Services Group, House Prices in America: 4th Quarter 2009 Update

Median Single-Family Home Prices

Area	2009	2010	2011p	Percent Change 2010 to 2011
MSA[1]	153.1	155.0	155.7	0.5
U.S. Average	172.1	173.1	166.2	-4.0

Note: Figures are median sales prices of existing single-family homes in thousands of dollars; (p) preliminary; n/a not available; (1) Metropolitan Statistical Area—see Appendix B for areas included
Source: National Association of Realtors, Median Sales Price of Existing Single-Family Homes for Metropolitan Areas, 4th Quarter 2011

Affordability Index of Existing Single-Family Homes

Area	2009	2010	2011p	Percent Change 2010 to 2011
MSA[1]	145.8	151.4	160.2	5.8

Note: The housing affordability index measures whether or not a typical family could qualify for a mortgage loan on a typical home. The higher the index, the greater the household purchasing power. An index of 100 is defined as the point where a median-income household has exactly enough income to qualify for the purchase of a median-priced existing single-family home, assuming a 20 percent downpayment and 25 percent of gross income devoted to mortgage principal and interest payments; (p) preliminary; n/a not available; (1) Metropolitan Statistical Area—see Appendix B for areas included
Source: National Association of Realtors, Affordability Index of Existing Single-Family Homes, 2011

Median Apartment Condo-Coop Home Prices

Area	2009	2010	2011p	Percent Change 2010 to 2011
MSA[1]	131.0	125.7	123.5	-1.8
U.S. Average	175.6	171.7	165.1	-3.8

Note: Figures are median sales prices of existing apartment condo-coop homes in thousands of dollars; (p) preliminary; n/a not available; (1) Metropolitan Statistical Area—see Appendix B for areas included
Source: National Association of Realtors, Median Sales Price of Existing Apartment Condo-Coop Homes for Metropolitan Areas, 4th Quarter 2011

Year Housing Structure Built

Area	2005 or Later	2000 -2004	1990 -1999	1980 -1989	1970 -1979	1960 -1969	1950 -1959	Before 1950	Median Year
City	5.5	8.0	9.0	14.3	26.7	15.4	11.6	9.4	1975
MSA[1]	9.8	13.4	14.6	17.2	21.7	10.0	7.4	5.9	1983
U.S.	5.0	8.6	14.0	14.1	16.3	11.3	11.2	19.6	1975

Note: Figures are percentages except for Median Year; (1) Figures cover the Houston-Sugar Land-Baytown, TX Metropolitan Statistical Area—see Appendix B for areas included
Source: U.S. Census Bureau, 2008-2010 American Community Survey 3-Year Estimates

HEALTH

Health Risk Data

Category	MSA[1] (%)	U.S. (%)
Adults who have been told they have high blood pressure[2]	26.5	28.7
Adults who have been told they have high blood cholesterol[2]	40.6	37.5
Adults who have been told they have diabetes[3]	8.5	8.7
Adults who have been told they have arthritis[2]	18.9	26.0
Adults who have been told they currently have asthma	4.9	9.1
Adults who are current smokers	16.2	17.3
Adults who are heavy drinkers[4]	6.1	5.0
Adults who are binge drinkers[5]	15.4	15.1
Adults who are overweight (BMI 25.0 - 29.9)	34.0	36.2
Adults who are obese (BMI 30.0 - 99.8)	29.1	27.5
Adults who participated in any physical activities in the past month	76.4	76.1
Adults 50+ who have ever had a sigmoidoscopy or colonoscopy	62.7	65.2
Women aged 40+ who have had a mammogram within the past two years	70.5	75.2
Men aged 40+ who have had a PSA test within the past two years	52.5	53.2
Adults aged 65+ who have had flu shot within the past year	64.2	67.5
Adults aged 18–64 who have any kind of health care coverage	72.7	82.2

Note: Data as of 2010 unless otherwise noted; (1) Figures cover the Houston-Sugar Land-Baytown, TX Metropolitan Statistical Area—see Appendix B for areas included; (2) Data as of 2009; (3) Figures do not include pregnancy-related, borderline, or pre-diabetes; (4) Heavy drinkers are classified as males having more than two drinks per day or females having more than one drink per day; (5) Binge drinkers are classified as males having five or more drinks on one occasion or females having four or more drinks on one occasion
Source: Centers for Disease Control and Prevention, Behaviorial Risk Factor Surveillance System, SMART: Selected Metropolitan/Micropolitan Area Risk Trends, 2009, 2010

Mortality Rates for the Top 10 Causes of Death in the U.S.

ICD-10[a] Sub-Chapter	ICD-10[a] Code	Age-Adjusted Mortality Rate[1] per 100,000 population	
		County[2]	U.S.
Malignant neoplasms	C00-C97	165.5	175.6
Ischaemic heart diseases	I20-I25	114.1	121.6
Other forms of heart disease	I30-I51	52.1	48.6
Chronic lower respiratory diseases	J40-J47	33.3	42.3
Cerebrovascular diseases	I60-I69	48.0	40.6
Organic, including symptomatic, mental disorders	F01-F09	32.9	26.7
Other degenerative diseases of the nervous system	G30-G31	21.0	24.7
Other external causes of accidental injury	W00-X59	26.2	24.4
Diabetes mellitus	E10-E14	22.5	21.7
Hypertensive diseases	I10-I15	19.4	18.2

Note: (a) ICD-10 = International Classification of Diseases 10th Revision; (1) Mortality rates are a three year average covering 2007-2009; (2) Figures cover Harris County
Source: Centers for Disease Control and Prevention, National Center for Health Statistics. Underlying Cause of Death 1999-2009 on CDC WONDER Online Database, released 2012. Data for year 2009 are compiled from the Multiple Cause of Death File 2009, Series 20 No. 2O, 2012, Data for year 2008 are compiled from the Multiple Cause of Death File 2008, Series 20 No. 2N, 2011, Data for year 2007 are compiled from Multiple Cause of Death File 2007, Series 20 No. 2M, 2010.

Mortality Rates for Selected Causes of Death

ICD-10[a] Sub-Chapter	ICD-10[a] Code	Age-Adjusted Mortality Rate[1] per 100,000 population	
		County[2]	U.S.
Assault	X85-Y09	10.0	5.7
Human immunodeficiency virus (HIV) disease	B20-B24	6.9	3.3
Influenza and pneumonia	J09-J18	15.3	16.4
Intentional self-harm	X60-X84	10.7	11.5
Malnutrition	E40-E46	1.5	0.8
Obesity and other hyperalimentation	E65-E68	1.4	1.6
Transport accidents	V01-V99	13.2	13.7
Viral hepatitis	B15-B19	2.3	2.2

Note: (a) ICD-10 = International Classification of Diseases 10th Revision; (1) Mortality rates are a three year average covering 2007-2009; (2) Figures cover Harris County
Source: Centers for Disease Control and Prevention, National Center for Health Statistics. Underlying Cause of Death 1999-2009 on CDC WONDER Online Database, released 2012. Data for year 2009 are compiled from the Multiple Cause of Death File 2009, Series 20 No. 2O, 2012, Data for year 2008 are compiled from the Multiple Cause of Death File 2008, Series 20 No. 2N, 2011, Data for year 2007 are compiled from Multiple Cause of Death File 2007, Series 20 No. 2M, 2010.

Distribution of Physicians and Dentists

Area[1]	Dentists[2]	D.O.[3]	M.D.[4]				
			Total	Family/ General Practice	Pediatrics	Medical Specialties	Surgical Specialties
Local (number)	1,620	317	7,232	772	573	2,708	1,700
Local (rate[5])	4.1	0.8	18.2	1.9	1.4	6.8	4.3
U.S. (rate[5])	4.5	1.9	18.3	2.5	1.4	6.8	4.1

Note: Data as of 2008 unless noted; (1) Local data covers Harris County; (2) Data as of 2007; (3) Doctor of Osteopathic Medicine; (4) Includes active, non-federal, patient-care, office-based Doctors of Medicine; (5) rate per 10,000 population
Source: Area Resource File (ARF). 2009-2010 Release. U.S. Department of Health and Human Services, Health Resources and Services Administration, Bureau of Health Professions, Rockville, MD, August 2010

Best Hospitals

According to *U.S. News,* the Houston-Sugar Land-Baytown, TX is home to nine of the best hospitals in the U.S.: **Cullen Eye Institute Baylor-Methodist Hospital** (1 specialty); **Memorial Hermann-Texas Medical Center** (2 specialties); **Menninger Clinic** (1 specialty); **Methodist Hospital** (10 specialties); **St. Luke's Episcopal Hospital** (5 specialties); **TIRR Memorial Hermann** (1 specialty); **Texas Heart Institute at St. Luke's Episcopal Hospital** (1 specialty); **Texas Orthopedic Hospital** (1 specialty); **University of Texas M.D. Anderson Cancer Center** (6 specialties). The hospitals listed were highly ranked in at least one adult specialty. *U.S. News Online, "America's Best Hospitals 2011-12"*

According to *U.S. News,* the Houston-Sugar Land-Baytown, TX is home to three of the best children's hospitals in the U.S.: **Children's Cancer Hospital-University of Texas M.D. Anderson Cancer Center** (1 specialty); **Children's Memorial Hermann Hospital** (1 specialty); **Texas Children's Hospital** (10 specialties). The hospitals listed were highly ranked in at least one pediatric specialty. *U.S. News Online, "America's Best Children's Hospitals 2011-12"*

EDUCATION

Public School District Statistics

District Name	Schls	Pupils	Pupil/ Teacher Ratio	Minority Pupils[1] (%)	Free Lunch Eligible[2] (%)	IEP[3] (%)
Aldine ISD	73	62,792	14.8	97.0	74.9	7.2
Alief ISD	46	45,553	14.8	96.2	68.5	7.7
Cypress-Fairbanks ISD	80	104,231	15.5	64.5	34.6	7.3
Galena Park ISD	24	21,536	13.7	94.0	66.8	8.6
Houston ISD	297	202,773	16.9	92.1	50.7	8.1
Kipp Inc Charter	12	3,864	16.6	99.1	82.0	3.8
North Forest ISD	11	7,665	15.3	99.3	99.6	8.2
Sheldon ISD	11	6,570	14.3	86.0	66.7	6.0
Southwest School	6	3,598	31.7	61.8	47.9	7.9
Spring Branch ISD	49	32,502	14.1	69.6	51.2	8.8
Spring ISD	37	35,350	15.0	84.3	58.2	8.6
Yes Preparatory Public Schools	7	3,374	15.2	98.9	57.2	4.6

Note: Table includes school districts with 2,000 or more students; (1) Percentage of students that are not non-Hispanic white; (2) Percentage of students that are eligible for the free lunch program; (3) Percentage of students that have an Individualized Education Program.
Source: U.S. Department of Education, National Center for Education Statistics, Common Core of Data, Local Education Agency (School District) Universe Survey: School Year 2009-2010; U.S. Department of Education, National Center for Education Statistics, Common Core of Data, Public Elementary/Secondary School Universe Survey: School Year 2009-2010

Top Public High Schools

High School Name	Rank[1]	Score[1]	Grad. Rate[2] (%)	College[3] (%)	AP/IB/ AICE[4] (%)	SAT/ ACT[5] (%)
Carnegie Vanguard	11	1.662	100	96	8.9	1801
Challenge Early College	327	0.325	99	95	1.6	1490
Clear Lake	267	0.414	94	94	2.4	1686
Michael E DeBakey High School for Health Professions	30	1.217	99	100	5.1	1829
Stratford	168	0.560	98	98	2.6	1647
YES Prep Public Schools - North Central	152	0.580	98	100	3.5	1541

Note: (1) Public schools are ranked from 1 to 500 based on the following self-reported statistics (with their corresponding weight in the final score). Schools that had fewer than 10 graduates, as well as those that were newly founded and did not have a graduating senior class in 2010 were excluded; (2) Four-year, on-time graduation rate (25%); (3) Percent of 2010 graduates who enrolled immediately in college (25%); (4) AP/IB/AICE tests per graduate (25%); (5) Average SAT and/or ACT score (10%); Average AP/IB/AICE exam score (10%); AP/IB/AICE courses offered per graduate (5%); (6) School is unranked, but has been identified by Newsweek as one of the nation's most elite public high schools.
Source: Newsweek Online, "Top High Schools 2011"

Highest Level of Education

Area	Less than H.S.	H.S. Diploma	Some College, No Deg.	Associate Degree	Bachelors Degree	Masters Degree	Profess. School Degree	Doctorate Degree
City	25.9	22.3	19.2	4.3	17.5	6.8	2.4	1.5
MSA[1]	19.6	23.9	22.3	5.9	18.7	6.6	1.8	1.2
U.S.	14.7	28.4	21.3	7.6	17.6	7.2	1.9	1.2

Note: Figures cover persons age 25 and over; (1) Figures cover the Houston-Sugar Land-Baytown, TX Metropolitan Statistical Area—see Appendix B for areas included
Source: U.S. Census Bureau, 2008-2010 American Community Survey 3-Year Estimates

Educational Attainment by Race

Area	High School Graduate or Higher (%)					Bachelor's Degree or Higher (%)				
	Total	White	Black	Asian	Hisp.[2]	Total	White	Black	Asian	Hisp.[2]
City	74.1	74.2	82.6	84.1	48.7	28.2	33.5	17.2	53.4	9.6
MSA[1]	80.4	81.6	86.6	85.6	55.2	28.4	30.0	21.7	51.6	10.7
U.S.	85.3	87.5	81.4	85.5	61.6	28.0	29.3	17.8	50.2	13.0

Note: Figures shown cover persons 25 years old and over; (1) Figures cover the Houston-Sugar Land-Baytown, TX Metropolitan Statistical Area—see Appendix B for areas included; (2) People of Hispanic origin can be of any race
Source: U.S. Census Bureau, 2008-2010 American Community Survey 3-Year Estimates

School Enrollment by Grade and Control

Area	Preschool (%)		Kindergarten (%)		Grades 1 - 4 (%)		Grades 5 - 8 (%)		Grades 9 - 12 (%)	
	Public	Private	Public	Private	Public	Private	Public	Private	Public	Private
City	68.7	31.3	92.3	7.7	93.7	6.3	93.5	6.5	94.3	5.7
MSA[1]	57.5	42.5	90.6	9.4	93.8	6.2	93.8	6.2	94.1	5.9
U.S.	55.4	44.6	87.1	12.9	89.4	10.6	89.5	10.5	90.4	9.6

Note: Figures shown cover persons 3 years old and over; (1) Figures cover the Houston-Sugar Land-Baytown, TX Metropolitan Statistical Area—see Appendix B for areas included
Source: U.S. Census Bureau, 2008-2010 American Community Survey 3-Year Estimates

Average Salaries of Public School Classroom Teachers

Area	2010-11		2011-12		Percent Change 2010-11 to 2011-12	Percent Change 2001-02 to 2011-12
	Dollars	Rank[1]	Dollars	Rank[1]		
Texas	48,638	31	49,017	31	0.78	24.90
U.S. Average	55,623	-	56,643	-	1.83	26.8

Note: (1) State rank ranges from 1 to 51 where 1 indicates highest salary.
Source: National Education Association, Rankings & Estimates: Rankings of the States 2011 and Estimates of School Statistics 2012, December 2011

Higher Education

Four-Year Colleges			Two-Year Colleges			Medical Schools[1]	Law Schools[2]	Voc/ Tech[3]
Public	Private Non-profit	Private For-profit	Public	Private Non-profit	Private For-profit			
6	8	9	1	3	12	2	3	34

Note: Figures cover institutions located within the city limits and include main campuses only; (1) includes schools accredited by the Liaison Committee on Medical Education and the American Osteopathic Association's Commission on Osteopathic College Accreditation; (2) includes American Bar Association-accredited law schools; (3) includes all schools with programs that are less than 2 years.
Source: National Center for Education Statistics, Integrated Postsecondary Education System (IPEDS) Peer Analysis System, 2011-12; Association of American Medical Colleges, Member List, April 23, 2012; American Osteopathic Association, Member List, April 23, 2012; Law School Admission Council, Official Guide to ABA-Approved Law Schools Online, April 23, 2012

According to *U.S. News & World Report,* the Houston-Sugar Land-Baytown, TX is home to one of the best national universities in the U.S.: **Rice University** (#17). The indicators used to capture academic quality fall into a number of categories: assessment by administrators at peer institutions; retention of students; faculty resources; student selectivity; financial resources; alumni giving; high school counselor ratings of colleges; and graduation rate.*U.S. News & World Report, "America's Best Colleges 2012"*

According to *Forbes,* the Houston-Sugar Land-Baytown, TX is home to one of the best business schools in the U.S.: **Rice (Jones)** (#45). The rankings are based on the return on investment that graduates of the Class of 2006 received (median salary five years after graduation). *Forbes, "Best Business Schools," August 3, 2011*

PRESIDENTIAL ELECTION

2008 Presidential Election Results

Area	Obama	McCain	Nader	Other
Harris County	50.4	48.8	0.1	0.7
U.S.	52.9	45.6	0.6	0.9

Note: Results are percentages and may not add to 100% due to rounding
Source: Dave Leip's Atlas of U.S. Presidential Elections, www.uselectionatlas.org

EMPLOYERS

Major Employers

Company Name	Industry
Christus Health Gulf Coast	Management consulting services
Conoco Phillips	Petroleum refining
Continental Airlines	Air trans scheduled
Dibellos Dynamic Orthotics and Prosthetics	Surgical appliances and supplies
El Paso E&P Company	Petroleum refining
F Charles Brunicardi MD	Accounting assoc
Grey Wolf Inc	Drilling oil and gas wells
Kellogg Brown &Root	Industrial plant construction
Mustang Engineers and Constructors	Construction management consultant
Philip Industrial Services	Environmental consultant
Philips Petroleum Company	Oil and gas exploration services
Quaker State Corp	Lubricating oils and greases
St Lukes Episcopal Health System	General medical/surgical hospitals
St Lukes Episcopal Hospital	General medical/surgical hospitals
Texas Childrens Hospital	Specialty hosp
The Methodist Hospital	General medical/surgical hospitals
Tracer Industries	Plumbing
Univ of Texas Medical Branch at Galveston	Accident and health ins
University of Houston System	University
University of Texas System	General medical/surgical hospitals
US Dept of Veteran Affairs	Administration of veterans affairs
Veterans Health Administration	Administration of veterans affairs

Note: Companies shown are located within the Houston-Sugar Land-Baytown, TX metropolitan area.
Source: Hoovers.com, data extracted April 25 2012

Best Companies to Work For

Camden Property Trust; EOG Resources; Men's Wearhouse; Methodist Hospital, headquartered in Houston, are among "The 100 Best Companies to Work For." To pick the 100 Best Companies to Work For, *Fortune* partnered with the Great Place to Work Institute. Two hundred eighty firms participated in this year's survey. Two-thirds of a company's score is based on the results of the Institute's Trust Index survey, which is sent to a random sample of employees from each company. The questions related to attitudes about management's credibility, job satisfaction, and camaraderie. The other third of the scoring is based on the company's responses to the Institute's Culture Audit, which includes detailed questions about pay and benefit programs, and a series of open-ended questions about hiring practices, internal communication, training, recognition programs, and diversity efforts. Any company that is at least five years old with more than 1,000 U.S. employees is eligible. *Fortune, "The 100 Best Companies to Work For," February 6, 2012*

The University of Texas MD Anderson Cancer Center, headquartered in Houston, is among the "50 Best Employers for Workers Over 50." Criteria: recruiting practices; opportunities for training, education, and career development; workplace accommodations; alternative work options, such as flexible scheduling, job sharing, and phased retirement; employee health and pension benefits; and retiree benefits. Employers with at least 50 employees based in the U.S. are eligible, including for-profit companies, not-for-profit organizations, and government employers. *AARP, "2011 AARP Best Employers for Workers Over 50"*

Baker Hughes; Transocean Ltd, headquartered in Houston, are among the "100 Best Places to Work in IT." To qualify, companies, both public and private, had to have a minimum of 50 IT employees and were selected based on average salary and bonus increases, the percentage of IT staffers promoted, IT staff turnover rates, training and development programs, and the percentage of women and minorities in IT staff and management positions. In addition, *Computerworld* looked at retention efforts, programs for recognizing and rewarding outstanding performances, and benefits such as flextime, elder care and child care, and reimbursement for college tuition and the cost of pursuing technology certifications. *Computerworld, "100 Best Places to Work in IT 2011"*

PUBLIC SAFETY

Crime Rate

Area	All Crimes	Violent Crimes				Property Crimes		
		Murder	Forcible Rape	Robbery	Aggrav. Assault	Burglary	Larceny -Theft	Motor Vehicle Theft
City	6,042.2	11.8	31.2	414.3	528.8	1,224.3	3,269.9	561.9
Suburbs[1]	3,653.1	4.5	22.5	127.8	240.5	821.0	2,185.5	251.3
Metro[2]	4,564.6	7.3	25.8	237.1	350.5	974.8	2,599.3	369.8
U.S.	3,345.5	4.8	27.5	119.1	252.3	699.6	2,003.5	238.8

Note: Figures are crimes per 100,000 population; (1) All areas within the metro area that are located outside the city limits; (2) Metropolitan Statistical Area—see Appendix B for areas included
Source: FBI Uniform Crime Reports, 2010

Hate Crimes

Area	Number of Quarters Reported	Bias Motivation				
		Race	Religion	Sexual Orientation	Ethnicity	Disability
City	4	5	0	6	2	0

Source: Federal Bureau of Investigation, Hate Crime Statistics 2010

Identity Theft Consumer Complaints

Area	Complaints	Complaints per 100,000 Population	Rank[2]
MSA[1]	6,294	111.8	58
U.S.	279,156	90.4	-

Note: (1) Metropolitan Statistical Area—see Appendix B for areas included; (2) Rank ranges from 1 to 384 where 1 indicates greatest number of identity theft complaints per 100,000 population
Source: Federal Trade Commission, Consumer Sentinel Network Data Book for January–December 2011

Fraud and Other Consumer Complaints

Area	Complaints	Complaints per 100,000 Population	Rank[2]
MSA[1]	23,534	418.2	266
U.S.	1,533,924	496.8	-

Note: (1) Metropolitan Statistical Area—see Appendix B for areas included; (2) Rank ranges from 1 to 384 where 1 indicates greatest number of fraud and other complaints per 100,000 population
Source: Federal Trade Commission, Consumer Sentinel Network Data Book for January–December 2011

RECREATION

Culture

Dance[1]	Theatre[1]	Instrumental Music[1]	Vocal Music[1]	Series/ Festivals	Museums	Zoos and Aquariums[2]
7	12	6	4	12	22	2

Note: (1) Number of professional performing groups; (2) AZA-accredited
Source: The Grey House Performing Arts Directory, 2011-2012; Official Museum Directory, 2011; American Association of Museums, AAM Member Museums, April 2012; Association of Zoos & Aquariums, AZA Member Zoos & Aquariums, April 2012

Professional Sports Teams

Team Name	League
Houston Astros	Major League Baseball (MLB)
Houston Dynamo	Major League Soccer (MLS)
Houston Rockets	National Basketball Association (NBA)
Houston Texans	National Football League (NFL)

Note: Includes teams located in the Houston metro area.
Source: Original research

CLIMATE

Average and Extreme Temperatures

Temperature	Jan	Feb	Mar	Apr	May	Jun	Jul	Aug	Sep	Oct	Nov	Dec	Yr.
Extreme High (°F)	84	91	91	95	97	103	104	107	102	94	89	83	107
Average High (°F)	61	65	73	79	85	91	93	93	89	81	72	65	79
Average Temp. (°F)	51	54	62	69	75	81	83	83	79	70	61	54	69
Average Low (°F)	41	43	51	58	65	71	73	73	68	58	50	43	58
Extreme Low (°F)	12	20	22	31	44	52	62	62	48	32	19	7	7

Note: Figures cover the years 1969-1990
Source: National Climatic Data Center, International Station Meteorological Climate Summary, 9/96

Average Precipitation/Snowfall/Humidity

Precip./Humidity	Jan	Feb	Mar	Apr	May	Jun	Jul	Aug	Sep	Oct	Nov	Dec	Yr.
Avg. Precip. (in.)	3.3	2.7	3.3	3.3	5.6	4.9	3.7	3.7	4.8	4.7	3.7	3.3	46.9
Avg. Snowfall (in.)	Tr	Tr	0	0	0	0	0	0	0	0	Tr	Tr	Tr
Avg. Rel. Hum. 6am (%)	85	86	87	89	91	92	93	93	93	91	89	86	90
Avg. Rel. Hum. 3pm (%)	58	55	54	54	57	56	55	55	57	53	55	57	55

Note: Figures cover the years 1969-1990; Tr = Trace amounts (<0.05 in. of rain; <0.5 in. of snow)
Source: National Climatic Data Center, International Station Meteorological Climate Summary, 9/96

Weather Conditions

Temperature			Daytime Sky			Precipitation		
32°F & below	45°F & below	90°F & above	Clear	Partly cloudy	Cloudy	0.01 inch or more precip.	0.1 inch or more snow/ice	Thunder-storms
21	87	96	83	168	114	101	1	62

Note: Figures are average number of days per year and cover the years 1969-1990
Source: National Climatic Data Center, International Station Meteorological Climate Summary, 9/96

HAZARDOUS WASTE

Superfund Sites

Houston has seven hazardous waste sites on the EPA's Superfund Final National Priorities List: **Jones Road Ground Water Plume; Many Diversified Interests, Inc.; Sol Lynn/Industrial Transformers; North Cavalcade Street; South Cavalcade Street; Geneva Industries/Fuhrmann Energy; Crystal Chemical Co.** *U.S. Environmental Protection Agency, Final National Priorities List, April 17, 2012*

AIR & WATER QUALITY

Air Quality Index

Area	Percent of Days when Air Quality was...[2]					AQI Statistics[2]	
	Good	Moderate	Unhealthy for Sensitive Groups	Unhealthy	Very Unhealthy	Maximum	Median
Area[1]	52.9	38.6	7.4	1.1	0.0	164	49

Note: Air Quality Index (AQI) is an index for reporting daily air quality. EPA calculates the AQI for five major air pollutants regulated by the Clean Air Act: ground-level ozone, particle pollution (aka particulate matter), carbon monoxide, sulfur dioxide, and nitrogen dioxide. The AQI runs from 0 to 500. The higher the AQI value, the greater the level of air pollution and the greater the health concern. There are six AQI categories: "Good" AQI is between 0 and 50. Air quality is considered satisfactory; "Moderate" AQI is between 51 and 100. Air quality is acceptable; "Unhealthy for Sensitive Groups" When AQI values are between 101 and 150, members of sensitive groups may experience health effects; "Unhealthy" When AQI values are between 151 and 200 everyone may begin to experience health effects; "Very Unhealthy" AQI values between 201 and 300 trigger a health alert; "Hazardous" AQI values over 300 trigger warnings of emergency conditions (not shown); (1) Data covers Harris County; (2) Based on 365 days with AQI data in 2011.
Source: U.S. Environmental Protection Agency, AirData Report, 2011

Air Quality Index Pollutants

Area	Percent of Days when AQI Pollutant was...[2]					
	Carbon Monoxide	Nitrogen Dioxide	Ozone	Sulfur Dioxide	Particulate Matter 2.5	Particulate Matter 10
Area[1]	0.0	10.7	32.9	5.2	44.1	7.1

Note: The Air Quality Index (AQI) is an index for reporting daily air quality. EPA calculates the AQI for five major air pollutants regulated by the Clean Air Act: ground-level ozone, particle pollution (also known as particulate matter), carbon monoxide, sulfur dioxide, and nitrogen dioxide. The AQI runs from 0 to 500. The higher the AQI value, the greater the level of air pollution and the greater the health concern; (1) Data covers Harris County; (2) Based on 365 days with AQI data in 2011.
Source: U.S. Environmental Protection Agency, AirData Report, 2011

Air Quality Index Trends

Area	Trend Sites (days)								All Sites (days)
	2003	2004	2005	2006	2007	2008	2009	2010	2010
MSA[1]	74	66	93	64	47	24	26	33	34

Note: Figures are the number of days the AQI value exceeded 100 in a given year. An AQI value greater than 100 indicates that air quality would have been in the unhealthful range on that day. Data from exceptional events are included. These counts are presented in two ways. First, the counts are based on sites having an adequate record of monitoring data during the trend period (trend sites). These counts represent the relative change in the number of days with AQI values greater than 100. In the last column, the counts are based on all sites with data in the most recent year (because it is possible for a site to have data in the most recent year but not enough data to be a trend site); (1) Data covers the Houston-Sugar Land-Baytown, TX—see Appendix B for areas included
Source: U.S. Environmental Protection Agency, Air Quality Index Information, "Number of Days with Air Quality Index Values Greater than 100 at Trend Sites, 2000-2010, and at All Sites in 2010"

Maximum Air Pollutant Concentrations: Particulate Matter, Ozone, CO and Lead

	Particulate Matter 10 (ug/m^3)	Particulate Matter 2.5 Wtd AM (ug/m^3)	Particulate Matter 2.5 24-Hr (ug/m^3)	Ozone (ppm)	Carbon Monoxide (ppm)	Lead (ug/m^3)
MSA[1] Level	82	12.3	24	0.088	2	0.01
NAAQS[2]	150	15	35	0.075	9	0.15
Met NAAQS[2]	Yes	Yes	Yes	No	Yes	Yes

Note: Data from exceptional events are not included; (1) Data covers the Houston-Sugar Land-Baytown, TX—see Appendix B for areas included; (2) National Ambient Air Quality Standards; ppm = parts per million; ug/m^3 = micrograms per cubic meter; n/a not available
Concentrations: Particulate Matter 10 (coarse particulate)—highest second maximum 24-hour concentration; Particulate Matter 2.5 Wtd AM (fine particulate)—highest weighted annual mean concentration; Particulate Matter 2.5 24-Hour (fine particulate)—highest 98th percentile 24-hour concentration; Ozone—highest fourth daily maximum 8-hour concentration; Carbon Monoxide—highest second maximum non-overlapping 8-hour concentration; Lead—maximum running 3-month average
Source: U.S. Environmental Protection Agency, CBSA Factbook 2010, Air Quality Statistics by City, 2010

Maximum Air Pollutant Concentrations: Nitrogen Dioxide and Sulfur Dioxide

	Nitrogen Dioxide AM (ppb)	Nitrogen Dioxide 1-Hr (ppb)	Sulfur Dioxide AM (ppb)	Sulfur Dioxide 1-Hr (ppb)	Sulfur Dioxide 24-Hr (ppb)
MSA[1] Level	14.941	60	2.336	45.6	13.8
NAAQS[2]	53	100	30	75	140
Met NAAQS[2]	Yes	Yes	Yes	Yes	Yes

Note: Data from exceptional events are not included; (1) Data covers the Houston-Sugar Land-Baytown, TX—see Appendix B for areas included; (2) National Ambient Air Quality Standards; ppb = parts per billion; n/a not available
Concentrations: Nitrogen Dioxide AM—highest arithmetic mean concentration; Nitrogen Dioxide 1-Hr—highest 98th percentile 1-hour daily maximum concentration; Sulfur Dioxide AM—highest annual mean concentration; Sulfur Dioxide 1-Hr—highest 99th percentile 1-hour daily maximum concentration; Sulfur Dioxide 24-Hr—highest second maximum 24-hour concentration
Source: U.S. Environmental Protection Agency, CBSA Factbook 2010, Air Quality Statistics by City, 2010

Drinking Water

Water System Name	Pop. Served	Primary Water Source Type	Violations[1]	
			Health Based	Monitoring/ Reporting
City of Houston	2,099,000	Surface	0	0

Note: (1) Based on violation data from January 1, 2011 to December 31, 2011 (includes unresolved violations from earlier years)
Source: U.S. Environmental Protection Agency, Office of Ground Water and Drinking Water, Safe Drinking Water Information System (based on data extracted April 18, 2012)

Huntsville, Alabama

Background

The seat of Madison County, Huntsville is richly evocative of the antebellum Deep South. It is also a uniquely cosmopolitan town that remains one of the South's fastest growing, with the highest per capita income in the Southeast.

Huntsville became the seat of Madison County, named for President James Madison, when that jurisdiction was created in 1808. Originally home to Cherokee and Chickasaw Indians, the Huntsville area was rich in forests and game animals. The town itself is named for John Hunt, a Virginia Revolutionary War veteran who built a cabin in 1805 on what is now the corner of Bank Street and Oak Avenue.

The fertility of the valley began to attract both smaller farmers and wealthy plantation investors. Leroy Pope, having donated land to the embryonic municipality, wished to rename it Twickenham, after a London suburb that was home to his relative, the poet Alexander Pope. However, resentment against all things British, which surged following the War of 1812, was sufficient to reestablish Huntsville under its original moniker.

Huntsville was the largest town in the Alabama Territory by 1819, the same year Alabama received statehood. The town was the site of the state's first constitutional convention and briefly served as the state capital. It quickly became a major hub for the sale and processing of corn, tobacco, and cotton, with the last crop becoming the economic mainstay. The establishment of textile mills allowed the town to benefit from both primary production and finished products. In 1852, the last leg of the Memphis and Charleston Railway was completed, establishing Huntsville as a major center in a larger regional marketplace. By the middle of the nineteenth century, the region's planters, merchants, and shippers had transformed Huntsville into one of the main commercial cities in the South.

Because many wealthy residents had remained loyal to the Union at the outset of the Civil War, the town was largely undamaged by occupying forces and, as a result, Huntsville boasts one of the largest collections of undamaged antebellum houses in the South. Walking tours of the Twickenham historic district offer the charms of the 1819 Weeden House Museum and the 1860 Huntsville Depot Museum. Restored nineteenth-century cabins and farm buildings are displayed at the mountaintop Burritt Museum and Park.

Huntsville's U.S. Space and Rocket Center, the state's largest tourist attraction, showcases space technology. It is also the home of Space Camp, providing residential and day camp eductional opportunities for children and adults designed to promote science, engineering, aviation and exploration. The Huntsville Botanical Garden, features year-long floral and aquatic gardens, and the Huntsville Museum of Art features both contemporary and classical exhibits.

The city's modern Von Braun Center hosts national and international trade shows and conventions and local sports teams; it also has a concert hall and playhouse. The city also has an outstanding symphony orchestra.

Institutions of higher learning include the University of Alabama in Huntsville (established 1950), and Oakwood College (1896), while Alabama A&M University (1875) is in nearby Normal, Alabama.

Redstone Arsenal, home to the U.S. Army Aviation and Missile Command, is the main engine that propelled Huntsville into the high-tech hub it is today, and is the United States' most crucial strategic and research site for the development and implementation of rocketry, aviation, and related programs. In 1950, German rocket scientists, most notably the famous Wernher von Braun, came to the Redstone Arsenal to develop rockets for the U.S. Army. Within the decade, the Redstone complex had developed the rocket that launched America's first satellite into space, and later, the rockets that put astronauts into space and eventually landed them on the moon.

Despite the economic downturn of the early 1990s, Huntsville has seen progress on the manufacturing front. More than forty Fortune 500 companies have operations in Huntsville. Since 2003, Toyota in Huntsville has produced that company's only V8 engines outside of Japan, and Target has two super centers in town.

Huntsville enjoys a mild, temperate climate. Only four to five weeks during the middle of winter see temperatures below freezing. While substantial winter weather and blizzards were frequent in the 1990s, Huntsville has now gone over 13 years without significant snowfall. Rainfall is fairly abundant.

Rankings

General Rankings

- The Huntsville metro area was selected one of America's "Best Cities" by *Kiplinger's Personal Finance*. Criteria: stable employment; income growth; cost of living; percentage of workforce in the creative class (scientists, engineers, educators, writers, artists, entertainers, etc.). *Kiplinger's Personal Finance, "Best Cities 2009: It's All About Jobs," July 2009*

- Huntsville appeared on RelocateAmerica's list of best places to live in America. The annual "Top 100 Places to Live" list recognizes the top communities as nominated by their residents & local businesses. RelocateAmerica's Research Group determines the list based on review of various data gathered for economic, employment, housing, education, industry, opportunity, environment and recreation along with feedback from area leaders and residents. *RelocateAmerica.com, "Top 100 Places to Live for 2011"*

- Huntsville was selected as one of the "Best Places to Live" by *Men's Journal*. Criteria: "18 towns were selected that are perfecting the art of living well—places where conservation is more important than development, bike makers and breweries and farmers thrive, and Whole Foods is considered a big-box store." *Men's Journal, "Best Place to Live 2011: Think Small, Live Big," April 2011*

Business/Finance Rankings

- The Huntsville metro area was identified as one of the 10 best cities for job growth in 2010 by *USAToday* based on data from *Moody's Economy.com*. The metro area was ranked #2. Criteria: one-year forecast change in jobs from the 4th quarter 2009 to the 4th quarter 2010. *USAToday, "Jobs May Rebound in 2010," April 7, 2010*

- Huntsville was selected as one of the "100 Best Places to Live and Launch" in the U.S. The city ranked #86. The editors at *Fortune Small Business* ranked 296 Census-designated metro areas by business friendliness (Launching Score, % New Businesses) and lifestyle offerings (Living Score). Then they picked the town within each of the top 100 metro areas that best blends business and pleasure. *Fortune Small Business, "100 Best Places to Live and Launch 2008," April 2008*

- *American City Business Journals* ranked America's 261 largest cities in terms of their resident's wealth. Huntsville ranked #129. Criteria: per capita income; median household income; percentage of households with annual incomes of $200,000 or more; median home value. *American City Business Journals, "Where the Money Is: America's Wealth Centers," August 18, 2008*

- The Huntsville metro area appeared on the Milken Institute "2011 Best Performing Metros" list. Rank: #8 out of 200 large metro areas. Criteria: job growth; wage and salary growth; high-tech output growth. *Milken Institute, "2011 Best Performing Metros"*

- The Huntsville metro area was selected as one of the best cities for entrepreneurs in America by *Inc. Magazine*. Criteria: job-growth data for 335 metro areas was analyzed for: recent growth trend; mid-term growth; long-term trend; current year growth. The Huntsville metro area ranked #5 among mid-sized metro areas and #32 overall. *Inc. Magazine, "The Best Cities for Doing Business," July 2008*

- *Forbes* ranked the 200 most populous metro areas in the U.S. in terms of the "Best Places for Business and Careers." The Huntsville metro area was ranked #17. Criteria: costs (business and living); job growth (past and projected); income growth; educational attainment; projected economic growth; crime; cultural and recreational opportunities; net migration patterns; number of highly ranked colleges. *Forbes, "Best Places for Business and Careers," June 2011*

Children/Family Rankings

- The Huntsville metro area was selected as one of the "Best Cities for Relocating Families" by Worldwide ERC and Primacy Relocation. The 2008 study looked at nearly 50 factors important to relocating families including: recent job growth; nearby top-ranked colleges; in-state tuition for four-year public colleges; population growth since 2000; pediatricians per 100,000 population; and a Green Living index. *Worldwide ERC and Primacy Relocation, "2008 Best Cities for Relocating Families"*

- Huntsville was chosen as one of America's "100 Best Communities for Young People." The winners were selected based upon detailed information provided about each community's efforts to fulfill five essential promises critical to the well-being of young people: caring adults who are actively involved in their lives; safe places in which to learn and grow; a healthy start toward adulthood; an effective education that builds marketable skills; and opportunities to help others. *America's Promise Alliance, "100 Best Communities for Young People, 2010"*

Education Rankings

- Huntsville was selected as one of "America's Geekiest Cities" by *Forbes.com*. The city ranked #4 of 20. Criteria: percentage of workers with jobs in science, technology, engineering and mathematics. *Forbes.com, "America's Geekiest Cities," August 5, 2011*

- Huntsville was identified as one of "America's Brainiest Bastions" by *Portfolio.com*. The metro area ranked #38 out of 200. *Portfolio.com* analyzed levels of educational attainment in the nation's 200 largest metropolitan areas. The editors established scores for five levels of educational attainment, based on relative earning power of adult workers age 25 or older. Scores were determined by comparing the median income for all workers with the median income for those workers at a specified educational level. *Portfolio.com, "America's Brainiest Bastions," December 1, 2010*

Environmental Rankings

- Huntsville was selected as one of 22 "Smarter Cities" for energy by the Natural Resources Defense Council. Criteria: investment in green power; energy efficiency measures; conservation. *Natural Resources Defense Council, "2010 Smarter Cities," July 19, 2010*

- Huntsville was selected as one of "America's 50 Greenest Cities" by *Popular Science*. The city ranked #18. Criteria: electricity; transportation; green living; recycling and green perspective. *Popular Science, February 2008*

- The Huntsville metro area appeared in *Country Home's* "Best Green Places" report. The area ranked #361 out of 379. Criteria: official energy policies; green power; green buildings; availability of fresh, locally grown food. *Country Home, "Best Green Places," 2008*

Health/Fitness Rankings

- The Huntsville metro area appeared in the 2011 Gallup-Healthways Well-Being Index. The index, based on interviews with more than 350,000 Americans, measured jobs, finances, physical health, emotional state of mind and communities. The metro area ranked #30 out of 190. Criteria: life evaluation; emotional health; work environment; physical health; healthy behaviors; basic access (basic needs optimal for a healthy life, such as access to food and medicine, having health insurance and feeling safe while walking at night). *Gallup-Healthways, "State of Well-Being 2011"*

Safety Rankings

- Allstate ranked the 193 largest cities in America in terms of driver safety. Huntsville ranked #5. In addition, drivers were 18.9% less likely to have had an accident compared to the national average. Allstate researchers analyzed internal property damage reported claims over a two-year period (from January 2008 to December 2009) to protect findings from external influences such as weather or road construction. A weighted average of the two-year numbers determined the annual percentages. The report defines an auto crash as any collision resulting in a property damage claim. *Allstate, "2011 Allstate America's Best Drivers Report™"*

- The National Insurance Crime Bureau ranked 366 metro areas in the U.S. in terms of per capita rates of vehicle theft. The Huntsville metro area ranked #145 (#1 = highest rate). Criteria: number of vehicle theft offenses per 100,000 inhabitants in 2010. *National Insurance Crime Bureau, "Hot Spots," June 21, 2011*

Seniors/Retirement Rankings

- Huntsville was selected as one of the best places to retire by *CNNMoney.com*. Criteria: low cost of living; low violent-crime rate; good medical care; large population over age 50; abundant amenities for retirees. *CNNMoney.com, "Best Places to Retire 2011"*

Sports/Recreation Rankings

- Huntsville appeared on the *Sporting News* list of the "Best Sports Cities" for 2011. The area ranked #255 out of 271 cities in the U.S. *Sporting News* takes a 12-month snapshot of each city's sports, putting a heavy premium on regular-season won-lost records (from the most recently completed season). Other criteria include: playoff berths, bowl appearances and tournament bids; championships; applicable power ratings; quality of competition; overall fan fervor (measured in part by attendance); abundance of teams (rewarding quality over quantity); stadium and arena quality; ticket availability and prices; franchise ownership; and marquee appeal of athletes. *Sporting News, "Best Sports Cities 2011," October 4, 2011*

- Huntsville was selected as one of the most playful cities in the U.S. by KaBOOM! The organization's Playful City USA initiative is a national recognition program that honors cities and towns across the nation for a vision, plan and commitment to creating an agenda for play. Cities were recognized based on a pledge to five specific commitments to play: creating a local play commission or task force; designing an annual action plan for play; conducting a play space audit; outlining a financial investment in play for the current fiscal year; and proclaiming and celebrating an annual "play day." *KaBOOM! National Campaign for Play, "2011 Playful City USA Communities"*

Business Environment

CITY FINANCES

City Government Finances

Component	2009 ($000)	2009 ($ per capita)
Total Revenues	807,060	4,711
Total Expenditures	838,685	4,895
Debt Outstanding	649,332	3,790
Cash and Securities[1]	381,511	2,227

Note: (1) Cash and security holdings of a government at the close of its fiscal year, including those of its dependent agencies, utilities, and liquor stores.
Source: U.S Census Bureau, State & Local Government Finances 2009

City Government Revenue by Source

Source	2009 ($000)	2009 ($ per capita)
General Revenue		
From Federal Government	3,081	18
From State Government	17,948	105
From Local Governments	2,095	12
Taxes		
Property	52,194	305
Sales and Gross Receipts	155,753	909
Personal Income	0	0
Corporate Income	0	0
Motor Vehicle License	0	0
Other Taxes	23,054	135
Current Charges	43,484	254
Liquor Store	0	0
Utility	484,551	2,828
Employee Retirement	0	0

Source: U.S Census Bureau, State & Local Government Finances 2009

City Government Expenditures by Function

Function	2009 ($000)	2009 ($ per capita)	2009 (%)
General Direct Expenditures			
Air Transportation	0	0	0.0
Corrections	0	0	0.0
Education	3,783	22	0.5
Employment Security Administration	0	0	0.0
Financial Administration	9,057	53	1.1
Fire Protection	27,788	162	3.3
General Public Buildings	8,503	50	1.0
Governmental Administration, Other	10,769	63	1.3
Health	1,586	9	0.2
Highways	25,963	152	3.1
Hospitals	0	0	0.0
Housing and Community Development	5,436	32	0.6
Interest on General Debt	25,790	151	3.1
Judicial and Legal	4,385	26	0.5
Libraries	5,468	32	0.7
Parking	1,854	11	0.2
Parks and Recreation	32,830	192	3.9
Police Protection	39,844	233	4.8
Public Welfare	0	0	0.0
Sewerage	25,357	148	3.0
Solid Waste Management	10,855	63	1.3
Veterans' Services	0	0	0.0
Liquor Store	0	0	0.0
Utility	518,584	3,027	61.8
Employee Retirement	0	0	0.0

Source: U.S Census Bureau, State & Local Government Finances 2009

Municipal Bond Ratings

Area	Moody's	S&P	Fitch
City	Aaa	AAA	n/a

Rating Systems (shown in declining order of credit quality): Moody's– Aaa, Aa, A, Baa, Ba, B, Caa, Ca, C (numerical modifiers 1, 2, and 3 are added to letter-rating); S&P– AAA, AA, A, BBB, BB, B, CCC, CC, C; Fitch– AAA, AA, A, BBB, BB, B, CCC, CC, C. Ratings may be modified by the addition of a plus or minus sign to show relative standing within the major rating categories.
Notes: n/a Not Available; w/d Withdrawn (1) Not Reviewed; (2) Issuer Rating/No General Obligation; (3) Standard and Poor's Issue Credit Rating (ICR) is a current opinion of an obliger with respect to a specific financial obligation, a specific class of financial obligations, or a specific financial program.
Source: City of Huntsville, Alabama, Comprehensive Annual Financial Report, Fiscal Year Ended September 30, 2010

DEMOGRAPHICS

Population Growth

Area	1990 Census	2000 Census	2010 Census	Population Growth (%) 1990-2000	Population Growth (%) 2000-2010
City	161,842	158,216	180,105	-2.2	13.8
MSA[1]	293,047	342,376	417,593	16.8	22.0
U.S.	248,709,873	281,421,906	308,745,538	13.2	9.7

Note: (1) Figures cover the Huntsville, AL Metropolitan Statistical Area—see Appendix B for areas included
Source: U.S. Census Bureau, 2010 Census

Household Size

Area	One	Two	Three	Four	Five	Six	Seven or More	Average Household Size
City	34.7	33.5	14.6	10.4	4.4	1.5	0.8	2.25
MSA[1]	27.8	33.8	16.8	13.4	5.5	1.8	0.9	2.45
U.S.	26.7	32.8	16.1	13.4	6.5	2.6	1.9	2.58

Note: (1) Figures cover the Huntsville, AL Metropolitan Statistical Area—see Appendix B for areas included
Source: U.S. Census Bureau, 2010 Census

Race

Area	White Alone[2] (%)	Black Alone[2] (%)	Asian Alone[2] (%)	AIAN[3] Alone[2] (%)	NHOPI[4] Alone[2] (%)	Other Race Alone[2] (%)	Two or More Races (%)
City	60.3	31.2	2.4	0.6	0.1	2.9	2.5
MSA[1]	70.6	21.7	2.2	0.7	0.1	2.3	2.3
U.S.	72.4	12.6	4.8	0.9	0.2	6.2	2.9

Note: (1) Figures cover the Huntsville, AL Metropolitan Statistical Area—see Appendix B for areas included; (2) Alone is defined as not being in combination with one or more other races; (3) American Indian and Alaska Native; (4) Native Hawaiian and Other Pacific Islander
Source: U.S. Census Bureau, 2010 Census

Hispanic or Latino Origin

Area	Hispanic or Latino (%)	Mexican (%)	Puerto Rican (%)	Cuban (%)	Other Hispanic or Latino (%)
City	5.8	4.0	0.6	0.1	1.1
MSA[1]	4.8	3.2	0.5	0.1	1.0
U.S.	16.3	10.3	1.5	0.6	4.0

Note: Persons of Hispanic or Latino origin can be of any race; (1) Figures cover the Huntsville, AL Metropolitan Statistical Area—see Appendix B for areas included
Source: U.S. Census Bureau, 2010 Census

Segregation

Type	Segregation Indices[1]				Percent Change		
	1990	2000	2010	2010 Rank[2]	1990-2000	1990-2010	2000-2010
Black/White	n/a	n/a	n/a	n/a	n/a	n/a	n/a
Asian/White	n/a	n/a	n/a	n/a	n/a	n/a	n/a
Hispanic/White	n/a	n/a	n/a	n/a	n/a	n/a	n/a

Note: Figures are based on an analysis of 1990, 2000, and 2010 Census Decennial Census tract data by William H. Frey, Brookings Institution and the University of Michigan Social Science Data Analysis Network. In this analysis all racial groups (whites, blacks, and asians) are non-Hispanic members of those races. Hispanics are shown as a separate category; All figures cover the Metropolitan Statistical Area (see Appendix B for areas included); (1) Segregation Indices are Dissimilarity Indices that measure the degree to which the minority group is distributed differently than whites across census tracts. They range from 0 (complete integration) to 100 (complete segregation) where the value indicates the percentage of the minority group that needs to move to be distributed exactly like whites; (2) Ranges from 1 (most segregated) to 102 (least segregated); n/a not available.
Source: www.CensusScope.org

Ancestry

Area	German	Irish	English	American	Italian	Polish	French[2]	Scottish	Dutch
City	8.6	9.4	10.1	10.2	2.5	1.0	2.3	2.5	1.2
MSA[1]	9.8	10.8	10.0	13.5	2.4	1.2	2.3	2.3	1.2
U.S.	16.1	11.6	8.8	6.1	5.7	3.2	3.0	1.9	1.6

Note: Figures are the percentage of the total population reporting a particular ancestry. The nine most commonly reported ancestries in the U.S. are shown. Figures include multiple ancestries (e.g. if a person reported being Irish and Italian, they were included in both columns); (1) Figures cover the Huntsville, AL Metropolitan Statistical Area—see Appendix B for areas included; (2) Excludes Basque
Source: U.S. Census Bureau, 2008-2010 American Community Survey 3-Year Estimates

Foreign-Born Population

Area	Percent of Population Born in								
	Any Foreign Country	Mexico	Asia	Europe	Carribean	South America	Central America[2]	Africa	Canada
City	7.0	2.4	1.9	0.9	0.6	0.1	0.3	0.6	0.1
MSA[1]	5.3	1.7	1.6	0.7	0.3	0.1	0.2	0.3	0.2
U.S.	12.8	3.8	3.6	1.6	1.2	0.9	1.0	0.5	0.3

Note: (1) Figures cover the Huntsville, AL Metropolitan Statistical Area—see Appendix B for areas included; (2) Excludes Mexico.
Source: U.S. Census Bureau, 2008-2010 American Community Survey 3-Year Estimates

Marital Status

Area	Never Married	Now Married[2]	Separated	Widowed	Divorced
City	33.8	43.9	3.0	6.1	13.2
MSA[1]	28.1	52.3	2.3	5.5	11.8
U.S.	31.6	49.6	2.2	6.1	10.7

Note: Figures are percentages and cover the population 15 years of age and older; (1) Figures cover the Huntsville, AL Metropolitan Statistical Area—see Appendix B for areas included; (2) Excludes separated
Source: U.S. Census Bureau, 2008-2010 American Community Survey 3-Year Estimates

Age

Area	Percent of Population							Median Age
	Under Age 5	Age 5 to 17	Age 18 to 34	Age 35 to 49	Age 50 to 64	Age 65 to 79	80 Years and Over	
City	6.2	15.3	26.8	19.3	18.3	10.4	3.8	36.5
MSA[1]	6.3	17.5	23.0	21.9	19.0	9.4	2.8	37.6
U.S.	6.5	17.5	23.2	20.7	19.0	9.4	3.6	37.2

Note: (1) Figures cover the Huntsville, AL Metropolitan Statistical Area—see Appendix B for areas included
Source: U.S. Census Bureau, 2010 Census

Male/Female Ratio

Area	Males	Females	Males per 100 Females
City	87,530	92,575	94.6
MSA[1]	206,230	211,363	97.6
U.S.	151,781,326	156,964,212	96.7

Note: (1) Figures cover the Huntsville, AL
Metropolitan Statistical Area—see Appendix B for areas included
Source: U.S. Census Bureau, 2010 Census

Religious Groups

Area	Catholic	Baptist	Non-Den.	Methodist[2]	Lutheran	LDS[3]	Pente-costal	Presby-terian[4]	Muslim[5]	Judaism
MSA[1]	4.0	27.6	3.2	7.5	0.7	1.2	1.2	1.7	0.2	0.2
U.S.	19.1	9.3	4.0	4.0	2.3	2.0	1.9	1.6	0.8	0.7

Note: Figures are the number of adherents as a percentage of the total population; (1) Figures cover the
Huntsville, AL Metropolitan Statistical Area—see Appendix B for areas included; (2) Methodist/Pietist;
(3) Latter Day Saints; (4) Reformed; (5) Figures are estimates
Source: Association of Statisticians of American Religious Bodies, 2010 U.S. Religion Census: Religious
Congregations & Membership Study

ECONOMY

Gross Metropolitan Product

Area	2007	2008	2009	2010	2010 Rank[2]
MSA[1]	18.3	19.1	19.7	20.5	97

Note: Figures are in billions of dollars; (1) Figures cover the Huntsville, AL Metropolitan Statistical Area—see
Appendix B for areas included; (2) Rank ranges from 1 to 363
Source: The United States Conference of Mayors, "U.S. Metro Economies: GMP and Employment Forecasts,"
June 2011

Economic Growth

Area	2007-2009 (%)	2010 (%)	2011 (%)	Rank[2]
MSA[1]	2.2	2.8	2.4	33
U.S.	-1.3	2.9	2.5	–

Note: Figures are real Gross Metropolitan Product growth rates and represent annual average percent change;
(1) Figures cover the Huntsville, AL Metropolitan Statistical Area—see Appendix B for areas included; (2) Rank
ranges from 1 to 363
Source: The United States Conference of Mayors, "U.S. Metro Economies: GMP and Employment Forecasts,"
June 2011

Metropolitan Area Exports

Area	2005	2006	2007	2008	2009	2010	2010 Rank[2]
MSA[1]	1,104.8	1,251.9	1,052.8	1,079.3	1,136.5	986.8	139

Note: Figures are in millions of dollars; (1) Figures cover the Huntsville, AL Metropolitan Statistical Area—see
Appendix B for areas included; (2) Rank ranges from 1 to 369
Source: U.S. Department of Commerce, International Trade Administration, Office of Trade & Industry
Information, Manufacturing & Services, data extracted April 2, 2012

INCOME

Income

Area	Per Capita ($)	Median Household ($)	Average Household ($)
City	29,582	47,238	68,304
MSA[1]	29,179	53,974	72,853
U.S.	26,942	51,222	70,116

Note: (1) Figures cover the Huntsville, AL Metropolitan Statistical Area—see Appendix B for areas included
Source: U.S. Census Bureau, 2008-2010 American Community Survey 3-Year Estimates

Household Income Distribution

Area	Percent of Households Earning							
	Under $15,000	$15,000 -24,999	$25,000 -34,999	$35,000 -49,999	$50,000 -74,999	$75,000 -99,000	$100,000 -149,999	$150,000 and up
City	15.3	12.5	11.1	13.1	16.7	10.7	12.2	8.3
MSA[1]	11.8	10.8	10.2	13.5	17.5	12.0	14.8	9.3
U.S.	13.0	11.0	10.6	14.2	18.5	12.1	12.2	8.4

Note: (1) Figures cover the Huntsville, AL Metropolitan Statistical Area—see Appendix B for areas included
Source: U.S. Census Bureau, 2008-2010 American Community Survey 3-Year Estimates

Poverty Rate

Area	All Ages	Under 18 Years Old	18 to 64 Years Old	65 Years and Over
City	16.4	24.4	15.7	7.1
MSA[1]	12.3	16.8	11.5	7.6
U.S.	14.4	20.1	13.1	9.4

Note: Figures are percentage of people whose income during the past 12 months was below the poverty level;
(1) Figures cover the Huntsville, AL Metropolitan Statistical Area—see Appendix B for areas included
Source: U.S. Census Bureau, 2008-2010 American Community Survey 3-Year Estimates

Personal Bankruptcy Filing Rate

Area	2006	2007	2008	2009	2010	2011
Madison County	3.19	3.65	4.45	4.94	5.11	4.81
U.S.	2.00	2.73	3.53	4.61	4.97	4.37

Note: Numbers are per 1,000 population and include Chapter 7 and Chapter 13 filings
Source: Federal Deposit Insurance Corporation, Regional Economic Conditions, March 9, 2012

EMPLOYMENT

Labor Force and Employment

Area	Civilian Labor Force			Workers Employed		
	Dec. 2010	Dec. 2011	% Chg.	Dec. 2010	Dec. 2011	% Chg.
City	90,774	91,862	1.2	84,297	85,874	1.9
MSA[1]	206,531	208,703	1.1	191,689	195,276	1.9
U.S.	153,156,000	153,373,000	0.1	139,159,000	140,681,000	1.1

Note: Data is not seasonally adjusted and covers workers 16 years of age and older;
(1) Metropolitan Statistical Area—see Appendix B for areas included
Source: Bureau of Labor Statistics, http://stats.bls.gov

Unemployment Rate

Area	2011											
	Jan.	Feb.	Mar.	Apr.	May	Jun.	Jul.	Aug.	Sep.	Oct.	Nov.	Dec.
City	8.2	7.7	7.4	7.5	7.9	9.0	8.6	8.2	8.1	7.4	6.8	6.5
MSA[1]	8.2	7.9	7.5	7.5	7.9	8.9	8.4	8.1	8.1	7.4	6.8	6.4
U.S.	9.8	9.5	9.2	8.7	8.7	9.3	9.3	9.1	8.8	8.5	8.2	8.3

Note: Data is not seasonally adjusted and covers workers 16 years of age and older; All figures are
percentages; (1) Metropolitan Statistical Area—see Appendix B for areas included
Source: Bureau of Labor Statistics, http://stats.bls.gov

Projected Unemployment Rate

Area	2010 (%)	2011 (%)	2012 (%)	2013 (%)
MSA[1]	7.7	7.7	7.0	6.5

Note: (1) Metropolitan Statistical Area—see Appendix B for areas included
Source: The United States Conference of Mayors, "U.S. Metro Economies: GMP and Employment Forecasts,"
June 2011

Employment by Occupation

Occupation Classification	City (%)	MSA[1] (%)	U.S. (%)
Management, Business, Science, and Arts	42.3	42.4	35.6
Natural Resources, Construction, and Maintenance	6.8	8.0	9.5
Production, Transportation, and Material Moving	10.4	11.9	12.1
Sales and Office	23.9	23.1	25.2
Service	16.6	14.6	17.6

Note: Figures cover employed civilians 16 years of age and older; (1) Figures cover the Huntsville, AL Metropolitan Statistical Area—see Appendix B for areas included
Source: U.S. Census Bureau, 2008-2010 American Community Survey 3-Year Estimates

Employment by Industry

Sector	MSA[1] Number of Employees	MSA[1] Percent of Total	U.S. Percent of Total
Construction	n/a	n/a	4.1
Education and Health Services	17,400	8.4	15.2
Financial Activities	6,100	2.9	5.8
Government	50,400	24.4	16.8
Information	2,500	1.2	2.0
Leisure and Hospitality	17,500	8.5	9.9
Manufacturing	21,900	10.6	8.9
Mining and Logging	n/a	n/a	0.6
Other Services	7,600	3.7	4.0
Professional and Business Services	45,900	22.2	13.3
Retail Trade	22,700	11.0	11.5
Transportation and Utilities	2,600	1.3	3.8
Wholesale Trade	5,500	2.7	4.2

Note: Figures cover non-farm employment as of December 2011 and are not seasonally adjusted; (1) Metropolitan Statistical Area—see Appendix B for areas included; n/a not available
Source: Bureau of Labor Statistics, http://stats.bls.gov

Occupations with Greatest Projected Employment Growth: 2008 – 2018

Occupation[1]	2008 Employment	2018 Projected Employment	Numeric Employment Change	Percent Employment Change
Retail Salespersons	61,560	71,470	9,910	16.1
Combined Food Preparation and Serving Workers, Including Fast Food	40,860	50,000	9,140	22.4
Registered Nurses	42,290	50,580	8,290	19.6
Team Assemblers	32,740	40,520	7,780	23.8
Customer Service Representatives	24,110	29,500	5,390	22.4
Truck Drivers, Heavy and Tractor-Trailer	38,050	42,910	4,860	12.8
Office Clerks, General	39,220	43,770	4,550	11.6
Waiters and Waitresses	28,680	33,040	4,360	15.2
Janitors and Cleaners, Except Maids and Housekeeping Cleaners	30,600	34,910	4,310	14.1
Bookkeeping, Accounting, and Auditing Clerks	32,440	36,680	4,240	13.1

Note: Projections cover Alabama; (1) Sorted by numeric employment change
Source: www.projectionscentral.com, State Occupational Projections, 2008–2018 Long-Term Projections

Fastest Growing Occupations: 2008 – 2018

Occupation[1]	2008 Employment	2018 Projected Employment	Numeric Employment Change	Percent Employment Change
Veterinary Technologists and Technicians	800	1,180	380	47.5
Computer Software Engineers, Applications	3,170	4,580	1,410	44.5
Network Systems and Data Communications Analysts	2,790	4,030	1,240	44.4
Occupational Therapist Assistants	380	530	150	39.5
Personal and Home Care Aides	3,440	4,780	1,340	39.0
Medical Assistants	6,770	9,320	2,550	37.7
Welding, Soldering, and Brazing Machine Setters, Operators, and Tenders	2,640	3,630	990	37.5
Home Health Aides	10,530	14,430	3,900	37.0
Skin Care Specialists	270	370	100	37.0
Aircraft Mechanics and Service Technicians	3,610	4,930	1,320	36.6

Note: Projections cover Alabama; (1) Sorted by percent employment change and excludes occupations with numeric employment change less than 100
Source: www.projectionscentral.com, State Occupational Projections, 2008–2018 Long-Term Projections

Average Wages

Occupation	$/Hr.	Occupation	$/Hr.
Accountants and Auditors	31.84	Maids and Housekeeping Cleaners	8.82
Automotive Mechanics	18.02	Maintenance and Repair Workers	19.82
Bookkeepers	15.77	Marketing Managers	55.76
Carpenters	15.15	Nuclear Medicine Technologists	n/a
Cashiers	8.95	Nurses, Licensed Practical	18.07
Clerks, General Office	10.91	Nurses, Registered	28.70
Clerks, Receptionists/Information	11.24	Nursing Aides/Orderlies/Attendants	11.24
Clerks, Shipping/Receiving	14.51	Packers and Packagers, Hand	10.42
Computer Programmers	38.31	Physical Therapists	37.50
Computer Support Specialists	21.89	Postal Service Mail Carriers	24.57
Computer Systems Analysts	42.27	Real Estate Brokers	25.73
Cooks, Restaurant	11.08	Retail Salespersons	11.31
Dentists	84.61	Sales Reps., Exc. Tech./Scientific	27.28
Electrical Engineers	49.02	Sales Reps., Tech./Scientific	36.21
Electricians	19.16	Secretaries, Exc. Legal/Med./Exec.	16.22
Financial Managers	53.23	Security Guards	13.18
First-Line Supervisors/Managers, Sales	18.35	Surgeons	n/a
Food Preparation Workers	9.06	Teacher Assistants	10.90
General and Operations Managers	59.83	Teachers, Elementary School	25.30
Hairdressers/Cosmetologists	12.52	Teachers, Secondary School	23.80
Internists	116.96	Telemarketers	n/a
Janitors and Cleaners	10.56	Truck Drivers, Heavy/Tractor-Trailer	17.13
Landscaping/Groundskeeping Workers	11.57	Truck Drivers, Light/Delivery Svcs.	15.28
Lawyers	66.29	Waiters and Waitresses	9.23

Note: Wage data covers the Huntsville, AL Metropolitan Statistical Area—see Appendix B for areas included. Hourly wages for elementary/secondary school teachers and teacher assistants were calculated by the editors from annual wage data assuming a 40 hour work week; n/a not available.
Source: Bureau of Labor Statistics, Metro Area Occupational Employment and Wage Estimates, May 2011

RESIDENTIAL REAL ESTATE

Building Permits

Area	Single-Family			Multi-Family			Total		
	2010	2011	Pct. Chg.	2010	2011	Pct. Chg.	2010	2011	Pct. Chg.
City	1,073	1,018	-5.1	0	4	-	1,073	1,022	-4.8
MSA[1]	2,275	2,015	-11.4	0	4	-	2,275	2,019	-11.3
U.S.	447,311	418,498	-6.4	157,299	205,563	30.7	604,610	624,061	3.2

Note: (1) Metropolitan Statistical Area—see Appendix B for areas included; figures represent new, privately-owned housing units authorized (unadjusted data); All permit data are based on estimates with imputation.
Source: U.S. Census Bureau, Manufacturing, Mining, and Construction Statistics, Building Permits, 2010, 2011

Homeownership Rate

Area	2005 (%)	2006 (%)	2007 (%)	2008 (%)	2009 (%)	2010 (%)	2011 (%)
MSA[1]	n/a	n/a	n/a	n/a	n/a	n/a	n/a
U.S.	68.9	68.8	68.1	67.8	67.4	66.9	66.1

Note: (1) Metropolitan Statistical Area—see Appendix B for areas included; n/a not available
Source: U.S. Census Bureau, Housing Vacancies and Homeownership Annual Statistics: 2011

Housing Vacancy Rates

Area	Gross Vacancy Rate[2] (%)			Year-Round Vacancy Rate[3] (%)			Rental Vacancy Rate[4] (%)			Homeowner Vacancy Rate[5] (%)		
	2009	2010	2011	2009	2010	2011	2009	2010	2011	2009	2010	2011
MSA[1]	n/a	n/a	n/a	n/a	n/a	n/a	n/a	n/a	n/a	n/a	n/a	n/a
U.S.	14.5	14.3	14.2	11.3	11.3	11.1	10.6	10.2	9.5	2.6	2.6	2.5

Note: (1) Metropolitan Statistical Area—see Appendix B for areas included; (2) The percentage of the total housing inventory that is vacant; (3) The percentage of the housing inventory (excluding seasonal units) that is year-round vacant; (4) The percentage of rental inventory that is vacant for rent; (5) The percentage of homeowner inventory that is vacant for sale; n/a not available
Source: U.S. Census Bureau, Housing Vacancies and Homeownership Annual Statistics: 2011

TAXES

State Corporate Income Tax Rates

State	Tax Rate (%)	Income Brackets ($)	Num. of Brackets	Financial Institution Tax Rate (%)[a]	Federal Income Tax Ded.
Alabama	6.5	Flat rate	1	6.5	Yes

Note: Tax rates as of January 1, 2012; (a) Rates listed are the corporate income tax rate applied to financial institutions or excise taxes based on income. Some states have other taxes based upon the value of deposits or shares.
Source: Federation of Tax Administrators, "State Corporate Income Tax Rates, 2012"

State Individual Income Tax Rates

State	Tax Rate (%)	Income Brackets ($)	Num. of Brackets	Personal Exempt. ($)[1] Single	Dependents	Fed. Inc. Tax Ded.
Alabama	2.0 - 5.0	500 (b) - 3,001 (b)	3	1,500	500 (e)	Yes

Note: Tax rates as of January 1, 2012; Local- and county-level taxes are not included; n/a not applicable; (1) Married joint filers generally receive double the single exemption; (b) For joint returns, taxes are twice the tax on half the couple's income; (e) In Alabama, the per-dependent exemption is $1,000 for taxpayers with state AGI of $20,000 or less, $500 with AGI from $20,001 to $100,000, and $300 with AGI over $100,000.
Source: Federation of Tax Administrators, "State Individual Income Tax Rates, 2012"

Various State and Local Tax Rates

State	State and Local Sales and Use (%)	State Sales and Use (%)	Gasoline[1] (¢/gal.)	Cigarette[2] ($/pack)	Spirits[3] ($/gal.)	Wine[4] ($/gal.)	Beer[5] ($/gal.)
Alabama	8.0	4.00	20.9	0.43	18.61 (f)	1.70 (k)	1.05 (n)

Note: All tax rates as of January 1, 2012 except beer, wine and spirits (September 1, 2011); (1) The American Petroleum Institute has developed a methodology for determining the average tax rate on a gallon of fuel. Rates may include any of the following: excise taxes, environmental fees, storage tank fees, other fees or taxes, general sales tax, and local taxes. In states where gasoline is subject to the general sales tax, or where the fuel tax is based on the average sale price, the average rate determined by API is sensitive to changes in the price of gasoline. States that fully or partially apply general sales taxes to gasoline: CA, CO, GA, IL, IN, MI, NY; (2) The federal excise tax of $1.0066 per pack and local taxes are not included; (3) Rates are those applicable to off-premise sales of 40% alcohol by volume (a.b.v.) distilled spirits in 750ml containers. Local excise taxes are excluded; (4) Rates are those applicable to off-premise sales of 11% a.b.v. non-carbonated wine in 750ml containers; (5) Rates are those applicable to off-premise sales of 4.7% a.b.v. beer in 12 ounce containers; (f) States where the government controls sales. In these "control states," products are subject to ad valorem mark-up and excise taxes. The excise tax rate is calculated using a methodology developed by the Distilled Spirits Council of the United States; (k) Includes $0.26 statewide local rate in Alabama; (n) Includes statewide local rate in Alabama ($0.52) and Georgia ($0.53).
Source: Tax Foundation, 2012 Facts & Figures: How Does Your State Compare?

State-Local Tax Burdens

Area	Rate (%)	Rank[1]	Per Capita Taxes Paid to Home State ($)	Total State and Local Per Capita Taxes Paid ($)	Per Capita Income ($)
Alabama	8.5	40	2,029	2,967	34,911
U.S. Average	9.8	-	3,057	4,160	42,539

Note: Figures cover 2009; (1) Rank ranges from 1 to 50 where 1 is highest tax burden
Source: Tax Foundation, State-Local Tax Burdens, All States, 2009

State Business Tax Climate Index Rankings

State	Overall Rank	Corporate Tax Index Rank	Individual Income Tax Index Rank	Sales Tax Index Rank	Unemployment Insurance Tax Index Rank	Property Tax Index Rank
Alabama	20	16	18	41	11	6

Note: The index is a measure of how each state's tax laws affect economic performance. The lower the rank, the more favorable a state's tax system is for business. States without a given tax are given a ranking of 1.
Source: Tax Foundation, Major Components of the State Business Tax Climate Index, FY 2012

COMMERCIAL UTILITIES

Typical Monthly Electric Bills

Area	Commercial Service ($/month)		Industrial Service ($/month)	
	1,500 kWh	40 kW demand 14,000 kWh	1,000 kW demand 200,000 kWh	50,000 kW demand 15,000,000 kWh
City	n/a	n/a	n/a	n/a
Average[1]	189	1,616	25,197	1,470,813

Note: Based on total rates in effect July 1, 2011; (1) average based on 184 utilities surveyed; n/a not available
Source: Edison Electric Institute, Typical Bills and Average Rates Report, Summer 2011

TRANSPORTATION

Means of Transportation to Work

Area	Car/Truck/Van Drove Alone	Car/Truck/Van Car-pooled	Public Transportation Bus	Public Transportation Subway	Public Transportation Railroad	Bicycle	Walked	Other Means	Worked at Home
City	83.5	9.9	0.7	0.0	0.0	0.1	1.1	1.5	3.1
MSA[1]	85.5	9.0	0.4	0.0	0.0	0.1	1.1	1.2	2.7
U.S.	76.0	10.2	2.7	1.7	0.5	0.5	2.8	1.3	4.2

Note: Figures are percentages and cover workers 16 years of age and older; (1) Figures cover the Huntsville, AL Metropolitan Statistical Area—see Appendix B for areas included
Source: U.S. Census Bureau, 2008-2010 American Community Survey 3-Year Estimates

Travel Time to Work

Area	Less Than 10 Minutes	10 to 19 Minutes	20 to 29 Minutes	30 to 44 Minutes	45 to 59 Minutes	60 to 89 Minutes	90 Minutes or More
City	16.1	43.7	25.6	10.8	1.4	1.2	1.2
MSA[1]	12.2	34.1	27.7	18.4	4.8	1.6	1.1
U.S.	13.9	30.1	20.8	19.8	7.5	5.5	2.5

Note: Figures are percentages and include workers 16 years old and over; (1) Figures cover the Huntsville, AL Metropolitan Statistical Area—see Appendix B for areas included
Source: U.S. Census Bureau, 2008-2010 American Community Survey 3-Year Estimates

Travel Time Index

Area	1985	1990	1995	2000	2005	2010
Urban Area[1]	n/a	n/a	n/a	n/a	n/a	n/a
Average[2]	1.11	1.16	1.18	1.21	1.25	1.20

Note: Travel Time Index—the ratio of travel time in the peak period to the travel time at free-flow conditions. A value of 1.30 indicates a 20-minute free-flow trip takes 26 minutes in the peak. Free-flow speeds (60 mph on freeways and 35 mph on principal arterials) are used as the comparison threshold; (1) Data for the Huntsville, AL urban area was not available; (2) average of 439 urban areas
Source: Texas Transportation Institute, Urban Mobility Report 2011, September 2011

Public Transportation

Agency Name / Mode of Transportation	Vehicles Operated in Maximum Service	Annual Unlinked Passenger Trips ('000)	Annual Passenger Miles ('000)
City of Huntsville - Public Transportation Division			
Bus (directly operated)	13	307.6	1,710.6
Demand Response (directly operated)	15	80.8	673.7

Source: Federal Transit Administration, National Transit Database, 2010

Air Transportation

Airport Name and Code / Type of Service	Passenger Airlines[1]	Passenger Enplanements	Freight Carriers[2]	Freight (lbs.)
Huntsville International (HSV)				
Domestic service (U.S. carriers - 2011)	18	614,275	9	7,257,424
International service (U.S. carriers - 2010)	1	31	8	67,237,369

Note: (1) Includes all U.S.-based major, minor and commuter airlines that carried at least one passenger during the year; (2) Includes all U.S.-based airlines and freight carriers that transported at least one pound of freight during the year
Source: Bureau of Transportation Statistics, The Intermodal Transportation Database, Air Carriers: T-100 Domestic Market (U.S. Carriers), 2011; Bureau of Transportation Statistics, The Intermodal Transportation Database, Air Carriers: T-100 International Market (U.S. Carriers), 2010

Other Transportation Statistics

Major Highways:	I-65
Amtrak Service:	No
Major Waterways/Ports:	Near the Tennessee River (12 miles)

Source: Amtrak.com; Google Maps

BUSINESSES

Major Business Headquarters

Company Name	Rankings	
	Fortune[1]	Forbes[2]
No companies listed	-	-

Note: (1) Fortune 500—companies that produce a 10-K are ranked 1 to 500 based on 2010 revenue; (2) all private companies with at least $2 billion in annual revenue are ranked 1 to 212; companies listed are headquartered in the city; dashes indicate no ranking
Source: Fortune, "Fortune 500," May 23, 2011; Forbes, "America's Largest Private Companies," November 16, 2011

Fast-Growing Businesses

According to *Inc.*, Huntsville is home to three of America's 500 fastest-growing private companies: **Connected Logistics** (#10); **Davis Strategic Innovations** (#301); **LocoX.com** (#473). Criteria: must be an independent, privately-held, for-profit, U.S. corporation, proprietorship or partnership; revenues must be at least $80,000 in 2007 and $2 million in 2010; must have four-year operating/sales history. Holding companies, regulated banks, and utilities were excluded. *Inc., "America's 500 Fastest-Growing Private Companies," September 2011*

According to *Initiative for a Competitive Inner City (ICIC)*, Huntsville is home to one of America's 100 fastest-growing "inner city" companies: **Bevilacqua Research Corporation** (#62). Companies were ranked by their five-year compound annual growth rate. Criteria for inclusion: company must be headquartered in or have 51 percent or more of its physical operations in an economically distressed urban area; must be an independent, for-profit corporation, partnership or proprietorship; must have 10 or more employees and have a five-year sales history that includes sales of at least $200,000 in the base year and at least $1 million in the current year with no decrease in sales over the two most recent years. *Initiative for a Competitive Inner City (ICIC), "Inner City 100 Companies, 2011"*

Minority Business Opportunity

Huntsville is home to one company which is on the *Black Enterprise* Industrial/Service 100 list (100 largest companies based on gross sales): **Tec-Masters** (#53). Criteria: operational in previous calendar year; at least 51% black-owned and manufactures/owns the product it sells or provides industrial or consumer services. Brokerages, real estate firms and firms that provide professional services are not eligible. *Black Enterprise, B.E. 100s, 2011*

Huntsville is home to one company which is on the *Black Enterprise* Auto Dealer 60 list (60 largest dealers based on gross sales): **Lexus of Huntsville** (#40). Criteria: company must be operational in previous calendar year and be at least 51% black-owned. *Black Enterprise, B.E. 100s, 2011*

Huntsville is home to three companies which are on the *Hispanic Business* 500 list (500 largest U.S. Hispanic-owned companies based on 2010 revenue): **COLSA Corp.** (#43); **Intuitive Research & Technology Corp.** (#69); **SEI Group** (#213). Companies included must show at least 51 percent ownership by Hispanic U.S. citizens, and must maintain headquarters in one of the 50 states or Washington, D.C. *Hispanic Business, "Hispanic Business 500," June 2011*

Huntsville is home to one company which is on the *Hispanic Business* Fastest-Growing 100 list (greatest sales growth from 2006 to 2010): **Intuitive Research & Technology Corp.** (#9). Companies included must show at least 51 percent ownership by Hispanic U.S. citizens, and must maintain headquarters in one of the 50 states or Washington, D.C. In addition, companies must have minimum revenues of $200,000 for calendar year 2005. *Hispanic Business, July/August 2011*

Minority- and Women-Owned Businesses

Group	All Firms		Firms with Paid Employees			
	Firms	Sales ($000)	Firms	Sales ($000)	Employees	Payroll ($000)
Asian	576	413,879	256	390,751	3,129	137,158
Black	2,007	268,991	157	243,092	1,821	77,246
Hispanic	207	260,684	45	254,977	1,705	111,457
Women	4,347	1,211,336	649	1,117,014	7,744	276,445
All Firms	14,555	28,244,278	4,604	27,652,214	122,186	5,233,410

Note: Figures cover firms located in the city; minority- and women-owned business are defined as firms in which the corresponding group own 51% or more of the stock or equity of the company
Source: U.S. Census Bureau, 2007 Economic Census, Survey of Business Owners

HOTELS

Hotels/Motels

Area	5 Star		4 Star		3 Star		2 Star		1 Star		Not Rated	
	Num.	Pct.[3]	Num.	Pct.[3]	Num.	Pct.[3]	Num.	Pct.[3]	Num.	Pct.[3]	Num.	Pct.[3]
City[1]	0	0.0	1	1.4	16	21.6	39	52.7	1	1.4	17	23.0
Total[2]	133	0.9	940	6.5	4,569	31.8	7,033	48.9	351	2.4	1,343	9.3

Note: (1) Figures cover Huntsville and vicinity; (2) Figures cover all 100 cities in this book; (3) Percentage of hotels which have a given star rating; Star ratings are determined by expedia.com and offer an indication of the general quality of a particular hotel.
Source: expedia.com, April 25, 2012

EVENT SITES

Major Stadiums, Arenas, and Auditoriums

Name	Max. Capacity
Joe W Davis Stadium	10,200
Von Braun Center Arena	10,000

Source: Original research

Living Environment

COST OF LIVING

Cost of Living Index

Composite Index	Groceries	Housing	Utilities	Trans-portation	Health Care	Misc. Goods/ Services
93.7	95.9	78.7	96.2	101.8	95.0	102.4

Note: U.S. = 100; Figures cover the Huntsville AL urban area.
Source: The Council for Community and Economic Research, ACCRA Cost of Living Index, 2011

Grocery Prices

Area[1]	T-Bone Steak ($/pound)	Frying Chicken ($/pound)	Whole Milk ($/half gal.)	Eggs ($/dozen)	Orange Juice ($/64 oz.)	Coffee ($/11.5 oz.)
City[2]	9.94	1.24	2.30	1.55	3.13	4.45
Avg.	9.25	1.18	2.22	1.66	3.19	4.40
Min.	6.70	0.88	1.31	0.95	2.46	2.94
Max.	14.30	2.16	3.50	3.18	4.75	6.83

Note: (1) Values for the local area are compared with the average, minimum and maximum values for all 335 areas in the Cost of Living Index; (2) Figures cover the Huntsville AL urban area; **T-Bone Steak** *(price per pound);* **Frying Chicken** *(price per pound, whole fryer);* **Whole Milk** *(half gallon carton);* **Eggs** *(price per dozen, Grade A, large);* **Orange Juice** *(64 oz. Tropicana or Florida Natural);* **Coffee** *(11.5 oz. can, vacuum-packed, Maxwell House, Hills Bros, or Folgers).*
Source: The Council for Community and Economic Research, ACCRA Cost of Living Index, 2011

Housing and Utility Costs

Area[1]	New Home Price ($)	Apartment Rent ($/month)	All Electric ($/month)	Part Electric ($/month)	Other Energy ($/month)	Telephone ($/month)
City[2]	221,338	726	142.62	-	-	30.38
Avg.	285,990	839	163.23	89.00	77.52	26.92
Min.	188,005	460	125.58	45.39	33.89	17.98
Max.	1,197,028	3,244	339.16	181.97	348.69	40.01

Note: (1) Values for the local area are compared with the average, minimum and maximum values for all 335 areas in the Cost of Living Index; (2) Figures cover the Huntsville AL urban area; **New Home Price** *(2,400 sf living area, 8,000 sf lot, in urban area with full utilities);* **Apartment Rent** *(950 sf 2 bedroom/1.5 or 2 bath, unfurnished, excluding all utilities except water);* **All Electric** *(average monthly cost for an all-electric home);* **Part Electric** *(average monthly cost for a part-electric home);* **Other Energy** *(average monthly cost for natural gas, fuel oil, coal, wood, and any other forms of energy except electricity);* **Telephone** *(price includes basic monthly rate for a private residential line plus additional local usage charges incurred by a family of four).*
Source: The Council for Community and Economic Research, ACCRA Cost of Living Index, 2011

Health Care, Transportation, and Other Costs

Area[1]	Doctor ($/visit)	Dentist ($/visit)	Optometrist ($/visit)	Gasoline ($/gallon)	Beauty Salon ($/visit)	Men's Shirt ($)
City[2]	71.67	79.17	106.00	3.48	35.66	21.18
Avg.	93.88	81.72	90.54	3.48	32.65	25.06
Min.	60.00	55.33	53.66	3.18	19.78	13.44
Max.	154.98	145.97	183.72	4.31	63.21	46.00

Note: (1) Values for the local area are compared with the average, minimum and maximum values for all 335 areas in the Cost of Living Index; (2) Figures cover the Huntsville AL urban area; **Doctor** *(general practitioners routine exam of an established patient);* **Dentist** *(adult teeth cleaning and periodic oral examination);* **Optometrist** *(full vision eye exam for established adult patient);* **Gasoline** *(one gallon regular unleaded, national brand, including all taxes, cash price at self-service pump if available);* **Beauty Salon** *(woman's shampoo, trim, and blow-dry);* **Men's Shirt** *(cotton/polyester dress shirt, pinpoint weave, long sleeves).*
Source: The Council for Community and Economic Research, ACCRA Cost of Living Index, 2011

HOUSING

House Price Index (HPI)

Area	National Ranking[2]	Quarterly Change (%)	One-Year Change (%)	Five-Year Change (%)
MSA[1]	94	0.62	-1.49	4.97
U.S.[3]	-	-0.10	-2.43	-19.16

Note: The HPI is a weighted repeat sales index. It measures average price changes in repeat sales or refinancings on the same properties. This information is obtained by reviewing repeat mortgage transactions on single-family properties whose mortgages have been purchased or securitized by Fannie Mae or Freddie Mac in January 1975; (1) Metropolitan/Micropolitan Statistical Area—see Appendix B for areas included; (2) Rankings are based on annual percentage change for all metro areas containing at least 15,000 transactions over the last 10 years and ranges from 1 to 306; (3) figures based on a weighted average of Census Division estimates using a purchase only index; all figures are for the period ending December 31, 2011
Source: Federal Housing Finance Agency, House Price Index, February 23, 2012

House Price Valuations

Area	Q4 2005		Q4 2006		Q4 2007		Q4 2008		Q4 2009	
	Price ($000)	Over-valuation	Price ($000)	Over-valuation	Price ($000)	Over-valuation	Price ($000)	Over-valuation	Price ($000)	Over-valuation
MSA[1]	117.4	-9.5	128.0	-7.2	133.0	-9.7	130.7	-13.4	135.4	-12.4

Note: Figures show the percentage of over- or under-valuation of single family homes relative to statistically normal house values (e.g. a value of 23.6 indicates that house values are 23.6% overvalued). Statistically normal house values are based on house prices, interest rates, household incomes, population densities, and any historical premiums or discounts metropolitan areas have exhibited over time; (1) Figures cover the Huntsville, AL - see Appendix B for areas included
Source: Global Insight/PNC Financial Services Group, House Prices in America: 4th Quarter 2009 Update

Median Single-Family Home Prices

Area	2009	2010	2011p	Percent Change 2010 to 2011
MSA[1]	n/a	n/a	172.8	n/a
U.S. Average	172.1	173.1	166.2	-4.0

Note: Figures are median sales prices of existing single-family homes in thousands of dollars; (p) preliminary; n/a not available; (1) Metropolitan Statistical Area—see Appendix B for areas included
Source: National Association of Realtors, Median Sales Price of Existing Single-Family Homes for Metropolitan Areas, 4th Quarter 2011

Affordability Index of Existing Single-Family Homes

Area	2009	2010	2011p	Percent Change 2010 to 2011
MSA[1]	n/a	n/a	117.4	n/a

Note: The housing affordability index measures whether or not a typical family could qualify for a mortgage loan on a typical home. The higher the index, the greater the household purchasing power. An index of 100 is defined as the point where a median-income household has exactly enough income to qualify for the purchase of a median-priced existing single-family home, assuming a 20 percent downpayment and 25 percent of gross income devoted to mortgage principal and interest payments; (p) preliminary; n/a not available; (1) Metropolitan Statistical Area—see Appendix B for areas included
Source: National Association of Realtors, Affordability Index of Existing Single-Family Homes, 2011

Median Apartment Condo-Coop Home Prices

Area	2009	2010	2011p	Percent Change 2010 to 2011
MSA[1]	n/a	n/a	n/a	n/a
U.S. Average	175.6	171.7	165.1	-3.8

Note: Figures are median sales prices of existing apartment condo-coop homes in thousands of dollars; (p) preliminary; n/a not available; (1) Metropolitan Statistical Area—see Appendix B for areas included
Source: National Association of Realtors, Median Sales Price of Existing Apartment Condo-Coop Homes for Metropolitan Areas, 4th Quarter 2011

Year Housing Structure Built

Area	2005 or Later	2000 -2004	1990 -1999	1980 -1989	1970 -1979	1960 -1969	1950 -1959	Before 1950	Median Year
City	7.5	6.1	11.2	16.2	17.5	23.8	10.4	7.4	1975
MSA[1]	9.6	10.7	18.8	18.3	14.2	15.3	7.1	6.0	1984
U.S.	5.0	8.6	14.0	14.1	16.3	11.3	11.2	19.6	1975

Note: Figures are percentages except for Median Year; (1) Figures cover the Huntsville, AL Metropolitan Statistical Area—see Appendix B for areas included
Source: U.S. Census Bureau, 2008-2010 American Community Survey 3-Year Estimates

HEALTH

Health Risk Data

Category	MSA[1] (%)	U.S. (%)
Adults who have been told they have high blood pressure[2]	n/a	28.7
Adults who have been told they have high blood cholesterol[2]	n/a	37.5
Adults who have been told they have diabetes[3]	n/a	8.7
Adults who have been told they have arthritis[2]	n/a	26.0
Adults who have been told they currently have asthma	n/a	9.1
Adults who are current smokers	n/a	17.3
Adults who are heavy drinkers[4]	n/a	5.0
Adults who are binge drinkers[5]	n/a	15.1
Adults who are overweight (BMI 25.0 - 29.9)	n/a	36.2
Adults who are obese (BMI 30.0 - 99.8)	n/a	27.5
Adults who participated in any physical activities in the past month	n/a	76.1
Adults 50+ who have ever had a sigmoidoscopy or colonoscopy	n/a	65.2
Women aged 40+ who have had a mammogram within the past two years	n/a	75.2
Men aged 40+ who have had a PSA test within the past two years	n/a	53.2
Adults aged 65+ who have had flu shot within the past year	n/a	67.5
Adults aged 18–64 who have any kind of health care coverage	n/a	82.2

Note: Data as of 2010 unless otherwise noted; n/a not available; (1) Figures cover the Huntsville, AL—see Appendix B for areas included; (2) Data as of 2009; (3) Figures do not include pregnancy-related, borderline, or pre-diabetes; (4) Heavy drinkers are classified as males having more than two drinks per day or females having more than one drink per day; (5) Binge drinkers are classified as males having five or more drinks on one occasion or females having four or more drinks on one occasion
Source: Centers for Disease Control and Prevention, Behaviorial Risk Factor Surveillance System, SMART: Selected Metropolitan/Micropolitan Area Risk Trends, 2009, 2010

Mortality Rates for the Top 10 Causes of Death in the U.S.

ICD-10[a] Sub-Chapter	ICD-10[a] Code	Age-Adjusted Mortality Rate[1] per 100,000 population	
		County[2]	U.S.
Malignant neoplasms	C00-C97	179.3	175.6
Ischaemic heart diseases	I20-I25	56.7	121.6
Other forms of heart disease	I30-I51	115.3	48.6
Chronic lower respiratory diseases	J40-J47	40.9	42.3
Cerebrovascular diseases	I60-I69	41.3	40.6
Organic, including symptomatic, mental disorders	F01-F09	31.8	26.7
Other degenerative diseases of the nervous system	G30-G31	32.0	24.7
Other external causes of accidental injury	W00-X59	20.1	24.4
Diabetes mellitus	E10-E14	29.0	21.7
Hypertensive diseases	I10-I15	18.7	18.2

Note: (a) ICD-10 = International Classification of Diseases 10th Revision; (1) Mortality rates are a three year average covering 2007-2009; (2) Figures cover Madison County
Source: Centers for Disease Control and Prevention, National Center for Health Statistics. Underlying Cause of Death 1999-2009 on CDC WONDER Online Database, released 2012. Data for year 2009 are compiled from the Multiple Cause of Death File 2009, Series 20 No. 2O, 2012, Data for year 2008 are compiled from the Multiple Cause of Death File 2008, Series 20 No. 2N, 2011, Data for year 2007 are compiled from Multiple Cause of Death File 2007, Series 20 No. 2M, 2010.

Mortality Rates for Selected Causes of Death

ICD-10[a] Sub-Chapter	ICD-10[a] Code	Age-Adjusted Mortality Rate[1] per 100,000 population	
		County[2]	U.S.
Assault	X85-Y09	5.9	5.7
Human immunodeficiency virus (HIV) disease	B20-B24	2.6	3.3
Influenza and pneumonia	J09-J18	18.3	16.4
Intentional self-harm	X60-X84	10.2	11.5
Malnutrition	E40-E46	*Unreliable	0.8
Obesity and other hyperalimentation	E65-E68	*0.0	1.6
Transport accidents	V01-V99	16.3	13.7
Viral hepatitis	B15-B19	*Unreliable	2.2

Note: (a) ICD-10 = International Classification of Diseases 10th Revision; (1) Mortality rates are a three year average covering 2007-2009; (2) Figures cover Madison County; (*) Unreliable data as per CDC
Source: Centers for Disease Control and Prevention, National Center for Health Statistics. Underlying Cause of Death 1999-2009 on CDC WONDER Online Database, released 2012. Data for year 2009 are compiled from the Multiple Cause of Death File 2009, Series 20 No. 2O, 2012, Data for year 2008 are compiled from the Multiple Cause of Death File 2008, Series 20 No. 2N, 2011, Data for year 2007 are compiled from Multiple Cause of Death File 2007, Series 20 No. 2M, 2010.

Distribution of Physicians and Dentists

Area[1]	Dentists[2]	D.O.[3]	M.D.[4]				
			Total	Family/ General Practice	Pediatrics	Medical Specialties	Surgical Specialties
Local (number)	138	29	670	118	44	222	162
Local (rate[5])	4.4	0.9	20.9	3.7	1.4	6.9	5.0
U.S. (rate[5])	4.5	1.9	18.3	2.5	1.4	6.8	4.1

Note: Data as of 2008 unless noted; (1) Local data covers Madison County; (2) Data as of 2007; (3) Doctor of Osteopathic Medicine; (4) Includes active, non-federal, patient-care, office-based Doctors of Medicine; (5) rate per 10,000 population
Source: Area Resource File (ARF). 2009-2010 Release. U.S. Department of Health and Human Services, Health Resources and Services Administration, Bureau of Health Professions, Rockville, MD, August 2010

EDUCATION

Public School District Statistics

District Name	Schls	Pupils	Pupil/ Teacher Ratio	Minority Pupils[1] (%)	Free Lunch Eligible[2] (%)	IEP[3] (%)
Huntsville City	50	23,374	13.4	52.6	40.2	10.9
Madison County	28	20,046	16.3	28.9	23.6	9.8

Note: Table includes school districts with 2,000 or more students; (1) Percentage of students that are not non-Hispanic white; (2) Percentage of students that are eligible for the free lunch program; (3) Percentage of students that have an Individualized Education Program.
Source: U.S. Department of Education, National Center for Education Statistics, Common Core of Data, Local Education Agency (School District) Universe Survey: School Year 2009-2010; U.S. Department of Education, National Center for Education Statistics, Common Core of Data, Public Elementary/Secondary School Universe Survey: School Year 2009-2010

Top Public High Schools

High School Name	Rank[1]	Score[1]	Grad. Rate[2] (%)	College[3] (%)	AP/IB/ AICE[4] (%)	SAT/ ACT[5] (%)
New Century Technology	500	0.081	95	88	1.3	NA

Note: (1) Public schools are ranked from 1 to 500 based on the following self-reported statistics (with their corresponding weight in the final score). Schools that had fewer than 10 graduates, as well as those that were newly founded and did not have a graduating senior class in 2010 were excluded; (2) Four-year, on-time graduation rate (25%); (3) Percent of 2010 graduates who enrolled immediately in college (25%); (4) AP/IB/AICE tests per graduate (25%); (5) Average SAT and/or ACT score (10%); Average AP/IB/AICE exam score (10%); AP/IB/AICE courses offered per graduate (5%); (6) School is unranked, but has been identified by Newsweek as one of the nation's most elite public high schools.
Source: Newsweek Online, "Top High Schools 2011"

Highest Level of Education

Area	Less than H.S.	H.S. Diploma	Some College, No Deg.	Associate Degree	Bachelors Degree	Masters Degree	Profess. School Degree	Doctorate Degree
City	12.6	20.2	23.1	6.4	23.9	9.5	2.4	1.8
MSA[1]	13.2	23.8	21.9	7.1	21.7	9.2	1.6	1.3
U.S.	14.7	28.4	21.3	7.6	17.6	7.2	1.9	1.2

Note: Figures cover persons age 25 and over; (1) Figures cover the Huntsville, AL Metropolitan Statistical Area—see Appendix B for areas included
Source: U.S. Census Bureau, 2008-2010 American Community Survey 3-Year Estimates

Educational Attainment by Race

Area	High School Graduate or Higher (%)					Bachelor's Degree or Higher (%)				
	Total	White	Black	Asian	Hisp.[2]	Total	White	Black	Asian	Hisp.[2]
City	87.4	89.8	81.2	89.8	47.3	37.6	42.7	21.6	67.2	12.0
MSA[1]	86.8	87.7	83.5	90.6	53.3	33.9	35.4	25.6	60.6	15.2
U.S.	85.3	87.5	81.4	85.5	61.6	28.0	29.3	17.8	50.2	13.0

Note: Figures shown cover persons 25 years old and over; (1) Figures cover the Huntsville, AL Metropolitan Statistical Area—see Appendix B for areas included; (2) People of Hispanic origin can be of any race
Source: U.S. Census Bureau, 2008-2010 American Community Survey 3-Year Estimates

School Enrollment by Grade and Control

Area	Preschool (%)		Kindergarten (%)		Grades 1 - 4 (%)		Grades 5 - 8 (%)		Grades 9 - 12 (%)	
	Public	Private	Public	Private	Public	Private	Public	Private	Public	Private
City	44.8	55.2	83.7	16.3	88.3	11.7	84.1	15.9	89.7	10.3
MSA[1]	45.4	54.6	88.3	11.7	87.9	12.1	84.6	15.4	88.9	11.1
U.S.	55.4	44.6	87.1	12.9	89.4	10.6	89.5	10.5	90.4	9.6

Note: Figures shown cover persons 3 years old and over; (1) Figures cover the Huntsville, AL Metropolitan Statistical Area—see Appendix B for areas included
Source: U.S. Census Bureau, 2008-2010 American Community Survey 3-Year Estimates

Average Salaries of Public School Classroom Teachers

Area	2010-11		2011-12		Percent Change 2010-11 to 2011-12	Percent Change 2001-02 to 2011-12
	Dollars	Rank[1]	Dollars	Rank[1]		
Alabama	47,803	32	48,003	40	0.42	29.10
U.S. Average	55,623	-	56,643	-	1.83	26.8

Note: (1) State rank ranges from 1 to 51 where 1 indicates highest salary.
Source: National Education Association, Rankings & Estimates: Rankings of the States 2011 and Estimates of School Statistics 2012, December 2011

Higher Education

Four-Year Colleges			Two-Year Colleges			Medical Schools[1]	Law Schools[2]	Voc/ Tech[3]
Public	Private Non-profit	Private For-profit	Public	Private Non-profit	Private For-profit			
1	2	1	1	0	0	0	0	0

Note: Figures cover institutions located within the city limits and include main campuses only; (1) includes schools accredited by the Liaison Committee on Medical Education and the American Osteopathic Association's Commission on Osteopathic College Accreditation; (2) includes American Bar Association-accredited law schools; (3) includes all schools with programs that are less than 2 years.
Source: National Center for Education Statistics, Integrated Postsecondary Education System (IPEDS) Peer Analysis System, 2011-12; Association of American Medical Colleges, Member List, April 23, 2012; American Osteopathic Association, Member List, April 23, 2012; Law School Admission Council, Official Guide to ABA-Approved Law Schools Online, April 23, 2012

According to *U.S. News & World Report*, the Huntsville, AL is home to one of the best national universities in the U.S.: **University of Alabama–Huntsville** (#190). The indicators used to capture academic quality fall into a number of categories: assessment by administrators at peer institutions; retention of students; faculty resources; student selectivity; financial resources; alumni giving; high school counselor ratings of colleges; and graduation rate. *U.S. News & World Report, "America's Best Colleges 2012"*

PRESIDENTIAL ELECTION

2008 Presidential Election Results

Area	Obama	McCain	Nader	Other
Madison County	41.9	56.9	0.3	0.9
U.S.	52.9	45.6	0.6	0.9

Note: Results are percentages and may not add to 100% due to rounding
Source: Dave Leip's Atlas of U.S. Presidential Elections, www.uselectionatlas.org

EMPLOYERS

Major Employers

Company Name	Industry
Avocent Corporation	Computer peripheral equip
City of Huntsville	Town council
City of Huntsville	Mayor's office
COLSA Corporation	Commercial research laboratory
County of Madison	Executive offices
Dynetics Inc	Engineering laboratory/except testing
General Dynamics C4 Systems Inc	Defense systems equipment
Healthcare Auth - City of Huntsville	General governement
Intergraph Process & Bldg Solutions Inc	Systems software development
Qualitest Products	Drugs and drug proprietaries
Science Applications Int'l Corporation	Computer processing services
Science Applications Int'l Corporation	Commercial research laboratory
Teledyne brown Engineering	Energy research
The Army United States Department Of	Army
The Boeing Company	Aircraft
The Boeing Company	Guided missiles/space vehicles
United States Department of the Army	Army

Note: Companies shown are located within the Huntsville, AL metropolitan area.
Source: Hoovers.com, data extracted April 25 2012

PUBLIC SAFETY

Crime Rate

Area	All Crimes	Violent Crimes				Property Crimes		
		Murder	Forcible Rape	Robbery	Aggrav. Assault	Burglary	Larceny -Theft	Motor Vehicle Theft
City	5,972.0	6.5	41.4	252.5	344.1	1,460.0	3,397.7	469.6
Suburbs[1]	2,326.0	4.3	17.1	43.7	139.2	586.3	1,407.3	128.1
Metro[2]	3,929.7	5.3	27.8	135.5	229.3	970.6	2,282.8	278.3
U.S.	3,345.5	4.8	27.5	119.1	252.3	699.6	2,003.5	238.8

Note: Figures are crimes per 100,000 population; (1) All areas within the metro area that are located outside the city limits; (2) Metropolitan Statistical Area—see Appendix B for areas included
Source: FBI Uniform Crime Reports, 2010

Hate Crimes

Area	Number of Quarters Reported	Bias Motivation				
		Race	Religion	Sexual Orientation	Ethnicity	Disability
City	4	0	0	0	0	0

Source: Federal Bureau of Investigation, Hate Crime Statistics 2010

Identity Theft Consumer Complaints

Area	Complaints	Complaints per 100,000 Population	Rank[2]
MSA[1]	323	83.5	153
U.S.	279,156	90.4	-

Note: (1) Metropolitan Statistical Area—see Appendix B for areas included; (2) Rank ranges from 1 to 384 where 1 indicates greatest number of identity theft complaints per 100,000 population
Source: Federal Trade Commission, Consumer Sentinel Network Data Book for January–December 2011

Fraud and Other Consumer Complaints

Area	Complaints	Complaints per 100,000 Population	Rank[2]
MSA[1]	2,075	536.7	105
U.S.	1,533,924	496.8	-

Note: (1) Metropolitan Statistical Area—see Appendix B for areas included; (2) Rank ranges from 1 to 384 where 1 indicates greatest number of fraud and other complaints per 100,000 population
Source: Federal Trade Commission, Consumer Sentinel Network Data Book for January–December 2011

RECREATION

Culture

Dance[1]	Theatre[1]	Instrumental Music[1]	Vocal Music[1]	Series/ Festivals	Museums	Zoos and Aquariums[2]
1	1	3	1	2	8	0

Note: (1) Number of professional performing groups; (2) AZA-accredited
Source: The Grey House Performing Arts Directory, 2011-2012; Official Museum Directory, 2011; American Association of Museums, AAM Member Museums, April 2012; Association of Zoos & Aquariums, AZA Member Zoos & Aquariums, April 2012

Professional Sports Teams

Team Name	League
No teams are located in the metro area	

Source: Original research

CLIMATE

Average and Extreme Temperatures

Temperature	Jan	Feb	Mar	Apr	May	Jun	Jul	Aug	Sep	Oct	Nov	Dec	Yr.
Extreme High (°F)	76	82	88	92	96	101	104	103	101	91	84	77	104
Average High (°F)	49	54	63	73	80	87	90	89	83	73	62	52	71
Average Temp. (°F)	39	44	52	61	69	76	80	79	73	62	51	43	61
Average Low (°F)	30	33	41	49	58	65	69	68	62	50	40	33	50
Extreme Low (°F)	-11	5	6	26	36	45	53	52	37	28	15	-3	-11

Note: Figures cover the years 1958-1995
Source: National Climatic Data Center, International Station Meteorological Climate Summary, 9/96

Average Precipitation/Snowfall/Humidity

Precip./Humidity	Jan	Feb	Mar	Apr	May	Jun	Jul	Aug	Sep	Oct	Nov	Dec	Yr.
Avg. Precip. (in.)	5.0	5.0	6.6	4.8	5.1	4.3	4.6	3.5	4.1	3.3	4.7	5.7	56.8
Avg. Snowfall (in.)	2	1	1	Tr	0	0	0	0	0	Tr	Tr	1	4
Avg. Rel. Hum. 7am (%)	82	81	79	78	79	81	84	86	85	86	84	81	82
Avg. Rel. Hum. 4pm (%)	60	56	51	46	51	53	56	55	54	51	55	60	54

Note: Figures cover the years 1958-1995; Tr = Trace amounts (<0.05 in. of rain; <0.5 in. of snow)
Source: National Climatic Data Center, International Station Meteorological Climate Summary, 9/96

Weather Conditions

Temperature			Daytime Sky			Precipitation		
10°F & below	32°F & below	90°F & above	Clear	Partly cloudy	Cloudy	0.01 inch or more precip.	0.1 inch or more snow/ice	Thunder-storms
2	66	49	70	118	177	116	2	54

Note: Figures are average number of days per year and cover the years 1958-1995
Source: National Climatic Data Center, International Station Meteorological Climate Summary, 9/96

HAZARDOUS WASTE

Superfund Sites

Huntsville has one hazardous waste site on the EPA's Superfund Final National Priorities List: **Redstone Arsenal (USARMY/NASA).** *U.S. Environmental Protection Agency, Final National Priorities List, April 17, 2012*

**AIR & WATER
QUALITY**

Air Quality Index

Area	Percent of Days when Air Quality was...[2]					AQI Statistics[2]	
	Good	Moderate	Unhealthy for Sensitive Groups	Unhealthy	Very Unhealthy	Maximum	Median
Area[1]	80.7	18.7	0.6	0.0	0.0	106	38

Note: Air Quality Index (AQI) is an index for reporting daily air quality. EPA calculates the AQI for five major air pollutants regulated by the Clean Air Act: ground-level ozone, particle pollution (aka particulate matter), carbon monoxide, sulfur dioxide, and nitrogen dioxide. The AQI runs from 0 to 500. The higher the AQI value, the greater the level of air pollution and the greater the health concern. There are six AQI categories: "Good" AQI is between 0 and 50. Air quality is considered satisfactory; "Moderate" AQI is between 51 and 100. Air quality is acceptable; "Unhealthy for Sensitive Groups" When AQI values are between 101 and 150, members of sensitive groups may experience health effects; "Unhealthy" When AQI values are between 151 and 200 everyone may begin to experience health effects; "Very Unhealthy" AQI values between 201 and 300 trigger a health alert; "Hazardous" AQI values over 300 trigger warnings of emergency conditions (not shown); (1) Data covers Madison County; (2) Based on 332 days with AQI data in 2011.
Source: U.S. Environmental Protection Agency, AirData Report, 2011

Air Quality Index Pollutants

Area	Percent of Days when AQI Pollutant was...[2]					
	Carbon Monoxide	Nitrogen Dioxide	Ozone	Sulfur Dioxide	Particulate Matter 2.5	Particulate Matter 10
Area[1]	0.0	0.0	62.3	0.0	21.7	16.0

Note: The Air Quality Index (AQI) is an index for reporting daily air quality. EPA calculates the AQI for five major air pollutants regulated by the Clean Air Act: ground-level ozone, particle pollution (also known as particulate matter), carbon monoxide, sulfur dioxide, and nitrogen dioxide. The AQI runs from 0 to 500. The higher the AQI value, the greater the level of air pollution and the greater the health concern; (1) Data covers Madison County; (2) Based on 332 days with AQI data in 2011.
Source: U.S. Environmental Protection Agency, AirData Report, 2011

Air Quality Index Trends

Area	Trend Sites (days)								All Sites (days)
	2003	2004	2005	2006	2007	2008	2009	2010	2010
MSA[1]	n/a	n/a	n/a	n/a	n/a	n/a	n/a	n/a	n/a

Note: Figures are the number of days the AQI value exceeded 100 in a given year. An AQI value greater than 100 indicates that air quality would have been in the unhealthful range on that day. Data from exceptional events are included. These counts are presented in two ways. First, the counts are based on sites having an adequate record of monitoring data during the trend period (trend sites). These counts represent the relative change in the number of days with AQI values greater than 100. In the last column, the counts are based on all sites with data in the most recent year (because it is possible for a site to have data in the most recent year but not enough data to be a trend site); (1) Data covers the Huntsville, AL—see Appendix B for areas included; n/a not available.
Source: U.S. Environmental Protection Agency, Air Quality Index Information, "Number of Days with Air Quality Index Values Greater than 100 at Trend Sites, 2000-2010, and at All Sites in 2010"

Maximum Air Pollutant Concentrations: Particulate Matter, Ozone, CO and Lead

	Particulate Matter 10 (ug/m^3)	Particulate Matter 2.5 Wtd AM (ug/m^3)	Particulate Matter 2.5 24-Hr (ug/m^3)	Ozone (ppm)	Carbon Monoxide (ppm)	Lead (ug/m^3)
MSA[1] Level	37	11.6	20	0.071	n/a	n/a
NAAQS[2]	150	15	35	0.075	9	0.15
Met NAAQS[2]	Yes	Yes	Yes	Yes	n/a	n/a

Note: Data from exceptional events are not included; (1) Data covers the Huntsville, AL—see Appendix B for areas included; (2) National Ambient Air Quality Standards; ppm = parts per million; ug/m^3 = micrograms per cubic meter; n/a not available
Concentrations: Particulate Matter 10 (coarse particulate)—highest second maximum 24-hour concentration; Particulate Matter 2.5 Wtd AM (fine particulate)—highest weighted annual mean concentration; Particulate Matter 2.5 24-Hour (fine particulate)—highest 98th percentile 24-hour concentration; Ozone—highest fourth daily maximum 8-hour concentration; Carbon Monoxide—highest second maximum non-overlapping 8-hour concentration; Lead—maximum running 3-month average
Source: U.S. Environmental Protection Agency, CBSA Factbook 2010, Air Quality Statistics by City, 2010

Maximum Air Pollutant Concentrations: Nitrogen Dioxide and Sulfur Dioxide

	Nitrogen Dioxide AM (ppb)	Nitrogen Dioxide 1-Hr (ppb)	Sulfur Dioxide AM (ppb)	Sulfur Dioxide 1-Hr (ppb)	Sulfur Dioxide 24-Hr (ppb)
MSA[1] Level	n/a	n/a	n/a	n/a	n/a
NAAQS[2]	53	100	30	75	140
Met NAAQS[2]	n/a	n/a	n/a	n/a	n/a

Note: Data from exceptional events are not included; (1) Data covers the Huntsville, AL—see Appendix B for areas included; (2) National Ambient Air Quality Standards; ppb = parts per billion; n/a not available
Concentrations: Nitrogen Dioxide AM—highest arithmetic mean concentration; Nitrogen Dioxide 1-Hr—highest 98th percentile 1-hour daily maximum concentration; Sulfur Dioxide AM—highest annual mean concentration; Sulfur Dioxide 1-Hr—highest 99th percentile 1-hour daily maximum concentration; Sulfur Dioxide 24-Hr—highest second maximum 24-hour concentration
Source: U.S. Environmental Protection Agency, CBSA Factbook 2010, Air Quality Statistics by City, 2010

Drinking Water

Water System Name	Pop. Served	Primary Water Source Type	Violations[1] Health Based	Violations[1] Monitoring/ Reporting
Huntsville Utilities	219,168	Surface	0	0

Note: (1) Based on violation data from January 1, 2011 to December 31, 2011 (includes unresolved violations from earlier years)
Source: U.S. Environmental Protection Agency, Office of Ground Water and Drinking Water, Safe Drinking Water Information System (based on data extracted April 18, 2012)

Jackson, Mississippi

Background

Jackson, located along the Pearl River in central-western Mississippi, is both the state capital and state's most populous city.

What is now Jackson was originally settled by a French Canadian trader named Louis LeFleur. The settlement was known as both Parkerville and LeFleur's Bluff before it became the state capital and renamed Jackson, after Andrew Jackson, the 7th President of the United States. The state legislature met for the first time in Jackson in 1822. The first railroads in the city were built in 1840, which connected Jackson to nearby cities including Vicksburg, Raymond and Brandon.

At the time of the Civil War, Jackson was a relatively small city but it still served as an important manufacturing center for the Confederate forces. In addition, several important battles took place in the city including the Battle of Jackson in 1863, which was won by the Union army.

The beginning of the twentieth century brought new industries and economic growth to Jackson. In the 1930s, the discovery of natural gas fields near Jackson was an important part of the city's economic prosperity. During World War II, Hawkins Field in Jackson became an important airbase and, in 1941, the Dutch Air Force relocated its Royal Netherlands Military Flying School there because Holland was occupied by Nazi forces.

The 1960s brought dramatic change to Jackson, primarily due to the Civil Rights Movement. The most noteworthy and tragic civil rights event that took place in Jackson was the 1963 assassination of Medgar Evers, a prominent civil rights activist and leader of the Mississippi chapter of the NAACP. Byron De La Beckwith, a white supremacist, was convicted for the murder in 1994.

Other notable events during this decade included the first successful lung transplant, performed in Jackson by Dr. James Hardy at the University of Mississippi Medical Center in 1963, and the Candlestick Park Tornado, which touched down in the Candlestick Shopping Center in 1966 killing nineteen people.

In 1997, Jackson voters elected Harvey Johnson, Jr., the city's first African-American mayor. One of his major proposals was a new convention center to attract businesses to the city. Jackson's original proposal failed, but the convention center was ultimately completed as part of a tax referendum designed to revitalize downtown Jackson. The $65 million facility opened in January of 2009 with over 330,000 square feet of usable space.

Other groups involved with the revitalization program include the Downtown Jackson Partners, comprised of corporate leaders, elected officials and citizens. Currently, over $1 billion in economic development projects are underway, including hotels, residential buildings, museums, a new Federal courthouse and a new Jackson Police Department Headquarters.

Transportation needs in Jackson are served by the Jackson-Evers International Airport, which was renamed in 2004 to honor the assassinated civil rights leader Medgar Evers. Airport Parkway, connecting downtown Jackson to the airport, with train service by Canadian National Railway, Kansas City Southern Railway, and Amtrak is scheduled to open in 2012.

Performing arts groups in Jackson include the Jackson Symphony Orchestra, Ballet Mississippi, the Mississippi Opera, the Mississippi Chorus and the New Stage Theatre. Other attractions include the Mississippi Museum of Art, the Russell C. Davis Planetarium, the Jackson State University Botanical Gardens and the Jackson Zoo. In addition, the city hosts the USA International Ballet Competition. The competition was founded in 1978 by Tahlia Mara and takes place every four years as part of the International Ballet Competition, which originated in Bulgaria in 1964. The next competition is scheduled for 2014, but a Gala Reunion occurred n the summer of 2012.

Major institutions of higher learning in Jackson include Tougaloo College, Jackson State University, Mississippi College School of Law and the University of Mississippi Medical Center, among others. While the city does not have any major professional sports teams, Millsap College is currently the summer home of the NFL's New Orleans Saints.

The climate in Jackson is generally very hot and humid during the summer and more mild during the winter. Rain is common during all seasons of the year and is usually accompanied by thunderstorms, which can be severe at times. Jackson does receive some snow, although it is generally light. More severe weather sometimes comes in the form of hail, strong winds and even tornadoes, such as the famed Candlestick Park Tornado of 1966.

Rankings

General Rankings

- *Men's Health Living* ranked 100 U.S. cities in terms of quality of life. Jackson was ranked #47 and received a grade of C. Criteria: number of fitness facilities; air quality; number of physicians; male/female ratio; education levels; household income; cost of living. *Men's Health Living, Spring 2008*

- Jackson appeared on RelocateAmerica's list of best places to live in America. The annual "Top 100 Places to Live" list recognizes the top communities as nominated by their residents & local businesses. RelocateAmerica's Research Group determines the list based on review of various data gathered for economic, employment, housing, education, industry, opportunity, environment and recreation along with feedback from area leaders and residents. *RelocateAmerica.com, "Top 100 Places to Live for 2011"*

Business/Finance Rankings

- Jackson was identified as one of the 20 weakest-performing metro areas during the recession and recovery from trough quarter through the third quarter of 2011. Criteria: percent change in employment; percentage point change in unemployment rate; percent change in gross metropolitan product; percent change in House Price Index. *Brookings Institution, MetroMonitor: Tracking Economic Recession and Recovery in America's 100 Largest Metropolitan Areas, December 2011*

- *American City Business Journals* ranked America's 261 largest cities in terms of their resident's wealth. Jackson ranked #249. Criteria: per capita income; median household income; percentage of households with annual incomes of $200,000 or more; median home value. *American City Business Journals, "Where the Money Is: America's Wealth Centers," August 18, 2008*

- The Jackson metro area appeared on the Milken Institute "2011 Best Performing Metros" list. Rank: #98 out of 200 large metro areas. Criteria: job growth; wage and salary growth; high-tech output growth. *Milken Institute, "2011 Best Performing Metros"*

- *Forbes* ranked the 200 most populous metro areas in the U.S. in terms of the "Best Places for Business and Careers." The Jackson metro area was ranked #159. Criteria: costs (business and living); job growth (past and projected); income growth; educational attainment; projected economic growth; crime; cultural and recreational opportunities; net migration patterns; number of highly ranked colleges. *Forbes, "Best Places for Business and Careers," June 2011*

Children/Family Rankings

- The Jackson metro area was selected as one of the "Best Cities for Relocating Families" by Worldwide ERC and Primacy Relocation. The 2008 study looked at nearly 50 factors important to relocating families including: recent job growth; nearby top-ranked colleges; in-state tuition for four-year public colleges; population growth since 2000; pediatricians per 100,000 population; and a Green Living index. *Worldwide ERC and Primacy Relocation, "2008 Best Cities for Relocating Families"*

Dating/Romance Rankings

- Jackson appeared on *Men's Health's* list of the most sex-happy cities in America. The city ranked #25 of 100. Criteria: condom sales; birth rates; sex toy sales; rates of chlamydia, gonorrhea, and syphilis. *Men's Health, "America's Most Sex-Happy Cities," October 2010*

- *Men's Health* ranked 100 U.S. cities in terms of best (and worst) marriages. Jackson was ranked #77 (#1 = worst). Criteria: rate of failed marriages; stringency of divorce laws; percentage of population who've split; number of licensed marriage and family therapists. *Men's Health, "Splitsville, USA," May 2010*

Education Rankings

- *Men's Health* ranked 100 U.S. cities in terms of their education levels. Jackson was ranked #72 (#1 = most educated city). Criteria: high school graduation rates; school enrollment; educational attainment; number of households who have outstanding student loans; number of households whose members have taken adult-education courses. *Men's Health, "Where School Is In: The Most and Least Educated Cities," September 12, 2011*

- Jackson was identified as one of the 100 "smartest" metro areas in the U.S. The area ranked #52. Criteria: the editors rated the collective brainpower of the 100 largest metro areas in the U.S. based on their residents' educational attainment. *American City Business Journals, April 14, 2008*

- Jackson was identified as one of "America's Brainiest Bastions" by *Portfolio.com*. The metro area ranked #89 out of 200. *Portfolio.com* analyzed levels of educational attainment in the nation's 200 largest metropolitan areas. The editors established scores for five levels of educational attainment, based on relative earning power of adult workers age 25 or older. Scores were determined by comparing the median income for all workers with the median income for those workers at a specified educational level. *Portfolio.com, "America's Brainiest Bastions," December 1, 2010*

Environmental Rankings

- Jackson was selected as one of 22 "Smarter Cities" for energy by the Natural Resources Defense Council. Criteria: investment in green power; energy efficiency measures; conservation. *Natural Resources Defense Council, "2010 Smarter Cities," July 19, 2010*

- 100 of the largest metro areas in the U.S. were analyzed in terms of their current drought severity. The Jackson metro area ranked #43 (#1 = driest). The rankings were based on statistics such as long-term precipitation trends and patterns and the Palmer drought indices. *Sperling's BestPlaces, www.BestPlaces.net, "America's Drought-Riskiest Cities," November 2007*

- The Jackson metro area appeared in *Country Home's* "Best Green Places" report. The area ranked #345 out of 379. Criteria: official energy policies; green power; green buildings; availability of fresh, locally grown food. *Country Home, "Best Green Places," 2008*

- Jackson was highlighted as one of the top 25 cleanest metro areas for short-term particle pollution (24-hour PM 2.5) in the U.S. Monitors in these cities reported no days with unhealthful PM 2.5 levels. *American Lung Association, State of the Air 2011*

Health/Fitness Rankings

- Jackson was identified as a "2011 Asthma Capital." The area ranked #87 out of the nation's 100 largest metropolitan areas. Twelve factors were used to identify the most challenging places to live for people with asthma: estimated prevalence; self-reported prevalence; crude death rate for asthma; annual pollen score; annual air quality; public smoking laws; number of board-certified asthma specialists; school inhaler access laws; rescue medication use; controller medication use; uninsured rate; poverty rate. *Asthma and Allergy Foundation of America, "2011 Asthma Capitals"*

- Jackson was identified as a "2011 Fall Allergy Capital." The area ranked #4 out of 100. Three groups of factors were used to identify the most severe cities for people with allergies during the fall season: annual pollen levels; medicine utilization; access to board-certified allergists. *Asthma and Allergy Foundation of America, "2011 Fall Allergy Capitals"*

- Jackson was identified as a "2012 Spring Allergy Capital." The area ranked #4 out of 100. Three groups of factors were used to identify the most severe cities for people with allergies during the spring season: annual pollen levels; medicine utilization; access to board-certified allergists. *Asthma and Allergy Foundation of America, "2012 Spring Allergy Capitals"*

- *Men's Health* examined 100 major U.S. cities and selected the best and worst cities for men. Jackson ranked #95. Criteria: 35 statistical parameters of long life in the categories of health, quality of life, and fitness. *Men's Health, "The 10 Best and Worst Cities for Men 2012," January/February 2012*

- Jackson was selected as one of the most accident-prone cities in America by *Men's Health*. The city ranked #7 of 10. Criteria: workplace accident rates; traffic fatalities; emergency room visits; accidental poisonings; incidents of drowning; fires; injury-producing falls. *Men's Health, "Ranking America's Cities: Accident City, USA," October 2009*

- *Men's Health* examined the nation's largest 100 cities and identified the cities with the best and worst teeth. Jackson was ranked among the ten worst at #5. Criteria: annual dentist visits; canceled appointments; regular flossers; fluoride usage; dental extractions. *Men's Health, April 2008*

- The Jackson metro area appeared in the 2011 Gallup-Healthways Well-Being Index. The index, based on interviews with more than 350,000 Americans, measured jobs, finances, physical health, emotional state of mind and communities. The metro area ranked #141 out of 190. Criteria: life evaluation; emotional health; work environment; physical health; healthy behaviors; basic access (basic needs optimal for a healthy life, such as access to food and medicine, having health insurance and feeling safe while walking at night). *Gallup-Healthways, "State of Well-Being 2011"*

- *Men's Health* ranked 100 U.S. cities in terms of their activity levels. Jackson was ranked #98 (#1 = most active city). Criteria: where and how often residents exercise; percentage of households that watch more than 15 hours of cable television a week and buy more than 11 video games a year; death rate from deep-vein thrombosis, a condition linked to sitting for extended periods of time. *Men's Health, "Where Sit Happens: The Most and Least Active Cities in America," June 20, 2011*

Real Estate Rankings

- Jackson was identified as one of the top 20 metro areas with the highest rate of house price appreciation in 2011. The area ranked #15 with a one-year price appreciation of 0.7% through the 4th quarter 2011. *Federal Housing Finance Agency, House Price Index, 4th Quarter 2011*

- The Center for Housing Policy ranked 210 U.S. metropolitan areas by the fair market rent for a two-bedroom unit. The Jackson metro area was ranked #125. (#1 = most expensive) with a rent of $788. Criteria: Fair Market Rent (FMR) in effect during the fourth quarter of 2009 based on HUD's fiscal year 2010 FMRs. *The Center for Housing Policy, "Paycheck to Paycheck: Most to Least Expensive Rental Markets in 2009"*

Safety Rankings

- Allstate ranked the 193 largest cities in America in terms of driver safety. Jackson ranked #90. In addition, drivers were 6.6% more likely to have had an accident compared to the national average. Allstate researchers analyzed internal property damage reported claims over a two-year period (from January 2008 to December 2009) to protect findings from external influences such as weather or road construction. A weighted average of the two-year numbers determined the annual percentages. The report defines an auto crash as any collision resulting in a property damage claim. *Allstate, "2011 Allstate America's Best Drivers Report™"*

- Jackson was identified as one of the least safe places in the U.S. in terms of its vulnerability to natural disasters and weather extremes. The city ranked #3 out of 10. Data was analyzed to show a metro areas' relative tendency to experience natural disasters (hail, tornadoes, high winds, hurricanes, earthquakes, and brush fires) or extreme weather (abundant rain or snowfall or days that are below freezing or above 90 degrees Fahrenheit). *Forbes, "Safest and Least Safe Places in the U.S.," August 30, 2005*

- Jackson was identified as one of the most dangerous mid-size cities in America by CQ Press. All 234 cities with populations of 100,000 to 499,999 that reported crime rates in 2010 for murder, rape, robbery, aggravated assault, burglary, and motor vehicle thefts were ranked. The city ranked #5 out of the top 10. *CQ Press, City Crime Rankings 2011-2012*

- The National Insurance Crime Bureau ranked 366 metro areas in the U.S. in terms of per capita rates of vehicle theft. The Jackson metro area ranked #19 (#1 = highest rate). Criteria: number of vehicle theft offenses per 100,000 inhabitants in 2010. *National Insurance Crime Bureau, "Hot Spots," June 21, 2011*

Seniors/Retirement Rankings

- The Jackson metro area was selected as one of the "10 Best Places for Single Seniors to Retire" by *U.S. News & World Report*. Criteria: metro areas with the most single seniors age 55 and over. *U.S. News & World Report, "10 Best Places for Single Seniors to Retire," November 1, 2010*

Sports/Recreation Rankings

- Jackson appeared on the *Sporting News* list of the "Best Sports Cities" for 2011. The area ranked #231 out of 271 cities in the U.S. *Sporting News* takes a 12-month snapshot of each city's sports, putting a heavy premium on regular-season won-lost records (from the most recently completed season). Other criteria include: playoff berths, bowl appearances and tournament bids; championships; applicable power ratings; quality of competition; overall fan fervor (measured in part by attendance); abundance of teams (rewarding quality over quantity); stadium and arena quality; ticket availability and prices; franchise ownership; and marquee appeal of athletes. *Sporting News, "Best Sports Cities 2011," October 4, 2011*

Women/Minorities Rankings

- *Women's Health* examined U.S. cities and identified the 100 best cities for women. Jackson was ranked #93. Criteria: 30 categories were examined from obesity and breast cancer rates to commuting times and hours spent working out. *Women's Health, "Best Cities for Women 2012"*

Miscellaneous Rankings

- *Men's Health* ranked 100 U.S. cities by their level of sadness. Jackson was ranked #78 (#1 = saddest city). Criteria: suicide rates; unemployment rates; percentage of households that use antidepressants; percent of population who report feeling blue all or most of the time. *Men's Health, "Frown Towns," November 28, 2011*

Business Environment

CITY FINANCES

City Government Finances

Component	2009 ($000)	2009 ($ per capita)
Total Revenues	244,221	1,390
Total Expenditures	255,992	1,457
Debt Outstanding	368,565	2,098
Cash and Securities[1]	180,925	1,030

Note: (1) Cash and security holdings of a government at the close of its fiscal year, including those of its dependent agencies, utilities, and liquor stores.
Source: U.S Census Bureau, State & Local Government Finances 2009

City Government Revenue by Source

Source	2009 ($000)	2009 ($ per capita)
General Revenue		
From Federal Government	18,980	108
From State Government	48,836	278
From Local Governments	968	6
Taxes		
Property	62,703	357
Sales and Gross Receipts	9,133	52
Personal Income	0	0
Corporate Income	0	0
Motor Vehicle License	0	0
Other Taxes	3,149	18
Current Charges	66,475	378
Liquor Store	0	0
Utility	20,409	116
Employee Retirement	0	0

Source: U.S Census Bureau, State & Local Government Finances 2009

City Government Expenditures by Function

Function	2009 ($000)	2009 ($ per capita)	2009 (%)
General Direct Expenditures			
Air Transportation	15,776	90	6.2
Corrections	2,388	14	0.9
Education	0	0	0.0
Employment Security Administration	0	0	0.0
Financial Administration	4,020	23	1.6
Fire Protection	19,741	112	7.7
General Public Buildings	2,871	16	1.1
Governmental Administration, Other	9,538	54	3.7
Health	844	5	0.3
Highways	19,293	110	7.5
Hospitals	0	0	0.0
Housing and Community Development	3,404	19	1.3
Interest on General Debt	8,761	50	3.4
Judicial and Legal	4,510	26	1.8
Libraries	0	0	0.0
Parking	0	0	0.0
Parks and Recreation	45,394	258	17.7
Police Protection	29,081	166	11.4
Public Welfare	844	5	0.3
Sewerage	23,697	135	9.3
Solid Waste Management	10,596	60	4.1
Veterans' Services	0	0	0.0
Liquor Store	0	0	0.0
Utility	30,493	174	11.9
Employee Retirement	0	0	0.0

Source: U.S Census Bureau, State & Local Government Finances 2009

Municipal Bond Ratings

Area	Moody's	S&P	Fitch
City	Aa2	AA-	n/a

Rating Systems (shown in declining order of credit quality): Moody's– Aaa, Aa, A, Baa, Ba, B, Caa, Ca, C (numerical modifiers 1, 2, and 3 are added to letter-rating); S&P– AAA, AA, A, BBB, BB, B, CCC, CC, C; Fitch– AAA, AA, A, BBB, BB, B, CCC, CC, C. Ratings may be modified by the addition of a plus or minus sign to show relative standing within the major rating categories.
Notes: n/a Not Available; w/d Withdrawn (1) Not Reviewed; (2) Issuer Rating/No General Obligation; (3) Standard and Poor's Issue Credit Rating (ICR) is a current opinion of an obliger with respect to a specific financial obligation, a specific class of financial obligations, or a specific financial program.
Source: City of Jackson, Mississippi, Comprehensive Annual Financial Report, Fiscal Year Ended September 30, 2010

DEMOGRAPHICS

Population Growth

Area	1990 Census	2000 Census	2010 Census	Population Growth (%) 1990-2000	Population Growth (%) 2000-2010
City	196,469	184,256	173,514	-6.2	-5.8
MSA[1]	446,941	497,197	539,057	11.2	8.4
U.S.	248,709,873	281,421,906	308,745,538	13.2	9.7

Note: (1) Figures cover the Jackson, MS Metropolitan Statistical Area—see Appendix B for areas included
Source: U.S. Census Bureau, 2010 Census

Household Size

Area	Persons in Household (%) One	Two	Three	Four	Five	Six	Seven or More	Average Household Size
City	30.2	28.0	16.9	12.4	6.9	3.1	2.5	2.60
MSA[1]	26.4	31.2	17.5	13.9	6.6	2.5	1.8	2.60
U.S.	26.7	32.8	16.1	13.4	6.5	2.6	1.9	2.58

Note: (1) Figures cover the Jackson, MS Metropolitan Statistical Area—see Appendix B for areas included
Source: U.S. Census Bureau, 2010 Census

Race

Area	White Alone[2] (%)	Black Alone[2] (%)	Asian Alone[2] (%)	AIAN[3] Alone[2] (%)	NHOPI[4] Alone[2] (%)	Other Race Alone[2] (%)	Two or More Races (%)
City	18.4	79.4	0.4	0.1	0.0	0.8	0.9
MSA[1]	49.1	47.7	1.1	0.2	0.0	1.1	0.9
U.S.	72.4	12.6	4.8	0.9	0.2	6.2	2.9

Note: (1) Figures cover the Jackson, MS Metropolitan Statistical Area—see Appendix B for areas included; (2) Alone is defined as not being in combination with one or more other races; (3) American Indian and Alaska Native; (4) Native Hawaiian and Other Pacific Islander
Source: U.S. Census Bureau, 2010 Census

Hispanic or Latino Origin

Area	Hispanic or Latino (%)	Mexican (%)	Puerto Rican (%)	Cuban (%)	Other Hispanic or Latino (%)
City	1.6	1.0	0.1	0.0	0.5
MSA[1]	2.1	1.3	0.1	0.0	0.7
U.S.	16.3	10.3	1.5	0.6	4.0

Note: Persons of Hispanic or Latino origin can be of any race; (1) Figures cover the Jackson, MS Metropolitan Statistical Area—see Appendix B for areas included
Source: U.S. Census Bureau, 2010 Census

Segregation

Type	Segregation Indices[1]				Percent Change		
	1990	2000	2010	2010 Rank[2]	1990-2000	1990-2010	2000-2010
Black/White	62.4	57.5	56.0	51	-5.0	-6.5	-1.5
Asian/White	35.3	38.0	38.9	63	2.7	3.6	1.0
Hispanic/White	26.2	31.6	42.9	52	5.4	16.7	11.4

Note: Figures are based on an analysis of 1990, 2000, and 2010 Census Decennial Census tract data by William H. Frey, Brookings Institution and the University of Michigan Social Science Data Analysis Network. In this analysis all racial groups (whites, blacks, and asians) are non-Hispanic members of those races. Hispanics are shown as a separate category; All figures cover the Metropolitan Statistical Area (see Appendix B for areas included); (1) Segregation Indices are Dissimilarity Indices that measure the degree to which the minority group is distributed differently than whites across census tracts. They range from 0 (complete integration) to 100 (complete segregation) where the value indicates the percentage of the minority group that needs to move to be distributed exactly like whites; (2) Ranges from 1 (most segregated) to 102 (least segregated); n/a not available.
Source: www.CensusScope.org

Ancestry

Area	German	Irish	English	American	Italian	Polish	French[2]	Scottish	Dutch
City	2.0	3.1	3.0	3.0	0.5	0.1	0.7	0.8	0.2
MSA[1]	5.2	8.3	7.6	7.4	1.3	0.4	1.9	1.8	0.5
U.S.	16.1	11.6	8.8	6.1	5.7	3.2	3.0	1.9	1.6

Note: Figures are the percentage of the total population reporting a particular ancestry. The nine most commonly reported ancestries in the U.S. are shown. Figures include multiple ancestries (e.g. if a person reported being Irish and Italian, they were included in both columns); (1) Figures cover the Jackson, MS Metropolitan Statistical Area—see Appendix B for areas included; (2) Excludes Basque
Source: U.S. Census Bureau, 2008-2010 American Community Survey 3-Year Estimates

Foreign-Born Population

Area	Percent of Population Born in								
	Any Foreign Country	Mexico	Asia	Europe	Carribean	South America	Central America[2]	Africa	Canada
City	n/a	n/a	n/a	n/a	n/a	n/a	n/a	n/a	n/a
MSA[1]	2.4	0.6	0.9	0.2	0.1	0.1	0.2	0.1	0.0
U.S.	12.8	3.8	3.6	1.6	1.2	0.9	1.0	0.5	0.3

Note: (1) Figures cover the Jackson, MS Metropolitan Statistical Area—see Appendix B for areas included; (2) Excludes Mexico.
Source: U.S. Census Bureau, 2008-2010 American Community Survey 3-Year Estimates

Marital Status

Area	Never Married	Now Married[2]	Separated	Widowed	Divorced
City	46.8	30.9	3.5	6.4	12.5
MSA[1]	34.5	44.8	2.8	6.2	11.6
U.S.	31.6	49.6	2.2	6.1	10.7

Note: Figures are percentages and cover the population 15 years of age and older; (1) Figures cover the Jackson, MS Metropolitan Statistical Area—see Appendix B for areas included; (2) Excludes separated
Source: U.S. Census Bureau, 2008-2010 American Community Survey 3-Year Estimates

Age

Area	Percent of Population							Median Age
	Under Age 5	Age 5 to 17	Age 18 to 34	Age 35 to 49	Age 50 to 64	Age 65 to 79	80 Years and Over	
City	7.8	19.6	27.6	18.1	17.0	7.1	2.8	31.2
MSA[1]	7.2	18.9	24.0	20.1	18.5	8.3	2.9	34.9
U.S.	6.5	17.5	23.2	20.7	19.0	9.4	3.6	37.2

Note: (1) Figures cover the Jackson, MS Metropolitan Statistical Area—see Appendix B for areas included
Source: U.S. Census Bureau, 2010 Census

Male/Female Ratio

Area	Males	Females	Males per 100 Females
City	80,615	92,899	86.8
MSA[1]	256,917	282,140	91.1
U.S.	151,781,326	156,964,212	96.7

Note: (1) Figures cover the Jackson, MS
Metropolitan Statistical Area—see Appendix B for areas included
Source: U.S. Census Bureau, 2010 Census

Religious Groups

Area	Catholic	Baptist	Non-Den.	Methodist[2]	Lutheran	LDS[3]	Pente-costal	Presby-terian[4]	Muslim[5]	Judaism
MSA[1]	3.2	34.5	7.7	10.5	0.2	0.7	2.1	2.0	0.1	0.3
U.S.	19.1	9.3	4.0	4.0	2.3	2.0	1.9	1.6	0.8	0.7

Note: Figures are the number of adherents as a percentage of the total population; (1) Figures cover the Jackson, MS Metropolitan Statistical Area—see Appendix B for areas included; (2) Methodist/Pietist; (3) Latter Day Saints; (4) Reformed; (5) Figures are estimates
Source: Association of Statisticians of American Religious Bodies, 2010 U.S. Religion Census: Religious Congregations & Membership Study

ECONOMY

Gross Metropolitan Product

Area	2007	2008	2009	2010	2010 Rank[2]
MSA[1]	23.1	23.8	23.5	24.1	88

Note: Figures are in billions of dollars; (1) Figures cover the Jackson, MS Metropolitan Statistical Area—see Appendix B for areas included; (2) Rank ranges from 1 to 363
Source: The United States Conference of Mayors, "U.S. Metro Economies: GMP and Employment Forecasts," June 2011

Economic Growth

Area	2007-2009 (%)	2010 (%)	2011 (%)	Rank[2]
MSA[1]	-0.4	1.9	1.9	120
U.S.	-1.3	2.9	2.5	–

Note: Figures are real Gross Metropolitan Product growth rates and represent annual average percent change; (1) Figures cover the Jackson, MS Metropolitan Statistical Area—see Appendix B for areas included; (2) Rank ranges from 1 to 363
Source: The United States Conference of Mayors, "U.S. Metro Economies: GMP and Employment Forecasts," June 2011

Metropolitan Area Exports

Area	2005	2006	2007	2008	2009	2010	2010 Rank[2]
MSA[1]	904.4	939.9	601.1	676.9	432.3	541.7	196

Note: Figures are in millions of dollars; (1) Figures cover the Jackson, MS Metropolitan Statistical Area—see Appendix B for areas included; (2) Rank ranges from 1 to 369
Source: U.S. Department of Commerce, International Trade Administration, Office of Trade & Industry Information, Manufacturing & Services, data extracted April 2, 2012

INCOME

Income

Area	Per Capita ($)	Median Household ($)	Average Household ($)
City	18,454	33,465	49,136
MSA[1]	23,237	45,116	61,506
U.S.	26,942	51,222	70,116

Note: (1) Figures cover the Jackson, MS Metropolitan Statistical Area—see Appendix B for areas included
Source: U.S. Census Bureau, 2008-2010 American Community Survey 3-Year Estimates

Household Income Distribution

Area				Percent of Households Earning				
	Under $15,000	$15,000 -24,999	$25,000 -34,999	$35,000 -49,999	$50,000 -74,999	$75,000 -99,000	$100,000 -149,999	$150,000 and up
City	22.8	15.8	13.3	15.3	15.0	7.5	6.3	4.1
MSA[1]	16.1	12.6	11.1	14.8	17.7	11.6	10.2	5.9
U.S.	13.0	11.0	10.6	14.2	18.5	12.1	12.2	8.4

Note: (1) Figures cover the Jackson, MS Metropolitan Statistical Area—see Appendix B for areas included
Source: U.S. Census Bureau, 2008-2010 American Community Survey 3-Year Estimates

Poverty Rate

Area	All Ages	Under 18 Years Old	18 to 64 Years Old	65 Years and Over
City	26.9	38.8	23.3	15.4
MSA[1]	18.2	26.3	16.1	11.0
U.S.	14.4	20.1	13.1	9.4

Note: Figures are percentage of people whose income during the past 12 months was below the poverty level;
(1) Figures cover the Jackson, MS Metropolitan Statistical Area—see Appendix B for areas included
Source: U.S. Census Bureau, 2008-2010 American Community Survey 3-Year Estimates

Personal Bankruptcy Filing Rate

Area	2006	2007	2008	2009	2010	2011
Hinds County	5.28	6.95	5.88	6.57	6.44	6.31
U.S.	2.00	2.73	3.53	4.61	4.97	4.37

Note: Numbers are per 1,000 population and include Chapter 7 and Chapter 13 filings
Source: Federal Deposit Insurance Corporation, Regional Economic Conditions, March 9, 2012

EMPLOYMENT

Labor Force and Employment

Area	Civilian Labor Force			Workers Employed		
	Dec. 2010	Dec. 2011	% Chg.	Dec. 2010	Dec. 2011	% Chg.
City	82,262	83,529	1.5	74,537	75,583	1.4
MSA[1]	269,419	273,599	1.6	248,550	252,036	1.4
U.S.	153,156,000	153,373,000	0.1	139,159,000	140,681,000	1.1

Note: Data is not seasonally adjusted and covers workers 16 years of age and older;
(1) Metropolitan Statistical Area—see Appendix B for areas included
Source: Bureau of Labor Statistics, http://stats.bls.gov

Unemployment Rate

Area	2011											
	Jan.	Feb.	Mar.	Apr.	May	Jun.	Jul.	Aug.	Sep.	Oct.	Nov.	Dec.
City	10.4	10.1	9.8	9.6	9.4	10.5	10.5	9.3	10.1	9.9	9.4	9.5
MSA[1]	8.6	8.5	8.2	8.0	7.8	8.8	8.8	7.7	8.6	8.4	7.8	7.9
U.S.	9.8	9.5	9.2	8.7	8.7	9.3	9.3	9.1	8.8	8.5	8.2	8.3

Note: Data is not seasonally adjusted and covers workers 16 years of age and older; All figures are
percentages; (1) Metropolitan Statistical Area—see Appendix B for areas included
Source: Bureau of Labor Statistics, http://stats.bls.gov

Projected Unemployment Rate

Area	2010 (%)	2011 (%)	2012 (%)	2013 (%)
MSA[1]	8.4	8.0	7.6	7.3

Note: (1) Metropolitan Statistical Area—see Appendix B for areas included
Source: The United States Conference of Mayors, "U.S. Metro Economies: GMP and Employment Forecasts,"
June 2011

Employment by Occupation

Occupation Classification	City (%)	MSA[1] (%)	U.S. (%)
Management, Business, Science, and Arts	30.4	35.9	35.6
Natural Resources, Construction, and Maintenance	7.0	9.5	9.5
Production, Transportation, and Material Moving	12.6	11.3	12.1
Sales and Office	26.3	25.6	25.2
Service	23.7	17.7	17.6

Note: Figures cover employed civilians 16 years of age and older; (1) Figures cover the Jackson, MS Metropolitan Statistical Area—see Appendix B for areas included
Source: U.S. Census Bureau, 2008-2010 American Community Survey 3-Year Estimates

Employment by Industry

Sector	MSA[1] Number of Employees	MSA[1] Percent of Total	U.S. Percent of Total
Construction	10,100	3.9	4.1
Education and Health Services	40,000	15.5	15.2
Financial Activities	15,300	5.9	5.8
Government	59,100	23.0	16.8
Information	4,300	1.7	2.0
Leisure and Hospitality	21,900	8.5	9.9
Manufacturing	16,200	6.3	8.9
Mining and Logging	900	0.3	0.6
Other Services	10,400	4.0	4.0
Professional and Business Services	28,900	11.2	13.3
Retail Trade	29,500	11.5	11.5
Transportation and Utilities	10,200	4.0	3.8
Wholesale Trade	10,500	4.1	4.2

Note: Figures cover non-farm employment as of December 2011 and are not seasonally adjusted; (1) Metropolitan Statistical Area—see Appendix B for areas included
Source: Bureau of Labor Statistics, http://stats.bls.gov

Occupations with Greatest Projected Employment Growth: 2008 – 2018

Occupation[1]	2008 Employment	2018 Projected Employment	Numeric Employment Change	Percent Employment Change
Registered Nurses	30,530	37,740	7,210	23.6
Cashiers	43,810	50,830	7,020	16.0
Retail Salespersons	38,400	45,390	6,990	18.2
Nursing Aides, Orderlies, and Attendants	21,010	26,390	5,380	25.6
Truck Drivers, Heavy and Tractor-Trailer	26,480	31,030	4,550	17.2
Customer Service Representatives	12,930	16,440	3,510	27.1
Stock Clerks and Order Fillers	18,040	21,160	3,120	17.3
Secretaries, Except Legal, Medical, and Executive	28,430	31,460	3,030	10.7
Bookkeeping, Accounting, and Auditing Clerks	20,360	23,280	2,920	14.3
Licensed Practical and Licensed Vocational Nurses	12,040	14,900	2,860	23.8

Note: Projections cover Mississippi; (1) Sorted by numeric employment change
Source: www.projectionscentral.com, State Occupational Projections, 2008–2018 Long-Term Projections

Fastest Growing Occupations: 2008 – 2018

Occupation[1]	2008 Employment	2018 Projected Employment	Numeric Employment Change	Percent Employment Change
Home Health Aides	4,400	6,760	2,360	53.6
Fitness Trainers and Aerobics Instructors	1,450	2,050	600	41.4
Computer Software Engineers, Applications	1,340	1,860	520	38.8
Computer Software Engineers, Systems Software	290	400	110	37.9
Aircraft Structure, Surfaces, Rigging, and Systems Assemblers	270	370	100	37.0
Physical Therapist Aides	420	570	150	35.7
Computer-Controlled Machine Tool Operators, Metal and Plastic	900	1,220	320	35.6
Industrial Engineers	2,360	3,170	810	34.3
Network Systems and Data Communications Analysts	620	830	210	33.9
Petroleum Engineers	300	400	100	33.3

Note: Projections cover Mississippi; (1) Sorted by percent employment change and excludes occupations with numeric employment change less than 100
Source: www.projectionscentral.com, State Occupational Projections, 2008–2018 Long-Term Projections

Average Wages

Occupation	$/Hr.	Occupation	$/Hr.
Accountants and Auditors	27.11	Maids and Housekeeping Cleaners	8.53
Automotive Mechanics	16.41	Maintenance and Repair Workers	14.27
Bookkeepers	16.10	Marketing Managers	42.99
Carpenters	14.11	Nuclear Medicine Technologists	26.13
Cashiers	8.86	Nurses, Licensed Practical	17.29
Clerks, General Office	11.51	Nurses, Registered	31.47
Clerks, Receptionists/Information	11.33	Nursing Aides/Orderlies/Attendants	9.48
Clerks, Shipping/Receiving	14.60	Packers and Packagers, Hand	9.45
Computer Programmers	26.73	Physical Therapists	34.15
Computer Support Specialists	21.39	Postal Service Mail Carriers	23.92
Computer Systems Analysts	26.99	Real Estate Brokers	n/a
Cooks, Restaurant	9.43	Retail Salespersons	12.64
Dentists	71.38	Sales Reps., Exc. Tech./Scientific	26.78
Electrical Engineers	36.57	Sales Reps., Tech./Scientific	n/a
Electricians	20.70	Secretaries, Exc. Legal/Med./Exec.	13.88
Financial Managers	38.79	Security Guards	11.69
First-Line Supervisors/Managers, Sales	17.71	Surgeons	88.21
Food Preparation Workers	8.36	Teacher Assistants	8.80
General and Operations Managers	49.11	Teachers, Elementary School	20.30
Hairdressers/Cosmetologists	13.13	Teachers, Secondary School	20.30
Internists	72.02	Telemarketers	14.52
Janitors and Cleaners	9.55	Truck Drivers, Heavy/Tractor-Trailer	17.55
Landscaping/Groundskeeping Workers	10.82	Truck Drivers, Light/Delivery Svcs.	14.71
Lawyers	55.86	Waiters and Waitresses	9.50

Note: Wage data covers the Jackson, MS Metropolitan Statistical Area—see Appendix B for areas included.
Hourly wages for elementary/secondary school teachers and teacher assistants were calculated by the editors from annual wage data assuming a 40 hour work week; n/a not available.
Source: Bureau of Labor Statistics, Metro Area Occupational Employment and Wage Estimates, May 2011

**RESIDENTIAL
REAL ESTATE**

Building Permits

Area	Single-Family			Multi-Family			Total		
	2010	2011	Pct. Chg.	2010	2011	Pct. Chg.	2010	2011	Pct. Chg.
City	42	148	252.4	88	153	73.9	130	301	131.5
MSA[1]	1,303	1,207	-7.4	88	153	73.9	1,391	1,360	-2.2
U.S.	447,311	418,498	-6.4	157,299	205,563	30.7	604,610	624,061	3.2

Note: (1) Metropolitan Statistical Area—see Appendix B for areas included; figures represent new, privately-owned housing units authorized (unadjusted data); All permit data are based on estimates with imputation.
Source: U.S. Census Bureau, Manufacturing, Mining, and Construction Statistics, Building Permits, 2010, 2011

Homeownership Rate

Area	2005 (%)	2006 (%)	2007 (%)	2008 (%)	2009 (%)	2010 (%)	2011 (%)
MSA[1]	n/a	n/a	n/a	n/a	n/a	n/a	n/a
U.S.	68.9	68.8	68.1	67.8	67.4	66.9	66.1

Note: (1) Metropolitan Statistical Area—see Appendix B for areas included; n/a not available
Source: U.S. Census Bureau, Housing Vacancies and Homeownership Annual Statistics: 2011

Housing Vacancy Rates

Area	Gross Vacancy Rate[2] (%)			Year-Round Vacancy Rate[3] (%)			Rental Vacancy Rate[4] (%)			Homeowner Vacancy Rate[5] (%)		
	2009	2010	2011	2009	2010	2011	2009	2010	2011	2009	2010	2011
MSA[1]	n/a	n/a	n/a	n/a	n/a	n/a	n/a	n/a	n/a	n/a	n/a	n/a
U.S.	14.5	14.3	14.2	11.3	11.3	11.1	10.6	10.2	9.5	2.6	2.6	2.5

Note: (1) Metropolitan Statistical Area—see Appendix B for areas included; (2) The percentage of the total housing inventory that is vacant; (3) The percentage of the housing inventory (excluding seasonal units) that is year-round vacant; (4) The percentage of rental inventory that is vacant for rent; (5) The percentage of homeowner inventory that is vacant for sale; n/a not available
Source: U.S. Census Bureau, Housing Vacancies and Homeownership Annual Statistics: 2011

TAXES

State Corporate Income Tax Rates

State	Tax Rate (%)	Income Brackets ($)	Num. of Brackets	Financial Institution Tax Rate (%)[a]	Federal Income Tax Ded.
Mississippi	3.0 - 5.0	5,000 - 10,001	3	3.0 - 5.0	No

Note: Tax rates as of January 1, 2012; (a) Rates listed are the corporate income tax rate applied to financial institutions or excise taxes based on income. Some states have other taxes based upon the value of deposits or shares.
Source: Federation of Tax Administrators, "State Corporate Income Tax Rates, 2012"

State Individual Income Tax Rates

State	Tax Rate (%)	Income Brackets ($)	Num. of Brackets	Personal Exempt. ($)[1] Single	Dependents	Fed. Inc. Tax Ded.
Mississippi	3.0 - 5.0	5,000 - 10,001	3	6,000	1,500	No

Note: Tax rates as of January 1, 2012; Local- and county-level taxes are not included; n/a not applicable; (1) Married joint filers generally receive double the single exemption
Source: Federation of Tax Administrators, "State Individual Income Tax Rates, 2012"

Various State and Local Tax Rates

State	State and Local Sales and Use (%)	State Sales and Use (%)	Gasoline[1] (¢/gal.)	Cigarette[2] ($/pack)	Spirits[3] ($/gal.)	Wine[4] ($/gal.)	Beer[5] ($/gal.)
Mississippi	7.0	7.00	18.8	0.68	8.43 (f)	- (j)	0.43

Note: All tax rates as of January 1, 2012 except beer, wine and spirits (September 1, 2011); (1) The American Petroleum Institute has developed a methodology for determining the average tax rate on a gallon of fuel. Rates may include any of the following: excise taxes, environmental fees, storage tank fees, other fees or taxes, general sales tax, and local taxes. In states where gasoline is subject to the general sales tax, or where the fuel tax is based on the average sale price, the average rate determined by API is sensitive to changes in the price of gasoline. States that fully or partially apply general sales taxes to gasoline: CA, CO, GA, IL, IN, MI, NY; (2) The federal excise tax of $1.0066 per pack and local taxes are not included; (3) Rates are those applicable to off-premise sales of 40% alcohol by volume (a.b.v.) distilled spirits in 750ml containers. Local excise taxes are excluded; (4) Rates are those applicable to off-premise sales of 11% a.b.v. non-carbonated wine in 750ml containers; (5) Rates are those applicable to off-premise sales of 4.7% a.b.v. beer in 12 ounce containers; (f) States where the government controls sales. In these "control states," products are subject to ad valorem mark-up and excise taxes. The excise tax rate is calculated using a methodology developed by the Distilled Spirits Council of the United States; (j) Control states, where the government controls all sales. Products can be subject to ad valorem mark-up and excise taxes.
Source: Tax Foundation, 2012 Facts & Figures: How Does Your State Compare?

State-Local Tax Burdens

Area	Rate (%)	Rank[1]	Per Capita Taxes Paid to Home State ($)	Total State and Local Per Capita Taxes Paid ($)	Per Capita Income ($)
Mississippi	8.7	36	1,863	2,678	30,689
U.S. Average	9.8	-	3,057	4,160	42,539

Note: Figures cover 2009; (1) Rank ranges from 1 to 50 where 1 is highest tax burden
Source: Tax Foundation, State-Local Tax Burdens, All States, 2009

State Business Tax Climate Index Rankings

State	Overall Rank	Corporate Tax Index Rank	Individual Income Tax Index Rank	Sales Tax Index Rank	Unemployment Insurance Tax Index Rank	Property Tax Index Rank
Mississippi	17	11	19	28	8	29

Note: The index is a measure of how each state's tax laws affect economic performance. The lower the rank, the more favorable a state's tax system is for business. States without a given tax are given a ranking of 1.
Source: Tax Foundation, Major Components of the State Business Tax Climate Index, FY 2012

COMMERCIAL UTILITIES

Typical Monthly Electric Bills

Area	Commercial Service ($/month)		Industrial Service ($/month)	
	1,500 kWh	40 kW demand 14,000 kWh	1,000 kW demand 200,000 kWh	50,000 kW demand 15,000,000 kWh
City	156	1,215	14,737	935,358
Average[1]	189	1,616	25,197	1,470,813

Note: Based on total rates in effect July 1, 2011; (1) average based on 184 utilities surveyed
Source: Edison Electric Institute, Typical Bills and Average Rates Report, Summer 2011

TRANSPORTATION

Means of Transportation to Work

Area	Car/Truck/Van Drove Alone	Car-pooled	Public Transportation Bus	Subway	Railroad	Bicycle	Walked	Other Means	Worked at Home
City	82.6	10.4	1.0	0.0	0.0	0.1	1.7	0.8	3.4
MSA[1]	84.4	9.6	0.5	0.0	0.0	0.1	1.3	1.0	3.2
U.S.	76.0	10.2	2.7	1.7	0.5	0.5	2.8	1.3	4.2

Note: Figures are percentages and cover workers 16 years of age and older; (1) Figures cover the Jackson, MS Metropolitan Statistical Area—see Appendix B for areas included
Source: U.S. Census Bureau, 2008-2010 American Community Survey 3-Year Estimates

Travel Time to Work

Area	Less Than 10 Minutes	10 to 19 Minutes	20 to 29 Minutes	30 to 44 Minutes	45 to 59 Minutes	60 to 89 Minutes	90 Minutes or More
City	9.7	41.0	29.5	15.7	1.8	1.3	0.9
MSA[1]	10.7	32.3	27.0	20.8	4.8	3.0	1.4
U.S.	13.9	30.1	20.8	19.8	7.5	5.5	2.5

Note: Figures are percentages and include workers 16 years old and over; (1) Figures cover the Jackson, MS Metropolitan Statistical Area—see Appendix B for areas included
Source: U.S. Census Bureau, 2008-2010 American Community Survey 3-Year Estimates

Travel Time Index

Area	1985	1990	1995	2000	2005	2010
Urban Area[1]	1.02	1.02	1.04	1.06	1.09	1.06
Average[2]	1.11	1.16	1.18	1.21	1.25	1.20

Note: Travel Time Index—the ratio of travel time in the peak period to the travel time at free-flow conditions. A value of 1.30 indicates a 20-minute free-flow trip takes 26 minutes in the peak. Free-flow speeds (60 mph on freeways and 35 mph on principal arterials) are used as the comparison threshold; (1) Covers the Jackson MS urban area; (2) average of 439 urban areas
Source: Texas Transportation Institute, Urban Mobility Report 2011, September 2011

Public Transportation

Agency Name / Mode of Transportation	Vehicles Operated in Maximum Service	Annual Unlinked Passenger Trips ('000)	Annual Passenger Miles ('000)
City of Jackson Transit System (JATRAN)			
Bus (directly operated)	27	520.6	807.0
Demand Response (directly operated)	8	24.8	222.4

Source: Federal Transit Administration, National Transit Database, 2010

Air Transportation

Airport Name and Code / Type of Service	Passenger Airlines[1]	Passenger Enplanements	Freight Carriers[2]	Freight (lbs.)
Jackson International (JAN)				
Domestic service (U.S. carriers - 2011)	14	615,148	8	6,953,316
International service (U.S. carriers - 2010)	0	0	0	0

Note: (1) Includes all U.S.-based major, minor and commuter airlines that carried at least one passenger during the year; (2) Includes all U.S.-based airlines and freight carriers that transported at least one pound of freight during the year
Source: Bureau of Transportation Statistics, The Intermodal Transportation Database, Air Carriers: T-100 Domestic Market (U.S. Carriers), 2011; Bureau of Transportation Statistics, The Intermodal Transportation Database, Air Carriers: T-100 International Market (U.S. Carriers), 2010

Other Transportation Statistics

Major Highways: I-20; I-55
Amtrak Service: Yes
Major Waterways/Ports: None
Source: Amtrak.com; Google Maps

BUSINESSES

Major Business Headquarters

Company Name	Rankings	
	Fortune[1]	Forbes[2]
No companies listed	-	-

Note: (1) Fortune 500—companies that produce a 10-K are ranked 1 to 500 based on 2010 revenue; (2) all private companies with at least $2 billion in annual revenue are ranked 1 to 212; companies listed are headquartered in the city; dashes indicate no ranking
Source: Fortune, "Fortune 500," May 23, 2011; Forbes, "America's Largest Private Companies," November 16, 2011

Fast-Growing Businesses

According to *Initiative for a Competitive Inner City (ICIC)*, Jackson is home to one of America's 100 fastest-growing "inner city" companies: **U.S. Coating Specialties & Supplies (#13)**. Companies were ranked by their five-year compound annual growth rate. Criteria for inclusion: company must be headquartered in or have 51 percent or more of its physical operations in an economically distressed urban area; must be an independent, for-profit corporation, partnership or proprietorship; must have 10 or more employees and have a five-year sales history that includes sales of at least $200,000 in the base year and at least $1 million in the current year with no decrease in sales over the two most recent years. *Initiative for a Competitive Inner City (ICIC), "Inner City 100 Companies, 2011"*

Minority- and Women-Owned Businesses

Group	All Firms		Firms with Paid Employees			
	Firms	Sales ($000)	Firms	Sales ($000)	Employees	Payroll ($000)
Asian	306	116,202	185	109,819	954	17,060
Black	6,447	247,563	283	138,044	2,017	44,947
Hispanic	49	16,856	20	15,783	204	3,961
Women	5,311	568,622	546	480,768	4,651	115,088
All Firms	382	3,742,687	379	3,740,645	16,329	546,236

Note: Figures cover firms located in the city; minority- and women-owned business are defined as firms in which the corresponding group own 51% or more of the stock or equity of the company
Source: U.S. Census Bureau, 2007 Economic Census, Survey of Business Owners

HOTELS

Hotels/Motels

Area	5 Star		4 Star		3 Star		2 Star		1 Star		Not Rated	
	Num.	Pct.[3]	Num.	Pct.[3]	Num.	Pct.[3]	Num.	Pct.[3]	Num.	Pct.[3]	Num.	Pct.[3]
City[1]	0	0.0	0	0.0	12	12.0	60	60.0	2	2.0	26	26.0
Total[2]	133	0.9	940	6.5	4,569	31.8	7,033	48.9	351	2.4	1,343	9.3

Note: (1) Figures cover Jackson and vicinity; (2) Figures cover all 100 cities in this book; (3) Percentage of hotels which have a given star rating; Star ratings are determined by expedia.com and offer an indication of the general quality of a particular hotel.
Source: expedia.com, April 25, 2012

EVENT SITES

Major Stadiums, Arenas, and Auditoriums

Name	Max. Capacity
Mississippi Coast Coliseum	15,000
Mississippi Veterans Memorial Stadium	60,492
Smith-Wills Stadium	5,200

Source: Original research

Convention Centers

Name	Overall Space (sq. ft.)	Exhibit Space (sq. ft.)	Meeting Space (sq. ft.)	Meeting Rooms
Jackson Cenvention Complex	330,000	n/a	60,000	n/a
Mississippi Telcom Center	120,000	n/a	n/a	n/a

Note: n/a not available
Source: Original research

Living Environment

COST OF LIVING

Cost of Living Index

Composite Index	Groceries	Housing	Utilities	Trans-portation	Health Care	Misc. Goods/ Services
96.7	91.3	95.1	124.3	94.9	98.4	91.7

Note: U.S. = 100; Figures cover the Jackson MS urban area.
Source: The Council for Community and Economic Research, ACCRA Cost of Living Index, 2011

Grocery Prices

Area[1]	T-Bone Steak ($/pound)	Frying Chicken ($/pound)	Whole Milk ($/half gal.)	Eggs ($/dozen)	Orange Juice ($/64 oz.)	Coffee ($/11.5 oz.)
City[2]	8.82	1.04	2.47	1.60	2.98	4.16
Avg.	9.25	1.18	2.22	1.66	3.19	4.40
Min.	6.70	0.88	1.31	0.95	2.46	2.94
Max.	14.30	2.16	3.50	3.18	4.75	6.83

Note: (1) Values for the local area are compared with the average, minimum and maximum values for all 335 areas in the Cost of Living Index; (2) Figures cover the Jackson MS urban area; **T-Bone Steak** *(price per pound);* **Frying Chicken** *(price per pound, whole fryer);* **Whole Milk** *(half gallon carton);* **Eggs** *(price per dozen, Grade A, large);* **Orange Juice** *(64 oz. Tropicana or Florida Natural);* **Coffee** *(11.5 oz. can, vacuum-packed, Maxwell House, Hills Bros, or Folgers).*
Source: The Council for Community and Economic Research, ACCRA Cost of Living Index, 2011

Housing and Utility Costs

Area[1]	New Home Price ($)	Apartment Rent ($/month)	All Electric ($/month)	Part Electric ($/month)	Other Energy ($/month)	Telephone ($/month)
City[2]	278,817	730	-	106.80	115.24	29.34
Avg.	285,990	839	163.23	89.00	77.52	26.92
Min.	188,005	460	125.58	45.39	33.89	17.98
Max.	1,197,028	3,244	339.16	181.97	348.69	40.01

Note: (1) Values for the local area are compared with the average, minimum and maximum values for all 335 areas in the Cost of Living Index; (2) Figures cover the Jackson MS urban area; **New Home Price** *(2,400 sf living area, 8,000 sf lot, in urban area with full utilities);* **Apartment Rent** *(950 sf 2 bedroom/1.5 or 2 bath, unfurnished, excluding all utilities except water);* **All Electric** *(average monthly cost for an all-electric home);* **Part Electric** *(average monthly cost for a part-electric home);* **Other Energy** *(average monthly cost for natural gas, fuel oil, coal, wood, and any other forms of energy except electricity);* **Telephone** *(price includes basic monthly rate for a private residential line plus additional local usage charges incurred by a family of four).*
Source: The Council for Community and Economic Research, ACCRA Cost of Living Index, 2011

Health Care, Transportation, and Other Costs

Area[1]	Doctor ($/visit)	Dentist ($/visit)	Optometrist ($/visit)	Gasoline ($/gallon)	Beauty Salon ($/visit)	Men's Shirt ($)
City[2]	86.10	87.33	82.32	3.31	28.92	16.10
Avg.	93.88	81.72	90.54	3.48	32.65	25.06
Min.	60.00	55.33	53.66	3.18	19.78	13.44
Max.	154.98	145.97	183.72	4.31	63.21	46.00

Note: (1) Values for the local area are compared with the average, minimum and maximum values for all 335 areas in the Cost of Living Index; (2) Figures cover the Jackson MS urban area; **Doctor** *(general practitioners routine exam of an established patient);* **Dentist** *(adult teeth cleaning and periodic oral examination);* **Optometrist** *(full vision eye exam for established adult patient);* **Gasoline** *(one gallon regular unleaded, national brand, including all taxes, cash price at self-service pump if available);* **Beauty Salon** *(woman's shampoo, trim, and blow-dry);* **Men's Shirt** *(cotton/polyester dress shirt, pinpoint weave, long sleeves).*
Source: The Council for Community and Economic Research, ACCRA Cost of Living Index, 2011

HOUSING

House Price Index (HPI)

Area	National Ranking[2]	Quarterly Change (%)	One-Year Change (%)	Five-Year Change (%)
MSA[1]	15	0.71	0.73	-0.07
U.S.[3]	-	-0.10	-2.43	-19.16

Note: The HPI is a weighted repeat sales index. It measures average price changes in repeat sales or refinancings on the same properties. This information is obtained by reviewing repeat mortgage transactions on single-family properties whose mortgages have been purchased or securitized by Fannie Mae or Freddie Mac in January 1975; (1) Metropolitan/Micropolitan Statistical Area—see Appendix B for areas included; (2) Rankings are based on annual percentage change for all metro areas containing at least 15,000 transactions over the last 10 years and ranges from 1 to 306; (3) figures based on a weighted average of Census Division estimates using a purchase only index; all figures are for the period ending December 31, 2011
Source: Federal Housing Finance Agency, House Price Index, February 23, 2012

House Price Valuations

Area	Q4 2005 Price ($000)	Q4 2005 Over-valuation	Q4 2006 Price ($000)	Q4 2006 Over-valuation	Q4 2007 Price ($000)	Q4 2007 Over-valuation	Q4 2008 Price ($000)	Q4 2008 Over-valuation	Q4 2009 Price ($000)	Q4 2009 Over-valuation
MSA[1]	99.9	-14.4	106.0	-12.9	105.7	-16.4	103.1	-19.4	101.6	-22.5

Note: Figures show the percentage of over- or under-valuation of single family homes relative to statistically normal house values (e.g. a value of 23.6 indicates that house values are 23.6% overvalued). Statistically normal house values are based on house prices, interest rates, household incomes, population densities, and any historical premiums or discounts metropolitan areas have exhibited over time; (1) Figures cover the Jackson, MS - see Appendix B for areas included
Source: Global Insight/PNC Financial Services Group, House Prices in America: 4th Quarter 2009 Update

Median Single-Family Home Prices

Area	2009	2010	2011p	Percent Change 2010 to 2011
MSA[1]	134.9	133.2	135.9	2.0
U.S. Average	172.1	173.1	166.2	-4.0

Note: Figures are median sales prices of existing single-family homes in thousands of dollars; (p) preliminary; n/a not available; (1) Metropolitan Statistical Area—see Appendix B for areas included
Source: National Association of Realtors, Median Sales Price of Existing Single-Family Homes for Metropolitan Areas, 4th Quarter 2011

Affordability Index of Existing Single-Family Homes

Area	2009	2010	2011p	Percent Change 2010 to 2011
MSA[1]	128.7	138.5	143.7	3.8

Note: The housing affordability index measures whether or not a typical family could qualify for a mortgage loan on a typical home. The higher the index, the greater the household purchasing power. An index of 100 is defined as the point where a median-income household has exactly enough income to qualify for the purchase of a median-priced existing single-family home, assuming a 20 percent downpayment and 25 percent of gross income devoted to mortgage principal and interest payments; (p) preliminary; n/a not available; (1) Metropolitan Statistical Area—see Appendix B for areas included
Source: National Association of Realtors, Affordability Index of Existing Single-Family Homes, 2011

Median Apartment Condo-Coop Home Prices

Area	2009	2010	2011p	Percent Change 2010 to 2011
MSA[1]	n/a	n/a	n/a	n/a
U.S. Average	175.6	171.7	165.1	-3.8

Note: Figures are median sales prices of existing apartment condo-coop homes in thousands of dollars; (p) preliminary; n/a not available; (1) Metropolitan Statistical Area—see Appendix B for areas included
Source: National Association of Realtors, Median Sales Price of Existing Apartment Condo-Coop Homes for Metropolitan Areas, 4th Quarter 2011

Year Housing Structure Built

Area	2005 or Later	2000 -2004	1990 -1999	1980 -1989	1970 -1979	1960 -1969	1950 -1959	Before 1950	Median Year
City	2.4	2.7	6.9	13.4	24.7	22.3	17.5	10.1	1970
MSA[1]	7.0	10.2	18.7	16.0	19.3	12.6	9.1	7.1	1981
U.S.	5.0	8.6	14.0	14.1	16.3	11.3	11.2	19.6	1975

Note: Figures are percentages except for Median Year; (1) Figures cover the Jackson, MS Metropolitan Statistical Area—see Appendix B for areas included
Source: U.S. Census Bureau, 2008-2010 American Community Survey 3-Year Estimates

HEALTH

Health Risk Data

Category	MSA[1] (%)	U.S. (%)
Adults who have been told they have high blood pressure[2]	36.4	28.7
Adults who have been told they have high blood cholesterol[2]	35.2	37.5
Adults who have been told they have diabetes[3]	11.7	8.7
Adults who have been told they have arthritis[2]	27.9	26.0
Adults who have been told they currently have asthma	6.3	9.1
Adults who are current smokers	19.4	17.3
Adults who are heavy drinkers[4]	2.6	5.0
Adults who are binge drinkers[5]	10.4	15.1
Adults who are overweight (BMI 25.0 - 29.9)	33.5	36.2
Adults who are obese (BMI 30.0 - 99.8)	33.3	27.5
Adults who participated in any physical activities in the past month	68.5	76.1
Adults 50+ who have ever had a sigmoidoscopy or colonoscopy	64.9	65.2
Women aged 40+ who have had a mammogram within the past two years	75.5	75.2
Men aged 40+ who have had a PSA test within the past two years	55.4	53.2
Adults aged 65+ who have had flu shot within the past year	65.7	67.5
Adults aged 18–64 who have any kind of health care coverage	81.6	82.2

Note: Data as of 2010 unless otherwise noted; (1) Figures cover the Jackson, MS Metropolitan Statistical Area—see Appendix B for areas included; (2) Data as of 2009; (3) Figures do not include pregnancy-related, borderline, or pre-diabetes; (4) Heavy drinkers are classified as males having more than two drinks per day or females having more than one drink per day; (5) Binge drinkers are classified as males having five or more drinks on one occasion or females having four or more drinks on one occasion
Source: Centers for Disease Control and Prevention, Behaviorial Risk Factor Surveillance System, SMART: Selected Metropolitan/Micropolitan Area Risk Trends, 2009, 2010

Mortality Rates for the Top 10 Causes of Death in the U.S.

ICD-10[a] Sub-Chapter	ICD-10[a] Code	Age-Adjusted Mortality Rate[1] per 100,000 population	
		County[2]	U.S.
Malignant neoplasms	C00-C97	162.6	175.6
Ischaemic heart diseases	I20-I25	104.9	121.6
Other forms of heart disease	I30-I51	79.1	48.6
Chronic lower respiratory diseases	J40-J47	36.1	42.3
Cerebrovascular diseases	I60-I69	45.2	40.6
Organic, including symptomatic, mental disorders	F01-F09	28.6	26.7
Other degenerative diseases of the nervous system	G30-G31	15.4	24.7
Other external causes of accidental injury	W00-X59	16.8	24.4
Diabetes mellitus	E10-E14	16.1	21.7
Hypertensive diseases	I10-I15	67.0	18.2

Note: (a) ICD-10 = International Classification of Diseases 10th Revision; (1) Mortality rates are a three year average covering 2007-2009; (2) Figures cover
Source: Centers for Disease Control and Prevention, National Center for Health Statistics. Underlying Cause of Death 1999-2009 on CDC WONDER Online Database, released 2012. Data for year 2009 are compiled from the Multiple Cause of Death File 2009, Series 20 No. 20, 2012, Data for year 2008 are compiled from the Multiple Cause of Death File 2008, Series 20 No. 2N, 2011, Data for year 2007 are compiled from Multiple Cause of Death File 2007, Series 20 No. 2M, 2010.

Mortality Rates for Selected Causes of Death

ICD-10[a] Sub-Chapter	ICD-10[a] Code	Age-Adjusted Mortality Rate[1] per 100,000 population	
		County[2]	U.S.
Assault	X85-Y09	21.4	5.7
Human immunodeficiency virus (HIV) disease	B20-B24	14.5	3.3
Influenza and pneumonia	J09-J18	16.9	16.4
Intentional self-harm	X60-X84	7.8	11.5
Malnutrition	E40-E46	*0.0	0.8
Obesity and other hyperalimentation	E65-E68	*Unreliable	1.6
Transport accidents	V01-V99	22.7	13.7
Viral hepatitis	B15-B19	*0.0	2.2

Note: (a) ICD-10 = International Classification of Diseases 10th Revision; (1) Mortality rates are a three year average covering 2007-2009; (2) Figures cover; (*) Unreliable data as per CDC
Source: Centers for Disease Control and Prevention, National Center for Health Statistics. Underlying Cause of Death 1999-2009 on CDC WONDER Online Database, released 2012. Data for year 2009 are compiled from the Multiple Cause of Death File 2009, Series 20 No. 2O, 2012, Data for year 2008 are compiled from the Multiple Cause of Death File 2008, Series 20 No. 2N, 2011, Data for year 2007 are compiled from Multiple Cause of Death File 2007, Series 20 No. 2M, 2010.

Distribution of Physicians and Dentists

Area[1]	Dentists[2]	D.O.[3]	M.D.[4]				
			Total	Family/ General Practice	Pediatrics	Medical Specialties	Surgical Specialties
Local (number)	123	18	683	62	45	250	183
Local (rate[5])	4.9	0.7	27.6	2.5	1.8	10.1	7.4
U.S. (rate[5])	4.5	1.9	18.3	2.5	1.4	6.8	4.1

Note: Data as of 2008 unless noted; (1) Local data covers Hinds County; (2) Data as of 2007; (3) Doctor of Osteopathic Medicine; (4) Includes active, non-federal, patient-care, office-based Doctors of Medicine; (5) rate per 10,000 population
Source: Area Resource File (ARF). 2009-2010 Release. U.S. Department of Health and Human Services, Health Resources and Services Administration, Bureau of Health Professions, Rockville, MD, August 2010

EDUCATION

Public School District Statistics

District Name	Schls	Pupils	Pupil/ Teacher Ratio	Minority Pupils[1] (%)	Free Lunch Eligible[2] (%)	IEP[3] (%)
Jackson Public School Dist	61	30,609	16.2	98.5	81.3	10.3

Note: Table includes school districts with 2,000 or more students; (1) Percentage of students that are not non-Hispanic white; (2) Percentage of students that are eligible for the free lunch program; (3) Percentage of students that have an Individualized Education Program.
Source: U.S. Department of Education, National Center for Education Statistics, Common Core of Data, Local Education Agency (School District) Universe Survey: School Year 2009-2010; U.S. Department of Education, National Center for Education Statistics, Common Core of Data, Public Elementary/Secondary School Universe Survey: School Year 2009-2010

Highest Level of Education

Area	Less than H.S.	H.S. Diploma	Some College, No Deg.	Associate Degree	Bachelors Degree	Masters Degree	Profess. School Degree	Doctorate Degree
City	18.1	25.5	22.9	6.7	15.9	6.8	2.8	1.2
MSA[1]	14.8	25.3	23.5	7.7	18.2	6.9	2.3	1.2
U.S.	14.7	28.4	21.3	7.6	17.6	7.2	1.9	1.2

Note: Figures cover persons age 25 and over; (1) Figures cover the Jackson, MS Metropolitan Statistical Area—see Appendix B for areas included
Source: U.S. Census Bureau, 2008-2010 American Community Survey 3-Year Estimates

Educational Attainment by Race

Area	High School Graduate or Higher (%)					Bachelor's Degree or Higher (%)				
	Total	White	Black	Asian	Hisp.[2]	Total	White	Black	Asian	Hisp.[2]
City	81.9	91.7	79.1	n/a	45.9	26.7	51.5	18.6	n/a	20.9
MSA[1]	85.2	90.6	79.1	80.3	48.9	28.7	35.5	19.4	62.0	16.0
U.S.	85.3	87.5	81.4	85.5	61.6	28.0	29.3	17.8	50.2	13.0

Note: Figures shown cover persons 25 years old and over; (1) Figures cover the Jackson, MS Metropolitan Statistical Area—see Appendix B for areas included; (2) People of Hispanic origin can be of any race
Source: U.S. Census Bureau, 2008-2010 American Community Survey 3-Year Estimates

School Enrollment by Grade and Control

Area	Preschool (%)		Kindergarten (%)		Grades 1 - 4 (%)		Grades 5 - 8 (%)		Grades 9 - 12 (%)	
	Public	Private	Public	Private	Public	Private	Public	Private	Public	Private
City	76.3	23.7	83.1	16.9	90.3	9.7	85.8	14.2	88.4	11.6
MSA[1]	59.9	40.1	84.3	15.7	86.1	13.9	83.3	16.7	86.2	13.8
U.S.	55.4	44.6	87.1	12.9	89.4	10.6	89.5	10.5	90.4	9.6

Note: Figures shown cover persons 3 years old and over; (1) Figures cover the Jackson, MS Metropolitan Statistical Area—see Appendix B for areas included
Source: U.S. Census Bureau, 2008-2010 American Community Survey 3-Year Estimates

Average Salaries of Public School Classroom Teachers

Area	2010-11		2011-12		Percent Change 2010-11 to 2011-12	Percent Change 2001-02 to 2011-12
	Dollars	Rank[1]	Dollars	Rank[1]		
Mississippi	41,975	50	41,646	50	-0.78	25.10
U.S. Average	55,623	-	56,643	-	1.83	26.8

Note: (1) State rank ranges from 1 to 51 where 1 indicates highest salary.
Source: National Education Association, Rankings & Estimates: Rankings of the States 2011 and Estimates of School Statistics 2012, December 2011

Higher Education

Four-Year Colleges			Two-Year Colleges			Medical Schools[1]	Law Schools[2]	Voc/ Tech[3]
Public	Private Non-profit	Private For-profit	Public	Private Non-profit	Private For-profit			
2	3	1	0	0	3	1	1	3

Note: Figures cover institutions located within the city limits and include main campuses only; (1) includes schools accredited by the Liaison Committee on Medical Education and the American Osteopathic Association's Commission on Osteopathic College Accreditation; (2) includes American Bar Association-accredited law schools; (3) includes all schools with programs that are less than 2 years.
Source: National Center for Education Statistics, Integrated Postsecondary Education System (IPEDS) Peer Analysis System, 2011-12; Association of American Medical Colleges, Member List, April 23, 2012; American Osteopathic Association, Member List, April 23, 2012; Law School Admission Council, Official Guide to ABA-Approved Law Schools Online, April 23, 2012

According to *U.S. News & World Report*, the Jackson, MS is home to one of the best liberal arts colleges in the U.S.: **Millsaps College** (#85). The indicators used to capture academic quality fall into a number of categories: assessment by administrators at peer institutions; retention of students; faculty resources; student selectivity; financial resources; alumni giving; high school counselor ratings of colleges; and graduation rate. *U.S. News & World Report*, "America's Best Colleges 2012"

PRESIDENTIAL ELECTION

2008 Presidential Election Results

Area	Obama	McCain	Nader	Other
Hinds County	69.2	30.3	0.1	0.4
U.S.	52.9	45.6	0.6	0.9

Note: Results are percentages and may not add to 100% due to rounding
Source: Dave Leip's Atlas of U.S. Presidential Elections, www.uselectionatlas.org

EMPLOYERS

Major Employers

Company Name	Industry
City of Jackson	Police protection/local government
County of Jackson	Executive offices
Entergy Nuclear	Electric services
Jackson HMA Inc	General medical/surgical hospitals
Jackson State University	Colleges/universities
Mississippi Baptist Health System	Hospital management
Mississippi State Dept of Health	Administration of public health programs
Pioneer Credit Recovery	Loan agents
River Oaks Hospital	General medical/surgical hospitals
Southern Capital Life Ins Company	Investment aid
Southern Farm Bureau Life Ins Company	Life insurance carriers
Southern Healthcare Agency Inc	Employee leasing service
St Dominic Jackson Memorial Hospital	General medical/surgical hospitals
Statewide Healthcare Services Inc	Visiting nurse association
Transportation Mississippi Dept Of	Regulation/administration of transportation
Transportation Mississippi Dept Of	Regulation administration of transportation
University of Mississippi Medical Center	General medical/surgical hospitals
Young Williams PC	Specialized legal service

Note: Companies shown are located within the Jackson, MS metropolitan area.
Source: Hoovers.com, data extracted April 25 2012

PUBLIC SAFETY

Crime Rate

Area	All Crimes	Violent Crimes				Property Crimes		
		Murder	Forcible Rape	Robbery	Aggrav. Assault	Burglary	Larceny -Theft	Motor Vehicle Theft
City	8,594.7	23.5	58.0	623.6	281.4	2,766.5	3,948.8	892.9
Suburbs[1]	2,118.5	4.3	19.9	28.8	92.2	513.6	1,326.1	133.6
Metro[2]	4,183.9	10.4	32.0	218.5	152.5	1,232.1	2,162.5	375.8
U.S.	3,345.5	4.8	27.5	119.1	252.3	699.6	2,003.5	238.8

Note: Figures are crimes per 100,000 population; (1) All areas within the metro area that are located outside the city limits; (2) Metropolitan Statistical Area—see Appendix B for areas included
Source: FBI Uniform Crime Reports, 2010

Hate Crimes

Area	Number of Quarters Reported	Bias Motivation				
		Race	Religion	Sexual Orientation	Ethnicity	Disability
City	n/a	n/a	n/a	n/a	n/a	n/a

Note: n/a not available.
Source: Federal Bureau of Investigation, Hate Crime Statistics 2010

Identity Theft Consumer Complaints

Area	Complaints	Complaints per 100,000 Population	Rank[2]
MSA[1]	672	125.8	31
U.S.	279,156	90.4	-

Note: (1) Metropolitan Statistical Area—see Appendix B for areas included; (2) Rank ranges from 1 to 384 where 1 indicates greatest number of identity theft complaints per 100,000 population
Source: Federal Trade Commission, Consumer Sentinel Network Data Book for January–December 2011

Fraud and Other Consumer Complaints

Area	Complaints	Complaints per 100,000 Population	Rank[2]
MSA[1]	1,969	368.7	342
U.S.	1,533,924	496.8	-

Note: (1) Metropolitan Statistical Area—see Appendix B for areas included; (2) Rank ranges from 1 to 384 where 1 indicates greatest number of fraud and other complaints per 100,000 population
Source: Federal Trade Commission, Consumer Sentinel Network Data Book for January–December 2011

RECREATION

Culture

Dance[1]	Theatre[1]	Instrumental Music[1]	Vocal Music[1]	Series/ Festivals	Museums	Zoos and Aquariums[2]
1	2	2	1	3	11	1

Note: (1) Number of professional perfoming groups; (2) AZA-accredited
Source: The Grey House Performing Arts Directory, 2011-2012; Official Museum Directory, 2011; American Association of Museums, AAM Member Museums, April 2012; Association of Zoos & Aquariums, AZA Member Zoos & Aquariums, April 2012

Professional Sports Teams

Team Name	League

No teams are located in the metro area
Source: Original research

CLIMATE

Average and Extreme Temperatures

Temperature	Jan	Feb	Mar	Apr	May	Jun	Jul	Aug	Sep	Oct	Nov	Dec	Yr.
Extreme High (°F)	82	85	89	94	99	105	106	102	104	95	88	84	106
Average High (°F)	56	60	69	77	84	90	92	92	87	78	68	59	76
Average Temp. (°F)	45	48	57	65	72	79	82	81	76	65	56	49	65
Average Low (°F)	34	36	44	52	60	68	71	70	65	52	44	37	53
Extreme Low (°F)	2	11	15	27	38	47	51	55	35	29	17	4	2

Note: Figures cover the years 1963-1990
Source: National Climatic Data Center, International Station Meteorological Climate Summary, 9/96

Average Precipitation/Snowfall/Humidity

Precip./Humidity	Jan	Feb	Mar	Apr	May	Jun	Jul	Aug	Sep	Oct	Nov	Dec	Yr.
Avg. Precip. (in.)	5.1	4.7	5.8	5.7	5.4	3.0	4.5	3.8	3.6	3.3	4.7	5.8	55.4
Avg. Snowfall (in.)	1	Tr	Tr	Tr	0	0	0	0	0	0	Tr	Tr	1
Avg. Rel. Hum. 6am (%)	87	87	88	90	92	92	93	94	94	93	90	87	91
Avg. Rel. Hum. 3pm (%)	59	54	51	50	53	52	56	56	55	49	52	58	54

Note: Figures cover the years 1963-1990; Tr = Trace amounts (<0.05 in. of rain; <0.5 in. of snow)
Source: National Climatic Data Center, International Station Meteorological Climate Summary, 9/96

Weather Conditions

Temperature			Daytime Sky			Precipitation		
10°F & below	32°F & below	90°F & above	Clear	Partly cloudy	Cloudy	0.01 inch or more precip.	0.1 inch or more snow/ice	Thunder-storms
1	50	84	103	144	118	106	2	68

Note: Figures are average number of days per year and cover the years 1963-1990
Source: National Climatic Data Center, International Station Meteorological Climate Summary, 9/96

HAZARDOUS WASTE

Superfund Sites

Jackson has no sites on the EPA's Superfund Final National Priorities List.
U.S. Environmental Protection Agency, Final National Priorities List, April 17, 2012

AIR & WATER QUALITY

Air Quality Index

Area	Percent of Days when Air Quality was...[2]					AQI Statistics[2]	
	Good	Moderate	Unhealthy for Sensitive Groups	Unhealthy	Very Unhealthy	Maximum	Median
Area[1]	68.5	30.7	0.8	0.0	0.0	124	43

Note: Air Quality Index (AQI) is an index for reporting daily air quality. EPA calculates the AQI for five major air pollutants regulated by the Clean Air Act: ground-level ozone, particle pollution (aka particulate matter), carbon monoxide, sulfur dioxide, and nitrogen dioxide. The AQI runs from 0 to 500. The higher the AQI value, the greater the level of air pollution and the greater the health concern. There are six AQI categories: "Good" AQI is between 0 and 50. Air quality is considered satisfactory; "Moderate" AQI is between 51 and 100. Air quality is acceptable; "Unhealthy for Sensitive Groups" When AQI values are between 101 and 150, members of sensitive groups may experience health effects; "Unhealthy" When AQI values are between 151 and 200 everyone may begin to experience health effects; "Very Unhealthy" AQI values between 201 and 300 trigger a health alert; "Hazardous" AQI values over 300 trigger warnings of emergency conditions (not shown); (1) Data covers Hinds County; (2) Based on 365 days with AQI data in 2011.
Source: U.S. Environmental Protection Agency, AirData Report, 2011

Air Quality Index Pollutants

Area	Percent of Days when AQI Pollutant was...[2]					
	Carbon Monoxide	Nitrogen Dioxide	Ozone	Sulfur Dioxide	Particulate Matter 2.5	Particulate Matter 10
Area[1]	0.0	0.0	34.8	0.0	65.2	0.0

Note: The Air Quality Index (AQI) is an index for reporting daily air quality. EPA calculates the AQI for five major air pollutants regulated by the Clean Air Act: ground-level ozone, particle pollution (also known as particulate matter), carbon monoxide, sulfur dioxide, and nitrogen dioxide. The AQI runs from 0 to 500. The higher the AQI value, the greater the level of air pollution and the greater the health concern; (1) Data covers Hinds County; (2) Based on 365 days with AQI data in 2011.
Source: U.S. Environmental Protection Agency, AirData Report, 2011

Air Quality Index Trends

Area	Trend Sites (days)								All Sites (days)
	2003	2004	2005	2006	2007	2008	2009	2010	2010
MSA[1]	n/a	n/a	n/a	n/a	n/a	n/a	n/a	n/a	n/a

Note: Figures are the number of days the AQI value exceeded 100 in a given year. An AQI value greater than 100 indicates that air quality would have been in the unhealthful range on that day. Data from exceptional events are included. These counts are presented in two ways. First, the counts are based on sites having an adequate record of monitoring data during the trend period (trend sites). These counts represent the relative change in the number of days with AQI values greater than 100. In the last column, the counts are based on all sites with data in the most recent year (because it is possible for a site to have data in the most recent year but not enough data to be a trend site); (1) Data covers the Jackson, MS—see Appendix B for areas included; n/a not available.
Source: U.S. Environmental Protection Agency, Air Quality Index Information, "Number of Days with Air Quality Index Values Greater than 100 at Trend Sites, 2000-2010, and at All Sites in 2010"

Maximum Air Pollutant Concentrations: Particulate Matter, Ozone, CO and Lead

	Particulate Matter 10 (ug/m^3)	Particulate Matter 2.5 Wtd AM (ug/m^3)	Particulate Matter 2.5 24-Hr (ug/m^3)	Ozone (ppm)	Carbon Monoxide (ppm)	Lead (ug/m^3)
MSA[1] Level	n/a	11.4	22	0.067	n/a	n/a
NAAQS[2]	150	15	35	0.075	9	0.15
Met NAAQS[2]	n/a	Yes	Yes	Yes	n/a	n/a

Note: Data from exceptional events are not included; (1) Data covers the Jackson, MS—see Appendix B for areas included; (2) National Ambient Air Quality Standards; ppm = parts per million; ug/m^3 = micrograms per cubic meter; n/a not available
Concentrations: Particulate Matter 10 (coarse particulate)—highest second maximum 24-hour concentration; Particulate Matter 2.5 Wtd AM (fine particulate)—highest weighted annual mean concentration; Particulate Matter 2.5 24-Hour (fine particulate)—highest 98th percentile 24-hour concentration; Ozone—highest fourth daily maximum 8-hour concentration; Carbon Monoxide—highest second maximum non-overlapping 8-hour concentration; Lead—maximum running 3-month average
Source: U.S. Environmental Protection Agency, CBSA Factbook 2010, Air Quality Statistics by City, 2010

Maximum Air Pollutant Concentrations: Nitrogen Dioxide and Sulfur Dioxide

	Nitrogen Dioxide AM (ppb)	Nitrogen Dioxide 1-Hr (ppb)	Sulfur Dioxide AM (ppb)	Sulfur Dioxide 1-Hr (ppb)	Sulfur Dioxide 24-Hr (ppb)
MSA[1] Level	n/a	n/a	n/a	n/a	n/a
NAAQS[2]	53	100	30	75	140
Met NAAQS[2]	n/a	n/a	n/a	n/a	n/a

Note: Data from exceptional events are not included; (1) Data covers the Jackson, MS—see Appendix B for areas included; (2) National Ambient Air Quality Standards; ppb = parts per billion; n/a not available
Concentrations: Nitrogen Dioxide AM—highest arithmetic mean concentration; Nitrogen Dioxide 1-Hr—highest 98th percentile 1-hour daily maximum concentration; Sulfur Dioxide AM—highest annual mean concentration; Sulfur Dioxide 1-Hr—highest 99th percentile 1-hour daily maximum concentration; Sulfur Dioxide 24-Hr—highest second maximum 24-hour concentration
Source: U.S. Environmental Protection Agency, CBSA Factbook 2010, Air Quality Statistics by City, 2010

Drinking Water

Water System Name	Pop. Served	Primary Water Source Type	Violations[1] Health Based	Violations[1] Monitoring/ Reporting
City of Jackson	175,930	Surface	0	1

Note: (1) Based on violation data from January 1, 2011 to December 31, 2011 (includes unresolved violations from earlier years)
Source: U.S. Environmental Protection Agency, Office of Ground Water and Drinking Water, Safe Drinking Water Information System (based on data extracted April 18, 2012)

Jacksonville, Florida

Background

Modern day Jacksonville is largely a product of the reconstruction that occurred during the 1940s after a fire had razed 147 city blocks a few decades earlier. Lying under the modern structures, however, is a history that dates back earlier than the settlement of Plymouth by the Pilgrims.

Located in the northeast part of Florida on the St. John's River, Jacksonville, the largest city in land area in the contiguous United States, was settled by English, Spanish, and French explorers from the sixteenth through the eighteenth centuries. Sites commemorating their presence include: Fort Caroline National Monument, marking the French settlement led by René de Goulaine Laudonniére in 1564; Spanish Pond one-quarter of a mile east of Fort Caroline, where Spanish forces led by Pedro Menendez captured the Fort; and Fort George Island, from which General James Oglethorpe led English attacks against the Spanish during the eighteenth century.

Jacksonville was attractive to these early settlers because of its easy access to the Atlantic Ocean, which meant a favorable port.

Today, Jacksonville remains an advantageous port and is home to Naval Air Station Jacksonville, a major employer in the area. In January of 2009 the Navy announced plans to station a nuclear powered-carrier at the Jacksonville Naval Base, Mayport. Construction has started to accommodate the large ship, which will arrive in 2014.

Jacksonville is the financial hub of Florida, and many companies have headquarters here, including the East Coast's largest rail network, CSX Transportation, Fidelity National Financial, and Winn-Dixie.

On the cultural front, Jacksonville boasts a range of options, including the Children's Museum, the Jacksonville Symphony Orchestra, the Gator Bowl, and beach facilities. In 2005, the city hosted Super Bowl XXXIX at the former Alltel Stadium (now Jacksonville Municipal Stadium), home of the NFL's Jacksonville Jaguars. The city also boasts the largest urban park system in the United States, providing services at more than 337 locations on more than 80,000 acres located throughout the city. The Jacksonville Jazz Festival, held every April, is the second-largest jazz festival in the nation. The city is home to several theaters, including Little Theatre, which, operating since 1919, is one of the oldest operating community theaters in the nation.

Jacksonville has more than 80,000 acres of parkland throughout the city, and is renowned for its outdoor recreational facilities. The city's most recent park, The Jacksonville Arboretum and Gardens, was opened in the fall of 2008.

Summers are long, warm, and relatively humid. Winters are generally mild, although periodic invasions of cold northern air bring the temperature down. Temperatures along the beaches rarely rise above 90 degrees. Summer coastal thunderstorms usually occur before noon, and move inland in the afternoons. The greatest rainfall, as localized thundershowers, occurs during the summer months. Although the area is in the hurricane belt, this section of the coast has been very fortunate in escaping hurricane-force winds.

Rankings

General Rankings

- *Men's Health Living* ranked 100 U.S. cities in terms of quality of life. Jacksonville was ranked #61 and received a grade of C-. Criteria: number of fitness facilities; air quality; number of physicians; male/female ratio; education levels; household income; cost of living. *Men's Health Living, Spring 2008*

- Jacksonville was selected as one of America's best cities by *Bloomberg Businessweek*. The city ranked #26 out of 50. Criteria: number of restaurants, bars and museums per capita; number of colleges, libraries, and professional sports teams; income, poverty, unemployment, crime, and foreclosure rates; percent of population with bachelor's degrees; public school performance; park acres per capita; air quality. *BusinessWeek, "America's 50 Best Cities," September 20, 2011*

Business/Finance Rankings

- Jacksonville was identified as one of the top 25 U.S. cities with the most credit card debt by credit reporting bureau Experian. The city was ranked #2. *Experian, March 4, 2011*

- *American City Business Journals* ranked America's 261 largest cities in terms of their resident's wealth. Jacksonville ranked #160. Criteria: per capita income; median household income; percentage of households with annual incomes of $200,000 or more; median home value. *American City Business Journals, "Where the Money Is: America's Wealth Centers," August 18, 2008*

- The Jacksonville metro area appeared on the Milken Institute "2011 Best Performing Metros" list. Rank: #134 out of 200 large metro areas. Criteria: job growth; wage and salary growth; high-tech output growth. *Milken Institute, "2011 Best Performing Metros"*

- The Jacksonville metro area was selected as one of the best cities for entrepreneurs in America by *Inc. Magazine*. Criteria: job-growth data for 335 metro areas was analyzed for: recent growth trend; mid-term growth; long-term trend; current year growth. The Jacksonville metro area ranked #19 among large metro areas and #102 overall. *Inc. Magazine, "The Best Cities for Doing Business," July 2008*

- Jacksonville was ranked #106 out of 145 regions worldwide in terms of its "Knowledge Competitiveness Index." The index attempts to measure the knowledge-based development taking place throughout the world and is based on 19 measures of economic performance that indicate a region's ability to translate its knowledge capacity into economic value. *Centre for International Competitiveness, World Knowledge Competitiveness Index 2008*

- *Forbes* ranked the 200 most populous metro areas in the U.S. in terms of the "Best Places for Business and Careers." The Jacksonville metro area was ranked #61. Criteria: costs (business and living); job growth (past and projected); income growth; educational attainment; projected economic growth; crime; cultural and recreational opportunities; net migration patterns; number of highly ranked colleges. *Forbes, "Best Places for Business and Careers," June 2011*

- Jacksonville appeared on *Kiplinger's Personal Finance* list of the "Top Ten Tax-Friendly Cities." The city was ranked #6. Criteria: income tax; sales tax; real estate and car/personal property tax. *Kiplinger's Personal Finance, March 1, 2009*

Children/Family Rankings

- Jacksonville was selected as one of the least safe cities for children in America by *Men's Health*. The city ranked #1 of 10. Criteria: accidental death rates for kids ages 5 to 14; number of car seat inspection locations per child; sex offenders per capita; percentage of abused children protected from further abuse; strength of child-restraint and bike-helmet laws. *Men's Health, "The Safest (and Least Safe) Cities for Children," September 2010*

- The Jacksonville metro area was selected as one of the "Best Cities for Relocating Families" by Worldwide ERC and Primacy Relocation. The 2008 study looked at nearly 50 factors important to relocating families including: recent job growth; nearby top-ranked colleges; in-state tuition for four-year public colleges; population growth since 2000; pediatricians per 100,000 population; and a Green Living index. *Worldwide ERC and Primacy Relocation, "2008 Best Cities for Relocating Families"*

- *Fit Pregnancy* magazine ranked the 50 best U.S. cities in which to have a baby. Jacksonville was ranked #11. Criteria: access to hospitals and doctors; affordability; birthing options; breastfeeding; child care; fertility laws/resources; maternal and infant health risk; parks/stroller friendliness; safety. *Fit Pregnancy, "The Best Cities in America to Have a Baby 2008"*

Culture/Performing Arts Rankings

- Jacksonville was selected as one of "America's Top 25 Arts Destinations." The city ranked #25 in the big city (population 500,000 and over) category. Criteria: readers' top choices for arts travel destinations based on the richness and variety of visual arts sites, activities and events. *American Style, "America's Top 25 Arts Destinations," May 2010*

Dating/Romance Rankings

- Jacksonville appeared on *Men's Health's* list of the most sex-happy cities in America. The city ranked #51 of 100. Criteria: condom sales; birth rates; sex toy sales; rates of chlamydia, gonorrhea, and syphilis. *Men's Health, "America's Most Sex-Happy Cities," October 2010*

- *Men's Health* ranked 100 U.S. cities in terms of best (and worst) marriages. Jacksonville was ranked #22 (#1 = worst). Criteria: rate of failed marriages; stringency of divorce laws; percentage of population who've split; number of licensed marriage and family therapists. *Men's Health, "Splitsville, USA," May 2010*

- Eli Lily and Company, in partnership with Sperling's BestPlaces, ranked the nation's 50 largest metro areas in terms of the "Most Romantic Cities for Baby Boomers." The Jacksonville metro area ranked #33. Criteria: marriage and divorce rates among baby boomers age 45 to 60; great restaurants; dance studios; chocolate, jewelry and flower sales. *Eli Lily and Company, "Most Romantic Cities for Baby Boomers," April 20, 2007*

- The Jacksonville metro area was selected as one of the "Best Cities for Relocating Singles" by Worldwide ERC and Primacy Relocation. The area ranked #22 out of the 100 largest metro areas in the U.S. Criteria: recent job growth; recent singles population growth; overall population growth; affordable rental housing; cost-of-living index; expanded arts and recreation opportunities; ratio of single men and single women; affordability of quality higher education (including state residency requirements); diversity index; climate; population density. *Worldwide ERC and Primacy Relocation, "2008 Best Cities for Relocating Singles"*

- *Forbes* ranked the 40 most populous urbanized areas in the U.S. in terms of the "Best Cities for Singles." The Jacksonville metro area ranked #40. Criteria: number of singles; cost of living alone; nightlife; culture; job growth; coolness; and online dating participation. *Forbes.com, "Best Cities for Singles," July 27, 2009*

Education Rankings

- *Men's Health* ranked 100 U.S. cities in terms of their education levels. Jacksonville was ranked #69 (#1 = most educated city). Criteria: high school graduation rates; school enrollment; educational attainment; number of households who have outstanding student loans; number of households whose members have taken adult-education courses. *Men's Health, "Where School Is In: The Most and Least Educated Cities," September 12, 2011*

- Jacksonville was selected as one of "America's Most Literate Cities." The city ranked #52 out of the 75 largest U.S. cities. Criteria: number of booksellers; library resources; Internet resources; educational attainment; periodical publishing resources; newspaper circulation. *Central Connecticut State University, "America's Most Literate Cities 2011"*

- Jacksonville was identified as one of the 100 "smartest" metro areas in the U.S. The area ranked #69. Criteria: the editors rated the collective brainpower of the 100 largest metro areas in the U.S. based on their residents' educational attainment. *American City Business Journals, April 14, 2008*

- Jacksonville was identified as one of "America's Brainiest Bastions" by *Portfolio.com*. The metro area ranked #91 out of 200. *Portfolio.com* analyzed levels of educational attainment in the nation's 200 largest metropolitan areas. The editors established scores for five levels of educational attainment, based on relative earning power of adult workers age 25 or older. Scores were determined by comparing the median income for all workers with the median income for those workers at a specified educational level. *Portfolio.com, "America's Brainiest Bastions," December 1, 2010*

Environmental Rankings

- Jacksonville was selected as one of 22 "Smarter Cities" for energy by the Natural Resources Defense Council. Criteria: investment in green power; energy efficiency measures; conservation. *Natural Resources Defense Council, "2010 Smarter Cities," July 19, 2010*

- *American City Business Journal* ranked 43 metropolitan areas in terms of their "greenness." The Jacksonville metro area ranked #27. Criteria: Forty-one metros in which *ACBJ* has business weeklies, plus Indianapolis and Cleveland, were ranked based on 20 different indicators such as adoption of green technologies, utilization of environmentally sound practices, and air and water quality. *American City Business Journals, "Green City Index," March 11, 2010*

- 100 of the largest metro areas in the U.S. were analyzed in terms of their current drought severity. The Jacksonville metro area ranked #11 (#1 = driest). The rankings were based on statistics such as long-term precipitation trends and patterns and the Palmer drought indices. *Sperling's BestPlaces, www.BestPlaces.net, "America's Drought-Riskiest Cities," November 2007*

- The Jacksonville metro area appeared in *Country Home's* "Best Green Places" report. The area ranked #283 out of 379. Criteria: official energy policies; green power; green buildings; availability of fresh, locally grown food. *Country Home, "Best Green Places," 2008*

Health/Fitness Rankings

- Jacksonville was given "Well City USA" status by The Wellness Councils of America, whose objective is to engage entire business communities in building healthy workforces. Well City status is met when a minimum of 20 employers who collectively employ at least 20% of the city's workforce become designated Well Workplaces within a three-year period. To date, eleven communities have achieved Well City USA status. *The Wellness Councils of America, Well City USA, 2012*

- Jacksonville was selected as one of the 25 fittest cities in America by *Men's Fitness Online*. It ranked #20 out of America's 50 largest cities. Criteria: fitness centers and sport stores; nutrition; sports participation; TV viewing; overweight/sedentary; junk food; air quality; geography; commute; parks and open space; city recreational facilities; access to healthcare; motivation; mayor and city initiatives; state obesity initiatives. *Men's Fitness, "The Fittest and Fattest Cities in America," March 5, 2012*

- Jacksonville was identified as a "2011 Asthma Capital." The area ranked #29 out of the nation's 100 largest metropolitan areas. Twelve factors were used to identify the most challenging places to live for people with asthma: estimated prevalence; self-reported prevalence; crude death rate for asthma; annual pollen score; annual air quality; public smoking laws; number of board-certified asthma specialists; school inhaler access laws; rescue medication use; controller medication use; uninsured rate; poverty rate. *Asthma and Allergy Foundation of America, "2011 Asthma Capitals"*

- Jacksonville was identified as a "2011 Fall Allergy Capital." The area ranked #44 out of 100. Three groups of factors were used to identify the most severe cities for people with allergies during the fall season: annual pollen levels; medicine utilization; access to board-certified allergists. *Asthma and Allergy Foundation of America, "2011 Fall Allergy Capitals"*

- Jacksonville was identified as a "2012 Spring Allergy Capital." The area ranked #48 out of 100. Three groups of factors were used to identify the most severe cities for people with allergies during the spring season: annual pollen levels; medicine utilization; access to board-certified allergists. *Asthma and Allergy Foundation of America, "2012 Spring Allergy Capitals"*

- *Men's Health* examined 100 major U.S. cities and selected the best and worst cities for men. Jacksonville ranked #81. Criteria: 35 statistical parameters of long life in the categories of health, quality of life, and fitness. *Men's Health, "The 10 Best and Worst Cities for Men 2012," January/February 2012*

- Jacksonville was selected as one of America's noisiest cities by *Men's Health*. The city ranked #10 of 10. Criteria: laws limiting excessive noise; traffic congestion levels; airports' overnight flight curfews; percentage of people who report sleeping seven hours or less. *Men's Health, "Ranking America's Cities: America's Noisiest Cities," May 2009*

- Jacksonville was selected as one of the most accident-prone cities in America by *Men's Health*. The city ranked #2 of 10. Criteria: workplace accident rates; traffic fatalities; emergency room visits; accidental poisonings; incidents of drowning; fires; injury-producing falls. *Men's Health, "Ranking America's Cities: Accident City, USA," October 2009*

- The Jacksonville metropolitan area was selected as one of the best metros for hospital care in America by *HealthGrades.com*. The rankings are based on a comprehensive study of patient death and complication rates in the nation's nearly 5,000 hospitals. Hospitals performing in the top 5% nationwide across 26 different medical procedures and diagnoses were identified. *HealthGrades.com* then ranked cities by the highest percentage of these Distinguished Hospitals for Clinical Excellence™. The Jacksonville metro area ranked #40. *HealthGrades.com, "America's Top 50 Cities for Hospital Care," January 21, 2012*

- The Jacksonville metro area appeared in the 2011 Gallup-Healthways Well-Being Index. The index, based on interviews with more than 350,000 Americans, measured jobs, finances, physical health, emotional state of mind and communities. The metro area ranked #153 out of 190. Criteria: life evaluation; emotional health; work environment; physical health; healthy behaviors; basic access (basic needs optimal for a healthy life, such as access to food and medicine, having health insurance and feeling safe while walking at night). *Gallup-Healthways, "State of Well-Being 2011"*

- The Jacksonville metro area was identified as one of "America's Most Stressful Cities" by *Sperling's BestPlaces*. The metro area ranked #4 out of 50. Criteria: unemployment rate; suicide rate; commute time; mental health; poor rest; alcohol use; violent crime rate; property crime rate; cloudy days annually. *Sperling's BestPlaces, www.BestPlaces.net, "Stressful Cities 2012*

- *Men's Health* ranked 100 U.S. cities in terms of their activity levels. Jacksonville was ranked #75 (#1 = most active city). Criteria: where and how often residents exercise; percentage of households that watch more than 15 hours of cable television a week and buy more than 11 video games a year; death rate from deep-vein thrombosis, a condition linked to sitting for extended periods of time. *Men's Health, "Where Sit Happens: The Most and Least Active Cities in America," June 20, 2011*

- 50 of the largest metro areas in the U.S. were analyzed in terms of their health and fitness by the American College of Sports Medicine in their "American Fitness Index." The Jacksonville metro area ranked #24 (#1 = healthiest). Criteria: preventative health behaviors; levels of chronic disease; health care access; community resources and policies that support physical activity. *American College of Sports Medicine, "Health and Community Fitness Status of the 50 Largest Metropolitan Areas," August 1, 2011*

- *The Daily Beast* identified the 30 U.S. metro areas with the worst smoking habits. The Jacksonville metro area ranked #20. Sixty urban centers with populations of more than one million were ranked based on the following criteria: number of smokers; number of cigarettes smoked per day; fewest attempts to quit. *The Daily Beast, "30 Cities With Smoking Problems," January 3, 2011*

Real Estate Rankings

- Jacksonville was selected as one of the best cities for renters by *Forbes*. The city ranked #2 out of 5. The 44 largest cities in the U.S. were rated on four criteria: average rent in the first quarter of 2011 and how much it changed year-over-year; vacancy rates; cost of renting versus buying. *Forbes, "Best and Worst Cities for Renters," June 20, 2011*

- Jacksonville was identified as one of 13 metro areas where home prices are falling dangerously. Criteria: home price change from October 2010 to September 2011; projected home price change through 2012. *Forbes.com, "Cities Where Home Prices are Falling Dangerously," January 10, 2012*

- Jacksonville was identified as one of the best cities for home buyers in the U.S. The area ranked #7 out of 10. The affordability of home ownership was calculated by comparing the cost of renting vs. owning. Criteria: cost to rent as a percent of after-tax mortgage payment. *Fortune, "The 10 Best Cities for Buyers," April 11, 2011*

- *Fortune* ranked the 100 largest metro areas in the U.S. in terms of projected median home price change in 2010. The Jacksonville metro area ranked #93. *Fortune, "The 2010 Housing Outlook," December 9, 2009*

- Jacksonville appeared on *ApartmentRatings.com* "Top Cities for Renters" list in 2009." The area ranked #30. Overall satisfaction ratings were ranked using thousands of user submitted scores for hundreds of apartment complexes located in the 100 most populated U.S. municipalities. *ApartmentRatings.com, "2009 Renter Satisfaction Rankings"*

- The Jacksonville metro area was identified as one of "America's 25 Weakest Housing Markets" by *Forbes*. The metro area ranked #6. Criteria: metro areas with populations over 500,000 were ranked based on projected home values through 2011. *Forbes.com, "America's 25 Weakest Housing Markets," January 7, 2009*

- The nation's largest metro areas were analyzed in terms of the best places to buy pre-foreclosures (short sales). The Jacksonville metro area ranked #6 out of 10. Criteria: at least 500 pre-foreclosure sales during the fourth quarter and a short sales increase of at least five percent from a year ago. The areas selected posted the biggest discounts on the sales of pre-foreclosure properties. *RealtyTrac, "Fourth Quarter and Year-End 2011 U.S. Foreclosure Sales Report: Shifting Towards Short Sales," February 28, 2012*

- The Jacksonville metro area appeared in a *Wall Street Journal* article ranking cities by "housing stress." The metro area was ranked #15 (#1 = most stress). Criteria: fraction of mortgage-holding homeowners with a monthly housing payment in excess of 30 percent of income; percentage of people without health insurance; unemployment rate. *The Wall Street Journal, "Which Cities Face Biggest Housing Risk," October 5, 2010*

- The Center for Housing Policy ranked 210 U.S. metropolitan areas by the fair market rent for a two-bedroom unit. The Jacksonville metro area was ranked #79. (#1 = most expensive) with a rent of $903. Criteria: Fair Market Rent (FMR) in effect during the fourth quarter of 2009 based on HUD's fiscal year 2010 FMRs. *The Center for Housing Policy, "Paycheck to Paycheck: Most to Least Expensive Rental Markets in 2009"*

- The Jacksonville metro area was identified as one of the markets with the worst expected performance in home prices over the next 12 months. *Local Market Monitor, "First Quarter Home Price Forecast for Largest US Markets," March 2, 2011*

- The Jacksonville metro area was identified as one of the best U.S. markets to invest in rental property" by HomeVestors and Local Market Monitor. The area ranked #18 out of 100. Criteria: risk-return premium relative to national average. *HomeVestors and Local Market Monitor, "Best 100 U.S. Markets to Invest in Rental Property," March 9, 2012*

Safety Rankings

- Symantec, the makers of Norton, in partnership with Sperling's BestPlaces, ranked the 50 largest cities in the U.S. in terms of their vulnerability to cybercrime. The city ranked #40. Criteria: number of cyberattacks and potential infections; level of Internet access; expenditures on smartphones and computer hardware/software; wireless hotspots; broadband connectivity; Internet usage; online purchases. *Symantec, "Riskiest Online Cities of 2012" February 15, 2012*

- Allstate ranked the 193 largest cities in America in terms of driver safety. Jacksonville ranked #73. In addition, drivers were 3.1% more likely to have had an accident compared to the national average. Allstate researchers analyzed internal property damage reported claims over a two-year period (from January 2008 to December 2009) to protect findings from external influences such as weather or road construction. A weighted average of the two-year numbers determined the annual percentages. The report defines an auto crash as any collision resulting in a property damage claim. *Allstate, "2011 Allstate America's Best Drivers Report™"*

- The National Insurance Crime Bureau ranked 366 metro areas in the U.S. in terms of per capita rates of vehicle theft. The Jacksonville metro area ranked #153 (#1 = highest rate). Criteria: number of vehicle theft offenses per 100,000 inhabitants in 2010. *National Insurance Crime Bureau, "Hot Spots," June 21, 2011*

- The Jacksonville metro area was identified as one of the most dangerous metro areas for pedestrians by Transportation for America. The metro area ranked #3 out of 52 metro areas with over 1 million residents. Criteria: area's population divided by the number of pedestrian fatalities in that area. *Transportation for America, "Dangerous by Design 2011"*

Seniors/Retirement Rankings

- Jacksonville was identified as one of the "100 Most Popular Retirement Towns" by *Topretirements.com* The list reflects the 100 cities (out of 815+ total cities reviewed) that visitors to the website are most interested in for retirement. *Topretirements.com, "100 Most Popular Retirement Towns," February 21, 2012*

- Jacksonville was selected as one of "The Best Retirement Places" by *Forbes*. The magazine considered a wide range of factors such as climate, availability of doctors, driving environment, and crime rates, but focused especially on tax burden and cost of living. *Forbes, "The Best Retirement Places," March 27, 2011*

Sports/Recreation Rankings

- Jacksonville appeared on the *Sporting News* list of the "Best Sports Cities" for 2011. The area ranked #44 out of 271 cities in the U.S. *Sporting News* takes a 12-month snapshot of each city's sports, putting a heavy premium on regular-season won-lost records (from the most recently completed season). Other criteria include: playoff berths, bowl appearances and tournament bids; championships; applicable power ratings; quality of competition; overall fan fervor (measured in part by attendance); abundance of teams (rewarding quality over quantity); stadium and arena quality; ticket availability and prices; franchise ownership; and marquee appeal of athletes. *Sporting News, "Best Sports Cities 2011," October 4, 2011*

- Scarborough Sports Marketing, a leading market research firm, identified the Jacksonville DMA (Designated Market Area) as one of the top markets for sports with more than 60% of adults reporting that they are "very" interested in any of the sports measured by Scarborough. *Scarborough Sports Marketing, October 1, 2008*

Transportation Rankings

- Jacksonville was identified as one of America's worst cities for speed traps by the National Motorists Association. The city ranked #12 out of 25. Criteria: speed trap locations per 100,000 residents. *National Motorists Association, September 2011*

- The Jacksonville metro area appeared on *Forbes* list of the best and worst cities for commuters. The metro area ranked #40 out of 60 (#1 is best). Criteria: travel time; road congestion; travel delays. *Forbes.com, "Best and Worst Cities for Commuters," February 16, 2010*

Women/Minorities Rankings

- *Women's Health* examined U.S. cities and identified the 100 best cities for women. Jacksonville was ranked #77. Criteria: 30 categories were examined from obesity and breast cancer rates to commuting times and hours spent working out. *Women's Health, "Best Cities for Women 2012"*

- Jacksonville was ranked #73 out of 100 metro areas in *SELF Magazine's* ranking of America's healthiest places for women." A panel of experts came up with more than 50 criteria including death and disease rates, environmental indicators, community resources, and lifestyle habits. *SELF Magazine, "Secrets of America's Healthiest Women," December 2008*

- Jacksonville appeared on *Black Enterprise's* list of the "Ten Best Cities for African Americans." The top picks were culled from more than 2,000 interactive surveys completed on *BlackEnterprise.com* and by editorial staff evaluation. The editors weighed the following criteria as it pertained to African Americans in each city: median household income; percentage of households earning more than $100,000; percentage of businesses owned; percentage of college graduates; unemployment rates; home loan rejections; and homeownership rates. *Black Enterprise, May 2007*

- The Jacksonville metro area appeared on *Forbes'* list of the "Best Cities for Minority Entrepreneurs." The area ranked #73 out of 10. Criteria: 52 metropolitan statistical areas were examined. For each ethnicity (African Americans, Asians and Hispanics), the editors measured housing affordability, population growth, income growth, and entrepreneurship (per capita self-employment). *Forbes, "Best Cities for Minority Entrepreneurs," March 23, 2011*

Miscellaneous Rankings

- *Men's Health* ranked 100 U.S. cities by their level of sadness. Jacksonville was ranked #88 (#1 = saddest city). Criteria: suicide rates; unemployment rates; percentage of households that use antidepressants; percent of population who report feeling blue all or most of the time. *Men's Health, "Frown Towns," November 28, 2011*

- Energizer Holdings, the makers of Edge® shave gel, in partnership with Sperling's BestPlaces, ranked 50 major metro areas in terms of everyday irritations. The Jacksonville metro area ranked #20. Criteria: humidity levels; weather conditions; incidence of traffic delays and congestion; average commute times; frequency of flight delays and cancellations; rates of sleeplessness; underemployment; pollens and allergens; pests; comedy clubs per capita. *Energizer Holdings, "Most Irritation Prone Cities," July 23, 2010*

- Mars Chocolate North America, the makers of COMBOS®, in partnership with Sperling's BestPlaces, ranked 50 major metro areas in terms of their "manliness." The Jacksonville metro area ranked #33. Criteria: number of professional sports teams; number of nearby NASCAR tracks and racing events; manly lifestyle; concentration of manly retail stores; manly occupations per capita; salty snack sales; "Board of Manliness" rankings. *Mars Chocolate North America, "America's Manliest Cities 2011," September 1, 2011*

- Jacksonville was selected as one of the best cities for shopping in the U.S. by *Forbes*. The city was ranked #9.Criteria: number of major shopping centers; retail locations; Consumer Price Index (CPI); combined state and local sales tax. *Forbes, "America's 25 Best Cities for Shopping," December 13, 2010*

- The Jacksonville metro area appeared in *AutoMD.com's* ranking of the "Best and Worst Cities for Auto Repair." The metro area ranked #2 (#1 is best). The 50 most-populated metro areas in the U.S. were ranked on three critical factors: repair affordability; price disparity range; shop integrity factor. *AutoMD.com, "Advocacy for Repair Shop Fairness Report," February 24, 2010*

Business Environment

CITY FINANCES

City Government Finances

Component	2009 ($000)	2009 ($ per capita)
Total Revenues	3,222,637	4,000
Total Expenditures	4,334,422	5,380
Debt Outstanding	12,341,016	15,319
Cash and Securities[1]	7,227,677	8,972

Note: (1) Cash and security holdings of a government at the close of its fiscal year, including those of its dependent agencies, utilities, and liquor stores.
Source: U.S Census Bureau, State & Local Government Finances 2009

City Government Revenue by Source

Source	2009 ($000)	2009 ($ per capita)
General Revenue		
From Federal Government	81,698	101
From State Government	170,202	211
From Local Governments	137	0
Taxes		
Property	477,369	593
Sales and Gross Receipts	387,924	482
Personal Income	0	0
Corporate Income	0	0
Motor Vehicle License	0	0
Other Taxes	19,478	24
Current Charges	431,752	536
Liquor Store	0	0
Utility	1,597,593	1,983
Employee Retirement	-372,540	-462

Source: U.S Census Bureau, State & Local Government Finances 2009

City Government Expenditures by Function

Function	2009 ($000)	2009 ($ per capita)	2009 (%)
General Direct Expenditures			
Air Transportation	59,265	74	1.4
Corrections	68,161	85	1.6
Education	0	0	0.0
Employment Security Administration	0	0	0.0
Financial Administration	57,034	71	1.3
Fire Protection	118,017	146	2.7
General Public Buildings	9,530	12	0.2
Governmental Administration, Other	23,046	29	0.5
Health	36,908	46	0.9
Highways	180,979	225	4.2
Hospitals	0	0	0.0
Housing and Community Development	19,751	25	0.5
Interest on General Debt	275,360	342	6.4
Judicial and Legal	35,570	44	0.8
Libraries	35,594	44	0.8
Parking	3,921	5	0.1
Parks and Recreation	51,840	64	1.2
Police Protection	257,402	320	5.9
Public Welfare	55,790	69	1.3
Sewerage	147,378	183	3.4
Solid Waste Management	70,967	88	1.6
Veterans' Services	0	0	0.0
Liquor Store	0	0	0.0
Utility	2,012,929	2,499	46.4
Employee Retirement	224,463	279	5.2

Source: U.S Census Bureau, State & Local Government Finances 2009

Municipal Bond Ratings

Area	Moody's	S&P	Fitch
City	Aa2	AA-	AA+

Rating Systems (shown in declining order of credit quality): Moody's– Aaa, Aa, A, Baa, Ba, B, Caa, Ca, C (numerical modifiers 1, 2, and 3 are added to letter-rating); S&P– AAA, AA, A, BBB, BB, B, CCC, CC, C; Fitch– AAA, AA, A, BBB, BB, B, CCC, CC, C. Ratings may be modified by the addition of a plus or minus sign to show relative standing within the major rating categories.
Notes: n/a Not Available; w/d Withdrawn (1) Not Reviewed; (2) Issuer Rating/No General Obligation; (3) Standard and Poor's Issue Credit Rating (ICR) is a current opinion of an obliger with respect to a specific financial obligation, a specific class of financial obligations, or a specific financial program.
Source: U.S. Census Bureau, 2012 Statistical Abstract, Bond Ratings for City Governments by Largest Cities: 2010

DEMOGRAPHICS

Population Growth

Area	1990 Census	2000 Census	2010 Census	Population Growth (%) 1990-2000	Population Growth (%) 2000-2010
City	635,221	735,617	821,784	15.8	11.7
MSA[1]	925,213	1,122,750	1,345,596	21.4	19.8
U.S.	248,709,873	281,421,906	308,745,538	13.2	9.7

Note: (1) Figures cover the Jacksonville, FL Metropolitan Statistical Area—see Appendix B for areas included
Source: U.S. Census Bureau, 2010 Census

Household Size

Area	One	Two	Three	Four	Five	Six	Seven or More	Average Household Size
City	28.2	32.5	17.4	12.8	5.6	2.2	1.3	2.48
MSA[1]	26.0	34.1	17.3	13.4	5.9	2.2	1.2	2.52
U.S.	26.7	32.8	16.1	13.4	6.5	2.6	1.9	2.58

Note: (1) Figures cover the Jacksonville, FL Metropolitan Statistical Area—see Appendix B for areas included
Source: U.S. Census Bureau, 2010 Census

Race

Area	White Alone[2] (%)	Black Alone[2] (%)	Asian Alone[2] (%)	AIAN[3] Alone[2] (%)	NHOPI[4] Alone[2] (%)	Other Race Alone[2] (%)	Two or More Races (%)
City	59.4	30.7	4.3	0.4	0.1	2.2	2.9
MSA[1]	69.9	21.8	3.4	0.4	0.1	1.8	2.6
U.S.	72.4	12.6	4.8	0.9	0.2	6.2	2.9

Note: (1) Figures cover the Jacksonville, FL Metropolitan Statistical Area—see Appendix B for areas included; (2) Alone is defined as not being in combination with one or more other races; (3) American Indian and Alaska Native; (4) Native Hawaiian and Other Pacific Islander
Source: U.S. Census Bureau, 2010 Census

Hispanic or Latino Origin

Area	Hispanic or Latino (%)	Mexican (%)	Puerto Rican (%)	Cuban (%)	Other Hispanic or Latino (%)
City	7.7	1.7	2.6	0.9	2.6
MSA[1]	6.9	1.5	2.3	0.7	2.3
U.S.	16.3	10.3	1.5	0.6	4.0

Note: Persons of Hispanic or Latino origin can be of any race; (1) Figures cover the Jacksonville, FL Metropolitan Statistical Area—see Appendix B for areas included
Source: U.S. Census Bureau, 2010 Census

Segregation

Type	Segregation Indices[1]				Percent Change		
	1990	2000	2010	2010 Rank[2]	1990-2000	1990-2010	2000-2010
Black/White	57.5	53.9	53.1	59	-3.6	-4.4	-0.8
Asian/White	34.2	37.0	37.5	71	2.8	3.2	0.4
Hispanic/White	22.1	26.6	27.6	98	4.6	5.5	1.0

Note: Figures are based on an analysis of 1990, 2000, and 2010 Census Decennial Census tract data by William H. Frey, Brookings Institution and the University of Michigan Social Science Data Analysis Network. In this analysis all racial groups (whites, blacks, and asians) are non-Hispanic members of those races. Hispanics are shown as a separate category; All figures cover the Metropolitan Statistical Area (see Appendix B for areas included); (1) Segregation Indices are Dissimilarity Indices that measure the degree to which the minority group is distributed differently than whites across census tracts. They range from 0 (complete integration) to 100 (complete segregation) where the value indicates the percentage of the minority group that needs to move to be distributed exactly like whites; (2) Ranges from 1 (most segregated) to 102 (least segregated); n/a not available.
Source: www.CensusScope.org

Ancestry

Area	German	Irish	English	American	Italian	Polish	French[2]	Scottish	Dutch
City	9.7	10.3	8.4	6.2	3.6	1.6	2.2	1.9	1.2
MSA[1]	11.8	12.2	10.1	8.0	4.8	2.0	2.6	2.1	1.3
U.S.	16.1	11.6	8.8	6.1	5.7	3.2	3.0	1.9	1.6

Note: Figures are the percentage of the total population reporting a particular ancestry. The nine most commonly reported ancestries in the U.S. are shown. Figures include multiple ancestries (e.g. if a person reported being Irish and Italian, they were included in both columns); (1) Figures cover the Jacksonville, FL Metropolitan Statistical Area—see Appendix B for areas included; (2) Excludes Basque
Source: U.S. Census Bureau, 2008-2010 American Community Survey 3-Year Estimates

Foreign-Born Population

Area	Percent of Population Born in								
	Any Foreign Country	Mexico	Asia	Europe	Carribean	South America	Central America[2]	Africa	Canada
City	9.4	0.6	3.3	1.7	1.5	1.0	0.5	0.6	0.2
MSA[1]	7.9	0.5	2.6	1.6	1.2	0.9	0.4	0.4	0.2
U.S.	12.8	3.8	3.6	1.6	1.2	0.9	1.0	0.5	0.3

Note: (1) Figures cover the Jacksonville, FL Metropolitan Statistical Area—see Appendix B for areas included; (2) Excludes Mexico.
Source: U.S. Census Bureau, 2008-2010 American Community Survey 3-Year Estimates

Marital Status

Area	Never Married	Now Married[2]	Separated	Widowed	Divorced
City	33.2	44.7	2.8	5.9	13.5
MSA[1]	29.9	48.8	2.4	5.9	13.0
U.S.	31.6	49.6	2.2	6.1	10.7

Note: Figures are percentages and cover the population 15 years of age and older; (1) Figures cover the Jacksonville, FL Metropolitan Statistical Area—see Appendix B for areas included; (2) Excludes separated
Source: U.S. Census Bureau, 2008-2010 American Community Survey 3-Year Estimates

Age

Area	Percent of Population							Median Age
	Under Age 5	Age 5 to 17	Age 18 to 34	Age 35 to 49	Age 50 to 64	Age 65 to 79	80 Years and Over	
City	7.0	16.9	25.4	21.1	18.7	8.0	2.9	35.5
MSA[1]	6.5	17.3	23.1	21.4	19.6	9.0	3.1	37.5
U.S.	6.5	17.5	23.2	20.7	19.0	9.4	3.6	37.2

Note: (1) Figures cover the Jacksonville, FL Metropolitan Statistical Area—see Appendix B for areas included
Source: U.S. Census Bureau, 2010 Census

Male/Female Ratio

Area	Males	Females	Males per 100 Females
City	398,294	423,490	94.1
MSA[1]	655,647	689,949	95.0
U.S.	151,781,326	156,964,212	96.7

Note: (1) Figures cover the Jacksonville, FL Metropolitan Statistical Area—see Appendix B for areas included
Source: U.S. Census Bureau, 2010 Census

Religious Groups

Area	Catholic	Baptist	Non-Den.	Methodist[2]	Lutheran	LDS[3]	Pente-costal	Presby-terian[4]	Muslim[5]	Judaism
MSA[1]	9.9	18.5	7.8	4.5	0.7	1.1	1.9	1.6	0.4	0.6
U.S.	19.1	9.3	4.0	4.0	2.3	2.0	1.9	1.6	0.8	0.7

Note: Figures are the number of adherents as a percentage of the total population; (1) Figures cover the Jacksonville, FL Metropolitan Statistical Area—see Appendix B for areas included; (2) Methodist/Pietist; (3) Latter Day Saints; (4) Reformed; (5) Figures are estimates
Source: Association of Statisticians of American Religious Bodies, 2010 U.S. Religion Census: Religious Congregations & Membership Study

ECONOMY

Gross Metropolitan Product

Area	2007	2008	2009	2010	2010 Rank[2]
MSA[1]	60.2	59.3	58.6	59.7	46

Note: Figures are in billions of dollars; (1) Figures cover the Jacksonville, FL Metropolitan Statistical Area—see Appendix B for areas included; (2) Rank ranges from 1 to 363
Source: The United States Conference of Mayors, "U.S. Metro Economies: GMP and Employment Forecasts," June 2011

Economic Growth

Area	2007-2009 (%)	2010 (%)	2011 (%)	Rank[2]
MSA[1]	-3.2	1.1	1.8	281
U.S.	-1.3	2.9	2.5	–

Note: Figures are real Gross Metropolitan Product growth rates and represent annual average percent change; (1) Figures cover the Jacksonville, FL Metropolitan Statistical Area—see Appendix B for areas included; (2) Rank ranges from 1 to 363
Source: The United States Conference of Mayors, "U.S. Metro Economies: GMP and Employment Forecasts," June 2011

Metropolitan Area Exports

Area	2005	2006	2007	2008	2009	2010	2010 Rank[2]
MSA[1]	1,200.6	1,445.9	1,709.3	1,973.5	1,634.4	1,940.5	89

Note: Figures are in millions of dollars; (1) Figures cover the Jacksonville, FL Metropolitan Statistical Area—see Appendix B for areas included; (2) Rank ranges from 1 to 369
Source: U.S. Department of Commerce, International Trade Administration, Office of Trade & Industry Information, Manufacturing & Services, data extracted April 2, 2012

INCOME

Income

Area	Per Capita ($)	Median Household ($)	Average Household ($)
City	24,478	47,356	61,797
MSA[1]	26,678	51,663	68,189
U.S.	26,942	51,222	70,116

Note: (1) Figures cover the Jacksonville, FL Metropolitan Statistical Area—see Appendix B for areas included
Source: U.S. Census Bureau, 2008-2010 American Community Survey 3-Year Estimates

Household Income Distribution

Area	Percent of Households Earning							
	Under $15,000	$15,000 -24,999	$25,000 -34,999	$35,000 -49,999	$50,000 -74,999	$75,000 -99,000	$100,000 -149,999	$150,000 and up
City	13.5	11.4	12.0	15.1	20.1	12.4	10.1	5.3
MSA[1]	11.9	10.2	11.1	14.9	20.3	12.8	11.8	7.0
U.S.	13.0	11.0	10.6	14.2	18.5	12.1	12.2	8.4

Note: (1) Figures cover the Jacksonville, FL Metropolitan Statistical Area—see Appendix B for areas included
Source: U.S. Census Bureau, 2008-2010 American Community Survey 3-Year Estimates

Poverty Rate

Area	All Ages	Under 18 Years Old	18 to 64 Years Old	65 Years and Over
City	15.2	22.0	13.5	9.8
MSA[1]	13.4	19.0	12.1	9.2
U.S.	14.4	20.1	13.1	9.4

Note: Figures are percentage of people whose income during the past 12 months was below the poverty level;
(1) Figures cover the Jacksonville, FL Metropolitan Statistical Area—see Appendix B for areas included
Source: U.S. Census Bureau, 2008-2010 American Community Survey 3-Year Estimates

Personal Bankruptcy Filing Rate

Area	2006	2007	2008	2009	2010	2011
Duval County	2.39	3.46	4.44	5.80	5.97	5.10
U.S.	2.00	2.73	3.53	4.61	4.97	4.37

Note: Numbers are per 1,000 population and include Chapter 7 and Chapter 13 filings
Source: Federal Deposit Insurance Corporation, Regional Economic Conditions, March 9, 2012

EMPLOYMENT

Labor Force and Employment

Area	Civilian Labor Force			Workers Employed		
	Dec. 2010	Dec. 2011	% Chg.	Dec. 2010	Dec. 2011	% Chg.
City	417,935	418,417	0.1	371,136	379,176	2.2
MSA[1]	688,236	688,514	0.0	611,911	625,167	2.2
U.S.	153,156,000	153,373,000	0.1	139,159,000	140,681,000	1.1

Note: Data is not seasonally adjusted and covers workers 16 years of age and older;
(1) Metropolitan Statistical Area—see Appendix B for areas included
Source: Bureau of Labor Statistics, http://stats.bls.gov

Unemployment Rate

Area	2011											
	Jan.	Feb.	Mar.	Apr.	May	Jun.	Jul.	Aug.	Sep.	Oct.	Nov.	Dec.
City	11.6	10.7	10.3	10.0	10.1	10.9	11.0	11.0	10.3	9.8	9.7	9.4
MSA[1]	11.5	10.6	10.2	9.8	9.7	10.4	10.5	10.4	10.0	9.6	9.5	9.2
U.S.	9.8	9.5	9.2	8.7	8.7	9.3	9.3	9.1	8.8	8.5	8.2	8.3

Note: Data is not seasonally adjusted and covers workers 16 years of age and older; All figures are
percentages; (1) Metropolitan Statistical Area—see Appendix B for areas included
Source: Bureau of Labor Statistics, http://stats.bls.gov

Projected Unemployment Rate

Area	2010 (%)	2011 (%)	2012 (%)	2013 (%)
MSA[1]	11.6	10.3	9.7	9.0

Note: (1) Metropolitan Statistical Area—see Appendix B for areas included
Source: The United States Conference of Mayors, "U.S. Metro Economies: GMP and Employment Forecasts,"
June 2011

Employment by Occupation

Occupation Classification	City (%)	MSA[1] (%)	U.S. (%)
Management, Business, Science, and Arts	32.8	34.6	35.6
Natural Resources, Construction, and Maintenance	8.8	9.1	9.5
Production, Transportation, and Material Moving	10.3	9.5	12.1
Sales and Office	30.3	29.2	25.2
Service	17.8	17.6	17.6

Note: Figures cover employed civilians 16 years of age and older; (1) Figures cover the Jacksonville, FL Metropolitan Statistical Area—see Appendix B for areas included
Source: U.S. Census Bureau, 2008-2010 American Community Survey 3-Year Estimates

Employment by Industry

Sector	MSA[1] Number of Employees	MSA[1] Percent of Total	U.S. Percent of Total
Construction	25,900	4.3	4.1
Education and Health Services	88,800	14.8	15.2
Financial Activities	58,400	9.7	5.8
Government	77,200	12.9	16.8
Information	9,600	1.6	2.0
Leisure and Hospitality	64,600	10.8	9.9
Manufacturing	26,800	4.5	8.9
Mining and Logging	300	<0.1	0.6
Other Services	23,000	3.8	4.0
Professional and Business Services	96,600	16.1	13.3
Retail Trade	73,300	12.2	11.5
Transportation and Utilities	30,700	5.1	3.8
Wholesale Trade	25,400	4.2	4.2

Note: Figures cover non-farm employment as of December 2011 and are not seasonally adjusted; (1) Metropolitan Statistical Area—see Appendix B for areas included
Source: Bureau of Labor Statistics, http://stats.bls.gov

Occupations with Greatest Projected Employment Growth: 2008 – 2018

Occupation[1]	2008 Employment	2018 Projected Employment	Numeric Employment Change	Percent Employment Change
Registered Nurses	151,100	187,380	36,280	24.0
Combined Food Preparation and Serving Workers, Including Fast Food	162,570	186,400	23,830	14.7
Customer Service Representatives	169,080	190,780	21,700	12.8
Nursing Aides, Orderlies, and Attendants	88,630	106,860	18,230	20.6
Home Health Aides	30,480	47,860	17,380	57.0
Postsecondary Teachers	70,790	85,380	14,590	20.6
Retail Salespersons	274,490	288,660	14,170	5.2
Elementary School Teachers, Except Special Education	74,130	86,390	12,260	16.5
Stock Clerks and Order Fillers	167,450	179,420	11,970	7.1
Accountants and Auditors	86,390	97,670	11,280	13.1

Note: Projections cover Florida; (1) Sorted by numeric employment change
Source: www.projectionscentral.com, State Occupational Projections, 2008–2018 Long-Term Projections

Fastest Growing Occupations: 2008 – 2018

Occupation[1]	2008 Employment	2018 Projected Employment	Numeric Employment Change	Percent Employment Change
Biomedical Engineers	520	840	320	61.5
Home Health Aides	30,480	47,860	17,380	57.0
Medical Scientists, Except Epidemiologists	2,640	3,870	1,230	46.6
Physician Assistants	3,900	5,490	1,590	40.8
Personal and Home Care Aides	13,890	19,430	5,540	39.9
Network Systems and Data Communications Analysts	21,550	30,110	8,560	39.7
Radiation Therapists	1,270	1,730	460	36.2
Dental Hygienists	9,030	11,890	2,860	31.7
Physical Therapist Assistants	3,550	4,660	1,110	31.3
Financial Examiners	610	800	190	31.1

Note: Projections cover Florida; (1) Sorted by percent employment change and excludes occupations with numeric employment change less than 100
Source: www.projectionscentral.com, State Occupational Projections, 2008–2018 Long-Term Projections

Average Wages

Occupation	$/Hr.	Occupation	$/Hr.
Accountants and Auditors	32.41	Maids and Housekeeping Cleaners	9.07
Automotive Mechanics	19.26	Maintenance and Repair Workers	16.49
Bookkeepers	16.24	Marketing Managers	56.19
Carpenters	16.70	Nuclear Medicine Technologists	34.06
Cashiers	9.17	Nurses, Licensed Practical	19.78
Clerks, General Office	13.06	Nurses, Registered	31.53
Clerks, Receptionists/Information	12.75	Nursing Aides/Orderlies/Attendants	11.48
Clerks, Shipping/Receiving	14.10	Packers and Packagers, Hand	9.62
Computer Programmers	34.13	Physical Therapists	46.78
Computer Support Specialists	21.65	Postal Service Mail Carriers	24.92
Computer Systems Analysts	36.27	Real Estate Brokers	31.18
Cooks, Restaurant	11.44	Retail Salespersons	11.67
Dentists	79.36	Sales Reps., Exc. Tech./Scientific	28.67
Electrical Engineers	40.92	Sales Reps., Tech./Scientific	38.14
Electricians	20.80	Secretaries, Exc. Legal/Med./Exec.	14.83
Financial Managers	57.19	Security Guards	10.26
First-Line Supervisors/Managers, Sales	20.25	Surgeons	n/a
Food Preparation Workers	9.52	Teacher Assistants	11.10
General and Operations Managers	49.47	Teachers, Elementary School	25.90
Hairdressers/Cosmetologists	12.38	Teachers, Secondary School	23.10
Internists	94.93	Telemarketers	12.03
Janitors and Cleaners	10.68	Truck Drivers, Heavy/Tractor-Trailer	17.52
Landscaping/Groundskeeping Workers	10.80	Truck Drivers, Light/Delivery Svcs.	14.95
Lawyers	46.99	Waiters and Waitresses	9.39

Note: Wage data covers the Jacksonville, FL Metropolitan Statistical Area—see Appendix B for areas included. Hourly wages for elementary/secondary school teachers and teacher assistants were calculated by the editors from annual wage data assuming a 40 hour work week; n/a not available.
Source: Bureau of Labor Statistics, Metro Area Occupational Employment and Wage Estimates, May 2011

RESIDENTIAL REAL ESTATE

Building Permits

Area	Single-Family			Multi-Family			Total		
	2010	2011	Pct. Chg.	2010	2011	Pct. Chg.	2010	2011	Pct. Chg.
City	1,397	957	-31.5	68	558	720.6	1,465	1,515	3.4
MSA[1]	3,387	3,245	-4.2	219	666	204.1	3,606	3,911	8.5
U.S.	447,311	418,498	-6.4	157,299	205,563	30.7	604,610	624,061	3.2

Note: (1) Metropolitan Statistical Area—see Appendix B for areas included; figures represent new, privately-owned housing units authorized (unadjusted data); All permit data are based on estimates with imputation.
Source: U.S. Census Bureau, Manufacturing, Mining, and Construction Statistics, Building Permits, 2010, 2011

Homeownership Rate

Area	2005 (%)	2006 (%)	2007 (%)	2008 (%)	2009 (%)	2010 (%)	2011 (%)
MSA[1]	67.9	70.0	70.9	72.1	72.6	70.0	68.0
U.S.	68.9	68.8	68.1	67.8	67.4	66.9	66.1

Note: (1) Metropolitan Statistical Area—see Appendix B for areas included
Source: U.S. Census Bureau, Housing Vacancies and Homeownership Annual Statistics: 2011

Housing Vacancy Rates

Area	Gross Vacancy Rate[2] (%)			Year-Round Vacancy Rate[3] (%)			Rental Vacancy Rate[4] (%)			Homeowner Vacancy Rate[5] (%)		
	2009	2010	2011	2009	2010	2011	2009	2010	2011	2009	2010	2011
MSA[1]	14.3	14.9	14.7	13.6	14.6	14.1	15.9	13.9	13.3	3.7	4.6	2.8
U.S.	14.5	14.3	14.2	11.3	11.3	11.1	10.6	10.2	9.5	2.6	2.6	2.5

Note: (1) Metropolitan Statistical Area—see Appendix B for areas included; (2) The percentage of the total housing inventory that is vacant; (3) The percentage of the housing inventory (excluding seasonal units) that is year-round vacant; (4) The percentage of rental inventory that is vacant for rent; (5) The percentage of homeowner inventory that is vacant for sale
Source: U.S. Census Bureau, Housing Vacancies and Homeownership Annual Statistics: 2011

TAXES

State Corporate Income Tax Rates

State	Tax Rate (%)	Income Brackets ($)	Num. of Brackets	Financial Institution Tax Rate (%)[a]	Federal Income Tax Ded.
Florida	5.5 (f)	Flat rate	1	5.5 (f)	No

Note: Tax rates as of January 1, 2012; (a) Rates listed are the corporate income tax rate applied to financial institutions or excise taxes based on income. Some states have other taxes based upon the value of deposits or shares; (f) An exemption of $5,000 is allowed. Florida's Alternative Minimum Tax rate is 3.3%.
Source: Federation of Tax Administrators, "State Corporate Income Tax Rates, 2012"

State Individual Income Tax Rates

State	Tax Rate (%)	Income Brackets ($)	Num. of Brackets	Personal Exempt. ($)[1] Single	Dependents	Fed. Inc. Tax Ded.
Florida – No State Income Tax						

Note: Tax rates as of January 1, 2012; Local- and county-level taxes are not included; n/a not applicable; (1) Married joint filers generally receive double the single exemption
Source: Federation of Tax Administrators, "State Individual Income Tax Rates, 2012"

Various State and Local Tax Rates

State	State and Local Sales and Use (%)	State Sales and Use (%)	Gasoline[1] (¢/gal.)	Cigarette[2] ($/pack)	Spirits[3] ($/gal.)	Wine[4] ($/gal.)	Beer[5] ($/gal.)
Florida	7.0	6.00	35.0	1.34	6.50	2.25	0.48

Note: All tax rates as of January 1, 2012 except beer, wine and spirits (September 1, 2011); (1) The American Petroleum Institute has developed a methodology for determining the average tax rate on a gallon of fuel. Rates may include any of the following: excise taxes, environmental fees, storage tank fees, other fees or taxes, general sales tax, and local taxes. In states where gasoline is subject to the general sales tax, or where the fuel tax is based on the average sale price, the average rate determined by API is sensitive to changes in the price of gasoline. States that fully or partially apply general sales taxes to gasoline: CA, CO, GA, IL, IN, MI, NY; (2) The federal excise tax of $1.0066 per pack and local taxes are not included; (3) Rates are those applicable to off-premise sales of 40% alcohol by volume (a.b.v.) distilled spirits in 750ml containers. Local excise taxes are excluded; (4) Rates are those applicable to off-premise sales of 11% a.b.v. non-carbonated wine in 750ml containers; (5) Rates are those applicable to off-premise sales of 4.7% a.b.v. beer in 12 ounce containers.
Source: Tax Foundation, 2012 Facts & Figures: How Does Your State Compare?

State-Local Tax Burdens

Area	Rate (%)	Rank[1]	Per Capita Taxes Paid to Home State ($)	Total State and Local Per Capita Taxes Paid ($)	Per Capita Income ($)
Florida	9.2	31	2,713	3,897	42,146
U.S. Average	9.8	-	3,057	4,160	42,539

Note: Figures cover 2009; (1) Rank ranges from 1 to 50 where 1 is highest tax burden
Source: Tax Foundation, State-Local Tax Burdens, All States, 2009

State Business Tax Climate Index Rankings

State	Overall Rank	Corporate Tax Index Rank	Individual Income Tax Index Rank	Sales Tax Index Rank	Unemployment Insurance Tax Index Rank	Property Tax Index Rank
Florida	5	12	1	19	5	24

Note: The index is a measure of how each state's tax laws affect economic performance. The lower the rank, the more favorable a state's tax system is for business. States without a given tax are given a ranking of 1.
Source: Tax Foundation, Major Components of the State Business Tax Climate Index, FY 2012

COMMERCIAL UTILITIES

Typical Monthly Electric Bills

Area	Commercial Service ($/month)		Industrial Service ($/month)	
	40 kW demand 5,000 kWh	500 kW demand 100,000 kWh	5,000 kW demand 1,500,000 kWh	70,000 kW demand 50,000,000 kWh
City	588	13,191	177,630	3,567,149

Note: Based on rates in effect January 1, 2011
Source: Memphis Light, Gas and Water, 2011 Utility Bill Comparisons for Selected U.S. Cities

TRANSPORTATION

Means of Transportation to Work

Area	Car/Truck/Van		Public Transportation			Bicycle	Walked	Other Means	Worked at Home
	Drove Alone	Car-pooled	Bus	Subway	Railroad				
City	81.0	10.7	1.6	0.0	0.0	0.4	1.8	0.9	3.6
MSA[1]	81.2	10.1	1.1	0.0	0.0	0.6	1.6	1.3	4.0
U.S.	76.0	10.2	2.7	1.7	0.5	0.5	2.8	1.3	4.2

Note: Figures are percentages and cover workers 16 years of age and older; (1) Figures cover the Jacksonville, FL Metropolitan Statistical Area—see Appendix B for areas included
Source: U.S. Census Bureau, 2008-2010 American Community Survey 3-Year Estimates

Travel Time to Work

Area	Less Than 10 Minutes	10 to 19 Minutes	20 to 29 Minutes	30 to 44 Minutes	45 to 59 Minutes	60 to 89 Minutes	90 Minutes or More
City	9.3	30.4	29.0	22.2	5.3	2.5	1.3
MSA[1]	10.4	27.5	25.2	23.4	8.3	3.6	1.5
U.S.	13.9	30.1	20.8	19.8	7.5	5.5	2.5

Note: Figures are percentages and include workers 16 years old and over; (1) Figures cover the Jacksonville, FL Metropolitan Statistical Area—see Appendix B for areas included
Source: U.S. Census Bureau, 2008-2010 American Community Survey 3-Year Estimates

Travel Time Index

Area	1985	1990	1995	2000	2005	2010
Urban Area[1]	1.07	1.11	1.16	1.13	1.17	1.09
Average[2]	1.11	1.16	1.18	1.21	1.25	1.20

Note: Travel Time Index—the ratio of travel time in the peak period to the travel time at free-flow conditions. A value of 1.30 indicates a 20-minute free-flow trip takes 26 minutes in the peak. Free-flow speeds (60 mph on freeways and 35 mph on principal arterials) are used as the comparison threshold; (1) Covers the Jacksonville FL urban area; (2) average of 439 urban areas
Source: Texas Transportation Institute, Urban Mobility Report 2011, September 2011

Public Transportation

Agency Name / Mode of Transportation	Vehicles Operated in Maximum Service	Annual Unlinked Passenger Trips ('000)	Annual Passenger Miles ('000)
Jacksonville Transportation Authority (JTA)			
Automated Guideway (directly operated)	7	470.4	191.2
Bus (directly operated)	135	10,443.1	60,297.0
Bus (purchased transportation)	20	314.3	1,904.9
Demand Response (purchased transportation)	75	369.6	3,643.9

Source: Federal Transit Administration, National Transit Database, 2010

Air Transportation

Airport Name and Code / Type of Service	Passenger Airlines[1]	Passenger Enplanements	Freight Carriers[2]	Freight (lbs.)
Jacksonville International (JAX)				
Domestic service (U.S. carriers - 2011)	32	2,699,547	14	75,256,205
International service (U.S. carriers - 2010)	5	320	0	0

Note: (1) Includes all U.S.-based major, minor and commuter airlines that carried at least one passenger during the year; (2) Includes all U.S.-based airlines and freight carriers that transported at least one pound of freight during the year
Source: Bureau of Transportation Statistics, The Intermodal Transportation Database, Air Carriers: T-100 Domestic Market (U.S. Carriers), 2011; Bureau of Transportation Statistics, The Intermodal Transportation Database, Air Carriers: T-100 International Market (U.S. Carriers), 2010

Other Transportation Statistics

Major Highways:	I-10; I-95
Amtrak Service:	Yes
Major Waterways/Ports:	St. Johns River

Source: Amtrak.com; Google Maps

BUSINESSES

Major Business Headquarters

Company Name	Rankings	
	Fortune[1]	Forbes[2]
CSX	230	-
Fidelity National Financial	398	-
Fidelity National Information Services	426	-
Winn-Dixie Stores	324	-

Note: (1) Fortune 500—companies that produce a 10-K are ranked 1 to 500 based on 2010 revenue; (2) all private companies with at least $2 billion in annual revenue are ranked 1 to 212; companies listed are headquartered in the city; dashes indicate no ranking
Source: Fortune, "Fortune 500," May 23, 2011; Forbes, "America's Largest Private Companies," November 16, 2011

Fast-Growing Businesses

According to *Inc.*, Jacksonville is home to three of America's 500 fastest-growing private companies: **A. Harold and Associates** (#36); **B3 Solutions** (#198); **SNS Logistics** (#200). Criteria: must be an independent, privately-held, for-profit, U.S. corporation, proprietorship or partnership; revenues must be at least $80,000 in 2007 and $2 million in 2010; must have four-year operating/sales history. Holding companies, regulated banks, and utilities were excluded. *Inc., "America's 500 Fastest-Growing Private Companies," September 2011*

According to Deloitte, Jacksonville is home to one of North America's 500 fastest-growing high-technology companies: **Web.com** (#475). Companies are ranked by percentage growth in revenue over a five-year period. Criteria for inclusion: company must be headquartered within North America; must own proprietary intellectual property or proprietary technology that contributes to a significant portion of the company's operating revenue, or devote a significant proportion of revenues to research and development of technology; must have been in business for a minumum of five years with 2006 operating revenues of at least $50,000 USD/CD and 2010 operating revenues of at least $5 million USD/CD. *Deloitte Touche Tohmatsu, 2011 Deloitte Technology Fast 500*[TM]

Minority Business Opportunity

Jacksonville is home to one company which is on the *Black Enterprise* Industrial/Service 100 list (100 largest companies based on gross sales): **Raven Transport Co.** (#50). Criteria: operational in previous calendar year; at least 51% black-owned and manufactures/owns the product it sells or provides industrial or consumer services. Brokerages, real estate firms and firms that provide professional services are not eligible. *Black Enterprise, B.E. 100s, 2011*

Jacksonville is home to one company which is on the *Black Enterprise* Auto Dealer 60 list (60 largest dealers based on gross sales): **Cadillac-Saab of Orange Park** (#47). Criteria: company must be operational in previous calendar year and be at least 51% black-owned. *Black Enterprise, B.E. 100s, 2011*

Jacksonville is home to one company which is on the *Hispanic Business* 500 list (500 largest U.S. Hispanic-owned companies based on 2010 revenue): **Information & Computing Services** (#231). Companies included must show at least 51 percent ownership by Hispanic U.S. citizens, and must maintain headquarters in one of the 50 states or Washington, D.C. *Hispanic Business, "Hispanic Business 500," June 2011*

Minority- and Women-Owned Businesses

Group	All Firms		Firms with Paid Employees			
	Firms	Sales ($000)	Firms	Sales ($000)	Employees	Payroll ($000)
Asian	3,275	683,318	873	590,497	5,392	124,476
Black	9,718	373,933	650	208,344	3,220	66,134
Hispanic	4,175	800,765	611	627,534	4,024	117,669
Women	19,155	3,802,252	3,059	3,403,581	22,636	698,117
All Firms	64,101	109,406,895	17,474	107,422,420	431,635	17,490,879

Note: Figures cover firms located in the city; minority- and women-owned business are defined as firms in which the corresponding group own 51% or more of the stock or equity of the company
Source: U.S. Census Bureau, 2007 Economic Census, Survey of Business Owners

HOTELS

Hotels/Motels

Area	5 Star		4 Star		3 Star		2 Star		1 Star		Not Rated	
	Num.	Pct.[3]	Num.	Pct.[3]	Num.	Pct.[3]	Num.	Pct.[3]	Num.	Pct.[3]	Num.	Pct.[3]
City[1]	1	0.6	9	5.2	49	28.5	100	58.1	2	1.2	11	6.4
Total[2]	133	0.9	940	6.5	4,569	31.8	7,033	48.9	351	2.4	1,343	9.3

Note: (1) Figures cover Jacksonville and vicinity; (2) Figures cover all 100 cities in this book; (3) Percentage of hotels which have a given star rating; Star ratings are determined by expedia.com and offer an indication of the general quality of a particular hotel.
Source: expedia.com, April 25, 2012

The Jacksonville, FL metro area is home to two of the best hotels in the U.S. according to *Travel & Leisure*: **Ritz-Carlton, Amelia Island** (#48); **One Ocean Resort** (#199). Criteria: service; location; rooms; food; and value. *Travel & Leisure, "T+L 500, The World's Best Hotels 2012"*

EVENT SITES

Major Stadiums, Arenas, and Auditoriums

Name	Max. Capacity
Baseball Grounds of Jacksonville	11,000
Florida Theatre	2,403
Jacksonville Municipal Stadium	77,000
Jacksonville Veterans Memorial Arena	15,000
Morocco Shrine Auditorium	3,000
Times-Union Center for the Performing Arts	2,979

Source: Original research

Convention Centers

Name	Overall Space (sq. ft.)	Exhibit Space (sq. ft.)	Meeting Space (sq. ft.)	Meeting Rooms
Prime F. Osborn III Convention Center	296,000	48,000	100,000	22

Source: Original research

Living Environment

COST OF LIVING

Cost of Living Index

Composite Index	Groceries	Housing	Utilities	Trans-portation	Health Care	Misc. Goods/ Services
94.0	100.5	82.9	101.5	106.4	88.5	95.2

Note: U.S. = 100; Figures cover the Jacksonville FL urban area.
Source: The Council for Community and Economic Research, ACCRA Cost of Living Index, 2011

Grocery Prices

Area[1]	T-Bone Steak ($/pound)	Frying Chicken ($/pound)	Whole Milk ($/half gal.)	Eggs ($/dozen)	Orange Juice ($/64 oz.)	Coffee ($/11.5 oz.)
City[2]	9.83	1.23	2.74	1.74	3.21	4.13
Avg.	9.25	1.18	2.22	1.66	3.19	4.40
Min.	6.70	0.88	1.31	0.95	2.46	2.94
Max.	14.30	2.16	3.50	3.18	4.75	6.83

Note: (1) Values for the local area are compared with the average, minimum and maximum values for all 335 areas in the Cost of Living Index; (2) Figures cover the Jacksonville FL urban area; **T-Bone Steak** (price per pound); **Frying Chicken** (price per pound, whole fryer); **Whole Milk** (half gallon carton); **Eggs** (price per dozen, Grade A, large); **Orange Juice** (64 oz. Tropicana or Florida Natural); **Coffee** (11.5 oz. can, vacuum-packed, Maxwell House, Hills Bros, or Folgers).
Source: The Council for Community and Economic Research, ACCRA Cost of Living Index, 2011

Housing and Utility Costs

Area[1]	New Home Price ($)	Apartment Rent ($/month)	All Electric ($/month)	Part Electric ($/month)	Other Energy ($/month)	Telephone ($/month)
City[2]	206,359	974	181.34	-	-	23.94
Avg.	285,990	839	163.23	89.00	77.52	26.92
Min.	188,005	460	125.58	45.39	33.89	17.98
Max.	1,197,028	3,244	339.16	181.97	348.69	40.01

Note: (1) Values for the local area are compared with the average, minimum and maximum values for all 335 areas in the Cost of Living Index; (2) Figures cover the Jacksonville FL urban area; **New Home Price** (2,400 sf living area, 8,000 sf lot, in urban area with full utilities); **Apartment Rent** (950 sf 2 bedroom/1.5 or 2 bath, unfurnished, excluding all utilities except water); **All Electric** (average monthly cost for an all-electric home); **Part Electric** (average monthly cost for a part-electric home); **Other Energy** (average monthly cost for natural gas, fuel oil, coal, wood, and any other forms of energy except electricity); **Telephone** (price includes basic monthly rate for a private residential line plus additional local usage charges incurred by a family of four).
Source: The Council for Community and Economic Research, ACCRA Cost of Living Index, 2011

Health Care, Transportation, and Other Costs

Area[1]	Doctor ($/visit)	Dentist ($/visit)	Optometrist ($/visit)	Gasoline ($/gallon)	Beauty Salon ($/visit)	Men's Shirt ($)
City[2]	69.07	81.07	67.49	3.39	42.37	20.95
Avg.	93.88	81.72	90.54	3.48	32.65	25.06
Min.	60.00	55.33	53.66	3.18	19.78	13.44
Max.	154.98	145.97	183.72	4.31	63.21	46.00

Note: (1) Values for the local area are compared with the average, minimum and maximum values for all 335 areas in the Cost of Living Index; (2) Figures cover the Jacksonville FL urban area; **Doctor** (general practitioners routine exam of an established patient); **Dentist** (adult teeth cleaning and periodic oral examination); **Optometrist** (full vision eye exam for established adult patient); **Gasoline** (one gallon regular unleaded, national brand, including all taxes, cash price at self-service pump if available); **Beauty Salon** (woman's shampoo, trim, and blow-dry); **Men's Shirt** (cotton/polyester dress shirt, pinpoint weave, long sleeves).
Source: The Council for Community and Economic Research, ACCRA Cost of Living Index, 2011

HOUSING

House Price Index (HPI)

Area	National Ranking[2]	Quarterly Change (%)	One-Year Change (%)	Five-Year Change (%)
MSA[1]	276	-1.29	-7.13	-33.76
U.S.[3]	-	-0.10	-2.43	-19.16

Note: The HPI is a weighted repeat sales index. It measures average price changes in repeat sales or refinancings on the same properties. This information is obtained by reviewing repeat mortgage transactions on single-family properties whose mortgages have been purchased or securitized by Fannie Mae or Freddie Mac in January 1975; (1) Metropolitan/Micropolitan Statistical Area—see Appendix B for areas included; (2) Rankings are based on annual percentage change for all metro areas containing at least 15,000 transactions over the last 10 years and ranges from 1 to 306; (3) figures based on a weighted average of Census Division estimates using a purchase only index; all figures are for the period ending December 31, 2011
Source: Federal Housing Finance Agency, House Price Index, February 23, 2012

House Price Valuations

Area	Q4 2005		Q4 2006		Q4 2007		Q4 2008		Q4 2009	
	Price ($000)	Over-valuation	Price ($000)	Over-valuation	Price ($000)	Over-valuation	Price ($000)	Over-valuation	Price ($000)	Over-valuation
MSA[1]	176.2	20.5	189.7	18.6	180.0	9.3	151.6	-8.4	137.1	-17.4

Note: Figures show the percentage of over- or under-valuation of single family homes relative to statistically normal house values (e.g. a value of 23.6 indicates that house values are 23.6% overvalued). Statistically normal house values are based on house prices, interest rates, household incomes, population densities, and any historical premiums or discounts metropolitan areas have exhibited over time; (1) Figures cover the Jacksonville, FL - see Appendix B for areas included
Source: Global Insight/PNC Financial Services Group, House Prices in America: 4th Quarter 2009 Update

Median Single-Family Home Prices

Area	2009	2010	2011[p]	Percent Change 2010 to 2011
MSA[1]	145.9	137.7	123.6	-10.2
U.S. Average	172.1	173.1	166.2	-4.0

Note: Figures are median sales prices of existing single-family homes in thousands of dollars; (p) preliminary; n/a not available; (1) Metropolitan Statistical Area—see Appendix B for areas included
Source: National Association of Realtors, Median Sales Price of Existing Single-Family Homes for Metropolitan Areas, 4th Quarter 2011

Affordability Index of Existing Single-Family Homes

Area	2009	2010	2011[p]	Percent Change 2010 to 2011
MSA[1]	128.4	144.0	167.8	16.5

Note: The housing affordability index measures whether or not a typical family could qualify for a mortgage loan on a typical home. The higher the index, the greater the household purchasing power. An index of 100 is defined as the point where a median-income household has exactly enough income to qualify for the purchase of a median-priced existing single-family home, assuming a 20 percent downpayment and 25 percent of gross income devoted to mortgage principal and interest payments; (p) preliminary; n/a not available; (1) Metropolitan Statistical Area—see Appendix B for areas included
Source: National Association of Realtors, Affordability Index of Existing Single-Family Homes, 2011

Median Apartment Condo-Coop Home Prices

Area	2009	2010	2011[p]	Percent Change 2010 to 2011
MSA[1]	104.8	69.5	65.5	-5.8
U.S. Average	175.6	171.7	165.1	-3.8

Note: Figures are median sales prices of existing apartment condo-coop homes in thousands of dollars; (p) preliminary; n/a not available; (1) Metropolitan Statistical Area—see Appendix B for areas included
Source: National Association of Realtors, Median Sales Price of Existing Apartment Condo-Coop Homes for Metropolitan Areas, 4th Quarter 2011

Year Housing Structure Built

Area	2005 or Later	2000 -2004	1990 -1999	1980 -1989	1970 -1979	1960 -1969	1950 -1959	Before 1950	Median Year
City	8.2	12.1	15.9	17.5	12.6	11.0	11.7	11.1	1982
MSA[1]	9.2	14.4	18.1	18.9	13.4	8.9	8.8	8.4	1986
U.S.	5.0	8.6	14.0	14.1	16.3	11.3	11.2	19.6	1975

Note: Figures are percentages except for Median Year; (1) Figures cover the Jacksonville, FL Metropolitan Statistical Area—see Appendix B for areas included
Source: U.S. Census Bureau, 2008-2010 American Community Survey 3-Year Estimates

HEALTH

Health Risk Data

Category	MSA[1] (%)	U.S. (%)
Adults who have been told they have high blood pressure[2]	26.8	28.7
Adults who have been told they have high blood cholesterol[2]	32.2	37.5
Adults who have been told they have diabetes[3]	9.3	8.7
Adults who have been told they have arthritis[2]	25.5	26.0
Adults who have been told they currently have asthma	10.1	9.1
Adults who are current smokers	17.7	17.3
Adults who are heavy drinkers[4]	6.4	5.0
Adults who are binge drinkers[5]	15.9	15.1
Adults who are overweight (BMI 25.0 - 29.9)	35.4	36.2
Adults who are obese (BMI 30.0 - 99.8)	26.0	27.5
Adults who participated in any physical activities in the past month	72.1	76.1
Adults 50+ who have ever had a sigmoidoscopy or colonoscopy	69.7	65.2
Women aged 40+ who have had a mammogram within the past two years	78.0	75.2
Men aged 40+ who have had a PSA test within the past two years	61.7	53.2
Adults aged 65+ who have had flu shot within the past year	64.3	67.5
Adults aged 18–64 who have any kind of health care coverage	82.8	82.2

Note: Data as of 2010 unless otherwise noted; (1) Figures cover the Jacksonville, FL Metropolitan Statistical Area—see Appendix B for areas included; (2) Data as of 2009; (3) Figures do not include pregnancy-related, borderline, or pre-diabetes; (4) Heavy drinkers are classified as males having more than two drinks per day or females having more than one drink per day; (5) Binge drinkers are classified as males having five or more drinks on one occasion or females having four or more drinks on one occasion
Source: Centers for Disease Control and Prevention, Behaviorial Risk Factor Surveillance System, SMART: Selected Metropolitan/Micropolitan Area Risk Trends, 2009, 2010

Mortality Rates for the Top 10 Causes of Death in the U.S.

ICD-10[a] Sub-Chapter	ICD-10[a] Code	Age-Adjusted Mortality Rate[1] per 100,000 population	
		County[2]	U.S.
Malignant neoplasms	C00-C97	203.4	175.6
Ischaemic heart diseases	I20-I25	130.5	121.6
Other forms of heart disease	I30-I51	47.9	48.6
Chronic lower respiratory diseases	J40-J47	52.7	42.3
Cerebrovascular diseases	I60-I69	44.2	40.6
Organic, including symptomatic, mental disorders	F01-F09	42.1	26.7
Other degenerative diseases of the nervous system	G30-G31	18.9	24.7
Other external causes of accidental injury	W00-X59	29.3	24.4
Diabetes mellitus	E10-E14	32.6	21.7
Hypertensive diseases	I10-I15	34.1	18.2

Note: (a) ICD-10 = International Classification of Diseases 10th Revision; (1) Mortality rates are a three year average covering 2007-2009; (2) Figures cover Duval County
Source: Centers for Disease Control and Prevention, National Center for Health Statistics. Underlying Cause of Death 1999-2009 on CDC WONDER Online Database, released 2012. Data for year 2009 are compiled from the Multiple Cause of Death File 2009, Series 20 No. 2O, 2012, Data for year 2008 are compiled from the Multiple Cause of Death File 2008, Series 20 No. 2N, 2011, Data for year 2007 are compiled from Multiple Cause of Death File 2007, Series 20 No. 2M, 2010.

Mortality Rates for Selected Causes of Death

ICD-10[a] Sub-Chapter	ICD-10[a] Code	Age-Adjusted Mortality Rate[1] per 100,000 population	
		County[2]	U.S.
Assault	X85-Y09	15.0	5.7
Human immunodeficiency virus (HIV) disease	B20-B24	12.0	3.3
Influenza and pneumonia	J09-J18	19.6	16.4
Intentional self-harm	X60-X84	15.4	11.5
Malnutrition	E40-E46	1.0	0.8
Obesity and other hyperalimentation	E65-E68	2.1	1.6
Transport accidents	V01-V99	16.9	13.7
Viral hepatitis	B15-B19	4.3	2.2

Note: (a) ICD-10 = International Classification of Diseases 10th Revision; (1) Mortality rates are a three year average covering 2007-2009; (2) Figures cover Duval County
Source: Centers for Disease Control and Prevention, National Center for Health Statistics. Underlying Cause of Death 1999-2009 on CDC WONDER Online Database, released 2012. Data for year 2009 are compiled from the Multiple Cause of Death File 2009, Series 20 No. 2O, 2012, Data for year 2008 are compiled from the Multiple Cause of Death File 2008, Series 20 No. 2N, 2011, Data for year 2007 are compiled from Multiple Cause of Death File 2007, Series 20 No. 2M, 2010.

Distribution of Physicians and Dentists

Area[1]	Dentists[2]	D.O.[3]	M.D.[4]				
			Total	Family/ General Practice	Pediatrics	Medical Specialties	Surgical Specialties
Local (number)	318	168	1,883	271	132	684	426
Local (rate[5])	3.7	2.0	22.1	3.2	1.5	8.0	5.0
U.S. (rate[5])	4.5	1.9	18.3	2.5	1.4	6.8	4.1

Note: Data as of 2008 unless noted; (1) Local data covers Duval County; (2) Data as of 2007; (3) Doctor of Osteopathic Medicine; (4) Includes active, non-federal, patient-care, office-based Doctors of Medicine; (5) rate per 10,000 population
Source: Area Resource File (ARF). 2009-2010 Release. U.S. Department of Health and Human Services, Health Resources and Services Administration, Bureau of Health Professions, Rockville, MD, August 2010

Best Hospitals

According to *U.S. News,* the Jacksonville, FL is home to one of the best hospitals in the U.S.: **Mayo Clinic** (2 specialties). The hospital listed was highly ranked in at least one adult specialty. *U.S. News Online, "America's Best Hospitals 2011-12"*

According to *U.S. News,* the Jacksonville, FL is home to one of the best children's hospitals in the U.S.: **Wolfson Children's Hospital** (3 specialties). The hospital listed was highly ranked in at least one pediatric specialty. *U.S. News Online, "America's Best Children's Hospitals 2011-12"*

EDUCATION

Public School District Statistics

District Name	Schls	Pupils	Pupil/ Teacher Ratio	Minority Pupils[1] (%)	Free Lunch Eligible[2] (%)	IEP[3] (%)
Duval	180	122,586	15.6	59.7	41.6	13.8

Note: Table includes school districts with 2,000 or more students; (1) Percentage of students that are not non-Hispanic white; (2) Percentage of students that are eligible for the free lunch program; (3) Percentage of students that have an Individualized Education Program.
Source: U.S. Department of Education, National Center for Education Statistics, Common Core of Data, Local Education Agency (School District) Universe Survey: School Year 2009-2010; U.S. Department of Education, National Center for Education Statistics, Common Core of Data, Public Elementary/Secondary School Universe Survey: School Year 2009-2010

Top Public High Schools

High School Name	Rank[1]	Score[1]	Grad. Rate[2] (%)	College[3] (%)	AP/IB/ AICE[4] (%)	SAT/ ACT[5] (%)
Douglas Anderson School of the Arts	129	0.637	96	89	6.2	1543
Stanton College Preparatory	4	2.175	99	99	11.8	1864
The PAXON School for Advanced Studies	170	0.556	72	98	8.8	1570

Note: (1) Public schools are ranked from 1 to 500 based on the following self-reported statistics (with their corresponding weight in the final score). Schools that had fewer than 10 graduates, as well as those that were newly founded and did not have a graduating senior class in 2010 were excluded; (2) Four-year, on-time graduation rate (25%); (3) Percent of 2010 graduates who enrolled immediately in college (25%); (4) AP/IB/AICE tests per graduate (25%); (5) Average SAT and/or ACT score (10%); Average AP/IB/AICE exam score (10%); AP/IB/AICE courses offered per graduate (5%); (6) School is unranked, but has been identified by Newsweek as one of the nation's most elite public high schools.
Source: Newsweek Online, "Top High Schools 2011"

Highest Level of Education

Area	Less than H.S.	H.S. Diploma	Some College, No Deg.	Associate Degree	Bachelors Degree	Masters Degree	Profess. School Degree	Doctorate Degree
City	13.2	29.7	24.8	8.6	16.3	5.2	1.5	0.7
MSA[1]	11.7	28.8	24.5	8.8	17.6	6.1	1.6	0.9
U.S.	14.7	28.4	21.3	7.6	17.6	7.2	1.9	1.2

Note: Figures cover persons age 25 and over; (1) Figures cover the Jacksonville, FL Metropolitan Statistical Area—see Appendix B for areas included
Source: U.S. Census Bureau, 2008-2010 American Community Survey 3-Year Estimates

Educational Attainment by Race

Area	High School Graduate or Higher (%)					Bachelor's Degree or Higher (%)				
	Total	White	Black	Asian	Hisp.[2]	Total	White	Black	Asian	Hisp.[2]
City	86.8	89.3	82.5	85.3	75.8	23.8	26.1	15.3	44.6	19.4
MSA[1]	88.3	90.2	82.6	86.7	77.8	26.2	28.4	15.4	45.5	20.5
U.S.	85.3	87.5	81.4	85.5	61.6	28.0	29.3	17.8	50.2	13.0

Note: Figures shown cover persons 25 years old and over; (1) Figures cover the Jacksonville, FL Metropolitan Statistical Area—see Appendix B for areas included; (2) People of Hispanic origin can be of any race
Source: U.S. Census Bureau, 2008-2010 American Community Survey 3-Year Estimates

School Enrollment by Grade and Control

Area	Preschool (%)		Kindergarten (%)		Grades 1 - 4 (%)		Grades 5 - 8 (%)		Grades 9 - 12 (%)	
	Public	Private	Public	Private	Public	Private	Public	Private	Public	Private
City	48.7	51.3	80.3	19.7	85.6	14.4	82.3	17.7	83.1	16.9
MSA[1]	47.7	52.3	85.1	14.9	86.7	13.3	84.5	15.5	87.0	13.0
U.S.	55.4	44.6	87.1	12.9	89.4	10.6	89.5	10.5	90.4	9.6

Note: Figures shown cover persons 3 years old and over; (1) Figures cover the Jacksonville, FL Metropolitan Statistical Area—see Appendix B for areas included
Source: U.S. Census Bureau, 2008-2010 American Community Survey 3-Year Estimates

Average Salaries of Public School Classroom Teachers

Area	2010-11		2011-12		Percent Change 2010-11 to 2011-12	Percent Change 2001-02 to 2011-12
	Dollars	Rank[1]	Dollars	Rank[1]		
Florida	45,732	45	46,232	46	1.09	17.70
U.S. Average	55,623	-	56,643	-	1.83	26.8

Note: (1) State rank ranges from 1 to 51 where 1 indicates highest salary.
Source: National Education Association, Rankings & Estimates: Rankings of the States 2011 and Estimates of School Statistics 2012, December 2011

Higher Education

Four-Year Colleges			Two-Year Colleges			Medical Schools[1]	Law Schools[2]	Voc/ Tech[3]
Public	Private Non-profit	Private For-profit	Public	Private Non-profit	Private For-profit			
2	4	5	0	0	9	0	1	9

Note: Figures cover institutions located within the city limits and include main campuses only; (1) includes schools accredited by the Liaison Committee on Medical Education and the American Osteopathic Association's Commission on Osteopathic College Accreditation; (2) includes American Bar Association-accredited law schools; (3) includes all schools with programs that are less than 2 years.
Source: National Center for Education Statistics, Integrated Postsecondary Education System (IPEDS) Peer Analysis System, 2011-12; Association of American Medical Colleges, Member List, April 23, 2012; American Osteopathic Association, Member List, April 23, 2012; Law School Admission Council, Official Guide to ABA-Approved Law Schools Online, April 23, 2012

PRESIDENTIAL ELECTION

2008 Presidential Election Results

Area	Obama	McCain	Nader	Other
Duval County	48.6	50.5	0.2	0.6
U.S.	52.9	45.6	0.6	0.9

Note: Results are percentages and may not add to 100% due to rounding
Source: Dave Leip's Atlas of U.S. Presidential Elections, www.uselectionatlas.org

EMPLOYERS

Major Employers

Company Name	Industry
Baptist Health System	Hospital management
Baptist Health System Foundation	Individual and family services
Baptist Health System Inc	General medical/surgical hospitals
Blue Cross Blue Shield of Florida	Hospital and medical service plans
Fidelity National Information Services	Prepackaged software
Jacksonville Electric Authority	Electric services
Kelley Clark	Food brokers
Mayo Clinic Jacksonville	General medical/surgical hospitals
Shands Jacksonville Medical Center	General medical/surgical hospitals
Southern Baptist Hospital of Florida	Hospital medical school affiliated with residency

Note: Companies shown are located within the Jacksonville, FL metropolitan area.
Source: Hoovers.com, data extracted April 25 2012

PUBLIC SAFETY

Crime Rate

Area	All Crimes	Violent Crimes				Property Crimes		
		Murder	Forcible Rape	Robbery	Aggrav. Assault	Burglary	Larceny -Theft	Motor Vehicle Theft
City	5,215.5	9.7	38.4	205.9	411.0	1,165.8	3,144.8	239.9
Suburbs[1]	2,948.0	3.2	19.1	57.8	308.4	534.9	1,925.7	98.9
Metro[2]	4,329.3	7.2	30.9	148.0	370.9	919.2	2,668.3	184.8
U.S.	3,345.5	4.8	27.5	119.1	252.3	699.6	2,003.5	238.8

Note: Figures are crimes per 100,000 population; (1) All areas within the metro area that are located outside the city limits; (2) Metropolitan Statistical Area—see Appendix B for areas included
Source: FBI Uniform Crime Reports, 2010

Hate Crimes

Area	Number of Quarters Reported	Bias Motivation				
		Race	Religion	Sexual Orientation	Ethnicity	Disability
City	4	0	0	0	0	0

Source: Federal Bureau of Investigation, Hate Crime Statistics 2010

Identity Theft Consumer Complaints

Area	Complaints	Complaints per 100,000 Population	Rank[2]
MSA[1]	1,411	108.5	69
U.S.	279,156	90.4	-

Note: (1) Metropolitan Statistical Area—see Appendix B for areas included; (2) Rank ranges from 1 to 384 where 1 indicates greatest number of identity theft complaints per 100,000 population
Source: Federal Trade Commission, Consumer Sentinel Network Data Book for January–December 2011

Fraud and Other Consumer Complaints

Area	Complaints	Complaints per 100,000 Population	Rank[2]
MSA[1]	7,463	573.7	66
U.S.	1,533,924	496.8	-

Note: (1) Metropolitan Statistical Area—see Appendix B for areas included; (2) Rank ranges from 1 to 384 where 1 indicates greatest number of fraud and other complaints per 100,000 population
Source: Federal Trade Commission, Consumer Sentinel Network Data Book for January–December 2011

RECREATION

Culture

Dance[1]	Theatre[1]	Instrumental Music[1]	Vocal Music[1]	Series/ Festivals	Museums	Zoos and Aquariums[2]
2	2	1	0	5	11	1

Note: (1) Number of professional perfoming groups; (2) AZA-accredited
Source: The Grey House Performing Arts Directory, 2011-2012; Official Museum Directory, 2011; American Association of Museums, AAM Member Museums, April 2012; Association of Zoos & Aquariums, AZA Member Zoos & Aquariums, April 2012

Professional Sports Teams

Team Name	League
Jacksonville Jaguars	National Football League (NFL)

Note: Includes teams located in the Jacksonville metro area.
Source: Original research

CLIMATE

Average and Extreme Temperatures

Temperature	Jan	Feb	Mar	Apr	May	Jun	Jul	Aug	Sep	Oct	Nov	Dec	Yr.
Extreme High (°F)	84	88	91	95	100	103	103	102	98	96	88	84	103
Average High (°F)	65	68	74	80	86	90	92	91	87	80	73	67	79
Average Temp. (°F)	54	57	62	69	75	80	83	82	79	71	62	56	69
Average Low (°F)	43	45	51	57	64	70	73	73	70	61	51	44	58
Extreme Low (°F)	7	22	23	34	45	47	61	63	48	36	21	11	7

Note: Figures cover the years 1948-1990
Source: National Climatic Data Center, International Station Meteorological Climate Summary, 9/96

Average Precipitation/Snowfall/Humidity

Precip./Humidity	Jan	Feb	Mar	Apr	May	Jun	Jul	Aug	Sep	Oct	Nov	Dec	Yr.
Avg. Precip. (in.)	3.0	3.7	3.8	3.0	3.6	5.3	6.2	7.4	7.8	3.7	2.0	2.6	52.0
Avg. Snowfall (in.)	Tr	Tr	Tr	0	0	0	0	0	0	0	0	Tr	0
Avg. Rel. Hum. 7am (%)	86	86	87	86	86	88	89	91	92	91	89	88	88
Avg. Rel. Hum. 4pm (%)	56	53	50	49	54	61	64	65	66	62	58	58	58

Note: Figures cover the years 1948-1990; Tr = Trace amounts (<0.05 in. of rain; <0.5 in. of snow)
Source: National Climatic Data Center, International Station Meteorological Climate Summary, 9/96

Weather Conditions

Temperature			Daytime Sky			Precipitation		
10°F & below	32°F & below	90°F & above	Clear	Partly cloudy	Cloudy	0.01 inch or more precip.	0.1 inch or more snow/ice	Thunder-storms
<1	16	83	86	181	98	114	1	65

Note: Figures are average number of days per year and cover the years 1948-1990
Source: National Climatic Data Center, International Station Meteorological Climate Summary, 9/96

**HAZARDOUS
WASTE**

Superfund Sites

Jacksonville has four hazardous waste sites on the EPA's Superfund Final National Priorities List: **Kerr-McGee Chemical Corp - Jacksonville; Cecil Field Naval Air Station; Jacksonville Naval Air Station; Pickettville Road Landfill**. *U.S. Environmental Protection Agency, Final National Priorities List, April 17, 2012*

**AIR & WATER
QUALITY**

Air Quality Index

Area	Percent of Days when Air Quality was...[2]					AQI Statistics[2]	
	Good	Moderate	Unhealthy for Sensitive Groups	Unhealthy	Very Unhealthy	Maximum	Median
Area[1]	83.6	14.2	1.4	0.8	0.0	173	38

Note: Air Quality Index (AQI) is an index for reporting daily air quality. EPA calculates the AQI for five major air pollutants regulated by the Clean Air Act: ground-level ozone, particle pollution (aka particulate matter), carbon monoxide, sulfur dioxide, and nitrogen dioxide. The AQI runs from 0 to 500. The higher the AQI value, the greater the level of air pollution and the greater the health concern. There are six AQI categories: "Good" AQI is between 0 and 50. Air quality is considered satisfactory; "Moderate" AQI is between 51 and 100. Air quality is acceptable; "Unhealthy for Sensitive Groups" When AQI values are between 101 and 150, members of sensitive groups may experience health effects; "Unhealthy" When AQI values are between 151 and 200 everyone may begin to experience health effects; "Very Unhealthy" AQI values between 201 and 300 trigger a health alert; "Hazardous" AQI values over 300 trigger warnings of emergency conditions (not shown); (1) Data covers Duval County; (2) Based on 365 days with AQI data in 2011.
Source: U.S. Environmental Protection Agency, AirData Report, 2011

Air Quality Index Pollutants

Area	Percent of Days when AQI Pollutant was...[2]					
	Carbon Monoxide	Nitrogen Dioxide	Ozone	Sulfur Dioxide	Particulate Matter 2.5	Particulate Matter 10
Area[1]	0.5	1.1	67.4	2.7	27.9	0.3

Note: The Air Quality Index (AQI) is an index for reporting daily air quality. EPA calculates the AQI for five major air pollutants regulated by the Clean Air Act: ground-level ozone, particle pollution (also known as particulate matter), carbon monoxide, sulfur dioxide, and nitrogen dioxide. The AQI runs from 0 to 500. The higher the AQI value, the greater the level of air pollution and the greater the health concern; (1) Data covers Duval County; (2) Based on 365 days with AQI data in 2011.
Source: U.S. Environmental Protection Agency, AirData Report, 2011

Air Quality Index Trends

Area	Trend Sites (days)								All Sites (days)
	2003	2004	2005	2006	2007	2008	2009	2010	2010
MSA[1]	10	15	20	35	16	10	3	15	16

Note: Figures are the number of days the AQI value exceeded 100 in a given year. An AQI value greater than 100 indicates that air quality would have been in the unhealthful range on that day. Data from exceptional events are included. These counts are presented in two ways. First, the counts are based on sites having an adequate record of monitoring data during the trend period (trend sites). These counts represent the relative change in the number of days with AQI values greater than 100. In the last column, the counts are based on all sites with data in the most recent year (because it is possible for a site to have data in the most recent year but not enough data to be a trend site); (1) Data covers the Jacksonville, FL—see Appendix B for areas included
Source: U.S. Environmental Protection Agency, Air Quality Index Information, "Number of Days with Air Quality Index Values Greater than 100 at Trend Sites, 2000-2010, and at All Sites in 2010"

Maximum Air Pollutant Concentrations: Particulate Matter, Ozone, CO and Lead

	Particulate Matter 10 (ug/m^3)	Particulate Matter 2.5 Wtd AM (ug/m^3)	Particulate Matter 2.5 24-Hr (ug/m^3)	Ozone (ppm)	Carbon Monoxide (ppm)	Lead (ug/m^3)
MSA[1] Level	62	9.4	20	0.068	2	n/a
NAAQS[2]	150	15	35	0.075	9	0.15
Met NAAQS[2]	Yes	Yes	Yes	Yes	Yes	n/a

Note: Data from exceptional events are not included; (1) Data covers the Jacksonville, FL—see Appendix B for areas included; (2) National Ambient Air Quality Standards; ppm = parts per million; ug/m^3 = micrograms per cubic meter; n/a not available
Concentrations: Particulate Matter 10 (coarse particulate)—highest second maximum 24-hour concentration; Particulate Matter 2.5 Wtd AM (fine particulate)—highest weighted annual mean concentration; Particulate Matter 2.5 24-Hour (fine particulate)—highest 98th percentile 24-hour concentration; Ozone—highest fourth daily maximum 8-hour concentration; Carbon Monoxide—highest second maximum non-overlapping 8-hour concentration; Lead—maximum running 3-month average
Source: U.S. Environmental Protection Agency, CBSA Factbook 2010, Air Quality Statistics by City, 2010

Maximum Air Pollutant Concentrations: Nitrogen Dioxide and Sulfur Dioxide

	Nitrogen Dioxide AM (ppb)	Nitrogen Dioxide 1-Hr (ppb)	Sulfur Dioxide AM (ppb)	Sulfur Dioxide 1-Hr (ppb)	Sulfur Dioxide 24-Hr (ppb)
MSA[1] Level	9.324	44	3.949	216	58.4
NAAQS[2]	53	100	30	75	140
Met NAAQS[2]	Yes	Yes	Yes	No	Yes

Note: Data from exceptional events are not included; (1) Data covers the Jacksonville, FL—see Appendix B for areas included; (2) National Ambient Air Quality Standards; ppb = parts per billion; n/a not available
Concentrations: Nitrogen Dioxide AM—highest arithmetic mean concentration; Nitrogen Dioxide 1-Hr—highest 98th percentile 1-hour daily maximum concentration; Sulfur Dioxide AM—highest annual mean concentration; Sulfur Dioxide 1-Hr—highest 99th percentile 1-hour daily maximum concentration; Sulfur Dioxide 24-Hr—highest second maximum 24-hour concentration
Source: U.S. Environmental Protection Agency, CBSA Factbook 2010, Air Quality Statistics by City, 2010

Drinking Water

Water System Name	Pop. Served	Primary Water Source Type	Violations[1] Health Based	Violations[1] Monitoring/ Reporting
JEA-Major Grid	800,000	Ground	0	0

Note: (1) Based on violation data from January 1, 2011 to December 31, 2011 (includes unresolved violations from earlier years)
Source: U.S. Environmental Protection Agency, Office of Ground Water and Drinking Water, Safe Drinking Water Information System (based on data extracted April 18, 2012)

Miami, Florida

Background

While the majority of Miami's residents used to be Caucasian of European descent, the rapidly growing city now consists of a majority of Latinos. The number of Cubans, Puerto Ricans, and Haitians give the city a flavorful mix with a Latin American and Caribbean accent. The City of Miami has three official languages: English, Spanish, and Haitian Creole.

Thanks to early pioneer Julia Tuttle, railroad magnate Henry Flagler extended the East Coast Railroad beyond Palm Beach. Within 15 years of that decision, Miami became known as the "Gold Coast." The land boom of the 1920s brought wealthy socialites, as well as African-Americans in search of work. Pink- and aquamarine-hued art deco hotels were squeezed onto a tiny tract of land called Miami Beach, and the population of the Miami metro area swelled.

Given Miami's origins in a tourist-oriented economy, many of the activities in which residents engage are "leisurely," including swimming, scuba diving, golf, tennis, and boating. For those who enjoy professional sports, the city is host to the following teams: the Miami Dolphins, football; the Florida Marlins, baseball; the Miami Heat, basketball; and the Florida Panthers, hockey. Cultural activities range from the Miami City Ballet and the Coconut Grove Playhouse to numerous art galleries and museums, including the Bass Museum of Art. Visits to the Villa Vizcaya, a gorgeous palazzo built by industrialist James Deering in the Italian Renaissance style, and to the Miami MetroZoo are popular pastimes.

Miami's prime location on Biscayne Bay in the southeastern United States makes it a perfect nexus for travel and trade. The Port of Miami is a bustling center for many cruise and cargo ships. The Port is also a base for the National Oceanic and Atmospheric Administration. The Miami International Airport is a busy destination point to and from many Latin-American and Caribbean countries.

Miami is still at the trading crossroads of the Western Hemisphere as the chief shipment point for exports and imports with Latin America and the Caribbean. One out of every three North American cruise passengers sails from Miami. Miami was also the host city of the 2003 Free Trade Area of the Americas negotiations, and is one of the leading candidates to become the trading bloc's headquarters.

The sultry, subtropical climate against a backdrop of Spanish, art deco, and modern architecture makes Miami a uniquely cosmopolitan city. The Art Deco Historic District, known as South Beach and located on the tip of Miami Beach, has recently developed an international reputation in the fashion, film, and music industries. Greater Miami is now a national center for film, television, and print production.

In recent years Miami has witnessed its largest real estate boom since the 1920s, especially in the newly created midtown, north of downtown and south of the Design District. Nearly 25,000 new residential units have been added to the downtown skyline since 2005.

Long, warm summers are typical, as are mild, dry winters. The marine influence is evidenced by the narrow daily range of temperature and the rapid warming of cold air masses. During the summer months, rainfall occurs in early morning near the ocean and in early afternoon further inland. Hurricanes occasionally affect the Miami area, usually in September and October, while destructive tornadoes are quite rare. Funnel clouds are occasionally sighted and a few touch the ground briefly, but significant destruction is unusual. Waterspouts are visible from the beaches during the summer months but seldom cause any damage. During June, July, and August, there are numerous beautiful, but dangerous, lightning events.

Rankings

General Rankings

- *Men's Health Living* ranked 100 U.S. cities in terms of quality of life. Miami was ranked #89 and received a grade of D. Criteria: number of fitness facilities; air quality; number of physicians; male/female ratio; education levels; household income; cost of living. *Men's Health Living, Spring 2008*

Business/Finance Rankings

- The Miami metro area was identified as one of 10 places with the fastest-growing wages in America. The area ranked #2. Criteria: private-sector wage growth between the 4th quarter of 2010 and the 4th quarter of 2011. *PayScale, "The 10 Cities with the Fastest-Growing Wages in America," January 12, 2012*

- The Miami metro area was identified as one of the most debt-ridden places in America by credit reporting agency Equifax. The metro area was ranked #4. Criteria: proportion of average yearly income owed to credit card companies. *Equifax, "The Most Debt-Ridden Cities in America," February 23, 2012*

- Experian ranked the top 20 major U.S. metropolitan areas by average debt per consumer. The Miami metro area was ranked #19. Criteria: average debt per consumer. Debt for this study includes credit cards, auto loans and personal loans. It does not include mortgages. *Experian, May 13, 2010*

- Miami was selected as one of the best places to start a business by *CNNMoney.com*. Criteria: compelling incentives to would-be entrepreneurs. *CNNMoney.com, "8 Great Cities to Start a Business," 2010*

- Miami was identified as one of America's most coupon-loving cities by *Coupons.com*. The city ranked #12 out of 25. Criteria: online coupon usage. *Coupons.com, "Top 25 Most Frugal Cities of 2011," February 23, 2012*

- Miami was identified as one of the top 25 U.S. cities with the most credit card debt by credit reporting bureau Experian. The city was ranked #23. *Experian, March 4, 2011*

- Miami was identified as one of the "Happiest Cities to Work in 2012" by *CareerBliss.com*, an online community for career advancement. The city ranked #1 out of 50. Criteria: independent company reviews from employees all over the country on: relationship with their boss and co-workers; work environment; job resources; growth opportunities; compensation; company culture; company reputation; daily tasks; job control over work performed on a daily basis. *CareerBliss.com, "Happiest and Unhappiest Cities to Work in 2012"*

- *American City Business Journals* ranked America's 261 largest cities in terms of their resident's wealth. Miami ranked #97. Criteria: per capita income; median household income; percentage of households with annual incomes of $200,000 or more; median home value. *American City Business Journals, "Where the Money Is: America's Wealth Centers," August 18, 2008*

- The Miami metro area appeared on the Milken Institute "2011 Best Performing Metros" list. Rank: #141 out of 200 large metro areas. Criteria: job growth; wage and salary growth; high-tech output growth. *Milken Institute, "2011 Best Performing Metros"*

- The Miami metro area was selected as one of the best cities for entrepreneurs in America by *Inc. Magazine*. Criteria: job-growth data for 335 metro areas was analyzed for: recent growth trend; mid-term growth; long-term trend; current year growth. The Miami metro area ranked #28 among large metro areas and #145 overall. *Inc. Magazine, "The Best Cities for Doing Business," July 2008*

- Miami was ranked #115 out of 145 regions worldwide in terms of its "Knowledge Competitiveness Index." The index attempts to measure the knowledge-based development taking place throughout the world and is based on 19 measures of economic performance that indicate a region's ability to translate its knowledge capacity into economic value. *Centre for International Competitiveness, World Knowledge Competitiveness Index 2008*

- *Forbes* ranked the 200 most populous metro areas in the U.S. in terms of the "Best Places for Business and Careers." The Miami metro area was ranked #152. Criteria: costs (business and living); job growth (past and projected); income growth; educational attainment; projected economic growth; crime; cultural and recreational opportunities; net migration patterns; number of highly ranked colleges. *Forbes, "Best Places for Business and Careers," June 2011*

Children/Family Rankings

- The Miami metro area was selected as one of the "Best Cities for Relocating Families" by Worldwide ERC and Primacy Relocation. The 2008 study looked at nearly 50 factors important to relocating families including: recent job growth; nearby top-ranked colleges; in-state tuition for four-year public colleges; population growth since 2000; pediatricians per 100,000 population; and a Green Living index. *Worldwide ERC and Primacy Relocation, "2008 Best Cities for Relocating Families"*

- *Fit Pregnancy* magazine ranked the 50 best U.S. cities in which to have a baby. Miami was ranked #23. Criteria: access to hospitals and doctors; affordability; birthing options; breastfeeding; child care; fertility laws/resources; maternal and infant health risk; parks/stroller friendliness; safety. *Fit Pregnancy, "The Best Cities in America to Have a Baby 2008"*

Culture/Performing Arts Rankings

- Miami was selected as one of "America's Top 25 Arts Destinations." The city ranked #12 in the mid-sized city (population 100,000 to 499,999) category. Criteria: readers' top choices for arts travel destinations based on the richness and variety of visual arts sites, activities and events. *American Style, "America's Top 25 Arts Destinations," May 2010*

Dating/Romance Rankings

- Miami was selected as one of the most romantic cities in America by *Amazon.com*. The city ranked #7 of 20. Criteria: per capita sales of romance novels and relationship books, romantic comedy movies, Barry White albums, and sexual wellness products. *Amazon.com, "America's Most Romantic Cities Revealed," February 14, 2012*

- Miami was selected as one of the best cities for single men by *Rent.com*. The city ranked #5 of 10. Criteria: high single female-to-male ratio; lively nightlife; low divorce rate; low cost of living. *Rent.com, "Top 10 Cities for Single Men," May 2, 2011*

- Miami was selected as one of "America's Best Cities for Dating" by *Yahoo! Travel*. Criteria: high proportion of singles; excellent dating venues and/or stunning natural settings. *Yahoo! Travel, "America's Best Cities for Dating," February 7, 2012*

- Miami appeared on *Men's Health's* list of the most sex-happy cities in America. The city ranked #88 of 100. Criteria: condom sales; birth rates; sex toy sales; rates of chlamydia, gonorrhea, and syphilis. *Men's Health, "America's Most Sex-Happy Cities," October 2010*

- *Men's Health* ranked 100 U.S. cities in terms of best (and worst) marriages. Miami was ranked #20 (#1 = worst). Criteria: rate of failed marriages; stringency of divorce laws; percentage of population who've split; number of licensed marriage and family therapists. *Men's Health, "Splitsville, USA," May 2010*

- Eli Lily and Company, in partnership with Sperling's BestPlaces, ranked the nation's 50 largest metro areas in terms of the "Most Romantic Cities for Baby Boomers." The Miami metro area ranked #49. Criteria: marriage and divorce rates among baby boomers age 45 to 60; great restaurants; dance studios; chocolate, jewelry and flower sales. *Eli Lily and Company, "Most Romantic Cities for Baby Boomers," April 20, 2007*

- The Miami metro area was selected as one of the "Best Cities for Relocating Singles" by Worldwide ERC and Primacy Relocation. The area ranked #26 out of the 100 largest metro areas in the U.S. Criteria: recent job growth; recent singles population growth; overall population growth; affordable rental housing; cost-of-living index; expanded arts and recreation opportunities; ratio of single men and single women; affordability of quality higher education (including state residency requirements); diversity index; climate; population density. *Worldwide ERC and Primacy Relocation, "2008 Best Cities for Relocating Singles"*

- *Forbes* ranked the 40 most populous urbanized areas in the U.S. in terms of the "Best Cities for Singles." The Miami metro area ranked #29. Criteria: number of singles; cost of living alone; nightlife; culture; job growth; coolness; and online dating participation. *Forbes.com, "Best Cities for Singles," July 27, 2009*

Education Rankings

- *Men's Health* ranked 100 U.S. cities in terms of their education levels. Miami was ranked #100 (#1 = most educated city). Criteria: high school graduation rates; school enrollment; educational attainment; number of households who have outstanding student loans; number of households whose members have taken adult-education courses. *Men's Health, "Where School Is In: The Most and Least Educated Cities," September 12, 2011*

- Miami was selected as one of the most well-read cities in America by *Amazon.com*. The city ranked #6 of 20. Cities with populations greater than 100,000 were evaluated based on per capita sales of books, magazines and newspapers. *Amazon.com, "Top 20 Most Well-Read Cities in America," June 4, 2011*

- Miami was selected as one of "America's Most Literate Cities." The city ranked #36 out of the 75 largest U.S. cities. Criteria: number of booksellers; library resources; Internet resources; educational attainment; periodical publishing resources; newspaper circulation. *Central Connecticut State University, "America's Most Literate Cities 2011"*

- Miami was identified as one of the 100 "smartest" metro areas in the U.S. The area ranked #61. Criteria: the editors rated the collective brainpower of the 100 largest metro areas in the U.S. based on their residents' educational attainment. *American City Business Journals, April 14, 2008*

- Miami was identified as one of "America's Brainiest Bastions" by *Portfolio.com*. The metro area ranked #118 out of 200. *Portfolio.com* analyzed levels of educational attainment in the nation's 200 largest metropolitan areas. The editors established scores for five levels of educational attainment, based on relative earning power of adult workers age 25 or older. Scores were determined by comparing the median income for all workers with the median income for those workers at a specified educational level. *Portfolio.com, "America's Brainiest Bastions," December 1, 2010*

Environmental Rankings

- The Miami was identified as one of North America's greenest metropolitan areas. The area ranked #22. The Green City Index is comprised of 31 indicators, and scores cities across nine categories: carbon dioxide; energy; land use; buildings; transport; water; waste; air quality; environmental governance. The 27 largest metropolitan areas in the U.S. and Canada were considered. *Economist Intelligence Unit, sponsored by Siemens, "U.S. and Canada Green City Index, 2011"*

- The Miami was identified as one of America's cities with the most ENERGY STAR certified buildings. The area ranked #21 out of 25. Criteria: number of ENERGY STAR labeled buildings in 2010. *U.S. Environmental Protection Agency, "Top Cities With the Most ENERGY STAR Certified Buildings," March 15, 2011*

- Miami was selected as one of 22 "Smarter Cities" for energy by the Natural Resources Defense Council. Criteria: investment in green power; energy efficiency measures; conservation. *Natural Resources Defense Council, "2010 Smarter Cities," July 19, 2010*

- Miami was selected as one of worst summer weather cities in the U.S. by the *Farmers' Almanac*. The city ranked #1 out of 5. Criteria: average summer and winter temperatures; humidity; precipitation; number of overcast days. The editors only considered cities with populations of 50,000 or more. *Farmers' Almanac, "America's Ten Worst Weather Cities," September 7, 2010*

- *American City Business Journal* ranked 43 metropolitan areas in terms of their "greenness." The Miami metro area ranked #30. Criteria: Forty-one metros in which *ACBJ* has business weeklies, plus Indianapolis and Cleveland, were ranked based on 20 different indicators such as adoption of green technologies, utilization of environmentally sound practices, and air and water quality. *American City Business Journals, "Green City Index," March 11, 2010*

- 100 of the largest metro areas in the U.S. were analyzed in terms of their current drought severity. The Miami metro area ranked #58 (#1 = driest). The rankings were based on statistics such as long-term precipitation trends and patterns and the Palmer drought indices. *Sperling's BestPlaces, www.BestPlaces.net, "America's Drought-Riskiest Cities," November 2007*

- The Miami metro area appeared in *Country Home's* "Best Green Places" report. The area ranked #121 out of 379. Criteria: official energy policies; green power; green buildings; availability of fresh, locally grown food. *Country Home, "Best Green Places," 2008*

- *WeatherBill.com* identified the 10 rainiest cities in the U.S. Miami ranked #7. The study ranked 195 cities in the contiguous 48 states by the amount of rainfall they received annually over a 30-year period. *WeatherBill.com, May 23, 2007*

Food/Drink Rankings

- Miami was identified as one of "America's Most Caffeinated Cities" by *Bundle.com*. The city was ranked #9 out of 10. The rankings were determined by examining consumer spending at 16 widely known coffee chains during the second quarter of 2011. *Bundle.com, "America's Most Caffeinated Cities," September 19, 2011*

Health/Fitness Rankings

- Miami was identified as one of the most walkable cities in the U.S. by *WalkScore.com*, a Seattle-based service that rates the convenience and transit access of 10,000 neighborhoods in 2,500 cities. The editors at Grey House Publishing used *WalkScore.com's* online service to look at the scores of 280 cities with populations greater than or equal to 100,000. The top 50 cities were selected. *WalkScore.com, April 2, 2012*

- The Miami metro area was selected as one of the worst cities for bed bugs in America by Rollins corporation, the owner of seven pest control companies, including Orkin. The area ranked #24 based on the number of bed bug treatments from January to December 2011. *Rollins, "The Top 50 U.S. Cities for Bed Bugs," March 19, 2012*

- Miami was selected as one of the 25 fattest cities in America by *Men's Fitness Online*. It ranked #12 out of America's 50 largest cities. Criteria: fitness centers and sport stores; nutrition; sports participation; TV viewing; overweight/sedentary; junk food; air quality; geography; commute; parks and open space; city recreational facilities; access to healthcare; motivation; mayor and city initiatives; state obesity initiatives. *Men's Fitness, "The Fittest and Fattest Cities in America," March 5, 2012*

- Miami was identified as a "2011 Asthma Capital." The area ranked #61 out of the nation's 100 largest metropolitan areas. Twelve factors were used to identify the most challenging places to live for people with asthma: estimated prevalence; self-reported prevalence; crude death rate for asthma; annual pollen score; annual air quality; public smoking laws; number of board-certified asthma specialists; school inhaler access laws; rescue medication use; controller medication use; uninsured rate; poverty rate. *Asthma and Allergy Foundation of America, "2011 Asthma Capitals"*

- Miami was identified as a "2011 Fall Allergy Capital." The area ranked #95 out of 100. Three groups of factors were used to identify the most severe cities for people with allergies during the fall season: annual pollen levels; medicine utilization; access to board-certified allergists. *Asthma and Allergy Foundation of America, "2011 Fall Allergy Capitals"*

- Miami was identified as a "2012 Spring Allergy Capital." The area ranked #71 out of 100. Three groups of factors were used to identify the most severe cities for people with allergies during the spring season: annual pollen levels; medicine utilization; access to board-certified allergists. *Asthma and Allergy Foundation of America, "2012 Spring Allergy Capitals"*

- *Men's Health* examined 100 major U.S. cities and selected the best and worst cities for men. Miami ranked #56. Criteria: 35 statistical parameters of long life in the categories of health, quality of life, and fitness. *Men's Health, "The 10 Best and Worst Cities for Men 2012," January/February 2012*

- Miami was selected as one of America's noisiest cities by *Men's Health*. The city ranked #5 of 10. Criteria: laws limiting excessive noise; traffic congestion levels; airports' overnight flight curfews; percentage of people who report sleeping seven hours or less. *Men's Health, "Ranking America's Cities: America's Noisiest Cities," May 2009*

- The Miami metropolitan area was selected as one of the best metros for hospital care in America by *HealthGrades.com*. The rankings are based on a comprehensive study of patient death and complication rates in the nation's nearly 5,000 hospitals. Hospitals performing in the top 5% nationwide across 26 different medical procedures and diagnoses were identified. *HealthGrades.com* then ranked cities by the highest percentage of these Distinguished Hospitals for Clinical Excellence™. The Miami metro area ranked #16. *HealthGrades.com, "America's Top 50 Cities for Hospital Care," January 21, 2012*

- The American Academy of Dermatology ranked 26 U.S. metropolitan regions in terms of their residents knowledge, attitude and behaviors towards tanning, sun protection and skin cancer detection. The Miami metro area ranked #13. The results of the study are based on an online survey of over 7,000 adults nationwide. *American Academy of Dermatology, "Suntelligence: How Sun Smart is Your City," May 3, 2010*

- The Miami metro area appeared in the 2011 Gallup-Healthways Well-Being Index. The index, based on interviews with more than 350,000 Americans, measured jobs, finances, physical health, emotional state of mind and communities. The metro area ranked #146 out of 190. Criteria: life evaluation; emotional health; work environment; physical health; healthy behaviors; basic access (basic needs optimal for a healthy life, such as access to food and medicine, having health insurance and feeling safe while walking at night). *Gallup-Healthways, "State of Well-Being 2011"*

- The Miami metro area was identified as one of "America's Most Stressful Cities" by *Sperling's BestPlaces*. The metro area ranked #3 out of 50. Criteria: unemployment rate; suicide rate; commute time; mental health; poor rest; alcohol use; violent crime rate; property crime rate; cloudy days annually. *Sperling's BestPlaces, www.BestPlaces.net, "Stressful Cities 2012*

- The Miami metro area was identified as one of "America's Most Stressful Cities" by *Forbes*. The metro area ranked #13 out of 40. Criteria: housing affordability; unemployment rate; cost of living; air quality; traffic congestion; sunny days; population density. *Forbes.com, "America's Most Stressful Cities," September 23, 2011*

- *Men's Health* ranked 100 U.S. cities in terms of their activity levels. Miami was ranked #12 (#1 = most active city). Criteria: where and how often residents exercise; percentage of households that watch more than 15 hours of cable television a week and buy more than 11 video games a year; death rate from deep-vein thrombosis, a condition linked to sitting for extended periods of time. *Men's Health, "Where Sit Happens: The Most and Least Active Cities in America," June 20, 2011*

- 50 of the largest metro areas in the U.S. were analyzed in terms of their health and fitness by the American College of Sports Medicine in their "American Fitness Index." The Miami metro area ranked #39 (#1 = healthiest). Criteria: preventative health behaviors; levels of chronic disease; health care access; community resources and policies that support physical activity. *American College of Sports Medicine, "Health and Community Fitness Status of the 50 Largest Metropolitan Areas," August 1, 2011*

- Miami was selected as one of the "20 Most Livable U.S. Cities for Wheelchair Users" by the Christopher & Dana Reeve Foundation. The city ranked #11. Criteria: Medicaid eligibility and spending; access to physicians and rehabilitation facilities; access to fitness facilities and recreation; access to paratransit; percentage of people living with disabilities who are employed; clean air; climate. *Christopher & Dana Reeve Foundation, "20 Most Livable U.S. Cities for Wheelchair Users," July 26, 2010*

Real Estate Rankings

- Miami was identified as one of the priciest cities to rent in the U.S. The area ranked #4 out of 10. Criteria: rent-to-income ratio. *CNBC, "Priciest Cities to Rent," March 14, 2012*

- Miami was identified as one of the "Top Turnaround Housing Markets for 2012." The area ranked #1 out of 10. Criteria: year-over-year median home price appreciation; year-over-year median inventory age; year-over-year inventory reduction. *AOL Real Estate, "Top Turnaround Housing Markets for 2012," February 4, 2012*

- *Fortune* ranked the 100 largest metro areas in the U.S. in terms of projected median home price change in 2010. The Miami metro area ranked #100. *Fortune, "The 2010 Housing Outlook," December 9, 2009*

- Miami was selected as one of the 10 best U.S. cities for real estate investment. The city ranked #8. *Association of Foreign Investors in Real Estate, "AFIRE News," January/February, 2011*

- The Miami metro area was identified as one of "The 15 Worst Housing Markets for the Next Five Years." Criteria: cities with home prices that are projected to appreciate at an annual rate of less than 1.5% rate between the second quarter 2011 and the second quarter 2016. *The Business Insider, "The 15 Worst Housing Markets for the Next Five Years," July 1, 2011*

- The Miami metro area was identified as one of the 10 best condo markets in the U.S. in 2011. The area ranked #3 out of 54 markets with a price appreciation of 6.3%. Criteria: year-over-year change of median sales price of existing apartment condo-coop homes between the 4th quarter of 2010 and the 4th quarter of 2011. *National Association of Realtors®, Median Sales Price of Existing Apartment Condo-Coop Homes for Metropolitan Areas, 4th Quarter 2011*

- Miami appeared on *ApartmentRatings.com* "Top Cities for Renters" list in 2009." The area ranked #76. Overall satisfaction ratings were ranked using thousands of user submitted scores for hundreds of apartment complexes located in the 100 most populated U.S. municipalities. *ApartmentRatings.com, "2009 Renter Satisfaction Rankings"*

- Miami appeared on *ApartmentRatings.com* "Top College Towns & Cities" for renters list in 2011." The area ranked #59 out of 87. Overall satisfaction ratings were ranked using thousands of user submitted scores for hundreds of apartment complexes located in cities and towns that are home to the 100 largest four-year institutions in the U.S. *ApartmentRatings.com, "2011 College Town Renter Satisfaction Rankings"*

- The Miami metro area was identified as one of "America's 25 Weakest Housing Markets" by *Forbes*. The metro area ranked #2. Criteria: metro areas with populations over 500,000 were ranked based on projected home values through 2011. *Forbes.com, "America's 25 Weakest Housing Markets," January 7, 2009*

- The Miami metro area appeared in a *Wall Street Journal* article ranking cities by "housing stress." The metro area was ranked #1 (#1 = most stress). Criteria: fraction of mortgage-holding homeowners with a monthly housing payment in excess of 30 percent of income; percentage of people without health insurance; unemployment rate. *The Wall Street Journal, "Which Cities Face Biggest Housing Risk," October 5, 2010*

- The Center for Housing Policy ranked 210 U.S. metropolitan areas by the fair market rent for a two-bedroom unit. The Miami metro area was ranked #26. (#1 = most expensive) with a rent of $1,206. Criteria: Fair Market Rent (FMR) in effect during the fourth quarter of 2009 based on HUD's fiscal year 2010 FMRs. *The Center for Housing Policy, "Paycheck to Paycheck: Most to Least Expensive Rental Markets in 2009"*

- The Miami metro area was identified as one of the top 20 cities in terms of decreasing home equity. The metro area was ranked #19. Criteria: percentage of home equity relative to the home's current value. *Forbes.com, "Where Americans are Losing Home Equity Most," May 1, 2010*

- The Miami metro area was identified as one of the best U.S. markets to invest in rental property" by HomeVestors and Local Market Monitor. The area ranked #33 out of 100. Criteria: risk-return premium relative to national average. *HomeVestors and Local Market Monitor, "Best 100 U.S. Markets to Invest in Rental Property," March 9, 2012*

Safety Rankings

- Symantec, the makers of Norton, in partnership with Sperling's BestPlaces, ranked the 50 largest cities in the U.S. in terms of their vulnerability to cybercrime. The city ranked #23. Criteria: number of cyberattacks and potential infections; level of Internet access; expenditures on smartphones and computer hardware/software; wireless hotspots; broadband connectivity; Internet usage; online purchases. *Symantec, "Riskiest Online Cities of 2012" February 15, 2012*

- Allstate ranked the 193 largest cities in America in terms of driver safety. Miami ranked #178. In addition, drivers were 43.1% more likely to have had an accident compared to the national average. Allstate researchers analyzed internal property damage reported claims over a two-year period (from January 2008 to December 2009) to protect findings from external influences such as weather or road construction. A weighted average of the two-year numbers determined the annual percentages. The report defines an auto crash as any collision resulting in a property damage claim. *Allstate, "2011 Allstate America's Best Drivers Report™"*

- Miami was identified as one of America's "11 Most Dangerous Cities" by *U.S. News & World Report*. The city ranked #7. Criteria: crime risk was calculated using the most recent seven years (2003-2009) of FBI crime reporting data. The data includes both property crimes and violent crimes. *U.S. News & World Report, "The 11 Most Dangerous Cities," February 16, 2011*

- Sperling's BestPlaces analyzed the tracks of tropical storms for the past 100 years and ranked which areas are most likely to be hit by a major hurricane. The Miami metro area ranked #1 out of 10. *Sperling's BestPlaces, www.bestplaces.net, February 2, 2006*

- The National Insurance Crime Bureau ranked 366 metro areas in the U.S. in terms of per capita rates of vehicle theft. The Miami metro area ranked #44 (#1 = highest rate). Criteria: number of vehicle theft offenses per 100,000 inhabitants in 2010. *National Insurance Crime Bureau, "Hot Spots," June 21, 2011*

- The Miami metro area was identified as one of the most dangerous metro areas for pedestrians by Transportation for America. The metro area ranked #4 out of 52 metro areas with over 1 million residents. Criteria: area's population divided by the number of pedestrian fatalities in that area. *Transportation for America, "Dangerous by Design 2011"*

Seniors/Retirement Rankings

- Bankers Life and Casualty Company, in partnership with Sperling's BestPlaces, ranked the nation's 50 largest metro areas in terms of the "Best U.S. Cities for Seniors." The Miami metro area ranked #35. Criteria: healthcare; transportation; housing; environment; economy; health and longevity; social and spiritual life; crime. *Bankers Life and Casualty Company, Center for a Secure Retirement, "Best U.S. Cities for Seniors 2011," September 2011*

- The Miami metro area was selected as one of the "10 Best Places for Single Seniors to Retire" by *U.S. News & World Report*. Criteria: metro areas with the most single seniors age 55 and over. *U.S. News & World Report, "10 Best Places for Single Seniors to Retire," November 1, 2010*

- Miami was identified as one of the "100 Most Popular Retirement Towns" by *Topretirements.com* The list reflects the 100 cities (out of 815+ total cities reviewed) that visitors to the website are most interested in for retirement. *Topretirements.com, "100 Most Popular Retirement Towns," February 21, 2012*

- The Miami metro area was selected as one of "The 10 Most Affordable Cities for Long-Term Care" by *U.S. News & World Report*. Criteria: costs at nursing homes, assisted living facilities, and adult day health care facilities; cost for licensed home health aides. *U.S. News & World Report, "The 10 Most Affordable Cities for Long-Term Care," May 17, 2010*

Sports/Recreation Rankings

- Miami appeared on the *Sporting News* list of the "Best Sports Cities" for 2011. The area ranked #9 out of 271 cities in the U.S. *Sporting News* takes a 12-month snapshot of each city's sports, putting a heavy premium on regular-season won-lost records (from the most recently completed season). Other criteria include: playoff berths, bowl appearances and tournament bids; championships; applicable power ratings; quality of competition; overall fan fervor (measured in part by attendance); abundance of teams (rewarding quality over quantity); stadium and arena quality; ticket availability and prices; franchise ownership; and marquee appeal of athletes. *Sporting News, "Best Sports Cities 2011," October 4, 2011*

- Miami was chosen as one of America's best cities for bicycling. The city ranked #44 out of 50. Criteria: number of segregated bike lanes, municipal bike racks, and bike boulevards; vibrant and diverse bike culture; smart, savvy bike shops; interviews with national and local advocates, bike shops and other experts. The editors only considered cities with populations of 100,000 or more. *Bicycling, "America's Best Bike Cities," April 2010*

Technology Rankings

- The Miami metro area was selected as one of "America's Most Wired Cities" by *Forbes*. The metro area was ranked #17 out of 20. Criteria: percentage of Internet users with high-speed access; number of companies providing high-speed Internet; number of public wireless hot spots. *Forbes, "America's Most Wired Cities," March 2, 2010*

Transportation Rankings

- The Miami metro area appeared on *Forbes* list of the best and worst cities for commuters. The metro area ranked #55 out of 60 (#1 is best). Criteria: travel time; road congestion; travel delays. *Forbes.com, "Best and Worst Cities for Commuters," February 16, 2010*

Women/Minorities Rankings

- *Women's Health* examined U.S. cities and identified the 100 best cities for women. Miami was ranked #56. Criteria: 30 categories were examined from obesity and breast cancer rates to commuting times and hours spent working out. *Women's Health, "Best Cities for Women 2012"*

- Miami was ranked #39 out of 100 metro areas in *SELF Magazine's* ranking of America's healthiest places for women." A panel of experts came up with more than 50 criteria including death and disease rates, environmental indicators, community resources, and lifestyle habits. *SELF Magazine, "Secrets of America's Healthiest Women," December 2008*

- The Miami metro area appeared on *Forbes'* list of the "Best Cities for Minority Entrepreneurs." The area ranked #39 out of 10. Criteria: 52 metropolitan statistical areas were examined. For each ethnicity (African Americans, Asians and Hispanics), the editors measured housing affordability, population growth, income growth, and entrepreneurship (per capita self-employment). *Forbes, "Best Cities for Minority Entrepreneurs," March 23, 2011*

- Miami was selected as one of the "Top 10 Cities for Hispanics." Criteria: the prospect of a good job; a safe place to raise a family; a manageable cost of living; the ability to buy and keep a home; a culture of inclusion where Hispanics are highly represented; resources to help start a business; the presence of Hispanic or Spanish-language media; representation of Hispanic needs on local government; a thriving arts and culture community; air quality; energy costs; city's state of health and rates of obesity. *Hispanic Magazine, August 2008*

Miscellaneous Rankings

- *Men's Health* ranked 100 U.S. cities by their level of sadness. Miami was ranked #93 (#1 = saddest city). Criteria: suicide rates; unemployment rates; percentage of households that use antidepressants; percent of population who report feeling blue all or most of the time. *Men's Health, "Frown Towns," November 28, 2011*

- Scarborough Research, a leading market research firm, identified the top local markets for lottery ticket purchasers. The Miami DMA (Designated Market Area) ranked in the top 13 with 48% of adults 18+ reporting that they purchased lottery tickets in the past 30 days. *Scarborough Research, January 30, 2012*

- Energizer Holdings, the makers of Edge® shave gel, in partnership with Sperling's BestPlaces, ranked 50 major metro areas in terms of everyday irritations. The Miami metro area ranked #14. Criteria: humidity levels; weather conditions; incidence of traffic delays and congestion; average commute times; frequency of flight delays and cancellations; rates of sleeplessness; underemployment; pollens and allergens; pests; comedy clubs per capita. *Energizer Holdings, "Most Irritation Prone Cities," July 23, 2010*

- Mars Chocolate North America, the makers of COMBOS®, in partnership with Sperling's BestPlaces, ranked 50 major metro areas in terms of their "manliness." The Miami metro area ranked #44. Criteria: number of professional sports teams; number of nearby NASCAR tracks and racing events; manly lifestyle; concentration of manly retail stores; manly occupations per capita; salty snack sales; "Board of Manliness" rankings. *Mars Chocolate North America, "America's Manliest Cities 2011," September 1, 2011*

- Miami was selected as one of the "Best Hair Cities" by *NaturallyCurly.com*. The city was ranked #7. Criteria: humidity levels; pollution; rainfall; average wind speeds; water hardness; beauty salons per capita. *NaturallyCurly.com, "Best/Worst Hair Cities," April 29, 2009*

- The Miami metro area was selected as one of "America's Greediest Cities" by *Forbes*. The area was ranked #10 out of 10. Criteria: number of Forbes 400 (*Forbes* annual list of the richest Americans) members per capita. *Forbes, "America's Greediest Cities," December 7, 2007*

- The Miami metro area appeared in *AutoMD.com's* ranking of the "Best and Worst Cities for Auto Repair." The metro area ranked #14 (#1 is best). The 50 most-populated metro areas in the U.S. were ranked on three critical factors: repair affordability; price disparity range; shop integrity factor. *AutoMD.com, "Advocacy for Repair Shop Fairness Report," February 24, 2010*

- Miami was identified as one of "America's Vainest Cities" by *Forbes.com*. The city ranked #3. Criteria: highest number of cosmetic surgeons per 100,000 people in America's 50 largest cities. *Forbes.com, "America's Vainest Cities," November 29, 2007*

- The Miami metro area was selected as one of "America's Most Miserable Cities" by *Forbes.com*. The metro area ranked #1 out of 10. Criteria: violent crime; unemployment; foreclosures; income and property taxes; home prices; political corruption; commute times; climate; pro sports team records. *Forbes.com, "America's Most Miserable Cities, 2012" February 2, 2012*

- Miami appeared on Procter & Gamble's list of the "Top-20 All-Time Sweatiest Cities." The city was ranked #7. The rankings are based on computer simulations of the amount of sweat a person of average height and weight would produce walking around for an hour in the average temperatures during the summer months, based on historical weather data during June, July and August from 2001-2008 for each city. *Procter & Gamble, Old Spice Press Release, "Top-20 All-Time Sweatiest Cities," July 1, 2009*

Business Environment

CITY FINANCES

City Government Finances

Component	2009 ($000)	2009 ($ per capita)
Total Revenues	500,709	1,222
Total Expenditures	872,548	2,130
Debt Outstanding	639,899	1,562
Cash and Securities[1]	2,497,305	6,095

Note: (1) Cash and security holdings of a government at the close of its fiscal year, including those of its dependent agencies, utilities, and liquor stores.
Source: U.S Census Bureau, State & Local Government Finances 2009

City Government Revenue by Source

Source	2009 ($000)	2009 ($ per capita)
General Revenue		
From Federal Government	50,108	122
From State Government	100,204	245
From Local Governments	58,250	142
Taxes		
Property	295,559	721
Sales and Gross Receipts	91,873	224
Personal Income	0	0
Corporate Income	0	0
Motor Vehicle License	0	0
Other Taxes	56,599	138
Current Charges	105,929	259
Liquor Store	0	0
Utility	0	0
Employee Retirement	-298,700	-729

Source: U.S Census Bureau, State & Local Government Finances 2009

City Government Expenditures by Function

Function	2009 ($000)	2009 ($ per capita)	2009 (%)
General Direct Expenditures			
Air Transportation	0	0	0.0
Corrections	0	0	0.0
Education	0	0	0.0
Employment Security Administration	0	0	0.0
Financial Administration	43,653	107	5.0
Fire Protection	141,598	346	16.2
General Public Buildings	0	0	0.0
Governmental Administration, Other	14,581	36	1.7
Health	0	0	0.0
Highways	42,317	103	4.8
Hospitals	0	0	0.0
Housing and Community Development	57,000	139	6.5
Interest on General Debt	27,207	66	3.1
Judicial and Legal	6,074	15	0.7
Libraries	0	0	0.0
Parking	20,800	51	2.4
Parks and Recreation	80,948	198	9.3
Police Protection	139,757	341	16.0
Public Welfare	0	0	0.0
Sewerage	12,791	31	1.5
Solid Waste Management	13,443	33	1.5
Veterans' Services	0	0	0.0
Liquor Store	0	0	0.0
Utility	0	0	0.0
Employee Retirement	148,173	362	17.0

Source: U.S Census Bureau, State & Local Government Finances 2009

Municipal Bond Ratings

Area	Moody's	S&P	Fitch
City	A2	A-	A

Rating Systems (shown in declining order of credit quality): Moody's– Aaa, Aa, A, Baa, Ba, B, Caa, Ca, C (numerical modifiers 1, 2, and 3 are added to letter-rating); S&P– AAA, AA, A, BBB, BB, B, CCC, CC, C; Fitch– AAA, AA, A, BBB, BB, B, CCC, CC, C. Ratings may be modified by the addition of a plus or minus sign to show relative standing within the major rating categories.
Notes: n/a Not Available; w/d Withdrawn (1) Not Reviewed; (2) Issuer Rating/No General Obligation; (3) Standard and Poor's Issue Credit Rating (ICR) is a current opinion of an obliger with respect to a specific financial obligation, a specific class of financial obligations, or a specific financial program.
Source: U.S. Census Bureau, 2012 Statistical Abstract, Bond Ratings for City Governments by Largest Cities: 2010

DEMOGRAPHICS

Population Growth

Area	1990 Census	2000 Census	2010 Census	Population Growth (%) 1990-2000	Population Growth (%) 2000-2010
City	358,843	362,470	399,457	1.0	10.2
MSA[1]	4,056,100	5,007,564	5,564,635	23.5	11.1
U.S.	248,709,873	281,421,906	308,745,538	13.2	9.7

Note: (1) Figures cover the Miami-Fort Lauderdale-Pompano Beach, FL Metropolitan Statistical Area—see Appendix B for areas included
Source: U.S. Census Bureau, 2010 Census

Household Size

Area	Persons in Household (%) One	Two	Three	Four	Five	Six	Seven or More	Average Household Size
City	33.3	28.8	16.2	11.0	5.6	2.7	2.4	2.47
MSA[1]	27.0	31.0	16.6	13.7	6.7	2.8	2.2	2.62
U.S.	26.7	32.8	16.1	13.4	6.5	2.6	1.9	2.58

Note: (1) Figures cover the Miami-Fort Lauderdale-Pompano Beach, FL Metropolitan Statistical Area—see Appendix B for areas included
Source: U.S. Census Bureau, 2010 Census

Race

Area	White Alone[2] (%)	Black Alone[2] (%)	Asian Alone[2] (%)	AIAN[3] Alone[2] (%)	NHOPI[4] Alone[2] (%)	Other Race Alone[2] (%)	Two or More Races (%)
City	72.6	19.2	1.0	0.3	0.0	4.2	2.7
MSA[1]	70.3	21.0	2.3	0.3	0.0	3.5	2.5
U.S.	72.4	12.6	4.8	0.9	0.2	6.2	2.9

Note: (1) Figures cover the Miami-Fort Lauderdale-Pompano Beach, FL Metropolitan Statistical Area—see Appendix B for areas included; (2) Alone is defined as not being in combination with one or more other races; (3) American Indian and Alaska Native; (4) Native Hawaiian and Other Pacific Islander
Source: U.S. Census Bureau, 2010 Census

Hispanic or Latino Origin

Area	Hispanic or Latino (%)	Mexican (%)	Puerto Rican (%)	Cuban (%)	Other Hispanic or Latino (%)
City	70.0	1.5	3.2	34.4	30.9
MSA[1]	41.6	2.4	3.7	17.7	17.8
U.S.	16.3	10.3	1.5	0.6	4.0

Note: Persons of Hispanic or Latino origin can be of any race; (1) Figures cover the Miami-Fort Lauderdale-Pompano Beach, FL Metropolitan Statistical Area—see Appendix B for areas included
Source: U.S. Census Bureau, 2010 Census

Segregation

Type	Segregation Indices[1]				Percent Change		
	1990	2000	2010	2010 Rank[2]	1990-2000	1990-2010	2000-2010
Black/White	71.4	69.2	64.8	23	-2.3	-6.6	-4.3
Asian/White	26.8	33.3	34.2	80	6.4	7.3	0.9
Hispanic/White	32.5	59.0	57.4	8	26.5	24.8	-1.6

Note: Figures are based on an analysis of 1990, 2000, and 2010 Census Decennial Census tract data by William H. Frey, Brookings Institution and the University of Michigan Social Science Data Analysis Network. In this analysis all racial groups (whites, blacks, and asians) are non-Hispanic members of those races. Hispanics are shown as a separate category; All figures cover the Metropolitan Statistical Area (see Appendix B for areas included); (1) Segregation Indices are Dissimilarity Indices that measure the degree to which the minority group is distributed differently than whites across census tracts. They range from 0 (complete integration) to 100 (complete segregation) where the value indicates the percentage of the minority group that needs to move to be distributed exactly like whites; (2) Ranges from 1 (most segregated) to 102 (least segregated); n/a not available.
Source: www.CensusScope.org

Ancestry

Area	German	Irish	English	American	Italian	Polish	French[2]	Scottish	Dutch
City	1.7	1.5	1.0	2.1	1.7	0.6	0.9	0.2	0.2
MSA[1]	5.8	5.5	3.8	4.2	5.6	2.5	1.6	0.8	0.6
U.S.	16.1	11.6	8.8	6.1	5.7	3.2	3.0	1.9	1.6

Note: Figures are the percentage of the total population reporting a particular ancestry. The nine most commonly reported ancestries in the U.S. are shown. Figures include multiple ancestries (e.g. if a person reported being Irish and Italian, they were included in both columns); (1) Figures cover the Miami-Fort Lauderdale-Pompano Beach, FL Metropolitan Statistical Area—see Appendix B for areas included; (2) Excludes Basque
Source: U.S. Census Bureau, 2008-2010 American Community Survey 3-Year Estimates

Foreign-Born Population

Area	Percent of Population Born in								
	Any Foreign Country	Mexico	Asia	Europe	Carribean	South America	Central America[2]	Africa	Canada
City	58.2	1.0	0.8	1.3	33.7	7.5	13.5	0.2	0.1
MSA[1]	38.1	1.2	1.9	2.2	19.6	7.7	4.5	0.3	0.6
U.S.	12.8	3.8	3.6	1.6	1.2	0.9	1.0	0.5	0.3

Note: (1) Figures cover the Miami-Fort Lauderdale-Pompano Beach, FL Metropolitan Statistical Area—see Appendix B for areas included; (2) Excludes Mexico.
Source: U.S. Census Bureau, 2008-2010 American Community Survey 3-Year Estimates

Marital Status

Area	Never Married	Now Married[2]	Separated	Widowed	Divorced
City	38.7	36.1	4.3	7.3	13.6
MSA[1]	32.5	44.9	2.9	7.1	12.6
U.S.	31.6	49.6	2.2	6.1	10.7

Note: Figures are percentages and cover the population 15 years of age and older; (1) Figures cover the Miami-Fort Lauderdale-Pompano Beach, FL Metropolitan Statistical Area—see Appendix B for areas included; (2) Excludes separated
Source: U.S. Census Bureau, 2008-2010 American Community Survey 3-Year Estimates

Age

Area	Percent of Population							Median Age
	Under Age 5	Age 5 to 17	Age 18 to 34	Age 35 to 49	Age 50 to 64	Age 65 to 79	80 Years and Over	
City	6.0	12.4	25.9	22.4	17.3	11.2	4.8	38.8
MSA[1]	5.8	15.8	21.8	22.1	18.6	10.9	5.0	39.8
U.S.	6.5	17.5	23.2	20.7	19.0	9.4	3.6	37.2

Note: (1) Figures cover the Miami-Fort Lauderdale-Pompano Beach, FL Metropolitan Statistical Area—see Appendix B for areas included
Source: U.S. Census Bureau, 2010 Census

Male/Female Ratio

Area	Males	Females	Males per 100 Females
City	198,927	200,530	99.2
MSA[1]	2,693,823	2,870,812	93.8
U.S.	151,781,326	156,964,212	96.7

Note: (1) Figures cover the Miami-Fort Lauderdale-Pompano Beach, FL
Metropolitan Statistical Area—see Appendix B for areas included
Source: U.S. Census Bureau, 2010 Census

Religious Groups

Area	Catholic	Baptist	Non-Den.	Methodist[2]	Lutheran	LDS[3]	Pente-costal	Presby-terian[4]	Muslim[5]	Judaism
MSA[1]	18.6	5.4	4.2	1.3	0.5	0.5	1.8	0.7	1.6	0.9
U.S.	19.1	9.3	4.0	4.0	2.3	2.0	1.9	1.6	0.8	0.7

Note: Figures are the number of adherents as a percentage of the total population; (1) Figures cover the
Miami-Fort Lauderdale-Pompano Beach, FL Metropolitan Statistical Area—see Appendix B for areas included;
(2) Methodist/Pietist; (3) Latter Day Saints; (4) Reformed; (5) Figures are estimates
Source: Association of Statisticians of American Religious Bodies, 2010 U.S. Religion Census: Religious
Congregations & Membership Study

ECONOMY

Gross Metropolitan Product

Area	2007	2008	2009	2010	2010 Rank[2]
MSA[1]	264.3	260.5	253.8	258.8	11

Note: Figures are in billions of dollars; (1) Figures cover the Miami-Fort Lauderdale-Pompano Beach, FL
Metropolitan Statistical Area—see Appendix B for areas included; (2) Rank ranges from 1 to 363
Source: The United States Conference of Mayors, "U.S. Metro Economies: GMP and Employment Forecasts,"
June 2011

Economic Growth

Area	2007-2009 (%)	2010 (%)	2011 (%)	Rank[2]
MSA[1]	-3.6	1.3	2.0	297
U.S.	-1.3	2.9	2.5	–

Note: Figures are real Gross Metropolitan Product growth rates and represent annual average percent change;
(1) Figures cover the Miami-Fort Lauderdale-Pompano Beach, FL Metropolitan Statistical Area—see Appendix
B for areas included; (2) Rank ranges from 1 to 363
Source: The United States Conference of Mayors, "U.S. Metro Economies: GMP and Employment Forecasts,"
June 2011

Metropolitan Area Exports

Area	2005	2006	2007	2008	2009	2010	2010 Rank[2]
MSA[1]	20,382.9	23,491.3	26,197.4	33,411.5	31,175.0	35,866.9	5

Note: Figures are in millions of dollars; (1) Figures cover the Miami-Fort Lauderdale-Pompano Beach, FL
Metropolitan Statistical Area—see Appendix B for areas included; (2) Rank ranges from 1 to 369
Source: U.S. Department of Commerce, International Trade Administration, Office of Trade & Industry
Information, Manufacturing & Services, data extracted April 2, 2012

INCOME

Income

Area	Per Capita ($)	Median Household ($)	Average Household ($)
City	19,723	28,506	48,561
MSA[1]	26,283	47,086	68,986
U.S.	26,942	51,222	70,116

Note: (1) Figures cover the Miami-Fort Lauderdale-Pompano Beach, FL Metropolitan Statistical Area—see
Appendix B for areas included
Source: U.S. Census Bureau, 2008-2010 American Community Survey 3-Year Estimates

Household Income Distribution

Area	Percent of Households Earning							
	Under $15,000	$15,000 -24,999	$25,000 -34,999	$35,000 -49,999	$50,000 -74,999	$75,000 -99,000	$100,000 -149,999	$150,000 and up
City	28.6	16.7	12.0	13.4	12.6	6.0	5.5	5.2
MSA[1]	14.7	11.9	11.3	14.5	17.7	10.7	10.9	8.4
U.S.	13.0	11.0	10.6	14.2	18.5	12.1	12.2	8.4

Note: (1) Figures cover the Miami-Fort Lauderdale-Pompano Beach, FL Metropolitan Statistical Area—see Appendix B for areas included
Source: U.S. Census Bureau, 2008-2010 American Community Survey 3-Year Estimates

Poverty Rate

Area	All Ages	Under 18 Years Old	18 to 64 Years Old	65 Years and Over
City	28.6	38.9	24.5	33.3
MSA[1]	15.5	20.7	13.8	15.0
U.S.	14.4	20.1	13.1	9.4

Note: Figures are percentage of people whose income during the past 12 months was below the poverty level; (1) Figures cover the Miami-Fort Lauderdale-Pompano Beach, FL Metropolitan Statistical Area—see Appendix B for areas included
Source: U.S. Census Bureau, 2008-2010 American Community Survey 3-Year Estimates

Personal Bankruptcy Filing Rate

Area	2006	2007	2008	2009	2010	2011
Miami-Dade County	n/a	n/a	n/a	n/a	n/a	n/a
U.S.	2.00	2.73	3.53	4.61	4.97	4.37

Note: Numbers are per 1,000 population and include Chapter 7 and Chapter 13 filings; n/a not available
Source: Federal Deposit Insurance Corporation, Regional Economic Conditions, March 9, 2012

EMPLOYMENT

Labor Force and Employment

Area	Civilian Labor Force			Workers Employed		
	Dec. 2010	Dec. 2011	% Chg.	Dec. 2010	Dec. 2011	% Chg.
City	200,338	200,590	0.1	172,181	178,782	3.8
MD[1]	1,253,036	1,279,120	2.1	1,098,081	1,148,960	4.6
U.S.	153,156,000	153,373,000	0.1	139,159,000	140,681,000	1.1

Note: Data is not seasonally adjusted and covers workers 16 years of age and older; (1) Metropolitan Division—see Appendix B for areas included
Source: Bureau of Labor Statistics, http://stats.bls.gov

Unemployment Rate

Area	2011											
	Jan.	Feb.	Mar.	Apr.	May	Jun.	Jul.	Aug.	Sep.	Oct.	Nov.	Dec.
City	13.0	12.7	13.2	14.2	14.6	14.8	13.3	13.4	12.2	11.3	10.0	10.9
MD[1]	11.6	11.4	11.7	12.2	12.3	12.4	11.5	11.4	10.8	10.7	9.5	10.2
U.S.	9.8	9.5	9.2	8.7	8.7	9.3	9.3	9.1	8.8	8.5	8.2	8.3

Note: Data is not seasonally adjusted and covers workers 16 years of age and older; All figures are percentages; (1) Metropolitan Division—see Appendix B for areas included
Source: Bureau of Labor Statistics, http://stats.bls.gov

Projected Unemployment Rate

Area	2010 (%)	2011 (%)	2012 (%)	2013 (%)
MSA[1]	12.1	11.3	10.6	9.7

Note: (1) Metropolitan Statistical Area—see Appendix B for areas included
Source: The United States Conference of Mayors, "U.S. Metro Economies: GMP and Employment Forecasts," June 2011

Employment by Occupation

Occupation Classification	City (%)	MSA[1] (%)	U.S. (%)
Management, Business, Science, and Arts	26.7	32.8	35.6
Natural Resources, Construction, and Maintenance	13.2	9.5	9.5
Production, Transportation, and Material Moving	11.3	8.9	12.1
Sales and Office	24.3	28.6	25.2
Service	24.5	20.2	17.6

Note: Figures cover employed civilians 16 years of age and older; (1) Figures cover the Miami-Fort Lauderdale-Pompano Beach, FL Metropolitan Statistical Area—see Appendix B for areas included
Source: U.S. Census Bureau, 2008-2010 American Community Survey 3-Year Estimates

Employment by Industry

Sector	MD[1] Number of Employees	MD[1] Percent of Total	U.S. Percent of Total
Construction	29,900	2.9	4.1
Education and Health Services	171,500	16.7	15.2
Financial Activities	62,400	6.1	5.8
Government	147,900	14.4	16.8
Information	17,900	1.7	2.0
Leisure and Hospitality	113,200	11.0	9.9
Manufacturing	35,600	3.5	8.9
Mining and Logging	400	<0.1	0.6
Other Services	40,500	3.9	4.0
Professional and Business Services	137,800	13.4	13.3
Retail Trade	136,500	13.3	11.5
Transportation and Utilities	62,100	6.0	3.8
Wholesale Trade	71,700	7.0	4.2

Note: Figures cover non-farm employment as of December 2011 and are not seasonally adjusted; (1) Metropolitan Division—see Appendix B for areas included
Source: Bureau of Labor Statistics, http://stats.bls.gov

Occupations with Greatest Projected Employment Growth: 2008 – 2018

Occupation[1]	2008 Employment	2018 Projected Employment	Numeric Employment Change	Percent Employment Change
Registered Nurses	151,100	187,380	36,280	24.0
Combined Food Preparation and Serving Workers, Including Fast Food	162,570	186,400	23,830	14.7
Customer Service Representatives	169,080	190,780	21,700	12.8
Nursing Aides, Orderlies, and Attendants	88,630	106,860	18,230	20.6
Home Health Aides	30,480	47,860	17,380	57.0
Postsecondary Teachers	70,790	85,380	14,590	20.6
Retail Salespersons	274,490	288,660	14,170	5.2
Elementary School Teachers, Except Special Education	74,130	86,390	12,260	16.5
Stock Clerks and Order Fillers	167,450	179,420	11,970	7.1
Accountants and Auditors	86,390	97,670	11,280	13.1

Note: Projections cover Florida; (1) Sorted by numeric employment change
Source: www.projectionscentral.com, State Occupational Projections, 2008–2018 Long-Term Projections

Fastest Growing Occupations: 2008 – 2018

Occupation[1]	2008 Employment	2018 Projected Employment	Numeric Employment Change	Percent Employment Change
Biomedical Engineers	520	840	320	61.5
Home Health Aides	30,480	47,860	17,380	57.0
Medical Scientists, Except Epidemiologists	2,640	3,870	1,230	46.6
Physician Assistants	3,900	5,490	1,590	40.8
Personal and Home Care Aides	13,890	19,430	5,540	39.9
Network Systems and Data Communications Analysts	21,550	30,110	8,560	39.7
Radiation Therapists	1,270	1,730	460	36.2
Dental Hygienists	9,030	11,890	2,860	31.7
Physical Therapist Assistants	3,550	4,660	1,110	31.3
Financial Examiners	610	800	190	31.1

Note: Projections cover Florida; (1) Sorted by percent employment change and excludes occupations with numeric employment change less than 100
Source: www.projectionscentral.com, State Occupational Projections, 2008–2018 Long-Term Projections

Average Wages

Occupation	$/Hr.	Occupation	$/Hr.
Accountants and Auditors	35.53	Maids and Housekeeping Cleaners	9.24
Automotive Mechanics	17.87	Maintenance and Repair Workers	15.63
Bookkeepers	16.28	Marketing Managers	61.78
Carpenters	17.28	Nuclear Medicine Technologists	31.68
Cashiers	9.41	Nurses, Licensed Practical	20.47
Clerks, General Office	12.50	Nurses, Registered	33.02
Clerks, Receptionists/Information	11.89	Nursing Aides/Orderlies/Attendants	10.61
Clerks, Shipping/Receiving	13.49	Packers and Packagers, Hand	9.42
Computer Programmers	36.56	Physical Therapists	36.47
Computer Support Specialists	22.06	Postal Service Mail Carriers	25.80
Computer Systems Analysts	40.96	Real Estate Brokers	45.70
Cooks, Restaurant	11.90	Retail Salespersons	11.31
Dentists	55.21	Sales Reps., Exc. Tech./Scientific	27.96
Electrical Engineers	42.83	Sales Reps., Tech./Scientific	40.36
Electricians	20.72	Secretaries, Exc. Legal/Med./Exec.	14.86
Financial Managers	65.40	Security Guards	11.47
First-Line Supervisors/Managers, Sales	20.34	Surgeons	116.44
Food Preparation Workers	9.60	Teacher Assistants	11.10
General and Operations Managers	52.48	Teachers, Elementary School	21.80
Hairdressers/Cosmetologists	11.92	Teachers, Secondary School	24.70
Internists	94.51	Telemarketers	11.43
Janitors and Cleaners	10.12	Truck Drivers, Heavy/Tractor-Trailer	19.33
Landscaping/Groundskeeping Workers	10.62	Truck Drivers, Light/Delivery Svcs.	14.37
Lawyers	69.52	Waiters and Waitresses	9.59

Note: Wage data covers the Miami-Miami Beach-Kendall, FL Metropolitan Division—see Appendix B for areas included. Hourly wages for elementary/secondary school teachers and teacher assistants were calculated by the editors from annual wage data assuming a 40 hour work week; n/a not available.
Source: Bureau of Labor Statistics, Metro Area Occupational Employment and Wage Estimates, May 2011

RESIDENTIAL REAL ESTATE

Building Permits

Area	Single-Family			Multi-Family			Total		
	2010	2011	Pct. Chg.	2010	2011	Pct. Chg.	2010	2011	Pct. Chg.
City	27	21	-22.2	685	266	-61.2	712	287	-59.7
MSA[1]	3,171	4,303	35.7	2,706	3,229	19.3	5,877	7,532	28.2
U.S.	447,311	418,498	-6.4	157,299	205,563	30.7	604,610	624,061	3.2

Note: (1) Metropolitan Statistical Area—see Appendix B for areas included; figures represent new, privately-owned housing units authorized (unadjusted data); All permit data are based on estimates with imputation.
Source: U.S. Census Bureau, Manufacturing, Mining, and Construction Statistics, Building Permits, 2010, 2011

Homeownership Rate

Area	2005 (%)	2006 (%)	2007 (%)	2008 (%)	2009 (%)	2010 (%)	2011 (%)
MSA[1]	69.2	67.4	66.6	66.0	67.1	63.8	64.2
U.S.	68.9	68.8	68.1	67.8	67.4	66.9	66.1

Note: (1) Metropolitan Statistical Area—see Appendix B for areas included
Source: U.S. Census Bureau, Housing Vacancies and Homeownership Annual Statistics: 2011

Housing Vacancy Rates

Area	Gross Vacancy Rate[2] (%)			Year-Round Vacancy Rate[3] (%)			Rental Vacancy Rate[4] (%)			Homeowner Vacancy Rate[5] (%)		
	2009	2010	2011	2009	2010	2011	2009	2010	2011	2009	2010	2011
MSA[1]	23.1	21.8	21.0	13.7	13.0	11.7	13.2	10.1	11.8	3.2	3.5	1.8
U.S.	14.5	14.3	14.2	11.3	11.3	11.1	10.6	10.2	9.5	2.6	2.6	2.5

Note: (1) Metropolitan Statistical Area—see Appendix B for areas included; (2) The percentage of the total housing inventory that is vacant; (3) The percentage of the housing inventory (excluding seasonal units) that is year-round vacant; (4) The percentage of rental inventory that is vacant for rent; (5) The percentage of homeowner inventory that is vacant for sale
Source: U.S. Census Bureau, Housing Vacancies and Homeownership Annual Statistics: 2011

TAXES

State Corporate Income Tax Rates

State	Tax Rate (%)	Income Brackets ($)	Num. of Brackets	Financial Institution Tax Rate (%)[a]	Federal Income Tax Ded.
Florida	5.5 (f)	Flat rate	1	5.5 (f)	No

Note: Tax rates as of January 1, 2012; (a) Rates listed are the corporate income tax rate applied to financial institutions or excise taxes based on income. Some states have other taxes based upon the value of deposits or shares; (f) An exemption of $5,000 is allowed. Florida's Alternative Minimum Tax rate is 3.3%.
Source: Federation of Tax Administrators, "State Corporate Income Tax Rates, 2012"

State Individual Income Tax Rates

State	Tax Rate (%)	Income Brackets ($)	Num. of Brackets	Personal Exempt. ($)[1] Single	Dependents	Fed. Inc. Tax Ded.
Florida – No State Income Tax						

Note: Tax rates as of January 1, 2012; Local- and county-level taxes are not included; n/a not applicable; (1) Married joint filers generally receive double the single exemption
Source: Federation of Tax Administrators, "State Individual Income Tax Rates, 2012"

Various State and Local Tax Rates

State	State and Local Sales and Use (%)	State Sales and Use (%)	Gasoline[1] (¢/gal.)	Cigarette[2] ($/pack)	Spirits[3] ($/gal.)	Wine[4] ($/gal.)	Beer[5] ($/gal.)
Florida	7.0	6.00	35.0	1.34	6.50	2.25	0.48

Note: All tax rates as of January 1, 2012 except beer, wine and spirits (September 1, 2011); (1) The American Petroleum Institute has developed a methodology for determining the average tax rate on a gallon of fuel. Rates may include any of the following: excise taxes, environmental fees, storage tank fees, other fees or taxes, general sales tax, and local taxes. In states where gasoline is subject to the general sales tax, or where the fuel tax is based on the average sale price, the average rate determined by API is sensitive to changes in the price of gasoline. States that fully or partially apply general sales taxes to gasoline: CA, CO, GA, IL, IN, MI, NY; (2) The federal excise tax of $1.0066 per pack and local taxes are not included; (3) Rates are those applicable to off-premise sales of 40% alcohol by volume (a.b.v.) distilled spirits in 750ml containers. Local excise taxes are excluded; (4) Rates are those applicable to off-premise sales of 11% a.b.v. non-carbonated wine in 750ml containers; (5) Rates are those applicable to off-premise sales of 4.7% a.b.v. beer in 12 ounce containers.
Source: Tax Foundation, 2012 Facts & Figures: How Does Your State Compare?

State-Local Tax Burdens

Area	Rate (%)	Rank[1]	Per Capita Taxes Paid to Home State ($)	Total State and Local Per Capita Taxes Paid ($)	Per Capita Income ($)
Florida	9.2	31	2,713	3,897	42,146
U.S. Average	9.8	-	3,057	4,160	42,539

Note: Figures cover 2009; (1) Rank ranges from 1 to 50 where 1 is highest tax burden
Source: Tax Foundation, State-Local Tax Burdens, All States, 2009

State Business Tax Climate Index Rankings

State	Overall Rank	Corporate Tax Index Rank	Individual Income Tax Index Rank	Sales Tax Index Rank	Unemployment Insurance Tax Index Rank	Property Tax Index Rank
Florida	5	12	1	19	5	24

Note: The index is a measure of how each state's tax laws affect economic performance. The lower the rank, the more favorable a state's tax system is for business. States without a given tax are given a ranking of 1.
Source: Tax Foundation, Major Components of the State Business Tax Climate Index, FY 2012

COMMERCIAL REAL ESTATE

Office Market

Market Area	Inventory (sq. ft.)	Vacant (sq. ft.)	Vac. Rate (%)	Under Constr. (sq. ft.)	Asking Rent ($/sf/yr) Class A	Class B
Miami-Dade County	46,734,453	8,815,997	18.9	322,276	37.50	26.89

Source: Grubb & Ellis, Office Markets Trends, 1st Quarter 2012

Industrial Market

Market Area	Inventory (sq. ft.)	Vacant (sq. ft.)	Vac. Rate (%)	Under Constr. (sq. ft.)	Asking Rent ($/sf/yr) WH/Dist	R&D/Flex
Miami	200,547,362	15,236,263	7.6	0	4.85	9.30

Source: Grubb & Ellis, Industrial Markets Trends, 4th Quarter 2011

COMMERCIAL UTILITIES

Typical Monthly Electric Bills

Area	Commercial Service ($/month) 1,500 kWh	40 kW demand 14,000 kWh	Industrial Service ($/month) 1,000 kW demand 200,000 kWh	50,000 kW demand 15,000,000 kWh
City	108	1,239	22,761	1,001,777
Average[1]	189	1,616	25,197	1,470,813

Note: Based on total rates in effect July 1, 2011; (1) average based on 184 utilities surveyed
Source: Edison Electric Institute, Typical Bills and Average Rates Report, Summer 2011

TRANSPORTATION

Means of Transportation to Work

Area	Car/Truck/Van Drove Alone	Car-pooled	Public Transportation Bus	Subway	Railroad	Bicycle	Walked	Other Means	Worked at Home
City	69.4	10.4	10.4	0.6	0.3	0.6	3.7	1.2	3.6
MSA[1]	78.3	10.0	3.1	0.2	0.2	0.5	1.8	1.4	4.4
U.S.	76.0	10.2	2.7	1.7	0.5	0.5	2.8	1.3	4.2

Note: Figures are percentages and cover workers 16 years of age and older; (1) Figures cover the Miami-Fort Lauderdale-Pompano Beach, FL Metropolitan Statistical Area—see Appendix B for areas included
Source: U.S. Census Bureau, 2008-2010 American Community Survey 3-Year Estimates

Travel Time to Work

Area	Less Than 10 Minutes	10 to 19 Minutes	20 to 29 Minutes	30 to 44 Minutes	45 to 59 Minutes	60 to 89 Minutes	90 Minutes or More
City	5.7	24.9	29.0	25.6	7.8	5.4	1.6
MSA[1]	8.1	25.6	22.9	26.9	8.8	5.9	1.9
U.S.	13.9	30.1	20.8	19.8	7.5	5.5	2.5

Note: Figures are percentages and include workers 16 years old and over; (1) Figures cover the Miami-Fort Lauderdale-Pompano Beach, FL Metropolitan Statistical Area—see Appendix B for areas included
Source: U.S. Census Bureau, 2008-2010 American Community Survey 3-Year Estimates

Travel Time Index

Area	1985	1990	1995	2000	2005	2010
Urban Area[1]	1.10	1.19	1.20	1.27	1.31	1.23
Average[2]	1.11	1.16	1.18	1.21	1.25	1.20

Note: Travel Time Index—the ratio of travel time in the peak period to the travel time at free-flow conditions. A value of 1.30 indicates a 20-minute free-flow trip takes 26 minutes in the peak. Free-flow speeds (60 mph on freeways and 35 mph on principal arterials) are used as the comparison threshold; (1) Covers the Miami FL urban area; (2) average of 439 urban areas
Source: Texas Transportation Institute, Urban Mobility Report 2011, September 2011

Public Transportation

Agency Name / Mode of Transportation	Vehicles Operated in Maximum Service	Annual Unlinked Passenger Trips ('000)	Annual Passenger Miles ('000)
Miami-Dade Transit (MDT)			
Automated Guideway (directly operated)	21	8,013.2	8,732.7
Bus (directly operated)	817	70,292.0	379,704.7
Demand Response (purchased transportation)	320	1,553.6	21,144.6
Heavy Rail (directly operated)	84	17,371.6	128,388.2
South Florida Regional Transportation Authority (TRI-Rail)			
Bus (purchased transportation)	18	444.3	1,523.9
Commuter Rail (purchased transportation)	34	3,606.1	104,575.6

Source: Federal Transit Administration, National Transit Database, 2010

Air Transportation

Airport Name and Code / Type of Service	Passenger Airlines[1]	Passenger Enplanements	Freight Carriers[2]	Freight (lbs.)
Miami International (MIA)				
Domestic service (U.S. carriers - 2011)	32	9,152,553	29	177,549,254
International service (U.S. carriers - 2010)	18	5,359,644	25	831,346,525

Note: (1) Includes all U.S.-based major, minor and commuter airlines that carried at least one passenger during the year; (2) Includes all U.S.-based airlines and freight carriers that transported at least one pound of freight during the year
Source: Bureau of Transportation Statistics, The Intermodal Transportation Database, Air Carriers: T-100 Domestic Market (U.S. Carriers), 2011; Bureau of Transportation Statistics, The Intermodal Transportation Database, Air Carriers: T-100 International Market (U.S. Carriers), 2010

Other Transportation Statistics

Major Highways: I-95
Amtrak Service: Yes
Major Waterways/Ports: Port of Miami; Atlantic Intracoastal Waterway
Source: Amtrak.com; Google Maps

BUSINESSES

Major Business Headquarters

Company Name	Rankings	
	Fortune[1]	Forbes[2]
Brightstar	-	70
Burger King	-	189
Ryder System	437	-
Southern Wine & Spirits	-	30
World Fuel Services	133	-

Note: (1) Fortune 500—companies that produce a 10-K are ranked 1 to 500 based on 2010 revenue; (2) all private companies with at least $2 billion in annual revenue are ranked 1 to 212; companies listed are headquartered in the city; dashes indicate no ranking
Source: Fortune, "Fortune 500," May 23, 2011; Forbes, "America's Largest Private Companies," November 16, 2011

Fast-Growing Businesses

According to *Inc.*, Miami is home to two of America's 500 fastest-growing private companies: **BrokersWeb.com** (#20); **PureFormulas.com** (#97). Criteria: must be an independent, privately-held, for-profit, U.S. corporation, proprietorship or partnership; revenues must be at least $80,000 in 2007 and $2 million in 2010; must have four-year operating/sales history. Holding companies, regulated banks, and utilities were excluded. *Inc., "America's 500 Fastest-Growing Private Companies," September 2011*

Minority Business Opportunity

Miami is home to 62 companies which are on the *Hispanic Business* 500 list (500 largest U.S. Hispanic-owned companies based on 2010 revenue): **Brightstar Corp.** (#1); **The Related Group of Florida** (#3); **Quirch Foods Co.** (#5); **First Equity Mortgage Bankers** (#32); **Precision Trading Corp.** (#35); **Headquarter Toyota** (#38); **MCM** (#52); **Refricenter of Miami** (#62); **Miami Automotive Retail** (#67); **Tire Group International** (#73); **South Dade Automotive** (#87); **Machado Garcia-Serra** (#88); **John Keeler & Co.** (#94); **CSA Group** (#102); **Century Metal & Supplies** (#111); **Kira** (#117); **Softech International** (#142); **Metric Engineering** (#144); **Solo Printing** (#147); **Everglades Steel Corp. & Medley Steel Corp.** (#148); **Fru-Veg Marketing** (#150); **The Intermarket Group** (#163); **Link Construction Group** (#173); **AZF Automotive Group** (#183); **Express Travel of Miami** (#191); **Original Impressions** (#204); **Roach Busters Bug Killers of America** (#207); **Ascendant Commercial Insurance** (#210); **Adonel Concrete Pumping & Finishing of S. FL** (#216); **Bermello Ajamil & Partners** (#226); **Saeg Engineering Group** (#227); **Granada Insurance Co.** (#236); **Jorda Enterprises** (#246); **Protec** (#263); **Vina & Son Food Distributor** (#264); **Nital Trading Co.** (#266); **Envirowaste Services Group** (#288); **Plastec USA** (#290); **South Miami Pharmacy** (#291); **Interamerican Bank** (#294); **Vista Color Corp.** (#296); **X-EETO** (#323); **Florida Lumber Co.** (#343); **Amtec Sales** (#345); **Rey's Pizza Corp.** (#350); **The Perishable Specialist** (#351); **Cherokee Enterprises** (#352); **Gancedo Lumber Co.** (#367); **A&P Consulting Transportation Engineers** (#373); **Island Dairy Distributors** (#376); **Wendium of Florida** (#383); **Tire Masters International** (#384); **Future Force Personnel** (#385); **American Fasteners Corp.** (#386); **Gem Paver Systems** (#408); **Farma International** (#416); **WONEF-Longwood** (#420); **South Florida Trading Corp.** (#422); **Honshy Electric Co.** (#425); **Meridian Partners** (#426); **Republica** (#434); **T&S Roofing Systems** (#470). Companies included must show at least 51 percent ownership by Hispanic U.S. citizens, and must maintain headquarters in one of the 50 states or Washington, D.C. *Hispanic Business, "Hispanic Business 500," June 2011*

Miami is home to 10 companies which are on the *Hispanic Business* Fastest-Growing 100 list (greatest sales growth from 2006 to 2010): **AZF Automotive Group** (#23); **Nital Trading Co.** (#24); **South Dade Automotive** (#36); **Cherokee Enterprises** (#41); **Softech International** (#44); **Machado Garcia-Serra** (#47); **Amtec Sales** (#49); **Envirowaste Services Group** (#58); **Century Metal & Supplies** (#61); **South Florida Trading Corp.** (#90). Companies included must show at least 51 percent ownership by Hispanic U.S. citizens, and must maintain headquarters in one of the 50 states or Washington, D.C. In addition, companies must have minimum revenues of $200,000 for calendar year 2005. *Hispanic Business, July/August 2011*

Minority- and Women-Owned Businesses

Group	All Firms		Firms with Paid Employees			
	Firms	Sales ($000)	Firms	Sales ($000)	Employees	Payroll ($000)
Asian	1,738	629,557	579	586,220	2,895	58,879
Black	9,448	492,059	588	337,832	4,470	75,101
Hispanic	53,234	11,975,646	6,317	10,407,324	35,426	1,127,862
Women	24,414	2,443,049	2,705	1,920,188	14,331	420,472
All Firms	85,143	65,730,894	15,127	62,998,520	321,378	15,801,777

Note: Figures cover firms located in the city; minority- and women-owned business are defined as firms in which the corresponding group own 51% or more of the stock or equity of the company
Source: U.S. Census Bureau, 2007 Economic Census, Survey of Business Owners

HOTELS

Hotels/Motels

Area	5 Star Num.	5 Star Pct.[3]	4 Star Num.	4 Star Pct.[3]	3 Star Num.	3 Star Pct.[3]	2 Star Num.	2 Star Pct.[3]	1 Star Num.	1 Star Pct.[3]	Not Rated Num.	Not Rated Pct.[3]
City[1]	9	2.5	63	17.3	149	40.9	114	31.3	6	1.6	23	6.3
Total[2]	133	0.9	940	6.5	4,569	31.8	7,033	48.9	351	2.4	1,343	9.3

Note: (1) Figures cover Miami and vicinity; (2) Figures cover all 100 cities in this book; (3) Percentage of hotels which have a given star rating; Star ratings are determined by expedia.com and offer an indication of the general quality of a particular hotel.
Source: expedia.com, April 25, 2012

The Miami-Miami Beach-Kendall, FL metro area is home to five of the best hotels in the U.S. according to *Travel & Leisure*: **The Setai** (#47); **Fairmont Turnberry Isle Resort & Club** (#92); **Mandarin Oriental, Miami** (#140); **Biltmore Hotel** (#155); **Ritz-Carlton, Key Biscayne** (#155). Criteria: service; location; rooms; food; and value. *Travel & Leisure, "T+L 500, The World's Best Hotels 2012"*

The Miami-Miami Beach-Kendall, FL metro area is home to three of the best hotels in the U.S. according to *Condé Nast Traveler*: **The Setai** (#32); **Epic Hotel** (#50); **Mandarin Oriental** (#75). The selections are based on over 25,000 responses to the magazine's annual Readers' Choice Survey. *Condé Nast Traveler, "2011 Readers' Choice Awards"*

EVENT SITES

Major Stadiums, Arenas, and Auditoriums

Name	Max. Capacity
American Airlines Arena	19,600
Arnold Hall and Coliseum, Fair Expo Center	7,460
Bayfront Park Amphitheater	6,500
Edwards Hall, Fair Expo Center	5,083
FIU Stadium	18,000
James L. Knight Center	4,646
Marlins Park	37,442
Sun Life Stadium	36,500
U.S. Century Bank Arena	5,000

Source: Original research

Convention Centers

Name	Overall Space (sq. ft.)	Exhibit Space (sq. ft.)	Meeting Space (sq. ft.)	Meeting Rooms
Coconut Grove Convention Center	n/a	n/a	150,000	n/a
Miami Beach Convention Center	1,000,000	100,000	500,000	70

Note: n/a not available
Source: Original research

Living Environment

COST OF LIVING

Cost of Living Index

Composite Index	Groceries	Housing	Utilities	Trans-portation	Health Care	Misc. Goods/ Services
107.2	107.4	112.0	94.3	109.0	106.3	106.4

Note: U.S. = 100; Figures cover the Miami-Dade County FL urban area.
Source: The Council for Community and Economic Research, ACCRA Cost of Living Index, 2011

Grocery Prices

Area[1]	T-Bone Steak ($/pound)	Frying Chicken ($/pound)	Whole Milk ($/half gal.)	Eggs ($/dozen)	Orange Juice ($/64 oz.)	Coffee ($/11.5 oz.)
City[2]	10.43	1.40	2.64	1.84	3.57	4.24
Avg.	9.25	1.18	2.22	1.66	3.19	4.40
Min.	6.70	0.88	1.31	0.95	2.46	2.94
Max.	14.30	2.16	3.50	3.18	4.75	6.83

Note: (1) Values for the local area are compared with the average, minimum and maximum values for all 335 areas in the Cost of Living Index; (2) Figures cover the Miami-Dade County FL urban area; **T-Bone Steak** *(price per pound);* **Frying Chicken** *(price per pound, whole fryer);* **Whole Milk** *(half gallon carton);* **Eggs** *(price per dozen, Grade A, large);* **Orange Juice** *(64 oz. Tropicana or Florida Natural);* **Coffee** *(11.5 oz. can, vacuum-packed, Maxwell House, Hills Bros, or Folgers).*
Source: The Council for Community and Economic Research, ACCRA Cost of Living Index, 2011

Housing and Utility Costs

Area[1]	New Home Price ($)	Apartment Rent ($/month)	All Electric ($/month)	Part Electric ($/month)	Other Energy ($/month)	Telephone ($/month)
City[2]	290,911	1,298	152.30	-	-	26.51
Avg.	285,990	839	163.23	89.00	77.52	26.92
Min.	188,005	460	125.58	45.39	33.89	17.98
Max.	1,197,028	3,244	339.16	181.97	348.69	40.01

Note: (1) Values for the local area are compared with the average, minimum and maximum values for all 335 areas in the Cost of Living Index; (2) Figures cover the Miami-Dade County FL urban area; **New Home Price** *(2,400 sf living area, 8,000 sf lot, in urban area with full utilities);* **Apartment Rent** *(950 sf 2 bedroom/1.5 or 2 bath, unfurnished, excluding all utilities except water);* **All Electric** *(average monthly cost for an all-electric home);* **Part Electric** *(average monthly cost for a part-electric home);* **Other Energy** *(average monthly cost for natural gas, fuel oil, coal, wood, and any other forms of energy except electricity);* **Telephone** *(price includes basic monthly rate for a private residential line plus additional local usage charges incurred by a family of four).*
Source: The Council for Community and Economic Research, ACCRA Cost of Living Index, 2011

Health Care, Transportation, and Other Costs

Area[1]	Doctor ($/visit)	Dentist ($/visit)	Optometrist ($/visit)	Gasoline ($/gallon)	Beauty Salon ($/visit)	Men's Shirt ($)
City[2]	100.88	89.24	82.47	3.58	46.97	22.26
Avg.	93.88	81.72	90.54	3.48	32.65	25.06
Min.	60.00	55.33	53.66	3.18	19.78	13.44
Max.	154.98	145.97	183.72	4.31	63.21	46.00

Note: (1) Values for the local area are compared with the average, minimum and maximum values for all 335 areas in the Cost of Living Index; (2) Figures cover the Miami-Dade County FL urban area; **Doctor** *(general practitioners routine exam of an established patient);* **Dentist** *(adult teeth cleaning and periodic oral examination);* **Optometrist** *(full vision eye exam for established adult patient);* **Gasoline** *(one gallon regular unleaded, national brand, including all taxes, cash price at self-service pump if available);* **Beauty Salon** *(woman's shampoo, trim, and blow-dry);* **Men's Shirt** *(cotton/polyester dress shirt, pinpoint weave, long sleeves).*
Source: The Council for Community and Economic Research, ACCRA Cost of Living Index, 2011

HOUSING

House Price Index (HPI)

Area	National Ranking[2]	Quarterly Change (%)	One-Year Change (%)	Five-Year Change (%)
MD[1]	251	0.74	-5.54	-43.62
U.S.[3]	-	-0.10	-2.43	-19.16

Note: The HPI is a weighted repeat sales index. It measures average price changes in repeat sales or refinancings on the same properties. This information is obtained by reviewing repeat mortgage transactions on single-family properties whose mortgages have been purchased or securitized by Fannie Mae or Freddie Mac in January 1975; (1) Metropolitan Division - see Appendix B for areas included; (2) Rankings are based on annual percentage change for all metro areas containing at least 15,000 transactions over the last 10 years and ranges from 1 to 306; (3) figures based on a weighted average of Census Division estimates using a purchase only index; all figures are for the period ending December 31, 2011
Source: Federal Housing Finance Agency, House Price Index, February 23, 2012

House Price Valuations

Area	Q4 2005 Price ($000)	Q4 2005 Over-valuation	Q4 2006 Price ($000)	Q4 2006 Over-valuation	Q4 2007 Price ($000)	Q4 2007 Over-valuation	Q4 2008 Price ($000)	Q4 2008 Over-valuation	Q4 2009 Price ($000)	Q4 2009 Over-valuation
MD[1]	281.3	49.4	307.2	48.8	307.4	45.0	206.9	-2.6	180.5	-15.6

Note: Figures show the percentage of over- or under-valuation of single family homes relative to statistically normal house values (e.g. a value of 23.6 indicates that house values are 23.6% overvalued). Statistically normal house values are based on house prices, interest rates, household incomes, population densities, and any historical premiums or discounts metropolitan areas have exhibited over time; (1) Figures cover the Miami-Miami Beach-Kendall, FL - see Appendix B for areas included
Source: Global Insight/PNC Financial Services Group, House Prices in America: 4th Quarter 2009 Update

Median Single-Family Home Prices

Area	2009	2010	2011p	Percent Change 2010 to 2011
MSA[1]	211.2	201.9	181.1	-10.3
U.S. Average	172.1	173.1	166.2	-4.0

Note: Figures are median sales prices of existing single-family homes in thousands of dollars; (p) preliminary; n/a not available; (1) Metropolitan Statistical Area—see Appendix B for areas included
Source: National Association of Realtors, Median Sales Price of Existing Single-Family Homes for Metropolitan Areas, 4th Quarter 2011

Affordability Index of Existing Single-Family Homes

Area	2009	2010	2011p	Percent Change 2010 to 2011
MSA[1]	97.5	107.0	125.3	17.1

Note: The housing affordability index measures whether or not a typical family could qualify for a mortgage loan on a typical home. The higher the index, the greater the household purchasing power. An index of 100 is defined as the point where a median-income household has exactly enough income to qualify for the purchase of a median-priced existing single-family home, assuming a 20 percent downpayment and 25 percent of gross income devoted to mortgage principal and interest payments; (p) preliminary; n/a not available; (1) Metropolitan Statistical Area—see Appendix B for areas included
Source: National Association of Realtors, Affordability Index of Existing Single-Family Homes, 2011

Median Apartment Condo-Coop Home Prices

Area	2009	2010	2011p	Percent Change 2010 to 2011
MSA[1]	107.4	92.2	84.0	-8.9
U.S. Average	175.6	171.7	165.1	-3.8

Note: Figures are median sales prices of existing apartment condo-coop homes in thousands of dollars; (p) preliminary; n/a not available; (1) Metropolitan Statistical Area—see Appendix B for areas included
Source: National Association of Realtors, Median Sales Price of Existing Apartment Condo-Coop Homes for Metropolitan Areas, 4th Quarter 2011

Year Housing Structure Built

Area	2005 or Later	2000 -2004	1990 -1999	1980 -1989	1970 -1979	1960 -1969	1950 -1959	Before 1950	Median Year
City	6.6	10.1	6.0	7.2	14.0	11.2	15.6	29.2	1965
MSA[1]	3.6	9.5	14.8	19.7	23.0	13.0	10.5	5.7	1979
U.S.	5.0	8.6	14.0	14.1	16.3	11.3	11.2	19.6	1975

Note: Figures are percentages except for Median Year; (1) Figures cover the Miami-Fort Lauderdale-Pompano Beach, FL Metropolitan Statistical Area—see Appendix B for areas included
Source: U.S. Census Bureau, 2008-2010 American Community Survey 3-Year Estimates

HEALTH

Health Risk Data

Category	MSA[1] (%)	U.S. (%)
Adults who have been told they have high blood pressure[2]	31.8	28.7
Adults who have been told they have high blood cholesterol[2]	38.2	37.5
Adults who have been told they have diabetes[3]	7.5	8.7
Adults who have been told they have arthritis[2]	22.1	26.0
Adults who have been told they currently have asthma	7.7	9.1
Adults who are current smokers	12.4	17.3
Adults who are heavy drinkers[4]	2.5	5.0
Adults who are binge drinkers[5]	13.3	15.1
Adults who are overweight (BMI 25.0 - 29.9)	37.5	36.2
Adults who are obese (BMI 30.0 - 99.8)	28.3	27.5
Adults who participated in any physical activities in the past month	75.9	76.1
Adults 50+ who have ever had a sigmoidoscopy or colonoscopy	66.5	65.2
Women aged 40+ who have had a mammogram within the past two years	79.6	75.2
Men aged 40+ who have had a PSA test within the past two years	58.8	53.2
Adults aged 65+ who have had flu shot within the past year	51.7	67.5
Adults aged 18–64 who have any kind of health care coverage	72.1	82.2

Note: Data as of 2010 unless otherwise noted; (1) Figures cover the Miami-Fort Lauderdale-Miami Beach, FL Metropolitan Statistical Area—see Appendix B for areas included; (2) Data as of 2009; (3) Figures do not include pregnancy-related, borderline, or pre-diabetes; (4) Heavy drinkers are classified as males having more than two drinks per day or females having more than one drink per day; (5) Binge drinkers are classified as males having five or more drinks on one occasion or females having four or more drinks on one occasion
Source: Centers for Disease Control and Prevention, Behaviorial Risk Factor Surveillance System, SMART: Selected Metropolitan/Micropolitan Area Risk Trends, 2009, 2010

Mortality Rates for the Top 10 Causes of Death in the U.S.

ICD-10[a] Sub-Chapter	ICD-10[a] Code	Age-Adjusted Mortality Rate[1] per 100,000 population	
		County[2]	U.S.
Malignant neoplasms	C00-C97	137.1	175.6
Ischaemic heart diseases	I20-I25	119.3	121.6
Other forms of heart disease	I30-I51	33.3	48.6
Chronic lower respiratory diseases	J40-J47	25.4	42.3
Cerebrovascular diseases	I60-I69	29.6	40.6
Organic, including symptomatic, mental disorders	F01-F09	18.7	26.7
Other degenerative diseases of the nervous system	G30-G31	23.8	24.7
Other external causes of accidental injury	W00-X59	15.5	24.4
Diabetes mellitus	E10-E14	22.5	21.7
Hypertensive diseases	I10-I15	19.3	18.2

Note: (a) ICD-10 = International Classification of Diseases 10th Revision; (1) Mortality rates are a three year average covering 2007-2009; (2) Figures cover Miami-Dade County
Source: Centers for Disease Control and Prevention, National Center for Health Statistics. Underlying Cause of Death 1999-2009 on CDC WONDER Online Database, released 2012. Data for year 2009 are compiled from the Multiple Cause of Death File 2009, Series 20 No. 2O, 2012, Data for year 2008 are compiled from the Multiple Cause of Death File 2008, Series 20 No. 2N, 2011, Data for year 2007 are compiled from Multiple Cause of Death File 2007, Series 20 No. 2M, 2010.

Mortality Rates for Selected Causes of Death

ICD-10[a] Sub-Chapter	ICD-10[a] Code	Age-Adjusted Mortality Rate[1] per 100,000 population	
		County[2]	U.S.
Assault	X85-Y09	9.7	5.7
Human immunodeficiency virus (HIV) disease	B20-B24	13.6	3.3
Influenza and pneumonia	J09-J18	8.4	16.4
Intentional self-harm	X60-X84	9.5	11.5
Malnutrition	E40-E46	0.2	0.8
Obesity and other hyperalimentation	E65-E68	1.4	1.6
Transport accidents	V01-V99	13.5	13.7
Viral hepatitis	B15-B19	2.2	2.2

Note: (a) ICD-10 = International Classification of Diseases 10th Revision; (1) Mortality rates are a three year average covering 2007-2009; (2) Figures cover Miami-Dade County
Source: Centers for Disease Control and Prevention, National Center for Health Statistics. Underlying Cause of Death 1999-2009 on CDC WONDER Online Database, released 2012. Data for year 2009 are compiled from the Multiple Cause of Death File 2009, Series 20 No. 2O, 2012, Data for year 2008 are compiled from the Multiple Cause of Death File 2008, Series 20 No. 2N, 2011, Data for year 2007 are compiled from Multiple Cause of Death File 2007, Series 20 No. 2M, 2010.

Distribution of Physicians and Dentists

Area[1]	Dentists[2]	D.O.[3]	M.D.[4]				
			Total	Family/General Practice	Pediatrics	Medical Specialties	Surgical Specialties
Local (number)	1,079	336	5,460	680	476	2,224	1,171
Local (rate[5])	4.4	1.4	22.0	2.7	1.9	9.0	4.7
U.S. (rate[5])	4.5	1.9	18.3	2.5	1.4	6.8	4.1

Note: Data as of 2008 unless noted; (1) Local data covers Miami-Dade County; (2) Data as of 2007; (3) Doctor of Osteopathic Medicine; (4) Includes active, non-federal, patient-care, office-based Doctors of Medicine; (5) rate per 10,000 population
Source: Area Resource File (ARF). 2009-2010 Release. U.S. Department of Health and Human Services, Health Resources and Services Administration, Bureau of Health Professions, Rockville, MD, August 2010

Best Hospitals

According to U.S. News, the Miami-Miami Beach-Kendall, FL is home to three of the best hospitals in the U.S.: **Bascom Palmer Eye Institute at the University of Miami** (1 specialty); **Mount Sinai Medical Center** (1 specialty); **University of Miami-Jackson Memorial Hospital** (4 specialties). The hospitals listed were highly ranked in at least one adult specialty. U.S. News Online, "America's Best Hospitals 2011-12"

According to U.S. News, the Miami-Miami Beach-Kendall, FL is home to two of the best children's hospitals in the U.S.: **Holtz Children's Hospital at UM-Jackson Memorial Hospital** (7 specialties); **Miami Children's Hospital** (10 specialties). The hospitals listed were highly ranked in at least one pediatric specialty. U.S. News Online, "America's Best Children's Hospitals 2011-12"

EDUCATION

Public School District Statistics

District Name	Schls	Pupils	Pupil/Teacher Ratio	Minority Pupils[1] (%)	Free Lunch Eligible[2] (%)	IEP[3] (%)
Dade	506	345,804	15.9	91.1	58.6	11.0

Note: Table includes school districts with 2,000 or more students; (1) Percentage of students that are not non-Hispanic white; (2) Percentage of students that are eligible for the free lunch program; (3) Percentage of students that have an Individualized Education Program.
Source: U.S. Department of Education, National Center for Education Statistics, Common Core of Data, Local Education Agency (School District) Universe Survey: School Year 2009-2010; U.S. Department of Education, National Center for Education Statistics, Common Core of Data, Public Elementary/Secondary School Universe Survey: School Year 2009-2010

Top Public High Schools

High School Name	Rank[1]	Score[1]	Grad. Rate[2] (%)	College[3] (%)	AP/IB/ AICE[4] (%)	SAT/ ACT[5] (%)
Coral Reef	53	0.994	98	98	6.2	1598
Maritime and Science Technology (MAST)	46	1.037	100	100	4.3	1721
Mater Lakes Academy	427	0.202	100	100	1.9	1358
School for Advanced Studies	28	1.276	100	100	7.3	1768

Note: (1) Public schools are ranked from 1 to 500 based on the following self-reported statistics (with their corresponding weight in the final score). Schools that had fewer than 10 graduates, as well as those that were newly founded and did not have a graduating senior class in 2010 were excluded; (2) Four-year, on-time graduation rate (25%); (3) Percent of 2010 graduates who enrolled immediately in college (25%); (4) AP/IB/AICE tests per graduate (25%); (5) Average SAT and/or ACT score (10%); Average AP/IB/AICE exam score (10%); AP/IB/AICE courses offered per graduate (5%); (6) School is unranked, but has been identified by Newsweek as one of the nation's most elite public high schools.
Source: Newsweek Online, "Top High Schools 2011"

Highest Level of Education

Area	Less than H.S.	H.S. Diploma	Some College, No Deg.	Associate Degree	Bachelors Degree	Masters Degree	Profess. School Degree	Doctorate Degree
City	32.0	28.0	10.3	7.2	14.1	4.6	2.6	1.3
MSA[1]	17.3	27.4	18.5	8.3	18.2	6.5	2.7	1.1
U.S.	14.7	28.4	21.3	7.6	17.6	7.2	1.9	1.2

Note: Figures cover persons age 25 and over; (1) Figures cover the Miami-Fort Lauderdale-Pompano Beach, FL Metropolitan Statistical Area—see Appendix B for areas included
Source: U.S. Census Bureau, 2008-2010 American Community Survey 3-Year Estimates

Educational Attainment by Race

Area	High School Graduate or Higher (%)					Bachelor's Degree or Higher (%)				
	Total	White	Black	Asian	Hisp.[2]	Total	White	Black	Asian	Hisp.[2]
City	68.0	69.5	61.2	84.9	64.8	22.6	25.1	9.8	60.4	19.3
MSA[1]	82.7	84.6	76.4	85.9	75.0	28.5	31.1	17.3	46.7	23.6
U.S.	85.3	87.5	81.4	85.5	61.6	28.0	29.3	17.8	50.2	13.0

Note: Figures shown cover persons 25 years old and over; (1) Figures cover the Miami-Fort Lauderdale-Pompano Beach, FL Metropolitan Statistical Area—see Appendix B for areas included; (2) People of Hispanic origin can be of any race
Source: U.S. Census Bureau, 2008-2010 American Community Survey 3-Year Estimates

School Enrollment by Grade and Control

Area	Preschool (%)		Kindergarten (%)		Grades 1 - 4 (%)		Grades 5 - 8 (%)		Grades 9 - 12 (%)	
	Public	Private	Public	Private	Public	Private	Public	Private	Public	Private
City	57.7	42.3	83.7	16.3	89.2	10.8	91.5	8.5	93.1	6.9
MSA[1]	44.6	55.4	82.0	18.0	87.2	12.8	87.3	12.7	88.1	11.9
U.S.	55.4	44.6	87.1	12.9	89.4	10.6	89.5	10.5	90.4	9.6

Note: Figures shown cover persons 3 years old and over; (1) Figures cover the Miami-Fort Lauderdale-Pompano Beach, FL Metropolitan Statistical Area—see Appendix B for areas included
Source: U.S. Census Bureau, 2008-2010 American Community Survey 3-Year Estimates

Average Salaries of Public School Classroom Teachers

Area	2010-11 Dollars	Rank[1]	2011-12 Dollars	Rank[1]	Percent Change 2010-11 to 2011-12	Percent Change 2001-02 to 2011-12
Florida	45,732	45	46,232	46	1.09	17.70
U.S. Average	55,623	-	56,643	-	1.83	26.8

Note: (1) State rank ranges from 1 to 51 where 1 indicates highest salary.
Source: National Education Association, Rankings & Estimates: Rankings of the States 2011 and Estimates of School Statistics 2012, December 2011

Higher Education

Four-Year Colleges			Two-Year Colleges			Medical Schools[1]	Law Schools[2]	Voc/ Tech[3]
Public	Private Non-profit	Private For-profit	Public	Private Non-profit	Private For-profit			
2	5	5	4	1	13	2	1	19

Note: Figures cover institutions located within the city limits and include main campuses only; (1) includes schools accredited by the Liaison Committee on Medical Education and the American Osteopathic Association's Commission on Osteopathic College Accreditation; (2) includes American Bar Association-accredited law schools; (3) includes all schools with programs that are less than 2 years.
Source: National Center for Education Statistics, Integrated Postsecondary Education System (IPEDS) Peer Analysis System, 2011-12; Association of American Medical Colleges, Member List, April 23, 2012; American Osteopathic Association, Member List, April 23, 2012; Law School Admission Council, Official Guide to ABA-Approved Law Schools Online, April 23, 2012

According to *U.S. News & World Report,* the Miami-Miami Beach-Kendall, FL is home to one of the best national universities in the U.S.: **University of Miami** (#38). The indicators used to capture academic quality fall into a number of categories: assessment by administrators at peer institutions; retention of students; faculty resources; student selectivity; financial resources; alumni giving; high school counselor ratings of colleges; and graduation rate.*U.S. News & World Report, "America's Best Colleges 2012"*

According to *Forbes,* the Miami-Miami Beach-Kendall, FL is home to one of the best business schools in the U.S.: **Miami** (#59). The rankings are based on the return on investment that graduates of the Class of 2006 received (median salary five years after graduation). *Forbes, "Best Business Schools," August 3, 2011*

PRESIDENTIAL ELECTION

2008 Presidential Election Results

Area	Obama	McCain	Nader	Other
Miami-Dade County	57.8	41.7	0.2	0.3
U.S.	52.9	45.6	0.6	0.9

Note: Results are percentages and may not add to 100% due to rounding
Source: Dave Leip's Atlas of U.S. Presidential Elections, www.uselectionatlas.org

EMPLOYERS

Major Employers

Company Name	Industry
Baptist Health South Florida	General medical and surgical hospitals
Baptist Hospital of Miami	General medical and surgical hospitals
County of Miami-Dade	Police protection, county government
County of Miami-Dade	Regulation, administration of transportation
County of, Palm Beach	County supervisors' and executives' office
Florida International University	Colleges and universities
Intercoastal Health Systems	Management services
Miami Dade College	Community college
Mount Sinai Medical Center of Florida	General medical and surgical hospitals
North Broward Hospital District	Hospital, ama approved residency
North Broward Hospital District	General and family practice, physician/surgeon
Royal Caribbean Cruises Ltd.	Computer processing services
Royal Caribbean Cruises Ltd.	Deep sea passenger transportation, except ferry
School Board of Palm Beach County	Public elementary and secondary schools
Style View Products	Storm doors of windows, metal
The Answer Group	Custom computer programming services
University of Miami	Colleges and universities
Veterans Health Administration	General medical and surgical hospitals

Note: Companies shown are located within the Miami-Fort Lauderdale-Pompano Beach, FL metropolitan area.
Source: Hoovers.com, data extracted April 25 2012

PUBLIC SAFETY

Crime Rate

Area	All Crimes	Violent Crimes				Property Crimes		
		Murder	Forcible Rape	Robbery	Aggrav. Assault	Burglary	Larceny -Theft	Motor Vehicle Theft
City	5,924.6	15.4	10.4	421.4	660.4	1,045.2	3,215.8	556.0
Suburbs[1]	5,303.1	7.5	23.6	196.9	426.2	888.3	3,354.8	405.9
Metro[2]	5,411.6	8.9	21.3	236.1	467.0	915.7	3,330.6	432.1
U.S.	3,345.5	4.8	27.5	119.1	252.3	699.6	2,003.5	238.8

Note: Figures are crimes per 100,000 population; (1) All areas within the metro area that are located outside the city limits; (2) Metropolitan Division—see Appendix B for areas included
Source: FBI Uniform Crime Reports, 2010

Hate Crimes

Area	Number of Quarters Reported	Bias Motivation				
		Race	Religion	Sexual Orientation	Ethnicity	Disability
City	4	0	0	0	0	0

Source: Federal Bureau of Investigation, Hate Crime Statistics 2010

Identity Theft Consumer Complaints

Area	Complaints	Complaints per 100,000 Population	Rank[2]
MSA[1]	17,546	324.1	1
U.S.	279,156	90.4	-

Note: (1) Metropolitan Statistical Area—see Appendix B for areas included; (2) Rank ranges from 1 to 384 where 1 indicates greatest number of identity theft complaints per 100,000 population
Source: Federal Trade Commission, Consumer Sentinel Network Data Book for January–December 2011

Fraud and Other Consumer Complaints

Area	Complaints	Complaints per 100,000 Population	Rank[2]
MSA[1]	25,320	467.7	197
U.S.	1,533,924	496.8	-

Note: (1) Metropolitan Statistical Area—see Appendix B for areas included; (2) Rank ranges from 1 to 384 where 1 indicates greatest number of fraud and other complaints per 100,000 population
Source: Federal Trade Commission, Consumer Sentinel Network Data Book for January–December 2011

RECREATION

Culture

Dance[1]	Theatre[1]	Instrumental Music[1]	Vocal Music[1]	Series/ Festivals	Museums	Zoos and Aquariums[2]
2	3	3	1	4	11	1

Note: (1) Number of professional perfoming groups; (2) AZA-accredited
Source: The Grey House Performing Arts Directory, 2011-2012; Official Museum Directory, 2011; American Association of Museums, AAM Member Museums, April 2012; Association of Zoos & Aquariums, AZA Member Zoos & Aquariums, April 2012

Professional Sports Teams

Team Name	League
Florida Panthers	National Hockey League (NHL)
Miami Dolphins	National Football League (NFL)
Miami Heat	National Basketball Association (NBA)
Miami Marlins	Major League Baseball (MLB)

Note: Includes teams located in the Miami-Fort Lauderdale metro area.
Source: Original research

CLIMATE

Average and Extreme Temperatures

Temperature	Jan	Feb	Mar	Apr	May	Jun	Jul	Aug	Sep	Oct	Nov	Dec	Yr.
Extreme High (°F)	88	89	92	96	95	98	98	98	97	95	89	87	98
Average High (°F)	75	77	79	82	85	88	89	90	88	85	80	77	83
Average Temp. (°F)	68	69	72	75	79	82	83	83	82	78	73	69	76
Average Low (°F)	59	60	64	68	72	75	76	76	76	72	66	61	69
Extreme Low (°F)	30	35	32	42	55	60	69	68	68	53	39	30	30

Note: Figures cover the years 1948-1990
Source: National Climatic Data Center, International Station Meteorological Climate Summary, 9/96

Average Precipitation/Snowfall/Humidity

Precip./Humidity	Jan	Feb	Mar	Apr	May	Jun	Jul	Aug	Sep	Oct	Nov	Dec	Yr.
Avg. Precip. (in.)	1.9	2.0	2.3	3.0	6.2	8.7	6.1	7.5	8.2	6.6	2.7	1.8	57.1
Avg. Snowfall (in.)	0	0	0	0	0	0	0	0	0	0	0	0	0
Avg. Rel. Hum. 7am (%)	84	84	82	80	81	84	84	86	88	87	85	84	84
Avg. Rel. Hum. 4pm (%)	59	57	57	57	62	68	66	67	69	65	63	60	63

Note: Figures cover the years 1948-1990; Tr = Trace amounts (<0.05 in. of rain; <0.5 in. of snow)
Source: National Climatic Data Center, International Station Meteorological Climate Summary, 9/96

Weather Conditions

Temperature			Daytime Sky			Precipitation		
32°F & below	45°F & below	90°F & above	Clear	Partly cloudy	Cloudy	0.01 inch or more precip.	0.1 inch or more snow/ice	Thunder-storms
< 1	7	55	48	263	54	128	0	74

Note: Figures are average number of days per year and cover the years 1948-1990
Source: National Climatic Data Center, International Station Meteorological Climate Summary, 9/96

HAZARDOUS WASTE

Superfund Sites

Miami has three hazardous waste sites on the EPA's Superfund Final National Priorities List: **Continental Cleaners; Airco Plating Co.; Miami Drum Services.** *U.S. Environmental Protection Agency, Final National Priorities List, April 17, 2012*

AIR & WATER QUALITY

Air Quality Index

Area	Percent of Days when Air Quality was...[2]					AQI Statistics[2]	
	Good	Moderate	Unhealthy for Sensitive Groups	Unhealthy	Very Unhealthy	Maximum	Median
Area[1]	89.9	9.6	0.5	0.0	0.0	109	36

Note: Air Quality Index (AQI) is an index for reporting daily air quality. EPA calculates the AQI for five major air pollutants regulated by the Clean Air Act: ground-level ozone, particle pollution (aka particulate matter), carbon monoxide, sulfur dioxide, and nitrogen dioxide. The AQI runs from 0 to 500. The higher the AQI value, the greater the level of air pollution and the greater the health concern. There are six AQI categories: "Good" AQI is between 0 and 50. Air quality is considered satisfactory; "Moderate" AQI is between 51 and 100. Air quality is acceptable; "Unhealthy for Sensitive Groups" When AQI values are between 101 and 150, members of sensitive groups may experience health effects; "Unhealthy" When AQI values are between 151 and 200 everyone may begin to experience health effects; "Very Unhealthy" AQI values between 201 and 300 trigger a health alert; "Hazardous" AQI values over 300 trigger warnings of emergency conditions (not shown); (1) Data covers Miami-Dade County; (2) Based on 365 days with AQI data in 2011.
Source: U.S. Environmental Protection Agency, AirData Report, 2011

Air Quality Index Pollutants

Area	Percent of Days when AQI Pollutant was...[2]					
	Carbon Monoxide	Nitrogen Dioxide	Ozone	Sulfur Dioxide	Particulate Matter 2.5	Particulate Matter 10
Area[1]	0.0	1.6	48.2	0.0	50.1	0.0

Note: The Air Quality Index (AQI) is an index for reporting daily air quality. EPA calculates the AQI for five major air pollutants regulated by the Clean Air Act: ground-level ozone, particle pollution (also known as particulate matter), carbon monoxide, sulfur dioxide, and nitrogen dioxide. The AQI runs from 0 to 500. The higher the AQI value, the greater the level of air pollution and the greater the health concern; (1) Data covers Miami-Dade County; (2) Based on 365 days with AQI data in 2011.
Source: U.S. Environmental Protection Agency, AirData Report, 2011

Air Quality Index Trends

Area	Trend Sites (days)								All Sites (days)
	2003	2004	2005	2006	2007	2008	2009	2010	2010
MSA[1]	4	11	4	12	10	5	2	4	4

Note: Figures are the number of days the AQI value exceeded 100 in a given year. An AQI value greater than 100 indicates that air quality would have been in the unhealthful range on that day. Data from exceptional events are included. These counts are presented in two ways. First, the counts are based on sites having an adequate record of monitoring data during the trend period (trend sites). These counts represent the relative change in the number of days with AQI values greater than 100. In the last column, the counts are based on all sites with data in the most recent year (because it is possible for a site to have data in the most recent year but not enough data to be a trend site); (1) Data covers the Miami-Fort Lauderdale-Pompano Beach, FL—see Appendix B for areas included
Source: U.S. Environmental Protection Agency, Air Quality Index Information, "Number of Days with Air Quality Index Values Greater than 100 at Trend Sites, 2000-2010, and at All Sites in 2010"

Maximum Air Pollutant Concentrations: Particulate Matter, Ozone, CO and Lead

	Particulate Matter 10 (ug/m³)	Particulate Matter 2.5 Wtd AM (ug/m³)	Particulate Matter 2.5 24-Hr (ug/m³)	Ozone (ppm)	Carbon Monoxide (ppm)	Lead (ug/m³)
MSA[1] Level	44	7.8	14	0.069	2	n/a
NAAQS[2]	150	15	35	0.075	9	0.15
Met NAAQS[2]	Yes	Yes	Yes	Yes	Yes	n/a

Note: Data from exceptional events are not included; (1) Data covers the Miami-Fort Lauderdale-Pompano Beach, FL—see Appendix B for areas included; (2) National Ambient Air Quality Standards; ppm = parts per million; ug/m³ = micrograms per cubic meter; n/a not available
Concentrations: Particulate Matter 10 (coarse particulate)—highest second maximum 24-hour concentration; Particulate Matter 2.5 Wtd AM (fine particulate)—highest weighted annual mean concentration; Particulate Matter 2.5 24-Hour (fine particulate)—highest 98th percentile 24-hour concentration; Ozone—highest fourth daily maximum 8-hour concentration; Carbon Monoxide—highest second maximum non-overlapping 8-hour concentration; Lead—maximum running 3-month average
Source: U.S. Environmental Protection Agency, CBSA Factbook 2010, Air Quality Statistics by City, 2010

Maximum Air Pollutant Concentrations: Nitrogen Dioxide and Sulfur Dioxide

	Nitrogen Dioxide AM (ppb)	Nitrogen Dioxide 1-Hr (ppb)	Sulfur Dioxide AM (ppb)	Sulfur Dioxide 1-Hr (ppb)	Sulfur Dioxide 24-Hr (ppb)
MSA[1] Level	9.651	49	0.831	38	5.9
NAAQS[2]	53	100	30	75	140
Met NAAQS[2]	Yes	Yes	Yes	Yes	Yes

Note: Data from exceptional events are not included; (1) Data covers the Miami-Fort Lauderdale-Pompano Beach, FL—see Appendix B for areas included; (2) National Ambient Air Quality Standards; ppb = parts per billion; n/a not available
Concentrations: Nitrogen Dioxide AM—highest arithmetic mean concentration; Nitrogen Dioxide 1-Hr—highest 98th percentile 1-hour daily maximum concentration; Sulfur Dioxide AM—highest annual mean concentration; Sulfur Dioxide 1-Hr—highest 99th percentile 1-hour daily maximum concentration; Sulfur Dioxide 24-Hr—highest second maximum 24-hour concentration
Source: U.S. Environmental Protection Agency, CBSA Factbook 2010, Air Quality Statistics by City, 2010

Drinking Water

Water System Name	Pop. Served	Primary Water Source Type	Violations[1]	
			Health Based	Monitoring/ Reporting
MDWASA - Main System	2,100,000	Ground	0	0

Note: (1) Based on violation data from January 1, 2011 to December 31, 2011 (includes unresolved violations from earlier years)

Source: U.S. Environmental Protection Agency, Office of Ground Water and Drinking Water, Safe Drinking Water Information System (based on data extracted April 18, 2012)

Murfreesboro, Tennessee

Background

Located in the geographic center of Tennessee just off I-24, thirty-four miles southeast of Nashville, Murfreesboro is the fast-growing seat of Rutherford County.

Founded in 1811 for the specific purpose of serving as the county's new seat, Murfreesboro was first called Cannonsburgh after a regional politician. However, the new town was sited on acreage owned by Capt. William Lytle, who asked that it be named in memory of his friend, Col. Hardy Murfree. Murfreesboro's central location made it the capital of Tennessee from 1818 to 1826.

A major Civil War battle was fought here that still can be remembered at the Stones River National Battlefield, now maintained by the National Park Service. Considered one of the war's bloodiest battles, it took place early in the conflict and the Union prevailed.

The centrally-located town is not only the retail hub for ten counties, but also home to one of two new award-winning Amazon fulfillment centers being opened in Tennessee. It is expected to bring 1,000 jobs to the county. The CiCi (Corporate Investment & Community Impact) Award was from Trade & Industry Development magazine.

The county's largest employer is Nissan Motor Manufacturing, located outside the city. The largest employers in the city proper include State Farm Insurance, Verizon Wireless call center, Alvin C. York VA Medical Center, and Middle Tennessee State University.

Established in 1911 as the Middle Tennessee Normal School, the university serves a diverse population of more than 26,000 students on its 800-acre campus.

The city clearly focuses on service, evident in the recent hiring of a Service Excellence Coordinator to help residents navigate government. In addition, a branch of Tennessee Technology Center is located here, which focuses on workforce development.

On deck for the city is the Murfreesboro Gateway, an extensive development that will include class A office space as well as an 18-hole golf course, and the new $300 million Middle Tennessee Medical Center. The city project will include two 25-acre sites reserved for corporate headquarters.

Currently headquartered in the city are Alpha Integration, Inc., Bioventures, Inc., ClaimTrust, Inc., B&W Wholesale Distributors, Inc., Barrett Firearms Manufacturing, and D&D Oil Company, Inc.

Life in Murfreesboro isn't all business. Recreational opportunities for residents include Sports*Com and Patterson Park Community Center with personal trainers, weight and fitness rooms, aquatics, sports teams for all ages, and McFadden Community Center with a gym, nursery school and the Rutherford County Food Bank. Parks include the Barfield Crescent Park Trail with its Disc Golf Course and paved and other types of trails, the Murfreesboro Greenway System that includes 12 miles of riverside trails, various pools, and cultural arts programs including the 305-seat Theatre at Patterson Park. Other family fun includes the local SkateCenter, the Lanes, Trains & Automobiles Entertainment Depot, and the Phazer Kraze Laser Tag. Murfreesboro has a popular dog park, and U.S. News and World Report gave the state Veteran's Home in Murfreesboro its highest rating—five stars—for all four quarters of 2011.

The climate here is moderate, with a relatively small amount of snow and July temperatures averaging less than eighty degrees. Come January, average lows are above thirty-five degrees.

Rankings

General Rankings

- The Nashville metro area was selected as one of 10 "Best Value Cities" for 2011 by *Kiplinger.com* The area ranked #3. Criteria: vibrant economy; low cost of living; abundant lifestyle amenities. *Kiplinger.com, "Best Value Cities 2011"*

Business/Finance Rankings

- Nashville was selected as one of the best metro areas for telecommuters in America. The area ranked #10 out of 11. Criteria: low cost of living; educational attainment; number of universities and libraries; literacy rates; personal fitness. *DailyFinance.com, "The 11 Best Cities for Telecommuters," December 2, 2010*

- The Nashville metro area appeared on the Milken Institute "2011 Best Performing Metros" list. Rank: #42 out of 200 large metro areas. Criteria: job growth; wage and salary growth; high-tech output growth. *Milken Institute, "2011 Best Performing Metros"*

- The Nashville metro area was selected as one of the best cities for entrepreneurs in America by *Inc. Magazine*. Criteria: job-growth data for 335 metro areas was analyzed for: recent growth trend; mid-term growth; long-term trend; current year growth. The Nashville metro area ranked #18 among large metro areas and #97 overall. *Inc. Magazine, "The Best Cities for Doing Business," July 2008*

- Nashville was ranked #92 out of 145 regions worldwide in terms of its "Knowledge Competitiveness Index." The index attempts to measure the knowledge-based development taking place throughout the world and is based on 19 measures of economic performance that indicate a region's ability to translate its knowledge capacity into economic value. *Centre for International Competitiveness, World Knowledge Competitiveness Index 2008*

- *Forbes* ranked the 200 most populous metro areas in the U.S. in terms of the "Best Places for Business and Careers." The Nashville metro area was ranked #6. Criteria: costs (business and living); job growth (past and projected); income growth; educational attainment; projected economic growth; crime; cultural and recreational opportunities; net migration patterns; number of highly ranked colleges. *Forbes, "Best Places for Business and Careers," June 2011*

Children/Family Rankings

- The Nashville metro area was selected as one of the "Best Cities for Relocating Families" by Worldwide ERC and Primacy Relocation. The 2008 study looked at nearly 50 factors important to relocating families including: recent job growth; nearby top-ranked colleges; in-state tuition for four-year public colleges; population growth since 2000; pediatricians per 100,000 population; and a Green Living index. *Worldwide ERC and Primacy Relocation, "2008 Best Cities for Relocating Families"*

Dating/Romance Rankings

- Murfreesboro was selected as one of the most romantic cities in America by *Amazon.com*. The city ranked #8 of 20. Criteria: per capita sales of romance novels and relationship books, romantic comedy movies, Barry White albums, and sexual wellness products. *Amazon.com, "America's Most Romantic Cities Revealed," February 14, 2012*

- Eli Lily and Company, in partnership with Sperling's BestPlaces, ranked the nation's 50 largest metro areas in terms of the "Most Romantic Cities for Baby Boomers." The Nashville metro area ranked #17. Criteria: marriage and divorce rates among baby boomers age 45 to 60; great restaurants; dance studios; chocolate, jewelry and flower sales. *Eli Lily and Company, "Most Romantic Cities for Baby Boomers," April 20, 2007*

- The Nashville metro area was selected as one of the "Best Cities for Relocating Singles" by Worldwide ERC and Primacy Relocation. The area ranked #41 out of the 100 largest metro areas in the U.S. Criteria: recent job growth; recent singles population growth; overall population growth; affordable rental housing; cost-of-living index; expanded arts and recreation opportunities; ratio of single men and single women; affordability of quality higher education (including state residency requirements); diversity index; climate; population density. *Worldwide ERC and Primacy Relocation, "2008 Best Cities for Relocating Singles"*

Education Rankings

- Nashville was identified as one of the 100 "smartest" metro areas in the U.S. The area ranked #59. Criteria: the editors rated the collective brainpower of the 100 largest metro areas in the U.S. based on their residents' educational attainment. *American City Business Journals, April 14, 2008*

- Nashville was identified as one of "America's Brainiest Bastions" by *Portfolio.com*. The metro area ranked #79 out of 200. *Portfolio.com* analyzed levels of educational attainment in the nation's 200 largest metropolitan areas. The editors established scores for five levels of educational attainment, based on relative earning power of adult workers age 25 or older. Scores were determined by comparing the median income for all workers with the median income for those workers at a specified educational level. *Portfolio.com, "America's Brainiest Bastions," December 1, 2010*

Environmental Rankings

- Murfreesboro was selected as one of 22 "Smarter Cities" for energy by the Natural Resources Defense Council. Criteria: investment in green power; energy efficiency measures; conservation. *Natural Resources Defense Council, "2010 Smarter Cities," July 19, 2010*

- *American City Business Journal* ranked 43 metropolitan areas in terms of their "greenness." The Nashville metro area ranked #34. Criteria: Forty-one metros in which *ACBJ* has business weeklies, plus Indianapolis and Cleveland, were ranked based on 20 different indicators such as adoption of green technologies, utilization of environmentally sound practices, and air and water quality. *American City Business Journals, "Green City Index," March 11, 2010*

- The Nashville metro area was selected as one of "America's Cleanest Cities" by *Forbes*. The metro area ranked #6 out of 10. Criteria: toxic releases; air and water quality; per capita spending on Superfund site cleanup. *Forbes.com, "America's Cleanest Cities 2011," March 11, 2011*

- 100 of the largest metro areas in the U.S. were analyzed in terms of their current drought severity. The Nashville metro area ranked #6 (#1 = driest). The rankings were based on statistics such as long-term precipitation trends and patterns and the Palmer drought indices. *Sperling's BestPlaces, www.BestPlaces.net, "America's Drought-Riskiest Cities," November 2007*

- The Nashville metro area appeared in *Country Home's* "Best Green Places" report. The area ranked #216 out of 379. Criteria: official energy policies; green power; green buildings; availability of fresh, locally grown food. *Country Home, "Best Green Places," 2008*

Health/Fitness Rankings

- The Nashville metro area was selected as one of the worst cities for bed bugs in America by Rollins corporation, the owner of seven pest control companies, including Orkin. The area ranked #40 based on the number of bed bug treatments from January to December 2011. *Rollins, "The Top 50 U.S. Cities for Bed Bugs," March 19, 2012*

- Nashville was identified as a "2011 Asthma Capital." The area ranked #10 out of the nation's 100 largest metropolitan areas. Twelve factors were used to identify the most challenging places to live for people with asthma: estimated prevalence; self-reported prevalence; crude death rate for asthma; annual pollen score; annual air quality; public smoking laws; number of board-certified asthma specialists; school inhaler access laws; rescue medication use; controller medication use; uninsured rate; poverty rate. *Asthma and Allergy Foundation of America, "2011 Asthma Capitals"*

- Nashville was identified as a "2011 Fall Allergy Capital." The area ranked #40 out of 100. Three groups of factors were used to identify the most severe cities for people with allergies during the fall season: annual pollen levels; medicine utilization; access to board-certified allergists. *Asthma and Allergy Foundation of America, "2011 Fall Allergy Capitals"*

- Nashville was identified as a "2012 Spring Allergy Capital." The area ranked #45 out of 100. Three groups of factors were used to identify the most severe cities for people with allergies during the spring season: annual pollen levels; medicine utilization; access to board-certified allergists. *Asthma and Allergy Foundation of America, "2012 Spring Allergy Capitals"*

- The makers of Breath Right Nasal Strips, in partnership with Sperling's BestPlaces, analyzed 50 metro areas and identified those U.S. cities most challenged by chronic nasal congestion. The Nashville metro area ranked #18. Criteria: tree, grass and weed pollens; molds and spores; air pollution; climate; smoking; purchase habits of congestion products; prescriptions of drugs for congestion relief; incidence of influenza. *Breathe Right Nasal Strips, "Most Congested Cities," October 3, 2011*

- The Nashville metro area appeared in the 2011 Gallup-Healthways Well-Being Index. The index, based on interviews with more than 350,000 Americans, measured jobs, finances, physical health, emotional state of mind and communities. The metro area ranked #48 out of 190. Criteria: life evaluation; emotional health; work environment; physical health; healthy behaviors; basic access (basic needs optimal for a healthy life, such as access to food and medicine, having health insurance and feeling safe while walking at night). *Gallup-Healthways, "State of Well-Being 2011"*

- The Nashville metro area was identified as one of "America's Most Stressful Cities" by *Sperling's BestPlaces*. The metro area ranked #30 out of 50. Criteria: unemployment rate; suicide rate; commute time; mental health; poor rest; alcohol use; violent crime rate; property crime rate; cloudy days annually. *Sperling's BestPlaces, www.BestPlaces.net, "Stressful Cities 2012*

- 50 of the largest metro areas in the U.S. were analyzed in terms of their health and fitness by the American College of Sports Medicine in their "American Fitness Index." The Nashville metro area ranked #31 (#1 = healthiest). Criteria: preventative health behaviors; levels of chronic disease; health care access; community resources and policies that support physical activity. *American College of Sports Medicine, "Health and Community Fitness Status of the 50 Largest Metropolitan Areas," August 1, 2011*

- *The Daily Beast* identified the 30 U.S. metro areas with the worst smoking habits. The Nashville metro area ranked #15. Sixty urban centers with populations of more than one million were ranked based on the following criteria: number of smokers; number of cigarettes smoked per day; fewest attempts to quit. *The Daily Beast, "30 Cities With Smoking Problems," January 3, 2011*

Real Estate Rankings

- *Fortune* ranked the 100 largest metro areas in the U.S. in terms of projected median home price change in 2010. The Nashville metro area ranked #48. *Fortune, "The 2010 Housing Outlook," December 9, 2009*

- The Nashville metro area was identified as one of the "Top 25 Real Estate Investment Markets" by *FinestExperts.com*. The metro area ranked #16. Over 10,000 real estate markets were analyzed to identify the most suitable places for real estate investors to seek stability and growth. Criteria: employment; rental markets; growth levels as offset by foreclosures. *FinestExperts.com, "Top 25 Real Estate Investment Markets," January 7, 2010*

- The nation's largest metro areas were analyzed in terms of the best places to buy bank-owned properties. The Nashville metro area ranked #9 out of 10. Criteria: at least 500 REO sales during the fourth quarter and an REO sales increase of at least five percent from a year ago. The areas selected posted the biggest discounts on the sales of bank-owned properties. *RealtyTrac, "Fourth Quarter and Year-End 2011 U.S. Foreclosure Sales Report: Shifting Towards Short Sales," February 28, 2012*

- The Nashville metro area appeared in a *Wall Street Journal* article ranking cities by "housing stress." The metro area was ranked #35 (#1 = most stress). Criteria: fraction of mortgage-holding homeowners with a monthly housing payment in excess of 30 percent of income; percentage of people without health insurance; unemployment rate. *The Wall Street Journal, "Which Cities Face Biggest Housing Risk," October 5, 2010*

- The Center for Housing Policy ranked 210 U.S. metropolitan areas by the fair market rent for a two-bedroom unit. The Nashville metro area was ranked #112. (#1 = most expensive) with a rent of $807. Criteria: Fair Market Rent (FMR) in effect during the fourth quarter of 2009 based on HUD's fiscal year 2010 FMRs. *The Center for Housing Policy, "Paycheck to Paycheck: Most to Least Expensive Rental Markets in 2009"*

- The Nashville metro area was identified as one of the markets with the best expected performance in home prices over the next 12 months. *Local Market Monitor, "First Quarter Home Price Forecast for Largest US Markets," March 2, 2011*

- The Nashville metro area was identified as one of the best U.S. markets to invest in rental property" by HomeVestors and Local Market Monitor. The area ranked #48 out of 100. Criteria: risk-return premium relative to national average. *HomeVestors and Local Market Monitor, "Best 100 U.S. Markets to Invest in Rental Property," March 9, 2012*

Safety Rankings

- The National Insurance Crime Bureau ranked 366 metro areas in the U.S. in terms of per capita rates of vehicle theft. The Nashville metro area ranked #158 (#1 = highest rate). Criteria: number of vehicle theft offenses per 100,000 inhabitants in 2010. *National Insurance Crime Bureau, "Hot Spots," June 21, 2011*

- The Nashville metro area was identified as one of the most dangerous metro areas for pedestrians by Transportation for America. The metro area ranked #14 out of 52 metro areas with over 1 million residents. Criteria: area's population divided by the number of pedestrian fatalities in that area. *Transportation for America, "Dangerous by Design 2011"*

Seniors/Retirement Rankings

- Bankers Life and Casualty Company, in partnership with Sperling's BestPlaces, ranked the nation's 50 largest metro areas in terms of the "Best U.S. Cities for Seniors." The Nashville metro area ranked #28. Criteria: healthcare; transportation; housing; environment; economy; health and longevity; social and spiritual life; crime. *Bankers Life and Casualty Company, Center for a Secure Retirement, "Best U.S. Cities for Seniors 2011," September 2011*

- The Nashville metro area was identified as one of "America's Most Affordable Places to Retire" by *Forbes*. The metro area ranked #10. Criteria: housing affordability; inflation; number of persons over 65 who are employed; net migration for persons over 65; percent of persons over 65 living below poverty level; doctors per capita; number of citizens tapping their Medicare benefits per thousand people. *Forbes.com, "America's Most Affordable Places to Retire," September 5, 2008*

- The Nashville metro area was selected as one of "America's Best Places to Grow Old" by *Forbes*. The area was ranked #10 out of 10. Criteria: housing affordability; inflationary pressures; number of persons over 65 who are currently employed; net migration for persons over 65; percent of seniors living below poverty level; doctors per capita; number of citizens tapping their Medicare benefits per 1,000 people. *Forbes, "America's Best Places to Grow Old," December 12, 2008*

Sports/Recreation Rankings

- Murfreesboro appeared on the *Sporting News* list of the "Best Sports Cities" for 2011. The area ranked #150 out of 271 cities in the U.S. *Sporting News* takes a 12-month snapshot of each city's sports, putting a heavy premium on regular-season won-lost records (from the most recently completed season). Other criteria include: playoff berths, bowl appearances and tournament bids; championships; applicable power ratings; quality of competition; overall fan fervor (measured in part by attendance); abundance of teams (rewarding quality over quantity); stadium and arena quality; ticket availability and prices; franchise ownership; and marquee appeal of athletes. *Sporting News, "Best Sports Cities 2011," October 4, 2011*

- The Nashville was selected as one of the best metro areas for golf in America by *Golf Digest*. The Nashville area was ranked #9 out of 20. Criteria: climate; cost of public golf; quality of public golf; accessibility. *Golf Digest, "The Top 20 Cities for Golf," October 2011*

Transportation Rankings

- The Nashville metro area appeared on *Forbes* list of the best and worst cities for commuters. The metro area ranked #49 out of 60 (#1 is best). Criteria: travel time; road congestion; travel delays. *Forbes.com, "Best and Worst Cities for Commuters," February 16, 2010*

Women/Minorities Rankings

- Nashville was ranked #56 out of 100 metro areas in *SELF Magazine's* ranking of America's healthiest places for women." A panel of experts came up with more than 50 criteria including death and disease rates, environmental indicators, community resources, and lifestyle habits. *SELF Magazine, "Secrets of America's Healthiest Women," December 2008*

- Nashville appeared on *Black Enterprise's* list of the "Ten Best Cities for African Americans." The top picks were culled from more than 2,000 interactive surveys completed on *BlackEnterprise.com* and by editorial staff evaluation. The editors weighed the following criteria as it pertained to African Americans in each city: median household income; percentage of households earning more than $100,000; percentage of businesses owned; percentage of college graduates; unemployment rates; home loan rejections; and homeownership rates. *Black Enterprise, May 2007*

- The Nashville metro area appeared on *Forbes'* list of the "Best Cities for Minority Entrepreneurs." The area ranked #56 out of 10. Criteria: 52 metropolitan statistical areas were examined. For each ethnicity (African Americans, Asians and Hispanics), the editors measured housing affordability, population growth, income growth, and entrepreneurship (per capita self-employment). *Forbes, "Best Cities for Minority Entrepreneurs," March 23, 2011*

Miscellaneous Rankings

- The Nashville metro area was selected as one of "The Best U.S. Cities for Bargain Shopping" by *Forbes*. The area ranked #9 out of 10. Criteria: number of outlet stores; gross leasable retail space in major malls; low consumer price index; low sales tax rate. Indicators were examined in the nation's 50 largest metropolitan areas. *Forbes, "The Best U.S. Cities for Bargain Shopping," January 20, 2012*

- Energizer Holdings, the makers of Edge® shave gel, in partnership with Sperling's BestPlaces, ranked 50 major metro areas in terms of everyday irritations. The Nashville metro area ranked #19. Criteria: humidity levels; weather conditions; incidence of traffic delays and congestion; average commute times; frequency of flight delays and cancellations; rates of sleeplessness; underemployment; pollens and allergens; pests; comedy clubs per capita. *Energizer Holdings, "Most Irritation Prone Cities," July 23, 2010*

- Mars Chocolate North America, the makers of COMBOS®, in partnership with Sperling's BestPlaces, ranked 50 major metro areas in terms of their "manliness." The Nashville metro area ranked #1. Criteria: number of professional sports teams; number of nearby NASCAR tracks and racing events; manly lifestyle; concentration of manly retail stores; manly occupations per capita; salty snack sales; "Board of Manliness" rankings. *Mars Chocolate North America, "America's Manliest Cities 2011," September 1, 2011*

Business Environment

CITY FINANCES

City Government Finances

Component	2009 ($000)	2009 ($ per capita)
Total Revenues	354,814	3,606
Total Expenditures	357,398	3,632
Debt Outstanding	342,983	3,485
Cash and Securities[1]	165,462	1,681

*Note: (1) Cash and security holdings of a government at the close of its fiscal
year, including those of its dependent agencies, utilities, and liquor stores.*
Source: U.S Census Bureau, State & Local Government Finances 2009

City Government Revenue by Source

Source	2009 ($000)	2009 ($ per capita)
General Revenue		
From Federal Government	9,321	95
From State Government	48,177	490
From Local Governments	52,707	536
Taxes		
Property	34,307	349
Sales and Gross Receipts	9,365	95
Personal Income	0	0
Corporate Income	0	0
Motor Vehicle License	0	0
Other Taxes	3,555	36
Current Charges	22,108	225
Liquor Store	0	0
Utility	160,685	1,633
Employee Retirement	0	0

Source: U.S Census Bureau, State & Local Government Finances 2009

City Government Expenditures by Function

Function	2009 ($000)	2009 ($ per capita)	2009 (%)
General Direct Expenditures			
Air Transportation	978	10	0.3
Corrections	0	0	0.0
Education	62,185	632	17.4
Employment Security Administration	0	0	0.0
Financial Administration	3,810	39	1.1
Fire Protection	15,064	153	4.2
General Public Buildings	0	0	0.0
Governmental Administration, Other	3,390	34	0.9
Health	0	0	0.0
Highways	26,661	271	7.5
Hospitals	0	0	0.0
Housing and Community Development	882	9	0.2
Interest on General Debt	3,346	34	0.9
Judicial and Legal	1,213	12	0.3
Libraries	682	7	0.2
Parking	141	1	0.0
Parks and Recreation	16,048	163	4.5
Police Protection	22,056	224	6.2
Public Welfare	137	1	0.0
Sewerage	8,380	85	2.3
Solid Waste Management	5,169	53	1.4
Veterans' Services	0	0	0.0
Liquor Store	0	0	0.0
Utility	180,010	1,829	50.4
Employee Retirement	0	0	0.0

Source: U.S Census Bureau, State & Local Government Finances 2009

Municipal Bond Ratings

Area	Moody's	S&P	Fitch
City	n/a	n/a	n/a

Rating Systems (shown in declining order of credit quality): Moody's– Aaa, Aa, A, Baa, Ba, B, Caa, Ca, C (numerical modifiers 1, 2, and 3 are added to letter-rating); S&P– AAA, AA, A, BBB, BB, B, CCC, CC, C; Fitch– AAA, AA, A, BBB, BB, B, CCC, CC, C. Ratings may be modified by the addition of a plus or minus sign to show relative standing within the major rating categories.
Notes: n/a Not Available; w/d Withdrawn (1) Not Reviewed; (2) Issuer Rating/No General Obligation; (3) Standard and Poor's Issue Credit Rating (ICR) is a current opinion of an obliger with respect to a specific financial obligation, a specific class of financial obligations, or a specific financial program.
Source: U.S. Census Bureau, 2012 Statistical Abstract, Bond Ratings for City Governments by Largest Cities: 2010

DEMOGRAPHICS

Population Growth

Area	1990 Census	2000 Census	2010 Census	Population Growth (%) 1990-2000	2000-2010
City	47,905	68,816	108,755	43.7	58.0
MSA[1]	1,048,218	1,311,789	1,589,934	25.1	21.2
U.S.	248,709,873	281,421,906	308,745,538	13.2	9.7

Note: (1) Figures cover the Nashville-Davidson—Murfreesboro—Franklin, TN Metropolitan Statistical Area—see Appendix B for areas included
Source: U.S. Census Bureau, 2010 Census

Household Size

Area	Persons in Household (%) One	Two	Three	Four	Five	Six	Seven or More	Average Household Size
City	27.3	32.3	17.6	14.4	5.6	1.8	1.0	2.49
MSA[1]	26.8	33.3	16.8	13.6	6.0	2.2	1.4	2.52
U.S.	26.7	32.8	16.1	13.4	6.5	2.6	1.9	2.58

Note: (1) Figures cover the Nashville-Davidson—Murfreesboro—Franklin, TN Metropolitan Statistical Area—see Appendix B for areas included
Source: U.S. Census Bureau, 2010 Census

Race

Area	White Alone[2] (%)	Black Alone[2] (%)	Asian Alone[2] (%)	AIAN[3] Alone[2] (%)	NHOPI[4] Alone[2] (%)	Other Race Alone[2] (%)	Two or More Races (%)
City	75.6	15.2	3.4	0.3	0.0	2.8	2.7
MSA[1]	76.9	15.2	2.3	0.3	0.1	3.2	2.1
U.S.	72.4	12.6	4.8	0.9	0.2	6.2	2.9

Note: (1) Figures cover the Nashville-Davidson—Murfreesboro—Franklin, TN Metropolitan Statistical Area—see Appendix B for areas included; (2) Alone is defined as not being in combination with one or more other races; (3) American Indian and Alaska Native; (4) Native Hawaiian and Other Pacific Islander
Source: U.S. Census Bureau, 2010 Census

Hispanic or Latino Origin

Area	Hispanic or Latino (%)	Mexican (%)	Puerto Rican (%)	Cuban (%)	Other Hispanic or Latino (%)
City	5.9	3.7	0.5	0.2	1.6
MSA[1]	6.6	4.1	0.4	0.2	1.9
U.S.	16.3	10.3	1.5	0.6	4.0

Note: Persons of Hispanic or Latino origin can be of any race; (1) Figures cover the Nashville-Davidson—Murfreesboro—Franklin, TN Metropolitan Statistical Area—see Appendix B for areas included
Source: U.S. Census Bureau, 2010 Census

Segregation

Type	Segregation Indices[1]				Percent Change		
	1990	2000	2010	2010 Rank[2]	1990-2000	1990-2010	2000-2010
Black/White	60.7	58.1	56.2	49	-2.6	-4.4	-1.9
Asian/White	45.2	44.4	41.0	51	-0.8	-4.2	-3.4
Hispanic/White	24.3	46.0	47.9	34	21.6	23.5	1.9

Note: Figures are based on an analysis of 1990, 2000, and 2010 Census Decennial Census tract data by William H. Frey, Brookings Institution and the University of Michigan Social Science Data Analysis Network. In this analysis all racial groups (whites, blacks, and asians) are non-Hispanic members of those races. Hispanics are shown as a separate category; All figures cover the Metropolitan Statistical Area (see Appendix B for areas included); (1) Segregation Indices are Dissimilarity Indices that measure the degree to which the minority group is distributed differently than whites across census tracts. They range from 0 (complete integration) to 100 (complete segregation) where the value indicates the percentage of the minority group that needs to move to be distributed exactly like whites; (2) Ranges from 1 (most segregated) to 102 (least segregated); n/a not available.
Source: www.CensusScope.org

Ancestry

Area	German	Irish	English	American	Italian	Polish	French[2]	Scottish	Dutch
City	12.5	11.4	9.7	12.3	2.8	1.2	2.4	2.4	1.3
MSA[1]	11.7	12.1	11.4	12.6	2.7	1.2	2.4	2.6	1.3
U.S.	16.1	11.6	8.8	6.1	5.7	3.2	3.0	1.9	1.6

Note: Figures are the percentage of the total population reporting a particular ancestry. The nine most commonly reported ancestries in the U.S. are shown. Figures include multiple ancestries (e.g. if a person reported being Irish and Italian, they were included in both columns); (1) Figures cover the Nashville-Davidson—Murfreesboro—Franklin, TN Metropolitan Statistical Area—see Appendix B for areas included; (2) Excludes Basque
Source: U.S. Census Bureau, 2008-2010 American Community Survey 3-Year Estimates

Foreign-Born Population

Area	Percent of Population Born in								
	Any Foreign Country	Mexico	Asia	Europe	Carribean	South America	Central America[2]	Africa	Canada
City	n/a	n/a	n/a	n/a	n/a	n/a	n/a	n/a	n/a
MSA[1]	7.5	2.2	2.2	0.6	0.2	0.3	0.9	0.8	0.2
U.S.	12.8	3.8	3.6	1.6	1.2	0.9	1.0	0.5	0.3

Note: (1) Figures cover the Nashville-Davidson—Murfreesboro—Franklin, TN Metropolitan Statistical Area—see Appendix B for areas included; (2) Excludes Mexico.
Source: U.S. Census Bureau, 2008-2010 American Community Survey 3-Year Estimates

Marital Status

Area	Never Married	Now Married[2]	Separated	Widowed	Divorced
City	39.5	43.9	1.7	4.7	10.3
MSA[1]	30.3	50.8	2.0	5.2	11.8
U.S.	31.6	49.6	2.2	6.1	10.7

Note: Figures are percentages and cover the population 15 years of age and older; (1) Figures cover the Nashville-Davidson—Murfreesboro—Franklin, TN Metropolitan Statistical Area—see Appendix B for areas included; (2) Excludes separated
Source: U.S. Census Bureau, 2008-2010 American Community Survey 3-Year Estimates

Age

Area	Percent of Population							Median Age
	Under Age 5	Age 5 to 17	Age 18 to 34	Age 35 to 49	Age 50 to 64	Age 65 to 79	80 Years and Over	
City	7.1	16.4	35.7	19.1	13.6	5.9	2.2	29.0
MSA[1]	6.9	17.5	24.6	21.9	18.4	8.0	2.7	35.7
U.S.	6.5	17.5	23.2	20.7	19.0	9.4	3.6	37.2

Note: (1) Figures cover the Nashville-Davidson—Murfreesboro—Franklin, TN Metropolitan Statistical Area—see Appendix B for areas included
Source: U.S. Census Bureau, 2010 Census

Male/Female Ratio

Area	Males	Females	Males per 100 Females
City	53,422	55,333	96.5
MSA[1]	777,473	812,461	95.7
U.S.	151,781,326	156,964,212	96.7

Note: (1) Figures cover the Nashville-Davidson—Murfreesboro—Franklin, TN Metropolitan Statistical Area—see Appendix B for areas included
Source: U.S. Census Bureau, 2010 Census

Religious Groups

Area	Catholic	Baptist	Non-Den.	Methodist[2]	Lutheran	LDS[3]	Pente-costal	Presby-terian[4]	Muslim[5]	Judaism
MSA[1]	4.1	25.3	5.8	6.1	0.4	0.8	2.2	2.1	0.2	0.4
U.S.	19.1	9.3	4.0	4.0	2.3	2.0	1.9	1.6	0.8	0.7

Note: Figures are the number of adherents as a percentage of the total population; (1) Figures cover the Nashville-Davidson—Murfreesboro—Franklin, TN Metropolitan Statistical Area—see Appendix B for areas included; (2) Methodist/Pietist; (3) Latter Day Saints; (4) Reformed; (5) Figures are estimates
Source: Association of Statisticians of American Religious Bodies, 2010 U.S. Religion Census: Religious Congregations & Membership Study

ECONOMY

Gross Metropolitan Product

Area	2007	2008	2009	2010	2010 Rank[2]
MSA[1]	75.4	77.9	76.4	80.3	40

Note: Figures are in billions of dollars; (1) Figures cover the Nashville-Davidson—Murfreesboro—Franklin, TN Metropolitan Statistical Area—see Appendix B for areas included; (2) Rank ranges from 1 to 363
Source: The United States Conference of Mayors, "U.S. Metro Economies: GMP and Employment Forecasts," June 2011

Economic Growth

Area	2007-2009 (%)	2010 (%)	2011 (%)	Rank[2]
MSA[1]	-1.3	4.2	2.7	173
U.S.	-1.3	2.9	2.5	–

Note: Figures are real Gross Metropolitan Product growth rates and represent annual average percent change; (1) Figures cover the Nashville-Davidson—Murfreesboro—Franklin, TN Metropolitan Statistical Area—see Appendix B for areas included; (2) Rank ranges from 1 to 363
Source: The United States Conference of Mayors, "U.S. Metro Economies: GMP and Employment Forecasts," June 2011

Metropolitan Area Exports

Area	2005	2006	2007	2008	2009	2010	2010 Rank[2]
MSA[1]	5,020.6	5,388.6	5,105.9	5,259.5	4,406.6	5,748.5	41

Note: Figures are in millions of dollars; (1) Figures cover the Nashville-Davidson—Murfreesboro—Franklin, TN Metropolitan Statistical Area—see Appendix B for areas included; (2) Rank ranges from 1 to 369
Source: U.S. Department of Commerce, International Trade Administration, Office of Trade & Industry Information, Manufacturing & Services, data extracted April 2, 2012

INCOME

Income

Area	Per Capita ($)	Median Household ($)	Average Household ($)
City	24,152	47,662	61,727
MSA[1]	26,953	50,837	68,640
U.S.	26,942	51,222	70,116

Note: (1) Figures cover the Nashville-Davidson—Murfreesboro—Franklin, TN Metropolitan Statistical Area—see Appendix B for areas included
Source: U.S. Census Bureau, 2008-2010 American Community Survey 3-Year Estimates

Household Income Distribution

Area	Percent of Households Earning							
	Under $15,000	$15,000 -24,999	$25,000 -34,999	$35,000 -49,999	$50,000 -74,999	$75,000 -99,000	$100,000 -149,999	$150,000 and up
City	14.7	10.7	10.2	16.4	17.8	12.9	12.3	5.1
MSA[1]	12.4	10.3	10.7	15.7	19.4	12.4	11.4	7.6
U.S.	13.0	11.0	10.6	14.2	18.5	12.1	12.2	8.4

Note: (1) Figures cover the Nashville-Davidson—Murfreesboro—Franklin, TN Metropolitan Statistical Area—see Appendix B for areas included
Source: U.S. Census Bureau, 2008-2010 American Community Survey 3-Year Estimates

Poverty Rate

Area	All Ages	Under 18 Years Old	18 to 64 Years Old	65 Years and Over
City	18.3	21.5	18.8	5.5
MSA[1]	13.9	19.6	12.4	9.3
U.S.	14.4	20.1	13.1	9.4

Note: Figures are percentage of people whose income during the past 12 months was below the poverty level; (1) Figures cover the Nashville-Davidson—Murfreesboro—Franklin, TN Metropolitan Statistical Area—see Appendix B for areas included
Source: U.S. Census Bureau, 2008-2010 American Community Survey 3-Year Estimates

Personal Bankruptcy Filing Rate

Area	2006	2007	2008	2009	2010	2011
Rutherford County	3.92	4.78	6.36	7.27	6.86	6.22
U.S.	2.00	2.73	3.53	4.61	4.97	4.37

Note: Numbers are per 1,000 population and include Chapter 7 and Chapter 13 filings
Source: Federal Deposit Insurance Corporation, Regional Economic Conditions, March 9, 2012

EMPLOYMENT

Labor Force and Employment

Area	Civilian Labor Force			Workers Employed		
	Dec. 2010	Dec. 2011	% Chg.	Dec. 2010	Dec. 2011	% Chg.
City	56,085	56,571	0.9	51,593	52,687	2.1
MSA[1]	823,775	831,576	0.9	758,483	774,567	2.1
U.S.	153,156,000	153,373,000	0.1	139,159,000	140,681,000	1.1

Note: Data is not seasonally adjusted and covers workers 16 years of age and older; (1) Metropolitan Statistical Area—see Appendix B for areas included
Source: Bureau of Labor Statistics, http://stats.bls.gov

Unemployment Rate

Area	2011											
	Jan.	Feb.	Mar.	Apr.	May	Jun.	Jul.	Aug.	Sep.	Oct.	Nov.	Dec.
City	8.9	8.8	8.4	8.7	8.9	9.7	9.2	9.2	9.0	7.9	7.4	6.9
MSA[1]	8.8	8.8	8.3	8.6	8.4	8.9	8.4	8.5	8.5	7.6	7.2	6.9
U.S.	9.8	9.5	9.2	8.7	8.7	9.3	9.3	9.1	8.8	8.5	8.2	8.3

Note: Data is not seasonally adjusted and covers workers 16 years of age and older; All figures are percentages; (1) Metropolitan Statistical Area—see Appendix B for areas included
Source: Bureau of Labor Statistics, http://stats.bls.gov

Projected Unemployment Rate

Area	2010 (%)	2011 (%)	2012 (%)	2013 (%)
MSA[1]	8.4	8.0	7.3	6.8

Note: (1) Metropolitan Statistical Area—see Appendix B for areas included
Source: The United States Conference of Mayors, "U.S. Metro Economies: GMP and Employment Forecasts," June 2011

Employment by Occupation

Occupation Classification	City (%)	MSA[1] (%)	U.S. (%)
Management, Business, Science, and Arts	36.3	37.0	35.6
Natural Resources, Construction, and Maintenance	7.8	8.8	9.5
Production, Transportation, and Material Moving	10.5	11.6	12.1
Sales and Office	27.1	27.0	25.2
Service	18.3	15.5	17.6

Note: Figures cover employed civilians 16 years of age and older; (1) Figures cover the
Nashville-Davidson—Murfreesboro—Franklin, TN Metropolitan Statistical Area—see Appendix B for areas
included
Source: U.S. Census Bureau, 2008-2010 American Community Survey 3-Year Estimates

Employment by Industry

Sector	MSA[1] Number of Employees	MSA[1] Percent of Total	U.S. Percent of Total
Construction	n/a	n/a	4.1
Education and Health Services	120,800	15.9	15.2
Financial Activities	46,600	6.1	5.8
Government	104,600	13.7	16.8
Information	18,800	2.5	2.0
Leisure and Hospitality	77,500	10.2	9.9
Manufacturing	62,900	8.3	8.9
Mining and Logging	n/a	n/a	0.6
Other Services	33,100	4.3	4.0
Professional and Business Services	110,500	14.5	13.3
Retail Trade	86,200	11.3	11.5
Transportation and Utilities	30,500	4.0	3.8
Wholesale Trade	36,900	4.8	4.2

Note: Figures cover non-farm employment as of December 2011 and are not seasonally adjusted;
(1) Metropolitan Statistical Area—see Appendix B for areas included; n/a not available
Source: Bureau of Labor Statistics, http://stats.bls.gov

Occupations with Greatest Projected Employment Growth: 2008 – 2018

Occupation[1]	2008 Employment	2018 Projected Employment	Numeric Employment Change	Percent Employment Change
Registered Nurses	61,600	71,750	10,150	16.5
Customer Service Representatives	55,110	63,610	8,500	15.4
Home Health Aides	13,700	21,800	8,100	59.1
Truck Drivers, Heavy and Tractor-Trailer	64,760	72,460	7,700	11.9
Combined Food Preparation and Serving Workers, Including Fast Food	64,590	71,850	7,260	11.2
Retail Salespersons	84,220	91,130	6,910	8.2
Office Clerks, General	65,370	71,770	6,400	9.8
Elementary School Teachers, Except Special Education	33,140	39,390	6,250	18.9
Nursing Aides, Orderlies, and Attendants	30,710	35,800	5,090	16.6
Licensed Practical and Licensed Vocational Nurses	25,390	30,390	5,000	19.7

Note: Projections cover Tennessee; (1) Sorted by numeric employment change
Source: www.projectionscentral.com, State Occupational Projections, 2008–2018 Long-Term Projections

Murfreesboro, Tennessee 439

Fastest Growing Occupations: 2008 – 2018

Occupation[1]	2008 Employment	2018 Projected Employment	Numeric Employment Change	Percent Employment Change
Biomedical Engineers	250	410	160	64.0
Home Health Aides	13,700	21,800	8,100	59.1
Network Systems and Data Communications Analysts	3,000	4,500	1,500	50.0
Medical Scientists, Except Epidemiologists	820	1,140	320	39.0
Physician Assistants	1,370	1,880	510	37.2
Commercial Pilots	350	480	130	37.1
Self-Enrichment Education Teachers	2,890	3,960	1,070	37.0
Financial Examiners	790	1,080	290	36.7
Psychiatric Aides	980	1,330	350	35.7
Personal and Home Care Aides	14,070	18,950	4,880	34.7

Note: Projections cover Tennessee; (1) Sorted by percent employment change and excludes occupations with numeric employment change less than 100
Source: www.projectionscentral.com, State Occupational Projections, 2008–2018 Long-Term Projections

Average Wages

Occupation	$/Hr.	Occupation	$/Hr.
Accountants and Auditors	29.64	Maids and Housekeeping Cleaners	9.10
Automotive Mechanics	17.30	Maintenance and Repair Workers	16.90
Bookkeepers	16.00	Marketing Managers	46.60
Carpenters	18.06	Nuclear Medicine Technologists	30.05
Cashiers	9.78	Nurses, Licensed Practical	18.81
Clerks, General Office	14.45	Nurses, Registered	30.99
Clerks, Receptionists/Information	12.64	Nursing Aides/Orderlies/Attendants	11.45
Clerks, Shipping/Receiving	13.85	Packers and Packagers, Hand	9.93
Computer Programmers	35.55	Physical Therapists	35.11
Computer Support Specialists	23.80	Postal Service Mail Carriers	24.48
Computer Systems Analysts	34.26	Real Estate Brokers	28.42
Cooks, Restaurant	11.15	Retail Salespersons	11.58
Dentists	70.70	Sales Reps., Exc. Tech./Scientific	28.49
Electrical Engineers	39.66	Sales Reps., Tech./Scientific	34.32
Electricians	20.54	Secretaries, Exc. Legal/Med./Exec.	14.84
Financial Managers	51.34	Security Guards	10.98
First-Line Supervisors/Managers, Sales	19.94	Surgeons	n/a
Food Preparation Workers	10.50	Teacher Assistants	10.90
General and Operations Managers	47.06	Teachers, Elementary School	22.30
Hairdressers/Cosmetologists	12.59	Teachers, Secondary School	22.70
Internists	82.01	Telemarketers	14.74
Janitors and Cleaners	9.99	Truck Drivers, Heavy/Tractor-Trailer	18.79
Landscaping/Groundskeeping Workers	11.26	Truck Drivers, Light/Delivery Svcs.	16.57
Lawyers	53.12	Waiters and Waitresses	9.18

Note: Wage data covers the Nashville-Davidson—Murfreesboro—Franklin, TN Metropolitan Statistical Area—see Appendix B for areas included. Hourly wages for elementary/secondary school teachers and teacher assistants were calculated by the editors from annual wage data assuming a 40 hour work week; n/a not available.
Source: Bureau of Labor Statistics, Metro Area Occupational Employment and Wage Estimates, May 2011

RESIDENTIAL REAL ESTATE

Building Permits

Area	Single-Family			Multi-Family			Total		
	2010	2011	Pct. Chg.	2010	2011	Pct. Chg.	2010	2011	Pct. Chg.
City	346	400	15.6	184	8	-95.7	530	408	-23.0
MSA[1]	3,938	4,100	4.1	1,154	1,294	12.1	5,092	5,394	5.9
U.S.	447,311	418,498	-6.4	157,299	205,563	30.7	604,610	624,061	3.2

Note: (1) Metropolitan Statistical Area—see Appendix B for areas included; figures represent new, privately-owned housing units authorized (unadjusted data); All permit data are based on estimates with imputation.
Source: U.S. Census Bureau, Manufacturing, Mining, and Construction Statistics, Building Permits, 2010, 2011

Homeownership Rate

Area	2005 (%)	2006 (%)	2007 (%)	2008 (%)	2009 (%)	2010 (%)	2011 (%)
MSA[1]	73.0	72.4	70.0	71.3	71.8	70.4	69.6
U.S.	68.9	68.8	68.1	67.8	67.4	66.9	66.1

Note: (1) Metropolitan Statistical Area—see Appendix B for areas included
Source: U.S. Census Bureau, Housing Vacancies and Homeownership Annual Statistics: 2011

Housing Vacancy Rates

Area	Gross Vacancy Rate[2] (%)			Year-Round Vacancy Rate[3] (%)			Rental Vacancy Rate[4] (%)			Homeowner Vacancy Rate[5] (%)		
	2009	2010	2011	2009	2010	2011	2009	2010	2011	2009	2010	2011
MSA[1]	8.7	10.9	9.0	8.1	10.5	8.3	8.3	8.2	8.2	1.9	2.4	2.2
U.S.	14.5	14.3	14.2	11.3	11.3	11.1	10.6	10.2	9.5	2.6	2.6	2.5

Note: (1) Metropolitan Statistical Area—see Appendix B for areas included; (2) The percentage of the total housing inventory that is vacant; (3) The percentage of the housing inventory (excluding seasonal units) that is year-round vacant; (4) The percentage of rental inventory that is vacant for rent; (5) The percentage of homeowner inventory that is vacant for sale
Source: U.S. Census Bureau, Housing Vacancies and Homeownership Annual Statistics: 2011

TAXES

State Corporate Income Tax Rates

State	Tax Rate (%)	Income Brackets ($)	Num. of Brackets	Financial Institution Tax Rate (%)[a]	Federal Income Tax Ded.
Tennessee	6.5	Flat rate	1	6.5	No

Note: Tax rates as of January 1, 2012; (a) Rates listed are the corporate income tax rate applied to financial institutions or excise taxes based on income. Some states have other taxes based upon the value of deposits or shares.
Source: Federation of Tax Administrators, "State Corporate Income Tax Rates, 2012"

State Individual Income Tax Rates

State	Tax Rate (%)	Income Brackets ($)	Num. of Brackets	Personal Exempt. ($)[1] Single	Dependents	Fed. Inc. Tax Ded.
Tennessee – State Income Tax of 6% on Dividends and Interest Income Only						

Note: Tax rates as of January 1, 2012; Local- and county-level taxes are not included; n/a not applicable; (1) Married joint filers generally receive double the single exemption
Source: Federation of Tax Administrators, "State Individual Income Tax Rates, 2012"

Various State and Local Tax Rates

State	State and Local Sales and Use (%)	State Sales and Use (%)	Gasoline[1] (¢/gal.)	Cigarette[2] ($/pack)	Spirits[3] ($/gal.)	Wine[4] ($/gal.)	Beer[5] ($/gal.)
Tennessee	9.75	7.00	21.4	0.62	4.46 (h)	1.27	0.14

Note: All tax rates as of January 1, 2012 except beer, wine and spirits (September 1, 2011); (1) The American Petroleum Institute has developed a methodology for determining the average tax rate on a gallon of fuel. Rates may include any of the following: excise taxes, environmental fees, storage tank fees, other fees or taxes, general sales tax, and local taxes. In states where gasoline is subject to the general sales tax, or where the fuel tax is based on the average sale price, the average rate determined by API is sensitive to changes in the price of gasoline. States that fully or partially apply general sales taxes to gasoline: CA, CO, GA, IL, IN, MI, NY; (2) The federal excise tax of $1.0066 per pack and local taxes are not included; (3) Rates are those applicable to off-premise sales of 40% alcohol by volume (a.b.v.) distilled spirits in 750ml containers. Local excise taxes are excluded; (4) Rates are those applicable to off-premise sales of 11% a.b.v. non-carbonated wine in 750ml containers; (5) Rates are those applicable to off-premise sales of 4.7% a.b.v. beer in 12 ounce containers; (h) Includes case fees and/or bottle fees which may vary with the size of the container.
Source: Tax Foundation, 2012 Facts & Figures: How Does Your State Compare?

State-Local Tax Burdens

Area	Rate (%)	Rank[1]	Per Capita Taxes Paid to Home State ($)	Total State and Local Per Capita Taxes Paid ($)	Per Capita Income ($)
Tennessee	7.6	47	1,851	2,752	36,157
U.S. Average	9.8	-	3,057	4,160	42,539

Note: Figures cover 2009; (1) Rank ranges from 1 to 50 where 1 is highest tax burden
Source: Tax Foundation, State-Local Tax Burdens, All States, 2009

State Business Tax Climate Index Rankings

State	Overall Rank	Corporate Tax Index Rank	Individual Income Tax Index Rank	Sales Tax Index Rank	Unemployment Insurance Tax Index Rank	Property Tax Index Rank
Tennessee	14	13	8	43	27	48

Note: The index is a measure of how each state's tax laws affect economic performance. The lower the rank, the more favorable a state's tax system is for business. States without a given tax are given a ranking of 1.
Source: Tax Foundation, Major Components of the State Business Tax Climate Index, FY 2012

COMMERCIAL UTILITIES

Typical Monthly Electric Bills

Area	Commercial Service ($/month)		Industrial Service ($/month)	
	1,500 kWh	40 kW demand 14,000 kWh	1,000 kW demand 200,000 kWh	50,000 kW demand 15,000,000 kWh
City	n/a	n/a	n/a	n/a
Average[1]	189	1,616	25,197	1,470,813

Note: Based on total rates in effect July 1, 2011; (1) average based on 184 utilities surveyed; n/a not available
Source: Edison Electric Institute, Typical Bills and Average Rates Report, Summer 2011

TRANSPORTATION

Means of Transportation to Work

Area	Car/Truck/Van		Public Transportation			Bicycle	Walked	Other Means	Worked at Home
	Drove Alone	Car-pooled	Bus	Subway	Railroad				
City	85.0	9.1	0.6	0.0	0.0	0.3	1.6	1.1	2.2
MSA[1]	81.2	10.7	1.0	0.0	0.1	0.2	1.3	1.0	4.5
U.S.	76.0	10.2	2.7	1.7	0.5	0.5	2.8	1.3	4.2

Note: Figures are percentages and cover workers 16 years of age and older; (1) Figures cover the Nashville-Davidson—Murfreesboro—Franklin, TN Metropolitan Statistical Area—see Appendix B for areas included
Source: U.S. Census Bureau, 2008-2010 American Community Survey 3-Year Estimates

Travel Time to Work

Area	Less Than 10 Minutes	10 to 19 Minutes	20 to 29 Minutes	30 to 44 Minutes	45 to 59 Minutes	60 to 89 Minutes	90 Minutes or More
City	14.4	33.8	16.8	17.4	10.4	5.4	1.9
MSA[1]	10.3	27.7	23.2	23.4	9.5	4.3	1.6
U.S.	13.9	30.1	20.8	19.8	7.5	5.5	2.5

Note: Figures are percentages and include workers 16 years old and over; (1) Figures cover the Nashville-Davidson—Murfreesboro—Franklin, TN Metropolitan Statistical Area—see Appendix B for areas included
Source: U.S. Census Bureau, 2008-2010 American Community Survey 3-Year Estimates

Travel Time Index

Area	1985	1990	1995	2000	2005	2010
Urban Area[1]	1.10	1.13	1.15	1.18	1.20	1.18
Average[2]	1.11	1.16	1.18	1.21	1.25	1.20

Note: Travel Time Index—the ratio of travel time in the peak period to the travel time at free-flow conditions. A value of 1.30 indicates a 20-minute free-flow trip takes 26 minutes in the peak. Free-flow speeds (60 mph on freeways and 35 mph on principal arterials) are used as the comparison threshold; (1) Covers the Nashville-Davidson TN urban area; (2) average of 439 urban areas
Source: Texas Transportation Institute, Urban Mobility Report 2011, September 2011

Public Transportation

Agency Name / Mode of Transportation	Vehicles Operated in Maximum Service	Annual Unlinked Passenger Trips ('000)	Annual Passenger Miles ('000)
City of Murfreesboro (Rover Public Transit)			
Bus (directly operated)	6	180.0	286.0
Demand Response (purchased transportation)	15	7.5	215.3

Source: Federal Transit Administration, National Transit Database, 2010

Air Transportation

Airport Name and Code / Type of Service	Passenger Airlines[1]	Passenger Enplanements	Freight Carriers[2]	Freight (lbs.)
Nashville Metropolitan (BNA)				
Domestic service (U.S. carriers - 2011)	40	4,647,288	19	48,386,088
International service (U.S. carriers - 2010)	10	3,149	0	0

Note: (1) Includes all U.S.-based major, minor and commuter airlines that carried at least one passenger during the year; (2) Includes all U.S.-based airlines and freight carriers that transported at least one pound of freight during the year
Source: Bureau of Transportation Statistics, The Intermodal Transportation Database, Air Carriers: T-100 Domestic Market (U.S. Carriers), 2011; Bureau of Transportation Statistics, The Intermodal Transportation Database, Air Carriers: T-100 International Market (U.S. Carriers), 2010

Other Transportation Statistics

Major Highways: I-24; SR-840 connecting to I-40 and I-65
Amtrak Service: No
Major Waterways/Ports: None
Source: Amtrak.com; Google Maps

BUSINESSES

Major Business Headquarters

Company Name	Rankings	
	Fortune[1]	Forbes[2]
No companies listed	-	-

Note: (1) Fortune 500—companies that produce a 10-K are ranked 1 to 500 based on 2010 revenue; (2) all private companies with at least $2 billion in annual revenue are ranked 1 to 212; companies listed are headquartered in the city; dashes indicate no ranking
Source: Fortune, "Fortune 500," May 23, 2011; Forbes, "America's Largest Private Companies," November 16, 2011

Minority- and Women-Owned Businesses

Group	All Firms		Firms with Paid Employees			
	Firms	Sales ($000)	Firms	Sales ($000)	Employees	Payroll ($000)
Asian	n/a	n/a	n/a	n/a	n/a	n/a
Black	n/a	n/a	n/a	n/a	n/a	n/a
Hispanic	n/a	n/a	n/a	n/a	n/a	n/a
Women	n/a	n/a	n/a	n/a	n/a	n/a
All Firms	1,934	2,789,376	312	2,716,049	7,705	331,658

Note: Figures cover firms located in the city; minority- and women-owned business are defined as firms in which the corresponding group own 51% or more of the stock or equity of the company; n/a not available
Source: U.S. Census Bureau, 2007 Economic Census, Survey of Business Owners

HOTELS

Hotels/Motels

Area	5 Star		4 Star		3 Star		2 Star		1 Star		Not Rated	
	Num.	Pct.[3]	Num.	Pct.[3]	Num.	Pct.[3]	Num.	Pct.[3]	Num.	Pct.[3]	Num.	Pct.[3]
City[1]	0	0.0	0	0.0	5	12.8	28	71.8	2	5.1	4	10.3
Total[2]	133	0.9	940	6.5	4,569	31.8	7,033	48.9	351	2.4	1,343	9.3

Note: (1) Figures cover Murfreesboro and vicinity; (2) Figures cover all 100 cities in this book; (3) Percentage of hotels which have a given star rating; Star ratings are determined by expedia.com and offer an indication of the general quality of a particular hotel.
Source: expedia.com, April 25, 2012

The Nashville-Davidson—Murfreesboro—Franklin, TN metro area is home to one of the best hotels in the U.S. according to *Travel & Leisure*: **Hermitage Hotel** (#91). Criteria: service; location; rooms; food; and value. *Travel & Leisure, "T+L 500, The World's Best Hotels 2012"*

EVENT SITES

Major Stadiums, Arenas, and Auditoriums

Name	Max. Capacity
Miller Coliseum	6,500

Source: Original research

Convention Centers

Name	Overall Space (sq. ft.)	Exhibit Space (sq. ft.)	Meeting Space (sq. ft.)	Meeting Rooms
Mid-Tn Expo Convention Center	n/a	n/a	n/a	n/a

Note: n/a not available
Source: Original research

Living Environment

COST OF LIVING

Cost of Living Index

Composite Index	Groceries	Housing	Utilities	Trans-portation	Health Care	Misc. Goods/ Services
88.2	94.7	78.4	84.0	95.6	89.2	93.0

Note: U.S. = 100; Figures cover the Murfreesboro-Smyrna TN urban area.
Source: The Council for Community and Economic Research, ACCRA Cost of Living Index, 2011

Grocery Prices

Area[1]	T-Bone Steak ($/pound)	Frying Chicken ($/pound)	Whole Milk ($/half gal.)	Eggs ($/dozen)	Orange Juice ($/64 oz.)	Coffee ($/11.5 oz.)
City[2]	8.41	1.06	1.76	1.40	2.80	4.00
Avg.	9.25	1.18	2.22	1.66	3.19	4.40
Min.	6.70	0.88	1.31	0.95	2.46	2.94
Max.	14.30	2.16	3.50	3.18	4.75	6.83

Note: (1) Values for the local area are compared with the average, minimum and maximum values for all 335 areas in the Cost of Living Index; (2) Figures cover the Murfreesboro-Smyrna TN urban area; **T-Bone Steak** *(price per pound);* **Frying Chicken** *(price per pound, whole fryer);* **Whole Milk** *(half gallon carton);* **Eggs** *(price per dozen, Grade A, large);* **Orange Juice** *(64 oz. Tropicana or Florida Natural);* **Coffee** *(11.5 oz. can, vacuum-packed, Maxwell House, Hills Bros, or Folgers).*
Source: The Council for Community and Economic Research, ACCRA Cost of Living Index, 2011

Housing and Utility Costs

Area[1]	New Home Price ($)	Apartment Rent ($/month)	All Electric ($/month)	Part Electric ($/month)	Other Energy ($/month)	Telephone ($/month)
City[2]	213,745	784	-	81.64	56.33	23.01
Avg.	285,990	839	163.23	89.00	77.52	26.92
Min.	188,005	460	125.58	45.39	33.89	17.98
Max.	1,197,028	3,244	339.16	181.97	348.69	40.01

Note: (1) Values for the local area are compared with the average, minimum and maximum values for all 335 areas in the Cost of Living Index; (2) Figures cover the Murfreesboro-Smyrna TN urban area; **New Home Price** *(2,400 sf living area, 8,000 sf lot, in urban area with full utilities);* **Apartment Rent** *(950 sf 2 bedroom/1.5 or 2 bath, unfurnished, excluding all utilities except water);* **All Electric** *(average monthly cost for an all-electric home);* **Part Electric** *(average monthly cost for a part-electric home);* **Other Energy** *(average monthly cost for natural gas, fuel oil, coal, wood, and any other forms of energy except electricity);* **Telephone** *(price includes basic monthly rate for a private residential line plus additional local usage charges incurred by a family of four).*
Source: The Council for Community and Economic Research, ACCRA Cost of Living Index, 2011

Health Care, Transportation, and Other Costs

Area[1]	Doctor ($/visit)	Dentist ($/visit)	Optometrist ($/visit)	Gasoline ($/gallon)	Beauty Salon ($/visit)	Men's Shirt ($)
City[2]	85.00	64.66	88.33	3.34	39.00	20.16
Avg.	93.88	81.72	90.54	3.48	32.65	25.06
Min.	60.00	55.33	53.66	3.18	19.78	13.44
Max.	154.98	145.97	183.72	4.31	63.21	46.00

Note: (1) Values for the local area are compared with the average, minimum and maximum values for all 335 areas in the Cost of Living Index; (2) Figures cover the Murfreesboro-Smyrna TN urban area; **Doctor** *(general practitioners routine exam of an established patient);* **Dentist** *(adult teeth cleaning and periodic oral examination);* **Optometrist** *(full vision eye exam for established adult patient);* **Gasoline** *(one gallon regular unleaded, national brand, including all taxes, cash price at self-service pump if available);* **Beauty Salon** *(woman's shampoo, trim, and blow-dry);* **Men's Shirt** *(cotton/polyester dress shirt, pinpoint weave, long sleeves).*
Source: The Council for Community and Economic Research, ACCRA Cost of Living Index, 2011

HOUSING

House Price Index (HPI)

Area	National Ranking[2]	Quarterly Change (%)	One-Year Change (%)	Five-Year Change (%)
MSA[1]	122	0.01	-1.98	-2.79
U.S.[3]	-	-0.10	-2.43	-19.16

Note: The HPI is a weighted repeat sales index. It measures average price changes in repeat sales or refinancings on the same properties. This information is obtained by reviewing repeat mortgage transactions on single-family properties whose mortgages have been purchased or securitized by Fannie Mae or Freddie Mac in January 1975; (1) Metropolitan/Micropolitan Statistical Area—see Appendix B for areas included; (2) Rankings are based on annual percentage change for all metro areas containing at least 15,000 transactions over the last 10 years and ranges from 1 to 306; (3) figures based on a weighted average of Census Division estimates using a purchase only index; all figures are for the period ending December 31, 2011
Source: Federal Housing Finance Agency, House Price Index, February 23, 2012

House Price Valuations

Area	Q4 2005 Price ($000)	Q4 2005 Over-valuation	Q4 2006 Price ($000)	Q4 2006 Over-valuation	Q4 2007 Price ($000)	Q4 2007 Over-valuation	Q4 2008 Price ($000)	Q4 2008 Over-valuation	Q4 2009 Price ($000)	Q4 2009 Over-valuation
MSA[1]	155.2	-3.2	168.8	-1.1	173.3	-2.6	167.7	-4.7	164.6	-8.0

Note: Figures show the percentage of over- or under-valuation of single family homes relative to statistically normal house values (e.g. a value of 23.6 indicates that house values are 23.6% overvalued). Statistically normal house values are based on house prices, interest rates, household incomes, population densities, and any historical premiums or discounts metropolitan areas have exhibited over time; (1) Figures cover the Nashville-Davidson—Murfreesboro—Franklin, TN - see Appendix B for areas included
Source: Global Insight/PNC Financial Services Group, House Prices in America: 4th Quarter 2009 Update

Median Single-Family Home Prices

Area	2009	2010	2011p	Percent Change 2010 to 2011
MSA[1]	147.9	153.8	151.9	-1.2
U.S. Average	172.1	173.1	166.2	-4.0

Note: Figures are median sales prices of existing single-family homes in thousands of dollars; (p) preliminary; n/a not available; (1) Metropolitan Statistical Area—see Appendix B for areas included
Source: National Association of Realtors, Median Sales Price of Existing Single-Family Homes for Metropolitan Areas, 4th Quarter 2011

Affordability Index of Existing Single-Family Homes

Area	2009	2010	2011p	Percent Change 2010 to 2011
MSA[1]	125.6	129.4	137.2	6.0

Note: The housing affordability index measures whether or not a typical family could qualify for a mortgage loan on a typical home. The higher the index, the greater the household purchasing power. An index of 100 is defined as the point where a median-income household has exactly enough income to qualify for the purchase of a median-priced existing single-family home, assuming a 20 percent downpayment and 25 percent of gross income devoted to mortgage principal and interest payments; (p) preliminary; n/a not available; (1) Metropolitan Statistical Area—see Appendix B for areas included
Source: National Association of Realtors, Affordability Index of Existing Single-Family Homes, 2011

Median Apartment Condo-Coop Home Prices

Area	2009	2010	2011p	Percent Change 2010 to 2011
MSA[1]	n/a	n/a	n/a	n/a
U.S. Average	175.6	171.7	165.1	-3.8

Note: Figures are median sales prices of existing apartment condo-coop homes in thousands of dollars; (p) preliminary; n/a not available; (1) Metropolitan Statistical Area—see Appendix B for areas included
Source: National Association of Realtors, Median Sales Price of Existing Apartment Condo-Coop Homes for Metropolitan Areas, 4th Quarter 2011

Year Housing Structure Built

Area	2005 or Later	2000 -2004	1990 -1999	1980 -1989	1970 -1979	1960 -1969	1950 -1959	Before 1950	Median Year
City	13.2	19.8	24.9	13.8	11.4	8.0	4.4	4.5	1993
MSA[1]	8.4	11.8	19.3	16.2	16.2	11.1	7.8	9.1	1984
U.S.	5.0	8.6	14.0	14.1	16.3	11.3	11.2	19.6	1975

Note: Figures are percentages except for Median Year; (1) Figures cover the Nashville-Davidson—Murfreesboro—Franklin, TN Metropolitan Statistical Area—see Appendix B for areas included
Source: U.S. Census Bureau, 2008-2010 American Community Survey 3-Year Estimates

HEALTH

Health Risk Data

Category	MSA[1] (%)	U.S. (%)
Adults who have been told they have high blood pressure[2]	26.3	28.7
Adults who have been told they have high blood cholesterol[2]	28.2	37.5
Adults who have been told they have diabetes[3]	8.7	8.7
Adults who have been told they have arthritis[2]	24.1	26.0
Adults who have been told they currently have asthma	5.6	9.1
Adults who are current smokers	17.4	17.3
Adults who are heavy drinkers[4]	1.0	5.0
Adults who are binge drinkers[5]	7.9	15.1
Adults who are overweight (BMI 25.0 - 29.9)	37.4	36.2
Adults who are obese (BMI 30.0 - 99.8)	24.7	27.5
Adults who participated in any physical activities in the past month	73.3	76.1
Adults 50+ who have ever had a sigmoidoscopy or colonoscopy	66.2	65.2
Women aged 40+ who have had a mammogram within the past two years	77.0	75.2
Men aged 40+ who have had a PSA test within the past two years	53.3	53.2
Adults aged 65+ who have had flu shot within the past year	69.3	67.5
Adults aged 18–64 who have any kind of health care coverage	84.0	82.2

Note: Data as of 2010 unless otherwise noted; (1) Figures cover the Nashville-Davidson—Murfreesboro, TN Metropolitan Statistical Area—see Appendix B for areas included; (2) Data as of 2009; (3) Figures do not include pregnancy-related, borderline, or pre-diabetes; (4) Heavy drinkers are classified as males having more than two drinks per day or females having more than one drink per day; (5) Binge drinkers are classified as males having five or more drinks on one occasion or females having four or more drinks on one occasion
Source: Centers for Disease Control and Prevention, Behaviorial Risk Factor Surveillance System, SMART: Selected Metropolitan/Micropolitan Area Risk Trends, 2009, 2010

Mortality Rates for the Top 10 Causes of Death in the U.S.

ICD-10[a] Sub-Chapter	ICD-10[a] Code	Age-Adjusted Mortality Rate[1] per 100,000 population	
		County[2]	U.S.
Malignant neoplasms	C00-C97	175.7	175.6
Ischaemic heart diseases	I20-I25	146.7	121.6
Other forms of heart disease	I30-I51	37.1	48.6
Chronic lower respiratory diseases	J40-J47	50.1	42.3
Cerebrovascular diseases	I60-I69	46.6	40.6
Organic, including symptomatic, mental disorders	F01-F09	21.3	26.7
Other degenerative diseases of the nervous system	G30-G31	35.7	24.7
Other external causes of accidental injury	W00-X59	25.6	24.4
Diabetes mellitus	E10-E14	19.5	21.7
Hypertensive diseases	I10-I15	20.7	18.2

Note: (a) ICD-10 = International Classification of Diseases 10th Revision; (1) Mortality rates are a three year average covering 2007-2009; (2) Figures cover Rutherford County
Source: Centers for Disease Control and Prevention, National Center for Health Statistics. Underlying Cause of Death 1999-2009 on CDC WONDER Online Database, released 2012. Data for year 2009 are compiled from the Multiple Cause of Death File 2009, Series 20 No. 2O, 2012, Data for year 2008 are compiled from the Multiple Cause of Death File 2008, Series 20 No. 2N, 2011, Data for year 2007 are compiled from Multiple Cause of Death File 2007, Series 20 No. 2M, 2010.

Mortality Rates for Selected Causes of Death

ICD-10[a] Sub-Chapter	ICD-10[a] Code	Age-Adjusted Mortality Rate[1] per 100,000 population	
		County[2]	U.S.
Assault	X85-Y09	5.1	5.7
Human immunodeficiency virus (HIV) disease	B20-B24	*Unreliable	3.3
Influenza and pneumonia	J09-J18	19.7	16.4
Intentional self-harm	X60-X84	12.2	11.5
Malnutrition	E40-E46	*0.0	0.8
Obesity and other hyperalimentation	E65-E68	*Unreliable	1.6
Transport accidents	V01-V99	12.0	13.7
Viral hepatitis	B15-B19	*Unreliable	2.2

Note: (a) ICD-10 = International Classification of Diseases 10th Revision; (1) Mortality rates are a three year average covering 2007-2009; (2) Figures cover Rutherford County; (*) Unreliable data as per CDC
Source: Centers for Disease Control and Prevention, National Center for Health Statistics. Underlying Cause of Death 1999-2009 on CDC WONDER Online Database, released 2012. Data for year 2009 are compiled from the Multiple Cause of Death File 2009, Series 20 No. 2O, 2012, Data for year 2008 are compiled from the Multiple Cause of Death File 2008, Series 20 No. 2N, 2011, Data for year 2007 are compiled from Multiple Cause of Death File 2007, Series 20 No. 2M, 2010.

Distribution of Physicians and Dentists

Area[1]	Dentists[2]	D.O.[3]	M.D.[4]				
			Total	Family/General Practice	Pediatrics	Medical Specialties	Surgical Specialties
Local (number)	82	6	278	33	26	108	78
Local (rate[5])	3.4	0.2	11.1	1.3	1.0	4.3	3.1
U.S. (rate[5])	4.5	1.9	18.3	2.5	1.4	6.8	4.1

Note: Data as of 2008 unless noted; (1) Local data covers Rutherford County; (2) Data as of 2007; (3) Doctor of Osteopathic Medicine; (4) Includes active, non-federal, patient-care, office-based Doctors of Medicine; (5) rate per 10,000 population
Source: Area Resource File (ARF). 2009-2010 Release. U.S. Department of Health and Human Services, Health Resources and Services Administration, Bureau of Health Professions, Rockville, MD, August 2010

Best Hospitals

According to *U.S. News,* the Nashville-Davidson—Murfreesboro—Franklin, TN is home to one of the best hospitals in the U.S.: **Vanderbilt University Medical Center** (11 specialties). The hospital listed was highly ranked in at least one adult specialty. *U.S. News Online, "America's Best Hospitals 2011-12"*

According to *U.S. News,* the Nashville-Davidson—Murfreesboro—Franklin, TN is home to one of the best children's hospitals in the U.S.: **Monroe Carell Jr. Children's Hospital at Vanderbilt** (10 specialties). The hospital listed was highly ranked in at least one pediatric specialty. *U.S. News Online, "America's Best Children's Hospitals 2011-12"*

EDUCATION

Public School District Statistics

District Name	Schls	Pupils	Pupil/Teacher Ratio	Minority Pupils[1] (%)	Free Lunch Eligible[2] (%)	IEP[3] (%)
Murfreesboro	12	7,078	14.2	40.5	41.2	11.4
Rutherford County	44	37,679	15.2	29.6	29.6	10.0

Note: Table includes school districts with 2,000 or more students; (1) Percentage of students that are not non-Hispanic white; (2) Percentage of students that are eligible for the free lunch program; (3) Percentage of students that have an Individualized Education Program.
Source: U.S. Department of Education, National Center for Education Statistics, Common Core of Data, Local Education Agency (School District) Universe Survey: School Year 2009-2010; U.S. Department of Education, National Center for Education Statistics, Common Core of Data, Public Elementary/Secondary School Universe Survey: School Year 2009-2010

Highest Level of Education

Area	Less than H.S.	H.S. Diploma	Some College, No Deg.	Associate Degree	Bachelors Degree	Masters Degree	Profess. School Degree	Doctorate Degree
City	10.5	24.5	23.3	7.0	23.6	8.0	1.3	1.7
MSA[1]	13.8	28.6	21.1	6.5	19.9	6.7	2.1	1.3
U.S.	14.7	28.4	21.3	7.6	17.6	7.2	1.9	1.2

Note: Figures cover persons age 25 and over; (1) Figures cover the Nashville-Davidson—Murfreesboro—Franklin, TN Metropolitan Statistical Area—see Appendix B for areas included
Source: U.S. Census Bureau, 2008-2010 American Community Survey 3-Year Estimates

Educational Attainment by Race

Area	High School Graduate or Higher (%)					Bachelor's Degree or Higher (%)				
	Total	White	Black	Asian	Hisp.[2]	Total	White	Black	Asian	Hisp.[2]
City	89.5	91.7	89.4	84.3	57.2	34.7	37.1	28.3	34.4	13.8
MSA[1]	86.2	87.5	82.8	86.6	56.7	30.0	31.4	22.6	45.2	11.9
U.S.	85.3	87.5	81.4	85.5	61.6	28.0	29.3	17.8	50.2	13.0

Note: Figures shown cover persons 25 years old and over; (1) Figures cover the Nashville-Davidson—Murfreesboro—Franklin, TN Metropolitan Statistical Area—see Appendix B for areas included; (2) People of Hispanic origin can be of any race
Source: U.S. Census Bureau, 2008-2010 American Community Survey 3-Year Estimates

School Enrollment by Grade and Control

Area	Preschool (%)		Kindergarten (%)		Grades 1 - 4 (%)		Grades 5 - 8 (%)		Grades 9 - 12 (%)	
	Public	Private	Public	Private	Public	Private	Public	Private	Public	Private
City	45.9	54.1	90.4	9.6	95.0	5.0	94.0	6.0	97.1	2.9
MSA[1]	44.0	56.0	84.7	15.3	87.6	12.4	85.2	14.8	84.8	15.2
U.S.	55.4	44.6	87.1	12.9	89.4	10.6	89.5	10.5	90.4	9.6

Note: Figures shown cover persons 3 years old and over; (1) Figures cover the Nashville-Davidson—Murfreesboro—Franklin, TN Metropolitan Statistical Area—see Appendix B for areas included
Source: U.S. Census Bureau, 2008-2010 American Community Survey 3-Year Estimates

Average Salaries of Public School Classroom Teachers

Area	2010-11		2011-12		Percent Change 2010-11 to 2011-12	Percent Change 2001-02 to 2011-12
	Dollars	Rank[1]	Dollars	Rank[1]		
Tennessee	45,891	44	46,613	43	1.57	21.00
U.S. Average	55,623	-	56,643	-	1.83	26.8

Note: (1) State rank ranges from 1 to 51 where 1 indicates highest salary.
Source: National Education Association, Rankings & Estimates: Rankings of the States 2011 and Estimates of School Statistics 2012, December 2011

Higher Education

Four-Year Colleges			Two-Year Colleges			Medical Schools[1]	Law Schools[2]	Voc/ Tech[3]
Public	Private Non-profit	Private For-profit	Public	Private Non-profit	Private For-profit			
1	0	1	1	0	0	0	0	1

Note: Figures cover institutions located within the city limits and include main campuses only; (1) includes schools accredited by the Liaison Committee on Medical Education and the American Osteopathic Association's Commission on Osteopathic College Accreditation; (2) includes American Bar Association-accredited law schools; (3) includes all schools with programs that are less than 2 years.
Source: National Center for Education Statistics, Integrated Postsecondary Education System (IPEDS) Peer Analysis System, 2011-12; Association of American Medical Colleges, Member List, April 23, 2012; American Osteopathic Association, Member List, April 23, 2012; Law School Admission Council, Official Guide to ABA-Approved Law Schools Online, April 23, 2012

According to *U.S. News & World Report*, the Nashville-Davidson—Murfreesboro—Franklin, TN is home to one of the best national universities in the U.S.: **Vanderbilt University** (#17). The indicators used to capture academic quality fall into a number of categories: assessment by administrators at peer institutions; retention of students; faculty resources; student selectivity; financial resources; alumni giving; high school counselor ratings of colleges; and graduation rate.*U.S. News & World Report, "America's Best Colleges 2012"*

According to *U.S. News & World Report,* the Nashville-Davidson—Murfreesboro—Franklin, TN is home to one of the best liberal arts colleges in the U.S.: **Fisk University** (#144). The indicators used to capture academic quality fall into a number of categories: assessment by administrators at peer institutions; retention of students; faculty resources; student selectivity; financial resources; alumni giving; high school counselor ratings of colleges; and graduation rate. *U.S. News & World Report, "America's Best Colleges 2012"*

According to *U.S. News & World Report,* the Nashville-Davidson—Murfreesboro—Franklin, TN is home to one of the best law schools in the U.S.: **Vanderbilt University** (#16). The rankings are based on a weighted average of 12 measures of quality: peer assessment score; assessment score by lawyers/judges; median LSAT scores; median undergrad GPA; acceptance rate; employment rates for graduates; placement success; bar passage rate; faculty resources; expenditures per student; student/faculty ratio; and library resources. *U.S. News & World Report, "America's Best Law Schools 2013"*

According to *Forbes,* the Nashville-Davidson—Murfreesboro—Franklin, TN is home to one of the best business schools in the U.S.: **Vanderbilt (Owen)** (#33). The rankings are based on the return on investment that graduates of the Class of 2006 received (median salary five years after graduation). *Forbes, "Best Business Schools," August 3, 2011*

PRESIDENTIAL ELECTION

2008 Presidential Election Results

Area	Obama	McCain	Nader	Other
Rutherford County	39.8	58.9	0.5	0.9
U.S.	52.9	45.6	0.6	0.9

Note: Results are percentages and may not add to 100% due to rounding
Source: Dave Leip's Atlas of U.S. Presidential Elections, www.uselectionatlas.org

EMPLOYERS

Major Employers

Company Name	Industry
AHOM Holdings Inc	Home health care services
Asurion Corporation	Business services nec
Baptist Hospital	General medical/surgical hospitals
Cannon County Knitting Mills Inc	Apparel and outerwear broadwoven fabrics
County of Rutherford	Public elementary and secondary schools
County of Sumner	Executive offices, local government
Gaylord Entertainment Company	Hotels/motels
Gaylord Opryland USA Inc	Hotels
Ingram Book Company	Books, periodicals, and newspapers
International Automotive	Automotive storage garage
LifeWay Christian Resources of the SBC	Religious organizations
Middle Tennessee State University	Colleges/universities
Newspaper Printing Corporation	Newspapers
Nissan North America Inc	Motor vehicles/car bodies
Primus Automotive Financial Services Inc	Automobile loans including insurance
Psychiatric Solutions Inc	Psychiatric clinic
State Industries Inc	Hot water heaters, household
State of Tennessee	Mentally handicapped home
Tennesee Department of Transportation	Regulation, administration of transportation
Vanderbilt Childrens Hospital	General medical/surgical hospitals
Vanderbilt University	Colleges/universities

Note: Companies shown are located within the Nashville-Davidson—Murfreesboro—Franklin, TN metropolitan area.
Source: Hoovers.com, data extracted April 25 2012

PUBLIC SAFETY

Crime Rate

Area	All Crimes	Violent Crimes				Property Crimes		
		Murder	Forcible Rape	Robbery	Aggrav. Assault	Burglary	Larceny -Theft	Motor Vehicle Theft
City	4,773.9	4.6	33.9	138.3	375.5	1,199.6	2,879.1	142.9
Suburbs[1]	3,978.1	6.3	41.6	138.9	463.0	820.9	2,314.4	192.9
Metro[2]	4,032.1	6.2	41.0	138.9	457.0	846.7	2,352.8	189.5
U.S.	3,345.5	4.8	27.5	119.1	252.3	699.6	2,003.5	238.8

Note: Figures are crimes per 100,000 population; (1) All areas within the metro area that are located outside the city limits; (2) Metropolitan Statistical Area—see Appendix B for areas included
Source: FBI Uniform Crime Reports, 2010

Hate Crimes

Area	Number of Quarters Reported	Bias Motivation				
		Race	Religion	Sexual Orientation	Ethnicity	Disability
City	4	2	0	1	0	0

Source: Federal Bureau of Investigation, Hate Crime Statistics 2010

Identity Theft Consumer Complaints

Area	Complaints	Complaints per 100,000 Population	Rank[2]
MSA[1]	1,156	76.0	187
U.S.	279,156	90.4	-

Note: (1) Metropolitan Statistical Area—see Appendix B for areas included; (2) Rank ranges from 1 to 384 where 1 indicates greatest number of identity theft complaints per 100,000 population
Source: Federal Trade Commission, Consumer Sentinel Network Data Book for January–December 2011

Fraud and Other Consumer Complaints

Area	Complaints	Complaints per 100,000 Population	Rank[2]
MSA[1]	7,962	523.3	121
U.S.	1,533,924	496.8	-

Note: (1) Metropolitan Statistical Area—see Appendix B for areas included; (2) Rank ranges from 1 to 384 where 1 indicates greatest number of fraud and other complaints per 100,000 population
Source: Federal Trade Commission, Consumer Sentinel Network Data Book for January–December 2011

RECREATION

Culture

Dance[1]	Theatre[1]	Instrumental Music[1]	Vocal Music[1]	Series/ Festivals	Museums	Zoos and Aquariums[2]
0	0	0	0	1	n/a	0

Note: (1) Number of professional performing groups; (2) AZA-accredited; n/a not available
Source: The Grey House Performing Arts Directory, 2011-2012; Official Museum Directory, 2011; American Association of Museums, AAM Member Museums, April 2012; Association of Zoos & Aquariums, AZA Member Zoos & Aquariums, April 2012

Professional Sports Teams

Team Name	League
Nashville Predators	National Hockey League (NHL)
Tennessee Titans	National Football League (NFL)

Note: Includes teams located in the Nashville metro area.
Source: Original research

CLIMATE

Average and Extreme Temperatures

Temperature	Jan	Feb	Mar	Apr	May	Jun	Jul	Aug	Sep	Oct	Nov	Dec	Yr.
Extreme High (°F)	78	84	86	91	95	106	107	104	105	94	84	79	107
Average High (°F)	47	51	60	71	79	87	90	89	83	72	60	50	70
Average Temp. (°F)	38	41	50	60	68	76	80	79	72	61	49	41	60
Average Low (°F)	28	31	39	48	57	65	69	68	61	48	39	31	49
Extreme Low (°F)	-17	-13	2	23	34	42	54	49	36	26	-1	-10	-17

Note: Figures cover the years 1948-1990
Source: National Climatic Data Center, International Station Meteorological Climate Summary, 9/96

Average Precipitation/Snowfall/Humidity

Precip./Humidity	Jan	Feb	Mar	Apr	May	Jun	Jul	Aug	Sep	Oct	Nov	Dec	Yr.
Avg. Precip. (in.)	4.4	4.2	5.0	4.1	4.6	3.7	3.8	3.3	3.2	2.6	3.9	4.6	47.4
Avg. Snowfall (in.)	4	3	1	Tr	0	0	0	0	0	Tr	1	1	11
Avg. Rel. Hum. 6am (%)	81	81	80	81	86	86	88	90	90	87	83	82	85
Avg. Rel. Hum. 3pm (%)	61	57	51	48	52	52	54	53	52	49	55	59	54

Note: Figures cover the years 1948-1990; Tr = Trace amounts (<0.05 in. of rain; <0.5 in. of snow)
Source: National Climatic Data Center, International Station Meteorological Climate Summary, 9/96

Weather Conditions

Temperature			Daytime Sky			Precipitation		
10°F & below	32°F & below	90°F & above	Clear	Partly cloudy	Cloudy	0.01 inch or more precip.	0.1 inch or more snow/ice	Thunder-storms
5	76	51	98	135	132	119	8	54

Note: Figures are average number of days per year and cover the years 1948-1990
Source: National Climatic Data Center, International Station Meteorological Climate Summary, 9/96

HAZARDOUS WASTE

Superfund Sites

Murfreesboro has no sites on the EPA's Superfund Final National Priorities List.
U.S. Environmental Protection Agency, Final National Priorities List, April 17, 2012

AIR & WATER QUALITY

Air Quality Index

Area	Percent of Days when Air Quality was...[2]					AQI Statistics[2]	
	Good	Moderate	Unhealthy for Sensitive Groups	Unhealthy	Very Unhealthy	Maximum	Median
Area[1]	88.9	11.1	0.0	0.0	0.0	84	40

Note: Air Quality Index (AQI) is an index for reporting daily air quality. EPA calculates the AQI for five major air pollutants regulated by the Clean Air Act: ground-level ozone, particle pollution (aka particulate matter), carbon monoxide, sulfur dioxide, and nitrogen dioxide. The AQI runs from 0 to 500. The higher the AQI value, the greater the level of air pollution and the greater the health concern. There are six AQI categories: "Good" AQI is between 0 and 50. Air quality is considered satisfactory; "Moderate" AQI is between 51 and 100. Air quality is acceptable; "Unhealthy for Sensitive Groups" When AQI values are between 101 and 150, members of sensitive groups may experience health effects; "Unhealthy" When AQI values are between 151 and 200 everyone may begin to experience health effects; "Very Unhealthy" AQI values between 201 and 300 trigger a health alert; "Hazardous" AQI values over 300 trigger warnings of emergency conditions (not shown); (1) Data covers Rutherford County; (2) Based on 243 days with AQI data in 2011.
Source: U.S. Environmental Protection Agency, AirData Report, 2011

Air Quality Index Pollutants

Area	Percent of Days when AQI Pollutant was...[2]					
	Carbon Monoxide	Nitrogen Dioxide	Ozone	Sulfur Dioxide	Particulate Matter 2.5	Particulate Matter 10
Area[1]	0.0	0.0	100.0	0.0	0.0	0.0

Note: The Air Quality Index (AQI) is an index for reporting daily air quality. EPA calculates the AQI for five major air pollutants regulated by the Clean Air Act: ground-level ozone, particle pollution (also known as particulate matter), carbon monoxide, sulfur dioxide, and nitrogen dioxide. The AQI runs from 0 to 500. The higher the AQI value, the greater the level of air pollution and the greater the health concern; (1) Data covers Rutherford County; (2) Based on 243 days with AQI data in 2011.
Source: U.S. Environmental Protection Agency, AirData Report, 2011

Air Quality Index Trends

Area	Trend Sites (days)								All Sites (days)
	2003	2004	2005	2006	2007	2008	2009	2010	2010
MSA[1]	23	7	29	17	37	11	1	10	10

Note: Figures are the number of days the AQI value exceeded 100 in a given year. An AQI value greater than 100 indicates that air quality would have been in the unhealthful range on that day. Data from exceptional events are included. These counts are presented in two ways. First, the counts are based on sites having an adequate record of monitoring data during the trend period (trend sites). These counts represent the relative change in the number of days with AQI values greater than 100. In the last column, the counts are based on all sites with data in the most recent year (because it is possible for a site to have data in the most recent year but not enough data to be a trend site); (1) Data covers the Nashville-Davidson—Murfreesboro—Franklin, TN—see Appendix B for areas included
Source: U.S. Environmental Protection Agency, Air Quality Index Information, "Number of Days with Air Quality Index Values Greater than 100 at Trend Sites, 2000-2010, and at All Sites in 2010"

Maximum Air Pollutant Concentrations: Particulate Matter, Ozone, CO and Lead

	Particulate Matter 10 (ug/m³)	Particulate Matter 2.5 Wtd AM (ug/m³)	Particulate Matter 2.5 24-Hr (ug/m³)	Ozone (ppm)	Carbon Monoxide (ppm)	Lead (ug/m³)
MSA[1] Level	42	11.8	24	0.078	2	n/a
NAAQS[2]	150	15	35	0.075	9	0.15
Met NAAQS[2]	Yes	Yes	Yes	No	Yes	n/a

Note: Data from exceptional events are not included; (1) Data covers the Nashville-Davidson—Murfreesboro—Franklin, TN—see Appendix B for areas included; (2) National Ambient Air Quality Standards; ppm = parts per million; ug/m³ = micrograms per cubic meter; n/a not available Concentrations: Particulate Matter 10 (coarse particulate)—highest second maximum 24-hour concentration; Particulate Matter 2.5 Wtd AM (fine particulate)—highest weighted annual mean concentration; Particulate Matter 2.5 24-Hour (fine particulate)—highest 98th percentile 24-hour concentration; Ozone—highest fourth daily maximum 8-hour concentration; Carbon Monoxide—highest second maximum non-overlapping 8-hour concentration; Lead—maximum running 3-month average
Source: U.S. Environmental Protection Agency, CBSA Factbook 2010, Air Quality Statistics by City, 2010

Maximum Air Pollutant Concentrations: Nitrogen Dioxide and Sulfur Dioxide

	Nitrogen Dioxide AM (ppb)	Nitrogen Dioxide 1-Hr (ppb)	Sulfur Dioxide AM (ppb)	Sulfur Dioxide 1-Hr (ppb)	Sulfur Dioxide 24-Hr (ppb)
MSA[1] Level	12.526	46	2.246	14	5.5
NAAQS[2]	53	100	30	75	140
Met NAAQS[2]	Yes	Yes	Yes	Yes	Yes

Note: Data from exceptional events are not included; (1) Data covers the Nashville-Davidson—Murfreesboro—Franklin, TN—see Appendix B for areas included; (2) National Ambient Air Quality Standards; ppb = parts per billion; n/a not available Concentrations: Nitrogen Dioxide AM—highest arithmetic mean concentration; Nitrogen Dioxide 1-Hr—highest 98th percentile 1-hour daily maximum concentration; Sulfur Dioxide AM—highest annual mean concentration; Sulfur Dioxide 1-Hr—highest 99th percentile 1-hour daily maximum concentration; Sulfur Dioxide 24-Hr—highest second maximum 24-hour concentration
Source: U.S. Environmental Protection Agency, CBSA Factbook 2010, Air Quality Statistics by City, 2010

Drinking Water

Water System Name	Pop. Served	Primary Water Source Type	Violations[1]	
			Health Based	Monitoring/ Reporting
Consolidated UD of Rutherford	134,591	Surface	0	0

Note: (1) Based on violation data from January 1, 2011 to December 31, 2011 (includes unresolved violations from earlier years)
Source: U.S. Environmental Protection Agency, Office of Ground Water and Drinking Water, Safe Drinking Water Information System (based on data extracted April 18, 2012)

Nashville, Tennessee

Background

Nashville, the capital of Tennessee, was founded on Christmas Day in 1779 by James Robertson and John Donelson, and sits in the minds of millions as the country music capital of the world. This is the place to record if you want to make it into the country music industry, and where the Grand Ole Opry—the longest-running radio show in the country—still captures the hearts of millions of devoted listeners. It is no wonder, given how profoundly this industry has touched people, names like Dolly, Chet, Loretta, Hank, and Johnny are more familiar than the city's true native sons: Andrew, James, and Sam. Jackson, Polk, and Houston, that is.

Nashville is home to Music Row, an area just to the southwest of downtown with hundreds of businesses related to the country music, gospel music, and contemporary Christian music industries. The USA Network's Nashville Star, a country music singing competition, is also held in the Acuff Theatre. The magnitude of Nashville's recording industry is impressive, but other industries are important to the city, such as health care management, automobile production, and printing and publishing.

Nashville is also a devoted patron of education. The Davidson Academy, forerunner of the George Peabody College for Teachers, was founded in Nashville, as were Vanderbilt and Fisk universities, the latter being the first private black university in the United States. Vanderbilt University and Medical Center is the region's largest non-governmental employer.

Nashville citizens take pride in their numerous museums, including the Adventure Science Center, with its Sudekum Planetarium; the Aaron Douglas Gallery at Fisk University, which features a remarkable collection of African-American art; and the Carl Van Vechten Gallery, also at Fisk University, home to works by Alfred Stieglitz, Picasso, Cezanne, and Georgia O'Keefe. The Cheekwood Botanical Garden and Museum of Art includes 55 acres of gardens and contemporary art galleries.

Gracing the city are majestic mansions and plantations that testify to the mid nineteenth-century splendor for which the South came to be famous. Known as the "Queen of the Tennessee Plantations," the Belle Meade Plantation is an 1853 Greek Revival mansion crowning a 5,400-acre thoroughbred stud farm and nursery. The Belmont Mansion, built in 1850 by Adelicia Acklen, one of the wealthiest women in America, is constructed in the style of an Italian villa and was originally intended to be the summer home of the Acklens. Travelers' Rest Plantation served as a haven for weary travelers, past and present, and is Nashville's oldest plantation home open to the public. It features docents dressed in period costume who explain and demonstrate life in the plantations' heyday. Carnton Plantation was the site of the Civil War's Battle of Franklin, and The Hermitage was the home of Andrew Jackson, the seventh president of the United States. Tennessee's historic State Capitol Building, completed in 1859, has had much of its interior restored to its nineteenth-century appearance.

The Nashville area comprises many urban, suburban, rural, and historic districts, which can differ immensely from each other. Most of the best restaurants, clubs, and shops are on the west side of the Cumberland River, however, the east side encompasses fine neighborhoods, interesting homes, plenty of shopping, and good food, as well. Outdoor activities include camping, fishing, hiking, and biking at the many scenic and accessible lakes in the region.

Located on the Cumberland River in central Tennessee, Nashville's average relative humidity is moderate, as is its weather, with great temperature extremes a rarity. The city is not in the most common path of storms that cross the country, but is in a zone of moderate frequency for thunderstorms.

Rankings

General Rankings

- *Men's Health Living* ranked 100 U.S. cities in terms of quality of life. Nashville was ranked #41 and received a grade of C. Criteria: number of fitness facilities; air quality; number of physicians; male/female ratio; education levels; household income; cost of living. *Men's Health Living, Spring 2008*

- Nashville was selected as one of America's best cities by *Bloomberg Businessweek*. The city ranked #28 out of 50. Criteria: number of restaurants, bars and museums per capita; number of colleges, libraries, and professional sports teams; income, poverty, unemployment, crime, and foreclosure rates; percent of population with bachelor's degrees; public school performance; park acres per capita; air quality. *BusinessWeek, "America's 50 Best Cities," September 20, 2011*

- Nashville was identified as one of the top places to live in the U.S. by Harris Interactive. The city ranked #11 out of 15. Criteria: 2,463 adults (age 18 and over) were polled and asked "if you could live in or near any city in the country except the one you live in or nearest to now, which city would you choose?" The poll was conducted online within the U.S. between September 14 and 20, 2010. *Harris Interactive, November 9, 2011*

- Nashville was selected as one of "America's Favorite Cities." The city ranked #10 in the "People" category. Respondents to an online survey were asked to rate 35 top urban destinations in the U.S. from a visitor's perspective. Criteria: attractive; friendly; stylish; intelligent; athletic/active; diverse. *Travelandleisure.com, "America's Favorite Cities 2010," November 2010*

- Nashville was selected as one of "America's Favorite Cities." The city ranked #5 in the "Nightlife" category. Respondents to an online survey were asked to rate 35 top urban destinations in the U.S. from a visitor's perspective. Criteria: cocktail hour; live music/concerts and bands; singles/bar scene. *Travelandleisure.com, "America's Favorite Cities 2010," November 2010*

- The Nashville metro area was selected as one of 10 "Best Value Cities" for 2011 by *Kiplinger.com* The area ranked #3. Criteria: vibrant economy; low cost of living; abundant lifestyle amenities. *Kiplinger.com, "Best Value Cities 2011"*

Business/Finance Rankings

- Nashville was identified as one of America's most coupon-loving cities by *Coupons.com*. The city ranked #10 out of 25. Criteria: online coupon usage. *Coupons.com, "Top 25 Most Frugal Cities of 2011," February 23, 2012*

- Nashville was identified as one of the "Unhappiest Cities to Work in 2012" by *CareerBliss.com*, an online community for career advancement. The city ranked #29 out of 30. Criteria: independent company reviews from employees all over the country on: relationship with their boss and co-workers; work environment; job resources; growth opportunities; compensation; company culture; company reputation; daily tasks; job control over work performed on a daily basis. *CareerBliss.com, "Happiest and Unhappiest Cities to Work in 2012"*

- Nashville was selected as one of the "100 Best Places to Live and Launch" in the U.S. The city ranked #79. The editors at *Fortune Small Business* ranked 296 Census-designated metro areas by business friendliness (Launching Score, % New Businesses) and lifestyle offerings (Living Score). Then they picked the town within each of the top 100 metro areas that best blends business and pleasure. *Fortune Small Business, "100 Best Places to Live and Launch 2008," April 2008*

- Nashville was selected as one of the best metro areas for telecommuters in America. The area ranked #10 out of 11. Criteria: low cost of living; educational attainment; number of universities and libraries; literacy rates; personal fitness. *DailyFinance.com, "The 11 Best Cities for Telecommuters," December 2, 2010*

- *American City Business Journals* ranked America's 261 largest cities in terms of their resident's wealth. Nashville ranked #161. Criteria: per capita income; median household income; percentage of households with annual incomes of $200,000 or more; median home value. *American City Business Journals, "Where the Money Is: America's Wealth Centers," August 18, 2008*

- The Nashville metro area appeared on the Milken Institute "2011 Best Performing Metros" list. Rank: #42 out of 200 large metro areas. Criteria: job growth; wage and salary growth; high-tech output growth. *Milken Institute, "2011 Best Performing Metros"*

- The Nashville metro area was selected as one of the best cities for entrepreneurs in America by *Inc. Magazine*. Criteria: job-growth data for 335 metro areas was analyzed for: recent growth trend; mid-term growth; long-term trend; current year growth. The Nashville metro area ranked #18 among large metro areas and #97 overall. *Inc. Magazine, "The Best Cities for Doing Business," July 2008*

- Nashville was ranked #92 out of 145 regions worldwide in terms of its "Knowledge Competitiveness Index." The index attempts to measure the knowledge-based development taking place throughout the world and is based on 19 measures of economic performance that indicate a region's ability to translate its knowledge capacity into economic value. *Centre for International Competitiveness, World Knowledge Competitiveness Index 2008*

- *Forbes* ranked the 200 most populous metro areas in the U.S. in terms of the "Best Places for Business and Careers." The Nashville metro area was ranked #6. Criteria: costs (business and living); job growth (past and projected); income growth; educational attainment; projected economic growth; crime; cultural and recreational opportunities; net migration patterns; number of highly ranked colleges. *Forbes, "Best Places for Business and Careers," June 2011*

Children/Family Rankings

- The Nashville metro area was selected as one of the "Best Cities for Relocating Families" by Worldwide ERC and Primacy Relocation. The 2008 study looked at nearly 50 factors important to relocating families including: recent job growth; nearby top-ranked colleges; in-state tuition for four-year public colleges; population growth since 2000; pediatricians per 100,000 population; and a Green Living index. *Worldwide ERC and Primacy Relocation, "2008 Best Cities for Relocating Families"*

- *Fit Pregnancy* magazine ranked the 50 best U.S. cities in which to have a baby. Nashville was ranked #33. Criteria: access to hospitals and doctors; affordability; birthing options; breastfeeding; child care; fertility laws/resources; maternal and infant health risk; parks/stroller friendliness; safety. *Fit Pregnancy, "The Best Cities in America to Have a Baby 2008"*

- Nashville was chosen as one of America's "100 Best Communities for Young People." The winners were selected based upon detailed information provided about each community's efforts to fulfill five essential promises critical to the well-being of young people: caring adults who are actively involved in their lives; safe places in which to learn and grow; a healthy start toward adulthood; an effective education that builds marketable skills; and opportunities to help others. *America's Promise Alliance, "100 Best Communities for Young People, 2010"*

Culture/Performing Arts Rankings

- Nashville was selected as one of "America's Top 25 Arts Destinations." The city ranked #18 in the big city (population 500,000 and over) category. Criteria: readers' top choices for arts travel destinations based on the richness and variety of visual arts sites, activities and events. *American Style, "America's Top 25 Arts Destinations," May 2010*

Dating/Romance Rankings

- Nashville appeared on *Men's Health's* list of the most sex-happy cities in America. The city ranked #18 of 100. Criteria: condom sales; birth rates; sex toy sales; rates of chlamydia, gonorrhea, and syphilis. *Men's Health, "America's Most Sex-Happy Cities," October 2010*

- *Men's Health* ranked 100 U.S. cities in terms of best (and worst) marriages. Nashville was ranked #43 (#1 = worst). Criteria: rate of failed marriages; stringency of divorce laws; percentage of population who've split; number of licensed marriage and family therapists. *Men's Health, "Splitsville, USA," May 2010*

- Eli Lily and Company, in partnership with Sperling's BestPlaces, ranked the nation's 50 largest metro areas in terms of the "Most Romantic Cities for Baby Boomers." The Nashville metro area ranked #17. Criteria: marriage and divorce rates among baby boomers age 45 to 60; great restaurants; dance studios; chocolate, jewelry and flower sales. *Eli Lily and Company, "Most Romantic Cities for Baby Boomers," April 20, 2007*

- The Nashville metro area was selected as one of the "Best Cities for Relocating Singles" by Worldwide ERC and Primacy Relocation. The area ranked #41 out of the 100 largest metro areas in the U.S. Criteria: recent job growth; recent singles population growth; overall population growth; affordable rental housing; cost-of-living index; expanded arts and recreation opportunities; ratio of single men and single women; affordability of quality higher education (including state residency requirements); diversity index; climate; population density. *Worldwide ERC and Primacy Relocation, "2008 Best Cities for Relocating Singles"*

Education Rankings

- *Men's Health* ranked 100 U.S. cities in terms of their education levels. Nashville was ranked #41 (#1 = most educated city). Criteria: high school graduation rates; school enrollment; educational attainment; number of households who have outstanding student loans; number of households whose members have taken adult-education courses. *Men's Health, "Where School Is In: The Most and Least Educated Cities," September 12, 2011*

- Nashville was selected as one of "America's Most Literate Cities." The city ranked #27 out of the 75 largest U.S. cities. Criteria: number of booksellers; library resources; Internet resources; educational attainment; periodical publishing resources; newspaper circulation. *Central Connecticut State University, "America's Most Literate Cities 2011"*

- Nashville was identified as one of the 100 "smartest" metro areas in the U.S. The area ranked #59. Criteria: the editors rated the collective brainpower of the 100 largest metro areas in the U.S. based on their residents' educational attainment. *American City Business Journals, April 14, 2008*

- Nashville was identified as one of "America's Brainiest Bastions" by *Portfolio.com*. The metro area ranked #79 out of 200. *Portfolio.com* analyzed levels of educational attainment in the nation's 200 largest metropolitan areas. The editors established scores for five levels of educational attainment, based on relative earning power of adult workers age 25 or older. Scores were determined by comparing the median income for all workers with the median income for those workers at a specified educational level. *Portfolio.com, "America's Brainiest Bastions," December 1, 2010*

Environmental Rankings

- Nashville was selected as one of 22 "Smarter Cities" for energy by the Natural Resources Defense Council. Criteria: investment in green power; energy efficiency measures; conservation. *Natural Resources Defense Council, "2010 Smarter Cities," July 19, 2010*

- *American City Business Journal* ranked 43 metropolitan areas in terms of their "greenness." The Nashville metro area ranked #34. Criteria: Forty-one metros in which *ACBJ* has business weeklies, plus Indianapolis and Cleveland, were ranked based on 20 different indicators such as adoption of green technologies, utilization of environmentally sound practices, and air and water quality. *American City Business Journals, "Green City Index," March 11, 2010*

- The Nashville metro area was selected as one of "America's Cleanest Cities" by *Forbes*. The metro area ranked #6 out of 10. Criteria: toxic releases; air and water quality; per capita spending on Superfund site cleanup. *Forbes.com, "America's Cleanest Cities 2011," March 11, 2011*

- 100 of the largest metro areas in the U.S. were analyzed in terms of their current drought severity. The Nashville metro area ranked #6 (#1 = driest). The rankings were based on statistics such as long-term precipitation trends and patterns and the Palmer drought indices. *Sperling's BestPlaces, www.BestPlaces.net, "America's Drought-Riskiest Cities," November 2007*

- The Nashville metro area appeared in *Country Home's* "Best Green Places" report. The area ranked #216 out of 379. Criteria: official energy policies; green power; green buildings; availability of fresh, locally grown food. *Country Home, "Best Green Places," 2008*

Food/Drink Rankings

- Nashville was selected as one of the seven best cities for barbeque by *U.S. News & World Report*. The city was ranked #6. *U.S. New & World Report, "America's Best BBQ Cities," February 29, 2012*

- Nashville was selected as one of America's best cities for hamburgers by the readers of *Travel + Leisure* in their annual America's Favorite Cities survey. The city was ranked #7 out of 10. Criteria:. *Travel + Leisure, "America's Best Burger Cities," May 2011*

Health/Fitness Rankings

- The Nashville metro area was selected as one of the worst cities for bed bugs in America by Rollins corporation, the owner of seven pest control companies, including Orkin. The area ranked #40 based on the number of bed bug treatments from January to December 2011. *Rollins, "The Top 50 U.S. Cities for Bed Bugs," March 19, 2012*

- Nashville was selected as one of the 25 fittest cities in America by *Men's Fitness Online*. It ranked #24 out of America's 50 largest cities. Criteria: fitness centers and sport stores; nutrition; sports participation; TV viewing; overweight/sedentary; junk food; air quality; geography; commute; parks and open space; city recreational facilities; access to healthcare; motivation; mayor and city initiatives; state obesity initiatives. *Men's Fitness, "The Fittest and Fattest Cities in America," March 5, 2012*

- Nashville was identified as a "2011 Asthma Capital." The area ranked #10 out of the nation's 100 largest metropolitan areas. Twelve factors were used to identify the most challenging places to live for people with asthma: estimated prevalence; self-reported prevalence; crude death rate for asthma; annual pollen score; annual air quality; public smoking laws; number of board-certified asthma specialists; school inhaler access laws; rescue medication use; controller medication use; uninsured rate; poverty rate. *Asthma and Allergy Foundation of America, "2011 Asthma Capitals"*

- Nashville was identified as a "2011 Fall Allergy Capital." The area ranked #40 out of 100. Three groups of factors were used to identify the most severe cities for people with allergies during the fall season: annual pollen levels; medicine utilization; access to board-certified allergists. *Asthma and Allergy Foundation of America, "2011 Fall Allergy Capitals"*

- Nashville was identified as a "2012 Spring Allergy Capital." The area ranked #45 out of 100. Three groups of factors were used to identify the most severe cities for people with allergies during the spring season: annual pollen levels; medicine utilization; access to board-certified allergists. *Asthma and Allergy Foundation of America, "2012 Spring Allergy Capitals"*

- *Men's Health* examined 100 major U.S. cities and selected the best and worst cities for men. Nashville ranked #66. Criteria: 35 statistical parameters of long life in the categories of health, quality of life, and fitness. *Men's Health, "The 10 Best and Worst Cities for Men 2012," January/February 2012*

- Nashville was selected as one of the most accident-prone cities in America by *Men's Health*. The city ranked #4 of 10. Criteria: workplace accident rates; traffic fatalities; emergency room visits; accidental poisonings; incidents of drowning; fires; injury-producing falls. *Men's Health, "Ranking America's Cities: Accident City, USA," October 2009*

- The makers of Breath Right Nasal Strips, in partnership with Sperling's BestPlaces, analyzed 50 metro areas and identified those U.S. cities most challenged by chronic nasal congestion. The Nashville metro area ranked #18. Criteria: tree, grass and weed pollens; molds and spores; air pollution; climate; smoking; purchase habits of congestion products; prescriptions of drugs for congestion relief; incidence of influenza. *Breathe Right Nasal Strips, "Most Congested Cities," October 3, 2011*

- *Men's Health* examined the nation's largest 100 cities and identified the cities with the best and worst teeth. Nashville was ranked among the ten best at #2. Criteria: annual dentist visits; canceled appointments; regular flossers; fluoride usage; dental extractions. *Men's Health, April 2008*

- The Nashville metro area appeared in the 2011 Gallup-Healthways Well-Being Index. The index, based on interviews with more than 350,000 Americans, measured jobs, finances, physical health, emotional state of mind and communities. The metro area ranked #48 out of 190. Criteria: life evaluation; emotional health; work environment; physical health; healthy behaviors; basic access (basic needs optimal for a healthy life, such as access to food and medicine, having health insurance and feeling safe while walking at night). *Gallup-Healthways, "State of Well-Being 2011"*

- The Nashville metro area was identified as one of "America's Most Stressful Cities" by *Sperling's BestPlaces*. The metro area ranked #30 out of 50. Criteria: unemployment rate; suicide rate; commute time; mental health; poor rest; alcohol use; violent crime rate; property crime rate; cloudy days annually. *Sperling's BestPlaces, www.BestPlaces.net, "Stressful Cities 2012*

- *Men's Health* ranked 100 U.S. cities in terms of their activity levels. Nashville was ranked #93 (#1 = most active city). Criteria: where and how often residents exercise; percentage of households that watch more than 15 hours of cable television a week and buy more than 11 video games a year; death rate from deep-vein thrombosis, a condition linked to sitting for extended periods of time. *Men's Health, "Where Sit Happens: The Most and Least Active Cities in America," June 20, 2011*

- 50 of the largest metro areas in the U.S. were analyzed in terms of their health and fitness by the American College of Sports Medicine in their "American Fitness Index." The Nashville metro area ranked #31 (#1 = healthiest). Criteria: preventative health behaviors; levels of chronic disease; health care access; community resources and policies that support physical activity. *American College of Sports Medicine, "Health and Community Fitness Status of the 50 Largest Metropolitan Areas," August 1, 2011*

- *The Daily Beast* identified the 30 U.S. metro areas with the worst smoking habits. The Nashville metro area ranked #15. Sixty urban centers with populations of more than one million were ranked based on the following criteria: number of smokers; number of cigarettes smoked per day; fewest attempts to quit. *The Daily Beast, "30 Cities With Smoking Problems," January 3, 2011*

Pet Rankings

- Nashville was selected as one of the best places to live with pets by *Livability.com*. The city was ranked #9. Criteria: pet-friendly parks and trails; quality veterinary care; active animal welfare groups; abundance of pet boutiques and retail shops; excellent quality of life for pet owners. *Livability.com, "Top 10 Pet Friendly Cities," October 20, 2010*

Real Estate Rankings

- Nashville was selected as one of five U.S. cities that may offer exceptional values for home buyers in this economy by *Kiplinger's Personal Finance*. The city ranked #3. Criteria: reasonable living costs; high quality of life; vibrant economies; great amenities. *Kiplinger's Personal Finance, "Best Cities for Housing Values, 2011" August 9, 2011*

- *Fortune* ranked the 100 largest metro areas in the U.S. in terms of projected median home price change in 2010. The Nashville metro area ranked #48. *Fortune, "The 2010 Housing Outlook," December 9, 2009*

- Nashville appeared on *ApartmentRatings.com* "Top Cities for Renters" list in 2009." The area ranked #44. Overall satisfaction ratings were ranked using thousands of user submitted scores for hundreds of apartment complexes located in the 100 most populated U.S. municipalities. *ApartmentRatings.com, "2009 Renter Satisfaction Rankings"*

- The Nashville metro area was identified as one of the "Top 25 Real Estate Investment Markets" by *FinestExperts.com*. The metro area ranked #16. Over 10,000 real estate markets were analyzed to identify the most suitable places for real estate investors to seek stability and growth. Criteria: employment; rental markets; growth levels as offset by foreclosures. *FinestExperts.com, "Top 25 Real Estate Investment Markets," January 7, 2010*

- The nation's largest metro areas were analyzed in terms of the best places to buy bank-owned properties. The Nashville metro area ranked #9 out of 10. Criteria: at least 500 REO sales during the fourth quarter and an REO sales increase of at least five percent from a year ago. The areas selected posted the biggest discounts on the sales of bank-owned properties. *RealtyTrac, "Fourth Quarter and Year-End 2011 U.S. Foreclosure Sales Report: Shifting Towards Short Sales," February 28, 2012*

- The Nashville metro area appeared in a *Wall Street Journal* article ranking cities by "housing stress." The metro area was ranked #35 (#1 = most stress). Criteria: fraction of mortgage-holding homeowners with a monthly housing payment in excess of 30 percent of income; percentage of people without health insurance; unemployment rate. *The Wall Street Journal, "Which Cities Face Biggest Housing Risk," October 5, 2010*

- The Center for Housing Policy ranked 210 U.S. metropolitan areas by the fair market rent for a two-bedroom unit. The Nashville metro area was ranked #112. (#1 = most expensive) with a rent of $807. Criteria: Fair Market Rent (FMR) in effect during the fourth quarter of 2009 based on HUD's fiscal year 2010 FMRs. *The Center for Housing Policy, "Paycheck to Paycheck: Most to Least Expensive Rental Markets in 2009"*

- The Nashville metro area was identified as one of the markets with the best expected performance in home prices over the next 12 months. *Local Market Monitor, "First Quarter Home Price Forecast for Largest US Markets," March 2, 2011*

- The Nashville metro area was identified as one of the best U.S. markets to invest in rental property" by HomeVestors and Local Market Monitor. The area ranked #48 out of 100. Criteria: risk-return premium relative to national average. *HomeVestors and Local Market Monitor, "Best 100 U.S. Markets to Invest in Rental Property," March 9, 2012*

Safety Rankings

- Symantec, the makers of Norton, in partnership with Sperling's BestPlaces, ranked the 50 largest cities in the U.S. in terms of their vulnerability to cybercrime. The city ranked #36. Criteria: number of cyberattacks and potential infections; level of Internet access; expenditures on smartphones and computer hardware/software; wireless hotspots; broadband connectivity; Internet usage; online purchases. *Symantec, "Riskiest Online Cities of 2012" February 15, 2012*

- Allstate ranked the 193 largest cities in America in terms of driver safety. Nashville ranked #30. In addition, drivers were 8.7% less likely to have had an accident compared to the national average. Allstate researchers analyzed internal property damage reported claims over a two-year period (from January 2008 to December 2009) to protect findings from external influences such as weather or road construction. A weighted average of the two-year numbers determined the annual percentages. The report defines an auto crash as any collision resulting in a property damage claim. *Allstate, "2011 Allstate America's Best Drivers Report™"*

- The National Insurance Crime Bureau ranked 366 metro areas in the U.S. in terms of per capita rates of vehicle theft. The Nashville metro area ranked #158 (#1 = highest rate). Criteria: number of vehicle theft offenses per 100,000 inhabitants in 2010. *National Insurance Crime Bureau, "Hot Spots," June 21, 2011*

- The Nashville metro area was identified as one of the most dangerous metro areas for pedestrians by Transportation for America. The metro area ranked #14 out of 52 metro areas with over 1 million residents. Criteria: area's population divided by the number of pedestrian fatalities in that area. *Transportation for America, "Dangerous by Design 2011"*

Seniors/Retirement Rankings

- Bankers Life and Casualty Company, in partnership with Sperling's BestPlaces, ranked the nation's 50 largest metro areas in terms of the "Best U.S. Cities for Seniors." The Nashville metro area ranked #28. Criteria: healthcare; transportation; housing; environment; economy; health and longevity; social and spiritual life; crime. *Bankers Life and Casualty Company, Center for a Secure Retirement, "Best U.S. Cities for Seniors 2011," September 2011*

- The Nashville metro area was identified as one of "America's Most Affordable Places to Retire" by *Forbes*. The metro area ranked #10. Criteria: housing affordability; inflation; number of persons over 65 who are employed; net migration for persons over 65; percent of persons over 65 living below poverty level; doctors per capita; number of citizens tapping their Medicare benefits per thousand people. *Forbes.com, "America's Most Affordable Places to Retire," September 5, 2008*

- The Nashville metro area was selected as one of "America's Best Places to Grow Old" by *Forbes*. The area was ranked #10 out of 10. Criteria: housing affordability; inflationary pressures; number of persons over 65 who are currently employed; net migration for persons over 65; percent of seniors living below poverty level; doctors per capita; number of citizens tapping their Medicare benefits per 1,000 people. *Forbes, "America's Best Places to Grow Old," December 12, 2008*

Sports/Recreation Rankings

- Nashville was selected as one of "10 Great Golf Cities" by *Livability.com*. The city was ranked #5. *Livability.com* searched 200 of the most livable cities in America to find the top 10 best lesser-known cities for golfers. *Livability.com, "Golf's Best Kept Secrets: 10 Great Golf Cities," March 2, 2010*

- Nashville appeared on the *Sporting News* list of the "Best Sports Cities" for 2011. The area ranked #16 out of 271 cities in the U.S. *Sporting News* takes a 12-month snapshot of each city's sports, putting a heavy premium on regular-season won-lost records (from the most recently completed season). Other criteria include: playoff berths, bowl appearances and tournament bids; championships; applicable power ratings; quality of competition; overall fan fervor (measured in part by attendance); abundance of teams (rewarding quality over quantity); stadium and arena quality; ticket availability and prices; franchise ownership; and marquee appeal of athletes. *Sporting News, "Best Sports Cities 2011," October 4, 2011*

- The Nashville was selected as one of the best metro areas for golf in America by *Golf Digest*. The Nashville area was ranked #9 out of 20. Criteria: climate; cost of public golf; quality of public golf; accessibility. *Golf Digest, "The Top 20 Cities for Golf," October 2011*

Technology Rankings

- Nashville was selected as a 2011 Digital Cities Survey winner. The city ranked #3 in the large city (250,000 or more population) category. The survey examined and assessed how city governments are utilizing information technology to operate and deliver quality service to their customers and citizens. Survey questions focused on implementation and adoption of online service delivery; planning and governance; and the infrastructure and architecture that make the transformation to digital government possible. *Center for Digital Government, "2011 Digital Cities Survey"*

Transportation Rankings

- The Nashville metro area appeared on *Forbes* list of the best and worst cities for commuters. The metro area ranked #49 out of 60 (#1 is best). Criteria: travel time; road congestion; travel delays. *Forbes.com, "Best and Worst Cities for Commuters," February 16, 2010*

Women/Minorities Rankings

- *Women's Health* examined U.S. cities and identified the 100 best cities for women. Nashville was ranked #64. Criteria: 30 categories were examined from obesity and breast cancer rates to commuting times and hours spent working out. *Women's Health, "Best Cities for Women 2012"*

- Nashville was ranked #56 out of 100 metro areas in *SELF Magazine's* ranking of America's healthiest places for women." A panel of experts came up with more than 50 criteria including death and disease rates, environmental indicators, community resources, and lifestyle habits. *SELF Magazine, "Secrets of America's Healthiest Women," December 2008*

- Nashville appeared on *Black Enterprise's* list of the "Ten Best Cities for African Americans." The top picks were culled from more than 2,000 interactive surveys completed on *BlackEnterprise.com* and by editorial staff evaluation. The editors weighed the following criteria as it pertained to African Americans in each city: median household income; percentage of households earning more than $100,000; percentage of businesses owned; percentage of college graduates; unemployment rates; home loan rejections; and homeownership rates. *Black Enterprise, May 2007*

- The Nashville metro area appeared on *Forbes'* list of the "Best Cities for Minority Entrepreneurs." The area ranked #56 out of 10. Criteria: 52 metropolitan statistical areas were examined. For each ethnicity (African Americans, Asians and Hispanics), the editors measured housing affordability, population growth, income growth, and entrepreneurship (per capita self-employment). *Forbes, "Best Cities for Minority Entrepreneurs," March 23, 2011*

Miscellaneous Rankings

- *Men's Health* ranked 100 U.S. cities by their level of sadness. Nashville was ranked #59 (#1 = saddest city). Criteria: suicide rates; unemployment rates; percentage of households that use antidepressants; percent of population who report feeling blue all or most of the time. *Men's Health, "Frown Towns," November 28, 2011*

- The Nashville metro area was selected as one of "The Best U.S. Cities for Bargain Shopping" by *Forbes*. The area ranked #9 out of 10. Criteria: number of outlet stores; gross leasable retail space in major malls; low consumer price index; low sales tax rate. Indicators were examined in the nation's 50 largest metropolitan areas. *Forbes, "The Best U.S. Cities for Bargain Shopping," January 20, 2012*

- Energizer Holdings, the makers of Edge® shave gel, in partnership with Sperling's BestPlaces, ranked 50 major metro areas in terms of everyday irritations. The Nashville metro area ranked #19. Criteria: humidity levels; weather conditions; incidence of traffic delays and congestion; average commute times; frequency of flight delays and cancellations; rates of sleeplessness; underemployment; pollens and allergens; pests; comedy clubs per capita. *Energizer Holdings, "Most Irritation Prone Cities," July 23, 2010*

- Mars Chocolate North America, the makers of COMBOS®, in partnership with Sperling's BestPlaces, ranked 50 major metro areas in terms of their "manliness." The Nashville metro area ranked #1. Criteria: number of professional sports teams; number of nearby NASCAR tracks and racing events; manly lifestyle; concentration of manly retail stores; manly occupations per capita; salty snack sales; "Board of Manliness" rankings. *Mars Chocolate North America, "America's Manliest Cities 2011," September 1, 2011*

- The Nashville metro area appeared in *AutoMD.com's* ranking of the "Best and Worst Cities for Auto Repair." The metro area ranked #11 (#1 is best). The 50 most-populated metro areas in the U.S. were ranked on three critical factors: repair affordability; price disparity range; shop integrity factor. *AutoMD.com, "Advocacy for Repair Shop Fairness Report," February 24, 2010*

- Nashville was identified as one of "America's Vainest Cities" by *Forbes.com*. The city ranked #6. Criteria: highest number of cosmetic surgeons per 100,000 people in America's 50 largest cities. *Forbes.com, "America's Vainest Cities," November 29, 2007*

Business Environment

CITY FINANCES

City Government Finances

Component	2009 ($000)	2009 ($ per capita)
Total Revenues	2,891,532	4,894
Total Expenditures	3,643,428	6,167
Debt Outstanding	3,757,131	6,359
Cash and Securities[1]	4,245,690	7,186

Note: (1) Cash and security holdings of a government at the close of its fiscal year, including those of its dependent agencies, utilities, and liquor stores.
Source: U.S Census Bureau, State & Local Government Finances 2009

City Government Revenue by Source

Source	2009 ($000)	2009 ($ per capita)
General Revenue		
From Federal Government	11,902	20
From State Government	488,506	827
From Local Governments	0	0
Taxes		
Property	775,404	1,312
Sales and Gross Receipts	336,066	569
Personal Income	0	0
Corporate Income	0	0
Motor Vehicle License	17,631	30
Other Taxes	38,598	65
Current Charges	270,399	458
Liquor Store	0	0
Utility	1,260,307	2,133
Employee Retirement	-476,358	-806

Source: U.S Census Bureau, State & Local Government Finances 2009

City Government Expenditures by Function

Function	2009 ($000)	2009 ($ per capita)	2009 (%)
General Direct Expenditures			
Air Transportation	0	0	0.0
Corrections	57,605	98	1.6
Education	769,435	1,302	21.1
Employment Security Administration	0	0	0.0
Financial Administration	23,508	40	0.6
Fire Protection	107,035	181	2.9
General Public Buildings	0	0	0.0
Governmental Administration, Other	22,397	38	0.6
Health	54,335	92	1.5
Highways	59,245	100	1.6
Hospitals	137,239	232	3.8
Housing and Community Development	0	0	0.0
Interest on General Debt	161,772	274	4.4
Judicial and Legal	62,057	105	1.7
Libraries	20,565	35	0.6
Parking	0	0	0.0
Parks and Recreation	78,563	133	2.2
Police Protection	170,609	289	4.7
Public Welfare	30,198	51	0.8
Sewerage	81,102	137	2.2
Solid Waste Management	19,798	34	0.5
Veterans' Services	0	0	0.0
Liquor Store	0	0	0.0
Utility	1,308,063	2,214	35.9
Employee Retirement	162,568	275	4.5

Source: U.S Census Bureau, State & Local Government Finances 2009

Municipal Bond Ratings

Area	Moody's	S&P	Fitch
City	Aa2	AA	AA

Rating Systems (shown in declining order of credit quality): Moody's– Aaa, Aa, A, Baa, Ba, B, Caa, Ca, C (numerical modifiers 1, 2, and 3 are added to letter-rating); S&P– AAA, AA, A, BBB, BB, B, CCC, CC, C; Fitch– AAA, AA, A, BBB, BB, B, CCC, CC, C. Ratings may be modified by the addition of a plus or minus sign to show relative standing within the major rating categories.
Notes: n/a Not Available; w/d Withdrawn (1) Not Reviewed; (2) Issuer Rating/No General Obligation; (3) Standard and Poor's Issue Credit Rating (ICR) is a current opinion of an obliger with respect to a specific financial obligation, a specific class of financial obligations, or a specific financial program.
Source: U.S. Census Bureau, 2012 Statistical Abstract, Bond Ratings for City Governments by Largest Cities: 2010

DEMOGRAPHICS

Population Growth

Area	1990 Census	2000 Census	2010 Census	Population Growth (%) 1990-2000	2000-2010
City	488,364	545,524	601,222	11.7	10.2
MSA[1]	1,048,218	1,311,789	1,589,934	25.1	21.2
U.S.	248,709,873	281,421,906	308,745,538	13.2	9.7

Note: (1) Figures cover the Nashville-Davidson—Murfreesboro—Franklin, TN Metropolitan Statistical Area—see Appendix B for areas included
Source: U.S. Census Bureau, 2010 Census

Household Size

Area	One	Two	Three	Four	Five	Six	Seven or More	Average Household Size
City	34.8	32.2	14.7	10.0	4.8	2.0	1.5	2.31
MSA[1]	26.8	33.3	16.8	13.6	6.0	2.2	1.4	2.52
U.S.	26.7	32.8	16.1	13.4	6.5	2.6	1.9	2.58

Note: (1) Figures cover the Nashville-Davidson—Murfreesboro—Franklin, TN Metropolitan Statistical Area—see Appendix B for areas included
Source: U.S. Census Bureau, 2010 Census

Race

Area	White Alone[2] (%)	Black Alone[2] (%)	Asian Alone[2] (%)	AIAN[3] Alone[2] (%)	NHOPI[4] Alone[2] (%)	Other Race Alone[2] (%)	Two or More Races (%)
City	60.5	28.4	3.1	0.3	0.1	5.1	2.5
MSA[1]	76.9	15.2	2.3	0.3	0.1	3.2	2.1
U.S.	72.4	12.6	4.8	0.9	0.2	6.2	2.9

Note: (1) Figures cover the Nashville-Davidson—Murfreesboro—Franklin, TN Metropolitan Statistical Area—see Appendix B for areas included; (2) Alone is defined as not being in combination with one or more other races; (3) American Indian and Alaska Native; (4) Native Hawaiian and Other Pacific Islander
Source: U.S. Census Bureau, 2010 Census

Hispanic or Latino Origin

Area	Hispanic or Latino (%)	Mexican (%)	Puerto Rican (%)	Cuban (%)	Other Hispanic or Latino (%)
City	10.0	6.1	0.5	0.3	3.1
MSA[1]	6.6	4.1	0.4	0.2	1.9
U.S.	16.3	10.3	1.5	0.6	4.0

Note: Persons of Hispanic or Latino origin can be of any race; (1) Figures cover the Nashville-Davidson—Murfreesboro—Franklin, TN Metropolitan Statistical Area—see Appendix B for areas included
Source: U.S. Census Bureau, 2010 Census

Segregation

Type	Segregation Indices[1]				Percent Change		
	1990	2000	2010	2010 Rank[2]	1990-2000	1990-2010	2000-2010
Black/White	60.7	58.1	56.2	49	-2.6	-4.4	-1.9
Asian/White	45.2	44.4	41.0	51	-0.8	-4.2	-3.4
Hispanic/White	24.3	46.0	47.9	34	21.6	23.5	1.9

*Note: Figures are based on an analysis of 1990, 2000, and 2010 Census Decennial Census tract data by William H. Frey, Brookings Institution and the University of Michigan Social Science Data Analysis Network. In this analysis all racial groups (whites, blacks, and asians) are non-Hispanic members of those races. Hispanics are shown as a separate category; All figures cover the Metropolitan Statistical Area (see Appendix B for areas included); (1) Segregation Indices are Dissimilarity Indices that measure the degree to which the minority group is distributed differently than whites across census tracts. They range from 0 (complete integration) to 100 (complete segregation) where the value indicates the percentage of the minority group that needs to move to be distributed exactly like whites; (2) Ranges from 1 (most segregated) to 102 (least segregated); n/a not available.
Source: www.CensusScope.org*

Ancestry

Area	German	Irish	English	American	Italian	Polish	French[2]	Scottish	Dutch
City	10.0	10.0	8.9	7.9	2.5	1.2	2.1	2.2	1.2
MSA[1]	11.7	12.1	11.4	12.6	2.7	1.2	2.4	2.6	1.3
U.S.	16.1	11.6	8.8	6.1	5.7	3.2	3.0	1.9	1.6

*Note: Figures are the percentage of the total population reporting a particular ancestry. The nine most commonly reported ancestries in the U.S. are shown. Figures include multiple ancestries (e.g. if a person reported being Irish and Italian, they were included in both columns); (1) Figures cover the Nashville-Davidson—Murfreesboro—Franklin, TN Metropolitan Statistical Area—see Appendix B for areas included; (2) Excludes Basque
Source: U.S. Census Bureau, 2008-2010 American Community Survey 3-Year Estimates*

Foreign-Born Population

Area	Percent of Population Born in								
	Any Foreign Country	Mexico	Asia	Europe	Carribean	South America	Central America[2]	Africa	Canada
City	12.3	4.0	3.4	0.8	0.4	0.3	1.3	1.9	0.1
MSA[1]	7.5	2.2	2.2	0.6	0.2	0.3	0.9	0.8	0.2
U.S.	12.8	3.8	3.6	1.6	1.2	0.9	1.0	0.5	0.3

*Note: (1) Figures cover the Nashville-Davidson—Murfreesboro—Franklin, TN Metropolitan Statistical Area—see Appendix B for areas included; (2) Excludes Mexico.
Source: U.S. Census Bureau, 2008-2010 American Community Survey 3-Year Estimates*

Marital Status

Area	Never Married	Now Married[2]	Separated	Widowed	Divorced
City	39.3	39.8	2.6	5.3	13.0
MSA[1]	30.3	50.8	2.0	5.2	11.8
U.S.	31.6	49.6	2.2	6.1	10.7

*Note: Figures are percentages and cover the population 15 years of age and older; (1) Figures cover the Nashville-Davidson—Murfreesboro—Franklin, TN Metropolitan Statistical Area—see Appendix B for areas included; (2) Excludes separated
Source: U.S. Census Bureau, 2008-2010 American Community Survey 3-Year Estimates*

Age

Area	Percent of Population							Median Age
	Under Age 5	Age 5 to 17	Age 18 to 34	Age 35 to 49	Age 50 to 64	Age 65 to 79	80 Years and Over	
City	7.2	14.5	30.3	20.5	17.2	7.3	2.9	33.7
MSA[1]	6.9	17.5	24.6	21.9	18.4	8.0	2.7	35.7
U.S.	6.5	17.5	23.2	20.7	19.0	9.4	3.6	37.2

*Note: (1) Figures cover the Nashville-Davidson—Murfreesboro—Franklin, TN Metropolitan Statistical Area—see Appendix B for areas included
Source: U.S. Census Bureau, 2010 Census*

Male/Female Ratio

Area	Males	Females	Males per 100 Females
City	291,294	309,928	94.0
MSA[1]	777,473	812,461	95.7
U.S.	151,781,326	156,964,212	96.7

Note: (1) Figures cover the Nashville-Davidson—Murfreesboro—Franklin, TN Metropolitan Statistical Area—see Appendix B for areas included
Source: U.S. Census Bureau, 2010 Census

Religious Groups

Area	Catholic	Baptist	Non-Den.	Methodist[2]	Lutheran	LDS[3]	Pentecostal	Presbyterian[4]	Muslim[5]	Judaism
MSA[1]	4.1	25.3	5.8	6.1	0.4	0.8	2.2	2.1	0.2	0.4
U.S.	19.1	9.3	4.0	4.0	2.3	2.0	1.9	1.6	0.8	0.7

Note: Figures are the number of adherents as a percentage of the total population; (1) Figures cover the Nashville-Davidson—Murfreesboro—Franklin, TN Metropolitan Statistical Area—see Appendix B for areas included; (2) Methodist/Pietist; (3) Latter Day Saints; (4) Reformed; (5) Figures are estimates
Source: Association of Statisticians of American Religious Bodies, 2010 U.S. Religion Census: Religious Congregations & Membership Study

ECONOMY

Gross Metropolitan Product

Area	2007	2008	2009	2010	2010 Rank[2]
MSA[1]	75.4	77.9	76.4	80.3	40

Note: Figures are in billions of dollars; (1) Figures cover the Nashville-Davidson—Murfreesboro—Franklin, TN Metropolitan Statistical Area—see Appendix B for areas included; (2) Rank ranges from 1 to 363
Source: The United States Conference of Mayors, "U.S. Metro Economies: GMP and Employment Forecasts," June 2011

Economic Growth

Area	2007-2009 (%)	2010 (%)	2011 (%)	Rank[2]
MSA[1]	-1.3	4.2	2.7	173
U.S.	-1.3	2.9	2.5	–

Note: Figures are real Gross Metropolitan Product growth rates and represent annual average percent change; (1) Figures cover the Nashville-Davidson—Murfreesboro—Franklin, TN Metropolitan Statistical Area—see Appendix B for areas included; (2) Rank ranges from 1 to 363
Source: The United States Conference of Mayors, "U.S. Metro Economies: GMP and Employment Forecasts," June 2011

Metropolitan Area Exports

Area	2005	2006	2007	2008	2009	2010	2010 Rank[2]
MSA[1]	5,020.6	5,388.6	5,105.9	5,259.5	4,406.6	5,748.5	41

Note: Figures are in millions of dollars; (1) Figures cover the Nashville-Davidson—Murfreesboro—Franklin, TN Metropolitan Statistical Area—see Appendix B for areas included; (2) Rank ranges from 1 to 369
Source: U.S. Department of Commerce, International Trade Administration, Office of Trade & Industry Information, Manufacturing & Services, data extracted April 2, 2012

INCOME

Income

Area	Per Capita ($)	Median Household ($)	Average Household ($)
City	26,153	44,630	61,792
MSA[1]	26,953	50,837	68,640
U.S.	26,942	51,222	70,116

Note: (1) Figures cover the Nashville-Davidson—Murfreesboro—Franklin, TN Metropolitan Statistical Area—see Appendix B for areas included
Source: U.S. Census Bureau, 2008-2010 American Community Survey 3-Year Estimates

Household Income Distribution

Area	Percent of Households Earning							
	Under $15,000	$15,000 -24,999	$25,000 -34,999	$35,000 -49,999	$50,000 -74,999	$75,000 -99,000	$100,000 -149,999	$150,000 and up
City	15.2	12.0	11.9	16.4	18.7	10.5	8.9	6.4
MSA[1]	12.4	10.3	10.7	15.7	19.4	12.4	11.4	7.6
U.S.	13.0	11.0	10.6	14.2	18.5	12.1	12.2	8.4

Note: (1) Figures cover the Nashville-Davidson—Murfreesboro—Franklin, TN Metropolitan Statistical Area—see Appendix B for areas included
Source: U.S. Census Bureau, 2008-2010 American Community Survey 3-Year Estimates

Poverty Rate

Area	All Ages	Under 18 Years Old	18 to 64 Years Old	65 Years and Over
City	18.8	30.3	16.3	10.4
MSA[1]	13.9	19.6	12.4	9.3
U.S.	14.4	20.1	13.1	9.4

Note: Figures are percentage of people whose income during the past 12 months was below the poverty level;
(1) Figures cover the Nashville-Davidson—Murfreesboro—Franklin, TN Metropolitan Statistical Area—see Appendix B for areas included
Source: U.S. Census Bureau, 2008-2010 American Community Survey 3-Year Estimates

Personal Bankruptcy Filing Rate

Area	2006	2007	2008	2009	2010	2011
Davidson County	4.67	5.49	6.61	7.29	6.84	6.51
U.S.	2.00	2.73	3.53	4.61	4.97	4.37

Note: Numbers are per 1,000 population and include Chapter 7 and Chapter 13 filings
Source: Federal Deposit Insurance Corporation, Regional Economic Conditions, March 9, 2012

EMPLOYMENT

Labor Force and Employment

Area	Civilian Labor Force			Workers Employed		
	Dec. 2010	Dec. 2011	% Chg.	Dec. 2010	Dec. 2011	% Chg.
City	332,223	334,839	0.8	305,276	311,750	2.1
MSA[1]	823,775	831,576	0.9	758,483	774,567	2.1
U.S.	153,156,000	153,373,000	0.1	139,159,000	140,681,000	1.1

Note: Data is not seasonally adjusted and covers workers 16 years of age and older;
(1) Metropolitan Statistical Area—see Appendix B for areas included
Source: Bureau of Labor Statistics, http://stats.bls.gov

Unemployment Rate

Area	2011											
	Jan.	Feb.	Mar.	Apr.	May	Jun.	Jul.	Aug.	Sep.	Oct.	Nov.	Dec.
City	8.6	8.7	8.3	8.8	8.5	9.1	8.5	8.8	8.7	7.8	7.3	6.9
MSA[1]	8.8	8.8	8.3	8.6	8.4	8.9	8.4	8.5	8.5	7.6	7.2	6.9
U.S.	9.8	9.5	9.2	8.7	8.7	9.3	9.3	9.1	8.8	8.5	8.2	8.3

Note: Data is not seasonally adjusted and covers workers 16 years of age and older; All figures are percentages; (1) Metropolitan Statistical Area—see Appendix B for areas included
Source: Bureau of Labor Statistics, http://stats.bls.gov

Projected Unemployment Rate

Area	2010 (%)	2011 (%)	2012 (%)	2013 (%)
MSA[1]	8.4	8.0	7.3	6.8

Note: (1) Metropolitan Statistical Area—see Appendix B for areas included
Source: The United States Conference of Mayors, "U.S. Metro Economies: GMP and Employment Forecasts," June 2011

Employment by Occupation

Occupation Classification	City (%)	MSA[1] (%)	U.S. (%)
Management, Business, Science, and Arts	37.5	37.0	35.6
Natural Resources, Construction, and Maintenance	7.6	8.8	9.5
Production, Transportation, and Material Moving	10.2	11.6	12.1
Sales and Office	27.2	27.0	25.2
Service	17.5	15.5	17.6

Note: Figures cover employed civilians 16 years of age and older; (1) Figures cover the Nashville-Davidson—Murfreesboro—Franklin, TN Metropolitan Statistical Area—see Appendix B for areas included
Source: U.S. Census Bureau, 2008-2010 American Community Survey 3-Year Estimates

Employment by Industry

Sector	MSA[1] Number of Employees	MSA[1] Percent of Total	U.S. Percent of Total
Construction	n/a	n/a	4.1
Education and Health Services	120,800	15.9	15.2
Financial Activities	46,600	6.1	5.8
Government	104,600	13.7	16.8
Information	18,800	2.5	2.0
Leisure and Hospitality	77,500	10.2	9.9
Manufacturing	62,900	8.3	8.9
Mining and Logging	n/a	n/a	0.6
Other Services	33,100	4.3	4.0
Professional and Business Services	110,500	14.5	13.3
Retail Trade	86,200	11.3	11.5
Transportation and Utilities	30,500	4.0	3.8
Wholesale Trade	36,900	4.8	4.2

Note: Figures cover non-farm employment as of December 2011 and are not seasonally adjusted; (1) Metropolitan Statistical Area—see Appendix B for areas included; n/a not available
Source: Bureau of Labor Statistics, http://stats.bls.gov

Occupations with Greatest Projected Employment Growth: 2008 – 2018

Occupation[1]	2008 Employment	2018 Projected Employment	Numeric Employment Change	Percent Employment Change
Registered Nurses	61,600	71,750	10,150	16.5
Customer Service Representatives	55,110	63,610	8,500	15.4
Home Health Aides	13,700	21,800	8,100	59.1
Truck Drivers, Heavy and Tractor-Trailer	64,760	72,460	7,700	11.9
Combined Food Preparation and Serving Workers, Including Fast Food	64,590	71,850	7,260	11.2
Retail Salespersons	84,220	91,130	6,910	8.2
Office Clerks, General	65,370	71,770	6,400	9.8
Elementary School Teachers, Except Special Education	33,140	39,390	6,250	18.9
Nursing Aides, Orderlies, and Attendants	30,710	35,800	5,090	16.6
Licensed Practical and Licensed Vocational Nurses	25,390	30,390	5,000	19.7

Note: Projections cover Tennessee; (1) Sorted by numeric employment change
Source: www.projectionscentral.com, State Occupational Projections, 2008–2018 Long-Term Projections

Fastest Growing Occupations: 2008 – 2018

Occupation[1]	2008 Employment	2018 Projected Employment	Numeric Employment Change	Percent Employment Change
Biomedical Engineers	250	410	160	64.0
Home Health Aides	13,700	21,800	8,100	59.1
Network Systems and Data Communications Analysts	3,000	4,500	1,500	50.0
Medical Scientists, Except Epidemiologists	820	1,140	320	39.0
Physician Assistants	1,370	1,880	510	37.2
Commercial Pilots	350	480	130	37.1
Self-Enrichment Education Teachers	2,890	3,960	1,070	37.0
Financial Examiners	790	1,080	290	36.7
Psychiatric Aides	980	1,330	350	35.7
Personal and Home Care Aides	14,070	18,950	4,880	34.7

Note: Projections cover Tennessee; (1) Sorted by percent employment change and excludes occupations with numeric employment change less than 100
Source: www.projectionscentral.com, State Occupational Projections, 2008–2018 Long-Term Projections

Average Wages

Occupation	$/Hr.	Occupation	$/Hr.
Accountants and Auditors	29.64	Maids and Housekeeping Cleaners	9.10
Automotive Mechanics	17.30	Maintenance and Repair Workers	16.90
Bookkeepers	16.00	Marketing Managers	46.60
Carpenters	18.06	Nuclear Medicine Technologists	30.05
Cashiers	9.78	Nurses, Licensed Practical	18.81
Clerks, General Office	14.45	Nurses, Registered	30.99
Clerks, Receptionists/Information	12.64	Nursing Aides/Orderlies/Attendants	11.45
Clerks, Shipping/Receiving	13.85	Packers and Packagers, Hand	9.93
Computer Programmers	35.55	Physical Therapists	35.11
Computer Support Specialists	23.80	Postal Service Mail Carriers	24.48
Computer Systems Analysts	34.26	Real Estate Brokers	28.42
Cooks, Restaurant	11.15	Retail Salespersons	11.58
Dentists	70.70	Sales Reps., Exc. Tech./Scientific	28.49
Electrical Engineers	39.66	Sales Reps., Tech./Scientific	34.32
Electricians	20.54	Secretaries, Exc. Legal/Med./Exec.	14.84
Financial Managers	51.34	Security Guards	10.98
First-Line Supervisors/Managers, Sales	19.94	Surgeons	n/a
Food Preparation Workers	10.50	Teacher Assistants	10.90
General and Operations Managers	47.06	Teachers, Elementary School	22.30
Hairdressers/Cosmetologists	12.59	Teachers, Secondary School	22.70
Internists	82.01	Telemarketers	14.74
Janitors and Cleaners	9.99	Truck Drivers, Heavy/Tractor-Trailer	18.79
Landscaping/Groundskeeping Workers	11.26	Truck Drivers, Light/Delivery Svcs.	16.57
Lawyers	53.12	Waiters and Waitresses	9.18

Note: Wage data covers the Nashville-Davidson—Murfreesboro—Franklin, TN Metropolitan Statistical Area—see Appendix B for areas included. Hourly wages for elementary/secondary school teachers and teacher assistants were calculated by the editors from annual wage data assuming a 40 hour work week; n/a not available.
Source: Bureau of Labor Statistics, Metro Area Occupational Employment and Wage Estimates, May 2011

RESIDENTIAL REAL ESTATE

Building Permits

Area	Single-Family			Multi-Family			Total		
	2010	2011	Pct. Chg.	2010	2011	Pct. Chg.	2010	2011	Pct. Chg.
City	n/a	n/a	n/a	n/a	n/a	n/a	n/a	n/a	n/a
MSA[1]	3,938	4,100	4.1	1,154	1,294	12.1	5,092	5,394	5.9
U.S.	447,311	418,498	-6.4	157,299	205,563	30.7	604,610	624,061	3.2

Note: (1) Metropolitan Statistical Area—see Appendix B for areas included; figures represent new, privately-owned housing units authorized (unadjusted data); All permit data are based on estimates with imputation.
Source: U.S. Census Bureau, Manufacturing, Mining, and Construction Statistics, Building Permits, 2010, 2011

Homeownership Rate

Area	2005 (%)	2006 (%)	2007 (%)	2008 (%)	2009 (%)	2010 (%)	2011 (%)
MSA[1]	73.0	72.4	70.0	71.3	71.8	70.4	69.6
U.S.	68.9	68.8	68.1	67.8	67.4	66.9	66.1

Note: (1) Metropolitan Statistical Area—see Appendix B for areas included
Source: U.S. Census Bureau, Housing Vacancies and Homeownership Annual Statistics: 2011

Housing Vacancy Rates

Area	Gross Vacancy Rate[2] (%)			Year-Round Vacancy Rate[3] (%)			Rental Vacancy Rate[4] (%)			Homeowner Vacancy Rate[5] (%)		
	2009	2010	2011	2009	2010	2011	2009	2010	2011	2009	2010	2011
MSA[1]	8.7	10.9	9.0	8.1	10.5	8.3	8.3	8.2	8.2	1.9	2.4	2.2
U.S.	14.5	14.3	14.2	11.3	11.3	11.1	10.6	10.2	9.5	2.6	2.6	2.5

Note: (1) Metropolitan Statistical Area—see Appendix B for areas included; (2) The percentage of the total housing inventory that is vacant; (3) The percentage of the housing inventory (excluding seasonal units) that is year-round vacant; (4) The percentage of rental inventory that is vacant for rent; (5) The percentage of homeowner inventory that is vacant for sale
Source: U.S. Census Bureau, Housing Vacancies and Homeownership Annual Statistics: 2011

TAXES

State Corporate Income Tax Rates

State	Tax Rate (%)	Income Brackets ($)	Num. of Brackets	Financial Institution Tax Rate (%)[a]	Federal Income Tax Ded.
Tennessee	6.5	Flat rate	1	6.5	No

Note: Tax rates as of January 1, 2012; (a) Rates listed are the corporate income tax rate applied to financial institutions or excise taxes based on income. Some states have other taxes based upon the value of deposits or shares.
Source: Federation of Tax Administrators, "State Corporate Income Tax Rates, 2012"

State Individual Income Tax Rates

State	Tax Rate (%)	Income Brackets ($)	Num. of Brackets	Personal Exempt. ($)[1] Single	Dependents	Fed. Inc. Tax Ded.

Tennessee – State Income Tax of 6% on Dividends and Interest Income Only

Note: Tax rates as of January 1, 2012; Local- and county-level taxes are not included; n/a not applicable; (1) Married joint filers generally receive double the single exemption
Source: Federation of Tax Administrators, "State Individual Income Tax Rates, 2012"

Various State and Local Tax Rates

State	State and Local Sales and Use (%)	State Sales and Use (%)	Gasoline[1] (¢/gal.)	Cigarette[2] ($/pack)	Spirits[3] ($/gal.)	Wine[4] ($/gal.)	Beer[5] ($/gal.)
Tennessee	9.25	7.00	21.4	0.62	4.46 (h)	1.27	0.14

Note: All tax rates as of January 1, 2012 except beer, wine and spirits (September 1, 2011); (1) The American Petroleum Institute has developed a methodology for determining the average tax rate on a gallon of fuel. Rates may include any of the following: excise taxes, environmental fees, storage tank fees, other fees or taxes, general sales tax, and local taxes. In states where gasoline is subject to the general sales tax, or where the fuel tax is based on the average sale price, the average rate determined by API is sensitive to changes in the price of gasoline. States that fully or partially apply general sales taxes to gasoline: CA, CO, GA, IL, IN, MI, NY; (2) The federal excise tax of $1.0066 per pack and local taxes are not included; (3) Rates are those applicable to off-premise sales of 40% alcohol by volume (a.b.v.) distilled spirits in 750ml containers. Local excise taxes are excluded; (4) Rates are those applicable to off-premise sales of 11% a.b.v. non-carbonated wine in 750ml containers; (5) Rates are those applicable to off-premise sales of 4.7% a.b.v. beer in 12 ounce containers; (h) Includes case fees and/or bottle fees which may vary with the size of the container.
Source: Tax Foundation, 2012 Facts & Figures: How Does Your State Compare?

State-Local Tax Burdens

Area	Rate (%)	Rank[1]	Per Capita Taxes Paid to Home State ($)	Total State and Local Per Capita Taxes Paid ($)	Per Capita Income ($)
Tennessee	7.6	47	1,851	2,752	36,157
U.S. Average	9.8	-	3,057	4,160	42,539

Note: Figures cover 2009; (1) Rank ranges from 1 to 50 where 1 is highest tax burden
Source: Tax Foundation, State-Local Tax Burdens, All States, 2009

State Business Tax Climate Index Rankings

State	Overall Rank	Corporate Tax Index Rank	Individual Income Tax Index Rank	Sales Tax Index Rank	Unemployment Insurance Tax Index Rank	Property Tax Index Rank
Tennessee	14	13	8	43	27	48

Note: The index is a measure of how each state's tax laws affect economic performance. The lower the rank, the more favorable a state's tax system is for business. States without a given tax are given a ranking of 1.
Source: Tax Foundation, Major Components of the State Business Tax Climate Index, FY 2012

COMMERCIAL UTILITIES

Typical Monthly Electric Bills

Area	Commercial Service ($/month)		Industrial Service ($/month)	
	40 kW demand 5,000 kWh	500 kW demand 100,000 kWh	5,000 kW demand 1,500,000 kWh	70,000 kW demand 50,000,000 kWh
City	548	13,025	165,609	3,389,740

Note: Based on rates in effect January 1, 2011
Source: Memphis Light, Gas and Water, 2011 Utility Bill Comparisons for Selected U.S. Cities

TRANSPORTATION

Means of Transportation to Work

Area	Car/Truck/Van		Public Transportation			Bicycle	Walked	Other Means	Worked at Home
	Drove Alone	Car-pooled	Bus	Subway	Railroad				
City	79.7	10.3	2.0	0.0	0.1	0.3	2.0	1.1	4.5
MSA[1]	81.2	10.7	1.0	0.0	0.1	0.2	1.3	1.0	4.5
U.S.	76.0	10.2	2.7	1.7	0.5	0.5	2.8	1.3	4.2

Note: Figures are percentages and cover workers 16 years of age and older; (1) Figures cover the Nashville-Davidson—Murfreesboro—Franklin, TN Metropolitan Statistical Area—see Appendix B for areas included
Source: U.S. Census Bureau, 2008-2010 American Community Survey 3-Year Estimates

Travel Time to Work

Area	Less Than 10 Minutes	10 to 19 Minutes	20 to 29 Minutes	30 to 44 Minutes	45 to 59 Minutes	60 to 89 Minutes	90 Minutes or More
City	9.2	31.3	29.0	22.5	5.1	1.7	1.2
MSA[1]	10.3	27.7	23.2	23.4	9.5	4.3	1.6
U.S.	13.9	30.1	20.8	19.8	7.5	5.5	2.5

Note: Figures are percentages and include workers 16 years old and over; (1) Figures cover the Nashville-Davidson—Murfreesboro—Franklin, TN Metropolitan Statistical Area—see Appendix B for areas included
Source: U.S. Census Bureau, 2008-2010 American Community Survey 3-Year Estimates

Travel Time Index

Area	1985	1990	1995	2000	2005	2010
Urban Area[1]	1.10	1.13	1.15	1.18	1.20	1.18
Average[2]	1.11	1.16	1.18	1.21	1.25	1.20

Note: Travel Time Index—the ratio of travel time in the peak period to the travel time at free-flow conditions. A value of 1.30 indicates a 20-minute free-flow trip takes 26 minutes in the peak. Free-flow speeds (60 mph on freeways and 35 mph on principal arterials) are used as the comparison threshold; (1) Covers the Nashville-Davidson TN urban area; (2) average of 439 urban areas
Source: Texas Transportation Institute, Urban Mobility Report 2011, September 2011

Public Transportation

Agency Name / Mode of Transportation	Vehicles Operated in Maximum Service	Annual Unlinked Passenger Trips ('000)	Annual Passenger Miles ('000)
Metropolitan Transit Authority (MTA)			
Bus (directly operated)	111	8,623.8	43,852.6
Demand Response (directly operated)	48	247.2	2,999.2
Demand Response Taxi (purchased transportation)	74	71.6	781.6

Source: Federal Transit Administration, National Transit Database, 2010

Air Transportation

Airport Name and Code / Type of Service	Passenger Airlines[1]	Passenger Enplanements	Freight Carriers[2]	Freight (lbs.)
Nashville International (BNA)				
Domestic service (U.S. carriers - 2011)	40	4,647,288	19	48,386,088
International service (U.S. carriers - 2010)	10	3,149	0	0

Note: (1) Includes all U.S.-based major, minor and commuter airlines that carried at least one passenger during the year; (2) Includes all U.S.-based airlines and freight carriers that transported at least one pound of freight during the year
Source: Bureau of Transportation Statistics, The Intermodal Transportation Database, Air Carriers: T-100 Domestic Market (U.S. Carriers), 2011; Bureau of Transportation Statistics, The Intermodal Transportation Database, Air Carriers: T-100 International Market (U.S. Carriers), 2010

Other Transportation Statistics

Major Highways:	I-24; I-40; I-65
Amtrak Service:	Bus connection
Major Waterways/Ports:	Cumberland River; Port of Nashville

Source: Amtrak.com; Google Maps

BUSINESSES

Major Business Headquarters

Company Name	Rankings	
	Fortune[1]	Forbes[2]
HCA Holdings	90	-

Note: (1) Fortune 500—companies that produce a 10-K are ranked 1 to 500 based on 2010 revenue; (2) all private companies with at least $2 billion in annual revenue are ranked 1 to 212; companies listed are headquartered in the city; dashes indicate no ranking
Source: Fortune, "Fortune 500," May 23, 2011; Forbes, "America's Largest Private Companies," November 16, 2011

Fast-Growing Businesses

According to *Inc.*, Nashville is home to one of America's 500 fastest-growing private companies: **Randa Solutions** (#388). Criteria: must be an independent, privately-held, for-profit, U.S. corporation, proprietorship or partnership; revenues must be at least $80,000 in 2007 and $2 million in 2010; must have four-year operating/sales history. Holding companies, regulated banks, and utilities were excluded. *Inc., "America's 500 Fastest-Growing Private Companies," September 2011*

According to *Initiative for a Competitive Inner City (ICIC)*, Nashville is home to three of America's 100 fastest-growing "inner city" companies: **Emma** (#10); **Centresource Interactive Agency** (#46); **Concept Technology** (#55). Companies were ranked by their five-year compound annual growth rate. Criteria for inclusion: company must be headquartered in or have 51 percent or more of its physical operations in an economically distressed urban area; must be an independent, for-profit corporation, partnership or proprietorship; must have 10 or more employees and have a five-year sales history that includes sales of at least $200,000 in the base year and at least $1 million in the current year with no decrease in sales over the two most recent years. *Initiative for a Competitive Inner City (ICIC), "Inner City 100 Companies, 2011"*

According to Deloitte, Nashville is home to one of North America's 500 fastest-growing high-technology companies: **Cumberland Pharmaceuticals** (#457). Companies are ranked by percentage growth in revenue over a five-year period. Criteria for inclusion: company must be headquartered within North America; must own proprietary intellectual property or proprietary technology that contributes to a significant portion of the company's operating revenue, or devote a significant proportion of revenues to research and development of technology; must have been in business for a minumum of five years with 2006 operating revenues of at least $50,000 USD/CD and 2010 operating revenues of at least $5 million USD/CD. *Deloitte Touche Tohmatsu, 2011 Deloitte Technology Fast 500*[TM]

Minority Business Opportunity

Nashville is home to one company which is on the *Black Enterprise* Industrial/Service 100 list (100 largest companies based on gross sales): **Zycron** (#86). Criteria: operational in previous calendar year; at least 51% black-owned and manufactures/owns the product it sells or provides industrial or consumer services. Brokerages, real estate firms and firms that provide professional services are not eligible. *Black Enterprise, B.E. 100s, 2011*

Nashville is home to one company which is on the *Black Enterprise* Bank 20 list (20 largest banks based on total assets, capital, deposits and loans, including mortgage-backed securities for the calendar year): **Citizens Savings Bank & Trust Company** (#17). Only commercial banks or savings and loans that are classified by the Federal Reserve as black institutions and have been fully operational for the previous calendar year were considered. *Black Enterprise, B.E. 100s, 2011*

Minority- and Women-Owned Businesses

Group	All Firms		Firms with Paid Employees			
	Firms	Sales ($000)	Firms	Sales ($000)	Employees	Payroll ($000)
Asian	n/a	n/a	n/a	n/a	n/a	n/a
Black	n/a	n/a	n/a	n/a	n/a	n/a
Hispanic	n/a	n/a	n/a	n/a	n/a	n/a
Women	n/a	n/a	n/a	n/a	n/a	n/a
All Firms						

Note: Figures cover firms located in the city; minority- and women-owned business are defined as firms in which the corresponding group own 51% or more of the stock or equity of the company; n/a not available
Source: U.S. Census Bureau, 2007 Economic Census, Survey of Business Owners

HOTELS

Hotels/Motels

Area	5 Star		4 Star		3 Star		2 Star		1 Star		Not Rated	
	Num.	Pct.[3]	Num.	Pct.[3]	Num.	Pct.[3]	Num.	Pct.[3]	Num.	Pct.[3]	Num.	Pct.[3]
City[1]	0	0.0	8	3.7	44	20.1	135	61.6	8	3.7	24	11.0
Total[2]	133	0.9	940	6.5	4,569	31.8	7,033	48.9	351	2.4	1,343	9.3

Note: (1) Figures cover Nashville and vicinity; (2) Figures cover all 100 cities in this book; (3) Percentage of hotels which have a given star rating; Star ratings are determined by expedia.com and offer an indication of the general quality of a particular hotel.
Source: expedia.com, April 25, 2012

The Nashville-Davidson—Murfreesboro—Franklin, TN metro area is home to one of the best hotels in the U.S. according to *Travel & Leisure*: **Hermitage Hotel** (#91). Criteria: service; location; rooms; food; and value. *Travel & Leisure, "T+L 500, The World's Best Hotels 2012"*

EVENT SITES

Major Stadiums, Arenas, and Auditoriums

Name	Max. Capacity
Bridgestone Arena	20,000
Gentry Complex, Tennessee State University	10,500
Grand Ole Opry House	4,400
Herschel Greer Stadium	10,139
LP Field	68,798
Nashville Municipal Auditorium	9,654
Vanderbilt Stadium at Dudley Field	39,790

Source: Original research

Convention Centers

Name	Overall Space (sq. ft.)	Exhibit Space (sq. ft.)	Meeting Space (sq. ft.)	Meeting Rooms
Nashville Convention Center	n/a	n/a	118,675	25

Note: n/a not available
Source: Original research

Living Environment

COST OF LIVING

Cost of Living Index

Composite Index	Groceries	Housing	Utilities	Trans-portation	Health Care	Misc. Goods/ Services
90.3	97.5	70.6	87.1	93.4	91.6	104.6

Note: U.S. = 100; Figures cover the Nashville-Franklin TN urban area.
Source: The Council for Community and Economic Research, ACCRA Cost of Living Index, 2011

Grocery Prices

Area[1]	T-Bone Steak ($/pound)	Frying Chicken ($/pound)	Whole Milk ($/half gal.)	Eggs ($/dozen)	Orange Juice ($/64 oz.)	Coffee ($/11.5 oz.)
City[2]	8.40	1.33	2.54	1.39	3.14	4.26
Avg.	9.25	1.18	2.22	1.66	3.19	4.40
Min.	6.70	0.88	1.31	0.95	2.46	2.94
Max.	14.30	2.16	3.50	3.18	4.75	6.83

Note: (1) Values for the local area are compared with the average, minimum and maximum values for all 335 areas in the Cost of Living Index; (2) Figures cover the Nashville-Franklin TN urban area; **T-Bone Steak** *(price per pound);* **Frying Chicken** *(price per pound, whole fryer);* **Whole Milk** *(half gallon carton);* **Eggs** *(price per dozen, Grade A, large);* **Orange Juice** *(64 oz. Tropicana or Florida Natural);* **Coffee** *(11.5 oz. can, vacuum-packed, Maxwell House, Hills Bros, or Folgers).*
Source: The Council for Community and Economic Research, ACCRA Cost of Living Index, 2011

Housing and Utility Costs

Area[1]	New Home Price ($)	Apartment Rent ($/month)	All Electric ($/month)	Part Electric ($/month)	Other Energy ($/month)	Telephone ($/month)
City[2]	188,005	795	-	82.30	60.69	23.86
Avg.	285,990	839	163.23	89.00	77.52	26.92
Min.	188,005	460	125.58	45.39	33.89	17.98
Max.	1,197,028	3,244	339.16	181.97	348.69	40.01

Note: (1) Values for the local area are compared with the average, minimum and maximum values for all 335 areas in the Cost of Living Index; (2) Figures cover the Nashville-Franklin TN urban area; **New Home Price** *(2,400 sf living area, 8,000 sf lot, in urban area with full utilities);* **Apartment Rent** *(950 sf 2 bedroom/1.5 or 2 bath, unfurnished, excluding all utilities except water);* **All Electric** *(average monthly cost for an all-electric home);* **Part Electric** *(average monthly cost for a part-electric home);* **Other Energy** *(average monthly cost for natural gas, fuel oil, coal, wood, and any other forms of energy except electricity);* **Telephone** *(price includes basic monthly rate for a private residential line plus additional local usage charges incurred by a family of four).*
Source: The Council for Community and Economic Research, ACCRA Cost of Living Index, 2011

Health Care, Transportation, and Other Costs

Area[1]	Doctor ($/visit)	Dentist ($/visit)	Optometrist ($/visit)	Gasoline ($/gallon)	Beauty Salon ($/visit)	Men's Shirt ($)
City[2]	81.47	78.78	86.47	3.34	29.00	24.20
Avg.	93.88	81.72	90.54	3.48	32.65	25.06
Min.	60.00	55.33	53.66	3.18	19.78	13.44
Max.	154.98	145.97	183.72	4.31	63.21	46.00

Note: (1) Values for the local area are compared with the average, minimum and maximum values for all 335 areas in the Cost of Living Index; (2) Figures cover the Nashville-Franklin TN urban area; **Doctor** *(general practitioners routine exam of an established patient);* **Dentist** *(adult teeth cleaning and periodic oral examination);* **Optometrist** *(full vision eye exam for established adult patient);* **Gasoline** *(one gallon regular unleaded, national brand, including all taxes, cash price at self-service pump if available);* **Beauty Salon** *(woman's shampoo, trim, and blow-dry);* **Men's Shirt** *(cotton/polyester dress shirt, pinpoint weave, long sleeves).*
Source: The Council for Community and Economic Research, ACCRA Cost of Living Index, 2011

HOUSING

House Price Index (HPI)

Area	National Ranking[2]	Quarterly Change (%)	One-Year Change (%)	Five-Year Change (%)
MSA[1]	122	0.01	-1.98	-2.79
U.S.[3]	-	-0.10	-2.43	-19.16

Note: The HPI is a weighted repeat sales index. It measures average price changes in repeat sales or refinancings on the same properties. This information is obtained by reviewing repeat mortgage transactions on single-family properties whose mortgages have been purchased or securitized by Fannie Mae or Freddie Mac in January 1975; (1) Metropolitan/Micropolitan Statistical Area—see Appendix B for areas included; (2) Rankings are based on annual percentage change for all metro areas containing at least 15,000 transactions over the last 10 years and ranges from 1 to 306; (3) figures based on a weighted average of Census Division estimates using a purchase only index; all figures are for the period ending December 31, 2011
Source: Federal Housing Finance Agency, House Price Index, February 23, 2012

House Price Valuations

Area	Q4 2005 Price ($000)	Q4 2005 Over-valuation	Q4 2006 Price ($000)	Q4 2006 Over-valuation	Q4 2007 Price ($000)	Q4 2007 Over-valuation	Q4 2008 Price ($000)	Q4 2008 Over-valuation	Q4 2009 Price ($000)	Q4 2009 Over-valuation
MSA[1]	155.2	-3.2	168.8	-1.1	173.3	-2.6	167.7	-4.7	164.6	-8.0

Note: Figures show the percentage of over- or under-valuation of single family homes relative to statistically normal house values (e.g. a value of 23.6 indicates that house values are 23.6% overvalued). Statistically normal house values are based on house prices, interest rates, household incomes, population densities, and any historical premiums or discounts metropolitan areas have exhibited over time; (1) Figures cover the Nashville-Davidson—Murfreesboro—Franklin, TN - see Appendix B for areas included
Source: Global Insight/PNC Financial Services Group, House Prices in America: 4th Quarter 2009 Update

Median Single-Family Home Prices

Area	2009	2010	2011[p]	Percent Change 2010 to 2011
MSA[1]	147.9	153.8	151.9	-1.2
U.S. Average	172.1	173.1	166.2	-4.0

Note: Figures are median sales prices of existing single-family homes in thousands of dollars; (p) preliminary; n/a not available; (1) Metropolitan Statistical Area—see Appendix B for areas included
Source: National Association of Realtors, Median Sales Price of Existing Single-Family Homes for Metropolitan Areas, 4th Quarter 2011

Affordability Index of Existing Single-Family Homes

Area	2009	2010	2011[p]	Percent Change 2010 to 2011
MSA[1]	125.6	129.4	137.2	6.0

Note: The housing affordability index measures whether or not a typical family could qualify for a mortgage loan on a typical home. The higher the index, the greater the household purchasing power. An index of 100 is defined as the point where a median-income household has exactly enough income to qualify for the purchase of a median-priced existing single-family home, assuming a 20 percent downpayment and 25 percent of gross income devoted to mortgage principal and interest payments; (p) preliminary; n/a not available; (1) Metropolitan Statistical Area—see Appendix B for areas included
Source: National Association of Realtors, Affordability Index of Existing Single-Family Homes, 2011

Median Apartment Condo-Coop Home Prices

Area	2009	2010	2011[p]	Percent Change 2010 to 2011
MSA[1]	n/a	n/a	n/a	n/a
U.S. Average	175.6	171.7	165.1	-3.8

Note: Figures are median sales prices of existing apartment condo-coop homes in thousands of dollars; (p) preliminary; n/a not available; (1) Metropolitan Statistical Area—see Appendix B for areas included
Source: National Association of Realtors, Median Sales Price of Existing Apartment Condo-Coop Homes for Metropolitan Areas, 4th Quarter 2011

Year Housing Structure Built

Area	2005 or Later	2000 -2004	1990 -1999	1980 -1989	1970 -1979	1960 -1969	1950 -1959	Before 1950	Median Year
City	5.9	7.6	12.2	16.6	18.9	14.7	11.7	12.5	1976
MSA[1]	8.4	11.8	19.3	16.2	16.2	11.1	7.8	9.1	1984
U.S.	5.0	8.6	14.0	14.1	16.3	11.3	11.2	19.6	1975

Note: Figures are percentages except for Median Year; (1) Figures cover the Nashville-Davidson—Murfreesboro—Franklin, TN Metropolitan Statistical Area—see Appendix B for areas included
Source: U.S. Census Bureau, 2008-2010 American Community Survey 3-Year Estimates

HEALTH

Health Risk Data

Category	MSA[1] (%)	U.S. (%)
Adults who have been told they have high blood pressure[2]	26.3	28.7
Adults who have been told they have high blood cholesterol[2]	28.2	37.5
Adults who have been told they have diabetes[3]	8.7	8.7
Adults who have been told they have arthritis[2]	24.1	26.0
Adults who have been told they currently have asthma	5.6	9.1
Adults who are current smokers	17.4	17.3
Adults who are heavy drinkers[4]	1.0	5.0
Adults who are binge drinkers[5]	7.9	15.1
Adults who are overweight (BMI 25.0 - 29.9)	37.4	36.2
Adults who are obese (BMI 30.0 - 99.8)	24.7	27.5
Adults who participated in any physical activities in the past month	73.3	76.1
Adults 50+ who have ever had a sigmoidoscopy or colonoscopy	66.2	65.2
Women aged 40+ who have had a mammogram within the past two years	77.0	75.2
Men aged 40+ who have had a PSA test within the past two years	53.3	53.2
Adults aged 65+ who have had flu shot within the past year	69.3	67.5
Adults aged 18–64 who have any kind of health care coverage	84.0	82.2

Note: Data as of 2010 unless otherwise noted; (1) Figures cover the Nashville-Davidson—Murfreesboro, TN Metropolitan Statistical Area—see Appendix B for areas included; (2) Data as of 2009; (3) Figures do not include pregnancy-related, borderline, or pre-diabetes; (4) Heavy drinkers are classified as males having more than two drinks per day or females having more than one drink per day; (5) Binge drinkers are classified as males having five or more drinks on one occasion or females having four or more drinks on one occasion
Source: Centers for Disease Control and Prevention, Behaviorial Risk Factor Surveillance System, SMART: Selected Metropolitan/Micropolitan Area Risk Trends, 2009, 2010

Mortality Rates for the Top 10 Causes of Death in the U.S.

ICD-10[a] Sub-Chapter	ICD-10[a] Code	Age-Adjusted Mortality Rate[1] per 100,000 population	
		County[2]	U.S.
Malignant neoplasms	C00-C97	187.4	175.6
Ischaemic heart diseases	I20-I25	139.4	121.6
Other forms of heart disease	I30-I51	35.9	48.6
Chronic lower respiratory diseases	J40-J47	47.2	42.3
Cerebrovascular diseases	I60-I69	46.4	40.6
Organic, including symptomatic, mental disorders	F01-F09	35.3	26.7
Other degenerative diseases of the nervous system	G30-G31	31.7	24.7
Other external causes of accidental injury	W00-X59	32.4	24.4
Diabetes mellitus	E10-E14	28.0	21.7
Hypertensive diseases	I10-I15	28.6	18.2

Note: (a) ICD-10 = International Classification of Diseases 10th Revision; (1) Mortality rates are a three year average covering 2007-2009; (2) Figures cover Davidson County
Source: Centers for Disease Control and Prevention, National Center for Health Statistics. Underlying Cause of Death 1999-2009 on CDC WONDER Online Database, released 2012. Data for year 2009 are compiled from the Multiple Cause of Death File 2009, Series 20 No. 2O, 2012, Data for year 2008 are compiled from the Multiple Cause of Death File 2008, Series 20 No. 2N, 2011, Data for year 2007 are compiled from Multiple Cause of Death File 2007, Series 20 No. 2M, 2010.

Mortality Rates for Selected Causes of Death

ICD-10[a] Sub-Chapter	ICD-10[a] Code	Age-Adjusted Mortality Rate[1] per 100,000 population	
		County[2]	U.S.
Assault	X85-Y09	11.4	5.7
Human immunodeficiency virus (HIV) disease	B20-B24	7.0	3.3
Influenza and pneumonia	J09-J18	16.7	16.4
Intentional self-harm	X60-X84	11.4	11.5
Malnutrition	E40-E46	*Unreliable	0.8
Obesity and other hyperalimentation	E65-E68	2.5	1.6
Transport accidents	V01-V99	12.4	13.7
Viral hepatitis	B15-B19	4.0	2.2

Note: (a) ICD-10 = International Classification of Diseases 10th Revision; (1) Mortality rates are a three year average covering 2007-2009; (2) Figures cover Davidson County; (*) Unreliable data as per CDC
Source: Centers for Disease Control and Prevention, National Center for Health Statistics. Underlying Cause of Death 1999-2009 on CDC WONDER Online Database, released 2012. Data for year 2009 are compiled from the Multiple Cause of Death File 2009, Series 20 No. 2O, 2012, Data for year 2008 are compiled from the Multiple Cause of Death File 2008, Series 20 No. 2N, 2011, Data for year 2007 are compiled from Multiple Cause of Death File 2007, Series 20 No. 2M, 2010.

Distribution of Physicians and Dentists

Area[1]	Dentists[2]	D.O.[3]	M.D.[4]				
			Total	Family/ General Practice	Pediatrics	Medical Specialties	Surgical Specialties
Local (number)	355	45	2,062	106	148	811	563
Local (rate[5])	5.7	0.7	32.8	1.7	2.4	12.9	9.0
U.S. (rate[5])	4.5	1.9	18.3	2.5	1.4	6.8	4.1

Note: Data as of 2008 unless noted; (1) Local data covers Davidson County; (2) Data as of 2007; (3) Doctor of Osteopathic Medicine; (4) Includes active, non-federal, patient-care, office-based Doctors of Medicine; (5) rate per 10,000 population
Source: Area Resource File (ARF). 2009-2010 Release. U.S. Department of Health and Human Services, Health Resources and Services Administration, Bureau of Health Professions, Rockville, MD, August 2010

Best Hospitals

According to *U.S. News,* the Nashville-Davidson—Murfreesboro—Franklin, TN is home to one of the best hospitals in the U.S.: **Vanderbilt University Medical Center** (11 specialties). The hospital listed was highly ranked in at least one adult specialty. *U.S. News Online, "America's Best Hospitals 2011-12"*

According to *U.S. News,* the Nashville-Davidson—Murfreesboro—Franklin, TN is home to one of the best children's hospitals in the U.S.: **Monroe Carell Jr. Children's Hospital at Vanderbilt** (10 specialties). The hospital listed was highly ranked in at least one pediatric specialty. *U.S. News Online, "America's Best Children's Hospitals 2011-12"*

EDUCATION

Public School District Statistics

District Name	Schls	Pupils	Pupil/ Teacher Ratio	Minority Pupils[1] (%)	Free Lunch Eligible[2] (%)	IEP[3] (%)
Davidson County	139	75,080	14.1	67.3	59.1	11.2

Note: Table includes school districts with 2,000 or more students; (1) Percentage of students that are not non-Hispanic white; (2) Percentage of students that are eligible for the free lunch program; (3) Percentage of students that have an Individualized Education Program.
Source: U.S. Department of Education, National Center for Education Statistics, Common Core of Data, Local Education Agency (School District) Universe Survey: School Year 2009-2010; U.S. Department of Education, National Center for Education Statistics, Common Core of Data, Public Elementary/Secondary School Universe Survey: School Year 2009-2010

Top Public High Schools

High School Name	Rank[1]	Score[1]	Grad. Rate[2] (%)	College[3] (%)	AP/IB/ AICE[4] (%)	SAT/ ACT[5] (%)
Hume-Fogg Academic Magnet	33	1.156	100	98	5.8	1826

Note: (1) Public schools are ranked from 1 to 500 based on the following self-reported statistics (with their corresponding weight in the final score). Schools that had fewer than 10 graduates, as well as those that were newly founded and did not have a graduating senior class in 2010 were excluded; (2) Four-year, on-time graduation rate (25%); (3) Percent of 2010 graduates who enrolled immediately in college (25%); (4) AP/IB/AICE tests per graduate (25%); (5) Average SAT and/or ACT score (10%); Average AP/IB/AICE exam score (10%); AP/IB/AICE courses offered per graduate (5%); (6) School is unranked, but has been identified by Newsweek as one of the nation's most elite public high schools.
Source: Newsweek Online, "Top High Schools 2011"

Highest Level of Education

Area	Less than H.S.	H.S. Diploma	Some College, No Deg.	Associate Degree	Bachelors Degree	Masters Degree	Profess. School Degree	Doctorate Degree
City	15.2	24.9	20.7	5.9	20.8	8.0	2.5	2.0
MSA[1]	13.8	28.6	21.1	6.5	19.9	6.7	2.1	1.3
U.S.	14.7	28.4	21.3	7.6	17.6	7.2	1.9	1.2

Note: Figures cover persons age 25 and over; (1) Figures cover the Nashville-Davidson—Murfreesboro—Franklin, TN Metropolitan Statistical Area—see Appendix B for areas included
Source: U.S. Census Bureau, 2008-2010 American Community Survey 3-Year Estimates

Educational Attainment by Race

Area	High School Graduate or Higher (%)					Bachelor's Degree or Higher (%)				
	Total	White	Black	Asian	Hisp.[2]	Total	White	Black	Asian	Hisp.[2]
City	84.8	87.3	82.0	85.2	51.2	33.3	37.8	22.6	46.8	9.6
MSA[1]	86.2	87.5	82.8	86.6	56.7	30.0	31.4	22.6	45.2	11.9
U.S.	85.3	87.5	81.4	85.5	61.6	28.0	29.3	17.8	50.2	13.0

Note: Figures shown cover persons 25 years old and over; (1) Figures cover the Nashville-Davidson—Murfreesboro—Franklin, TN Metropolitan Statistical Area—see Appendix B for areas included; (2) People of Hispanic origin can be of any race
Source: U.S. Census Bureau, 2008-2010 American Community Survey 3-Year Estimates

School Enrollment by Grade and Control

Area	Preschool (%)		Kindergarten (%)		Grades 1 - 4 (%)		Grades 5 - 8 (%)		Grades 9 - 12 (%)	
	Public	Private	Public	Private	Public	Private	Public	Private	Public	Private
City	50.3	49.7	78.6	21.4	84.2	15.8	80.1	19.9	81.6	18.4
MSA[1]	44.0	56.0	84.7	15.3	87.6	12.4	85.2	14.8	84.8	15.2
U.S.	55.4	44.6	87.1	12.9	89.4	10.6	89.5	10.5	90.4	9.6

Note: Figures shown cover persons 3 years old and over; (1) Figures cover the Nashville-Davidson—Murfreesboro—Franklin, TN Metropolitan Statistical Area—see Appendix B for areas included
Source: U.S. Census Bureau, 2008-2010 American Community Survey 3-Year Estimates

Average Salaries of Public School Classroom Teachers

Area	2010-11		2011-12		Percent Change 2010-11 to 2011-12	Percent Change 2001-02 to 2011-12
	Dollars	Rank[1]	Dollars	Rank[1]		
Tennessee	45,891	44	46,613	43	1.57	21.00
U.S. Average	55,623	-	56,643	-	1.83	26.8

Note: (1) State rank ranges from 1 to 51 where 1 indicates highest salary.
Source: National Education Association, Rankings & Estimates: Rankings of the States 2011 and Estimates of School Statistics 2012, December 2011

Higher Education

Four-Year Colleges			Two-Year Colleges			Medical Schools[1]	Law Schools[2]	Voc/ Tech[3]
Public	Private Non-profit	Private For-profit	Public	Private Non-profit	Private For-profit			
1	10	6	2	2	5	2	1	5

Note: Figures cover institutions located within the city limits and include main campuses only; (1) includes schools accredited by the Liaison Committee on Medical Education and the American Osteopathic Association's Commission on Osteopathic College Accreditation; (2) includes American Bar Association-accredited law schools; (3) includes all schools with programs that are less than 2 years.
Source: National Center for Education Statistics, Integrated Postsecondary Education System (IPEDS) Peer Analysis System, 2011-12; Association of American Medical Colleges, Member List, April 23, 2012; American Osteopathic Association, Member List, April 23, 2012; Law School Admission Council, Official Guide to ABA-Approved Law Schools Online, April 23, 2012

According to *U.S. News & World Report,* the Nashville-Davidson—Murfreesboro—Franklin, TN is home to one of the best national universities in the U.S.: **Vanderbilt University** (#17). The indicators used to capture academic quality fall into a number of categories: assessment by administrators at peer institutions; retention of students; faculty resources; student selectivity; financial resources; alumni giving; high school counselor ratings of colleges; and graduation rate.*U.S. News & World Report, "America's Best Colleges 2012"*

According to *U.S. News & World Report,* the Nashville-Davidson—Murfreesboro—Franklin, TN is home to one of the best liberal arts colleges in the U.S.: **Fisk University** (#144). The indicators used to capture academic quality fall into a number of categories: assessment by administrators at peer institutions; retention of students; faculty resources; student selectivity; financial resources; alumni giving; high school counselor ratings of colleges; and graduation rate.*U.S. News & World Report, "America's Best Colleges 2012"*

According to *U.S. News & World Report,* the Nashville-Davidson—Murfreesboro—Franklin, TN is home to one of the best law schools in the U.S.: **Vanderbilt University** (#16). The rankings are based on a weighted average of 12 measures of quality: peer assessment score; assessment score by lawyers/judges; median LSAT scores; median undergrad GPA; acceptance rate; employment rates for graduates; placement success; bar passage rate; faculty resources; expenditures per student; student/faculty ratio; and library resources. *U.S. News & World Report, "America's Best Law Schools 2013"*

According to *Forbes,* the Nashville-Davidson—Murfreesboro—Franklin, TN is home to one of the best business schools in the U.S.: **Vanderbilt (Owen)** (#33). The rankings are based on the return on investment that graduates of the Class of 2006 received (median salary five years after graduation). *Forbes, "Best Business Schools," August 3, 2011*

PRESIDENTIAL ELECTION

2008 Presidential Election Results

Area	Obama	McCain	Nader	Other
Davidson County	59.9	38.9	0.4	0.8
U.S.	52.9	45.6	0.6	0.9

Note: Results are percentages and may not add to 100% due to rounding
Source: Dave Leip's Atlas of U.S. Presidential Elections, www.uselectionatlas.org

EMPLOYERS

Major Employers

Company Name	Industry
AHOM Holdings Inc	Home health care services
Asurion Corporation	Business services nec
Baptist Hospital	General medical/surgical hospitals
Cannon County Knitting Mills Inc	Apparel and outerwear broadwoven fabrics
County of Rutherford	Public elementary and secondary schools
County of Sumner	Executive offices, local government
Gaylord Entertainment Company	Hotels/motels
Gaylord Opryland USA Inc	Hotels
Ingram Book Company	Books, periodicals, and newspapers
International Automotive	Automotive storage garage
LifeWay Christian Resources of the SBC	Religious organizations
Middle Tennessee State University	Colleges/universities
Newspaper Printing Corporation	Newspapers
Nissan North America Inc	Motor vehicles/car bodies
Primus Automotive Financial Services Inc	Automobile loans including insurance
Psychiatric Solutions Inc	Psychiatric clinic
State Industries Inc	Hot water heaters, household
State of Tennessee	Mentally handicapped home
Tennesee Department of Transportation	Regulation, administration of transportation
Vanderbilt Childrens Hospital	General medical/surgical hospitals
Vanderbilt University	Colleges/universities

Note: Companies shown are located within the Nashville-Davidson—Murfreesboro—Franklin, TN metropolitan area.
Source: Hoovers.com, data extracted April 25 2012

Best Companies to Work For

HCA, headquartered in Nashville, is among the "100 Best Places to Work in IT." To qualify, companies, both public and private, had to have a minimum of 50 IT employees and were selected based on average salary and bonus increases, the percentage of IT staffers promoted, IT staff turnover rates, training and development programs, and the percentage of women and minorities in IT staff and management positions. In addition, *Computerworld* looked at retention efforts, programs for recognizing and rewarding outstanding performances, and benefits such as flextime, elder care and child care, and reimbursement for college tuition and the cost of pursuing technology certifications. *Computerworld, "100 Best Places to Work in IT 2011"*

PUBLIC SAFETY

Crime Rate

Area	All Crimes	Violent Crimes				Property Crimes		
		Murder	Forcible Rape	Robbery	Aggrav. Assault	Burglary	Larceny -Theft	Motor Vehicle Theft
City	6,086.0	8.9	59.5	294.8	771.6	1,254.3	3,387.8	309.1
Suburbs[1]	2,756.0	4.5	29.5	42.0	261.6	593.4	1,709.7	115.2
Metro[2]	4,032.1	6.2	41.0	138.9	457.0	846.7	2,352.8	189.5
U.S.	3,345.5	4.8	27.5	119.1	252.3	699.6	2,003.5	238.8

Note: Figures are crimes per 100,000 population; (1) All areas within the metro area that are located outside the city limits; (2) Metropolitan Statistical Area—see Appendix B for areas included
Source: FBI Uniform Crime Reports, 2010

Hate Crimes

Area	Number of Quarters Reported	Bias Motivation				
		Race	Religion	Sexual Orientation	Ethnicity	Disability
City	4	6	0	1	1	0

Source: Federal Bureau of Investigation, Hate Crime Statistics 2010

Identity Theft Consumer Complaints

Area	Complaints	Complaints per 100,000 Population	Rank[2]
MSA[1]	1,156	76.0	187
U.S.	279,156	90.4	-

Note: (1) Metropolitan Statistical Area—see Appendix B for areas included; (2) Rank ranges from 1 to 384 where 1 indicates greatest number of identity theft complaints per 100,000 population
Source: Federal Trade Commission, Consumer Sentinel Network Data Book for January–December 2011

Fraud and Other Consumer Complaints

Area	Complaints	Complaints per 100,000 Population	Rank[2]
MSA[1]	7,962	523.3	121
U.S.	1,533,924	496.8	-

Note: (1) Metropolitan Statistical Area—see Appendix B for areas included; (2) Rank ranges from 1 to 384 where 1 indicates greatest number of fraud and other complaints per 100,000 population
Source: Federal Trade Commission, Consumer Sentinel Network Data Book for January–December 2011

RECREATION

Culture

Dance[1]	Theatre[1]	Instrumental Music[1]	Vocal Music[1]	Series/ Festivals	Museums	Zoos and Aquariums[2]
1	7	1	2	5	14	1

Note: (1) Number of professional performing groups; (2) AZA-accredited
Source: The Grey House Performing Arts Directory, 2011-2012; Official Museum Directory, 2011; American Association of Museums, AAM Member Museums, April 2012; Association of Zoos & Aquariums, AZA Member Zoos & Aquariums, April 2012

Professional Sports Teams

Team Name	League
Nashville Predators	National Hockey League (NHL)
Tennessee Titans	National Football League (NFL)

Note: Includes teams located in the Nashville metro area.
Source: Original research

CLIMATE

Average and Extreme Temperatures

Temperature	Jan	Feb	Mar	Apr	May	Jun	Jul	Aug	Sep	Oct	Nov	Dec	Yr.
Extreme High (°F)	78	84	86	91	95	106	107	104	105	94	84	79	107
Average High (°F)	47	51	60	71	79	87	90	89	83	72	60	50	70
Average Temp. (°F)	38	41	50	60	68	76	80	79	72	61	49	41	60
Average Low (°F)	28	31	39	48	57	65	69	68	61	48	39	31	49
Extreme Low (°F)	-17	-13	2	23	34	42	54	49	36	26	-1	-10	-17

Note: Figures cover the years 1948-1990
Source: National Climatic Data Center, International Station Meteorological Climate Summary, 9/96

Average Precipitation/Snowfall/Humidity

Precip./Humidity	Jan	Feb	Mar	Apr	May	Jun	Jul	Aug	Sep	Oct	Nov	Dec	Yr.
Avg. Precip. (in.)	4.4	4.2	5.0	4.1	4.6	3.7	3.8	3.3	3.2	2.6	3.9	4.6	47.4
Avg. Snowfall (in.)	4	3	1	Tr	0	0	0	0	0	Tr	1	1	11
Avg. Rel. Hum. 6am (%)	81	81	80	81	86	86	88	90	90	87	83	82	85
Avg. Rel. Hum. 3pm (%)	61	57	51	48	52	52	54	53	52	49	55	59	54

Note: Figures cover the years 1948-1990; Tr = Trace amounts (<0.05 in. of rain; <0.5 in. of snow)
Source: National Climatic Data Center, International Station Meteorological Climate Summary, 9/96

Weather Conditions

Temperature			Daytime Sky			Precipitation		
10°F & below	32°F & below	90°F & above	Clear	Partly cloudy	Cloudy	0.01 inch or more precip.	0.1 inch or more snow/ice	Thunder-storms
5	76	51	98	135	132	119	8	54

Note: Figures are average number of days per year and cover the years 1948-1990
Source: National Climatic Data Center, International Station Meteorological Climate Summary, 9/96

**HAZARDOUS
WASTE**

Superfund Sites

Nashville has no sites on the EPA's Superfund Final National Priorities List.
U.S. Environmental Protection Agency, Final National Priorities List, April 17, 2012

**AIR & WATER
QUALITY**

Air Quality Index

Area	Percent of Days when Air Quality was...[2]					AQI Statistics[2]	
	Good	Moderate	Unhealthy for Sensitive Groups	Unhealthy	Very Unhealthy	Maximum	Median
Area[1]	74.2	24.9	0.8	0.0	0.0	124	41

Note: Air Quality Index (AQI) is an index for reporting daily air quality. EPA calculates the AQI for five major air pollutants regulated by the Clean Air Act: ground-level ozone, particle pollution (aka particulate matter), carbon monoxide, sulfur dioxide, and nitrogen dioxide. The AQI runs from 0 to 500. The higher the AQI value, the greater the level of air pollution and the greater the health concern. There are six AQI categories: "Good" AQI is between 0 and 50. Air quality is considered satisfactory; "Moderate" AQI is between 51 and 100. Air quality is acceptable; "Unhealthy for Sensitive Groups" When AQI values are between 101 and 150, members of sensitive groups may experience health effects; "Unhealthy" When AQI values are between 151 and 200 everyone may begin to experience health effects; "Very Unhealthy" AQI values between 201 and 300 trigger a health alert; "Hazardous" AQI values over 300 trigger warnings of emergency conditions (not shown); (1) Data covers Davidson County; (2) Based on 365 days with AQI data in 2011.
Source: U.S. Environmental Protection Agency, AirData Report, 2011

Air Quality Index Pollutants

Area	Percent of Days when AQI Pollutant was...[2]					
	Carbon Monoxide	Nitrogen Dioxide	Ozone	Sulfur Dioxide	Particulate Matter 2.5	Particulate Matter 10
Area[1]	0.0	9.9	30.4	0.0	59.5	0.3

Note: The Air Quality Index (AQI) is an index for reporting daily air quality. EPA calculates the AQI for five major air pollutants regulated by the Clean Air Act: ground-level ozone, particle pollution (also known as particulate matter), carbon monoxide, sulfur dioxide, and nitrogen dioxide. The AQI runs from 0 to 500. The higher the AQI value, the greater the level of air pollution and the greater the health concern; (1) Data covers Davidson County; (2) Based on 365 days with AQI data in 2011.
Source: U.S. Environmental Protection Agency, AirData Report, 2011

Air Quality Index Trends

Area	Trend Sites (days)								All Sites (days)
	2003	2004	2005	2006	2007	2008	2009	2010	2010
MSA[1]	23	7	29	17	37	11	1	10	10

Note: Figures are the number of days the AQI value exceeded 100 in a given year. An AQI value greater than 100 indicates that air quality would have been in the unhealthful range on that day. Data from exceptional events are included. These counts are presented in two ways. First, the counts are based on sites having an adequate record of monitoring data during the trend period (trend sites). These counts represent the relative change in the number of days with AQI values greater than 100. In the last column, the counts are based on all sites with data in the most recent year (because it is possible for a site to have data in the most recent year but not enough data to be a trend site); (1) Data covers the Nashville-Davidson—Murfreesboro—Franklin, TN—see Appendix B for areas included
Source: U.S. Environmental Protection Agency, Air Quality Index Information, "Number of Days with Air Quality Index Values Greater than 100 at Trend Sites, 2000-2010, and at All Sites in 2010"

Maximum Air Pollutant Concentrations: Particulate Matter, Ozone, CO and Lead

	Particulate Matter 10 (ug/m³)	Particulate Matter 2.5 Wtd AM (ug/m³)	Particulate Matter 2.5 24-Hr (ug/m³)	Ozone (ppm)	Carbon Monoxide (ppm)	Lead (ug/m³)
MSA[1] Level	42	11.8	24	0.078	2	n/a
NAAQS[2]	150	15	35	0.075	9	0.15
Met NAAQS[2]	Yes	Yes	Yes	No	Yes	n/a

Note: Data from exceptional events are not included; (1) Data covers the Nashville-Davidson—Murfreesboro—Franklin, TN—see Appendix B for areas included; (2) National Ambient Air Quality Standards; ppm = parts per million; ug/m³ = micrograms per cubic meter; n/a not available
Concentrations: Particulate Matter 10 (coarse particulate)—highest second maximum 24-hour concentration; Particulate Matter 2.5 Wtd AM (fine particulate)—highest weighted annual mean concentration; Particulate Matter 2.5 24-Hour (fine particulate)—highest 98th percentile 24-hour concentration; Ozone—highest fourth daily maximum 8-hour concentration; Carbon Monoxide—highest second maximum non-overlapping 8-hour concentration; Lead—maximum running 3-month average
Source: U.S. Environmental Protection Agency, CBSA Factbook 2010, Air Quality Statistics by City, 2010

Maximum Air Pollutant Concentrations: Nitrogen Dioxide and Sulfur Dioxide

	Nitrogen Dioxide AM (ppb)	Nitrogen Dioxide 1-Hr (ppb)	Sulfur Dioxide AM (ppb)	Sulfur Dioxide 1-Hr (ppb)	Sulfur Dioxide 24-Hr (ppb)
MSA[1] Level	12.526	46	2.246	14	5.5
NAAQS[2]	53	100	30	75	140
Met NAAQS[2]	Yes	Yes	Yes	Yes	Yes

Note: Data from exceptional events are not included; (1) Data covers the Nashville-Davidson—Murfreesboro—Franklin, TN—see Appendix B for areas included; (2) National Ambient Air Quality Standards; ppb = parts per billion; n/a not available
Concentrations: Nitrogen Dioxide AM—highest arithmetic mean concentration; Nitrogen Dioxide 1-Hr—highest 98th percentile 1-hour daily maximum concentration; Sulfur Dioxide AM—highest annual mean concentration; Sulfur Dioxide 1-Hr—highest 99th percentile 1-hour daily maximum concentration; Sulfur Dioxide 24-Hr—highest second maximum 24-hour concentration
Source: U.S. Environmental Protection Agency, CBSA Factbook 2010, Air Quality Statistics by City, 2010

Drinking Water

Water System Name	Pop. Served	Primary Water Source Type	Violations[1] Health Based	Violations[1] Monitoring/ Reporting
Nashville Water Dept #1	582,341	Surface	0	0

Note: (1) Based on violation data from January 1, 2011 to December 31, 2011 (includes unresolved violations from earlier years)
Source: U.S. Environmental Protection Agency, Office of Ground Water and Drinking Water, Safe Drinking Water Information System (based on data extracted April 18, 2012)

New Orleans, Louisiana

Background

New Orleans, the old port city upriver from the mouth of the Mississippi River, is on a par with San Francisco and New York City as one of the United States' most interesting cities. The birthplace of jazz is rich in unique local history, distinctive neighborhoods, and an unmistakably individual character.

The failure of the federal levees following Hurricane Katrina in 2005 brought New Orleans to its knees and put 80 percent of the city under floodwaters for weeks. The Crescent City's revival since then is a testament to her unique spirit, an influx of federal dollars, and an outpouring from volunteers ranging from church groups to spring breakers who returned year after year to help rebuild.

New Orleans was founded on behalf of France by the brothers Le Moyne, Sieurs d'Iberville, and de Bienville, in 1718. Despite early travesties such as disease, starvation, and an unwilling working class, New Orleans nevertheless emerged as a genteel antebellum slave society, fashioning itself after the rigid social hierarchy of Versailles. Even after New Orleans was ceded to Spain after the French & Indian War, this unequal lifestyle, however gracious, persisted.

The port city briefly returned to French control, then became a crown jewel in the 1803 Louisiana Purchase to the U.S. The transfer of control changed New Orleans's Old World isolation. American settlers introduced aggressive business acumen to the area, as well as the idea of respect for the self-made man. As trade opened up with countries around the world, this made for a happy union. New Orleans became "Queen City of the South," growing prosperous from adventurous riverboat traders and speculators, as well as the cotton trade.

Today, much of the city's Old World charm remains, resulting from a polyglot of Southern, Creole, African-American, and European cultures. New Orleans' fine and native cuisine, indigenous music, unique festivals, and sultry, pleasing atmosphere, drew more than eight million visitors in 2010.

A major pillar of the city's economy is the enormous tourism trade that includes the Ernest N. Morial Convention Center's numerous convention goers who fill more than 35,000 rooms. A second economic pillar is the Port of New Orleans, one of the nation's leading general cargo ports. In recent years, it has seen $400 million invested in new facilities.

In addition, an influx of mostly young people who arrived after Hurrican Katrina is giving rise to a new start-up spirit. Plus, state tax breaks have helped to turn New Orleans into "Hollywood South," where 35 films were produced in the last few years. New Orleans has given birth to a mother lode of cultural phenomena: Dixieland jazz, musicians Louis Armstrong, Mahalia Jackson, Dr. John, and chefs Emeril Lagasse and John Besh. The city is well aware of its "cultural economy," which employs 12.5 percent of the local workforce. Popular tourist draws include the annual Mardi Gras celebration—which spans two long weekends leading up to Fat Tuesday—and the annual New Orleans Jazz & Heritage Festival. The Louisiana Superdome—renovated and renamed to the Mercedes Benz Superdome, is home to the 2010 Super Bowl champion New Orleans Saints, and will host the 2013 Super Bowl. A new, nearly $75 million Consolidated Rental Car Facility project is expanding rental capacity and bring scattered facilities under one roof at the Louis Armstrong New Orleans International Airport.

In addition, an effort to boost medical services—and a medical economy that suffered after the hurricane—is underway with a major new Louisiana State University teaching/Veterans Administration hospital under construction with a completion date of 2013.

In his 2011 state of the city address, Mayor Mitch Landrieu said more than $13 billion in investments would unfold in coming years for bridge, airport, road and hospital repairs. School rebuilding was set for a $1.8 billion influx. Since Katrina, the majority of New Orleans public schools have become charter schools—a major experiment that is seeing some success. Higher education campuses include Tulane University (including a med school and law school), Loyola University, and the University of New Orleans. Louisiana State University has a medical school campus downtown.

Cultural amenities include the New Orleans Museum of Art located in the live-oak filled City Park, the Ogden Museum of Southern Art, and Audubon Park, designed by John Charles Olmsted (nephew and business partner of Frederick Law Olmsted) with its golf course and the Audubon Zoo.

The New Orleans metro area is virtually surrounded by water, which influences its climate. Between mid-June and September, temperatures are kept down by near-daily sporadic thunderstorms. Cold spells sometimes reach the area in winter but seldom last. Frequent and sometimes heavy rains are typical. Hurricane season officially runs from June 1 to November 30 but typically reaches its height in late summer.

Rankings

General Rankings

- New Orleans was selected as one of America's best cities by *Bloomberg Businessweek*. The city ranked #29 out of 50. Criteria: number of restaurants, bars and museums per capita; number of colleges, libraries, and professional sports teams; income, poverty, unemployment, crime, and foreclosure rates; percent of population with bachelor's degrees; public school performance; park acres per capita; air quality. *BusinessWeek, "America's 50 Best Cities," September 20, 2011*

- New Orleans was identified as one of seven American cities that have lost the most people in the past decade. The city ranked #1. Criteria: population change 2000-2009; percent population change 2000-2009; home vacancy rates. *24/7 Wall St., "American Cities that are Running Out of People," January 1, 2011*

- New Orleans was selected as one of "America's Favorite Cities." The city ranked #1 in the "Nightlife" category. Respondents to an online survey were asked to rate 35 top urban destinations in the U.S. from a visitor's perspective. Criteria: cocktail hour; live music/concerts and bands; singles/bar scene. *Travelandleisure.com, "America's Favorite Cities 2010," November 2010*

- New Orleans was selected as one of the "Best Places to Live" by *Men's Journal*. Criteria: "18 towns were selected that are perfecting the art of living well—places where conservation is more important than development, bike makers and breweries and farmers thrive, and Whole Foods is considered a big-box store." *Men's Journal, "Best Place to Live 2011: Think Small, Live Big," April 2011*

- New Orleans appeared on *Travel + Leisure's* list of the ten best cities in the continental U.S. and Canada. The city was ranked #6. Criteria: activities/attractions; culture/arts; restaurants/food; people; and value. *Travel + Leisure, "The World's Best Awards 2011"*

Business/Finance Rankings

- New Orleans was identified as one of the 20 strongest-performing metro areas during the recession and recovery from trough quarter through the third quarter of 2011. Criteria: percent change in employment; percentage point change in unemployment rate; percent change in gross metropolitan product; percent change in House Price Index. *Brookings Institution, MetroMonitor: Tracking Economic Recession and Recovery in America's 100 Largest Metropolitan Areas, December 2011*

- New Orleans was selected as one of the best places to ride out a recession in the U.S. by *BusinessWeek*. Twenty cities were identified as places where large portions of the population worked in anticyclical industries such as government, health care, education, agriculture, and legal services. *BusinessWeek, "Some Cities Will Be Safer in a Recession," October 14, 2008*

- New Orleans was identified as one of America's most coupon-loving cities by *Coupons.com*. The city ranked #22 out of 25. Criteria: online coupon usage. *Coupons.com, "Top 25 Most Frugal Cities of 2011," February 23, 2012*

- New Orleans was identified as one of the "Happiest Cities to Work in 2012" by *CareerBliss.com*, an online community for career advancement. The city ranked #11 out of 50. Criteria: independent company reviews from employees all over the country on: relationship with their boss and co-workers; work environment; job resources; growth opportunities; compensation; company culture; company reputation; daily tasks; job control over work performed on a daily basis. *CareerBliss.com, "Happiest and Unhappiest Cities to Work in 2012"*

- *American City Business Journals* ranked America's 261 largest cities in terms of their resident's wealth. New Orleans ranked #98. Criteria: per capita income; median household income; percentage of households with annual incomes of $200,000 or more; median home value. *American City Business Journals, "Where the Money Is: America's Wealth Centers," August 18, 2008*

- The New Orleans metro area appeared on the Milken Institute "2011 Best Performing Metros" list. Rank: #101 out of 200 large metro areas. Criteria: job growth; wage and salary growth; high-tech output growth. *Milken Institute, "2011 Best Performing Metros"*

- The New Orleans metro area was selected as one of the best cities for entrepreneurs in America by *Inc. Magazine*. Criteria: job-growth data for 335 metro areas was analyzed for: recent growth trend; mid-term growth; long-term trend; current year growth. The New Orleans metro area ranked #13 among large metro areas and #60 overall. *Inc. Magazine, "The Best Cities for Doing Business," July 2008*

- *Forbes* ranked the 200 most populous metro areas in the U.S. in terms of the "Best Places for Business and Careers." The New Orleans metro area was ranked #143. Criteria: costs (business and living); job growth (past and projected); income growth; educational attainment; projected economic growth; crime; cultural and recreational opportunities; net migration patterns; number of highly ranked colleges. *Forbes, "Best Places for Business and Careers," June 2011*

Children/Family Rankings

- New Orleans was selected as one of the least safe cities for children in America by *Men's Health*. The city ranked #2 of 10. Criteria: accidental death rates for kids ages 5 to 14; number of car seat inspection locations per child; sex offenders per capita; percentage of abused children protected from further abuse; strength of child-restraint and bike-helmet laws. *Men's Health, "The Safest (and Least Safe) Cities for Children," September 2010*

- New Orleans was selected as one of the 10 worst cities to raise children in the U.S. by *KidFriendlyCities.org*. Criteria: education; environment; health; employment; crime; diversity; cost of living. *KidFriendlyCities.org, "Top Rated Kid/Family Friendly Cities 2009"*

- The New Orleans metro area was selected as one of the "Best Cities for Relocating Families" by Worldwide ERC and Primacy Relocation. The 2008 study looked at nearly 50 factors important to relocating families including: recent job growth; nearby top-ranked colleges; in-state tuition for four-year public colleges; population growth since 2000; pediatricians per 100,000 population; and a Green Living index. *Worldwide ERC and Primacy Relocation, "2008 Best Cities for Relocating Families"*

Culture/Performing Arts Rankings

- New Orleans was selected as one of 10 best U.S. cities to be a moviemaker. The city was ranked #1. Criteria: cost of living; average salary; unemployment rate; job growth; median home price; crime rate; number of film schools, festivals, movie-related vendors and local movie theaters; current production scene (i.e. production days, size of talent pool); financial incentives for shooting in a particular area. *MovieMaker Magazine, "Top 10 Cities to be a Moviemaker: 2012," January 16, 2012*

- New Orleans was selected as one of "America's Top 25 Arts Destinations." The city ranked #2 in the mid-sized city (population 100,000 to 499,999) category. Criteria: readers' top choices for arts travel destinations based on the richness and variety of visual arts sites, activities and events. *American Style, "America's Top 25 Arts Destinations," May 2010*

Dating/Romance Rankings

- New Orleans was selected as one of the best cities for single men by *Rent.com*. The city ranked #7 of 10. Criteria: high single female-to-male ratio; lively nightlife; low divorce rate; low cost of living. *Rent.com, "Top 10 Cities for Single Men," May 2, 2011*

- New Orleans was selected as one of "America's Best Cities for Dating" by *Yahoo! Travel*. Criteria: high proportion of singles; excellent dating venues and/or stunning natural settings. *Yahoo! Travel, "America's Best Cities for Dating," February 7, 2012*

- New Orleans appeared on *Men's Health's* list of the most sex-happy cities in America. The city ranked #46 of 100. Criteria: condom sales; birth rates; sex toy sales; rates of chlamydia, gonorrhea, and syphilis. *Men's Health, "America's Most Sex-Happy Cities," October 2010*

- *Men's Health* ranked 100 U.S. cities in terms of best (and worst) marriages. New Orleans was ranked #88 (#1 = worst). Criteria: rate of failed marriages; stringency of divorce laws; percentage of population who've split; number of licensed marriage and family therapists. *Men's Health, "Splitsville, USA," May 2010*

- The New Orleans metro area was selected as one of the "Best Cities for Relocating Singles" by Worldwide ERC and Primacy Relocation. The area ranked #19 out of the 100 largest metro areas in the U.S. Criteria: recent job growth; recent singles population growth; overall population growth; affordable rental housing; cost-of-living index; expanded arts and recreation opportunities; ratio of single men and single women; affordability of quality higher education (including state residency requirements); diversity index; climate; population density. *Worldwide ERC and Primacy Relocation, "2008 Best Cities for Relocating Singles"*

Education Rankings

- *Men's Health* ranked 100 U.S. cities in terms of their education levels. New Orleans was ranked #60 (#1 = most educated city). Criteria: high school graduation rates; school enrollment; educational attainment; number of households who have outstanding student loans; number of households whose members have taken adult-education courses. *Men's Health, "Where School Is In: The Most and Least Educated Cities," September 12, 2011*

- New Orleans was selected as one of "America's Most Literate Cities." The city ranked #17 out of the 75 largest U.S. cities. Criteria: number of booksellers; library resources; Internet resources; educational attainment; periodical publishing resources; newspaper circulation. *Central Connecticut State University, "America's Most Literate Cities 2011"*

- New Orleans was identified as one of the 100 "smartest" metro areas in the U.S. The area ranked #78. Criteria: the editors rated the collective brainpower of the 100 largest metro areas in the U.S. based on their residents' educational attainment. *American City Business Journals, April 14, 2008*

- New Orleans was identified as one of "America's Brainiest Bastions" by *Portfolio.com*. The metro area ranked #123 out of 200. *Portfolio.com* analyzed levels of educational attainment in the nation's 200 largest metropolitan areas. The editors established scores for five levels of educational attainment, based on relative earning power of adult workers age 25 or older. Scores were determined by comparing the median income for all workers with the median income for those workers at a specified educational level. *Portfolio.com, "America's Brainiest Bastions," December 1, 2010*

Environmental Rankings

- Scarborough Research, a leading market research firm, identified the top local markets for green appliance households. The New Orleans DMA (Designated Market Area) ranked in the top 16 with 36% of consumers reporting that they own an energy-efficient appliance. *Scarborough Research, March 23, 2010*

- New Orleans was selected as one of 22 "Smarter Cities" for energy by the Natural Resources Defense Council. Criteria: investment in green power; energy efficiency measures; conservation. *Natural Resources Defense Council, "2010 Smarter Cities," July 19, 2010*

- New Orleans was selected as one of worst summer weather cities in the U.S. by the *Farmers' Almanac*. The city ranked #2 out of 5. Criteria: average summer and winter temperatures; humidity; precipitation; number of overcast days. The editors only considered cities with populations of 50,000 or more. *Farmers' Almanac, "America's Ten Worst Weather Cities," September 7, 2010*

- 100 of the largest metro areas in the U.S. were analyzed in terms of their current drought severity. The New Orleans metro area ranked #65 (#1 = driest). The rankings were based on statistics such as long-term precipitation trends and patterns and the Palmer drought indices. *Sperling's BestPlaces, www.BestPlaces.net, "America's Drought-Riskiest Cities," November 2007*

- The New Orleans metro area appeared in *Country Home's* "Best Green Places" report. The area ranked #304 out of 379. Criteria: official energy policies; green power; green buildings; availability of fresh, locally grown food. *Country Home, "Best Green Places," 2008*

Food/Drink Rankings

- New Orleans was selected as one of "America's Favorite Cities." The city ranked #1 in the "Food/Dining" category. Respondents to an online survey were asked to rate 35 top urban destinations in the U.S. from a visitor's perspective. Criteria: big-name restaurants; ethnic food; farmers' markets; neighborhood joints and cafes. *Travelandleisure.com, "America's Favorite Cities 2010," November 2010*

Health/Fitness Rankings

- The American Podiatric Medical Association and *Prevention* magazine ranked 100 American cities based on walkability. Nineteen walking criteria were evaluated including the percentage of adults who walk to work, number of parks per square mile, number of trails for walking and hiking, air pollution, use of mass transit, crime rate, pedestrian fatalities, and percentage of adults who walk for fitness. New Orleans ranked #22. *Prevention, "The Best Walking Cities of 2009," May 2009; American Podiatric Medical Association, "2009 Best Fitness-Walking Cities," April 7, 2009*

- New Orleans was selected as one of the 25 fattest cities in America by *Men's Fitness Online*. It ranked #19 out of America's 50 largest cities. Criteria: fitness centers and sport stores; nutrition; sports participation; TV viewing; overweight/sedentary; junk food; air quality; geography; commute; parks and open space; city recreational facilities; access to healthcare; motivation; mayor and city initiatives; state obesity initiatives. *Men's Fitness, "The Fittest and Fattest Cities in America," March 5, 2012*

- New Orleans was identified as one of "The 8 Most Artery-Clogging Cities in America." The metro area ranked #4. Criteria: obesity rates; heart disease rates. *Prevention, "The 8 Most Artery-Clogging Cities in America," December 2011*

- New Orleans was identified as a "2011 Asthma Capital." The area ranked #76 out of the nation's 100 largest metropolitan areas. Twelve factors were used to identify the most challenging places to live for people with asthma: estimated prevalence; self-reported prevalence; crude death rate for asthma; annual pollen score; annual air quality; public smoking laws; number of board-certified asthma specialists; school inhaler access laws; rescue medication use; controller medication use; uninsured rate; poverty rate. *Asthma and Allergy Foundation of America, "2011 Asthma Capitals"*

- New Orleans was identified as a "2011 Fall Allergy Capital." The area ranked #28 out of 100. Three groups of factors were used to identify the most severe cities for people with allergies during the fall season: annual pollen levels; medicine utilization; access to board-certified allergists. *Asthma and Allergy Foundation of America, "2011 Fall Allergy Capitals"*

- New Orleans was identified as a "2012 Spring Allergy Capital." The area ranked #14 out of 100. Three groups of factors were used to identify the most severe cities for people with allergies during the spring season: annual pollen levels; medicine utilization; access to board-certified allergists. *Asthma and Allergy Foundation of America, "2012 Spring Allergy Capitals"*

- *Men's Health* examined 100 major U.S. cities and selected the best and worst cities for men. New Orleans ranked #70. Criteria: 35 statistical parameters of long life in the categories of health, quality of life, and fitness. *Men's Health, "The 10 Best and Worst Cities for Men 2012," January/February 2012*

- The makers of Breath Right Nasal Strips, in partnership with Sperling's BestPlaces, analyzed 50 metro areas and identified those U.S. cities most challenged by chronic nasal congestion. The New Orleans metro area ranked #3. Criteria: tree, grass and weed pollens; molds and spores; air pollution; climate; smoking; purchase habits of congestion products; prescriptions of drugs for congestion relief; incidence of influenza. *Breathe Right Nasal Strips, "Most Congested Cities," October 3, 2011*

- The New Orleans metro area appeared in the 2011 Gallup-Healthways Well-Being Index. The index, based on interviews with more than 350,000 Americans, measured jobs, finances, physical health, emotional state of mind and communities. The metro area ranked #147 out of 190. Criteria: life evaluation; emotional health; work environment; physical health; healthy behaviors; basic access (basic needs optimal for a healthy life, such as access to food and medicine, having health insurance and feeling safe while walking at night). *Gallup-Healthways, "State of Well-Being 2011"*

- *Men's Health* ranked 100 U.S. cities in terms of their activity levels. New Orleans was ranked #68 (#1 = most active city). Criteria: where and how often residents exercise; percentage of households that watch more than 15 hours of cable television a week and buy more than 11 video games a year; death rate from deep-vein thrombosis, a condition linked to sitting for extended periods of time. *Men's Health, "Where Sit Happens: The Most and Least Active Cities in America," June 20, 2011*

- 50 of the largest metro areas in the U.S. were analyzed in terms of their health and fitness by the American College of Sports Medicine in their "American Fitness Index." The New Orleans metro area ranked #41 (#1 = healthiest). Criteria: preventative health behaviors; levels of chronic disease; health care access; community resources and policies that support physical activity. *American College of Sports Medicine, "Health and Community Fitness Status of the 50 Largest Metropolitan Areas," August 1, 2011*

- New Orleans was selected as one of the "20 Most Livable U.S. Cities for Wheelchair Users" by the Christopher & Dana Reeve Foundation. The city ranked #18. Criteria: Medicaid eligibility and spending; access to physicians and rehabilitation facilities; access to fitness facilities and recreation; access to paratransit; percentage of people living with disabilities who are employed; clean air; climate. *Christopher & Dana Reeve Foundation, "20 Most Livable U.S. Cities for Wheelchair Users," July 26, 2010*

- *The Daily Beast* identified the 30 U.S. metro areas with the worst smoking habits. The New Orleans metro area ranked #24. Sixty urban centers with populations of more than one million were ranked based on the following criteria: number of smokers; number of cigarettes smoked per day; fewest attempts to quit. *The Daily Beast, "30 Cities With Smoking Problems," January 3, 2011*

Real Estate Rankings

- The New Orleans metro area was identified as one of ten places where real estate is ripe for a rebound by *Forbes*. Criteria: change in home price over the past 12 months and three years; unemployment rates; 12-month job-growth projections; population change from 2006 through 2009; new home construction rates for the third quarter of 2011 as compared to the same quarter in 2010. *Forbes.com, "Cities Where Real Estate is Ripe for a Rebound," January 12, 2012*

- *Fortune* ranked the 100 largest metro areas in the U.S. in terms of projected median home price change in 2010. The New Orleans metro area ranked #23. *Fortune, "The 2010 Housing Outlook," December 9, 2009*

- The New Orleans metro area was identified as one of the 25 worst housing markets in the U.S. in 2011. The area ranked #25 out of 149 markets with a home price appreciation of -10.5%. Criteria: year-over-year change of median sales price of existing single-family homes between the 4th quarter of 2010 and the 4th quarter of 2011. *National Association of Realtors®, Median Sales Price of Existing Single-Family Homes for Metropolitan Areas, 4th Quarter 2011*

- The New Orleans metro area was identified as one of the 10 best condo markets in the U.S. in 2011. The area ranked #6 out of 54 markets with a price appreciation of 3.1%. Criteria: year-over-year change of median sales price of existing apartment condo-coop homes between the 4th quarter of 2010 and the 4th quarter of 2011. *National Association of Realtors®, Median Sales Price of Existing Apartment Condo-Coop Homes for Metropolitan Areas, 4th Quarter 2011*

- New Orleans appeared on *ApartmentRatings.com* "Top Cities for Renters" list in 2009." The area ranked #72. Overall satisfaction ratings were ranked using thousands of user submitted scores for hundreds of apartment complexes located in the 100 most populated U.S. municipalities. *ApartmentRatings.com, "2009 Renter Satisfaction Rankings"*

- New Orleans appeared on *CNNMoney.com's* list of "Foreclosure Hotspots." The list includes the 10 cities with the fastest-growing foreclosure rates out of the 100 worst-hit places. *CNNMoney.com, "Foreclosure Hotspots," February 14, 2011*

- The New Orleans metro area was identified as one of the "Top 25 Real Estate Investment Markets" by *FinestExperts.com*. The metro area ranked #8. Over 10,000 real estate markets were analyzed to identify the most suitable places for real estate investors to seek stability and growth. Criteria: employment; rental markets; growth levels as offset by foreclosures. *FinestExperts.com, "Top 25 Real Estate Investment Markets," January 7, 2010*

- The New Orleans metro area appeared in a *Wall Street Journal* article ranking cities by "housing stress." The metro area was ranked #14 (#1 = most stress). Criteria: fraction of mortgage-holding homeowners with a monthly housing payment in excess of 30 percent of income; percentage of people without health insurance; unemployment rate. *The Wall Street Journal, "Which Cities Face Biggest Housing Risk," October 5, 2010*

- The Center for Housing Policy ranked 210 U.S. metropolitan areas by the fair market rent for a two-bedroom unit. The New Orleans metro area was ranked #58. (#1 = most expensive) with a rent of $982. Criteria: Fair Market Rent (FMR) in effect during the fourth quarter of 2009 based on HUD's fiscal year 2010 FMRs. *The Center for Housing Policy, "Paycheck to Paycheck: Most to Least Expensive Rental Markets in 2009"*

- The New Orleans metro area was identified as one of the best U.S. markets to invest in rental property" by HomeVestors and Local Market Monitor. The area ranked #86 out of 100. Criteria: risk-return premium relative to national average. *HomeVestors and Local Market Monitor, "Best 100 U.S. Markets to Invest in Rental Property," March 9, 2012*

Safety Rankings

- Allstate ranked the 193 largest cities in America in terms of driver safety. New Orleans ranked #156. In addition, drivers were 29.3% more likely to have had an accident compared to the national average. Allstate researchers analyzed internal property damage reported claims over a two-year period (from January 2008 to December 2009) to protect findings from external influences such as weather or road construction. A weighted average of the two-year numbers determined the annual percentages. The report defines an auto crash as any collision resulting in a property damage claim. *Allstate, "2011 Allstate America's Best Drivers Report™"*

- New Orleans was identified as one of the most dangerous mid-size cities in America by CQ Press. All 234 cities with populations of 100,000 to 499,999 that reported crime rates in 2010 for murder, rape, robbery, aggravated assault, burglary, and motor vehicle thefts were ranked. The city ranked #8 out of the top 10. *CQ Press, City Crime Rankings 2011-2012*

- Sperling's BestPlaces analyzed the tracks of tropical storms for the past 100 years and ranked which areas are most likely to be hit by a major hurricane. The New Orleans metro area ranked #9 out of 10. *Sperling's BestPlaces, www.bestplaces.net, February 2, 2006*

- The National Insurance Crime Bureau ranked 366 metro areas in the U.S. in terms of per capita rates of vehicle theft. The New Orleans metro area ranked #32 (#1 = highest rate). Criteria: number of vehicle theft offenses per 100,000 inhabitants in 2010. *National Insurance Crime Bureau, "Hot Spots," June 21, 2011*

- The New Orleans metro area was identified as one of the most dangerous metro areas for pedestrians by Transportation for America. The metro area ranked #15 out of 52 metro areas with over 1 million residents. Criteria: area's population divided by the number of pedestrian fatalities in that area. *Transportation for America, "Dangerous by Design 2011"*

Seniors/Retirement Rankings

- Bankers Life and Casualty Company, in partnership with Sperling's BestPlaces, ranked the nation's 50 largest metro areas in terms of the "Best U.S. Cities for Seniors." The New Orleans metro area ranked #30. Criteria: healthcare; transportation; housing; environment; economy; health and longevity; social and spiritual life; crime. *Bankers Life and Casualty Company, Center for a Secure Retirement, "Best U.S. Cities for Seniors 2011," September 2011*

- The New Orleans metro area was selected as one of the "10 Best Places for Single Seniors to Retire" by *U.S. News & World Report.* Criteria: metro areas with the most single seniors age 55 and over. *U.S. News & World Report, "10 Best Places for Single Seniors to Retire," November 1, 2010*

- New Orleans was selected as one of "10 Historic Places to Retire" by *U.S. News & World Report.* The editors looked for places filled with museums, libraries, and national historic monuments that also offer a good quality of life and plenty of amenities for seniors. *U.S. News & World Report, "10 Historic Places to Retire," September 6, 2010*

- The New Orleans metro area was selected as one of the "Best Places for Military Retirees" by *U.S. News & World Report*. The area ranked #9 out of 10. Criteria: climate; health resources; health indicators; crime levels; local school performance; recreational resources; arts and culture; airport and mass transit resources; susceptibility to natural disasters; military facilities and base amenities; VA medical services; tax policies affecting military pensions, unemployment trends; higher education resources; overall affordability; housing costs; home price trends; economic stability. *U.S. News & World Report, "Best Places for Military Retirees," December 8, 2010*

Sports/Recreation Rankings

- New Orleans appeared on the *Sporting News* list of the "Best Sports Cities" for 2011. The area ranked #22 out of 271 cities in the U.S. *Sporting News* takes a 12-month snapshot of each city's sports, putting a heavy premium on regular-season won-lost records (from the most recently completed season). Other criteria include: playoff berths, bowl appearances and tournament bids; championships; applicable power ratings; quality of competition; overall fan fervor (measured in part by attendance); abundance of teams (rewarding quality over quantity); stadium and arena quality; ticket availability and prices; franchise ownership; and marquee appeal of athletes. *Sporting News, "Best Sports Cities 2011," October 4, 2011*

- New Orleans was chosen as a bicycle friendly community by the League of American Bicyclists. A Bicycle Friendly Community welcomes cyclists by providing safe accommodation for cycling and encouraging people to bike for transportation and recreation. There are four award levels: Platinum; Gold; Silver; and Bronze. The community achieved an award level of Bronze. *League of American Bicyclists, "Bicycle Friendly Community Master List 2011"*

Technology Rankings

- The New Orleans metro area was selected as one of "America's Most Wired Cities" by *Forbes*. The metro area was ranked #13 out of 20. Criteria: percentage of Internet users with high-speed access; number of companies providing high-speed Internet; number of public wireless hot spots. *Forbes, "America's Most Wired Cities," March 2, 2010*

Transportation Rankings

- New Orleans was identified as one of America's worst cities for speed traps by the National Motorists Association. The city ranked #16 out of 25. Criteria: speed trap locations per 100,000 residents. *National Motorists Association, September 2011*

- The New Orleans metro area appeared on *Forbes* list of the best and worst cities for commuters. The metro area ranked #32 out of 60 (#1 is best). Criteria: travel time; road congestion; travel delays. *Forbes.com, "Best and Worst Cities for Commuters," February 16, 2010*

Women/Minorities Rankings

- *Women's Health* examined U.S. cities and identified the 100 best cities for women. New Orleans was ranked #70. Criteria: 30 categories were examined from obesity and breast cancer rates to commuting times and hours spent working out. *Women's Health, "Best Cities for Women 2012"*

- New Orleans was ranked #61 out of 100 metro areas in *SELF Magazine's* ranking of America's healthiest places for women." A panel of experts came up with more than 50 criteria including death and disease rates, environmental indicators, community resources, and lifestyle habits. *SELF Magazine, "Secrets of America's Healthiest Women," December 2008*

- The New Orleans metro area appeared on *Forbes'* list of the "Best Cities for Minority Entrepreneurs." The area ranked #61 out of 10. Criteria: 52 metropolitan statistical areas were examined. For each ethnicity (African Americans, Asians and Hispanics), the editors measured housing affordability, population growth, income growth, and entrepreneurship (per capita self-employment). *Forbes, "Best Cities for Minority Entrepreneurs," March 23, 2011*

Miscellaneous Rankings

- *Men's Health* ranked 100 U.S. cities by their level of sadness. New Orleans was ranked #44 (#1 = saddest city). Criteria: suicide rates; unemployment rates; percentage of households that use antidepressants; percent of population who report feeling blue all or most of the time. *Men's Health, "Frown Towns," November 28, 2011*

- The New Orleans metro area was selected as one of "The Best U.S. Cities for Bargain Shopping" by *Forbes*. The area ranked #10 out of 10. Criteria: number of outlet stores; gross leasable retail space in major malls; low consumer price index; low sales tax rate. Indicators were examined in the nation's 50 largest metropolitan areas. *Forbes, "The Best U.S. Cities for Bargain Shopping," January 20, 2012*

- Energizer Holdings, the makers of Edge® shave gel, in partnership with Sperling's BestPlaces, ranked 50 major metro areas in terms of everyday irritations. The New Orleans metro area ranked #31. Criteria: humidity levels; weather conditions; incidence of traffic delays and congestion; average commute times; frequency of flight delays and cancellations; rates of sleeplessness; underemployment; pollens and allergens; pests; comedy clubs per capita. *Energizer Holdings, "Most Irritation Prone Cities," July 23, 2010*

- Mars Chocolate North America, the makers of COMBOS®, in partnership with Sperling's BestPlaces, ranked 50 major metro areas in terms of their "manliness." The New Orleans metro area ranked #17. Criteria: number of professional sports teams; number of nearby NASCAR tracks and racing events; manly lifestyle; concentration of manly retail stores; manly occupations per capita; salty snack sales; "Board of Manliness" rankings. *Mars Chocolate North America, "America's Manliest Cities 2011," September 1, 2011*

- New Orleans was selected as one of the "Worst Hair Cities" by *NaturallyCurly.com*. The city was ranked #10. Criteria: humidity levels; pollution; rainfall; average wind speeds; water hardness; beauty salons per capita. *NaturallyCurly.com, "Best/Worst Hair Cities," April 29, 2009*

- New Orleans was selected as one of "America's Best Cities for Hipsters" by *Travel + Leisure*. The city was ranked #4 out of 10. Criteria: live music; coffee bars; independent boutiques; best microbrews; offbeat and tech-savvy locals. *Travel + Leisure, "America's Best Cities for Hipsters," April 11, 2012*

- The New Orleans metro area appeared in *AutoMD.com's* ranking of the "Best and Worst Cities for Auto Repair." The metro area ranked #32 (#1 is best). The 50 most-populated metro areas in the U.S. were ranked on three critical factors: repair affordability; price disparity range; shop integrity factor. *AutoMD.com, "Advocacy for Repair Shop Fairness Report," February 24, 2010*

- New Orleans appeared on Procter & Gamble's list of the "Top-20 All-Time Sweatiest Cities." The city was ranked #6. The rankings are based on computer simulations of the amount of sweat a person of average height and weight would produce walking around for an hour in the average temperatures during the summer months, based on historical weather data during June, July and August from 2001-2008 for each city. *Procter & Gamble, Old Spice Press Release, "Top-20 All-Time Sweatiest Cities," July 1, 2009*

Business Environment

CITY FINANCES

City Government Finances

Component	2009 ($000)	2009 ($ per capita)
Total Revenues	1,220,291	5,103
Total Expenditures	1,630,489	6,819
Debt Outstanding	2,038,603	8,525
Cash and Securities[1]	2,015,108	8,427

Note: (1) Cash and security holdings of a government at the close of its fiscal year, including those of its dependent agencies, utilities, and liquor stores.
Source: U.S Census Bureau, State & Local Government Finances 2009

City Government Revenue by Source

Source	2009 ($000)	2009 ($ per capita)
General Revenue		
From Federal Government	404,410	1,691
From State Government	88,364	370
From Local Governments	250	1
Taxes		
Property	215,803	902
Sales and Gross Receipts	199,353	834
Personal Income	0	0
Corporate Income	0	0
Motor Vehicle License	1,675	7
Other Taxes	28,545	119
Current Charges	269,204	1,126
Liquor Store	0	0
Utility	44,970	188
Employee Retirement	-156,812	-656

Source: U.S Census Bureau, State & Local Government Finances 2009

City Government Expenditures by Function

Function	2009 ($000)	2009 ($ per capita)	2009 (%)
General Direct Expenditures			
Air Transportation	70,358	294	4.3
Corrections	64,115	268	3.9
Education	0	0	0.0
Employment Security Administration	0	0	0.0
Financial Administration	55,392	232	3.4
Fire Protection	66,574	278	4.1
General Public Buildings	9,412	39	0.6
Governmental Administration, Other	90,471	378	5.5
Health	18,393	77	1.1
Highways	21,236	89	1.3
Hospitals	0	0	0.0
Housing and Community Development	232,047	970	14.2
Interest on General Debt	112,007	468	6.9
Judicial and Legal	43,197	181	2.6
Libraries	6,363	27	0.4
Parking	2,688	11	0.2
Parks and Recreation	70,581	295	4.3
Police Protection	137,042	573	8.4
Public Welfare	0	0	0.0
Sewerage	128,926	539	7.9
Solid Waste Management	47,727	200	2.9
Veterans' Services	0	0	0.0
Liquor Store	0	0	0.0
Utility	89,642	375	5.5
Employee Retirement	84,424	353	5.2

Source: U.S Census Bureau, State & Local Government Finances 2009

Municipal Bond Ratings

Area	Moody's	S&P	Fitch
City	Baa3	BBB	A-

Rating Systems (shown in declining order of credit quality): Moody's– Aaa, Aa, A, Baa, Ba, B, Caa, Ca, C (numerical modifiers 1, 2, and 3 are added to letter-rating); S&P– AAA, AA, A, BBB, BB, B, CCC, CC, C; Fitch– AAA, AA, A, BBB, BB, B, CCC, CC, C. Ratings may be modified by the addition of a plus or minus sign to show relative standing within the major rating categories.
Notes: n/a Not Available; w/d Withdrawn (1) Not Reviewed; (2) Issuer Rating/No General Obligation; (3) Standard and Poor's Issue Credit Rating (ICR) is a current opinion of an obliger with respect to a specific financial obligation, a specific class of financial obligations, or a specific financial program.
Source: U.S. Census Bureau, 2012 Statistical Abstract, Bond Ratings for City Governments by Largest Cities: 2010

DEMOGRAPHICS

Population Growth

Area	1990 Census	2000 Census	2010 Census	Population Growth (%) 1990-2000	Population Growth (%) 2000-2010
City	496,938	484,674	343,829	-2.5	-29.1
MSA[1]	1,264,391	1,316,510	1,167,764	4.1	-11.3
U.S.	248,709,873	281,421,906	308,745,538	13.2	9.7

Note: (1) Figures cover the New Orleans-Metairie-Kenner, LA Metropolitan Statistical Area—see Appendix B for areas included
Source: U.S. Census Bureau, 2010 Census

Household Size

Area	Persons in Household (%) One	Two	Three	Four	Five	Six	Seven or More	Average Household Size
City	35.9	29.9	15.4	10.0	5.1	2.1	1.6	2.33
MSA[1]	28.4	31.2	17.2	13.0	6.3	2.4	1.6	2.52
U.S.	26.7	32.8	16.1	13.4	6.5	2.6	1.9	2.58

Note: (1) Figures cover the New Orleans-Metairie-Kenner, LA Metropolitan Statistical Area—see Appendix B for areas included
Source: U.S. Census Bureau, 2010 Census

Race

Area	White Alone[2] (%)	Black Alone[2] (%)	Asian Alone[2] (%)	AIAN[3] Alone[2] (%)	NHOPI[4] Alone[2] (%)	Other Race Alone[2] (%)	Two or More Races (%)
City	33.0	60.2	2.9	0.3	0.0	1.9	1.7
MSA[1]	58.2	34.0	2.7	0.4	0.0	2.6	1.9
U.S.	72.4	12.6	4.8	0.9	0.2	6.2	2.9

Note: (1) Figures cover the New Orleans-Metairie-Kenner, LA Metropolitan Statistical Area—see Appendix B for areas included; (2) Alone is defined as not being in combination with one or more other races; (3) American Indian and Alaska Native; (4) Native Hawaiian and Other Pacific Islander
Source: U.S. Census Bureau, 2010 Census

Hispanic or Latino Origin

Area	Hispanic or Latino (%)	Mexican (%)	Puerto Rican (%)	Cuban (%)	Other Hispanic or Latino (%)
City	5.2	1.3	0.3	0.4	3.4
MSA[1]	7.9	1.8	0.4	0.6	5.1
U.S.	16.3	10.3	1.5	0.6	4.0

Note: Persons of Hispanic or Latino origin can be of any race; (1) Figures cover the New Orleans-Metairie-Kenner, LA Metropolitan Statistical Area—see Appendix B for areas included
Source: U.S. Census Bureau, 2010 Census

Segregation

Type	Segregation Indices[1]				Percent Change		
	1990	2000	2010	2010 Rank[2]	1990-2000	1990-2010	2000-2010
Black/White	68.3	69.2	63.9	28	0.9	-4.4	-5.3
Asian/White	49.6	50.4	48.6	9	0.8	-1.0	-1.8
Hispanic/White	31.1	35.6	38.3	74	4.5	7.2	2.7

Note: Figures are based on an analysis of 1990, 2000, and 2010 Census Decennial Census tract data by William H. Frey, Brookings Institution and the University of Michigan Social Science Data Analysis Network. In this analysis all racial groups (whites, blacks, and asians) are non-Hispanic members of those races. Hispanics are shown as a separate category; All figures cover the Metropolitan Statistical Area (see Appendix B for areas included); (1) Segregation Indices are Dissimilarity Indices that measure the degree to which the minority group is distributed differently than whites across census tracts. They range from 0 (complete integration) to 100 (complete segregation) where the value indicates the percentage of the minority group that needs to move to be distributed exactly like whites; (2) Ranges from 1 (most segregated) to 102 (least segregated); n/a not available.
Source: www.CensusScope.org

Ancestry

Area	German	Irish	English	American	Italian	Polish	French[2]	Scottish	Dutch
City	6.9	5.6	4.3	2.8	3.4	0.7	6.2	1.1	0.3
MSA[1]	12.5	8.5	5.4	4.6	9.0	0.6	15.7	1.0	0.4
U.S.	16.1	11.6	8.8	6.1	5.7	3.2	3.0	1.9	1.6

Note: Figures are the percentage of the total population reporting a particular ancestry. The nine most commonly reported ancestries in the U.S. are shown. Figures include multiple ancestries (e.g. if a person reported being Irish and Italian, they were included in both columns); (1) Figures cover the New Orleans-Metairie-Kenner, LA Metropolitan Statistical Area—see Appendix B for areas included; (2) Excludes Basque
Source: U.S. Census Bureau, 2008-2010 American Community Survey 3-Year Estimates

Foreign-Born Population

Area	Percent of Population Born in								
	Any Foreign Country	Mexico	Asia	Europe	Carribean	South America	Central America[2]	Africa	Canada
City	5.7	0.5	1.9	0.8	0.2	0.5	1.4	0.4	0.1
MSA[1]	7.1	0.8	2.0	0.6	0.5	0.5	2.4	0.2	0.1
U.S.	12.8	3.8	3.6	1.6	1.2	0.9	1.0	0.5	0.3

Note: (1) Figures cover the New Orleans-Metairie-Kenner, LA Metropolitan Statistical Area—see Appendix B for areas included; (2) Excludes Mexico.
Source: U.S. Census Bureau, 2008-2010 American Community Survey 3-Year Estimates

Marital Status

Area	Never Married	Now Married[2]	Separated	Widowed	Divorced
City	45.8	33.6	2.8	6.1	11.7
MSA[1]	34.6	44.5	2.6	6.6	11.7
U.S.	31.6	49.6	2.2	6.1	10.7

Note: Figures are percentages and cover the population 15 years of age and older; (1) Figures cover the New Orleans-Metairie-Kenner, LA Metropolitan Statistical Area—see Appendix B for areas included; (2) Excludes separated
Source: U.S. Census Bureau, 2008-2010 American Community Survey 3-Year Estimates

Age

Area	Percent of Population							Median Age
	Under Age 5	Age 5 to 17	Age 18 to 34	Age 35 to 49	Age 50 to 64	Age 65 to 79	80 Years and Over	
City	6.4	14.9	29.2	19.2	19.4	8.0	3.0	34.6
MSA[1]	6.6	16.8	24.1	20.2	20.1	8.9	3.3	37.1
U.S.	6.5	17.5	23.2	20.7	19.0	9.4	3.6	37.2

Note: (1) Figures cover the New Orleans-Metairie-Kenner, LA Metropolitan Statistical Area—see Appendix B for areas included
Source: U.S. Census Bureau, 2010 Census

New Orleans, Louisiana

Male/Female Ratio

Area	Males	Females	Males per 100 Females
City	166,248	177,581	93.6
MSA[1]	568,375	599,389	94.8
U.S.	151,781,326	156,964,212	96.7

Note: (1) Figures cover the New Orleans-Metairie-Kenner, LA
Metropolitan Statistical Area—see Appendix B for areas included
Source: U.S. Census Bureau, 2010 Census

Religious Groups

Area	Catholic	Baptist	Non-Den.	Methodist[2]	Lutheran	LDS[3]	Pente-costal	Presby-terian[4]	Muslim[5]	Judaism
MSA[1]	31.6	8.4	3.7	2.7	0.8	0.6	2.1	0.5	0.5	0.5
U.S.	19.1	9.3	4.0	4.0	2.3	2.0	1.9	1.6	0.8	0.7

Note: Figures are the number of adherents as a percentage of the total population; (1) Figures cover the New
Orleans-Metairie-Kenner, LA Metropolitan Statistical Area—see Appendix B for areas included;
(2) Methodist/Pietist; (3) Latter Day Saints; (4) Reformed; (5) Figures are estimates
Source: Association of Statisticians of American Religious Bodies, 2010 U.S. Religion Census: Religious
Congregations & Membership Study

ECONOMY

Gross Metropolitan Product

Area	2007	2008	2009	2010	2010 Rank[2]
MSA[1]	67.3	69.6	66.9	70.7	41

Note: Figures are in billions of dollars; (1) Figures cover the New Orleans-Metairie-Kenner, LA Metropolitan
Statistical Area—see Appendix B for areas included; (2) Rank ranges from 1 to 363
Source: The United States Conference of Mayors, "U.S. Metro Economies: GMP and Employment Forecasts,"
June 2011

Economic Growth

Area	2007-2009 (%)	2010 (%)	2011 (%)	Rank[2]
MSA[1]	2.3	6.0	2.5	31
U.S.	-1.3	2.9	2.5	–

Note: Figures are real Gross Metropolitan Product growth rates and represent annual average percent change;
(1) Figures cover the New Orleans-Metairie-Kenner, LA Metropolitan Statistical Area—see Appendix B for
areas included; (2) Rank ranges from 1 to 363
Source: The United States Conference of Mayors, "U.S. Metro Economies: GMP and Employment Forecasts,"
June 2011

Metropolitan Area Exports

Area	2005	2006	2007	2008	2009	2010	2010 Rank[2]
MSA[1]	4,857.8	6,717.2	8,449.1	12,664.5	10,145.1	13,964.9	19

Note: Figures are in millions of dollars; (1) Figures cover the New Orleans-Metairie-Kenner, LA Metropolitan
Statistical Area—see Appendix B for areas included; (2) Rank ranges from 1 to 369
Source: U.S. Department of Commerce, International Trade Administration, Office of Trade & Industry
Information, Manufacturing & Services, data extracted April 2, 2012

INCOME

Income

Area	Per Capita ($)	Median Household ($)	Average Household ($)
City	24,721	36,208	57,174
MSA[1]	25,870	46,210	64,705
U.S.	26,942	51,222	70,116

Note: (1) Figures cover the New Orleans-Metairie-Kenner, LA Metropolitan Statistical Area—see Appendix B
for areas included
Source: U.S. Census Bureau, 2008-2010 American Community Survey 3-Year Estimates

Household Income Distribution

Area	Percent of Households Earning							
	Under $15,000	$15,000 -24,999	$25,000 -34,999	$35,000 -49,999	$50,000 -74,999	$75,000 -99,000	$100,000 -149,999	$150,000 and up
City	22.6	14.7	11.5	13.7	15.1	8.0	8.2	6.3
MSA[1]	15.4	12.3	11.2	14.5	17.2	11.0	11.4	7.0
U.S.	13.0	11.0	10.6	14.2	18.5	12.1	12.2	8.4

Note: (1) Figures cover the New Orleans-Metairie-Kenner, LA Metropolitan Statistical Area—see Appendix B for areas included
Source: U.S. Census Bureau, 2008-2010 American Community Survey 3-Year Estimates

Poverty Rate

Area	All Ages	Under 18 Years Old	18 to 64 Years Old	65 Years and Over
City	25.8	39.1	23.0	16.5
MSA[1]	16.4	23.9	14.7	11.1
U.S.	14.4	20.1	13.1	9.4

Note: Figures are percentage of people whose income during the past 12 months was below the poverty level; (1) Figures cover the New Orleans-Metairie-Kenner, LA Metropolitan Statistical Area—see Appendix B for areas included
Source: U.S. Census Bureau, 2008-2010 American Community Survey 3-Year Estimates

Personal Bankruptcy Filing Rate

Area	2006	2007	2008	2009	2010	2011
Orleans Parish	1.18	1.42	1.59	2.12	2.31	2.30
U.S.	2.00	2.73	3.53	4.61	4.97	4.37

Note: Numbers are per 1,000 population and include Chapter 7 and Chapter 13 filings
Source: Federal Deposit Insurance Corporation, Regional Economic Conditions, March 9, 2012

EMPLOYMENT

Labor Force and Employment

Area	Civilian Labor Force			Workers Employed		
	Dec. 2010	Dec. 2011	% Chg.	Dec. 2010	Dec. 2011	% Chg.
City	148,131	144,947	-2.1	135,477	133,707	-1.3
MSA[1]	541,914	531,205	-2.0	503,787	497,205	-1.3
U.S.	153,156,000	153,373,000	0.1	139,159,000	140,681,000	1.1

Note: Data is not seasonally adjusted and covers workers 16 years of age and older; (1) Metropolitan Statistical Area—see Appendix B for areas included
Source: Bureau of Labor Statistics, http://stats.bls.gov

Unemployment Rate

Area	2011											
	Jan.	Feb.	Mar.	Apr.	May	Jun.	Jul.	Aug.	Sep.	Oct.	Nov.	Dec.
City	10.0	9.0	9.1	8.4	9.3	9.6	9.7	9.1	8.6	8.7	7.8	7.8
MSA[1]	8.4	7.8	7.9	7.2	8.0	8.0	7.8	7.3	6.9	7.1	6.5	6.4
U.S.	9.8	9.5	9.2	8.7	8.7	9.3	9.3	9.1	8.8	8.5	8.2	8.3

Note: Data is not seasonally adjusted and covers workers 16 years of age and older; All figures are percentages; (1) Metropolitan Statistical Area—see Appendix B for areas included
Source: Bureau of Labor Statistics, http://stats.bls.gov

Projected Unemployment Rate

Area	2010 (%)	2011 (%)	2012 (%)	2013 (%)
MSA[1]	8.7	8.9	8.3	7.6

Note: (1) Metropolitan Statistical Area—see Appendix B for areas included
Source: The United States Conference of Mayors, "U.S. Metro Economies: GMP and Employment Forecasts," June 2011

Employment by Occupation

Occupation Classification	City (%)	MSA[1] (%)	U.S. (%)
Management, Business, Science, and Arts	38.2	34.5	35.6
Natural Resources, Construction, and Maintenance	8.5	11.9	9.5
Production, Transportation, and Material Moving	9.1	10.2	12.1
Sales and Office	21.5	25.1	25.2
Service	22.6	18.3	17.6

Note: Figures cover employed civilians 16 years of age and older; (1) Figures cover the New Orleans-Metairie-Kenner, LA Metropolitan Statistical Area—see Appendix B for areas included
Source: U.S. Census Bureau, 2008-2010 American Community Survey 3-Year Estimates

Employment by Industry

Sector	MSA[1] Number of Employees	MSA[1] Percent of Total	U.S. Percent of Total
Construction	28,000	5.3	4.1
Education and Health Services	78,800	14.9	15.2
Financial Activities	25,000	4.7	5.8
Government	82,700	15.6	16.8
Information	7,600	1.4	2.0
Leisure and Hospitality	73,000	13.8	9.9
Manufacturing	31,500	6.0	8.9
Mining and Logging	6,800	1.3	0.6
Other Services	18,400	3.5	4.0
Professional and Business Services	69,600	13.1	13.3
Retail Trade	58,600	11.1	11.5
Transportation and Utilities	25,800	4.9	3.8
Wholesale Trade	23,500	4.4	4.2

Note: Figures cover non-farm employment as of December 2011 and are not seasonally adjusted;
(1) Metropolitan Statistical Area—see Appendix B for areas included
Source: Bureau of Labor Statistics, http://stats.bls.gov

Occupations with Greatest Projected Employment Growth: 2008 – 2018

Occupation[1]	2008 Employment	2018 Projected Employment	Numeric Employment Change	Percent Employment Change
Registered Nurses	40,090	50,110	10,020	25.0
Retail Salespersons	60,700	67,300	6,600	10.9
Food Preparation Workers	31,350	37,830	6,480	20.7
Personal and Home Care Aides	13,700	19,680	5,980	43.6
Customer Service Representatives	24,390	30,090	5,700	23.4
Waiters and Waitresses	33,360	38,630	5,270	15.8
Home Health Aides	11,340	16,560	5,220	46.0
Nursing Aides, Orderlies, and Attendants	25,560	30,640	5,080	19.9
Elementary School Teachers, Except Special Education	27,100	30,660	3,560	13.1
Combined Food Preparation and Serving Workers, Including Fast Food	13,250	16,490	3,240	24.5

Note: Projections cover Louisiana; (1) Sorted by numeric employment change
Source: www.projectionscentral.com, State Occupational Projections, 2008–2018 Long-Term Projections

Fastest Growing Occupations: 2008 – 2018

Occupation[1]	2008 Employment	2018 Projected Employment	Numeric Employment Change	Percent Employment Change
Home Health Aides	11,340	16,560	5,220	46.0
Personal and Home Care Aides	13,700	19,680	5,980	43.6
Network Systems and Data Communications Analysts	1,320	1,890	570	43.2
Skin Care Specialists	440	600	160	36.4
Pharmacy Technicians	4,620	6,230	1,610	34.8
Medical Assistants	4,530	6,080	1,550	34.2
Physical Therapist Assistants	840	1,120	280	33.3
Computer Software Engineers, Applications	1,210	1,610	400	33.1
Health Educators	400	520	120	30.0
Manicurists and Pedicurists	570	740	170	29.8

Note: Projections cover Louisiana; (1) Sorted by percent employment change and excludes occupations with numeric employment change less than 100
Source: www.projectionscentral.com, State Occupational Projections, 2008–2018 Long-Term Projections

Average Wages

Occupation	$/Hr.	Occupation	$/Hr.
Accountants and Auditors	31.66	Maids and Housekeeping Cleaners	9.55
Automotive Mechanics	18.89	Maintenance and Repair Workers	17.54
Bookkeepers	16.95	Marketing Managers	42.58
Carpenters	18.29	Nuclear Medicine Technologists	32.59
Cashiers	9.24	Nurses, Licensed Practical	20.38
Clerks, General Office	12.09	Nurses, Registered	32.72
Clerks, Receptionists/Information	11.64	Nursing Aides/Orderlies/Attendants	11.18
Clerks, Shipping/Receiving	15.28	Packers and Packagers, Hand	11.49
Computer Programmers	28.87	Physical Therapists	37.57
Computer Support Specialists	23.18	Postal Service Mail Carriers	25.16
Computer Systems Analysts	29.30	Real Estate Brokers	n/a
Cooks, Restaurant	11.36	Retail Salespersons	12.01
Dentists	74.29	Sales Reps., Exc. Tech./Scientific	28.99
Electrical Engineers	47.05	Sales Reps., Tech./Scientific	31.55
Electricians	22.16	Secretaries, Exc. Legal/Med./Exec.	14.64
Financial Managers	46.42	Security Guards	12.18
First-Line Supervisors/Managers, Sales	18.54	Surgeons	120.03
Food Preparation Workers	9.00	Teacher Assistants	10.70
General and Operations Managers	54.57	Teachers, Elementary School	23.60
Hairdressers/Cosmetologists	11.63	Teachers, Secondary School	23.80
Internists	n/a	Telemarketers	14.84
Janitors and Cleaners	10.36	Truck Drivers, Heavy/Tractor-Trailer	19.44
Landscaping/Groundskeeping Workers	10.94	Truck Drivers, Light/Delivery Svcs.	16.87
Lawyers	55.05	Waiters and Waitresses	9.55

Note: Wage data covers the New Orleans-Metairie-Kenner, LA Metropolitan Statistical Area—see Appendix B for areas included. Hourly wages for elementary/secondary school teachers and teacher assistants were calculated by the editors from annual wage data assuming a 40 hour work week; n/a not available.
Source: Bureau of Labor Statistics, Metro Area Occupational Employment and Wage Estimates, May 2011

RESIDENTIAL REAL ESTATE

Building Permits

Area	Single-Family			Multi-Family			Total		
	2010	2011	Pct. Chg.	2010	2011	Pct. Chg.	2010	2011	Pct. Chg.
City	820	717	-12.6	260	377	45.0	1,080	1,094	1.3
MSA[1]	1,875	1,945	3.7	296	383	29.4	2,171	2,328	7.2
U.S.	447,311	418,498	-6.4	157,299	205,563	30.7	604,610	624,061	3.2

Note: (1) Metropolitan Statistical Area—see Appendix B for areas included; figures represent new, privately-owned housing units authorized (unadjusted data); All permit data are based on estimates with imputation.
Source: U.S. Census Bureau, Manufacturing, Mining, and Construction Statistics, Building Permits, 2010, 2011

Homeownership Rate

Area	2005 (%)	2006 (%)	2007 (%)	2008 (%)	2009 (%)	2010 (%)	2011 (%)
MSA[1]	71.2	70.3	67.8	68.0	68.2	66.9	63.9
U.S.	68.9	68.8	68.1	67.8	67.4	66.9	66.1

Note: (1) Metropolitan Statistical Area—see Appendix B for areas included
Source: U.S. Census Bureau, Housing Vacancies and Homeownership Annual Statistics: 2011

Housing Vacancy Rates

Area	Gross Vacancy Rate[2] (%)			Year-Round Vacancy Rate[3] (%)			Rental Vacancy Rate[4] (%)			Homeowner Vacancy Rate[5] (%)		
	2009	2010	2011	2009	2010	2011	2009	2010	2011	2009	2010	2011
MSA[1]	16.1	14.6	10.7	15.9	14.4	10.3	18.0	15.2	13.1	2.5	2.6	2.1
U.S.	14.5	14.3	14.2	11.3	11.3	11.1	10.6	10.2	9.5	2.6	2.6	2.5

Note: (1) Metropolitan Statistical Area—see Appendix B for areas included; (2) The percentage of the total housing inventory that is vacant; (3) The percentage of the housing inventory (excluding seasonal units) that is year-round vacant; (4) The percentage of rental inventory that is vacant for rent; (5) The percentage of homeowner inventory that is vacant for sale
Source: U.S. Census Bureau, Housing Vacancies and Homeownership Annual Statistics: 2011

TAXES

State Corporate Income Tax Rates

State	Tax Rate (%)	Income Brackets ($)	Num. of Brackets	Financial Institution Tax Rate (%)[a]	Federal Income Tax Ded.
Louisiana	4.0 - 8.0	25,000 - 200,001	5	4.0 - 8.0	Yes

Note: Tax rates as of January 1, 2012; (a) Rates listed are the corporate income tax rate applied to financial institutions or excise taxes based on income. Some states have other taxes based upon the value of deposits or shares.
Source: Federation of Tax Administrators, "State Corporate Income Tax Rates, 2012"

State Individual Income Tax Rates

State	Tax Rate (%)	Income Brackets ($)	Num. of Brackets	Personal Exempt. ($)[1] Single	Dependents	Fed. Inc. Tax Ded.
Louisiana	2.0 - 6.0	12,500 (b)-50,001 (b)	3	4,500 (j)	1,000	Yes

Note: Tax rates as of January 1, 2012; Local- and county-level taxes are not included; n/a not applicable; (1) Married joint filers generally receive double the single exemption; (b) For joint returns, taxes are twice the tax on half the couple's income; (j) The amounts reported for Louisiana are a combined personal exemption-standard deduction.
Source: Federation of Tax Administrators, "State Individual Income Tax Rates, 2012"

Various State and Local Tax Rates

State	State and Local Sales and Use (%)	State Sales and Use (%)	Gasoline[1] (¢/gal.)	Cigarette[2] ($/pack)	Spirits[3] ($/gal.)	Wine[4] ($/gal.)	Beer[5] ($/gal.)
Louisiana	8.75	4.00	20.0	0.36	2.50	0.11	0.32

Note: All tax rates as of January 1, 2012 except beer, wine and spirits (September 1, 2011); (1) The American Petroleum Institute has developed a methodology for determining the average tax rate on a gallon of fuel. Rates may include any of the following: excise taxes, environmental fees, storage tank fees, other fees or taxes, general sales tax, and local taxes. In states where gasoline is subject to the general sales tax, or where the fuel tax is based on the average sale price, the average rate determined by API is sensitive to changes in the price of gasoline. States that fully or partially apply general sales taxes to gasoline: CA, CO, GA, IL, IN, MI, NY; (2) The federal excise tax of $1.0066 per pack and local taxes are not included; (3) Rates are those applicable to off-premise sales of 40% alcohol by volume (a.b.v.) distilled spirits in 750ml containers. Local excise taxes are excluded; (4) Rates are those applicable to off-premise sales of 11% a.b.v. non-carbonated wine in 750ml containers; (5) Rates are those applicable to off-premise sales of 4.7% a.b.v. beer in 12 ounce containers.
Source: Tax Foundation, 2012 Facts & Figures: How Does Your State Compare?

State-Local Tax Burdens

Area	Rate (%)	Rank[1]	Per Capita Taxes Paid to Home State ($)	Total State and Local Per Capita Taxes Paid ($)	Per Capita Income ($)
Louisiana	8.2	42	2,034	3,037	37,109
U.S. Average	9.8	-	3,057	4,160	42,539

Note: Figures cover 2009; (1) Rank ranges from 1 to 50 where 1 is highest tax burden
Source: Tax Foundation, State-Local Tax Burdens, All States, 2009

State Business Tax Climate Index Rankings

State	Overall Rank	Corporate Tax Index Rank	Individual Income Tax Index Rank	Sales Tax Index Rank	Unemployment Insurance Tax Index Rank	Property Tax Index Rank
Louisiana	32	17	24	49	4	23

Note: The index is a measure of how each state's tax laws affect economic performance. The lower the rank, the more favorable a state's tax system is for business. States without a given tax are given a ranking of 1.
Source: Tax Foundation, Major Components of the State Business Tax Climate Index, FY 2012

COMMERCIAL UTILITIES

Typical Monthly Electric Bills

Area	Commercial Service ($/month)		Industrial Service ($/month)	
	1,500 kWh	40 kW demand 14,000 kWh	1,000 kW demand 200,000 kWh	50,000 kW demand 15,000,000 kWh
City	156	1,360	21,443	1,390,389
Average[1]	189	1,616	25,197	1,470,813

Note: Based on total rates in effect July 1, 2011; (1) average based on 184 utilities surveyed
Source: Edison Electric Institute, Typical Bills and Average Rates Report, Summer 2011

TRANSPORTATION

Means of Transportation to Work

Area	Car/Truck/Van Drove Alone	Car-pooled	Public Transportation Bus	Subway	Railroad	Bicycle	Walked	Other Means	Worked at Home
City	68.4	12.2	6.2	0.0	0.0	1.8	5.3	2.6	3.4
MSA[1]	78.3	11.5	2.5	0.0	0.0	0.7	2.5	1.8	2.7
U.S.	76.0	10.2	2.7	1.7	0.5	0.5	2.8	1.3	4.2

Note: Figures are percentages and cover workers 16 years of age and older; (1) Figures cover the New Orleans-Metairie-Kenner, LA Metropolitan Statistical Area—see Appendix B for areas included
Source: U.S. Census Bureau, 2008-2010 American Community Survey 3-Year Estimates

Travel Time to Work

Area	Less Than 10 Minutes	10 to 19 Minutes	20 to 29 Minutes	30 to 44 Minutes	45 to 59 Minutes	60 to 89 Minutes	90 Minutes or More
City	10.8	35.9	24.4	18.6	4.8	3.6	1.9
MSA[1]	11.0	32.2	21.2	20.6	7.5	5.2	2.4
U.S.	13.9	30.1	20.8	19.8	7.5	5.5	2.5

Note: Figures are percentages and include workers 16 years old and over; (1) Figures cover the New Orleans-Metairie-Kenner, LA Metropolitan Statistical Area—see Appendix B for areas included
Source: U.S. Census Bureau, 2008-2010 American Community Survey 3-Year Estimates

Travel Time Index

Area	1985	1990	1995	2000	2005	2010
Urban Area[1]	1.18	1.18	1.19	1.19	1.19	1.17
Average[2]	1.11	1.16	1.18	1.21	1.25	1.20

Note: Travel Time Index—the ratio of travel time in the peak period to the travel time at free-flow conditions. A value of 1.30 indicates a 20-minute free-flow trip takes 26 minutes in the peak. Free-flow speeds (60 mph on freeways and 35 mph on principal arterials) are used as the comparison threshold; (1) Covers the New Orleans LA urban area; (2) average of 439 urban areas
Source: Texas Transportation Institute, Urban Mobility Report 2011, September 2011

Public Transportation

Agency Name / Mode of Transportation	Vehicles Operated in Maximum Service	Annual Unlinked Passenger Trips ('000)	Annual Passenger Miles ('000)
New Orleans Regional Transit Authority (NORTA)			
Bus (purchased transportation)	62	9,096.5	31,752.9
Demand Response (purchased transportation)	29	162.5	1,324.8
Light Rail (purchased transportation)	21	6,784.7	15,384.4

Source: Federal Transit Administration, National Transit Database, 2010

Air Transportation

Airport Name and Code / Type of Service	Passenger Airlines[1]	Passenger Enplanements	Freight Carriers[2]	Freight (lbs.)
New Orleans International (MSY)				
Domestic service (U.S. carriers - 2011)	36	4,219,681	14	46,067,457
International service (U.S. carriers - 2010)	9	8,142	3	10,323

Note: (1) Includes all U.S.-based major, minor and commuter airlines that carried at least one passenger during the year; (2) Includes all U.S.-based airlines and freight carriers that transported at least one pound of freight during the year
Source: Bureau of Transportation Statistics, The Intermodal Transportation Database, Air Carriers: T-100 Domestic Market (U.S. Carriers), 2011; Bureau of Transportation Statistics, The Intermodal Transportation Database, Air Carriers: T-100 International Market (U.S. Carriers), 2010

Other Transportation Statistics

Major Highways:	I-10; I-59
Amtrak Service:	Yes
Major Waterways/Ports:	Port of New Orleans; Mississippi River

Source: Amtrak.com; Google Maps

BUSINESSES

Major Business Headquarters

Company Name	Rankings	
	Fortune[1]	Forbes[2]
Entergy	213	-

Note: (1) Fortune 500—companies that produce a 10-K are ranked 1 to 500 based on 2010 revenue; (2) all private companies with at least $2 billion in annual revenue are ranked 1 to 212; companies listed are headquartered in the city; dashes indicate no ranking
Source: Fortune, "Fortune 500," May 23, 2011; Forbes, "America's Largest Private Companies," November 16, 2011

Fast-Growing Businesses

According to *Inc.*, New Orleans is home to one of America's 500 fastest-growing private companies: **Search Influence** (#418). Criteria: must be an independent, privately-held, for-profit, U.S. corporation, proprietorship or partnership; revenues must be at least $80,000 in 2007 and $2 million in 2010; must have four-year operating/sales history. Holding companies, regulated banks, and utilities were excluded. *Inc., "America's 500 Fastest-Growing Private Companies," September 2011*

According to *Initiative for a Competitive Inner City (ICIC)*, New Orleans is home to two of America's 100 fastest-growing "inner city" companies: **Perez, APC** (#5); **NewBath** (#14). Companies were ranked by their five-year compound annual growth rate. Criteria for inclusion: company must be headquartered in or have 51 percent or more of its physical operations in an economically distressed urban area; must be an independent, for-profit corporation, partnership or proprietorship; must have 10 or more employees and have a five-year sales history that includes sales of at least $200,000 in the base year and at least $1 million in the current year with no decrease in sales over the two most recent years. *Initiative for a Competitive Inner City (ICIC), "Inner City 100 Companies, 2011"*

Minority Business Opportunity

New Orleans is home to one company which is on the *Black Enterprise* Bank 20 list (20 largest banks based on total assets, capital, deposits and loans, including mortgage-backed securities for the calendar year): **Liberty Bank and Trust Company** (#5). Only commercial banks or savings and loans that are classified by the Federal Reserve as black institutions and have been fully operational for the previous calendar year were considered. *Black Enterprise, B.E. 100s, 2011*

New Orleans is home to one company which is on the *Hispanic Business* 500 list (500 largest U.S. Hispanic-owned companies based on 2010 revenue): **Pan-American Life Insurance Group** (#12). Companies included must show at least 51 percent ownership by Hispanic U.S. citizens, and must maintain headquarters in one of the 50 states or Washington, D.C. *Hispanic Business, "Hispanic Business 500," June 2011*

New Orleans is home to one company which is on the *Hispanic Business* Fastest-Growing 100 list (greatest sales growth from 2006 to 2010): **Pan-American Life Insurance Group** (#97). Companies included must show at least 51 percent ownership by Hispanic U.S. citizens, and must maintain headquarters in one of the 50 states or Washington, D.C. In addition, companies must have minimum revenues of $200,000 for calendar year 2005. *Hispanic Business, July/August 2011*

Minority- and Women-Owned Businesses

Group	All Firms		Firms with Paid Employees			
	Firms	Sales ($000)	Firms	Sales ($000)	Employees	Payroll ($000)
Asian	1,403	310,414	388	268,702	1,755	39,419
Black	7,843	497,070	391	345,949	4,728	104,339
Hispanic	1,103	107,771	137	77,257	970	23,102
Women	8,245	1,418,443	1,048	1,236,470	9,907	300,668
All Firms	61	(w)	40	(w)	1,000 - 2,499	(w)

Note: Figures cover firms located in the city; minority- and women-owned business are defined as firms in which the corresponding group own 51% or more of the stock or equity of the company
Source: U.S. Census Bureau, 2007 Economic Census, Survey of Business Owners

HOTELS

Hotels/Motels

Area	5 Star		4 Star		3 Star		2 Star		1 Star		Not Rated	
	Num.	Pct.[3]	Num.	Pct.[3]	Num.	Pct.[3]	Num.	Pct.[3]	Num.	Pct.[3]	Num.	Pct.[3]
City[1]	0	0.0	22	11.5	81	42.4	69	36.1	6	3.1	13	6.8
Total[2]	133	0.9	940	6.5	4,569	31.8	7,033	48.9	351	2.4	1,343	9.3

Note: (1) Figures cover New Orleans and vicinity; (2) Figures cover all 100 cities in this book; (3) Percentage of hotels which have a given star rating; Star ratings are determined by expedia.com and offer an indication of the general quality of a particular hotel.
Source: expedia.com, April 25, 2012

The New Orleans-Metairie-Kenner, LA metro area is home to four of the best hotels in the U.S. according to *Travel & Leisure*: **Windsor Court Hotel** (#40); **The Roosevelt Hotel, New Orleans** (#55); **Loews New Orleans Hotel** (#136); **Ritz-Carlton, New Orleans** (#154). Criteria: service; location; rooms; food; and value. *Travel & Leisure, "T+L 500, The World's Best Hotels 2012"*

The New Orleans-Metairie-Kenner, LA metro area is home to two of the best hotels in the U.S. according to *Condé Nast Traveler*: **Windsor Court Hotel** (#80); **Omni Royal Orleans** (#87). The selections are based on over 25,000 responses to the magazine's annual Readers' Choice Survey. *Condé Nast Traveler, "2011 Readers' Choice Awards"*

EVENT SITES

Major Stadiums, Arenas, and Auditoriums

Name	Max. Capacity
Lakefront Arena	10,000
Louisiana Superdome	76,468
New Orleans Cultural Center	8,500
Tad Gormley Stadium/Alerion Field	26,500
The Conference Auditorium at the Morial Center	4,000

Source: Original research

Convention Centers

Name	Overall Space (sq. ft.)	Exhibit Space (sq. ft.)	Meeting Space (sq. ft.)	Meeting Rooms
Ernest N. Morial Convention Center	3,000,000	n/a	1,100,000	n/a

Note: n/a not available
Source: Original research

Living Environment

COST OF LIVING

Cost of Living Index

Composite Index	Groceries	Housing	Utilities	Trans-portation	Health Care	Misc. Goods/Services
95.7	95.9	95.2	89.3	99.1	91.2	97.7

Note: U.S. = 100; Figures cover the Slidell-St. Tammany Parish LA urban area.
Source: The Council for Community and Economic Research, ACCRA Cost of Living Index, 2011

Grocery Prices

Area[1]	T-Bone Steak ($/pound)	Frying Chicken ($/pound)	Whole Milk ($/half gal.)	Eggs ($/dozen)	Orange Juice ($/64 oz.)	Coffee ($/11.5 oz.)
City[2]	9.07	1.07	2.76	1.67	3.13	3.99
Avg.	9.25	1.18	2.22	1.66	3.19	4.40
Min.	6.70	0.88	1.31	0.95	2.46	2.94
Max.	14.30	2.16	3.50	3.18	4.75	6.83

Note: (1) Values for the local area are compared with the average, minimum and maximum values for all 335 areas in the Cost of Living Index; (2) Figures cover the Slidell-St. Tammany Parish LA urban area; **T-Bone Steak** *(price per pound);* **Frying Chicken** *(price per pound, whole fryer);* **Whole Milk** *(half gallon carton);* **Eggs** *(price per dozen, Grade A, large);* **Orange Juice** *(64 oz. Tropicana or Florida Natural);* **Coffee** *(11.5 oz. can, vacuum-packed, Maxwell House, Hills Bros, or Folgers).*
Source: The Council for Community and Economic Research, ACCRA Cost of Living Index, 2011

Housing and Utility Costs

Area[1]	New Home Price ($)	Apartment Rent ($/month)	All Electric ($/month)	Part Electric ($/month)	Other Energy ($/month)	Telephone ($/month)
City[2]	252,394	988	146.02	-	-	24.58
Avg.	285,990	839	163.23	89.00	77.52	26.92
Min.	188,005	460	125.58	45.39	33.89	17.98
Max.	1,197,028	3,244	339.16	181.97	348.69	40.01

Note: (1) Values for the local area are compared with the average, minimum and maximum values for all 335 areas in the Cost of Living Index; (2) Figures cover the Slidell-St. Tammany Parish LA urban area; **New Home Price** *(2,400 sf living area, 8,000 sf lot, in urban area with full utilities);* **Apartment Rent** *(950 sf 2 bedroom/1.5 or 2 bath, unfurnished, excluding all utilities except water);* **All Electric** *(average monthly cost for an all-electric home);* **Part Electric** *(average monthly cost for a part-electric home);* **Other Energy** *(average monthly cost for natural gas, fuel oil, coal, wood, and any other forms of energy except electricity);* **Telephone** *(price includes basic monthly rate for a private residential line plus additional local usage charges incurred by a family of four).*
Source: The Council for Community and Economic Research, ACCRA Cost of Living Index, 2011

Health Care, Transportation, and Other Costs

Area[1]	Doctor ($/visit)	Dentist ($/visit)	Optometrist ($/visit)	Gasoline ($/gallon)	Beauty Salon ($/visit)	Men's Shirt ($)
City[2]	81.57	68.39	73.40	3.39	37.95	27.58
Avg.	93.88	81.72	90.54	3.48	32.65	25.06
Min.	60.00	55.33	53.66	3.18	19.78	13.44
Max.	154.98	145.97	183.72	4.31	63.21	46.00

Note: (1) Values for the local area are compared with the average, minimum and maximum values for all 335 areas in the Cost of Living Index; (2) Figures cover the Slidell-St. Tammany Parish LA urban area; **Doctor** *(general practitioners routine exam of an established patient);* **Dentist** *(adult teeth cleaning and periodic oral examination);* **Optometrist** *(full vision eye exam for established adult patient);* **Gasoline** *(one gallon regular unleaded, national brand, including all taxes, cash price at self-service pump if available);* **Beauty Salon** *(woman's shampoo, trim, and blow-dry);* **Men's Shirt** *(cotton/polyester dress shirt, pinpoint weave, long sleeves).*
Source: The Council for Community and Economic Research, ACCRA Cost of Living Index, 2011

HOUSING

House Price Index (HPI)

Area	National Ranking[2]	Quarterly Change (%)	One-Year Change (%)	Five-Year Change (%)
MSA[1]	41	0.89	-0.36	-7.18
U.S.[3]	-	-0.10	-2.43	-19.16

Note: The HPI is a weighted repeat sales index. It measures average price changes in repeat sales or refinancings on the same properties. This information is obtained by reviewing repeat mortgage transactions on single-family properties whose mortgages have been purchased or securitized by Fannie Mae or Freddie Mac in January 1975; (1) Metropolitan/Micropolitan Statistical Area—see Appendix B for areas included; (2) Rankings are based on annual percentage change for all metro areas containing at least 15,000 transactions over the last 10 years and ranges from 1 to 306; (3) figures based on a weighted average of Census Division estimates using a purchase only index; all figures are for the period ending December 31, 2011
Source: Federal Housing Finance Agency, House Price Index, February 23, 2012

House Price Valuations

Area	Q4 2005 Price ($000)	Q4 2005 Over-valuation	Q4 2006 Price ($000)	Q4 2006 Over-valuation	Q4 2007 Price ($000)	Q4 2007 Over-valuation	Q4 2008 Price ($000)	Q4 2008 Over-valuation	Q4 2009 Price ($000)	Q4 2009 Over-valuation
MSA[1]	142.5	-30.2	156.1	-6.0	154.4	-9.8	149.0	-12.4	145.5	-12.5

Note: Figures show the percentage of over- or under-valuation of single family homes relative to statistically normal house values (e.g. a value of 23.6 indicates that house values are 23.6% overvalued). Statistically normal house values are based on house prices, interest rates, household incomes, population densities, and any historical premiums or discounts metropolitan areas have exhibited over time; (1) Figures cover the New Orleans-Metairie-Kenner, LA - see Appendix B for areas included
Source: Global Insight/PNC Financial Services Group, House Prices in America: 4th Quarter 2009 Update

Median Single-Family Home Prices

Area	2009	2010	2011p	Percent Change 2010 to 2011
MSA[1]	160.1	159.7	153.0	-4.2
U.S. Average	172.1	173.1	166.2	-4.0

Note: Figures are median sales prices of existing single-family homes in thousands of dollars; (p) preliminary; n/a not available; (1) Metropolitan Statistical Area—see Appendix B for areas included
Source: National Association of Realtors, Median Sales Price of Existing Single-Family Homes for Metropolitan Areas, 4th Quarter 2011

Affordability Index of Existing Single-Family Homes

Area	2009	2010	2011p	Percent Change 2010 to 2011
MSA[1]	132.5	139.4	160.1	14.8

Note: The housing affordability index measures whether or not a typical family could qualify for a mortgage loan on a typical home. The higher the index, the greater the household purchasing power. An index of 100 is defined as the point where a median-income household has exactly enough income to qualify for the purchase of a median-priced existing single-family home, assuming a 20 percent downpayment and 25 percent of gross income devoted to mortgage principal and interest payments; (p) preliminary; n/a not available; (1) Metropolitan Statistical Area—see Appendix B for areas included
Source: National Association of Realtors, Affordability Index of Existing Single-Family Homes, 2011

Median Apartment Condo-Coop Home Prices

Area	2009	2010	2011p	Percent Change 2010 to 2011
MSA[1]	171.5	175.7	167.6	-4.6
U.S. Average	175.6	171.7	165.1	-3.8

Note: Figures are median sales prices of existing apartment condo-coop homes in thousands of dollars; (p) preliminary; n/a not available; (1) Metropolitan Statistical Area—see Appendix B for areas included
Source: National Association of Realtors, Median Sales Price of Existing Apartment Condo-Coop Homes for Metropolitan Areas, 4th Quarter 2011

Year Housing Structure Built

Area	2005 or Later	2000 -2004	1990 -1999	1980 -1989	1970 -1979	1960 -1969	1950 -1959	Before 1950	Median Year
City	3.3	3.2	3.8	7.5	13.7	12.7	11.6	44.2	1955
MSA[1]	5.1	6.5	9.8	14.5	20.0	14.7	10.0	19.5	1973
U.S.	5.0	8.6	14.0	14.1	16.3	11.3	11.2	19.6	1975

Note: Figures are percentages except for Median Year; (1) Figures cover the New Orleans-Metairie-Kenner, LA Metropolitan Statistical Area—see Appendix B for areas included
Source: U.S. Census Bureau, 2008-2010 American Community Survey 3-Year Estimates

HEALTH

Health Risk Data

Category	MSA[1] (%)	U.S. (%)
Adults who have been told they have high blood pressure[2]	36.1	28.7
Adults who have been told they have high blood cholesterol[2]	35.0	37.5
Adults who have been told they have diabetes[3]	11.0	8.7
Adults who have been told they have arthritis[2]	24.2	26.0
Adults who have been told they currently have asthma	7.1	9.1
Adults who are current smokers	20.3	17.3
Adults who are heavy drinkers[4]	5.4	5.0
Adults who are binge drinkers[5]	16.8	15.1
Adults who are overweight (BMI 25.0 - 29.9)	37.2	36.2
Adults who are obese (BMI 30.0 - 99.8)	32.6	27.5
Adults who participated in any physical activities in the past month	73.1	76.1
Adults 50+ who have ever had a sigmoidoscopy or colonoscopy	66.7	65.2
Women aged 40+ who have had a mammogram within the past two years	75.8	75.2
Men aged 40+ who have had a PSA test within the past two years	60.8	53.2
Adults aged 65+ who have had flu shot within the past year	64.3	67.5
Adults aged 18–64 who have any kind of health care coverage	75.7	82.2

Note: Data as of 2010 unless otherwise noted; (1) Figures cover the New Orleans-Metairie-Kenner, LA Metropolitan Statistical Area—see Appendix B for areas included; (2) Data as of 2009; (3) Figures do not include pregnancy-related, borderline, or pre-diabetes; (4) Heavy drinkers are classified as males having more than two drinks per day or females having more than one drink per day; (5) Binge drinkers are classified as males having five or more drinks on one occasion or females having four or more drinks on one occasion
Source: Centers for Disease Control and Prevention, Behaviorial Risk Factor Surveillance System, SMART: Selected Metropolitan/Micropolitan Area Risk Trends, 2009, 2010

Mortality Rates for the Top 10 Causes of Death in the U.S.

ICD-10[a] Sub-Chapter	ICD-10[a] Code	Age-Adjusted Mortality Rate[1] per 100,000 population County[2]	U.S.
Malignant neoplasms	C00-C97	183.8	175.6
Ischaemic heart diseases	I20-I25	91.7	121.6
Other forms of heart disease	I30-I51	51.2	48.6
Chronic lower respiratory diseases	J40-J47	25.2	42.3
Cerebrovascular diseases	I60-I69	42.6	40.6
Organic, including symptomatic, mental disorders	F01-F09	19.5	26.7
Other degenerative diseases of the nervous system	G30-G31	17.6	24.7
Other external causes of accidental injury	W00-X59	29.9	24.4
Diabetes mellitus	E10-E14	24.3	21.7
Hypertensive diseases	I10-I15	58.0	18.2

Note: (a) ICD-10 = International Classification of Diseases 10th Revision; (1) Mortality rates are a three year average covering 2007-2009; (2) Figures cover Orleans Parish
Source: Centers for Disease Control and Prevention, National Center for Health Statistics. Underlying Cause of Death 1999-2009 on CDC WONDER Online Database, released 2012. Data for year 2009 are compiled from the Multiple Cause of Death File 2009, Series 20 No. 2O, 2012, Data for year 2008 are compiled from the Multiple Cause of Death File 2008, Series 20 No. 2N, 2011, Data for year 2007 are compiled from Multiple Cause of Death File 2007, Series 20 No. 2M, 2010.

Mortality Rates for Selected Causes of Death

ICD-10[a] Sub-Chapter	ICD-10[a] Code	Age-Adjusted Mortality Rate[1] per 100,000 population	
		County[2]	U.S.
Assault	X85-Y09	52.7	5.7
Human immunodeficiency virus (HIV) disease	B20-B24	19.5	3.3
Influenza and pneumonia	J09-J18	12.0	16.4
Intentional self-harm	X60-X84	10.1	11.5
Malnutrition	E40-E46	*Unreliable	0.8
Obesity and other hyperalimentation	E65-E68	*Unreliable	1.6
Transport accidents	V01-V99	15.4	13.7
Viral hepatitis	B15-B19	3.5	2.2

Note: (a) ICD-10 = International Classification of Diseases 10th Revision; (1) Mortality rates are a three year average covering 2007-2009; (2) Figures cover Orleans Parish; (*) Unreliable data as per CDC
Source: Centers for Disease Control and Prevention, National Center for Health Statistics. Underlying Cause of Death 1999-2009 on CDC WONDER Online Database, released 2012. Data for year 2009 are compiled from the Multiple Cause of Death File 2009, Series 20 No. 2O, 2012, Data for year 2008 are compiled from the Multiple Cause of Death File 2008, Series 20 No. 2N, 2011, Data for year 2007 are compiled from Multiple Cause of Death File 2007, Series 20 No. 2M, 2010.

Distribution of Physicians and Dentists

Area[1]	Dentists[2]	D.O.[3]	M.D.[4]				
			Total	Family/ General Practice	Pediatrics	Medical Specialties	Surgical Specialties
Local (number)	99	26	1,082	62	77	399	269
Local (rate[5])	3.4	0.8	32.1	1.8	2.3	11.9	8.0
U.S. (rate[5])	4.5	1.9	18.3	2.5	1.4	6.8	4.1

Note: Data as of 2008 unless noted; (1) Local data covers Orleans Parish; (2) Data as of 2007; (3) Doctor of Osteopathic Medicine; (4) Includes active, non-federal, patient-care, office-based Doctors of Medicine; (5) rate per 10,000 population
Source: Area Resource File (ARF). 2009-2010 Release. U.S. Department of Health and Human Services, Health Resources and Services Administration, Bureau of Health Professions, Rockville, MD, August 2010

Best Hospitals

According to *U.S. News,* the New Orleans-Metairie-Kenner, LA is home to two of the best hospitals in the U.S.: **Ochsner Medical Center** (7 specialties); **Tulane University Hospital and Clinic** (1 specialty). The hospitals listed were highly ranked in at least one adult specialty. *U.S. News Online, "America's Best Hospitals 2011-12"*

EDUCATION

Public School District Statistics

District Name	Schls	Pupils	Pupil/ Teacher Ratio	Minority Pupils[1] (%)	Free Lunch Eligible[2] (%)	IEP[3] (%)
Orleans Parish	18	10,287	14.4	84.1	58.7	9.0
RSD-Algiers Charter Schls Assn (ACSA)	7	3,902	15.4	99.3	81.6	8.6
Recovery School District-LDE	34	11,872	13.9	99.1	85.3	12.7

Note: Table includes school districts with 2,000 or more students; (1) Percentage of students that are not non-Hispanic white; (2) Percentage of students that are eligible for the free lunch program; (3) Percentage of students that have an Individualized Education Program.
Source: U.S. Department of Education, National Center for Education Statistics, Common Core of Data, Local Education Agency (School District) Universe Survey: School Year 2009-2010; U.S. Department of Education, National Center for Education Statistics, Common Core of Data, Public Elementary/Secondary School Universe Survey: School Year 2009-2010

Top Public High Schools

High School Name	Rank[1]	Score[1]	Grad. Rate[2] (%)	College[3] (%)	AP/IB/ AICE[4] (%)	SAT/ ACT[5] (%)
Benjamin Franklin	27	1.278	100	100	5.5	1883

Note: (1) Public schools are ranked from 1 to 500 based on the following self-reported statistics (with their corresponding weight in the final score). Schools that had fewer than 10 graduates, as well as those that were newly founded and did not have a graduating senior class in 2010 were excluded; (2) Four-year, on-time graduation rate (25%); (3) Percent of 2010 graduates who enrolled immediately in college (25%); (4) AP/IB/AICE tests per graduate (25%); (5) Average SAT and/or ACT score (10%); Average AP/IB/AICE exam score (10%); AP/IB/AICE courses offered per graduate (5%); (6) School is unranked, but has been identified by Newsweek as one of the nation's most elite public high schools.
Source: Newsweek Online, "Top High Schools 2011"

Highest Level of Education

Area	Less than H.S.	H.S. Diploma	Some College, No Deg.	Associate Degree	Bachelors Degree	Masters Degree	Profess. School Degree	Doctorate Degree
City	15.3	26.4	21.9	4.2	18.5	8.0	3.7	2.0
MSA[1]	15.4	30.2	22.9	5.3	17.0	5.7	2.3	1.1
U.S.	14.7	28.4	21.3	7.6	17.6	7.2	1.9	1.2

Note: Figures cover persons age 25 and over; (1) Figures cover the New Orleans-Metairie-Kenner, LA Metropolitan Statistical Area—see Appendix B for areas included
Source: U.S. Census Bureau, 2008-2010 American Community Survey 3-Year Estimates

Educational Attainment by Race

Area	High School Graduate or Higher (%)					Bachelor's Degree or Higher (%)				
	Total	White	Black	Asian	Hisp.[2]	Total	White	Black	Asian	Hisp.[2]
City	84.7	94.1	80.0	65.2	72.2	32.2	57.1	15.5	34.2	31.7
MSA[1]	84.6	88.5	79.4	70.7	71.8	26.2	31.7	14.9	31.5	20.2
U.S.	85.3	87.5	81.4	85.5	61.6	28.0	29.3	17.8	50.2	13.0

Note: Figures shown cover persons 25 years old and over; (1) Figures cover the New Orleans-Metairie-Kenner, LA Metropolitan Statistical Area—see Appendix B for areas included; (2) People of Hispanic origin can be of any race
Source: U.S. Census Bureau, 2008-2010 American Community Survey 3-Year Estimates

School Enrollment by Grade and Control

Area	Preschool (%)		Kindergarten (%)		Grades 1 - 4 (%)		Grades 5 - 8 (%)		Grades 9 - 12 (%)	
	Public	Private	Public	Private	Public	Private	Public	Private	Public	Private
City	51.2	48.8	64.6	35.4	76.4	23.6	72.0	28.0	78.0	22.0
MSA[1]	50.4	49.6	67.6	32.4	75.5	24.5	72.9	27.1	74.0	26.0
U.S.	55.4	44.6	87.1	12.9	89.4	10.6	89.5	10.5	90.4	9.6

Note: Figures shown cover persons 3 years old and over; (1) Figures cover the New Orleans-Metairie-Kenner, LA Metropolitan Statistical Area—see Appendix B for areas included
Source: U.S. Census Bureau, 2008-2010 American Community Survey 3-Year Estimates

Average Salaries of Public School Classroom Teachers

Area	2010-11		2011-12		Percent Change 2010-11 to 2011-12	Percent Change 2001-02 to 2011-12
	Dollars	Rank[1]	Dollars	Rank[1]		
Louisiana	49,006	28	50,179	28	2.39	38.10
U.S. Average	55,623	-	56,643	-	1.83	26.8

Note: (1) State rank ranges from 1 to 51 where 1 indicates highest salary.
Source: National Education Association, Rankings & Estimates: Rankings of the States 2011 and Estimates of School Statistics 2012, December 2011

Higher Education

Four-Year Colleges			Two-Year Colleges			Medical Schools[1]	Law Schools[2]	Voc/ Tech[3]
Public	Private Non-profit	Private For-profit	Public	Private Non-profit	Private For-profit			
3	7	0	1	0	1	2	2	5

Note: Figures cover institutions located within the city limits and include main campuses only; (1) includes schools accredited by the Liaison Committee on Medical Education and the American Osteopathic Association's Commission on Osteopathic College Accreditation; (2) includes American Bar Association-accredited law schools; (3) includes all schools with programs that are less than 2 years.
Source: National Center for Education Statistics, Integrated Postsecondary Education System (IPEDS) Peer Analysis System, 2011-12; Association of American Medical Colleges, Member List, April 23, 2012; American Osteopathic Association, Member List, April 23, 2012; Law School Admission Council, Official Guide to ABA-Approved Law Schools Online, April 23, 2012

According to *U.S. News & World Report,* the New Orleans-Metairie-Kenner, LA is home to one of the best national universities in the U.S.: **Tulane University** (#50). The indicators used to capture academic quality fall into a number of categories: assessment by administrators at peer institutions; retention of students; faculty resources; student selectivity; financial resources; alumni giving; high school counselor ratings of colleges; and graduation rate.*U.S. News & World Report, "America's Best Colleges 2012"*

According to *Forbes,* the New Orleans-Metairie-Kenner, LA is home to one of the best business schools in the U.S.: **Tulane (Freeman)** (#52). The rankings are based on the return on investment that graduates of the Class of 2006 received (median salary five years after graduation). *Forbes, "Best Business Schools," August 3, 2011*

PRESIDENTIAL ELECTION

2008 Presidential Election Results

Area	Obama	McCain	Nader	Other
Orleans Parish	79.4	19.1	0.3	1.2
U.S.	52.9	45.6	0.6	0.9

Note: Results are percentages and may not add to 100% due to rounding
Source: Dave Leip's Atlas of U.S. Presidential Elections, www.uselectionatlas.org

EMPLOYERS

Major Employers

Company Name	Industry
Alton Ochsner Medical Foundation	Home health care services
Avondale Industries of New York Inc	Barges, building and repair
Capital One, National Association	National commercial banks
Chevron USA Inc	Filling stations, gasoline
Childrens Hospital	Childrens hospital
East Jefferson Hospital	General medical/surgical hospitals
Jazz Casino Company LJC	Casino hotel
Lockheed Martin Corporation	Tanks, standard or custom fabricated metal plate 0
Louisiana State University System	University
Medical Center of Louisiana at New Orleans	General medical/surgical hospitals
NASA George C Marshall Space Flight Center	Space flight operations
Ochsner Clinic Foundation	General medical/surgical hospitals
Ochsner Foundation Hospital	General medical/surgical hospitals
St Tammany Parish Hospital	General medical/surgical hospitals
Tulane University	Colleges/universities
United States Department of the Army	Army
United States Dept of Agriculture	Regulation of agricultural marketing
United States Postal Service	Us postal service
University Healthcare System LC	General medical/surgical hospitals
US Army Corps of Engineers	Army
West Jefferson Medical Center	General medical/surgical hospitals

Note: Companies shown are located within the New Orleans-Metairie-Kenner, LA metropolitan area.
Source: Hoovers.com, data extracted April 25 2012

Best Companies to Work For

Ochsner Health System, headquartered in New Orleans, is among the "50 Best Employers for Workers Over 50." Criteria: recruiting practices; opportunities for training, education, and career development; workplace accommodations; alternative work options, such as flexible scheduling, job sharing, and phased retirement; employee health and pension benefits; and retiree benefits. Employers with at least 50 employees based in the U.S. are eligible, including for-profit companies, not-for-profit organizations, and government employers. *AARP, "2011 AARP Best Employers for Workers Over 50"*

PUBLIC SAFETY

Crime Rate

Area	All Crimes	Violent Crimes				Property Crimes		
		Murder	Forcible Rape	Robbery	Aggrav. Assault	Burglary	Larceny -Theft	Motor Vehicle Theft
City	4,276.5	49.1	40.4	267.5	370.7	1,037.0	1,835.4	676.4
Suburbs[1]	n/a	8.9	19.3	78.9	249.2	634.3	2,145.3	n/a
Metro[2]	n/a	20.8	25.6	134.8	285.3	753.7	2,053.4	n/a
U.S.	3,345.5	4.8	27.5	119.1	252.3	699.6	2,003.5	238.8

Note: Figures are crimes per 100,000 population; (1) All areas within the metro area that are located outside the city limits; (2) Metropolitan Statistical Area—see Appendix B for areas included
Source: FBI Uniform Crime Reports, 2010

Hate Crimes

Area	Number of Quarters Reported	Bias Motivation				
		Race	Religion	Sexual Orientation	Ethnicity	Disability
City	2	0	0	0	0	0

Source: Federal Bureau of Investigation, Hate Crime Statistics 2010

Identity Theft Consumer Complaints

Area	Complaints	Complaints per 100,000 Population	Rank[2]
MSA[1]	979	95.0	110
U.S.	279,156	90.4	-

Note: (1) Metropolitan Statistical Area—see Appendix B for areas included; (2) Rank ranges from 1 to 384 where 1 indicates greatest number of identity theft complaints per 100,000 population
Source: Federal Trade Commission, Consumer Sentinel Network Data Book for January–December 2011

Fraud and Other Consumer Complaints

Area	Complaints	Complaints per 100,000 Population	Rank[2]
MSA[1]	5,207	505.4	144
U.S.	1,533,924	496.8	-

Note: (1) Metropolitan Statistical Area—see Appendix B for areas included; (2) Rank ranges from 1 to 384 where 1 indicates greatest number of fraud and other complaints per 100,000 population
Source: Federal Trade Commission, Consumer Sentinel Network Data Book for January–December 2011

RECREATION

Culture

Dance[1]	Theatre[1]	Instrumental Music[1]	Vocal Music[1]	Series/ Festivals	Museums	Zoos and Aquariums[2]
2	5	3	2	5	16	2

Note: (1) Number of professional perfoming groups; (2) AZA-accredited
Source: The Grey House Performing Arts Directory, 2011-2012; Official Museum Directory, 2011; American Association of Museums, AAM Member Museums, April 2012; Association of Zoos & Aquariums, AZA Member Zoos & Aquariums, April 2012

Professional Sports Teams

Team Name	League
New Orleans Hornets	National Basketball Association (NBA)
New Orleans Saints	National Football League (NFL)

Note: Includes teams located in the New Orleans metro area.
Source: Original research

CLIMATE

Average and Extreme Temperatures

Temperature	Jan	Feb	Mar	Apr	May	Jun	Jul	Aug	Sep	Oct	Nov	Dec	Yr.
Extreme High (°F)	83	85	89	92	96	100	101	102	101	92	87	84	102
Average High (°F)	62	65	71	78	85	89	91	90	87	80	71	64	78
Average Temp. (°F)	53	56	62	69	75	81	82	82	79	70	61	55	69
Average Low (°F)	43	46	52	59	66	71	73	73	70	59	51	45	59
Extreme Low (°F)	14	19	25	32	41	50	60	60	42	35	24	11	11

Note: Figures cover the years 1948-1990
Source: National Climatic Data Center, International Station Meteorological Climate Summary, 9/96

Average Precipitation/Snowfall/Humidity

Precip./Humidity	Jan	Feb	Mar	Apr	May	Jun	Jul	Aug	Sep	Oct	Nov	Dec	Yr.
Avg. Precip. (in.)	4.7	5.6	5.2	4.7	4.4	5.4	6.4	5.9	5.5	2.8	4.4	5.5	60.6
Avg. Snowfall (in.)	Tr	Tr	Tr	0	0	0	0	0	0	0	0	Tr	Tr
Avg. Rel. Hum. 6am (%)	85	84	84	88	89	89	91	91	89	87	86	85	88
Avg. Rel. Hum. 3pm (%)	62	59	57	57	58	61	66	65	63	56	59	62	60

Note: Figures cover the years 1948-1990; Tr = Trace amounts (<0.05 in. of rain; <0.5 in. of snow)
Source: National Climatic Data Center, International Station Meteorological Climate Summary, 9/96

Weather Conditions

Temperature			Daytime Sky			Precipitation		
10°F & below	32°F & below	90°F & above	Clear	Partly cloudy	Cloudy	0.01 inch or more precip.	0.1 inch or more snow/ice	Thunder-storms
0	13	70	90	169	106	114	1	69

Note: Figures are average number of days per year and cover the years 1948-1990
Source: National Climatic Data Center, International Station Meteorological Climate Summary, 9/96

HAZARDOUS WASTE

Superfund Sites

New Orleans has one hazardous waste site on the EPA's Superfund Final National Priorities List: **Agriculture Street Landfill**. *U.S. Environmental Protection Agency, Final National Priorities List, April 17, 2012*

AIR & WATER QUALITY

Air Quality Index

Area	Percent of Days when Air Quality was...[2]					AQI Statistics[2]	
	Good	Moderate	Unhealthy for Sensitive Groups	Unhealthy	Very Unhealthy	Maximum	Median
Area[1]	89.6	9.9	0.3	0.3	0.0	155	34

Note: Air Quality Index (AQI) is an index for reporting daily air quality. EPA calculates the AQI for five major air pollutants regulated by the Clean Air Act: ground-level ozone, particle pollution (aka particulate matter), carbon monoxide, sulfur dioxide, and nitrogen dioxide. The AQI runs from 0 to 500. The higher the AQI value, the greater the level of air pollution and the greater the health concern. There are six AQI categories: "Good" AQI is between 0 and 50. Air quality is considered satisfactory; "Moderate" AQI is between 51 and 100. Air quality is acceptable; "Unhealthy for Sensitive Groups" When AQI values are between 101 and 150, members of sensitive groups may experience health effects; "Unhealthy" When AQI values are between 151 and 200 everyone may begin to experience health effects; "Very Unhealthy" AQI values between 201 and 300 trigger a health alert; "Hazardous" AQI values over 300 trigger warnings of emergency conditions (not shown); (1) Data covers Orleans Parish; (2) Based on 365 days with AQI data in 2011.
Source: U.S. Environmental Protection Agency, AirData Report, 2011

Air Quality Index Pollutants

Area	Percent of Days when AQI Pollutant was...[2]					
	Carbon Monoxide	Nitrogen Dioxide	Ozone	Sulfur Dioxide	Particulate Matter 2.5	Particulate Matter 10
Area[1]	0.0	0.0	70.1	0.0	25.8	4.1

Note: The Air Quality Index (AQI) is an index for reporting daily air quality. EPA calculates the AQI for five major air pollutants regulated by the Clean Air Act: ground-level ozone, particle pollution (also known as particulate matter), carbon monoxide, sulfur dioxide, and nitrogen dioxide. The AQI runs from 0 to 500. The higher the AQI value, the greater the level of air pollution and the greater the health concern; (1) Data covers Orleans Parish; (2) Based on 365 days with AQI data in 2011.
Source: U.S. Environmental Protection Agency, AirData Report, 2011

Air Quality Index Trends

Area	Trend Sites (days)								All Sites (days)
	2003	2004	2005	2006	2007	2008	2009	2010	2010
MSA[1]	15	12	13	13	17	2	6	8	66

Note: Figures are the number of days the AQI value exceeded 100 in a given year. An AQI value greater than 100 indicates that air quality would have been in the unhealthful range on that day. Data from exceptional events are included. These counts are presented in two ways. First, the counts are based on sites having an adequate record of monitoring data during the trend period (trend sites). These counts represent the relative change in the number of days with AQI values greater than 100. In the last column, the counts are based on all sites with data in the most recent year (because it is possible for a site to have data in the most recent year but not enough data to be a trend site); (1) Data covers the New Orleans-Metairie-Kenner, LA—see Appendix B for areas included
Source: U.S. Environmental Protection Agency, Air Quality Index Information, "Number of Days with Air Quality Index Values Greater than 100 at Trend Sites, 2000-2010, and at All Sites in 2010"

Maximum Air Pollutant Concentrations: Particulate Matter, Ozone, CO and Lead

	Particulate Matter 10 (ug/m^3)	Particulate Matter 2.5 Wtd AM (ug/m^3)	Particulate Matter 2.5 24-Hr (ug/m^3)	Ozone (ppm)	Carbon Monoxide (ppm)	Lead (ug/m^3)
MSA[1] Level	73	10.1	19	0.081	n/a	n/a
NAAQS[2]	150	15	35	0.075	9	0.15
Met NAAQS[2]	Yes	Yes	Yes	No	n/a	n/a

Note: Data from exceptional events are not included; (1) Data covers the New Orleans-Metairie-Kenner, LA—see Appendix B for areas included; (2) National Ambient Air Quality Standards; ppm = parts per million; ug/m^3 = micrograms per cubic meter; n/a not available
Concentrations: Particulate Matter 10 (coarse particulate)—highest second maximum 24-hour concentration; Particulate Matter 2.5 Wtd AM (fine particulate)—highest weighted annual mean concentration; Particulate Matter 2.5 24-Hour (fine particulate)—highest 98th percentile 24-hour concentration; Ozone—highest fourth daily maximum 8-hour concentration; Carbon Monoxide—highest second maximum non-overlapping 8-hour concentration; Lead—maximum running 3-month average
Source: U.S. Environmental Protection Agency, CBSA Factbook 2010, Air Quality Statistics by City, 2010

Maximum Air Pollutant Concentrations: Nitrogen Dioxide and Sulfur Dioxide

	Nitrogen Dioxide AM (ppb)	Nitrogen Dioxide 1-Hr (ppb)	Sulfur Dioxide AM (ppb)	Sulfur Dioxide 1-Hr (ppb)	Sulfur Dioxide 24-Hr (ppb)
MSA[1] Level	7.759	47	7.743	248	75.6
NAAQS[2]	53	100	30	75	140
Met NAAQS[2]	Yes	Yes	Yes	No	Yes

Note: Data from exceptional events are not included; (1) Data covers the New Orleans-Metairie-Kenner, LA—see Appendix B for areas included; (2) National Ambient Air Quality Standards; ppb = parts per billion; n/a not available
Concentrations: Nitrogen Dioxide AM—highest arithmetic mean concentration; Nitrogen Dioxide 1-Hr—highest 98th percentile 1-hour daily maximum concentration; Sulfur Dioxide AM—highest annual mean concentration; Sulfur Dioxide 1-Hr—highest 99th percentile 1-hour daily maximum concentration; Sulfur Dioxide 24-Hr—highest second maximum 24-hour concentration
Source: U.S. Environmental Protection Agency, CBSA Factbook 2010, Air Quality Statistics by City, 2010

Drinking Water

Water System Name	Pop. Served	Primary Water Source Type	Violations[1]	
			Health Based	Monitoring/ Reporting
New Orleans Carrollton WW	428,000	Surface	0	0

Note: (1) Based on violation data from January 1, 2011 to December 31, 2011 (includes unresolved violations from earlier years)
Source: U.S. Environmental Protection Agency, Office of Ground Water and Drinking Water, Safe Drinking Water Information System (based on data extracted April 18, 2012)

Orlando, Florida

Background

The city of Orlando can hold the viewer aghast with its rampant tourism. Not only is it home to the worldwide tourist attractions of Disney World, Epcot Center, and Sea World, but Orlando and its surrounding area also host such institutions as Medieval Times Dinner & Tournament, Wet-N-Wild, Ripley's Believe It or Not Museum, and Sleuths Mystery Dinner Shows, as well as thousands of T-shirt, citrus, and shell vendor shacks.

Orlando has its own high-tech corridor because of the University of Central Florida's College of Optics and Photonics. Manufacturing, government, business service, health care, high-tech research, and tourism supply significant numbers of jobs. Xenerga, a new biodiesel fuel manufacturer, built its flagship plant in Orlando with plans for dozens more sites across the United States. Other major employees in Orlando include Lockheed-Martin, General Dynamics, Mitsubishi, AT&T, Boeing, and Hewlett Packard.

Aside from the glitz that pumps most of the money into its economy, Orlando is also called "The City Beautiful." The warm climate and abundant rains produce a variety of lush flora and fauna, which provide an attractive setting for the many young people who settle in the area, spending their nights in the numerous jazz clubs, restaurants, and pubs along Orange Avenue and Church Street. Stereotypically the land of orange juice and sunshine, Orlando is becoming the city for young job seekers and professionals.

This genteel setting is a far cry from Orlando's rough-and-tumble origins. The city started out as a makeshift campsite in the middle of a cotton plantation. The Civil War and devastating rains brought an end to the cotton trade, and its settlers turned to raising livestock. The transition to a new livelihood did not insure any peace and serenity. Rustling, chaotic brawls, and senseless shootings were everyday occurrences. Martial law had to be imposed by a few large ranch families.

The greatest impetus toward modernity came from the installation of Cape Canaveral, 50 miles away, which brought missile assembly and electronic component production to the area, and Walt Disney World, created out of 27,000 acres of unexplored swampland, which set the tone for Orlando as a tourist-oriented economy.

Orlando is also a major film production site. Nickelodeon, the world's largest teleproduction studio dedicated to children's television programming, is based there, as are the Golf Channel, Sun Sports, House of Moves, and the America Channel. Disney's biggest theme-park competitor, Universal Studios, is also based in Orlando.

The city is also home to a variety of arts and entertainment facilities, including the Amway Arena, part of the Orlando Centroplex, home to the NBA's Orlando Magic and the Orlando Sharks of the Indoor Soccer League. The city vies with Chicago and Las Vegas for hosting the most convention attendees in the United States.

Orlando is surrounded by many lakes. Its relative humidity remains high year-round, though in winter the humidity may drop. June through September is the rainy season, during which time, scattered afternoon thunderstorms are an almost daily occurrence. During the winter months rainfall is light and the afternoons are most pleasant. Hurricanes are not usually considered a threat to the area.

Rankings

General Rankings

- The Orlando metro area was identified as one of the 10 most popular big cities by Pew Research Center. The results are based on a telephone survey of 2,260 adults conducted during October 2008. The report explored a range of attitudes related to where Americans live, where they would like to live, and why. *Pew Research Center, "For Nearly Half of America, Grass is Greener Somewhere Else," January 29, 2009*

- *Men's Health Living* ranked 100 U.S. cities in terms of quality of life. Orlando was ranked #71 and received a grade of D+. Criteria: number of fitness facilities; air quality; number of physicians; male/female ratio; education levels; household income; cost of living. *Men's Health Living, Spring 2008*

- Orlando was identified as one of the top places to live in the U.S. by Harris Interactive. The city ranked #12 out of 15. Criteria: 2,463 adults (age 18 and over) were polled and asked "if you could live in or near any city in the country except the one you live in or nearest to now, which city would you choose?" The poll was conducted online within the U.S. between September 14 and 20, 2010. *Harris Interactive, November 9, 2011*

Business/Finance Rankings

- Experian ranked the top 20 major U.S. metropolitan areas by average debt per consumer. The Orlando metro area was ranked #10. Criteria: average debt per consumer. Debt for this study includes credit cards, auto loans and personal loans. It does not include mortgages. *Experian, May 13, 2010*

- Orlando was identified as one of the top 25 U.S. cities with the most credit card debt by credit reporting bureau Experian. The city was ranked #25. *Experian, March 4, 2011*

- Orlando was identified as one of the "Happiest Cities to Work in 2012" by *CareerBliss.com*, an online community for career advancement. The city ranked #34 out of 50. Criteria: independent company reviews from employees all over the country on: relationship with their boss and co-workers; work environment; job resources; growth opportunities; compensation; company culture; company reputation; daily tasks; job control over work performed on a daily basis. *CareerBliss.com, "Happiest and Unhappiest Cities to Work in 2012"*

- Orlando was selected as one of the "100 Best Places to Live and Launch" in the U.S. The city ranked #73. The editors at *Fortune Small Business* ranked 296 Census-designated metro areas by business friendliness (Launching Score, % New Businesses) and lifestyle offerings (Living Score). Then they picked the town within each of the top 100 metro areas that best blends business and pleasure. *Fortune Small Business, "100 Best Places to Live and Launch 2008," April 2008*

- *American City Business Journals* ranked America's 261 largest cities in terms of their resident's wealth. Orlando ranked #124. Criteria: per capita income; median household income; percentage of households with annual incomes of $200,000 or more; median home value. *American City Business Journals, "Where the Money Is: America's Wealth Centers," August 18, 2008*

- The Orlando metro area appeared on the Milken Institute "2011 Best Performing Metros" list. Rank: #96 out of 200 large metro areas. Criteria: job growth; wage and salary growth; high-tech output growth. *Milken Institute, "2011 Best Performing Metros"*

- The Orlando metro area was selected as one of the best cities for entrepreneurs in America by *Inc. Magazine*. Criteria: job-growth data for 335 metro areas was analyzed for: recent growth trend; mid-term growth; long-term trend; current year growth. The Orlando metro area ranked #6 among large metro areas and #45 overall. *Inc. Magazine, "The Best Cities for Doing Business," July 2008*

- Orlando was ranked #103 out of 145 regions worldwide in terms of its "Knowledge Competitiveness Index." The index attempts to measure the knowledge-based development taking place throughout the world and is based on 19 measures of economic performance that indicate a region's ability to translate its knowledge capacity into economic value. *Centre for International Competitiveness, World Knowledge Competitiveness Index 2008*

- *Forbes* ranked the 200 most populous metro areas in the U.S. in terms of the "Best Places for Business and Careers." The Orlando metro area was ranked #72. Criteria: costs (business and living); job growth (past and projected); income growth; educational attainment; projected economic growth; crime; cultural and recreational opportunities; net migration patterns; number of highly ranked colleges. *Forbes, "Best Places for Business and Careers," June 2011*

Children/Family Rankings

- Orlando was selected as one of the 10 worst cities to raise children in the U.S. by *KidFriendlyCities.org.* Criteria: education; environment; health; employment; crime; diversity; cost of living. *KidFriendlyCities.org, "Top Rated Kid/Family Friendly Cities 2009"*

- The Orlando metro area was selected as one of the "Best Cities for Relocating Families" by Worldwide ERC and Primacy Relocation. The 2008 study looked at nearly 50 factors important to relocating families including: recent job growth; nearby top-ranked colleges; in-state tuition for four-year public colleges; population growth since 2000; pediatricians per 100,000 population; and a Green Living index. *Worldwide ERC and Primacy Relocation, "2008 Best Cities for Relocating Families"*

Dating/Romance Rankings

- Orlando was selected as one of the most romantic cities in America by *Amazon.com.* The city ranked #4 of 20. Criteria: per capita sales of romance novels and relationship books, romantic comedy movies, Barry White albums, and sexual wellness products. *Amazon.com, "America's Most Romantic Cities Revealed," February 14, 2012*

- Orlando appeared on *Men's Health's* list of the most sex-happy cities in America. The city ranked #71 of 100. Criteria: condom sales; birth rates; sex toy sales; rates of chlamydia, gonorrhea, and syphilis. *Men's Health, "America's Most Sex-Happy Cities," October 2010*

- *Men's Health* ranked 100 U.S. cities in terms of best (and worst) marriages. Orlando was ranked #18 (#1 = worst). Criteria: rate of failed marriages; stringency of divorce laws; percentage of population who've split; number of licensed marriage and family therapists. *Men's Health, "Splitsville, USA," May 2010*

- Eli Lily and Company, in partnership with Sperling's BestPlaces, ranked the nation's 50 largest metro areas in terms of the "Most Romantic Cities for Baby Boomers." The Orlando metro area ranked #19. Criteria: marriage and divorce rates among baby boomers age 45 to 60; great restaurants; dance studios; chocolate, jewelry and flower sales. *Eli Lily and Company, "Most Romantic Cities for Baby Boomers," April 20, 2007*

- The Orlando metro area was selected as one of the "Best Cities for Relocating Singles" by Worldwide ERC and Primacy Relocation. The area ranked #13 out of the 100 largest metro areas in the U.S. Criteria: recent job growth; recent singles population growth; overall population growth; affordable rental housing; cost-of-living index; expanded arts and recreation opportunities; ratio of single men and single women; affordability of quality higher education (including state residency requirements); diversity index; climate; population density. *Worldwide ERC and Primacy Relocation, "2008 Best Cities for Relocating Singles"*

- *Forbes* ranked the 40 most populous urbanized areas in the U.S. in terms of the "Best Cities for Singles." The Orlando metro area ranked #26. Criteria: number of singles; cost of living alone; nightlife; culture; job growth; coolness; and online dating participation. *Forbes.com, "Best Cities for Singles," July 27, 2009*

Education Rankings

- *Men's Health* ranked 100 U.S. cities in terms of their education levels. Orlando was ranked #53 (#1 = most educated city). Criteria: high school graduation rates; school enrollment; educational attainment; number of households who have outstanding student loans; number of households whose members have taken adult-education courses. *Men's Health, "Where School Is In: The Most and Least Educated Cities," September 12, 2011*

- Orlando was selected as one of the most well-read cities in America by *Amazon.com.* The city ranked #12 of 20. Cities with populations greater than 100,000 were evaluated based on per capita sales of books, magazines and newspapers. *Amazon.com, "Top 20 Most Well-Read Cities in America," June 4, 2011*

- Orlando was identified as one of the 100 "smartest" metro areas in the U.S. The area ranked #47. Criteria: the editors rated the collective brainpower of the 100 largest metro areas in the U.S. based on their residents' educational attainment. *American City Business Journals, April 14, 2008*

- Orlando was identified as one of "America's Brainiest Bastions" by *Portfolio.com*. The metro area ranked #115 out of 200. *Portfolio.com* analyzed levels of educational attainment in the nation's 200 largest metropolitan areas. The editors established scores for five levels of educational attainment, based on relative earning power of adult workers age 25 or older. Scores were determined by comparing the median income for all workers with the median income for those workers at a specified educational level. *Portfolio.com, "America's Brainiest Bastions," December 1, 2010*

Environmental Rankings

- The Orlando was identified as one of North America's greenest metropolitan areas. The area ranked #18. The Green City Index is comprised of 31 indicators, and scores cities across nine categories: carbon dioxide; energy; land use; buildings; transport; water; waste; air quality; environmental governance. The 27 largest metropolitan areas in the U.S. and Canada were considered. *Economist Intelligence Unit, sponsored by Siemens, "U.S. and Canada Green City Index, 2011"*

- The Orlando metro area was identified as one of "The Ten Biggest American Cities that are Running Out of Water" by *24/7 Wall St.* The metro area ranked #10 out of 10. *24/7 Wall St.* did an analysis of the water supply and consumption in the 30 largest metropolitan areas in the U.S. Criteria include: projected water demand as a share of available precipitation; groundwater use as a share or projected available precipitation; susceptibility to drought; projected increase in freshwater withdrawals; projected increase in summer water deficit. *24/7 Wall St., "The Ten Biggest American Cities that are Running Out of Water," November 1, 2010*

- Scarborough Research, a leading market research firm, identified the top local markets for green appliance households. The Orlando DMA (Designated Market Area) ranked in the top 16 with 35% of consumers reporting that they own an energy-efficient appliance. *Scarborough Research, March 23, 2010*

- Orlando was selected as one of 22 "Smarter Cities" for energy by the Natural Resources Defense Council. Criteria: investment in green power; energy efficiency measures; conservation. *Natural Resources Defense Council, "2010 Smarter Cities," July 19, 2010*

- *American City Business Journal* ranked 43 metropolitan areas in terms of their "greenness." The Orlando metro area ranked #28. Criteria: Forty-one metros in which *ACBJ* has business weeklies, plus Indianapolis and Cleveland, were ranked based on 20 different indicators such as adoption of green technologies, utilization of environmentally sound practices, and air and water quality. *American City Business Journals, "Green City Index," March 11, 2010*

- The Orlando metro area was selected as one of "America's Cleanest Cities" by *Forbes*. The metro area ranked #4 out of 10. Criteria: toxic releases; air and water quality; per capita spending on Superfund site cleanup. *Forbes.com, "America's Cleanest Cities 2011," March 11, 2011*

- 100 of the largest metro areas in the U.S. were analyzed in terms of their current drought severity. The Orlando metro area ranked #15 (#1 = driest). The rankings were based on statistics such as long-term precipitation trends and patterns and the Palmer drought indices. *Sperling's BestPlaces, www.BestPlaces.net, "America's Drought-Riskiest Cities," November 2007*

- The Orlando metro area appeared in *Country Home's* "Best Green Places" report. The area ranked #236 out of 379. Criteria: official energy policies; green power; green buildings; availability of fresh, locally grown food. *Country Home, "Best Green Places," 2008*

- Orlando was highlighted as one of the top 25 cleanest metro areas for year-round particle pollution (Annual PM 2.5) in the U.S. The area ranked #24. *American Lung Association, State of the Air 2011*

Health/Fitness Rankings

- Orlando was identified as a "2011 Asthma Capital." The area ranked #26 out of the nation's 100 largest metropolitan areas. Twelve factors were used to identify the most challenging places to live for people with asthma: estimated prevalence; self-reported prevalence; crude death rate for asthma; annual pollen score; annual air quality; public smoking laws; number of board-certified asthma specialists; school inhaler access laws; rescue medication use; controller medication use; uninsured rate; poverty rate. *Asthma and Allergy Foundation of America, "2011 Asthma Capitals"*

- Orlando was identified as a "2011 Fall Allergy Capital." The area ranked #71 out of 100. Three groups of factors were used to identify the most severe cities for people with allergies during the fall season: annual pollen levels; medicine utilization; access to board-certified allergists. *Asthma and Allergy Foundation of America, "2011 Fall Allergy Capitals"*

- Orlando was identified as a "2012 Spring Allergy Capital." The area ranked #80 out of 100. Three groups of factors were used to identify the most severe cities for people with allergies during the spring season: annual pollen levels; medicine utilization; access to board-certified allergists. *Asthma and Allergy Foundation of America, "2012 Spring Allergy Capitals"*

- *Men's Health* examined 100 major U.S. cities and selected the best and worst cities for men. Orlando ranked #55. Criteria: 35 statistical parameters of long life in the categories of health, quality of life, and fitness. *Men's Health, "The 10 Best and Worst Cities for Men 2012," January/February 2012*

- The Orlando metro area appeared in the 2011 Gallup-Healthways Well-Being Index. The index, based on interviews with more than 350,000 Americans, measured jobs, finances, physical health, emotional state of mind and communities. The metro area ranked #144 out of 190. Criteria: life evaluation; emotional health; work environment; physical health; healthy behaviors; basic access (basic needs optimal for a healthy life, such as access to food and medicine, having health insurance and feeling safe while walking at night). *Gallup-Healthways, "State of Well-Being 2011"*

- The Orlando metro area was identified as one of "America's Most Stressful Cities" by *Sperling's BestPlaces*. The metro area ranked #6 out of 50. Criteria: unemployment rate; suicide rate; commute time; mental health; poor rest; alcohol use; violent crime rate; property crime rate; cloudy days annually. *Sperling's BestPlaces, www.BestPlaces.net, "Stressful Cities 2012*

- *Men's Health* ranked 100 U.S. cities in terms of their activity levels. Orlando was ranked #48 (#1 = most active city). Criteria: where and how often residents exercise; percentage of households that watch more than 15 hours of cable television a week and buy more than 11 video games a year; death rate from deep-vein thrombosis, a condition linked to sitting for extended periods of time. *Men's Health, "Where Sit Happens: The Most and Least Active Cities in America," June 20, 2011*

- 50 of the largest metro areas in the U.S. were analyzed in terms of their health and fitness by the American College of Sports Medicine in their "American Fitness Index." The Orlando metro area ranked #19 (#1 = healthiest). Criteria: preventative health behaviors; levels of chronic disease; health care access; community resources and policies that support physical activity. *American College of Sports Medicine, "Health and Community Fitness Status of the 50 Largest Metropolitan Areas," August 1, 2011*

- Orlando was selected as one of the "20 Most Livable U.S. Cities for Wheelchair Users" by the Christopher & Dana Reeve Foundation. The city ranked #9. Criteria: Medicaid eligibility and spending; access to physicians and rehabilitation facilities; access to fitness facilities and recreation; access to paratransit; percentage of people living with disabilities who are employed; clean air; climate. *Christopher & Dana Reeve Foundation, "20 Most Livable U.S. Cities for Wheelchair Users," July 26, 2010*

Real Estate Rankings

- Orlando was identified as one of 13 metro areas where home prices are falling dangerously. Criteria: home price change from October 2010 to September 2011; projected home price change through 2012. *Forbes.com, "Cities Where Home Prices are Falling Dangerously," January 10, 2012*

- Orlando was identified as one of the "Top Turnaround Housing Markets for 2012." The area ranked #3 out of 10. Criteria: year-over-year median home price appreciation; year-over-year median inventory age; year-over-year inventory reduction. *AOL Real Estate, "Top Turnaround Housing Markets for 2012," February 4, 2012*

- Orlando was identified as one of the best cities for home buyers in the U.S. The area ranked #2 out of 10. The affordability of home ownership was calculated by comparing the cost of renting vs. owning. Criteria: cost to rent as a percent of after-tax mortgage payment. *Fortune, "The 10 Best Cities for Buyers," April 11, 2011*

- *Fortune* ranked the 100 largest metro areas in the U.S. in terms of projected median home price change in 2010. The Orlando metro area ranked #99. *Fortune, "The 2010 Housing Outlook," December 9, 2009*

- Orlando appeared on *ApartmentRatings.com* "Top College Towns & Cities" for renters list in 2011." The area ranked #62 out of 87. Overall satisfaction ratings were ranked using thousands of user submitted scores for hundreds of apartment complexes located in cities and towns that are home to the 100 largest four-year institutions in the U.S. *ApartmentRatings.com, "2011 College Town Renter Satisfaction Rankings"*

- The Orlando metro area was identified as one of "America's 25 Weakest Housing Markets" by *Forbes.* The metro area ranked #9. Criteria: metro areas with populations over 500,000 were ranked based on projected home values through 2011. *Forbes.com, "America's 25 Weakest Housing Markets," January 7, 2009*

- The Orlando metro area appeared in a *Wall Street Journal* article ranking cities by "housing stress." The metro area was ranked #6 (#1 = most stress). Criteria: fraction of mortgage-holding homeowners with a monthly housing payment in excess of 30 percent of income; percentage of people without health insurance; unemployment rate. *The Wall Street Journal, "Which Cities Face Biggest Housing Risk," October 5, 2010*

- The Center for Housing Policy ranked 210 U.S. metropolitan areas by the fair market rent for a two-bedroom unit. The Orlando metro area was ranked #48. (#1 = most expensive) with a rent of $1,052. Criteria: Fair Market Rent (FMR) in effect during the fourth quarter of 2009 based on HUD's fiscal year 2010 FMRs. *The Center for Housing Policy, "Paycheck to Paycheck: Most to Least Expensive Rental Markets in 2009"*

- The Orlando metro area was identified as one of the top 20 cities in terms of decreasing home equity. The metro area was ranked #13. Criteria: percentage of home equity relative to the home's current value. *Forbes.com, "Where Americans are Losing Home Equity Most," May 1, 2010*

- The Orlando metro area was identified as one of the markets with the worst expected performance in home prices over the next 12 months. *Local Market Monitor, "First Quarter Home Price Forecast for Largest US Markets," March 2, 2011*

- The Orlando metro area was identified as one of the best U.S. markets to invest in rental property" by HomeVestors and Local Market Monitor. The area ranked #3 out of 100. Criteria: risk-return premium relative to national average. *HomeVestors and Local Market Monitor, "Best 100 U.S. Markets to Invest in Rental Property," March 9, 2012*

Safety Rankings

- Allstate ranked the 193 largest cities in America in terms of driver safety. Orlando ranked #149. In addition, drivers were 25.5% more likely to have had an accident compared to the national average. Allstate researchers analyzed internal property damage reported claims over a two-year period (from January 2008 to December 2009) to protect findings from external influences such as weather or road construction. A weighted average of the two-year numbers determined the annual percentages. The report defines an auto crash as any collision resulting in a property damage claim. *Allstate, "2011 Allstate America's Best Drivers Report™"*

- Orlando was identified as one of America's "11 Most Dangerous Cities" by *U.S. News & World Report.* The city ranked #3. Criteria: crime risk was calculated using the most recent seven years (2003-2009) of FBI crime reporting data. The data includes both property crimes and violent crimes. *U.S. News & World Report, "The 11 Most Dangerous Cities," February 16, 2011*

- The National Insurance Crime Bureau ranked 366 metro areas in the U.S. in terms of per capita rates of vehicle theft. The Orlando metro area ranked #100 (#1 = highest rate). Criteria: number of vehicle theft offenses per 100,000 inhabitants in 2010. *National Insurance Crime Bureau, "Hot Spots," June 21, 2011*

- The Orlando metro area was identified as one of the most dangerous metro areas for pedestrians by Transportation for America. The metro area ranked #1 out of 52 metro areas with over 1 million residents. Criteria: area's population divided by the number of pedestrian fatalities in that area. *Transportation for America, "Dangerous by Design 2011"*

Seniors/Retirement Rankings

- Bankers Life and Casualty Company, in partnership with Sperling's BestPlaces, ranked the nation's 50 largest metro areas in terms of the "Best U.S. Cities for Seniors." The Orlando metro area ranked #46. Criteria: healthcare; transportation; housing; environment; economy; health and longevity; social and spiritual life; crime. *Bankers Life and Casualty Company, Center for a Secure Retirement, "Best U.S. Cities for Seniors 2011," September 2011*

- Orlando was identified as one of the "100 Most Popular Retirement Towns" by *Topretirements.com* The list reflects the 100 cities (out of 815+ total cities reviewed) that visitors to the website are most interested in for retirement. *Topretirements.com, "100 Most Popular Retirement Towns," February 21, 2012*

- Orlando was selected as one of "Seven Places to Retire During an Economic Downturn." The city ranked #3. The editors at *Smart Money* selected seven recession-proof places soon-to-be retirees should consider. *SmartMoney.com, "Seven Places to Retire During an Economic Downturn," February 29, 2008*

Sports/Recreation Rankings

- Orlando appeared on the *Sporting News* list of the "Best Sports Cities" for 2011. The area ranked #34 out of 271 cities in the U.S. *Sporting News* takes a 12-month snapshot of each city's sports, putting a heavy premium on regular-season won-lost records (from the most recently completed season). Other criteria include: playoff berths, bowl appearances and tournament bids; championships; applicable power ratings; quality of competition; overall fan fervor (measured in part by attendance); abundance of teams (rewarding quality over quantity); stadium and arena quality; ticket availability and prices; franchise ownership; and marquee appeal of athletes. *Sporting News, "Best Sports Cities 2011," October 4, 2011*

- Orlando was chosen as a bicycle friendly community by the League of American Bicyclists. A Bicycle Friendly Community welcomes cyclists by providing safe accommodation for cycling and encouraging people to bike for transportation and recreation. There are four award levels: Platinum; Gold; Silver; and Bronze. The community achieved an award level of Bronze. *League of American Bicyclists, "Bicycle Friendly Community Master List 2011"*

- Orlando was selected as one of the most playful cities in the U.S. by KaBOOM! The organization's Playful City USA initiative is a national recognition program that honors cities and towns across the nation for a vision, plan and commitment to creating an agenda for play. Cities were recognized based on a pledge to five specific commitments to play: creating a local play commission or task force; designing an annual action plan for play; conducting a play space audit; outlining a financial investment in play for the current fiscal year; and proclaiming and celebrating an annual "play day." *KaBOOM! National Campaign for Play, "2011 Playful City USA Communities"*

- The Orlando was selected as one of the best metro areas for golf in America by *Golf Digest*. The Orlando area was ranked #6 out of 20. Criteria: climate; cost of public golf; quality of public golf; accessibility. *Golf Digest, "The Top 20 Cities for Golf," October 2011*

- *Golf.com* and the research arm of the National Golf Foundation analyzed the 50 largest metropolitan areas in the U.S. in terms of golf. The Orlando metro area ranked #5. Criteria: weather; affordability; quality of courses; accessibility; number of courses designed by esteemed architects; availability; crowdedness. *Golf.com, November 15, 2007*

Technology Rankings

- The Orlando metro area was selected as one of "America's Most Wired Cities" by *Forbes*. The metro area was ranked #9 out of 20. Criteria: percentage of Internet users with high-speed access; number of companies providing high-speed Internet; number of public wireless hot spots. *Forbes, "America's Most Wired Cities," March 2, 2010*

Transportation Rankings

- Orlando appeared on *Trapster.com's* list of the 10 most-active U.S. cities for speed traps. The city ranked #7 of 10. *Trapster.com* is a community platform accessed online and via smartphone app that alerts drivers to traps, hazards and other traffic issues nearby. *Trapster.com, "Speeders Beware: Cities With the Most Speed Traps," February 10, 2012*

- Orlando was identified as one of America's worst cities for speed traps by the National Motorists Association. The city ranked #3 out of 25. Criteria: speed trap locations per 100,000 residents. *National Motorists Association, September 2011*

- The Orlando metro area appeared on *Forbes* list of the best and worst cities for commuters. The metro area ranked #57 out of 60 (#1 is best). Criteria: travel time; road congestion; travel delays. *Forbes.com, "Best and Worst Cities for Commuters," February 16, 2010*

Women/Minorities Rankings

- *Women's Health* examined U.S. cities and identified the 100 best cities for women. Orlando was ranked #52. Criteria: 30 categories were examined from obesity and breast cancer rates to commuting times and hours spent working out. *Women's Health, "Best Cities for Women 2012"*

- Orlando was ranked #57 out of 100 metro areas in *SELF Magazine's* ranking of America's healthiest places for women." A panel of experts came up with more than 50 criteria including death and disease rates, environmental indicators, community resources, and lifestyle habits. *SELF Magazine, "Secrets of America's Healthiest Women," December 2008*

- Orlando was selected as one of the "Gayest Cities in America" by *The Advocate*. The city ranked #2 out of 15. *The Advocate* used several different measures to establish "per capita queerness"—including a city's number of teams entered in the Gay Softball World Series, gay bookstores, openly gay elected officials and semifinalists in the International Mr. Leather Contest. *The Advocate, "Gayest Cities in America, 2012" January 2012*

- The Orlando metro area appeared on *Forbes'* list of the "Best Cities for Minority Entrepreneurs." The area ranked #2 out of 10. Criteria: 52 metropolitan statistical areas were examined. For each ethnicity (African Americans, Asians and Hispanics), the editors measured housing affordability, population growth, income growth, and entrepreneurship (per capita self-employment). *Forbes, "Best Cities for Minority Entrepreneurs," March 23, 2011*

Miscellaneous Rankings

- *Men's Health* ranked 100 U.S. cities by their level of sadness. Orlando was ranked #82 (#1 = saddest city). Criteria: suicide rates; unemployment rates; percentage of households that use antidepressants; percent of population who report feeling blue all or most of the time. *Men's Health, "Frown Towns," November 28, 2011*

- Scarborough Research, a leading market research firm, identified the top local markets for lottery ticket purchasers. The Orlando DMA (Designated Market Area) ranked in the top 13 with 48% of adults 18+ reporting that they purchased lottery tickets in the past 30 days. *Scarborough Research, January 30, 2012*

- The Orlando metro area was selected as one of "The Best U.S. Cities for Bargain Shopping" by *Forbes*. The area ranked #1 out of 10. Criteria: number of outlet stores; gross leasable retail space in major malls; low consumer price index; low sales tax rate. Indicators were examined in the nation's 50 largest metropolitan areas. *Forbes, "The Best U.S. Cities for Bargain Shopping," January 20, 2012*

- Energizer Holdings, the makers of Edge® shave gel, in partnership with Sperling's BestPlaces, ranked 50 major metro areas in terms of everyday irritations. The Orlando metro area ranked #11. Criteria: humidity levels; weather conditions; incidence of traffic delays and congestion; average commute times; frequency of flight delays and cancellations; rates of sleeplessness; underemployment; pollens and allergens; pests; comedy clubs per capita. *Energizer Holdings, "Most Irritation Prone Cities," July 23, 2010*

- Mars Chocolate North America, the makers of COMBOS®, in partnership with Sperling's BestPlaces, ranked 50 major metro areas in terms of their "manliness." The Orlando metro area ranked #30. Criteria: number of professional sports teams; number of nearby NASCAR tracks and racing events; manly lifestyle; concentration of manly retail stores; manly occupations per capita; salty snack sales; "Board of Manliness" rankings. *Mars Chocolate North America, "America's Manliest Cities 2011," September 1, 2011*

- Orlando appeared on Procter & Gamble's list of the "Top-20 All-Time Sweatiest Cities." The city was ranked #10. The rankings are based on computer simulations of the amount of sweat a person of average height and weight would produce walking around for an hour in the average temperatures during the summer months, based on historical weather data during June, July and August from 2001-2008 for each city. *Procter & Gamble, Old Spice Press Release, "Top-20 All-Time Sweatiest Cities," July 1, 2009*

- Orlando was selected as one of America's "10 Meanest Cities" by the National Coalition for the Homeless and The National Law Center on Homelessness & Poverty. The city was ranked #3. Criteria: the number of anti-homeless laws; the enforcement of those laws and severity of penalties; the general political climate towards homeless people; local advocate support for the meanest designation; the city's history of criminalization measures; and the existence of pending or recently enacted criminalization legislation in the city. *National Coalition for the Homeless and The National Law Center on Homelessness & Poverty, "Homes Not Handcuffs: The Criminalization of Homelessness in U.S. Cities," July 2009*

Business Environment

City Government Finances

Component	2009 ($000)	2009 ($ per capita)
Total Revenues	539,846	2,369
Total Expenditures	652,402	2,863
Debt Outstanding	927,097	4,068
Cash and Securities[1]	1,493,528	6,553

Note: (1) Cash and security holdings of a government at the close of its fiscal year, including those of its dependent agencies, utilities, and liquor stores.
Source: U.S Census Bureau, State & Local Government Finances 2009

City Government Revenue by Source

Source	2009 ($000)	2009 ($ per capita)
General Revenue		
From Federal Government	15,304	67
From State Government	60,655	266
From Local Governments	87,524	384
Taxes		
Property	121,496	533
Sales and Gross Receipts	56,341	247
Personal Income	0	0
Corporate Income	0	0
Motor Vehicle License	0	0
Other Taxes	70,766	311
Current Charges	157,297	690
Liquor Store	0	0
Utility	58	0
Employee Retirement	-89,895	-394

Source: U.S Census Bureau, State & Local Government Finances 2009

City Government Expenditures by Function

Function	2009 ($000)	2009 ($ per capita)	2009 (%)
General Direct Expenditures			
Air Transportation	0	0	0.0
Corrections	0	0	0.0
Education	0	0	0.0
Employment Security Administration	0	0	0.0
Financial Administration	42,718	187	6.5
Fire Protection	84,461	371	12.9
General Public Buildings	6,174	27	0.9
Governmental Administration, Other	17,119	75	2.6
Health	0	0	0.0
Highways	54,714	240	8.4
Hospitals	0	0	0.0
Housing and Community Development	11,252	49	1.7
Interest on General Debt	24,696	108	3.8
Judicial and Legal	3,760	16	0.6
Libraries	0	0	0.0
Parking	14,868	65	2.3
Parks and Recreation	60,967	268	9.3
Police Protection	124,043	544	19.0
Public Welfare	0	0	0.0
Sewerage	62,756	275	9.6
Solid Waste Management	24,632	108	3.8
Veterans' Services	0	0	0.0
Liquor Store	0	0	0.0
Utility	0	0	0.0
Employee Retirement	31,113	137	4.8

Source: U.S Census Bureau, State & Local Government Finances 2009

Municipal Bond Ratings

Area	Moody's	S&P	Fitch
City	Aa1	AA	AAA

Rating Systems (shown in declining order of credit quality): Moody's– Aaa, Aa, A, Baa, Ba, B, Caa, Ca, C (numerical modifiers 1, 2, and 3 are added to letter-rating); S&P– AAA, AA, A, BBB, BB, B, CCC, CC, C; Fitch– AAA, AA, A, BBB, BB, B, CCC, CC, C. Ratings may be modified by the addition of a plus or minus sign to show relative standing within the major rating categories.

Notes: n/a Not Available; w/d Withdrawn (1) Not Reviewed; (2) Issuer Rating/No General Obligation; (3) Standard and Poor's Issue Credit Rating (ICR) is a current opinion of an obliger with respect to a specific financial obligation, a specific class of financial obligations, or a specific financial program.

Source: City of Orlando, Florida, Comprehensive Annual Financial Report, Fiscal Year Ended September 30, 2010

DEMOGRAPHICS

Population Growth

Area	1990 Census	2000 Census	2010 Census	Population Growth (%) 1990-2000	2000-2010
City	161,172	185,951	238,300	15.4	28.2
MSA[1]	1,224,852	1,644,561	2,134,411	34.3	29.8
U.S.	248,709,873	281,421,906	308,745,538	13.2	9.7

Note: (1) Figures cover the Orlando-Kissimmee-Sanford, FL Metropolitan Statistical Area—see Appendix B for areas included
Source: U.S. Census Bureau, 2010 Census

Household Size

Area	Persons in Household (%) One	Two	Three	Four	Five	Six	Seven or More	Average Household Size
City	34.6	32.2	15.3	10.4	4.6	1.8	1.2	2.29
MSA[1]	24.1	33.4	17.3	14.2	6.7	2.6	1.6	2.62
U.S.	26.7	32.8	16.1	13.4	6.5	2.6	1.9	2.58

Note: (1) Figures cover the Orlando-Kissimmee-Sanford, FL Metropolitan Statistical Area—see Appendix B for areas included
Source: U.S. Census Bureau, 2010 Census

Race

Area	White Alone[2] (%)	Black Alone[2] (%)	Asian Alone[2] (%)	AIAN[3] Alone[2] (%)	NHOPI[4] Alone[2] (%)	Other Race Alone[2] (%)	Two or More Races (%)
City	57.6	28.1	3.8	0.4	0.1	6.8	3.4
MSA[1]	70.0	16.2	4.0	0.4	0.1	6.1	3.2
U.S.	72.4	12.6	4.8	0.9	0.2	6.2	2.9

Note: (1) Figures cover the Orlando-Kissimmee-Sanford, FL Metropolitan Statistical Area—see Appendix B for areas included; (2) Alone is defined as not being in combination with one or more other races; (3) American Indian and Alaska Native; (4) Native Hawaiian and Other Pacific Islander
Source: U.S. Census Bureau, 2010 Census

Hispanic or Latino Origin

Area	Hispanic or Latino (%)	Mexican (%)	Puerto Rican (%)	Cuban (%)	Other Hispanic or Latino (%)
City	25.4	1.8	13.1	1.8	8.7
MSA[1]	25.2	3.0	12.6	1.7	7.9
U.S.	16.3	10.3	1.5	0.6	4.0

Note: Persons of Hispanic or Latino origin can be of any race; (1) Figures cover the Orlando-Kissimmee-Sanford, FL Metropolitan Statistical Area—see Appendix B for areas included
Source: U.S. Census Bureau, 2010 Census

Segregation

Type	Segregation Indices[1]				Percent Change		
	1990	2000	2010	2010 Rank[2]	1990-2000	1990-2010	2000-2010
Black/White	59.1	55.9	50.7	69	-3.2	-8.4	-5.2
Asian/White	29.4	35.4	33.9	81	6.0	4.6	-1.4
Hispanic/White	29.2	38.7	40.2	64	9.5	11.0	1.5

Note: Figures are based on an analysis of 1990, 2000, and 2010 Census Decennial Census tract data by William H. Frey, Brookings Institution and the University of Michigan Social Science Data Analysis Network. In this analysis all racial groups (whites, blacks, and asians) are non-Hispanic members of those races. Hispanics are shown as a separate category; All figures cover the Metropolitan Statistical Area (see Appendix B for areas included); (1) Segregation Indices are Dissimilarity Indices that measure the degree to which the minority group is distributed differently than whites across census tracts. They range from 0 (complete integration) to 100 (complete segregation) where the value indicates the percentage of the minority group that needs to move to be distributed exactly like whites; (2) Ranges from 1 (most segregated) to 102 (least segregated); n/a not available.
Source: www.CensusScope.org

Ancestry

Area	German	Irish	English	American	Italian	Polish	French[2]	Scottish	Dutch
City	8.5	8.5	6.2	4.4	5.5	1.7	1.9	1.6	0.8
MSA[1]	11.1	9.4	7.8	7.0	6.0	2.3	2.5	1.6	1.2
U.S.	16.1	11.6	8.8	6.1	5.7	3.2	3.0	1.9	1.6

Note: Figures are the percentage of the total population reporting a particular ancestry. The nine most commonly reported ancestries in the U.S. are shown. Figures include multiple ancestries (e.g. if a person reported being Irish and Italian, they were included in both columns); (1) Figures cover the Orlando-Kissimmee-Sanford, FL Metropolitan Statistical Area—see Appendix B for areas included; (2) Excludes Basque
Source: U.S. Census Bureau, 2008-2010 American Community Survey 3-Year Estimates

Foreign-Born Population

Area	Percent of Population Born in								
	Any Foreign Country	Mexico	Asia	Europe	Carribean	South America	Central America[2]	Africa	Canada
City	18.3	1.2	2.6	1.5	6.0	5.1	0.8	0.7	0.3
MSA[1]	16.2	1.4	2.8	1.7	4.7	3.7	0.9	0.5	0.4
U.S.	12.8	3.8	3.6	1.6	1.2	0.9	1.0	0.5	0.3

Note: (1) Figures cover the Orlando-Kissimmee-Sanford, FL Metropolitan Statistical Area—see Appendix B for areas included; (2) Excludes Mexico.
Source: U.S. Census Bureau, 2008-2010 American Community Survey 3-Year Estimates

Marital Status

Area	Never Married	Now Married[2]	Separated	Widowed	Divorced
City	43.1	35.7	3.7	4.4	13.1
MSA[1]	32.6	48.0	2.6	5.4	11.5
U.S.	31.6	49.6	2.2	6.1	10.7

Note: Figures are percentages and cover the population 15 years of age and older; (1) Figures cover the Orlando-Kissimmee-Sanford, FL Metropolitan Statistical Area—see Appendix B for areas included; (2) Excludes separated
Source: U.S. Census Bureau, 2008-2010 American Community Survey 3-Year Estimates

Age

Area	Percent of Population							Median Age
	Under Age 5	Age 5 to 17	Age 18 to 34	Age 35 to 49	Age 50 to 64	Age 65 to 79	80 Years and Over	
City	7.1	14.9	31.7	21.9	15.0	6.7	2.7	32.8
MSA[1]	6.2	17.2	24.9	21.5	17.8	9.2	3.2	36.3
U.S.	6.5	17.5	23.2	20.7	19.0	9.4	3.6	37.2

Note: (1) Figures cover the Orlando-Kissimmee-Sanford, FL Metropolitan Statistical Area—see Appendix B for areas included
Source: U.S. Census Bureau, 2010 Census

Male/Female Ratio

Area	Males	Females	Males per 100 Females
City	115,883	122,417	94.7
MSA[1]	1,044,696	1,089,715	95.9
U.S.	151,781,326	156,964,212	96.7

Note: (1) Figures cover the Orlando-Kissimmee-Sanford, FL Metropolitan Statistical Area—see Appendix B for areas included
Source: U.S. Census Bureau, 2010 Census

Religious Groups

Area	Catholic	Baptist	Non-Den.	Methodist[2]	Lutheran	LDS[3]	Pente-costal	Presby-terian[4]	Muslim[5]	Judaism
MSA[1]	13.2	7.0	5.7	3.0	0.9	1.0	3.2	1.4	0.3	1.3
U.S.	19.1	9.3	4.0	4.0	2.3	2.0	1.9	1.6	0.8	0.7

Note: Figures are the number of adherents as a percentage of the total population; (1) Figures cover the Orlando-Kissimmee-Sanford, FL Metropolitan Statistical Area—see Appendix B for areas included; (2) Methodist/Pietist; (3) Latter Day Saints; (4) Reformed; (5) Figures are estimates
Source: Association of Statisticians of American Religious Bodies, 2010 U.S. Religion Census: Religious Congregations & Membership Study

ECONOMY

Gross Metropolitan Product

Area	2007	2008	2009	2010	2010 Rank[2]
MSA[1]	104.1	103.6	101.2	103.6	29

Note: Figures are in billions of dollars; (1) Figures cover the Orlando-Kissimmee-Sanford, FL Metropolitan Statistical Area—see Appendix B for areas included; (2) Rank ranges from 1 to 363
Source: The United States Conference of Mayors, "U.S. Metro Economies: GMP and Employment Forecasts," June 2011

Economic Growth

Area	2007-2009 (%)	2010 (%)	2011 (%)	Rank[2]
MSA[1]	-3.1	1.8	2.4	277
U.S.	-1.3	2.9	2.5	–

Note: Figures are real Gross Metropolitan Product growth rates and represent annual average percent change; (1) Figures cover the Orlando-Kissimmee-Sanford, FL Metropolitan Statistical Area—see Appendix B for areas included; (2) Rank ranges from 1 to 363
Source: The United States Conference of Mayors, "U.S. Metro Economies: GMP and Employment Forecasts," June 2011

Metropolitan Area Exports

Area	2005	2006	2007	2008	2009	2010	2010 Rank[2]
MSA[1]	2,183.2	2,474.3	3,045.1	3,388.0	2,947.1	3,453.6	61

Note: Figures are in millions of dollars; (1) Figures cover the Orlando-Kissimmee-Sanford, FL Metropolitan Statistical Area—see Appendix B for areas included; (2) Rank ranges from 1 to 369
Source: U.S. Department of Commerce, International Trade Administration, Office of Trade & Industry Information, Manufacturing & Services, data extracted April 2, 2012

INCOME

Income

Area	Per Capita ($)	Median Household ($)	Average Household ($)
City	24,643	40,669	57,840
MSA[1]	24,530	48,450	65,091
U.S.	26,942	51,222	70,116

Note: (1) Figures cover the Orlando-Kissimmee-Sanford, FL Metropolitan Statistical Area—see Appendix B for areas included
Source: U.S. Census Bureau, 2008-2010 American Community Survey 3-Year Estimates

Household Income Distribution

Area	Percent of Households Earning							
	Under $15,000	$15,000 -24,999	$25,000 -34,999	$35,000 -49,999	$50,000 -74,999	$75,000 -99,000	$100,000 -149,999	$150,000 and up
City	14.5	13.8	13.2	18.4	17.9	8.6	7.7	6.0
MSA[1]	11.5	11.5	12.4	16.0	19.9	11.3	10.7	6.8
U.S.	13.0	11.0	10.6	14.2	18.5	12.1	12.2	8.4

Note: (1) Figures cover the Orlando-Kissimmee-Sanford, FL Metropolitan Statistical Area—see Appendix B for areas included
Source: U.S. Census Bureau, 2008-2010 American Community Survey 3-Year Estimates

Poverty Rate

Area	All Ages	Under 18 Years Old	18 to 64 Years Old	65 Years and Over
City	17.7	24.3	16.2	13.9
MSA[1]	13.6	18.5	12.7	8.9
U.S.	14.4	20.1	13.1	9.4

Note: Figures are percentage of people whose income during the past 12 months was below the poverty level;
(1) Figures cover the Orlando-Kissimmee-Sanford, FL Metropolitan Statistical Area—see Appendix B for areas included
Source: U.S. Census Bureau, 2008-2010 American Community Survey 3-Year Estimates

Personal Bankruptcy Filing Rate

Area	2006	2007	2008	2009	2010	2011
Orange County	1.17	2.14	3.83	6.51	7.70	6.40
U.S.	2.00	2.73	3.53	4.61	4.97	4.37

Note: Numbers are per 1,000 population and include Chapter 7 and Chapter 13 filings
Source: Federal Deposit Insurance Corporation, Regional Economic Conditions, March 9, 2012

EMPLOYMENT

Labor Force and Employment

Area	Civilian Labor Force			Workers Employed		
	Dec. 2010	Dec. 2011	% Chg.	Dec. 2010	Dec. 2011	% Chg.
City	136,757	135,243	-1.1	121,383	122,868	1.2
MSA[1]	1,125,039	1,113,686	-1.0	996,137	1,008,325	1.2
U.S.	153,156,000	153,373,000	0.1	139,159,000	140,681,000	1.1

Note: Data is not seasonally adjusted and covers workers 16 years of age and older;
(1) Metropolitan Statistical Area—see Appendix B for areas included
Source: Bureau of Labor Statistics, http://stats.bls.gov

Unemployment Rate

Area	2011											
	Jan.	Feb.	Mar.	Apr.	May	Jun.	Jul.	Aug.	Sep.	Oct.	Nov.	Dec.
City	11.5	10.6	10.2	9.7	9.7	10.2	10.3	10.3	10.0	9.7	9.4	9.2
MSA[1]	11.8	10.8	10.4	10.0	9.9	10.4	10.5	10.4	10.2	9.8	9.7	9.5
U.S.	9.8	9.5	9.2	8.7	8.7	9.3	9.3	9.1	8.8	8.5	8.2	8.3

Note: Data is not seasonally adjusted and covers workers 16 years of age and older; All figures are percentages; (1) Metropolitan Statistical Area—see Appendix B for areas included
Source: Bureau of Labor Statistics, http://stats.bls.gov

Projected Unemployment Rate

Area	2010 (%)	2011 (%)	2012 (%)	2013 (%)
MSA[1]	11.8	10.3	9.6	8.8

Note: (1) Metropolitan Statistical Area—see Appendix B for areas included
Source: The United States Conference of Mayors, "U.S. Metro Economies: GMP and Employment Forecasts," June 2011

Employment by Occupation

Occupation Classification	City (%)	MSA[1] (%)	U.S. (%)
Management, Business, Science, and Arts	33.8	34.2	35.6
Natural Resources, Construction, and Maintenance	7.3	8.6	9.5
Production, Transportation, and Material Moving	8.5	8.5	12.1
Sales and Office	28.0	28.6	25.2
Service	22.4	20.2	17.6

Note: Figures cover employed civilians 16 years of age and older; (1) Figures cover the Orlando-Kissimmee-Sanford, FL Metropolitan Statistical Area—see Appendix B for areas included
Source: U.S. Census Bureau, 2008-2010 American Community Survey 3-Year Estimates

Employment by Industry

Sector	MSA[1] Number of Employees	MSA[1] Percent of Total	U.S. Percent of Total
Construction	43,500	4.2	4.1
Education and Health Services	124,500	12.1	15.2
Financial Activities	65,100	6.3	5.8
Government	117,500	11.5	16.8
Information	23,800	2.3	2.0
Leisure and Hospitality	208,900	20.4	9.9
Manufacturing	37,800	3.7	8.9
Mining and Logging	200	<0.1	0.6
Other Services	47,600	4.6	4.0
Professional and Business Services	162,600	15.8	13.3
Retail Trade	125,700	12.3	11.5
Transportation and Utilities	31,300	3.1	3.8
Wholesale Trade	37,600	3.7	4.2

Note: Figures cover non-farm employment as of December 2011 and are not seasonally adjusted; (1) Metropolitan Statistical Area—see Appendix B for areas included
Source: Bureau of Labor Statistics, http://stats.bls.gov

Occupations with Greatest Projected Employment Growth: 2008 – 2018

Occupation[1]	2008 Employment	2018 Projected Employment	Numeric Employment Change	Percent Employment Change
Registered Nurses	151,100	187,380	36,280	24.0
Combined Food Preparation and Serving Workers, Including Fast Food	162,570	186,400	23,830	14.7
Customer Service Representatives	169,080	190,780	21,700	12.8
Nursing Aides, Orderlies, and Attendants	88,630	106,860	18,230	20.6
Home Health Aides	30,480	47,860	17,380	57.0
Postsecondary Teachers	70,790	85,380	14,590	20.6
Retail Salespersons	274,490	288,660	14,170	5.2
Elementary School Teachers, Except Special Education	74,130	86,390	12,260	16.5
Stock Clerks and Order Fillers	167,450	179,420	11,970	7.1
Accountants and Auditors	86,390	97,670	11,280	13.1

Note: Projections cover Florida; (1) Sorted by numeric employment change
Source: www.projectionscentral.com, State Occupational Projections, 2008–2018 Long-Term Projections

Fastest Growing Occupations: 2008 – 2018

Occupation[1]	2008 Employment	2018 Projected Employment	Numeric Employment Change	Percent Employment Change
Biomedical Engineers	520	840	320	61.5
Home Health Aides	30,480	47,860	17,380	57.0
Medical Scientists, Except Epidemiologists	2,640	3,870	1,230	46.6
Physician Assistants	3,900	5,490	1,590	40.8
Personal and Home Care Aides	13,890	19,430	5,540	39.9
Network Systems and Data Communications Analysts	21,550	30,110	8,560	39.7
Radiation Therapists	1,270	1,730	460	36.2
Dental Hygienists	9,030	11,890	2,860	31.7
Physical Therapist Assistants	3,550	4,660	1,110	31.3
Financial Examiners	610	800	190	31.1

Note: Projections cover Florida; (1) Sorted by percent employment change and excludes occupations with numeric employment change less than 100
Source: www.projectionscentral.com, State Occupational Projections, 2008–2018 Long-Term Projections

Average Wages

Occupation	$/Hr.	Occupation	$/Hr.
Accountants and Auditors	30.31	Maids and Housekeeping Cleaners	9.50
Automotive Mechanics	16.88	Maintenance and Repair Workers	14.88
Bookkeepers	15.51	Marketing Managers	51.91
Carpenters	16.27	Nuclear Medicine Technologists	33.19
Cashiers	8.98	Nurses, Licensed Practical	18.83
Clerks, General Office	13.05	Nurses, Registered	28.25
Clerks, Receptionists/Information	11.70	Nursing Aides/Orderlies/Attendants	11.78
Clerks, Shipping/Receiving	12.62	Packers and Packagers, Hand	11.28
Computer Programmers	33.08	Physical Therapists	38.75
Computer Support Specialists	20.38	Postal Service Mail Carriers	24.96
Computer Systems Analysts	38.82	Real Estate Brokers	58.00
Cooks, Restaurant	11.78	Retail Salespersons	11.47
Dentists	62.52	Sales Reps., Exc. Tech./Scientific	26.15
Electrical Engineers	35.26	Sales Reps., Tech./Scientific	42.08
Electricians	18.63	Secretaries, Exc. Legal/Med./Exec.	14.78
Financial Managers	56.61	Security Guards	11.10
First-Line Supervisors/Managers, Sales	20.19	Surgeons	107.08
Food Preparation Workers	9.67	Teacher Assistants	10.80
General and Operations Managers	47.91	Teachers, Elementary School	24.40
Hairdressers/Cosmetologists	11.18	Teachers, Secondary School	24.70
Internists	n/a	Telemarketers	11.87
Janitors and Cleaners	10.13	Truck Drivers, Heavy/Tractor-Trailer	16.98
Landscaping/Groundskeeping Workers	10.77	Truck Drivers, Light/Delivery Svcs.	14.67
Lawyers	60.74	Waiters and Waitresses	11.28

Note: Wage data covers the Orlando-Kissimmee-Sanford, FL Metropolitan Statistical Area—see Appendix B for areas included. Hourly wages for elementary/secondary school teachers and teacher assistants were calculated by the editors from annual wage data assuming a 40 hour work week; n/a not available.
Source: Bureau of Labor Statistics, Metro Area Occupational Employment and Wage Estimates, May 2011

RESIDENTIAL REAL ESTATE

Building Permits

Area	Single-Family			Multi-Family			Total		
	2010	2011	Pct. Chg.	2010	2011	Pct. Chg.	2010	2011	Pct. Chg.
City	224	308	37.5	336	637	89.6	560	945	68.8
MSA[1]	4,221	4,533	7.4	1,033	1,972	90.9	5,254	6,505	23.8
U.S.	447,311	418,498	-6.4	157,299	205,563	30.7	604,610	624,061	3.2

Note: (1) Metropolitan Statistical Area—see Appendix B for areas included; figures represent new, privately-owned housing units authorized (unadjusted data); All permit data are based on estimates with imputation.
Source: U.S. Census Bureau, Manufacturing, Mining, and Construction Statistics, Building Permits, 2010, 2011

Homeownership Rate

Area	2005 (%)	2006 (%)	2007 (%)	2008 (%)	2009 (%)	2010 (%)	2011 (%)
MSA[1]	70.5	71.1	71.8	70.5	72.4	70.8	68.6
U.S.	68.9	68.8	68.1	67.8	67.4	66.9	66.1

Note: (1) Metropolitan Statistical Area—see Appendix B for areas included
Source: U.S. Census Bureau, Housing Vacancies and Homeownership Annual Statistics: 2011

Housing Vacancy Rates

Area	Gross Vacancy Rate[2] (%)			Year-Round Vacancy Rate[3] (%)			Rental Vacancy Rate[4] (%)			Homeowner Vacancy Rate[5] (%)		
	2009	2010	2011	2009	2010	2011	2009	2010	2011	2009	2010	2011
MSA[1]	21.2	19.9	20.1	17.5	16.6	14.0	22.8	19.0	19.0	5.8	5.9	2.5
U.S.	14.5	14.3	14.2	11.3	11.3	11.1	10.6	10.2	9.5	2.6	2.6	2.5

Note: (1) Metropolitan Statistical Area—see Appendix B for areas included; (2) The percentage of the total housing inventory that is vacant; (3) The percentage of the housing inventory (excluding seasonal units) that is year-round vacant; (4) The percentage of rental inventory that is vacant for rent; (5) The percentage of homeowner inventory that is vacant for sale
Source: U.S. Census Bureau, Housing Vacancies and Homeownership Annual Statistics: 2011

TAXES

State Corporate Income Tax Rates

State	Tax Rate (%)	Income Brackets ($)	Num. of Brackets	Financial Institution Tax Rate (%)[a]	Federal Income Tax Ded.
Florida	5.5 (f)	Flat rate	1	5.5 (f)	No

Note: Tax rates as of January 1, 2012; (a) Rates listed are the corporate income tax rate applied to financial institutions or excise taxes based on income. Some states have other taxes based upon the value of deposits or shares; (f) An exemption of $5,000 is allowed. Florida's Alternative Minimum Tax rate is 3.3%.
Source: Federation of Tax Administrators, "State Corporate Income Tax Rates, 2012"

State Individual Income Tax Rates

State	Tax Rate (%)	Income Brackets ($)	Num. of Brackets	Personal Exempt. ($)[1] Single	Personal Exempt. ($)[1] Dependents	Fed. Inc. Tax Ded.
Florida – No State Income Tax						

Note: Tax rates as of January 1, 2012; Local- and county-level taxes are not included; n/a not applicable; (1) Married joint filers generally receive double the single exemption
Source: Federation of Tax Administrators, "State Individual Income Tax Rates, 2012"

Various State and Local Tax Rates

State	State and Local Sales and Use (%)	State Sales and Use (%)	Gasoline[1] (¢/gal.)	Cigarette[2] ($/pack)	Spirits[3] ($/gal.)	Wine[4] ($/gal.)	Beer[5] ($/gal.)
Florida	6.5	6.00	35.0	1.34	6.50	2.25	0.48

Note: All tax rates as of January 1, 2012 except beer, wine and spirits (September 1, 2011); (1) The American Petroleum Institute has developed a methodology for determining the average tax rate on a gallon of fuel. Rates may include any of the following: excise taxes, environmental fees, storage tank fees, other fees or taxes, general sales tax, and local taxes. In states where gasoline is subject to the general sales tax, or where the fuel tax is based on the average sale price, the average rate determined by API is sensitive to changes in the price of gasoline. States that fully or partially apply general sales taxes to gasoline: CA, CO, GA, IL, IN, MI, NY; (2) The federal excise tax of $1.0066 per pack and local taxes are not included; (3) Rates are those applicable to off-premise sales of 40% alcohol by volume (a.b.v.) distilled spirits in 750ml containers. Local excise taxes are excluded; (4) Rates are those applicable to off-premise sales of 11% a.b.v. non-carbonated wine in 750ml containers; (5) Rates are those applicable to off-premise sales of 4.7% a.b.v. beer in 12 ounce containers.
Source: Tax Foundation, 2012 Facts & Figures: How Does Your State Compare?

State-Local Tax Burdens

Area	Rate (%)	Rank[1]	Per Capita Taxes Paid to Home State ($)	Total State and Local Per Capita Taxes Paid ($)	Per Capita Income ($)
Florida	9.2	31	2,713	3,897	42,146
U.S. Average	9.8	-	3,057	4,160	42,539

Note: Figures cover 2009; (1) Rank ranges from 1 to 50 where 1 is highest tax burden
Source: Tax Foundation, State-Local Tax Burdens, All States, 2009

State Business Tax Climate Index Rankings

State	Overall Rank	Corporate Tax Index Rank	Individual Income Tax Index Rank	Sales Tax Index Rank	Unemployment Insurance Tax Index Rank	Property Tax Index Rank
Florida	5	12	1	19	5	24

Note: The index is a measure of how each state's tax laws affect economic performance. The lower the rank, the more favorable a state's tax system is for business. States without a given tax are given a ranking of 1.
Source: Tax Foundation, Major Components of the State Business Tax Climate Index, FY 2012

COMMERCIAL REAL ESTATE

Office Market

Market Area	Inventory (sq. ft.)	Vacant (sq. ft.)	Vac. Rate (%)	Under Constr. (sq. ft.)	Asking Rent ($/sf/yr) Class A	Class B
Orlando	55,293,136	9,668,640	17.5	489,211	22.35	18.05

Source: Grubb & Ellis, Office Markets Trends, 4th Quarter 2011

Industrial Market

Market Area	Inventory (sq. ft.)	Vacant (sq. ft.)	Vac. Rate (%)	Under Constr. (sq. ft.)	Asking Rent ($/sf/yr) WH/Dist	R&D/Flex
Orlando	182,577,460	19,804,668	10.8	0	4.47	8.63

Source: Grubb & Ellis, Industrial Markets Trends, 4th Quarter 2011

COMMERCIAL UTILITIES

Typical Monthly Electric Bills

Area	Commercial Service ($/month) 1,500 kWh	40 kW demand 14,000 kWh	Industrial Service ($/month) 1,000 kW demand 200,000 kWh	50,000 kW demand 15,000,000 kWh
City	108	1,239	22,761	1,001,777
Average[1]	189	1,616	25,197	1,470,813

Note: Based on total rates in effect July 1, 2011; (1) average based on 184 utilities surveyed
Source: Edison Electric Institute, Typical Bills and Average Rates Report, Summer 2011

TRANSPORTATION

Means of Transportation to Work

Area	Car/Truck/Van Drove Alone	Car-pooled	Public Transportation Bus	Subway	Railroad	Bicycle	Walked	Other Means	Worked at Home
City	78.3	10.2	4.0	0.0	0.0	0.4	1.7	1.5	3.9
MSA[1]	81.4	9.3	1.7	0.0	0.0	0.4	1.1	1.7	4.6
U.S.	76.0	10.2	2.7	1.7	0.5	0.5	2.8	1.3	4.2

Note: Figures are percentages and cover workers 16 years of age and older; (1) Figures cover the Orlando-Kissimmee-Sanford, FL Metropolitan Statistical Area—see Appendix B for areas included
Source: U.S. Census Bureau, 2008-2010 American Community Survey 3-Year Estimates

Travel Time to Work

Area	Less Than 10 Minutes	10 to 19 Minutes	20 to 29 Minutes	30 to 44 Minutes	45 to 59 Minutes	60 to 89 Minutes	90 Minutes or More
City	8.4	32.3	26.3	22.1	6.1	2.9	1.8
MSA[1]	8.5	26.9	23.4	26.0	9.1	4.3	1.8
U.S.	13.9	30.1	20.8	19.8	7.5	5.5	2.5

Note: Figures are percentages and include workers 16 years old and over; (1) Figures cover the Orlando-Kissimmee-Sanford, FL Metropolitan Statistical Area—see Appendix B for areas included
Source: U.S. Census Bureau, 2008-2010 American Community Survey 3-Year Estimates

Travel Time Index

Area	1985	1990	1995	2000	2005	2010
Urban Area[1]	1.11	1.18	1.19	1.23	1.22	1.18
Average[2]	1.11	1.16	1.18	1.21	1.25	1.20

Note: Travel Time Index—the ratio of travel time in the peak period to the travel time at free-flow conditions. A value of 1.30 indicates a 20-minute free-flow trip takes 26 minutes in the peak. Free-flow speeds (60 mph on freeways and 35 mph on principal arterials) are used as the comparison threshold; (1) Covers the Orlando FL urban area; (2) average of 439 urban areas
Source: Texas Transportation Institute, Urban Mobility Report 2011, September 2011

Public Transportation

Agency Name / Mode of Transportation	Vehicles Operated in Maximum Service	Annual Unlinked Passenger Trips ('000)	Annual Passenger Miles ('000)
Central Florida Regional Transportation Authority (Lynx)			
Bus (directly operated)	223	24,780.7	133,309.6
Demand Response (purchased transportation)	174	749.6	8,825.5
Vanpool (purchased transportation)	67	189.6	6,159.7

Source: Federal Transit Administration, National Transit Database, 2010

Air Transportation

Airport Name and Code / Type of Service	Passenger Airlines[1]	Passenger Enplanements	Freight Carriers[2]	Freight (lbs.)
Orlando International (MCO)				
Domestic service (U.S. carriers - 2011)	33	15,550,060	18	118,879,689
International service (U.S. carriers - 2010)	14	272,645	3	5,811

Note: (1) Includes all U.S.-based major, minor and commuter airlines that carried at least one passenger during the year; (2) Includes all U.S.-based airlines and freight carriers that transported at least one pound of freight during the year
Source: Bureau of Transportation Statistics, The Intermodal Transportation Database, Air Carriers: T-100 Domestic Market (U.S. Carriers), 2011; Bureau of Transportation Statistics, The Intermodal Transportation Database, Air Carriers: T-100 International Market (U.S. Carriers), 2010

Other Transportation Statistics

Major Highways:	I-4
Amtrak Service:	Yes
Major Waterways/Ports:	None

Source: Amtrak.com; Google Maps

BUSINESSES

Major Business Headquarters

Company Name	Rankings	
	Fortune[1]	Forbes[2]
Darden Restaurants	332	-

Note: (1) Fortune 500—companies that produce a 10-K are ranked 1 to 500 based on 2010 revenue; (2) all private companies with at least $2 billion in annual revenue are ranked 1 to 212; companies listed are headquartered in the city; dashes indicate no ranking
Source: Fortune, "Fortune 500," May 23, 2011; Forbes, "America's Largest Private Companies," November 16, 2011

Fast-Growing Businesses

According to *Inc.*, Orlando is home to three of America's 500 fastest-growing private companies: **Vertiglo** (#16); **Dignitas Technologies** (#410); **AA Metals** (#464). Criteria: must be an independent, privately-held, for-profit, U.S. corporation, proprietorship or partnership; revenues must be at least $80,000 in 2007 and $2 million in 2010; must have four-year operating/sales history. Holding companies, regulated banks, and utilities were excluded.
Inc., "America's 500 Fastest-Growing Private Companies," September 2011

According to Deloitte, Orlando is home to one of North America's 500 fastest-growing high-technology companies: **API Technologies Corp.** (#260). Companies are ranked by percentage growth in revenue over a five-year period. Criteria for inclusion: company must be headquartered within North America; must own proprietary intellectual property or proprietary technology that contributes to a significant portion of the company's operating revenue, or devote a significant proportion of revenues to research and development of technology; must have been in business for a minumum of five years with 2006 operating revenues of at least $50,000 USD/CD and 2010 operating revenues of at least $5 million USD/CD. *Deloitte Touche Tohmatsu, 2011 Deloitte Technology Fast 500*[TM]

Minority Business Opportunity

Orlando is home to two companies which are on the *Black Enterprise* Auto Dealer 60 list (60 largest dealers based on gross sales): **Boyland Auto Group** (#4); **Massey Automotive Group** (#29). Criteria: company must be operational in previous calendar year and be at least 51% black-owned. *Black Enterprise, B.E. 100s, 2011*

Orlando is home to seven companies which are on the *Hispanic Business* 500 list (500 largest U.S. Hispanic-owned companies based on 2010 revenue): **Greenway Ford** (#6); **Jardon & Howard Technologies** (#134); **Advanced Xerographics Imaging Systems** (#187); **Exterior Walls** (#251); **T&G Constructors** (#258); **US Aluminum Services Corp.** (#471); **Moreno Peelen Pinto & Clark** (#485). Companies included must show at least 51 percent ownership by Hispanic U.S. citizens, and must maintain headquarters in one of the 50 states or Washington, D.C. *Hispanic Business, "Hispanic Business 500," June 2011*

Orlando is home to three companies which are on the *Hispanic Business* Fastest-Growing 100 list (greatest sales growth from 2006 to 2010): **US Aluminum Services Corp.** (#12); **Moreno Peelen Pinto & Clark** (#86); **Exterior Walls** (#99). Companies included must show at least 51 percent ownership by Hispanic U.S. citizens, and must maintain headquarters in one of the 50 states or Washington, D.C. In addition, companies must have minimum revenues of $200,000 for calendar year 2005. *Hispanic Business, July/August 2011*

Minority- and Women-Owned Businesses

Group	All Firms		Firms with Paid Employees			
	Firms	Sales ($000)	Firms	Sales ($000)	Employees	Payroll ($000)
Asian	1,522	774,833	467	715,806	2,957	77,699
Black	3,685	676,406	267	594,074	4,180	237,447
Hispanic	5,698	763,059	625	612,670	4,149	111,111
Women	8,731	1,491,871	1,376	1,231,467	9,795	283,759
All Firms	30,564	47,965,704	9,019	46,886,322	239,814	9,467,514

Note: Figures cover firms located in the city; minority- and women-owned business are defined as firms in which the corresponding group own 51% or more of the stock or equity of the company
Source: U.S. Census Bureau, 2007 Economic Census, Survey of Business Owners

HOTELS

Hotels/Motels

Area	5 Star		4 Star		3 Star		2 Star		1 Star		Not Rated	
	Num.	Pct.[3]	Num.	Pct.[3]	Num.	Pct.[3]	Num.	Pct.[3]	Num.	Pct.[3]	Num.	Pct.[3]
City[1]	3	0.6	40	8.3	202	42.1	184	38.3	7	1.5	44	9.2
Total[2]	133	0.9	940	6.5	4,569	31.8	7,033	48.9	351	2.4	1,343	9.3

Note: (1) Figures cover Orlando and vicinity; (2) Figures cover all 100 cities in this book; (3) Percentage of hotels which have a given star rating; Star ratings are determined by expedia.com and offer an indication of the general quality of a particular hotel.
Source: expedia.com, April 25, 2012

The Orlando-Kissimmee-Sanford, FL metro area is home to four of the best hotels in the U.S. according to *Travel & Leisure*: **Waldorf Astoria, Orlando** (#51); **Ritz-Carlton Orlando, Grande Lakes** (#165); **Hilton Orlando Bonnet Creek** (#182); **Disney's Animal Kingdom Lodge** (#186). Criteria: service; location; rooms; food; and value. *Travel & Leisure, "T+L 500, The World's Best Hotels 2012"*

The Orlando-Kissimmee-Sanford, FL metro area is home to two of the best hotels in the U.S. according to *Condé Nast Traveler*: **Waldorf Astoria Orlando** (#17); **Grand Bohemian Hotel** (#87). The selections are based on over 25,000 responses to the magazine's annual Readers' Choice Survey. *Condé Nast Traveler, "2011 Readers' Choice Awards"*

EVENT SITES

Major Stadiums, Arenas, and Auditoriums

Name	Max. Capacity
Amway Arena	17,282
Bob Carr Performing Arts Centre	2,518
Bright House Networks Stadium	45,301
The Florida Citrus Bowl	70,000
Tinker Field	5,000
U.C.F. Arena at Knights Plaza	10,000

Source: Original research

Convention Centers

Name	Overall Space (sq. ft.)	Exhibit Space (sq. ft.)	Meeting Space (sq. ft.)	Meeting Rooms
Orange County Convention Center	n/a	n/a	2,100,000	74

Note: n/a not available
Source: Original research

Living Environment

COST OF LIVING

Cost of Living Index

Composite Index	Groceries	Housing	Utilities	Trans-portation	Health Care	Misc. Goods/ Services
97.3	100.2	79.7	107.8	99.2	94.2	108.1

Note: U.S. = 100; Figures cover the Orlando FL urban area.
Source: The Council for Community and Economic Research, ACCRA Cost of Living Index, 2011

Grocery Prices

Area[1]	T-Bone Steak ($/pound)	Frying Chicken ($/pound)	Whole Milk ($/half gal.)	Eggs ($/dozen)	Orange Juice ($/64 oz.)	Coffee ($/11.5 oz.)
City[2]	9.03	1.25	2.65	1.71	3.28	4.27
Avg.	9.25	1.18	2.22	1.66	3.19	4.40
Min.	6.70	0.88	1.31	0.95	2.46	2.94
Max.	14.30	2.16	3.50	3.18	4.75	6.83

*Note: (1) Values for the local area are compared with the average, minimum and maximum values for all 335 areas in the Cost of Living Index; (2) Figures cover the Orlando FL urban area; **T-Bone Steak** (price per pound); **Frying Chicken** (price per pound, whole fryer); **Whole Milk** (half gallon carton); **Eggs** (price per dozen, Grade A, large); **Orange Juice** (64 oz. Tropicana or Florida Natural); **Coffee** (11.5 oz. can, vacuum-packed, Maxwell House, Hills Bros, or Folgers).*
Source: The Council for Community and Economic Research, ACCRA Cost of Living Index, 2011

Housing and Utility Costs

Area[1]	New Home Price ($)	Apartment Rent ($/month)	All Electric ($/month)	Part Electric ($/month)	Other Energy ($/month)	Telephone ($/month)
City[2]	209,687	817	179.04	-	-	28.95
Avg.	285,990	839	163.23	89.00	77.52	26.92
Min.	188,005	460	125.58	45.39	33.89	17.98
Max.	1,197,028	3,244	339.16	181.97	348.69	40.01

*Note: (1) Values for the local area are compared with the average, minimum and maximum values for all 335 areas in the Cost of Living Index; (2) Figures cover the Orlando FL urban area; **New Home Price** (2,400 sf living area, 8,000 sf lot, in urban area with full utilities); **Apartment Rent** (950 sf 2 bedroom/1.5 or 2 bath, unfurnished, excluding all utilities except water); **All Electric** (average monthly cost for an all-electric home); **Part Electric** (average monthly cost for a part-electric home); **Other Energy** (average monthly cost for natural gas, fuel oil, coal, wood, and any other forms of energy except electricity); **Telephone** (price includes basic monthly rate for a private residential line plus additional local usage charges incurred by a family of four).*
Source: The Council for Community and Economic Research, ACCRA Cost of Living Index, 2011

Health Care, Transportation, and Other Costs

Area[1]	Doctor ($/visit)	Dentist ($/visit)	Optometrist ($/visit)	Gasoline ($/gallon)	Beauty Salon ($/visit)	Men's Shirt ($)
City[2]	77.70	76.16	71.75	3.48	41.54	35.81
Avg.	93.88	81.72	90.54	3.48	32.65	25.06
Min.	60.00	55.33	53.66	3.18	19.78	13.44
Max.	154.98	145.97	183.72	4.31	63.21	46.00

*Note: (1) Values for the local area are compared with the average, minimum and maximum values for all 335 areas in the Cost of Living Index; (2) Figures cover the Orlando FL urban area; **Doctor** (general practitioners routine exam of an established patient); **Dentist** (adult teeth cleaning and periodic oral examination); **Optometrist** (full vision eye exam for established adult patient); **Gasoline** (one gallon regular unleaded, national brand, including all taxes, cash price at self-service pump if available); **Beauty Salon** (woman's shampoo, trim, and blow-dry); **Men's Shirt** (cotton/polyester dress shirt, pinpoint weave, long sleeves).*
Source: The Council for Community and Economic Research, ACCRA Cost of Living Index, 2011

HOUSING

House Price Index (HPI)

Area	National Ranking[2]	Quarterly Change (%)	One-Year Change (%)	Five-Year Change (%)
MSA[1]	281	0.93	-7.54	-45.20
U.S.[3]	-	-0.10	-2.43	-19.16

Note: The HPI is a weighted repeat sales index. It measures average price changes in repeat sales or refinancings on the same properties. This information is obtained by reviewing repeat mortgage transactions on single-family properties whose mortgages have been purchased or securitized by Fannie Mae or Freddie Mac in January 1975; (1) Metropolitan/Micropolitan Statistical Area—see Appendix B for areas included; (2) Rankings are based on annual percentage change for all metro areas containing at least 15,000 transactions over the last 10 years and ranges from 1 to 306; (3) figures based on a weighted average of Census Division estimates using a purchase only index; all figures are for the period ending December 31, 2011
Source: Federal Housing Finance Agency, House Price Index, February 23, 2012

House Price Valuations

Area	Q4 2005		Q4 2006		Q4 2007		Q4 2008		Q4 2009	
	Price ($000)	Over-valuation	Price ($000)	Over-valuation	Price ($000)	Over-valuation	Price ($000)	Over-valuation	Price ($000)	Over-valuation
MSA[1]	205.6	28.6	220.5	29.0	203.9	17.6	156.0	-9.5	135.3	-20.4

Note: Figures show the percentage of over- or under-valuation of single family homes relative to statistically normal house values (e.g. a value of 23.6 indicates that house values are 23.6% overvalued). Statistically normal house values are based on house prices, interest rates, household incomes, population densities, and any historical premiums or discounts metropolitan areas have exhibited over time; (1) Figures cover the Orlando-Kissimmee-Sanford, FL - see Appendix B for areas included
Source: Global Insight/PNC Financial Services Group, House Prices in America: 4th Quarter 2009 Update

Median Single-Family Home Prices

Area	2009	2010	2011[p]	Percent Change 2010 to 2011
MSA[1]	147.4	134.7	124.9	-7.3
U.S. Average	172.1	173.1	166.2	-4.0

Note: Figures are median sales prices of existing single-family homes in thousands of dollars; (p) preliminary; n/a not available; (1) Metropolitan Statistical Area—see Appendix B for areas included
Source: National Association of Realtors, Median Sales Price of Existing Single-Family Homes for Metropolitan Areas, 4th Quarter 2011

Affordability Index of Existing Single-Family Homes

Area	2009	2010	2011[p]	Percent Change 2010 to 2011
MSA[1]	112.8	130.0	146.1	12.4

Note: The housing affordability index measures whether or not a typical family could qualify for a mortgage loan on a typical home. The higher the index, the greater the household purchasing power. An index of 100 is defined as the point where a median-income household has exactly enough income to qualify for the purchase of a median-priced existing single-family home, assuming a 20 percent downpayment and 25 percent of gross income devoted to mortgage principal and interest payments; (p) preliminary; n/a not available; (1) Metropolitan Statistical Area—see Appendix B for areas included
Source: National Association of Realtors, Affordability Index of Existing Single-Family Homes, 2011

Median Apartment Condo-Coop Home Prices

Area	2009	2010	2011[p]	Percent Change 2010 to 2011
MSA[1]	n/a	n/a	n/a	n/a
U.S. Average	175.6	171.7	165.1	-3.8

Note: Figures are median sales prices of existing apartment condo-coop homes in thousands of dollars; (p) preliminary; n/a not available; (1) Metropolitan Statistical Area—see Appendix B for areas included
Source: National Association of Realtors, Median Sales Price of Existing Apartment Condo-Coop Homes for Metropolitan Areas, 4th Quarter 2011

Year Housing Structure Built

Area	2005 or Later	2000 -2004	1990 -1999	1980 -1989	1970 -1979	1960 -1969	1950 -1959	Before 1950	Median Year
City	7.7	15.0	15.8	19.8	13.8	8.9	10.9	8.1	1984
MSA[1]	8.2	17.6	21.3	22.5	14.1	7.1	5.9	3.3	1989
U.S.	5.0	8.6	14.0	14.1	16.3	11.3	11.2	19.6	1975

Note: Figures are percentages except for Median Year; (1) Figures cover the Orlando-Kissimmee-Sanford, FL Metropolitan Statistical Area—see Appendix B for areas included
Source: U.S. Census Bureau, 2008-2010 American Community Survey 3-Year Estimates

HEALTH

Health Risk Data

Category	MSA[1] (%)	U.S. (%)
Adults who have been told they have high blood pressure[2]	27.3	28.7
Adults who have been told they have high blood cholesterol[2]	35.3	37.5
Adults who have been told they have diabetes[3]	11.3	8.7
Adults who have been told they have arthritis[2]	24.3	26.0
Adults who have been told they currently have asthma	8.6	9.1
Adults who are current smokers	15.8	17.3
Adults who are heavy drinkers[4]	5.2	5.0
Adults who are binge drinkers[5]	13.8	15.1
Adults who are overweight (BMI 25.0 - 29.9)	37.4	36.2
Adults who are obese (BMI 30.0 - 99.8)	28.3	27.5
Adults who participated in any physical activities in the past month	74.7	76.1
Adults 50+ who have ever had a sigmoidoscopy or colonoscopy	66.0	65.2
Women aged 40+ who have had a mammogram within the past two years	72.5	75.2
Men aged 40+ who have had a PSA test within the past two years	62.4	53.2
Adults aged 65+ who have had flu shot within the past year	61.4	67.5
Adults aged 18–64 who have any kind of health care coverage	77.7	82.2

Note: Data as of 2010 unless otherwise noted; (1) Figures cover the Orlando-Kissimmee, FL Metropolitan Statistical Area—see Appendix B for areas included; (2) Data as of 2009; (3) Figures do not include pregnancy-related, borderline, or pre-diabetes; (4) Heavy drinkers are classified as males having more than two drinks per day or females having more than one drink per day; (5) Binge drinkers are classified as males having five or more drinks on one occasion or females having four or more drinks on one occasion
Source: Centers for Disease Control and Prevention, Behaviorial Risk Factor Surveillance System, SMART: Selected Metropolitan/Micropolitan Area Risk Trends, 2009, 2010

Mortality Rates for the Top 10 Causes of Death in the U.S.

ICD-10[a] Sub-Chapter	ICD-10[a] Code	Age-Adjusted Mortality Rate[1] per 100,000 population County[2]	U.S.
Malignant neoplasms	C00-C97	173.5	175.6
Ischaemic heart diseases	I20-I25	111.4	121.6
Other forms of heart disease	I30-I51	41.8	48.6
Chronic lower respiratory diseases	J40-J47	42.6	42.3
Cerebrovascular diseases	I60-I69	37.0	40.6
Organic, including symptomatic, mental disorders	F01-F09	25.0	26.7
Other degenerative diseases of the nervous system	G30-G31	23.9	24.7
Other external causes of accidental injury	W00-X59	19.9	24.4
Diabetes mellitus	E10-E14	22.8	21.7
Hypertensive diseases	I10-I15	16.9	18.2

Note: (a) ICD-10 = International Classification of Diseases 10th Revision; (1) Mortality rates are a three year average covering 2007-2009; (2) Figures cover Orange County
Source: Centers for Disease Control and Prevention, National Center for Health Statistics. Underlying Cause of Death 1999-2009 on CDC WONDER Online Database, released 2012. Data for year 2009 are compiled from the Multiple Cause of Death File 2009, Series 20 No. 2O, 2012, Data for year 2008 are compiled from the Multiple Cause of Death File 2008, Series 20 No. 2N, 2011, Data for year 2007 are compiled from Multiple Cause of Death File 2007, Series 20 No. 2M, 2010.

Mortality Rates for Selected Causes of Death

ICD-10[a] Sub-Chapter	ICD-10[a] Code	Age-Adjusted Mortality Rate[1] per 100,000 population	
		County[2]	U.S.
Assault	X85-Y09	9.0	5.7
Human immunodeficiency virus (HIV) disease	B20-B24	7.5	3.3
Influenza and pneumonia	J09-J18	11.4	16.4
Intentional self-harm	X60-X84	11.7	11.5
Malnutrition	E40-E46	*0.0	0.8
Obesity and other hyperalimentation	E65-E68	0.9	1.6
Transport accidents	V01-V99	14.5	13.7
Viral hepatitis	B15-B19	2.0	2.2

Note: (a) ICD-10 = International Classification of Diseases 10th Revision; (1) Mortality rates are a three year average covering 2007-2009; (2) Figures cover Orange County; (*) Unreliable data as per CDC
Source: Centers for Disease Control and Prevention, National Center for Health Statistics. Underlying Cause of Death 1999-2009 on CDC WONDER Online Database, released 2012. Data for year 2009 are compiled from the Multiple Cause of Death File 2009, Series 20 No. 2O, 2012, Data for year 2008 are compiled from the Multiple Cause of Death File 2008, Series 20 No. 2N, 2011, Data for year 2007 are compiled from Multiple Cause of Death File 2007, Series 20 No. 2M, 2010.

Distribution of Physicians and Dentists

Area[1]	Dentists[2]	D.O.[3]	M.D.[4]				
			Total	Family/General Practice	Pediatrics	Medical Specialties	Surgical Specialties
Local (number)	427	206	2,124	264	192	820	462
Local (rate[5])	4.0	1.9	19.7	2.5	1.8	7.6	4.3
U.S. (rate[5])	4.5	1.9	18.3	2.5	1.4	6.8	4.1

Note: Data as of 2008 unless noted; (1) Local data covers Orange County; (2) Data as of 2007; (3) Doctor of Osteopathic Medicine; (4) Includes active, non-federal, patient-care, office-based Doctors of Medicine; (5) rate per 10,000 population
Source: Area Resource File (ARF). 2009-2010 Release. U.S. Department of Health and Human Services, Health Resources and Services Administration, Bureau of Health Professions, Rockville, MD, August 2010

Best Hospitals

According to *U.S. News*, the Orlando-Kissimmee-Sanford, FL is home to one of the best hospitals in the U.S.: **Florida Hospital** (2 specialties). The hospital listed was highly ranked in at least one adult specialty. *U.S. News Online, "America's Best Hospitals 2011-12"*

According to *U.S. News*, the Orlando-Kissimmee-Sanford, FL is home to one of the best children's hospitals in the U.S.: **Arnold Palmer Medical Center** (2 specialties). The hospital listed was highly ranked in at least one pediatric specialty. *U.S. News Online, "America's Best Children's Hospitals 2011-12"*

EDUCATION

Public School District Statistics

District Name	Schls	Pupils	Pupil/Teacher Ratio	Minority Pupils[1] (%)	Free Lunch Eligible[2] (%)	IEP[3] (%)
Orange	240	173,259	16.2	67.2	42.2	13.1

Note: Table includes school districts with 2,000 or more students; (1) Percentage of students that are not non-Hispanic white; (2) Percentage of students that are eligible for the free lunch program; (3) Percentage of students that have an Individualized Education Program.
Source: U.S. Department of Education, National Center for Education Statistics, Common Core of Data, Local Education Agency (School District) Universe Survey: School Year 2009-2010; U.S. Department of Education, National Center for Education Statistics, Common Core of Data, Public Elementary/Secondary School Universe Survey: School Year 2009-2010

Highest Level of Education

Area	Less than H.S.	H.S. Diploma	Some College, No Deg.	Associate Degree	Bachelors Degree	Masters Degree	Profess. School Degree	Doctorate Degree
City	12.8	26.7	19.9	9.5	21.3	6.8	2.1	0.9
MSA[1]	12.4	29.0	21.7	9.6	18.5	6.3	1.6	0.8
U.S.	14.7	28.4	21.3	7.6	17.6	7.2	1.9	1.2

Note: Figures cover persons age 25 and over; (1) Figures cover the Orlando-Kissimmee-Sanford, FL Metropolitan Statistical Area—see Appendix B for areas included
Source: U.S. Census Bureau, 2008-2010 American Community Survey 3-Year Estimates

Educational Attainment by Race

Area	High School Graduate or Higher (%)					Bachelor's Degree or Higher (%)				
	Total	White	Black	Asian	Hisp.[2]	Total	White	Black	Asian	Hisp.[2]
City	87.2	91.6	79.2	82.8	78.1	31.1	38.2	15.8	42.5	18.9
MSA[1]	87.6	89.5	81.3	86.3	79.2	27.3	28.8	18.2	44.1	18.4
U.S.	85.3	87.5	81.4	85.5	61.6	28.0	29.3	17.8	50.2	13.0

Note: Figures shown cover persons 25 years old and over; (1) Figures cover the Orlando-Kissimmee-Sanford, FL Metropolitan Statistical Area—see Appendix B for areas included; (2) People of Hispanic origin can be of any race
Source: U.S. Census Bureau, 2008-2010 American Community Survey 3-Year Estimates

School Enrollment by Grade and Control

Area	Preschool (%)		Kindergarten (%)		Grades 1 - 4 (%)		Grades 5 - 8 (%)		Grades 9 - 12 (%)	
	Public	Private	Public	Private	Public	Private	Public	Private	Public	Private
City	41.4	58.6	85.3	14.7	88.5	11.5	88.0	12.0	88.3	11.7
MSA[1]	44.9	55.1	82.3	17.7	87.4	12.6	89.1	10.9	90.2	9.8
U.S.	55.4	44.6	87.1	12.9	89.4	10.6	89.5	10.5	90.4	9.6

Note: Figures shown cover persons 3 years old and over; (1) Figures cover the Orlando-Kissimmee-Sanford, FL Metropolitan Statistical Area—see Appendix B for areas included
Source: U.S. Census Bureau, 2008-2010 American Community Survey 3-Year Estimates

Average Salaries of Public School Classroom Teachers

Area	2010-11		2011-12		Percent Change 2010-11 to 2011-12	Percent Change 2001-02 to 2011-12
	Dollars	Rank[1]	Dollars	Rank[1]		
Florida	45,732	45	46,232	46	1.09	17.70
U.S. Average	55,623	-	56,643	-	1.83	26.8

Note: (1) State rank ranges from 1 to 51 where 1 indicates highest salary.
Source: National Education Association, Rankings & Estimates: Rankings of the States 2011 and Estimates of School Statistics 2012, December 2011

Higher Education

Four-Year Colleges			Two-Year Colleges			Medical Schools[1]	Law Schools[2]	Voc/ Tech[3]
Public	Private Non-profit	Private For-profit	Public	Private Non-profit	Private For-profit			
2	2	5	2	0	9	1	2	1

Note: Figures cover institutions located within the city limits and include main campuses only; (1) includes schools accredited by the Liaison Committee on Medical Education and the American Osteopathic Association's Commission on Osteopathic College Accreditation; (2) includes American Bar Association-accredited law schools; (3) includes all schools with programs that are less than 2 years.
Source: National Center for Education Statistics, Integrated Postsecondary Education System (IPEDS) Peer Analysis System, 2011-12; Association of American Medical Colleges, Member List, April 23, 2012; American Osteopathic Association, Member List, April 23, 2012; Law School Admission Council, Official Guide to ABA-Approved Law Schools Online, April 23, 2012

According to *U.S. News & World Report,* the Orlando-Kissimmee-Sanford, FL is home to one of the best national universities in the U.S.: **University of Central Florida** (#177). The indicators used to capture academic quality fall into a number of categories: assessment by administrators at peer institutions; retention of students; faculty resources; student selectivity; financial resources; alumni giving; high school counselor ratings of colleges; and graduation rate.*U.S. News & World Report, "America's Best Colleges 2012"*

According to *Forbes,* the Orlando-Kissimmee-Sanford, FL is home to one of the best business schools in the U.S.: **Rollins (Crummer)** (#46). The rankings are based on the return on investment that graduates of the Class of 2006 received (median salary five years after graduation). *Forbes, "Best Business Schools," August 3, 2011*

PRESIDENTIAL ELECTION

2008 Presidential Election Results

Area	Obama	McCain	Nader	Other
Orange County	59.0	40.4	0.2	0.4
U.S.	52.9	45.6	0.6	0.9

Note: Results are percentages and may not add to 100% due to rounding
Source: Dave Leip's Atlas of U.S. Presidential Elections, www.uselectionatlas.org

EMPLOYERS

Major Employers

Company Name	Industry
Adventist Health System/Sunbelt	General medical and surgical hospitals
Airtran Airways	Air passenger carrier, scheduled
Central Florida Health Alliance	Hospital management
Children & Families, Florida Department	Individual and family services
Cnl Lifestyle Properties	Real estate agents and managers
Connexions	Communication services, nec
Florida Hospital Medical Center	General medical and surgical hospitals
Gaylord Palms Resort & Conv Ctr	Hotel franchised
Leesburg Regional Medical Center	General medical and surgical hospitals
Lockheed Martin Corporation	Aircraft
Marriott International	Hotels and motels
Orlando Health	General medical and surgical hospitals
Rosen 9939	Hotels
Sea World of Florida	Theme park, amusement
Sears Termite & Pest Control	Pest control in structures
Siemens Energy	Power plant construction
Universal City Florida Partners	Amusement parks
University of Central Florida	Colleges and universities
Winter Park Healthcare Group, Ltd	Hospital affiliated with ama residency

Note: Companies shown are located within the Orlando-Kissimmee-Sanford, FL metropolitan area.
Source: Hoovers.com, data extracted April 25 2012

Best Companies to Work For

Darden Restaurants, headquartered in Orlando, is among "The 100 Best Companies to Work For." To pick the 100 Best Companies to Work For, *Fortune* partnered with the Great Place to Work Institute. Two hundred eighty firms participated in this year's survey. Two-thirds of a company's score is based on the results of the Institute's Trust Index survey, which is sent to a random sample of employees from each company. The questions related to attitudes about management's credibility, job satisfaction, and camaraderie. The other third of the scoring is based on the company's responses to the Institute's Culture Audit, which includes detailed questions about pay and benefit programs, and a series of open-ended questions about hiring practices, internal communication, training, recognition programs, and diversity efforts. Any company that is at least five years old with more than 1,000 U.S. employees is eligible. *Fortune, "The 100 Best Companies to Work For," February 6, 2012*

PUBLIC SAFETY

Crime Rate

Area	All Crimes	Violent Crimes				Property Crimes		
		Murder	Forcible Rape	Robbery	Aggrav. Assault	Burglary	Larceny -Theft	Motor Vehicle Theft
City	7,550.9	7.5	47.0	279.7	737.2	1,671.4	4,311.4	496.6
Suburbs[1]	3,783.3	4.5	31.2	126.8	393.0	918.9	2,098.4	210.5
Metro[2]	4,208.2	4.8	33.0	144.1	431.8	1,003.8	2,348.0	242.7
U.S.	3,345.5	4.8	27.5	119.1	252.3	699.6	2,003.5	238.8

Note: Figures are crimes per 100,000 population; (1) All areas within the metro area that are located outside the city limits; (2) Metropolitan Statistical Area—see Appendix B for areas included
Source: FBI Uniform Crime Reports, 2010

Hate Crimes

Area	Number of Quarters Reported	Bias Motivation				
		Race	Religion	Sexual Orientation	Ethnicity	Disability
City	4	4	0	2	1	0

Source: Federal Bureau of Investigation, Hate Crime Statistics 2010

Identity Theft Consumer Complaints

Area	Complaints	Complaints per 100,000 Population	Rank[2]
MSA[1]	2,989	147.1	12
U.S.	279,156	90.4	-

Note: (1) Metropolitan Statistical Area—see Appendix B for areas included; (2) Rank ranges from 1 to 384 where 1 indicates greatest number of identity theft complaints per 100,000 population
Source: Federal Trade Commission, Consumer Sentinel Network Data Book for January–December 2011

Fraud and Other Consumer Complaints

Area	Complaints	Complaints per 100,000 Population	Rank[2]
MSA[1]	10,947	538.6	103
U.S.	1,533,924	496.8	-

Note: (1) Metropolitan Statistical Area—see Appendix B for areas included; (2) Rank ranges from 1 to 384 where 1 indicates greatest number of fraud and other complaints per 100,000 population
Source: Federal Trade Commission, Consumer Sentinel Network Data Book for January–December 2011

RECREATION

Culture

Dance[1]	Theatre[1]	Instrumental Music[1]	Vocal Music[1]	Series/ Festivals	Museums	Zoos and Aquariums[2]
2	5	3	1	1	6	3

Note: (1) Number of professional performing groups; (2) AZA-accredited
Source: The Grey House Performing Arts Directory, 2011-2012; Official Museum Directory, 2011; American Association of Museums, AAM Member Museums, April 2012; Association of Zoos & Aquariums, AZA Member Zoos & Aquariums, April 2012

Professional Sports Teams

Team Name	League
Orlando Magic	National Basketball Association (NBA)

Note: Includes teams located in the Orlando metro area.
Source: Original research

CLIMATE

Average and Extreme Temperatures

Temperature	Jan	Feb	Mar	Apr	May	Jun	Jul	Aug	Sep	Oct	Nov	Dec	Yr.
Extreme High (°F)	86	89	90	95	100	100	99	100	98	95	89	90	100
Average High (°F)	70	72	77	82	87	90	91	91	89	83	78	72	82
Average Temp. (°F)	59	62	67	72	77	81	82	82	81	75	68	62	72
Average Low (°F)	48	51	56	60	66	71	73	74	72	66	58	51	62
Extreme Low (°F)	19	29	25	38	51	53	64	65	57	44	32	20	19

Note: Figures cover the years 1952-1990
Source: National Climatic Data Center, International Station Meteorological Climate Summary, 9/96

Average Precipitation/Snowfall/Humidity

Precip./Humidity	Jan	Feb	Mar	Apr	May	Jun	Jul	Aug	Sep	Oct	Nov	Dec	Yr.
Avg. Precip. (in.)	2.3	2.8	3.4	2.0	3.2	7.0	7.2	5.8	5.8	2.7	3.5	2.0	47.7
Avg. Snowfall (in.)	Tr	0	0	0	0	0	0	0	0	0	0	0	Tr
Avg. Rel. Hum. 7am (%)	87	87	88	87	88	89	90	92	92	89	89	87	89
Avg. Rel. Hum. 4pm (%)	53	51	49	47	51	61	65	66	66	59	56	55	57

Note: Figures cover the years 1952-1990; Tr = Trace amounts (<0.05 in. of rain; <0.5 in. of snow)
Source: National Climatic Data Center, International Station Meteorological Climate Summary, 9/96

Weather Conditions

Temperature			Daytime Sky			Precipitation		
32°F & below	45°F & below	90°F & above	Clear	Partly cloudy	Cloudy	0.01 inch or more precip.	0.1 inch or more snow/ice	Thunder-storms
3	35	90	76	208	81	115	0	80

Note: Figures are average number of days per year and cover the years 1952-1990
Source: National Climatic Data Center, International Station Meteorological Climate Summary, 9/96

HAZARDOUS WASTE

Superfund Sites

Orlando has two hazardous waste sites on the EPA's Superfund Final National Priorities List: **Chevron Chemical Co. (Ortho Division); City Industries, Inc.** *U.S. Environmental Protection Agency, Final National Priorities List, April 17, 2012*

AIR & WATER QUALITY

Air Quality Index

Area	Percent of Days when Air Quality was...[2]					AQI Statistics[2]	
	Good	Moderate	Unhealthy for Sensitive Groups	Unhealthy	Very Unhealthy	Maximum	Median
Area[1]	87.9	10.1	1.9	0.0	0.0	111	36

Note: Air Quality Index (AQI) is an index for reporting daily air quality. EPA calculates the AQI for five major air pollutants regulated by the Clean Air Act: ground-level ozone, particle pollution (aka particulate matter), carbon monoxide, sulfur dioxide, and nitrogen dioxide. The AQI runs from 0 to 500. The higher the AQI value, the greater the level of air pollution and the greater the health concern. There are six AQI categories: "Good" AQI is between 0 and 50. Air quality is considered satisfactory; "Moderate" AQI is between 51 and 100. Air quality is acceptable; "Unhealthy for Sensitive Groups" When AQI values are between 101 and 150, members of sensitive groups may experience health effects; "Unhealthy" When AQI values are between 151 and 200 everyone may begin to experience health effects; "Very Unhealthy" AQI values between 201 and 300 trigger a health alert; "Hazardous" AQI values over 300 trigger warnings of emergency conditions (not shown); (1) Data covers Orange County; (2) Based on 365 days with AQI data in 2011.
Source: U.S. Environmental Protection Agency, AirData Report, 2011

Air Quality Index Pollutants

Area	Percent of Days when AQI Pollutant was...[2]					
	Carbon Monoxide	Nitrogen Dioxide	Ozone	Sulfur Dioxide	Particulate Matter 2.5	Particulate Matter 10
Area[1]	0.0	0.5	68.8	0.0	30.7	0.0

Note: The Air Quality Index (AQI) is an index for reporting daily air quality. EPA calculates the AQI for five major air pollutants regulated by the Clean Air Act: ground-level ozone, particle pollution (also known as particulate matter), carbon monoxide, sulfur dioxide, and nitrogen dioxide. The AQI runs from 0 to 500. The higher the AQI value, the greater the level of air pollution and the greater the health concern; (1) Data covers Orange County; (2) Based on 365 days with AQI data in 2011.
Source: U.S. Environmental Protection Agency, AirData Report, 2011

Air Quality Index Trends

Area	Trend Sites (days)								All Sites (days)
	2003	2004	2005	2006	2007	2008	2009	2010	2010
MSA[1]	8	6	10	8	11	2	1	2	2

Note: Figures are the number of days the AQI value exceeded 100 in a given year. An AQI value greater than 100 indicates that air quality would have been in the unhealthful range on that day. Data from exceptional events are included. These counts are presented in two ways. First, the counts are based on sites having an adequate record of monitoring data during the trend period (trend sites). These counts represent the relative change in the number of days with AQI values greater than 100. In the last column, the counts are based on all sites with data in the most recent year (because it is possible for a site to have data in the most recent year but not enough data to be a trend site); (1) Data covers the Orlando-Kissimmee-Sanford, FL—see Appendix B for areas included
Source: U.S. Environmental Protection Agency, Air Quality Index Information, "Number of Days with Air Quality Index Values Greater than 100 at Trend Sites, 2000-2010, and at All Sites in 2010"

Maximum Air Pollutant Concentrations: Particulate Matter, Ozone, CO and Lead

	Particulate Matter 10 (ug/m³)	Particulate Matter 2.5 Wtd AM (ug/m³)	Particulate Matter 2.5 24-Hr (ug/m³)	Ozone (ppm)	Carbon Monoxide (ppm)	Lead (ug/m³)
MSA[1] Level	46	7.6	14	0.071	1	n/a
NAAQS[2]	150	15	35	0.075	9	0.15
Met NAAQS[2]	Yes	Yes	Yes	Yes	Yes	n/a

Note: Data from exceptional events are not included; (1) Data covers the Orlando-Kissimmee-Sanford, FL—see Appendix B for areas included; (2) National Ambient Air Quality Standards; ppm = parts per million; ug/m³ = micrograms per cubic meter; n/a not available
Concentrations: Particulate Matter 10 (coarse particulate)—highest second maximum 24-hour concentration; Particulate Matter 2.5 Wtd AM (fine particulate)—highest weighted annual mean concentration; Particulate Matter 2.5 24-Hour (fine particulate)—highest 98th percentile 24-hour concentration; Ozone—highest fourth daily maximum 8-hour concentration; Carbon Monoxide—highest second maximum non-overlapping 8-hour concentration; Lead—maximum running 3-month average
Source: U.S. Environmental Protection Agency, CBSA Factbook 2010, Air Quality Statistics by City, 2010

Maximum Air Pollutant Concentrations: Nitrogen Dioxide and Sulfur Dioxide

	Nitrogen Dioxide AM (ppb)	Nitrogen Dioxide 1-Hr (ppb)	Sulfur Dioxide AM (ppb)	Sulfur Dioxide 1-Hr (ppb)	Sulfur Dioxide 24-Hr (ppb)
MSA[1] Level	5.627	40	0.157	7	2.2
NAAQS[2]	53	100	30	75	140
Met NAAQS[2]	Yes	Yes	Yes	Yes	Yes

Note: Data from exceptional events are not included; (1) Data covers the Orlando-Kissimmee-Sanford, FL—see Appendix B for areas included; (2) National Ambient Air Quality Standards; ppb = parts per billion; n/a not available
Concentrations: Nitrogen Dioxide AM—highest arithmetic mean concentration; Nitrogen Dioxide 1-Hr—highest 98th percentile 1-hour daily maximum concentration; Sulfur Dioxide AM—highest annual mean concentration; Sulfur Dioxide 1-Hr—highest 99th percentile 1-hour daily maximum concentration; Sulfur Dioxide 24-Hr—highest second maximum 24-hour concentration
Source: U.S. Environmental Protection Agency, CBSA Factbook 2010, Air Quality Statistics by City, 2010

Drinking Water

Water System Name	Pop. Served	Primary Water Source Type	Violations[1] Health Based	Violations[1] Monitoring/ Reporting
Orlando Utilities Commission	426,452	Ground	0	0

Note: (1) Based on violation data from January 1, 2011 to December 31, 2011 (includes unresolved violations from earlier years)
Source: U.S. Environmental Protection Agency, Office of Ground Water and Drinking Water, Safe Drinking Water Information System (based on data extracted April 18, 2012)

Pembroke Pines, Florida

Background

Once a dairy pasture, Pembroke Pines was incorporated in 1960 in a vote taken in a resident's garage when the town was less than one square mile in size. Over the years, the residential city grew in a westward direction—away from the North Perry Airport and the South Florida State Hospital—and received an unexpected population boost after Hurricane Andrew hit Homestead, Florida in 1992. According to the city's history, numerous displaced residents headed north to Pembroke Pines and its new subdivisions then under construction.

Located on Florida's east coast just southwest of Fort Lauderdale and inland from Hollywood and the beaches, Pembroke Pines is the second most populous city in Broward County. In 2008 and 2010, it was named first in Florida in BusinessWeek's Best Places in the United States to Raise Your Kids. The city's charter school system of three elementary, two middle, and one high school received recognition when Pembroke Pines Charter Middle School was given a Blue Ribbon School designation from the U.S. Dept. of Education in 2009.

A residential community boasting populations of retirees as well as young families, the city is easily accessible from land, sea and air. Whole Foods Markets opened a new store here in 2012, and major businesses and agencies in the city include Claire's Stores Inc., Cintas Corporation, Bergeron Land Development, Broward College, the US Dept. of Homeland Security, the US Postal Services, Nautilus Corporation, and Homan Enterprises. Memorial Healthcare System, the South Florida healthcare provider, has a significant presence in Pembroke Pines with Memorial Hospital West, Memorial Hospital Pembroke, an urgent care center, a same day surgery center, a fitness center, a rehabilitation center, and Memorial Manor—a nursing home care center. Keiser University, with its career-focused programs, has a campus here.

Pembroke Pines has two business parks, the Bergeron Park of Commerce (with its Bergeron Business Plaza) and Chapel Trail Corporate Park.

The city provides abundant recreational opportunities such as the Pembroke Lakes Golf and Racquet Club, replete with restaurant and pro shop. In addition, the city operates nearly twenty parks, including the West Pines Soccer Park & Nature Preserve, home to a sprint soccer league and summer soccer camp. The Walter C. Young Resource Center offers a wealth of recreational amenities, from paddleball and tennis to track and a gymnasium (and a co-ed adult kickball league). At Fletcher Park—home to softball fields, and a batting cage—the arts are on deck with music classes and an art camp.

Culturally, the residents of Pembroke Pines have access to the multitude of offerings around Broward County as well as those of Miami-Dade. Closer to home, Studio 18 is a unique space that offers exhibitions, lectures classrooms, workshops, and studio space to juried artists. Broward County's River of Grass ArtsPark in Pembroke Pines also includes the 450-seat Susan B. Katz Theater of the Performing Arts, where shows such as The Producers are performed.

Pembroke Pines sees its hottest temperatures and wettest days in June, July and August, while January—its coolest month- averages a pleasant 75 degrees.

Rankings

Business/Finance Rankings

- The Miami metro area was identified as one of 10 places with the fastest-growing wages in America. The area ranked #2. Criteria: private-sector wage growth between the 4th quarter of 2010 and the 4th quarter of 2011. *PayScale, "The 10 Cities with the Fastest-Growing Wages in America," January 12, 2012*

- The Miami metro area was identified as one of the most debt-ridden places in America by credit reporting agency Equifax. The metro area was ranked #4. Criteria: proportion of average yearly income owed to credit card companies. *Equifax, "The Most Debt-Ridden Cities in America," February 23, 2012*

- Experian ranked the top 20 major U.S. metropolitan areas by average debt per consumer. The Miami metro area was ranked #19. Criteria: average debt per consumer. Debt for this study includes credit cards, auto loans and personal loans. It does not include mortgages. *Experian, May 13, 2010*

- *American City Business Journals* ranked America's 261 largest cities in terms of their resident's wealth. Pembroke Pines ranked #66. Criteria: per capita income; median household income; percentage of households with annual incomes of $200,000 or more; median home value. *American City Business Journals, "Where the Money Is: America's Wealth Centers," August 18, 2008*

- The Fort Lauderdale metro area appeared on the Milken Institute "2011 Best Performing Metros" list. Rank: #172 out of 200 large metro areas. Criteria: job growth; wage and salary growth; high-tech output growth. *Milken Institute, "2011 Best Performing Metros"*

- The Fort Lauderdale metro area was selected as one of the best cities for entrepreneurs in America by *Inc. Magazine*. Criteria: job-growth data for 335 metro areas was analyzed for: recent growth trend; mid-term growth; long-term trend; current year growth. The Fort Lauderdale metro area ranked #27 among large metro areas and #144 overall. *Inc. Magazine, "The Best Cities for Doing Business," July 2008*

- Fort Lauderdale was ranked #115 out of 145 regions worldwide in terms of its "Knowledge Competitiveness Index." The index attempts to measure the knowledge-based development taking place throughout the world and is based on 19 measures of economic performance that indicate a region's ability to translate its knowledge capacity into economic value. *Centre for International Competitiveness, World Knowledge Competitiveness Index 2008*

- *Forbes* ranked the 200 most populous metro areas in the U.S. in terms of the "Best Places for Business and Careers." The Fort Lauderdale metro area was ranked #184. Criteria: costs (business and living); job growth (past and projected); income growth; educational attainment; projected economic growth; crime; cultural and recreational opportunities; net migration patterns; number of highly ranked colleges. *Forbes, "Best Places for Business and Careers," June 2011*

Children/Family Rankings

- The Fort Lauderdale metro area was selected as one of the "Best Cities for Relocating Families" by Worldwide ERC and Primacy Relocation. The 2008 study looked at nearly 50 factors important to relocating families including: recent job growth; nearby top-ranked colleges; in-state tuition for four-year public colleges; population growth since 2000; pediatricians per 100,000 population; and a Green Living index. *Worldwide ERC and Primacy Relocation, "2008 Best Cities for Relocating Families"*

Dating/Romance Rankings

- Eli Lily and Company, in partnership with Sperling's BestPlaces, ranked the nation's 50 largest metro areas in terms of the "Most Romantic Cities for Baby Boomers." The Miami metro area ranked #49. Criteria: marriage and divorce rates among baby boomers age 45 to 60; great restaurants; dance studios; chocolate, jewelry and flower sales. *Eli Lily and Company, "Most Romantic Cities for Baby Boomers," April 20, 2007*

- The Fort Lauderdale metro area was selected as one of the "Best Cities for Relocating Singles" by Worldwide ERC and Primacy Relocation. The area ranked #24 out of the 100 largest metro areas in the U.S. Criteria: recent job growth; recent singles population growth; overall population growth; affordable rental housing; cost-of-living index; expanded arts and recreation opportunities; ratio of single men and single women; affordability of quality higher education (including state residency requirements); diversity index; climate; population density. *Worldwide ERC and Primacy Relocation, "2008 Best Cities for Relocating Singles"*

- *Forbes* ranked the 40 most populous urbanized areas in the U.S. in terms of the "Best Cities for Singles." The Miami metro area ranked #29. Criteria: number of singles; cost of living alone; nightlife; culture; job growth; coolness; and online dating participation. *Forbes.com, "Best Cities for Singles," July 27, 2009*

Education Rankings

- Fort Lauderdale was identified as one of the 100 "smartest" metro areas in the U.S. The area ranked #61. Criteria: the editors rated the collective brainpower of the 100 largest metro areas in the U.S. based on their residents' educational attainment. *American City Business Journals, April 14, 2008*

- Fort Lauderdale was identified as one of "America's Brainiest Bastions" by *Portfolio.com*. The metro area ranked #118 out of 200. *Portfolio.com* analyzed levels of educational attainment in the nation's 200 largest metropolitan areas. The editors established scores for five levels of educational attainment, based on relative earning power of adult workers age 25 or older. Scores were determined by comparing the median income for all workers with the median income for those workers at a specified educational level. *Portfolio.com, "America's Brainiest Bastions," December 1, 2010*

Environmental Rankings

- The Miami was identified as one of North America's greenest metropolitan areas. The area ranked #22. The Green City Index is comprised of 31 indicators, and scores cities across nine categories: carbon dioxide; energy; land use; buildings; transport; water; waste; air quality; environmental governance. The 27 largest metropolitan areas in the U.S. and Canada were considered. *Economist Intelligence Unit, sponsored by Siemens, "U.S. and Canada Green City Index, 2011"*

- The Miami was identified as one of America's cities with the most ENERGY STAR certified buildings. The area ranked #21 out of 25. Criteria: number of ENERGY STAR labeled buildings in 2010. *U.S. Environmental Protection Agency, "Top Cities With the Most ENERGY STAR Certified Buildings," March 15, 2011*

- Pembroke Pines was selected as one of 22 "Smarter Cities" for energy by the Natural Resources Defense Council. Criteria: investment in green power; energy efficiency measures; conservation. *Natural Resources Defense Council, "2010 Smarter Cities," July 19, 2010*

- *American City Business Journal* ranked 43 metropolitan areas in terms of their "greenness." The Fort Lauderdale metro area ranked #30. Criteria: Forty-one metros in which *ACBJ* has business weeklies, plus Indianapolis and Cleveland, were ranked based on 20 different indicators such as adoption of green technologies, utilization of environmentally sound practices, and air and water quality. *American City Business Journals, "Green City Index," March 11, 2010*

- 100 of the largest metro areas in the U.S. were analyzed in terms of their current drought severity. The Fort Lauderdale metro area ranked #58 (#1 = driest). The rankings were based on statistics such as long-term precipitation trends and patterns and the Palmer drought indices. *Sperling's BestPlaces, www.BestPlaces.net, "America's Drought-Riskiest Cities," November 2007*

- The Fort Lauderdale metro area appeared in *Country Home's* "Best Green Places" report. The area ranked #219 out of 379. Criteria: official energy policies; green power; green buildings; availability of fresh, locally grown food. *Country Home, "Best Green Places," 2008*

Health/Fitness Rankings

- The Fort Lauderdale metro area was selected as one of the worst cities for bed bugs in America by Rollins corporation, the owner of seven pest control companies, including Orkin. The area ranked #24 based on the number of bed bug treatments from January to December 2011. *Rollins, "The Top 50 U.S. Cities for Bed Bugs," March 19, 2012*

- Miami was identified as a "2011 Asthma Capital." The area ranked #61 out of the nation's 100 largest metropolitan areas. Twelve factors were used to identify the most challenging places to live for people with asthma: estimated prevalence; self-reported prevalence; crude death rate for asthma; annual pollen score; annual air quality; public smoking laws; number of board-certified asthma specialists; school inhaler access laws; rescue medication use; controller medication use; uninsured rate; poverty rate. *Asthma and Allergy Foundation of America, "2011 Asthma Capitals"*

- Miami was identified as a "2011 Fall Allergy Capital." The area ranked #95 out of 100. Three groups of factors were used to identify the most severe cities for people with allergies during the fall season: annual pollen levels; medicine utilization; access to board-certified allergists. *Asthma and Allergy Foundation of America, "2011 Fall Allergy Capitals"*

- Miami was identified as a "2012 Spring Allergy Capital." The area ranked #71 out of 100. Three groups of factors were used to identify the most severe cities for people with allergies during the spring season: annual pollen levels; medicine utilization; access to board-certified allergists. *Asthma and Allergy Foundation of America, "2012 Spring Allergy Capitals"*

- The Fort Lauderdale metropolitan area was selected as one of the best metros for hospital care in America by *HealthGrades.com*. The rankings are based on a comprehensive study of patient death and complication rates in the nation's nearly 5,000 hospitals. Hospitals performing in the top 5% nationwide across 26 different medical procedures and diagnoses were identified. *HealthGrades.com* then ranked cities by the highest percentage of these Distinguished Hospitals for Clinical Excellence™. The Fort Lauderdale metro area ranked #16. *HealthGrades.com, "America's Top 50 Cities for Hospital Care," January 21, 2012*

- The American Academy of Dermatology ranked 26 U.S. metropolitan regions in terms of their residents knowledge, attitude and behaviors towards tanning, sun protection and skin cancer detection. The Miami metro area ranked #13. The results of the study are based on an online survey of over 7,000 adults nationwide. *American Academy of Dermatology, "Suntelligence: How Sun Smart is Your City," May 3, 2010*

- The Miami metro area appeared in the 2011 Gallup-Healthways Well-Being Index. The index, based on interviews with more than 350,000 Americans, measured jobs, finances, physical health, emotional state of mind and communities. The metro area ranked #146 out of 190. Criteria: life evaluation; emotional health; work environment; physical health; healthy behaviors; basic access (basic needs optimal for a healthy life, such as access to food and medicine, having health insurance and feeling safe while walking at night). *Gallup-Healthways, "State of Well-Being 2011"*

- The Fort Lauderdale metro area was identified as one of "America's Most Stressful Cities" by *Sperling's BestPlaces*. The metro area ranked #11 out of 50. Criteria: unemployment rate; suicide rate; commute time; mental health; poor rest; alcohol use; violent crime rate; property crime rate; cloudy days annually. *Sperling's BestPlaces, www.BestPlaces.net, "Stressful Cities 2012*

- The Miami metro area was identified as one of "America's Most Stressful Cities" by *Forbes*. The metro area ranked #13 out of 40. Criteria: housing affordability; unemployment rate; cost of living; air quality; traffic congestion; sunny days; population density. *Forbes.com, "America's Most Stressful Cities," September 23, 2011*

- 50 of the largest metro areas in the U.S. were analyzed in terms of their health and fitness by the American College of Sports Medicine in their "American Fitness Index." The Miami metro area ranked #39 (#1 = healthiest). Criteria: preventative health behaviors; levels of chronic disease; health care access; community resources and policies that support physical activity. *American College of Sports Medicine, "Health and Community Fitness Status of the 50 Largest Metropolitan Areas," August 1, 2011*

Real Estate Rankings

- Miami was identified as one of the priciest cities to rent in the U.S. The area ranked #4 out of 10. Criteria: rent-to-income ratio. *CNBC, "Priciest Cities to Rent," March 14, 2012*

- Fort Lauderdale was identified as one of the "Top Turnaround Housing Markets for 2012." The area ranked #8 out of 10. Criteria: year-over-year median home price appreciation; year-over-year median inventory age; year-over-year inventory reduction. *AOL Real Estate, "Top Turnaround Housing Markets for 2012," February 4, 2012*

- *Fortune* ranked the 100 largest metro areas in the U.S. in terms of projected median home price change in 2010. The Fort Lauderdale metro area ranked #98. *Fortune, "The 2010 Housing Outlook," December 9, 2009*

- The Fort Lauderdale metro area was identified as one of "The 15 Worst Housing Markets for the Next Five Years." Criteria: cities with home prices that are projected to appreciate at an annual rate of less than 1.5% rate between the second quarter 2011 and the second quarter 2016. *The Business Insider, "The 15 Worst Housing Markets for the Next Five Years," July 1, 2011*

- The Miami metro area was identified as one of the 10 best condo markets in the U.S. in 2011. The area ranked #3 out of 54 markets with a price appreciation of 6.3%. Criteria: year-over-year change of median sales price of existing apartment condo-coop homes between the 4th quarter of 2010 and the 4th quarter of 2011. *National Association of Realtors®, Median Sales Price of Existing Apartment Condo-Coop Homes for Metropolitan Areas, 4th Quarter 2011*

- The Fort Lauderdale metro area was identified as one of "America's 25 Weakest Housing Markets" by *Forbes*. The metro area ranked #4. Criteria: metro areas with populations over 500,000 were ranked based on projected home values through 2011. *Forbes.com, "America's 25 Weakest Housing Markets," January 7, 2009*

- The Fort Lauderdale metro area appeared in a *Wall Street Journal* article ranking cities by "housing stress." The metro area was ranked #1 (#1 = most stress). Criteria: fraction of mortgage-holding homeowners with a monthly housing payment in excess of 30 percent of income; percentage of people without health insurance; unemployment rate. *The Wall Street Journal, "Which Cities Face Biggest Housing Risk," October 5, 2010*

- The Center for Housing Policy ranked 210 U.S. metropolitan areas by the fair market rent for a two-bedroom unit. The Fort Lauderdale metro area was ranked #14. (#1 = most expensive) with a rent of $1,358. Criteria: Fair Market Rent (FMR) in effect during the fourth quarter of 2009 based on HUD's fiscal year 2010 FMRs. *The Center for Housing Policy, "Paycheck to Paycheck: Most to Least Expensive Rental Markets in 2009"*

- The Fort Lauderdale metro area was identified as one of the top 20 cities in terms of decreasing home equity. The metro area was ranked #17. Criteria: percentage of home equity relative to the home's current value. *Forbes.com, "Where Americans are Losing Home Equity Most," May 1, 2010*

- The Fort Lauderdale metro area was identified as one of the markets with the best expected performance in home prices over the next 12 months. *Local Market Monitor, "First Quarter Home Price Forecast for Largest US Markets," March 2, 2011*

- The Fort Lauderdale metro area was identified as one of the best U.S. markets to invest in rental property" by HomeVestors and Local Market Monitor. The area ranked #12 out of 100. Criteria: risk-return premium relative to national average. *HomeVestors and Local Market Monitor, "Best 100 U.S. Markets to Invest in Rental Property," March 9, 2012*

Safety Rankings

- Sperling's BestPlaces analyzed the tracks of tropical storms for the past 100 years and ranked which areas are most likely to be hit by a major hurricane. The Fort Lauderdale metro area ranked #1 out of 10. *Sperling's BestPlaces, www.bestplaces.net, February 2, 2006*

- The National Insurance Crime Bureau ranked 366 metro areas in the U.S. in terms of per capita rates of vehicle theft. The Fort Lauderdale metro area ranked #44 (#1 = highest rate). Criteria: number of vehicle theft offenses per 100,000 inhabitants in 2010. *National Insurance Crime Bureau, "Hot Spots," June 21, 2011*

- The Miami metro area was identified as one of the most dangerous metro areas for pedestrians by Transportation for America. The metro area ranked #4 out of 52 metro areas with over 1 million residents. Criteria: area's population divided by the number of pedestrian fatalities in that area. *Transportation for America, "Dangerous by Design 2011"*

Seniors/Retirement Rankings

- Bankers Life and Casualty Company, in partnership with Sperling's BestPlaces, ranked the nation's 50 largest metro areas in terms of the "Best U.S. Cities for Seniors." The Fort Lauderdale metro area ranked #43. Criteria: healthcare; transportation; housing; environment; economy; health and longevity; social and spiritual life; crime. *Bankers Life and Casualty Company, Center for a Secure Retirement, "Best U.S. Cities for Seniors 2011," September 2011*

- The Fort Lauderdale metro area was selected as one of the "10 Best Places for Single Seniors to Retire" by *U.S. News & World Report.* Criteria: metro areas with the most single seniors age 55 and over. *U.S. News & World Report, "10 Best Places for Single Seniors to Retire," November 1, 2010*

- The Fort Lauderdale metro area was selected as one of "The 10 Most Affordable Cities for Long-Term Care" by *U.S. News & World Report.* Criteria: costs at nursing homes, assisted living facilities, and adult day health care facilities; cost for licensed home health aides. *U.S. News & World Report, "The 10 Most Affordable Cities for Long-Term Care," May 17, 2010*

Technology Rankings

- The Fort Lauderdale metro area was selected as one of "America's Most Wired Cities" by *Forbes.* The metro area was ranked #17 out of 20. Criteria: percentage of Internet users with high-speed access; number of companies providing high-speed Internet; number of public wireless hot spots. *Forbes, "America's Most Wired Cities," March 2, 2010*

Transportation Rankings

- The Fort Lauderdale metro area appeared on *Forbes* list of the best and worst cities for commuters. The metro area ranked #55 out of 60 (#1 is best). Criteria: travel time; road congestion; travel delays. *Forbes.com, "Best and Worst Cities for Commuters," February 16, 2010*

Women/Minorities Rankings

- Fort Lauderdale was ranked #40 out of 100 metro areas in *SELF Magazine's* ranking of America's healthiest places for women." A panel of experts came up with more than 50 criteria including death and disease rates, environmental indicators, community resources, and lifestyle habits. *SELF Magazine, "Secrets of America's Healthiest Women," December 2008*

- The Miami metro area appeared on *Forbes'* list of the "Best Cities for Minority Entrepreneurs." The area ranked #40 out of 10. Criteria: 52 metropolitan statistical areas were examined. For each ethnicity (African Americans, Asians and Hispanics), the editors measured housing affordability, population growth, income growth, and entrepreneurship (per capita self-employment). *Forbes, "Best Cities for Minority Entrepreneurs," March 23, 2011*

Miscellaneous Rankings

- Scarborough Research, a leading market research firm, identified the top local markets for lottery ticket purchasers. The Miami DMA (Designated Market Area) ranked in the top 13 with 48% of adults 18+ reporting that they purchased lottery tickets in the past 30 days. *Scarborough Research, January 30, 2012*

- Energizer Holdings, the makers of Edge® shave gel, in partnership with Sperling's BestPlaces, ranked 50 major metro areas in terms of everyday irritations. The Miami metro area ranked #14. Criteria: humidity levels; weather conditions; incidence of traffic delays and congestion; average commute times; frequency of flight delays and cancellations; rates of sleeplessness; underemployment; pollens and allergens; pests; comedy clubs per capita. *Energizer Holdings, "Most Irritation Prone Cities," July 23, 2010*

- Mars Chocolate North America, the makers of COMBOS®, in partnership with Sperling's BestPlaces, ranked 50 major metro areas in terms of their "manliness." The Miami metro area ranked #44. Criteria: number of professional sports teams; number of nearby NASCAR tracks and racing events; manly lifestyle; concentration of manly retail stores; manly occupations per capita; salty snack sales; "Board of Manliness" rankings. *Mars Chocolate North America, "America's Manliest Cities 2011," September 1, 2011*

- The Miami metro area was selected as one of "America's Greediest Cities" by *Forbes*. The area was ranked #10 out of 10. Criteria: number of Forbes 400 (*Forbes* annual list of the richest Americans) members per capita. *Forbes, "America's Greediest Cities," December 7, 2007*

- The Fort Lauderdale metro area was selected as one of "America's Most Miserable Cities" by *Forbes.com*. The metro area ranked #7 out of 10. Criteria: violent crime; unemployment; foreclosures; income and property taxes; home prices; political corruption; commute times; climate; pro sports team records. *Forbes.com, "America's Most Miserable Cities, 2012" February 2, 2012*

Business Environment

CITY FINANCES

City Government Finances

Component	2009 ($000)	2009 ($ per capita)
Total Revenues	178,887	1,218
Total Expenditures	266,324	1,814
Debt Outstanding	400,595	2,728
Cash and Securities[1]	548,640	3,737

Note: (1) Cash and security holdings of a government at the close of its fiscal year, including those of its dependent agencies, utilities, and liquor stores.
Source: U.S Census Bureau, State & Local Government Finances 2009

City Government Revenue by Source

Source	2009 ($000)	2009 ($ per capita)
General Revenue		
From Federal Government	6,372	43
From State Government	15,385	105
From Local Governments	1,540	10
Taxes		
Property	52,343	356
Sales and Gross Receipts	37,961	259
Personal Income	0	0
Corporate Income	0	0
Motor Vehicle License	0	0
Other Taxes	8,887	61
Current Charges	25,588	174
Liquor Store	0	0
Utility	16,344	111
Employee Retirement	-52,427	-357

Source: U.S Census Bureau, State & Local Government Finances 2009

City Government Expenditures by Function

Function	2009 ($000)	2009 ($ per capita)	2009 (%)
General Direct Expenditures			
Air Transportation	0	0	0.0
Corrections	0	0	0.0
Education	0	0	0.0
Employment Security Administration	0	0	0.0
Financial Administration	1,824	12	0.7
Fire Protection	23,538	160	8.8
General Public Buildings	3,241	22	1.2
Governmental Administration, Other	12,692	86	4.8
Health	0	0	0.0
Highways	26,995	184	10.1
Hospitals	0	0	0.0
Housing and Community Development	10,530	72	4.0
Interest on General Debt	18,335	125	6.9
Judicial and Legal	0	0	0.0
Libraries	0	0	0.0
Parking	0	0	0.0
Parks and Recreation	19,414	132	7.3
Police Protection	26,974	184	10.1
Public Welfare	2,397	16	0.9
Sewerage	28,850	196	10.8
Solid Waste Management	0	0	0.0
Veterans' Services	0	0	0.0
Liquor Store	0	0	0.0
Utility	10,548	72	4.0
Employee Retirement	12,759	87	4.8

Source: U.S Census Bureau, State & Local Government Finances 2009

Municipal Bond Ratings

Area	Moody's	S&P	Fitch
City	n/a	n/a	n/a

Rating Systems (shown in declining order of credit quality): Moody's– Aaa, Aa, A, Baa, Ba, B, Caa, Ca, C (numerical modifiers 1, 2, and 3 are added to letter-rating); S&P– AAA, AA, A, BBB, BB, B, CCC, CC, C; Fitch– AAA, AA, A, BBB, BB, B, CCC, CC, C. Ratings may be modified by the addition of a plus or minus sign to show relative standing within the major rating categories.
Notes: n/a Not Available; w/d Withdrawn (1) Not Reviewed; (2) Issuer Rating/No General Obligation; (3) Standard and Poor's Issue Credit Rating (ICR) is a current opinion of an obliger with respect to a specific financial obligation, a specific class of financial obligations, or a specific financial program.
Source: U.S. Census Bureau, 2012 Statistical Abstract, Bond Ratings for City Governments by Largest Cities: 2010

DEMOGRAPHICS

Population Growth

Area	1990 Census	2000 Census	2010 Census	Population Growth (%) 1990-2000	Population Growth (%) 2000-2010
City	66,095	137,427	154,750	107.9	12.6
MSA[1]	4,056,100	5,007,564	5,564,635	23.5	11.1
U.S.	248,709,873	281,421,906	308,745,538	13.2	9.7

Note: (1) Figures cover the Miami-Fort Lauderdale-Pompano Beach, FL Metropolitan Statistical Area—see Appendix B for areas included
Source: U.S. Census Bureau, 2010 Census

Household Size

Area	Persons in Household (%) One	Two	Three	Four	Five	Six	Seven or More	Average Household Size
City	24.0	29.0	18.4	17.2	7.4	2.5	1.5	2.70
MSA[1]	27.0	31.0	16.6	13.7	6.7	2.8	2.2	2.62
U.S.	26.7	32.8	16.1	13.4	6.5	2.6	1.9	2.58

Note: (1) Figures cover the Miami-Fort Lauderdale-Pompano Beach, FL Metropolitan Statistical Area—see Appendix B for areas included
Source: U.S. Census Bureau, 2010 Census

Race

Area	White Alone[2] (%)	Black Alone[2] (%)	Asian Alone[2] (%)	AIAN[3] Alone[2] (%)	NHOPI[4] Alone[2] (%)	Other Race Alone[2] (%)	Two or More Races (%)
City	67.3	19.8	4.9	0.3	0.0	4.4	3.3
MSA[1]	70.3	21.0	2.3	0.3	0.0	3.5	2.5
U.S.	72.4	12.6	4.8	0.9	0.2	6.2	2.9

Note: (1) Figures cover the Miami-Fort Lauderdale-Pompano Beach, FL Metropolitan Statistical Area—see Appendix B for areas included; (2) Alone is defined as not being in combination with one or more other races; (3) American Indian and Alaska Native; (4) Native Hawaiian and Other Pacific Islander
Source: U.S. Census Bureau, 2010 Census

Hispanic or Latino Origin

Area	Hispanic or Latino (%)	Mexican (%)	Puerto Rican (%)	Cuban (%)	Other Hispanic or Latino (%)
City	41.4	1.1	6.8	12.8	20.7
MSA[1]	41.6	2.4	3.7	17.7	17.8
U.S.	16.3	10.3	1.5	0.6	4.0

Note: Persons of Hispanic or Latino origin can be of any race; (1) Figures cover the Miami-Fort Lauderdale-Pompano Beach, FL Metropolitan Statistical Area—see Appendix B for areas included
Source: U.S. Census Bureau, 2010 Census

Segregation

Type	Segregation Indices[1]				Percent Change		
	1990	2000	2010	2010 Rank[2]	1990-2000	1990-2010	2000-2010
Black/White	71.4	69.2	64.8	23	-2.3	-6.6	-4.3
Asian/White	26.8	33.3	34.2	80	6.4	7.3	0.9
Hispanic/White	32.5	59.0	57.4	8	26.5	24.8	-1.6

Note: Figures are based on an analysis of 1990, 2000, and 2010 Census Decennial Census tract data by William H. Frey, Brookings Institution and the University of Michigan Social Science Data Analysis Network. In this analysis all racial groups (whites, blacks, and asians) are non-Hispanic members of those races. Hispanics are shown as a separate category; All figures cover the Metropolitan Statistical Area (see Appendix B for areas included); (1) Segregation Indices are Dissimilarity Indices that measure the degree to which the minority group is distributed differently than whites across census tracts. They range from 0 (complete integration) to 100 (complete segregation) where the value indicates the percentage of the minority group that needs to move to be distributed exactly like whites; (2) Ranges from 1 (most segregated) to 102 (least segregated); n/a not available.
Source: www.CensusScope.org

Ancestry

Area	German	Irish	English	American	Italian	Polish	French[2]	Scottish	Dutch
City	5.2	5.5	3.1	5.1	6.1	2.4	1.4	0.7	0.9
MSA[1]	5.8	5.5	3.8	4.2	5.6	2.5	1.6	0.8	0.6
U.S.	16.1	11.6	8.8	6.1	5.7	3.2	3.0	1.9	1.6

Note: Figures are the percentage of the total population reporting a particular ancestry. The nine most commonly reported ancestries in the U.S. are shown. Figures include multiple ancestries (e.g. if a person reported being Irish and Italian, they were included in both columns); (1) Figures cover the Miami-Fort Lauderdale-Pompano Beach, FL Metropolitan Statistical Area—see Appendix B for areas included; (2) Excludes Basque
Source: U.S. Census Bureau, 2008-2010 American Community Survey 3-Year Estimates

Foreign-Born Population

Area	Percent of Population Born in								
	Any Foreign Country	Mexico	Asia	Europe	Carribean	South America	Central America[2]	Africa	Canada
City	36.7	0.5	4.1	1.8	15.8	11.0	2.2	0.6	0.5
MSA[1]	38.1	1.2	1.9	2.2	19.6	7.7	4.5	0.3	0.6
U.S.	12.8	3.8	3.6	1.6	1.2	0.9	1.0	0.5	0.3

Note: (1) Figures cover the Miami-Fort Lauderdale-Pompano Beach, FL Metropolitan Statistical Area—see Appendix B for areas included; (2) Excludes Mexico.
Source: U.S. Census Bureau, 2008-2010 American Community Survey 3-Year Estimates

Marital Status

Area	Never Married	Now Married[2]	Separated	Widowed	Divorced
City	29.0	48.4	2.8	7.9	12.0
MSA[1]	32.5	44.9	2.9	7.1	12.6
U.S.	31.6	49.6	2.2	6.1	10.7

Note: Figures are percentages and cover the population 15 years of age and older; (1) Figures cover the Miami-Fort Lauderdale-Pompano Beach, FL Metropolitan Statistical Area—see Appendix B for areas included; (2) Excludes separated
Source: U.S. Census Bureau, 2008-2010 American Community Survey 3-Year Estimates

Age

Area	Percent of Population							Median Age
	Under Age 5	Age 5 to 17	Age 18 to 34	Age 35 to 49	Age 50 to 64	Age 65 to 79	80 Years and Over	
City	5.7	18.1	20.2	23.3	18.0	9.7	5.1	39.5
MSA[1]	5.8	15.8	21.8	22.1	18.6	10.9	5.0	39.8
U.S.	6.5	17.5	23.2	20.7	19.0	9.4	3.6	37.2

Note: (1) Figures cover the Miami-Fort Lauderdale-Pompano Beach, FL Metropolitan Statistical Area—see Appendix B for areas included
Source: U.S. Census Bureau, 2010 Census

Male/Female Ratio

Area	Males	Females	Males per 100 Females
City	71,515	83,235	85.9
MSA[1]	2,693,823	2,870,812	93.8
U.S.	151,781,326	156,964,212	96.7

Note: (1) Figures cover the Miami-Fort Lauderdale-Pompano Beach, FL
Metropolitan Statistical Area—see Appendix B for areas included
Source: U.S. Census Bureau, 2010 Census

Religious Groups

Area	Catholic	Baptist	Non-Den.	Methodist[2]	Lutheran	LDS[3]	Pentecostal	Presbyterian[4]	Muslim[5]	Judaism
MSA[1]	18.6	5.4	4.2	1.3	0.5	0.5	1.8	0.7	1.6	0.9
U.S.	19.1	9.3	4.0	4.0	2.3	2.0	1.9	1.6	0.8	0.7

Note: Figures are the number of adherents as a percentage of the total population; (1) Figures cover the
Miami-Fort Lauderdale-Pompano Beach, FL Metropolitan Statistical Area—see Appendix B for areas included;
(2) Methodist/Pietist; (3) Latter Day Saints; (4) Reformed; (5) Figures are estimates
Source: Association of Statisticians of American Religious Bodies, 2010 U.S. Religion Census: Religious
Congregations & Membership Study

ECONOMY

Gross Metropolitan Product

Area	2007	2008	2009	2010	2010 Rank[2]
MSA[1]	264.3	260.5	253.8	258.8	11

Note: Figures are in billions of dollars; (1) Figures cover the Miami-Fort Lauderdale-Pompano Beach, FL
Metropolitan Statistical Area—see Appendix B for areas included; (2) Rank ranges from 1 to 363
Source: The United States Conference of Mayors, "U.S. Metro Economies: GMP and Employment Forecasts,"
June 2011

Economic Growth

Area	2007-2009 (%)	2010 (%)	2011 (%)	Rank[2]
MSA[1]	-3.6	1.3	2.0	297
U.S.	-1.3	2.9	2.5	–

Note: Figures are real Gross Metropolitan Product growth rates and represent annual average percent change;
(1) Figures cover the Miami-Fort Lauderdale-Pompano Beach, FL Metropolitan Statistical Area—see Appendix
B for areas included; (2) Rank ranges from 1 to 363
Source: The United States Conference of Mayors, "U.S. Metro Economies: GMP and Employment Forecasts,"
June 2011

Metropolitan Area Exports

Area	2005	2006	2007	2008	2009	2010	2010 Rank[2]
MSA[1]	20,382.9	23,491.3	26,197.4	33,411.5	31,175.0	35,866.9	5

Note: Figures are in millions of dollars; (1) Figures cover the Miami-Fort Lauderdale-Pompano Beach, FL
Metropolitan Statistical Area—see Appendix B for areas included; (2) Rank ranges from 1 to 369
Source: U.S. Department of Commerce, International Trade Administration, Office of Trade & Industry
Information, Manufacturing & Services, data extracted April 2, 2012

INCOME

Income

Area	Per Capita ($)	Median Household ($)	Average Household ($)
City	26,976	59,968	74,235
MSA[1]	26,283	47,086	68,986
U.S.	26,942	51,222	70,116

Note: (1) Figures cover the Miami-Fort Lauderdale-Pompano Beach, FL Metropolitan Statistical Area—see
Appendix B for areas included
Source: U.S. Census Bureau, 2008-2010 American Community Survey 3-Year Estimates

Household Income Distribution

Area	Percent of Households Earning							
	Under $15,000	$15,000 -24,999	$25,000 -34,999	$35,000 -49,999	$50,000 -74,999	$75,000 -99,000	$100,000 -149,999	$150,000 and up
City	9.4	9.8	8.9	13.2	18.9	14.7	15.5	9.6
MSA[1]	14.7	11.9	11.3	14.5	17.7	10.7	10.9	8.4
U.S.	13.0	11.0	10.6	14.2	18.5	12.1	12.2	8.4

Note: (1) Figures cover the Miami-Fort Lauderdale-Pompano Beach, FL Metropolitan Statistical Area—see Appendix B for areas included
Source: U.S. Census Bureau, 2008-2010 American Community Survey 3-Year Estimates

Poverty Rate

Area	All Ages	Under 18 Years Old	18 to 64 Years Old	65 Years and Over
City	7.9	9.8	6.7	10.3
MSA[1]	15.5	20.7	13.8	15.0
U.S.	14.4	20.1	13.1	9.4

Note: Figures are percentage of people whose income during the past 12 months was below the poverty level;
(1) Figures cover the Miami-Fort Lauderdale-Pompano Beach, FL Metropolitan Statistical Area—see Appendix B for areas included
Source: U.S. Census Bureau, 2008-2010 American Community Survey 3-Year Estimates

Personal Bankruptcy Filing Rate

Area	2006	2007	2008	2009	2010	2011
Broward County	1.34	2.24	3.75	5.48	6.89	5.98
U.S.	2.00	2.73	3.53	4.61	4.97	4.37

Note: Numbers are per 1,000 population and include Chapter 7 and Chapter 13 filings
Source: Federal Deposit Insurance Corporation, Regional Economic Conditions, March 9, 2012

EMPLOYMENT

Labor Force and Employment

Area	Civilian Labor Force			Workers Employed		
	Dec. 2010	Dec. 2011	% Chg.	Dec. 2010	Dec. 2011	% Chg.
City	82,381	81,684	-0.8	74,479	75,293	1.1
MD[1]	985,607	978,951	-0.7	885,009	894,687	1.1
U.S.	153,156,000	153,373,000	0.1	139,159,000	140,681,000	1.1

Note: Data is not seasonally adjusted and covers workers 16 years of age and older;
(1) Metropolitan Division—see Appendix B for areas included
Source: Bureau of Labor Statistics, http://stats.bls.gov

Unemployment Rate

Area	2011											
	Jan.	Feb.	Mar.	Apr.	May	Jun.	Jul.	Aug.	Sep.	Oct.	Nov.	Dec.
City	10.0	9.1	8.7	8.3	8.3	9.0	9.0	9.0	8.7	8.3	8.2	7.8
MD[1]	10.5	9.7	9.3	8.9	9.0	9.6	9.7	9.5	9.4	8.9	8.9	8.6
U.S.	9.8	9.5	9.2	8.7	8.7	9.3	9.3	9.1	8.8	8.5	8.2	8.3

Note: Data is not seasonally adjusted and covers workers 16 years of age and older; All figures are percentages; (1) Metropolitan Division—see Appendix B for areas included
Source: Bureau of Labor Statistics, http://stats.bls.gov

Projected Unemployment Rate

Area	2010 (%)	2011 (%)	2012 (%)	2013 (%)
MSA[1]	12.1	11.3	10.6	9.7

Note: (1) Metropolitan Statistical Area—see Appendix B for areas included
Source: The United States Conference of Mayors, "U.S. Metro Economies: GMP and Employment Forecasts," June 2011

Employment by Occupation

Occupation Classification	City (%)	MSA[1] (%)	U.S. (%)
Management, Business, Science, and Arts	39.5	32.8	35.6
Natural Resources, Construction, and Maintenance	5.9	9.5	9.5
Production, Transportation, and Material Moving	6.8	8.9	12.1
Sales and Office	32.8	28.6	25.2
Service	14.9	20.2	17.6

Note: Figures cover employed civilians 16 years of age and older; (1) Figures cover the Miami-Fort Lauderdale-Pompano Beach, FL Metropolitan Statistical Area—see Appendix B for areas included
Source: U.S. Census Bureau, 2008-2010 American Community Survey 3-Year Estimates

Employment by Industry

Sector	MD[1] Number of Employees	MD[1] Percent of Total	U.S. Percent of Total
Construction	27,700	3.8	4.1
Education and Health Services	97,800	13.6	15.2
Financial Activities	53,100	7.4	5.8
Government	100,200	13.9	16.8
Information	16,600	2.3	2.0
Leisure and Hospitality	80,200	11.1	9.9
Manufacturing	27,300	3.8	8.9
Mining and Logging	n/a	n/a	0.6
Other Services	31,000	4.3	4.0
Professional and Business Services	119,600	16.6	13.3
Retail Trade	100,400	14.0	11.5
Transportation and Utilities	22,200	3.1	3.8
Wholesale Trade	43,400	6.0	4.2

Note: Figures cover non-farm employment as of December 2011 and are not seasonally adjusted; (1) Metropolitan Division—see Appendix B for areas included; n/a not available
Source: Bureau of Labor Statistics, http://stats.bls.gov

Occupations with Greatest Projected Employment Growth: 2008 – 2018

Occupation[1]	2008 Employment	2018 Projected Employment	Numeric Employment Change	Percent Employment Change
Registered Nurses	151,100	187,380	36,280	24.0
Combined Food Preparation and Serving Workers, Including Fast Food	162,570	186,400	23,830	14.7
Customer Service Representatives	169,080	190,780	21,700	12.8
Nursing Aides, Orderlies, and Attendants	88,630	106,860	18,230	20.6
Home Health Aides	30,480	47,860	17,380	57.0
Postsecondary Teachers	70,790	85,380	14,590	20.6
Retail Salespersons	274,490	288,660	14,170	5.2
Elementary School Teachers, Except Special Education	74,130	86,390	12,260	16.5
Stock Clerks and Order Fillers	167,450	179,420	11,970	7.1
Accountants and Auditors	86,390	97,670	11,280	13.1

Note: Projections cover Florida; (1) Sorted by numeric employment change
Source: www.projectionscentral.com, State Occupational Projections, 2008–2018 Long-Term Projections

Fastest Growing Occupations: 2008 – 2018

Occupation[1]	2008 Employment	2018 Projected Employment	Numeric Employment Change	Percent Employment Change
Biomedical Engineers	520	840	320	61.5
Home Health Aides	30,480	47,860	17,380	57.0
Medical Scientists, Except Epidemiologists	2,640	3,870	1,230	46.6
Physician Assistants	3,900	5,490	1,590	40.8
Personal and Home Care Aides	13,890	19,430	5,540	39.9
Network Systems and Data Communications Analysts	21,550	30,110	8,560	39.7
Radiation Therapists	1,270	1,730	460	36.2
Dental Hygienists	9,030	11,890	2,860	31.7
Physical Therapist Assistants	3,550	4,660	1,110	31.3
Financial Examiners	610	800	190	31.1

Note: Projections cover Florida; (1) Sorted by percent employment change and excludes occupations with numeric employment change less than 100
Source: www.projectionscentral.com, State Occupational Projections, 2008–2018 Long-Term Projections

Average Wages

Occupation	$/Hr.	Occupation	$/Hr.
Accountants and Auditors	31.08	Maids and Housekeeping Cleaners	9.74
Automotive Mechanics	18.77	Maintenance and Repair Workers	16.02
Bookkeepers	16.79	Marketing Managers	53.59
Carpenters	21.04	Nuclear Medicine Technologists	34.17
Cashiers	9.93	Nurses, Licensed Practical	20.12
Clerks, General Office	12.92	Nurses, Registered	32.78
Clerks, Receptionists/Information	13.00	Nursing Aides/Orderlies/Attendants	11.94
Clerks, Shipping/Receiving	13.55	Packers and Packagers, Hand	9.51
Computer Programmers	31.99	Physical Therapists	41.16
Computer Support Specialists	22.73	Postal Service Mail Carriers	25.81
Computer Systems Analysts	37.90	Real Estate Brokers	22.28
Cooks, Restaurant	11.70	Retail Salespersons	11.49
Dentists	60.26	Sales Reps., Exc. Tech./Scientific	30.80
Electrical Engineers	37.94	Sales Reps., Tech./Scientific	41.23
Electricians	18.76	Secretaries, Exc. Legal/Med./Exec.	15.08
Financial Managers	61.20	Security Guards	10.24
First-Line Supervisors/Managers, Sales	21.21	Surgeons	111.34
Food Preparation Workers	10.13	Teacher Assistants	10.30
General and Operations Managers	51.16	Teachers, Elementary School	n/a
Hairdressers/Cosmetologists	13.47	Teachers, Secondary School	n/a
Internists	118.93	Telemarketers	11.62
Janitors and Cleaners	9.95	Truck Drivers, Heavy/Tractor-Trailer	18.90
Landscaping/Groundskeeping Workers	10.73	Truck Drivers, Light/Delivery Svcs.	15.92
Lawyers	58.17	Waiters and Waitresses	9.70

Note: Wage data covers the Fort Lauderdale-Pompano Beach-Deerfield Beach, FL Metropolitan Division—see Appendix B for areas included. Hourly wages for elementary/secondary school teachers and teacher assistants were calculated by the editors from annual wage data assuming a 40 hour work week; n/a not available.
Source: Bureau of Labor Statistics, Metro Area Occupational Employment and Wage Estimates, May 2011

RESIDENTIAL REAL ESTATE

Building Permits

Area	Single-Family			Multi-Family			Total		
	2010	2011	Pct. Chg.	2010	2011	Pct. Chg.	2010	2011	Pct. Chg.
City	68	44	-35.3	0	0	-	68	44	-35.3
MSA[1]	3,171	4,303	35.7	2,706	3,229	19.3	5,877	7,532	28.2
U.S.	447,311	418,498	-6.4	157,299	205,563	30.7	604,610	624,061	3.2

Note: (1) Metropolitan Statistical Area—see Appendix B for areas included; figures represent new, privately-owned housing units authorized (unadjusted data); All permit data are based on estimates with imputation.
Source: U.S. Census Bureau, Manufacturing, Mining, and Construction Statistics, Building Permits, 2010, 2011

Homeownership Rate

Area	2005 (%)	2006 (%)	2007 (%)	2008 (%)	2009 (%)	2010 (%)	2011 (%)
MSA[1]	69.2	67.4	66.6	66.0	67.1	63.8	64.2
U.S.	68.9	68.8	68.1	67.8	67.4	66.9	66.1

Note: (1) Metropolitan Statistical Area—see Appendix B for areas included
Source: U.S. Census Bureau, Housing Vacancies and Homeownership Annual Statistics: 2011

Housing Vacancy Rates

Area	Gross Vacancy Rate[2] (%)			Year-Round Vacancy Rate[3] (%)			Rental Vacancy Rate[4] (%)			Homeowner Vacancy Rate[5] (%)		
	2009	2010	2011	2009	2010	2011	2009	2010	2011	2009	2010	2011
MSA[1]	23.1	21.8	21.0	13.7	13.0	11.7	13.2	10.1	11.8	3.2	3.5	1.8
U.S.	14.5	14.3	14.2	11.3	11.3	11.1	10.6	10.2	9.5	2.6	2.6	2.5

Note: (1) Metropolitan Statistical Area—see Appendix B for areas included; (2) The percentage of the total housing inventory that is vacant; (3) The percentage of the housing inventory (excluding seasonal units) that is year-round vacant; (4) The percentage of rental inventory that is vacant for rent; (5) The percentage of homeowner inventory that is vacant for sale
Source: U.S. Census Bureau, Housing Vacancies and Homeownership Annual Statistics: 2011

TAXES

State Corporate Income Tax Rates

State	Tax Rate (%)	Income Brackets ($)	Num. of Brackets	Financial Institution Tax Rate (%)[a]	Federal Income Tax Ded.
Florida	5.5 (f)	Flat rate	1	5.5 (f)	No

Note: Tax rates as of January 1, 2012; (a) Rates listed are the corporate income tax rate applied to financial institutions or excise taxes based on income. Some states have other taxes based upon the value of deposits or shares; (f) An exemption of $5,000 is allowed. Florida's Alternative Minimum Tax rate is 3.3%.
Source: Federation of Tax Administrators, "State Corporate Income Tax Rates, 2012"

State Individual Income Tax Rates

State	Tax Rate (%)	Income Brackets ($)	Num. of Brackets	Personal Exempt. ($)[1] Single	Dependents	Fed. Inc. Tax Ded.

Florida – No State Income Tax

Note: Tax rates as of January 1, 2012; Local- and county-level taxes are not included; n/a not applicable; (1) Married joint filers generally receive double the single exemption
Source: Federation of Tax Administrators, "State Individual Income Tax Rates, 2012"

Various State and Local Tax Rates

State	State and Local Sales and Use (%)	State Sales and Use (%)	Gasoline[1] (¢/gal.)	Cigarette[2] ($/pack)	Spirits[3] ($/gal.)	Wine[4] ($/gal.)	Beer[5] ($/gal.)
Florida	6.0	6.00	35.0	1.34	6.50	2.25	0.48

Note: All tax rates as of January 1, 2012 except beer, wine and spirits (September 1, 2011); (1) The American Petroleum Institute has developed a methodology for determining the average tax rate on a gallon of fuel. Rates may include any of the following: excise taxes, environmental fees, storage tank fees, other fees or taxes, general sales tax, and local taxes. In states where gasoline is subject to the general sales tax, or where the fuel tax is based on the average sale price, the average rate determined by API is sensitive to changes in the price of gasoline. States that fully or partially apply general sales taxes to gasoline: CA, CO, GA, IL, IN, MI, NY; (2) The federal excise tax of $1.0066 per pack and local taxes are not included; (3) Rates are those applicable to off-premise sales of 40% alcohol by volume (a.b.v.) distilled spirits in 750ml containers. Local excise taxes are excluded; (4) Rates are those applicable to off-premise sales of 11% a.b.v. non-carbonated wine in 750ml containers; (5) Rates are those applicable to off-premise sales of 4.7% a.b.v. beer in 12 ounce containers.
Source: Tax Foundation, 2012 Facts & Figures: How Does Your State Compare?

State-Local Tax Burdens

Area	Rate (%)	Rank[1]	Per Capita Taxes Paid to Home State ($)	Total State and Local Per Capita Taxes Paid ($)	Per Capita Income ($)
Florida	9.2	31	2,713	3,897	42,146
U.S. Average	9.8	-	3,057	4,160	42,539

Note: Figures cover 2009; (1) Rank ranges from 1 to 50 where 1 is highest tax burden
Source: Tax Foundation, State-Local Tax Burdens, All States, 2009

State Business Tax Climate Index Rankings

State	Overall Rank	Corporate Tax Index Rank	Individual Income Tax Index Rank	Sales Tax Index Rank	Unemployment Insurance Tax Index Rank	Property Tax Index Rank
Florida	5	12	1	19	5	24

Note: The index is a measure of how each state's tax laws affect economic performance. The lower the rank, the more favorable a state's tax system is for business. States without a given tax are given a ranking of 1.
Source: Tax Foundation, Major Components of the State Business Tax Climate Index, FY 2012

COMMERCIAL REAL ESTATE

Office Market

Market Area	Inventory (sq. ft.)	Vacant (sq. ft.)	Vac. Rate (%)	Under Constr. (sq. ft.)	Asking Rent ($/sf/yr)	
					Class A	Class B
Broward County	33,616,916	5,796,398	17.2	0	30.47	22.80

Source: Grubb & Ellis, Office Markets Trends, 4th Quarter 2011

Industrial Market

Market Area	Inventory (sq. ft.)	Vacant (sq. ft.)	Vac. Rate (%)	Under Constr. (sq. ft.)	Asking Rent ($/sf/yr)	
					WH/Dist	R&D/Flex
Broward County	102,631,597	9,972,142	9.7	0	6.08	9.89

Source: Grubb & Ellis, Industrial Markets Trends, 4th Quarter 2011

COMMERCIAL UTILITIES

Typical Monthly Electric Bills

Area	Commercial Service ($/month)		Industrial Service ($/month)	
	1,500 kWh	40 kW demand 14,000 kWh	1,000 kW demand 200,000 kWh	50,000 kW demand 15,000,000 kWh
City	108	1,239	22,761	1,001,777
Average[1]	189	1,616	25,197	1,470,813

Note: Based on total rates in effect July 1, 2011; (1) average based on 184 utilities surveyed
Source: Edison Electric Institute, Typical Bills and Average Rates Report, Summer 2011

TRANSPORTATION

Means of Transportation to Work

Area	Car/Truck/Van		Public Transportation			Bicycle	Walked	Other Means	Worked at Home
	Drove Alone	Car-pooled	Bus	Subway	Railroad				
City	84.6	9.0	1.1	0.0	0.1	0.1	0.5	0.8	3.8
MSA[1]	78.3	10.0	3.1	0.2	0.2	0.5	1.8	1.4	4.4
U.S.	76.0	10.2	2.7	1.7	0.5	0.5	2.8	1.3	4.2

Note: Figures are percentages and cover workers 16 years of age and older; (1) Figures cover the Miami-Fort Lauderdale-Pompano Beach, FL Metropolitan Statistical Area—see Appendix B for areas included
Source: U.S. Census Bureau, 2008-2010 American Community Survey 3-Year Estimates

Travel Time to Work

Area	Less Than 10 Minutes	10 to 19 Minutes	20 to 29 Minutes	30 to 44 Minutes	45 to 59 Minutes	60 to 89 Minutes	90 Minutes or More
City	7.1	21.2	21.5	27.7	13.9	6.7	1.9
MSA[1]	8.1	25.6	22.9	26.9	8.8	5.9	1.9
U.S.	13.9	30.1	20.8	19.8	7.5	5.5	2.5

Note: Figures are percentages and include workers 16 years old and over; (1) Figures cover the Miami-Fort Lauderdale-Pompano Beach, FL Metropolitan Statistical Area—see Appendix B for areas included
Source: U.S. Census Bureau, 2008-2010 American Community Survey 3-Year Estimates

Travel Time Index

Area	1985	1990	1995	2000	2005	2010
Urban Area[1]	1.10	1.19	1.20	1.27	1.31	1.23
Average[2]	1.11	1.16	1.18	1.21	1.25	1.20

Note: Travel Time Index—the ratio of travel time in the peak period to the travel time at free-flow conditions. A value of 1.30 indicates a 20-minute free-flow trip takes 26 minutes in the peak. Free-flow speeds (60 mph on freeways and 35 mph on principal arterials) are used as the comparison threshold; (1) Covers the Miami FL urban area; (2) average of 439 urban areas
Source: Texas Transportation Institute, Urban Mobility Report 2011, September 2011

Public Transportation

Agency Name / Mode of Transportation	Vehicles Operated in Maximum Service	Annual Unlinked Passenger Trips ('000)	Annual Passenger Miles ('000)
Broward County Transportation Department (BCT)			
Bus (directly operated)	249	36,585.3	172,113.5
Demand Response (purchased transportation)	231	769.2	7,384.5

Source: Federal Transit Administration, National Transit Database, 2010

Air Transportation

Airport Name and Code / Type of Service	Passenger Airlines[1]	Passenger Enplanements	Freight Carriers[2]	Freight (lbs.)
Miami International (MIA)				
Domestic service (U.S. carriers - 2011)	32	9,152,553	29	177,549,254
International service (U.S. carriers - 2010)	18	5,359,644	25	831,346,525

Note: (1) Includes all U.S.-based major, minor and commuter airlines that carried at least one passenger during the year; (2) Includes all U.S.-based airlines and freight carriers that transported at least one pound of freight during the year
Source: Bureau of Transportation Statistics, The Intermodal Transportation Database, Air Carriers: T-100 Domestic Market (U.S. Carriers), 2011; Bureau of Transportation Statistics, The Intermodal Transportation Database, Air Carriers: T-100 International Market (U.S. Carriers), 2010

Other Transportation Statistics

Major Highways:	I-75; CR-820 connecting to I-95 and FL Turnpike
Amtrak Service:	Yes (station is located in Hollywood)
Major Waterways/Ports:	Near Atlantic Ocean (10 miles)

Source: Amtrak.com; Google Maps

BUSINESSES

Major Business Headquarters

Company Name	Rankings	
	Fortune[1]	Forbes[2]
No companies listed	-	-

Note: (1) Fortune 500—companies that produce a 10-K are ranked 1 to 500 based on 2010 revenue; (2) all private companies with at least $2 billion in annual revenue are ranked 1 to 212; companies listed are headquartered in the city; dashes indicate no ranking
Source: Fortune, "Fortune 500," May 23, 2011; Forbes, "America's Largest Private Companies," November 16, 2011

Minority- and Women-Owned Businesses

Group	All Firms		Firms with Paid Employees			
	Firms	Sales ($000)	Firms	Sales ($000)	Employees	Payroll ($000)
Asian	958	140,340	184	87,933	948	17,668
Black	3,209	125,692	(s)	(s)	(s)	(s)
Hispanic	6,844	687,607	689	480,926	3,218	100,916
Women	6,031	337,152	626	158,543	1,925	46,069
All Firms	18,865	7,033,614	3,267	6,423,121	31,712	917,477

Note: Figures cover firms located in the city; minority- and women-owned business are defined as firms in which the corresponding group own 51% or more of the stock or equity of the company; (s) estimates are suppressed when publication standards are not met
Source: U.S. Census Bureau, 2007 Economic Census, Survey of Business Owners

HOTELS

Hotels/Motels

Area	5 Star		4 Star		3 Star		2 Star		1 Star		Not Rated	
	Num.	Pct.[3]	Num.	Pct.[3]	Num.	Pct.[3]	Num.	Pct.[3]	Num.	Pct.[3]	Num.	Pct.[3]
City[1]	0	0.0	2	4.8	15	35.7	23	54.8	0	0.0	2	4.8
Total[2]	133	0.9	940	6.5	4,569	31.8	7,033	48.9	351	2.4	1,343	9.3

Note: (1) Figures cover Pembroke Pines and vicinity; (2) Figures cover all 100 cities in this book; (3) Percentage of hotels which have a given star rating; Star ratings are determined by expedia.com and offer an indication of the general quality of a particular hotel.
Source: expedia.com, April 25, 2012

EVENT SITES

Convention Centers

Name	Overall Space (sq. ft.)	Exhibit Space (sq. ft.)	Meeting Space (sq. ft.)	Meeting Rooms
Pines Conference Center	n/a	n/a	n/a	n/a

Note: n/a not available
Source: Original research

Living Environment

COST OF LIVING

Cost of Living Index

Composite Index	Groceries	Housing	Utilities	Trans-portation	Health Care	Misc. Goods/ Services
111.1	106.8	128.7	94.3	108.2	103.1	104.9

Note: U.S. = 100; Figures cover the Fort Lauderdale FL urban area.
Source: The Council for Community and Economic Research, ACCRA Cost of Living Index, 2011

Grocery Prices

Area[1]	T-Bone Steak ($/pound)	Frying Chicken ($/pound)	Whole Milk ($/half gal.)	Eggs ($/dozen)	Orange Juice ($/64 oz.)	Coffee ($/11.5 oz.)
City[2]	10.38	1.40	2.69	1.87	3.16	4.20
Avg.	9.25	1.18	2.22	1.66	3.19	4.40
Min.	6.70	0.88	1.31	0.95	2.46	2.94
Max.	14.30	2.16	3.50	3.18	4.75	6.83

Note: (1) Values for the local area are compared with the average, minimum and maximum values for all 335 areas in the Cost of Living Index; (2) Figures cover the Fort Lauderdale FL urban area; **T-Bone Steak** (price per pound); **Frying Chicken** (price per pound, whole fryer); **Whole Milk** (half gallon carton); **Eggs** (price per dozen, Grade A, large); **Orange Juice** (64 oz. Tropicana or Florida Natural); **Coffee** (11.5 oz. can, vacuum-packed, Maxwell House, Hills Bros, or Folgers).
Source: The Council for Community and Economic Research, ACCRA Cost of Living Index, 2011

Housing and Utility Costs

Area[1]	New Home Price ($)	Apartment Rent ($/month)	All Electric ($/month)	Part Electric ($/month)	Other Energy ($/month)	Telephone ($/month)
City[2]	350,825	1,339	152.30	-	-	26.51
Avg.	285,990	839	163.23	89.00	77.52	26.92
Min.	188,005	460	125.58	45.39	33.89	17.98
Max.	1,197,028	3,244	339.16	181.97	348.69	40.01

Note: (1) Values for the local area are compared with the average, minimum and maximum values for all 335 areas in the Cost of Living Index; (2) Figures cover the Fort Lauderdale FL urban area; **New Home Price** (2,400 sf living area, 8,000 sf lot, in urban area with full utilities); **Apartment Rent** (950 sf 2 bedroom/1.5 or 2 bath, unfurnished, excluding all utilities except water); **All Electric** (average monthly cost for an all-electric home); **Part Electric** (average monthly cost for a part-electric home); **Other Energy** (average monthly cost for natural gas, fuel oil, coal, wood, and any other forms of energy except electricity); **Telephone** (price includes basic monthly rate for a private residential line plus additional local usage charges incurred by a family of four).
Source: The Council for Community and Economic Research, ACCRA Cost of Living Index, 2011

Health Care, Transportation, and Other Costs

Area[1]	Doctor ($/visit)	Dentist ($/visit)	Optometrist ($/visit)	Gasoline ($/gallon)	Beauty Salon ($/visit)	Men's Shirt ($)
City[2]	82.10	88.82	101.81	3.56	45.61	23.10
Avg.	93.88	81.72	90.54	3.48	32.65	25.06
Min.	60.00	55.33	53.66	3.18	19.78	13.44
Max.	154.98	145.97	183.72	4.31	63.21	46.00

Note: (1) Values for the local area are compared with the average, minimum and maximum values for all 335 areas in the Cost of Living Index; (2) Figures cover the Fort Lauderdale FL urban area; **Doctor** (general practitioners routine exam of an established patient); **Dentist** (adult teeth cleaning and periodic oral examination); **Optometrist** (full vision eye exam for established adult patient); **Gasoline** (one gallon regular unleaded, national brand, including all taxes, cash price at self-service pump if available); **Beauty Salon** (woman's shampoo, trim, and blow-dry); **Men's Shirt** (cotton/polyester dress shirt, pinpoint weave, long sleeves).
Source: The Council for Community and Economic Research, ACCRA Cost of Living Index, 2011

HOUSING

House Price Index (HPI)

Area	National Ranking[2]	Quarterly Change (%)	One-Year Change (%)	Five-Year Change (%)
MD[1]	203	0.71	-3.99	-44.84
U.S.[3]	-	-0.10	-2.43	-19.16

Note: The HPI is a weighted repeat sales index. It measures average price changes in repeat sales or refinancings on the same properties. This information is obtained by reviewing repeat mortgage transactions on single-family properties whose mortgages have been purchased or securitized by Fannie Mae or Freddie Mac in January 1975; (1) Metropolitan Division - see Appendix B for areas included; (2) Rankings are based on annual percentage change for all metro areas containing at least 15,000 transactions over the last 10 years and ranges from 1 to 306; (3) figures based on a weighted average of Census Division estimates using a purchase only index; all figures are for the period ending December 31, 2011
Source: Federal Housing Finance Agency, House Price Index, February 23, 2012

House Price Valuations

Area	Q4 2005 Price ($000)	Q4 2005 Over-valuation	Q4 2006 Price ($000)	Q4 2006 Over-valuation	Q4 2007 Price ($000)	Q4 2007 Over-valuation	Q4 2008 Price ($000)	Q4 2008 Over-valuation	Q4 2009 Price ($000)	Q4 2009 Over-valuation
MD[1]	259.4	41.9	268.7	39.5	237.6	22.1	161.2	-16.5	146.6	-24.0

Note: Figures show the percentage of over- or under-valuation of single family homes relative to statistically normal house values (e.g. a value of 23.6 indicates that house values are 23.6% overvalued). Statistically normal house values are based on house prices, interest rates, household incomes, population densities, and any historical premiums or discounts metropolitan areas have exhibited over time; (1) Figures cover the Fort Lauderdale-Pompano Beach-Deerfield Beach, FL - see Appendix B for areas included
Source: Global Insight/PNC Financial Services Group, House Prices in America: 4th Quarter 2009 Update

Median Single-Family Home Prices

Area	2009	2010	2011p	Percent Change 2010 to 2011
MSA[1]	211.2	201.9	181.1	-10.3
U.S. Average	172.1	173.1	166.2	-4.0

Note: Figures are median sales prices of existing single-family homes in thousands of dollars; (p) preliminary; n/a not available; (1) Metropolitan Statistical Area—see Appendix B for areas included
Source: National Association of Realtors, Median Sales Price of Existing Single-Family Homes for Metropolitan Areas, 4th Quarter 2011

Affordability Index of Existing Single-Family Homes

Area	2009	2010	2011p	Percent Change 2010 to 2011
MSA[1]	97.5	107.0	125.3	17.1

Note: The housing affordability index measures whether or not a typical family could qualify for a mortgage loan on a typical home. The higher the index, the greater the household purchasing power. An index of 100 is defined as the point where a median-income household has exactly enough income to qualify for the purchase of a median-priced existing single-family home, assuming a 20 percent downpayment and 25 percent of gross income devoted to mortgage principal and interest payments; (p) preliminary; n/a not available; (1) Metropolitan Statistical Area—see Appendix B for areas included
Source: National Association of Realtors, Affordability Index of Existing Single-Family Homes, 2011

Median Apartment Condo-Coop Home Prices

Area	2009	2010	2011p	Percent Change 2010 to 2011
MSA[1]	107.4	92.2	84.0	-8.9
U.S. Average	175.6	171.7	165.1	-3.8

Note: Figures are median sales prices of existing apartment condo-coop homes in thousands of dollars; (p) preliminary; n/a not available; (1) Metropolitan Statistical Area—see Appendix B for areas included
Source: National Association of Realtors, Median Sales Price of Existing Apartment Condo-Coop Homes for Metropolitan Areas, 4th Quarter 2011

Year Housing Structure Built

Area	2005 or Later	2000 -2004	1990 -1999	1980 -1989	1970 -1979	1960 -1969	1950 -1959	Before 1950	Median Year
City	1.6	11.9	41.1	22.0	15.7	5.5	1.9	0.3	1991
MSA[1]	3.6	9.5	14.8	19.7	23.0	13.0	10.5	5.7	1979
U.S.	5.0	8.6	14.0	14.1	16.3	11.3	11.2	19.6	1975

Note: Figures are percentages except for Median Year; (1) Figures cover the Miami-Fort Lauderdale-Pompano Beach, FL Metropolitan Statistical Area—see Appendix B for areas included
Source: U.S. Census Bureau, 2008-2010 American Community Survey 3-Year Estimates

HEALTH

Health Risk Data

Category	MSA[1] (%)	U.S. (%)
Adults who have been told they have high blood pressure[2]	31.8	28.7
Adults who have been told they have high blood cholesterol[2]	38.2	37.5
Adults who have been told they have diabetes[3]	7.5	8.7
Adults who have been told they have arthritis[2]	22.1	26.0
Adults who have been told they currently have asthma	7.7	9.1
Adults who are current smokers	12.4	17.3
Adults who are heavy drinkers[4]	2.5	5.0
Adults who are binge drinkers[5]	13.3	15.1
Adults who are overweight (BMI 25.0 - 29.9)	37.5	36.2
Adults who are obese (BMI 30.0 - 99.8)	28.3	27.5
Adults who participated in any physical activities in the past month	75.9	76.1
Adults 50+ who have ever had a sigmoidoscopy or colonoscopy	66.5	65.2
Women aged 40+ who have had a mammogram within the past two years	79.6	75.2
Men aged 40+ who have had a PSA test within the past two years	58.8	53.2
Adults aged 65+ who have had flu shot within the past year	51.7	67.5
Adults aged 18–64 who have any kind of health care coverage	72.1	82.2

Note: Data as of 2010 unless otherwise noted; (1) Figures cover the Miami-Fort Lauderdale-Miami Beach, FL Metropolitan Statistical Area—see Appendix B for areas included; (2) Data as of 2009; (3) Figures do not include pregnancy-related, borderline, or pre-diabetes; (4) Heavy drinkers are classified as males having more than two drinks per day or females having more than one drink per day; (5) Binge drinkers are classified as males having five or more drinks on one occasion or females having four or more drinks on one occasion
Source: Centers for Disease Control and Prevention, Behaviorial Risk Factor Surveillance System, SMART: Selected Metropolitan/Micropolitan Area Risk Trends, 2009, 2010

Mortality Rates for the Top 10 Causes of Death in the U.S.

ICD-10[a] Sub-Chapter	ICD-10[a] Code	Age-Adjusted Mortality Rate[1] per 100,000 population County[2]	U.S.
Malignant neoplasms	C00-C97	161.7	175.6
Ischaemic heart diseases	I20-I25	111.8	121.6
Other forms of heart disease	I30-I51	34.4	48.6
Chronic lower respiratory diseases	J40-J47	32.2	42.3
Cerebrovascular diseases	I60-I69	35.1	40.6
Organic, including symptomatic, mental disorders	F01-F09	11.7	26.7
Other degenerative diseases of the nervous system	G30-G31	28.5	24.7
Other external causes of accidental injury	W00-X59	24.4	24.4
Diabetes mellitus	E10-E14	16.6	21.7
Hypertensive diseases	I10-I15	15.8	18.2

Note: (a) ICD-10 = International Classification of Diseases 10th Revision; (1) Mortality rates are a three year average covering 2007-2009; (2) Figures cover Broward County
Source: Centers for Disease Control and Prevention, National Center for Health Statistics. Underlying Cause of Death 1999-2009 on CDC WONDER Online Database, released 2012. Data for year 2009 are compiled from the Multiple Cause of Death File 2009, Series 20 No. 2O, 2012, Data for year 2008 are compiled from the Multiple Cause of Death File 2008, Series 20 No. 2N, 2011, Data for year 2007 are compiled from Multiple Cause of Death File 2007, Series 20 No. 2M, 2010.

Mortality Rates for Selected Causes of Death

ICD-10[a] Sub-Chapter	ICD-10[a] Code	Age-Adjusted Mortality Rate[1] per 100,000 population	
		County[2]	U.S.
Assault	X85-Y09	5.7	5.7
Human immunodeficiency virus (HIV) disease	B20-B24	11.7	3.3
Influenza and pneumonia	J09-J18	6.8	16.4
Intentional self-harm	X60-X84	12.4	11.5
Malnutrition	E40-E46	*Unreliable	0.8
Obesity and other hyperalimentation	E65-E68	1.8	1.6
Transport accidents	V01-V99	13.7	13.7
Viral hepatitis	B15-B19	2.4	2.2

Note: (a) ICD-10 = International Classification of Diseases 10th Revision; (1) Mortality rates are a three year average covering 2007-2009; (2) Figures cover Broward County; (*) Unreliable data as per CDC
Source: Centers for Disease Control and Prevention, National Center for Health Statistics. Underlying Cause of Death 1999-2009 on CDC WONDER Online Database, released 2012. Data for year 2009 are compiled from the Multiple Cause of Death File 2009, Series 20 No. 2O, 2012, Data for year 2008 are compiled from the Multiple Cause of Death File 2008, Series 20 No. 2N, 2011, Data for year 2007 are compiled from Multiple Cause of Death File 2007, Series 20 No. 2M, 2010.

Distribution of Physicians and Dentists

Area[1]	Dentists[2]	D.O.[3]	M.D.[4]				
			Total	Family/General Practice	Pediatrics	Medical Specialties	Surgical Specialties
Local (number)	878	592	3,416	279	284	1,463	787
Local (rate[5])	5.0	3.4	19.5	1.6	1.6	8.3	4.5
U.S. (rate[5])	4.5	1.9	18.3	2.5	1.4	6.8	4.1

Note: Data as of 2008 unless noted; (1) Local data covers Broward County; (2) Data as of 2007; (3) Doctor of Osteopathic Medicine; (4) Includes active, non-federal, patient-care, office-based Doctors of Medicine; (5) rate per 10,000 population
Source: Area Resource File (ARF). 2009-2010 Release. U.S. Department of Health and Human Services, Health Resources and Services Administration, Bureau of Health Professions, Rockville, MD, August 2010

Best Hospitals

According to *U.S. News,* the Fort Lauderdale-Pompano Beach-Deerfield Beach, FL is home to one of the best hospitals in the U.S.: **Cleveland Clinic Florida** (1 specialty). The hospital listed was highly ranked in at least one adult specialty. *U.S. News Online, "America's Best Hospitals 2011-12"*

EDUCATION

Public School District Statistics

District Name	Schls	Pupils	Pupil/Teacher Ratio	Minority Pupils[1] (%)	Free Lunch Eligible[2] (%)	IEP[3] (%)
Broward	308	256,137	14.4	73.0	43.8	12.3

Note: Table includes school districts with 2,000 or more students; (1) Percentage of students that are not non-Hispanic white; (2) Percentage of students that are eligible for the free lunch program; (3) Percentage of students that have an Individualized Education Program.
Source: U.S. Department of Education, National Center for Education Statistics, Common Core of Data, Local Education Agency (School District) Universe Survey: School Year 2009-2010; U.S. Department of Education, National Center for Education Statistics, Common Core of Data, Public Elementary/Secondary School Universe Survey: School Year 2009-2010

Highest Level of Education

Area	Less than H.S.	H.S. Diploma	Some College, No Deg.	Associate Degree	Bachelors Degree	Masters Degree	Profess. School Degree	Doctorate Degree
City	11.6	24.7	21.5	10.4	20.3	8.7	1.5	1.1
MSA[1]	17.3	27.4	18.5	8.3	18.2	6.5	2.7	1.1
U.S.	14.7	28.4	21.3	7.6	17.6	7.2	1.9	1.2

Note: Figures cover persons age 25 and over; (1) Figures cover the Miami-Fort Lauderdale-Pompano Beach, FL Metropolitan Statistical Area—see Appendix B for areas included
Source: U.S. Census Bureau, 2008-2010 American Community Survey 3-Year Estimates

Educational Attainment by Race

Area	High School Graduate or Higher (%)					Bachelor's Degree or Higher (%)				
	Total	White	Black	Asian	Hisp.[2]	Total	White	Black	Asian	Hisp.[2]
City	88.4	88.0	89.5	87.4	84.9	31.7	29.8	33.4	52.2	29.4
MSA[1]	82.7	84.6	76.4	85.9	75.0	28.5	31.1	17.3	46.7	23.6
U.S.	85.3	87.5	81.4	85.5	61.6	28.0	29.3	17.8	50.2	13.0

Note: Figures shown cover persons 25 years old and over; (1) Figures cover the Miami-Fort Lauderdale-Pompano Beach, FL Metropolitan Statistical Area—see Appendix B for areas included; (2) People of Hispanic origin can be of any race
Source: U.S. Census Bureau, 2008-2010 American Community Survey 3-Year Estimates

School Enrollment by Grade and Control

Area	Preschool (%)		Kindergarten (%)		Grades 1 - 4 (%)		Grades 5 - 8 (%)		Grades 9 - 12 (%)	
	Public	Private	Public	Private	Public	Private	Public	Private	Public	Private
City	27.6	72.4	83.2	16.8	89.6	10.4	90.9	9.1	87.6	12.4
MSA[1]	44.6	55.4	82.0	18.0	87.2	12.8	87.3	12.7	88.1	11.9
U.S.	55.4	44.6	87.1	12.9	89.4	10.6	89.5	10.5	90.4	9.6

Note: Figures shown cover persons 3 years old and over; (1) Figures cover the Miami-Fort Lauderdale-Pompano Beach, FL Metropolitan Statistical Area—see Appendix B for areas included
Source: U.S. Census Bureau, 2008-2010 American Community Survey 3-Year Estimates

Average Salaries of Public School Classroom Teachers

Area	2010-11		2011-12		Percent Change 2010-11 to 2011-12	Percent Change 2001-02 to 2011-12
	Dollars	Rank[1]	Dollars	Rank[1]		
Florida	45,732	45	46,232	46	1.09	17.70
U.S. Average	55,623	-	56,643	-	1.83	26.8

Note: (1) State rank ranges from 1 to 51 where 1 indicates highest salary.
Source: National Education Association, Rankings & Estimates: Rankings of the States 2011 and Estimates of School Statistics 2012, December 2011

Higher Education

Four-Year Colleges			Two-Year Colleges			Medical Schools[1]	Law Schools[2]	Voc/ Tech[3]
Public	Private Non-profit	Private For-profit	Public	Private Non-profit	Private For-profit			
0	0	1	0	0	2	0	0	0

Note: Figures cover institutions located within the city limits and include main campuses only; (1) includes schools accredited by the Liaison Committee on Medical Education and the American Osteopathic Association's Commission on Osteopathic College Accreditation; (2) includes American Bar Association-accredited law schools; (3) includes all schools with programs that are less than 2 years.
Source: National Center for Education Statistics, Integrated Postsecondary Education System (IPEDS) Peer Analysis System, 2011-12; Association of American Medical Colleges, Member List, April 23, 2012; American Osteopathic Association, Member List, April 23, 2012; Law School Admission Council, Official Guide to ABA-Approved Law Schools Online, April 23, 2012

PRESIDENTIAL ELECTION

2008 Presidential Election Results

Area	Obama	McCain	Nader	Other
Broward County	67.0	32.3	0.2	0.4
U.S.	52.9	45.6	0.6	0.9

Note: Results are percentages and may not add to 100% due to rounding
Source: Dave Leip's Atlas of U.S. Presidential Elections, www.uselectionatlas.org

EMPLOYERS

Major Employers

Company Name	Industry
Baptist Health South Florida	General medical and surgical hospitals
Baptist Hospital of Miami	General medical and surgical hospitals
County of Miami-Dade	Police protection, county government
County of Miami-Dade	Regulation, administration of transportation
County of, Palm Beach	County supervisors' and executives' office
Florida International University	Colleges and universities
Intercoastal Health Systems	Management services
Miami Dade College	Community college
Mount Sinai Medical Center of Florida	General medical and surgical hospitals
North Broward Hospital District	Hospital, ama approved residency
North Broward Hospital District	General and family practice, physician/surgeon
Royal Caribbean Cruises Ltd.	Computer processing services
Royal Caribbean Cruises Ltd.	Deep sea passenger transportation, except ferry
School Board of Palm Beach County	Public elementary and secondary schools
Style View Products	Storm doors of windows, metal
The Answer Group	Custom computer programming services
University of Miami	Colleges and universities
Veterans Health Administration	General medical and surgical hospitals

Note: Companies shown are located within the Miami-Fort Lauderdale-Pompano Beach, FL metropolitan area.
Source: Hoovers.com, data extracted April 25 2012

PUBLIC SAFETY

Crime Rate

Area	All Crimes	Violent Crimes				Property Crimes		
		Murder	Forcible Rape	Robbery	Aggrav. Assault	Burglary	Larceny -Theft	Motor Vehicle Theft
City	3,598.4	2.7	8.1	62.4	114.0	747.9	2,456.2	207.0
Suburbs[1]	4,388.7	3.6	26.2	186.6	293.6	996.0	2,612.3	270.4
Metro[2]	4,323.2	3.5	24.7	176.3	278.7	975.5	2,599.4	265.1
U.S.	3,345.5	4.8	27.5	119.1	252.3	699.6	2,003.5	238.8

Note: Figures are crimes per 100,000 population; (1) All areas within the metro area that are located outside the city limits; (2) Metropolitan Division—see Appendix B for areas included
Source: FBI Uniform Crime Reports, 2010

Hate Crimes

Area	Number of Quarters Reported	Bias Motivation				
		Race	Religion	Sexual Orientation	Ethnicity	Disability
City	4	0	0	0	0	0

Source: Federal Bureau of Investigation, Hate Crime Statistics 2010

Identity Theft Consumer Complaints

Area	Complaints	Complaints per 100,000 Population	Rank[2]
MSA[1]	17,546	324.1	1
U.S.	279,156	90.4	-

Note: (1) Metropolitan Statistical Area—see Appendix B for areas included; (2) Rank ranges from 1 to 384 where 1 indicates greatest number of identity theft complaints per 100,000 population
Source: Federal Trade Commission, Consumer Sentinel Network Data Book for January–December 2011

Fraud and Other Consumer Complaints

Area	Complaints	Complaints per 100,000 Population	Rank[2]
MSA[1]	25,320	467.7	197
U.S.	1,533,924	496.8	-

Note: (1) Metropolitan Statistical Area—see Appendix B for areas included; (2) Rank ranges from 1 to 384 where 1 indicates greatest number of fraud and other complaints per 100,000 population
Source: Federal Trade Commission, Consumer Sentinel Network Data Book for January–December 2011

RECREATION

Culture

Dance[1]	Theatre[1]	Instrumental Music[1]	Vocal Music[1]	Series/ Festivals	Museums	Zoos and Aquariums[2]
0	0	0	0	0	n/a	0

Note: (1) Number of professional performing groups; (2) AZA-accredited; n/a not available
Source: The Grey House Performing Arts Directory, 2011-2012; Official Museum Directory, 2011; American Association of Museums, AAM Member Museums, April 2012; Association of Zoos & Aquariums, AZA Member Zoos & Aquariums, April 2012

Professional Sports Teams

Team Name	League
Florida Panthers	National Hockey League (NHL)
Miami Dolphins	National Football League (NFL)
Miami Heat	National Basketball Association (NBA)
Miami Marlins	Major League Baseball (MLB)

Note: Includes teams located in the Miami-Fort Lauderdale metro area.
Source: Original research

CLIMATE

Average and Extreme Temperatures

Temperature	Jan	Feb	Mar	Apr	May	Jun	Jul	Aug	Sep	Oct	Nov	Dec	Yr.
Extreme High (°F)	88	89	92	96	95	98	98	98	97	95	89	87	98
Average High (°F)	75	77	79	82	85	88	89	90	88	85	80	77	83
Average Temp. (°F)	68	69	72	75	79	82	83	83	82	78	73	69	76
Average Low (°F)	59	60	64	68	72	75	76	76	76	72	66	61	69
Extreme Low (°F)	30	35	32	42	55	60	69	68	68	53	39	30	30

Note: Figures cover the years 1948-1990
Source: National Climatic Data Center, International Station Meteorological Climate Summary, 9/96

Average Precipitation/Snowfall/Humidity

Precip./Humidity	Jan	Feb	Mar	Apr	May	Jun	Jul	Aug	Sep	Oct	Nov	Dec	Yr.
Avg. Precip. (in.)	1.9	2.0	2.3	3.0	6.2	8.7	6.1	7.5	8.2	6.6	2.7	1.8	57.1
Avg. Snowfall (in.)	0	0	0	0	0	0	0	0	0	0	0	0	0
Avg. Rel. Hum. 7am (%)	84	84	82	80	81	84	84	86	88	87	85	84	84
Avg. Rel. Hum. 4pm (%)	59	57	57	57	62	68	66	67	69	65	63	60	63

Note: Figures cover the years 1948-1990; Tr = Trace amounts (<0.05 in. of rain; <0.5 in. of snow)
Source: National Climatic Data Center, International Station Meteorological Climate Summary, 9/96

Weather Conditions

Temperature			Daytime Sky			Precipitation		
32°F & below	45°F & below	90°F & above	Clear	Partly cloudy	Cloudy	0.01 inch or more precip.	0.1 inch or more snow/ice	Thunder-storms
<1	7	55	48	263	54	128	0	74

Note: Figures are average number of days per year and cover the years 1948-1990
Source: National Climatic Data Center, International Station Meteorological Climate Summary, 9/96

HAZARDOUS WASTE

Superfund Sites

Pembroke Pines has no sites on the EPA's Superfund Final National Priorities List.
U.S. Environmental Protection Agency, Final National Priorities List, April 17, 2012

**AIR & WATER
QUALITY**

Air Quality Index

| Area | Percent of Days when Air Quality was...[2] | | | | | AQI Statistics[2] | |
	Good	Moderate	Unhealthy for Sensitive Groups	Unhealthy	Very Unhealthy	Maximum	Median
Area[1]	95.9	4.1	0.0	0.0	0.0	100	34

Note: Air Quality Index (AQI) is an index for reporting daily air quality. EPA calculates the AQI for five major air pollutants regulated by the Clean Air Act: ground-level ozone, particle pollution (aka particulate matter), carbon monoxide, sulfur dioxide, and nitrogen dioxide. The AQI runs from 0 to 500. The higher the AQI value, the greater the level of air pollution and the greater the health concern. There are six AQI categories: "Good" AQI is between 0 and 50. Air quality is considered satisfactory; "Moderate" AQI is between 51 and 100. Air quality is acceptable; "Unhealthy for Sensitive Groups" When AQI values are between 101 and 150, members of sensitive groups may experience health effects; "Unhealthy" When AQI values are between 151 and 200 everyone may begin to experience health effects; "Very Unhealthy" AQI values between 201 and 300 trigger a health alert; "Hazardous" AQI values over 300 trigger warnings of emergency conditions (not shown); (1) Data covers Broward County; (2) Based on 365 days with AQI data in 2011.
Source: U.S. Environmental Protection Agency, AirData Report, 2011

Air Quality Index Pollutants

| Area | Percent of Days when AQI Pollutant was...[2] | | | | | |
	Carbon Monoxide	Nitrogen Dioxide	Ozone	Sulfur Dioxide	Particulate Matter 2.5	Particulate Matter 10
Area[1]	0.0	6.8	56.4	0.0	36.7	0.0

Note: The Air Quality Index (AQI) is an index for reporting daily air quality. EPA calculates the AQI for five major air pollutants regulated by the Clean Air Act: ground-level ozone, particle pollution (also known as particulate matter), carbon monoxide, sulfur dioxide, and nitrogen dioxide. The AQI runs from 0 to 500. The higher the AQI value, the greater the level of air pollution and the greater the health concern; (1) Data covers Broward County; (2) Based on 365 days with AQI data in 2011.
Source: U.S. Environmental Protection Agency, AirData Report, 2011

Air Quality Index Trends

| Area | Trend Sites (days) | | | | | | | | All Sites (days) |
	2003	2004	2005	2006	2007	2008	2009	2010	2010
MSA[1]	4	11	4	12	10	5	2	4	4

Note: Figures are the number of days the AQI value exceeded 100 in a given year. An AQI value greater than 100 indicates that air quality would have been in the unhealthful range on that day. Data from exceptional events are included. These counts are presented in two ways. First, the counts are based on sites having an adequate record of monitoring data during the trend period (trend sites). These counts represent the relative change in the number of days with AQI values greater than 100. In the last column, the counts are based on all sites with data in the most recent year (because it is possible for a site to have data in the most recent year but not enough data to be a trend site); (1) Data covers the Miami-Fort Lauderdale-Pompano Beach, FL—see Appendix B for areas included
Source: U.S. Environmental Protection Agency, Air Quality Index Information, "Number of Days with Air Quality Index Values Greater than 100 at Trend Sites, 2000-2010, and at All Sites in 2010"

Maximum Air Pollutant Concentrations: Particulate Matter, Ozone, CO and Lead

	Particulate Matter 10 (ug/m^3)	Particulate Matter 2.5 Wtd AM (ug/m^3)	Particulate Matter 2.5 24-Hr (ug/m^3)	Ozone (ppm)	Carbon Monoxide (ppm)	Lead (ug/m^3)
MSA[1] Level	44	7.8	14	0.069	2	n/a
NAAQS[2]	150	15	35	0.075	9	0.15
Met NAAQS[2]	Yes	Yes	Yes	Yes	Yes	n/a

Note: Data from exceptional events are not included; (1) Data covers the Miami-Fort Lauderdale-Pompano Beach, FL—see Appendix B for areas included; (2) National Ambient Air Quality Standards; ppm = parts per million; ug/m^3 = micrograms per cubic meter; n/a not available
Concentrations: Particulate Matter 10 (coarse particulate)—highest second maximum 24-hour concentration; Particulate Matter 2.5 Wtd AM (fine particulate)—highest weighted annual mean concentration; Particulate Matter 2.5 24-Hour (fine particulate)—highest 98th percentile 24-hour concentration; Ozone—highest fourth daily maximum 8-hour concentration; Carbon Monoxide—highest second maximum non-overlapping 8-hour concentration; Lead—maximum running 3-month average
Source: U.S. Environmental Protection Agency, CBSA Factbook 2010, Air Quality Statistics by City, 2010

Maximum Air Pollutant Concentrations: Nitrogen Dioxide and Sulfur Dioxide

	Nitrogen Dioxide AM (ppb)	Nitrogen Dioxide 1-Hr (ppb)	Sulfur Dioxide AM (ppb)	Sulfur Dioxide 1-Hr (ppb)	Sulfur Dioxide 24-Hr (ppb)
MSA[1] Level	9.651	49	0.831	38	5.9
NAAQS[2]	53	100	30	75	140
Met NAAQS[2]	Yes	Yes	Yes	Yes	Yes

Note: Data from exceptional events are not included; (1) Data covers the Miami-Fort Lauderdale-Pompano Beach, FL—see Appendix B for areas included; (2) National Ambient Air Quality Standards; ppb = parts per billion; n/a not available
Concentrations: Nitrogen Dioxide AM—highest arithmetic mean concentration; Nitrogen Dioxide 1-Hr—highest 98th percentile 1-hour daily maximum concentration; Sulfur Dioxide AM—highest annual mean concentration; Sulfur Dioxide 1-Hr—highest 99th percentile 1-hour daily maximum concentration; Sulfur Dioxide 24-Hr—highest second maximum 24-hour concentration
Source: U.S. Environmental Protection Agency, CBSA Factbook 2010, Air Quality Statistics by City, 2010

Drinking Water

Water System Name	Pop. Served	Primary Water Source Type	Violations[1] Health Based	Violations[1] Monitoring/ Reporting
City of Pembroke Pines	156,254	Ground	0	2

Note: (1) Based on violation data from January 1, 2011 to December 31, 2011 (includes unresolved violations from earlier years)
Source: U.S. Environmental Protection Agency, Office of Ground Water and Drinking Water, Safe Drinking Water Information System (based on data extracted April 18, 2012)

Plano, Texas

Background

Plano, just 20 miles north of downtown Dallas, is the largest city in Collin County. Its location, and the performance of its municipal government and local economy, help to explain why Plano proudly presents itself as a good choice for families and businesses of all types.

The city was first settled in the 1840s during the era of the Republic of Texas, mostly by migrants from Kentucky and Tennessee who were seeking new hunting and grazing areas. In 1846, William Foreman, an early entrepreneur, established a sawmill and gristmill at the site, and later a store and cotton gin. Such improvements began to attract new settlers and, by 1850, residents decided they needed an official post office. Their first application requesting the name Fillmore to the federal government, in honor of the president of the United States, was rejected, and in its place, Foreman's name was proposed. This alternative, however, was also rejected, and finally, the descriptive Plano (Spanish for plain) was suggested and adopted.

Cattle and other livestock were the mainstay of Plano's early economy, but gradually farmers began to exploit the rich, black soil of the area. Population and economic growth was slow and steady until the Civil War, but afterwards, with the growth of railroads and the adjacent towns, Plano began to assume its modern form. In 1872, with the completion of the Houston and Texas Railroad, Plano's economy took off, and the city was incorporated in 1873. Although for much its early life, Plano had been dependent on agriculture, all manner of building and business flourished toward the end of the nineteenth century. It was said locally that virtually anything could be bought, sold, or traded in the city. By the mid-twentieth century, Plano had almost completed its conversion from farming to trading, and by the 1960s, the expansion of Dallas had exerted a significant effect.

With the historic shift of manufacturing and labor from the North to the South, Plano achieved its economic maturity.

Today, Plano is headquarters of several large corporations, such as Pizza Hut, Frito Lay, J.C. Penney, Dr. Pepper Snapple Group, HP Enterprise ServicesDell, Rent-A-Center, and Ericsson.

The Plano Independent School District (PISD) serves the City of Plano, portions of Dallas and Richardson, the City of Parker, portions of Allen and Murphy, Carrollton, Garland, Lucas, and Wylie. The schools have consistently garnered awards, and the school district itself most recently garnered an "exemplary" rating from the Texas Education Agency in preliminary 2010 ratings.

In and around Plano are numerous institutions of higher learning, including Austin College, Collin College Spring Creek Campus and Courtyard Center, Dallas Baptist University-Frisco, Richland College, SMU-in-Plano, University of North Texas Irving, University of North Texas Denton, and the University of Texas Southwestern Medical School.

There are more than 65 parks and numerous acres of park land in the city. Also in Plano is the Southfork Ranch, set of the iconic 1980s TV show "Dallas."

Plano can be hot in the summer. The good news, though, is that there is plenty of sunshine. Winters are generally mild, and cold snaps are infrequent and short-lived. Rainfall is relatively plentiful and usually falls more often at night than during daytime.

Rankings

General Rankings

- Plano was selected as one of America's best cities by *Bloomberg Businessweek*. The city ranked #11 out of 50. Criteria: number of restaurants, bars and museums per capita; number of colleges, libraries, and professional sports teams; income, poverty, unemployment, crime, and foreclosure rates; percent of population with bachelor's degrees; public school performance; park acres per capita; air quality. *BusinessWeek, "America's 50 Best Cities," September 20, 2011*

Business/Finance Rankings

- Dallas was identified as one of the 20 strongest-performing metro areas during the recession and recovery from trough quarter through the third quarter of 2011. Criteria: percent change in employment; percentage point change in unemployment rate; percent change in gross metropolitan product; percent change in House Price Index. *Brookings Institution, MetroMonitor: Tracking Economic Recession and Recovery in America's 100 Largest Metropolitan Areas, December 2011*

- The Dallas metro area was identified as one of 10 "Cities Where the Recession is Easing." The metro area was ranked #3. Criteria: job growth; goods produced; home sale prices; unemployment rates. *Forbes.com, "Cities Where the Recession is Easing," March 3, 2010*

- The Dallas metro area was identified as one of five places with the worst wage growth in America. The area ranked #4. Criteria: private-sector wage growth between the 4th quarter of 2010 and the 4th quarter of 2011. *PayScale, "Five Worst Cities for Wage Growth," January 12, 2012*

- The Dallas metro area was identified as one of the most affordable major metropolitan areas in America by *Forbes*. The metro area was ranked #14 out of 15. Criteria: median asking price of homes for sale; median salaries of workers with bachelor's degrees or higher compared to a cost-of-living index; unemployment rates. *Forbes.com, "The Most Affordable Cities in America," January 7, 2011*

- Experian ranked the top 20 major U.S. metropolitan areas by average debt per consumer. The Dallas metro area was ranked #2. Criteria: average debt per consumer. Debt for this study includes credit cards, auto loans and personal loans. It does not include mortgages. *Experian, May 13, 2010*

- The Dallas metro area was identified as one of the "Best U.S. Cities for Earning a Living" by *Forbes*. The metro area ranked #8. Criteria: median income; cost of living; job growth; number of companies on *Forbes* 400 best big company and 200 best small company lists. *Forbes.com, "Best U.S. Cities for Earning a Living," August 21, 2008*

- Dallas was cited as one of America's top metros for new and expanded facility projects in 2011. The area ranked #4 in the large metro area category (population over 1 million). *Site Selection, "2011 Top Metros," March 2012*

- *American City Business Journals* ranked America's 261 largest cities in terms of their resident's wealth. Plano ranked #22. Criteria: per capita income; median household income; percentage of households with annual incomes of $200,000 or more; median home value. *American City Business Journals, "Where the Money Is: America's Wealth Centers," August 18, 2008*

- The Dallas metro area appeared on the Milken Institute "2011 Best Performing Metros" list. Rank: #20 out of 200 large metro areas. Criteria: job growth; wage and salary growth; high-tech output growth. *Milken Institute, "2011 Best Performing Metros"*

- The Dallas metro area was selected as one of the best cities for entrepreneurs in America by *Inc. Magazine*. Criteria: job-growth data for 335 metro areas was analyzed for: recent growth trend; mid-term growth; long-term trend; current year growth. The Dallas metro area ranked #12 among large metro areas and #57 overall. *Inc. Magazine, "The Best Cities for Doing Business," July 2008*

- Dallas was ranked #52 out of 145 regions worldwide in terms of its "Knowledge Competitiveness Index." The index attempts to measure the knowledge-based development taking place throughout the world and is based on 19 measures of economic performance that indicate a region's ability to translate its knowledge capacity into economic value. *Centre for International Competitiveness, World Knowledge Competitiveness Index 2008*

- *Forbes* ranked the 200 most populous metro areas in the U.S. in terms of the "Best Places for Business and Careers." The Dallas metro area was ranked #10. Criteria: costs (business and living); job growth (past and projected); income growth; educational attainment; projected economic growth; crime; cultural and recreational opportunities; net migration patterns; number of highly ranked colleges. *Forbes, "Best Places for Business and Careers," June 2011*

Children/Family Rankings

- Plano was identified as one of the best cities for raising a family by *24/7 Wall St.* The city ranked #7. The nation's 100 largest cities were evaluated on the following criteria: large public outdoor spaces; top hospitals; strong schools; low unemployment; high educational attainment; low violent crime rates. *24/7 Wall St., "The 10 Best U.S. Cities for Raising a Family," January 13, 2012*

- The Dallas metro area was selected as one of the "Best Cities for Relocating Families" by Worldwide ERC and Primacy Relocation. The 2008 study looked at nearly 50 factors important to relocating families including: recent job growth; nearby top-ranked colleges; in-state tuition for four-year public colleges; population growth since 2000; pediatricians per 100,000 population; and a Green Living index. *Worldwide ERC and Primacy Relocation, "2008 Best Cities for Relocating Families"*

Dating/Romance Rankings

- Eli Lily and Company, in partnership with Sperling's BestPlaces, ranked the nation's 50 largest metro areas in terms of the "Most Romantic Cities for Baby Boomers." The Dallas metro area ranked #9. Criteria: marriage and divorce rates among baby boomers age 45 to 60; great restaurants; dance studios; chocolate, jewelry and flower sales. *Eli Lily and Company, "Most Romantic Cities for Baby Boomers," April 20, 2007*

- The Dallas metro area was selected as one of the "Best Cities for Relocating Singles" by Worldwide ERC and Primacy Relocation. The area ranked #37 out of the 100 largest metro areas in the U.S. Criteria: recent job growth; recent singles population growth; overall population growth; affordable rental housing; cost-of-living index; expanded arts and recreation opportunities; ratio of single men and single women; affordability of quality higher education (including state residency requirements); diversity index; climate; population density. *Worldwide ERC and Primacy Relocation, "2008 Best Cities for Relocating Singles"*

- *Forbes* ranked the 40 most populous urbanized areas in the U.S. in terms of the "Best Cities for Singles." The Dallas metro area ranked #17. Criteria: number of singles; cost of living alone; nightlife; culture; job growth; coolness; and online dating participation. *Forbes.com, "Best Cities for Singles," July 27, 2009*

Education Rankings

- *Men's Health* ranked 100 U.S. cities in terms of their education levels. Plano was ranked #2 (#1 = most educated city). Criteria: high school graduation rates; school enrollment; educational attainment; number of households who have outstanding student loans; number of households whose members have taken adult-education courses. *Men's Health, "Where School Is In: The Most and Least Educated Cities," September 12, 2011*

- Plano was selected as one of "America's Most Literate Cities." The city ranked #46 out of the 75 largest U.S. cities. Criteria: number of booksellers; library resources; Internet resources; educational attainment; periodical publishing resources; newspaper circulation. *Central Connecticut State University, "America's Most Literate Cities 2011"*

- Dallas was identified as one of the 100 "smartest" metro areas in the U.S. The area ranked #72. Criteria: the editors rated the collective brainpower of the 100 largest metro areas in the U.S. based on their residents' educational attainment. *American City Business Journals, April 14, 2008*

- Plano was identified as one of America's most inventive cities by *The Daily Beast*. The city ranked #10 out of 25. The 200 largest cities in the U.S. were ranked by the number of patents (applied and approved) per capita. *The Daily Beast, "The 25 Most Inventive Cities," October 2, 2011*

- Dallas was identified as one of "America's Brainiest Bastions" by *Portfolio.com*. The metro area ranked #96 out of 200. *Portfolio.com* analyzed levels of educational attainment in the nation's 200 largest metropolitan areas. The editors established scores for five levels of educational attainment, based on relative earning power of adult workers age 25 or older. Scores were determined by comparing the median income for all workers with the median income for those workers at a specified educational level. *Portfolio.com, "America's Brainiest Bastions," December 1, 2010*

Environmental Rankings

- The Dallas was identified as one of North America's greenest metropolitan areas. The area ranked #17. The Green City Index is comprised of 31 indicators, and scores cities across nine categories: carbon dioxide; energy; land use; buildings; transport; water; waste; air quality; environmental governance. The 27 largest metropolitan areas in the U.S. and Canada were considered. *Economist Intelligence Unit, sponsored by Siemens, "U.S. and Canada Green City Index, 2011"*

- The Dallas was identified as one of America's cities with the most ENERGY STAR certified buildings. The area ranked #10 out of 25. Criteria: number of ENERGY STAR labeled buildings in 2010. *U.S. Environmental Protection Agency, "Top Cities With the Most ENERGY STAR Certified Buildings," March 15, 2011*

- Plano was selected as one of 22 "Smarter Cities" for energy by the Natural Resources Defense Council. Criteria: investment in green power; energy efficiency measures; conservation. *Natural Resources Defense Council, "2010 Smarter Cities," July 19, 2010*

- *American City Business Journal* ranked 43 metropolitan areas in terms of their "greenness." The Dallas metro area ranked #37. Criteria: Forty-one metros in which *ACBJ* has business weeklies, plus Indianapolis and Cleveland, were ranked based on 20 different indicators such as adoption of green technologies, utilization of environmentally sound practices, and air and water quality. *American City Business Journals, "Green City Index," March 11, 2010*

- 100 of the largest metro areas in the U.S. were analyzed in terms of their current drought severity. The Dallas metro area ranked #97 (#1 = driest). The rankings were based on statistics such as long-term precipitation trends and patterns and the Palmer drought indices. *Sperling's BestPlaces, www.BestPlaces.net, "America's Drought-Riskiest Cities," November 2007*

- The Dallas metro area appeared in *Country Home's* "Best Green Places" report. The area ranked #94 out of 379. Criteria: official energy policies; green power; green buildings; availability of fresh, locally grown food. *Country Home, "Best Green Places," 2008*

- Dallas was highlighted as one of the 25 most ozone-polluted metro areas in the U.S. The area ranked #12. *American Lung Association, State of the Air 2011*

Health/Fitness Rankings

- The Dallas metro area was selected as one of the worst cities for bed bugs in America by Rollins corporation, the owner of seven pest control companies, including Orkin. The area ranked #7 based on the number of bed bug treatments from January to December 2011. *Rollins, "The Top 50 U.S. Cities for Bed Bugs," March 19, 2012*

- Dallas was identified as one of "The 8 Most Artery-Clogging Cities in America." The metro area ranked #5. Criteria: obesity rates; heart disease rates. *Prevention, "The 8 Most Artery-Clogging Cities in America," December 2011*

- Dallas was identified as a "2011 Asthma Capital." The area ranked #34 out of the nation's 100 largest metropolitan areas. Twelve factors were used to identify the most challenging places to live for people with asthma: estimated prevalence; self-reported prevalence; crude death rate for asthma; annual pollen score; annual air quality; public smoking laws; number of board-certified asthma specialists; school inhaler access laws; rescue medication use; controller medication use; uninsured rate; poverty rate. *Asthma and Allergy Foundation of America, "2011 Asthma Capitals"*

- Dallas was identified as a "2011 Fall Allergy Capital." The area ranked #22 out of 100. Three groups of factors were used to identify the most severe cities for people with allergies during the fall season: annual pollen levels; medicine utilization; access to board-certified allergists. *Asthma and Allergy Foundation of America, "2011 Fall Allergy Capitals"*

- Dallas was identified as a "2012 Spring Allergy Capital." The area ranked #24 out of 100. Three groups of factors were used to identify the most severe cities for people with allergies during the spring season: annual pollen levels; medicine utilization; access to board-certified allergists. *Asthma and Allergy Foundation of America, "2012 Spring Allergy Capitals"*

- *Men's Health* examined 100 major U.S. cities and selected the best and worst cities for men. Plano ranked #3. Criteria: 35 statistical parameters of long life in the categories of health, quality of life, and fitness. *Men's Health, "The 10 Best and Worst Cities for Men 2012," January/February 2012*

- *Men's Health* examined 100 U.S. cities and selected the best and worst cities for women. Plano was ranked among the ten best at #1. Criteria: dozens of statistical parameters of long life in the categories of health, quality of life, and fitness. *Men's Health, "The 10 Best and Worst Cities for Women 2011," January/February 2011*

- The makers of Breath Right Nasal Strips, in partnership with Sperling's BestPlaces, analyzed 50 metro areas and identified those U.S. cities most challenged by chronic nasal congestion. The Dallas metro area ranked #7. Criteria: tree, grass and weed pollens; molds and spores; air pollution; climate; smoking; purchase habits of congestion products; prescriptions of drugs for congestion relief; incidence of influenza. *Breathe Right Nasal Strips, "Most Congested Cities," October 3, 2011*

- The American Academy of Dermatology ranked 26 U.S. metropolitan regions in terms of their residents knowledge, attitude and behaviors towards tanning, sun protection and skin cancer detection. The Dallas metro area ranked #11. The results of the study are based on an online survey of over 7,000 adults nationwide. *American Academy of Dermatology, "Suntelligence: How Sun Smart is Your City," May 3, 2010*

- The Dallas metro area appeared in the 2011 Gallup-Healthways Well-Being Index. The index, based on interviews with more than 350,000 Americans, measured jobs, finances, physical health, emotional state of mind and communities. The metro area ranked #64 out of 190. Criteria: life evaluation; emotional health; work environment; physical health; healthy behaviors; basic access (basic needs optimal for a healthy life, such as access to food and medicine, having health insurance and feeling safe while walking at night). *Gallup-Healthways, "State of Well-Being 2011"*

- The Dallas metro area was identified as one of "America's Most Stressful Cities" by *Sperling's BestPlaces*. The metro area ranked #43 out of 50. Criteria: unemployment rate; suicide rate; commute time; mental health; poor rest; alcohol use; violent crime rate; property crime rate; cloudy days annually. *Sperling's BestPlaces, www.BestPlaces.net, "Stressful Cities 2012*

- The Dallas metro area was identified as one of "America's Most Stressful Cities" by *Forbes*. The metro area ranked #9 out of 40. Criteria: housing affordability; unemployment rate; cost of living; air quality; traffic congestion; sunny days; population density. *Forbes.com, "America's Most Stressful Cities," September 23, 2011*

- *Men's Health* ranked 100 U.S. cities in terms of their activity levels. Plano was ranked #64 (#1 = most active city). Criteria: where and how often residents exercise; percentage of households that watch more than 15 hours of cable television a week and buy more than 11 video games a year; death rate from deep-vein thrombosis, a condition linked to sitting for extended periods of time. *Men's Health, "Where Sit Happens: The Most and Least Active Cities in America," June 20, 2011*

- 50 of the largest metro areas in the U.S. were analyzed in terms of their health and fitness by the American College of Sports Medicine in their "American Fitness Index." The Dallas metro area ranked #40 (#1 = healthiest). Criteria: preventative health behaviors; levels of chronic disease; health care access; community resources and policies that support physical activity. *American College of Sports Medicine, "Health and Community Fitness Status of the 50 Largest Metropolitan Areas," August 1, 2011*

Real Estate Rankings

- *Fortune* ranked the 100 largest metro areas in the U.S. in terms of projected median home price change in 2010. The Dallas metro area ranked #13. *Fortune, "The 2010 Housing Outlook," December 9, 2009*

- Plano appeared on *ApartmentRatings.com* "Top Cities for Renters" list in 2009." The area ranked #14. Overall satisfaction ratings were ranked using thousands of user submitted scores for hundreds of apartment complexes located in the 100 most populated U.S. municipalities. *ApartmentRatings.com, "2009 Renter Satisfaction Rankings"*

- The Dallas metro area was identified as one of the "Top 25 Real Estate Investment Markets" by *FinestExperts.com*. The metro area ranked #1. Over 10,000 real estate markets were analyzed to identify the most suitable places for real estate investors to seek stability and growth. Criteria: employment; rental markets; growth levels as offset by foreclosures. *FinestExperts.com, "Top 25 Real Estate Investment Markets," January 7, 2010*

- The Dallas metro area was identified as one of "America's Best Housing Markets" by *Forbes*. The metro area ranked #9. Criteria: housing affordability; rising home prices; percentage of foreclosures. *Forbes.com, "America's Best Housing Markets," February 19, 2010*

- The Dallas metro area appeared in a *Wall Street Journal* article ranking cities by "housing stress." The metro area was ranked #22 (#1 = most stress). Criteria: fraction of mortgage-holding homeowners with a monthly housing payment in excess of 30 percent of income; percentage of people without health insurance; unemployment rate. *The Wall Street Journal, "Which Cities Face Biggest Housing Risk," October 5, 2010*

- The Center for Housing Policy ranked 210 U.S. metropolitan areas by the fair market rent for a two-bedroom unit. The Dallas metro area was ranked #82. (#1 = most expensive) with a rent of $894. Criteria: Fair Market Rent (FMR) in effect during the fourth quarter of 2009 based on HUD's fiscal year 2010 FMRs. *The Center for Housing Policy, "Paycheck to Paycheck: Most to Least Expensive Rental Markets in 2009"*

- The Dallas metro area was identified as one of the markets with the best expected performance in home prices over the next 12 months. *Local Market Monitor, "First Quarter Home Price Forecast for Largest US Markets," March 2, 2011*

- The Dallas metro area was identified as one of the best U.S. markets to invest in rental property" by HomeVestors and Local Market Monitor. The area ranked #14 out of 100. Criteria: risk-return premium relative to national average. *HomeVestors and Local Market Monitor, "Best 100 U.S. Markets to Invest in Rental Property," March 9, 2012*

Safety Rankings

- Allstate ranked the 193 largest cities in America in terms of driver safety. Plano ranked #153. In addition, drivers were 27.2% more likely to have had an accident compared to the national average. Allstate researchers analyzed internal property damage reported claims over a two-year period (from January 2008 to December 2009) to protect findings from external influences such as weather or road construction. A weighted average of the two-year numbers determined the annual percentages. The report defines an auto crash as any collision resulting in a property damage claim. *Allstate, "2011 Allstate America's Best Drivers Report™"*

- Dallas was identified as one of the least safe places in the U.S. in terms of its vulnerability to natural disasters and weather extremes. The city ranked #2 out of 10. Data was analyzed to show a metro areas' relative tendency to experience natural disasters (hail, tornadoes, high winds, hurricanes, earthquakes, and brush fires) or extreme weather (abundant rain or snowfall or days that are below freezing or above 90 degrees Fahrenheit). *Forbes, "Safest and Least Safe Places in the U.S.," August 30, 2005*

- Plano was selected as one of "America's Safest Cities" by *Forbes*. The city ranked #1 out of 10. Criteria: violent crime rates; traffic fatalities per 100,000 residents. The editors only considered cities with populations above 250,000. *Forbes, "America's Safest Cities," December 15, 2011*

- The National Insurance Crime Bureau ranked 366 metro areas in the U.S. in terms of per capita rates of vehicle theft. The Dallas metro area ranked #47 (#1 = highest rate). Criteria: number of vehicle theft offenses per 100,000 inhabitants in 2010. *National Insurance Crime Bureau, "Hot Spots," June 21, 2011*

- The Dallas metro area was identified as one of the most dangerous metro areas for pedestrians by Transportation for America. The metro area ranked #10 out of 52 metro areas with over 1 million residents. Criteria: area's population divided by the number of pedestrian fatalities in that area. *Transportation for America, "Dangerous by Design 2011"*

Seniors/Retirement Rankings

- Bankers Life and Casualty Company, in partnership with Sperling's BestPlaces, ranked the nation's 50 largest metro areas in terms of the "Best U.S. Cities for Seniors." The Dallas metro area ranked #29. Criteria: healthcare; transportation; housing; environment; economy; health and longevity; social and spiritual life; crime. *Bankers Life and Casualty Company, Center for a Secure Retirement, "Best U.S. Cities for Seniors 2011," September 2011*

- The Dallas metro area was identified as one of "America's Most Affordable Places to Retire" by *Forbes*. The metro area ranked #2. Criteria: housing affordability; inflation; number of persons over 65 who are employed; net migration for persons over 65; percent of persons over 65 living below poverty level; doctors per capita; number of citizens tapping their Medicare benefits per thousand people. *Forbes.com, "America's Most Affordable Places to Retire," September 5, 2008*

- The Dallas metro area was selected as one of "America's Best Places to Grow Old" by *Forbes*. The area was ranked #2 out of 10. Criteria: housing affordability; inflationary pressures; number of persons over 65 who are currently employed; net migration for persons over 65; percent of seniors living below poverty level; doctors per capita; number of citizens tapping their Medicare benefits per 1,000 people. *Forbes, "America's Best Places to Grow Old," December 12, 2008*

- The Dallas metro area was selected as one of "The 10 Most Affordable Cities for Long-Term Care" by *U.S. News & World Report*. Criteria: costs at nursing homes, assisted living facilities, and adult day health care facilities; cost for licensed home health aides. *U.S. News & World Report, "The 10 Most Affordable Cities for Long-Term Care," May 17, 2010*

Sports/Recreation Rankings

- The Dallas was selected as one of the best metro areas for golf in America by *Golf Digest*. The Dallas area was ranked #1 out of 20. Criteria: climate; cost of public golf; quality of public golf; accessibility. *Golf Digest, "The Top 20 Cities for Golf," October 2011*

- *Golf.com* and the research arm of the National Golf Foundation analyzed the 50 largest metropolitan areas in the U.S. in terms of golf. The Dallas metro area ranked #4. Criteria: weather; affordability; quality of courses; accessibility; number of courses designed by esteemed architects; availability; crowdedness. *Golf.com, November 15, 2007*

Technology Rankings

- Scarborough Research, a leading market research firm, identified the Dallas DMA (Designated Market Area) as one of the top markets for text messaging with more than 50% of cell phone subscribers age 18+ utilizing the text messaging feature on their phone. *Scarborough Research, November 24, 2008*

Transportation Rankings

- The Dallas metro area appeared on *Forbes* list of the best and worst cities for commuters. The metro area ranked #56 out of 60 (#1 is best). Criteria: travel time; road congestion; travel delays. *Forbes.com, "Best and Worst Cities for Commuters," February 16, 2010*

Women/Minorities Rankings

- *Women's Health* examined U.S. cities and identified the 100 best cities for women. Plano was ranked #6. Criteria: 30 categories were examined from obesity and breast cancer rates to commuting times and hours spent working out. *Women's Health, "Best Cities for Women 2012"*

- Dallas was ranked #68 out of 100 metro areas in *SELF Magazine's* ranking of America's healthiest places for women." A panel of experts came up with more than 50 criteria including death and disease rates, environmental indicators, community resources, and lifestyle habits. *SELF Magazine, "Secrets of America's Healthiest Women," December 2008*

- Dallas appeared on *Black Enterprise's* list of the "Ten Best Cities for African Americans." The top picks were culled from more than 2,000 interactive surveys completed on *BlackEnterprise.com* and by editorial staff evaluation. The editors weighed the following criteria as it pertained to African Americans in each city: median household income; percentage of households earning more than $100,000; percentage of businesses owned; percentage of college graduates; unemployment rates; home loan rejections; and homeownership rates. *Black Enterprise, May 2007*

- The Dallas metro area appeared on *Forbes'* list of the "Best Cities for Minority Entrepreneurs." The area ranked #68 out of 10. Criteria: 52 metropolitan statistical areas were examined. For each ethnicity (African Americans, Asians and Hispanics), the editors measured housing affordability, population growth, income growth, and entrepreneurship (per capita self-employment). *Forbes, "Best Cities for Minority Entrepreneurs," March 23, 2011*

Miscellaneous Rankings

- *Men's Health* ranked 100 U.S. cities by their level of sadness. Plano was ranked #10 (#1 = saddest city). Criteria: suicide rates; unemployment rates; percentage of households that use antidepressants; percent of population who report feeling blue all or most of the time. *Men's Health, "Frown Towns," November 28, 2011*

- Energizer Holdings, the makers of Edge® shave gel, in partnership with Sperling's BestPlaces, ranked 50 major metro areas in terms of everyday irritations. The Dallas metro area ranked #13. Criteria: humidity levels; weather conditions; incidence of traffic delays and congestion; average commute times; frequency of flight delays and cancellations; rates of sleeplessness; underemployment; pollens and allergens; pests; comedy clubs per capita. *Energizer Holdings, "Most Irritation Prone Cities," July 23, 2010*

- Mars Chocolate North America, the makers of COMBOS®, in partnership with Sperling's BestPlaces, ranked 50 major metro areas in terms of their "manliness." The Dallas metro area ranked #21. Criteria: number of professional sports teams; number of nearby NASCAR tracks and racing events; manly lifestyle; concentration of manly retail stores; manly occupations per capita; salty snack sales; "Board of Manliness" rankings. *Mars Chocolate North America, "America's Manliest Cities 2011," September 1, 2011*

- The Dallas metro area was selected as one of "America's Greediest Cities" by *Forbes*. The area was ranked #7 out of 10. Criteria: number of Forbes 400 (*Forbes* annual list of the richest Americans) members per capita. *Forbes, "America's Greediest Cities," December 7, 2007*

Business Environment

CITY FINANCES

City Government Finances

Component	2009 ($000)	2009 ($ per capita)
Total Revenues	404,307	1,550
Total Expenditures	394,628	1,513
Debt Outstanding	372,424	1,428
Cash and Securities[1]	260,941	1,001

Note: (1) Cash and security holdings of a government at the close of its fiscal year, including those of its dependent agencies, utilities, and liquor stores.
Source: U.S Census Bureau, State & Local Government Finances 2009

City Government Revenue by Source

Source	2009 ($000)	2009 ($ per capita)
General Revenue		
From Federal Government	0	0
From State Government	3,722	14
From Local Governments	714	3
Taxes		
Property	124,265	476
Sales and Gross Receipts	97,776	375
Personal Income	0	0
Corporate Income	0	0
Motor Vehicle License	0	0
Other Taxes	5,236	20
Current Charges	92,037	353
Liquor Store	0	0
Utility	53,310	204
Employee Retirement	84	0

Source: U.S Census Bureau, State & Local Government Finances 2009

City Government Expenditures by Function

Function	2009 ($000)	2009 ($ per capita)	2009 (%)
General Direct Expenditures			
Air Transportation	0	0	0.0
Corrections	0	0	0.0
Education	0	0	0.0
Employment Security Administration	0	0	0.0
Financial Administration	5,202	20	1.3
Fire Protection	50,651	194	12.8
General Public Buildings	10,412	40	2.6
Governmental Administration, Other	8,208	31	2.1
Health	2,972	11	0.8
Highways	18,877	72	4.8
Hospitals	0	0	0.0
Housing and Community Development	0	0	0.0
Interest on General Debt	16,009	61	4.1
Judicial and Legal	6,099	23	1.5
Libraries	10,500	40	2.7
Parking	0	0	0.0
Parks and Recreation	40,150	154	10.2
Police Protection	54,752	210	13.9
Public Welfare	0	0	0.0
Sewerage	10,842	42	2.7
Solid Waste Management	21,825	84	5.5
Veterans' Services	0	0	0.0
Liquor Store	0	0	0.0
Utility	24,067	92	6.1
Employee Retirement	201	1	0.1

Source: U.S Census Bureau, State & Local Government Finances 2009

Municipal Bond Ratings

Area	Moody's	S&P	Fitch
City	Aaa	AAA	AAA

Rating Systems (shown in declining order of credit quality): Moody's– Aaa, Aa, A, Baa, Ba, B, Caa, Ca, C (numerical modifiers 1, 2, and 3 are added to letter-rating); S&P– AAA, AA, A, BBB, BB, B, CCC, CC, C; Fitch– AAA, AA, A, BBB, BB, B, CCC, CC, C. Ratings may be modified by the addition of a plus or minus sign to show relative standing within the major rating categories.
Notes: n/a Not Available; w/d Withdrawn (1) Not Reviewed; (2) Issuer Rating/No General Obligation; (3) Standard and Poor's Issue Credit Rating (ICR) is a current opinion of an obliger with respect to a specific financial obligation, a specific class of financial obligations, or a specific financial program.
Source: U.S. Census Bureau, 2012 Statistical Abstract, Bond Ratings for City Governments by Largest Cities: 2010

DEMOGRAPHICS

Population Growth

Area	1990 Census	2000 Census	2010 Census	Population Growth (%) 1990-2000	Population Growth (%) 2000-2010
City	128,507	222,030	259,841	72.8	17.0
MSA[1]	3,989,294	5,161,544	6,371,773	29.4	23.4
U.S.	248,709,873	281,421,906	308,745,538	13.2	9.7

Note: (1) Figures cover the Dallas-Fort Worth-Arlington, TX Metropolitan Statistical Area—see Appendix B for areas included
Source: U.S. Census Bureau, 2010 Census

Household Size

Area	One	Two	Three	Four	Five	Six	Seven or More	Average Household Size
City	24.4	31.8	17.5	16.4	6.3	2.3	1.3	2.61
MSA[1]	24.8	29.6	16.7	15.2	7.9	3.3	2.5	2.74
U.S.	26.7	32.8	16.1	13.4	6.5	2.6	1.9	2.58

Note: (1) Figures cover the Dallas-Fort Worth-Arlington, TX Metropolitan Statistical Area—see Appendix B for areas included
Source: U.S. Census Bureau, 2010 Census

Race

Area	White Alone[2] (%)	Black Alone[2] (%)	Asian Alone[2] (%)	AIAN[3] Alone[2] (%)	NHOPI[4] Alone[2] (%)	Other Race Alone[2] (%)	Two or More Races (%)
City	66.9	7.6	16.9	0.4	0.1	5.1	3.0
MSA[1]	65.3	15.1	5.4	0.7	0.1	10.6	2.8
U.S.	72.4	12.6	4.8	0.9	0.2	6.2	2.9

Note: (1) Figures cover the Dallas-Fort Worth-Arlington, TX Metropolitan Statistical Area—see Appendix B for areas included; (2) Alone is defined as not being in combination with one or more other races; (3) American Indian and Alaska Native; (4) Native Hawaiian and Other Pacific Islander
Source: U.S. Census Bureau, 2010 Census

Hispanic or Latino Origin

Area	Hispanic or Latino (%)	Mexican (%)	Puerto Rican (%)	Cuban (%)	Other Hispanic or Latino (%)
City	14.7	10.6	0.5	0.2	3.5
MSA[1]	27.5	22.9	0.5	0.2	3.9
U.S.	16.3	10.3	1.5	0.6	4.0

Note: Persons of Hispanic or Latino origin can be of any race; (1) Figures cover the Dallas-Fort Worth-Arlington, TX Metropolitan Statistical Area—see Appendix B for areas included
Source: U.S. Census Bureau, 2010 Census

Segregation

Type	Segregation Indices[1]				Percent Change		
	1990	2000	2010	2010 Rank[2]	1990-2000	1990-2010	2000-2010
Black/White	62.8	59.8	56.6	48	-3.1	-6.2	-3.2
Asian/White	41.8	45.6	46.6	19	3.8	4.8	1.0
Hispanic/White	48.8	52.3	50.3	24	3.5	1.5	-2.0

Note: Figures are based on an analysis of 1990, 2000, and 2010 Census Decennial Census tract data by William H. Frey, Brookings Institution and the University of Michigan Social Science Data Analysis Network. In this analysis all racial groups (whites, blacks, and asians) are non-Hispanic members of those races. Hispanics are shown as a separate category; All figures cover the Metropolitan Statistical Area (see Appendix B for areas included); (1) Segregation Indices are Dissimilarity Indices that measure the degree to which the minority group is distributed differently than whites across census tracts. They range from 0 (complete integration) to 100 (complete segregation) where the value indicates the percentage of the minority group that needs to move to be distributed exactly like whites; (2) Ranges from 1 (most segregated) to 102 (least segregated); n/a not available.
Source: www.CensusScope.org

Ancestry

Area	German	Irish	English	American	Italian	Polish	French[2]	Scottish	Dutch
City	12.9	10.0	8.7	7.3	3.7	1.7	2.9	2.5	0.9
MSA[1]	11.1	8.6	8.2	6.0	2.3	1.1	2.2	1.8	1.1
U.S.	16.1	11.6	8.8	6.1	5.7	3.2	3.0	1.9	1.6

Note: Figures are the percentage of the total population reporting a particular ancestry. The nine most commonly reported ancestries in the U.S. are shown. Figures include multiple ancestries (e.g. if a person reported being Irish and Italian, they were included in both columns); (1) Figures cover the Dallas-Fort Worth-Arlington, TX Metropolitan Statistical Area—see Appendix B for areas included; (2) Excludes Basque
Source: U.S. Census Bureau, 2008-2010 American Community Survey 3-Year Estimates

Foreign-Born Population

Area	Percent of Population Born in								
	Any Foreign Country	Mexico	Asia	Europe	Carribean	South America	Central America[2]	Africa	Canada
City	24.1	4.9	13.1	1.6	0.3	1.2	1.1	1.3	0.4
MSA[1]	17.5	9.3	4.2	0.8	0.2	0.5	1.3	0.9	0.2
U.S.	12.8	3.8	3.6	1.6	1.2	0.9	1.0	0.5	0.3

Note: (1) Figures cover the Dallas-Fort Worth-Arlington, TX Metropolitan Statistical Area—see Appendix B for areas included; (2) Excludes Mexico.
Source: U.S. Census Bureau, 2008-2010 American Community Survey 3-Year Estimates

Marital Status

Area	Never Married	Now Married[2]	Separated	Widowed	Divorced
City	26.6	58.7	1.6	3.5	9.6
MSA[1]	30.4	51.6	2.6	4.5	10.9
U.S.	31.6	49.6	2.2	6.1	10.7

Note: Figures are percentages and cover the population 15 years of age and older; (1) Figures cover the Dallas-Fort Worth-Arlington, TX Metropolitan Statistical Area—see Appendix B for areas included; (2) Excludes separated
Source: U.S. Census Bureau, 2008-2010 American Community Survey 3-Year Estimates

Age

Area	Percent of Population							Median Age
	Under Age 5	Age 5 to 17	Age 18 to 34	Age 35 to 49	Age 50 to 64	Age 65 to 79	80 Years and Over	
City	6.3	19.6	21.0	24.8	19.5	6.9	1.9	37.2
MSA[1]	7.8	20.0	24.3	22.5	16.6	6.7	2.1	33.5
U.S.	6.5	17.5	23.2	20.7	19.0	9.4	3.6	37.2

Note: (1) Figures cover the Dallas-Fort Worth-Arlington, TX Metropolitan Statistical Area—see Appendix B for areas included
Source: U.S. Census Bureau, 2010 Census

Male/Female Ratio

Area	Males	Females	Males per 100 Females
City	127,078	132,763	95.7
MSA[1]	3,141,634	3,230,139	97.3
U.S.	151,781,326	156,964,212	96.7

Note: (1) Figures cover the Dallas-Fort Worth-Arlington, TX
Metropolitan Statistical Area—see Appendix B for areas included
Source: U.S. Census Bureau, 2010 Census

Religious Groups

Area	Catholic	Baptist	Non-Den.	Methodist[2]	Lutheran	LDS[3]	Pente-costal	Presby-terian[4]	Muslim[5]	Judaism
MSA[1]	13.3	18.7	7.8	5.3	0.8	1.2	2.2	1.0	0.4	2.4
U.S.	19.1	9.3	4.0	4.0	2.3	2.0	1.9	1.6	0.8	0.7

Note: Figures are the number of adherents as a percentage of the total population; (1) Figures cover the
Dallas-Fort Worth-Arlington, TX Metropolitan Statistical Area—see Appendix B for areas included;
(2) Methodist/Pietist; (3) Latter Day Saints; (4) Reformed; (5) Figures are estimates
Source: Association of Statisticians of American Religious Bodies, 2010 U.S. Religion Census: Religious
Congregations & Membership Study

ECONOMY

Gross Metropolitan Product

Area	2007	2008	2009	2010	2010 Rank[2]
MSA[1]	358.1	370.8	358.3	376.8	6

Note: Figures are in billions of dollars; (1) Figures cover the Dallas-Fort Worth-Arlington, TX Metropolitan
Statistical Area—see Appendix B for areas included; (2) Rank ranges from 1 to 363
Source: The United States Conference of Mayors, "U.S. Metro Economies: GMP and Employment Forecasts,"
June 2011

Economic Growth

Area	2007-2009 (%)	2010 (%)	2011 (%)	Rank[2]
MSA[1]	-0.3	5.0	4.1	114
U.S.	-1.3	2.9	2.5	–

Note: Figures are real Gross Metropolitan Product growth rates and represent annual average percent change;
(1) Figures cover the Dallas-Fort Worth-Arlington, TX Metropolitan Statistical Area—see Appendix B for areas
included; (2) Rank ranges from 1 to 363
Source: The United States Conference of Mayors, "U.S. Metro Economies: GMP and Employment Forecasts,"
June 2011

Metropolitan Area Exports

Area	2005	2006	2007	2008	2009	2010	2010 Rank[2]
MSA[1]	20,541.2	22,461.6	22,079.1	22,503.7	19,881.8	22,500.4	11

Note: Figures are in millions of dollars; (1) Figures cover the Dallas-Fort Worth-Arlington, TX Metropolitan
Statistical Area—see Appendix B for areas included; (2) Rank ranges from 1 to 369
Source: U.S. Department of Commerce, International Trade Administration, Office of Trade & Industry
Information, Manufacturing & Services, data extracted April 2, 2012

INCOME

Income

Area	Per Capita ($)	Median Household ($)	Average Household ($)
City	39,482	80,210	104,026
MSA[1]	28,035	55,740	76,630
U.S.	26,942	51,222	70,116

Note: (1) Figures cover the Dallas-Fort Worth-Arlington, TX Metropolitan Statistical Area—see Appendix B for
areas included
Source: U.S. Census Bureau, 2008-2010 American Community Survey 3-Year Estimates

Household Income Distribution

Area	Percent of Households Earning							
	Under $15,000	$15,000 -24,999	$25,000 -34,999	$35,000 -49,999	$50,000 -74,999	$75,000 -99,000	$100,000 -149,999	$150,000 and up
City	5.7	7.1	6.7	10.5	16.9	13.6	19.7	19.8
MSA[1]	10.3	10.1	10.2	14.0	18.7	12.5	13.8	10.2
U.S.	13.0	11.0	10.6	14.2	18.5	12.1	12.2	8.4

Note: (1) Figures cover the Dallas-Fort Worth-Arlington, TX Metropolitan Statistical Area—see Appendix B for areas included
Source: U.S. Census Bureau, 2008-2010 American Community Survey 3-Year Estimates

Poverty Rate

Area	All Ages	Under 18 Years Old	18 to 64 Years Old	65 Years and Over
City	7.9	11.1	6.7	6.9
MSA[1]	14.0	20.1	12.0	8.7
U.S.	14.4	20.1	13.1	9.4

Note: Figures are percentage of people whose income during the past 12 months was below the poverty level;
(1) Figures cover the Dallas-Fort Worth-Arlington, TX Metropolitan Statistical Area—see Appendix B for areas included
Source: U.S. Census Bureau, 2008-2010 American Community Survey 3-Year Estimates

Personal Bankruptcy Filing Rate

Area	2006	2007	2008	2009	2010	2011
Collin County	1.95	2.47	2.84	3.49	3.85	3.26
U.S.	2.00	2.73	3.53	4.61	4.97	4.37

Note: Numbers are per 1,000 population and include Chapter 7 and Chapter 13 filings
Source: Federal Deposit Insurance Corporation, Regional Economic Conditions, March 9, 2012

EMPLOYMENT

Labor Force and Employment

Area	Civilian Labor Force			Workers Employed		
	Dec. 2010	Dec. 2011	% Chg.	Dec. 2010	Dec. 2011	% Chg.
City	147,581	149,299	1.2	137,656	140,283	1.9
MD[1]	2,158,513	2,180,878	1.0	1,985,464	2,023,344	1.9
U.S.	153,156,000	153,373,000	0.1	139,159,000	140,681,000	1.1

Note: Data is not seasonally adjusted and covers workers 16 years of age and older;
(1) Metropolitan Division—see Appendix B for areas included
Source: Bureau of Labor Statistics, http://stats.bls.gov

Unemployment Rate

Area	2011											
	Jan.	Feb.	Mar.	Apr.	May	Jun.	Jul.	Aug.	Sep.	Oct.	Nov.	Dec.
City	7.4	7.1	7.2	6.9	7.1	7.6	7.4	7.2	7.3	6.9	6.4	6.0
MD[1]	8.5	8.2	8.1	7.7	7.9	8.7	8.7	8.4	8.4	8.1	7.5	7.2
U.S.	9.8	9.5	9.2	8.7	8.7	9.3	9.3	9.1	8.8	8.5	8.2	8.3

Note: Data is not seasonally adjusted and covers workers 16 years of age and older; All figures are percentages; (1) Metropolitan Division—see Appendix B for areas included
Source: Bureau of Labor Statistics, http://stats.bls.gov

Projected Unemployment Rate

Area	2010 (%)	2011 (%)	2012 (%)	2013 (%)
MSA[1]	8.4	8.1	7.7	7.2

Note: (1) Metropolitan Statistical Area—see Appendix B for areas included
Source: The United States Conference of Mayors, "U.S. Metro Economies: GMP and Employment Forecasts," June 2011

Employment by Occupation

Occupation Classification	City (%)	MSA[1] (%)	U.S. (%)
Management, Business, Science, and Arts	51.9	36.4	35.6
Natural Resources, Construction, and Maintenance	4.6	10.1	9.5
Production, Transportation, and Material Moving	4.7	11.6	12.1
Sales and Office	26.6	26.8	25.2
Service	12.2	15.2	17.6

Note: Figures cover employed civilians 16 years of age and older; (1) Figures cover the Dallas-Fort Worth-Arlington, TX Metropolitan Statistical Area—see Appendix B for areas included
Source: U.S. Census Bureau, 2008-2010 American Community Survey 3-Year Estimates

Employment by Industry

Sector	MD[1] Number of Employees	MD[1] Percent of Total	U.S. Percent of Total
Construction	n/a	n/a	4.1
Education and Health Services	254,000	12.2	15.2
Financial Activities	184,600	8.9	5.8
Government	275,100	13.2	16.8
Information	65,100	3.1	2.0
Leisure and Hospitality	200,700	9.6	9.9
Manufacturing	167,000	8.0	8.9
Mining and Logging	n/a	n/a	0.6
Other Services	71,300	3.4	4.0
Professional and Business Services	352,400	16.9	13.3
Retail Trade	216,400	10.4	11.5
Transportation and Utilities	78,800	3.8	3.8
Wholesale Trade	121,700	5.8	4.2

Note: Figures cover non-farm employment as of December 2011 and are not seasonally adjusted; (1) Metropolitan Division—see Appendix B for areas included; n/a not available
Source: Bureau of Labor Statistics, http://stats.bls.gov

Occupations with Greatest Projected Employment Growth: 2008 – 2018

Occupation[1]	2008 Employment	2018 Projected Employment	Numeric Employment Change	Percent Employment Change
Combined Food Preparation and Serving Workers, Including Fast Food	247,750	326,190	78,440	31.7
Elementary School Teachers, Except Special Education	156,930	218,030	61,100	38.9
Retail Salespersons	361,780	416,090	54,310	15.0
Registered Nurses	166,240	219,880	53,640	32.3
Home Health Aides	92,660	143,720	51,060	55.1
Customer Service Representatives	217,250	267,290	50,040	23.0
Waiters and Waitresses	192,340	237,660	45,320	23.6
Personal and Home Care Aides	94,530	138,530	44,000	46.5
Office Clerks, General	239,400	279,000	39,600	16.5
Cashiers	276,070	312,940	36,870	13.4

Note: Projections cover Texas; (1) Sorted by numeric employment change
Source: www.projectionscentral.com, State Occupational Projections, 2008–2018 Long-Term Projections

Fastest Growing Occupations: 2008 – 2018

Occupation[1]	2008 Employment	2018 Projected Employment	Numeric Employment Change	Percent Employment Change
Biomedical Engineers	650	1,150	500	76.9
Home Health Aides	92,660	143,720	51,060	55.1
Network Systems and Data Communications Analysts	19,160	29,490	10,330	53.9
Petroleum Engineers	13,440	20,140	6,700	49.9
Athletic Trainers	1,560	2,300	740	47.4
Personal and Home Care Aides	94,530	138,530	44,000	46.5
Electrical and Electronics Repairers, Powerhouse, Substation, and Relay	1,550	2,260	710	45.8
Financial Examiners	2,150	3,130	980	45.6
Medical Scientists, Except Epidemiologists	3,670	5,320	1,650	45.0
Biochemists and Biophysicists	740	1,060	320	43.2

Note: Projections cover Texas; (1) Sorted by percent employment change and excludes occupations with numeric employment change less than 100
Source: www.projectionscentral.com, State Occupational Projections, 2008–2018 Long-Term Projections

Average Wages

Occupation	$/Hr.	Occupation	$/Hr.
Accountants and Auditors	35.62	Maids and Housekeeping Cleaners	9.01
Automotive Mechanics	17.75	Maintenance and Repair Workers	16.80
Bookkeepers	18.20	Marketing Managers	62.63
Carpenters	15.57	Nuclear Medicine Technologists	31.31
Cashiers	9.39	Nurses, Licensed Practical	21.67
Clerks, General Office	14.88	Nurses, Registered	32.86
Clerks, Receptionists/Information	12.90	Nursing Aides/Orderlies/Attendants	11.46
Clerks, Shipping/Receiving	14.09	Packers and Packagers, Hand	10.61
Computer Programmers	41.54	Physical Therapists	45.67
Computer Support Specialists	28.05	Postal Service Mail Carriers	25.10
Computer Systems Analysts	41.07	Real Estate Brokers	49.69
Cooks, Restaurant	10.09	Retail Salespersons	12.80
Dentists	98.53	Sales Reps., Exc. Tech./Scientific	32.42
Electrical Engineers	46.14	Sales Reps., Tech./Scientific	50.79
Electricians	21.29	Secretaries, Exc. Legal/Med./Exec.	15.88
Financial Managers	59.28	Security Guards	12.77
First-Line Supervisors/Managers, Sales	20.33	Surgeons	n/a
Food Preparation Workers	9.15	Teacher Assistants	11.30
General and Operations Managers	59.82	Teachers, Elementary School	26.40
Hairdressers/Cosmetologists	14.08	Teachers, Secondary School	27.90
Internists	79.49	Telemarketers	12.69
Janitors and Cleaners	10.27	Truck Drivers, Heavy/Tractor-Trailer	19.42
Landscaping/Groundskeeping Workers	10.86	Truck Drivers, Light/Delivery Svcs.	16.73
Lawyers	68.66	Waiters and Waitresses	9.75

Note: Wage data covers the Dallas-Plano-Irving, TX Metropolitan Division—see Appendix B for areas included. Hourly wages for elementary/secondary school teachers and teacher assistants were calculated by the editors from annual wage data assuming a 40 hour work week; n/a not available.
Source: Bureau of Labor Statistics, Metro Area Occupational Employment and Wage Estimates, May 2011

RESIDENTIAL REAL ESTATE

Building Permits

Area	Single-Family			Multi-Family			Total		
	2010	2011	Pct. Chg.	2010	2011	Pct. Chg.	2010	2011	Pct. Chg.
City	311	349	12.2	303	673	122.1	614	1,022	66.4
MSA[1]	14,420	14,039	-2.6	5,138	10,788	110.0	19,558	24,827	26.9
U.S.	447,311	418,498	-6.4	157,299	205,563	30.7	604,610	624,061	3.2

Note: (1) Metropolitan Statistical Area—see Appendix B for areas included; figures represent new, privately-owned housing units authorized (unadjusted data); All permit data are based on estimates with imputation.
Source: U.S. Census Bureau, Manufacturing, Mining, and Construction Statistics, Building Permits, 2010, 2011

Homeownership Rate

Area	2005 (%)	2006 (%)	2007 (%)	2008 (%)	2009 (%)	2010 (%)	2011 (%)
MSA[1]	62.3	60.7	60.9	60.9	61.6	63.8	62.6
U.S.	68.9	68.8	68.1	67.8	67.4	66.9	66.1

Note: (1) Metropolitan Statistical Area—see Appendix B for areas included
Source: U.S. Census Bureau, Housing Vacancies and Homeownership Annual Statistics: 2011

Housing Vacancy Rates

Area	Gross Vacancy Rate[2] (%)			Year-Round Vacancy Rate[3] (%)			Rental Vacancy Rate[4] (%)			Homeowner Vacancy Rate[5] (%)		
	2009	2010	2011	2009	2010	2011	2009	2010	2011	2009	2010	2011
MSA[1]	9.4	10.5	9.8	9.3	10.4	9.6	11.7	13.5	11.8	2.1	2.3	2.0
U.S.	14.5	14.3	14.2	11.3	11.3	11.1	10.6	10.2	9.5	2.6	2.6	2.5

Note: (1) Metropolitan Statistical Area—see Appendix B for areas included; (2) The percentage of the total housing inventory that is vacant; (3) The percentage of the housing inventory (excluding seasonal units) that is year-round vacant; (4) The percentage of rental inventory that is vacant for rent; (5) The percentage of homeowner inventory that is vacant for sale
Source: U.S. Census Bureau, Housing Vacancies and Homeownership Annual Statistics: 2011

TAXES

State Corporate Income Tax Rates

State	Tax Rate (%)	Income Brackets ($)	Num. of Brackets	Financial Institution Tax Rate (%)[a]	Federal Income Tax Ded.
Texas	(x)	–	–	(x)	No

Note: Tax rates as of January 1, 2012; (a) Rates listed are the corporate income tax rate applied to financial institutions or excise taxes based on income. Some states have other taxes based upon the value of deposits or shares; (x) Texas imposes a Franchise Tax, otherwise known as margin tax, imposed on entities with more than $1,000,000 total revenues at rate of 1%, or 0.5% for entities primarily engaged in retail or wholesale trade, on lesser of 70% of total revenues or 100%of gross receipts after deductions for either compensation or cost of goods sold.
Source: Federation of Tax Administrators, "State Corporate Income Tax Rates, 2012"

State Individual Income Tax Rates

State	Tax Rate (%)	Income Brackets ($)	Num. of Brackets	Personal Exempt. ($)[1] Single	Dependents	Fed. Inc. Tax Ded.
Texas – No State Income Tax						

Note: Tax rates as of January 1, 2012; Local- and county-level taxes are not included; n/a not applicable; (1) Married joint filers generally receive double the single exemption
Source: Federation of Tax Administrators, "State Individual Income Tax Rates, 2012"

Various State and Local Tax Rates

State	State and Local Sales and Use (%)	State Sales and Use (%)	Gasoline[1] (¢/gal.)	Cigarette[2] ($/pack)	Spirits[3] ($/gal.)	Wine[4] ($/gal.)	Beer[5] ($/gal.)
Texas	8.25	6.25	20.0	1.41	2.40	0.20	0.20

Note: All tax rates as of January 1, 2012 except beer, wine and spirits (September 1, 2011); (1) The American Petroleum Institute has developed a methodology for determining the average tax rate on a gallon of fuel. Rates may include any of the following: excise taxes, environmental fees, storage tank fees, other fees or taxes, general sales tax, and local taxes. In states where gasoline is subject to the general sales tax, or where the fuel tax is based on the average sale price, the average rate determined by API is sensitive to changes in the price of gasoline. States that fully or partially apply general sales taxes to gasoline: CA, CO, GA, IL, IN, MI, NY; (2) The federal excise tax of $1.0066 per pack and local taxes are not included; (3) Rates are those applicable to off-premise sales of 40% alcohol by volume (a.b.v.) distilled spirits in 750ml containers. Local excise taxes are excluded; (4) Rates are those applicable to off-premise sales of 11% a.b.v. non-carbonated wine in 750ml containers; (5) Rates are those applicable to off-premise sales of 4.7% a.b.v. beer in 12 ounce containers.
Source: Tax Foundation, 2012 Facts & Figures: How Does Your State Compare?

State-Local Tax Burdens

Area	Rate (%)	Rank[1]	Per Capita Taxes Paid to Home State ($)	Total State and Local Per Capita Taxes Paid ($)	Per Capita Income ($)
Texas	7.9	45	2,248	3,197	40,498
U.S. Average	9.8	-	3,057	4,160	42,539

Note: Figures cover 2009; (1) Rank ranges from 1 to 50 where 1 is highest tax burden
Source: Tax Foundation, State-Local Tax Burdens, All States, 2009

State Business Tax Climate Index Rankings

State	Overall Rank	Corporate Tax Index Rank	Individual Income Tax Index Rank	Sales Tax Index Rank	Unemployment Insurance Tax Index Rank	Property Tax Index Rank
Texas	9	37	7	35	15	31

Note: The index is a measure of how each state's tax laws affect economic performance. The lower the rank, the more favorable a state's tax system is for business. States without a given tax are given a ranking of 1.
Source: Tax Foundation, Major Components of the State Business Tax Climate Index, FY 2012

COMMERCIAL REAL ESTATE

Office Market

Market Area	Inventory (sq. ft.)	Vacant (sq. ft.)	Vac. Rate (%)	Under Constr. (sq. ft.)	Asking Rent ($/sf/yr) Class A	Class B
Dallas-Fort Worth	190,863,123	41,477,914	21.7	615,600	22.92	17.72

Source: Grubb & Ellis, Office Markets Trends, 4th Quarter 2011

Industrial Market

Market Area	Inventory (sq. ft.)	Vacant (sq. ft.)	Vac. Rate (%)	Under Constr. (sq. ft.)	Asking Rent ($/sf/yr) WH/Dist	R&D/Flex
Dallas-Fort Worth	663,801,566	69,153,380	10.4	725,976	3.50	6.47

Source: Grubb & Ellis, Industrial Markets Trends, 4th Quarter 2011

COMMERCIAL UTILITIES

Typical Monthly Electric Bills

Area	Commercial Service ($/month) 1,500 kWh	40 kW demand 14,000 kWh	Industrial Service ($/month) 1,000 kW demand 200,000 kWh	50,000 kW demand 15,000,000 kWh
City	n/a	n/a	n/a	n/a
Average[1]	189	1,616	25,197	1,470,813

Note: Based on total rates in effect July 1, 2011; (1) average based on 184 utilities surveyed; n/a not available
Source: Edison Electric Institute, Typical Bills and Average Rates Report, Summer 2011

TRANSPORTATION

Means of Transportation to Work

Area	Car/Truck/Van Drove Alone	Car-pooled	Public Transportation Bus	Subway	Railroad	Bicycle	Walked	Other Means	Worked at Home
City	82.0	6.7	0.6	0.4	0.6	0.1	0.7	1.8	7.1
MSA[1]	80.8	10.6	1.1	0.1	0.2	0.2	1.3	1.4	4.3
U.S.	76.0	10.2	2.7	1.7	0.5	0.5	2.8	1.3	4.2

Note: Figures are percentages and cover workers 16 years of age and older; (1) Figures cover the Dallas-Fort Worth-Arlington, TX Metropolitan Statistical Area—see Appendix B for areas included
Source: U.S. Census Bureau, 2008-2010 American Community Survey 3-Year Estimates

Travel Time to Work

Area	Less Than 10 Minutes	10 to 19 Minutes	20 to 29 Minutes	30 to 44 Minutes	45 to 59 Minutes	60 to 89 Minutes	90 Minutes or More
City	9.6	28.3	22.3	24.5	9.3	5.1	1.0
MSA[1]	10.2	27.1	21.4	24.5	9.5	5.6	1.7
U.S.	13.9	30.1	20.8	19.8	7.5	5.5	2.5

Note: Figures are percentages and include workers 16 years old and over; (1) Figures cover the Dallas-Fort Worth-Arlington, TX Metropolitan Statistical Area—see Appendix B for areas included
Source: U.S. Census Bureau, 2008-2010 American Community Survey 3-Year Estimates

Travel Time Index

Area	1985	1990	1995	2000	2005	2010
Urban Area[1]	1.07	1.11	1.14	1.20	1.27	1.23
Average[2]	1.11	1.16	1.18	1.21	1.25	1.20

Note: Travel Time Index—the ratio of travel time in the peak period to the travel time at free-flow conditions. A value of 1.30 indicates a 20-minute free-flow trip takes 26 minutes in the peak. Free-flow speeds (60 mph on freeways and 35 mph on principal arterials) are used as the comparison threshold; (1) Covers the Dallas-Fort Worth-Arlington TX urban area; (2) average of 439 urban areas
Source: Texas Transportation Institute, Urban Mobility Report 2011, September 2011

Public Transportation

Agency Name / Mode of Transportation	Vehicles Operated in Maximum Service	Annual Unlinked Passenger Trips ('000)	Annual Passenger Miles ('000)
Dallas Area Rapid Transit (DART)			
Bus (directly operated)	556	37,693.4	164,323.6
Commuter Rail (purchased transportation)	36	2,432.2	43,689.3
Demand Response (purchased transportation)	197	1,136.0	13,896.9
Light Rail (directly operated)	76	17,799.2	125,403.0
Vanpool (directly operated)	177	924.6	36,784.7

Source: Federal Transit Administration, National Transit Database, 2010

Air Transportation

Airport Name and Code / Type of Service	Passenger Airlines[1]	Passenger Enplanements	Freight Carriers[2]	Freight (lbs.)
Dallas-Fort Worth International (DFW)				
Domestic service (U.S. carriers - 2011)	35	24,839,278	22	310,694,455
International service (U.S. carriers - 2010)	12	2,209,457	7	72,348,682
Dallas Love Field (DAL)				
Domestic service (U.S. carriers - 2011)	25	3,849,150	6	9,050,237
International service (U.S. carriers - 2010)	6	677	1	14,019

Note: (1) Includes all U.S.-based major, minor and commuter airlines that carried at least one passenger during the year; (2) Includes all U.S.-based airlines and freight carriers that transported at least one pound of freight during the year
Source: Bureau of Transportation Statistics, The Intermodal Transportation Database, Air Carriers: T-100 Domestic Market (U.S. Carriers), 2011; Bureau of Transportation Statistics, The Intermodal Transportation Database, Air Carriers: T-100 International Market (U.S. Carriers), 2010

Other Transportation Statistics

Major Highways:	I-20; I-30; I-35E; I-45
Amtrak Service:	No
Major Waterways/Ports:	None

Source: Amtrak.com; Google Maps

BUSINESSES

Major Business Headquarters

Company Name	Rankings	
	Fortune[1]	Forbes[2]
Dr Pepper Snapple Group	404	-
J.C. Penney	146	-

Note: (1) Fortune 500—companies that produce a 10-K are ranked 1 to 500 based on 2010 revenue; (2) all private companies with at least $2 billion in annual revenue are ranked 1 to 212; companies listed are headquartered in the city; dashes indicate no ranking
Source: Fortune, "Fortune 500," May 23, 2011; Forbes, "America's Largest Private Companies," November 16, 2011

Fast-Growing Businesses

According to Deloitte, Plano is home to one of North America's 500 fastest-growing high-technology companies: **Dairy.com** (#494). Companies are ranked by percentage growth in revenue over a five-year period. Criteria for inclusion: company must be headquartered within North America; must own proprietary intellectual property or proprietary technology that contributes to a significant portion of the company's operating revenue, or devote a significant proportion of revenues to research and development of technology; must have been in business for a minumum of five years with 2006 operating revenues of at least $50,000 USD/CD and 2010 operating revenues of at least $5 million USD/CD. *Deloitte Touche Tohmatsu, 2011 Deloitte Technology Fast 500*[TM]

Minority- and Women-Owned Businesses

Group	All Firms		Firms with Paid Employees			
	Firms	Sales ($000)	Firms	Sales ($000)	Employees	Payroll ($000)
Asian	n/a	n/a	n/a	n/a	n/a	n/a
Black	n/a	n/a	n/a	n/a	n/a	n/a
Hispanic	n/a	n/a	n/a	n/a	n/a	n/a
Women	n/a	n/a	n/a	n/a	n/a	n/a
All Firms	3,220	613,481	389	513,266	3,939	103,480

Note: Figures cover firms located in the city; minority- and women-owned business are defined as firms in which the corresponding group own 51% or more of the stock or equity of the company; n/a not available
Source: U.S. Census Bureau, 2007 Economic Census, Survey of Business Owners

HOTELS

Hotels/Motels

Area	5 Star		4 Star		3 Star		2 Star		1 Star		Not Rated	
	Num.	Pct.[3]	Num.	Pct.[3]	Num.	Pct.[3]	Num.	Pct.[3]	Num.	Pct.[3]	Num.	Pct.[3]
City[1]	0	0.0	2	4.8	17	40.5	23	54.8	0	0.0	0	0.0
Total[2]	133	0.9	940	6.5	4,569	31.8	7,033	48.9	351	2.4	1,343	9.3

Note: (1) Figures cover Plano and vicinity; (2) Figures cover all 100 cities in this book; (3) Percentage of hotels which have a given star rating; Star ratings are determined by expedia.com and offer an indication of the general quality of a particular hotel.
Source: expedia.com, April 25, 2012

The Dallas-Plano-Irving, TX metro area is home to two of the best hotels in the U.S. according to *Travel & Leisure*: **Rosewood Mansion on Turtle Creek** (#30); **Rosewood Crescent Hotel** (#152). Criteria: service; location; rooms; food; and value. *Travel & Leisure, "T+L 500, The World's Best Hotels 2012"*

The Dallas-Plano-Irving, TX metro area is home to two of the best hotels in the U.S. according to *Condé Nast Traveler*: **Rosewood Crescent Hotel** (#9); **Rosewood Mansion on Turtle Creek** (#13). The selections are based on over 25,000 responses to the magazine's annual Readers' Choice Survey. *Condé Nast Traveler, "2011 Readers' Choice Awards"*

Living Environment

COST OF LIVING

Cost of Living Index

Composite Index	Groceries	Housing	Utilities	Trans-portation	Health Care	Misc. Goods/ Services
96.7	101.8	85.1	106.3	102.3	103.2	99.2

Note: U.S. = 100; Figures cover the Plano TX urban area.
Source: The Council for Community and Economic Research, ACCRA Cost of Living Index, 2011

Grocery Prices

Area[1]	T-Bone Steak ($/pound)	Frying Chicken ($/pound)	Whole Milk ($/half gal.)	Eggs ($/dozen)	Orange Juice ($/64 oz.)	Coffee ($/11.5 oz.)
City[2]	8.94	1.05	2.09	1.70	3.50	4.98
Avg.	9.25	1.18	2.22	1.66	3.19	4.40
Min.	6.70	0.88	1.31	0.95	2.46	2.94
Max.	14.30	2.16	3.50	3.18	4.75	6.83

Note: (1) Values for the local area are compared with the average, minimum and maximum values for all 335 areas in the Cost of Living Index; (2) Figures cover the Plano TX urban area; **T-Bone Steak** *(price per pound);* **Frying Chicken** *(price per pound, whole fryer);* **Whole Milk** *(half gallon carton);* **Eggs** *(price per dozen, Grade A, large);* **Orange Juice** *(64 oz. Tropicana or Florida Natural);* **Coffee** *(11.5 oz. can, vacuum-packed, Maxwell House, Hills Bros, or Folgers).*
Source: The Council for Community and Economic Research, ACCRA Cost of Living Index, 2011

Housing and Utility Costs

Area[1]	New Home Price ($)	Apartment Rent ($/month)	All Electric ($/month)	Part Electric ($/month)	Other Energy ($/month)	Telephone ($/month)
City[2]	226,303	930	-	134.72	51.47	26.01
Avg.	285,990	839	163.23	89.00	77.52	26.92
Min.	188,005	460	125.58	45.39	33.89	17.98
Max.	1,197,028	3,244	339.16	181.97	348.69	40.01

Note: (1) Values for the local area are compared with the average, minimum and maximum values for all 335 areas in the Cost of Living Index; (2) Figures cover the Plano TX urban area; **New Home Price** *(2,400 sf living area, 8,000 sf lot, in urban area with full utilities);* **Apartment Rent** *(950 sf 2 bedroom/1.5 or 2 bath, unfurnished, excluding all utilities except water);* **All Electric** *(average monthly cost for an all-electric home);* **Part Electric** *(average monthly cost for a part-electric home);* **Other Energy** *(average monthly cost for natural gas, fuel oil, coal, wood, and any other forms of energy except electricity);* **Telephone** *(price includes basic monthly rate for a private residential line plus additional local usage charges incurred by a family of four).*
Source: The Council for Community and Economic Research, ACCRA Cost of Living Index, 2011

Health Care, Transportation, and Other Costs

Area[1]	Doctor ($/visit)	Dentist ($/visit)	Optometrist ($/visit)	Gasoline ($/gallon)	Beauty Salon ($/visit)	Men's Shirt ($)
City[2]	91.01	92.67	69.67	3.39	33.04	22.25
Avg.	93.88	81.72	90.54	3.48	32.65	25.06
Min.	60.00	55.33	53.66	3.18	19.78	13.44
Max.	154.98	145.97	183.72	4.31	63.21	46.00

Note: (1) Values for the local area are compared with the average, minimum and maximum values for all 335 areas in the Cost of Living Index; (2) Figures cover the Plano TX urban area; **Doctor** *(general practitioners routine exam of an established patient);* **Dentist** *(adult teeth cleaning and periodic oral examination);* **Optometrist** *(full vision eye exam for established adult patient);* **Gasoline** *(one gallon regular unleaded, national brand, including all taxes, cash price at self-service pump if available);* **Beauty Salon** *(woman's shampoo, trim, and blow-dry);* **Men's Shirt** *(cotton/polyester dress shirt, pinpoint weave, long sleeves).*
Source: The Council for Community and Economic Research, ACCRA Cost of Living Index, 2011

HOUSING

House Price Index (HPI)

Area	National Ranking[2]	Quarterly Change (%)	One-Year Change (%)	Five-Year Change (%)
MD[1]	91	-0.11	-1.44	1.58
U.S.[3]	-	-0.10	-2.43	-19.16

Note: The HPI is a weighted repeat sales index. It measures average price changes in repeat sales or refinancings on the same properties. This information is obtained by reviewing repeat mortgage transactions on single-family properties whose mortgages have been purchased or securitized by Fannie Mae or Freddie Mac in January 1975; (1) Metropolitan Division - see Appendix B for areas included; (2) Rankings are based on annual percentage change for all metro areas containing at least 15,000 transactions over the last 10 years and ranges from 1 to 306; (3) figures based on a weighted average of Census Division estimates using a purchase only index; all figures are for the period ending December 31, 2011
Source: Federal Housing Finance Agency, House Price Index, February 23, 2012

House Price Valuations

Area	Q4 2005 Price ($000)	Q4 2005 Over-valuation	Q4 2006 Price ($000)	Q4 2006 Over-valuation	Q4 2007 Price ($000)	Q4 2007 Over-valuation	Q4 2008 Price ($000)	Q4 2008 Over-valuation	Q4 2009 Price ($000)	Q4 2009 Over-valuation
MD[1]	127.1	-20.5	131.9	-22.2	134.1	-24.6	136.4	-24.0	137.1	-23.1

Note: Figures show the percentage of over- or under-valuation of single family homes relative to statistically normal house values (e.g. a value of 23.6 indicates that house values are 23.6% overvalued). Statistically normal house values are based on house prices, interest rates, household incomes, population densities, and any historical premiums or discounts metropolitan areas have exhibited over time; (1) Figures cover the Dallas-Plano-Irving, TX - see Appendix B for areas included
Source: Global Insight/PNC Financial Services Group, House Prices in America: 4th Quarter 2009 Update

Median Single-Family Home Prices

Area	2009	2010	2011[p]	Percent Change 2010 to 2011
MSA[1]	140.5	143.8	148.9	3.5
U.S. Average	172.1	173.1	166.2	-4.0

Note: Figures are median sales prices of existing single-family homes in thousands of dollars; (p) preliminary; n/a not available; (1) Metropolitan Statistical Area—see Appendix B for areas included
Source: National Association of Realtors, Median Sales Price of Existing Single-Family Homes for Metropolitan Areas, 4th Quarter 2011

Affordability Index of Existing Single-Family Homes

Area	2009	2010	2011[p]	Percent Change 2010 to 2011
MSA[1]	145.7	150.0	152.5	1.7

Note: The housing affordability index measures whether or not a typical family could qualify for a mortgage loan on a typical home. The higher the index, the greater the household purchasing power. An index of 100 is defined as the point where a median-income household has exactly enough income to qualify for the purchase of a median-priced existing single-family home, assuming a 20 percent downpayment and 25 percent of gross income devoted to mortgage principal and interest payments; (p) preliminary; n/a not available; (1) Metropolitan Statistical Area—see Appendix B for areas included
Source: National Association of Realtors, Affordability Index of Existing Single-Family Homes, 2011

Median Apartment Condo-Coop Home Prices

Area	2009	2010	2011[p]	Percent Change 2010 to 2011
MSA[1]	130.5	132.6	126.0	-5.0
U.S. Average	175.6	171.7	165.1	-3.8

Note: Figures are median sales prices of existing apartment condo-coop homes in thousands of dollars; (p) preliminary; n/a not available; (1) Metropolitan Statistical Area—see Appendix B for areas included
Source: National Association of Realtors, Median Sales Price of Existing Apartment Condo-Coop Homes for Metropolitan Areas, 4th Quarter 2011

Year Housing Structure Built

Area	2005 or Later	2000 -2004	1990 -1999	1980 -1989	1970 -1979	1960 -1969	1950 -1959	Before 1950	Median Year
City	5.1	10.7	35.9	28.0	15.7	3.3	0.8	0.6	1990
MSA[1]	8.6	13.9	16.9	20.1	15.5	10.1	8.4	6.5	1985
U.S.	5.0	8.6	14.0	14.1	16.3	11.3	11.2	19.6	1975

Note: Figures are percentages except for Median Year; (1) Figures cover the Dallas-Fort Worth-Arlington, TX Metropolitan Statistical Area—see Appendix B for areas included
Source: U.S. Census Bureau, 2008-2010 American Community Survey 3-Year Estimates

HEALTH

Health Risk Data

Category	MSA[1] (%)	U.S. (%)
Adults who have been told they have high blood pressure[2]	25.4	28.7
Adults who have been told they have high blood cholesterol[2]	41.8	37.5
Adults who have been told they have diabetes[3]	8.1	8.7
Adults who have been told they have arthritis[2]	18.5	26.0
Adults who have been told they currently have asthma	8.4	9.1
Adults who are current smokers	14.6	17.3
Adults who are heavy drinkers[4]	4.5	5.0
Adults who are binge drinkers[5]	13.2	15.1
Adults who are overweight (BMI 25.0 - 29.9)	29.8	36.2
Adults who are obese (BMI 30.0 - 99.8)	33.8	27.5
Adults who participated in any physical activities in the past month	73.6	76.1
Adults 50+ who have ever had a sigmoidoscopy or colonoscopy	60.5	65.2
Women aged 40+ who have had a mammogram within the past two years	77.2	75.2
Men aged 40+ who have had a PSA test within the past two years	65.2	53.2
Adults aged 65+ who have had flu shot within the past year	68.3	67.5
Adults aged 18–64 who have any kind of health care coverage	75.6	82.2

Note: Data as of 2010 unless otherwise noted; (1) Figures cover the Dallas-Plano-Irving, TX Metropolitan Division—see Appendix B for areas included; (2) Data as of 2009; (3) Figures do not include pregnancy-related, borderline, or pre-diabetes; (4) Heavy drinkers are classified as males having more than two drinks per day or females having more than one drink per day; (5) Binge drinkers are classified as males having five or more drinks on one occasion or females having four or more drinks on one occasion
Source: Centers for Disease Control and Prevention, Behaviorial Risk Factor Surveillance System, SMART: Selected Metropolitan/Micropolitan Area Risk Trends, 2009, 2010

Mortality Rates for the Top 10 Causes of Death in the U.S.

ICD-10[a] Sub-Chapter	ICD-10[a] Code	Age-Adjusted Mortality Rate[1] per 100,000 population	
		County[2]	U.S.
Malignant neoplasms	C00-C97	136.8	175.6
Ischaemic heart diseases	I20-I25	93.0	121.6
Other forms of heart disease	I30-I51	44.1	48.6
Chronic lower respiratory diseases	J40-J47	31.7	42.3
Cerebrovascular diseases	I60-I69	36.5	40.6
Organic, including symptomatic, mental disorders	F01-F09	40.0	26.7
Other degenerative diseases of the nervous system	G30-G31	33.9	24.7
Other external causes of accidental injury	W00-X59	20.1	24.4
Diabetes mellitus	E10-E14	10.0	21.7
Hypertensive diseases	I10-I15	10.2	18.2

Note: (a) ICD-10 = International Classification of Diseases 10th Revision; (1) Mortality rates are a three year average covering 2007-2009; (2) Figures cover Collin County
Source: Centers for Disease Control and Prevention, National Center for Health Statistics. Underlying Cause of Death 1999-2009 on CDC WONDER Online Database, released 2012. Data for year 2009 are compiled from the Multiple Cause of Death File 2009, Series 20 No. 2O, 2012, Data for year 2008 are compiled from the Multiple Cause of Death File 2008, Series 20 No. 2N, 2011, Data for year 2007 are compiled from Multiple Cause of Death File 2007, Series 20 No. 2M, 2010.

Mortality Rates for Selected Causes of Death

ICD-10[a] Sub-Chapter	ICD-10[a] Code	Age-Adjusted Mortality Rate[1] per 100,000 population	
		County[2]	U.S.
Assault	X85-Y09	1.5	5.7
Human immunodeficiency virus (HIV) disease	B20-B24	0.9	3.3
Influenza and pneumonia	J09-J18	11.7	16.4
Intentional self-harm	X60-X84	7.8	11.5
Malnutrition	E40-E46	*0.0	0.8
Obesity and other hyperalimentation	E65-E68	*Unreliable	1.6
Transport accidents	V01-V99	8.1	13.7
Viral hepatitis	B15-B19	*Unreliable	2.2

Note: (a) ICD-10 = International Classification of Diseases 10th Revision; (1) Mortality rates are a three year average covering 2007-2009; (2) Figures cover Collin County; (*) Unreliable data as per CDC
Source: Centers for Disease Control and Prevention, National Center for Health Statistics. Underlying Cause of Death 1999-2009 on CDC WONDER Online Database, released 2012. Data for year 2009 are compiled from the Multiple Cause of Death File 2009, Series 20 No. 2O, 2012, Data for year 2008 are compiled from the Multiple Cause of Death File 2008, Series 20 No. 2N, 2011, Data for year 2007 are compiled from Multiple Cause of Death File 2007, Series 20 No. 2M, 2010.

Distribution of Physicians and Dentists

Area[1]	Dentists[2]	D.O.[3]	M.D.[4]				
			Total	Family/ General Practice	Pediatrics	Medical Specialties	Surgical Specialties
Local (number)	415	109	1,427	176	135	562	305
Local (rate[5])	5.7	1.4	18.7	2.3	1.8	7.4	4.0
U.S. (rate[5])	4.5	1.9	18.3	2.5	1.4	6.8	4.1

Note: Data as of 2008 unless noted; (1) Local data covers Collin County; (2) Data as of 2007; (3) Doctor of Osteopathic Medicine; (4) Includes active, non-federal, patient-care, office-based Doctors of Medicine; (5) rate per 10,000 population
Source: Area Resource File (ARF). 2009-2010 Release. U.S. Department of Health and Human Services, Health Resources and Services Administration, Bureau of Health Professions, Rockville, MD, August 2010

Best Hospitals

According to *U.S. News,* the Dallas-Plano-Irving, TX is home to three of the best hospitals in the U.S.: **Baylor University Medical Center** (4 specialties); **Parkland Memorial Hospital** (2 specialties); **University of Texas Southwestern Medical Center** (6 specialties). The hospitals listed were highly ranked in at least one adult specialty. *U.S. News Online, "America's Best Hospitals 2011-12"*

According to *U.S. News,* the Dallas-Plano-Irving, TX is home to two of the best children's hospitals in the U.S.: **Children's Medical Center Dallas** (9 specialties); **Children's Medical Center-Texas Scottish Rite Hospital for Children** (1 specialty). The hospitals listed were highly ranked in at least one pediatric specialty. *U.S. News Online, "America's Best Children's Hospitals 2011-12"*

EDUCATION

Public School District Statistics

District Name	Schls	Pupils	Pupil/ Teacher Ratio	Minority Pupils[1] (%)	Free Lunch Eligible[2] (%)	IEP[3] (%)
Plano ISD	76	54,939	13.9	51.0	18.9	10.7

Note: Table includes school districts with 2,000 or more students; (1) Percentage of students that are not non-Hispanic white; (2) Percentage of students that are eligible for the free lunch program; (3) Percentage of students that have an Individualized Education Program.
Source: U.S. Department of Education, National Center for Education Statistics, Common Core of Data, Local Education Agency (School District) Universe Survey: School Year 2009-2010; U.S. Department of Education, National Center for Education Statistics, Common Core of Data, Public Elementary/Secondary School Universe Survey: School Year 2009-2010

Top Public High Schools

High School Name	Rank[1]	Score[1]	Grad. Rate[2] (%)	College[3] (%)	AP/IB/ AICE[4] (%)	SAT/ ACT[5] (%)
Plano East	461	0.141	95	85	2.2	1640
Plano West	98	0.780	99	95	2.9	1748

Note: (1) Public schools are ranked from 1 to 500 based on the following self-reported statistics (with their corresponding weight in the final score). Schools that had fewer than 10 graduates, as well as those that were newly founded and did not have a graduating senior class in 2010 were excluded; (2) Four-year, on-time graduation rate (25%); (3) Percent of 2010 graduates who enrolled immediately in college (25%); (4) AP/IB/AICE tests per graduate (25%); (5) Average SAT and/or ACT score (10%); Average AP/IB/AICE exam score (10%); AP/IB/AICE courses offered per graduate (5%); (6) School is unranked, but has been identified by Newsweek as one of the nation's most elite public high schools.
Source: Newsweek Online, "Top High Schools 2011"

Highest Level of Education

Area	Less than H.S.	H.S. Diploma	Some College, No Deg.	Associate Degree	Bachelors Degree	Masters Degree	Profess. School Degree	Doctorate Degree
City	6.8	14.1	18.8	6.4	34.8	14.9	2.1	2.0
MSA[1]	17.1	23.0	22.7	6.4	20.9	7.4	1.6	1.0
U.S.	14.7	28.4	21.3	7.6	17.6	7.2	1.9	1.2

Note: Figures cover persons age 25 and over; (1) Figures cover the Dallas-Fort Worth-Arlington, TX Metropolitan Statistical Area—see Appendix B for areas included
Source: U.S. Census Bureau, 2008-2010 American Community Survey 3-Year Estimates

Educational Attainment by Race

Area	High School Graduate or Higher (%)					Bachelor's Degree or Higher (%)				
	Total	White	Black	Asian	Hisp.[2]	Total	White	Black	Asian	Hisp.[2]
City	93.2	92.6	96.6	96.1	66.3	53.9	50.7	47.4	76.1	22.6
MSA[1]	82.9	85.4	87.2	87.8	51.7	30.9	33.2	22.2	55.8	10.5
U.S.	85.3	87.5	81.4	85.5	61.6	28.0	29.3	17.8	50.2	13.0

Note: Figures shown cover persons 25 years old and over; (1) Figures cover the Dallas-Fort Worth-Arlington, TX Metropolitan Statistical Area—see Appendix B for areas included; (2) People of Hispanic origin can be of any race
Source: U.S. Census Bureau, 2008-2010 American Community Survey 3-Year Estimates

School Enrollment by Grade and Control

Area	Preschool (%)		Kindergarten (%)		Grades 1 - 4 (%)		Grades 5 - 8 (%)		Grades 9 - 12 (%)	
	Public	Private	Public	Private	Public	Private	Public	Private	Public	Private
City	43.6	56.4	86.8	13.2	89.4	10.6	89.0	11.0	91.2	8.8
MSA[1]	51.9	48.1	89.1	10.9	91.6	8.4	92.4	7.6	92.6	7.4
U.S.	55.4	44.6	87.1	12.9	89.4	10.6	89.5	10.5	90.4	9.6

Note: Figures shown cover persons 3 years old and over; (1) Figures cover the Dallas-Fort Worth-Arlington, TX Metropolitan Statistical Area—see Appendix B for areas included
Source: U.S. Census Bureau, 2008-2010 American Community Survey 3-Year Estimates

Average Salaries of Public School Classroom Teachers

Area	2010-11		2011-12		Percent Change 2010-11 to 2011-12	Percent Change 2001-02 to 2011-12
	Dollars	Rank[1]	Dollars	Rank[1]		
Texas	48,638	31	49,017	31	0.78	24.90
U.S. Average	55,623	-	56,643	-	1.83	26.8

Note: (1) State rank ranges from 1 to 51 where 1 indicates highest salary.
Source: National Education Association, Rankings & Estimates: Rankings of the States 2011 and Estimates of School Statistics 2012, December 2011

Higher Education

Four-Year Colleges			Two-Year Colleges			Medical Schools[1]	Law Schools[2]	Voc/ Tech[3]
Public	Private Non-profit	Private For-profit	Public	Private Non-profit	Private For-profit			
0	0	0	0	0	0	0	0	0

Note: Figures cover institutions located within the city limits and include main campuses only; (1) includes schools accredited by the Liaison Committee on Medical Education and the American Osteopathic Association's Commission on Osteopathic College Accreditation; (2) includes American Bar Association-accredited law schools; (3) includes all schools with programs that are less than 2 years.
Source: National Center for Education Statistics, Integrated Postsecondary Education System (IPEDS) Peer Analysis System, 2011-12; Association of American Medical Colleges, Member List, April 23, 2012; American Osteopathic Association, Member List, April 23, 2012; Law School Admission Council, Official Guide to ABA-Approved Law Schools Online, April 23, 2012

According to *U.S. News & World Report,* the Dallas-Plano-Irving, TX is home to two of the best national universities in the U.S.: **Southern Methodist University** (#62); **University of Texas–Dallas** (#143). The indicators used to capture academic quality fall into a number of categories: assessment by administrators at peer institutions; retention of students; faculty resources; student selectivity; financial resources; alumni giving; high school counselor ratings of colleges; and graduation rate.*U.S. News & World Report, "America's Best Colleges 2012"*

According to *Forbes,* the Dallas-Plano-Irving, TX is home to one of the best business schools in the U.S.: **SMU (Cox)** (#25). The rankings are based on the return on investment that graduates of the Class of 2006 received (median salary five years after graduation). *Forbes, "Best Business Schools," August 3, 2011*

PRESIDENTIAL ELECTION

2008 Presidential Election Results

Area	Obama	McCain	Nader	Other
Collin County	36.7	62.2	0.1	1.1
U.S.	52.9	45.6	0.6	0.9

Note: Results are percentages and may not add to 100% due to rounding
Source: Dave Leip's Atlas of U.S. Presidential Elections, www.uselectionatlas.org

EMPLOYERS

Major Employers

Company Name	Industry
AMR Corporation	Air transportation, scheduled
Associates First Capital Corporation	Mortgage bankers
Baylor University Medical Center	General medical and surgical hospitals
Children's Medical Center Dallas	Specialty hospitals, except psychiatric
Combat Support Associates	Engineering services
County of Dallas	County supervisors' and executives' office
Dallas County Hospital District	General medical and surgical hospitals
Fort Worth Independent School District	Public elementary and secondary schools
Housewares Holding Company	Toasters, electric: household
HP Enterprise Services	Computer integrated systems design
J.C. Penney Company	Department stores
JCP Publications Corp.	Department stores
L-3 Communications Corporation	Business economic service
Odyssey HealthCare	Home health care services
Romano's Macaroni Grill	Italian restaurant
SFG Management Limited Liability	Milk processing (pasteurizing, homogenizing, bottling)
Texas Instruments Incorporated	Semiconductors and related devices
University of North Texas	Colleges and universities
University of Texas SW Medical Center	Accident and health insurance
Verizon Business Global	Telephone communication, except radio

Note: Companies shown are located within the Dallas-Fort Worth-Arlington, TX metropolitan area.
Source: Hoovers.com, data extracted April 25 2012

PUBLIC SAFETY

Crime Rate

Area	All Crimes	Violent Crimes				Property Crimes		
		Murder	Forcible Rape	Robbery	Aggrav. Assault	Burglary	Larceny -Theft	Motor Vehicle Theft
City	2,594.5	1.4	19.0	54.6	105.7	444.6	1,830.4	138.7
Suburbs[1]	3,901.1	4.9	26.8	147.8	189.4	938.4	2,238.1	355.9
Metro[2]	3,818.8	4.7	26.3	141.9	184.1	907.2	2,212.4	342.2
U.S.	3,345.5	4.8	27.5	119.1	252.3	699.6	2,003.5	238.8

Note: Figures are crimes per 100,000 population; (1) All areas within the metro area that are located outside the city limits; (2) Metropolitan Division—see Appendix B for areas included
Source: FBI Uniform Crime Reports, 2010

Hate Crimes

Area	Number of Quarters Reported	Bias Motivation				
		Race	Religion	Sexual Orientation	Ethnicity	Disability
City	4	0	3	0	1	0

Source: Federal Bureau of Investigation, Hate Crime Statistics 2010

Identity Theft Consumer Complaints

Area	Complaints	Complaints per 100,000 Population	Rank[2]
MSA[1]	7,171	116.7	47
U.S.	279,156	90.4	-

Note: (1) Metropolitan Statistical Area—see Appendix B for areas included; (2) Rank ranges from 1 to 384 where 1 indicates greatest number of identity theft complaints per 100,000 population
Source: Federal Trade Commission, Consumer Sentinel Network Data Book for January–December 2011

Fraud and Other Consumer Complaints

Area	Complaints	Complaints per 100,000 Population	Rank[2]
MSA[1]	30,244	492.2	163
U.S.	1,533,924	496.8	-

Note: (1) Metropolitan Statistical Area—see Appendix B for areas included; (2) Rank ranges from 1 to 384 where 1 indicates greatest number of fraud and other complaints per 100,000 population
Source: Federal Trade Commission, Consumer Sentinel Network Data Book for January–December 2011

RECREATION

Culture

Dance[1]	Theatre[1]	Instrumental Music[1]	Vocal Music[1]	Series/ Festivals	Museums	Zoos and Aquariums[2]
0	1	0	0	0	2	0

Note: (1) Number of professional performing groups; (2) AZA-accredited
Source: The Grey House Performing Arts Directory, 2011-2012; Official Museum Directory, 2011; American Association of Museums, AAM Member Museums, April 2012; Association of Zoos & Aquariums, AZA Member Zoos & Aquariums, April 2012

Professional Sports Teams

Team Name	League
Dallas Cowboys	National Football League (NFL)
Dallas Mavericks	National Basketball Association (NBA)
Dallas Stars	National Hockey League (NHL)
FC Dallas	Major League Soccer (MLS)
Texas Rangers	Major League Baseball (MLB)

Note: Includes teams located in the Dallas-Fort Worth metro area.
Source: Original research

CLIMATE

Average and Extreme Temperatures

Temperature	Jan	Feb	Mar	Apr	May	Jun	Jul	Aug	Sep	Oct	Nov	Dec	Yr.
Extreme High (°F)	85	90	100	100	101	112	111	109	107	101	91	87	112
Average High (°F)	55	60	68	76	84	92	96	96	89	79	67	58	77
Average Temp. (°F)	45	50	57	66	74	82	86	86	79	68	56	48	67
Average Low (°F)	35	39	47	56	64	72	76	75	68	57	46	38	56
Extreme Low (°F)	-2	9	12	30	39	53	58	58	42	24	16	0	-2

Note: Figures cover the years 1945-1993
Source: National Climatic Data Center, International Station Meteorological Climate Summary, 9/96

Average Precipitation/Snowfall/Humidity

Precip./Humidity	Jan	Feb	Mar	Apr	May	Jun	Jul	Aug	Sep	Oct	Nov	Dec	Yr.
Avg. Precip. (in.)	1.9	2.3	2.6	3.8	4.9	3.4	2.1	2.3	2.9	3.3	2.3	2.1	33.9
Avg. Snowfall (in.)	1	1	Tr	Tr	0	0	0	0	0	Tr	Tr	Tr	3
Avg. Rel. Hum. 6am (%)	78	77	75	77	82	81	77	76	80	79	78	77	78
Avg. Rel. Hum. 3pm (%)	53	51	47	49	51	48	43	41	46	46	48	51	48

Note: Figures cover the years 1945-1993; Tr = Trace amounts (<0.05 in. of rain; <0.5 in. of snow)
Source: National Climatic Data Center, International Station Meteorological Climate Summary, 9/96

Weather Conditions

Temperature			Daytime Sky			Precipitation		
10°F & below	32°F & below	90°F & above	Clear	Partly cloudy	Cloudy	0.01 inch or more precip.	0.1 inch or more snow/ice	Thunder-storms
1	34	102	108	160	97	78	2	49

Note: Figures are average number of days per year and cover the years 1945-1993
Source: National Climatic Data Center, International Station Meteorological Climate Summary, 9/96

HAZARDOUS WASTE

Superfund Sites

Plano has no sites on the EPA's Superfund Final National Priorities List.
U.S. Environmental Protection Agency, Final National Priorities List, April 17, 2012

AIR & WATER QUALITY

Air Quality Index

Area	Percent of Days when Air Quality was...[2]					AQI Statistics[2]	
	Good	Moderate	Unhealthy for Sensitive Groups	Unhealthy	Very Unhealthy	Maximum	Median
Area[1]	78.7	14.9	6.4	0.0	0.0	150	36

Note: Air Quality Index (AQI) is an index for reporting daily air quality. EPA calculates the AQI for five major air pollutants regulated by the Clean Air Act: ground-level ozone, particle pollution (aka particulate matter), carbon monoxide, sulfur dioxide, and nitrogen dioxide. The AQI runs from 0 to 500. The higher the AQI value, the greater the level of air pollution and the greater the health concern. There are six AQI categories: "Good" AQI is between 0 and 50. Air quality is considered satisfactory; "Moderate" AQI is between 51 and 100. Air quality is acceptable; "Unhealthy for Sensitive Groups" When AQI values are between 101 and 150, members of sensitive groups may experience health effects; "Unhealthy" When AQI values are between 151 and 200 everyone may begin to experience health effects; "Very Unhealthy" AQI values between 201 and 300 trigger a health alert; "Hazardous" AQI values over 300 trigger warnings of emergency conditions (not shown); (1) Data covers Collin County; (2) Based on 362 days with AQI data in 2011.
Source: U.S. Environmental Protection Agency, AirData Report, 2011

Air Quality Index Pollutants

Area	Percent of Days when AQI Pollutant was...[2]					
	Carbon Monoxide	Nitrogen Dioxide	Ozone	Sulfur Dioxide	Particulate Matter 2.5	Particulate Matter 10
Area[1]	0.0	0.0	100.0	0.0	0.0	0.0

Note: The Air Quality Index (AQI) is an index for reporting daily air quality. EPA calculates the AQI for five major air pollutants regulated by the Clean Air Act: ground-level ozone, particle pollution (also known as particulate matter), carbon monoxide, sulfur dioxide, and nitrogen dioxide. The AQI runs from 0 to 500. The higher the AQI value, the greater the level of air pollution and the greater the health concern; (1) Data covers Collin County; (2) Based on 362 days with AQI data in 2011.
Source: U.S. Environmental Protection Agency, AirData Report, 2011

Air Quality Index Trends

Area	Trend Sites (days)								All Sites (days)
	2003	2004	2005	2006	2007	2008	2009	2010	2010
MSA[1]	49	50	80	54	34	30	32	15	18

Note: Figures are the number of days the AQI value exceeded 100 in a given year. An AQI value greater than 100 indicates that air quality would have been in the unhealthful range on that day. Data from exceptional events are included. These counts are presented in two ways. First, the counts are based on sites having an adequate record of monitoring data during the trend period (trend sites). These counts represent the relative change in the number of days with AQI values greater than 100. In the last column, the counts are based on all sites with data in the most recent year (because it is possible for a site to have data in the most recent year but not enough data to be a trend site); (1) Data covers the Dallas-Fort Worth-Arlington, TX—see Appendix B for areas included
Source: U.S. Environmental Protection Agency, Air Quality Index Information, "Number of Days with Air Quality Index Values Greater than 100 at Trend Sites, 2000-2010, and at All Sites in 2010"

Maximum Air Pollutant Concentrations: Particulate Matter, Ozone, CO and Lead

	Particulate Matter 10 (ug/m³)	Particulate Matter 2.5 Wtd AM (ug/m³)	Particulate Matter 2.5 24-Hr (ug/m³)	Ozone (ppm)	Carbon Monoxide (ppm)	Lead (ug/m³)
MSA[1] Level	62	10.8	25	0.085	2	0.77
NAAQS[2]	150	15	35	0.075	9	0.15
Met NAAQS[2]	Yes	Yes	Yes	No	Yes	No

Note: Data from exceptional events are not included; (1) Data covers the Dallas-Fort Worth-Arlington, TX—see Appendix B for areas included; (2) National Ambient Air Quality Standards; ppm = parts per million; ug/m³ = micrograms per cubic meter; n/a not available
Concentrations: Particulate Matter 10 (coarse particulate)—highest second maximum 24-hour concentration; Particulate Matter 2.5 Wtd AM (fine particulate)—highest weighted annual mean concentration; Particulate Matter 2.5 24-Hour (fine particulate)—highest 98th percentile 24-hour concentration; Ozone—highest fourth daily maximum 8-hour concentration; Carbon Monoxide—highest second maximum non-overlapping 8-hour concentration; Lead—maximum running 3-month average
Source: U.S. Environmental Protection Agency, CBSA Factbook 2010, Air Quality Statistics by City, 2010

Maximum Air Pollutant Concentrations: Nitrogen Dioxide and Sulfur Dioxide

	Nitrogen Dioxide AM (ppb)	Nitrogen Dioxide 1-Hr (ppb)	Sulfur Dioxide AM (ppb)	Sulfur Dioxide 1-Hr (ppb)	Sulfur Dioxide 24-Hr (ppb)
MSA[1] Level	13.186	56.9	0.808	17.3	4.5
NAAQS[2]	53	100	30	75	140
Met NAAQS[2]	Yes	Yes	Yes	Yes	Yes

Note: Data from exceptional events are not included; (1) Data covers the Dallas-Fort Worth-Arlington, TX—see Appendix B for areas included; (2) National Ambient Air Quality Standards; ppb = parts per billion; n/a not available
Concentrations: Nitrogen Dioxide AM—highest arithmetic mean concentration; Nitrogen Dioxide 1-Hr—highest 98th percentile 1-hour daily maximum concentration; Sulfur Dioxide AM—highest annual mean concentration; Sulfur Dioxide 1-Hr—highest 99th percentile 1-hour daily maximum concentration; Sulfur Dioxide 24-Hr—highest second maximum 24-hour concentration
Source: U.S. Environmental Protection Agency, CBSA Factbook 2010, Air Quality Statistics by City, 2010

Drinking Water

Water System Name	Pop. Served	Primary Water Source Type	Violations[1]	
			Health Based	Monitoring/ Reporting
City of Plano	260,000	Purchased Surface	1	0

Note: (1) Based on violation data from January 1, 2011 to December 31, 2011 (includes unresolved violations from earlier years)
Source: U.S. Environmental Protection Agency, Office of Ground Water and Drinking Water, Safe Drinking Water Information System (based on data extracted April 18, 2012)

Round Rock, Texas

Background

Located twenty miles north of bustling, techie and hip Austin, Round Rock, one of the nation's fastest growing cities, is located on I-35, partly in Texas Hill Country and partly in Blackland Prairie, and named for the round rock that marks an old fording area along Brushy Creek—the creek being the town's first namesake. In 1845, the name was changed to Round Rock and the area near the rock is now called Old Town. Round Rock is located on the old Chisholm Trail, the cattle herding trail mapped out by Jesse Chisholm—and expanded from the Southwest to the Midwest.

Round Rock is the home of Dell Inc. and, with 13,000 employees, the city's largest employer. As if to underscore Round Rock's contemporary appeal, IKEA, another major employer, is installing solar energy panels at their Round Rock location, the company's largest solar unit.

Sears has a large call center here, Emerson Process Management headquarters its automation process systems division here, and TECO Westinghouse is headquartered in Round Rock. Signaling the city's economic diversity, Michael Angelo's Gourmet Foods also is headquartered in Round Rock.

They city has earned a slew of awards in recent years, from best town in 2010 to second-safest Texas city in 2011.

Higher education is actively being nurtured in the city via a planned collaboration that puts satellite campuses in close physical proximity to one another. Austin Community College operates a new campus alongside the Texas State Round Rock Higher Education Center and Seton Hospital Williamson. Texas A&M has built a new Health Science Center College of Medicine here, which offers clinical training to third- and fourth-year students. It's part of the large Avery Center, a mixed-use development just east of I-35 that will include residences, churches, and even a YMCA.

In addition, Texas State University's San Marcos Round Rock Higher Education Center offers undergraduate, graduate, and a BS in nursing degrees, and the local Round Rock Independent School District is working through Austin Community College to offer dual credit courses.

The school district, which includes portions of the cities of Austin and Cedar Park serves approximately 45,000 ethnically diverse students and has seen a 15% enrollment increase in the last five years.

Round Rock calls itself the Sports Capital of Texas and offers wide-ranging opportunities for recreation. The Austin Sports Arena in town offers leagues for hockey, volleyball, lacrosse, dodgeball, and more. The 570-acre Old Settlers Park provides 20 baseball fields, disc golf, soccer, cricket, two football fields, a five-field softball complex, picnic area, playgrounds, and an aquatic center. The city also operates the Clay Madsen Recreation Center, with two gyms and a lap pool, as well as the Forest Creek Golf Club.

Memorial Park, along Brushy Creek, is home to "the" round rock, and leads to Chisholm Trail Park, where the city memorializes its cattle-driving culture in bronze sculptures. Also keeping an eye on the past is the Old Settlers Association of Williamson, which hosts a village park and events.

In 2011 the city undertook Arts and Culture in Public Spaces planning, an effort to coordinate and boost these activities in the city. In addition to the wealth of cultural opportunities in nearby Austin, Round rock also has its local arts council with events and a gallery called Round Rock Arts, the Round Rock Symphony, and the Williamson Museum, focused on local culture. The city also has developed into a regional shopping destination with a number of shopping centers and malls.

The climate is sunny and hot, with summers heating well into the 90s. May is the rainiest month. Winters are very mild.

Rankings

General Rankings

- The Austin metro area was selected as one of the best cities to relocate to in America by Sperling's BestPlaces. The metro area ranked #5 out of 10. Criteria: unemployment; cost of living; crime rates; population health; cultural events; economic stability. *Sperling's BestPlaces, www.BestPlaces.net, "The Best Cities to Relocate to in America," October 2010*

- The Austin metro area was selected one of America's "Best Cities to Live, Work and Play" by *Kiplinger's Personal Finance*. Criteria: population growth; percentage of workforce in the creative class (scientists, engineers, educators, writers, artists, entertainers, etc.); job quality; income growth; cost of living. *Kiplinger's Personal Finance, "Best Cities to Live, Work and Play," July 2008*

- The Austin metro area was selected one of America's "Best Cities" by *Kiplinger's Personal Finance*. Criteria: stable employment; income growth; cost of living; percentage of workforce in the creative class (scientists, engineers, educators, writers, artists, entertainers, etc.). *Kiplinger's Personal Finance, "Best Cities 2009: It's All About Jobs," July 2009*

- Round Rock appeared on RelocateAmerica's list of best places to live in America. The annual "Top 100 Places to Live" list recognizes the top communities as nominated by their residents & local businesses. RelocateAmerica's Research Group determines the list based on review of various data gathered for economic, employment, housing, education, industry, opportunity, environment and recreation along with feedback from area leaders and residents. *RelocateAmerica.com, "Top 100 Places to Live for 2011"*

Business/Finance Rankings

- *Forbes* ranked the largest metro areas in the U.S. in terms of the "Best Cities for Young Professionals." The Austin metro area ranked #11out of 15. Criteria: job growth; unemployment rate; median salary of college graduates age 24 to 34; cost of living; number of small businesses per capita; number of large companies; percentage of population 25 years of age and older with college degrees. *Forbes.com, "America's Best Cities for Young Professionals," July 12, 2011*

- The Austin metro area was identified as one of 10 "Cities Where the Recession is Easing." The metro area was ranked #1. Criteria: job growth; goods produced; home sale prices; unemployment rates. *Forbes.com, "Cities Where the Recession is Easing," March 3, 2010*

- Austin was selected as one of the best metro areas for telecommuters in America. The area ranked #1 out of 11. Criteria: low cost of living; educational attainment; number of universities and libraries; literacy rates; personal fitness. *DailyFinance.com, "The 11 Best Cities for Telecommuters," December 2, 2010*

- The Austin metro area appeared on the Milken Institute "2011 Best Performing Metros" list. Rank: #4 out of 200 large metro areas. Criteria: job growth; wage and salary growth; high-tech output growth. *Milken Institute, "2011 Best Performing Metros"*

- The Austin metro area was selected as one of the best cities for entrepreneurs in America by *Inc. Magazine*. Criteria: job-growth data for 335 metro areas was analyzed for: recent growth trend; mid-term growth; long-term trend; current year growth. The Austin metro area ranked #2 among large metro areas and #19 overall. *Inc. Magazine, "The Best Cities for Doing Business," July 2008*

- Austin was ranked #42 out of 145 regions worldwide in terms of its "Knowledge Competitiveness Index." The index attempts to measure the knowledge-based development taking place throughout the world and is based on 19 measures of economic performance that indicate a region's ability to translate its knowledge capacity into economic value. *Centre for International Competitiveness, World Knowledge Competitiveness Index 2008*

- *Forbes* ranked the 200 most populous metro areas in the U.S. in terms of the "Best Places for Business and Careers." The Austin metro area was ranked #7. Criteria: costs (business and living); job growth (past and projected); income growth; educational attainment; projected economic growth; crime; cultural and recreational opportunities; net migration patterns; number of highly ranked colleges. *Forbes, "Best Places for Business and Careers," June 2011*

Children/Family Rankings

- The Austin metro area was selected as one of the "Best Cities for Relocating Families" by Worldwide ERC and Primacy Relocation. The 2008 study looked at nearly 50 factors important to relocating families including: recent job growth; nearby top-ranked colleges; in-state tuition for four-year public colleges; population growth since 2000; pediatricians per 100,000 population; and a Green Living index. *Worldwide ERC and Primacy Relocation, "2008 Best Cities for Relocating Families"*

Dating/Romance Rankings

- Eli Lily and Company, in partnership with Sperling's BestPlaces, ranked the nation's 50 largest metro areas in terms of the "Most Romantic Cities for Baby Boomers." The Austin metro area ranked #32. Criteria: marriage and divorce rates among baby boomers age 45 to 60; great restaurants; dance studios; chocolate, jewelry and flower sales. *Eli Lily and Company, "Most Romantic Cities for Baby Boomers," April 20, 2007*

- The Austin metro area was selected as one of the "Best Cities for Relocating Singles" by Worldwide ERC and Primacy Relocation. The area ranked #33 out of the 100 largest metro areas in the U.S. Criteria: recent job growth; recent singles population growth; overall population growth; affordable rental housing; cost-of-living index; expanded arts and recreation opportunities; ratio of single men and single women; affordability of quality higher education (including state residency requirements); diversity index; climate; population density. *Worldwide ERC and Primacy Relocation, "2008 Best Cities for Relocating Singles"*

- *Forbes* ranked the 40 most populous urbanized areas in the U.S. in terms of the "Best Cities for Singles." The Austin metro area ranked #11. Criteria: number of singles; cost of living alone; nightlife; culture; job growth; coolness; and online dating participation. *Forbes.com, "Best Cities for Singles," July 27, 2009*

Education Rankings

- Austin was identified as one of the 100 "smartest" metro areas in the U.S. The area ranked #12. Criteria: the editors rated the collective brainpower of the 100 largest metro areas in the U.S. based on their residents' educational attainment. *American City Business Journals, April 14, 2008*

- Austin was identified as one of "America's Smartest Cities" by *The Daily Beast*. The metro area ranked #7 out of 55. The editors ranked metropolitan areas with one million or more residents on the following criteria: percentage of residents over age 25 with bachelor's or graduate degrees; non-fiction book sales; ratio of institutions of higher education; libraries per capita. *The Daily Beast, "America's Smartest Cities," October 24, 2010*

- Austin was identified as one of "America's Brainiest Bastions" by *Portfolio.com*. The metro area ranked #22 out of 200. *Portfolio.com* analyzed levels of educational attainment in the nation's 200 largest metropolitan areas. The editors established scores for five levels of educational attainment, based on relative earning power of adult workers age 25 or older. Scores were determined by comparing the median income for all workers with the median income for those workers at a specified educational level. *Portfolio.com, "America's Brainiest Bastions," December 1, 2010*

- Austin was identified as one of "America's Smartest Cities" by *CNNMoney.com*. The area ranked #6. Criteria: percentage of residents with bachelors or graduate degrees. *CNNMoney.com, "America's Smartest Cities," October 1, 2010*

Environmental Rankings

- The Austin was identified as one of America's cities with the most ENERGY STAR certified buildings. The area ranked #18 out of 25. Criteria: number of ENERGY STAR labeled buildings in 2010. *U.S. Environmental Protection Agency, "Top Cities With the Most ENERGY STAR Certified Buildings," March 15, 2011*

- Round Rock was selected as one of 22 "Smarter Cities" for energy by the Natural Resources Defense Council. Criteria: investment in green power; energy efficiency measures; conservation. *Natural Resources Defense Council, "2010 Smarter Cities," July 19, 2010*

- *American City Business Journal* ranked 43 metropolitan areas in terms of their "greenness." The Austin metro area ranked #4. Criteria: Forty-one metros in which *ACBJ* has business weeklies, plus Indianapolis and Cleveland, were ranked based on 20 different indicators such as adoption of green technologies, utilization of environmentally sound practices, and air and water quality. *American City Business Journals, "Green City Index," March 11, 2010*

- 100 of the largest metro areas in the U.S. were analyzed in terms of their current drought severity. The Austin metro area ranked #98 (#1 = driest). The rankings were based on statistics such as long-term precipitation trends and patterns and the Palmer drought indices. *Sperling's BestPlaces, www.BestPlaces.net, "America's Drought-Riskiest Cities," November 2007*

- The Austin metro area appeared in *Country Home's* "Best Green Places" report. The area ranked #33 out of 379. Criteria: official energy policies; green power; green buildings; availability of fresh, locally grown food. *Country Home, "Best Green Places," 2008*

- Austin was highlighted as one of the top 25 cleanest metro areas for short-term particle pollution (24-hour PM 2.5) in the U.S. Monitors in these cities reported no days with unhealthful PM 2.5 levels. *American Lung Association, State of the Air 2011*

Health/Fitness Rankings

- Austin was identified as a "2011 Asthma Capital." The area ranked #94 out of the nation's 100 largest metropolitan areas. Twelve factors were used to identify the most challenging places to live for people with asthma: estimated prevalence; self-reported prevalence; crude death rate for asthma; annual pollen score; annual air quality; public smoking laws; number of board-certified asthma specialists; school inhaler access laws; rescue medication use; controller medication use; uninsured rate; poverty rate. *Asthma and Allergy Foundation of America, "2011 Asthma Capitals"*

- Austin was identified as a "2011 Fall Allergy Capital." The area ranked #42 out of 100. Three groups of factors were used to identify the most severe cities for people with allergies during the fall season: annual pollen levels; medicine utilization; access to board-certified allergists. *Asthma and Allergy Foundation of America, "2011 Fall Allergy Capitals"*

- Austin was identified as a "2012 Spring Allergy Capital." The area ranked #26 out of 100. Three groups of factors were used to identify the most severe cities for people with allergies during the spring season: annual pollen levels; medicine utilization; access to board-certified allergists. *Asthma and Allergy Foundation of America, "2012 Spring Allergy Capitals"*

- The makers of Breath Right Nasal Strips, in partnership with Sperling's BestPlaces, analyzed 50 metro areas and identified those U.S. cities most challenged by chronic nasal congestion. The Austin metro area ranked #14. Criteria: tree, grass and weed pollens; molds and spores; air pollution; climate; smoking; purchase habits of congestion products; prescriptions of drugs for congestion relief; incidence of influenza. *Breathe Right Nasal Strips, "Most Congested Cities," October 3, 2011*

- The Austin metropolitan area was selected as one of the best metros for hospital care in America by *HealthGrades.com*. The rankings are based on a comprehensive study of patient death and complication rates in the nation's nearly 5,000 hospitals. Hospitals performing in the top 5% nationwide across 26 different medical procedures and diagnoses were identified. *HealthGrades.com* then ranked cities by the highest percentage of these Distinguished Hospitals for Clinical Excellence™. The Austin metro area ranked #45. *HealthGrades.com, "America's Top 50 Cities for Hospital Care," January 21, 2012*

- The Austin metro area appeared in the 2011 Gallup-Healthways Well-Being Index. The index, based on interviews with more than 350,000 Americans, measured jobs, finances, physical health, emotional state of mind and communities. The metro area ranked #36 out of 190. Criteria: life evaluation; emotional health; work environment; physical health; healthy behaviors; basic access (basic needs optimal for a healthy life, such as access to food and medicine, having health insurance and feeling safe while walking at night). *Gallup-Healthways, "State of Well-Being 2011"*

- The Austin metro area was identified as one of "America's Most Stressful Cities" by *Sperling's BestPlaces*. The metro area ranked #38 out of 50. Criteria: unemployment rate; suicide rate; commute time; mental health; poor rest; alcohol use; violent crime rate; property crime rate; cloudy days annually. *Sperling's BestPlaces, www.BestPlaces.net, "Stressful Cities 2012*

- 50 of the largest metro areas in the U.S. were analyzed in terms of their health and fitness by the American College of Sports Medicine in their "American Fitness Index." The Austin metro area ranked #10 (#1 = healthiest). Criteria: preventative health behaviors; levels of chronic disease; health care access; community resources and policies that support physical activity. *American College of Sports Medicine, "Health and Community Fitness Status of the 50 Largest Metropolitan Areas," August 1, 2011*

Real Estate Rankings

- The Austin metro area was identified as one of ten places where real estate is ripe for a rebound by *Forbes*. Criteria: change in home price over the past 12 months and three years; unemployment rates; 12-month job-growth projections; population change from 2006 through 2009; new home construction rates for the third quarter of 2011 as compared to the same quarter in 2010. *Forbes.com, "Cities Where Real Estate is Ripe for a Rebound," January 12, 2012*

- *Fortune* ranked the 100 largest metro areas in the U.S. in terms of projected median home price change in 2010. The Austin metro area ranked #26. *Fortune, "The 2010 Housing Outlook," December 9, 2009*

- Austin was identified as one of the top 20 metro areas with the highest rate of house price appreciation in 2011. The area ranked #18 with a one-year price appreciation of 0.6% through the 4th quarter 2011. *Federal Housing Finance Agency, House Price Index, 4th Quarter 2011*

- The Austin metro area was identified as one of "The 15 Worst Housing Markets for the Next Five Years." Criteria: cities with home prices that are projected to appreciate at an annual rate of less than 1.5% rate between the second quarter 2011 and the second quarter 2016. *The Business Insider, "The 15 Worst Housing Markets for the Next Five Years," July 1, 2011*

- The Austin metro area was identified as one of the 10 best condo markets in the U.S. in 2011. The area ranked #5 out of 54 markets with a price appreciation of 5.0%. Criteria: year-over-year change of median sales price of existing apartment condo-coop homes between the 4th quarter of 2010 and the 4th quarter of 2011. *National Association of Realtors®, Median Sales Price of Existing Apartment Condo-Coop Homes for Metropolitan Areas, 4th Quarter 2011*

- The Austin metro area was identified as one of "America's Best Housing Markets" by *Forbes*. The metro area ranked #10. Criteria: housing affordability; rising home prices; percentage of foreclosures. *Forbes.com, "America's Best Housing Markets," February 19, 2010*

- The Austin metro area appeared in a *Wall Street Journal* article ranking cities by "housing stress." The metro area was ranked #26 (#1 = most stress). Criteria: fraction of mortgage-holding homeowners with a monthly housing payment in excess of 30 percent of income; percentage of people without health insurance; unemployment rate. *The Wall Street Journal, "Which Cities Face Biggest Housing Risk," October 5, 2010*

- The Center for Housing Policy ranked 210 U.S. metropolitan areas by the fair market rent for a two-bedroom unit. The Austin metro area was ranked #65. (#1 = most expensive) with a rent of $954. Criteria: Fair Market Rent (FMR) in effect during the fourth quarter of 2009 based on HUD's fiscal year 2010 FMRs. *The Center for Housing Policy, "Paycheck to Paycheck: Most to Least Expensive Rental Markets in 2009"*

- The Austin metro area was identified as one of the best U.S. markets to invest in rental property" by HomeVestors and Local Market Monitor. The area ranked #25 out of 100. Criteria: risk-return premium relative to national average. *HomeVestors and Local Market Monitor, "Best 100 U.S. Markets to Invest in Rental Property," March 9, 2012*

Safety Rankings

- Farmers Insurance Group of Companies, in partnership with Sperling's BestPlaces, ranked 379 metro areas and identified the "Most Secure U.S. Places to Live." The Austin metro area ranked #10 out of the top 20 in the large metro area category (500,000 or more residents). Criteria: crime statistics; extreme weather; risk of natural disasters; housing depreciation; foreclosures; environmental hazards; terrorist threats; air quality; life expectancy; mortality rates from cancer and motor vehicle accidents; job loss numbers. *Farmers Insurance Group, "Most Secure U.S. Places to Live 2011," December 15, 2011*

- The National Insurance Crime Bureau ranked 366 metro areas in the U.S. in terms of per capita rates of vehicle theft. The Austin metro area ranked #122 (#1 = highest rate). Criteria: number of vehicle theft offenses per 100,000 inhabitants in 2010. *National Insurance Crime Bureau, "Hot Spots," June 21, 2011*

- The Austin metro area was identified as one of the most dangerous metro areas for pedestrians by Transportation for America. The metro area ranked #18 out of 52 metro areas with over 1 million residents. Criteria: area's population divided by the number of pedestrian fatalities in that area. *Transportation for America, "Dangerous by Design 2011"*

Seniors/Retirement Rankings

- Bankers Life and Casualty Company, in partnership with Sperling's BestPlaces, ranked the nation's 50 largest metro areas in terms of the "Best U.S. Cities for Seniors." The Austin metro area ranked #24. Criteria: healthcare; transportation; housing; environment; economy; health and longevity; social and spiritual life; crime. *Bankers Life and Casualty Company, Center for a Secure Retirement, "Best U.S. Cities for Seniors 2011," September 2011*

- USAA and *Military.com*, in partnership with Sperling's BestPlaces, ranked 379 metropolitan areas in terms of which are the best places for military retirees. The metro area ranked #4 out of 10. Criteria: military skill related jobs; unemployment rate; number of federal government jobs; volume of DoD contracts; number of small businesses; number of veteran-owned businesses; military installation proximity/amenities; Veteran's Affairs hospitals; affordability; military pension taxation; presence of colleges/universities; sales tax; climate; crime level. *USAA and Military.com, "2011 Best Places for Military Retirement: Second Careers*

- The Austin metro area was selected as one of the "Best Places for Military Retirees" by *U.S. News & World Report*. The area ranked #3 out of 10. Criteria: climate; health resources; health indicators; crime levels; local school performance; recreational resources; arts and culture; airport and mass transit resources; susceptibility to natural disasters; military facilities and base amenities; VA medical services; tax policies affecting military pensions, unemployment trends; higher education resources; overall affordability; housing costs; home price trends; economic stability. *U.S. News & World Report, "Best Places for Military Retirees," December 8, 2010*

Sports/Recreation Rankings

- *Golf.com* and the research arm of the National Golf Foundation analyzed the 50 largest metropolitan areas in the U.S. in terms of golf. The Austin metro area ranked #1. Criteria: weather; affordability; quality of courses; accessibility; number of courses designed by esteemed architects; availability; crowdedness. *Golf.com, November 15, 2007*

Technology Rankings

- The Austin metro area was selected as one of "America's Most Wired Cities" by *Forbes*. The metro area was ranked #20 out of 20. Criteria: percentage of Internet users with high-speed access; number of companies providing high-speed Internet; number of public wireless hot spots. *Forbes, "America's Most Wired Cities," March 2, 2010*

- The Austin metro area was selected as one of "America's Most Innovative Cities" by *Forbes*. The metro area was ranked #2 out of 20. Criteria: patents per capita; venture capital investment per capita; ratio of high-tech, science and "creative" jobs. *Forbes, "America's Most Innovative Cities," May 24, 2010*

- The Austin metro area was identified as one of the "Top 14 Nano Metros" in the U.S. by the Project on Emerging Nanotechnologies. The metro area is home to 24 companies, universities, government laboratories and/or organizations working in nanotechnology. *Project on Emerging Nanotechnologies, "Nano Metros 2009"*

Transportation Rankings

- The Austin metro area appeared on *Forbes* list of the best and worst cities for commuters. The metro area ranked #27 out of 60 (#1 is best). Criteria: travel time; road congestion; travel delays. *Forbes.com, "Best and Worst Cities for Commuters," February 16, 2010*

Women/Minorities Rankings

- Austin was ranked #36 out of 100 metro areas in *SELF Magazine's* ranking of America's healthiest places for women." A panel of experts came up with more than 50 criteria including death and disease rates, environmental indicators, community resources, and lifestyle habits. *SELF Magazine, "Secrets of America's Healthiest Women," December 2008*

- The Austin metro area appeared on *Forbes'* list of the "Best Cities for Minority Entrepreneurs." The area ranked #36 out of 10. Criteria: 52 metropolitan statistical areas were examined. For each ethnicity (African Americans, Asians and Hispanics), the editors measured housing affordability, population growth, income growth, and entrepreneurship (per capita self-employment). *Forbes, "Best Cities for Minority Entrepreneurs," March 23, 2011*

Miscellaneous Rankings

- The Austin metro area was selected as one of "The Best U.S. Cities for Bargain Shopping" by *Forbes*. The area ranked #2 out of 10. Criteria: number of outlet stores; gross leasable retail space in major malls; low consumer price index; low sales tax rate. Indicators were examined in the nation's 50 largest metropolitan areas. *Forbes, "The Best U.S. Cities for Bargain Shopping," January 20, 2012*

- Energizer Holdings, the makers of Edge® shave gel, in partnership with Sperling's BestPlaces, ranked 50 major metro areas in terms of everyday irritations. The Austin metro area ranked #32. Criteria: humidity levels; weather conditions; incidence of traffic delays and congestion; average commute times; frequency of flight delays and cancellations; rates of sleeplessness; underemployment; pollens and allergens; pests; comedy clubs per capita. *Energizer Holdings, "Most Irritation Prone Cities," July 23, 2010*

Business Environment

CITY FINANCES

City Government Finances

Component	2009 ($000)	2009 ($ per capita)
Total Revenues	171,281	1,766
Total Expenditures	176,093	1,816
Debt Outstanding	211,100	2,176
Cash and Securities[1]	258,423	2,664

Note: (1) Cash and security holdings of a government at the close of its fiscal year, including those of its dependent agencies, utilities, and liquor stores.
Source: U.S Census Bureau, State & Local Government Finances 2009

City Government Revenue by Source

Source	2009 ($000)	2009 ($ per capita)
General Revenue		
From Federal Government	543	6
From State Government	1,159	12
From Local Governments	4,978	51
Taxes		
Property	27,687	285
Sales and Gross Receipts	77,293	797
Personal Income	0	0
Corporate Income	0	0
Motor Vehicle License	0	0
Other Taxes	6,810	70
Current Charges	17,455	180
Liquor Store	0	0
Utility	20,160	208
Employee Retirement	0	0

Source: U.S Census Bureau, State & Local Government Finances 2009

City Government Expenditures by Function

Function	2009 ($000)	2009 ($ per capita)	2009 (%)
General Direct Expenditures			
Air Transportation	0	0	0.0
Corrections	0	0	0.0
Education	0	0	0.0
Employment Security Administration	0	0	0.0
Financial Administration	2,744	28	1.6
Fire Protection	10,404	107	5.9
General Public Buildings	5,664	58	3.2
Governmental Administration, Other	2,993	31	1.7
Health	409	4	0.2
Highways	33,177	342	18.8
Hospitals	0	0	0.0
Housing and Community Development	494	5	0.3
Interest on General Debt	9,086	94	5.2
Judicial and Legal	1,413	15	0.8
Libraries	2,178	22	1.2
Parking	0	0	0.0
Parks and Recreation	21,848	225	12.4
Police Protection	23,939	247	13.6
Public Welfare	216	2	0.1
Sewerage	14,826	153	8.4
Solid Waste Management	109	1	0.1
Veterans' Services	0	0	0.0
Liquor Store	0	0	0.0
Utility	39,478	407	22.4
Employee Retirement	0	0	0.0

Source: U.S Census Bureau, State & Local Government Finances 2009

Municipal Bond Ratings

Area	Moody's	S&P	Fitch
City	n/a	n/a	n/a

Rating Systems (shown in declining order of credit quality): Moody's– Aaa, Aa, A, Baa, Ba, B, Caa, Ca, C (numerical modifiers 1, 2, and 3 are added to letter-rating); S&P– AAA, AA, A, BBB, BB, B, CCC, CC, C; Fitch– AAA, AA, A, BBB, BB, B, CCC, CC, C. Ratings may be modified by the addition of a plus or minus sign to show relative standing within the major rating categories.
Notes: n/a Not Available; w/d Withdrawn (1) Not Reviewed; (2) Issuer Rating/No General Obligation; (3) Standard and Poor's Issue Credit Rating (ICR) is a current opinion of an obliger with respect to a specific financial obligation, a specific class of financial obligations, or a specific financial program.
Source: U.S. Census Bureau, 2012 Statistical Abstract, Bond Ratings for City Governments by Largest Cities: 2010

DEMOGRAPHICS

Population Growth

Area	1990 Census	2000 Census	2010 Census	Population Growth (%) 1990-2000	2000-2010
City	32,854	61,136	99,887	86.1	63.4
MSA[1]	846,217	1,249,763	1,716,289	47.7	37.3
U.S.	248,709,873	281,421,906	308,745,538	13.2	9.7

Note: (1) Figures cover the Austin-Round Rock-San Marcos, TX Metropolitan Statistical Area—see Appendix B for areas included
Source: U.S. Census Bureau, 2010 Census

Household Size

Area	One	Two	Three	Four	Five	Six	Seven or More	Average Household Size
City	20.8	28.7	18.9	18.2	8.4	3.1	2.0	2.84
MSA[1]	27.3	32.0	16.0	13.7	6.4	2.6	2.0	2.58
U.S.	26.7	32.8	16.1	13.4	6.5	2.6	1.9	2.58

Note: (1) Figures cover the Austin-Round Rock-San Marcos, TX Metropolitan Statistical Area—see Appendix B for areas included
Source: U.S. Census Bureau, 2010 Census

Race

Area	White Alone[2] (%)	Black Alone[2] (%)	Asian Alone[2] (%)	AIAN[3] Alone[2] (%)	NHOPI[4] Alone[2] (%)	Other Race Alone[2] (%)	Two or More Races (%)
City	70.8	9.8	5.2	0.7	0.1	9.7	3.8
MSA[1]	72.9	7.4	4.8	0.8	0.1	10.9	3.2
U.S.	72.4	12.6	4.8	0.9	0.2	6.2	2.9

Note: (1) Figures cover the Austin-Round Rock-San Marcos, TX Metropolitan Statistical Area—see Appendix B for areas included; (2) Alone is defined as not being in combination with one or more other races; (3) American Indian and Alaska Native; (4) Native Hawaiian and Other Pacific Islander
Source: U.S. Census Bureau, 2010 Census

Hispanic or Latino Origin

Area	Hispanic or Latino (%)	Mexican (%)	Puerto Rican (%)	Cuban (%)	Other Hispanic or Latino (%)
City	29.0	23.4	0.9	0.3	4.4
MSA[1]	31.4	26.2	0.6	0.3	4.3
U.S.	16.3	10.3	1.5	0.6	4.0

Note: Persons of Hispanic or Latino origin can be of any race; (1) Figures cover the Austin-Round Rock-San Marcos, TX Metropolitan Statistical Area—see Appendix B for areas included
Source: U.S. Census Bureau, 2010 Census

Segregation

Type	Segregation Indices[1]				Percent Change		
	1990	2000	2010	2010 Rank[2]	1990-2000	1990-2010	2000-2010
Black/White	54.1	52.1	50.1	70	-1.9	-4.0	-2.1
Asian/White	39.4	42.3	41.2	49	2.9	1.8	-1.2
Hispanic/White	41.7	45.6	43.2	51	3.9	1.5	-2.4

Note: Figures are based on an analysis of 1990, 2000, and 2010 Census Decennial Census tract data by William H. Frey, Brookings Institution and the University of Michigan Social Science Data Analysis Network. In this analysis all racial groups (whites, blacks, and asians) are non-Hispanic members of those races. Hispanics are shown as a separate category; All figures cover the Metropolitan Statistical Area (see Appendix B for areas included); (1) Segregation Indices are Dissimilarity Indices that measure the degree to which the minority group is distributed differently than whites across census tracts. They range from 0 (complete integration) to 100 (complete segregation) where the value indicates the percentage of the minority group that needs to move to be distributed exactly like whites; (2) Ranges from 1 (most segregated) to 102 (least segregated); n/a not available.
Source: www.CensusScope.org

Ancestry

Area	German	Irish	English	American	Italian	Polish	French[2]	Scottish	Dutch
City	16.7	11.3	9.9	4.1	2.8	1.7	3.0	2.0	1.1
MSA[1]	15.6	9.5	9.5	3.6	2.7	1.6	2.9	2.5	1.1
U.S.	16.1	11.6	8.8	6.1	5.7	3.2	3.0	1.9	1.6

Note: Figures are the percentage of the total population reporting a particular ancestry. The nine most commonly reported ancestries in the U.S. are shown. Figures include multiple ancestries (e.g. if a person reported being Irish and Italian, they were included in both columns); (1) Figures cover the Austin-Round Rock-San Marcos, TX Metropolitan Statistical Area—see Appendix B for areas included; (2) Excludes Basque
Source: U.S. Census Bureau, 2008-2010 American Community Survey 3-Year Estimates

Foreign-Born Population

Area	Percent of Population Born in								
	Any Foreign Country	Mexico	Asia	Europe	Carribean	South America	Central America[2]	Africa	Canada
City	n/a	n/a	n/a	n/a	n/a	n/a	n/a	n/a	n/a
MSA[1]	14.6	7.6	3.6	1.0	0.2	0.4	1.1	0.4	0.3
U.S.	12.8	3.8	3.6	1.6	1.2	0.9	1.0	0.5	0.3

Note: (1) Figures cover the Austin-Round Rock-San Marcos, TX Metropolitan Statistical Area—see Appendix B for areas included; (2) Excludes Mexico.
Source: U.S. Census Bureau, 2008-2010 American Community Survey 3-Year Estimates

Marital Status

Area	Never Married	Now Married[2]	Separated	Widowed	Divorced
City	29.2	53.8	2.5	3.0	11.6
MSA[1]	34.8	49.2	1.9	3.6	10.4
U.S.	31.6	49.6	2.2	6.1	10.7

Note: Figures are percentages and cover the population 15 years of age and older; (1) Figures cover the Austin-Round Rock-San Marcos, TX Metropolitan Statistical Area—see Appendix B for areas included; (2) Excludes separated
Source: U.S. Census Bureau, 2008-2010 American Community Survey 3-Year Estimates

Age

Area	Percent of Population							Median Age
	Under Age 5	Age 5 to 17	Age 18 to 34	Age 35 to 49	Age 50 to 64	Age 65 to 79	80 Years and Over	
City	8.8	22.3	24.4	25.1	14.1	4.2	1.2	32.0
MSA[1]	7.4	17.9	28.6	22.1	15.9	6.1	2.0	32.6
U.S.	6.5	17.5	23.2	20.7	19.0	9.4	3.6	37.2

Note: (1) Figures cover the Austin-Round Rock-San Marcos, TX Metropolitan Statistical Area—see Appendix B for areas included
Source: U.S. Census Bureau, 2010 Census

Male/Female Ratio

Area	Males	Females	Males per 100 Females
City	49,139	50,748	96.8
MSA[1]	860,101	856,188	100.5
U.S.	151,781,326	156,964,212	96.7

*Note: (1) Figures cover the Austin-Round Rock-San Marcos, TX
Metropolitan Statistical Area—see Appendix B for areas included
Source: U.S. Census Bureau, 2010 Census*

Religious Groups

Area	Catholic	Baptist	Non-Den.	Methodist[2]	Lutheran	LDS[3]	Pentecostal	Presbyterian[4]	Muslim[5]	Judaism
MSA[1]	16.0	10.3	4.5	3.6	2.0	1.2	0.8	1.1	0.3	1.2
U.S.	19.1	9.3	4.0	4.0	2.3	2.0	1.9	1.6	0.8	0.7

*Note: Figures are the number of adherents as a percentage of the total population; (1) Figures cover the
Austin-Round Rock-San Marcos, TX Metropolitan Statistical Area—see Appendix B for areas included;
(2) Methodist/Pietist; (3) Latter Day Saints; (4) Reformed; (5) Figures are estimates
Source: Association of Statisticians of American Religious Bodies, 2010 U.S. Religion Census: Religious
Congregations & Membership Study*

ECONOMY

Gross Metropolitan Product

Area	2007	2008	2009	2010	2010 Rank[2]
MSA[1]	76.4	79.8	78.8	84.2	37

*Note: Figures are in billions of dollars; (1) Figures cover the Austin-Round Rock-San Marcos, TX Metropolitan
Statistical Area—see Appendix B for areas included; (2) Rank ranges from 1 to 363
Source: The United States Conference of Mayors, "U.S. Metro Economies: GMP and Employment Forecasts,"
June 2011*

Economic Growth

Area	2007-2009 (%)	2010 (%)	2011 (%)	Rank[2]
MSA[1]	1.7	6.7	3.0	41
U.S.	-1.3	2.9	2.5	–

*Note: Figures are real Gross Metropolitan Product growth rates and represent annual average percent change;
(1) Figures cover the Austin-Round Rock-San Marcos, TX Metropolitan Statistical Area—see Appendix B for
areas included; (2) Rank ranges from 1 to 363
Source: The United States Conference of Mayors, "U.S. Metro Economies: GMP and Employment Forecasts,"
June 2011*

Metropolitan Area Exports

Area	2005	2006	2007	2008	2009	2010	2010 Rank[2]
MSA[1]	7,687.0	8,204.6	8,428.6	7,405.5	5,963.7	8,867.8	31

*Note: Figures are in millions of dollars; (1) Figures cover the Austin-Round Rock-San Marcos, TX Metropolitan
Statistical Area—see Appendix B for areas included; (2) Rank ranges from 1 to 369
Source: U.S. Department of Commerce, International Trade Administration, Office of Trade & Industry
Information, Manufacturing & Services, data extracted April 2, 2012*

INCOME

Income

Area	Per Capita ($)	Median Household ($)	Average Household ($)
City	27,502	62,664	76,488
MSA[1]	29,482	56,732	76,321
U.S.	26,942	51,222	70,116

*Note: (1) Figures cover the Austin-Round Rock-San Marcos, TX Metropolitan Statistical Area—see Appendix B
for areas included
Source: U.S. Census Bureau, 2008-2010 American Community Survey 3-Year Estimates*

Household Income Distribution

Area	Percent of Households Earning							
	Under $15,000	$15,000 -24,999	$25,000 -34,999	$35,000 -49,999	$50,000 -74,999	$75,000 -99,000	$100,000 -149,999	$150,000 and up
City	4.5	8.0	10.1	15.0	21.8	15.4	16.6	8.5
MSA[1]	11.0	9.0	9.7	14.2	18.9	12.9	14.0	10.2
U.S.	13.0	11.0	10.6	14.2	18.5	12.1	12.2	8.4

Note: (1) Figures cover the Austin-Round Rock-San Marcos, TX Metropolitan Statistical Area—see Appendix B for areas included
Source: U.S. Census Bureau, 2008-2010 American Community Survey 3-Year Estimates

Poverty Rate

Area	All Ages	Under 18 Years Old	18 to 64 Years Old	65 Years and Over
City	7.6	10.8	6.3	4.2
MSA[1]	14.5	18.5	13.9	7.1
U.S.	14.4	20.1	13.1	9.4

Note: Figures are percentage of people whose income during the past 12 months was below the poverty level;
(1) Figures cover the Austin-Round Rock-San Marcos, TX Metropolitan Statistical Area—see Appendix B for areas included
Source: U.S. Census Bureau, 2008-2010 American Community Survey 3-Year Estimates

Personal Bankruptcy Filing Rate

Area	2006	2007	2008	2009	2010	2011
Williamson County	1.65	2.02	2.02	2.52	2.50	2.26
U.S.	2.00	2.73	3.53	4.61	4.97	4.37

Note: Numbers are per 1,000 population and include Chapter 7 and Chapter 13 filings
Source: Federal Deposit Insurance Corporation, Regional Economic Conditions, March 9, 2012

EMPLOYMENT

Labor Force and Employment

Area	Civilian Labor Force			Workers Employed		
	Dec. 2010	Dec. 2011	% Chg.	Dec. 2010	Dec. 2011	% Chg.
City	53,943	54,845	1.7	50,395	51,605	2.4
MSA[1]	902,646	918,215	1.7	840,510	860,696	2.4
U.S.	153,156,000	153,373,000	0.1	139,159,000	140,681,000	1.1

Note: Data is not seasonally adjusted and covers workers 16 years of age and older;
(1) Metropolitan Statistical Area—see Appendix B for areas included
Source: Bureau of Labor Statistics, http://stats.bls.gov

Unemployment Rate

Area	2011											
	Jan.	Feb.	Mar.	Apr.	May	Jun.	Jul.	Aug.	Sep.	Oct.	Nov.	Dec.
City	7.0	6.6	6.7	6.2	6.5	7.4	7.3	6.9	7.0	6.7	6.1	5.9
MSA[1]	7.3	6.9	6.8	6.5	6.8	7.6	7.6	7.4	7.5	7.1	6.6	6.3
U.S.	9.8	9.5	9.2	8.7	8.7	9.3	9.3	9.1	8.8	8.5	8.2	8.3

Note: Data is not seasonally adjusted and covers workers 16 years of age and older; All figures are percentages; (1) Metropolitan Statistical Area—see Appendix B for areas included
Source: Bureau of Labor Statistics, http://stats.bls.gov

Projected Unemployment Rate

Area	2010 (%)	2011 (%)	2012 (%)	2013 (%)
MSA[1]	7.3	6.9	6.6	6.3

Note: (1) Metropolitan Statistical Area—see Appendix B for areas included
Source: The United States Conference of Mayors, "U.S. Metro Economies: GMP and Employment Forecasts," June 2011

Employment by Occupation

Occupation Classification	City (%)	MSA[1] (%)	U.S. (%)
Management, Business, Science, and Arts	41.5	42.8	35.6
Natural Resources, Construction, and Maintenance	7.2	9.5	9.5
Production, Transportation, and Material Moving	8.6	7.1	12.1
Sales and Office	27.3	24.8	25.2
Service	15.4	15.8	17.6

Note: Figures cover employed civilians 16 years of age and older; (1) Figures cover the Austin-Round Rock-San Marcos, TX Metropolitan Statistical Area—see Appendix B for areas included
Source: U.S. Census Bureau, 2008-2010 American Community Survey 3-Year Estimates

Employment by Industry

Sector	MSA[1] Number of Employees	MSA[1] Percent of Total	U.S. Percent of Total
Construction	n/a	n/a	4.1
Education and Health Services	92,400	11.6	15.2
Financial Activities	45,300	5.7	5.8
Government	167,400	20.9	16.8
Information	20,300	2.5	2.0
Leisure and Hospitality	91,600	11.5	9.9
Manufacturing	50,900	6.4	8.9
Mining and Logging	n/a	n/a	0.6
Other Services	33,700	4.2	4.0
Professional and Business Services	116,500	14.6	13.3
Retail Trade	86,400	10.8	11.5
Transportation and Utilities	13,700	1.7	3.8
Wholesale Trade	42,500	5.3	4.2

Note: Figures cover non-farm employment as of December 2011 and are not seasonally adjusted; (1) Metropolitan Statistical Area—see Appendix B for areas included; n/a not available
Source: Bureau of Labor Statistics, http://stats.bls.gov

Occupations with Greatest Projected Employment Growth: 2008 – 2018

Occupation[1]	2008 Employment	2018 Projected Employment	Numeric Employment Change	Percent Employment Change
Combined Food Preparation and Serving Workers, Including Fast Food	247,750	326,190	78,440	31.7
Elementary School Teachers, Except Special Education	156,930	218,030	61,100	38.9
Retail Salespersons	361,780	416,090	54,310	15.0
Registered Nurses	166,240	219,880	53,640	32.3
Home Health Aides	92,660	143,720	51,060	55.1
Customer Service Representatives	217,250	267,290	50,040	23.0
Waiters and Waitresses	192,340	237,660	45,320	23.6
Personal and Home Care Aides	94,530	138,530	44,000	46.5
Office Clerks, General	239,400	279,000	39,600	16.5
Cashiers	276,070	312,940	36,870	13.4

Note: Projections cover Texas; (1) Sorted by numeric employment change
Source: www.projectionscentral.com, State Occupational Projections, 2008–2018 Long-Term Projections

Fastest Growing Occupations: 2008 – 2018

Occupation[1]	2008 Employment	2018 Projected Employment	Numeric Employment Change	Percent Employment Change
Biomedical Engineers	650	1,150	500	76.9
Home Health Aides	92,660	143,720	51,060	55.1
Network Systems and Data Communications Analysts	19,160	29,490	10,330	53.9
Petroleum Engineers	13,440	20,140	6,700	49.9
Athletic Trainers	1,560	2,300	740	47.4
Personal and Home Care Aides	94,530	138,530	44,000	46.5
Electrical and Electronics Repairers, Powerhouse, Substation, and Relay	1,550	2,260	710	45.8
Financial Examiners	2,150	3,130	980	45.6
Medical Scientists, Except Epidemiologists	3,670	5,320	1,650	45.0
Biochemists and Biophysicists	740	1,060	320	43.2

Note: Projections cover Texas; (1) Sorted by percent employment change and excludes occupations with numeric employment change less than 100
Source: www.projectionscentral.com, State Occupational Projections, 2008–2018 Long-Term Projections

Average Wages

Occupation	$/Hr.	Occupation	$/Hr.
Accountants and Auditors	33.31	Maids and Housekeeping Cleaners	9.22
Automotive Mechanics	22.03	Maintenance and Repair Workers	16.02
Bookkeepers	18.23	Marketing Managers	65.36
Carpenters	15.60	Nuclear Medicine Technologists	32.42
Cashiers	9.71	Nurses, Licensed Practical	21.93
Clerks, General Office	15.47	Nurses, Registered	33.09
Clerks, Receptionists/Information	12.65	Nursing Aides/Orderlies/Attendants	11.00
Clerks, Shipping/Receiving	14.00	Packers and Packagers, Hand	11.36
Computer Programmers	38.53	Physical Therapists	38.51
Computer Support Specialists	26.47	Postal Service Mail Carriers	25.00
Computer Systems Analysts	40.99	Real Estate Brokers	45.04
Cooks, Restaurant	10.93	Retail Salespersons	12.19
Dentists	90.89	Sales Reps., Exc. Tech./Scientific	33.93
Electrical Engineers	45.14	Sales Reps., Tech./Scientific	39.52
Electricians	19.31	Secretaries, Exc. Legal/Med./Exec.	15.34
Financial Managers	57.82	Security Guards	11.96
First-Line Supervisors/Managers, Sales	19.65	Surgeons	n/a
Food Preparation Workers	9.75	Teacher Assistants	12.00
General and Operations Managers	54.61	Teachers, Elementary School	24.40
Hairdressers/Cosmetologists	10.68	Teachers, Secondary School	25.10
Internists	100.65	Telemarketers	15.46
Janitors and Cleaners	10.51	Truck Drivers, Heavy/Tractor-Trailer	16.34
Landscaping/Groundskeeping Workers	11.79	Truck Drivers, Light/Delivery Svcs.	16.12
Lawyers	47.69	Waiters and Waitresses	8.82

Note: Wage data covers the Austin-Round Rock-San Marcos, TX Metropolitan Statistical Area—see Appendix B for areas included. Hourly wages for elementary/secondary school teachers and teacher assistants were calculated by the editors from annual wage data assuming a 40 hour work week; n/a not available.
Source: Bureau of Labor Statistics, Metro Area Occupational Employment and Wage Estimates, May 2011

RESIDENTIAL REAL ESTATE

Building Permits

Area	Single-Family			Multi-Family			Total		
	2010	2011	Pct. Chg.	2010	2011	Pct. Chg.	2010	2011	Pct. Chg.
City	253	259	2.4	0	0	-	253	259	2.4
MSA[1]	6,200	6,231	0.5	2,586	4,008	55.0	8,786	10,239	16.5
U.S.	447,311	418,498	-6.4	157,299	205,563	30.7	604,610	624,061	3.2

Note: (1) Metropolitan Statistical Area—see Appendix B for areas included; figures represent new, privately-owned housing units authorized (unadjusted data); All permit data are based on estimates with imputation.
Source: U.S. Census Bureau, Manufacturing, Mining, and Construction Statistics, Building Permits, 2010, 2011

Homeownership Rate

Area	2005 (%)	2006 (%)	2007 (%)	2008 (%)	2009 (%)	2010 (%)	2011 (%)
MSA[1]	63.9	66.7	66.4	65.5	64.0	65.8	58.4
U.S.	68.9	68.8	68.1	67.8	67.4	66.9	66.1

Note: (1) Metropolitan Statistical Area—see Appendix B for areas included
Source: U.S. Census Bureau, Housing Vacancies and Homeownership Annual Statistics: 2011

Housing Vacancy Rates

Area	Gross Vacancy Rate[2] (%)			Year-Round Vacancy Rate[3] (%)			Rental Vacancy Rate[4] (%)			Homeowner Vacancy Rate[5] (%)		
	2009	2010	2011	2009	2010	2011	2009	2010	2011	2009	2010	2011
MSA[1]	12.8	15.8	12.6	12.7	15.7	11.7	12.2	11.8	6.4	1.6	1.9	0.6
U.S.	14.5	14.3	14.2	11.3	11.3	11.1	10.6	10.2	9.5	2.6	2.6	2.5

Note: (1) Metropolitan Statistical Area—see Appendix B for areas included; (2) The percentage of the total housing inventory that is vacant; (3) The percentage of the housing inventory (excluding seasonal units) that is year-round vacant; (4) The percentage of rental inventory that is vacant for rent; (5) The percentage of homeowner inventory that is vacant for sale
Source: U.S. Census Bureau, Housing Vacancies and Homeownership Annual Statistics: 2011

TAXES

State Corporate Income Tax Rates

State	Tax Rate (%)	Income Brackets ($)	Num. of Brackets	Financial Institution Tax Rate (%)[a]	Federal Income Tax Ded.
Texas	(x)	–	-	(x)	No

Note: Tax rates as of January 1, 2012; (a) Rates listed are the corporate income tax rate applied to financial institutions or excise taxes based on income. Some states have other taxes based upon the value of deposits or shares; (x) Texas imposes a Franchise Tax, otherwise known as margin tax, imposed on entities with more than $1,000,000 total revenues at rate of 1%, or 0.5% for entities primarily engaged in retail or wholesale trade, on lesser of 70% of total revenues or 100% of gross receipts after deductions for either compensation or cost of goods sold.
Source: Federation of Tax Administrators, "State Corporate Income Tax Rates, 2012"

State Individual Income Tax Rates

State	Tax Rate (%)	Income Brackets ($)	Num. of Brackets	Personal Exempt. ($)[1] Single	Dependents	Fed. Inc. Tax Ded.

Texas – No State Income Tax

Note: Tax rates as of January 1, 2012; Local- and county-level taxes are not included; n/a not applicable; (1) Married joint filers generally receive double the single exemption
Source: Federation of Tax Administrators, "State Individual Income Tax Rates, 2012"

Various State and Local Tax Rates

State	State and Local Sales and Use (%)	State Sales and Use (%)	Gasoline[1] (¢/gal.)	Cigarette[2] ($/pack)	Spirits[3] ($/gal.)	Wine[4] ($/gal.)	Beer[5] ($/gal.)
Texas	8.25	6.25	20.0	1.41	2.40	0.20	0.20

Note: All tax rates as of January 1, 2012 except beer, wine and spirits (September 1, 2011); (1) The American Petroleum Institute has developed a methodology for determining the average tax rate on a gallon of fuel. Rates may include any of the following: excise taxes, environmental fees, storage tank fees, other fees or taxes, general sales tax, and local taxes. In states where gasoline is subject to the general sales tax, or where the fuel tax is based on the average sale price, the average rate determined by API is sensitive to changes in the price of gasoline. States that fully or partially apply general sales taxes to gasoline: CA, CO, GA, IL, IN, MI, NY; (2) The federal excise tax of $1.0066 per pack and local taxes are not included; (3) Rates are those applicable to off-premise sales of 40% alcohol by volume (a.b.v.) distilled spirits in 750ml containers. Local excise taxes are excluded; (4) Rates are those applicable to off-premise sales of 11% a.b.v. non-carbonated wine in 750ml containers; (5) Rates are those applicable to off-premise sales of 4.7% a.b.v. beer in 12 ounce containers.
Source: Tax Foundation, 2012 Facts & Figures: How Does Your State Compare?

State-Local Tax Burdens

Area	Rate (%)	Rank[1]	Per Capita Taxes Paid to Home State ($)	Total State and Local Per Capita Taxes Paid ($)	Per Capita Income ($)
Texas	7.9	45	2,248	3,197	40,498
U.S. Average	9.8	-	3,057	4,160	42,539

Note: Figures cover 2009; (1) Rank ranges from 1 to 50 where 1 is highest tax burden
Source: Tax Foundation, State-Local Tax Burdens, All States, 2009

State Business Tax Climate Index Rankings

State	Overall Rank	Corporate Tax Index Rank	Individual Income Tax Index Rank	Sales Tax Index Rank	Unemployment Insurance Tax Index Rank	Property Tax Index Rank
Texas	9	37	7	35	15	31

Note: The index is a measure of how each state's tax laws affect economic performance. The lower the rank, the more favorable a state's tax system is for business. States without a given tax are given a ranking of 1.
Source: Tax Foundation, Major Components of the State Business Tax Climate Index, FY 2012

COMMERCIAL REAL ESTATE

Office Market

Market Area	Inventory (sq. ft.)	Vacant (sq. ft.)	Vac. Rate (%)	Under Constr. (sq. ft.)	Asking Rent ($/sf/yr) Class A	Asking Rent ($/sf/yr) Class B
Austin	43,215,201	6,639,265	15.4	23,000	28.85	21.15

Source: Grubb & Ellis, Office Markets Trends, 4th Quarter 2011

Industrial Market

Market Area	Inventory (sq. ft.)	Vacant (sq. ft.)	Vac. Rate (%)	Under Constr. (sq. ft.)	Asking Rent ($/sf/yr) WH/Dist	Asking Rent ($/sf/yr) R&D/Flex
Austin	77,110,746	9,620,024	12.5	72,000	5.57	9.43

Source: Grubb & Ellis, Industrial Markets Trends, 4th Quarter 2011

COMMERCIAL UTILITIES

Typical Monthly Electric Bills

Area	Commercial Service ($/month) 1,500 kWh	Commercial Service ($/month) 40 kW demand 14,000 kWh	Industrial Service ($/month) 1,000 kW demand 200,000 kWh	Industrial Service ($/month) 50,000 kW demand 15,000,000 kWh
City	n/a	n/a	n/a	n/a
Average[1]	189	1,616	25,197	1,470,813

Note: Based on total rates in effect July 1, 2011; (1) average based on 184 utilities surveyed; n/a not available
Source: Edison Electric Institute, Typical Bills and Average Rates Report, Summer 2011

TRANSPORTATION

Means of Transportation to Work

Area	Car/Truck/Van Drove Alone	Car/Truck/Van Car-pooled	Public Transportation Bus	Public Transportation Subway	Public Transportation Railroad	Bicycle	Walked	Other Means	Worked at Home
City	78.5	12.6	0.1	0.0	0.0	0.4	1.3	1.0	6.2
MSA[1]	74.9	11.4	2.6	0.0	0.0	0.7	1.8	2.2	6.5
U.S.	76.0	10.2	2.7	1.7	0.5	0.5	2.8	1.3	4.2

Note: Figures are percentages and cover workers 16 years of age and older; (1) Figures cover the Austin-Round Rock-San Marcos, TX Metropolitan Statistical Area—see Appendix B for areas included
Source: U.S. Census Bureau, 2008-2010 American Community Survey 3-Year Estimates

Travel Time to Work

Area	Less Than 10 Minutes	10 to 19 Minutes	20 to 29 Minutes	30 to 44 Minutes	45 to 59 Minutes	60 to 89 Minutes	90 Minutes or More
City	11.5	36.0	22.5	18.0	7.8	3.0	1.1
MSA[1]	10.9	30.1	22.9	22.0	7.9	4.4	1.7
U.S.	13.9	30.1	20.8	19.8	7.5	5.5	2.5

Note: Figures are percentages and include workers 16 years old and over; (1) Figures cover the Austin-Round Rock-San Marcos, TX Metropolitan Statistical Area—see Appendix B for areas included
Source: U.S. Census Bureau, 2008-2010 American Community Survey 3-Year Estimates

Travel Time Index

Area	1985	1990	1995	2000	2005	2010
Urban Area[1]	1.11	1.14	1.20	1.23	1.32	1.28
Average[2]	1.11	1.16	1.18	1.21	1.25	1.20

Note: Travel Time Index—the ratio of travel time in the peak period to the travel time at free-flow conditions. A value of 1.30 indicates a 20-minute free-flow trip takes 26 minutes in the peak. Free-flow speeds (60 mph on freeways and 35 mph on principal arterials) are used as the comparison threshold; (1) Covers the Austin TX urban area; (2) average of 439 urban areas
Source: Texas Transportation Institute, Urban Mobility Report 2011, September 2011

Public Transportation

Agency Name / Mode of Transportation	Vehicles Operated in Maximum Service	Annual Unlinked Passenger Trips ('000)	Annual Passenger Miles ('000)
Capital Area Rural Transportation System (CARTS)	n/a	n/a	n/a

Source: Federal Transit Administration, National Transit Database, 2010

Air Transportation

Airport Name and Code / Type of Service	Passenger Airlines[1]	Passenger Enplanements	Freight Carriers[2]	Freight (lbs.)
Austin-Bergstrom International (AUS)				
Domestic service (U.S. carriers - 2011)	33	4,412,298	18	74,894,957
International service (U.S. carriers - 2010)	9	5,376	3	7,763,158

Note: (1) Includes all U.S.-based major, minor and commuter airlines that carried at least one passenger during the year; (2) Includes all U.S.-based airlines and freight carriers that transported at least one pound of freight during the year
Source: Bureau of Transportation Statistics, The Intermodal Transportation Database, Air Carriers: T-100 Domestic Market (U.S. Carriers), 2011; Bureau of Transportation Statistics, The Intermodal Transportation Database, Air Carriers: T-100 International Market (U.S. Carriers), 2010

Other Transportation Statistics

Major Highways: I-35; SR-79
Amtrak Service: Yes (stations located in Austin and Taylor)
Major Waterways/Ports: Near Colorado River

Source: Amtrak.com; Google Maps

BUSINESSES

Major Business Headquarters

Company Name	Rankings	
	Fortune[1]	Forbes[2]
Dell	41	-

Note: (1) Fortune 500—companies that produce a 10-K are ranked 1 to 500 based on 2010 revenue; (2) all private companies with at least $2 billion in annual revenue are ranked 1 to 212; companies listed are headquartered in the city; dashes indicate no ranking
Source: Fortune, "Fortune 500," May 23, 2011; Forbes, "America's Largest Private Companies," November 16, 2011

Minority- and Women-Owned Businesses

Group	All Firms		Firms with Paid Employees			
	Firms	Sales ($000)	Firms	Sales ($000)	Employees	Payroll ($000)
Asian	n/a	n/a	n/a	n/a	n/a	n/a
Black	n/a	n/a	n/a	n/a	n/a	n/a
Hispanic	n/a	n/a	n/a	n/a	n/a	n/a
Women	n/a	n/a	n/a	n/a	n/a	n/a
All Firms	12,140	6,496,832	2,975	6,008,436	27,498	1,264,434

Note: Figures cover firms located in the city; minority- and women-owned business are defined as firms in which the corresponding group own 51% or more of the stock or equity of the company; n/a not available
Source: U.S. Census Bureau, 2007 Economic Census, Survey of Business Owners

HOTELS

Hotels/Motels

Area	5 Star		4 Star		3 Star		2 Star		1 Star		Not Rated	
	Num.	Pct.[3]	Num.	Pct.[3]	Num.	Pct.[3]	Num.	Pct.[3]	Num.	Pct.[3]	Num.	Pct.[3]
City[1]	0	0.0	1	2.3	18	40.9	23	52.3	0	0.0	2	4.5
Total[2]	133	0.9	940	6.5	4,569	31.8	7,033	48.9	351	2.4	1,343	9.3

Note: (1) Figures cover Round Rock and vicinity; (2) Figures cover all 100 cities in this book; (3) Percentage of hotels which have a given star rating; Star ratings are determined by expedia.com and offer an indication of the general quality of a particular hotel.
Source: expedia.com, April 25, 2012

The Austin-Round Rock-San Marcos, TX metro area is home to one of the best hotels in the U.S. according to *Travel & Leisure*: **Four Seasons Hotel, Austin** (#181). Criteria: service; location; rooms; food; and value. *Travel & Leisure, "T+L 500, The World's Best Hotels 2012"*

EVENT SITES

Convention Centers

Name	Overall Space (sq. ft.)	Exhibit Space (sq. ft.)	Meeting Space (sq. ft.)	Meeting Rooms
Wingate by Wyndham Hotel & Conference Center	15,000	n/a	n/a	n/a

Note: n/a not available
Source: Original research

Living Environment

COST OF LIVING

Cost of Living Index

Composite Index	Groceries	Housing	Utilities	Trans-portation	Health Care	Misc. Goods/ Services
88.7	82.1	76.1	104.9	88.7	93.9	96.6

Note: U.S. = 100; Figures cover the Round Rock TX urban area.
Source: The Council for Community and Economic Research, ACCRA Cost of Living Index, 2011

Grocery Prices

Area[1]	T-Bone Steak ($/pound)	Frying Chicken ($/pound)	Whole Milk ($/half gal.)	Eggs ($/dozen)	Orange Juice ($/64 oz.)	Coffee ($/11.5 oz.)
City[2]	8.79	0.99	2.33	1.28	2.70	3.27
Avg.	9.25	1.18	2.22	1.66	3.19	4.40
Min.	6.70	0.88	1.31	0.95	2.46	2.94
Max.	14.30	2.16	3.50	3.18	4.75	6.83

Note: (1) Values for the local area are compared with the average, minimum and maximum values for all 335 areas in the Cost of Living Index; (2) Figures cover the Round Rock TX urban area; T-Bone Steak (price per pound); Frying Chicken (price per pound, whole fryer); Whole Milk (half gallon carton); Eggs (price per dozen, Grade A, large); Orange Juice (64 oz. Tropicana or Florida Natural); Coffee (11.5 oz. can, vacuum-packed, Maxwell House, Hills Bros, or Folgers).
Source: The Council for Community and Economic Research, ACCRA Cost of Living Index, 2011

Housing and Utility Costs

Area[1]	New Home Price ($)	Apartment Rent ($/month)	All Electric ($/month)	Part Electric ($/month)	Other Energy ($/month)	Telephone ($/month)
City[2]	210,266	761	-	119.07	49.29	29.72
Avg.	285,990	839	163.23	89.00	77.52	26.92
Min.	188,005	460	125.58	45.39	33.89	17.98
Max.	1,197,028	3,244	339.16	181.97	348.69	40.01

Note: (1) Values for the local area are compared with the average, minimum and maximum values for all 335 areas in the Cost of Living Index; (2) Figures cover the Round Rock TX urban area; New Home Price (2,400 sf living area, 8,000 sf lot, in urban area with full utilities); Apartment Rent (950 sf 2 bedroom/1.5 or 2 bath, unfurnished, excluding all utilities except water); All Electric (average monthly cost for an all-electric home); Part Electric (average monthly cost for a part-electric home); Other Energy (average monthly cost for natural gas, fuel oil, coal, wood, and any other forms of energy except electricity); Telephone (price includes basic monthly rate for a private residential line plus additional local usage charges incurred by a family of four).
Source: The Council for Community and Economic Research, ACCRA Cost of Living Index, 2011

Health Care, Transportation, and Other Costs

Area[1]	Doctor ($/visit)	Dentist ($/visit)	Optometrist ($/visit)	Gasoline ($/gallon)	Beauty Salon ($/visit)	Men's Shirt ($)
City[2]	70.96	91.23	75.69	3.36	29.33	20.61
Avg.	93.88	81.72	90.54	3.48	32.65	25.06
Min.	60.00	55.33	53.66	3.18	19.78	13.44
Max.	154.98	145.97	183.72	4.31	63.21	46.00

Note: (1) Values for the local area are compared with the average, minimum and maximum values for all 335 areas in the Cost of Living Index; (2) Figures cover the Round Rock TX urban area; Doctor (general practitioners routine exam of an established patient); Dentist (adult teeth cleaning and periodic oral examination); Optometrist (full vision eye exam for established adult patient); Gasoline (one gallon regular unleaded, national brand, including all taxes, cash price at self-service pump if available); Beauty Salon (woman's shampoo, trim, and blow-dry); Men's Shirt (cotton/polyester dress shirt, pinpoint weave, long sleeves).
Source: The Council for Community and Economic Research, ACCRA Cost of Living Index, 2011

HOUSING

House Price Index (HPI)

Area	National Ranking[2]	Quarterly Change (%)	One-Year Change (%)	Five-Year Change (%)
MSA[1]	18	0.87	0.60	9.27
U.S.[3]	-	-0.10	-2.43	-19.16

Note: The HPI is a weighted repeat sales index. It measures average price changes in repeat sales or refinancings on the same properties. This information is obtained by reviewing repeat mortgage transactions on single-family properties whose mortgages have been purchased or securitized by Fannie Mae or Freddie Mac in January 1975; (1) Metropolitan/Micropolitan Statistical Area—see Appendix B for areas included; (2) Rankings are based on annual percentage change for all metro areas containing at least 15,000 transactions over the last 10 years and ranges from 1 to 306; (3) figures based on a weighted average of Census Division estimates using a purchase only index; all figures are for the period ending December 31, 2011
Source: Federal Housing Finance Agency, House Price Index, February 23, 2012

House Price Valuations

Area	Q4 2005 Price ($000)	Q4 2005 Over-valuation	Q4 2006 Price ($000)	Q4 2006 Over-valuation	Q4 2007 Price ($000)	Q4 2007 Over-valuation	Q4 2008 Price ($000)	Q4 2008 Over-valuation	Q4 2009 Price ($000)	Q4 2009 Over-valuation
MSA[1]	148.8	-10.8	163.3	-7.1	174.1	-4.4	177.4	-2.9	177.0	-2.2

Note: Figures show the percentage of over- or under-valuation of single family homes relative to statistically normal house values (e.g. a value of 23.6 indicates that house values are 23.6% overvalued). Statistically normal house values are based on house prices, interest rates, household incomes, population densities, and any historical premiums or discounts metropolitan areas have exhibited over time; (1) Figures cover the Austin-Round Rock-San Marcos, TX - see Appendix B for areas included
Source: Global Insight/PNC Financial Services Group, House Prices in America: 4th Quarter 2009 Update

Median Single-Family Home Prices

Area	2009	2010	2011p	Percent Change 2010 to 2011
MSA[1]	187.4	193.6	193.1	-0.3
U.S. Average	172.1	173.1	166.2	-4.0

Note: Figures are median sales prices of existing single-family homes in thousands of dollars; (p) preliminary; n/a not available; (1) Metropolitan Statistical Area—see Appendix B for areas included
Source: National Association of Realtors, Median Sales Price of Existing Single-Family Homes for Metropolitan Areas, 4th Quarter 2011

Affordability Index of Existing Single-Family Homes

Area	2009	2010	2011p	Percent Change 2010 to 2011
MSA[1]	97.1	99.6	104.6	5.0

Note: The housing affordability index measures whether or not a typical family could qualify for a mortgage loan on a typical home. The higher the index, the greater the household purchasing power. An index of 100 is defined as the point where a median-income household has exactly enough income to qualify for the purchase of a median-priced existing single-family home, assuming a 20 percent downpayment and 25 percent of gross income devoted to mortgage principal and interest payments; (p) preliminary; n/a not available; (1) Metropolitan Statistical Area—see Appendix B for areas included
Source: National Association of Realtors, Affordability Index of Existing Single-Family Homes, 2011

Median Apartment Condo-Coop Home Prices

Area	2009	2010	2011p	Percent Change 2010 to 2011
MSA[1]	150.9	155.5	168.8	8.6
U.S. Average	175.6	171.7	165.1	-3.8

Note: Figures are median sales prices of existing apartment condo-coop homes in thousands of dollars; (p) preliminary; n/a not available; (1) Metropolitan Statistical Area—see Appendix B for areas included
Source: National Association of Realtors, Median Sales Price of Existing Apartment Condo-Coop Homes for Metropolitan Areas, 4th Quarter 2011

Year Housing Structure Built

Area	2005 or Later	2000 -2004	1990 -1999	1980 -1989	1970 -1979	1960 -1969	1950 -1959	Before 1950	Median Year
City	14.7	23.8	28.1	19.9	10.3	1.3	1.3	0.4	1996
MSA[1]	12.1	16.6	20.5	19.9	15.5	5.9	4.5	5.1	1990
U.S.	5.0	8.6	14.0	14.1	16.3	11.3	11.2	19.6	1975

Note: Figures are percentages except for Median Year; (1) Figures cover the Austin-Round Rock-San Marcos, TX Metropolitan Statistical Area—see Appendix B for areas included
Source: U.S. Census Bureau, 2008-2010 American Community Survey 3-Year Estimates

HEALTH

Health Risk Data

Category	MSA[1] (%)	U.S. (%)
Adults who have been told they have high blood pressure[2]	27.8	28.7
Adults who have been told they have high blood cholesterol[2]	37.9	37.5
Adults who have been told they have diabetes[3]	5.7	8.7
Adults who have been told they have arthritis[2]	18.6	26.0
Adults who have been told they currently have asthma	7.0	9.1
Adults who are current smokers	10.4	17.3
Adults who are heavy drinkers[4]	5.0	5.0
Adults who are binge drinkers[5]	18.4	15.1
Adults who are overweight (BMI 25.0 - 29.9)	37.1	36.2
Adults who are obese (BMI 30.0 - 99.8)	27.0	27.5
Adults who participated in any physical activities in the past month	80.7	76.1
Adults 50+ who have ever had a sigmoidoscopy or colonoscopy	71.4	65.2
Women aged 40+ who have had a mammogram within the past two years	75.0	75.2
Men aged 40+ who have had a PSA test within the past two years	n/a	53.2
Adults aged 65+ who have had flu shot within the past year	71.1	67.5
Adults aged 18–64 who have any kind of health care coverage	86.5	82.2

Note: Data as of 2010 unless otherwise noted; n/a not available; (1) Figures cover the Austin-Round Rock, TX Metropolitan Statistical Area—see Appendix B for areas included; (2) Data as of 2009; (3) Figures do not include pregnancy-related, borderline, or pre-diabetes; (4) Heavy drinkers are classified as males having more than two drinks per day or females having more than one drink per day; (5) Binge drinkers are classified as males having five or more drinks on one occasion or females having four or more drinks on one occasion
Source: Centers for Disease Control and Prevention, Behavioral Risk Factor Surveillance System, SMART: Selected Metropolitan/Micropolitan Area Risk Trends, 2009, 2010

Mortality Rates for the Top 10 Causes of Death in the U.S.

ICD-10[a] Sub-Chapter	ICD-10[a] Code	Age-Adjusted Mortality Rate[1] per 100,000 population	
		County[2]	U.S.
Malignant neoplasms	C00-C97	136.9	175.6
Ischaemic heart diseases	I20-I25	70.1	121.6
Other forms of heart disease	I30-I51	44.5	48.6
Chronic lower respiratory diseases	J40-J47	31.2	42.3
Cerebrovascular diseases	I60-I69	31.6	40.6
Organic, including symptomatic, mental disorders	F01-F09	27.6	26.7
Other degenerative diseases of the nervous system	G30-G31	30.9	24.7
Other external causes of accidental injury	W00-X59	17.4	24.4
Diabetes mellitus	E10-E14	10.9	21.7
Hypertensive diseases	I10-I15	8.2	18.2

Note: (a) ICD-10 = International Classification of Diseases 10th Revision; (1) Mortality rates are a three year average covering 2007-2009; (2) Figures cover Williamson County
Source: Centers for Disease Control and Prevention, National Center for Health Statistics. Underlying Cause of Death 1999-2009 on CDC WONDER Online Database, released 2012. Data for year 2009 are compiled from the Multiple Cause of Death File 2009, Series 20 No. 2O, 2012, Data for year 2008 are compiled from the Multiple Cause of Death File 2008, Series 20 No. 2N, 2011, Data for year 2007 are compiled from Multiple Cause of Death File 2007, Series 20 No. 2M, 2010.

Mortality Rates for Selected Causes of Death

ICD-10[a] Sub-Chapter	ICD-10[a] Code	Age-Adjusted Mortality Rate[1] per 100,000 population	
		County[2]	U.S.
Assault	X85-Y09	1.8	5.7
Human immunodeficiency virus (HIV) disease	B20-B24	*0.0	3.3
Influenza and pneumonia	J09-J18	11.9	16.4
Intentional self-harm	X60-X84	9.7	11.5
Malnutrition	E40-E46	*0.0	0.8
Obesity and other hyperalimentation	E65-E68	*Unreliable	1.6
Transport accidents	V01-V99	11.0	13.7
Viral hepatitis	B15-B19	*Unreliable	2.2

Note: (a) ICD-10 = International Classification of Diseases 10th Revision; (1) Mortality rates are a three year average covering 2007-2009; (2) Figures cover Williamson County; (*) Unreliable data as per CDC
Source: Centers for Disease Control and Prevention, National Center for Health Statistics. Underlying Cause of Death 1999-2009 on CDC WONDER Online Database, released 2012. Data for year 2009 are compiled from the Multiple Cause of Death File 2009, Series 20 No. 2O, 2012, Data for year 2008 are compiled from the Multiple Cause of Death File 2008, Series 20 No. 2N, 2011, Data for year 2007 are compiled from Multiple Cause of Death File 2007, Series 20 No. 2M, 2010.

Distribution of Physicians and Dentists

Area[1]	Dentists[2]	D.O.[3]	M.D.[4]				
			Total	Family/ General Practice	Pediatrics	Medical Specialties	Surgical Specialties
Local (number)	144	54	432	97	47	143	98
Local (rate[5])	3.9	1.4	10.9	2.5	1.2	3.6	2.5
U.S. (rate[5])	4.5	1.9	18.3	2.5	1.4	6.8	4.1

Note: Data as of 2008 unless noted; (1) Local data covers Williamson County; (2) Data as of 2007; (3) Doctor of Osteopathic Medicine; (4) Includes active, non-federal, patient-care, office-based Doctors of Medicine; (5) rate per 10,000 population
Source: Area Resource File (ARF). 2009-2010 Release. U.S. Department of Health and Human Services, Health Resources and Services Administration, Bureau of Health Professions, Rockville, MD, August 2010

EDUCATION

Public School District Statistics

District Name	Schls	Pupils	Pupil/ Teacher Ratio	Minority Pupils[1] (%)	Free Lunch Eligible[2] (%)	IEP[3] (%)
Round Rock ISD	51	43,008	14.7	49.0	22.3	7.7

Note: Table includes school districts with 2,000 or more students; (1) Percentage of students that are not non-Hispanic white; (2) Percentage of students that are eligible for the free lunch program; (3) Percentage of students that have an Individualized Education Program.
Source: U.S. Department of Education, National Center for Education Statistics, Common Core of Data, Local Education Agency (School District) Universe Survey: School Year 2009-2010; U.S. Department of Education, National Center for Education Statistics, Common Core of Data, Public Elementary/Secondary School Universe Survey: School Year 2009-2010

Highest Level of Education

Area	Less than H.S.	H.S. Diploma	Some College, No Deg.	Associate Degree	Bachelors Degree	Masters Degree	Profess. School Degree	Doctorate Degree
City	10.5	19.9	26.8	8.8	23.8	8.6	0.7	0.9
MSA[1]	12.7	19.7	22.0	6.4	25.5	9.7	2.3	1.7
U.S.	14.7	28.4	21.3	7.6	17.6	7.2	1.9	1.2

Note: Figures cover persons age 25 and over; (1) Figures cover the Austin-Round Rock-San Marcos, TX Metropolitan Statistical Area—see Appendix B for areas included
Source: U.S. Census Bureau, 2008-2010 American Community Survey 3-Year Estimates

Educational Attainment by Race

Area	High School Graduate or Higher (%)					Bachelor's Degree or Higher (%)				
	Total	White	Black	Asian	Hisp.[2]	Total	White	Black	Asian	Hisp.[2]
City	89.5	89.7	93.3	89.4	70.0	34.0	34.6	23.5	64.0	15.9
MSA[1]	87.3	90.5	87.9	91.6	64.5	39.2	42.5	21.8	66.4	16.9
U.S.	85.3	87.5	81.4	85.5	61.6	28.0	29.3	17.8	50.2	13.0

Note: Figures shown cover persons 25 years old and over; (1) Figures cover the Austin-Round Rock-San Marcos, TX Metropolitan Statistical Area—see Appendix B for areas included; (2) People of Hispanic origin can be of any race
Source: U.S. Census Bureau, 2008-2010 American Community Survey 3-Year Estimates

School Enrollment by Grade and Control

Area	Preschool (%)		Kindergarten (%)		Grades 1 - 4 (%)		Grades 5 - 8 (%)		Grades 9 - 12 (%)	
	Public	Private	Public	Private	Public	Private	Public	Private	Public	Private
City	46.3	53.7	94.8	5.2	94.9	5.1	92.2	7.8	95.3	4.7
MSA[1]	50.0	50.0	90.8	9.2	92.4	7.6	93.0	7.0	93.2	6.8
U.S.	55.4	44.6	87.1	12.9	89.4	10.6	89.5	10.5	90.4	9.6

Note: Figures shown cover persons 3 years old and over; (1) Figures cover the Austin-Round Rock-San Marcos, TX Metropolitan Statistical Area—see Appendix B for areas included
Source: U.S. Census Bureau, 2008-2010 American Community Survey 3-Year Estimates

Average Salaries of Public School Classroom Teachers

Area	2010-11		2011-12		Percent Change 2010-11 to 2011-12	Percent Change 2001-02 to 2011-12
	Dollars	Rank[1]	Dollars	Rank[1]		
Texas	48,638	31	49,017	31	0.78	24.90
U.S. Average	55,623	-	56,643	-	1.83	26.8

Note: (1) State rank ranges from 1 to 51 where 1 indicates highest salary.
Source: National Education Association, Rankings & Estimates: Rankings of the States 2011 and Estimates of School Statistics 2012, December 2011

Higher Education

Four-Year Colleges			Two-Year Colleges			Medical Schools[1]	Law Schools[2]	Voc/ Tech[3]
Public	Private Non-profit	Private For-profit	Public	Private Non-profit	Private For-profit			
0	0	0	0	0	0	0	0	2

Note: Figures cover institutions located within the city limits and include main campuses only; (1) includes schools accredited by the Liaison Committee on Medical Education and the American Osteopathic Association's Commission on Osteopathic College Accreditation; (2) includes American Bar Association-accredited law schools; (3) includes all schools with programs that are less than 2 years.
Source: National Center for Education Statistics, Integrated Postsecondary Education System (IPEDS) Peer Analysis System, 2011-12; Association of American Medical Colleges, Member List, April 23, 2012; American Osteopathic Association, Member List, April 23, 2012; Law School Admission Council, Official Guide to ABA-Approved Law Schools Online, April 23, 2012

According to *U.S. News & World Report*, the Austin-Round Rock-San Marcos, TX is home to one of the best national universities in the U.S.: **University of Texas–Austin** (#45). The indicators used to capture academic quality fall into a number of categories: assessment by administrators at peer institutions; retention of students; faculty resources; student selectivity; financial resources; alumni giving; high school counselor ratings of colleges; and graduation rate.*U.S. News & World Report, "America's Best Colleges 2012"*

According to *U.S. News & World Report*, the Austin-Round Rock-San Marcos, TX is home to one of the best liberal arts colleges in the U.S.: **Southwestern University** (#71). The indicators used to capture academic quality fall into a number of categories: assessment by administrators at peer institutions; retention of students; faculty resources; student selectivity; financial resources; alumni giving; high school counselor ratings of colleges; and graduation rate.*U.S. News & World Report, "America's Best Colleges 2012"*

According to *U.S. News & World Report,* the Austin-Round Rock-San Marcos, TX is home to one of the best law schools in the U.S.: **University of Texas–Austin** (#16). The rankings are based on a weighted average of 12 measures of quality: peer assessment score; assessment score by lawyers/judges; median LSAT scores; median undergrad GPA; acceptance rate; employment rates for graduates; placement success; bar passage rate; faculty resources; expenditures per student; student/faculty ratio; and library resources. *U.S. News & World Report,* "*America's Best Law Schools 2013*"

According to *Forbes,* the Austin-Round Rock-San Marcos, TX is home to one of the best business schools in the U.S.: **Texas-Austin (McCombs)** (#17). The rankings are based on the return on investment that graduates of the Class of 2006 received (median salary five years after graduation). *Forbes, "Best Business Schools," August 3, 2011*

PRESIDENTIAL ELECTION

2008 Presidential Election Results

Area	Obama	McCain	Nader	Other
Williamson County	42.5	55.5	0.1	1.9
U.S.	52.9	45.6	0.6	0.9

Note: Results are percentages and may not add to 100% due to rounding
Source: Dave Leip's Atlas of U.S. Presidential Elections, www.uselectionatlas.org

EMPLOYERS

Major Employers

Company Name	Industry
3M Company	Tape, pressure sensitive: made from purchased materials
Attorney General, Texas	Attorney general's office
Dell	Electronic computers
Dell USA Corporation	Business management
Environmental Quality, Texas Comm On	Air, water, & solid waste management
Environmental Quality, Texas Comm On	Air, water, and solid waste management
Freescale Semiconductor	Semiconductors and related devices
Freescale Semiconductor	Electronic research
Hospital Housekeeping Systems GP	Cleaning service, industrial or commercial
Internal Revenue Service	Taxation department, government
Legislative Office, Texas	Legislative bodies
Nextel of Texas	Radiotelephone communication
Pleasant Hill Preservation LP	Apartment building operators
State Farm	Automobile insurance
Texas Department of Public Safety	Public order and safety statistics centers
Texas Department of State Health Services	Administration of public health programs
Texas State University-San Marcos	Colleges and universities
Texas Workforce Commission	Administration of social and manpower programs
Univ of Texas System	Academy
Univ of Texas System	Generation, electric power
University of Texas at Austin	University

Note: Companies shown are located within the Austin-Round Rock-San Marcos, TX metropolitan area.
Source: Hoovers.com, data extracted April 25 2012

Best Companies to Work For

Dell, headquartered in Round Rock, is among the "100 Best Companies for Working Mothers." Criteria: workforce profile; benefits; child care; women's issues and advancement; flexible work; paid time off and leave; company culture; and work-life programs. This year *Working Mother* gave particular weight to workforce profile, paid time off and company culture. *Working Mother, "100 Best Companies 2011"*

PUBLIC SAFETY

Crime Rate

Area	All Crimes	Violent Crimes				Property Crimes		
		Murder	Forcible Rape	Robbery	Aggrav. Assault	Burglary	Larceny -Theft	Motor Vehicle Theft
City	2,819.1	0.0	23.4	31.5	49.5	417.6	2,207.0	90.0
Suburbs[1]	4,207.9	3.7	24.7	87.5	227.1	777.1	2,911.6	176.3
Metro[2]	4,119.9	3.4	24.7	84.0	215.8	754.3	2,866.9	170.8
U.S.	3,345.5	4.8	27.5	119.1	252.3	699.6	2,003.5	238.8

Note: Figures are crimes per 100,000 population; (1) All areas within the metro area that are located outside the city limits; (2) Metropolitan Statistical Area—see Appendix B for areas included
Source: FBI Uniform Crime Reports, 2010

Hate Crimes

Area	Number of Quarters Reported	Bias Motivation				
		Race	Religion	Sexual Orientation	Ethnicity	Disability
City	4	1	0	0	1	0

Source: Federal Bureau of Investigation, Hate Crime Statistics 2010

Identity Theft Consumer Complaints

Area	Complaints	Complaints per 100,000 Population	Rank[2]
MSA[1]	1,367	85.5	143
U.S.	279,156	90.4	-

Note: (1) Metropolitan Statistical Area—see Appendix B for areas included; (2) Rank ranges from 1 to 384 where 1 indicates greatest number of identity theft complaints per 100,000 population
Source: Federal Trade Commission, Consumer Sentinel Network Data Book for January–December 2011

Fraud and Other Consumer Complaints

Area	Complaints	Complaints per 100,000 Population	Rank[2]
MSA[1]	8,347	522.3	122
U.S.	1,533,924	496.8	-

Note: (1) Metropolitan Statistical Area—see Appendix B for areas included; (2) Rank ranges from 1 to 384 where 1 indicates greatest number of fraud and other complaints per 100,000 population
Source: Federal Trade Commission, Consumer Sentinel Network Data Book for January–December 2011

RECREATION

Culture

Dance[1]	Theatre[1]	Instrumental Music[1]	Vocal Music[1]	Series/ Festivals	Museums	Zoos and Aquariums[2]
0	0	0	0	0	n/a	0

Note: (1) Number of professional performing groups; (2) AZA-accredited; n/a not available
Source: The Grey House Performing Arts Directory, 2011-2012; Official Museum Directory, 2011; American Association of Museums, AAM Member Museums, April 2012; Association of Zoos & Aquariums, AZA Member Zoos & Aquariums, April 2012

Professional Sports Teams

Team Name	League

No teams are located in the metro area
Source: Original research

CLIMATE

Average and Extreme Temperatures

Temperature	Jan	Feb	Mar	Apr	May	Jun	Jul	Aug	Sep	Oct	Nov	Dec	Yr.
Extreme High (°F)	90	97	98	98	100	105	109	106	104	98	91	90	109
Average High (°F)	60	64	72	79	85	91	95	96	90	81	70	63	79
Average Temp. (°F)	50	53	61	69	75	82	85	85	80	70	60	52	69
Average Low (°F)	39	43	50	58	65	72	74	74	69	59	49	41	58
Extreme Low (°F)	-2	7	18	35	43	53	64	61	47	32	20	4	-2

Note: Figures cover the years 1948-1990
Source: National Climatic Data Center, International Station Meteorological Climate Summary, 9/96

Average Precipitation/Snowfall/Humidity

Precip./Humidity	Jan	Feb	Mar	Apr	May	Jun	Jul	Aug	Sep	Oct	Nov	Dec	Yr.
Avg. Precip. (in.)	1.6	2.3	1.8	2.9	4.3	3.5	1.9	1.9	3.3	3.5	2.1	1.9	31.1
Avg. Snowfall (in.)	1	Tr	Tr	0	0	0	0	0	0	0	Tr	Tr	1
Avg. Rel. Hum. 6am (%)	79	80	79	83	88	89	88	87	86	84	81	79	84
Avg. Rel. Hum. 3pm (%)	53	51	47	50	53	49	43	42	47	47	49	51	48

Note: Figures cover the years 1948-1990; Tr = Trace amounts (<0.05 in. of rain; <0.5 in. of snow)
Source: National Climatic Data Center, International Station Meteorological Climate Summary, 9/96

Weather Conditions

Temperature			Daytime Sky			Precipitation		
10°F & below	32°F & below	90°F & above	Clear	Partly cloudy	Cloudy	0.01 inch or more precip.	0.1 inch or more snow/ice	Thunder-storms
< 1	20	111	105	148	112	83	1	41

Note: Figures are average number of days per year and cover the years 1948-1990
Source: National Climatic Data Center, International Station Meteorological Climate Summary, 9/96

HAZARDOUS WASTE

Superfund Sites

Round Rock has no sites on the EPA's Superfund Final National Priorities List.
U.S. Environmental Protection Agency, Final National Priorities List, April 17, 2012

AIR & WATER QUALITY

Air Quality Index

Area	Percent of Days when Air Quality was...[2]					AQI Statistics[2]	
	Good	Moderate	Unhealthy for Sensitive Groups	Unhealthy	Very Unhealthy	Maximum	Median
Area[1]	n/a	n/a	n/a	n/a	n/a	n/a	n/a

Note: Air Quality Index (AQI) is an index for reporting daily air quality. EPA calculates the AQI for five major air pollutants regulated by the Clean Air Act: ground-level ozone, particle pollution (aka particulate matter), carbon monoxide, sulfur dioxide, and nitrogen dioxide. The AQI runs from 0 to 500. The higher the AQI value, the greater the level of air pollution and the greater the health concern. There are six AQI categories: "Good" AQI is between 0 and 50. Air quality is considered satisfactory; "Moderate" AQI is between 51 and 100. Air quality is acceptable; "Unhealthy for Sensitive Groups" When AQI values are between 101 and 150, members of sensitive groups may experience health effects; "Unhealthy" When AQI values are between 151 and 200 everyone may begin to experience health effects; "Very Unhealthy" AQI values between 201 and 300 trigger a health alert; "Hazardous" AQI values over 300 trigger warnings of emergency conditions (not shown); (1) Data covers Williamson County; (2) Based on n/a days with AQI data in 2011.
Source: U.S. Environmental Protection Agency, AirData Report, 2011

Air Quality Index Pollutants

Area	Percent of Days when AQI Pollutant was...[2]					
	Carbon Monoxide	Nitrogen Dioxide	Ozone	Sulfur Dioxide	Particulate Matter 2.5	Particulate Matter 10
Area[1]	n/a	n/a	n/a	n/a	n/a	n/a

Note: The Air Quality Index (AQI) is an index for reporting daily air quality. EPA calculates the AQI for five major air pollutants regulated by the Clean Air Act: ground-level ozone, particle pollution (also known as particulate matter), carbon monoxide, sulfur dioxide, and nitrogen dioxide. The AQI runs from 0 to 500. The higher the AQI value, the greater the level of air pollution and the greater the health concern; (1) Data covers Williamson County; (2) Based on n/a days with AQI data in 2011.
Source: U.S. Environmental Protection Agency, AirData Report, 2011

Air Quality Index Trends

| Area | Trend Sites (days) | | | | | | | | All Sites (days) |
	2003	2004	2005	2006	2007	2008	2009	2010	2010
MSA[1]	10	10	11	14	4	2	4	2	3

Note: Figures are the number of days the AQI value exceeded 100 in a given year. An AQI value greater than 100 indicates that air quality would have been in the unhealthful range on that day. Data from exceptional events are included. These counts are presented in two ways. First, the counts are based on sites having an adequate record of monitoring data during the trend period (trend sites). These counts represent the relative change in the number of days with AQI values greater than 100. In the last column, the counts are based on all sites with data in the most recent year (because it is possible for a site to have data in the most recent year but not enough data to be a trend site); (1) Data covers the Austin-Round Rock-San Marcos, TX—see Appendix B for areas included
Source: U.S. Environmental Protection Agency, Air Quality Index Information, "Number of Days with Air Quality Index Values Greater than 100 at Trend Sites, 2000-2010, and at All Sites in 2010"

Maximum Air Pollutant Concentrations: Particulate Matter, Ozone, CO and Lead

	Particulate Matter 10 (ug/m³)	Particulate Matter 2.5 Wtd AM (ug/m³)	Particulate Matter 2.5 24-Hr (ug/m³)	Ozone (ppm)	Carbon Monoxide (ppm)	Lead (ug/m³)
MSA[1] Level	34	10	19	0.074	0	n/a
NAAQS[2]	150	15	35	0.075	9	0.15
Met NAAQS[2]	Yes	Yes	Yes	Yes	Yes	n/a

Note: Data from exceptional events are not included; (1) Data covers the Austin-Round Rock-San Marcos, TX—see Appendix B for areas included; (2) National Ambient Air Quality Standards; ppm = parts per million; ug/m³ = micrograms per cubic meter; n/a not available
Concentrations: Particulate Matter 10 (coarse particulate)—highest second maximum 24-hour concentration; Particulate Matter 2.5 Wtd AM (fine particulate)—highest weighted annual mean concentration; Particulate Matter 2.5 24-Hour (fine particulate)—highest 98th percentile 24-hour concentration; Ozone—highest fourth daily maximum 8-hour concentration; Carbon Monoxide—highest second maximum non-overlapping 8-hour concentration; Lead—maximum running 3-month average
Source: U.S. Environmental Protection Agency, CBSA Factbook 2010, Air Quality Statistics by City, 2010

Maximum Air Pollutant Concentrations: Nitrogen Dioxide and Sulfur Dioxide

	Nitrogen Dioxide AM (ppb)	Nitrogen Dioxide 1-Hr (ppb)	Sulfur Dioxide AM (ppb)	Sulfur Dioxide 1-Hr (ppb)	Sulfur Dioxide 24-Hr (ppb)
MSA[1] Level	3.314	21.1	n/a	n/a	n/a
NAAQS[2]	53	100	30	75	140
Met NAAQS[2]	Yes	Yes	n/a	n/a	n/a

Note: Data from exceptional events are not included; (1) Data covers the Austin-Round Rock-San Marcos, TX—see Appendix B for areas included; (2) National Ambient Air Quality Standards; ppb = parts per billion; n/a not available
Concentrations: Nitrogen Dioxide AM—highest arithmetic mean concentration; Nitrogen Dioxide 1-Hr—highest 98th percentile 1-hour daily maximum concentration; Sulfur Dioxide AM—highest annual mean concentration; Sulfur Dioxide 1-Hr—highest 99th percentile 1-hour daily maximum concentration; Sulfur Dioxide 24-Hr—highest second maximum 24-hour concentration
Source: U.S. Environmental Protection Agency, CBSA Factbook 2010, Air Quality Statistics by City, 2010

Drinking Water

Water System Name	Pop. Served	Primary Water Source Type	Violations[1] Health Based	Violations[1] Monitoring/Reporting
City of Round Rock	94,156	Surface	0	0

Note: (1) Based on violation data from January 1, 2011 to December 31, 2011 (includes unresolved violations from earlier years)
Source: U.S. Environmental Protection Agency, Office of Ground Water and Drinking Water, Safe Drinking Water Information System (based on data extracted April 18, 2012)

San Antonio, Texas

Background

San Antonio is a charming preservation of its Mexican-Spanish heritage. Walking along its famous Paseo Del Rio at night, with cream-colored stucco structures, sea shell ornamented facades, and gently illuminating tiny lights is very romantic.

Emotional intensity is nothing new to San Antonio. The city began in the early eighteenth century as a cohesion of different Spanish missions, whose zealous aim was to convert the Coahuiltecan natives to Christianity, and to European ways of farming. A debilitating epidemic, however, killed most of the natives, as well as the missions' goal, causing the city to be abandoned.

In 1836, San Antonio became the site of interest again, when a small band of American soldiers were unable to successfully defend themselves against an army of 4,000 Mexican soldiers, led by General Antonio de Lopez Santa Anna. Fighting desperately from within the walls of the Mission San Antonio de Valero, or The Alamo, all 183 men were killed. This inspired the cry "Remember the Alamo" from the throats of every American soldier led by General Sam Houston, who was determined to wrest Texas territory and independence from Mexico.

Despite the Anglo victory over the Mexicans more than 150 years ago, the Mexican culture and its influence remain strong. We see evidence of this in the architecture, the Franciscan educational system, the variety of Spanish-language media, and the racial composition of the population, in which over half the city's residents are Latino.

This picturesque and practical blend of old and new makes San Antonio unique among American cities.

The city continues to draw tourists who come to visit not just the Alamo, but the nearby theme parks like Six Flags Fiesta Texas and SeaWorld, or to take in the famed River Walk, the charming promenade of shops, restaurants, and pubs. In addition, the city has used ingenuity to diversify its traditional economy. For instance, Kelly Air Force Base, which was decommissioned in 2001, was developed into a successful, nearly 5,000-acre business park, called Kelly USA. The name has since changed to Port San Antonio and a warehouse on the site was used to house refugees from Hurricane Katrina. Businesses at the port receive favorable property tax and pay no state, city or corporate income taxes.

Toyota is a major employer in the city. Since 2003, Toyota's San Antonio plant has produced Tundra trucks and other Toyota products. Other top employers include Clear Channel Communication, Whataburger, NuStar Energy and Valero Energy.

San Antonio's location on the edge of the Gulf Coastal Plains exposes it to a modified subtropical climate. Summers are hot, although extremely high temperatures are rare. Winters are mild. Since the city is only 140 miles from the Gulf of Mexico, tropical storms occasionally occur, bringing strong winds and heavy rains. Relative humidity is high in the morning, but tends to drop by late afternoon.

Rankings

General Rankings

- The San Antonio metro area was identified as one of the 10 most popular big cities by Pew Research Center. The results are based on a telephone survey of 2,260 adults conducted during October 2008. The report explored a range of attitudes related to where Americans live, where they would like to live, and why. *Pew Research Center, "For Nearly Half of America, Grass is Greener Somewhere Else," January 29, 2009*

- *Men's Health Living* ranked 100 U.S. cities in terms of quality of life. San Antonio was ranked #43 and received a grade of C. Criteria: number of fitness facilities; air quality; number of physicians; male/female ratio; education levels; household income; cost of living. *Men's Health Living, Spring 2008*

- San Antonio was selected as one of America's best cities by *Bloomberg Businessweek*. The city ranked #40 out of 50. Criteria: number of restaurants, bars and museums per capita; number of colleges, libraries, and professional sports teams; income, poverty, unemployment, crime, and foreclosure rates; percent of population with bachelor's degrees; public school performance; park acres per capita; air quality. *BusinessWeek, "America's 50 Best Cities," September 20, 2011*

- San Antonio appeared on RelocateAmerica's list of best places to live in America. The annual "Top 100 Places to Live" list recognizes the top communities as nominated by their residents & local businesses. RelocateAmerica's Research Group determines the list based on review of various data gathered for economic, employment, housing, education, industry, opportunity, environment and recreation along with feedback from area leaders and residents. *RelocateAmerica.com, "Top 100 Places to Live for 2011"*

Business/Finance Rankings

- The San Antonio metro area was identified as one of 10 "Cities Where the Recession is Easing." The metro area was ranked #7. Criteria: job growth; goods produced; home sale prices; unemployment rates. *Forbes.com, "Cities Where the Recession is Easing," March 3, 2010*

- San Antonio was identified as one of the top 25 U.S. cities with the most credit card debt by credit reporting bureau Experian. The city was ranked #1. *Experian, March 4, 2011*

- San Antonio was identified as one of the "Happiest Cities to Work in 2012" by *CareerBliss.com*, an online community for career advancement. The city ranked #9 out of 50. Criteria: independent company reviews from employees all over the country on: relationship with their boss and co-workers; work environment; job resources; growth opportunities; compensation; company culture; company reputation; daily tasks; job control over work performed on a daily basis. *CareerBliss.com, "Happiest and Unhappiest Cities to Work in 2012"*

- San Antonio was selected as one of the "100 Best Places to Live and Launch" in the U.S. The city ranked #34. The editors at *Fortune Small Business* ranked 296 Census-designated metro areas by business friendliness (Launching Score, % New Businesses) and lifestyle offerings (Living Score). Then they picked the town within each of the top 100 metro areas that best blends business and pleasure. *Fortune Small Business, "100 Best Places to Live and Launch 2008," April 2008*

- *American City Business Journals* ranked America's 261 largest cities in terms of their resident's wealth. San Antonio ranked #215. Criteria: per capita income; median household income; percentage of households with annual incomes of $200,000 or more; median home value. *American City Business Journals, "Where the Money Is: America's Wealth Centers," August 18, 2008*

- The San Antonio metro area appeared on the Milken Institute "2011 Best Performing Metros" list. Rank: #1 out of 200 large metro areas. Criteria: job growth; wage and salary growth; high-tech output growth. *Milken Institute, "2011 Best Performing Metros"*

- The San Antonio metro area was selected as one of the best cities for entrepreneurs in America by *Inc. Magazine*. Criteria: job-growth data for 335 metro areas was analyzed for: recent growth trend; mid-term growth; long-term trend; current year growth. The San Antonio metro area ranked #7 among large metro areas and #48 overall. *Inc. Magazine, "The Best Cities for Doing Business," July 2008*

- San Antonio was ranked #88 out of 145 regions worldwide in terms of its "Knowledge Competitiveness Index." The index attempts to measure the knowledge-based development taking place throughout the world and is based on 19 measures of economic performance that indicate a region's ability to translate its knowledge capacity into economic value. *Centre for International Competitiveness, World Knowledge Competitiveness Index 2008*

- *Forbes* ranked the 200 most populous metro areas in the U.S. in terms of the "Best Places for Business and Careers." The San Antonio metro area was ranked #8. Criteria: costs (business and living); job growth (past and projected); income growth; educational attainment; projected economic growth; crime; cultural and recreational opportunities; net migration patterns; number of highly ranked colleges. *Forbes, "Best Places for Business and Careers," June 2011*

Children/Family Rankings

- San Antonio was selected as one of the 10 worst cities to raise children in the U.S. by *KidFriendlyCities.org*. Criteria: education; environment; health; employment; crime; diversity; cost of living. *KidFriendlyCities.org, "Top Rated Kid/Family Friendly Cities 2009"*

- The San Antonio metro area was selected as one of the "Best Cities for Relocating Families" by Worldwide ERC and Primacy Relocation. The 2008 study looked at nearly 50 factors important to relocating families including: recent job growth; nearby top-ranked colleges; in-state tuition for four-year public colleges; population growth since 2000; pediatricians per 100,000 population; and a Green Living index. *Worldwide ERC and Primacy Relocation, "2008 Best Cities for Relocating Families"*

- *Fit Pregnancy* magazine ranked the 50 best U.S. cities in which to have a baby. San Antonio was ranked #38. Criteria: access to hospitals and doctors; affordability; birthing options; breastfeeding; child care; fertility laws/resources; maternal and infant health risk; parks/stroller friendliness; safety. *Fit Pregnancy, "The Best Cities in America to Have a Baby 2008"*

Culture/Performing Arts Rankings

- San Antonio was selected as one of "America's Top 25 Arts Destinations." The city ranked #21 in the big city (population 500,000 and over) category. Criteria: readers' top choices for arts travel destinations based on the richness and variety of visual arts sites, activities and events. *American Style, "America's Top 25 Arts Destinations," May 2010*

Dating/Romance Rankings

- San Antonio was selected as one of the best cities for single men by *Rent.com*. The city ranked #3 of 10. Criteria: high single female-to-male ratio; lively nightlife; low divorce rate; low cost of living. *Rent.com, "Top 10 Cities for Single Men," May 2, 2011*

- San Antonio appeared on *Men's Health's* list of the most sex-happy cities in America. The city ranked #15 of 100. Criteria: condom sales; birth rates; sex toy sales; rates of chlamydia, gonorrhea, and syphilis. *Men's Health, "America's Most Sex-Happy Cities," October 2010*

- *Men's Health* ranked 100 U.S. cities in terms of best (and worst) marriages. San Antonio was ranked #91 (#1 = worst). Criteria: rate of failed marriages; stringency of divorce laws; percentage of population who've split; number of licensed marriage and family therapists. *Men's Health, "Splitsville, USA," May 2010*

- Eli Lily and Company, in partnership with Sperling's BestPlaces, ranked the nation's 50 largest metro areas in terms of the "Most Romantic Cities for Baby Boomers." The San Antonio metro area ranked #31. Criteria: marriage and divorce rates among baby boomers age 45 to 60; great restaurants; dance studios; chocolate, jewelry and flower sales. *Eli Lily and Company, "Most Romantic Cities for Baby Boomers," April 20, 2007*

- The San Antonio metro area was selected as one of the "Best Cities for Relocating Singles" by Worldwide ERC and Primacy Relocation. The area ranked #61 out of the 100 largest metro areas in the U.S. Criteria: recent job growth; recent singles population growth; overall population growth; affordable rental housing; cost-of-living index; expanded arts and recreation opportunities; ratio of single men and single women; affordability of quality higher education (including state residency requirements); diversity index; climate; population density. *Worldwide ERC and Primacy Relocation, "2008 Best Cities for Relocating Singles"*

- *Forbes* ranked the 40 most populous urbanized areas in the U.S. in terms of the "Best Cities for Singles." The San Antonio metro area ranked #27. Criteria: number of singles; cost of living alone; nightlife; culture; job growth; coolness; and online dating participation. *Forbes.com, "Best Cities for Singles," July 27, 2009*

Education Rankings

- *Men's Health* ranked 100 U.S. cities in terms of their education levels. San Antonio was ranked #76 (#1 = most educated city). Criteria: high school graduation rates; school enrollment; educational attainment; number of households who have outstanding student loans; number of households whose members have taken adult-education courses. *Men's Health, "Where School Is In: The Most and Least Educated Cities," September 12, 2011*

- San Antonio was selected as one of "America's Most Literate Cities." The city ranked #66 out of the 75 largest U.S. cities. Criteria: number of booksellers; library resources; Internet resources; educational attainment; periodical publishing resources; newspaper circulation. *Central Connecticut State University, "America's Most Literate Cities 2011"*

- San Antonio was identified as one of the 100 "smartest" metro areas in the U.S. The area ranked #86. Criteria: the editors rated the collective brainpower of the 100 largest metro areas in the U.S. based on their residents' educational attainment. *American City Business Journals, April 14, 2008*

- San Antonio was identified as one of "America's Brainiest Bastions" by *Portfolio.com*. The metro area ranked #140 out of 200. *Portfolio.com* analyzed levels of educational attainment in the nation's 200 largest metropolitan areas. The editors established scores for five levels of educational attainment, based on relative earning power of adult workers age 25 or older. Scores were determined by comparing the median income for all workers with the median income for those workers at a specified educational level. *Portfolio.com, "America's Brainiest Bastions," December 1, 2010*

Environmental Rankings

- The San Antonio metro area was identified as one of "The Ten Biggest American Cities that are Running Out of Water" by *24/7 Wall St.* The metro area ranked #4 out of 10. *24/7 Wall St.* did an analysis of the water supply and consumption in the 30 largest metropolitan areas in the U.S. Criteria include: projected water demand as a share of available precipitation; groundwater use as a share or projected available precipitation; susceptibility to drought; projected increase in freshwater withdrawals; projected increase in summer water deficit. *24/7 Wall St., "The Ten Biggest American Cities that are Running Out of Water," November 1, 2010*

- San Antonio was selected as one of 22 "Smarter Cities" for energy by the Natural Resources Defense Council. Criteria: investment in green power; energy efficiency measures; conservation. *Natural Resources Defense Council, "2010 Smarter Cities," July 19, 2010*

- *American City Business Journal* ranked 43 metropolitan areas in terms of their "greenness." The San Antonio metro area ranked #19. Criteria: Forty-one metros in which *ACBJ* has business weeklies, plus Indianapolis and Cleveland, were ranked based on 20 different indicators such as adoption of green technologies, utilization of environmentally sound practices, and air and water quality. *American City Business Journals, "Green City Index," March 11, 2010*

- 100 of the largest metro areas in the U.S. were analyzed in terms of their current drought severity. The San Antonio metro area ranked #99 (#1 = driest). The rankings were based on statistics such as long-term precipitation trends and patterns and the Palmer drought indices. *Sperling's BestPlaces, www.BestPlaces.net, "America's Drought-Riskiest Cities," November 2007*

- The San Antonio metro area appeared in *Country Home's* "Best Green Places" report. The area ranked #114 out of 379. Criteria: official energy policies; green power; green buildings; availability of fresh, locally grown food. *Country Home, "Best Green Places," 2008*

Food/Drink Rankings

- San Antonio was identified as one of "America's Drunkest Cities of 2011" by *The Daily Beast*. The city ranked #5 out of 25. Criteria: binge drinking; drinks consumed per month. *The Daily Beast, "Tipsy Towns: Where are America's Drunkest Cities?," December 31, 2011*

- San Antonio was selected as one of "America's Favorite Cities." The city ranked #10 in the "Food/Dining" category. Respondents to an online survey were asked to rate 35 top urban destinations in the U.S. from a visitor's perspective. Criteria: big-name restaurants; ethnic food; farmers' markets; neighborhood joints and cafes. *Travelandleisure.com, "America's Favorite Cities 2010," November 2010*

- San Antonio was selected as one of the "Top 10 Places to Eat Classic American Chow." *USA Weekend, "Summer Travel Report," May 18-20, 2007*

Health/Fitness Rankings

- San Antonio was selected as one of the 25 fittest cities in America by *Men's Fitness Online*. It ranked #25 out of America's 50 largest cities. Criteria: fitness centers and sport stores; nutrition; sports participation; TV viewing; overweight/sedentary; junk food; air quality; geography; commute; parks and open space; city recreational facilities; access to healthcare; motivation; mayor and city initiatives; state obesity initiatives. *Men's Fitness, "The Fittest and Fattest Cities in America," March 5, 2012*

- San Antonio was identified as a "2011 Asthma Capital." The area ranked #22 out of the nation's 100 largest metropolitan areas. Twelve factors were used to identify the most challenging places to live for people with asthma: estimated prevalence; self-reported prevalence; crude death rate for asthma; annual pollen score; annual air quality; public smoking laws; number of board-certified asthma specialists; school inhaler access laws; rescue medication use; controller medication use; uninsured rate; poverty rate. *Asthma and Allergy Foundation of America, "2011 Asthma Capitals"*

- San Antonio was identified as a "2011 Fall Allergy Capital." The area ranked #15 out of 100. Three groups of factors were used to identify the most severe cities for people with allergies during the fall season: annual pollen levels; medicine utilization; access to board-certified allergists. *Asthma and Allergy Foundation of America, "2011 Fall Allergy Capitals"*

- San Antonio was identified as a "2012 Spring Allergy Capital." The area ranked #9 out of 100. Three groups of factors were used to identify the most severe cities for people with allergies during the spring season: annual pollen levels; medicine utilization; access to board-certified allergists. *Asthma and Allergy Foundation of America, "2012 Spring Allergy Capitals"*

- *Men's Health* examined 100 major U.S. cities and selected the best and worst cities for men. San Antonio ranked #41. Criteria: 35 statistical parameters of long life in the categories of health, quality of life, and fitness. *Men's Health, "The 10 Best and Worst Cities for Men 2012," January/February 2012*

- The makers of Breath Right Nasal Strips, in partnership with Sperling's BestPlaces, analyzed 50 metro areas and identified those U.S. cities most challenged by chronic nasal congestion. The San Antonio metro area ranked #6. Criteria: tree, grass and weed pollens; molds and spores; air pollution; climate; smoking; purchase habits of congestion products; prescriptions of drugs for congestion relief; incidence of influenza. *Breathe Right Nasal Strips, "Most Congested Cities," October 3, 2011*

- The San Antonio metro area appeared in the 2011 Gallup-Healthways Well-Being Index. The index, based on interviews with more than 350,000 Americans, measured jobs, finances, physical health, emotional state of mind and communities. The metro area ranked #55 out of 190. Criteria: life evaluation; emotional health; work environment; physical health; healthy behaviors; basic access (basic needs optimal for a healthy life, such as access to food and medicine, having health insurance and feeling safe while walking at night). *Gallup-Healthways, "State of Well-Being 2011"*

- The San Antonio metro area was identified as one of "America's Most Stressful Cities" by *Sperling's BestPlaces*. The metro area ranked #40 out of 50. Criteria: unemployment rate; suicide rate; commute time; mental health; poor rest; alcohol use; violent crime rate; property crime rate; cloudy days annually. *Sperling's BestPlaces, www.BestPlaces.net, "Stressful Cities 2012*

- *Men's Health* ranked 100 U.S. cities in terms of their activity levels. San Antonio was ranked #66 (#1 = most active city). Criteria: where and how often residents exercise; percentage of households that watch more than 15 hours of cable television a week and buy more than 11 video games a year; death rate from deep-vein thrombosis, a condition linked to sitting for extended periods of time. *Men's Health, "Where Sit Happens: The Most and Least Active Cities in America," June 20, 2011*

- 50 of the largest metro areas in the U.S. were analyzed in terms of their health and fitness by the American College of Sports Medicine in their "American Fitness Index." The San Antonio metro area ranked #43 (#1 = healthiest). Criteria: preventative health behaviors; levels of chronic disease; health care access; community resources and policies that support physical activity. *American College of Sports Medicine, "Health and Community Fitness Status of the 50 Largest Metropolitan Areas," August 1, 2011*

- *The Daily Beast* identified the 30 U.S. metro areas with the worst smoking habits. The San Antonio metro area ranked #17. Sixty urban centers with populations of more than one million were ranked based on the following criteria: number of smokers; number of cigarettes smoked per day; fewest attempts to quit. *The Daily Beast, "30 Cities With Smoking Problems," January 3, 2011*

Real Estate Rankings

- *Fortune* ranked the 100 largest metro areas in the U.S. in terms of projected median home price change in 2010. The San Antonio metro area ranked #28. *Fortune, "The 2010 Housing Outlook," December 9, 2009*

- San Antonio appeared on *ApartmentRatings.com* "Top Cities for Renters" list in 2009." The area ranked #82. Overall satisfaction ratings were ranked using thousands of user submitted scores for hundreds of apartment complexes located in the 100 most populated U.S. municipalities. *ApartmentRatings.com, "2009 Renter Satisfaction Rankings"*

- San Antonio appeared on *ApartmentRatings.com* "Top College Towns & Cities" for renters list in 2011." The area ranked #72 out of 87. Overall satisfaction ratings were ranked using thousands of user submitted scores for hundreds of apartment complexes located in cities and towns that are home to the 100 largest four-year institutions in the U.S. *ApartmentRatings.com, "2011 College Town Renter Satisfaction Rankings"*

- The San Antonio metro area was identified as one of the "Top 25 Real Estate Investment Markets" by *FinestExperts.com*. The metro area ranked #10. Over 10,000 real estate markets were analyzed to identify the most suitable places for real estate investors to seek stability and growth. Criteria: employment; rental markets; growth levels as offset by foreclosures. *FinestExperts.com, "Top 25 Real Estate Investment Markets," January 7, 2010*

- The San Antonio metro area appeared in a *Wall Street Journal* article ranking cities by "housing stress." The metro area was ranked #24 (#1 = most stress). Criteria: fraction of mortgage-holding homeowners with a monthly housing payment in excess of 30 percent of income; percentage of people without health insurance; unemployment rate. *The Wall Street Journal, "Which Cities Face Biggest Housing Risk," October 5, 2010*

- The Center for Housing Policy ranked 210 U.S. metropolitan areas by the fair market rent for a two-bedroom unit. The San Antonio metro area was ranked #118. (#1 = most expensive) with a rent of $796. Criteria: Fair Market Rent (FMR) in effect during the fourth quarter of 2009 based on HUD's fiscal year 2010 FMRs. *The Center for Housing Policy, "Paycheck to Paycheck: Most to Least Expensive Rental Markets in 2009"*

- The San Antonio metro area was identified as one of the markets with the best expected performance in home prices over the next 12 months. *Local Market Monitor, "First Quarter Home Price Forecast for Largest US Markets," March 2, 2011*

- The San Antonio metro area was identified as one of the best U.S. markets to invest in rental property" by HomeVestors and Local Market Monitor. The area ranked #24 out of 100. Criteria: risk-return premium relative to national average. *HomeVestors and Local Market Monitor, "Best 100 U.S. Markets to Invest in Rental Property," March 9, 2012*

Safety Rankings

- Symantec, the makers of Norton, in partnership with Sperling's BestPlaces, ranked the 50 largest cities in the U.S. in terms of their vulnerability to cybercrime. The city ranked #43. Criteria: number of cyberattacks and potential infections; level of Internet access; expenditures on smartphones and computer hardware/software; wireless hotspots; broadband connectivity; Internet usage; online purchases. *Symantec, "Riskiest Online Cities of 2012" February 15, 2012*

- Allstate ranked the 193 largest cities in America in terms of driver safety. San Antonio ranked #142. In addition, drivers were 23.3% more likely to have had an accident compared to the national average. Allstate researchers analyzed internal property damage reported claims over a two-year period (from January 2008 to December 2009) to protect findings from external influences such as weather or road construction. A weighted average of the two-year numbers determined the annual percentages. The report defines an auto crash as any collision resulting in a property damage claim. *Allstate, "2011 Allstate America's Best Drivers Report™"*

- The National Insurance Crime Bureau ranked 366 metro areas in the U.S. in terms of per capita rates of vehicle theft. The San Antonio metro area ranked #53 (#1 = highest rate). Criteria: number of vehicle theft offenses per 100,000 inhabitants in 2010. *National Insurance Crime Bureau, "Hot Spots," June 21, 2011*

- The San Antonio metro area was identified as one of the most dangerous metro areas for pedestrians by Transportation for America. The metro area ranked #24 out of 52 metro areas with over 1 million residents. Criteria: area's population divided by the number of pedestrian fatalities in that area. *Transportation for America, "Dangerous by Design 2011"*

Seniors/Retirement Rankings

- Bankers Life and Casualty Company, in partnership with Sperling's BestPlaces, ranked the nation's 50 largest metro areas in terms of the "Best U.S. Cities for Seniors." The San Antonio metro area ranked #34. Criteria: healthcare; transportation; housing; environment; economy; health and longevity; social and spiritual life; crime. *Bankers Life and Casualty Company, Center for a Secure Retirement, "Best U.S. Cities for Seniors 2011," September 2011*

- USAA and *Military.com*, in partnership with Sperling's BestPlaces, ranked 379 metropolitan areas in terms of which are the best places for military retirees. The metro area ranked #5 out of 10. Criteria: military skill related jobs; unemployment rate; number of federal government jobs; volume of DoD contracts; number of small businesses; number of veteran-owned businesses; military installation proximity/amenities; Veteran's Affairs hospitals; affordability; military pension taxation; presence of colleges/universities; sales tax; climate; crime level. *USAA and Military.com, "2011 Best Places for Military Retirement: Second Careers*

- San Antonio was selected as one of "5 Great Places to Retire" by *Fortune*. The city ranked #3. Criteria: cost of living; culture; tax rates; health care; attractive real estate markets that have come down significantly in price. *Fortune, "5 Great Places to Retire," June 14, 2010*

- San Antonio was identified as one of the "100 Most Popular Retirement Towns" by *Topretirements.com* The list reflects the 100 cities (out of 815+ total cities reviewed) that visitors to the website are most interested in for retirement. *Topretirements.com, "100 Most Popular Retirement Towns," February 21, 2012*

- San Antonio was selected as one of "The 10 Best Places to Retire" by *Topretirements.com*. Editors analyzed their "100 Most Popular Retirement Towns" against 12 important retirement criteria: college town; large number of active adult communities; adult education/cultural opportunities; healthcare options; employment opportunities; income tax for retirees; property tax; climate; cost of housing; crime; walkability/attractiveness of downtown; wow factor. *Topretirements.com, "The 10 Best Places to Retire," February 28, 2012*

- San Antonio was selected as one of "Seven Places to Retire During an Economic Downturn." The city ranked #6. The editors at *Smart Money* selected seven recession-proof places soon-to-be retirees should consider. *SmartMoney.com, "Seven Places to Retire During an Economic Downturn," February 29, 2008*

- The San Antonio metro area was selected as one of "The 10 Most Affordable Cities for Long-Term Care" by *U.S. News & World Report*. Criteria: costs at nursing homes, assisted living facilities, and adult day health care facilities; cost for licensed home health aides. *U.S. News & World Report, "The 10 Most Affordable Cities for Long-Term Care," May 17, 2010*

Sports/Recreation Rankings

- San Antonio appeared on the *Sporting News* list of the "Best Sports Cities" for 2011. The area ranked #39 out of 271 cities in the U.S. *Sporting News* takes a 12-month snapshot of each city's sports, putting a heavy premium on regular-season won-lost records (from the most recently completed season). Other criteria include: playoff berths, bowl appearances and tournament bids; championships; applicable power ratings; quality of competition; overall fan fervor (measured in part by attendance); abundance of teams (rewarding quality over quantity); stadium and arena quality; ticket availability and prices; franchise ownership; and marquee appeal of athletes. *Sporting News, "Best Sports Cities 2011," October 4, 2011*

- Scarborough Sports Marketing, a leading market research firm, identified the San Antonio DMA (Designated Market Area) as one of the top markets for sports with more than 60% of adults reporting that they are "very" interested in any of the sports measured by Scarborough. *Scarborough Sports Marketing, October 1, 2008*

- San Antonio was chosen as a bicycle friendly community by the League of American Bicyclists. A Bicycle Friendly Community welcomes cyclists by providing safe accommodation for cycling and encouraging people to bike for transportation and recreation. There are four award levels: Platinum; Gold; Silver; and Bronze. The community achieved an award level of Bronze. *League of American Bicyclists, "Bicycle Friendly Community Master List 2011"*

- San Antonio was selected as one of the most playful cities in the U.S. by KaBOOM! The organization's Playful City USA initiative is a national recognition program that honors cities and towns across the nation for a vision, plan and commitment to creating an agenda for play. Cities were recognized based on a pledge to five specific commitments to play: creating a local play commission or task force; designing an annual action plan for play; conducting a play space audit; outlining a financial investment in play for the current fiscal year; and proclaiming and celebrating an annual "play day." *KaBOOM! National Campaign for Play, "2011 Playful City USA Communities"*

Technology Rankings

- San Antonio was selected as a 2011 Digital Cities Survey winner. The city ranked #10 in the large city (250,000 or more population) category. The survey examined and assessed how city governments are utilizing information technology to operate and deliver quality service to their customers and citizens. Survey questions focused on implementation and adoption of online service delivery; planning and governance; and the infrastructure and architecture that make the transformation to digital government possible. *Center for Digital Government, "2011 Digital Cities Survey"*

Transportation Rankings

- San Antonio was identified as one of America's worst cities for speed traps by the National Motorists Association. The city ranked #13 out of 25. Criteria: speed trap locations per 100,000 residents. *National Motorists Association, September 2011*

- The San Antonio metro area appeared on *Forbes* list of the best and worst cities for commuters. The metro area ranked #23 out of 60 (#1 is best). Criteria: travel time; road congestion; travel delays. *Forbes.com, "Best and Worst Cities for Commuters," February 16, 2010*

Women/Minorities Rankings

- *Women's Health* examined U.S. cities and identified the 100 best cities for women. San Antonio was ranked #44. Criteria: 30 categories were examined from obesity and breast cancer rates to commuting times and hours spent working out. *Women's Health, "Best Cities for Women 2012"*

- San Antonio was ranked #76 out of 100 metro areas in *SELF Magazine's* ranking of America's healthiest places for women." A panel of experts came up with more than 50 criteria including death and disease rates, environmental indicators, community resources, and lifestyle habits. *SELF Magazine, "Secrets of America's Healthiest Women," December 2008*

- San Antonio was selected as one of the 25 healthiest cities for Latinas by *Latina Magazine*. The city ranked #13. Criteria: U.S. cities with populations over 500,000 residents were evaluated on the following criteria: percentage of 18-34 year-olds per city; Latino college graduation rates; number of colleges and universities; affordability; housing costs; income growth over time; average salary; percentage of singles; climate; safety; how the city's diversity compares to the national average; opportunities for minority entrepreneurs. *Latina Magazine, "Top 15 U.S. Cities for Young Latinos to Live In," August 19, 2011*

- The San Antonio metro area appeared on *Forbes'* list of the "Best Cities for Minority Entrepreneurs." The area ranked #13 out of 10. Criteria: 52 metropolitan statistical areas were examined. For each ethnicity (African Americans, Asians and Hispanics), the editors measured housing affordability, population growth, income growth, and entrepreneurship (per capita self-employment). *Forbes, "Best Cities for Minority Entrepreneurs," March 23, 2011*

- San Antonio was selected as one of the "Top 10 Cities for Hispanics." Criteria: the prospect of a good job; a safe place to raise a family; a manageable cost of living; the ability to buy and keep a home; a culture of inclusion where Hispanics are highly represented; resources to help start a business; the presence of Hispanic or Spanish-language media; representation of Hispanic needs on local government; a thriving arts and culture community; air quality; energy costs; city's state of health and rates of obesity. *Hispanic Magazine, August 2008*

Miscellaneous Rankings

- *Men's Health* ranked 100 U.S. cities by their level of sadness. San Antonio was ranked #33 (#1 = saddest city). Criteria: suicide rates; unemployment rates; percentage of households that use antidepressants; percent of population who report feeling blue all or most of the time. *Men's Health, "Frown Towns," November 28, 2011*

- Energizer Holdings, the makers of Edge® shave gel, in partnership with Sperling's BestPlaces, ranked 50 major metro areas in terms of everyday irritations. The San Antonio metro area ranked #29. Criteria: humidity levels; weather conditions; incidence of traffic delays and congestion; average commute times; frequency of flight delays and cancellations; rates of sleeplessness; underemployment; pollens and allergens; pests; comedy clubs per capita. *Energizer Holdings, "Most Irritation Prone Cities," July 23, 2010*

- San Antonio was selected as one of the best cities for shopping in the U.S. by *Forbes*. The city was ranked #8.Criteria: number of major shopping centers; retail locations; Consumer Price Index (CPI); combined state and local sales tax. *Forbes, "America's 25 Best Cities for Shopping," December 13, 2010*

- The San Antonio metro area appeared in *AutoMD.com's* ranking of the "Best and Worst Cities for Auto Repair." The metro area ranked #4 (#1 is best). The 50 most-populated metro areas in the U.S. were ranked on three critical factors: repair affordability; price disparity range; shop integrity factor. *AutoMD.com, "Advocacy for Repair Shop Fairness Report," February 24, 2010*

- *Men's Health* examined the nation's largest 100 cities and identified "America's Most Political Cities." San Antonio was ranked among the ten least political at #8. Criteria: percentage of active registered voters; percentage of ballots counted of active registration; percentage of income donated to 2008 presidential election; campaign spending; percentage of registrants who voted in the 2008 primaries; percentage of voters in the 2004/2006 Senate election; percentage of voters in the 2004-2007 gubernatorial election. *Men's Health, "Ranking America's Cities: America's Most Political Cities," October 2008*

- San Antonio appeared on Procter & Gamble's list of the "Top-20 All-Time Sweatiest Cities." The city was ranked #2. The rankings are based on computer simulations of the amount of sweat a person of average height and weight would produce walking around for an hour in the average temperatures during the summer months, based on historical weather data during June, July and August from 2001-2008 for each city. *Procter & Gamble, Old Spice Press Release, "Top-20 All-Time Sweatiest Cities," July 1, 2009*

Business Environment

CITY FINANCES

City Government Finances

Component	2009 ($000)	2009 ($ per capita)
Total Revenues	3,686,520	2,774
Total Expenditures	4,679,421	3,521
Debt Outstanding	7,309,501	5,500
Cash and Securities[1]	4,010,006	3,017

Note: (1) Cash and security holdings of a government at the close of its fiscal year, including those of its dependent agencies, utilities, and liquor stores.
Source: U.S Census Bureau, State & Local Government Finances 2009

City Government Revenue by Source

Source	2009 ($000)	2009 ($ per capita)
General Revenue		
From Federal Government	54,852	41
From State Government	112,634	85
From Local Governments	41,174	31
Taxes		
Property	349,555	263
Sales and Gross Receipts	319,917	241
Personal Income	0	0
Corporate Income	0	0
Motor Vehicle License	0	0
Other Taxes	39,770	30
Current Charges	515,880	388
Liquor Store	0	0
Utility	2,276,912	1,713
Employee Retirement	-253,809	-191

Source: U.S Census Bureau, State & Local Government Finances 2009

City Government Expenditures by Function

Function	2009 ($000)	2009 ($ per capita)	2009 (%)
General Direct Expenditures			
Air Transportation	125,630	95	2.7
Corrections	0	0	0.0
Education	35	< 1	< 0.1
Employment Security Administration	0	0	0.0
Financial Administration	24,121	18	0.5
Fire Protection	184,721	139	3.9
General Public Buildings	12,077	9	0.3
Governmental Administration, Other	12,058	9	0.3
Health	42,504	32	0.9
Highways	130,536	98	2.8
Hospitals	0	0	0.0
Housing and Community Development	47,389	36	1.0
Interest on General Debt	28,137	21	0.6
Judicial and Legal	18,870	14	0.4
Libraries	31,704	24	0.7
Parking	9,685	7	0.2
Parks and Recreation	177,209	133	3.8
Police Protection	266,671	201	5.7
Public Welfare	124,846	94	2.7
Sewerage	250,040	188	5.3
Solid Waste Management	79,964	60	1.7
Veterans' Services	0	0	0.0
Liquor Store	0	0	0.0
Utility	2,864,255	2,155	61.2
Employee Retirement	90,105	68	1.9

Source: U.S Census Bureau, State & Local Government Finances 2009

Municipal Bond Ratings

Area	Moody's	S&P	Fitch
City	Aa1	AAA	AAA

Rating Systems (shown in declining order of credit quality): Moody's– Aaa, Aa, A, Baa, Ba, B, Caa, Ca, C (numerical modifiers 1, 2, and 3 are added to letter-rating); S&P– AAA, AA, A, BBB, BB, B, CCC, CC, C; Fitch– AAA, AA, A, BBB, BB, B, CCC, CC, C. Ratings may be modified by the addition of a plus or minus sign to show relative standing within the major rating categories.

Notes: n/a Not Available; w/d Withdrawn (1) Not Reviewed; (2) Issuer Rating/No General Obligation; (3) Standard and Poor's Issue Credit Rating (ICR) is a current opinion of an obliger with respect to a specific financial obligation, a specific class of financial obligations, or a specific financial program.
Source: U.S. Census Bureau, 2012 Statistical Abstract, Bond Ratings for City Governments by Largest Cities: 2010

DEMOGRAPHICS

Population Growth

Area	1990 Census	2000 Census	2010 Census	Population Growth (%) 1990-2000	Population Growth (%) 2000-2010
City	997,258	1,144,646	1,327,407	14.8	16.0
MSA[1]	1,407,745	1,711,703	2,142,508	21.6	25.2
U.S.	248,709,873	281,421,906	308,745,538	13.2	9.7

Note: (1) Figures cover the San Antonio-New Braunfels, TX Metropolitan Statistical Area—see Appendix B for areas included
Source: U.S. Census Bureau, 2010 Census

Household Size

Area	Persons in Household (%) One	Two	Three	Four	Five	Six	Seven or More	Average Household Size
City	26.9	28.5	16.6	14.0	7.8	3.5	2.7	2.71
MSA[1]	24.3	30.3	16.8	14.6	7.9	3.4	2.6	2.74
U.S.	26.7	32.8	16.1	13.4	6.5	2.6	1.9	2.58

Note: (1) Figures cover the San Antonio-New Braunfels, TX Metropolitan Statistical Area—see Appendix B for areas included
Source: U.S. Census Bureau, 2010 Census

Race

Area	White Alone[2] (%)	Black Alone[2] (%)	Asian Alone[2] (%)	AIAN[3] Alone[2] (%)	NHOPI[4] Alone[2] (%)	Other Race Alone[2] (%)	Two or More Races (%)
City	72.6	6.9	2.4	0.9	0.1	13.7	3.4
MSA[1]	75.5	6.6	2.1	0.8	0.1	11.6	3.3
U.S.	72.4	12.6	4.8	0.9	0.2	6.2	2.9

Note: (1) Figures cover the San Antonio-New Braunfels, TX Metropolitan Statistical Area—see Appendix B for areas included; (2) Alone is defined as not being in combination with one or more other races; (3) American Indian and Alaska Native; (4) Native Hawaiian and Other Pacific Islander
Source: U.S. Census Bureau, 2010 Census

Hispanic or Latino Origin

Area	Hispanic or Latino (%)	Mexican (%)	Puerto Rican (%)	Cuban (%)	Other Hispanic or Latino (%)
City	63.2	53.2	1.0	0.2	8.9
MSA[1]	54.1	45.3	1.0	0.2	7.6
U.S.	16.3	10.3	1.5	0.6	4.0

Note: Persons of Hispanic or Latino origin can be of any race; (1) Figures cover the San Antonio-New Braunfels, TX Metropolitan Statistical Area—see Appendix B for areas included
Source: U.S. Census Bureau, 2010 Census

Segregation

Type	Segregation Indices[1]				Percent Change		
	1990	2000	2010	2010 Rank[2]	1990-2000	1990-2010	2000-2010
Black/White	56.1	52.8	49.0	73	-3.3	-7.1	-3.8
Asian/White	33.8	35.4	38.3	66	1.6	4.5	2.9
Hispanic/White	52.1	49.7	46.1	43	-2.4	-6.0	-3.6

Note: Figures are based on an analysis of 1990, 2000, and 2010 Census Decennial Census tract data by William H. Frey, Brookings Institution and the University of Michigan Social Science Data Analysis Network. In this analysis all racial groups (whites, blacks, and asians) are non-Hispanic members of those races. Hispanics are shown as a separate category; All figures cover the Metropolitan Statistical Area (see Appendix B for areas included); (1) Segregation Indices are Dissimilarity Indices that measure the degree to which the minority group is distributed differently than whites across census tracts. They range from 0 (complete integration) to 100 (complete segregation) where the value indicates the percentage of the minority group that needs to move to be distributed exactly like whites; (2) Ranges from 1 (most segregated) to 102 (least segregated); n/a not available.
Source: www.CensusScope.org

Ancestry

Area	German	Irish	English	American	Italian	Polish	French[2]	Scottish	Dutch
City	8.5	5.1	4.5	3.7	1.9	1.1	1.7	1.2	0.5
MSA[1]	12.3	6.7	5.8	3.9	2.0	1.7	2.1	1.4	0.8
U.S.	16.1	11.6	8.8	6.1	5.7	3.2	3.0	1.9	1.6

Note: Figures are the percentage of the total population reporting a particular ancestry. The nine most commonly reported ancestries in the U.S. are shown. Figures include multiple ancestries (e.g. if a person reported being Irish and Italian, they were included in both columns); (1) Figures cover the San Antonio-New Braunfels, TX Metropolitan Statistical Area—see Appendix B for areas included; (2) Excludes Basque
Source: U.S. Census Bureau, 2008-2010 American Community Survey 3-Year Estimates

Foreign-Born Population

Area	Percent of Population Born in								
	Any Foreign Country	Mexico	Asia	Europe	Carribean	South America	Central America[2]	Africa	Canada
City	13.8	9.6	1.9	0.7	0.2	0.3	0.6	0.3	0.1
MSA[1]	11.6	7.7	1.7	0.7	0.2	0.3	0.6	0.2	0.1
U.S.	12.8	3.8	3.6	1.6	1.2	0.9	1.0	0.5	0.3

Note: (1) Figures cover the San Antonio-New Braunfels, TX Metropolitan Statistical Area—see Appendix B for areas included; (2) Excludes Mexico.
Source: U.S. Census Bureau, 2008-2010 American Community Survey 3-Year Estimates

Marital Status

Area	Never Married	Now Married[2]	Separated	Widowed	Divorced
City	34.5	44.5	3.1	5.6	12.3
MSA[1]	30.8	49.7	2.7	5.4	11.3
U.S.	31.6	49.6	2.2	6.1	10.7

Note: Figures are percentages and cover the population 15 years of age and older; (1) Figures cover the San Antonio-New Braunfels, TX Metropolitan Statistical Area—see Appendix B for areas included; (2) Excludes separated
Source: U.S. Census Bureau, 2008-2010 American Community Survey 3-Year Estimates

Age

Area	Percent of Population							Median Age
	Under Age 5	Age 5 to 17	Age 18 to 34	Age 35 to 49	Age 50 to 64	Age 65 to 79	80 Years and Over	
City	7.6	19.2	26.3	20.1	16.4	7.6	2.9	32.7
MSA[1]	7.3	19.5	24.3	20.5	17.3	8.1	2.8	34.1
U.S.	6.5	17.5	23.2	20.7	19.0	9.4	3.6	37.2

Note: (1) Figures cover the San Antonio-New Braunfels, TX Metropolitan Statistical Area—see Appendix B for areas included
Source: U.S. Census Bureau, 2010 Census

Male/Female Ratio

Area	Males	Females	Males per 100 Females
City	647,690	679,717	95.3
MSA[1]	1,052,485	1,090,023	96.6
U.S.	151,781,326	156,964,212	96.7

Note: (1) Figures cover the San Antonio-New Braunfels, TX
Metropolitan Statistical Area—see Appendix B for areas included
Source: U.S. Census Bureau, 2010 Census

Religious Groups

Area	Catholic	Baptist	Non-Den.	Methodist[2]	Lutheran	LDS[3]	Pente-costal	Presby-terian[4]	Muslim[5]	Judaism
MSA[1]	28.4	8.5	6.0	3.1	1.7	1.4	1.3	0.8	0.2	1.0
U.S.	19.1	9.3	4.0	4.0	2.3	2.0	1.9	1.6	0.8	0.7

Note: Figures are the number of adherents as a percentage of the total population; (1) Figures cover the San
Antonio-New Braunfels, TX Metropolitan Statistical Area—see Appendix B for areas included;
(2) Methodist/Pietist; (3) Latter Day Saints; (4) Reformed; (5) Figures are estimates
Source: Association of Statisticians of American Religious Bodies, 2010 U.S. Religion Census: Religious
Congregations & Membership Study

ECONOMY

Gross Metropolitan Product

Area	2007	2008	2009	2010	2010 Rank[2]
MSA[1]	75.9	78.2	78.1	82.7	38

Note: Figures are in billions of dollars; (1) Figures cover the San Antonio-New Braunfels, TX Metropolitan
Statistical Area—see Appendix B for areas included; (2) Rank ranges from 1 to 363
Source: The United States Conference of Mayors, "U.S. Metro Economies: GMP and Employment Forecasts,"
June 2011

Economic Growth

Area	2007-2009 (%)	2010 (%)	2011 (%)	Rank[2]
MSA[1]	0.0	5.1	2.6	101
U.S.	-1.3	2.9	2.5	–

Note: Figures are real Gross Metropolitan Product growth rates and represent annual average percent change;
(1) Figures cover the San Antonio-New Braunfels, TX Metropolitan Statistical Area—see Appendix B for areas
included; (2) Rank ranges from 1 to 363
Source: The United States Conference of Mayors, "U.S. Metro Economies: GMP and Employment Forecasts,"
June 2011

Metropolitan Area Exports

Area	2005	2006	2007	2008	2009	2010	2010 Rank[2]
MSA[1]	2,347.0	3,093.7	3,567.8	5,049.5	4,390.0	6,416.2	37

Note: Figures are in millions of dollars; (1) Figures cover the San Antonio-New Braunfels, TX Metropolitan
Statistical Area—see Appendix B for areas included; (2) Rank ranges from 1 to 369
Source: U.S. Department of Commerce, International Trade Administration, Office of Trade & Industry
Information, Manufacturing & Services, data extracted April 2, 2012

INCOME

Income

Area	Per Capita ($)	Median Household ($)	Average Household ($)
City	21,613	42,656	58,406
MSA[1]	23,641	49,112	65,016
U.S.	26,942	51,222	70,116

Note: (1) Figures cover the San Antonio-New Braunfels, TX Metropolitan Statistical Area—see Appendix B for
areas included
Source: U.S. Census Bureau, 2008-2010 American Community Survey 3-Year Estimates

Household Income Distribution

Area	Under $15,000	$15,000 -24,999	$25,000 -34,999	$35,000 -49,999	$50,000 -74,999	$75,000 -99,000	$100,000 -149,999	$150,000 and up
City	16.7	12.8	12.0	15.0	18.0	10.7	9.1	5.5
MSA[1]	14.1	11.2	11.0	14.5	18.9	12.3	11.1	6.9
U.S.	13.0	11.0	10.6	14.2	18.5	12.1	12.2	8.4

Note: (1) Figures cover the San Antonio-New Braunfels, TX Metropolitan Statistical Area—see Appendix B for areas included
Source: U.S. Census Bureau, 2008-2010 American Community Survey 3-Year Estimates

Poverty Rate

Area	All Ages	Under 18 Years Old	18 to 64 Years Old	65 Years and Over
City	19.7	28.4	17.0	13.9
MSA[1]	16.4	23.3	14.2	11.7
U.S.	14.4	20.1	13.1	9.4

Note: Figures are percentage of people whose income during the past 12 months was below the poverty level; (1) Figures cover the San Antonio-New Braunfels, TX Metropolitan Statistical Area—see Appendix B for areas included
Source: U.S. Census Bureau, 2008-2010 American Community Survey 3-Year Estimates

Personal Bankruptcy Filing Rate

Area	2006	2007	2008	2009	2010	2011
Bexar County	1.46	1.73	1.91	2.39	2.32	2.05
U.S.	2.00	2.73	3.53	4.61	4.97	4.37

Note: Numbers are per 1,000 population and include Chapter 7 and Chapter 13 filings
Source: Federal Deposit Insurance Corporation, Regional Economic Conditions, March 9, 2012

EMPLOYMENT

Labor Force and Employment

Area	Civilian Labor Force			Workers Employed		
	Dec. 2010	Dec. 2011	% Chg.	Dec. 2010	Dec. 2011	% Chg.
City	646,232	649,341	0.5	602,179	607,078	0.8
MSA[1]	989,732	992,776	0.3	918,035	925,503	0.8
U.S.	153,156,000	153,373,000	0.1	139,159,000	140,681,000	1.1

Note: Data is not seasonally adjusted and covers workers 16 years of age and older; (1) Metropolitan Statistical Area—see Appendix B for areas included
Source: Bureau of Labor Statistics, http://stats.bls.gov

Unemployment Rate

Area	2011											
	Jan.	Feb.	Mar.	Apr.	May	Jun.	Jul.	Aug.	Sep.	Oct.	Nov.	Dec.
City	7.4	7.0	7.0	6.8	7.1	7.9	8.0	7.6	7.7	7.3	6.7	6.5
MSA[1]	7.8	7.4	7.3	7.0	7.3	8.1	8.2	7.9	8.0	7.5	7.0	6.8
U.S.	9.8	9.5	9.2	8.7	8.7	9.3	9.3	9.1	8.8	8.5	8.2	8.3

Note: Data is not seasonally adjusted and covers workers 16 years of age and older; All figures are percentages; (1) Metropolitan Statistical Area—see Appendix B for areas included
Source: Bureau of Labor Statistics, http://stats.bls.gov

Projected Unemployment Rate

Area	2010 (%)	2011 (%)	2012 (%)	2013 (%)
MSA[1]	7.7	7.4	7.0	6.6

Note: (1) Metropolitan Statistical Area—see Appendix B for areas included
Source: The United States Conference of Mayors, "U.S. Metro Economies: GMP and Employment Forecasts," June 2011

Employment by Occupation

Occupation Classification	City (%)	MSA[1] (%)	U.S. (%)
Management, Business, Science, and Arts	31.8	34.1	35.6
Natural Resources, Construction, and Maintenance	10.5	10.7	9.5
Production, Transportation, and Material Moving	10.2	10.2	12.1
Sales and Office	27.7	27.0	25.2
Service	19.8	18.1	17.6

Note: Figures cover employed civilians 16 years of age and older; (1) Figures cover the San Antonio-New Braunfels, TX Metropolitan Statistical Area—see Appendix B for areas included
Source: U.S. Census Bureau, 2008-2010 American Community Survey 3-Year Estimates

Employment by Industry

Sector	MSA[1] Number of Employees	MSA[1] Percent of Total	U.S. Percent of Total
Construction	40,300	4.7	4.1
Education and Health Services	132,800	15.5	15.2
Financial Activities	69,600	8.1	5.8
Government	159,800	18.7	16.8
Information	18,100	2.1	2.0
Leisure and Hospitality	104,300	12.2	9.9
Manufacturing	46,500	5.4	8.9
Mining and Logging	3,200	0.4	0.6
Other Services	31,700	3.7	4.0
Professional and Business Services	100,100	11.7	13.3
Retail Trade	100,300	11.7	11.5
Transportation and Utilities	21,000	2.5	3.8
Wholesale Trade	28,900	3.4	4.2

Note: Figures cover non-farm employment as of December 2011 and are not seasonally adjusted; (1) Metropolitan Statistical Area—see Appendix B for areas included
Source: Bureau of Labor Statistics, http://stats.bls.gov

Occupations with Greatest Projected Employment Growth: 2008 – 2018

Occupation[1]	2008 Employment	2018 Projected Employment	Numeric Employment Change	Percent Employment Change
Combined Food Preparation and Serving Workers, Including Fast Food	247,750	326,190	78,440	31.7
Elementary School Teachers, Except Special Education	156,930	218,030	61,100	38.9
Retail Salespersons	361,780	416,090	54,310	15.0
Registered Nurses	166,240	219,880	53,640	32.3
Home Health Aides	92,660	143,720	51,060	55.1
Customer Service Representatives	217,250	267,290	50,040	23.0
Waiters and Waitresses	192,340	237,660	45,320	23.6
Personal and Home Care Aides	94,530	138,530	44,000	46.5
Office Clerks, General	239,400	279,000	39,600	16.5
Cashiers	276,070	312,940	36,870	13.4

Note: Projections cover Texas; (1) Sorted by numeric employment change
Source: www.projectionscentral.com, State Occupational Projections, 2008–2018 Long-Term Projections

Fastest Growing Occupations: 2008 – 2018

Occupation[1]	2008 Employment	2018 Projected Employment	Numeric Employment Change	Percent Employment Change
Biomedical Engineers	650	1,150	500	76.9
Home Health Aides	92,660	143,720	51,060	55.1
Network Systems and Data Communications Analysts	19,160	29,490	10,330	53.9
Petroleum Engineers	13,440	20,140	6,700	49.9
Athletic Trainers	1,560	2,300	740	47.4
Personal and Home Care Aides	94,530	138,530	44,000	46.5
Electrical and Electronics Repairers, Powerhouse, Substation, and Relay	1,550	2,260	710	45.8
Financial Examiners	2,150	3,130	980	45.6
Medical Scientists, Except Epidemiologists	3,670	5,320	1,650	45.0
Biochemists and Biophysicists	740	1,060	320	43.2

Note: Projections cover Texas; (1) Sorted by percent employment change and excludes occupations with numeric employment change less than 100
Source: www.projectionscentral.com, State Occupational Projections, 2008–2018 Long-Term Projections

Average Wages

Occupation	$/Hr.	Occupation	$/Hr.
Accountants and Auditors	32.20	Maids and Housekeeping Cleaners	9.32
Automotive Mechanics	17.23	Maintenance and Repair Workers	14.22
Bookkeepers	16.88	Marketing Managers	61.38
Carpenters	15.25	Nuclear Medicine Technologists	31.18
Cashiers	9.26	Nurses, Licensed Practical	20.43
Clerks, General Office	13.07	Nurses, Registered	33.17
Clerks, Receptionists/Information	11.79	Nursing Aides/Orderlies/Attendants	11.70
Clerks, Shipping/Receiving	13.92	Packers and Packagers, Hand	10.67
Computer Programmers	37.36	Physical Therapists	45.48
Computer Support Specialists	24.98	Postal Service Mail Carriers	24.92
Computer Systems Analysts	41.42	Real Estate Brokers	29.54
Cooks, Restaurant	9.69	Retail Salespersons	11.50
Dentists	93.56	Sales Reps., Exc. Tech./Scientific	27.20
Electrical Engineers	39.74	Sales Reps., Tech./Scientific	42.93
Electricians	20.08	Secretaries, Exc. Legal/Med./Exec.	15.20
Financial Managers	56.50	Security Guards	11.40
First-Line Supervisors/Managers, Sales	20.41	Surgeons	98.05
Food Preparation Workers	9.13	Teacher Assistants	10.50
General and Operations Managers	49.92	Teachers, Elementary School	26.60
Hairdressers/Cosmetologists	11.23	Teachers, Secondary School	27.10
Internists	111.63	Telemarketers	10.94
Janitors and Cleaners	10.02	Truck Drivers, Heavy/Tractor-Trailer	15.74
Landscaping/Groundskeeping Workers	11.50	Truck Drivers, Light/Delivery Svcs.	14.27
Lawyers	45.71	Waiters and Waitresses	9.36

Note: Wage data covers the San Antonio-New Braunfels, TX Metropolitan Statistical Area—see Appendix B for areas included. Hourly wages for elementary/secondary school teachers and teacher assistants were calculated by the editors from annual wage data assuming a 40 hour work week; n/a not available.
Source: Bureau of Labor Statistics, Metro Area Occupational Employment and Wage Estimates, May 2011

RESIDENTIAL REAL ESTATE

Building Permits

Area	Single-Family			Multi-Family			Total		
	2010	2011	Pct. Chg.	2010	2011	Pct. Chg.	2010	2011	Pct. Chg.
City	2,337	1,594	-31.8	1,237	2,476	100.2	3,574	4,070	13.9
MSA[1]	5,144	4,410	-14.3	1,721	2,717	57.9	6,865	7,127	3.8
U.S.	447,311	418,498	-6.4	157,299	205,563	30.7	604,610	624,061	3.2

Note: (1) Metropolitan Statistical Area—see Appendix B for areas included; figures represent new, privately-owned housing units authorized (unadjusted data); All permit data are based on estimates with imputation.
Source: U.S. Census Bureau, Manufacturing, Mining, and Construction Statistics, Building Permits, 2010, 2011

Homeownership Rate

Area	2005 (%)	2006 (%)	2007 (%)	2008 (%)	2009 (%)	2010 (%)	2011 (%)
MSA[1]	66.0	62.6	62.4	66.1	69.8	70.1	66.5
U.S.	68.9	68.8	68.1	67.8	67.4	66.9	66.1

Note: (1) Metropolitan Statistical Area—see Appendix B for areas included
Source: U.S. Census Bureau, Housing Vacancies and Homeownership Annual Statistics: 2011

Housing Vacancy Rates

Area	Gross Vacancy Rate[2] (%)			Year-Round Vacancy Rate[3] (%)			Rental Vacancy Rate[4] (%)			Homeowner Vacancy Rate[5] (%)		
	2009	2010	2011	2009	2010	2011	2009	2010	2011	2009	2010	2011
MSA[1]	10.6	11.1	11.2	10.3	10.6	10.2	12.1	14.0	9.2	1.2	1.6	1.5
U.S.	14.5	14.3	14.2	11.3	11.3	11.1	10.6	10.2	9.5	2.6	2.6	2.5

Note: (1) Metropolitan Statistical Area—see Appendix B for areas included; (2) The percentage of the total housing inventory that is vacant; (3) The percentage of the housing inventory (excluding seasonal units) that is year-round vacant; (4) The percentage of rental inventory that is vacant for rent; (5) The percentage of homeowner inventory that is vacant for sale
Source: U.S. Census Bureau, Housing Vacancies and Homeownership Annual Statistics: 2011

TAXES

State Corporate Income Tax Rates

State	Tax Rate (%)	Income Brackets ($)	Num. of Brackets	Financial Institution Tax Rate (%)[a]	Federal Income Tax Ded.
Texas	(x)	–	-	(x)	No

Note: Tax rates as of January 1, 2012; (a) Rates listed are the corporate income tax rate applied to financial institutions or excise taxes based on income. Some states have other taxes based upon the value of deposits or shares; (x) Texas imposes a Franchise Tax, otherwise known as margin tax, imposed on entities with more than $1,000,000 total revenues at rate of 1%, or 0.5% for entities primarily engaged in retail or wholesale trade, on lesser of 70% of total revenues or 100% of gross receipts after deductions for either compensation or cost of goods sold.
Source: Federation of Tax Administrators, "State Corporate Income Tax Rates, 2012"

State Individual Income Tax Rates

State	Tax Rate (%)	Income Brackets ($)	Num. of Brackets	Personal Exempt. ($)[1] Single	Dependents	Fed. Inc. Tax Ded.

Texas – No State Income Tax

Note: Tax rates as of January 1, 2012; Local- and county-level taxes are not included; n/a not applicable; (1) Married joint filers generally receive double the single exemption
Source: Federation of Tax Administrators, "State Individual Income Tax Rates, 2012"

Various State and Local Tax Rates

State	State and Local Sales and Use (%)	State Sales and Use (%)	Gasoline[1] (¢/gal.)	Cigarette[2] ($/pack)	Spirits[3] ($/gal.)	Wine[4] ($/gal.)	Beer[5] ($/gal.)
Texas	8.125	6.25	20.0	1.41	2.40	0.20	0.20

Note: All tax rates as of January 1, 2012 except beer, wine and spirits (September 1, 2011); (1) The American Petroleum Institute has developed a methodology for determining the average tax rate on a gallon of fuel. Rates may include any of the following: excise taxes, environmental fees, storage tank fees, other fees or taxes, general sales tax, and local taxes. In states where gasoline is subject to the general sales tax, or where the fuel tax is based on the average sale price, the average rate determined by API is sensitive to changes in the price of gasoline. States that fully or partially apply general sales taxes to gasoline: CA, CO, GA, IL, IN, MI, NY; (2) The federal excise tax of $1.0066 per pack and local taxes are not included; (3) Rates are those applicable to off-premise sales of 40% alcohol by volume (a.b.v.) distilled spirits in 750ml containers. Local excise taxes are excluded; (4) Rates are those applicable to off-premise sales of 11% a.b.v. non-carbonated wine in 750ml containers; (5) Rates are those applicable to off-premise sales of 4.7% a.b.v. beer in 12 ounce containers.
Source: Tax Foundation, 2012 Facts & Figures: How Does Your State Compare?

State-Local Tax Burdens

Area	Rate (%)	Rank[1]	Per Capita Taxes Paid to Home State ($)	Total State and Local Per Capita Taxes Paid ($)	Per Capita Income ($)
Texas	7.9	45	2,248	3,197	40,498
U.S. Average	9.8	-	3,057	4,160	42,539

Note: Figures cover 2009; (1) Rank ranges from 1 to 50 where 1 is highest tax burden
Source: Tax Foundation, State-Local Tax Burdens, All States, 2009

State Business Tax Climate Index Rankings

State	Overall Rank	Corporate Tax Index Rank	Individual Income Tax Index Rank	Sales Tax Index Rank	Unemployment Insurance Tax Index Rank	Property Tax Index Rank
Texas	9	37	7	35	15	31

Note: The index is a measure of how each state's tax laws affect economic performance. The lower the rank, the more favorable a state's tax system is for business. States without a given tax are given a ranking of 1.
Source: Tax Foundation, Major Components of the State Business Tax Climate Index, FY 2012

COMMERCIAL REAL ESTATE

Office Market

Market Area	Inventory (sq. ft.)	Vacant (sq. ft.)	Vac. Rate (%)	Under Constr. (sq. ft.)	Asking Rent ($/sf/yr) Class A	Class B
San Antonio	25,813,575	4,454,802	17.3	130,110	25.33	18.86

Source: Grubb & Ellis, Office Markets Trends, 4th Quarter 2011

Industrial Market

Market Area	Inventory (sq. ft.)	Vacant (sq. ft.)	Vac. Rate (%)	Under Constr. (sq. ft.)	Asking Rent ($/sf/yr) WH/Dist	R&D/Flex
San Antonio	68,415,329	7,199,144	10.5	250,000	4.18	7.54

Source: Grubb & Ellis, Industrial Markets Trends, 4th Quarter 2011

COMMERCIAL UTILITIES

Typical Monthly Electric Bills

Area	Commercial Service ($/month) 1,500 kWh	40 kW demand 14,000 kWh	Industrial Service ($/month) 1,000 kW demand 200,000 kWh	50,000 kW demand 15,000,000 kWh
City	n/a	n/a	n/a	n/a
Average[1]	189	1,616	25,197	1,470,813

Note: Based on total rates in effect July 1, 2011; (1) average based on 184 utilities surveyed; n/a not available
Source: Edison Electric Institute, Typical Bills and Average Rates Report, Summer 2011

TRANSPORTATION

Means of Transportation to Work

Area	Car/Truck/Van Drove Alone	Car-pooled	Bus	Subway	Railroad	Bicycle	Walked	Other Means	Worked at Home
City	78.9	11.5	3.3	0.0	0.0	0.1	2.1	1.5	2.6
MSA[1]	79.2	11.7	2.2	0.0	0.0	0.1	2.0	1.4	3.4
U.S.	76.0	10.2	2.7	1.7	0.5	0.5	2.8	1.3	4.2

Note: Figures are percentages and cover workers 16 years of age and older; (1) Figures cover the San Antonio-New Braunfels, TX Metropolitan Statistical Area—see Appendix B for areas included
Source: U.S. Census Bureau, 2008-2010 American Community Survey 3-Year Estimates

Travel Time to Work

Area	Less Than 10 Minutes	10 to 19 Minutes	20 to 29 Minutes	30 to 44 Minutes	45 to 59 Minutes	60 to 89 Minutes	90 Minutes or More
City	10.2	32.0	26.6	22.4	4.7	2.5	1.6
MSA[1]	10.7	29.4	24.0	23.1	7.3	3.8	1.8
U.S.	13.9	30.1	20.8	19.8	7.5	5.5	2.5

Note: Figures are percentages and include workers 16 years old and over; (1) Figures cover the San Antonio-New Braunfels, TX Metropolitan Statistical Area—see Appendix B for areas included
Source: U.S. Census Bureau, 2008-2010 American Community Survey 3-Year Estimates

Travel Time Index

Area	1985	1990	1995	2000	2005	2010
Urban Area[1]	1.06	1.06	1.09	1.18	1.21	1.18
Average[2]	1.11	1.16	1.18	1.21	1.25	1.20

Note: Travel Time Index—the ratio of travel time in the peak period to the travel time at free-flow conditions. A value of 1.30 indicates a 20-minute free-flow trip takes 26 minutes in the peak. Free-flow speeds (60 mph on freeways and 35 mph on principal arterials) are used as the comparison threshold; (1) Covers the San Antonio TX urban area; (2) average of 439 urban areas
Source: Texas Transportation Institute, Urban Mobility Report 2011, September 2011

Public Transportation

Agency Name / Mode of Transportation	Vehicles Operated in Maximum Service	Annual Unlinked Passenger Trips ('000)	Annual Passenger Miles ('000)
VIA Metropolitan Transit (VIA)			
Bus (directly operated)	349	41,323.1	173,370.4
Demand Response (directly operated)	91	529.9	5,979.9
Demand Response (purchased transportation)	97	524.2	6,018.5
Vanpool (purchased transportation)	72	129.4	8,417.1

Source: Federal Transit Administration, National Transit Database, 2010

Air Transportation

Airport Name and Code / Type of Service	Passenger Airlines[1]	Passenger Enplanements	Freight Carriers[2]	Freight (lbs.)
San Antonio International (SAT)				
Domestic service (U.S. carriers - 2011)	33	3,882,240	19	114,477,345
International service (U.S. carriers - 2010)	11	5,405	8	10,153,656

Note: (1) Includes all U.S.-based major, minor and commuter airlines that carried at least one passenger during the year; (2) Includes all U.S.-based airlines and freight carriers that transported at least one pound of freight during the year
Source: Bureau of Transportation Statistics, The Intermodal Transportation Database, Air Carriers: T-100 Domestic Market (U.S. Carriers), 2011; Bureau of Transportation Statistics, The Intermodal Transportation Database, Air Carriers: T-100 International Market (U.S. Carriers), 2010

Other Transportation Statistics

Major Highways:	I-10; I-35; I-37
Amtrak Service:	Yes
Major Waterways/Ports:	None

Source: Amtrak.com; Google Maps

BUSINESSES

Major Business Headquarters

Company Name	Rankings	
	Fortune[1]	Forbes[2]
CC Media Holdings	391	-
HE Butt Grocery	-	12
NuStar Energy	497	-
Tesoro	128	-
United Services Automobile Assn.	145	-
Valero Energy	24	-

Note: (1) Fortune 500—companies that produce a 10-K are ranked 1 to 500 based on 2010 revenue; (2) all private companies with at least $2 billion in annual revenue are ranked 1 to 212; companies listed are headquartered in the city; dashes indicate no ranking
Source: Fortune, "Fortune 500," May 23, 2011; Forbes, "America's Largest Private Companies," November 16, 2011

Fast-Growing Businesses

According to *Inc.*, San Antonio is home to four of America's 500 fastest-growing private companies: **One Source Networks** (#9); **The Armando Montelongo Company** (#19); **InGenesis Diversified Healthcare Solutions** (#126); **TeleQuality Communications** (#232). Criteria: must be an independent, privately-held, for-profit, U.S. corporation, proprietorship or partnership; revenues must be at least $80,000 in 2007 and $2 million in 2010; must have four-year operating/sales history. Holding companies, regulated banks, and utilities were excluded. *Inc., "America's 500 Fastest-Growing Private Companies," September 2011*

According to *Initiative for a Competitive Inner City (ICIC)*, San Antonio is home to two of America's 100 fastest-growing "inner city" companies: **J. R. Ramon & Sons** (#54); **Webhead** (#65). Companies were ranked by their five-year compound annual growth rate. Criteria for inclusion: company must be headquartered in or have 51 percent or more of its physical operations in an economically distressed urban area; must be an independent, for-profit corporation, partnership or proprietorship; must have 10 or more employees and have a five-year sales history that includes sales of at least $200,000 in the base year and at least $1 million in the current year with no decrease in sales over the two most recent years. *Initiative for a Competitive Inner City (ICIC), "Inner City 100 Companies, 2011"*

Minority Business Opportunity

San Antonio is home to one company which is on the *Black Enterprise* Industrial/Service 100 list (100 largest companies based on gross sales): **Millennium Steel of Texas** (#27). Criteria: operational in previous calendar year; at least 51% black-owned and manufactures/owns the product it sells or provides industrial or consumer services. Brokerages, real estate firms and firms that provide professional services are not eligible. *Black Enterprise, B.E. 100s, 2011*

San Antonio is home to 13 companies which are on the *Hispanic Business* 500 list (500 largest U.S. Hispanic-owned companies based on 2010 revenue): **Genesis Networks Enterprises** (#10); **Ancira Enterprises** (#11); **The Alamo Travel Group** (#51); **InGenesis** (#97); **P3S Corporation** (#179); **Maldonado Nursery & Landscaping** (#209); **Davila Pharmacy** (#225); **Garcia Foods** (#270); **Kell Munoz Architects** (#303); **Cacheaux Cavazos & Newton** (#364); **J.R. Ramon & Sons** (#423); **Inventiva** (#424); **IDC** (#453). Companies included must show at least 51 percent ownership by Hispanic U.S. citizens, and must maintain headquarters in one of the 50 states or Washington, D.C. *Hispanic Business, "Hispanic Business 500," June 2011*

San Antonio is home to six companies which are on the *Hispanic Business* Fastest-Growing 100 list (greatest sales growth from 2006 to 2010): **P3S Corp.** (#4); **Genesis Networks Enterprises** (#5); **InGenesis** (#6); **IDC** (#64); **The Alamo Travel Group** (#72); **Cacheaux Cavazo & Newton** (#89). Companies included must show at least 51 percent ownership by Hispanic U.S. citizens, and must maintain headquarters in one of the 50 states or Washington, D.C. In addition, companies must have minimum revenues of $200,000 for calendar year 2005. *Hispanic Business, July/August 2011*

Minority- and Women-Owned Businesses

Group	All Firms		Firms with Paid Employees			
	Firms	Sales ($000)	Firms	Sales ($000)	Employees	Payroll ($000)
Asian	n/a	n/a	n/a	n/a	n/a	n/a
Black	n/a	n/a	n/a	n/a	n/a	n/a
Hispanic	n/a	n/a	n/a	n/a	n/a	n/a
Women	n/a	n/a	n/a	n/a	n/a	n/a
All Firms	481	21,376				

Note: Figures cover firms located in the city; minority- and women-owned business are defined as firms in which the corresponding group own 51% or more of the stock or equity of the company; n/a not available
Source: U.S. Census Bureau, 2007 Economic Census, Survey of Business Owners

HOTELS

Hotels/Motels

Area	5 Star		4 Star		3 Star		2 Star		1 Star		Not Rated	
	Num.	Pct.[3]	Num.	Pct.[3]	Num.	Pct.[3]	Num.	Pct.[3]	Num.	Pct.[3]	Num.	Pct.[3]
City[1]	0	0.0	20	6.6	85	28.2	165	54.8	10	3.3	21	7.0
Total[2]	133	0.9	940	6.5	4,569	31.8	7,033	48.9	351	2.4	1,343	9.3

Note: (1) Figures cover San Antonio and vicinity; (2) Figures cover all 100 cities in this book; (3) Percentage of hotels which have a given star rating; Star ratings are determined by expedia.com and offer an indication of the general quality of a particular hotel.
Source: expedia.com, April 25, 2012

The San Antonio-New Braunfels, TX metro area is home to three of the best hotels in the U.S. according to *Travel & Leisure*: **Mokara Hotel & Spa** (#41); **JW Marriott San Antonio Hill Country Resort & Spa** (#106); **Omni La Mansion del Rio** (#197). Criteria: service; location; rooms; food; and value. *Travel & Leisure, "T+L 500, The World's Best Hotels 2012"*

The San Antonio-New Braunfels, TX metro area is home to four of the best hotels in the U.S. according to *Condé Nast Traveler*: **Mokara Hotel & Spa** (#23); **Omni La Mansión Del Rio** (#43); **Hotel Valencia Riverwalk** (#54); **Hotel Contessa** (#60). The selections are based on over 25,000 responses to the magazine's annual Readers' Choice Survey. *Condé Nast Traveler, "2011 Readers' Choice Awards"*

EVENT SITES

Major Stadiums, Arenas, and Auditoriums

Name	Max. Capacity
AT&T Center	18,797
Alamodome	65,000
Freeman Coliseum	12,000
Municipal Auditorium/San Antonio Convention Facilities	4,884
Nelson W. Wolff Municipal Stadium	9,200
Verizon Wireless Amphitheatre	20,000

Source: Original research

Convention Centers

Name	Overall Space (sq. ft.)	Exhibit Space (sq. ft.)	Meeting Space (sq. ft.)	Meeting Rooms
Henry B. Gonzalez Convention Center	1,300,000	n/a	440,000	59

Note: n/a not available
Source: Original research

Living Environment

COST OF LIVING

Cost of Living Index

Composite Index	Groceries	Housing	Utilities	Trans-portation	Health Care	Misc. Goods/ Services
93.2	84.6	91.4	85.8	102.2	97.2	97.2

Note: U.S. = 100; Figures cover the San Antonio TX urban area.
Source: The Council for Community and Economic Research, ACCRA Cost of Living Index, 2011

Grocery Prices

Area[1]	T-Bone Steak ($/pound)	Frying Chicken ($/pound)	Whole Milk ($/half gal.)	Eggs ($/dozen)	Orange Juice ($/64 oz.)	Coffee ($/11.5 oz.)
City[2]	9.00	1.03	2.08	1.35	3.01	3.51
Avg.	9.25	1.18	2.22	1.66	3.19	4.40
Min.	6.70	0.88	1.31	0.95	2.46	2.94
Max.	14.30	2.16	3.50	3.18	4.75	6.83

Note: (1) Values for the local area are compared with the average, minimum and maximum values for all 335 areas in the Cost of Living Index; (2) Figures cover the San Antonio TX urban area; **T-Bone Steak** *(price per pound);* **Frying Chicken** *(price per pound, whole fryer);* **Whole Milk** *(half gallon carton);* **Eggs** *(price per dozen, Grade A, large);* **Orange Juice** *(64 oz. Tropicana or Florida Natural);* **Coffee** *(11.5 oz. can, vacuum-packed, Maxwell House, Hills Bros, or Folgers).*
Source: The Council for Community and Economic Research, ACCRA Cost of Living Index, 2011

Housing and Utility Costs

Area[1]	New Home Price ($)	Apartment Rent ($/month)	All Electric ($/month)	Part Electric ($/month)	Other Energy ($/month)	Telephone ($/month)
City[2]	237,886	993	-	92.63	38.54	26.01
Avg.	285,990	839	163.23	89.00	77.52	26.92
Min.	188,005	460	125.58	45.39	33.89	17.98
Max.	1,197,028	3,244	339.16	181.97	348.69	40.01

Note: (1) Values for the local area are compared with the average, minimum and maximum values for all 335 areas in the Cost of Living Index; (2) Figures cover the San Antonio TX urban area; **New Home Price** *(2,400 sf living area, 8,000 sf lot, in urban area with full utilities);* **Apartment Rent** *(950 sf 2 bedroom/1.5 or 2 bath, unfurnished, excluding all utilities except water);* **All Electric** *(average monthly cost for an all-electric home);* **Part Electric** *(average monthly cost for a part-electric home);* **Other Energy** *(average monthly cost for natural gas, fuel oil, coal, wood, and any other forms of energy except electricity);* **Telephone** *(price includes basic monthly rate for a private residential line plus additional local usage charges incurred by a family of four).*
Source: The Council for Community and Economic Research, ACCRA Cost of Living Index, 2011

Health Care, Transportation, and Other Costs

Area[1]	Doctor ($/visit)	Dentist ($/visit)	Optometrist ($/visit)	Gasoline ($/gallon)	Beauty Salon ($/visit)	Men's Shirt ($)
City[2]	84.47	79.55	86.08	3.35	42.94	34.31
Avg.	93.88	81.72	90.54	3.48	32.65	25.06
Min.	60.00	55.33	53.66	3.18	19.78	13.44
Max.	154.98	145.97	183.72	4.31	63.21	46.00

Note: (1) Values for the local area are compared with the average, minimum and maximum values for all 335 areas in the Cost of Living Index; (2) Figures cover the San Antonio TX urban area; **Doctor** *(general practitioners routine exam of an established patient);* **Dentist** *(adult teeth cleaning and periodic oral examination);* **Optometrist** *(full vision eye exam for established adult patient);* **Gasoline** *(one gallon regular unleaded, national brand, including all taxes, cash price at self-service pump if available);* **Beauty Salon** *(woman's shampoo, trim, and blow-dry);* **Men's Shirt** *(cotton/polyester dress shirt, pinpoint weave, long sleeves).*
Source: The Council for Community and Economic Research, ACCRA Cost of Living Index, 2011

HOUSING

House Price Index (HPI)

Area	National Ranking[2]	Quarterly Change (%)	One-Year Change (%)	Five-Year Change (%)
MSA[1]	77	-0.11	-1.20	4.49
U.S.[3]	-	-0.10	-2.43	-19.16

Note: The HPI is a weighted repeat sales index. It measures average price changes in repeat sales or refinancings on the same properties. This information is obtained by reviewing repeat mortgage transactions on single-family properties whose mortgages have been purchased or securitized by Fannie Mae or Freddie Mac in January 1975; (1) Metropolitan/Micropolitan Statistical Area—see Appendix B for areas included; (2) Rankings are based on annual percentage change for all metro areas containing at least 15,000 transactions over the last 10 years and ranges from 1 to 306; (3) figures based on a weighted average of Census Division estimates using a purchase only index; all figures are for the period ending December 31, 2011
Source: Federal Housing Finance Agency, House Price Index, February 23, 2012

House Price Valuations

Area	Q4 2005 Price ($000)	Q4 2005 Over-valuation	Q4 2006 Price ($000)	Q4 2006 Over-valuation	Q4 2007 Price ($000)	Q4 2007 Over-valuation	Q4 2008 Price ($000)	Q4 2008 Over-valuation	Q4 2009 Price ($000)	Q4 2009 Over-valuation
MSA[1]	99.0	-12.2	106.4	-10.1	113.5	-7.8	110.7	-11.1	111.6	-10.9

Note: Figures show the percentage of over- or under-valuation of single family homes relative to statistically normal house values (e.g. a value of 23.6 indicates that house values are 23.6% overvalued). Statistically normal house values are based on house prices, interest rates, household incomes, population densities, and any historical premiums or discounts metropolitan areas have exhibited over time; (1) Figures cover the San Antonio-New Braunfels, TX - see Appendix B for areas included
Source: Global Insight/PNC Financial Services Group, House Prices in America: 4th Quarter 2009 Update

Median Single-Family Home Prices

Area	2009	2010	2011p	Percent Change 2010 to 2011
MSA[1]	149.3	151.0	152.5	1.0
U.S. Average	172.1	173.1	166.2	-4.0

Note: Figures are median sales prices of existing single-family homes in thousands of dollars; (p) preliminary; n/a not available; (1) Metropolitan Statistical Area—see Appendix B for areas included
Source: National Association of Realtors, Median Sales Price of Existing Single-Family Homes for Metropolitan Areas, 4th Quarter 2011

Affordability Index of Existing Single-Family Homes

Area	2009	2010	2011p	Percent Change 2010 to 2011
MSA[1]	114.3	120.0	126.2	5.2

Note: The housing affordability index measures whether or not a typical family could qualify for a mortgage loan on a typical home. The higher the index, the greater the household purchasing power. An index of 100 is defined as the point where a median-income household has exactly enough income to qualify for the purchase of a median-priced existing single-family home, assuming a 20 percent downpayment and 25 percent of gross income devoted to mortgage principal and interest payments; (p) preliminary; n/a not available; (1) Metropolitan Statistical Area—see Appendix B for areas included
Source: National Association of Realtors, Affordability Index of Existing Single-Family Homes, 2011

Median Apartment Condo-Coop Home Prices

Area	2009	2010	2011p	Percent Change 2010 to 2011
MSA[1]	n/a	n/a	n/a	n/a
U.S. Average	175.6	171.7	165.1	-3.8

Note: Figures are median sales prices of existing apartment condo-coop homes in thousands of dollars; (p) preliminary; n/a not available; (1) Metropolitan Statistical Area—see Appendix B for areas included
Source: National Association of Realtors, Median Sales Price of Existing Apartment Condo-Coop Homes for Metropolitan Areas, 4th Quarter 2011

Year Housing Structure Built

Area	2005 or Later	2000 -2004	1990 -1999	1980 -1989	1970 -1979	1960 -1969	1950 -1959	Before 1950	Median Year
City	6.8	10.7	13.3	17.3	18.4	10.9	11.1	11.5	1979
MSA[1]	10.2	12.2	15.4	16.8	17.1	9.5	8.8	10.0	1983
U.S.	5.0	8.6	14.0	14.1	16.3	11.3	11.2	19.6	1975

Note: Figures are percentages except for Median Year; (1) Figures cover the San Antonio-New Braunfels, TX Metropolitan Statistical Area—see Appendix B for areas included
Source: U.S. Census Bureau, 2008-2010 American Community Survey 3-Year Estimates

HEALTH

Health Risk Data

Category	MSA[1] (%)	U.S. (%)
Adults who have been told they have high blood pressure[2]	27.7	28.7
Adults who have been told they have high blood cholesterol[2]	34.7	37.5
Adults who have been told they have diabetes[3]	9.2	8.7
Adults who have been told they have arthritis[2]	24.9	26.0
Adults who have been told they currently have asthma	6.1	9.1
Adults who are current smokers	17.0	17.3
Adults who are heavy drinkers[4]	8.2	5.0
Adults who are binge drinkers[5]	19.4	15.1
Adults who are overweight (BMI 25.0 - 29.9)	33.5	36.2
Adults who are obese (BMI 30.0 - 99.8)	29.8	27.5
Adults who participated in any physical activities in the past month	73.5	76.1
Adults 50+ who have ever had a sigmoidoscopy or colonoscopy	67.7	65.2
Women aged 40+ who have had a mammogram within the past two years	70.1	75.2
Men aged 40+ who have had a PSA test within the past two years	53.6	53.2
Adults aged 65+ who have had flu shot within the past year	67.6	67.5
Adults aged 18–64 who have any kind of health care coverage	80.1	82.2

Note: Data as of 2010 unless otherwise noted; (1) Figures cover the San Antonio, TX Metropolitan Statistical Area—see Appendix B for areas included; (2) Data as of 2009; (3) Figures do not include pregnancy-related, borderline, or pre-diabetes; (4) Heavy drinkers are classified as males having more than two drinks per day or females having more than one drink per day; (5) Binge drinkers are classified as males having five or more drinks on one occasion or females having four or more drinks on one occasion
Source: Centers for Disease Control and Prevention, Behaviorial Risk Factor Surveillance System, SMART: Selected Metropolitan/Micropolitan Area Risk Trends, 2009, 2010

Mortality Rates for the Top 10 Causes of Death in the U.S.

ICD-10[a] Sub-Chapter	ICD-10[a] Code	Age-Adjusted Mortality Rate[1] per 100,000 population	
		County[2]	U.S.
Malignant neoplasms	C00-C97	158.9	175.6
Ischaemic heart diseases	I20-I25	110.0	121.6
Other forms of heart disease	I30-I51	47.3	48.6
Chronic lower respiratory diseases	J40-J47	36.1	42.3
Cerebrovascular diseases	I60-I69	44.5	40.6
Organic, including symptomatic, mental disorders	F01-F09	30.6	26.7
Other degenerative diseases of the nervous system	G30-G31	22.7	24.7
Other external causes of accidental injury	W00-X59	29.9	24.4
Diabetes mellitus	E10-E14	27.8	21.7
Hypertensive diseases	I10-I15	15.1	18.2

Note: (a) ICD-10 = International Classification of Diseases 10th Revision; (1) Mortality rates are a three year average covering 2007-2009; (2) Figures cover Bexar County
Source: Centers for Disease Control and Prevention, National Center for Health Statistics. Underlying Cause of Death 1999-2009 on CDC WONDER Online Database, released 2012. Data for year 2009 are compiled from the Multiple Cause of Death File 2009, Series 20 No. 2O, 2012, Data for year 2008 are compiled from the Multiple Cause of Death File 2008, Series 20 No. 2N, 2011, Data for year 2007 are compiled from Multiple Cause of Death File 2007, Series 20 No. 2M, 2010.

Mortality Rates for Selected Causes of Death

ICD-10[a] Sub-Chapter	ICD-10[a] Code	Age-Adjusted Mortality Rate[1] per 100,000 population	
		County[2]	U.S.
Assault	X85-Y09	8.2	5.7
Human immunodeficiency virus (HIV) disease	B20-B24	3.8	3.3
Influenza and pneumonia	J09-J18	13.2	16.4
Intentional self-harm	X60-X84	10.2	11.5
Malnutrition	E40-E46	1.2	0.8
Obesity and other hyperalimentation	E65-E68	1.7	1.6
Transport accidents	V01-V99	12.8	13.7
Viral hepatitis	B15-B19	3.1	2.2

Note: (a) ICD-10 = International Classification of Diseases 10th Revision; (1) Mortality rates are a three year average covering 2007-2009; (2) Figures cover Bexar County
Source: Centers for Disease Control and Prevention, National Center for Health Statistics. Underlying Cause of Death 1999-2009 on CDC WONDER Online Database, released 2012. Data for year 2009 are compiled from the Multiple Cause of Death File 2009, Series 20 No. 2O, 2012, Data for year 2008 are compiled from the Multiple Cause of Death File 2008, Series 20 No. 2N, 2011, Data for year 2007 are compiled from Multiple Cause of Death File 2007, Series 20 No. 2M, 2010.

Distribution of Physicians and Dentists

Area[1]	Dentists[2]	D.O.[3]	M.D.[4]				
			Total	Family/ General Practice	Pediatrics	Medical Specialties	Surgical Specialties
Local (number)	737	278	3,354	437	245	1,177	770
Local (rate[5])	4.6	1.7	20.7	2.7	1.5	7.3	4.7
U.S. (rate[5])	4.5	1.9	18.3	2.5	1.4	6.8	4.1

Note: Data as of 2008 unless noted; (1) Local data covers Bexar County; (2) Data as of 2007; (3) Doctor of Osteopathic Medicine; (4) Includes active, non-federal, patient-care, office-based Doctors of Medicine; (5) rate per 10,000 population
Source: Area Resource File (ARF). 2009-2010 Release. U.S. Department of Health and Human Services, Health Resources and Services Administration, Bureau of Health Professions, Rockville, MD, August 2010

Best Hospitals

According to *U.S. News*, the San Antonio-New Braunfels, TX is home to one of the best hospitals in the U.S.: **University Hospital** (2 specialties). The hospital listed was highly ranked in at least one adult specialty. *U.S. News Online, "America's Best Hospitals 2011-12"*

EDUCATION

Public School District Statistics

District Name	Schls	Pupils	Pupil/ Teacher Ratio	Minority Pupils[1] (%)	Free Lunch Eligible[2] (%)	IEP[3] (%)
Alamo Heights ISD	6	4,762	14.2	39.3	17.8	5.5
East Central ISD	15	9,292	16.2	74.9	51.5	10.6
Edgewood ISD	22	12,392	15.8	99.4	8.5	10.3
Harlandale ISD	30	14,521	14.9	96.9	0.0	9.7
North East ISD	75	65,498	15.0	63.2	34.3	10.2
Northside ISD	106	92,335	15.6	76.6	39.7	12.2
San Antonio ISD	100	55,327	16.3	97.3	39.6	10.6
School of Excellence in Education	8	2,087	19.0	93.5	67.7	8.8
South San Antonio ISD	20	9,974	14.6	97.8	11.0	8.6
Southside ISD	8	5,216	14.4	89.1	68.7	10.1
Southwest ISD	14	11,531	16.3	93.5	71.5	10.9

Note: Table includes school districts with 2,000 or more students; (1) Percentage of students that are not non-Hispanic white; (2) Percentage of students that are eligible for the free lunch program; (3) Percentage of students that have an Individualized Education Program.
Source: U.S. Department of Education, National Center for Education Statistics, Common Core of Data, Local Education Agency (School District) Universe Survey: School Year 2009-2010; U.S. Department of Education, National Center for Education Statistics, Common Core of Data, Public Elementary/Secondary School Universe Survey: School Year 2009-2010

Top Public High Schools

High School Name	Rank[1]	Score[1]	Grad. Rate[2] (%)	College[3] (%)	AP/IB/ AICE[4] (%)	SAT/ ACT[5] (%)
Communications Arts	80	0.821	100	80	6.7	1664
Northside Health Careers	142	0.608	100	98	3.1	1129
Ronald Reagan	228	0.477	98	100	3.0	1095

Note: (1) Public schools are ranked from 1 to 500 based on the following self-reported statistics (with their corresponding weight in the final score). Schools that had fewer than 10 graduates, as well as those that were newly founded and did not have a graduating senior class in 2010 were excluded; (2) Four-year, on-time graduation rate (25%); (3) Percent of 2010 graduates who enrolled immediately in college (25%); (4) AP/IB/AICE tests per graduate (25%); (5) Average SAT and/or ACT score (10%); Average AP/IB/AICE exam score (10%); AP/IB/AICE courses offered per graduate (5%); (6) School is unranked, but has been identified by Newsweek as one of the nation's most elite public high schools.
Source: Newsweek Online, "Top High Schools 2011"

Highest Level of Education

Area	Less than H.S.	H.S. Diploma	Some College, No Deg.	Associate Degree	Bachelors Degree	Masters Degree	Profess. School Degree	Doctorate Degree
City	20.6	25.2	24.0	6.6	15.0	5.9	1.8	0.9
MSA[1]	17.8	25.4	24.4	7.1	16.1	6.5	1.7	0.9
U.S.	14.7	28.4	21.3	7.6	17.6	7.2	1.9	1.2

Note: Figures cover persons age 25 and over; (1) Figures cover the San Antonio-New Braunfels, TX Metropolitan Statistical Area—see Appendix B for areas included
Source: U.S. Census Bureau, 2008-2010 American Community Survey 3-Year Estimates

Educational Attainment by Race

Area	High School Graduate or Higher (%)					Bachelor's Degree or Higher (%)				
	Total	White	Black	Asian	Hisp.[2]	Total	White	Black	Asian	Hisp.[2]
City	79.4	80.7	85.5	87.6	70.0	23.6	25.1	19.9	53.1	12.8
MSA[1]	82.2	83.5	87.5	86.4	71.0	25.3	26.6	22.7	50.1	13.3
U.S.	85.3	87.5	81.4	85.5	61.6	28.0	29.3	17.8	50.2	13.0

Note: Figures shown cover persons 25 years old and over; (1) Figures cover the San Antonio-New Braunfels, TX Metropolitan Statistical Area—see Appendix B for areas included; (2) People of Hispanic origin can be of any race
Source: U.S. Census Bureau, 2008-2010 American Community Survey 3-Year Estimates

School Enrollment by Grade and Control

Area	Preschool (%)		Kindergarten (%)		Grades 1 - 4 (%)		Grades 5 - 8 (%)		Grades 9 - 12 (%)	
	Public	Private	Public	Private	Public	Private	Public	Private	Public	Private
City	68.0	32.0	89.4	10.6	93.5	6.5	92.8	7.2	93.0	7.0
MSA[1]	64.1	35.9	89.5	10.5	92.6	7.4	92.3	7.7	93.3	6.7
U.S.	55.4	44.6	87.1	12.9	89.4	10.6	89.5	10.5	90.4	9.6

Note: Figures shown cover persons 3 years old and over; (1) Figures cover the San Antonio-New Braunfels, TX Metropolitan Statistical Area—see Appendix B for areas included
Source: U.S. Census Bureau, 2008-2010 American Community Survey 3-Year Estimates

Average Salaries of Public School Classroom Teachers

Area	2010-11		2011-12		Percent Change 2010-11 to 2011-12	Percent Change 2001-02 to 2011-12
	Dollars	Rank[1]	Dollars	Rank[1]		
Texas	48,638	31	49,017	31	0.78	24.90
U.S. Average	55,623	-	56,643	-	1.83	26.8

Note: (1) State rank ranges from 1 to 51 where 1 indicates highest salary.
Source: National Education Association, Rankings & Estimates: Rankings of the States 2011 and Estimates of School Statistics 2012, December 2011

Higher Education

Four-Year Colleges			Two-Year Colleges			Medical Schools[1]	Law Schools[2]	Voc/ Tech[3]
Public	Private Non-profit	Private For-profit	Public	Private Non-profit	Private For-profit			
2	6	7	4	0	8	1	1	14

Note: Figures cover institutions located within the city limits and include main campuses only; (1) includes schools accredited by the Liaison Committee on Medical Education and the American Osteopathic Association's Commission on Osteopathic College Accreditation; (2) includes American Bar Association-accredited law schools; (3) includes all schools with programs that are less than 2 years.
Source: National Center for Education Statistics, Integrated Postsecondary Education System (IPEDS) Peer Analysis System, 2011-12; Association of American Medical Colleges, Member List, April 23, 2012; American Osteopathic Association, Member List, April 23, 2012; Law School Admission Council, Official Guide to ABA-Approved Law Schools Online, April 23, 2012

PRESIDENTIAL ELECTION

2008 Presidential Election Results

Area	Obama	McCain	Nader	Other
Bexar County	52.2	46.7	0.0	1.0
U.S.	52.9	45.6	0.6	0.9

Note: Results are percentages and may not add to 100% due to rounding
Source: Dave Leip's Atlas of U.S. Presidential Elections, www.uselectionatlas.org

EMPLOYERS

Major Employers

Company Name	Industry
Air Force, United States Dept of the	Air force
Baptist Health Systems	Hospital, ama approved residency
Baptist Health Systems	Hospital, med school affiliated with nursing & residency
Boeing Aerospace Operations	Aviation school
Boeing Aerospace Operations	Aircraft and heavy equipment repair services
Christus Santa Rosa Health Care Corp	General medical and surgical hospitals
Continental Automotive Systems	Semiconductors and related devices
Diamond Shamrock Refining & Marketing Co	Gasoline service stations
Northside Independent School District	Personal service agents, brokers and bureaus
Pacific Telesis Group	Telephone communication, except radio
Season Group USA	Electronic circuits
Southwest Research Institute	Commercial physical research
The Scooter Store, Ltd	Medical and hospital equipment
Toyota Motor Manufacturing, Texas	Motor vehicles and car bodies
U of Texas Health Science Center	University
University Health System	General medical and surgical hospitals
University of Texas at San Antonio	University
USAA	Fire, marine, and casualty insurance
Valero Services	Petroleum refining
Veterans Health Administration	Administration of veterans' affairs

Note: Companies shown are located within the San Antonio-New Braunfels, TX metropolitan area.
Source: Hoovers.com, data extracted April 25 2012

Best Companies to Work For

NuStar Energy; Rackspace Hosting; USAA, headquartered in San Antonio, are among "The 100 Best Companies to Work For." To pick the 100 Best Companies to Work For, *Fortune* partnered with the Great Place to Work Institute. Two hundred eighty firms participated in this year's survey. Two-thirds of a company's score is based on the results of the Institute's Trust Index survey, which is sent to a random sample of employees from each company. The questions related to attitudes about management's credibility, job satisfaction, and camaraderie. The other third of the scoring is based on the company's responses to the Institute's Culture Audit, which includes detailed questions about pay and benefit programs, and a series of open-ended questions about hiring practices, internal communication, training, recognition programs, and diversity efforts. Any company that is at least five years old with more than 1,000 U.S. employees is eligible. *Fortune, "The 100 Best Companies to Work For," February 6, 2012*

San Antonio Lighthouse for the Blind, headquartered in San Antonio, is among the "50 Best Employers for Workers Over 50." Criteria: recruiting practices; opportunities for training, education, and career development; workplace accommodations; alternative work options, such as flexible scheduling, job sharing, and phased retirement; employee health and pension benefits; and retiree benefits. Employers with at least 50 employees based in the U.S. are eligible, including for-profit companies, not-for-profit organizations, and government employers. *AARP, "2011 AARP Best Employers for Workers Over 50"*

GlobalScape; Rackspace US; USAA, headquartered in San Antonio, are among the "100 Best Places to Work in IT." To qualify, companies, both public and private, had to have a minimum of 50 IT employees and were selected based on average salary and bonus increases, the percentage of IT staffers promoted, IT staff turnover rates, training and development programs, and the percentage of women and minorities in IT staff and management positions. In addition, *Computerworld* looked at retention efforts, programs for recognizing and rewarding outstanding performances, and benefits such as flextime, elder care and child care, and reimbursement for college tuition and the cost of pursuing technology certifications. *Computerworld, "100 Best Places to Work in IT 2011"*

PUBLIC SAFETY

Crime Rate

Area	All Crimes	Violent Crimes				Property Crimes		
		Murder	Forcible Rape	Robbery	Aggrav. Assault	Burglary	Larceny -Theft	Motor Vehicle Theft
City	6,952.1	5.7	33.5	169.5	397.1	1,242.7	4,697.2	406.3
Suburbs[1]	3,304.7	2.7	30.7	44.6	168.1	736.4	2,183.8	138.5
Metro[2]	5,717.1	4.7	32.6	127.2	319.5	1,071.3	3,846.2	315.6
U.S.	3,345.5	4.8	27.5	119.1	252.3	699.6	2,003.5	238.8

Note: Figures are crimes per 100,000 population; (1) All areas within the metro area that are located outside the city limits; (2) Metropolitan Statistical Area—see Appendix B for areas included
Source: FBI Uniform Crime Reports, 2010

Hate Crimes

Area	Number of Quarters Reported	Bias Motivation				
		Race	Religion	Sexual Orientation	Ethnicity	Disability
City	4	2	0	2	1	0

Source: Federal Bureau of Investigation, Hate Crime Statistics 2010

Identity Theft Consumer Complaints

Area	Complaints	Complaints per 100,000 Population	Rank[2]
MSA[1]	2,048	102.9	86
U.S.	279,156	90.4	-

Note: (1) Metropolitan Statistical Area—see Appendix B for areas included; (2) Rank ranges from 1 to 384 where 1 indicates greatest number of identity theft complaints per 100,000 population
Source: Federal Trade Commission, Consumer Sentinel Network Data Book for January–December 2011

Fraud and Other Consumer Complaints

Area	Complaints	Complaints per 100,000 Population	Rank[2]
MSA[1]	8,607	432.4	247
U.S.	1,533,924	496.8	-

Note: (1) Metropolitan Statistical Area—see Appendix B for areas included; (2) Rank ranges from 1 to 384 where 1 indicates greatest number of fraud and other complaints per 100,000 population
Source: Federal Trade Commission, Consumer Sentinel Network Data Book for January–December 2011

RECREATION

Culture

Dance[1]	Theatre[1]	Instrumental Music[1]	Vocal Music[1]	Series/ Festivals	Museums	Zoos and Aquariums[2]
1	4	3	1	5	15	2

Note: (1) Number of professional performing groups; (2) AZA-accredited
Source: The Grey House Performing Arts Directory, 2011-2012; Official Museum Directory, 2011; American Association of Museums, AAM Member Museums, April 2012; Association of Zoos & Aquariums, AZA Member Zoos & Aquariums, April 2012

Professional Sports Teams

Team Name	League
San Antonio Spurs	National Basketball Association (NBA)

Note: Includes teams located in the San Antonio metro area.
Source: Original research

CLIMATE

Average and Extreme Temperatures

Temperature	Jan	Feb	Mar	Apr	May	Jun	Jul	Aug	Sep	Oct	Nov	Dec	Yr.
Extreme High (°F)	89	97	100	100	103	105	106	108	103	98	94	90	108
Average High (°F)	62	66	74	80	86	92	95	95	90	82	71	64	80
Average Temp. (°F)	51	55	62	70	76	82	85	85	80	71	60	53	69
Average Low (°F)	39	43	50	58	66	72	74	74	69	59	49	41	58
Extreme Low (°F)	0	6	19	31	43	53	62	61	46	33	21	6	0

Note: Figures cover the years 1948-1990
Source: National Climatic Data Center, International Station Meteorological Climate Summary, 9/96

Average Precipitation/Snowfall/Humidity

Precip./Humidity	Jan	Feb	Mar	Apr	May	Jun	Jul	Aug	Sep	Oct	Nov	Dec	Yr.
Avg. Precip. (in.)	1.5	1.8	1.5	2.6	3.8	3.6	2.0	2.5	3.3	3.2	2.3	1.4	29.6
Avg. Snowfall (in.)	1	Tr	Tr	0	0	0	0	0	0	0	Tr	Tr	1
Avg. Rel. Hum. 6am (%)	79	80	79	82	87	87	87	86	85	83	81	79	83
Avg. Rel. Hum. 3pm (%)	51	48	45	48	51	48	43	42	47	46	48	49	47

Note: Figures cover the years 1948-1990; Tr = Trace amounts (<0.05 in. of rain; <0.5 in. of snow)
Source: National Climatic Data Center, International Station Meteorological Climate Summary, 9/96

Weather Conditions

Temperature			Daytime Sky			Precipitation		
32°F & below	45°F & below	90°F & above	Clear	Partly cloudy	Cloudy	0.01 inch or more precip.	0.1 inch or more snow/ice	Thunder-storms
23	91	112	97	153	115	81	1	36

Note: Figures are average number of days per year and cover the years 1948-1990
Source: National Climatic Data Center, International Station Meteorological Climate Summary, 9/96

HAZARDOUS WASTE

Superfund Sites

San Antonio has no sites on the EPA's Superfund Final National Priorities List.
U.S. Environmental Protection Agency, Final National Priorities List, April 17, 2012

**AIR & WATER
QUALITY**

Air Quality Index

Area	Percent of Days when Air Quality was...[2]					AQI Statistics[2]	
	Good	Moderate	Unhealthy for Sensitive Groups	Unhealthy	Very Unhealthy	Maximum	Median
Area[1]	71.8	25.2	3.0	0.0	0.0	140	40

Note: Air Quality Index (AQI) is an index for reporting daily air quality. EPA calculates the AQI for five major air pollutants regulated by the Clean Air Act: ground-level ozone, particle pollution (aka particulate matter), carbon monoxide, sulfur dioxide, and nitrogen dioxide. The AQI runs from 0 to 500. The higher the AQI value, the greater the level of air pollution and the greater the health concern. There are six AQI categories: "Good" AQI is between 0 and 50. Air quality is considered satisfactory; "Moderate" AQI is between 51 and 100. Air quality is acceptable; "Unhealthy for Sensitive Groups" When AQI values are between 101 and 150, members of sensitive groups may experience health effects; "Unhealthy" When AQI values are between 151 and 200 everyone may begin to experience health effects; "Very Unhealthy" AQI values between 201 and 300 trigger a health alert; "Hazardous" AQI values over 300 trigger warnings of emergency conditions (not shown); (1) Data covers Bexar County; (2) Based on 365 days with AQI data in 2011.
Source: U.S. Environmental Protection Agency, AirData Report, 2011

Air Quality Index Pollutants

Area	Percent of Days when AQI Pollutant was...[2]					
	Carbon Monoxide	Nitrogen Dioxide	Ozone	Sulfur Dioxide	Particulate Matter 2.5	Particulate Matter 10
Area[1]	0.0	0.8	63.8	0.0	35.1	0.3

Note: The Air Quality Index (AQI) is an index for reporting daily air quality. EPA calculates the AQI for five major air pollutants regulated by the Clean Air Act: ground-level ozone, particle pollution (also known as particulate matter), carbon monoxide, sulfur dioxide, and nitrogen dioxide. The AQI runs from 0 to 500. The higher the AQI value, the greater the level of air pollution and the greater the health concern; (1) Data covers Bexar County; (2) Based on 365 days with AQI data in 2011.
Source: U.S. Environmental Protection Agency, AirData Report, 2011

Air Quality Index Trends

Area	Trend Sites (days)								All Sites (days)
	2003	2004	2005	2006	2007	2008	2009	2010	2010
MSA[1]	21	15	15	21	3	9	3	4	4

Note: Figures are the number of days the AQI value exceeded 100 in a given year. An AQI value greater than 100 indicates that air quality would have been in the unhealthful range on that day. Data from exceptional events are included. These counts are presented in two ways. First, the counts are based on sites having an adequate record of monitoring data during the trend period (trend sites). These counts represent the relative change in the number of days with AQI values greater than 100. In the last column, the counts are based on all sites with data in the most recent year (because it is possible for a site to have data in the most recent year but not enough data to be a trend site); (1) Data covers the San Antonio-New Braunfels, TX—see Appendix B for areas included
Source: U.S. Environmental Protection Agency, Air Quality Index Information, "Number of Days with Air Quality Index Values Greater than 100 at Trend Sites, 2000-2010, and at All Sites in 2010"

Maximum Air Pollutant Concentrations: Particulate Matter, Ozone, CO and Lead

	Particulate Matter 10 (ug/m^3)	Particulate Matter 2.5 Wtd AM (ug/m^3)	Particulate Matter 2.5 24-Hr (ug/m^3)	Ozone (ppm)	Carbon Monoxide (ppm)	Lead (ug/m^3)
MSA[1] Level	55	8.7	16	0.078	1	n/a
NAAQS[2]	150	15	35	0.075	9	0.15
Met NAAQS[2]	Yes	Yes	Yes	No	Yes	n/a

Note: Data from exceptional events are not included; (1) Data covers the San Antonio-New Braunfels, TX—see Appendix B for areas included; (2) National Ambient Air Quality Standards; ppm = parts per million; ug/m^3 = micrograms per cubic meter; n/a not available
Concentrations: Particulate Matter 10 (coarse particulate)—highest second maximum 24-hour concentration; Particulate Matter 2.5 Wtd AM (fine particulate)—highest weighted annual mean concentration; Particulate Matter 2.5 24-Hour (fine particulate)—highest 98th percentile 24-hour concentration; Ozone—highest fourth daily maximum 8-hour concentration; Carbon Monoxide—highest second maximum non-overlapping 8-hour concentration; Lead—maximum running 3-month average
Source: U.S. Environmental Protection Agency, CBSA Factbook 2010, Air Quality Statistics by City, 2010

Maximum Air Pollutant Concentrations: Nitrogen Dioxide and Sulfur Dioxide

	Nitrogen Dioxide AM (ppb)	Nitrogen Dioxide 1-Hr (ppb)	Sulfur Dioxide AM (ppb)	Sulfur Dioxide 1-Hr (ppb)	Sulfur Dioxide 24-Hr (ppb)
MSA[1] Level	3.831	31.9	n/a	n/a	n/a
NAAQS[2]	53	100	30	75	140
Met NAAQS[2]	Yes	Yes	n/a	n/a	n/a

Note: Data from exceptional events are not included; (1) Data covers the San Antonio-New Braunfels, TX—see Appendix B for areas included; (2) National Ambient Air Quality Standards; ppb = parts per billion; n/a not available
Concentrations: Nitrogen Dioxide AM—highest arithmetic mean concentration; Nitrogen Dioxide 1-Hr—highest 98th percentile 1-hour daily maximum concentration; Sulfur Dioxide AM—highest annual mean concentration; Sulfur Dioxide 1-Hr—highest 99th percentile 1-hour daily maximum concentration; Sulfur Dioxide 24-Hr—highest second maximum 24-hour concentration
Source: U.S. Environmental Protection Agency, CBSA Factbook 2010, Air Quality Statistics by City, 2010

Drinking Water

Water System Name	Pop. Served	Primary Water Source Type	Violations[1] Health Based	Violations[1] Monitoring/ Reporting
San Antonio Water System	1,342,747	Purchased Surface	0	0

Note: (1) Based on violation data from January 1, 2011 to December 31, 2011 (includes unresolved violations from earlier years)
Source: U.S. Environmental Protection Agency, Office of Ground Water and Drinking Water, Safe Drinking Water Information System (based on data extracted April 18, 2012)

Savannah, Georgia

Background

Savannah, at the mouth of the Savannah River on the border between Georgia and South Carolina, is Georgia's second fastest-growing city. It was established in 1733 when General James Oglethorpe landed with a group of settlers in the sailing vessel Anne, after a voyage of more than three months. City Hall now stands at the spot where Oglethorpe and his followers first camped on a small bluff overlooking the river.

Savannah is unique among American cities in that it was extensively planned while Oglethorpe was still in England. Each new settler was given a package of property, including a town lot, a garden space, and an outlying farm area. The town was planned in quadrants, the north and south for residences, and the east and west for public buildings.

The quadrant design was inspired in part by considerations of public defense, given the unsettled character of relations with Native Americans, but in fact an early treaty between the settlers and the Creek Indian Chief Tomochichi allowed Savannah to develop quite peacefully, with little of the hostility between Europeans and Indians that marred much of the development elsewhere in the colonies.

Savannah was taken by the British during the American Revolution, and in the patriotic siege that followed, many lives were lost. Count Pulaski, among other Revolutionary heroes, lost his life during the battle, but Savannah was eventually retaken in 1782 by the American Generals Nathaniel Greene and Anthony Wayne.

In the post-Revolutionary period, Savannah grew dramatically, its economic strength being driven in large part by Eli Whitney's cotton gin. As the world's leader in the cotton trade, Savannah also hosted a great development in export activity, and the first American steamboat built in the United States to cross the Atlantic was launched in its busy port.

Savannah's physical structure had been saved from the worst ravages of war, but the destruction of the area's infrastructure slowed its further development for an extended period, and "sleepy" became a common adjective applied to the once-vibrant economic center. In the long period of slow recovery that followed, one of the great Savannah success stories was the establishment of the Girl Scouts in 1912 by Juliette Gordon Low.

In 1954, an extensive fire destroyed a large portion of the historic City Market, and the area was bulldozed to make room for a parking garage. The Historic Savannah Foundation has worked unceasingly since then to maintain and improve Savannah's considerable architectural charms.

As a result, Savannah's Historic District was designated a Registered National Historic Landmark. Savannah has also been one of the favored sites for movie makers for decades. More than forty major movies have been filmed in Savannah including *Roots* (1976), *East of Eden* (1980), *Forrest Gump* (1994), *Midnight in the Garden of Good and Evil* (1997) and *The Legend of Bagger Vance* (2000), and a segment of the Colbert Report (2005).

Tourism, military services, port operations, and arts & culture industries are major employers in the city. Savannah's port facilities, operated by the Georgia Ports Authority, have seen notable growth in container tonnage in recent years. Garden City Terminal is the fourth largest container port in the United States, and the largest single-terminal operation in North America. Military installations in the area include Hunter Army Airfield and Fort Stewart military bases, employing a combined 42,000 people. Museums include Juliette Gordon Low Museum, Telfair Museum of Art and the Mighty 8th Air Forth Museum.

In addition, the city's beauty draws not just tourists, but conventioneers. The Savannah International Trade & Convention Center is a state-of-the-art facility with more than 100,000 square feet of exhibition space, accommodating nearly 10,000 people.

Colleges and universities in the city include the Savannah College of Art and Design, Savannah State University, and South University.

Savannah's climate is subtropical, with hot summers and mild winters, making the city an ideal locale for all-year outside activities.

Rankings

General Rankings

- Savannah was selected as one of "America's Favorite Cities." The city ranked #1 in the "Quality of Life and Visitor Experience" category. Respondents to an online survey were asked to rate 35 top urban destinations in the U.S. from a visitor's perspective. Criteria: noteworthy neighborhoods; skyline/views; public parks and outdoor access; cleanliness; public transportation and pedestrian friendliness; safety; weather; peace and quiet; people-watching; environmental friendliness. *Travelandleisure.com, "America's Favorite Cities 2010," November 2010*

- Savannah was selected as one of "America's Favorite Cities." The city ranked #1 in the "People" category. Respondents to an online survey were asked to rate 35 top urban destinations in the U.S. from a visitor's perspective. Criteria: attractive; friendly; stylish; intelligent; athletic/active; diverse. *Travelandleisure.com, "America's Favorite Cities 2010," November 2010*

- Savannah was selected as one of "America's Favorite Cities." The city ranked #9 in the "Nightlife" category. Respondents to an online survey were asked to rate 35 top urban destinations in the U.S. from a visitor's perspective. Criteria: cocktail hour; live music/concerts and bands; singles/bar scene. *Travelandleisure.com, "America's Favorite Cities 2010," November 2010*

- Savannah appeared on *Travel + Leisure's* list of the ten best cities in the continental U.S. and Canada. The city was ranked #7. Criteria: activities/attractions; culture/arts; restaurants/food; people; and value. *Travel + Leisure, "The World's Best Awards 2011"*

- *Condé Nast Traveler* polled thousands of readers for travel satisfaction. American cities were ranked based on the following criteria: friendliness; atmosphere/ambiance; culture/sites; restaurants; lodging; and shopping. Savannah appeared in the top 10, ranking #7. *Condé Nast Traveler, 2011 Readers' Choice Awards*

Business/Finance Rankings

- Savannah was identified as one of the top 25 U.S. cities with the most credit card debt by credit reporting bureau Experian. The city was ranked #21. *Experian, March 4, 2011*

- Savannah was selected as one of the "100 Best Places to Live and Launch" in the U.S. The city ranked #99. The editors at *Fortune Small Business* ranked 296 Census-designated metro areas by business friendliness (Launching Score, % New Businesses) and lifestyle offerings (Living Score). Then they picked the town within each of the top 100 metro areas that best blends business and pleasure. *Fortune Small Business, "100 Best Places to Live and Launch 2008," April 2008*

- *American City Business Journals* ranked America's 261 largest cities in terms of their resident's wealth. Savannah ranked #229. Criteria: per capita income; median household income; percentage of households with annual incomes of $200,000 or more; median home value. *American City Business Journals, "Where the Money Is: America's Wealth Centers," August 18, 2008*

- The Savannah metro area appeared on the Milken Institute "2011 Best Performing Metros" list. Rank: #70 out of 200 large metro areas. Criteria: job growth; wage and salary growth; high-tech output growth. *Milken Institute, "2011 Best Performing Metros"*

- The Savannah metro area was selected as one of the best cities for entrepreneurs in America by *Inc. Magazine.* Criteria: job-growth data for 335 metro areas was analyzed for: recent growth trend; mid-term growth; long-term trend; current year growth. The Savannah metro area ranked #3 among mid-sized metro areas and #15 overall. *Inc. Magazine, "The Best Cities for Doing Business," July 2008*

- *Forbes* ranked the 200 most populous metro areas in the U.S. in terms of the "Best Places for Business and Careers." The Savannah metro area was ranked #120. Criteria: costs (business and living); job growth (past and projected); income growth; educational attainment; projected economic growth; crime; cultural and recreational opportunities; net migration patterns; number of highly ranked colleges. *Forbes, "Best Places for Business and Careers," June 2011*

Culture/Performing Arts Rankings

- Savannah was selected as one of "America's Favorite Cities." The city ranked #6 in the "Culture" category. Respondents to an online survey were asked to rate 35 top urban destinations in the U.S. from a visitor's perspective. Criteria: classical music; live music/bands; theater; museums/galleries; historical sites/monuments. *Travelandleisure.com, "America's Favorite Cities 2010," November 2010*

- Savannah was selected as one of "America's Top 25 Arts Destinations." The city ranked #6 in the mid-sized city (population 100,000 to 499,999) category. Criteria: readers' top choices for arts travel destinations based on the richness and variety of visual arts sites, activities and events. *American Style, "America's Top 25 Arts Destinations," May 2010*

Education Rankings

- Savannah was identified as one of "America's Brainiest Bastions" by *Portfolio.com*. The metro area ranked #107 out of 200. *Portfolio.com* analyzed levels of educational attainment in the nation's 200 largest metropolitan areas. The editors established scores for five levels of educational attainment, based on relative earning power of adult workers age 25 or older. Scores were determined by comparing the median income for all workers with the median income for those workers at a specified educational level. *Portfolio.com, "America's Brainiest Bastions," December 1, 2010*

Environmental Rankings

- Savannah was selected as one of 22 "Smarter Cities" for energy by the Natural Resources Defense Council. Criteria: investment in green power; energy efficiency measures; conservation. *Natural Resources Defense Council, "2010 Smarter Cities," July 19, 2010*

- The Savannah metro area appeared in *Country Home's* "Best Green Places" report. The area ranked #277 out of 379. Criteria: official energy policies; green power; green buildings; availability of fresh, locally grown food. *Country Home, "Best Green Places," 2008*

- Savannah was highlighted as one of the cleanest metro areas for ozone air pollution in the U.S. The list represents cities with no monitored ozone air pollution in unhealthful ranges. *American Lung Association, State of the Air 2011*

Food/Drink Rankings

- Savannah was selected as one of "America's Favorite Cities." The city ranked #8 in the "Food/Dining" category. Respondents to an online survey were asked to rate 35 top urban destinations in the U.S. from a visitor's perspective. Criteria: big-name restaurants; ethnic food; farmers' markets; neighborhood joints and cafes. *Travelandleisure.com, "America's Favorite Cities 2010," November 2010*

- Savannah was selected as one of America's best cities for hamburgers by the readers of *Travel + Leisure* in their annual America's Favorite Cities survey. The city was ranked #10 out of 10. Criteria:. *Travel + Leisure, "America's Best Burger Cities," May 2011*

Health/Fitness Rankings

- The Savannah metro area appeared in the 2011 Gallup-Healthways Well-Being Index. The index, based on interviews with more than 350,000 Americans, measured jobs, finances, physical health, emotional state of mind and communities. The metro area ranked #76 out of 190. Criteria: life evaluation; emotional health; work environment; physical health; healthy behaviors; basic access (basic needs optimal for a healthy life, such as access to food and medicine, having health insurance and feeling safe while walking at night). *Gallup-Healthways, "State of Well-Being 2011"*

Real Estate Rankings

- Savannah appeared on *CNNMoney.com's* list of "Foreclosure Hotspots." The list includes the 10 cities with the fastest-growing foreclosure rates out of the 100 worst-hit places. *CNNMoney.com, "Foreclosure Hotspots," February 14, 2011*

- The Savannah metro area was identified as one of the markets with the worst expected performance in home prices over the next 12 months. *Local Market Monitor, "First Quarter Home Price Forecast for Smallest US Markets," March 2, 2011*

Safety Rankings

- Allstate ranked the 193 largest cities in America in terms of driver safety. Savannah ranked #114. In addition, drivers were 12.2% more likely to have had an accident compared to the national average. Allstate researchers analyzed internal property damage reported claims over a two-year period (from January 2008 to December 2009) to protect findings from external influences such as weather or road construction. A weighted average of the two-year numbers determined the annual percentages. The report defines an auto crash as any collision resulting in a property damage claim. *Allstate, "2011 Allstate America's Best Drivers Report™"*

- The National Insurance Crime Bureau ranked 366 metro areas in the U.S. in terms of per capita rates of vehicle theft. The Savannah metro area ranked #90 (#1 = highest rate). Criteria: number of vehicle theft offenses per 100,000 inhabitants in 2010. *National Insurance Crime Bureau, "Hot Spots," June 21, 2011*

Seniors/Retirement Rankings

- Savannah was selected as one of "10 Historic Places to Retire" by *U.S. News & World Report*. The editors looked for places filled with museums, libraries, and national historic monuments that also offer a good quality of life and plenty of amenities for seniors. *U.S. News & World Report, "10 Historic Places to Retire," September 6, 2010*

Sports/Recreation Rankings

- Savannah appeared on the *Sporting News* list of the "Best Sports Cities" for 2011. The area ranked #225 out of 271 cities in the U.S. *Sporting News* takes a 12-month snapshot of each city's sports, putting a heavy premium on regular-season won-lost records (from the most recently completed season). Other criteria include: playoff berths, bowl appearances and tournament bids; championships; applicable power ratings; quality of competition; overall fan fervor (measured in part by attendance); abundance of teams (rewarding quality over quantity); stadium and arena quality; ticket availability and prices; franchise ownership; and marquee appeal of athletes. *Sporting News, "Best Sports Cities 2011," October 4, 2011*

- Savannah was selected as one of the most playful cities in the U.S. by KaBOOM! The organization's Playful City USA initiative is a national recognition program that honors cities and towns across the nation for a vision, plan and commitment to creating an agenda for play. Cities were recognized based on a pledge to five specific commitments to play: creating a local play commission or task force; designing an annual action plan for play; conducting a play space audit; outlining a financial investment in play for the current fiscal year; and proclaiming and celebrating an annual "play day." *KaBOOM! National Campaign for Play, "2011 Playful City USA Communities"*

Miscellaneous Rankings

- Savannah was selected as one of the "Top 10 Cities to Defy Death" by *Livability.com*. The city was ranked #9. The editors scoured the U.S. for the best adventure cities. Criteria includes: extreme sports; surfing; rock-climbing; haunted cities. *Livability.com, "Top 10 Cities to Defy Death," February 22, 2011*

- Savannah was selected as one of America's best-mannered cities. The area ranked #2. The general public determined the winners by casting votes online and by mail. *The Charleston School of Protocol and Etiquette, "2010 Most Mannerly City in America Contest," February 7, 2011*

Business Environment

CITY FINANCES

City Government Finances

Component	2009 ($000)	2009 ($ per capita)
Total Revenues	309,474	2,375
Total Expenditures	401,310	3,079
Debt Outstanding	192,537	1,477
Cash and Securities[1]	481,221	3,692

Note: (1) Cash and security holdings of a government at the close of its fiscal year, including those of its dependent agencies, utilities, and liquor stores.
Source: U.S Census Bureau, State & Local Government Finances 2009

City Government Revenue by Source

Source	2009 ($000)	2009 ($ per capita)
General Revenue		
From Federal Government	14,110	108
From State Government	14,907	114
From Local Governments	70,014	537
Taxes		
Property	59,072	453
Sales and Gross Receipts	35,923	276
Personal Income	0	0
Corporate Income	0	0
Motor Vehicle License	0	0
Other Taxes	10,500	81
Current Charges	91,970	706
Liquor Store	0	0
Utility	35,207	270
Employee Retirement	-49,816	-382

Source: U.S Census Bureau, State & Local Government Finances 2009

City Government Expenditures by Function

Function	2009 ($000)	2009 ($ per capita)	2009 (%)
General Direct Expenditures			
Air Transportation	21,154	162	5.3
Corrections	0	0	0.0
Education	0	0	0.0
Employment Security Administration	0	0	0.0
Financial Administration	5,581	43	1.4
Fire Protection	28,039	215	7.0
General Public Buildings	21,849	168	5.4
Governmental Administration, Other	5,746	44	1.4
Health	0	0	0.0
Highways	16,461	126	4.1
Hospitals	0	0	0.0
Housing and Community Development	26,210	201	6.5
Interest on General Debt	5,171	40	1.3
Judicial and Legal	2,171	17	0.5
Libraries	0	0	0.0
Parking	5,562	43	1.4
Parks and Recreation	28,027	215	7.0
Police Protection	60,570	465	15.1
Public Welfare	1,008	8	0.3
Sewerage	43,916	337	10.9
Solid Waste Management	29,853	229	7.4
Veterans' Services	0	0	0.0
Liquor Store	0	0	0.0
Utility	46,278	355	11.5
Employee Retirement	14,490	111	3.6

Source: U.S Census Bureau, State & Local Government Finances 2009

Municipal Bond Ratings

Area	Moody's	S&P	Fitch
City	Aa3	AA	n/a

Rating Systems (shown in declining order of credit quality): Moody's– Aaa, Aa, A, Baa, Ba, B, Caa, Ca, C (numerical modifiers 1, 2, and 3 are added to letter-rating); S&P– AAA, AA, A, BBB, BB, B, CCC, CC, C; Fitch– AAA, AA, A, BBB, BB, B, CCC, CC, C. Ratings may be modified by the addition of a plus or minus sign to show relative standing within the major rating categories.
Notes: n/a Not Available; w/d Withdrawn (1) Not Reviewed; (2) Issuer Rating/No General Obligation; (3) Standard and Poor's Issue Credit Rating (ICR) is a current opinion of an obliger with respect to a specific financial obligation, a specific class of financial obligations, or a specific financial program.
Source: City of Savannah, Georgia, Comprehensive Annual Financial Report, Fiscal Year Ended December 31, 2009

DEMOGRAPHICS

Population Growth

Area	1990 Census	2000 Census	2010 Census	Population Growth (%) 1990-2000	Population Growth (%) 2000-2010
City	138,038	131,510	136,286	-4.7	3.6
MSA[1]	258,060	293,000	347,611	13.5	18.6
U.S.	248,709,873	281,421,906	308,745,538	13.2	9.7

Note: (1) Figures cover the Savannah, GA Metropolitan Statistical Area—see Appendix B for areas included
Source: U.S. Census Bureau, 2010 Census

Household Size

Area	Persons in Household (%) One	Two	Three	Four	Five	Six	Seven or More	Average Household Size
City	32.7	31.1	16.2	10.5	5.5	2.3	1.7	2.40
MSA[1]	26.2	33.4	17.4	13.1	6.1	2.3	1.4	2.53
U.S.	26.7	32.8	16.1	13.4	6.5	2.6	1.9	2.58

Note: (1) Figures cover the Savannah, GA Metropolitan Statistical Area—see Appendix B for areas included
Source: U.S. Census Bureau, 2010 Census

Race

Area	White Alone[2] (%)	Black Alone[2] (%)	Asian Alone[2] (%)	AIAN[3] Alone[2] (%)	NHOPI[4] Alone[2] (%)	Other Race Alone[2] (%)	Two or More Races (%)
City	38.3	55.4	2.0	0.3	0.1	1.8	2.1
MSA[1]	59.7	33.9	2.1	0.3	0.1	1.9	2.1
U.S.	72.4	12.6	4.8	0.9	0.2	6.2	2.9

Note: (1) Figures cover the Savannah, GA Metropolitan Statistical Area—see Appendix B for areas included; (2) Alone is defined as not being in combination with one or more other races; (3) American Indian and Alaska Native; (4) Native Hawaiian and Other Pacific Islander
Source: U.S. Census Bureau, 2010 Census

Hispanic or Latino Origin

Area	Hispanic or Latino (%)	Mexican (%)	Puerto Rican (%)	Cuban (%)	Other Hispanic or Latino (%)
City	4.7	2.1	1.0	0.2	1.4
MSA[1]	5.0	2.3	1.1	0.2	1.4
U.S.	16.3	10.3	1.5	0.6	4.0

Note: Persons of Hispanic or Latino origin can be of any race; (1) Figures cover the Savannah, GA Metropolitan Statistical Area—see Appendix B for areas included
Source: U.S. Census Bureau, 2010 Census

Segregation

Type	Segregation Indices[1]				Percent Change		
	1990	2000	2010	2010 Rank[2]	1990-2000	1990-2010	2000-2010
Black/White	n/a	n/a	n/a	n/a	n/a	n/a	n/a
Asian/White	n/a	n/a	n/a	n/a	n/a	n/a	n/a
Hispanic/White	n/a	n/a	n/a	n/a	n/a	n/a	n/a

Note: Figures are based on an analysis of 1990, 2000, and 2010 Census Decennial Census tract data by William H. Frey, Brookings Institution and the University of Michigan Social Science Data Analysis Network. In this analysis all racial groups (whites, blacks, and asians) are non-Hispanic members of those races. Hispanics are shown as a separate category; All figures cover the Metropolitan Statistical Area (see Appendix B for areas included); (1) Segregation Indices are Dissimilarity Indices that measure the degree to which the minority group is distributed differently than whites across census tracts. They range from 0 (complete integration) to 100 (complete segregation) where the value indicates the percentage of the minority group that needs to move to be distributed exactly like whites; (2) Ranges from 1 (most segregated) to 102 (least segregated); n/a not available.
Source: www.CensusScope.org

Ancestry

Area	German	Irish	English	American	Italian	Polish	French[2]	Scottish	Dutch
City	5.1	7.3	5.8	2.7	2.0	0.6	1.0	0.9	0.5
MSA[1]	9.3	10.6	9.5	5.5	2.8	1.1	1.8	2.0	1.1
U.S.	16.1	11.6	8.8	6.1	5.7	3.2	3.0	1.9	1.6

Note: Figures are the percentage of the total population reporting a particular ancestry. The nine most commonly reported ancestries in the U.S. are shown. Figures include multiple ancestries (e.g. if a person reported being Irish and Italian, they were included in both columns); (1) Figures cover the Savannah, GA Metropolitan Statistical Area—see Appendix B for areas included; (2) Excludes Basque
Source: U.S. Census Bureau, 2008-2010 American Community Survey 3-Year Estimates

Foreign-Born Population

Area	Percent of Population Born in								
	Any Foreign Country	Mexico	Asia	Europe	Carribean	South America	Central America[2]	Africa	Canada
City	n/a	n/a	n/a	n/a	n/a	n/a	n/a	n/a	n/a
MSA[1]	5.2	1.4	1.8	0.6	0.3	0.3	0.4	0.2	0.1
U.S.	12.8	3.8	3.6	1.6	1.2	0.9	1.0	0.5	0.3

Note: (1) Figures cover the Savannah, GA Metropolitan Statistical Area—see Appendix B for areas included; (2) Excludes Mexico.
Source: U.S. Census Bureau, 2008-2010 American Community Survey 3-Year Estimates

Marital Status

Area	Never Married	Now Married[2]	Separated	Widowed	Divorced
City	47.3	31.0	2.4	7.6	11.7
MSA[1]	34.8	46.4	1.9	5.9	11.1
U.S.	31.6	49.6	2.2	6.1	10.7

Note: Figures are percentages and cover the population 15 years of age and older; (1) Figures cover the Savannah, GA Metropolitan Statistical Area—see Appendix B for areas included; (2) Excludes separated
Source: U.S. Census Bureau, 2008-2010 American Community Survey 3-Year Estimates

Age

Area	Percent of Population							Median Age
	Under Age 5	Age 5 to 17	Age 18 to 34	Age 35 to 49	Age 50 to 64	Age 65 to 79	80 Years and Over	
City	7.1	15.2	32.4	17.2	16.4	8.0	3.6	31.3
MSA[1]	7.0	17.1	26.7	19.6	18.0	8.6	3.0	34.3
U.S.	6.5	17.5	23.2	20.7	19.0	9.4	3.6	37.2

Note: (1) Figures cover the Savannah, GA Metropolitan Statistical Area—see Appendix B for areas included
Source: U.S. Census Bureau, 2010 Census

Male/Female Ratio

Area	Males	Females	Males per 100 Females
City	65,301	70,985	92.0
MSA[1]	168,573	179,038	94.2
U.S.	151,781,326	156,964,212	96.7

Note: (1) Figures cover the Savannah, GA
Metropolitan Statistical Area—see Appendix B for areas included
Source: U.S. Census Bureau, 2010 Census

Religious Groups

Area	Catholic	Baptist	Non-Den.	Methodist[2]	Lutheran	LDS[3]	Pente-costal	Presby-terian[4]	Muslim[5]	Judaism
MSA[1]	7.1	19.7	6.9	8.9	1.6	1.0	2.4	1.0	0.8	0.2
U.S.	19.1	9.3	4.0	4.0	2.3	2.0	1.9	1.6	0.8	0.7

Note: Figures are the number of adherents as a percentage of the total population; (1) Figures cover the Savannah, GA Metropolitan Statistical Area—see Appendix B for areas included; (2) Methodist/Pietist; (3) Latter Day Saints; (4) Reformed; (5) Figures are estimates
Source: Association of Statisticians of American Religious Bodies, 2010 U.S. Religion Census: Religious Congregations & Membership Study

ECONOMY

Gross Metropolitan Product

Area	2007	2008	2009	2010	2010 Rank[2]
MSA[1]	13.0	13.1	12.9	13.3	145

Note: Figures are in billions of dollars; (1) Figures cover the Savannah, GA Metropolitan Statistical Area—see Appendix B for areas included; (2) Rank ranges from 1 to 363
Source: The United States Conference of Mayors, "U.S. Metro Economies: GMP and Employment Forecasts," June 2011

Economic Growth

Area	2007-2009 (%)	2010 (%)	2011 (%)	Rank[2]
MSA[1]	-2.9	1.4	1.5	262
U.S.	-1.3	2.9	2.5	–

Note: Figures are real Gross Metropolitan Product growth rates and represent annual average percent change; (1) Figures cover the Savannah, GA Metropolitan Statistical Area—see Appendix B for areas included; (2) Rank ranges from 1 to 363
Source: The United States Conference of Mayors, "U.S. Metro Economies: GMP and Employment Forecasts," June 2011

Metropolitan Area Exports

Area	2005	2006	2007	2008	2009	2010	2010 Rank[2]
MSA[1]	1,647.9	1,951.1	2,520.2	3,598.5	2,724.7	3,459.1	60

Note: Figures are in millions of dollars; (1) Figures cover the Savannah, GA Metropolitan Statistical Area—see Appendix B for areas included; (2) Rank ranges from 1 to 369
Source: U.S. Department of Commerce, International Trade Administration, Office of Trade & Industry Information, Manufacturing & Services, data extracted April 2, 2012

INCOME

Income

Area	Per Capita ($)	Median Household ($)	Average Household ($)
City	19,464	32,699	47,361
MSA[1]	24,660	47,505	62,789
U.S.	26,942	51,222	70,116

Note: (1) Figures cover the Savannah, GA Metropolitan Statistical Area—see Appendix B for areas included
Source: U.S. Census Bureau, 2008-2010 American Community Survey 3-Year Estimates

Household Income Distribution

Area	Percent of Households Earning							
	Under $15,000	$15,000 -24,999	$25,000 -34,999	$35,000 -49,999	$50,000 -74,999	$75,000 -99,000	$100,000 -149,999	$150,000 and up
City	23.3	15.5	13.9	13.6	16.1	8.0	6.7	2.9
MSA[1]	14.4	11.9	11.2	14.4	19.0	11.6	11.8	5.7
U.S.	13.0	11.0	10.6	14.2	18.5	12.1	12.2	8.4

Note: (1) Figures cover the Savannah, GA Metropolitan Statistical Area—see Appendix B for areas included
Source: U.S. Census Bureau, 2008-2010 American Community Survey 3-Year Estimates

Poverty Rate

Area	All Ages	Under 18 Years Old	18 to 64 Years Old	65 Years and Over
City	24.6	33.1	22.9	17.1
MSA[1]	15.7	21.2	14.4	10.7
U.S.	14.4	20.1	13.1	9.4

Note: Figures are percentage of people whose income during the past 12 months was below the poverty level;
(1) Figures cover the Savannah, GA Metropolitan Statistical Area—see Appendix B for areas included
Source: U.S. Census Bureau, 2008-2010 American Community Survey 3-Year Estimates

Personal Bankruptcy Filing Rate

Area	2006	2007	2008	2009	2010	2011
Chatham County	4.85	5.26	6.33	6.98	6.53	6.28
U.S.	2.00	2.73	3.53	4.61	4.97	4.37

Note: Numbers are per 1,000 population and include Chapter 7 and Chapter 13 filings
Source: Federal Deposit Insurance Corporation, Regional Economic Conditions, March 9, 2012

EMPLOYMENT

Labor Force and Employment

Area	Civilian Labor Force			Workers Employed		
	Dec. 2010	Dec. 2011	% Chg.	Dec. 2010	Dec. 2011	% Chg.
City	63,625	64,361	1.2	56,977	57,626	1.1
MSA[1]	175,491	177,044	0.9	159,717	161,537	1.1
U.S.	153,156,000	153,373,000	0.1	139,159,000	140,681,000	1.1

Note: Data is not seasonally adjusted and covers workers 16 years of age and older;
(1) Metropolitan Statistical Area—see Appendix B for areas included
Source: Bureau of Labor Statistics, http://stats.bls.gov

Unemployment Rate

Area	2011											
	Jan.	Feb.	Mar.	Apr.	May	Jun.	Jul.	Aug.	Sep.	Oct.	Nov.	Dec.
City	10.7	10.3	9.9	9.5	9.8	11.4	11.3	11.4	11.2	10.6	9.9	10.5
MSA[1]	9.2	9.1	8.6	8.4	8.5	9.5	9.3	9.5	9.3	9.0	8.4	8.8
U.S.	9.8	9.5	9.2	8.7	8.7	9.3	9.3	9.1	8.8	8.5	8.2	8.3

Note: Data is not seasonally adjusted and covers workers 16 years of age and older; All figures are
percentages; (1) Metropolitan Statistical Area—see Appendix B for areas included
Source: Bureau of Labor Statistics, http://stats.bls.gov

Projected Unemployment Rate

Area	2010 (%)	2011 (%)	2012 (%)	2013 (%)
MSA[1]	9.4	8.7	8.0	7.3

Note: (1) Metropolitan Statistical Area—see Appendix B for areas included
Source: The United States Conference of Mayors, "U.S. Metro Economies: GMP and Employment Forecasts,"
June 2011

Employment by Occupation

Occupation Classification	City (%)	MSA[1] (%)	U.S. (%)
Management, Business, Science, and Arts	30.9	33.3	35.6
Natural Resources, Construction, and Maintenance	8.6	10.1	9.5
Production, Transportation, and Material Moving	13.1	13.0	12.1
Sales and Office	23.8	24.5	25.2
Service	23.6	19.1	17.6

Note: Figures cover employed civilians 16 years of age and older; (1) Figures cover the Savannah, GA Metropolitan Statistical Area—see Appendix B for areas included
Source: U.S. Census Bureau, 2008-2010 American Community Survey 3-Year Estimates

Employment by Industry

Sector	MSA[1] Number of Employees	MSA[1] Percent of Total	U.S. Percent of Total
Construction	n/a	n/a	4.1
Education and Health Services	23,900	15.9	15.2
Financial Activities	5,100	3.4	5.8
Government	23,000	15.3	16.8
Information	1,400	0.9	2.0
Leisure and Hospitality	19,600	13.0	9.9
Manufacturing	14,300	9.5	8.9
Mining and Logging	n/a	n/a	0.6
Other Services	6,800	4.5	4.0
Professional and Business Services	17,400	11.6	13.3
Retail Trade	17,700	11.8	11.5
Transportation and Utilities	9,900	6.6	3.8
Wholesale Trade	5,600	3.7	4.2

Note: Figures cover non-farm employment as of December 2011 and are not seasonally adjusted; (1) Metropolitan Statistical Area—see Appendix B for areas included; n/a not available
Source: Bureau of Labor Statistics, http://stats.bls.gov

Occupations with Greatest Projected Employment Growth: 2008 – 2018

Occupation[1]	2008 Employment	2018 Projected Employment	Numeric Employment Change	Percent Employment Change
Combined Food Preparation and Serving Workers, Including Fast Food	102,970	134,890	31,920	31.0
Retail Salespersons	156,260	186,090	29,830	19.1
Registered Nurses	66,610	90,440	23,830	35.8
Customer Service Representatives	99,680	122,990	23,310	23.4
Janitors and Cleaners, Except Maids and Housekeeping Cleaners	78,880	95,000	16,120	20.4
Waiters and Waitresses	66,470	82,520	16,050	24.1
Elementary School Teachers, Except Special Education	46,730	61,680	14,950	32.0
Office Clerks, General	86,710	101,420	14,710	17.0
Postsecondary Teachers	36,460	49,930	13,470	36.9
Management Analysts	50,150	62,340	12,190	24.3

Note: Projections cover Georgia; (1) Sorted by numeric employment change
Source: www.projectionscentral.com, State Occupational Projections, 2008–2018 Long-Term Projections

Fastest Growing Occupations: 2008 – 2018

Occupation[1]	2008 Employment	2018 Projected Employment	Numeric Employment Change	Percent Employment Change
Marriage and Family Therapists	260	470	210	80.8
Home Health Aides	11,010	18,230	7,220	65.6
Shoe and Leather Workers and Repairers	290	470	180	62.1
Skin Care Specialists	1,740	2,780	1,040	59.8
Actors	1,150	1,760	610	53.0
Network Systems and Data Communications Analysts	7,800	11,850	4,050	51.9
Makeup Artists, Theatrical and Performance	270	410	140	51.9
Manicurists and Pedicurists	540	810	270	50.0
Mental Health Counselors	1,860	2,730	870	46.8
Physical Therapist Assistants	1,030	1,510	480	46.6

Note: Projections cover Georgia; (1) Sorted by percent employment change and excludes occupations with numeric employment change less than 100
Source: www.projectionscentral.com, State Occupational Projections, 2008–2018 Long-Term Projections

Average Wages

Occupation	$/Hr.	Occupation	$/Hr.
Accountants and Auditors	32.41	Maids and Housekeeping Cleaners	8.61
Automotive Mechanics	18.85	Maintenance and Repair Workers	15.51
Bookkeepers	16.56	Marketing Managers	49.22
Carpenters	19.40	Nuclear Medicine Technologists	n/a
Cashiers	9.20	Nurses, Licensed Practical	18.32
Clerks, General Office	11.24	Nurses, Registered	29.22
Clerks, Receptionists/Information	11.80	Nursing Aides/Orderlies/Attendants	10.72
Clerks, Shipping/Receiving	14.96	Packers and Packagers, Hand	9.73
Computer Programmers	31.16	Physical Therapists	42.69
Computer Support Specialists	23.14	Postal Service Mail Carriers	24.12
Computer Systems Analysts	32.95	Real Estate Brokers	n/a
Cooks, Restaurant	9.62	Retail Salespersons	11.37
Dentists	79.03	Sales Reps., Exc. Tech./Scientific	27.05
Electrical Engineers	41.86	Sales Reps., Tech./Scientific	34.62
Electricians	24.40	Secretaries, Exc. Legal/Med./Exec.	14.67
Financial Managers	46.08	Security Guards	13.87
First-Line Supervisors/Managers, Sales	17.54	Surgeons	118.18
Food Preparation Workers	10.05	Teacher Assistants	11.60
General and Operations Managers	45.29	Teachers, Elementary School	24.10
Hairdressers/Cosmetologists	12.98	Teachers, Secondary School	23.50
Internists	104.42	Telemarketers	8.97
Janitors and Cleaners	10.57	Truck Drivers, Heavy/Tractor-Trailer	18.62
Landscaping/Groundskeeping Workers	12.43	Truck Drivers, Light/Delivery Svcs.	15.26
Lawyers	52.91	Waiters and Waitresses	9.05

Note: Wage data covers the Savannah, GA Metropolitan Statistical Area—see Appendix B for areas included. Hourly wages for elementary/secondary school teachers and teacher assistants were calculated by the editors from annual wage data assuming a 40 hour work week; n/a not available.
Source: Bureau of Labor Statistics, Metro Area Occupational Employment and Wage Estimates, May 2011

RESIDENTIAL REAL ESTATE

Building Permits

Area	Single-Family			Multi-Family			Total		
	2010	2011	Pct. Chg.	2010	2011	Pct. Chg.	2010	2011	Pct. Chg.
City	241	197	-18.3	279	250	-10.4	520	447	-14.0
MSA[1]	1,020	1,049	2.8	281	576	105.0	1,301	1,625	24.9
U.S.	447,311	418,498	-6.4	157,299	205,563	30.7	604,610	624,061	3.2

Note: (1) Metropolitan Statistical Area—see Appendix B for areas included; figures represent new, privately-owned housing units authorized (unadjusted data); All permit data are based on estimates with imputation.
Source: U.S. Census Bureau, Manufacturing, Mining, and Construction Statistics, Building Permits, 2010, 2011

Homeownership Rate

Area	2005 (%)	2006 (%)	2007 (%)	2008 (%)	2009 (%)	2010 (%)	2011 (%)
MSA[1]	n/a	n/a	n/a	n/a	n/a	n/a	n/a
U.S.	68.9	68.8	68.1	67.8	67.4	66.9	66.1

Note: (1) Metropolitan Statistical Area—see Appendix B for areas included; n/a not available
Source: U.S. Census Bureau, Housing Vacancies and Homeownership Annual Statistics: 2011

Housing Vacancy Rates

Area	Gross Vacancy Rate[2] (%)			Year-Round Vacancy Rate[3] (%)			Rental Vacancy Rate[4] (%)			Homeowner Vacancy Rate[5] (%)		
	2009	2010	2011	2009	2010	2011	2009	2010	2011	2009	2010	2011
MSA[1]	n/a	n/a	n/a	n/a	n/a	n/a	n/a	n/a	n/a	n/a	n/a	n/a
U.S.	14.5	14.3	14.2	11.3	11.3	11.1	10.6	10.2	9.5	2.6	2.6	2.5

Note: (1) Metropolitan Statistical Area—see Appendix B for areas included; (2) The percentage of the total housing inventory that is vacant; (3) The percentage of the housing inventory (excluding seasonal units) that is year-round vacant; (4) The percentage of rental inventory that is vacant for rent; (5) The percentage of homeowner inventory that is vacant for sale; n/a not available
Source: U.S. Census Bureau, Housing Vacancies and Homeownership Annual Statistics: 2011

TAXES

State Corporate Income Tax Rates

State	Tax Rate (%)	Income Brackets ($)	Num. of Brackets	Financial Institution Tax Rate (%)[a]	Federal Income Tax Ded.
Georgia	6.0	Flat rate	1	6.0	No

Note: Tax rates as of January 1, 2012; (a) Rates listed are the corporate income tax rate applied to financial institutions or excise taxes based on income. Some states have other taxes based upon the value of deposits or shares.
Source: Federation of Tax Administrators, "State Corporate Income Tax Rates, 2012"

State Individual Income Tax Rates

State	Tax Rate (%)	Income Brackets ($)	Num. of Brackets	Personal Exempt. ($)[1] Single	Dependents	Fed. Inc. Tax Ded.
Georgia	1.0 - 6.0	750 (h) - 7,001 (h)	6	2,700	3,000	No

Note: Tax rates as of January 1, 2012; Local- and county-level taxes are not included; n/a not applicable; (1) Married joint filers generally receive double the single exemption; (h) The Georgia income brackets reported are for single individuals. For married couples filing jointly, the same tax rates apply to income brackets ranging from $1,000, to $10,000.
Source: Federation of Tax Administrators, "State Individual Income Tax Rates, 2012"

Various State and Local Tax Rates

State	State and Local Sales and Use (%)	State Sales and Use (%)	Gasoline[1] (¢/gal.)	Cigarette[2] ($/pack)	Spirits[3] ($/gal.)	Wine[4] ($/gal.)	Beer[5] ($/gal.)
Georgia	7.0	4.00	29.4	0.37	3.79	1.51	1.01 (n)

Note: All tax rates as of January 1, 2012 except beer, wine and spirits (September 1, 2011); (1) The American Petroleum Institute has developed a methodology for determining the average tax rate on a gallon of fuel. Rates may include any of the following: excise taxes, environmental fees, storage tank fees, other fees or taxes, general sales tax, and local taxes. In states where gasoline is subject to the general sales tax, or where the fuel tax is based on the average sale price, the average rate determined by API is sensitive to changes in the price of gasoline. States that fully or partially apply general sales taxes to gasoline: CA, CO, GA, IL, IN, MI, NY; (2) The federal excise tax of $1.0066 per pack and local taxes are not included; (3) Rates are those applicable to off-premise sales of 40% alcohol by volume (a.b.v.) distilled spirits in 750ml containers. Local excise taxes are excluded; (4) Rates are those applicable to off-premise sales of 11% a.b.v. non-carbonated wine in 750ml containers; (5) Rates are those applicable to off-premise sales of 4.7% a.b.v. beer in 12 ounce containers; (n) Includes statewide local rate in Alabama ($0.52) and Georgia ($0.53).
Source: Tax Foundation, 2012 Facts & Figures: How Does Your State Compare?

State-Local Tax Burdens

Area	Rate (%)	Rank[1]	Per Capita Taxes Paid to Home State ($)	Total State and Local Per Capita Taxes Paid ($)	Per Capita Income ($)
Georgia	9.1	32	2,411	3,350	36,738
U.S. Average	9.8	-	3,057	4,160	42,539

Note: Figures cover 2009; (1) Rank ranges from 1 to 50 where 1 is highest tax burden
Source: Tax Foundation, State-Local Tax Burdens, All States, 2009

State Business Tax Climate Index Rankings

State	Overall Rank	Corporate Tax Index Rank	Individual Income Tax Index Rank	Sales Tax Index Rank	Unemployment Insurance Tax Index Rank	Property Tax Index Rank
Georgia	34	9	40	12	22	39

Note: The index is a measure of how each state's tax laws affect economic performance. The lower the rank, the more favorable a state's tax system is for business. States without a given tax are given a ranking of 1.
Source: Tax Foundation, Major Components of the State Business Tax Climate Index, FY 2012

COMMERCIAL UTILITIES

Typical Monthly Electric Bills

Area	Commercial Service ($/month)		Industrial Service ($/month)	
	1,500 kWh	40 kW demand 14,000 kWh	1,000 kW demand 200,000 kWh	50,000 kW demand 15,000,000 kWh
City	252	1,660	31,345	1,601,449
Average[1]	189	1,616	25,197	1,470,813

Note: Based on total rates in effect July 1, 2011; (1) average based on 184 utilities surveyed
Source: Edison Electric Institute, Typical Bills and Average Rates Report, Summer 2011

TRANSPORTATION

Means of Transportation to Work

Area	Car/Truck/Van		Public Transportation			Bicycle	Walked	Other Means	Worked at Home
	Drove Alone	Car-pooled	Bus	Subway	Railroad				
City	75.2	11.5	4.4	0.0	0.0	0.7	3.6	1.2	3.4
MSA[1]	80.8	10.4	1.9	0.0	0.0	0.4	1.7	1.2	3.8
U.S.	76.0	10.2	2.7	1.7	0.5	0.5	2.8	1.3	4.2

Note: Figures are percentages and cover workers 16 years of age and older; (1) Figures cover the Savannah, GA Metropolitan Statistical Area—see Appendix B for areas included
Source: U.S. Census Bureau, 2008-2010 American Community Survey 3-Year Estimates

Travel Time to Work

Area	Less Than 10 Minutes	10 to 19 Minutes	20 to 29 Minutes	30 to 44 Minutes	45 to 59 Minutes	60 to 89 Minutes	90 Minutes or More
City	10.1	45.2	27.9	12.1	2.1	2.0	0.5
MSA[1]	9.5	34.6	27.4	19.9	5.4	2.2	1.0
U.S.	13.9	30.1	20.8	19.8	7.5	5.5	2.5

Note: Figures are percentages and include workers 16 years old and over; (1) Figures cover the Savannah, GA Metropolitan Statistical Area—see Appendix B for areas included
Source: U.S. Census Bureau, 2008-2010 American Community Survey 3-Year Estimates

Travel Time Index

Area	1985	1990	1995	2000	2005	2010
Urban Area[1]	n/a	n/a	n/a	n/a	n/a	n/a
Average[2]	1.11	1.16	1.18	1.21	1.25	1.20

Note: Travel Time Index—the ratio of travel time in the peak period to the travel time at free-flow conditions. A value of 1.30 indicates a 20-minute free-flow trip takes 26 minutes in the peak. Free-flow speeds (60 mph on freeways and 35 mph on principal arterials) are used as the comparison threshold; (1) Data for the Savannah, GA urban area was not available; (2) average of 439 urban areas
Source: Texas Transportation Institute, Urban Mobility Report 2011, September 2011

Public Transportation

Agency Name / Mode of Transportation	Vehicles Operated in Maximum Service	Annual Unlinked Passenger Trips ('000)	Annual Passenger Miles ('000)
Chatham Area Transit Authority (CAT)			
Bus (directly operated)	50	3,348.0	12,075.6
Demand Response (directly operated)	20	36.5	366.2
Demand Response (purchased transportation)	19	34.4	285.9
Ferryboat (directly operated)	2	459.5	181.2

Source: Federal Transit Administration, National Transit Database, 2010

Air Transportation

Airport Name and Code / Type of Service	Passenger Airlines[1]	Passenger Enplanements	Freight Carriers[2]	Freight (lbs.)
Savannah International (SAV)				
Domestic service (U.S. carriers - 2011)	23	785,029	12	5,418,530
International service (U.S. carriers - 2010)	3	93	0	0

Note: (1) Includes all U.S.-based major, minor and commuter airlines that carried at least one passenger during the year; (2) Includes all U.S.-based airlines and freight carriers that transported at least one pound of freight during the year
Source: Bureau of Transportation Statistics, The Intermodal Transportation Database, Air Carriers: T-100 Domestic Market (U.S. Carriers), 2011; Bureau of Transportation Statistics, The Intermodal Transportation Database, Air Carriers: T-100 International Market (U.S. Carriers), 2010

Other Transportation Statistics

Major Highways: I-16; I-95
Amtrak Service: Yes
Major Waterways/Ports: Savannah River (Atlantic Ocean)
Source: Amtrak.com; Google Maps

BUSINESSES

Major Business Headquarters

Company Name	Rankings	
	Fortune[1]	Forbes[2]
Colonial Group	-	59

Note: (1) Fortune 500—companies that produce a 10-K are ranked 1 to 500 based on 2010 revenue; (2) all private companies with at least $2 billion in annual revenue are ranked 1 to 212; companies listed are headquartered in the city; dashes indicate no ranking
Source: Fortune, "Fortune 500," May 23, 2011; Forbes, "America's Largest Private Companies," November 16, 2011

Minority- and Women-Owned Businesses

Group	All Firms		Firms with Paid Employees			
	Firms	Sales ($000)	Firms	Sales ($000)	Employees	Payroll ($000)
Asian	639	240,363	290	222,341	3,076	38,001
Black	4,185	316,962	211	193,454	839	21,492
Hispanic	139	47,330	39	39,932	727	6,988
Women	4,332	717,594	628	633,948	7,500	147,281
All Firms	13,717	14,667,749	3,975	14,215,679	89,726	2,944,187

Note: Figures cover firms located in the city; minority- and women-owned business are defined as firms in which the corresponding group own 51% or more of the stock or equity of the company
Source: U.S. Census Bureau, 2007 Economic Census, Survey of Business Owners

HOTELS

Hotels/Motels

Area	5 Star		4 Star		3 Star		2 Star		1 Star		Not Rated	
	Num.	Pct.[3]	Num.	Pct.[3]	Num.	Pct.[3]	Num.	Pct.[3]	Num.	Pct.[3]	Num.	Pct.[3]
City[1]	0	0.0	6	3.9	42	27.1	83	53.5	4	2.6	20	12.9
Total[2]	133	0.9	940	6.5	4,569	31.8	7,033	48.9	351	2.4	1,343	9.3

Note: (1) Figures cover Savannah and vicinity; (2) Figures cover all 100 cities in this book; (3) Percentage of hotels which have a given star rating; Star ratings are determined by expedia.com and offer an indication of the general quality of a particular hotel.
Source: expedia.com, April 25, 2012

The Savannah, GA metro area is home to one of the best hotels in the U.S. according to *Travel & Leisure*: **Mansion on Forsyth Park** (#144). Criteria: service; location; rooms; food; and value. *Travel & Leisure, "T+L 500, The World's Best Hotels 2012"*

The Savannah, GA metro area is home to one of the best hotels in the U.S. according to *Condé Nast Traveler*: **Avia Savannah** (#91). The selections are based on over 25,000 responses to the magazine's annual Readers' Choice Survey. *Condé Nast Traveler, "2011 Readers' Choice Awards"*

EVENT SITES

Major Stadiums, Arenas, and Auditoriums

Name	Max. Capacity
Grayson Stadium	8,000
Johnny Mercer Theatre, Savannah Civic Center	2,506
MLK Jr. Arena, Savannah Civic Center	9,600

Source: Original research

Convention Centers

Name	Overall Space (sq. ft.)	Exhibit Space (sq. ft.)	Meeting Space (sq. ft.)	Meeting Rooms
Savannah Intl Trade & Convention Center	330,000	50,000	100,000	13

Source: Original research

Living Environment

COST OF LIVING

Cost of Living Index

Composite Index	Groceries	Housing	Utilities	Trans-portation	Health Care	Misc. Goods/Services
91.6	97.1	77.2	100.6	97.7	93.2	97.1

Note: U.S. = 100; Figures cover the Savannah GA urban area.
Source: The Council for Community and Economic Research, ACCRA Cost of Living Index, 2011

Grocery Prices

Area[1]	T-Bone Steak ($/pound)	Frying Chicken ($/pound)	Whole Milk ($/half gal.)	Eggs ($/dozen)	Orange Juice ($/64 oz.)	Coffee ($/11.5 oz.)
City[2]	9.67	1.18	2.22	1.57	2.93	4.20
Avg.	9.25	1.18	2.22	1.66	3.19	4.40
Min.	6.70	0.88	1.31	0.95	2.46	2.94
Max.	14.30	2.16	3.50	3.18	4.75	6.83

Note: (1) Values for the local area are compared with the average, minimum and maximum values for all 335 areas in the Cost of Living Index; (2) Figures cover the Savannah GA urban area; **T-Bone Steak** *(price per pound);* **Frying Chicken** *(price per pound, whole fryer);* **Whole Milk** *(half gallon carton);* **Eggs** *(price per dozen, Grade A, large);* **Orange Juice** *(64 oz. Tropicana or Florida Natural);* **Coffee** *(11.5 oz. can, vacuum-packed, Maxwell House, Hills Bros, or Folgers).*
Source: The Council for Community and Economic Research, ACCRA Cost of Living Index, 2011

Housing and Utility Costs

Area[1]	New Home Price ($)	Apartment Rent ($/month)	All Electric ($/month)	Part Electric ($/month)	Other Energy ($/month)	Telephone ($/month)
City[2]	210,203	731	165.86	-	-	27.39
Avg.	285,990	839	163.23	89.00	77.52	26.92
Min.	188,005	460	125.58	45.39	33.89	17.98
Max.	1,197,028	3,244	339.16	181.97	348.69	40.01

Note: (1) Values for the local area are compared with the average, minimum and maximum values for all 335 areas in the Cost of Living Index; (2) Figures cover the Savannah GA urban area; **New Home Price** *(2,400 sf living area, 8,000 sf lot, in urban area with full utilities);* **Apartment Rent** *(950 sf 2 bedroom/1.5 or 2 bath, unfurnished, excluding all utilities except water);* **All Electric** *(average monthly cost for an all-electric home);* **Part Electric** *(average monthly cost for a part-electric home);* **Other Energy** *(average monthly cost for natural gas, fuel oil, coal, wood, and any other forms of energy except electricity);* **Telephone** *(price includes basic monthly rate for a private residential line plus additional local usage charges incurred by a family of four).*
Source: The Council for Community and Economic Research, ACCRA Cost of Living Index, 2011

Health Care, Transportation, and Other Costs

Area[1]	Doctor ($/visit)	Dentist ($/visit)	Optometrist ($/visit)	Gasoline ($/gallon)	Beauty Salon ($/visit)	Men's Shirt ($)
City[2]	87.56	71.83	74.62	3.46	37.71	19.58
Avg.	93.88	81.72	90.54	3.48	32.65	25.06
Min.	60.00	55.33	53.66	3.18	19.78	13.44
Max.	154.98	145.97	183.72	4.31	63.21	46.00

Note: (1) Values for the local area are compared with the average, minimum and maximum values for all 335 areas in the Cost of Living Index; (2) Figures cover the Savannah GA urban area; **Doctor** *(general practitioners routine exam of an established patient);* **Dentist** *(adult teeth cleaning and periodic oral examination);* **Optometrist** *(full vision eye exam for established adult patient);* **Gasoline** *(one gallon regular unleaded, national brand, including all taxes, cash price at self-service pump if available);* **Beauty Salon** *(woman's shampoo, trim, and blow-dry);* **Men's Shirt** *(cotton/polyester dress shirt, pinpoint weave, long sleeves).*
Source: The Council for Community and Economic Research, ACCRA Cost of Living Index, 2011

HOUSING

House Price Index (HPI)

Area	National Ranking[2]	Quarterly Change (%)	One-Year Change (%)	Five-Year Change (%)
MSA[1]	205	1.61	-4.00	-15.99
U.S.[3]	-	-0.10	-2.43	-19.16

Note: The HPI is a weighted repeat sales index. It measures average price changes in repeat sales or refinancings on the same properties. This information is obtained by reviewing repeat mortgage transactions on single-family properties whose mortgages have been purchased or securitized by Fannie Mae or Freddie Mac in January 1975; (1) Metropolitan/Micropolitan Statistical Area—see Appendix B for areas included; (2) Rankings are based on annual percentage change for all metro areas containing at least 15,000 transactions over the last 10 years and ranges from 1 to 306; (3) figures based on a weighted average of Census Division estimates using a purchase only index; all figures are for the period ending December 31, 2011
Source: Federal Housing Finance Agency, House Price Index, February 23, 2012

House Price Valuations

Area	Q4 2005 Price ($000)	Q4 2005 Over-valuation	Q4 2006 Price ($000)	Q4 2006 Over-valuation	Q4 2007 Price ($000)	Q4 2007 Over-valuation	Q4 2008 Price ($000)	Q4 2008 Over-valuation	Q4 2009 Price ($000)	Q4 2009 Over-valuation
MSA[1]	137.6	11.8	150.0	13.8	148.7	7.2	135.5	-2.4	135.3	-3.0

Note: Figures show the percentage of over- or under-valuation of single family homes relative to statistically normal house values (e.g. a value of 23.6 indicates that house values are 23.6% overvalued). Statistically normal house values are based on house prices, interest rates, household incomes, population densities, and any historical premiums or discounts metropolitan areas have exhibited over time; (1) Figures cover the Savannah, GA - see Appendix B for areas included
Source: Global Insight/PNC Financial Services Group, House Prices in America: 4th Quarter 2009 Update

Median Single-Family Home Prices

Area	2009	2010	2011p	Percent Change 2010 to 2011
MSA[1]	n/a	n/a	n/a	n/a
U.S. Average	172.1	173.1	166.2	-4.0

Note: Figures are median sales prices of existing single-family homes in thousands of dollars; (p) preliminary; n/a not available; (1) Metropolitan Statistical Area—see Appendix B for areas included
Source: National Association of Realtors, Median Sales Price of Existing Single-Family Homes for Metropolitan Areas, 4th Quarter 2011

Affordability Index of Existing Single-Family Homes

Area	2009	2010	2011p	Percent Change 2010 to 2011
MSA[1]	n/a	n/a	n/a	n/a

Note: The housing affordability index measures whether or not a typical family could qualify for a mortgage loan on a typical home. The higher the index, the greater the household purchasing power. An index of 100 is defined as the point where a median-income household has exactly enough income to qualify for the purchase of a median-priced existing single-family home, assuming a 20 percent downpayment and 25 percent of gross income devoted to mortgage principal and interest payments; (p) preliminary; n/a not available; (1) Metropolitan Statistical Area—see Appendix B for areas included
Source: National Association of Realtors, Affordability Index of Existing Single-Family Homes, 2011

Median Apartment Condo-Coop Home Prices

Area	2009	2010	2011p	Percent Change 2010 to 2011
MSA[1]	n/a	n/a	n/a	n/a
U.S. Average	175.6	171.7	165.1	-3.8

Note: Figures are median sales prices of existing apartment condo-coop homes in thousands of dollars; (p) preliminary; n/a not available; (1) Metropolitan Statistical Area—see Appendix B for areas included
Source: National Association of Realtors, Median Sales Price of Existing Apartment Condo-Coop Homes for Metropolitan Areas, 4th Quarter 2011

Year Housing Structure Built

Area	2005 or Later	2000 -2004	1990 -1999	1980 -1989	1970 -1979	1960 -1969	1950 -1959	Before 1950	Median Year
City	6.1	4.9	7.5	10.8	16.3	15.0	15.2	24.2	1967
MSA[1]	10.7	12.8	17.2	14.9	12.9	9.7	8.5	13.3	1984
U.S.	5.0	8.6	14.0	14.1	16.3	11.3	11.2	19.6	1975

Note: Figures are percentages except for Median Year; (1) Figures cover the Savannah, GA Metropolitan Statistical Area—see Appendix B for areas included
Source: U.S. Census Bureau, 2008-2010 American Community Survey 3-Year Estimates

HEALTH

Health Risk Data

Category	MSA[1] (%)	U.S. (%)
Adults who have been told they have high blood pressure[2]	n/a	28.7
Adults who have been told they have high blood cholesterol[2]	n/a	37.5
Adults who have been told they have diabetes[3]	n/a	8.7
Adults who have been told they have arthritis[2]	n/a	26.0
Adults who have been told they currently have asthma	n/a	9.1
Adults who are current smokers	n/a	17.3
Adults who are heavy drinkers[4]	n/a	5.0
Adults who are binge drinkers[5]	n/a	15.1
Adults who are overweight (BMI 25.0 - 29.9)	n/a	36.2
Adults who are obese (BMI 30.0 - 99.8)	n/a	27.5
Adults who participated in any physical activities in the past month	n/a	76.1
Adults 50+ who have ever had a sigmoidoscopy or colonoscopy	n/a	65.2
Women aged 40+ who have had a mammogram within the past two years	n/a	75.2
Men aged 40+ who have had a PSA test within the past two years	n/a	53.2
Adults aged 65+ who have had flu shot within the past year	n/a	67.5
Adults aged 18–64 who have any kind of health care coverage	n/a	82.2

Note: Data as of 2010 unless otherwise noted; n/a not available; (1) Figures cover the Savannah, GA—see Appendix B for areas included; (2) Data as of 2009; (3) Figures do not include pregnancy-related, borderline, or pre-diabetes; (4) Heavy drinkers are classified as males having more than two drinks per day or females having more than one drink per day; (5) Binge drinkers are classified as males having five or more drinks on one occasion or females having four or more drinks on one occasion
Source: Centers for Disease Control and Prevention, Behaviorial Risk Factor Surveillance System, SMART: Selected Metropolitan/Micropolitan Area Risk Trends, 2009, 2010

Mortality Rates for the Top 10 Causes of Death in the U.S.

ICD-10[a] Sub-Chapter	ICD-10[a] Code	Age-Adjusted Mortality Rate[1] per 100,000 population	
		County[2]	U.S.
Malignant neoplasms	C00-C97	180.5	175.6
Ischaemic heart diseases	I20-I25	95.5	121.6
Other forms of heart disease	I30-I51	97.2	48.6
Chronic lower respiratory diseases	J40-J47	42.0	42.3
Cerebrovascular diseases	I60-I69	42.2	40.6
Organic, including symptomatic, mental disorders	F01-F09	26.2	26.7
Other degenerative diseases of the nervous system	G30-G31	20.8	24.7
Other external causes of accidental injury	W00-X59	27.4	24.4
Diabetes mellitus	E10-E14	12.7	21.7
Hypertensive diseases	I10-I15	21.9	18.2

Note: (a) ICD-10 = International Classification of Diseases 10th Revision; (1) Mortality rates are a three year average covering 2007-2009; (2) Figures cover Chatham County
Source: Centers for Disease Control and Prevention, National Center for Health Statistics. Underlying Cause of Death 1999-2009 on CDC WONDER Online Database, released 2012. Data for year 2009 are compiled from the Multiple Cause of Death File 2009, Series 20 No. 2O, 2012, Data for year 2008 are compiled from the Multiple Cause of Death File 2008, Series 20 No. 2N, 2011, Data for year 2007 are compiled from Multiple Cause of Death File 2007, Series 20 No. 2M, 2010.

Mortality Rates for Selected Causes of Death

ICD-10[a] Sub-Chapter	ICD-10[a] Code	Age-Adjusted Mortality Rate[1] per 100,000 population	
		County[2]	U.S.
Assault	X85-Y09	12.1	5.7
Human immunodeficiency virus (HIV) disease	B20-B24	12.0	3.3
Influenza and pneumonia	J09-J18	18.4	16.4
Intentional self-harm	X60-X84	12.4	11.5
Malnutrition	E40-E46	*0.0	0.8
Obesity and other hyperalimentation	E65-E68	*Unreliable	1.6
Transport accidents	V01-V99	15.9	13.7
Viral hepatitis	B15-B19	*Unreliable	2.2

Note: (a) ICD-10 = International Classification of Diseases 10th Revision; (1) Mortality rates are a three year average covering 2007-2009; (2) Figures cover Chatham County; (*) Unreliable data as per CDC
Source: Centers for Disease Control and Prevention, National Center for Health Statistics. Underlying Cause of Death 1999-2009 on CDC WONDER Online Database, released 2012. Data for year 2009 are compiled from the Multiple Cause of Death File 2009, Series 20 No. 2O, 2012, Data for year 2008 are compiled from the Multiple Cause of Death File 2008, Series 20 No. 2N, 2011, Data for year 2007 are compiled from Multiple Cause of Death File 2007, Series 20 No. 2M, 2010.

Distribution of Physicians and Dentists

Area[1]	Dentists[2]	D.O.[3]	M.D.[4]				
			Total	Family/ General Practice	Pediatrics	Medical Specialties	Surgical Specialties
Local (number)	114	33	671	67	48	238	185
Local (rate[5])	4.6	1.3	26.7	2.7	1.9	9.5	7.4
U.S. (rate[5])	4.5	1.9	18.3	2.5	1.4	6.8	4.1

Note: Data as of 2008 unless noted; (1) Local data covers Chatham County; (2) Data as of 2007; (3) Doctor of Osteopathic Medicine; (4) Includes active, non-federal, patient-care, office-based Doctors of Medicine; (5) rate per 10,000 population
Source: Area Resource File (ARF). 2009-2010 Release. U.S. Department of Health and Human Services, Health Resources and Services Administration, Bureau of Health Professions, Rockville, MD, August 2010

EDUCATION

Public School District Statistics

District Name	Schls	Pupils	Pupil/ Teacher Ratio	Minority Pupils[1] (%)	Free Lunch Eligible[2] (%)	IEP[3] (%)
Chatham County	58	34,668	12.9	72.4	61.5	10.6

Note: Table includes school districts with 2,000 or more students; (1) Percentage of students that are not non-Hispanic white; (2) Percentage of students that are eligible for the free lunch program; (3) Percentage of students that have an Individualized Education Program.
Source: U.S. Department of Education, National Center for Education Statistics, Common Core of Data, Local Education Agency (School District) Universe Survey: School Year 2009-2010; U.S. Department of Education, National Center for Education Statistics, Common Core of Data, Public Elementary/Secondary School Universe Survey: School Year 2009-2010

Top Public High Schools

High School Name	Rank[1]	Score[1]	Grad. Rate[2] (%)	College[3] (%)	AP/IB/ AICE[4] (%)	SAT/ ACT[5] (%)
Savannah Arts Academy	107	0.737	100	98	2.5	1712

Note: (1) Public schools are ranked from 1 to 500 based on the following self-reported statistics (with their corresponding weight in the final score). Schools that had fewer than 10 graduates, as well as those that were newly founded and did not have a graduating senior class in 2010 were excluded; (2) Four-year, on-time graduation rate (25%); (3) Percent of 2010 graduates who enrolled immediately in college (25%); (4) AP/IB/AICE tests per graduate (25%); (5) Average SAT and/or ACT score (10%); Average AP/IB/AICE exam score (10%); AP/IB/AICE courses offered per graduate (5%); (6) School is unranked, but has been identified by Newsweek as one of the nation's most elite public high schools.
Source: Newsweek Online, "Top High Schools 2011"

Highest Level of Education

Area	Less than H.S.	H.S. Diploma	Some College, No Deg.	Associate Degree	Bachelors Degree	Masters Degree	Profess. School Degree	Doctorate Degree
City	15.8	32.7	21.4	6.7	15.7	5.7	1.0	1.0
MSA[1]	12.4	30.5	22.9	7.0	17.8	6.7	1.7	1.0
U.S.	14.7	28.4	21.3	7.6	17.6	7.2	1.9	1.2

Note: Figures cover persons age 25 and over; (1) Figures cover the Savannah, GA Metropolitan Statistical Area—see Appendix B for areas included
Source: U.S. Census Bureau, 2008-2010 American Community Survey 3-Year Estimates

Educational Attainment by Race

Area	High School Graduate or Higher (%)					Bachelor's Degree or Higher (%)				
	Total	White	Black	Asian	Hisp.[2]	Total	White	Black	Asian	Hisp.[2]
City	84.2	90.3	79.4	78.2	63.7	23.5	36.3	12.4	33.0	18.3
MSA[1]	87.6	90.6	82.3	80.9	70.4	27.2	33.0	14.6	31.1	19.8
U.S.	85.3	87.5	81.4	85.5	61.6	28.0	29.3	17.8	50.2	13.0

Note: Figures shown cover persons 25 years old and over; (1) Figures cover the Savannah, GA Metropolitan Statistical Area—see Appendix B for areas included; (2) People of Hispanic origin can be of any race
Source: U.S. Census Bureau, 2008-2010 American Community Survey 3-Year Estimates

School Enrollment by Grade and Control

Area	Preschool (%)		Kindergarten (%)		Grades 1 - 4 (%)		Grades 5 - 8 (%)		Grades 9 - 12 (%)	
	Public	Private	Public	Private	Public	Private	Public	Private	Public	Private
City	71.9	28.1	86.4	13.6	90.4	9.6	89.7	10.3	91.1	8.9
MSA[1]	58.7	41.3	84.1	15.9	86.2	13.8	85.5	14.5	86.0	14.0
U.S.	55.4	44.6	87.1	12.9	89.4	10.6	89.5	10.5	90.4	9.6

Note: Figures shown cover persons 3 years old and over; (1) Figures cover the Savannah, GA Metropolitan Statistical Area—see Appendix B for areas included
Source: U.S. Census Bureau, 2008-2010 American Community Survey 3-Year Estimates

Average Salaries of Public School Classroom Teachers

Area	2010-11		2011-12		Percent Change 2010-11 to 2011-12	Percent Change 2001-02 to 2011-12
	Dollars	Rank[1]	Dollars	Rank[1]		
Georgia	52,815	22	52,938	23	0.23	20.10
U.S. Average	55,623	-	56,643	-	1.83	26.8

Note: (1) State rank ranges from 1 to 51 where 1 indicates highest salary.
Source: National Education Association, Rankings & Estimates: Rankings of the States 2011 and Estimates of School Statistics 2012, December 2011

Higher Education

Four-Year Colleges			Two-Year Colleges			Medical Schools[1]	Law Schools[2]	Voc/ Tech[3]
Public	Private Non-profit	Private For-profit	Public	Private Non-profit	Private For-profit			
2	1	3	1	0	0	0	0	1

Note: Figures cover institutions located within the city limits and include main campuses only; (1) includes schools accredited by the Liaison Committee on Medical Education and the American Osteopathic Association's Commission on Osteopathic College Accreditation; (2) includes American Bar Association-accredited law schools; (3) includes all schools with programs that are less than 2 years.
Source: National Center for Education Statistics, Integrated Postsecondary Education System (IPEDS) Peer Analysis System, 2011-12; Association of American Medical Colleges, Member List, April 23, 2012; American Osteopathic Association, Member List, April 23, 2012; Law School Admission Council, Official Guide to ABA-Approved Law Schools Online, April 23, 2012

PRESIDENTIAL ELECTION

2008 Presidential Election Results

Area	Obama	McCain	Nader	Other
Chatham County	56.8	42.4	0.0	0.7
U.S.	52.9	45.6	0.6	0.9

Note: Results are percentages and may not add to 100% due to rounding
Source: Dave Leip's Atlas of U.S. Presidential Elections, www.uselectionatlas.org

EMPLOYERS

Major Employers

Company Name	Industry
Armstrong Atlantic State University	University
Candler Hospital	General medical and surgical hospitals
City of Savannah	City and town managers' office
City of Savannah	Police protection, local government
Georgia Dept of Public Health	Administration of public health programs
Great Dane Trailers	Trailer parts and accessories
Gulfstream Aerospace Corporation	Aircraft
Honeywell International	Aircraft/aerospace flight instruments & guidance systems
International Paper Company	Paper mills
Kapstone Paper and Packaging Corporation	Stationery stores
Memorial Health University Medical Center	General medical and surgical hospitals
Netjets International	Air transportation, nonscheduled
Saint Joseph's Hospital	General medical and surgical hospitals
Savannah College of Art & Design	Professional schools
Savannah State University	University
St. Joseph's/Candler Health System	General medical and surgical hospitals
The Sullivan Group	Employment agencies
United Parcel Service	Mailing and messenger services
Wal-Mart Stores	Department stores, discount
Wells Fargo Insurance Services USA	Insurance brokers, nec

Note: Companies shown are located within the Savannah, GA metropolitan area.
Source: Hoovers.com, data extracted April 25 2012

PUBLIC SAFETY

Crime Rate

Area	All Crimes	Violent Crimes				Property Crimes		
		Murder	Forcible Rape	Robbery	Aggrav. Assault	Burglary	Larceny -Theft	Motor Vehicle Theft
City	4,766.4	9.5	14.2	215.4	160.9	1,210.9	2,859.4	296.1
Suburbs[1]	2,836.9	1.6	30.8	53.7	160.5	645.0	1,784.8	160.5
Metro[2]	4,042.6	6.5	20.5	154.8	160.7	998.6	2,456.3	245.2
U.S.	3,345.5	4.8	27.5	119.1	252.3	699.6	2,003.5	238.8

Note: Figures are crimes per 100,000 population; (1) All areas within the metro area that are located outside the city limits; (2) Metropolitan Statistical Area—see Appendix B for areas included
Source: FBI Uniform Crime Reports, 2010

Hate Crimes

Area	Number of Quarters Reported	Bias Motivation				
		Race	Religion	Sexual Orientation	Ethnicity	Disability
Area[2]	4	0	0	0	0	0

Note: (2) Figures cover Savannah-Chatham Metropolitan.
Source: Federal Bureau of Investigation, Hate Crime Statistics 2010

Identity Theft Consumer Complaints

Area	Complaints	Complaints per 100,000 Population	Rank[2]
MSA[1]	492	149.4	9
U.S.	279,156	90.4	-

Note: (1) Metropolitan Statistical Area—see Appendix B for areas included; (2) Rank ranges from 1 to 384 where 1 indicates greatest number of identity theft complaints per 100,000 population
Source: Federal Trade Commission, Consumer Sentinel Network Data Book for January–December 2011

Fraud and Other Consumer Complaints

Area	Complaints	Complaints per 100,000 Population	Rank[2]
MSA[1]	1,869	567.5	70
U.S.	1,533,924	496.8	-

Note: (1) Metropolitan Statistical Area—see Appendix B for areas included; (2) Rank ranges from 1 to 384 where 1 indicates greatest number of fraud and other complaints per 100,000 population
Source: Federal Trade Commission, Consumer Sentinel Network Data Book for January–December 2011

RECREATION

Culture

Dance[1]	Theatre[1]	Instrumental Music[1]	Vocal Music[1]	Series/Festivals	Museums	Zoos and Aquariums[2]
0	0	0	0	3	12	0

Note: (1) Number of professional perfoming groups; (2) AZA-accredited
Source: The Grey House Performing Arts Directory, 2011-2012; Official Museum Directory, 2011; American Association of Museums, AAM Member Museums, April 2012; Association of Zoos & Aquariums, AZA Member Zoos & Aquariums, April 2012

Professional Sports Teams

Team Name	League
No teams are located in the metro area	

Source: Original research

CLIMATE

Average and Extreme Temperatures

Temperature	Jan	Feb	Mar	Apr	May	Jun	Jul	Aug	Sep	Oct	Nov	Dec	Yr.
Extreme High (°F)	84	86	91	95	100	104	105	104	98	97	89	83	105
Average High (°F)	60	64	70	78	84	89	92	90	86	78	70	62	77
Average Temp. (°F)	49	53	59	66	74	79	82	81	77	68	59	52	67
Average Low (°F)	38	41	48	54	62	69	72	72	68	57	47	40	56
Extreme Low (°F)	3	14	20	32	39	51	61	57	43	28	15	9	3

Note: Figures cover the years 1950-1995
Source: National Climatic Data Center, International Station Meteorological Climate Summary, 9/96

Average Precipitation/Snowfall/Humidity

Precip./Humidity	Jan	Feb	Mar	Apr	May	Jun	Jul	Aug	Sep	Oct	Nov	Dec	Yr.
Avg. Precip. (in.)	3.5	3.1	3.9	3.2	4.2	5.6	6.8	7.2	5.0	2.9	2.2	2.7	50.3
Avg. Snowfall (in.)	Tr	Tr	Tr	0	0	0	0	0	0	0	Tr	Tr	Tr
Avg. Rel. Hum. 7am (%)	83	82	83	84	85	87	88	91	91	88	86	83	86
Avg. Rel. Hum. 4pm (%)	53	50	49	48	52	58	61	63	62	55	53	54	55

Note: Figures cover the years 1950-1995; Tr = Trace amounts (<0.05 in. of rain; <0.5 in. of snow)
Source: National Climatic Data Center, International Station Meteorological Climate Summary, 9/96

Weather Conditions

Temperature			Daytime Sky			Precipitation		
10°F & below	32°F & below	90°F & above	Clear	Partly cloudy	Cloudy	0.01 inch or more precip.	0.1 inch or more snow/ice	Thunder-storms
< 1	29	70	97	155	113	111	< 1	63

Note: Figures are average number of days per year and cover the years 1950-1995
Source: National Climatic Data Center, International Station Meteorological Climate Summary, 9/96

HAZARDOUS WASTE

Superfund Sites

Savannah has no sites on the EPA's Superfund Final National Priorities List.
U.S. Environmental Protection Agency, Final National Priorities List, April 17, 2012

AIR & WATER
QUALITY

Air Quality Index

Area	Percent of Days when Air Quality was...[2]					AQI Statistics[2]	
	Good	Moderate	Unhealthy for Sensitive Groups	Unhealthy	Very Unhealthy	Maximum	Median
Area[1]	60.5	36.7	2.2	0.5	0.0	155	46

Note: Air Quality Index (AQI) is an index for reporting daily air quality. EPA calculates the AQI for five major air pollutants regulated by the Clean Air Act: ground-level ozone, particle pollution (aka particulate matter), carbon monoxide, sulfur dioxide, and nitrogen dioxide. The AQI runs from 0 to 500. The higher the AQI value, the greater the level of air pollution and the greater the health concern. There are six AQI categories: "Good" AQI is between 0 and 50. Air quality is considered satisfactory; "Moderate" AQI is between 51 and 100. Air quality is acceptable; "Unhealthy for Sensitive Groups" When AQI values are between 101 and 150, members of sensitive groups may experience health effects; "Unhealthy" When AQI values are between 151 and 200 everyone may begin to experience health effects; "Very Unhealthy" AQI values between 201 and 300 trigger a health alert; "Hazardous" AQI values over 300 trigger warnings of emergency conditions (not shown); (1) Data covers Chatham County; (2) Based on 365 days with AQI data in 2011.
Source: U.S. Environmental Protection Agency, AirData Report, 2011

Air Quality Index Pollutants

Area	Percent of Days when AQI Pollutant was...[2]					
	Carbon Monoxide	Nitrogen Dioxide	Ozone	Sulfur Dioxide	Particulate Matter 2.5	Particulate Matter 10
Area[1]	0.0	0.0	23.8	27.9	48.2	0.0

Note: The Air Quality Index (AQI) is an index for reporting daily air quality. EPA calculates the AQI for five major air pollutants regulated by the Clean Air Act: ground-level ozone, particle pollution (also known as particulate matter), carbon monoxide, sulfur dioxide, and nitrogen dioxide. The AQI runs from 0 to 500. The higher the AQI value, the greater the level of air pollution and the greater the health concern; (1) Data covers Chatham County; (2) Based on 365 days with AQI data in 2011.
Source: U.S. Environmental Protection Agency, AirData Report, 2011

Air Quality Index Trends

Area	Trend Sites (days)								All Sites (days)
	2003	2004	2005	2006	2007	2008	2009	2010	2010
MSA[1]	n/a	n/a	n/a	n/a	n/a	n/a	n/a	n/a	n/a

Note: Figures are the number of days the AQI value exceeded 100 in a given year. An AQI value greater than 100 indicates that air quality would have been in the unhealthful range on that day. Data from exceptional events are included. These counts are presented in two ways. First, the counts are based on sites having an adequate record of monitoring data during the trend period (trend sites). These counts represent the relative change in the number of days with AQI values greater than 100. In the last column, the counts are based on all sites with data in the most recent year (because it is possible for a site to have data in the most recent year but not enough data to be a trend site); (1) Data covers the Savannah, GA—see Appendix B for areas included; n/a not available.
Source: U.S. Environmental Protection Agency, Air Quality Index Information, "Number of Days with Air Quality Index Values Greater than 100 at Trend Sites, 2000-2010, and at All Sites in 2010"

Maximum Air Pollutant Concentrations: Particulate Matter, Ozone, CO and Lead

	Particulate Matter 10 (ug/m³)	Particulate Matter 2.5 Wtd AM (ug/m³)	Particulate Matter 2.5 24-Hr (ug/m³)	Ozone (ppm)	Carbon Monoxide (ppm)	Lead (ug/m³)
MSA[1] Level	33	10.5	24	0.065	n/a	n/a
NAAQS[2]	150	15	35	0.075	9	0.15
Met NAAQS[2]	Yes	Yes	Yes	Yes	n/a	n/a

Note: Data from exceptional events are not included; (1) Data covers the Savannah, GA—see Appendix B for areas included; (2) National Ambient Air Quality Standards; ppm = parts per million; ug/m³ = micrograms per cubic meter; n/a not available
Concentrations: Particulate Matter 10 (coarse particulate)—highest second maximum 24-hour concentration; Particulate Matter 2.5 Wtd AM (fine particulate)—highest weighted annual mean concentration; Particulate Matter 2.5 24-Hour (fine particulate)—highest 98th percentile 24-hour concentration; Ozone—highest fourth daily maximum 8-hour concentration; Carbon Monoxide—highest second maximum non-overlapping 8-hour concentration; Lead—maximum running 3-month average
Source: U.S. Environmental Protection Agency, CBSA Factbook 2010, Air Quality Statistics by City, 2010

Maximum Air Pollutant Concentrations: Nitrogen Dioxide and Sulfur Dioxide

	Nitrogen Dioxide AM (ppb)	Nitrogen Dioxide 1-Hr (ppb)	Sulfur Dioxide AM (ppb)	Sulfur Dioxide 1-Hr (ppb)	Sulfur Dioxide 24-Hr (ppb)
MSA[1] Level	n/a	n/a	3.42	83	33.2
NAAQS[2]	53	100	30	75	140
Met NAAQS[2]	n/a	n/a	Yes	No	Yes

Note: Data from exceptional events are not included; (1) Data covers the Savannah, GA—see Appendix B for areas included; (2) National Ambient Air Quality Standards; ppb = parts per billion; n/a not available
Concentrations: Nitrogen Dioxide AM—highest arithmetic mean concentration; Nitrogen Dioxide 1-Hr—highest 98th percentile 1-hour daily maximum concentration; Sulfur Dioxide AM—highest annual mean concentration; Sulfur Dioxide 1-Hr—highest 99th percentile 1-hour daily maximum concentration; Sulfur Dioxide 24-Hr—highest second maximum 24-hour concentration
Source: U.S. Environmental Protection Agency, CBSA Factbook 2010, Air Quality Statistics by City, 2010

Drinking Water

Water System Name	Pop. Served	Primary Water Source Type	Violations[1] Health Based	Violations[1] Monitoring/ Reporting
Savannah-Main	163,688	Ground	0	1

Note: (1) Based on violation data from January 1, 2011 to December 31, 2011 (includes unresolved violations from earlier years)
Source: U.S. Environmental Protection Agency, Office of Ground Water and Drinking Water, Safe Drinking Water Information System (based on data extracted April 18, 2012)

Tampa, Florida

Background

Although Tampa was visited by Spanish explorers, such as Ponce de Leon and Hernando de Soto as early as 1521, this city, located on the mouth of the Hillsborough River on Tampa Bay, did not see significant growth until the mid-nineteenth century.

Like many cities in northern Florida such as Jacksonville, Tampa was a fort during the Seminole War, and during the Civil War it was captured by the Union Army. Later, Tampa enjoyed prosperity and development when the railroad transported tourists from up north to enjoy the warmth and sunshine of Florida.

Two historical events in the late nineteenth century set Tampa apart from other Florida cities. First, Tampa played a significant role during the Spanish-American War in 1898 as a chief port of embarkation for American troops to Cuba. During that time, Colonel Theodore Roosevelt occupied a Tampa hotel as his military headquarters. Second, a cigar factory in nearby Ybor City, named after owner Vicente Martinez Ybor, was the site where Jose Marti (the George Washington of Cuba) exhorted workers to take up arms against the tyranny of Spanish rule in the late 1800s.

Today, Tampa enjoys its role as a U.S. port and is host to many cruise ships. Major industries in and around Tampa include services, retail trade, government and finance, insurance and real estate. Like most of Florida, its economy is also heavily based on tourism. Significant employers include the Hillsborough County School District, WellCare Health Plan, Raymond James Financial, the University of South Florida, Hillsborough County Government, and MacDill Air Force Base. It is also home to servers at Wikipedia, the online encyclopedia.

The city boasts NFL's Tampa Bay Buccaneers, the Devil Rays baseball team, and the NHL's Lightning. Other attractions include Florida's Latin Quarter known as Ybor City (a National Historic Landmark District), Busch Gardens, and a Museum of Science and Industry. MacDill Air Force Base also hosts a popular air show every year. Tampa will host the 2012 Republican National Convention.

Tampa has received high marks in various surveys throughout the years, including being top cleanest and outdoor cities, as well as the best place for 20-somethings.

Winters are mild, while summers are long, warm, and humid. Freezing temperatures occur on one or two mornings per year during November through March. A dramatic feature of the Tampa climate is the summer thunderstorm season. Most occur during the late afternoon, sometimes causing temperatures to drop dramatically. The area is vulnerable to tidal surges, as the land has an elevation of less than 15 feet above sea level. The city has not experienced a direct hit from a hurricane since the 1930s.

Rankings

General Rankings

- The Tampa metro area was identified as one of the 10 most popular big cities by Pew Research Center. The results are based on a telephone survey of 2,260 adults conducted during October 2008. The report explored a range of attitudes related to where Americans live, where they would like to live, and why. *Pew Research Center, "For Nearly Half of America, Grass is Greener Somewhere Else," January 29, 2009*

- *Men's Health Living* ranked 100 U.S. cities in terms of quality of life. Tampa was ranked #72 and received a grade of D+. Criteria: number of fitness facilities; air quality; number of physicians; male/female ratio; education levels; household income; cost of living. *Men's Health Living, Spring 2008*

- Tampa was selected as one of America's best cities by *Bloomberg Businessweek*. The city ranked #47 out of 50. Criteria: number of restaurants, bars and museums per capita; number of colleges, libraries, and professional sports teams; income, poverty, unemployment, crime, and foreclosure rates; percent of population with bachelor's degrees; public school performance; park acres per capita; air quality. *BusinessWeek, "America's 50 Best Cities," September 20, 2011*

Business/Finance Rankings

- The Tampa metro area was identified as one of five places with the worst wage growth in America. The area ranked #3. Criteria: private-sector wage growth between the 4th quarter of 2010 and the 4th quarter of 2011. *PayScale, "Five Worst Cities for Wage Growth," January 12, 2012*

- Experian ranked the top 20 major U.S. metropolitan areas by average debt per consumer. The Tampa metro area was ranked #8. Criteria: average debt per consumer. Debt for this study includes credit cards, auto loans and personal loans. It does not include mortgages. *Experian, May 13, 2010*

- Tampa was identified as one of America's most coupon-loving cities by *Coupons.com*. The city ranked #2 out of 25. Criteria: online coupon usage. *Coupons.com, "Top 25 Most Frugal Cities of 2011," February 23, 2012*

- Tampa was cited as one of America's top metros for new and expanded facility projects in 2011. The area ranked #10 in the large metro area category (population over 1 million). *Site Selection, "2011 Top Metros," March 2012*

- Tampa was identified as one of the "Happiest Cities to Work in 2012" by *CareerBliss.com*, an online community for career advancement. The city ranked #20 out of 50. Criteria: independent company reviews from employees all over the country on: relationship with their boss and co-workers; work environment; job resources; growth opportunities; compensation; company culture; company reputation; daily tasks; job control over work performed on a daily basis. *CareerBliss.com, "Happiest and Unhappiest Cities to Work in 2012"*

- *American City Business Journals* ranked America's 261 largest cities in terms of their resident's wealth. Tampa ranked #81. Criteria: per capita income; median household income; percentage of households with annual incomes of $200,000 or more; median home value. *American City Business Journals, "Where the Money Is: America's Wealth Centers," August 18, 2008*

- The Tampa metro area appeared on the Milken Institute "2011 Best Performing Metros" list. Rank: #153 out of 200 large metro areas. Criteria: job growth; wage and salary growth; high-tech output growth. *Milken Institute, "2011 Best Performing Metros"*

- Tampa was ranked #98 out of 145 regions worldwide in terms of its "Knowledge Competitiveness Index." The index attempts to measure the knowledge-based development taking place throughout the world and is based on 19 measures of economic performance that indicate a region's ability to translate its knowledge capacity into economic value. *Centre for International Competitiveness, World Knowledge Competitiveness Index 2008*

- *Forbes* ranked the 200 most populous metro areas in the U.S. in terms of the "Best Places for Business and Careers." The Tampa metro area was ranked #74. Criteria: costs (business and living); job growth (past and projected); income growth; educational attainment; projected economic growth; crime; cultural and recreational opportunities; net migration patterns; number of highly ranked colleges. *Forbes, "Best Places for Business and Careers," June 2011*

Children/Family Rankings

- Underwriters Laboratories (UL), in partnership with Sperling's BestPlaces, ranked the 50 largest cities in the U.S. in terms of the safest for families with young children. Each city was measured on 25 criteria encompassing child-focused, safety-oriented behaviors and regulatory best practices. The study filtered out cities with the highest crime rates and considered air quality, incidence of child pedestrian accidents, injuries and drowning. The study also focused on accessibility to hospitals; response time for fire and police personnel; and laws, codes and regulations that address smoking, home inspections, smoke and carbon monoxide alarms, pool safety and bike helmets. The top 10 cities had the highest frequency or values in these categories. *Underwriters Laboratories, "Safest Cities for Families with Young Children," September 29, 2010*

- The Tampa metro area was selected as one of the "Best Cities for Relocating Families" by Worldwide ERC and Primacy Relocation. The 2008 study looked at nearly 50 factors important to relocating families including: recent job growth; nearby top-ranked colleges; in-state tuition for four-year public colleges; population growth since 2000; pediatricians per 100,000 population; and a Green Living index. *Worldwide ERC and Primacy Relocation, "2008 Best Cities for Relocating Families"*

- Tampa was chosen as one of America's "100 Best Communities for Young People." The winners were selected based upon detailed information provided about each community's efforts to fulfill five essential promises critical to the well-being of young people: caring adults who are actively involved in their lives; safe places in which to learn and grow; a healthy start toward adulthood; an effective education that builds marketable skills; and opportunities to help others. *America's Promise Alliance, "100 Best Communities for Young People, 2010"*

Culture/Performing Arts Rankings

- Tampa was selected as one of "America's Top 25 Arts Destinations." The city ranked #11 in the mid-sized city (population 100,000 to 499,999) category. Criteria: readers' top choices for arts travel destinations based on the richness and variety of visual arts sites, activities and events. *American Style, "America's Top 25 Arts Destinations," May 2010*

Dating/Romance Rankings

- Tampa appeared on *Men's Health's* list of the most sex-happy cities in America. The city ranked #83 of 100. Criteria: condom sales; birth rates; sex toy sales; rates of chlamydia, gonorrhea, and syphilis. *Men's Health, "America's Most Sex-Happy Cities," October 2010*

- *Men's Health* ranked 100 U.S. cities in terms of best (and worst) marriages. Tampa was ranked #12 (#1 = worst). Criteria: rate of failed marriages; stringency of divorce laws; percentage of population who've split; number of licensed marriage and family therapists. *Men's Health, "Splitsville, USA," May 2010*

- Eli Lily and Company, in partnership with Sperling's BestPlaces, ranked the nation's 50 largest metro areas in terms of the "Most Romantic Cities for Baby Boomers." The Tampa metro area ranked #44. Criteria: marriage and divorce rates among baby boomers age 45 to 60; great restaurants; dance studios; chocolate, jewelry and flower sales. *Eli Lily and Company, "Most Romantic Cities for Baby Boomers," April 20, 2007*

- The Tampa metro area was selected as one of the "Best Cities for Relocating Singles" by Worldwide ERC and Primacy Relocation. The area ranked #11 out of the 100 largest metro areas in the U.S. Criteria: recent job growth; recent singles population growth; overall population growth; affordable rental housing; cost-of-living index; expanded arts and recreation opportunities; ratio of single men and single women; affordability of quality higher education (including state residency requirements); diversity index; climate; population density. *Worldwide ERC and Primacy Relocation, "2008 Best Cities for Relocating Singles"*

- *Forbes* ranked the 40 most populous urbanized areas in the U.S. in terms of the "Best Cities for Singles." The Tampa metro area ranked #33. Criteria: number of singles; cost of living alone; nightlife; culture; job growth; coolness; and online dating participation. *Forbes.com, "Best Cities for Singles," July 27, 2009*

Education Rankings

- *Men's Health* ranked 100 U.S. cities in terms of their education levels. Tampa was ranked #51 (#1 = most educated city). Criteria: high school graduation rates; school enrollment; educational attainment; number of households who have outstanding student loans; number of households whose members have taken adult-education courses. *Men's Health, "Where School Is In: The Most and Least Educated Cities," September 12, 2011*

- Tampa was selected as one of "America's Most Literate Cities." The city ranked #25 out of the 75 largest U.S. cities. Criteria: number of booksellers; library resources; Internet resources; educational attainment; periodical publishing resources; newspaper circulation. *Central Connecticut State University, "America's Most Literate Cities 2011"*

- Tampa was identified as one of the 100 "smartest" metro areas in the U.S. The area ranked #64. Criteria: the editors rated the collective brainpower of the 100 largest metro areas in the U.S. based on their residents' educational attainment. *American City Business Journals, April 14, 2008*

- Tampa was identified as one of "America's Brainiest Bastions" by *Portfolio.com*. The metro area ranked #134 out of 200. *Portfolio.com* analyzed levels of educational attainment in the nation's 200 largest metropolitan areas. The editors established scores for five levels of educational attainment, based on relative earning power of adult workers age 25 or older. Scores were determined by comparing the median income for all workers with the median income for those workers at a specified educational level. *Portfolio.com, "America's Brainiest Bastions," December 1, 2010*

Environmental Rankings

- Tampa was selected as one of 22 "Smarter Cities" for energy by the Natural Resources Defense Council. Criteria: investment in green power; energy efficiency measures; conservation. *Natural Resources Defense Council, "2010 Smarter Cities," July 19, 2010*

- *American City Business Journal* ranked 43 metropolitan areas in terms of their "greenness." The Tampa metro area ranked #41. Criteria: Forty-one metros in which *ACBJ* has business weeklies, plus Indianapolis and Cleveland, were ranked based on 20 different indicators such as adoption of green technologies, utilization of environmentally sound practices, and air and water quality. *American City Business Journals, "Green City Index," March 11, 2010*

- 100 of the largest metro areas in the U.S. were analyzed in terms of their current drought severity. The Tampa metro area ranked #16 (#1 = driest). The rankings were based on statistics such as long-term precipitation trends and patterns and the Palmer drought indices. *Sperling's BestPlaces, www.BestPlaces.net, "America's Drought-Riskiest Cities," November 2007*

- The Tampa metro area appeared in *Country Home's* "Best Green Places" report. The area ranked #176 out of 379. Criteria: official energy policies; green power; green buildings; availability of fresh, locally grown food. *Country Home, "Best Green Places," 2008*

Health/Fitness Rankings

- Tampa was selected as one of the 25 fattest cities in America by *Men's Fitness Online*. It ranked #5 out of America's 50 largest cities. Criteria: fitness centers and sport stores; nutrition; sports participation; TV viewing; overweight/sedentary; junk food; air quality; geography; commute; parks and open space; city recreational facilities; access to healthcare; motivation; mayor and city initiatives; state obesity initiatives. *Men's Fitness, "The Fittest and Fattest Cities in America," March 5, 2012*

- Tampa was identified as a "2011 Asthma Capital." The area ranked #86 out of the nation's 100 largest metropolitan areas. Twelve factors were used to identify the most challenging places to live for people with asthma: estimated prevalence; self-reported prevalence; crude death rate for asthma; annual pollen score; annual air quality; public smoking laws; number of board-certified asthma specialists; school inhaler access laws; rescue medication use; controller medication use; uninsured rate; poverty rate. *Asthma and Allergy Foundation of America, "2011 Asthma Capitals"*

- Tampa was identified as a "2011 Fall Allergy Capital." The area ranked #66 out of 100. Three groups of factors were used to identify the most severe cities for people with allergies during the fall season: annual pollen levels; medicine utilization; access to board-certified allergists. *Asthma and Allergy Foundation of America, "2011 Fall Allergy Capitals"*

- Tampa was identified as a "2012 Spring Allergy Capital." The area ranked #65 out of 100. Three groups of factors were used to identify the most severe cities for people with allergies during the spring season: annual pollen levels; medicine utilization; access to board-certified allergists. *Asthma and Allergy Foundation of America, "2012 Spring Allergy Capitals"*

- *Men's Health* examined 100 major U.S. cities and selected the best and worst cities for men. Tampa ranked #82. Criteria: 35 statistical parameters of long life in the categories of health, quality of life, and fitness. *Men's Health, "The 10 Best and Worst Cities for Men 2012," January/February 2012*

- The makers of Breath Right Nasal Strips, in partnership with Sperling's BestPlaces, analyzed 50 metro areas and identified those U.S. cities most challenged by chronic nasal congestion. The Tampa metro area ranked #19. Criteria: tree, grass and weed pollens; molds and spores; air pollution; climate; smoking; purchase habits of congestion products; prescriptions of drugs for congestion relief; incidence of influenza. *Breathe Right Nasal Strips, "Most Congested Cities," October 3, 2011*

- The American Academy of Dermatology ranked 26 U.S. metropolitan regions in terms of their residents knowledge, attitude and behaviors towards tanning, sun protection and skin cancer detection. The Tampa metro area ranked #4. The results of the study are based on an online survey of over 7,000 adults nationwide. *American Academy of Dermatology, "Suntelligence: How Sun Smart is Your City," May 3, 2010*

- The Tampa metro area appeared in the 2011 Gallup-Healthways Well-Being Index. The index, based on interviews with more than 350,000 Americans, measured jobs, finances, physical health, emotional state of mind and communities. The metro area ranked #139 out of 190. Criteria: life evaluation; emotional health; work environment; physical health; healthy behaviors; basic access (basic needs optimal for a healthy life, such as access to food and medicine, having health insurance and feeling safe while walking at night). *Gallup-Healthways, "State of Well-Being 2011"*

- The Tampa metro area was identified as one of "America's Most Stressful Cities" by *Sperling's BestPlaces.* The metro area ranked #1 out of 50. Criteria: unemployment rate; suicide rate; commute time; mental health; poor rest; alcohol use; violent crime rate; property crime rate; cloudy days annually. *Sperling's BestPlaces, www.BestPlaces.net, "Stressful Cities 2012*

- *Men's Health* ranked 100 U.S. cities in terms of their activity levels. Tampa was ranked #67 (#1 = most active city). Criteria: where and how often residents exercise; percentage of households that watch more than 15 hours of cable television a week and buy more than 11 video games a year; death rate from deep-vein thrombosis, a condition linked to sitting for extended periods of time. *Men's Health, "Where Sit Happens: The Most and Least Active Cities in America," June 20, 2011*

- 50 of the largest metro areas in the U.S. were analyzed in terms of their health and fitness by the American College of Sports Medicine in their "American Fitness Index." The Tampa metro area ranked #30 (#1 = healthiest). Criteria: preventative health behaviors; levels of chronic disease; health care access; community resources and policies that support physical activity. *American College of Sports Medicine, "Health and Community Fitness Status of the 50 Largest Metropolitan Areas," August 1, 2011*

- Tampa was selected as one of the "20 Most Livable U.S. Cities for Wheelchair Users" by the Christopher & Dana Reeve Foundation. The city ranked #12. Criteria: Medicaid eligibility and spending; access to physicians and rehabilitation facilities; access to fitness facilities and recreation; access to paratransit; percentage of people living with disabilities who are employed; clean air; climate. *Christopher & Dana Reeve Foundation, "20 Most Livable U.S. Cities for Wheelchair Users," July 26, 2010*

- *The Daily Beast* identified the 30 U.S. metro areas with the worst smoking habits. The Tampa metro area ranked #19. Sixty urban centers with populations of more than one million were ranked based on the following criteria: number of smokers; number of cigarettes smoked per day; fewest attempts to quit. *The Daily Beast, "30 Cities With Smoking Problems," January 3, 2011*

Pet Rankings

- Tampa was selected as one of the "Top 10 Cat-Friendly Cities" in the U.S. The area ranked #1. Criteria: cat ownership per capita; level of veterinary care; microchipping; cat-friendly local ordinances. *CATalyst Council, "Top 10 Cat-Friendly Cities," March 27, 2009*

Real Estate Rankings

- Tampa was identified as one of the best cities for home buyers in the U.S. The area ranked #5 out of 10. The affordability of home ownership was calculated by comparing the cost of renting vs. owning. Criteria: cost to rent as a percent of after-tax mortgage payment. *Fortune, "The 10 Best Cities for Buyers," April 11, 2011*

- *Fortune* ranked the 100 largest metro areas in the U.S. in terms of projected median home price change in 2010. The Tampa metro area ranked #94. *Fortune, "The 2010 Housing Outlook," December 9, 2009*

- The Tampa metro area was identified as one of the 25 best housing markets in the U.S. in 2011. The area ranked #14 out of 149 markets with a home price appreciation of 3.0%. Criteria: year-over-year change of median sales price of existing single-family homes between the 4th quarter of 2010 and the 4th quarter of 2011. *National Association of Realtors®, Median Sales Price of Existing Single-Family Homes for Metropolitan Areas, 4th Quarter 2011*

- The Tampa metro area was identified as one of the 10 worst condo markets in the U.S. in 2011. The area ranked #2 out of 54 markets with a price appreciation of -23.8%. Criteria: year-over-year change of median sales price of existing apartment condo-coop homes between the 4th quarter of 2010 and the 4th quarter of 2011. *National Association of Realtors®, Median Sales Price of Existing Apartment Condo-Coop Homes for Metropolitan Areas, 4th Quarter 2011*

- Tampa appeared on *ApartmentRatings.com* "Top Cities for Renters" list in 2009." The area ranked #79. Overall satisfaction ratings were ranked using thousands of user submitted scores for hundreds of apartment complexes located in the 100 most populated U.S. municipalities. *ApartmentRatings.com, "2009 Renter Satisfaction Rankings"*

- Tampa appeared on *ApartmentRatings.com* "Top College Towns & Cities" for renters list in 2011." The area ranked #71 out of 87. Overall satisfaction ratings were ranked using thousands of user submitted scores for hundreds of apartment complexes located in cities and towns that are home to the 100 largest four-year institutions in the U.S. *ApartmentRatings.com, "2011 College Town Renter Satisfaction Rankings"*

- The Tampa metro area was identified as one of "America's 25 Weakest Housing Markets" by *Forbes*. The metro area ranked #14. Criteria: metro areas with populations over 500,000 were ranked based on projected home values through 2011. *Forbes.com, "America's 25 Weakest Housing Markets," January 7, 2009*

- The Tampa metro area appeared in a *Wall Street Journal* article ranking cities by "housing stress." The metro area was ranked #7 (#1 = most stress). Criteria: fraction of mortgage-holding homeowners with a monthly housing payment in excess of 30 percent of income; percentage of people without health insurance; unemployment rate. *The Wall Street Journal, "Which Cities Face Biggest Housing Risk," October 5, 2010*

- The Center for Housing Policy ranked 210 U.S. metropolitan areas by the fair market rent for a two-bedroom unit. The Tampa metro area was ranked #63. (#1 = most expensive) with a rent of $959. Criteria: Fair Market Rent (FMR) in effect during the fourth quarter of 2009 based on HUD's fiscal year 2010 FMRs. *The Center for Housing Policy, "Paycheck to Paycheck: Most to Least Expensive Rental Markets in 2009"*

- The Tampa metro area was identified as one of the markets with the worst expected performance in home prices over the next 12 months. *Local Market Monitor, "First Quarter Home Price Forecast for Largest US Markets," March 2, 2011*

- The Tampa metro area was identified as one of the best U.S. markets to invest in rental property" by HomeVestors and Local Market Monitor. The area ranked #11 out of 100. Criteria: risk-return premium relative to national average. *HomeVestors and Local Market Monitor, "Best 100 U.S. Markets to Invest in Rental Property," March 9, 2012*

Safety Rankings

- Allstate ranked the 193 largest cities in America in terms of driver safety. Tampa ranked #176. In addition, drivers were 41.7% more likely to have had an accident compared to the national average. Allstate researchers analyzed internal property damage reported claims over a two-year period (from January 2008 to December 2009) to protect findings from external influences such as weather or road construction. A weighted average of the two-year numbers determined the annual percentages. The report defines an auto crash as any collision resulting in a property damage claim. *Allstate, "2011 Allstate America's Best Drivers Report™"*

- Sperling's BestPlaces analyzed the tracks of tropical storms for the past 100 years and ranked which areas are most likely to be hit by a major hurricane. The Tampa metro area ranked #4 out of 10. *Sperling's BestPlaces, www.bestplaces.net, February 2, 2006*

- The National Insurance Crime Bureau ranked 366 metro areas in the U.S. in terms of per capita rates of vehicle theft. The Tampa metro area ranked #129 (#1 = highest rate). Criteria: number of vehicle theft offenses per 100,000 inhabitants in 2010. *National Insurance Crime Bureau, "Hot Spots," June 21, 2011*

- The Tampa metro area was identified as one of the most dangerous metro areas for pedestrians by Transportation for America. The metro area ranked #2 out of 52 metro areas with over 1 million residents. Criteria: area's population divided by the number of pedestrian fatalities in that area. *Transportation for America, "Dangerous by Design 2011"*

Seniors/Retirement Rankings

- Bankers Life and Casualty Company, in partnership with Sperling's BestPlaces, ranked the nation's 50 largest metro areas in terms of the "Best U.S. Cities for Seniors." The Tampa metro area ranked #44. Criteria: healthcare; transportation; housing; environment; economy; health and longevity; social and spiritual life; crime. *Bankers Life and Casualty Company, Center for a Secure Retirement, "Best U.S. Cities for Seniors 2011," September 2011*

- Tampa was identified as one of the "100 Most Popular Retirement Towns" by *Topretirements.com* The list reflects the 100 cities (out of 815+ total cities reviewed) that visitors to the website are most interested in for retirement. *Topretirements.com, "100 Most Popular Retirement Towns," February 21, 2012*

Sports/Recreation Rankings

- Tampa appeared on the *Sporting News* list of the "Best Sports Cities" for 2011. The area ranked #10 out of 271 cities in the U.S. *Sporting News* takes a 12-month snapshot of each city's sports, putting a heavy premium on regular-season won-lost records (from the most recently completed season). Other criteria include: playoff berths, bowl appearances and tournament bids; championships; applicable power ratings; quality of competition; overall fan fervor (measured in part by attendance); abundance of teams (rewarding quality over quantity); stadium and arena quality; ticket availability and prices; franchise ownership; and marquee appeal of athletes. *Sporting News, "Best Sports Cities 2011," October 4, 2011*

- Tampa was selected as one of the five best boat cities in the U.S. The city ranked #4. Criteria: climate; scenery; fishing; boat communities with water access. *Best Boat News, "The 5 Best Boat Cities to Live In (in the U.S.)," April 16, 2010*

- Tampa was chosen as one of America's 10 best places to live and boat. Criteria: boating opportunities; boat-friendly regulations; water access; availability of waterfront homes; health of the local economy; and overall lifestyle for boaters. *Boating Magazine, "10 Best Places to Live and Boat," June 2010*

- The Tampa was selected as one of the best metro areas for golf in America by *Golf Digest*. The Tampa area was ranked #4 out of 20. Criteria: climate; cost of public golf; quality of public golf; accessibility. *Golf Digest, "The Top 20 Cities for Golf," October 2011*

Technology Rankings

- Tampa was selected as one of the best cities for broadband by Ookla, the company behind the broadband speed testing site Speedtest.net. The city ranked #6 out of 10. Criteria: U.S. cities were ranked based on their 30-day average speeds. Only cities with more than 75,000 people connecting for more than three months were measured. *Ookla, "The Top 10 Cities With the Best Broadband," May 25, 2010*

Transportation Rankings

- Tampa was identified as one of America's worst cities for speed traps by the National Motorists Association. The city ranked #7 out of 25. Criteria: speed trap locations per 100,000 residents. *National Motorists Association, September 2011*

- The Tampa metro area appeared on *Forbes* list of the best and worst cities for commuters. The metro area ranked #60 out of 60 (#1 is best). Criteria: travel time; road congestion; travel delays. *Forbes.com, "Best and Worst Cities for Commuters," February 16, 2010*

Women/Minorities Rankings

- *Women's Health* examined U.S. cities and identified the 100 best cities for women. Tampa was ranked #74. Criteria: 30 categories were examined from obesity and breast cancer rates to commuting times and hours spent working out. *Women's Health, "Best Cities for Women 2012"*

- Tampa was ranked #71 out of 100 metro areas in *SELF Magazine's* ranking of America's healthiest places for women." A panel of experts came up with more than 50 criteria including death and disease rates, environmental indicators, community resources, and lifestyle habits. *SELF Magazine, "Secrets of America's Healthiest Women," December 2008*

- The Tampa metro area appeared on *Forbes'* list of the "Best Cities for Minority Entrepreneurs." The area ranked #71 out of 10. Criteria: 52 metropolitan statistical areas were examined. For each ethnicity (African Americans, Asians and Hispanics), the editors measured housing affordability, population growth, income growth, and entrepreneurship (per capita self-employment). *Forbes, "Best Cities for Minority Entrepreneurs," March 23, 2011*

Miscellaneous Rankings

- *Men's Health* ranked 100 U.S. cities by their level of sadness. Tampa was ranked #97 (#1 = saddest city). Criteria: suicide rates; unemployment rates; percentage of households that use antidepressants; percent of population who report feeling blue all or most of the time. *Men's Health, "Frown Towns," November 28, 2011*

- Energizer Holdings, the makers of Edge® shave gel, in partnership with Sperling's BestPlaces, ranked 50 major metro areas in terms of everyday irritations. The Tampa metro area ranked #7. Criteria: humidity levels; weather conditions; incidence of traffic delays and congestion; average commute times; frequency of flight delays and cancellations; rates of sleeplessness; underemployment; pollens and allergens; pests; comedy clubs per capita. *Energizer Holdings, "Most Irritation Prone Cities," July 23, 2010*

- Mars Chocolate North America, the makers of COMBOS®, in partnership with Sperling's BestPlaces, ranked 50 major metro areas in terms of their "manliness." The Tampa metro area ranked #39. Criteria: number of professional sports teams; number of nearby NASCAR tracks and racing events; manly lifestyle; concentration of manly retail stores; manly occupations per capita; salty snack sales; "Board of Manliness" rankings. *Mars Chocolate North America, "America's Manliest Cities 2011," September 1, 2011*

- Tampa appeared on Procter & Gamble's list of the "Top-20 All-Time Sweatiest Cities." The city was ranked #9. The rankings are based on computer simulations of the amount of sweat a person of average height and weight would produce walking around for an hour in the average temperatures during the summer months, based on historical weather data during June, July and August from 2001-2008 for each city. *Procter & Gamble, Old Spice Press Release, "Top-20 All-Time Sweatiest Cities," July 1, 2009*

Business Environment

CITY FINANCES

City Government Finances

Component	2009 ($000)	2009 ($ per capita)
Total Revenues	561,744	1,668
Total Expenditures	744,870	2,211
Debt Outstanding	1,536,299	4,561
Cash and Securities[1]	2,740,873	8,137

Note: (1) Cash and security holdings of a government at the close of its fiscal year, including those of its dependent agencies, utilities, and liquor stores.
Source: U.S Census Bureau, State & Local Government Finances 2009

City Government Revenue by Source

Source	2009 ($000)	2009 ($ per capita)
General Revenue		
From Federal Government	28,391	84
From State Government	66,454	197
From Local Governments	31,760	94
Taxes		
Property	163,637	486
Sales and Gross Receipts	115,822	344
Personal Income	0	0
Corporate Income	0	0
Motor Vehicle License	0	0
Other Taxes	44,099	131
Current Charges	199,077	591
Liquor Store	0	0
Utility	71,589	213
Employee Retirement	-221,856	-659

Source: U.S Census Bureau, State & Local Government Finances 2009

City Government Expenditures by Function

Function	2009 ($000)	2009 ($ per capita)	2009 (%)
General Direct Expenditures			
Air Transportation	0	0	0.0
Corrections	0	0	0.0
Education	0	0	0.0
Employment Security Administration	0	0	0.0
Financial Administration	10,328	31	1.4
Fire Protection	58,211	173	7.8
General Public Buildings	11,733	35	1.6
Governmental Administration, Other	4,695	14	0.6
Health	0	0	0.0
Highways	82,926	246	11.1
Hospitals	0	0	0.0
Housing and Community Development	27,514	82	3.7
Interest on General Debt	31,543	94	4.2
Judicial and Legal	3,336	10	0.4
Libraries	0	0	0.0
Parking	17,048	51	2.3
Parks and Recreation	39,567	117	5.3
Police Protection	139,076	413	18.7
Public Welfare	0	0	0.0
Sewerage	89,645	266	12.0
Solid Waste Management	62,072	184	8.3
Veterans' Services	0	0	0.0
Liquor Store	0	0	0.0
Utility	91,463	272	12.3
Employee Retirement	55,286	164	7.4

Source: U.S Census Bureau, State & Local Government Finances 2009

Municipal Bond Ratings

Area	Moody's	S&P	Fitch
City	Aa2	(1)	n/a

Rating Systems (shown in declining order of credit quality): Moody's– Aaa, Aa, A, Baa, Ba, B, Caa, Ca, C (numerical modifiers 1, 2, and 3 are added to letter-rating); S&P– AAA, AA, A, BBB, BB, B, CCC, CC, C; Fitch– AAA, AA, A, BBB, BB, B, CCC, CC, C. Ratings may be modified by the addition of a plus or minus sign to show relative standing within the major rating categories.

Notes: n/a Not Available; w/d Withdrawn (1) Not Reviewed; (2) Issuer Rating/No General Obligation; (3) Standard and Poor's Issue Credit Rating (ICR) is a current opinion of an obliger with respect to a specific financial obligation, a specific class of financial obligations, or a specific financial program.
Source: U.S. Census Bureau, 2012 Statistical Abstract, Bond Ratings for City Governments by Largest Cities: 2010

DEMOGRAPHICS

Population Growth

Area	1990 Census	2000 Census	2010 Census	Population Growth (%) 1990-2000	Population Growth (%) 2000-2010
City	279,960	303,447	335,709	8.4	10.6
MSA[1]	2,067,959	2,395,997	2,783,243	15.9	16.2
U.S.	248,709,873	281,421,906	308,745,538	13.2	9.7

Note: (1) Figures cover the Tampa-St. Petersburg-Clearwater, FL Metropolitan Statistical Area—see Appendix B for areas included
Source: U.S. Census Bureau, 2010 Census

Household Size

Area	One	Two	Three	Four	Five	Six	Seven or More	Average Household Size
City	33.6	30.5	15.5	11.5	5.2	2.1	1.5	2.38
MSA[1]	29.9	35.7	15.0	11.4	5.0	1.9	1.2	2.37
U.S.	26.7	32.8	16.1	13.4	6.5	2.6	1.9	2.58

Note: (1) Figures cover the Tampa-St. Petersburg-Clearwater, FL Metropolitan Statistical Area—see Appendix B for areas included
Source: U.S. Census Bureau, 2010 Census

Race

Area	White Alone[2] (%)	Black Alone[2] (%)	Asian Alone[2] (%)	AIAN[3] Alone[2] (%)	NHOPI[4] Alone[2] (%)	Other Race Alone[2] (%)	Two or More Races (%)
City	62.9	26.2	3.4	0.4	0.1	3.8	3.2
MSA[1]	78.8	11.8	2.9	0.4	0.1	3.4	2.6
U.S.	72.4	12.6	4.8	0.9	0.2	6.2	2.9

Note: (1) Figures cover the Tampa-St. Petersburg-Clearwater, FL Metropolitan Statistical Area—see Appendix B for areas included; (2) Alone is defined as not being in combination with one or more other races; (3) American Indian and Alaska Native; (4) Native Hawaiian and Other Pacific Islander
Source: U.S. Census Bureau, 2010 Census

Hispanic or Latino Origin

Area	Hispanic or Latino (%)	Mexican (%)	Puerto Rican (%)	Cuban (%)	Other Hispanic or Latino (%)
City	23.1	2.9	7.2	6.3	6.7
MSA[1]	16.2	3.6	5.2	2.9	4.5
U.S.	16.3	10.3	1.5	0.6	4.0

Note: Persons of Hispanic or Latino origin can be of any race; (1) Figures cover the Tampa-St. Petersburg-Clearwater, FL Metropolitan Statistical Area—see Appendix B for areas included
Source: U.S. Census Bureau, 2010 Census

Segregation

Type	Segregation Indices[1]				Percent Change		
	1990	2000	2010	2010 Rank[2]	1990-2000	1990-2010	2000-2010
Black/White	69.7	64.6	56.2	50	-5.1	-13.5	-8.3
Asian/White	33.8	35.4	35.3	78	1.6	1.5	-0.1
Hispanic/White	45.3	44.4	40.7	62	-0.9	-4.6	-3.7

Note: Figures are based on an analysis of 1990, 2000, and 2010 Census Decennial Census tract data by William H. Frey, Brookings Institution and the University of Michigan Social Science Data Analysis Network. In this analysis all racial groups (whites, blacks, and asians) are non-Hispanic members of those races. Hispanics are shown as a separate category; All figures cover the Metropolitan Statistical Area (see Appendix B for areas included); (1) Segregation Indices are Dissimilarity Indices that measure the degree to which the minority group is distributed differently than whites across census tracts. They range from 0 (complete integration) to 100 (complete segregation) where the value indicates the percentage of the minority group that needs to move to be distributed exactly like whites; (2) Ranges from 1 (most segregated) to 102 (least segregated); n/a not available.
Source: www.CensusScope.org

Ancestry

Area	German	Irish	English	American	Italian	Polish	French[2]	Scottish	Dutch
City	9.8	8.5	6.8	3.5	6.4	2.0	2.0	1.5	1.0
MSA[1]	15.4	13.4	10.3	6.4	8.6	3.4	3.4	2.1	1.4
U.S.	16.1	11.6	8.8	6.1	5.7	3.2	3.0	1.9	1.6

Note: Figures are the percentage of the total population reporting a particular ancestry. The nine most commonly reported ancestries in the U.S. are shown. Figures include multiple ancestries (e.g. if a person reported being Irish and Italian, they were included in both columns); (1) Figures cover the Tampa-St. Petersburg-Clearwater, FL Metropolitan Statistical Area—see Appendix B for areas included; (2) Excludes Basque
Source: U.S. Census Bureau, 2008-2010 American Community Survey 3-Year Estimates

Foreign-Born Population

Area	Percent of Population Born in								
	Any Foreign Country	Mexico	Asia	Europe	Carribean	South America	Central America[2]	Africa	Canada
City	15.0	1.5	2.3	1.4	5.8	1.5	1.2	0.7	0.5
MSA[1]	12.2	1.4	2.2	2.4	3.0	1.5	0.6	0.4	0.7
U.S.	12.8	3.8	3.6	1.6	1.2	0.9	1.0	0.5	0.3

Note: (1) Figures cover the Tampa-St. Petersburg-Clearwater, FL Metropolitan Statistical Area—see Appendix B for areas included; (2) Excludes Mexico.
Source: U.S. Census Bureau, 2008-2010 American Community Survey 3-Year Estimates

Marital Status

Area	Never Married	Now Married[2]	Separated	Widowed	Divorced
City	39.7	37.4	3.5	5.1	14.3
MSA[1]	29.0	47.1	2.4	7.5	14.0
U.S.	31.6	49.6	2.2	6.1	10.7

Note: Figures are percentages and cover the population 15 years of age and older; (1) Figures cover the Tampa-St. Petersburg-Clearwater, FL Metropolitan Statistical Area—see Appendix B for areas included; (2) Excludes separated
Source: U.S. Census Bureau, 2008-2010 American Community Survey 3-Year Estimates

Age

Area	Percent of Population							Median Age
	Under Age 5	Age 5 to 17	Age 18 to 34	Age 35 to 49	Age 50 to 64	Age 65 to 79	80 Years and Over	
City	6.4	16.2	27.9	21.4	17.2	7.9	3.1	34.6
MSA[1]	5.6	15.6	20.8	20.7	20.1	12.2	5.1	41.2
U.S.	6.5	17.5	23.2	20.7	19.0	9.4	3.6	37.2

Note: (1) Figures cover the Tampa-St. Petersburg-Clearwater, FL Metropolitan Statistical Area—see Appendix B for areas included
Source: U.S. Census Bureau, 2010 Census

Male/Female Ratio

Area	Males	Females	Males per 100 Females
City	164,061	171,648	95.6
MSA[1]	1,347,513	1,435,730	93.9
U.S.	151,781,326	156,964,212	96.7

Note: (1) Figures cover the Tampa-St. Petersburg-Clearwater, FL Metropolitan Statistical Area—see Appendix B for areas included
Source: U.S. Census Bureau, 2010 Census

Religious Groups

Area	Catholic	Baptist	Non-Den.	Methodist[2]	Lutheran	LDS[3]	Pente-costal	Presby-terian[4]	Muslim[5]	Judaism
MSA[1]	10.9	7.1	3.8	3.5	1.0	0.6	2.1	1.0	0.5	1.3
U.S.	19.1	9.3	4.0	4.0	2.3	2.0	1.9	1.6	0.8	0.7

Note: Figures are the number of adherents as a percentage of the total population; (1) Figures cover the Tampa-St. Petersburg-Clearwater, FL Metropolitan Statistical Area—see Appendix B for areas included; (2) Methodist/Pietist; (3) Latter Day Saints; (4) Reformed; (5) Figures are estimates
Source: Association of Statisticians of American Religious Bodies, 2010 U.S. Religion Census: Religious Congregations & Membership Study

ECONOMY

Gross Metropolitan Product

Area	2007	2008	2009	2010	2010 Rank[2]
MSA[1]	114.1	112.6	111.9	113.9	24

Note: Figures are in billions of dollars; (1) Figures cover the Tampa-St. Petersburg-Clearwater, FL Metropolitan Statistical Area—see Appendix B for areas included; (2) Rank ranges from 1 to 363
Source: The United States Conference of Mayors, "U.S. Metro Economies: GMP and Employment Forecasts," June 2011

Economic Growth

Area	2007-2009 (%)	2010 (%)	2011 (%)	Rank[2]
MSA[1]	-2.7	1.0	1.9	255
U.S.	-1.3	2.9	2.5	–

Note: Figures are real Gross Metropolitan Product growth rates and represent annual average percent change; (1) Figures cover the Tampa-St. Petersburg-Clearwater, FL Metropolitan Statistical Area—see Appendix B for areas included; (2) Rank ranges from 1 to 363
Source: The United States Conference of Mayors, "U.S. Metro Economies: GMP and Employment Forecasts," June 2011

Metropolitan Area Exports

Area	2005	2006	2007	2008	2009	2010	2010 Rank[2]
MSA[1]	4,423.8	4,738.5	5,711.2	7,153.5	6,463.6	6,633.6	36

Note: Figures are in millions of dollars; (1) Figures cover the Tampa-St. Petersburg-Clearwater, FL Metropolitan Statistical Area—see Appendix B for areas included; (2) Rank ranges from 1 to 369
Source: U.S. Department of Commerce, International Trade Administration, Office of Trade & Industry Information, Manufacturing & Services, data extracted April 2, 2012

INCOME

Income

Area	Per Capita ($)	Median Household ($)	Average Household ($)
City	27,186	42,359	65,617
MSA[1]	25,801	45,104	61,685
U.S.	26,942	51,222	70,116

Note: (1) Figures cover the Tampa-St. Petersburg-Clearwater, FL Metropolitan Statistical Area—see Appendix B for areas included
Source: U.S. Census Bureau, 2008-2010 American Community Survey 3-Year Estimates

Household Income Distribution

Area	Percent of Households Earning							
	Under $15,000	$15,000 -24,999	$25,000 -34,999	$35,000 -49,999	$50,000 -74,999	$75,000 -99,000	$100,000 -149,999	$150,000 and up
City	17.3	13.1	11.5	15.1	16.1	9.1	9.0	8.8
MSA[1]	13.2	13.0	12.2	16.2	18.8	10.9	9.5	6.1
U.S.	13.0	11.0	10.6	14.2	18.5	12.1	12.2	8.4

Note: (1) Figures cover the Tampa-St. Petersburg-Clearwater, FL Metropolitan Statistical Area—see Appendix B for areas included
Source: U.S. Census Bureau, 2008-2010 American Community Survey 3-Year Estimates

Poverty Rate

Area	All Ages	Under 18 Years Old	18 to 64 Years Old	65 Years and Over
City	19.9	30.4	16.9	15.1
MSA[1]	14.1	20.4	13.4	8.8
U.S.	14.4	20.1	13.1	9.4

Note: Figures are percentage of people whose income during the past 12 months was below the poverty level; (1) Figures cover the Tampa-St. Petersburg-Clearwater, FL Metropolitan Statistical Area—see Appendix B for areas included
Source: U.S. Census Bureau, 2008-2010 American Community Survey 3-Year Estimates

Personal Bankruptcy Filing Rate

Area	2006	2007	2008	2009	2010	2011
Hillsborough County	1.80	2.76	4.09	5.55	6.26	4.92
U.S.	2.00	2.73	3.53	4.61	4.97	4.37

Note: Numbers are per 1,000 population and include Chapter 7 and Chapter 13 filings
Source: Federal Deposit Insurance Corporation, Regional Economic Conditions, March 9, 2012

EMPLOYMENT

Labor Force and Employment

Area	Civilian Labor Force			Workers Employed		
	Dec. 2010	Dec. 2011	% Chg.	Dec. 2010	Dec. 2011	% Chg.
City	162,264	163,252	0.6	143,133	147,016	2.7
MSA[1]	1,298,265	1,301,885	0.3	1,140,498	1,171,437	2.7
U.S.	153,156,000	153,373,000	0.1	139,159,000	140,681,000	1.1

Note: Data is not seasonally adjusted and covers workers 16 years of age and older; (1) Metropolitan Statistical Area—see Appendix B for areas included
Source: Bureau of Labor Statistics, http://stats.bls.gov

Unemployment Rate

Area	2011											
	Jan.	Feb.	Mar.	Apr.	May	Jun.	Jul.	Aug.	Sep.	Oct.	Nov.	Dec.
City	12.2	11.3	11.0	10.5	10.7	11.3	11.3	11.0	10.8	10.2	10.2	9.9
MSA[1]	12.5	11.5	11.0	10.6	10.6	11.1	11.1	11.0	10.8	10.4	10.3	10.0
U.S.	9.8	9.5	9.2	8.7	8.7	9.3	9.3	9.1	8.8	8.5	8.2	8.3

Note: Data is not seasonally adjusted and covers workers 16 years of age and older; All figures are percentages; (1) Metropolitan Statistical Area—see Appendix B for areas included
Source: Bureau of Labor Statistics, http://stats.bls.gov

Projected Unemployment Rate

Area	2010 (%)	2011 (%)	2012 (%)	2013 (%)
MSA[1]	12.5	10.9	10.1	9.2

Note: (1) Metropolitan Statistical Area—see Appendix B for areas included
Source: The United States Conference of Mayors, "U.S. Metro Economies: GMP and Employment Forecasts," June 2011

Employment by Occupation

Occupation Classification	City (%)	MSA[1] (%)	U.S. (%)
Management, Business, Science, and Arts	37.5	35.4	35.6
Natural Resources, Construction, and Maintenance	7.4	8.8	9.5
Production, Transportation, and Material Moving	8.3	9.0	12.1
Sales and Office	28.0	29.4	25.2
Service	18.7	17.3	17.6

Note: Figures cover employed civilians 16 years of age and older; (1) Figures cover the Tampa-St. Petersburg-Clearwater, FL Metropolitan Statistical Area—see Appendix B for areas included
Source: U.S. Census Bureau, 2008-2010 American Community Survey 3-Year Estimates

Employment by Industry

Sector	MSA[1] Number of Employees	MSA[1] Percent of Total	U.S. Percent of Total
Construction	49,200	4.3	4.1
Education and Health Services	184,600	16.0	15.2
Financial Activities	92,500	8.0	5.8
Government	158,000	13.7	16.8
Information	26,000	2.3	2.0
Leisure and Hospitality	128,800	11.2	9.9
Manufacturing	59,700	5.2	8.9
Mining and Logging	500	<0.1	0.6
Other Services	44,000	3.8	4.0
Professional and Business Services	192,100	16.6	13.3
Retail Trade	146,000	12.7	11.5
Transportation and Utilities	26,200	2.3	3.8
Wholesale Trade	46,400	4.0	4.2

Note: Figures cover non-farm employment as of December 2011 and are not seasonally adjusted;
(1) Metropolitan Statistical Area—see Appendix B for areas included
Source: Bureau of Labor Statistics, http://stats.bls.gov

Occupations with Greatest Projected Employment Growth: 2008 – 2018

Occupation[1]	2008 Employment	2018 Projected Employment	Numeric Employment Change	Percent Employment Change
Registered Nurses	151,100	187,380	36,280	24.0
Combined Food Preparation and Serving Workers, Including Fast Food	162,570	186,400	23,830	14.7
Customer Service Representatives	169,080	190,780	21,700	12.8
Nursing Aides, Orderlies, and Attendants	88,630	106,860	18,230	20.6
Home Health Aides	30,480	47,860	17,380	57.0
Postsecondary Teachers	70,790	85,380	14,590	20.6
Retail Salespersons	274,490	288,660	14,170	5.2
Elementary School Teachers, Except Special Education	74,130	86,390	12,260	16.5
Stock Clerks and Order Fillers	167,450	179,420	11,970	7.1
Accountants and Auditors	86,390	97,670	11,280	13.1

Note: Projections cover Florida; (1) Sorted by numeric employment change
Source: www.projectionscentral.com, State Occupational Projections, 2008–2018 Long-Term Projections

Fastest Growing Occupations: 2008 – 2018

Occupation[1]	2008 Employment	2018 Projected Employment	Numeric Employment Change	Percent Employment Change
Biomedical Engineers	520	840	320	61.5
Home Health Aides	30,480	47,860	17,380	57.0
Medical Scientists, Except Epidemiologists	2,640	3,870	1,230	46.6
Physician Assistants	3,900	5,490	1,590	40.8
Personal and Home Care Aides	13,890	19,430	5,540	39.9
Network Systems and Data Communications Analysts	21,550	30,110	8,560	39.7
Radiation Therapists	1,270	1,730	460	36.2
Dental Hygienists	9,030	11,890	2,860	31.7
Physical Therapist Assistants	3,550	4,660	1,110	31.3
Financial Examiners	610	800	190	31.1

Note: Projections cover Florida; (1) Sorted by percent employment change and excludes occupations with numeric employment change less than 100
Source: www.projectionscentral.com, State Occupational Projections, 2008–2018 Long-Term Projections

Average Wages

Occupation	$/Hr.	Occupation	$/Hr.
Accountants and Auditors	30.06	Maids and Housekeeping Cleaners	8.98
Automotive Mechanics	17.49	Maintenance and Repair Workers	15.64
Bookkeepers	15.71	Marketing Managers	51.71
Carpenters	17.16	Nuclear Medicine Technologists	31.56
Cashiers	8.99	Nurses, Licensed Practical	20.00
Clerks, General Office	12.82	Nurses, Registered	31.80
Clerks, Receptionists/Information	12.52	Nursing Aides/Orderlies/Attendants	11.52
Clerks, Shipping/Receiving	13.17	Packers and Packagers, Hand	9.58
Computer Programmers	34.50	Physical Therapists	38.77
Computer Support Specialists	21.13	Postal Service Mail Carriers	24.78
Computer Systems Analysts	39.51	Real Estate Brokers	28.72
Cooks, Restaurant	10.45	Retail Salespersons	12.11
Dentists	89.88	Sales Reps., Exc. Tech./Scientific	28.26
Electrical Engineers	35.43	Sales Reps., Tech./Scientific	40.55
Electricians	18.16	Secretaries, Exc. Legal/Med./Exec.	14.37
Financial Managers	55.17	Security Guards	10.90
First-Line Supervisors/Managers, Sales	21.18	Surgeons	90.41
Food Preparation Workers	9.37	Teacher Assistants	10.90
General and Operations Managers	52.79	Teachers, Elementary School	26.40
Hairdressers/Cosmetologists	10.53	Teachers, Secondary School	28.10
Internists	110.77	Telemarketers	12.22
Janitors and Cleaners	10.04	Truck Drivers, Heavy/Tractor-Trailer	17.86
Landscaping/Groundskeeping Workers	10.87	Truck Drivers, Light/Delivery Svcs.	16.05
Lawyers	52.36	Waiters and Waitresses	10.07

Note: Wage data covers the Tampa-St. Petersburg-Clearwater, FL Metropolitan Statistical Area—see Appendix B for areas included. Hourly wages for elementary/secondary school teachers and teacher assistants were calculated by the editors from annual wage data assuming a 40 hour work week; n/a not available.
Source: Bureau of Labor Statistics, Metro Area Occupational Employment and Wage Estimates, May 2011

RESIDENTIAL REAL ESTATE

Building Permits

Area	Single-Family			Multi-Family			Total		
	2010	2011	Pct. Chg.	2010	2011	Pct. Chg.	2010	2011	Pct. Chg.
City	455	590	29.7	643	104	-83.8	1,098	694	-36.8
MSA[1]	4,396	4,511	2.6	2,105	1,831	-13.0	6,501	6,342	-2.4
U.S.	447,311	418,498	-6.4	157,299	205,563	30.7	604,610	624,061	3.2

Note: (1) Metropolitan Statistical Area—see Appendix B for areas included; figures represent new, privately-owned housing units authorized (unadjusted data); All permit data are based on estimates with imputation.
Source: U.S. Census Bureau, Manufacturing, Mining, and Construction Statistics, Building Permits, 2010, 2011

Homeownership Rate

Area	2005 (%)	2006 (%)	2007 (%)	2008 (%)	2009 (%)	2010 (%)	2011 (%)
MSA[1]	71.7	71.6	72.9	70.5	68.3	68.3	68.3
U.S.	68.9	68.8	68.1	67.8	67.4	66.9	66.1

Note: (1) Metropolitan Statistical Area—see Appendix B for areas included
Source: U.S. Census Bureau, Housing Vacancies and Homeownership Annual Statistics: 2011

Housing Vacancy Rates

Area	Gross Vacancy Rate[2] (%)			Year-Round Vacancy Rate[3] (%)			Rental Vacancy Rate[4] (%)			Homeowner Vacancy Rate[5] (%)		
	2009	2010	2011	2009	2010	2011	2009	2010	2011	2009	2010	2011
MSA[1]	20.5	20.2	20.4	14.7	14.2	14.5	12.4	12.6	11.7	4.1	4.0	3.8
U.S.	14.5	14.3	14.2	11.3	11.3	11.1	10.6	10.2	9.5	2.6	2.6	2.5

Note: (1) Metropolitan Statistical Area—see Appendix B for areas included; (2) The percentage of the total housing inventory that is vacant; (3) The percentage of the housing inventory (excluding seasonal units) that is year-round vacant; (4) The percentage of rental inventory that is vacant for rent; (5) The percentage of homeowner inventory that is vacant for sale
Source: U.S. Census Bureau, Housing Vacancies and Homeownership Annual Statistics: 2011

TAXES

State Corporate Income Tax Rates

State	Tax Rate (%)	Income Brackets ($)	Num. of Brackets	Financial Institution Tax Rate (%)[a]	Federal Income Tax Ded.
Florida	5.5 (f)	Flat rate	1	5.5 (f)	No

Note: Tax rates as of January 1, 2012; (a) Rates listed are the corporate income tax rate applied to financial institutions or excise taxes based on income. Some states have other taxes based upon the value of deposits or shares; (f) An exemption of $5,000 is allowed. Florida's Alternative Minimum Tax rate is 3.3%.
Source: Federation of Tax Administrators, "State Corporate Income Tax Rates, 2012"

State Individual Income Tax Rates

State	Tax Rate (%)	Income Brackets ($)	Num. of Brackets	Personal Exempt. ($)[1]		Fed. Inc. Tax Ded.
				Single	Dependents	
Florida – No State Income Tax						

Note: Tax rates as of January 1, 2012; Local- and county-level taxes are not included; n/a not applicable; (1) Married joint filers generally receive double the single exemption
Source: Federation of Tax Administrators, "State Individual Income Tax Rates, 2012"

Various State and Local Tax Rates

State	State and Local Sales and Use (%)	State Sales and Use (%)	Gasoline[1] (¢/gal.)	Cigarette[2] ($/pack)	Spirits[3] ($/gal.)	Wine[4] ($/gal.)	Beer[5] ($/gal.)
Florida	7.0	6.00	35.0	1.34	6.50	2.25	0.48

Note: All tax rates as of January 1, 2012 except beer, wine and spirits (September 1, 2011); (1) The American Petroleum Institute has developed a methodology for determining the average tax rate on a gallon of fuel. Rates may include any of the following: excise taxes, environmental fees, storage tank fees, other fees or taxes, general sales tax, and local taxes. In states where gasoline is subject to the general sales tax, or where the fuel tax is based on the average sale price, the average rate determined by API is sensitive to changes in the price of gasoline. States that fully or partially apply general sales taxes to gasoline: CA, CO, GA, IL, IN, MI, NY; (2) The federal excise tax of $1.0066 per pack and local taxes are not included; (3) Rates are those applicable to off-premise sales of 40% alcohol by volume (a.b.v.) distilled spirits in 750ml containers. Local excise taxes are excluded; (4) Rates are those applicable to off-premise sales of 11% a.b.v. non-carbonated wine in 750ml containers; (5) Rates are those applicable to off-premise sales of 4.7% a.b.v. beer in 12 ounce containers.
Source: Tax Foundation, 2012 Facts & Figures: How Does Your State Compare?

State-Local Tax Burdens

Area	Rate (%)	Rank[1]	Per Capita Taxes Paid to Home State ($)	Total State and Local Per Capita Taxes Paid ($)	Per Capita Income ($)
Florida	9.2	31	2,713	3,897	42,146
U.S. Average	9.8	-	3,057	4,160	42,539

Note: Figures cover 2009; (1) Rank ranges from 1 to 50 where 1 is highest tax burden
Source: Tax Foundation, State-Local Tax Burdens, All States, 2009

State Business Tax Climate Index Rankings

State	Overall Rank	Corporate Tax Index Rank	Individual Income Tax Index Rank	Sales Tax Index Rank	Unemployment Insurance Tax Index Rank	Property Tax Index Rank
Florida	5	12	1	19	5	24

Note: The index is a measure of how each state's tax laws affect economic performance. The lower the rank, the more favorable a state's tax system is for business. States without a given tax are given a ranking of 1.
Source: Tax Foundation, Major Components of the State Business Tax Climate Index, FY 2012

COMMERCIAL REAL ESTATE

Office Market

Market Area	Inventory (sq. ft.)	Vacant (sq. ft.)	Vac. Rate (%)	Under Constr. (sq. ft.)	Asking Rent ($/sf/yr) Class A	Class B
Tampa	69,391,318	13,290,212	19.2	0	23.24	18.16

Source: Grubb & Ellis, Office Markets Trends, 4th Quarter 2011

Industrial Market

Market Area	Inventory (sq. ft.)	Vacant (sq. ft.)	Vac. Rate (%)	Under Constr. (sq. ft.)	Asking Rent ($/sf/yr) WH/Dist	R&D/Flex
Tampa	269,387,380	27,991,912	10.4	40,159	4.60	7.58

Source: Grubb & Ellis, Industrial Markets Trends, 4th Quarter 2011

COMMERCIAL UTILITIES

Typical Monthly Electric Bills

Area	Commercial Service ($/month) 1,500 kWh	40 kW demand 14,000 kWh	Industrial Service ($/month) 1,000 kW demand 200,000 kWh	50,000 kW demand 15,000,000 kWh
City	113	1,449	23,474	1,489,289
Average[1]	189	1,616	25,197	1,470,813

Note: Based on total rates in effect July 1, 2011; (1) average based on 184 utilities surveyed
Source: Edison Electric Institute, Typical Bills and Average Rates Report, Summer 2011

TRANSPORTATION

Means of Transportation to Work

Area	Car/Truck/Van Drove Alone	Car-pooled	Public Transportation Bus	Subway	Railroad	Bicycle	Walked	Other Means	Worked at Home
City	76.7	9.6	3.1	0.0	0.0	1.3	2.9	1.1	5.3
MSA[1]	80.3	9.4	1.4	0.0	0.0	0.7	1.5	1.4	5.2
U.S.	76.0	10.2	2.7	1.7	0.5	0.5	2.8	1.3	4.2

Note: Figures are percentages and cover workers 16 years of age and older; (1) Figures cover the Tampa-St. Petersburg-Clearwater, FL Metropolitan Statistical Area—see Appendix B for areas included
Source: U.S. Census Bureau, 2008-2010 American Community Survey 3-Year Estimates

Travel Time to Work

Area	Less Than 10 Minutes	10 to 19 Minutes	20 to 29 Minutes	30 to 44 Minutes	45 to 59 Minutes	60 to 89 Minutes	90 Minutes or More
City	13.6	34.8	22.7	19.9	4.6	2.9	1.5
MSA[1]	11.0	29.7	22.4	22.1	8.2	4.8	1.9
U.S.	13.9	30.1	20.8	19.8	7.5	5.5	2.5

Note: Figures are percentages and include workers 16 years old and over; (1) Figures cover the Tampa-St. Petersburg-Clearwater, FL Metropolitan Statistical Area—see Appendix B for areas included
Source: U.S. Census Bureau, 2008-2010 American Community Survey 3-Year Estimates

Travel Time Index

Area	1985	1990	1995	2000	2005	2010
Urban Area[1]	1.14	1.17	1.18	1.15	1.18	1.16
Average[2]	1.11	1.16	1.18	1.21	1.25	1.20

Note: Travel Time Index—the ratio of travel time in the peak period to the travel time at free-flow conditions. A value of 1.30 indicates a 20-minute free-flow trip takes 26 minutes in the peak. Free-flow speeds (60 mph on freeways and 35 mph on principal arterials) are used as the comparison threshold; (1) Covers the Tampa-St. Petersburg FL urban area; (2) average of 439 urban areas
Source: Texas Transportation Institute, Urban Mobility Report 2011, September 2011

Public Transportation

Agency Name / Mode of Transportation	Vehicles Operated in Maximum Service	Annual Unlinked Passenger Trips ('000)	Annual Passenger Miles ('000)
Hillsborough Area Regional Transit Authority (HART)			
Bus (directly operated)	161	12,665.4	60,062.4
Demand Response (directly operated)	30	104.4	909.1
Light Rail (directly operated)	4	502.0	789.2
Vanpool (purchased transportation)	30	66.4	2,515.6

Source: Federal Transit Administration, National Transit Database, 2010

Air Transportation

Airport Name and Code / Type of Service	Passenger Airlines[1]	Passenger Enplanements	Freight Carriers[2]	Freight (lbs.)
Tampa International (TPA)				
Domestic service (U.S. carriers - 2011)	34	7,952,534	12	75,510,105
International service (U.S. carriers - 2010)	6	8,527	3	75,748

Note: (1) Includes all U.S.-based major, minor and commuter airlines that carried at least one passenger during the year; (2) Includes all U.S.-based airlines and freight carriers that transported at least one pound of freight during the year
Source: Bureau of Transportation Statistics, The Intermodal Transportation Database, Air Carriers: T-100 Domestic Market (U.S. Carriers), 2011; Bureau of Transportation Statistics, The Intermodal Transportation Database, Air Carriers: T-100 International Market (U.S. Carriers), 2010

Other Transportation Statistics

Major Highways:	I-4; I-75
Amtrak Service:	Yes
Major Waterways/Ports:	Port of Tampa

Source: Amtrak.com; Google Maps

BUSINESSES

Major Business Headquarters

Company Name	Rankings	
	Fortune[1]	Forbes[2]
OSI Restaurant Partners	-	107
WellCare Health Plans	420	-

Note: (1) Fortune 500—companies that produce a 10-K are ranked 1 to 500 based on 2010 revenue; (2) all private companies with at least $2 billion in annual revenue are ranked 1 to 212; companies listed are headquartered in the city; dashes indicate no ranking
Source: Fortune, "Fortune 500," May 23, 2011; Forbes, "America's Largest Private Companies," November 16, 2011

Fast-Growing Businesses

According to *Inc.*, Tampa is home to two of America's 500 fastest-growing private companies: **The Cybrix Group** (#55); **Digital Legal Tampa** (#495). Criteria: must be an independent, privately-held, for-profit, U.S. corporation, proprietorship or partnership; revenues must be at least $80,000 in 2007 and $2 million in 2010; must have four-year operating/sales history. Holding companies, regulated banks, and utilities were excluded. *Inc., "America's 500 Fastest-Growing Private Companies," September 2011*

According to Deloitte, Tampa is home to one of North America's 500 fastest-growing high-technology companies: **Acclaris** (#302). Companies are ranked by percentage growth in revenue over a five-year period. Criteria for inclusion: company must be headquartered within North America; must own proprietary intellectual property or proprietary technology that contributes to a significant portion of the company's operating revenue, or devote a significant proportion of revenues to research and development of technology; must have been in business for a minumum of five years with 2006 operating revenues of at least $50,000 USD/CD and 2010 operating revenues of at least $5 million USD/CD. *Deloitte Touche Tohmatsu, 2011 Deloitte Technology Fast 500*[TM]

Minority Business Opportunity

Tampa is home to one company which is on the *Black Enterprise* Auto Dealer 60 list (60 largest dealers based on gross sales): **March Hodge Automotive** (#3). Criteria: company must be operational in previous calendar year and be at least 51% black-owned. *Black Enterprise, B.E. 100s, 2011*

Tampa is home to three companies which are on the *Hispanic Business* 500 list (500 largest U.S. Hispanic-owned companies based on 2010 revenue): **J2 Engineering** (#76); **Paul J. Sierra Construction** (#254); **Apex Office Products** (#326). Companies included must show at least 51 percent ownership by Hispanic U.S. citizens, and must maintain headquarters in one of the 50 states or Washington, D.C. *Hispanic Business, "Hispanic Business 500," June 2011*

Minority- and Women-Owned Businesses

Group	All Firms		Firms with Paid Employees			
	Firms	Sales ($000)	Firms	Sales ($000)	Employees	Payroll ($000)
Asian	1,552	605,434	521	483,557	3,663	95,944
Black	4,378	455,594	338	351,483	2,814	63,365
Hispanic	7,947	1,642,003	1,395	1,338,467	7,318	288,902
Women	10,798	3,708,549	1,626	3,373,231	13,263	369,989
All Firms	38,662	67,668,675	11,085	66,207,395	301,427	13,045,436

Note: Figures cover firms located in the city; minority- and women-owned business are defined as firms in which the corresponding group own 51% or more of the stock or equity of the company
Source: U.S. Census Bureau, 2007 Economic Census, Survey of Business Owners

HOTELS

Hotels/Motels

Area	5 Star		4 Star		3 Star		2 Star		1 Star		Not Rated	
	Num.	Pct.[3]	Num.	Pct.[3]	Num.	Pct.[3]	Num.	Pct.[3]	Num.	Pct.[3]	Num.	Pct.[3]
City[1]	0	0.0	7	4.6	51	33.3	85	55.6	2	1.3	8	5.2
Total[2]	133	0.9	940	6.5	4,569	31.8	7,033	48.9	351	2.4	1,343	9.3

Note: (1) Figures cover Tampa and vicinity; (2) Figures cover all 100 cities in this book; (3) Percentage of hotels which have a given star rating; Star ratings are determined by expedia.com and offer an indication of the general quality of a particular hotel.
Source: expedia.com, April 25, 2012

The Tampa-St. Petersburg-Clearwater, FL metro area is home to one of the best hotels in the U.S. according to *Travel & Leisure*: **Sandpearl Resort** (#122). Criteria: service; location; rooms; food; and value. *Travel & Leisure, "T+L 500, The World's Best Hotels 2012"*

EVENT SITES

Major Stadiums, Arenas, and Auditoriums

Name	Max. Capacity
George M Steinbrenner Field	11,000
Plant City Stadium	6,700
Raymond James Stadium	65,000
St. Pete Times Forum	21,500
USF Sun Dome	10,411

Source: Original research

Convention Centers

Name	Overall Space (sq. ft.)	Exhibit Space (sq. ft.)	Meeting Space (sq. ft.)	Meeting Rooms
Tampa Convention Center	600,000	42,000	200,000	36

Source: Original research

Living Environment

COST OF LIVING

Cost of Living Index

Composite Index	Groceries	Housing	Utilities	Trans-portation	Health Care	Misc. Goods/ Services
91.9	98.2	79.0	96.7	102.9	93.6	95.2

Note: U.S. = 100; Figures cover the Tampa FL urban area.
Source: The Council for Community and Economic Research, ACCRA Cost of Living Index, 2011

Grocery Prices

Area[1]	T-Bone Steak ($/pound)	Frying Chicken ($/pound)	Whole Milk ($/half gal.)	Eggs ($/dozen)	Orange Juice ($/64 oz.)	Coffee ($/11.5 oz.)
City[2]	9.32	1.17	2.57	1.66	3.11	3.84
Avg.	9.25	1.18	2.22	1.66	3.19	4.40
Min.	6.70	0.88	1.31	0.95	2.46	2.94
Max.	14.30	2.16	3.50	3.18	4.75	6.83

Note: (1) Values for the local area are compared with the average, minimum and maximum values for all 335 areas in the Cost of Living Index; (2) Figures cover the Tampa FL urban area; **T-Bone Steak** *(price per pound);* **Frying Chicken** *(price per pound, whole fryer);* **Whole Milk** *(half gallon carton);* **Eggs** *(price per dozen, Grade A, large);* **Orange Juice** *(64 oz. Tropicana or Florida Natural);* **Coffee** *(11.5 oz. can, vacuum-packed, Maxwell House, Hills Bros, or Folgers).*
Source: The Council for Community and Economic Research, ACCRA Cost of Living Index, 2011

Housing and Utility Costs

Area[1]	New Home Price ($)	Apartment Rent ($/month)	All Electric ($/month)	Part Electric ($/month)	Other Energy ($/month)	Telephone ($/month)
City[2]	212,171	790	164.70	-	-	24.95
Avg.	285,990	839	163.23	89.00	77.52	26.92
Min.	188,005	460	125.58	45.39	33.89	17.98
Max.	1,197,028	3,244	339.16	181.97	348.69	40.01

Note: (1) Values for the local area are compared with the average, minimum and maximum values for all 335 areas in the Cost of Living Index; (2) Figures cover the Tampa FL urban area; **New Home Price** *(2,400 sf living area, 8,000 sf lot, in urban area with full utilities);* **Apartment Rent** *(950 sf 2 bedroom/1.5 or 2 bath, unfurnished, excluding all utilities except water);* **All Electric** *(average monthly cost for an all-electric home);* **Part Electric** *(average monthly cost for a part-electric home);* **Other Energy** *(average monthly cost for natural gas, fuel oil, coal, wood, and any other forms of energy except electricity);* **Telephone** *(price includes basic monthly rate for a private residential line plus additional local usage charges incurred by a family of four).*
Source: The Council for Community and Economic Research, ACCRA Cost of Living Index, 2011

Health Care, Transportation, and Other Costs

Area[1]	Doctor ($/visit)	Dentist ($/visit)	Optometrist ($/visit)	Gasoline ($/gallon)	Beauty Salon ($/visit)	Men's Shirt ($)
City[2]	78.56	76.67	80.19	3.46	34.23	20.20
Avg.	93.88	81.72	90.54	3.48	32.65	25.06
Min.	60.00	55.33	53.66	3.18	19.78	13.44
Max.	154.98	145.97	183.72	4.31	63.21	46.00

Note: (1) Values for the local area are compared with the average, minimum and maximum values for all 335 areas in the Cost of Living Index; (2) Figures cover the Tampa FL urban area; **Doctor** *(general practitioners routine exam of an established patient);* **Dentist** *(adult teeth cleaning and periodic oral examination);* **Optometrist** *(full vision eye exam for established adult patient);* **Gasoline** *(one gallon regular unleaded, national brand, including all taxes, cash price at self-service pump if available);* **Beauty Salon** *(woman's shampoo, trim, and blow-dry);* **Men's Shirt** *(cotton/polyester dress shirt, pinpoint weave, long sleeves).*
Source: The Council for Community and Economic Research, ACCRA Cost of Living Index, 2011

HOUSING

House Price Index (HPI)

Area	National Ranking[2]	Quarterly Change (%)	One-Year Change (%)	Five-Year Change (%)
MSA[1]	236	-0.17	-4.97	-40.26
U.S.[3]	-	-0.10	-2.43	-19.16

Note: The HPI is a weighted repeat sales index. It measures average price changes in repeat sales or refinancings on the same properties. This information is obtained by reviewing repeat mortgage transactions on single-family properties whose mortgages have been purchased or securitized by Fannie Mae or Freddie Mac in January 1975; (1) Metropolitan/Micropolitan Statistical Area—see Appendix B for areas included; (2) Rankings are based on annual percentage change for all metro areas containing at least 15,000 transactions over the last 10 years and ranges from 1 to 306; (3) figures based on a weighted average of Census Division estimates using a purchase only index; all figures are for the period ending December 31, 2011
Source: Federal Housing Finance Agency, House Price Index, February 23, 2012

House Price Valuations

Area	Q4 2005 Price ($000)	Q4 2005 Over-valuation	Q4 2006 Price ($000)	Q4 2006 Over-valuation	Q4 2007 Price ($000)	Q4 2007 Over-valuation	Q4 2008 Price ($000)	Q4 2008 Over-valuation	Q4 2009 Price ($000)	Q4 2009 Over-valuation
MSA[1]	181.8	30.2	188.8	26.4	169.9	11.8	130.8	-13.6	120.4	-19.9

Note: Figures show the percentage of over- or under-valuation of single family homes relative to statistically normal house values (e.g. a value of 23.6 indicates that house values are 23.6% overvalued). Statistically normal house values are based on house prices, interest rates, household incomes, population densities, and any historical premiums or discounts metropolitan areas have exhibited over time; (1) Figures cover the Tampa-St. Petersburg-Clearwater, FL - see Appendix B for areas included
Source: Global Insight/PNC Financial Services Group, House Prices in America: 4th Quarter 2009 Update

Median Single-Family Home Prices

Area	2009	2010	2011[p]	Percent Change 2010 to 2011
MSA[1]	140.7	134.2	127.8	-4.8
U.S. Average	172.1	173.1	166.2	-4.0

Note: Figures are median sales prices of existing single-family homes in thousands of dollars; (p) preliminary; n/a not available; (1) Metropolitan Statistical Area—see Appendix B for areas included
Source: National Association of Realtors, Median Sales Price of Existing Single-Family Homes for Metropolitan Areas, 4th Quarter 2011

Affordability Index of Existing Single-Family Homes

Area	2009	2010	2011[p]	Percent Change 2010 to 2011
MSA[1]	127.1	140.4	154.4	10.0

Note: The housing affordability index measures whether or not a typical family could qualify for a mortgage loan on a typical home. The higher the index, the greater the household purchasing power. An index of 100 is defined as the point where a median-income household has exactly enough income to qualify for the purchase of a median-priced existing single-family home, assuming a 20 percent downpayment and 25 percent of gross income devoted to mortgage principal and interest payments; (p) preliminary; n/a not available; (1) Metropolitan Statistical Area—see Appendix B for areas included
Source: National Association of Realtors, Affordability Index of Existing Single-Family Homes, 2011

Median Apartment Condo-Coop Home Prices

Area	2009	2010	2011[p]	Percent Change 2010 to 2011
MSA[1]	107.1	91.1	69.1	-24.1
U.S. Average	175.6	171.7	165.1	-3.8

Note: Figures are median sales prices of existing apartment condo-coop homes in thousands of dollars; (p) preliminary; n/a not available; (1) Metropolitan Statistical Area—see Appendix B for areas included
Source: National Association of Realtors, Median Sales Price of Existing Apartment Condo-Coop Homes for Metropolitan Areas, 4th Quarter 2011

Year Housing Structure Built

Area	2005 or Later	2000 -2004	1990 -1999	1980 -1989	1970 -1979	1960 -1969	1950 -1959	Before 1950	Median Year
City	6.0	10.3	10.3	13.2	15.1	13.1	17.0	14.9	1973
MSA[1]	5.2	10.5	14.4	22.8	21.9	11.3	9.1	4.8	1981
U.S.	5.0	8.6	14.0	14.1	16.3	11.3	11.2	19.6	1975

Note: Figures are percentages except for Median Year; (1) Figures cover the Tampa-St. Petersburg-Clearwater, FL Metropolitan Statistical Area—see Appendix B for areas included
Source: U.S. Census Bureau, 2008-2010 American Community Survey 3-Year Estimates

HEALTH

Health Risk Data

Category	MSA[1] (%)	U.S. (%)
Adults who have been told they have high blood pressure[2]	30.7	28.7
Adults who have been told they have high blood cholesterol[2]	39.9	37.5
Adults who have been told they have diabetes[3]	11.9	8.7
Adults who have been told they have arthritis[2]	29.7	26.0
Adults who have been told they currently have asthma	9.4	9.1
Adults who are current smokers	20.5	17.3
Adults who are heavy drinkers[4]	5.3	5.0
Adults who are binge drinkers[5]	16.1	15.1
Adults who are overweight (BMI 25.0 - 29.9)	38.2	36.2
Adults who are obese (BMI 30.0 - 99.8)	26.3	27.5
Adults who participated in any physical activities in the past month	77.9	76.1
Adults 50+ who have ever had a sigmoidoscopy or colonoscopy	68.0	65.2
Women aged 40+ who have had a mammogram within the past two years	77.6	75.2
Men aged 40+ who have had a PSA test within the past two years	68.3	53.2
Adults aged 65+ who have had flu shot within the past year	63.4	67.5
Adults aged 18–64 who have any kind of health care coverage	80.9	82.2

Note: Data as of 2010 unless otherwise noted; (1) Figures cover the Tampa-St. Petersburg-Clearwater, FL Metropolitan Statistical Area—see Appendix B for areas included; (2) Data as of 2009; (3) Figures do not include pregnancy-related, borderline, or pre-diabetes; (4) Heavy drinkers are classified as males having more than two drinks per day or females having more than one drink per day; (5) Binge drinkers are classified as males having five or more drinks on one occasion or females having four or more drinks on one occasion
Source: Centers for Disease Control and Prevention, Behaviorial Risk Factor Surveillance System, SMART: Selected Metropolitan/Micropolitan Area Risk Trends, 2009, 2010

Mortality Rates for the Top 10 Causes of Death in the U.S.

ICD-10[a] Sub-Chapter	ICD-10[a] Code	Age-Adjusted Mortality Rate[1] per 100,000 population	
		County[2]	U.S.
Malignant neoplasms	C00-C97	177.1	175.6
Ischaemic heart diseases	I20-I25	128.4	121.6
Other forms of heart disease	I30-I51	30.1	48.6
Chronic lower respiratory diseases	J40-J47	47.1	42.3
Cerebrovascular diseases	I60-I69	37.1	40.6
Organic, including symptomatic, mental disorders	F01-F09	32.1	26.7
Other degenerative diseases of the nervous system	G30-G31	28.0	24.7
Other external causes of accidental injury	W00-X59	35.6	24.4
Diabetes mellitus	E10-E14	27.2	21.7
Hypertensive diseases	I10-I15	29.4	18.2

Note: (a) ICD-10 = International Classification of Diseases 10th Revision; (1) Mortality rates are a three year average covering 2007-2009; (2) Figures cover Hillsborough County
Source: Centers for Disease Control and Prevention, National Center for Health Statistics. Underlying Cause of Death 1999-2009 on CDC WONDER Online Database, released 2012. Data for year 2009 are compiled from the Multiple Cause of Death File 2009, Series 20 No. 2O, 2012, Data for year 2008 are compiled from the Multiple Cause of Death File 2008, Series 20 No. 2N, 2011, Data for year 2007 are compiled from Multiple Cause of Death File 2007, Series 20 No. 2M, 2010.

Mortality Rates for Selected Causes of Death

ICD-10[a] Sub-Chapter	ICD-10[a] Code	Age-Adjusted Mortality Rate[1] per 100,000 population	
		County[2]	U.S.
Assault	X85-Y09	5.9	5.7
Human immunodeficiency virus (HIV) disease	B20-B24	6.6	3.3
Influenza and pneumonia	J09-J18	8.6	16.4
Intentional self-harm	X60-X84	13.9	11.5
Malnutrition	E40-E46	0.6	0.8
Obesity and other hyperalimentation	E65-E68	1.8	1.6
Transport accidents	V01-V99	14.9	13.7
Viral hepatitis	B15-B19	3.6	2.2

Note: (a) ICD-10 = International Classification of Diseases 10th Revision; (1) Mortality rates are a three year average covering 2007-2009; (2) Figures cover Hillsborough County
Source: Centers for Disease Control and Prevention, National Center for Health Statistics. Underlying Cause of Death 1999-2009 on CDC WONDER Online Database, released 2012. Data for year 2009 are compiled from the Multiple Cause of Death File 2009, Series 20 No. 2O, 2012, Data for year 2008 are compiled from the Multiple Cause of Death File 2008, Series 20 No. 2N, 2011, Data for year 2007 are compiled from Multiple Cause of Death File 2007, Series 20 No. 2M, 2010.

Distribution of Physicians and Dentists

Area[1]	Dentists[2]	D.O.[3]	M.D.[4]				
			Total	Family/ General Practice	Pediatrics	Medical Specialties	Surgical Specialties
Local (number)	487	271	2,617	209	225	1,043	601
Local (rate[5])	4.2	2.3	22.2	1.8	1.9	8.8	5.1
U.S. (rate[5])	4.5	1.9	18.3	2.5	1.4	6.8	4.1

Note: Data as of 2008 unless noted; (1) Local data covers Hillsborough County; (2) Data as of 2007; (3) Doctor of Osteopathic Medicine; (4) Includes active, non-federal, patient-care, office-based Doctors of Medicine; (5) rate per 10,000 population
Source: Area Resource File (ARF). 2009-2010 Release. U.S. Department of Health and Human Services, Health Resources and Services Administration, Bureau of Health Professions, Rockville, MD, August 2010

Best Hospitals

According to *U.S. News,* the Tampa-St. Petersburg-Clearwater, FL is home to two of the best hospitals in the U.S.: **Moffitt Cancer Center** (1 specialty); **Tampa General Hospital** (7 specialties). The hospitals listed were highly ranked in at least one adult specialty. *U.S. News Online, "America's Best Hospitals 2011-12"*

According to *U.S. News,* the Tampa-St. Petersburg-Clearwater, FL is home to one of the best children's hospitals in the U.S.: **All Children's Hospital** (2 specialties). The hospital listed was highly ranked in at least one pediatric specialty. *U.S. News Online, "America's Best Children's Hospitals 2011-12"*

EDUCATION

Public School District Statistics

District Name	Schls	Pupils	Pupil/ Teacher Ratio	Minority Pupils[1] (%)	Free Lunch Eligible[2] (%)	IEP[3] (%)
Hillsborough	292	193,265	13.5	58.6	44.6	15.2

Note: Table includes school districts with 2,000 or more students; (1) Percentage of students that are not non-Hispanic white; (2) Percentage of students that are eligible for the free lunch program; (3) Percentage of students that have an Individualized Education Program.
Source: U.S. Department of Education, National Center for Education Statistics, Common Core of Data, Local Education Agency (School District) Universe Survey: School Year 2009-2010; U.S. Department of Education, National Center for Education Statistics, Common Core of Data, Public Elementary/Secondary School Universe Survey: School Year 2009-2010

Top Public High Schools

High School Name	Rank[1]	Score[1]	Grad. Rate[2] (%)	College[3] (%)	AP/IB/ AICE[4] (%)	SAT/ ACT[5] (%)
C Leon King	293	0.378	89	84	5.7	1613

Note: (1) Public schools are ranked from 1 to 500 based on the following self-reported statistics (with their corresponding weight in the final score). Schools that had fewer than 10 graduates, as well as those that were newly founded and did not have a graduating senior class in 2010 were excluded; (2) Four-year, on-time graduation rate (25%); (3) Percent of 2010 graduates who enrolled immediately in college (25%); (4) AP/IB/AICE tests per graduate (25%); (5) Average SAT and/or ACT score (10%); Average AP/IB/AICE exam score (10%); AP/IB/AICE courses offered per graduate (5%); (6) School is unranked, but has been identified by Newsweek as one of the nation's most elite public high schools.
Source: Newsweek Online, "Top High Schools 2011"

Highest Level of Education

Area	Less than H.S.	H.S. Diploma	Some College, No Deg.	Associate Degree	Bachelors Degree	Masters Degree	Profess. School Degree	Doctorate Degree
City	15.4	27.0	18.0	7.9	19.6	7.3	3.4	1.3
MSA[1]	13.2	30.8	21.7	8.8	17.1	5.8	1.7	0.9
U.S.	14.7	28.4	21.3	7.6	17.6	7.2	1.9	1.2

Note: Figures cover persons age 25 and over; (1) Figures cover the Tampa-St. Petersburg-Clearwater, FL Metropolitan Statistical Area—see Appendix B for areas included
Source: U.S. Census Bureau, 2008-2010 American Community Survey 3-Year Estimates

Educational Attainment by Race

Area	High School Graduate or Higher (%)					Bachelor's Degree or Higher (%)				
	Total	White	Black	Asian	Hisp.[2]	Total	White	Black	Asian	Hisp.[2]
City	84.6	87.6	78.2	84.9	71.8	31.7	37.2	13.3	59.5	16.2
MSA[1]	86.8	87.9	80.6	84.0	74.2	25.5	25.9	17.7	47.3	16.8
U.S.	85.3	87.5	81.4	85.5	61.6	28.0	29.3	17.8	50.2	13.0

Note: Figures shown cover persons 25 years old and over; (1) Figures cover the Tampa-St. Petersburg-Clearwater, FL Metropolitan Statistical Area—see Appendix B for areas included; (2) People of Hispanic origin can be of any race
Source: U.S. Census Bureau, 2008-2010 American Community Survey 3-Year Estimates

School Enrollment by Grade and Control

Area	Preschool (%)		Kindergarten (%)		Grades 1 - 4 (%)		Grades 5 - 8 (%)		Grades 9 - 12 (%)	
	Public	Private	Public	Private	Public	Private	Public	Private	Public	Private
City	56.3	43.7	86.9	13.1	91.4	8.6	87.4	12.6	93.5	6.5
MSA[1]	54.8	45.2	86.4	13.6	88.7	11.3	88.6	11.4	91.6	8.4
U.S.	55.4	44.6	87.1	12.9	89.4	10.6	89.5	10.5	90.4	9.6

Note: Figures shown cover persons 3 years old and over; (1) Figures cover the Tampa-St. Petersburg-Clearwater, FL Metropolitan Statistical Area—see Appendix B for areas included
Source: U.S. Census Bureau, 2008-2010 American Community Survey 3-Year Estimates

Average Salaries of Public School Classroom Teachers

Area	2010-11		2011-12		Percent Change 2010-11 to 2011-12	Percent Change 2001-02 to 2011-12
	Dollars	Rank[1]	Dollars	Rank[1]		
Florida	45,732	45	46,232	46	1.09	17.70
U.S. Average	55,623	-	56,643	-	1.83	26.8

Note: (1) State rank ranges from 1 to 51 where 1 indicates highest salary.
Source: National Education Association, Rankings & Estimates: Rankings of the States 2011 and Estimates of School Statistics 2012, December 2011

Higher Education

Four-Year Colleges			Two-Year Colleges			Medical Schools[1]	Law Schools[2]	Voc/ Tech[3]
Public	Private Non-profit	Private For-profit	Public	Private Non-profit	Private For-profit			
1	2	8	3	0	5	1	0	5

Note: Figures cover institutions located within the city limits and include main campuses only; (1) includes schools accredited by the Liaison Committee on Medical Education and the American Osteopathic Association's Commission on Osteopathic College Accreditation; (2) includes American Bar Association-accredited law schools; (3) includes all schools with programs that are less than 2 years.
Source: National Center for Education Statistics, Integrated Postsecondary Education System (IPEDS) Peer Analysis System, 2011-12; Association of American Medical Colleges, Member List, April 23, 2012; American Osteopathic Association, Member List, April 23, 2012; Law School Admission Council, Official Guide to ABA-Approved Law Schools Online, April 23, 2012

According to *U.S. News & World Report,* the Tampa-St. Petersburg-Clearwater, FL is home to one of the best national universities in the U.S.: **University of South Florida** (#181). The indicators used to capture academic quality fall into a number of categories: assessment by administrators at peer institutions; retention of students; faculty resources; student selectivity; financial resources; alumni giving; high school counselor ratings of colleges; and graduation rate.*U.S. News & World Report, "America's Best Colleges 2012"*

According to *U.S. News & World Report,* the Tampa-St. Petersburg-Clearwater, FL is home to one of the best liberal arts colleges in the U.S.: **Eckerd College** (#144). The indicators used to capture academic quality fall into a number of categories: assessment by administrators at peer institutions; retention of students; faculty resources; student selectivity; financial resources; alumni giving; high school counselor ratings of colleges; and graduation rate.*U.S. News & World Report, "America's Best Colleges 2012"*

PRESIDENTIAL ELECTION

2008 Presidential Election Results

Area	Obama	McCain	Nader	Other
Hillsborough County	53.1	45.9	0.4	0.7
U.S.	52.9	45.6	0.6	0.9

Note: Results are percentages and may not add to 100% due to rounding
Source: Dave Leip's Atlas of U.S. Presidential Elections, www.uselectionatlas.org

EMPLOYERS

Major Employers

Company Name	Industry
American Staff Management	Employee leasing service
City of Tampa	County supervisor of education, except school board
Diversified Maintenance Systems	Building and maintenance services, nec
Florida Hospital Tampa Bay Division	General medical and surgical hospitals
Granite Services International	Help supply services
H. Lee Moffitt Cancer Center	Physicians' office, including specialists
Honeywell International	Aircraft engines and engine parts
JPMorgan Chase Bank National Association	National commerical banks
Morton Plant Hospital Association	General medical and surgical hospitals
Raymond James & Associates	Security brokers and dealers
Seven-One-Seven Parking Services	Valet parking
SHC Holding	Convalescent home with continuous care
Sykes Enterprisesorporated	Business services, nec
Tech Data Corporation	Computers, peripherals, and software
United States Postal Service	Us postal service
University of South Florida	Colleges and universities
Usani Sub	Television broadcasting stations
Verizon Data Services	Data processing service
Veterans Health Administration	Administration of veterans' affairs
Veterans Health Administration	General medical and surgical hospitals

Note: Companies shown are located within the Tampa-St. Petersburg-Clearwater, FL metropolitan area.
Source: Hoovers.com, data extracted April 25 2012

Best Companies to Work For

Moffitt Cancer Center, headquartered in Tampa, is among the "100 Best Companies for Working Mothers." Criteria: workforce profile; benefits; child care; women's issues and advancement; flexible work; paid time off and leave; company culture; and work-life programs. This year *Working Mother* gave particular weight to workforce profile, paid time off and company culture. *Working Mother, "100 Best Companies 2011"*

H. Lee Moffitt Cancer Center & Research Institute, headquartered in Tampa, is among the "100 Best Places to Work in IT." To qualify, companies, both public and private, had to have a minimum of 50 IT employees and were selected based on average salary and bonus increases, the percentage of IT staffers promoted, IT staff turnover rates, training and development programs, and the percentage of women and minorities in IT staff and management positions. In addition, *Computerworld* looked at retention efforts, programs for recognizing and rewarding outstanding performances, and benefits such as flextime, elder care and child care, and reimbursement for college tuition and the cost of pursuing technology certifications. *Computerworld, "100 Best Places to Work in IT 2011"*

PUBLIC SAFETY

Crime Rate

Area	All Crimes	Violent Crimes				Property Crimes		
		Murder	Forcible Rape	Robbery	Aggrav. Assault	Burglary	Larceny -Theft	Motor Vehicle Theft
City	3,916.6	7.8	13.5	196.6	405.9	900.2	2,151.6	240.9
Suburbs[1]	3,883.0	3.8	28.4	115.8	334.3	840.3	2,363.5	196.8
Metro[2]	3,887.2	4.3	26.6	125.9	343.3	847.8	2,337.1	202.3
U.S.	3,345.5	4.8	27.5	119.1	252.3	699.6	2,003.5	238.8

Note: Figures are crimes per 100,000 population; (1) All areas within the metro area that are located outside the city limits; (2) Metropolitan Statistical Area—see Appendix B for areas included
Source: FBI Uniform Crime Reports, 2010

Hate Crimes

Area	Number of Quarters Reported	Bias Motivation				
		Race	Religion	Sexual Orientation	Ethnicity	Disability
City	4	0	0	0	0	0

Source: Federal Bureau of Investigation, Hate Crime Statistics 2010

Identity Theft Consumer Complaints

Area	Complaints	Complaints per 100,000 Population	Rank[2]
MSA[1]	4,255	156.2	7
U.S.	279,156	90.4	-

Note: (1) Metropolitan Statistical Area—see Appendix B for areas included; (2) Rank ranges from 1 to 384 where 1 indicates greatest number of identity theft complaints per 100,000 population
Source: Federal Trade Commission, Consumer Sentinel Network Data Book for January–December 2011

Fraud and Other Consumer Complaints

Area	Complaints	Complaints per 100,000 Population	Rank[2]
MSA[1]	14,798	543.3	96
U.S.	1,533,924	496.8	-

Note: (1) Metropolitan Statistical Area—see Appendix B for areas included; (2) Rank ranges from 1 to 384 where 1 indicates greatest number of fraud and other complaints per 100,000 population
Source: Federal Trade Commission, Consumer Sentinel Network Data Book for January–December 2011

RECREATION

Culture

Dance[1]	Theatre[1]	Instrumental Music[1]	Vocal Music[1]	Series/ Festivals	Museums	Zoos and Aquariums[2]
0	5	0	2	0	8	3

Note: (1) Number of professional performing groups; (2) AZA-accredited
Source: The Grey House Performing Arts Directory, 2011-2012; Official Museum Directory, 2011; American Association of Museums, AAM Member Museums, April 2012; Association of Zoos & Aquariums, AZA Member Zoos & Aquariums, April 2012

Professional Sports Teams

Team Name	League
Tampa Bay Buccaneers	National Football League (NFL)
Tampa Bay Lightning	National Hockey League (NHL)
Tampa Bay Rays	Major League Baseball (MLB)

Note: Includes teams located in the Tampa-Saint Petersburg metro area.
Source: Original research

CLIMATE

Average and Extreme Temperatures

Temperature	Jan	Feb	Mar	Apr	May	Jun	Jul	Aug	Sep	Oct	Nov	Dec	Yr.
Extreme High (°F)	85	88	91	93	98	99	97	98	96	94	90	86	99
Average High (°F)	70	72	76	82	87	90	90	90	89	84	77	72	82
Average Temp. (°F)	60	62	67	72	78	81	82	83	81	75	68	62	73
Average Low (°F)	50	52	56	61	67	73	74	74	73	66	57	52	63
Extreme Low (°F)	21	24	29	40	49	53	63	67	57	40	23	18	18

Note: Figures cover the years 1948-1990
Source: National Climatic Data Center, International Station Meteorological Climate Summary, 9/96

Average Precipitation/Snowfall/Humidity

Precip./Humidity	Jan	Feb	Mar	Apr	May	Jun	Jul	Aug	Sep	Oct	Nov	Dec	Yr.
Avg. Precip. (in.)	2.1	2.8	3.5	1.8	3.0	5.6	7.3	7.9	6.5	2.3	1.8	2.1	46.7
Avg. Snowfall (in.)	Tr	Tr	Tr	0	0	0	0	0	0	0	0	Tr	Tr
Avg. Rel. Hum. 7am (%)	87	87	86	86	85	86	88	90	91	89	88	87	88
Avg. Rel. Hum. 4pm (%)	56	55	54	51	52	60	65	66	64	57	56	57	58

Note: Figures cover the years 1948-1990; Tr = Trace amounts (<0.05 in. of rain; <0.5 in. of snow)
Source: National Climatic Data Center, International Station Meteorological Climate Summary, 9/96

Weather Conditions

Temperature			Daytime Sky			Precipitation		
32°F & below	45°F & below	90°F & above	Clear	Partly cloudy	Cloudy	0.01 inch or more precip.	0.1 inch or more snow/ice	Thunder-storms
3	35	85	81	204	80	107	< 1	87

Note: Figures are average number of days per year and cover the years 1948-1990
Source: National Climatic Data Center, International Station Meteorological Climate Summary, 9/96

HAZARDOUS WASTE

Superfund Sites

Tampa has eight hazardous waste sites on the EPA's Superfund Final National Priorities List: **Raleigh Street Dump; Alaric Area Ground Water Plume; Southern Solvents, Inc.; MRI Corp (Tampa); Stauffer Chemical Co (Tampa); Helena Chemical Co. (Tampa Plant); Peak Oil Co./Bay Drum Co.; Reeves Southeastern Galvanizing Corp.** U.S. Environmental Protection Agency, Final National Priorities List, April 17, 2012

**AIR & WATER
QUALITY**

Air Quality Index

Area	Percent of Days when Air Quality was...[2]					AQI Statistics[2]	
	Good	Moderate	Unhealthy for Sensitive Groups	Unhealthy	Very Unhealthy	Maximum	Median
Area[1]	75.1	21.4	3.6	0.0	0.0	119	41

*Note: Air Quality Index (AQI) is an index for reporting daily air quality. EPA calculates the AQI for five major air pollutants regulated by the Clean Air Act: ground-level ozone, particle pollution (aka particulate matter), carbon monoxide, sulfur dioxide, and nitrogen dioxide. The AQI runs from 0 to 500. The higher the AQI value, the greater the level of air pollution and the greater the health concern. There are six AQI categories: "Good" AQI is between 0 and 50. Air quality is considered satisfactory; "Moderate" AQI is between 51 and 100. Air quality is acceptable; "Unhealthy for Sensitive Groups" When AQI values are between 101 and 150, members of sensitive groups may experience health effects; "Unhealthy" When AQI values are between 151 and 200 everyone may begin to experience health effects; "Very Unhealthy" AQI values between 201 and 300 trigger a health alert; "Hazardous" AQI values over 300 trigger warnings of emergency conditions (not shown); (1) Data covers Hillsborough County; (2) Based on 365 days with AQI data in 2011.
Source: U.S. Environmental Protection Agency, AirData Report, 2011*

Air Quality Index Pollutants

Area	Percent of Days when AQI Pollutant was...[2]					
	Carbon Monoxide	Nitrogen Dioxide	Ozone	Sulfur Dioxide	Particulate Matter 2.5	Particulate Matter 10
Area[1]	0.0	0.0	54.0	11.8	32.6	1.6

*Note: The Air Quality Index (AQI) is an index for reporting daily air quality. EPA calculates the AQI for five major air pollutants regulated by the Clean Air Act: ground-level ozone, particle pollution (also known as particulate matter), carbon monoxide, sulfur dioxide, and nitrogen dioxide. The AQI runs from 0 to 500. The higher the AQI value, the greater the level of air pollution and the greater the health concern; (1) Data covers Hillsborough County; (2) Based on 365 days with AQI data in 2011.
Source: U.S. Environmental Protection Agency, AirData Report, 2011*

Air Quality Index Trends

Area	Trend Sites (days)								All Sites (days)
	2003	2004	2005	2006	2007	2008	2009	2010	2010
MSA[1]	87	50	47	38	47	24	18	11	12

*Note: Figures are the number of days the AQI value exceeded 100 in a given year. An AQI value greater than 100 indicates that air quality would have been in the unhealthful range on that day. Data from exceptional events are included. These counts are presented in two ways. First, the counts are based on sites having an adequate record of monitoring data during the trend period (trend sites). These counts represent the relative change in the number of days with AQI values greater than 100. In the last column, the counts are based on all sites with data in the most recent year (because it is possible for a site to have data in the most recent year but not enough data to be a trend site); (1) Data covers the Tampa-St. Petersburg-Clearwater, FL—see Appendix B for areas included
Source: U.S. Environmental Protection Agency, Air Quality Index Information, "Number of Days with Air Quality Index Values Greater than 100 at Trend Sites, 2000-2010, and at All Sites in 2010"*

Maximum Air Pollutant Concentrations: Particulate Matter, Ozone, CO and Lead

	Particulate Matter 10 (ug/m³)	Particulate Matter 2.5 Wtd AM (ug/m³)	Particulate Matter 2.5 24-Hr (ug/m³)	Ozone (ppm)	Carbon Monoxide (ppm)	Lead (ug/m³)
MSA[1] Level	62	8.1	16	0.072	1	0.73
NAAQS[2]	150	15	35	0.075	9	0.15
Met NAAQS[2]	Yes	Yes	Yes	Yes	Yes	No

*Note: Data from exceptional events are not included; (1) Data covers the Tampa-St. Petersburg-Clearwater, FL—see Appendix B for areas included; (2) National Ambient Air Quality Standards; ppm = parts per million; ug/m³ = micrograms per cubic meter; n/a not available
Concentrations: Particulate Matter 10 (coarse particulate)—highest second maximum 24-hour concentration; Particulate Matter 2.5 Wtd AM (fine particulate)—highest weighted annual mean concentration; Particulate Matter 2.5 24-Hour (fine particulate)—highest 98th percentile 24-hour concentration; Ozone—highest fourth daily maximum 8-hour concentration; Carbon Monoxide—highest second maximum non-overlapping 8-hour concentration; Lead—maximum running 3-month average
Source: U.S. Environmental Protection Agency, CBSA Factbook 2010, Air Quality Statistics by City, 2010*

Maximum Air Pollutant Concentrations: Nitrogen Dioxide and Sulfur Dioxide

	Nitrogen Dioxide AM (ppb)	Nitrogen Dioxide 1-Hr (ppb)	Sulfur Dioxide AM (ppb)	Sulfur Dioxide 1-Hr (ppb)	Sulfur Dioxide 24-Hr (ppb)
MSA[1] Level	6.079	38	2.852	104	28.7
NAAQS[2]	53	100	30	75	140
Met NAAQS[2]	Yes	Yes	Yes	No	Yes

Note: Data from exceptional events are not included; (1) Data covers the Tampa-St. Petersburg-Clearwater, FL—see Appendix B for areas included; (2) National Ambient Air Quality Standards; ppb = parts per billion; n/a not available
Concentrations: Nitrogen Dioxide AM—highest arithmetic mean concentration; Nitrogen Dioxide 1-Hr—highest 98th percentile 1-hour daily maximum concentration; Sulfur Dioxide AM—highest annual mean concentration; Sulfur Dioxide 1-Hr—highest 99th percentile 1-hour daily maximum concentration; Sulfur Dioxide 24-Hr—highest second maximum 24-hour concentration
Source: U.S. Environmental Protection Agency, CBSA Factbook 2010, Air Quality Statistics by City, 2010

Drinking Water

Water System Name	Pop. Served	Primary Water Source Type	Violations[1] Health Based	Violations[1] Monitoring/ Reporting
City of Tampa Water Department	667,313	Surface	0	0

Note: (1) Based on violation data from January 1, 2011 to December 31, 2011 (includes unresolved violations from earlier years)
Source: U.S. Environmental Protection Agency, Office of Ground Water and Drinking Water, Safe Drinking Water Information System (based on data extracted April 18, 2012)

Appendix A: Counties

Albuquerque, NM
Bernalillo County

Alexandria, VA
Alexandria Independent City

Anchorage, AK
Anchorage County

Ann Arbor, MI
Washtenaw County

Athens, GA
Clarke County

Atlanta, GA
Fulton County

Austin, TX
Travis County

Baltimore, MD
Baltimore Independent City

Bellevue, WA
King County

Billings, MT
Yellowstone County

Boise City, ID
Ada County

Boston, MA
Suffolk County

Boulder, CO
Boulder County

Broken Arrow, OK
Tulsa County

Cambridge, MA
Middlesex County

Cape Coral, FL
Lee County

Carlsbad, CA
San Diego County

Cary, NC
Wake County

Cedar Rapids, IA
Linn County

Charleston, SC
Charleston County

Charlotte, NC
Mecklenburg County

Chesapeake, VA
Chesapeake Independent City

Chicago, IL
Cook County

Clarksville, TN
Montgomery County

Colorado Springs, CO
El Paso County

Columbia, MD
Howard County

Columbia, MO
Boone County

Columbia, SC
Richland County

Columbus, OH
Franklin County

Dallas, TX
Dallas County

Denver, CO
Denver County

Durham, NC
Durham County

Edison, NJ
Middlesex County

El Paso, TX
El Paso County

Fargo, ND
Cass County

Fort Collins, CO
Larimer County

Fort Worth, TX
Tarrant County

Gilbert, AZ
Maricopa County

Green Bay, WI
Brown County

Henderson, NV
Clark County

High Point, NC
Guilford County

Honolulu, HI
Honolulu County

Houston, TX
Harris County

Huntington, NY
Suffolk County

Huntsville, AL
Madison County

Indianapolis, IN
Marion County

Irvine, CA
Orange County

Jackson, MS
Hinds County

Jacksonville, FL
Duval County

Jersey City, NJ
Hudson County

Kansas City, MO
Jackson County

Kenosha, WI
Kenosha County

Las Vegas, NV
Clark County

Lexington, KY
Fayette County

Lincoln, NE
Lancaster County

Little Rock, AR
Pulaski County

Los Angeles, CA
Los Angeles County

Madison, WI
Dane County

Manchester, NH
Hillsborough County

Miami, FL
Miami-Dade County

Minneapolis, MN
Hennepin County

Murfreesboro, TN
Rutherford County

Naperville, IL
DuPage County

Nashville, TN
Davidson County

New Orleans, LA
Orleans Parish

New York, NY
Bronx, Kings, New York, Queens, and
Richmond Counties

Norman, OK
Cleveland County

Olathe, KS
Johnson County

Omaha, NE
Douglas County

Orlando, FL
Orange County

Overland Park, KS
Johnson County

Oyster Bay, NY
Nassau County

Pembroke Pines, FL
Broward County

Philadelphia, PA
Philadelphia County

Phoenix, AZ
Maricopa County

Pittsburgh, PA
Allegheny County

Plano, TX
Collin County

Portland, OR
Multnomah County

Providence, RI
Providence County

Provo, UT
Utah County

Raleigh, NC
Wake County

Richmond, VA
Richmond Independent City

Roseville, CA
Placer County

Round Rock, TX
Williamson County

San Antonio, TX
Bexar County

San Diego, CA
San Diego County

San Francisco, CA
San Francisco County

San Jose, CA
Santa Clara County

Savannah, GA
Chatham County

Scottsdale, AZ
Maricopa County

Seattle, WA
King County

Sioux Falls, SD
Minnehaha County

Stamford, CT
Fairfield County

Sterling Heights, MI
Macomb County

Sunnyvale, CA
Santa Clara County

Tampa, FL
Hillsborough County

Temecula, CA
Riverside County

Thousand Oaks, CA
Ventura County

Virginia Beach, VA
Virginia Beach Independent City

Washington, DC
District of Columbia

*Note: In cases where a city's population is
split over multiple counties (except New York),
data in this book reflects the county where the
majority of the population resides.*

Appendix B: Metropolitan Area Definitions

Metropolitan Statistical Areas (MSA), Metropolitan Divisions (MD), New England City and Town Areas (NECTA), and New England City and Town Area Divisions (NECTAD)

Albuquerque, NM MSA
Bernalillo, Sandoval, Torrance, and Valencia Counties

Alexandria, VA
See Washington, DC

Anchorage, AK MSA
Anchorage Municipality and Matanuska-Susitna Borough

Ann Arbor, MI MSA
Washtenaw County

Athens-Clarke County, GA MSA
Clarke, Madison, Oconee, and Oglethorpe Counties

Atlanta-Sandy Springs-Marietta, GA MSA
Barrow, Bartow, Butts, Carroll, Cherokee, Clayton, Cobb, Coweta, Dawson, DeKalb, Douglas, Fayette, Forsyth, Fulton, Gwinnett, Haralson, Heard, Henry, Jasper, Lamar, Meriwether, Newton, Paulding, Pickens, Pike, Rockdale, Spalding, and Walton Counties

Austin-Round Rock-San Marcos, TX MSA
Bastrop, Caldwell, Hays, Travis, and Williamson Counties

Baltimore-Towson, MD MSA
Baltimore city; Anne Arundel, Baltimore, Carroll, Harford, Howard, and Queen's Counties

Bellevue, WA
See Seattle, WA

Billings, MT MSA
Carbon and Yellowstone Counties

Boise City-Nampa, ID MSA
Ada, Boise, Canyon, Gem, and Owyhee Counties

Boston, MA
Boston-Cambridge-Quincy, MA-NH MSA
Essex, Middlesex, Norfolk, Plymouth, and Suffolk Counties, MA; Rockingham and Strafford Counties, NH
Boston-Quincy, MA MD
Norfolk, Plymouth, and Suffolk Counties
Boston-Cambridge-Quincy, MA-NH NECTA
Includes 155 cities and towns in Massachusetts and 38 cities and towns in New Hampshire

Boston-Cambridge-Quincy, MA NECTA Division
Includes 97 cities and towns in Massachusetts

Boulder, CO MSA
Boulder County

Bridgeport, CT
Bridgeport-Stamford-Norwalk, CT MSA
Fairfield County
Bridgeport-Stamford-Norwalk, CT NECTA
Includes 25 cities and towns in Connecticut

Broken Arrow, OK
See Tulsa, OK MSA

Cambridge, MA
See Boston, MA

Cape Coral-Fort Myers, FL MSA
Lee County

Carlsbad, CA
See San Diego-Carlsbad-San Marcos, CA MSA

Cary, NC
See Raleigh-Cary, NC MSA

Cedar Rapids, IA, MSA
Benton, Jones, and Linn Counties

Charleston-North Charleston-Summerville, SC MSA
Berkeley, Charleston, and Dorchester Counties

Charlotte-Gastonia-Rock Hill, NC-SC MSA
Anson, Cabarrus, Gaston, Mecklenburg, and Union Counties, NC; York County, SC

Chattanooga, TN-GA MSA
Catoosa, Dade, and Walker Counties, GA; Hamilton, Marion, and Sequatchie Counties, TN

Chesapeake, VA
See Virginia Beach-Norfolk-Newport News, VA-NC MSA

Chicago, IL
Chicago-Joliet-Naperville, IL-IN-WI MSA
Cook, DeKalb, DuPage, Grundy, Kane, Kendall, Lake, McHenry, and Will Counties, IL; Jasper, Lake, Newton, and Porter Counties, IN; Kenosha County, WI

Chicago-Joliet-Naperville, IL MD
Cook, DeKalb, DuPage, Grundy, Kane, Kendall, McHenry, and Will Counties
Lake County-Kenosha County, IL-WI MD
Lake County, IL; Kenosha County, WI

Clarksville, TN-KY MSA
Mongomery and Stewart Counties, TN; Christian and Trigg Counties, KY

Colorado Springs, CO MSA
El Paso and Teller Counties

Columbia, MD
See Baltimore-Towson, MD MSA

Columbia, MO MSA
Boone and Howard Counties

Columbia, SC MSA
Calhoun, Fairfield, Kershaw, Lexington, Richland, and Saluda Counties

Columbus, OH MSA
Delaware, Fairfield, Franklin, Licking, Madison, Morrow, Pickaway, and Union Counties

Dallas, TX
Dallas-Fort Worth-Arlington, TX MSA
Collin, Dallas, Delta, Denton, Ellis, Hunt, Johnson, Kaufman, Parker, Rockwall, Tarrant, and Wise Counties
Dallas-Plano-Irving, TX MD
Collin, Dallas, Delta, Denton, Ellis, Hunt, Kaufman, and Rockwall Counties

Denver-Aurora-Broomfield, CO MSA
Adams, Arapahoe, Broomfield, Clear Creek, Denver, Douglas, Elbert, Gilpin, Jefferson, and Park Counties

Detroit, MI
Detroit-Warren-Livonia, MI MSA
Lapeer, Livingston, Macomb, Oakland, and St. Clair, and Wayne Counties
Warren-Troy-Farmington Hills, MI MD
Lapeer, Livingston, Macomb, Oakland, and St. Clair Counties

Durham-Chapel Hill, NC MSA
Chatham, Durham, Orange, and and Person Counties

Edison, NJ
Edison-New Brunswick, NJ MD
Hunterdon, Middlesex and Somerset Counties

See also New York-Northern New Jersey-Long Island, NY-NJ-PA MSA

El Paso, TX MSA
El Paso County

Eugene-Springfield, OR MSA
Lane County

Fargo, ND-MN MSA
Cass County, ND; Clay County, MN

Fort Collins-Loveland, CO MSA
Larimer County

Fort Lauderdale, FL
Fort Lauderdale-Pompano Beach-Deerfield Beach, FL MD
Broward County
See also Miami-Fort Lauderdale-Miami Beach, FL MSA

Fort Worth, TX
Fort Worth-Arlington, TX MD
Johnson, Parker, Tarrant, and Wise Counties
See also Dallas-Fort Worth-Arlington, TX MSA

Gilbert, AZ
See Phoenix, AZ MSA

Green Bay, WI MSA
Brown, Kewaunee, and Oconto Counties

Greensboro-High Point, NC MSA
Guilford, Randolph, and Rockingham Counties

Henderson, NV
See Las Vegas-Paradise, NV MSA

High Point, NC
See Greensboro-High Point, NC MSA

Honolulu, HI MSA
Honolulu County

Houston-Sugar Land-Baytown, TX MSA
Austin, Brazoria, Chambers, Fort Bend, Galveston, Harris, Liberty, Montgomery, San Jacinto, and Waller Counties

Huntington, NY
Nassau-Suffolk, NY MD
Nassau and Suffolk Counties
See also New York, NY

Huntsville, AL MSA
Limestone and Madison Counties

Indianapolis-Carmel, IN MSA
Boone, Brown, Hamilton, Hancock, Hendricks, Johnson, Marion, Morgan, Putnam, and Shelby Counties

Irvine, CA
Santa Ana-Anaheim-Irvine, CA MD

Orange County
See also Los Angeles, CA

Jackson, MS MSA
Copiah, Hinds, Madison, Rankin and Simpson Counties, MS

Jacksonville, FL MSA
Baker, Clay, Duval, Nassau, and St. Johns Counties

Jersey City, NJ
New York-White Plains-Wayne, NY-NJ MD
Bergen, Hudson, and Passaic Counties, NJ; Bronx, Kings, New York, Putnam, Queens, Richmond, Rockland, and Westchester Counties, NY
See also New York, NY

Kansas City, MO-KS MSA
Franklin, Johnson, Leavenworth, Linn, Miami, and Wyandotte Counties, KS; Bates, Caldwell, Cass, Clay, Clinton, Jackson, Lafayette, Platte, and Ray Counties, MO

Kenosha, WA
Lake County-Kenosha County, IL-WI MD
Lake County, IL; Kenosha County, WI
See also Chicago, IL

Las Vegas-Paradise, NV MSA
Clark County

Lexington-Fayette, KY MSA
Bourbon, Clark, Fayette, Jessamine, Scott, and Woodford Counties

Lincoln, NE MSA
Lancaster and Seward Counties

Little Rock-North Little Rock-Conway, AR MSA
Faulkner, Grant, Lonoke, Perry, Pulaski and Saline Counties, AR

Los Angeles, CA
Los Angeles-Long Beach-Santa Ana, CA MSA
Los Angeles and Orange Counties
Los Angeles-Long Beach-Glendale, CA MD
Los Angeles County
Santa Ana-Anaheim-Irvine, CA MD
Orange County

Madison, WI MSA
Columbia, Dane, and Iowa Counties

Manchester-Nashua, NH MSA
Hillsborough County
Manchester, NH NECTA
Includes 9 cities and towns in New Hampshire

Miami, FL
Miami-Fort Lauderdale-Pompano Beach, FL MSA
Broward, Miami-Dade, and Palm Beach Counties
Miami-Miami Beach-Kendall, FL MD
Miami-Dade County

Minneapolis-St. Paul-Bloomington, MN-WI MSA
Anoka, Carver, Chisago, Dakota, Hennepin, Isanti, Ramsey, Scott, Sherburne, Washington, and Wright Counties, MN; Pierce and St. Croix Counties, WI

Murfreesboro, TN
See Nashville-Davidson—Murfreesboro—Franklin, TN MSA

Naperville, IL
See Chicago, IL

Nashville-Davidson—Murfreesboro—Franklin, TN MSA
Cannon, Cheatham, Davidson, Dickson, Hickman, Macon, Robertson, Rutherford, Smith, Sumner, Trousdale, Williamson, and Wilson Counties

New Orleans-Metarie-Kenner, LA MSA
Jefferson, Orleans, Plaquemines, St. Bernard, St. Charles, St. John the Baptist, and St. Tammany Parish

New York, NY
Nassau-Suffolk, NY MD
Nassau and Suffolk Counties
New York-Northern New Jersey-Long Island, NY-NJ-PA MSA
Bergen, Essex, Hudson, Hunterdon, Middlesex, Monmouth, Morris, Ocean, Passaic, Somerset, Sussex, and Union Counties, NJ; Bronx, Kings, Nassau, New York, Putnam, Queens, Richmond, Rockland, Suffolk, and Westchester Counties, NY; Pike County, PA
New York-Wayne-White Plains, NY-NJ MD
Bergen, Hudson, and Passaic Counties, NJ; Bronx, Kings, New York, Putnam, Queens, Richmond, Rockland, and Westchester Counties, NY

Norman, OK
See Oklahoma City, OK MSA

Oakland, CA
Oakland-Fremont-Hayward, CA MD
Alameda and Contra Costa Counties
See also San Francisco-Oakland-Fremont, CA MSA

Oklahoma City, OK MSA
Canadian, Cleveland, Grady, Lincoln, Logan, McClain, and Oklahoma Counties

Olathe, KS
See Kansas City, MO-KS MSA

Omaha-Council Bluffs, NE-IA MSA
Harrison, Mills, and Pottawattamie Counties, IA; Cass, Douglas, Sarpy, Saunders, and Washington Counties, NE

Orlando-Kissimmee-Sanford, FL MSA
Lake, Orange, Osceola, and Seminole Counties

Overland Park, KS
See Kansas City, MO-KS MSA

Oyster Bay, NY
Nassau-Suffolk, NY MD
Nassau and Suffolk Counties
See also New York, NY

Oxnard-Thousand Oaks-Ventura, CA MSA
Ventura County

Pembroke Pines, FL
Fort Lauderdale-Pompano Beach-Deerfield Beach, FL MD
Broward County
See also Miami, FL

Philadelphia, PA
Philadelphia-Camden-Wilmington, PA-NJ-DE-MD MSA
New Castle County, DE; Cecil County, MD; Burlington, Camden, Gloucester, and Salem Counties, NJ; Bucks, Chester, Delaware, Montgomery, and Philadelphia Counties, PA
Philadelphia, PA MD
Bucks, Chester, Delaware, Montgomery, and Philadelphia Counties

Phoenix-Mesa-Glendale, AZ MSA
Maricopa and Pinal Counties

Pittsburgh, PA MSA
Allegheny, Armstrong, Beaver, Butler, Fayette, Washington, and Westmoreland Counties

Plano, TX
Dallas-Plano-Irving, TX MD
Collin, Dallas, Delta, Denton, Ellis, Hunt, Kaufman, and Rockwall Counties
See also Dallas, TX

Portland-Vancouver-Hillsboro, OR-WA MSA
Clackamas, Columbia, Multnomah, Washington, and Yamhill Counties, OR; Clark and Skamania Counties, WA

Providence-New Bedford-Fall River, RI-MA MSA
Bristol County, MA; Bristol, Kent, Newport, Providence, and Washington Counties, RI

Providence-Fall River-Warwick, RI-MA NECTA
Includes 12 cities and towns in Massachusetts and 37 cities and towns in Rhode Island

Provo-Orem, UT MSA
Juab and Utah Counties

Raleigh-Cary, NC MSA
Franklin, Johnston, and Wake Counties

Richmond, VA MSA
Petersburg, Colonial Heights, Hopewell, and Richmond cities; Amelia, Caroline, Charles City, Chesterfield, Cumberland, Dinwiddie, Goochland, Hanover, Henrico, King William, King and Queen, Louisa, New Kent, Powhatan, Prince George, and Sussex Counties

Riverside-San Bernardino-Ontario, CA MSA
Riverside and San Bernardino Counties

Roseville, CA
See Sacramento—Arden-Arcade—Roseville, CA MSA

Round Rock, TX
See Austin-Round Rock-San Marcos, TX MSA

Sacramento—Arden-Arcade—Roseville, CA MSA
El Dorado, Placer, Sacramento, and Yolo Counties

San Antonio-New Braunfels, TX MSA
Atascosa, Bandera, Bexar, Comal, Guadalupe, Kendall, Medina, and Wilson Counties

San Diego-Carlsbad-San Marcos, CA MSA
San Diego County

San Francisco, CA
San Francisco-Oakland-Fremont, CA MSA
Alameda, Contra Costa, Marin, San Francisco, and San Mateo Counties
San Francisco-San Mateo-Redwood City, CA MD
Marin, San Francisco, and San Mateo Counties

San Jose-Sunnyvale-Santa Clara, CA MSA
San Benito and Santa Clara Counties

Savannah, GA MSA
Bryan, Chatham, and Effingham Counties

Scottsdale, AZ
See Phoenix-Mesa-Glendale, AZ MSA

Seattle, WA
Seattle-Tacoma-Bellevue, WA MSA
King, Pierce, and Snohomish Counties

Seattle-Bellevue-Everett, WA MD
King and Snohomish Counties

Sioux Falls, SD MSA
Lincoln, McCook, Minnehaha, and Turner Counties

Stamford, CT
See Bridgeport, CT

Sterling Heights, MI
Warren-Troy-Farmington Hills, MI MD
Lapeer, Livingston, Macomb, Oakland, and St. Clair Counties
See also Detroit, MI

Sunnyvale, CA
See San Jose-Sunnyvale-Santa Clara, CA MSA

Tampa-St. Petersburg-Clearwater, FL MSA
Hernando, Hillsborough, Pasco, and Pinellas Counties

Temecula, CA
See Riverside-San Bernardino-Ontario, CA MSA

Thousand Oaks, CA
See Oxnard-Thousand Oaks-Ventura, CA MSA

Tulsa, OK MSA
Creek, Okmulgee, Osage, Pawnee, Rogers, Tulsa, and Wagoner Counties

Virginia Beach-Norfolk-Newport News, VA-NC MSA
Currituck County, NC; Chesapeake, Hampton, Newport News, Norfolk, Poquoson, Portsmouth, Suffolk, Virginia Beach and Williamsburg cities, VA; Gloucester, Isle of Wight, James City, Mathews, Surry, and York Counties, VA

Washington, DC
Washington-Arlington-Alexandria, DC-VA-MD-WV MSA
District of Columbia; Calvert, Charles, Frederick, Montgomery, and Prince George's Counties, MD; Alexandria, Fairfax, Falls Church, Fredericksburg, Manassas Park, and Manassas cities, VA; Arlington, Clarke, Fairfax, Fauquier, Loudoun, Prince William, Spotsylvania, Stafford, and Warren Counties, VA; Jefferson County, WV
Washington-Arlington-Alexandria, DC-VA-MD-WV MD
District of Columbia; Calvert, Charles, and Prince George's Counties, MD; Alexandria, Fairfax, Falls Church, Fredericksburg, Manassas Park, and Manassas cities, VA; Arlington, Clarke, Fairfax, Fauquier, Loudoun, Prince William, Spotsylvania, Stafford, and Warren Counties, VA; Jefferson County, WV

Appendix C: Chambers of Commerce & Economic Development Offices

Albuquerque, NM

Albuquerque Chamber of Commerce
P.O. Box 25100
Albuquerque, NM 87125
Phone: (505) 764-3700
Fax: (505) 764-3714
www.abqchamber.com

Albuquerque Economic Development Dept
851 University Blvd SE
Suite 203
Albuquerque, NM 87106
Phone: (505) 246-6200
Fax: (505) 246-6219
www.cabq.gov/econdev

Alexandria, VA

Alexandria Chamber of Commerce
801 N Fairfax St
Suite 402
Alexandria, VA 22314
Phone: (703) 739-3810
Fax: (703) 739-3805
www.alexchamber.com

Anchorage, AK

Anchorage Chamber of Commerce
1016 W Sixth Avenue
Suite 303
Anchorage, AK 99501
Phone: (907) 272-2401
Fax: (907) 272-4117
www.anchoragechamber.org

Anchorage Economic Development
Department
900 W 5th Avenue
Suite 300
Anchorage, AK 99501
Phone: (907) 258-3700
Fax: (907) 258-6646
www.aedcweb.com/aedcdig

Ann Arbor, MI

Ann Arbor Area Chamber of Commerce
115 West Huron
3rd Floor
Ann Arbor, MI 48104
Phone: (734) 665-4433
Fax: (734) 665-4191
www.annarborchamber.org

Ann Arbor Economic Development
Department
201 S Division
Suite 430
Ann Arbor, MI 48104
Phone: (734) 761-9317
www.annarborspark.org

Athens, GA

Athens Area Chamber of Commerce
246 W Hancock Avenue
Athens, GA 30601
Phone: (706) 549-6800
Fax: (706) 549-5636
www.aacoc.org

Athens-Clarke Economic Development
150 E. Hancock Avenue
P.O. Box 1692
Athens, GA 30603
Phone: (706) 613-3810
Fax: (706) 613-3812
www.athensbusiness.org/contact.aspx

Atlanta, GA

Metro Atlanta Chamber of Commerce
235 Andrew Young International Blvd NW
Atlanta, GA 30303
Phone: (404) 880-9000
Fax: (404) 586-8464
www.metroatlantachamber.com

Austin, TX

Greater Austin Chamber of Commerce
210 Barton Springs Road
Suite 400
Austin, TX 78704
Phone: (512) 478-9383
Fax: (512) 478-6389
www.austin-chamber.org

Baltimore, MD

Baltimore City Chamber of Commerce
312 Martin Luther King Jr Blvd
Baltimore, MD 21201
Phone: (410) 837-7101
Fax: (410) 837-7104
www.baltimorecitychamber.com

City of Baltimore Development Corporation
36 South Charles Street
Suite 1600
Baltimore, MD 21201
Phone: (410) 837-9305
Fax: (410) 837-6363
www.baltimoredevelopment.com

Bellevue, WA

Bellevue Chamber of Commerce
302 Bellevue Square
Bellevue, WA 98004
Phone: (425) 454-2464
www.bellevuechamber.org

Billings, MT

Billings Area Chamber of Commerce
815 S 27th St
Billings, MT 59101
Phone: (406) 245-4111
Fax: (406) 2457333
www.billingschamber.com

Boise City, ID

Boise Metro Chamber of Commerce
250 S 5th Street
Suite 800
Boise City, ID 83701
Phone: (208) 472-5200
Fax: (208) 472-5201
www.bisechamber.org

Boston, MA

Greater Boston Chamber of Commerce
265 Franklin Street
12th Floor
Boston, MA 02110
Phone: (617) 227-4500
Fax: (617) 227-7505
www.bostonchamber.com

Boulder, CO

Boulder Chamber of Commerce
2440 Pearl Street
Boulder, CO 80302
Phone: (303) 442-1044
Fax: (303) 938-8837
www.boulderchamber.com

City of Boulder Economic Vitality Program
P.O. Box 791
Boulder, CO 80306
Phone: (303) 441-3090
www.bouldercolorado.gov

Broken Arrow, OK

The Broken Arrow Area
Chamber of Commerce
210 N Main Street
Suite C
Broken Arrow, OK 74013
Phone: (918) 251-1518
Fax: (918)251-1777
www.brokenarrow.com

Cambridge, MA

Cambridge Chamber of Commerce
859 Massachusetts Ave
Cambridge, MA 02139
Phone: (617) 876-4100
www.cambridgechamber.org

Cape Coral, FL

Chamber of Commerce of Cape Coral
2051 Cape Coral Parkway East
Cape Coral, FL 33904
Phone: (239) 549-6900
Fax: (239) 549-9609
www.capecoralchamber.com

Carlsbad, CA

The City of Carlsbad Chamber of Commerce
5934 Priestly Dr.
Carlsbad, CA 92008
Phone: (760) 931-8400
Fax: (760) 931-9153
www.carlsbad.org

Cary, NC

Cary Chamber of Commerce
307 North Academy St
Cary, NC 27513
Phone: (919) 467-1016
www.carychamber.com

Cedar Rapids, IA

Cedar Rapids Chamber of Commerce
424 First Avenue NE
Cedar Rapids, IA 52401
Phone: (319) 398-5317
Fax: (319) 398-5228
www.cedarrapids.org

Cedar Rapids Economic Development
50 Second Avenue Bridge
Sixth Floor
Cedar Rapids, IA 52401-1256
Phone: (319) 286-5041
Fax: (319) 286-5141
www.cedar-rapids.org

Cedar Rapids Metro Economic Alliance
424 First Avenue NE
Cedar Rapids, IA 52401-1196
Phone: (319) 398-5317
www.cedarrapids.org

Charleston, SC

Charleston Metro Chamber of Commerce
P.O. Box 975
Charleston, SC 29402
Phone: (843) 577-2510
www.charlestonchamber.net

Charlotte, NC

Charlotte Chamber of Commerce
330 S Tryon Street
P.O. Box 32785
Charlotte, NC 28232
Phone: (704) 378-1300
Fax: (704) 374-1903
www.charlottechamber.com

Charlotte Regional Partnership
1001 Morehead Square Drive
Suite 200
Charlotte, NC 28203
Phone: (704) 347-8942
Fax: (704) 347-8981
www.charlotteusa.com

Chesapeake, VA

Hampton Roads Chamber of Commerce
500 East Main Street
Suite 700
Chesapeake, VA 23510
Phone: (757) 622-2312
Fax: (757) 664-2558
www.hamptonroadschamber.com

Chicago, IL

Chicagoland Chamber of Commerce
200 E Randolph Street
Suite 2200
Chicago, IL 60601-6436
Phone: (312) 494-6700
Fax: (312) 861-0660
www.chicagolandchamber.org

City of Chicago Department of Planning and Development
City Hall, Room 1000
121 North La Salle Street
Chicago, IL 60602
Phone: (312) 744-4190
Fax: (312) 744-2271
egov.cityofchicago.org

Clarksville, TN

Clarksville Area Chamber of Commerce
25 Jefferson Street
Suite 300
Clarksville, TN 37040
Phone: (931) 647-2331
www.clarksvillechamber.com

Colorado Springs, CO

Greater Colorado Springs Chamber of Commerce
6 S. Tejon Street
Suite 700
Colorado Springs, CO 80903
Phone: (719) 635-1551
Fax: (719) 635-1571
gcsco.wliinc3.com

Greater Colorado Springs Economic Development Corp
90 South Cascade Avenue
Suite 1050
Colorado Springs, CO 80903
Phone: (719) 471-8183
Fax: (719) 471-9733
www.coloradosprings.org

Columbia, MD

Howard County Chamber of Commerce
5560 Sterrett Pl.
Suite 105
Columbia, MD 21044
Phone: (410) 730-4111
Fax: (410) 730-4584
www.howardchamber.com

Columbia, MO

Columbia Chamber of Commerce
300 South Providence Rd.
PO Box 1016
Columbia, MO 65205-1016
Phone: (573) 874-1132
Fax: (573)443-3986
www.columbiamochamber.com

Columbia, SC

City of Columbia Office of Economic Development
1201 Main Street
Suite 250
Columbia, SC 29201
Phone: (803) 734-2700
Fax: (803) 734-2702
www.columbiascdevelopment.com

Columbia Chamber of Commerce
930 Richmond Street
Columbia, SC 20201
Phone: (803) 733-1110
Fax: (803) 733-1149
www.columbiachamber.com

Columbus, OH

Greater Columbus Chamber
37 North High Street
Columbus, OH 43215
Phone: (614) 221-1321
Fax: (614) 221-1408
www.columbus.org

Dallas, TX

City of Dallas Economic Development Department
1500 Marilla Street
5C South
Dallas, TX 75201
Phone: (214) 670-1685
Fax: (214) 670-0158
www.dallas-edd.org

Greater Dallas Chamber of Commerce
700 North Pearl Street
Suite1200
Dallas, TX 75201
Phone: (214) 746-6600
Fax: (214) 746-6799
www.dallaschamber.org

Denver, CO

Denver Metro Chamber of Commerce
1445 Market Street
Denver, CO 80202
Phone: (303) 534-8500
Fax: (303) 534-3200
www.denverchamber.org

Downtown Denver Partnership
511 16th Street
Suite 200
Denver, CO 80202
Phone: (303) 534-6161
Fax: (303) 534-2803
www.downtowndenver.com

Durham, NC

Durham Chamber of Commerce
PO Box 3829
Durham, NC 27702
Phone: (919) 682-2133
Fax: (919) 688-8351
www.durhamchamber.org

North Carolina Institute of Minority Economic
Development
114 W Parish Street
Durham, NC 27701
Phone: (919) 956-8889
Fax: (919) 688-7668
www.ncimed.com

Edison, NJ

Edison Chamber of Commerce
336 Raritan Center Parkway
Campus Plaza 6
Edison, NJ 08837
Phone: (732) 738-9482
Fax: (732) 738-9485
www.edisonchamber.com

El Paso, TX

City of El Paso Department of Economic
Development
2 Civic Center Plaza
El Paso, TX 79901
Phone: (915) 541-4000
Fax: (915) 541-1316
www.elpasotexas.gov

Greater El Paso Chamber of Commerce
10 Civic Center Plaza
El Paso, TX 79901
Phone: (915) 534-0500
Fax: (915) 534-0510
www.elpaso.org

Fargo, ND

Chamber of Commerce of Fargo Moorhead
202 First Avenue North
Fargo, ND 56560
Phone: (218) 233-1100
Fax: (218) 233-1200
www.fmchamber.com

Greater Fargo-Moorhead Economic
Development Corporation
51 Broadway, Suite 500
Fargo, ND 58102
Phone: (701) 364-1900
Fax: (701) 293-7819
www.gfmedc.com

Fort Collins, CO

Fort Collins Chamber of Commerce
225 South Meldrum
Fort Collins, CO 80521
Phone: (970) 482-3746
Fax: (970) 482-3774
www.fcchamber.org

Fort Worth, TX

City of Fort Worth Economic Development
City Hall
900 Monroe Street, Suite 301
Fort Worth, TX 76102
Phone: (817) 392-6103
Fax: (817) 392-2431
www.fortworthgov.org

Fort Worth Chamber of Commerce
777 Taylor Street
Suite 900
Fort Worth, TX 76102-4997
Phone: (817) 336-2491
Fax: (817) 877-4034
www.fortworthchamber.com

Gilbert, AZ

Gilbert Chamber of Commerce
119 North Gilbert Road
Suite 101
Gilbert, AZ 85299-0527
Phone: (480) 892-0056
Fax: (480) 892-1980
www.gilbertaz.com

Green Bay, WI

Economic Development
100 N Jefferson St
Room 202
Green Bay, WI 54301
Phone: (920) 448-3397
Fax: (920) 448-3063
www.ci.green-bay.wi.us

Green Bay Area Chamber of Commerce
300 N. Broadway
Suite 3A
Green Bay, WI 54305-1660
Phone: (920) 437-8704
Fax: (920) 593-3468
www.titletown.org

Henderson, NV

Henderson Chamber of Commerce
590 S. Boulder Highway
Henderson, NV 89015
Phone: (702) 565-8951
www.hendersonchamber.com

High Point, NC

High Point Chamber of Commerce
1634 N. Main Street
High Point, NC 27262
Phone: (336) 882-5000
Fax: (336) 889-9499
www.highpointchamber.org

Honolulu, HI

The Chamber of Commerce of Hawaii
1132 Bishop Street
Suite 402
Honolulu, HI 96813
Phone: (808) 545-4300
Fax: (808) 545-4369
www.cochawaii.com

Houston, TX

Greater Houston Partnership
1200 Smith Street
Suite 700
Houston, TX 77002-4400
Phone: (713) 844-3600
Fax: (713) 844-0200
www.houston.org

Huntington, NY

Huntington Chamber of Commerce
164 Main Street
Huntington, NY 11743
Phone: (631) 423-6100
Fax: (631) 351-8276
www.huntingtonchamber.com

Huntsville, AL

Chamber of Commerce of Huntsville/Madison
County
225 Church Street
Huntsville, AL 35801
Phone: (256) 535-2000
Fax: (256) 535-2015
www.huntsvillealabamausa.com

Indianapolis, IN

Greater Indianapolis Chamber of Commerce
111 Monument Circle
Suite 1950
Indianapolis, IN 46204
Phone: (317) 464-2222
Fax: (317) 464-2217
www.indychamber.com

The Indy Partnership
111 Monument Circle
Suite 1800
Indianapolis, IN 46204
Phone: (317) 236-6262
Fax: (317) 236-6275
www.indypartnership.com

Irvine, CA

Irvine Chamber of Commerce
2485 McCabe Way
Suite 150
Irvine, CA 92614
Phone: (949) 660-9112
Fax: (949) 660-0829
www.irvinechamber.com

Jackson, MS

MetroJackson Chamber of Commerce
PO Box 22548
Jackson, MS 39225
Phone: (601) 948-7575
Fax: (601) 352-5539
www.metrochamber.com

Jacksonville, FL

Jacksonville Chamber of Commerce
3 Independent Drive
Jacksonville, FL 32202
Phone: (904) 366-6600
Fax: (904) 632-0617
www.myjaxchamber.com

Jersey City, NJ

Hudson County Chamber of Commerce
857 Bergen Avenue
3rd Floor
Jersey City, NJ 7306
Phone: (201) 386-0699
Fax: (201) 386-8480
www.hudsonchamber.org

Kansas City, MO

Greater Kansas City Chamber of Commerce
2600 Commerce Tower
911 Main Street
Kansas City, MO 64105
Phone: (816) 221-2424
Fax: (816) 221-7440
www.kcchamber.com

Kansas City Area Development Council
2600 Commerce Tower
911 Main Street
Kansas City, MO 64105
Phone: (816) 221-2121
Fax: (816) 842-2865
www.thinkkc.com

Kenosha, WI

Kenosha Area Chamber of Commerce
600 52nd Street
Suite 130
Kenosha, WI 53140-3423
Phone: (262) 654-1234
Fax: (262) 654-4655
www.kenoshaareachamber.com

Las Vegas, NV

Las Vegas Chamber of Commerce
6671 Las Vegas Blvd South
Suite 300
Las Vegas, NV 89119
Phone: (702) 735-1616
Fax: (702) 735-0406
www.lvchamber.org

Las Vegas Office of Business Development
400 Stewart Avenue
City Hall
Las Vegas, NV 89101
Phone: (702) 229-6011
Fax: (702) 385-3128
www.lasvegasnevada.gov

Lexington, KY

Greater Lexington Chamber of Commerce
330 East Main Street
Suite 100
Lexington, KY 40507
Phone: (859) 254-4447
Fax: (859) 233-3304
www.commercelexington.com

Lexington Downtown Development Authority
101 East Vine Street
Suite 500
Lexington, KY 40507
Phone: (859) 425-2296
Fax: (859) 425-2292
www.lexingtondda.com

Lincoln, NE

Lincoln Chamber of Commerce
1135 M Street
Suite 200
Lincoln, NE 68508
Phone: (402) 436-2350
Fax: (402) 436-2360
www.lcoc.com

Little Rock, AR

Little Rock Regional Chamber of Commerce
One Chamber Plaza
Little Rock, AR 72201-1618
Phone: (501) 374-2001
www.littlerockchamber.com

Los Angeles, CA

Los Angeles Area Chamber of Commerce
350 South Bixel Street
Los Angeles, CA 90017
Phone: (213) 580-7500
Fax: (213) 580-7511
www.lachamber.org

Los Angeles County Economic Development
Corporation
444 South Flower Street
34th Floor
Los Angeles, CA 90071
Phone: (213) 622-4300
Fax: (213) 622-7100
www.laedc.org

Madison, WI

Greater Madison Chamber of Commerce
615 East Washington Avenue
P.O. Box 71
Madison, WI 53701-0071
Phone: (608) 256-8348
Fax: (608) 256-0333
www.greatermadisonchamber.com

Manchester, NH

Greater Manchester Chamber of Commerce
889 Elm Street
Manchester, NH 03101
Phone: (603) 666-6600
Fax: (603) 626-0910
www.manchester-chamber.org

Manchester Economic Development Office
One City Hall Plaza
Manchester, NH 03101
Phone: (603) 624-6505
Fax: (603) 624-6308
www.yourmanchesternh.com

Miami, FL

Greater Miami Chamber of Commerce
1601 Biscayne Boulevard
Ballroom Level
Miami, FL 33132-1260
Phone: (305) 350-7700
Fax: (305) 374-6902
www.greatermiami.com

The Beacon Council
80 Southwest 8th Street
Suite 2400
Miami, FL 33130
Phone: (305) 579-1300
Fax: (305) 375-0271
www.beaconcouncil.com

Minneapolis, MN

Minneapolis Community Development
Agency
Crown Roller Mill
105 5th Avenue South, Suite 200
Minneapolis, MN 55401
Phone: (612) 673-5095
Fax: (612) 673-5100
www.ci.minneapolis.mn.us

Murfreesboro, TN

Rutherford County Chamber of Commerce
3050 Medical Center Parkway
Murfreesboro, TN 37129
Phone: (615) 893-6565
Fax: (615) 890-7600
www.rutherfordchamber.org

Naperville, IL

Naperville Chamber of Commerce
55 S Main St #351
Naperville, IL 60540
Phone: (630) 355-4141
www.naperville.net

Nashville, TN

Community Development Department
312 Eighth Avenue North
Eleventh Floor
Nashville, TN 37243
Phone: (615) 741-2626
Fax: (615) 532-8715
www.state.tn.us

Nashville Area Chamber of Commerce
211 Commerce Street
Suite 100
Nashville, TN 37201
Phone: (615) 743-3000
Fax: (615) 256-3074
www.nashvillechamber.cm

Tennessee Valley Authority Economic
Development Corp.
P.O. Box 292409
Nashville, TN 37229-2409
Phone: (615) 232-6225
www.tvaed.com

New Orleans, LA

New Orleans Chamber of Commerce
1515 Poydras St
Suite 1010
New Orleans, LA 70112
Phone: (504) 799-4260
Fax: (504) 799-4259
neworleanschamber.org

New York, NY

New York City Economic Development
Corporation
110 William Street
New York, NY 10038
Phone: (212) 619-5000
www.nycedc.com

The Partnership for New York City
One Battery Park Plaza
5th Floor
New York, NY 10004
Phone: (212) 493-7400
Fax: (212) 344-3344
www.pfnyc.org

Norman, OK

Norman Chamber of Commerce
115 E. Gray
Norman, OK 73070
Phone: (405) 321-7260
Fax: (405) 360-4679
www.normanchamber.com

Olathe, KS

Olathe Chamber of Commerce
18001 W. 106th St.
Suite 160
Olathe, KS 66061-0098
Phone: (913) 764-1050
Fax: (913) 782-4636
www.olathe.org

Omaha, NE

Omaha Chamber of Commerce
1301 Harney Street
Omaha, NE 68102
Phone: (402) 346-5000
Fax: (402) 346-7050
www.omahachamber.org

Orlando, FL

Metro Orlando Economic Development
Commission of Mid-Florida
301 East Pine Street
Suite 900
Orlando, FL 32801
Phone: (407) 422-7159
Fax: (407) 425.6428
www.orlandoedc.com

Orlando Regional Chamber of Commerce
75 South Ivanhoe Boulevard
PO Box 1234
Orlando, FL 32802
Phone: (407) 425-1234
Fax: (407) 839-5020
www.orlando.org

Overland Park, KS

Overland Park Chamber of Commerce
9001 W 110th St
Suite 150
Overland Park, KS 66210
Phone: (913) 491-3600
www.opks.org

Oyster Bay, NY

Historic Oyster Bay Chamber of Commerce
PO Box 21
Oyster Bay, NY 11771
Phone: (516) 922-6464
www.visitoysterbay.com

Pembroke Pines, FL

Miramar Pembroke Pines Regional Chamber
of Commerce
10100 Pines Boulevard
4th Floor
Pembroke Pines, FL 33026
Phone: (954) 432-9808
Fax: (954) 432-9193
www.miramarpembrokepines.org

Philadelphia, PA

Greater Philadelphia Chamber of Commerce
200 South Broad Street
Suite 700
Philadelphia, PA 19102
Phone: (215) 545-1234
Fax: (215) 790-3600
www.greaterphilachamber.com

Phoenix, AZ

Greater Phoenix Chamber of Commerce
201 North Central Avenue
27th Floor
Phoenix, AZ 85073
Phone: (602) 495-2195
Fax: (602) 495-8913
www.phoenixchamber.com

Greater Phoenix Economic Council
2 North Central Avenue
Suite 2500
Phoenix, AZ 85004
Phone: (602) 256-7700
Fax: (602) 256-7744
www.gpec.org

Pittsburgh, PA

Allegheny County Industrial Development
Authority
425 6th Avenue
Suite 800
Pittsburgh, PA 15219
Phone: (412) 350-1067
Fax: (412) 642-2217
www.alleghenycounty.us

Greater Pittsburgh Chamber of Commerce
425 6th Avenue
12th Floor
Pittsburgh, PA 15219
Phone: (412) 392-4500
Fax: (412) 392-4520
www.alleghenyconference.org

Plano, TX

Plano Chamber of Commerce
1200 E 15th St
Plano, TX 75074
Phone: (972) 424-7547
Fax: (972) 422-5182
www.planochamber.org

Portland, OR

Portland Business Alliance
200 SW Market Street
Suite 1770
Portland, OR 97201
Phone: (503) 224-8684
Fax: (503) 323-9186
www.portlandalliance.com

Providence, RI

Greater Providence Chamber of Commerce
30 Exchange Terrace
Fourth Floor
Providence, RI 02903
Phone: (401) 521-5000
Fax: (401) 351-2090
www.provchamber.com

Rhode Island Economic Development
Corporation
Providence City Hall
25 Dorrance Street
Providence, RI 02903
Phone: (401) 421-7740
Fax: (401) 751-0203
www.providenceri.com

Provo, UT

Provo-Orem Chamber of Commerce
51 South University Avenue
Suite 215
Provo, UT 84601
Phone: (801) 851-2555
Fax: (801) 851-2557
www.thechamber.org/

Raleigh, NC

Greater Raleigh Chamber of Commerce
800 South Salisbury Street
Raleigh, NC 27601-2978
Phone: (919) 664-7000
Fax: (919) 664-7099
www.raleighchamber.org

Richmond, VA

Greater Richmond Chamber of Commerce
P.O. Box 12280
Richmond, VA 23241-2280
Phone: (804) 648-1234
Fax: (804) 783-9366
www.grcc.com/

Greater Richmond Partnership
901 East Byrd Street
Suite 801
Richmond, VA 23219-4070
Phone: (804) 643-3227
Fax: (804) 343-7167
www.grpva.com/New_pages/home_ted.shtm

Roseville, CA

Roseville Chamber of Commerce
650 Douglas Blvd.
Roseville, CA 95678
Phone: (916) 783-8136
www.rosevillechamber.com

Round Rock, TX

Round Rock Chamber
212 East Main St.
Round Rock, TX 78664
Phone: (512) 255-5805
Fax: (512) 255-3345
www.roundrockchamber.org

San Antonio, TX

San Antonio Economic Development
Department
P.O. Box 839966
San Antonio, TX 78283-3966
Phone: (210) 207-8080
Fax: (210) 207-8151
www.sanantonio.gov/edd

The Greater San Antonio Chamber of
Commerce
602 E. Commerce Street
San Antonio, TX 78205
Phone: (210) 229-2100
Fax: (210) 229-1600
www.sachamber.org

San Diego, CA

San Diego Economic Development
Corporation
401 B Street
Suite 1100
San Diego, CA 92101
Phone: (619) 234-8484
Fax: (619) 234-1935
www.sandiegobusiness.org

San Diego Regional Chamber of Commerce
402 West Broadway
Suite 1000
San Diego, CA 92101-3585
Phone: (619) 544-1300
Fax: (619) 744-7481
www.sdchamber.org

San Francisco, CA

San Francisco Chamber of Commerce
235 Montgomery Street
12th Floor
San Francisco, CA 94104
Phone: (415) 392-4520
Fax: (415) 392-0485
www.sfchamber.com

San Jose, CA

Office of Economic Development
60 South Market Street
Suite 470
San Jose, CA 95113
Phone: (408) 277-5880
Fax: (408) 277-3615
www.sba.gov

San Jose-Silicone Valley Chamber of
Commerce
310 South First Street
San Jose, CA 95113
Phone: (408) 291-5250
Fax: (408) 286-5019
www.sjchamber.com

Savannah, GA

Economic Development Authority
131 Hutchinson Island Road
4th Floor
Savannah, GA 31421
Phone: (912) 447-8450
Fax: (912) 447-8455
www.Seda.org

Savannah Chamber of Commerce
101 E. Bay Street
Savannah, GA 31402
Phone: (912) 644-6400
Fax: (912) 644-6499
www.savannahchamber.com

Scottsdale, AZ

Scottsdale Area Chamber of Commerce
4725 N. Scottsdale Rd.
#210
Scottsdale, AZ 85251-4498
Phone: (480) 355-2700
Fax: (480) 355-2710
www.scottsdalechamber.com

Seattle, WA

Greater Seattle Chamber of Commerce
1301 Fifth Avenue
Suite 2500
Seattle, WA 98101
Phone: (206) 389-7200
Fax: (206) 389-7288
www.seattlechamber.com

Sioux Falls, SD

Sioux Falls Area Chamber of Commerce
200 N. Phillips Avenue
Suite 102
Sioux Falls, SD 57104
Phone: (605) 336-1620
Fax: (605) 336-6499
www.siouxfallschamber.com

Stamford, CT

Stamford Chamber of Commerce
733 Summer Street
Stamford, CT 6901
Phone: (203) 359-4761
Fax: (203) 363-5069
www.stamfordchamber.com

Sterling Heights, MI

Sterling Heights Regional Chamber of
Commerce & Industry
12900 Hall Road
Suite 100
Sterling Heights, MI 48313
Phone: (586) 731-5400
Fax: (586) 731-3521
www.suscc.com

Sunnyvale, CA

Sunnyvale Chamber of Commerce
260 S. Sunnyvale Ave.
Suite 402
Sunnyvale, CA 94086
Phone: (408) 736-4971
Fax: (408) 736-1919
www.svcoc.org

Tampa, FL

Greater Tampa Chamber of Commerce
P.O. Box 420
Tampa, FL 33601-0420
Phone: (813) 276-9401
Fax: (813) 229-7855
www.tampachamber.com

Temecula, CA

Temecula Valley Chamber of Commerce
26790 Ynez Court
Suite A
Temecula, CA 92591
Phone: (951) 676-5090
Fax: (951) 694-0201
www.temecula.org

Thousand Oaks, CA

Greater Conejo Valley Chamber of Commerce
600 Hampshire Rd.
Suite 200
Thousand Oaks, CA 91361
Phone: (805) 370-0035
Fax: (805) 370-1083
www.conejochamber.org

Virginia Beach, VA

Hampton Roads Chamber of Commerce
500 East Main St
Suite 700
Virginia Beach, VA 23510
Phone: (757) 664-2531
www.hamptonroadschamber.com

Washington, DC

District of Columbia Chamber of Commerce
1213 K Street NW
Washington, DC 20005
Phone: (202) 347-7201
Fax: (202) 638-6762
www.dcchamber.org

District of Columbia Office of Planning and
Economic Development
J.A. Wilson Building
1350 Pennsylvania Ave NW, Suite 317
Washington, DC 20004
Phone: (202) 727-6365
Fax: (202) 727-6703
dcbiz.dc.gov/dmped/site/default.asp

Appendix D: State Departments of Labor

Alabama

Jim Bennett, Commissioner
Alabama Department of Labor
P.O. Box 303500
Montgomery, AL 36130-3500
Phone: (334) 242-3072
www.Alalabor.state.al.us

Alaska

Clark Bishop, Commissioner
Dept of Labor and Workforce Devel.
P.O. Box 11149
Juneau, AK 99822-2249
Phone: (907) 465-2700
www.labor.state.AK.us

Arizona

Brian C. Delfs, Director
Arizona Industrial Commission
800 West Washington Street
Phoenix, AZ 85007
Phone: (602) 542-4515
www.ica.state.AZ.us

Arkansas

James Salkeld, Director
Department of Labor
10421 West Markham
Little Rock, AR 72205
Phone: (501) 682-4500
www.Arkansas.gov/labor

California

Victoria Bradshaw, Director
Labor and Workforce Development
445 Golden Gate Ave., 10th Floor
San Francisco, CA 94102
Phone: (916) 263-1811
www.labor.CA.gov

Colorado

Donald J. Mares, Executive Director
Dept of Labor and Employment
633 17th St., 2nd Floor
Denver, CO 80202-3660
Phone: (888) 390-7936
www.COworkforce.com

Connecticut

Patricia H. Mayfield, Commissioner
Department of Labor
200 Folly Brook Blvd.
Wethersfield, CT 06109-1114
Phone: (860) 263-6000
www.CT.gov/dol

Delaware

Thomas B. Sharp, Secretary of Labor
Department of Labor
4425 N. Market St., 4th Floor
Wilmington, DE 19802
Phone: (302) 451-3423
www.Delawareworks.com

District of Columbia

Ms. Summer Spencer, Director
Employment Services Department
614 New York Ave., NE, Suite 300
Washington, DC 20002
Phone: (202) 671-1900
www.DOES.DC.gov

Florida

Monesia T. Brown, Director
Agency for Workforce Innovation
The Caldwell Building
107 East Madison St. Suite 100
Tallahassee, FL 32399-4120
Phone: (800) 342-3450
www.Floridajobs.org

Georgia

Michael Thurmond, Commissioner
Department of Labor
Sussex Place, Room 600
148 Andrew Young Intl Blvd., NE
Atlanta, GA 30303
Phone: (404) 656-3011
www.dol.state.GA.us

Hawaii

Director
Dept of Labor & Industrial Relations
830 Punchbowl Street
Honolulu, HI 96813
Phone: (808) 586-8842
wwwHawaii.gov/labor

Idaho

Robert B. Madsen, Director
Department of Labor
317 W. Main St.
Boise, ID 83735-0001
Phone: (208) 332-3579
www.labor.Idaho.gov

Illinois

Catherine M. Shannon, Director
Department of Labor
160 N. LaSalle Street, 13th Floor
Suite C-1300
Chicago, IL 60601
Phone: (312) 793-2800
www.state.IL.us/agency/idol

Indiana

Lori Torres, Dept of Labor
Indiana Government Center South
402 W. Washington Street
Room W195
Indianapolis, IN 46204
Phone: (317) 232-2655
www.IN.gov/labor

Iowa

David Neil, Labor Commissioner
Iowa Workforce Development
1000 East Grand Avenue
Des Moines, IA 50319-0209
Phone: (515) 242-5870
www.Iowaworkforce.org/labor

Kansas

Jim Garner, Secretary
Department of Labor
401 S.W. Topeka Blvd.
Topeka, KS 66603-3182
Phone: (785) 296-5000
www.dol.KS.gov

Kentucky

Philip Anderson, Commissioner
Department of Labor
1047 U.S. Hwy 127 South, Suite 4
Frankfort, KY 40601-4381
Phone: (502) 564-3070
www.labor.KY.gov

Louisiana

John Warner Smith, Secretary
Department of Labor
P.O. Box 94094
Baton Rouge, LA 70804-9094
Phone: (225) 342-3111
www.LAworks.net

Maine

Laura Fortman, Commissioner
Department of Labor
45 Commerce Street
Augusta, ME 04330
Phone: (207) 623-7900
www.state.ME.us/labor

Maryland

Tom Perez, Secretary
Department of Labor and Industry
500 N. Calvert Street
Suite 401
Baltimore, MD 21202
Phone: (410) 767-2357
www.dllr.state.MD.us

Massachusetts

Greg Noel, Secretary
Dept of Labor & Work Force Devel.
One Ashburton Place
Room 2112
Boston, MA 02108
Phone: (617) 626-7100
www.Mass.gov/eolwd

Michigan

Keith Cooley, Director
Dept of Labor & Economic Growth
P.O. Box 30004
Lansing, MI 48909
Phone: (517) 335-0400
www.Michigan.gov/cis

Minnesota

Steven A. Sviggum, Commissioner
Dept of Labor and Industry
443 Lafayette Road North
Saint Paul, MN 55155
Phone: (651) 284-5070
www.doli.state.MN.us

Mississippi

Tommye Dale Favre, Executive Director
Dept of Employment Security
P.O. Box 1699
Jackson, MS 39215-1699
Phone: (601) 321-6000
www.mdes.MS.gov

Missouri

Todd Smith, Director
Labor and Industrial Relations
P.O. Box 599
3315 W. Truman Boulevard
Jefferson City, MO 65102-0599
Phone: (573) 751-7500
www.dolir.MO.gov/lirc

Montana

Keith Kelly, Commissioner
Dept of Labor and Industry
P.O. Box 1728
Helena, MT 59624-1728
Phone: (406) 444-9091
www.dli.MT.gov

Nebraska

Fernando Lecuona, Commissioner
Department of Labor
550 South 16th Street
Box 94600
Lincoln, NE 68509-4600
Phone: (402) 471-9000
www.Nebraskaworkforce.com

Nevada

Michael Tanchek, Commissioner
Dept of Business and Industry
555 E. Washington Ave.
Suite 4100
Las Vegas, NV 89101-1050
Phone: (702) 486-2650
www.laborcommissioner.com

New Hampshire

George N. Copadis, Commissioner
Department of Labor
State Office Park South
95 Pleasant Street
Concord, NH 03301
Phone: (603) 271-3176
www.labor.state.NH.us

New Jersey

David Socolow, Commissioner
Department of Labor
John Fitch Plaza, 13th Floor
Suite D
Trenton, NJ 08625-0110
Phone: (609) 777-3200
lwd.dol.state.nj.us/labor

New Mexico

Betty D. Sparrow, Secretary
Department of Labor
401 Broadway, NE
Albuquerque, NM 87103-1928
Phone: (505) 841-8450
www.dol.state.NM.us

New York

M. Patricia Smith, Commissioner
Department of Labor
State Office Bldg. # 12
W.A. Harriman Campus
Albany, NY 12240
Phone: (518) 457-5519
www.labor.state.NY.us

North Carolina

Cherie K. Berry, Commissioner
Department of Labor
4 West Edenton Street
Raleigh, NC 27601-1092
Phone: (919) 733-7166
www.nclabor.com

North Dakota

Lisa Fair McEvers, Commissioner
Department of Labor
State Capitol Building
600 East Boulevard, Dept 406
Bismark, ND 58505-0340
Phone: (701) 328-2660
www.nd.gov/labor

Ohio

Kimberly A. Zurz, Director
Department of Commerce
77 South High Street, 22nd Floor
Columbus, OH 43215
Phone: (614) 644-2239
www.com.state.OH.us

Oklahoma

Lloyd Fields, Commissioner
Department of Labor
4001 N. Lincoln Blvd.
Oklahoma City, OK 73105-5212
Phone: (405) 528-1500
www.state.OK.us/~okdol

Oregon

Dan Gardner, Commissioner
Bureau of Labor and Industries
800 NE Oregon St., #32
Portland, OR 97232
Phone: (971) 673-0761
www.Oregon.gov/boli

Pennsylvania

Stephen M. Schmerin, Secretary
Dept of Labor and Industry
1700 Labor and Industry Bldg
7th and Forster Streets
Harrisburg, PA 17120
Phone: (717) 787-5279
www.dli.state.PA.us

Rhode Island

Adelita S. Orefice, Director
Department of Labor and Training
1511 Pontiac Avenue
Cranston, RI 02920
Phone: (401) 462-8000
www.dlt.state.RI.us

South Carolina

Adrienne R. Youmans, Director
Dept of Labor, Licensing & Regulations
P.O. Box 11329
Columbia, SC 29211-1329
Phone: (803) 896-4300
www.llr.state.SC.us

South Dakota

Pamela S. Roberts, Secretary
Department of Labor
700 Governors Drive
Pierre, SD 57501-2291
Phone: (605) 773-3682
www.state.SD.us

Tennessee

James G. Neeley, Commissioner
Dept of Labor & Workforce Development
Andrew Johnson Tower
710 James Robertson Pkwy
Nashville, TN 37243-0655
Phone: (615) 741-6642
www.state.TN.us/labor-wfd

Texas

Ronald Congleton, Labor Commissioner
Texas Workforce Commission
101 East 15th St.
Austin, TX 78778
Phone: (512) 475-2670
www.twc.state.TX.us

Utah

Sherrie Hayashi, Commissioner
Utah Labor Commission
P.O. Box 146610
Salt Lake City, UT 84114-6610
Phone: (801) 530-6800
Laborcommission.Utah.gov

Vermont

Patricia Moulton Pow, Commissioner
Department of Labor
5 Green Mountain Drive
P.O. Box 488
Montpelier, VT 05601-0488
Phone: (802) 828-4000
www.labor.verMont.gov

Virginia

C. Ray Davenport, Commissioner
Dept of Labor and Industry
Powers-Taylor Building
13 S. 13th Street
Richmond, VA 23219
Phone: (804) 371-2327
www.doli.Virginia.gov

Washington

Judy Schurke, Acting Director
Dept of Labor and Industries
P.O. Box 44001
Olympia, WA 98504-4001
Phone: (360) 902-4200
www.lni.WA.gov

West Virginia

David Mullens, Commissioner
Division of Labor
State Capitol Complex, Building #6
1900 Kanawha Blvd.
Charleston, WV 25305
Phone: (304) 558-7890
www.labor.state.WV.us

Wisconsin

Roberta Gassman, Secretary
Dept of Workforce Development
201 E. Washington Ave., #A400
P.O. Box 7946
Madison, WI 53707-7946
Phone: (608) 266-6861
www.dwd.state.WI.us

Wyoming

Cynthia Pomeroy, Director
Department of Employment
1510 East Pershing Blvd.
Cheyenne, WY 82002
Phone: (307) 777-7261
www.doe.state.WY.us

*Source: U.S. Department of Labor
http://www.dol.gov/esa/contacts/state_of.htm*

Appendix E: Comparative Statistics

Population Growth: City

City	1990 Census	2000 Census	2010 Census	Population Growth (%)	
				1990-2000	2000-2010
Albuquerque, NM	388,375	448,607	545,852	15.5	21.7
Alexandria, VA	111,526	128,283	139,966	15.0	9.1
Anchorage, AK	226,338	260,283	291,826	15.0	12.1
Ann Arbor, MI	111,018	114,024	113,934	2.7	-0.1
Athens, GA	86,561	100,266	115,452	15.8	15.1
Atlanta, GA	394,092	416,474	420,003	5.7	0.8
Austin, TX	499,053	656,562	790,390	31.6	20.4
Baltimore, MD	736,014	651,154	620,961	-11.5	-4.6
Bellevue, WA	99,057	109,569	122,363	10.6	11.7
Billings, MT	81,812	89,847	104,170	9.8	15.9
Boise City, ID	144,317	185,787	205,671	28.7	10.7
Boston, MA	574,283	589,141	617,594	2.6	4.8
Boulder, CO	87,737	94,673	97,385	7.9	2.9
Broken Arrow, OK	59,372	74,859	98,850	26.1	32.0
Cambridge, MA	95,959	101,355	105,162	5.6	3.8
Cape Coral, FL	75,507	102,286	154,305	35.5	50.9
Carlsbad, CA	62,753	78,247	105,328	24.7	34.6
Cary, NC	49,835	94,536	135,234	89.7	43.1
Cedar Rapids, IA	110,829	120,758	126,326	9.0	4.6
Charleston, SC	96,102	96,650	120,083	0.6	24.2
Charlotte, NC	428,283	540,828	731,424	26.3	35.2
Chesapeake, VA	151,976	199,184	222,209	31.1	11.6
Chicago, IL	2,783,726	2,896,016	2,695,598	4.0	-6.9
Clarksville, TN	78,569	103,455	132,929	31.7	28.5
Colorado Spgs., CO	283,798	360,890	416,427	27.2	15.4
Columbia, MD	76,649	88,254	99,615	15.1	12.9
Columbia, MO	71,069	84,531	108,500	18.9	28.4
Columbia, SC	115,475	116,278	129,272	0.7	11.2
Columbus, OH	648,656	711,470	787,033	9.7	10.6
Dallas, TX	1,006,971	1,188,580	1,197,816	18.0	0.8
Denver, CO	467,153	554,636	600,158	18.7	8.2
Durham, NC	151,737	187,035	228,330	23.3	22.1
Edison, NJ	88,680	97,687	99,967	10.2	2.3
El Paso, TX	515,541	563,662	649,121	9.3	15.2
Fargo, ND	74,372	90,599	105,549	21.8	16.5
Ft. Collins, CO	89,555	118,652	143,986	32.5	21.4
Ft. Worth, TX	448,311	534,694	741,206	19.3	38.6
Gilbert, AZ	33,229	109,697	208,453	230.1	90.0
Green Bay, WI	96,466	102,313	104,057	6.1	1.7
Henderson, NV	66,093	175,381	257,729	165.4	47.0
High Point, NC	72,061	85,839	104,371	19.1	21.6
Honolulu, HI	376,465	371,657	337,256	-1.3	-9.3
Houston, TX	1,697,610	1,953,631	2,099,451	15.1	7.5
Huntington, NY	191,474	195,289	203,264	2.0	4.1
Huntsville, AL	161,842	158,216	180,105	-2.2	13.8
Indianapolis, IN	730,993	781,870	820,445	7.0	4.9
Irvine, CA	111,754	143,072	212,375	28.0	48.4
Jackson, MS	196,469	184,256	173,514	-6.2	-5.8
Jacksonville, FL	635,221	735,617	821,784	15.8	11.7
Jersey City, NJ	228,543	240,055	247,597	5.0	3.1
Kansas City, MO	434,967	441,545	459,787	1.5	4.1
Kenosha, WI	81,575	90,352	99,218	10.8	9.8
Las Vegas, NV	261,374	478,434	583,756	83.0	22.0
Lexington, KY	225,366	260,512	295,803	15.6	13.5
Lincoln, NE	193,629	225,581	258,379	16.5	14.5

Table continued on next page.

City	1990 Census	2000 Census	2010 Census	Population Growth (%) 1990-2000	2000-2010
Little Rock, AR	177,519	183,133	193,524	3.2	5.7
Los Angeles, CA	3,487,671	3,694,820	3,792,621	5.9	2.6
Madison, WI	193,451	208,054	233,209	7.5	12.1
Manchester, NH	99,567	107,006	109,565	7.5	2.4
Miami, FL	358,843	362,470	399,457	1.0	10.2
Minneapolis, MN	368,383	382,618	382,578	3.9	0.0
Murfreesboro, TN	47,905	68,816	108,755	43.7	58.0
Naperville, IL	90,506	128,358	141,853	41.8	10.5
Nashville, TN	488,364	545,524	601,222	11.7	10.2
New Orleans, LA	496,938	484,674	343,829	-2.5	-29.1
New York, NY	7,322,552	8,008,278	8,175,133	9.4	2.1
Norman, OK	80,071	95,694	110,925	19.5	15.9
Olathe, KS	64,592	92,962	125,872	43.9	35.4
Omaha, NE	371,972	390,007	408,958	4.8	4.9
Orlando, FL	161,172	185,951	238,300	15.4	28.2
Overland Park, KS	111,803	149,080	173,372	33.3	16.3
Oyster Bay, NY	293,200	293,925	293,214	0.2	-0.2
Pembroke Pines, FL	66,095	137,427	154,750	107.9	12.6
Philadelphia, PA	1,585,577	1,517,550	1,526,006	-4.3	0.6
Phoenix, AZ	989,873	1,321,045	1,445,632	33.5	9.4
Pittsburgh, PA	369,785	334,563	305,704	-9.5	-8.6
Plano, TX	128,507	222,030	259,841	72.8	17.0
Portland, OR	485,833	529,121	583,776	8.9	10.3
Providence, RI	160,734	173,618	178,042	8.0	2.5
Provo, UT	87,148	105,166	112,488	20.7	7.0
Raleigh, NC	226,841	276,093	403,892	21.7	46.3
Richmond, VA	202,783	197,790	204,214	-2.5	3.2
Roseville, CA	44,692	79,921	118,788	78.8	48.6
Round Rock, TX	32,854	61,136	99,887	86.1	63.4
San Antonio, TX	997,258	1,144,646	1,327,407	14.8	16.0
San Diego, CA	1,111,048	1,223,400	1,307,402	10.1	6.9
San Francisco, CA	723,959	776,733	805,235	7.3	3.7
San Jose, CA	784,324	894,943	945,942	14.1	5.7
Savannah, GA	138,038	131,510	136,286	-4.7	3.6
Scottsdale, AZ	130,300	202,705	217,385	55.6	7.2
Seattle, WA	516,262	563,374	608,660	9.1	8.0
Sioux Falls, SD	102,262	123,975	153,888	21.2	24.1
Stamford, CT	108,087	117,083	122,643	8.3	4.7
Sterling Hgts, MI	117,810	124,471	129,699	5.7	4.2
Sunnyvale, CA	117,242	131,760	140,081	12.4	6.3
Tampa, FL	279,960	303,447	335,709	8.4	10.6
Temecula, CA	27,078	57,716	100,097	113.1	73.4
Thousand Oaks, CA	104,661	117,005	126,683	11.8	8.3
Virginia Beach, VA	393,069	425,257	437,994	8.2	3.0
Washington, DC	606,900	572,059	601,723	-5.7	5.2
U.S.	248,709,873	281,421,906	308,745,538	13.2	9.7

Source: U.S. Census Bureau, 2010 Census

Population Growth: Metro Area

Metro Area	1990 Census	2000 Census	2010 Census	Population Growth (%)	
				1990-2000	2000-2010
Albuquerque, NM	599,416	729,649	887,077	21.7	21.6
Alexandria, VA	4,122,914	4,796,183	5,582,170	16.3	16.4
Anchorage, AK	266,021	319,605	380,821	20.1	19.2
Ann Arbor, MI	282,937	322,895	344,791	14.1	6.8
Athens, GA	136,025	166,079	192,541	22.1	15.9
Atlanta, GA	3,069,411	4,247,981	5,268,860	38.4	24.0
Austin, TX	846,217	1,249,763	1,716,289	47.7	37.3
Baltimore, MD	2,382,172	2,552,994	2,710,489	7.2	6.2
Bellevue, WA	2,559,164	3,043,878	3,439,809	18.9	13.0
Billings, MT	121,499	138,904	158,050	14.3	13.8
Boise City, ID	319,596	464,840	616,561	45.4	32.6
Boston, MA	4,133,895	4,391,344	4,552,402	6.2	3.7
Boulder, CO	208,898	269,758	294,567	29.1	9.2
Broken Arrow, OK	761,019	859,532	937,478	12.9	9.1
Cambridge, MA	4,133,895	4,391,344	4,552,402	6.2	3.7
Cape Coral, FL	335,113	440,888	618,754	31.6	40.3
Carlsbad, CA	2,498,016	2,813,833	3,095,313	12.6	10.0
Cary, NC	541,081	797,071	1,130,490	47.3	41.8
Cedar Rapids, IA	210,640	237,230	257,940	12.6	8.7
Charleston, SC	506,875	549,033	664,607	8.3	21.1
Charlotte, NC	1,024,331	1,330,448	1,758,038	29.9	32.1
Chesapeake, VA	1,449,389	1,576,370	1,671,683	8.8	6.0
Chicago, IL	8,182,076	9,098,316	9,461,105	11.2	4.0
Clarksville, TN	189,277	232,000	273,949	22.6	18.1
Colorado Spgs., CO	409,482	537,484	645,613	31.3	20.1
Columbia, MD	2,382,172	2,552,994	2,710,489	7.2	6.2
Columbia, MO	122,010	145,666	172,786	19.4	18.6
Columbia, SC	548,325	647,158	767,598	18.0	18.6
Columbus, OH	1,405,176	1,612,694	1,836,536	14.8	13.9
Dallas, TX	3,989,294	5,161,544	6,371,773	29.4	23.4
Denver, CO	1,666,935	2,179,296	2,543,482	30.7	16.7
Durham, NC	344,646	426,493	504,357	23.7	18.3
Edison, NJ	16,845,992	18,323,002	18,897,109	8.8	3.1
El Paso, TX	591,610	679,622	800,647	14.9	17.8
Fargo, ND	153,296	174,367	208,777	13.7	19.7
Ft. Collins, CO	186,136	251,494	299,630	35.1	19.1
Ft. Worth, TX	3,989,294	5,161,544	6,371,773	29.4	23.4
Gilbert, AZ	2,238,480	3,251,876	4,192,887	45.3	28.9
Green Bay, WI	243,698	282,599	306,241	16.0	8.4
Henderson, NV	741,459	1,375,765	1,951,269	85.5	41.8
High Point, NC	540,257	643,430	723,801	19.1	12.5
Honolulu, HI	836,231	876,156	953,207	4.8	8.8
Houston, TX	3,767,335	4,715,407	5,946,800	25.2	26.1
Huntington, NY	16,845,992	18,323,002	18,897,109	8.8	3.1
Huntsville, AL	293,047	342,376	417,593	16.8	22.0
Indianapolis, IN	1,294,217	1,525,104	1,756,241	17.8	15.2
Irvine, CA	11,273,720	12,365,627	12,828,837	9.7	3.7
Jackson, MS	446,941	497,197	539,057	11.2	8.4
Jacksonville, FL	925,213	1,122,750	1,345,596	21.4	19.8
Jersey City, NJ	16,845,992	18,323,002	18,897,109	8.8	3.1
Kansas City, MO	1,636,528	1,836,038	2,035,334	12.2	10.9
Kenosha, WI	8,182,076	9,098,316	9,461,105	11.2	4.0
Las Vegas, NV	741,459	1,375,765	1,951,269	85.5	41.8
Lexington, KY	348,428	408,326	472,099	17.2	15.6
Lincoln, NE	229,091	266,787	302,157	16.5	13.3

Table continued on next page.

Metro Area	1990 Census	2000 Census	2010 Census	Population Growth (%)	
				1990-2000	2000-2010
Little Rock, AR	535,034	610,518	699,757	14.1	14.6
Los Angeles, CA	11,273,720	12,365,627	12,828,837	9.7	3.7
Madison, WI	432,323	501,774	568,593	16.1	13.3
Manchester, NH	336,073	380,841	400,721	13.3	5.2
Miami, FL	4,056,100	5,007,564	5,564,635	23.5	11.1
Minneapolis, MN	2,538,834	2,968,806	3,279,833	16.9	10.5
Murfreesboro, TN	1,048,218	1,311,789	1,589,934	25.1	21.2
Naperville, IL	8,182,076	9,098,316	9,461,105	11.2	4.0
Nashville, TN	1,048,218	1,311,789	1,589,934	25.1	21.2
New Orleans, LA	1,264,391	1,316,510	1,167,764	4.1	-11.3
New York, NY	16,845,992	18,323,002	18,897,109	8.8	3.1
Norman, OK	971,042	1,095,421	1,252,987	12.8	14.4
Olathe, KS	1,636,528	1,836,038	2,035,334	12.2	10.9
Omaha, NE	685,797	767,041	865,350	11.8	12.8
Orlando, FL	1,224,852	1,644,561	2,134,411	34.3	29.8
Overland Park, KS	1,636,528	1,836,038	2,035,334	12.2	10.9
Oyster Bay, NY	16,845,992	18,323,002	18,897,109	8.8	3.1
Pembroke Pines, FL	4,056,100	5,007,564	5,564,635	23.5	11.1
Philadelphia, PA	5,435,470	5,687,147	5,965,343	4.6	4.9
Phoenix, AZ	2,238,480	3,251,876	4,192,887	45.3	28.9
Pittsburgh, PA	2,468,289	2,431,087	2,356,285	-1.5	-3.1
Plano, TX	3,989,294	5,161,544	6,371,773	29.4	23.4
Portland, OR	1,523,741	1,927,881	2,226,009	26.5	15.5
Providence, RI	1,509,789	1,582,997	1,600,852	4.8	1.1
Provo, UT	269,407	376,774	526,810	39.9	39.8
Raleigh, NC	541,081	797,071	1,130,490	47.3	41.8
Richmond, VA	949,244	1,096,957	1,258,251	15.6	14.7
Roseville, CA	1,481,126	1,796,857	2,149,127	21.3	19.6
Round Rock, TX	846,217	1,249,763	1,716,289	47.7	37.3
San Antonio, TX	1,407,745	1,711,703	2,142,508	21.6	25.2
San Diego, CA	2,498,016	2,813,833	3,095,313	12.6	10.0
San Francisco, CA	3,686,592	4,123,740	4,335,391	11.9	5.1
San Jose, CA	1,534,280	1,735,819	1,836,911	13.1	5.8
Savannah, GA	258,060	293,000	347,611	13.5	18.6
Scottsdale, AZ	2,238,480	3,251,876	4,192,887	45.3	28.9
Seattle, WA	2,559,164	3,043,878	3,439,809	18.9	13.0
Sioux Falls, SD	153,500	187,093	228,261	21.9	22.0
Stamford, CT	827,645	882,567	916,829	6.6	3.9
Sterling Hgts, MI	4,248,699	4,452,557	4,296,250	4.8	-3.5
Sunnyvale, CA	1,534,280	1,735,819	1,836,911	13.1	5.8
Tampa, FL	2,067,959	2,395,997	2,783,243	15.9	16.2
Temecula, CA	2,588,793	3,254,821	4,224,851	25.7	29.8
Thousand Oaks, CA	669,016	753,197	823,318	12.6	9.3
Virginia Beach, VA	1,449,389	1,576,370	1,671,683	8.8	6.0
Washington, DC	4,122,914	4,796,183	5,582,170	16.3	16.4
U.S.	248,709,873	281,421,906	308,745,538	13.2	9.7

Note: Figures cover the Metropolitan Statistical Area (MSA)—see Appendix B for areas included
Source: U.S. Census Bureau, 2010 Census

Household Size: City

City	Persons in Household (%)							Average Household Size
	One	Two	Three	Four	Five	Six	Seven or More	
Albuquerque, NM	31.9	32.1	15.1	11.9	5.6	2.1	1.3	2.40
Alexandria, VA	43.4	31.9	11.7	7.8	3.1	1.3	0.8	2.03
Anchorage, AK	24.9	32.6	17.1	13.8	6.5	2.8	2.3	2.64
Ann Arbor, MI	37.4	33.9	13.2	9.7	3.4	1.5	0.9	2.17
Athens, GA	30.6	34.1	15.9	11.9	4.5	1.8	1.2	2.37
Atlanta, GA	44.0	29.1	11.9	8.0	3.8	1.6	1.5	2.11
Austin, TX	34.0	31.4	14.4	11.2	5.0	2.2	1.8	2.37
Baltimore, MD	36.1	28.7	15.4	9.8	5.3	2.5	2.3	2.38
Bellevue, WA	28.1	34.8	16.4	13.7	4.7	1.6	0.8	2.41
Billings, MT	32.6	34.7	14.6	10.7	4.8	1.6	0.9	2.29
Boise City, ID	30.6	34.9	15.4	11.5	4.7	1.9	1.1	2.36
Boston, MA	37.1	30.9	14.6	9.6	4.6	1.8	1.4	2.26
Boulder, CO	35.8	34.7	14.3	10.7	3.2	0.9	0.4	2.16
Broken Arrow, OK	19.2	34.7	18.3	16.4	7.4	2.7	1.2	2.72
Cambridge, MA	40.7	34.8	13.7	7.2	2.4	0.7	0.4	2.00
Cape Coral, FL	21.4	39.8	16.7	13.2	5.8	2.1	1.0	2.53
Carlsbad, CA	23.9	35.6	16.7	15.6	5.6	1.8	0.8	2.53
Cary, NC	23.9	32.0	17.1	17.9	6.4	2.0	0.8	2.61
Cedar Rapids, IA	32.5	34.4	14.4	11.3	4.8	1.7	0.9	2.31
Charleston, SC	34.6	35.5	14.9	9.5	3.6	1.1	0.7	2.18
Charlotte, NC	30.3	30.8	16.1	13.0	6.0	2.3	1.5	2.48
Chesapeake, VA	19.8	32.0	20.2	16.7	7.1	2.8	1.4	2.75
Chicago, IL	35.0	27.4	14.2	10.8	6.3	3.1	3.2	2.52
Clarksville, TN	23.7	31.4	19.6	14.6	6.8	2.5	1.3	2.63
Colorado Spgs., CO	29.6	33.2	15.6	12.5	5.7	2.2	1.2	2.44
Columbia, MD	27.7	32.1	16.9	14.3	5.7	2.0	1.3	2.50
Columbia, MO	32.0	32.9	16.3	12.8	4.0	1.4	0.7	2.32
Columbia, SC	38.0	31.9	14.6	9.3	4.0	1.4	0.9	2.18
Columbus, OH	35.1	31.4	14.9	10.4	4.9	2.0	1.3	2.31
Dallas, TX	33.9	27.2	13.8	11.4	7.0	3.5	3.3	2.57
Denver, CO	40.6	30.4	11.7	8.9	4.4	2.0	2.0	2.22
Durham, NC	33.7	32.0	15.5	10.7	4.8	2.1	1.3	2.34
Edison, NJ	20.4	27.7	21.2	19.7	6.6	2.8	1.5	2.80
El Paso, TX	21.5	26.0	18.5	16.8	10.0	4.3	3.0	2.95
Fargo, ND	36.6	34.4	13.9	9.8	3.7	1.1	0.5	2.15
Ft. Collins, CO	28.4	35.6	16.8	12.6	4.3	1.5	0.7	2.37
Ft. Worth, TX	26.5	27.4	16.3	14.6	8.3	3.8	3.0	2.77
Gilbert, AZ	16.1	30.0	18.1	19.6	9.6	4.2	2.3	3.00
Green Bay, WI	32.4	32.8	14.6	11.0	5.3	2.2	1.7	2.39
Henderson, NV	24.2	37.2	15.9	12.8	5.9	2.5	1.4	2.53
High Point, NC	29.8	31.7	16.5	12.8	5.5	2.3	1.4	2.46
Honolulu, HI	32.9	31.1	14.9	10.2	5.0	2.6	3.4	2.51
Houston, TX	31.0	27.6	15.1	12.3	7.3	3.6	3.1	2.64
Huntington, NY	18.5	31.2	17.5	18.6	8.9	3.0	2.3	2.89
Huntsville, AL	34.7	33.5	14.6	10.4	4.4	1.5	0.8	2.25
Indianapolis, IN	32.0	31.3	15.5	11.4	5.7	2.4	1.6	2.42
Irvine, CA	23.4	31.4	18.7	18.0	5.8	1.9	0.8	2.61
Jackson, MS	30.2	28.0	16.9	12.4	6.9	3.1	2.5	2.60
Jacksonville, FL	28.2	32.5	17.4	12.8	5.6	2.2	1.3	2.48
Jersey City, NJ	30.2	29.2	17.5	12.4	6.1	2.6	2.0	2.53
Kansas City, MO	34.7	31.1	14.6	10.7	5.2	2.2	1.5	2.34
Kenosha, WI	28.8	29.4	16.7	14.2	6.6	2.6	1.6	2.56
Las Vegas, NV	26.0	31.1	15.7	12.9	7.5	3.7	3.1	2.71
Lexington, KY	32.7	33.6	15.4	11.5	4.5	1.5	0.8	2.30

Table continued on next page.

City	Persons in Household (%)							Average Household Size
	One	Two	Three	Four	Five	Six	Seven or More	
Lincoln, NE	31.3	33.8	14.9	11.8	5.2	1.9	1.0	2.36
Little Rock, AR	34.8	31.6	15.0	10.7	4.9	1.8	1.1	2.30
Los Angeles, CA	28.3	27.0	15.2	13.2	7.7	4.0	4.6	2.81
Madison, WI	36.2	34.8	13.6	9.8	3.6	1.2	0.7	2.17
Manchester, NH	32.4	32.8	16.0	11.3	4.7	1.7	1.2	2.34
Miami, FL	33.3	28.8	16.2	11.0	5.6	2.7	2.4	2.47
Minneapolis, MN	40.3	30.3	12.5	9.0	4.0	1.8	2.1	2.23
Murfreesboro, TN	27.3	32.3	17.6	14.4	5.6	1.8	1.0	2.49
Naperville, IL	20.5	29.1	18.2	20.3	8.7	2.4	0.9	2.79
Nashville, TN	34.8	32.2	14.7	10.0	4.8	2.0	1.5	2.31
New Orleans, LA	35.9	29.9	15.4	10.0	5.1	2.1	1.6	2.33
New York, NY	32.0	27.6	16.0	12.1	6.4	3.0	2.9	2.57
Norman, OK	30.7	34.5	16.1	11.8	4.5	1.6	0.8	2.33
Olathe, KS	20.0	30.7	18.1	18.6	8.3	2.8	1.4	2.80
Omaha, NE	32.3	31.3	14.5	11.5	6.0	2.5	1.9	2.45
Orlando, FL	34.6	32.2	15.3	10.4	4.6	1.8	1.2	2.29
Overland Park, KS	29.8	33.5	14.9	13.6	5.7	1.8	0.8	2.41
Oyster Bay, NY	17.9	29.9	18.4	20.1	9.1	3.0	1.6	2.89
Pembroke Pines, FL	24.0	29.0	18.4	17.2	7.4	2.5	1.5	2.70
Philadelphia, PA	34.1	28.2	15.8	11.2	5.9	2.6	2.1	2.45
Phoenix, AZ	27.1	28.8	15.3	13.3	7.9	4.0	3.7	2.77
Pittsburgh, PA	41.7	31.7	13.4	7.9	3.2	1.2	0.7	2.07
Plano, TX	24.4	31.8	17.5	16.4	6.3	2.3	1.3	2.61
Portland, OR	34.5	33.7	14.3	10.3	4.1	1.7	1.4	2.28
Providence, RI	31.7	26.5	16.2	12.6	7.1	3.3	2.7	2.60
Provo, UT	12.8	29.5	18.8	18.3	8.7	7.6	4.2	3.24
Raleigh, NC	32.8	31.8	15.5	12.0	4.9	1.8	1.2	2.36
Richmond, VA	37.9	32.0	14.6	8.7	3.9	1.6	1.2	2.20
Roseville, CA	24.5	32.4	16.4	16.0	7.0	2.4	1.3	2.62
Round Rock, TX	20.8	28.7	18.9	18.2	8.4	3.1	2.0	2.84
San Antonio, TX	26.9	28.5	16.6	14.0	7.8	3.5	2.7	2.71
San Diego, CA	28.0	31.6	15.6	13.0	6.4	2.9	2.6	2.60
San Francisco, CA	38.6	31.4	13.3	8.9	3.7	1.8	2.3	2.26
San Jose, CA	19.7	27.0	17.7	17.3	8.8	4.4	5.2	3.09
Savannah, GA	32.7	31.1	16.2	10.5	5.5	2.3	1.7	2.40
Scottsdale, AZ	34.4	39.4	12.0	9.3	3.4	1.1	0.5	2.14
Seattle, WA	41.3	33.3	12.2	8.5	2.8	1.0	0.9	2.06
Sioux Falls, SD	30.6	33.6	15.0	12.4	5.4	2.0	1.1	2.40
Stamford, CT	28.9	30.2	16.4	13.6	6.2	2.6	2.1	2.56
Sterling Hgts, MI	26.5	31.3	16.0	14.6	7.2	2.8	1.6	2.61
Sunnyvale, CA	25.2	31.0	18.8	15.5	5.4	2.3	1.8	2.61
Tampa, FL	33.6	30.5	15.5	11.5	5.2	2.1	1.5	2.38
Temecula, CA	13.8	27.1	19.2	21.6	11.1	4.5	2.6	3.15
Thousand Oaks, CA	21.2	32.8	17.6	17.1	7.0	2.6	1.8	2.73
Virginia Beach, VA	23.3	33.3	18.9	14.8	6.2	2.3	1.2	2.60
Washington, DC	44.0	29.2	12.3	7.6	3.7	1.7	1.5	2.11
U.S.	26.7	32.8	16.1	13.4	6.5	2.6	1.9	2.58

U.S. Census Bureau, 2010 Census

Household Size: Metro Area

Metro Area	Persons in Household (%)							Average Household Size
	One	Two	Three	Four	Five	Six	Seven or More	
Albuquerque, NM	28.5	32.8	15.5	12.6	6.3	2.5	1.7	2.51
Alexandria, VA	27.0	30.1	16.5	14.3	6.9	2.9	2.3	2.64
Anchorage, AK	24.3	32.8	16.9	13.8	6.7	3.0	2.4	2.67
Ann Arbor, MI	30.6	33.9	15.1	12.4	5.1	1.9	1.0	2.38
Athens, GA	26.5	34.2	16.9	13.7	5.4	2.0	1.3	2.50
Atlanta, GA	25.3	30.2	17.3	15.1	7.2	2.9	2.1	2.68
Austin, TX	27.3	32.0	16.0	13.7	6.4	2.6	2.0	2.58
Baltimore, MD	27.4	31.8	17.0	13.7	6.1	2.4	1.6	2.54
Bellevue, WA	28.4	33.2	15.9	13.3	5.5	2.2	1.5	2.49
Billings, MT	29.8	36.0	14.7	11.5	5.2	1.8	1.0	2.37
Boise City, ID	23.6	33.9	15.7	14.1	7.3	3.3	2.0	2.67
Boston, MA	28.5	31.6	16.4	14.1	6.1	2.1	1.2	2.50
Boulder, CO	29.0	34.8	15.7	13.2	4.8	1.6	0.9	2.39
Broken Arrow, OK	27.3	33.9	15.8	12.8	6.3	2.5	1.5	2.51
Cambridge, MA	28.5	31.6	16.4	14.1	6.1	2.1	1.2	2.50
Cape Coral, FL	26.7	42.7	12.9	9.8	4.7	1.9	1.2	2.35
Carlsbad, CA	24.0	31.2	16.5	14.5	7.4	3.3	3.0	2.75
Cary, NC	25.6	32.3	17.1	15.2	6.3	2.2	1.3	2.57
Cedar Rapids, IA	28.6	35.9	14.7	12.7	5.5	1.9	0.8	2.40
Charleston, SC	26.4	34.3	17.2	13.0	5.7	2.1	1.2	2.49
Charlotte, NC	25.9	32.1	17.0	14.6	6.5	2.3	1.4	2.58
Chesapeake, VA	25.0	33.4	18.3	13.9	6.0	2.2	1.2	2.55
Chicago, IL	27.2	29.3	15.9	14.3	7.5	3.2	2.5	2.68
Clarksville, TN	23.6	32.6	18.7	14.5	6.7	2.5	1.4	2.62
Colorado Spgs., CO	25.9	33.8	16.3	13.8	6.4	2.5	1.3	2.55
Columbia, MD	27.4	31.8	17.0	13.7	6.1	2.4	1.6	2.54
Columbia, MO	28.7	34.3	16.6	13.2	4.7	1.7	0.8	2.40
Columbia, SC	27.5	33.3	17.1	13.1	5.7	2.1	1.2	2.48
Columbus, OH	28.4	33.2	16.0	13.2	5.9	2.1	1.2	2.47
Dallas, TX	24.8	29.6	16.7	15.2	7.9	3.3	2.5	2.74
Denver, CO	29.1	32.6	15.1	13.2	6.0	2.4	1.7	2.50
Durham, NC	29.8	34.5	15.8	12.0	4.9	1.9	1.1	2.39
Edison, NJ	27.6	28.5	16.7	14.5	7.2	3.0	2.6	2.67
El Paso, TX	19.8	24.9	18.5	17.5	11.0	4.8	3.5	3.06
Fargo, ND	31.4	34.5	14.8	12.1	5.0	1.4	0.7	2.32
Ft. Collins, CO	25.9	38.0	15.9	12.7	4.9	1.8	0.9	2.42
Ft. Worth, TX	24.8	29.6	16.7	15.2	7.9	3.3	2.5	2.74
Gilbert, AZ	25.4	33.2	14.8	13.2	7.3	3.4	2.8	2.68
Green Bay, WI	27.2	36.0	15.1	13.1	5.6	1.9	1.1	2.45
Henderson, NV	25.3	32.0	15.9	13.0	7.4	3.5	2.8	2.70
High Point, NC	28.6	34.1	16.6	12.4	5.3	1.9	1.1	2.43
Honolulu, HI	22.8	29.4	17.2	13.9	7.5	4.0	5.2	2.95
Houston, TX	23.5	28.6	17.0	15.6	8.6	3.8	2.9	2.83
Huntington, NY	27.6	28.5	16.7	14.5	7.2	3.0	2.6	2.67
Huntsville, AL	27.8	33.8	16.8	13.4	5.5	1.8	0.9	2.45
Indianapolis, IN	27.0	32.7	16.3	13.8	6.5	2.4	1.3	2.53
Irvine, CA	23.4	27.0	16.3	15.3	8.7	4.4	4.9	2.98
Jackson, MS	26.4	31.2	17.5	13.9	6.6	2.5	1.8	2.60
Jacksonville, FL	26.0	34.1	17.3	13.4	5.9	2.2	1.2	2.52
Jersey City, NJ	27.6	28.5	16.7	14.5	7.2	3.0	2.6	2.67
Kansas City, MO	27.8	33.2	15.8	13.3	6.2	2.4	1.4	2.51
Kenosha, WI	27.2	29.3	15.9	14.3	7.5	3.2	2.5	2.68
Las Vegas, NV	25.3	32.0	15.9	13.0	7.4	3.5	2.8	2.70
Lexington, KY	29.3	34.1	16.4	12.5	5.1	1.7	0.9	2.39

Table continued on next page.

| Metro Area | Persons in Household (%) | | | | | | | Average Household Size |
	One	Two	Three	Four	Five	Six	Seven or More	
Lincoln, NE	29.8	34.7	14.9	12.2	5.4	2.0	1.1	2.40
Little Rock, AR	27.7	34.2	16.8	12.7	5.5	2.0	1.1	2.45
Los Angeles, CA	23.4	27.0	16.3	15.3	8.7	4.4	4.9	2.98
Madison, WI	29.9	35.8	14.8	12.4	4.8	1.5	0.8	2.35
Manchester, NH	25.3	34.0	17.0	14.7	5.9	2.0	1.0	2.53
Miami, FL	27.0	31.0	16.6	13.7	6.7	2.8	2.2	2.62
Minneapolis, MN	27.5	33.1	15.5	14.1	6.1	2.2	1.6	2.53
Murfreesboro, TN	26.8	33.3	16.8	13.6	6.0	2.2	1.4	2.52
Naperville, IL	27.2	29.3	15.9	14.3	7.5	3.2	2.5	2.68
Nashville, TN	26.8	33.3	16.8	13.6	6.0	2.2	1.4	2.52
New Orleans, LA	28.4	31.2	17.2	13.0	6.3	2.4	1.6	2.52
New York, NY	27.6	28.5	16.7	14.5	7.2	3.0	2.6	2.67
Norman, OK	27.8	33.5	16.0	12.8	6.1	2.3	1.4	2.49
Olathe, KS	27.8	33.2	15.8	13.3	6.2	2.4	1.4	2.51
Omaha, NE	27.5	33.0	15.6	13.3	6.6	2.5	1.5	2.54
Orlando, FL	24.1	33.4	17.3	14.2	6.7	2.6	1.6	2.62
Overland Park, KS	27.8	33.2	15.8	13.3	6.2	2.4	1.4	2.51
Oyster Bay, NY	27.6	28.5	16.7	14.5	7.2	3.0	2.6	2.67
Pembroke Pines, FL	27.0	31.0	16.6	13.7	6.7	2.8	2.2	2.62
Philadelphia, PA	27.4	31.0	16.8	14.2	6.6	2.5	1.6	2.56
Phoenix, AZ	25.4	33.2	14.8	13.2	7.3	3.4	2.8	2.68
Pittsburgh, PA	31.9	34.7	15.3	11.5	4.5	1.4	0.6	2.29
Plano, TX	24.8	29.6	16.7	15.2	7.9	3.3	2.5	2.74
Portland, OR	27.0	34.1	15.8	13.2	5.8	2.4	1.7	2.52
Providence, RI	28.9	32.1	16.7	13.6	5.7	2.0	1.1	2.46
Provo, UT	11.7	25.2	16.4	17.0	13.1	9.5	7.0	3.57
Raleigh, NC	25.6	32.3	17.1	15.2	6.3	2.2	1.3	2.57
Richmond, VA	26.6	33.5	17.4	13.6	5.7	2.0	1.2	2.50
Roseville, CA	24.8	32.1	16.2	14.2	7.0	3.1	2.5	2.68
Round Rock, TX	27.3	32.0	16.0	13.7	6.4	2.6	2.0	2.58
San Antonio, TX	24.3	30.3	16.8	14.6	7.9	3.4	2.6	2.74
San Diego, CA	24.0	31.2	16.5	14.5	7.4	3.3	3.0	2.75
San Francisco, CA	28.0	30.8	16.1	13.7	6.2	2.7	2.6	2.61
San Jose, CA	21.6	28.9	17.7	16.9	7.7	3.6	3.7	2.91
Savannah, GA	26.2	33.4	17.4	13.1	6.1	2.3	1.4	2.53
Scottsdale, AZ	25.4	33.2	14.8	13.2	7.3	3.4	2.8	2.68
Seattle, WA	28.4	33.2	15.9	13.3	5.5	2.2	1.5	2.49
Sioux Falls, SD	27.4	34.5	15.3	13.4	6.2	2.1	1.0	2.48
Stamford, CT	24.9	30.0	17.0	16.2	7.6	2.7	1.6	2.68
Sterling Hgts, MI	28.8	31.2	16.1	13.5	6.3	2.4	1.6	2.53
Sunnyvale, CA	21.6	28.9	17.7	16.9	7.7	3.6	3.7	2.91
Tampa, FL	29.9	35.7	15.0	11.4	5.0	1.9	1.2	2.37
Temecula, CA	18.5	27.1	16.1	16.4	10.8	5.6	5.6	3.20
Thousand Oaks, CA	19.9	29.3	16.9	16.3	8.6	4.1	4.9	3.04
Virginia Beach, VA	25.0	33.4	18.3	13.9	6.0	2.2	1.2	2.55
Washington, DC	27.0	30.1	16.5	14.3	6.9	2.9	2.3	2.64
U.S.	26.7	32.8	16.1	13.4	6.5	2.6	1.9	2.58

Note: Figures cover the Metropolitan Statistical Area (MSA)—see Appendix B for areas included
Source: U.S. Census Bureau, 2010 Census

Race: City

City	White Alone[1] (%)	Black Alone[1] (%)	Asian Alone[1] (%)	AIAN[2] Alone[1] (%)	NHOPI[3] Alone[1] (%)	Other Race Alone[1] (%)	Two or More Races (%)
Albuquerque, NM	69.7	3.3	2.6	4.6	0.1	15.0	4.6
Alexandria, VA	60.9	21.8	6.0	0.4	0.1	7.1	3.7
Anchorage, AK	66.0	5.6	8.1	7.9	2.0	2.3	8.1
Ann Arbor, MI	73.0	7.7	14.4	0.3	0.0	1.0	3.6
Athens, GA	61.8	26.6	4.2	0.2	0.1	5.0	2.2
Atlanta, GA	38.4	54.0	3.1	0.2	0.0	2.2	2.0
Austin, TX	68.3	8.1	6.3	0.9	0.1	12.9	3.4
Baltimore, MD	29.6	63.7	2.3	0.4	0.0	1.8	2.1
Bellevue, WA	62.6	2.3	27.6	0.4	0.2	3.1	3.9
Billings, MT	89.6	0.8	0.7	4.4	0.1	1.4	2.9
Boise City, ID	89.0	1.5	3.2	0.7	0.2	2.5	3.0
Boston, MA	53.9	24.4	8.9	0.4	0.0	8.4	3.9
Boulder, CO	88.0	0.9	4.7	0.4	0.1	3.2	2.6
Broken Arrow, OK	79.3	4.3	3.6	5.2	0.0	2.2	5.4
Cambridge, MA	66.6	11.7	15.1	0.2	0.0	2.1	4.3
Cape Coral, FL	88.2	4.3	1.5	0.3	0.1	3.3	2.3
Carlsbad, CA	82.8	1.3	7.1	0.5	0.2	4.0	4.2
Cary, NC	73.1	8.0	13.1	0.4	0.0	2.8	2.6
Cedar Rapids, IA	88.0	5.6	2.2	0.3	0.1	0.9	2.9
Charleston, SC	70.2	25.4	1.6	0.2	0.1	1.0	1.5
Charlotte, NC	50.0	35.0	5.0	0.5	0.1	6.8	2.7
Chesapeake, VA	62.6	29.8	2.9	0.4	0.1	1.2	3.0
Chicago, IL	45.0	32.9	5.5	0.5	0.0	13.4	2.7
Clarksville, TN	65.6	23.2	2.3	0.6	0.5	2.8	5.1
Colorado Spgs., CO	78.8	6.3	3.0	1.0	0.3	5.5	5.1
Columbia, MD	55.5	25.3	11.4	0.4	0.0	2.8	4.4
Columbia, MO	79.0	11.3	5.2	0.3	0.1	1.1	3.1
Columbia, SC	51.7	42.2	2.2	0.3	0.1	1.5	2.0
Columbus, OH	61.5	28.0	4.1	0.3	0.1	2.9	3.3
Dallas, TX	50.7	25.0	2.9	0.7	0.0	18.1	2.6
Denver, CO	68.9	10.2	3.4	1.4	0.1	11.9	4.1
Durham, NC	42.5	41.0	5.1	0.5	0.1	8.3	2.7
Edison, NJ	44.1	7.0	43.2	0.2	0.0	2.7	2.7
El Paso, TX	80.8	3.4	1.2	0.7	0.1	11.0	2.7
Fargo, ND	90.2	2.7	3.0	1.4	0.0	0.6	2.1
Ft. Collins, CO	89.0	1.2	2.9	0.6	0.1	3.0	3.1
Ft. Worth, TX	61.1	18.9	3.7	0.6	0.1	12.4	3.1
Gilbert, AZ	81.8	3.4	5.8	0.8	0.2	4.5	3.5
Green Bay, WI	77.9	3.5	4.0	4.1	0.1	7.2	3.1
Henderson, NV	76.9	5.1	7.2	0.7	0.6	4.8	4.8
High Point, NC	53.6	33.0	6.1	0.6	0.0	4.4	2.3
Honolulu, HI	17.9	1.5	54.8	0.2	8.4	0.8	16.3
Houston, TX	50.5	23.7	6.0	0.7	0.1	15.7	3.3
Huntington, NY	84.2	4.7	5.0	0.2	0.0	3.9	2.1
Huntsville, AL	60.3	31.2	2.4	0.6	0.1	2.9	2.5
Indianapolis, IN	61.8	27.5	2.1	0.3	0.0	5.5	2.8
Irvine, CA	50.5	1.8	39.2	0.2	0.2	2.8	5.5
Jackson, MS	18.4	79.4	0.4	0.1	0.0	0.8	0.9
Jacksonville, FL	59.4	30.7	4.3	0.4	0.1	2.2	2.9
Jersey City, NJ	32.7	25.8	23.7	0.5	0.1	12.8	4.4
Kansas City, MO	59.2	29.9	2.5	0.5	0.2	4.5	3.2
Kenosha, WI	77.1	10.0	1.7	0.6	0.1	6.8	3.8
Las Vegas, NV	62.1	11.1	6.1	0.7	0.6	14.5	4.9
Lexington, KY	75.7	14.5	3.2	0.3	0.0	3.7	2.5

Table continued on next page.

City	White Alone[1] (%)	Black Alone[1] (%)	Asian Alone[1] (%)	AIAN[2] Alone[1] (%)	NHOPI[3] Alone[1] (%)	Other Race Alone[1] (%)	Two or More Races (%)
Lincoln, NE	86.0	3.8	3.8	0.8	0.1	2.5	3.0
Little Rock, AR	48.9	42.3	2.7	0.4	0.1	3.9	1.7
Los Angeles, CA	49.8	9.6	11.3	0.7	0.1	23.8	4.6
Madison, WI	78.9	7.3	7.4	0.4	0.0	2.9	3.1
Manchester, NH	86.1	4.1	3.7	0.3	0.1	3.1	2.7
Miami, FL	72.6	19.2	1.0	0.3	0.0	4.2	2.7
Minneapolis, MN	63.8	18.6	5.6	2.0	0.0	5.6	4.4
Murfreesboro, TN	75.6	15.2	3.4	0.3	0.0	2.8	2.7
Naperville, IL	76.5	4.7	14.9	0.1	0.0	1.5	2.3
Nashville, TN	60.5	28.4	3.1	0.3	0.1	5.1	2.5
New Orleans, LA	33.0	60.2	2.9	0.3	0.0	1.9	1.7
New York, NY	44.0	25.5	12.7	0.7	0.1	13.0	4.0
Norman, OK	79.7	4.3	3.8	4.7	0.1	1.9	5.5
Olathe, KS	83.1	5.3	4.1	0.4	0.1	4.1	3.0
Omaha, NE	73.1	13.7	2.4	0.8	0.1	6.9	3.0
Orlando, FL	57.6	28.1	3.8	0.4	0.1	6.8	3.4
Overland Park, KS	84.4	4.3	6.3	0.3	0.0	2.1	2.5
Oyster Bay, NY	85.0	2.3	9.1	0.2	0.0	1.9	1.6
Pembroke Pines, FL	67.3	19.8	4.9	0.3	0.0	4.4	3.3
Philadelphia, PA	41.0	43.4	6.3	0.5	0.0	5.9	2.8
Phoenix, AZ	65.9	6.5	3.2	2.2	0.2	18.5	3.6
Pittsburgh, PA	66.0	26.1	4.4	0.2	0.0	0.8	2.5
Plano, TX	66.9	7.6	16.9	0.4	0.1	5.1	3.0
Portland, OR	76.1	6.3	7.1	1.0	0.5	4.2	4.7
Providence, RI	49.8	16.0	6.4	1.4	0.1	19.8	6.5
Provo, UT	84.8	0.7	2.5	0.8	1.1	6.6	3.4
Raleigh, NC	57.5	29.3	4.3	0.5	0.0	5.7	2.6
Richmond, VA	40.8	50.6	2.3	0.3	0.1	3.6	2.3
Roseville, CA	79.3	2.0	8.4	0.7	0.3	4.3	5.0
Round Rock, TX	70.8	9.8	5.2	0.7	0.1	9.7	3.8
San Antonio, TX	72.6	6.9	2.4	0.9	0.1	13.7	3.4
San Diego, CA	58.9	6.7	15.9	0.6	0.5	12.3	5.1
San Francisco, CA	48.5	6.1	33.3	0.5	0.4	6.6	4.7
San Jose, CA	42.8	3.2	32.0	0.9	0.4	15.7	5.0
Savannah, GA	38.3	55.4	2.0	0.3	0.1	1.8	2.1
Scottsdale, AZ	89.3	1.7	3.3	0.8	0.1	2.5	2.3
Seattle, WA	69.5	7.9	13.8	0.8	0.4	2.4	5.1
Sioux Falls, SD	86.8	4.2	1.8	2.7	0.1	2.0	2.5
Stamford, CT	65.0	13.9	7.9	0.3	0.1	9.7	3.2
Sterling Hgts, MI	85.1	5.2	6.7	0.2	0.0	0.5	2.2
Sunnyvale, CA	43.0	2.0	40.9	0.5	0.5	8.7	4.5
Tampa, FL	62.9	26.2	3.4	0.4	0.1	3.8	3.2
Temecula, CA	70.8	4.1	9.8	1.1	0.4	7.9	5.9
Thousand Oaks, CA	80.3	1.3	8.7	0.4	0.1	5.4	3.8
Virginia Beach, VA	67.7	19.6	6.1	0.4	0.2	2.0	4.0
Washington, DC	38.5	50.7	3.5	0.3	0.1	4.1	2.9
U.S.	72.4	12.6	4.8	0.9	0.2	6.2	2.9

Note: (1) Alone is defined as not being in combination with one or more other races; (2) American Indian and Alaska Native; (3) Native Hawaiian and Other Pacific Islander
Source: U.S. Census Bureau, 2010 Census

Race: Metro Area

Metro Area	White Alone[1] (%)	Black Alone[1] (%)	Asian Alone[1] (%)	AIAN[2] Alone[1] (%)	NHOPI[3] Alone[1] (%)	Other Race Alone[1] (%)	Two or More Races (%)
Albuquerque, NM	69.6	2.7	2.0	5.9	0.1	15.4	4.3
Alexandria, VA	54.8	25.8	9.3	0.4	0.1	6.0	3.7
Anchorage, AK	70.4	4.5	6.5	7.4	1.6	2.0	7.7
Ann Arbor, MI	74.5	12.7	7.9	0.3	0.0	1.2	3.4
Athens, GA	71.4	19.5	3.2	0.2	0.0	3.7	1.9
Atlanta, GA	55.4	32.4	4.8	0.3	0.1	4.5	2.4
Austin, TX	72.9	7.4	4.8	0.8	0.1	10.9	3.2
Baltimore, MD	62.1	28.7	4.5	0.3	0.1	1.7	2.5
Bellevue, WA	71.9	5.6	11.4	1.1	0.8	3.8	5.3
Billings, MT	91.1	0.6	0.6	3.8	0.1	1.1	2.7
Boise City, ID	87.9	0.9	1.8	0.9	0.2	5.4	2.9
Boston, MA	78.8	7.3	6.5	0.2	0.0	4.6	2.6
Boulder, CO	87.2	0.9	4.1	0.6	0.1	4.5	2.7
Broken Arrow, OK	70.9	8.4	1.8	8.3	0.1	4.2	6.4
Cambridge, MA	78.8	7.3	6.5	0.2	0.0	4.6	2.6
Cape Coral, FL	83.0	8.3	1.4	0.4	0.1	4.9	2.1
Carlsbad, CA	64.0	5.1	10.9	0.9	0.5	13.6	5.1
Cary, NC	67.5	20.2	4.4	0.5	0.0	5.0	2.4
Cedar Rapids, IA	92.0	3.4	1.5	0.3	0.1	0.6	2.1
Charleston, SC	65.6	27.7	1.6	0.5	0.1	2.5	2.1
Charlotte, NC	65.1	24.0	3.1	0.5	0.1	5.0	2.2
Chesapeake, VA	59.6	31.3	3.5	0.4	0.1	1.7	3.4
Chicago, IL	65.4	17.4	5.6	0.4	0.0	8.8	2.4
Clarksville, TN	73.2	18.3	1.6	0.6	0.4	2.1	3.8
Colorado Spgs., CO	80.3	6.0	2.7	1.0	0.3	4.8	5.0
Columbia, MD	62.1	28.7	4.5	0.3	0.1	1.7	2.5
Columbia, MO	83.3	9.1	3.6	0.4	0.1	0.9	2.8
Columbia, SC	60.4	33.2	1.7	0.4	0.1	2.3	2.0
Columbus, OH	77.5	14.9	3.1	0.2	0.1	1.7	2.5
Dallas, TX	65.3	15.1	5.4	0.7	0.1	10.6	2.8
Denver, CO	78.0	5.6	3.7	1.0	0.1	8.0	3.6
Durham, NC	59.3	27.1	4.4	0.5	0.0	6.3	2.4
Edison, NJ	59.2	17.8	9.9	0.5	0.0	9.3	3.2
El Paso, TX	82.1	3.1	1.0	0.8	0.1	10.5	2.5
Fargo, ND	92.0	2.0	2.1	1.3	0.0	0.6	2.0
Ft. Collins, CO	90.5	0.8	1.9	0.7	0.1	3.2	2.6
Ft. Worth, TX	65.3	15.1	5.4	0.7	0.1	10.6	2.8
Gilbert, AZ	73.0	5.0	3.3	2.4	0.2	12.7	3.5
Green Bay, WI	88.4	1.8	2.3	2.4	0.0	3.1	2.0
Henderson, NV	60.9	10.5	8.7	0.7	0.7	13.5	5.1
High Point, NC	65.0	25.5	2.9	0.5	0.0	3.8	2.1
Honolulu, HI	20.8	2.0	43.9	0.3	9.5	1.1	22.3
Houston, TX	60.2	17.2	6.5	0.6	0.1	12.3	3.0
Huntington, NY	59.2	17.8	9.9	0.5	0.0	9.3	3.2
Huntsville, AL	70.6	21.7	2.2	0.7	0.1	2.3	2.3
Indianapolis, IN	77.0	15.0	2.3	0.3	0.0	3.2	2.2
Irvine, CA	52.8	7.1	14.7	0.7	0.3	20.1	4.4
Jackson, MS	49.1	47.7	1.1	0.2	0.0	1.1	0.9
Jacksonville, FL	69.9	21.8	3.4	0.4	0.1	1.8	2.6
Jersey City, NJ	59.2	17.8	9.9	0.5	0.0	9.3	3.2
Kansas City, MO	78.4	12.5	2.3	0.5	0.2	3.3	2.8
Kenosha, WI	65.4	17.4	5.6	0.4	0.0	8.8	2.4
Las Vegas, NV	60.9	10.5	8.7	0.7	0.7	13.5	5.1
Lexington, KY	81.4	10.8	2.3	0.2	0.0	3.0	2.2

Table continued on next page.

Metro Area	White Alone[1] (%)	Black Alone[1] (%)	Asian Alone[1] (%)	AIAN[2] Alone[1] (%)	NHOPI[3] Alone[1] (%)	Other Race Alone[1] (%)	Two or More Races (%)
Lincoln, NE	87.7	3.3	3.3	0.7	0.1	2.3	2.7
Little Rock, AR	71.6	22.2	1.5	0.5	0.1	2.4	1.9
Los Angeles, CA	52.8	7.1	14.7	0.7	0.3	20.1	4.4
Madison, WI	86.4	4.6	4.1	0.4	0.0	2.2	2.3
Manchester, NH	90.4	2.1	3.2	0.2	0.0	2.1	2.0
Miami, FL	70.3	21.0	2.3	0.3	0.0	3.5	2.5
Minneapolis, MN	81.0	7.4	5.7	0.7	0.0	2.3	2.8
Murfreesboro, TN	76.9	15.2	2.3	0.3	0.1	3.2	2.1
Naperville, IL	65.4	17.4	5.6	0.4	0.0	8.8	2.4
Nashville, TN	76.9	15.2	2.3	0.3	0.1	3.2	2.1
New Orleans, LA	58.2	34.0	2.7	0.4	0.0	2.6	1.9
New York, NY	59.2	17.8	9.9	0.5	0.0	9.3	3.2
Norman, OK	71.9	10.4	2.8	4.1	0.1	5.5	5.2
Olathe, KS	78.4	12.5	2.3	0.5	0.2	3.3	2.8
Omaha, NE	82.5	7.9	2.1	0.6	0.1	4.3	2.6
Orlando, FL	70.0	16.2	4.0	0.4	0.1	6.1	3.2
Overland Park, KS	78.4	12.5	2.3	0.5	0.2	3.3	2.8
Oyster Bay, NY	59.2	17.8	9.9	0.5	0.0	9.3	3.2
Pembroke Pines, FL	70.3	21.0	2.3	0.3	0.0	3.5	2.5
Philadelphia, PA	68.2	20.8	5.0	0.3	0.0	3.4	2.3
Phoenix, AZ	73.0	5.0	3.3	2.4	0.2	12.7	3.5
Pittsburgh, PA	87.8	8.4	1.8	0.1	0.0	0.4	1.6
Plano, TX	65.3	15.1	5.4	0.7	0.1	10.6	2.8
Portland, OR	81.0	2.9	5.7	0.9	0.5	4.9	4.1
Providence, RI	83.8	4.9	2.5	0.5	0.0	5.1	3.1
Provo, UT	89.5	0.5	1.3	0.6	0.7	4.6	2.7
Raleigh, NC	67.5	20.2	4.4	0.5	0.0	5.0	2.4
Richmond, VA	62.0	29.8	3.1	0.4	0.1	2.3	2.3
Roseville, CA	64.7	7.4	11.9	1.0	0.7	8.4	5.9
Round Rock, TX	72.9	7.4	4.8	0.8	0.1	10.9	3.2
San Antonio, TX	75.5	6.6	2.1	0.8	0.1	11.6	3.3
San Diego, CA	64.0	5.1	10.9	0.9	0.5	13.6	5.1
San Francisco, CA	51.7	8.4	23.2	0.6	0.7	9.9	5.5
San Jose, CA	47.5	2.6	31.1	0.8	0.4	12.8	4.9
Savannah, GA	59.7	33.9	2.1	0.3	0.1	1.9	2.1
Scottsdale, AZ	73.0	5.0	3.3	2.4	0.2	12.7	3.5
Seattle, WA	71.9	5.6	11.4	1.1	0.8	3.8	5.3
Sioux Falls, SD	90.2	3.0	1.3	2.0	0.1	1.4	2.0
Stamford, CT	74.8	10.8	4.6	0.3	0.0	6.8	2.6
Sterling Hgts, MI	70.1	22.8	3.3	0.3	0.0	1.2	2.2
Sunnyvale, CA	47.5	2.6	31.1	0.8	0.4	12.8	4.9
Tampa, FL	78.8	11.8	2.9	0.4	0.1	3.4	2.6
Temecula, CA	58.9	7.6	6.1	1.1	0.3	21.0	4.9
Thousand Oaks, CA	68.7	1.8	6.7	1.0	0.2	17.0	4.5
Virginia Beach, VA	59.6	31.3	3.5	0.4	0.1	1.7	3.4
Washington, DC	54.8	25.8	9.3	0.4	0.1	6.0	3.7
U.S.	72.4	12.6	4.8	0.9	0.2	6.2	2.9

Note: (1) Figures cover the Metropolitan Statistical Area (MSA)—see Appendix B for areas included; (1) Alone is defined as not being in combination with one or more other races; (2) American Indian and Alaska Native; (3) Native Hawaiian and Other Pacific Islander
Source: U.S. Census Bureau, 2010 Census

Hispanic Origin: City

City	Hispanic or Latino (%)	Mexican (%)	Puerto Rican (%)	Cuban (%)	Other Hispanic or Latino (%)
Albuquerque, NM	46.7	26.8	0.5	0.5	18.9
Alexandria, VA	16.1	1.7	1.1	0.3	13.0
Anchorage, AK	7.6	3.9	0.9	0.2	2.5
Ann Arbor, MI	4.1	1.8	0.4	0.2	1.7
Athens, GA	10.5	6.6	0.6	0.3	3.0
Atlanta, GA	5.2	2.8	0.5	0.3	1.5
Austin, TX	35.1	29.1	0.5	0.4	5.1
Baltimore, MD	4.2	1.3	0.5	0.1	2.3
Bellevue, WA	7.0	4.7	0.2	0.1	2.0
Billings, MT	5.2	4.0	0.2	0.0	0.9
Boise City, ID	7.1	5.4	0.2	0.1	1.4
Boston, MA	17.5	1.0	4.9	0.4	11.2
Boulder, CO	8.7	6.1	0.3	0.2	2.2
Broken Arrow, OK	6.5	4.4	0.4	0.1	1.5
Cambridge, MA	7.6	1.4	1.6	0.4	4.3
Cape Coral, FL	19.5	1.8	4.7	6.4	6.6
Carlsbad, CA	13.3	10.2	0.4	0.2	2.5
Cary, NC	7.7	3.7	0.9	0.4	2.7
Cedar Rapids, IA	3.3	2.3	0.2	0.0	0.7
Charleston, SC	2.9	1.3	0.4	0.1	1.0
Charlotte, NC	13.1	5.6	1.0	0.4	6.1
Chesapeake, VA	4.4	1.6	1.2	0.2	1.3
Chicago, IL	28.9	21.4	3.8	0.3	3.3
Clarksville, TN	9.3	4.1	3.0	0.2	2.0
Colorado Spgs., CO	16.1	10.6	1.1	0.2	4.1
Columbia, MD	7.9	2.0	1.1	0.2	4.5
Columbia, MO	3.4	2.1	0.3	0.2	0.9
Columbia, SC	4.3	1.9	1.0	0.2	1.3
Columbus, OH	5.6	3.3	0.6	0.1	1.6
Dallas, TX	42.4	36.7	0.3	0.2	5.2
Denver, CO	31.8	24.9	0.4	0.2	6.4
Durham, NC	14.2	7.7	0.7	0.2	5.6
Edison, NJ	8.1	1.2	2.6	0.6	3.8
El Paso, TX	80.7	74.9	0.9	0.1	4.8
Fargo, ND	2.2	1.5	0.1	0.0	0.5
Ft. Collins, CO	10.1	6.9	0.3	0.1	2.8
Ft. Worth, TX	34.1	29.6	0.8	0.2	3.5
Gilbert, AZ	14.9	11.4	0.7	0.2	2.6
Green Bay, WI	13.4	10.7	0.9	0.1	1.7
Henderson, NV	14.9	9.9	0.9	0.6	3.5
High Point, NC	8.5	4.9	0.8	0.2	2.5
Honolulu, HI	5.4	1.7	1.6	0.1	2.1
Houston, TX	43.8	32.1	0.4	0.4	10.9
Huntington, NY	11.0	0.7	2.1	0.3	7.9
Huntsville, AL	5.8	4.0	0.6	0.1	1.1
Indianapolis, IN	9.4	6.9	0.4	0.1	2.0
Irvine, CA	9.2	6.0	0.3	0.2	2.7
Jackson, MS	1.6	1.0	0.1	0.0	0.5
Jacksonville, FL	7.7	1.7	2.6	0.9	2.6
Jersey City, NJ	27.6	1.8	10.4	0.7	14.7
Kansas City, MO	10.0	7.8	0.3	0.3	1.6
Kenosha, WI	16.3	12.5	1.7	0.1	2.0
Las Vegas, NV	31.5	24.0	0.9	0.9	5.7
Lexington, KY	6.9	5.1	0.3	0.2	1.3
Lincoln, NE	6.3	4.7	0.2	0.1	1.3

Table continued on next page.

City	Hispanic or Latino (%)	Mexican (%)	Puerto Rican (%)	Cuban (%)	Other Hispanic or Latino (%)
Little Rock, AR	6.8	5.0	0.2	0.1	1.5
Los Angeles, CA	48.5	31.9	0.4	0.4	15.8
Madison, WI	6.8	4.5	0.5	0.1	1.7
Manchester, NH	8.1	1.7	3.0	0.1	3.2
Miami, FL	70.0	1.5	3.2	34.4	30.9
Minneapolis, MN	10.5	7.0	0.4	0.1	3.0
Murfreesboro, TN	5.9	3.7	0.5	0.2	1.6
Naperville, IL	5.3	3.4	0.6	0.2	1.2
Nashville, TN	10.0	6.1	0.5	0.3	3.1
New Orleans, LA	5.2	1.3	0.3	0.4	3.4
New York, NY	28.6	3.9	8.9	0.5	15.3
Norman, OK	6.4	4.2	0.4	0.1	1.7
Olathe, KS	10.2	7.9	0.4	0.1	1.8
Omaha, NE	13.1	10.4	0.2	0.1	2.3
Orlando, FL	25.4	1.8	13.1	1.8	8.7
Overland Park, KS	6.3	4.4	0.2	0.1	1.5
Oyster Bay, NY	7.5	0.5	1.6	0.3	5.0
Pembroke Pines, FL	41.4	1.1	6.8	12.8	20.7
Philadelphia, PA	12.3	1.0	8.0	0.3	3.0
Phoenix, AZ	40.8	35.9	0.6	0.3	4.0
Pittsburgh, PA	2.3	0.7	0.4	0.1	1.0
Plano, TX	14.7	10.6	0.5	0.2	3.5
Portland, OR	9.4	6.7	0.3	0.4	2.0
Providence, RI	38.1	1.8	8.3	0.3	27.7
Provo, UT	15.2	10.2	0.3	0.1	4.6
Raleigh, NC	11.4	5.9	1.1	0.3	4.1
Richmond, VA	6.3	2.0	0.7	0.2	3.3
Roseville, CA	14.6	11.0	0.5	0.1	3.0
Round Rock, TX	29.0	23.4	0.9	0.3	4.4
San Antonio, TX	63.2	53.2	1.0	0.2	8.9
San Diego, CA	28.8	24.9	0.6	0.2	3.0
San Francisco, CA	15.1	7.4	0.5	0.2	6.9
San Jose, CA	33.2	28.4	0.5	0.1	4.1
Savannah, GA	4.7	2.1	1.0	0.2	1.4
Scottsdale, AZ	8.8	6.6	0.4	0.1	1.7
Seattle, WA	6.6	4.1	0.3	0.2	2.0
Sioux Falls, SD	4.4	2.2	0.2	0.1	1.9
Stamford, CT	23.8	2.0	2.8	0.3	18.6
Sterling Hgts, MI	1.9	1.2	0.2	0.1	0.5
Sunnyvale, CA	18.9	14.2	0.4	0.1	4.2
Tampa, FL	23.1	2.9	7.2	6.3	6.7
Temecula, CA	24.7	19.9	1.0	0.2	3.6
Thousand Oaks, CA	16.8	11.6	0.4	0.2	4.7
Virginia Beach, VA	6.6	1.9	2.2	0.2	2.3
Washington, DC	9.1	1.4	0.5	0.3	6.9
U.S.	16.3	10.3	1.5	0.6	4.0

Note: Persons of Hispanic or Latino origin can be of any race
Source: U.S. Census Bureau, 2010 Census

Hispanic Origin: Metro Area

Metro Area	Hispanic or Latino (%)	Mexican (%)	Puerto Rican (%)	Cuban (%)	Other Hispanic or Latino (%)
Albuquerque, NM	46.7	26.0	0.5	0.4	19.8
Alexandria, VA	13.8	2.1	0.9	0.3	10.6
Anchorage, AK	6.7	3.5	0.8	0.2	2.2
Ann Arbor, MI	4.0	2.1	0.4	0.1	1.4
Athens, GA	8.0	5.0	0.4	0.2	2.3
Atlanta, GA	10.4	6.0	0.8	0.3	3.3
Austin, TX	31.4	26.2	0.6	0.3	4.3
Baltimore, MD	4.6	1.2	0.7	0.1	2.5
Bellevue, WA	9.0	6.4	0.5	0.1	2.0
Billings, MT	4.5	3.5	0.2	0.0	0.8
Boise City, ID	12.6	10.5	0.2	0.1	1.8
Boston, MA	9.0	0.6	2.5	0.2	5.7
Boulder, CO	13.3	10.3	0.3	0.1	2.6
Broken Arrow, OK	8.4	6.6	0.3	0.1	1.4
Cambridge, MA	9.0	0.6	2.5	0.2	5.7
Cape Coral, FL	18.3	5.5	4.0	3.3	5.5
Carlsbad, CA	32.0	28.1	0.7	0.2	3.1
Cary, NC	10.1	5.9	0.9	0.3	3.1
Cedar Rapids, IA	2.4	1.6	0.2	0.0	0.5
Charleston, SC	5.4	3.1	0.7	0.1	1.5
Charlotte, NC	9.8	4.8	0.9	0.3	3.8
Chesapeake, VA	5.4	1.7	1.6	0.2	1.8
Chicago, IL	20.7	16.3	2.0	0.2	2.1
Clarksville, TN	6.8	3.2	2.0	0.2	1.4
Colorado Spgs., CO	14.7	9.5	1.2	0.2	3.8
Columbia, MD	4.6	1.2	0.7	0.1	2.5
Columbia, MO	2.9	1.8	0.3	0.1	0.7
Columbia, SC	5.1	2.7	0.9	0.1	1.3
Columbus, OH	3.6	2.0	0.4	0.1	1.1
Dallas, TX	27.5	22.9	0.5	0.2	3.9
Denver, CO	22.5	16.7	0.4	0.1	5.2
Durham, NC	11.3	6.7	0.6	0.2	3.8
Edison, NJ	22.9	3.0	6.2	0.7	13.0
El Paso, TX	82.2	76.6	0.8	0.1	4.7
Fargo, ND	2.4	1.7	0.1	0.0	0.5
Ft. Collins, CO	10.6	7.7	0.3	0.1	2.5
Ft. Worth, TX	27.5	22.9	0.5	0.2	3.9
Gilbert, AZ	29.5	25.5	0.6	0.2	3.2
Green Bay, WI	6.2	4.8	0.5	0.0	0.9
Henderson, NV	29.1	21.7	0.9	1.1	5.5
High Point, NC	7.6	5.2	0.5	0.2	1.7
Honolulu, HI	8.1	2.3	2.9	0.1	2.9
Houston, TX	35.3	26.6	0.5	0.3	7.9
Huntington, NY	22.9	3.0	6.2	0.7	13.0
Huntsville, AL	4.8	3.2	0.5	0.1	1.0
Indianapolis, IN	6.2	4.4	0.3	0.1	1.4
Irvine, CA	44.4	34.1	0.4	0.4	9.6
Jackson, MS	2.1	1.3	0.1	0.0	0.7
Jacksonville, FL	6.9	1.5	2.3	0.7	2.3
Jersey City, NJ	22.9	3.0	6.2	0.7	13.0
Kansas City, MO	8.2	6.4	0.3	0.1	1.4
Kenosha, WI	20.7	16.3	2.0	0.2	2.1
Las Vegas, NV	29.1	21.7	0.9	1.1	5.5
Lexington, KY	5.9	4.4	0.3	0.1	1.0
Lincoln, NE	5.6	4.2	0.2	0.1	1.2

Table continued on next page.

Metro Area	Hispanic or Latino (%)	Mexican (%)	Puerto Rican (%)	Cuban (%)	Other Hispanic or Latino (%)
Little Rock, AR	4.8	3.5	0.2	0.1	1.0
Los Angeles, CA	44.4	34.1	0.4	0.4	9.6
Madison, WI	5.4	3.7	0.4	0.1	1.2
Manchester, NH	5.3	1.1	1.8	0.1	2.3
Miami, FL	41.6	2.4	3.7	17.7	17.8
Minneapolis, MN	5.4	3.7	0.3	0.1	1.4
Murfreesboro, TN	6.6	4.1	0.4	0.2	1.9
Naperville, IL	20.7	16.3	2.0	0.2	2.1
Nashville, TN	6.6	4.1	0.4	0.2	1.9
New Orleans, LA	7.9	1.8	0.4	0.6	5.1
New York, NY	22.9	3.0	6.2	0.7	13.0
Norman, OK	11.3	9.1	0.3	0.1	1.8
Olathe, KS	8.2	6.4	0.3	0.1	1.4
Omaha, NE	9.0	7.0	0.2	0.1	1.7
Orlando, FL	25.2	3.0	12.6	1.7	7.9
Overland Park, KS	8.2	6.4	0.3	0.1	1.4
Oyster Bay, NY	22.9	3.0	6.2	0.7	13.0
Pembroke Pines, FL	41.6	2.4	3.7	17.7	17.8
Philadelphia, PA	7.8	1.7	4.0	0.2	2.0
Phoenix, AZ	29.5	25.5	0.6	0.2	3.2
Pittsburgh, PA	1.3	0.5	0.3	0.1	0.5
Plano, TX	27.5	22.9	0.5	0.2	3.9
Portland, OR	10.9	8.5	0.3	0.2	1.9
Providence, RI	10.2	0.7	3.3	0.1	6.1
Provo, UT	10.7	7.2	0.2	0.1	3.2
Raleigh, NC	10.1	5.9	0.9	0.3	3.1
Richmond, VA	5.0	1.7	0.8	0.2	2.4
Roseville, CA	20.2	16.4	0.6	0.1	3.1
Round Rock, TX	31.4	26.2	0.6	0.3	4.3
San Antonio, TX	54.1	45.3	1.0	0.2	7.6
San Diego, CA	32.0	28.1	0.7	0.2	3.1
San Francisco, CA	21.7	14.2	0.7	0.2	6.6
San Jose, CA	27.8	23.4	0.4	0.1	3.9
Savannah, GA	5.0	2.3	1.1	0.2	1.4
Scottsdale, AZ	29.5	25.5	0.6	0.2	3.2
Seattle, WA	9.0	6.4	0.5	0.1	2.0
Sioux Falls, SD	3.4	1.8	0.2	0.0	1.4
Stamford, CT	16.9	2.1	5.5	0.4	9.0
Sterling Hgts, MI	3.9	2.8	0.4	0.1	0.6
Sunnyvale, CA	27.8	23.4	0.4	0.1	3.9
Tampa, FL	16.2	3.6	5.2	2.9	4.5
Temecula, CA	47.3	40.6	0.7	0.3	5.7
Thousand Oaks, CA	40.3	35.6	0.4	0.2	4.1
Virginia Beach, VA	5.4	1.7	1.6	0.2	1.8
Washington, DC	13.8	2.1	0.9	0.3	10.6
U.S.	16.3	10.3	1.5	0.6	4.0

Note: Persons of Hispanic or Latino origin can be of any race; Figures cover the Metropolitan Statistical Area (MSA)—see Appendix B for areas included
Source: U.S. Census Bureau, 2010 Census

Age: City

City	Percent of Population							Median Age
	Under Age 5	Age 5 to 17	Age 18 to 34	Age 35 to 49	Age 50 to 64	Age 65 to 79	80 Years and Over	
Albuquerque, NM	7.0	17.0	25.9	19.8	18.3	8.6	3.5	35.1
Alexandria, VA	7.1	10.0	31.6	24.6	17.5	6.6	2.5	35.6
Anchorage, AK	7.5	18.4	26.8	21.1	18.9	5.8	1.5	32.9
Ann Arbor, MI	4.3	10.1	47.2	14.9	14.1	6.5	2.9	27.8
Athens, GA	6.0	11.5	47.4	14.4	12.3	6.1	2.3	25.8
Atlanta, GA	6.4	13.0	34.1	21.2	15.5	7.2	2.6	32.9
Austin, TX	7.3	14.9	35.2	21.0	14.5	5.1	1.9	31.0
Baltimore, MD	6.6	14.9	29.3	19.3	18.2	8.4	3.4	34.4
Bellevue, WA	5.6	15.6	24.1	22.0	18.8	9.7	4.3	38.5
Billings, MT	7.0	15.6	24.5	18.4	19.5	9.9	5.1	37.5
Boise City, ID	6.4	16.3	26.8	20.3	19.0	7.8	3.4	35.3
Boston, MA	5.2	11.5	40.2	18.4	14.6	7.1	2.9	30.8
Boulder, CO	4.1	9.8	45.1	17.1	15.0	6.0	2.9	28.7
Broken Arrow, OK	7.2	20.2	21.6	21.6	19.0	7.9	2.5	35.7
Cambridge, MA	4.3	7.1	49.5	16.3	13.3	6.9	2.6	30.2
Cape Coral, FL	5.4	17.1	17.8	21.3	21.5	12.9	4.1	42.4
Carlsbad, CA	6.0	18.1	18.0	23.5	20.4	9.2	4.8	40.4
Cary, NC	7.0	20.8	19.7	26.1	17.8	6.6	2.1	36.6
Cedar Rapids, IA	6.7	16.8	26.1	19.3	18.0	8.8	4.3	35.3
Charleston, SC	6.3	11.7	35.4	17.5	16.9	8.6	3.7	32.5
Charlotte, NC	7.6	17.7	27.7	22.8	15.8	6.2	2.3	33.2
Chesapeake, VA	6.5	19.4	21.7	22.7	19.4	7.9	2.5	37.0
Chicago, IL	6.9	16.2	30.3	20.4	15.9	7.5	2.8	32.9
Clarksville, TN	9.6	18.9	32.5	18.9	12.9	5.6	1.6	28.6
Colorado Spgs., CO	7.1	17.9	25.1	20.6	18.4	8.0	2.9	34.9
Columbia, MD	6.4	17.6	22.6	22.6	20.0	8.4	2.5	37.5
Columbia, MO	6.0	12.9	43.5	15.7	13.5	5.7	2.8	26.8
Columbia, SC	5.4	11.5	43.6	16.4	14.4	6.0	2.7	28.1
Columbus, OH	7.6	15.6	33.0	19.7	15.5	6.2	2.4	31.2
Dallas, TX	8.6	17.9	28.8	20.7	15.1	6.4	2.5	31.8
Denver, CO	7.3	14.2	30.9	21.1	16.3	7.2	3.2	33.7
Durham, NC	7.7	15.0	32.4	20.5	15.5	6.1	2.7	32.1
Edison, NJ	6.4	16.2	22.3	22.8	19.6	8.8	3.8	38.1
El Paso, TX	7.9	21.3	24.0	19.6	16.1	8.1	3.1	32.5
Fargo, ND	6.4	12.9	37.7	16.8	16.0	6.5	3.6	30.2
Ft. Collins, CO	5.7	14.2	38.3	17.8	15.2	6.0	2.8	29.6
Ft. Worth, TX	9.0	20.3	26.6	21.2	14.7	6.0	2.2	31.2
Gilbert, AZ	8.5	23.6	22.7	24.6	14.5	5.0	1.0	31.9
Green Bay, WI	7.7	16.9	27.0	19.5	17.5	7.6	3.7	33.7
Henderson, NV	5.9	16.8	20.8	21.9	20.4	11.6	2.7	39.6
High Point, NC	7.1	18.2	23.6	21.5	17.7	8.3	3.6	35.8
Honolulu, HI	4.9	12.5	24.1	20.3	20.4	11.3	6.5	41.3
Houston, TX	8.1	17.7	28.8	20.4	16.0	6.7	2.4	32.1
Huntington, NY	5.3	19.5	15.6	22.9	21.4	10.8	4.6	42.5
Huntsville, AL	6.2	15.3	26.8	19.3	18.3	10.4	3.8	36.5
Indianapolis, IN	7.6	17.4	26.9	20.2	17.5	7.5	3.0	33.7
Irvine, CA	5.7	15.9	30.1	23.0	16.7	6.5	2.1	33.9
Jackson, MS	7.8	19.6	27.6	18.1	17.0	7.1	2.8	31.2
Jacksonville, FL	7.0	16.9	25.4	21.1	18.7	8.0	2.9	35.5
Jersey City, NJ	7.1	14.1	32.4	21.7	15.6	6.9	2.2	33.2
Kansas City, MO	7.5	16.6	26.4	20.3	18.1	7.9	3.2	34.6
Kenosha, WI	7.6	19.2	25.3	21.2	15.9	7.1	3.7	33.5
Las Vegas, NV	7.2	18.4	23.1	21.9	17.3	9.3	2.7	35.9
Lexington, KY	6.5	14.7	30.8	20.1	17.4	7.6	2.9	33.7

Table continued on next page.

City	Percent of Population							Median Age
	Under Age 5	Age 5 to 17	Age 18 to 34	Age 35 to 49	Age 50 to 64	Age 65 to 79	80 Years and Over	
Lincoln, NE	7.2	15.5	31.7	18.1	16.8	7.4	3.4	31.8
Little Rock, AR	7.0	17.2	25.8	20.0	18.8	7.8	3.6	35.1
Los Angeles, CA	6.6	16.4	28.3	21.9	16.3	7.4	3.1	34.1
Madison, WI	5.8	11.7	39.1	17.6	16.2	6.5	3.1	30.9
Manchester, NH	6.7	14.9	27.0	21.1	18.5	7.8	4.0	36.0
Miami, FL	6.0	12.4	25.9	22.4	17.3	11.2	4.8	38.8
Minneapolis, MN	6.9	13.3	36.2	19.9	15.7	5.6	2.4	31.4
Murfreesboro, TN	7.1	16.4	35.7	19.1	13.6	5.9	2.2	29.0
Naperville, IL	5.8	22.9	17.7	24.8	20.1	6.1	2.5	37.9
Nashville, TN	7.2	14.5	30.3	20.5	17.2	7.3	2.9	33.7
New Orleans, LA	6.4	14.9	29.2	19.2	19.4	8.0	3.0	34.6
New York, NY	6.3	15.3	27.7	21.0	17.5	8.7	3.5	35.5
Norman, OK	5.8	14.0	37.4	16.8	15.9	7.3	2.7	29.6
Olathe, KS	8.9	21.1	23.5	23.6	15.8	5.1	2.0	32.9
Omaha, NE	7.5	17.6	26.8	19.1	17.6	7.9	3.4	33.5
Orlando, FL	7.1	14.9	31.7	21.9	15.0	6.7	2.7	32.8
Overland Park, KS	6.4	18.4	21.7	21.7	19.5	8.4	3.9	37.8
Oyster Bay, NY	4.9	18.2	16.8	21.9	21.9	10.8	5.5	43.1
Pembroke Pines, FL	5.7	18.1	20.2	23.3	18.0	9.7	5.1	39.5
Philadelphia, PA	6.6	15.9	29.5	18.8	17.1	8.5	3.7	33.5
Phoenix, AZ	8.3	20.0	25.9	21.3	16.1	6.3	2.1	32.2
Pittsburgh, PA	4.9	11.3	35.8	16.3	17.8	8.9	4.8	33.2
Plano, TX	6.3	19.6	21.0	24.8	19.5	6.9	1.9	37.2
Portland, OR	6.0	13.1	29.3	22.6	18.5	7.1	3.3	35.8
Providence, RI	6.9	16.4	36.5	17.7	13.7	5.8	2.9	28.5
Provo, UT	8.5	13.9	54.5	9.8	7.5	4.0	1.8	23.3
Raleigh, NC	7.2	15.9	32.3	21.7	14.7	5.8	2.4	31.9
Richmond, VA	6.3	12.3	35.3	17.7	17.3	7.5	3.6	32.0
Roseville, CA	6.8	19.5	21.2	22.4	16.7	9.1	4.3	36.8
Round Rock, TX	8.8	22.3	24.4	25.1	14.1	4.2	1.2	32.0
San Antonio, TX	7.6	19.2	26.3	20.1	16.4	7.6	2.9	32.7
San Diego, CA	6.2	15.2	30.7	20.9	16.4	7.5	3.2	33.6
San Francisco, CA	4.4	9.0	30.5	23.8	18.7	9.3	4.3	38.5
San Jose, CA	7.3	17.6	24.8	23.4	16.9	7.5	2.6	35.2
Savannah, GA	7.1	15.2	32.4	17.2	16.4	8.0	3.6	31.3
Scottsdale, AZ	4.2	13.6	18.9	20.4	22.9	14.4	5.6	45.4
Seattle, WA	5.3	10.1	32.6	23.1	18.1	7.2	3.6	36.1
Sioux Falls, SD	8.0	16.6	27.4	19.9	17.1	7.4	3.5	33.6
Stamford, CT	6.8	14.8	25.2	22.5	17.7	8.7	4.4	37.1
Sterling Hgts, MI	5.5	16.2	21.2	20.9	21.0	10.8	4.4	40.4
Sunnyvale, CA	8.0	14.4	26.3	23.9	16.2	7.9	3.3	35.6
Tampa, FL	6.4	16.2	27.9	21.4	17.2	7.9	3.1	34.6
Temecula, CA	7.0	23.6	21.3	24.3	15.9	6.0	1.8	33.4
Thousand Oaks, CA	5.2	18.5	17.9	22.5	21.2	10.4	4.2	41.5
Virginia Beach, VA	6.7	17.4	26.1	21.3	18.0	7.9	2.7	34.9
Washington, DC	5.4	11.3	35.2	19.8	16.8	8.1	3.3	33.8
U.S.	6.5	17.5	23.2	20.7	19.0	9.4	3.6	37.2

Source: U.S. Census Bureau, 2010 Census

Age: Metro Area

Metro Area	Percent of Population							Median Age
	Under Age 5	Age 5 to 17	Age 18 to 34	Age 35 to 49	Age 50 to 64	Age 65 to 79	80 Years and Over	
Albuquerque, NM	6.8	17.8	23.6	20.0	19.5	9.1	3.2	36.4
Alexandria, VA	6.7	17.1	24.6	23.0	18.5	7.4	2.6	36.1
Anchorage, AK	7.6	19.1	25.5	21.2	19.2	5.9	1.5	33.3
Ann Arbor, MI	5.6	15.3	31.2	19.6	18.2	7.3	2.8	33.3
Athens, GA	6.0	14.9	35.7	17.7	15.7	7.6	2.5	29.9
Atlanta, GA	7.2	19.3	23.6	23.6	17.4	6.9	2.0	34.9
Austin, TX	7.4	17.9	28.6	22.1	15.9	6.1	2.0	32.6
Baltimore, MD	6.2	16.8	23.2	21.3	19.8	9.0	3.6	38.1
Bellevue, WA	6.5	16.4	24.5	22.5	19.3	7.7	3.1	36.8
Billings, MT	6.7	16.8	22.0	19.2	21.0	10.0	4.4	39.0
Boise City, ID	7.8	20.2	23.2	20.5	17.4	8.0	2.9	34.1
Boston, MA	5.6	16.0	24.0	21.8	19.6	9.1	4.0	38.5
Boulder, CO	5.6	15.7	27.6	21.4	19.7	7.4	2.7	35.8
Broken Arrow, OK	7.1	18.5	22.6	20.0	19.1	9.5	3.4	36.5
Cambridge, MA	5.6	16.0	24.0	21.8	19.6	9.1	4.0	38.5
Cape Coral, FL	5.3	14.2	18.3	18.0	20.7	17.5	6.0	45.6
Carlsbad, CA	6.6	16.8	27.1	20.7	17.5	7.9	3.4	34.6
Cary, NC	7.3	18.9	23.9	23.9	17.0	6.8	2.2	34.9
Cedar Rapids, IA	6.6	17.9	22.5	20.5	19.0	9.5	4.1	37.5
Charleston, SC	6.9	16.4	26.2	20.3	18.7	8.8	2.7	35.4
Charlotte, NC	7.2	18.7	23.4	23.3	17.3	7.6	2.5	35.4
Chesapeake, VA	6.5	17.0	26.0	20.5	18.4	8.5	3.0	35.4
Chicago, IL	6.7	18.4	23.8	21.3	18.3	8.1	3.3	35.8
Clarksville, TN	8.8	18.8	28.5	19.2	15.1	7.4	2.2	30.7
Colorado Spgs., CO	7.2	18.8	24.6	20.8	18.6	7.7	2.4	34.6
Columbia, MD	6.2	16.8	23.2	21.3	19.8	9.0	3.6	38.1
Columbia, MO	6.2	14.9	35.4	17.6	16.2	6.9	2.8	30.0
Columbia, SC	6.5	17.0	25.7	20.5	18.9	8.6	2.8	35.7
Columbus, OH	6.9	17.8	25.1	21.5	18.1	7.8	2.8	35.1
Dallas, TX	7.8	20.0	24.3	22.5	16.6	6.7	2.1	33.5
Denver, CO	7.1	17.8	24.0	22.3	18.7	7.4	2.6	35.7
Durham, NC	6.5	15.5	27.9	20.5	18.3	8.1	3.1	35.0
Edison, NJ	6.2	16.6	23.7	21.7	18.8	9.2	3.9	37.6
El Paso, TX	8.1	22.0	24.5	19.6	15.6	7.5	2.7	31.3
Fargo, ND	6.9	15.3	32.5	18.2	16.7	7.0	3.4	31.5
Ft. Collins, CO	5.9	15.5	28.0	19.0	19.7	8.7	3.2	35.5
Ft. Worth, TX	7.8	20.0	24.3	22.5	16.6	6.7	2.1	33.5
Gilbert, AZ	7.5	19.0	24.0	20.5	16.8	9.1	3.2	34.7
Green Bay, WI	6.7	17.9	22.3	21.2	19.5	8.9	3.6	37.7
Henderson, NV	7.1	17.9	24.3	21.9	17.5	8.9	2.4	35.5
High Point, NC	6.2	17.3	22.9	21.3	19.2	9.6	3.6	37.8
Honolulu, HI	6.4	15.7	24.4	20.1	18.9	9.9	4.7	37.8
Houston, TX	7.9	20.0	24.7	21.6	17.2	6.6	2.0	33.2
Huntington, NY	6.2	16.6	23.7	21.7	18.8	9.2	3.9	37.6
Huntsville, AL	6.3	17.5	23.0	21.9	19.0	9.4	2.8	37.6
Indianapolis, IN	7.3	18.9	23.1	21.7	18.2	7.9	2.9	35.5
Irvine, CA	6.5	17.9	25.4	21.9	17.2	7.9	3.1	35.1
Jackson, MS	7.2	18.9	24.0	20.1	18.5	8.3	2.9	34.9
Jacksonville, FL	6.5	17.3	23.1	21.4	19.6	9.0	3.1	37.5
Jersey City, NJ	6.2	16.6	23.7	21.7	18.8	9.2	3.9	37.6
Kansas City, MO	7.2	18.5	22.3	21.1	19.0	8.6	3.4	36.5
Kenosha, WI	6.7	18.4	23.8	21.3	18.3	8.1	3.3	35.8
Las Vegas, NV	7.1	17.9	24.3	21.9	17.5	8.9	2.4	35.5
Lexington, KY	6.6	16.1	27.2	20.8	18.3	8.1	3.0	35.1

Table continued on next page.

Metro Area	Percent of Population							Median Age
	Under Age 5	Age 5 to 17	Age 18 to 34	Age 35 to 49	Age 50 to 64	Age 65 to 79	80 Years and Over	
Lincoln, NE	7.0	16.1	29.7	18.4	17.6	7.7	3.4	32.8
Little Rock, AR	6.9	17.6	24.3	20.4	18.7	9.1	3.1	35.9
Los Angeles, CA	6.5	17.9	25.4	21.9	17.2	7.9	3.1	35.1
Madison, WI	6.2	15.8	27.6	20.6	18.9	7.6	3.2	35.3
Manchester, NH	5.9	17.5	20.8	23.2	20.6	8.5	3.4	39.3
Miami, FL	5.8	15.8	21.8	22.1	18.6	10.9	5.0	39.8
Minneapolis, MN	6.9	18.1	23.7	21.8	18.9	7.6	3.1	36.0
Murfreesboro, TN	6.9	17.5	24.6	21.9	18.4	8.0	2.7	35.7
Naperville, IL	6.7	18.4	23.8	21.3	18.3	8.1	3.3	35.8
Nashville, TN	6.9	17.5	24.6	21.9	18.4	8.0	2.7	35.7
New Orleans, LA	6.6	16.8	24.1	20.2	20.1	8.9	3.3	37.1
New York, NY	6.2	16.6	23.7	21.7	18.8	9.2	3.9	37.6
Norman, OK	7.3	17.7	25.5	19.5	18.2	8.7	3.1	34.6
Olathe, KS	7.2	18.5	22.3	21.1	19.0	8.6	3.4	36.5
Omaha, NE	7.6	18.6	24.2	20.3	18.1	8.0	3.1	34.6
Orlando, FL	6.2	17.2	24.9	21.5	17.8	9.2	3.2	36.3
Overland Park, KS	7.2	18.5	22.3	21.1	19.0	8.6	3.4	36.5
Oyster Bay, NY	6.2	16.6	23.7	21.7	18.8	9.2	3.9	37.6
Pembroke Pines, FL	5.8	15.8	21.8	22.1	18.6	10.9	5.0	39.8
Philadelphia, PA	6.2	17.1	23.0	20.9	19.5	9.2	4.1	38.1
Phoenix, AZ	7.5	19.0	24.0	20.5	16.8	9.1	3.2	34.7
Pittsburgh, PA	5.1	15.0	20.7	19.8	22.0	11.5	5.8	42.6
Plano, TX	7.8	20.0	24.3	22.5	16.6	6.7	2.1	33.5
Portland, OR	6.5	17.2	23.8	21.7	19.4	8.1	3.3	36.7
Providence, RI	5.5	16.1	22.7	21.2	20.1	9.6	4.8	39.6
Provo, UT	11.3	24.0	32.6	15.3	10.3	4.9	1.7	24.6
Raleigh, NC	7.3	18.9	23.9	23.9	17.0	6.8	2.2	34.9
Richmond, VA	6.2	17.1	22.9	21.6	20.0	8.9	3.3	38.0
Roseville, CA	6.7	18.2	23.9	20.5	18.7	8.6	3.4	36.0
Round Rock, TX	7.4	17.9	28.6	22.1	15.9	6.1	2.0	32.6
San Antonio, TX	7.3	19.5	24.3	20.5	17.3	8.1	2.8	34.1
San Diego, CA	6.6	16.8	27.1	20.7	17.5	7.9	3.4	34.6
San Francisco, CA	6.0	15.2	23.9	22.8	19.5	8.9	3.7	38.3
San Jose, CA	7.0	17.3	23.9	23.3	17.5	8.0	3.1	36.1
Savannah, GA	7.0	17.1	26.7	19.6	18.0	8.6	3.0	34.3
Scottsdale, AZ	7.5	19.0	24.0	20.5	16.8	9.1	3.2	34.7
Seattle, WA	6.5	16.4	24.5	22.5	19.3	7.7	3.1	36.8
Sioux Falls, SD	8.0	18.0	24.7	20.4	17.7	7.7	3.5	34.5
Stamford, CT	6.2	18.6	19.4	22.8	19.5	9.2	4.3	39.5
Sterling Hgts, MI	6.0	18.3	20.4	21.6	20.5	9.2	4.0	39.1
Sunnyvale, CA	7.0	17.3	23.9	23.3	17.5	8.0	3.1	36.1
Tampa, FL	5.6	15.6	20.8	20.7	20.1	12.2	5.1	41.2
Temecula, CA	7.6	21.1	24.2	20.4	16.2	7.7	2.7	32.7
Thousand Oaks, CA	6.7	19.0	22.7	21.1	18.8	8.4	3.3	36.2
Virginia Beach, VA	6.5	17.0	26.0	20.5	18.4	8.5	3.0	35.4
Washington, DC	6.7	17.1	24.6	23.0	18.5	7.4	2.6	36.1
U.S.	6.5	17.5	23.2	20.7	19.0	9.4	3.6	37.2

Note: Figures cover the Metropolitan Statistical Area (MSA)—see Appendix B for areas included
Source: U.S. Census Bureau, 2010 Census

Segregation

Area	Black/White		Asian/White		Hispanic/White	
	Index[1]	Rank[2]	Index[1]	Rank[2]	Index[1]	Rank[2]
Albuquerque, NM	30.9	99	28.5	93	36.4	79
Alexandria, VA	62.3	32	38.9	64	48.3	32
Anchorage, AK	n/a	n/a	n/a	n/a	n/a	n/a
Ann Arbor, MI	n/a	n/a	n/a	n/a	n/a	n/a
Athens, GA	n/a	n/a	n/a	n/a	n/a	n/a
Atlanta, GA	59.0	41	48.5	10	49.5	27
Austin, TX	50.1	70	41.2	49	43.2	51
Baltimore, MD	65.4	19	43.6	33	39.8	67
Bellevue, WA	49.1	72	37.6	69	32.8	87
Billings, MT	n/a	n/a	n/a	n/a	n/a	n/a
Boise City, ID	30.2	101	27.6	95	36.2	80
Boston, MA	64.0	27	45.4	23	59.6	5
Boulder, CO	n/a	n/a	n/a	n/a	n/a	n/a
Broken Arrow, OK	56.6	47	42.6	40	45.3	45
Cambridge, MA	64.0	27	45.4	23	59.6	5
Cape Coral, FL	61.6	35	25.3	96	40.2	63
Carlsbad, CA	51.2	68	48.2	13	49.6	25
Cary, NC	42.1	87	46.7	16	37.1	76
Cedar Rapids, IA	n/a	n/a	n/a	n/a	n/a	n/a
Charleston, SC	41.5	88	33.4	84	39.8	66
Charlotte, NC	53.8	56	43.6	34	47.6	35
Chesapeake, VA	47.8	76	34.3	79	32.2	90
Chicago, IL	76.4	3	44.9	26	56.3	10
Clarksville, TN	n/a	n/a	n/a	n/a	n/a	n/a
Colorado Spgs., CO	39.3	92	24.1	98	30.3	95
Columbia, MD	65.4	19	43.6	33	39.8	67
Columbia, MO	n/a	n/a	n/a	n/a	n/a	n/a
Columbia, SC	48.8	74	41.9	46	34.9	82
Columbus, OH	62.2	33	43.3	35	41.5	59
Dallas, TX	56.6	48	46.6	19	50.3	24
Denver, CO	62.6	31	33.4	83	48.8	31
Durham, NC	48.1	75	44.0	30	48.0	33
Edison, NJ	78.0	2	51.9	3	62.0	3
El Paso, TX	30.7	100	22.2	100	43.3	50
Fargo, ND	n/a	n/a	n/a	n/a	n/a	n/a
Ft. Collins, CO	n/a	n/a	n/a	n/a	n/a	n/a
Ft. Worth, TX	56.6	48	46.6	19	50.3	24
Gilbert, AZ	43.6	86	32.7	85	49.3	28
Green Bay, WI	n/a	n/a	n/a	n/a	n/a	n/a
Henderson, NV	37.6	94	28.8	92	42.0	58
High Point, NC	54.7	53	47.7	14	41.1	61
Honolulu, HI	36.9	95	42.1	44	31.9	91
Houston, TX	61.4	36	50.4	7	52.5	18
Huntington, NY	78.0	2	51.9	3	62.0	3
Huntsville, AL	n/a	n/a	n/a	n/a	n/a	n/a
Indianapolis, IN	66.4	15	41.6	47	47.3	37
Irvine, CA	67.8	10	48.4	12	62.2	2
Jackson, MS	56.0	51	38.9	63	42.9	52
Jacksonville, FL	53.1	59	37.5	71	27.6	98
Jersey City, NJ	78.0	2	51.9	3	62.0	3
Kansas City, MO	61.2	39	38.4	65	44.4	48
Kenosha, WI	76.4	3	44.9	26	56.3	10
Las Vegas, NV	37.6	94	28.8	92	42.0	58
Lexington, KY	n/a	n/a	n/a	n/a	n/a	n/a
Lincoln, NE	n/a	n/a	n/a	n/a	n/a	n/a

Table continued on next page.

Area	Black/White		Asian/White		Hispanic/White	
	Index[1]	Rank[2]	Index[1]	Rank[2]	Index[1]	Rank[2]
Little Rock, AR	58.8	42	39.7	59	39.7	68
Los Angeles, CA	67.8	10	48.4	12	62.2	2
Madison, WI	49.6	71	44.2	29	40.1	65
Manchester, NH	n/a	n/a	n/a	n/a	n/a	n/a
Miami, FL	64.8	23	34.2	80	57.4	8
Minneapolis, MN	52.9	60	42.8	39	42.5	54
Murfreesboro, TN	56.2	49	41.0	51	47.9	34
Naperville, IL	76.4	3	44.9	26	56.3	10
Nashville, TN	56.2	49	41.0	51	47.9	34
New Orleans, LA	63.9	28	48.6	9	38.3	74
New York, NY	78.0	2	51.9	3	62.0	3
Norman, OK	51.4	67	39.2	60	47.0	38
Olathe, KS	61.2	39	38.4	65	44.4	48
Omaha, NE	61.3	38	36.3	74	48.8	30
Orlando, FL	50.7	69	33.9	81	40.2	64
Overland Park, KS	61.2	39	38.4	65	44.4	48
Oyster Bay, NY	78.0	2	51.9	3	62.0	3
Pembroke Pines, FL	64.8	23	34.2	80	57.4	8
Philadelphia, PA	68.4	9	42.3	42	55.1	12
Phoenix, AZ	43.6	86	32.7	85	49.3	28
Pittsburgh, PA	65.8	17	52.4	2	28.6	97
Plano, TX	56.6	48	46.6	19	50.3	24
Portland, OR	46.0	81	35.8	75	34.3	83
Providence, RI	53.5	57	40.1	55	60.1	4
Provo, UT	21.9	102	28.2	94	30.9	93
Raleigh, NC	42.1	87	46.7	16	37.1	76
Richmond, VA	52.4	63	43.9	32	44.9	46
Roseville, CA	56.9	46	49.9	8	38.9	71
Round Rock, TX	50.1	70	41.2	49	43.2	51
San Antonio, TX	49.0	73	38.3	66	46.1	43
San Diego, CA	51.2	68	48.2	13	49.6	25
San Francisco, CA	62.0	34	46.6	18	49.6	26
San Jose, CA	40.9	89	45.0	25	47.6	36
Savannah, GA	n/a	n/a	n/a	n/a	n/a	n/a
Scottsdale, AZ	43.6	86	32.7	85	49.3	28
Seattle, WA	49.1	72	37.6	69	32.8	87
Sioux Falls, SD	n/a	n/a	n/a	n/a	n/a	n/a
Stamford, CT	67.5	12	31.4	86	59.2	6
Sterling Hgts, MI	75.3	4	50.6	6	43.3	49
Sunnyvale, CA	40.9	89	45.0	25	47.6	36
Tampa, FL	56.2	50	35.3	78	40.7	62
Temecula, CA	45.7	82	40.7	53	42.4	55
Thousand Oaks, CA	39.9	91	31.2	87	54.6	13
Virginia Beach, VA	47.8	76	34.3	79	32.2	90
Washington, DC	62.3	32	38.9	64	48.3	32

Note: Figures are based on an analysis of 1990, 2000, and 2010 Census Decennial Census tract data by William H. Frey, Brookings Institution and the University of Michigan Social Science Data Analysis Network. In this analysis all racial groups (whites, blacks, and asians) are non-Hispanic members of those races. Hispanics are shown as a separate category; All figures cover the Metropolitan Statistical Area (see Appendix B for areas included); (1) Segregation Indices are Dissimilarity Indices that measure the degree to which the minority group is distributed differently than whites across census tracts. They range from 0 (complete integration) to 100 (complete [segregation] where the value indicates the percentage of the minority group that needs to move to be distributed exactly like whites; (2) Ranges from 1 (most segregated) to 102 (least segregated); n/a not available.
Source: www.CensusScope.org

Religious Groups

Area[1]	Catholic	Baptist	Non-Den.	Methodist[2]	Lutheran	LDS[3]	Pentecostal	Presbyterian[4]	Muslim[5]	Judaism
Albuquerque, NM	27.2	3.8	4.2	1.5	1.0	2.4	1.5	1.1	0.3	0.2
Alexandria, VA	14.5	7.3	4.9	4.5	1.3	1.2	1.1	1.4	1.2	2.4
Anchorage, AK	6.9	5.0	6.4	1.4	1.9	5.1	1.9	0.7	0.1	0.2
Ann Arbor, MI	12.4	2.2	1.6	3.1	2.9	0.9	1.9	3.0	0.9	1.3
Athens, GA	4.4	16.3	2.3	8.4	0.4	0.8	2.8	2.0	0.2	0.4
Atlanta, GA	7.5	17.5	6.9	7.9	0.5	0.8	2.6	1.8	0.6	0.8
Austin, TX	16.0	10.3	4.5	3.6	2.0	1.2	0.8	1.1	0.3	1.2
Baltimore, MD	16.7	4.2	4.8	6.1	2.1	0.5	1.1	1.3	1.8	0.5
Bellevue, WA	12.3	2.2	5.0	1.2	2.1	3.3	2.8	1.4	0.5	0.5
Billings, MT	12.1	2.5	3.8	2.1	6.1	4.9	4.1	1.8	0.1	0.0
Boise City, ID	8.0	2.9	4.2	2.1	1.2	15.9	2.3	0.6	0.1	0.1
Boston, MA	44.4	1.2	1.0	1.0	0.4	0.4	0.6	1.6	1.4	0.4
Boulder, CO	20.1	2.3	4.8	1.8	3.1	3.0	0.5	2.0	0.8	0.1
Broken Arrow, OK	5.8	22.9	7.6	9.2	0.8	1.2	3.3	1.3	0.3	0.3
Cambridge, MA	44.4	1.2	1.0	1.0	0.4	0.4	0.6	1.6	1.4	0.4
Cape Coral, FL	16.2	5.0	3.0	2.5	1.2	0.5	4.4	1.4	0.2	0.9
Carlsbad, CA	25.9	2.0	4.8	1.1	1.0	2.3	1.0	0.9	0.5	0.7
Cary, NC	9.2	12.1	6.0	6.7	0.9	0.9	2.3	2.3	0.3	0.9
Cedar Rapids, IA	18.8	2.4	3.0	7.3	11.3	0.9	1.8	3.3	0.1	0.5
Charleston, SC	6.2	12.4	7.1	10.0	1.1	1.0	2.0	2.4	0.3	0.2
Charlotte, NC	5.9	17.3	6.8	8.6	1.3	0.8	3.3	4.5	0.3	0.2
Chesapeake, VA	6.4	11.6	6.2	5.3	0.7	0.9	1.9	2.0	0.4	2.1
Chicago, IL	34.2	3.2	4.5	1.9	3.0	0.4	1.2	1.9	0.8	3.3
Clarksville, TN	4.1	30.9	2.3	6.2	0.6	1.5	1.8	1.1	n/a	0.1
Colorado Spgs., CO	8.4	4.3	7.4	2.4	2.0	3.0	1.1	2.1	0.1	0.1
Columbia, MD	16.7	4.2	4.8	6.1	2.1	0.5	1.1	1.3	1.8	0.5
Columbia, MO	6.6	14.7	5.4	4.3	1.7	1.4	1.1	2.3	0.3	0.3
Columbia, SC	3.1	18.1	5.2	9.4	3.4	1.1	2.7	3.3	0.2	0.1
Columbus, OH	11.8	5.3	3.6	4.7	2.4	0.7	2.0	2.0	0.5	0.8
Dallas, TX	13.3	18.7	7.8	5.3	0.8	1.2	2.2	1.0	0.4	2.4
Denver, CO	16.1	3.0	4.6	1.7	2.1	2.4	1.2	1.6	0.6	0.6
Durham, NC	5.1	13.9	5.6	8.1	0.5	0.8	1.4	2.5	0.6	0.5
Edison, NJ	36.9	1.9	1.8	1.3	0.8	0.4	0.9	1.1	4.8	2.3
El Paso, TX	43.2	3.8	5.0	0.9	0.3	1.6	1.4	0.2	0.2	0.1
Fargo, ND	17.4	0.4	0.5	3.3	32.5	0.6	1.5	1.9	0.0	0.1
Ft. Collins, CO	11.8	2.2	6.4	4.4	3.5	3.0	4.7	1.9	0.0	0.1
Ft. Worth, TX	13.3	18.7	7.8	5.3	0.8	1.2	2.2	1.0	0.4	2.4
Gilbert, AZ	13.4	3.5	5.2	1.0	1.6	6.1	2.9	0.6	0.3	0.2
Green Bay, WI	42.0	0.7	3.4	2.2	12.7	0.4	0.6	1.0	0.1	0.1
Henderson, NV	18.1	3.0	3.1	0.4	0.7	6.4	1.5	0.2	0.3	0.1
High Point, NC	2.7	12.8	7.4	9.9	0.7	0.8	2.5	3.2	0.4	0.6
Honolulu, HI	18.2	1.9	2.2	0.8	0.3	5.1	4.2	1.5	0.1	0.0
Houston, TX	17.1	16.0	7.3	4.9	1.1	1.1	1.5	0.9	0.4	2.7
Huntington, NY	36.9	1.9	1.8	1.3	0.8	0.4	0.9	1.1	4.8	2.3
Huntsville, AL	4.0	27.6	3.2	7.5	0.7	1.2	1.2	1.7	0.2	0.2
Indianapolis, IN	10.5	10.3	7.2	5.0	1.7	0.7	1.6	1.7	0.4	0.2
Irvine, CA	33.8	2.8	3.6	1.1	0.7	1.7	1.8	0.9	1.0	0.7
Jackson, MS	3.2	34.5	7.7	10.5	0.2	0.7	2.1	2.0	0.1	0.3
Jacksonville, FL	9.9	18.5	7.8	4.5	0.7	1.1	1.9	1.6	0.4	0.6
Jersey City, NJ	36.9	1.9	1.8	1.3	0.8	0.4	0.9	1.1	4.8	2.3
Kansas City, MO	12.7	13.2	5.2	5.9	2.3	2.5	2.6	1.6	0.4	0.3
Kenosha, WI	34.2	3.2	4.5	1.9	3.0	0.4	1.2	1.9	0.8	3.3
Las Vegas, NV	18.1	3.0	3.1	0.4	0.7	6.4	1.5	0.2	0.3	0.1
Lexington, KY	6.8	24.9	2.4	5.9	0.4	1.1	2.1	1.4	0.3	0.1
Lincoln, NE	14.8	2.4	1.9	7.2	11.3	1.2	1.4	3.9	0.2	0.2

Table continued on next page.

Area[1]	Catholic	Baptist	Non-Den.	Methodist[2]	Lutheran	LDS[3]	Pentecostal	Presbyterian[4]	Muslim[5]	Judaism
Little Rock, AR	4.5	25.9	6.1	7.3	0.5	0.9	2.9	0.9	0.1	0.1
Los Angeles, CA	33.8	2.8	3.6	1.1	0.7	1.7	1.8	0.9	1.0	0.7
Madison, WI	21.8	1.1	1.6	3.7	12.8	0.5	0.4	2.2	0.5	0.5
Manchester, NH	31.2	1.4	2.4	1.2	0.5	0.6	0.5	2.0	0.5	0.3
Miami, FL	18.6	5.4	4.2	1.3	0.5	0.5	1.8	0.7	1.6	0.9
Minneapolis, MN	21.7	2.5	3.0	2.8	14.5	0.6	1.8	1.9	0.7	0.4
Murfreesboro, TN	4.1	25.3	5.8	6.1	0.4	0.8	2.2	2.1	0.2	0.4
Naperville, IL	34.2	3.2	4.5	1.9	3.0	0.4	1.2	1.9	0.8	3.3
Nashville, TN	4.1	25.3	5.8	6.1	0.4	0.8	2.2	2.1	0.2	0.4
New Orleans, LA	31.6	8.4	3.7	2.7	0.8	0.6	2.1	0.5	0.5	0.5
New York, NY	36.9	1.9	1.8	1.3	0.8	0.4	0.9	1.1	4.8	2.3
Norman, OK	6.4	25.4	7.1	10.6	0.7	1.3	3.2	1.0	0.1	0.2
Olathe, KS	12.7	13.2	5.2	5.9	2.3	2.5	2.6	1.6	0.4	0.3
Omaha, NE	21.6	4.6	1.8	3.9	7.9	1.8	1.3	2.3	0.4	0.5
Orlando, FL	13.2	7.0	5.7	3.0	0.9	1.0	3.2	1.4	0.3	1.3
Overland Park, KS	12.7	13.2	5.2	5.9	2.3	2.5	2.6	1.6	0.4	0.3
Oyster Bay, NY	36.9	1.9	1.8	1.3	0.8	0.4	0.9	1.1	4.8	2.3
Pembroke Pines, FL	18.6	5.4	4.2	1.3	0.5	0.5	1.8	0.7	1.6	0.9
Philadelphia, PA	33.5	3.9	2.9	3.0	1.9	0.3	0.9	2.1	1.4	1.3
Phoenix, AZ	13.4	3.5	5.2	1.0	1.6	6.1	2.9	0.6	0.3	0.2
Pittsburgh, PA	32.8	2.3	2.8	5.7	3.4	0.4	1.1	4.7	0.7	0.3
Plano, TX	13.3	18.7	7.8	5.3	0.8	1.2	2.2	1.0	0.4	2.4
Portland, OR	10.6	2.3	4.5	1.0	1.6	3.8	2.0	1.0	0.3	0.1
Providence, RI	47.0	1.4	1.2	0.8	0.5	0.3	0.6	1.0	0.7	0.1
Provo, UT	1.3	0.1	0.1	0.2	0.0	88.6	0.1	0.1	n/a	n/a
Raleigh, NC	9.2	12.1	6.0	6.7	0.9	0.9	2.3	2.3	0.3	0.9
Richmond, VA	6.0	19.9	5.5	6.1	0.6	1.0	1.8	2.1	0.4	2.8
Roseville, CA	16.2	3.2	4.0	1.8	0.8	3.4	2.0	0.8	0.3	0.8
Round Rock, TX	16.0	10.3	4.5	3.6	2.0	1.2	0.8	1.1	0.3	1.2
San Antonio, TX	28.4	8.5	6.0	3.1	1.7	1.4	1.3	0.8	0.2	1.0
San Diego, CA	25.9	2.0	4.8	1.1	1.0	2.3	1.0	0.9	0.5	0.7
San Francisco, CA	20.8	2.5	2.5	2.0	0.6	1.6	1.2	1.1	0.9	1.2
San Jose, CA	26.0	1.4	4.3	1.1	0.6	1.4	1.2	0.7	0.7	1.0
Savannah, GA	7.1	19.7	6.9	8.9	1.6	1.0	2.4	1.0	0.8	0.2
Scottsdale, AZ	13.4	3.5	5.2	1.0	1.6	6.1	2.9	0.6	0.3	0.2
Seattle, WA	12.3	2.2	5.0	1.2	2.1	3.3	2.8	1.4	0.5	0.5
Sioux Falls, SD	14.9	3.0	1.5	3.9	21.4	0.7	1.1	6.2	0.1	0.3
Stamford, CT	44.1	2.0	2.4	2.1	0.8	0.5	1.2	3.0	2.0	0.6
Sterling Hgts, MI	21.4	4.5	5.0	2.1	3.1	0.4	1.3	1.4	0.8	1.9
Sunnyvale, CA	26.0	1.4	4.3	1.1	0.6	1.4	1.2	0.7	0.7	1.0
Tampa, FL	10.9	7.1	3.8	3.5	1.0	0.6	2.1	1.0	0.5	1.3
Temecula, CA	24.8	2.6	5.5	0.6	0.5	2.5	1.6	0.6	0.1	0.6
Thousand Oaks, CA	28.2	1.9	4.1	1.1	1.5	2.5	1.3	0.7	0.7	0.4
Virginia Beach, VA	6.4	11.6	6.2	5.3	0.7	0.9	1.9	2.0	0.4	2.1
Washington, DC	14.5	7.3	4.9	4.5	1.3	1.2	1.1	1.4	1.2	2.4
U.S.	19.1	9.3	4.0	4.0	2.3	2.0	1.9	1.6	0.8	0.7

Note: Figures are the number of adherents as a percentage of the total population; (1) Figures cover the Metropolitan Statistical Area—see Appendix B for areas included; (2) Methodist/Pietist; (3) Latter Day Saints; (4) Reformed; (5) Figures are estimates
Source: Association of Statisticians of American Religious Bodies, 2010 U.S. Religion Census: Religious Congregations & Membership Study

Ancestry: City

City	German	Irish	English	American	Italian	Polish	French[1]	Scottish	Dutch
Albuquerque, NM	11.5	8.8	7.1	2.4	3.4	1.5	2.3	1.9	1.1
Alexandria, VA	12.5	11.4	10.5	2.9	5.0	2.5	2.0	2.7	1.2
Anchorage, AK	19.5	12.2	9.4	3.5	3.6	2.8	3.7	3.3	2.1
Ann Arbor, MI	19.7	10.1	11.4	4.0	4.4	6.8	3.7	3.0	1.8
Athens, GA	9.2	8.6	9.8	8.3	2.2	1.8	1.9	3.6	1.1
Atlanta, GA	6.4	5.4	6.6	6.1	1.9	1.3	1.7	1.9	0.7
Austin, TX	12.5	8.6	9.4	2.8	2.7	1.6	2.9	2.6	1.0
Baltimore, MD	7.6	6.4	3.8	2.1	3.1	2.4	0.9	0.8	0.5
Bellevue, WA	14.4	8.4	10.3	2.2	3.3	2.1	3.1	2.9	1.6
Billings, MT	30.2	13.7	10.4	10.0	2.8	1.6	3.6	3.0	1.8
Boise City, ID	17.7	12.3	15.0	8.1	3.5	1.6	2.9	3.1	1.9
Boston, MA	4.8	16.8	5.5	1.7	8.5	2.8	2.4	1.4	0.5
Boulder, CO	23.4	13.9	16.2	2.0	7.1	4.4	4.1	4.7	2.6
Broken Arrow, OK	16.2	11.6	10.6	7.9	2.3	1.8	2.4	2.2	2.4
Cambridge, MA	9.3	15.1	9.7	1.5	8.8	4.1	3.1	2.6	1.1
Cape Coral, FL	17.0	14.0	8.9	12.3	10.9	4.3	3.4	1.8	1.6
Carlsbad, CA	16.8	11.4	17.5	3.1	7.2	3.9	3.6	2.4	1.9
Cary, NC	15.4	11.5	13.0	7.5	7.2	3.5	2.1	2.8	1.3
Cedar Rapids, IA	39.0	18.4	9.2	4.1	2.4	1.2	3.3	1.6	3.4
Charleston, SC	12.9	11.2	12.4	9.6	4.1	1.9	2.9	3.5	1.2
Charlotte, NC	10.0	7.5	8.0	4.1	4.0	1.5	1.7	2.5	1.0
Chesapeake, VA	10.4	10.5	10.5	15.8	4.1	2.0	2.2	2.2	0.7
Chicago, IL	7.6	7.6	2.4	1.3	3.9	6.4	0.9	0.6	0.6
Clarksville, TN	13.2	10.6	6.9	12.4	2.9	1.3	2.3	1.6	1.0
Colorado Spgs., CO	22.0	13.2	12.1	4.5	5.5	2.5	3.8	2.8	1.8
Columbia, MD	14.4	11.7	8.8	3.7	4.7	4.3	2.3	2.0	1.2
Columbia, MO	28.2	12.9	11.2	3.7	3.5	2.0	3.5	2.7	1.5
Columbia, SC	8.4	8.4	9.3	7.0	2.4	1.2	2.1	2.6	0.8
Columbus, OH	21.0	13.2	7.3	3.8	5.1	2.4	1.9	1.8	1.4
Dallas, TX	6.1	4.8	5.3	2.7	1.4	0.8	1.4	1.2	0.6
Denver, CO	14.7	10.0	8.4	3.3	4.4	2.2	2.6	1.9	1.4
Durham, NC	8.6	6.0	8.0	4.2	2.7	1.7	1.5	2.2	0.8
Edison, NJ	6.0	7.4	2.0	2.7	10.3	5.5	0.8	0.6	0.4
El Paso, TX	3.9	2.5	2.2	3.7	1.2	0.5	0.7	0.5	0.3
Fargo, ND	43.8	9.8	4.3	1.3	1.2	2.9	5.1	1.0	0.9
Ft. Collins, CO	29.7	14.9	12.8	3.3	5.7	2.7	2.9	3.1	2.9
Ft. Worth, TX	9.4	7.3	6.7	6.6	1.8	0.9	1.6	1.6	0.8
Gilbert, AZ	22.8	13.0	13.8	3.4	5.9	3.6	3.3	2.0	1.6
Green Bay, WI	33.7	9.4	3.6	2.4	2.2	9.7	5.5	0.6	3.9
Henderson, NV	17.0	12.8	11.5	4.8	8.9	3.8	2.9	2.3	1.8
High Point, NC	9.1	7.0	8.2	5.5	2.4	0.9	1.1	1.7	0.7
Honolulu, HI	4.1	3.5	3.3	0.6	1.5	0.8	1.1	0.8	0.6
Houston, TX	5.7	4.0	4.3	2.3	1.5	0.9	1.6	1.0	0.5
Huntington, NY	16.1	21.5	5.9	3.0	27.1	6.5	1.4	1.1	1.1
Huntsville, AL	8.6	9.4	10.1	10.2	2.5	1.0	2.3	2.5	1.2
Indianapolis, IN	18.2	11.3	7.9	5.7	2.4	1.5	1.8	1.6	1.5
Irvine, CA	9.1	6.3	6.6	2.1	3.5	1.8	2.2	1.5	0.8
Jackson, MS	2.0	3.1	3.0	3.0	0.5	0.1	0.7	0.8	0.2
Jacksonville, FL	9.7	10.3	8.4	6.2	3.6	1.6	2.2	1.9	1.2
Jersey City, NJ	3.5	5.1	1.7	0.7	5.0	2.4	0.6	0.5	0.3
Kansas City, MO	17.8	11.7	7.8	11.8	3.6	1.3	2.3	1.7	1.5
Kenosha, WI	28.7	12.0	6.3	2.1	11.0	8.4	2.8	1.2	1.5
Las Vegas, NV	11.2	8.6	6.9	2.4	6.2	2.8	2.1	1.5	1.0
Lexington, KY	14.0	13.6	12.6	14.4	3.1	1.4	2.1	2.8	1.3
Lincoln, NE	43.7	14.4	9.6	3.6	1.7	2.9	2.5	1.8	2.6
Little Rock, AR	9.1	8.2	9.8	4.3	1.6	0.6	2.1	1.9	1.0

Table continued on next page.

City	German	Irish	English	American	Italian	Polish	French[1]	Scottish	Dutch
Los Angeles, CA	4.8	3.8	3.4	1.5	2.7	1.6	1.2	0.7	0.5
Madison, WI	35.6	13.5	8.8	2.0	4.3	5.5	2.8	1.8	2.3
Manchester, NH	5.3	21.1	10.4	2.4	8.9	5.1	21.2	2.8	0.3
Miami, FL	1.7	1.5	1.0	2.1	1.7	0.6	0.9	0.2	0.2
Minneapolis, MN	23.7	11.2	6.2	1.3	2.5	3.8	3.3	1.5	1.5
Murfreesboro, TN	12.5	11.4	9.7	12.3	2.8	1.2	2.4	2.4	1.3
Naperville, IL	22.8	17.1	8.0	2.0	10.6	11.4	2.1	1.9	1.7
Nashville, TN	10.0	10.0	8.9	7.9	2.5	1.2	2.1	2.2	1.2
New Orleans, LA	6.9	5.6	4.3	2.8	3.4	0.7	6.2	1.1	0.3
New York, NY	3.3	5.0	1.8	2.4	7.6	2.7	0.8	0.5	0.3
Norman, OK	18.0	15.6	12.2	6.7	2.8	1.5	2.4	3.0	1.5
Olathe, KS	31.1	14.4	12.1	4.9	4.0	2.0	3.0	2.1	2.1
Omaha, NE	29.4	17.2	8.3	3.0	4.8	4.2	2.6	1.2	1.5
Orlando, FL	8.5	8.5	6.2	4.4	5.5	1.7	1.9	1.6	0.8
Overland Park, KS	29.4	16.2	13.9	5.5	3.9	2.5	3.4	3.0	2.1
Oyster Bay, NY	13.8	20.8	4.1	3.2	30.2	6.4	1.3	0.8	0.3
Pembroke Pines, FL	5.2	5.5	3.1	5.1	6.1	2.4	1.4	0.7	0.9
Philadelphia, PA	8.1	12.7	3.0	1.3	8.3	3.9	0.8	0.6	0.4
Phoenix, AZ	12.8	9.0	7.0	3.7	4.1	2.4	2.1	1.5	1.2
Pittsburgh, PA	21.2	16.2	5.3	2.8	13.1	7.4	1.3	1.8	0.6
Plano, TX	12.9	10.0	8.7	7.3	3.7	1.7	2.9	2.5	0.9
Portland, OR	19.2	12.4	11.8	4.2	4.2	2.2	3.6	3.5	1.9
Providence, RI	4.0	9.4	4.6	0.6	11.3	2.6	3.7	0.9	0.4
Provo, UT	11.0	5.3	28.3	2.7	2.5	0.7	2.2	5.8	1.2
Raleigh, NC	9.8	8.0	10.2	9.2	3.8	1.9	1.8	2.9	1.0
Richmond, VA	7.5	6.7	8.2	3.9	3.1	1.6	1.7	2.2	0.6
Roseville, CA	18.5	15.2	12.4	3.1	7.6	2.2	3.2	2.2	1.3
Round Rock, TX	16.7	11.3	9.9	4.1	2.8	1.7	3.0	2.0	1.1
San Antonio, TX	8.5	5.1	4.5	3.7	1.9	1.1	1.7	1.2	0.5
San Diego, CA	10.9	8.3	7.0	2.3	4.7	2.1	2.3	1.9	1.1
San Francisco, CA	8.2	7.9	5.5	1.0	4.8	2.1	2.3	1.6	0.9
San Jose, CA	6.7	4.8	4.5	1.1	4.4	0.9	1.5	0.9	0.8
Savannah, GA	5.1	7.3	5.8	2.7	2.0	0.6	1.0	0.9	0.5
Scottsdale, AZ	20.4	14.6	12.6	4.2	8.4	4.8	3.5	3.1	2.0
Seattle, WA	16.0	11.9	11.3	2.7	4.4	2.5	3.3	3.8	1.9
Sioux Falls, SD	41.5	11.8	5.8	3.4	1.5	1.6	2.0	1.0	6.2
Stamford, CT	5.4	8.7	4.6	1.5	14.1	5.6	1.8	1.3	0.5
Sterling Hgts, MI	16.3	8.5	6.6	4.0	10.0	16.9	3.8	1.5	1.0
Sunnyvale, CA	7.9	6.1	5.7	1.3	3.4	1.4	2.2	1.4	0.8
Tampa, FL	9.8	8.5	6.8	3.5	6.4	2.0	2.0	1.5	1.0
Temecula, CA	12.3	11.6	9.7	1.6	7.5	3.5	3.0	2.1	1.8
Thousand Oaks, CA	14.4	12.9	10.7	4.1	9.2	3.8	2.9	2.5	1.8
Virginia Beach, VA	13.5	12.1	10.3	11.9	7.0	2.6	2.6	2.5	1.5
Washington, DC	6.8	7.1	5.3	1.3	3.0	1.9	1.7	1.3	0.6
U.S.	16.1	11.6	8.8	6.1	5.7	3.2	3.0	1.9	1.6

Note: Figures are the percentage of the total population reporting a particular ancestry. The nine most commonly reported ancestries in the U.S. are shown. Figures include multiple ancestries (e.g. if a person reported being Irish and Italian, they were included in both columns); (1) Excludes Basque
Source: U.S. Census Bureau, 2008-2010 American Community Survey 3-Year Estimates

Ancestry: Metro Area

Metro Area	German	Irish	English	American	Italian	Polish	French[1]	Scottish	Dutch
Albuquerque, NM	11.8	8.5	7.3	2.7	3.3	1.5	2.4	1.9	1.0
Alexandria, VA	11.4	9.8	8.4	3.8	4.5	2.4	2.0	1.9	0.9
Anchorage, AK	20.9	12.9	10.3	3.7	3.8	2.9	4.0	3.5	2.6
Ann Arbor, MI	21.6	11.9	12.1	5.1	4.3	7.2	3.8	3.0	2.1
Athens, GA	9.2	9.6	11.3	13.2	2.0	1.5	1.7	3.4	1.2
Atlanta, GA	8.1	8.2	8.1	8.9	2.7	1.3	1.6	1.9	0.9
Austin, TX	15.6	9.5	9.5	3.6	2.7	1.6	2.9	2.5	1.1
Baltimore, MD	19.2	14.2	9.0	4.2	6.5	4.7	1.9	1.8	1.0
Bellevue, WA	18.1	11.7	11.1	3.3	3.8	2.1	3.5	3.1	2.0
Billings, MT	30.7	13.7	11.4	10.9	2.5	1.8	3.3	3.1	2.2
Boise City, ID	17.7	10.1	14.2	12.7	3.0	1.4	2.7	3.1	2.1
Boston, MA	6.6	24.6	11.4	3.0	14.7	3.9	6.2	2.8	0.7
Boulder, CO	23.7	14.3	14.4	3.0	6.2	3.9	4.0	4.3	2.4
Broken Arrow, OK	15.2	13.1	9.3	7.8	1.8	1.0	2.4	2.1	2.2
Cambridge, MA	6.6	24.6	11.4	3.0	14.7	3.9	6.2	2.8	0.7
Cape Coral, FL	16.0	12.5	10.7	12.0	8.0	3.7	3.1	2.2	1.4
Carlsbad, CA	12.3	9.0	8.7	2.3	4.6	2.1	2.6	1.9	1.3
Cary, NC	11.4	9.9	11.5	10.8	4.9	2.3	2.0	2.8	1.1
Cedar Rapids, IA	42.7	18.6	9.9	4.2	2.1	1.2	3.2	1.9	3.6
Charleston, SC	12.0	10.4	9.6	11.7	3.5	1.8	2.7	2.6	1.0
Charlotte, NC	13.0	9.7	9.0	7.9	4.1	1.7	1.9	2.6	1.3
Chesapeake, VA	11.2	10.0	10.6	11.0	4.6	2.0	2.2	2.2	1.1
Chicago, IL	16.6	12.3	4.7	2.2	7.2	9.9	1.6	1.0	1.3
Clarksville, TN	12.3	11.0	8.8	15.0	2.6	1.2	2.2	1.6	1.2
Colorado Spgs., CO	22.4	13.5	12.1	5.1	5.1	2.7	3.7	2.8	1.9
Columbia, MD	19.2	14.2	9.0	4.2	6.5	4.7	1.9	1.8	1.0
Columbia, MO	28.4	13.4	11.4	5.9	3.1	1.6	3.3	2.7	1.8
Columbia, SC	11.9	9.0	9.1	12.4	2.4	1.1	1.8	2.0	0.9
Columbus, OH	26.6	15.3	10.1	6.6	5.6	2.6	2.2	2.3	1.9
Dallas, TX	11.1	8.6	8.2	6.0	2.3	1.1	2.2	1.8	1.1
Denver, CO	20.6	12.0	10.8	4.7	5.3	2.7	3.1	2.5	1.8
Durham, NC	10.8	8.8	11.9	6.1	3.0	2.0	2.1	2.9	1.1
Edison, NJ	7.7	11.1	3.3	2.9	14.3	4.5	1.1	0.8	0.7
El Paso, TX	3.6	2.4	1.9	3.5	1.1	0.5	0.6	0.4	0.2
Fargo, ND	43.1	9.1	4.9	1.5	1.1	3.2	4.7	1.2	1.1
Ft. Collins, CO	31.1	14.8	13.6	3.7	5.0	2.7	3.3	3.2	2.6
Ft. Worth, TX	11.1	8.6	8.2	6.0	2.3	1.1	2.2	1.8	1.1
Gilbert, AZ	16.0	10.5	9.3	5.1	4.9	2.8	2.7	1.9	1.5
Green Bay, WI	40.7	9.6	4.0	3.1	2.2	10.9	5.8	0.8	5.6
Henderson, NV	11.1	8.7	7.2	2.7	6.2	2.5	2.2	1.5	1.1
High Point, NC	9.7	7.5	9.4	8.7	2.3	1.1	1.4	2.2	1.1
Honolulu, HI	5.7	4.4	3.7	0.7	1.8	0.8	1.3	0.9	0.7
Houston, TX	9.5	6.5	6.1	4.3	2.2	1.2	2.6	1.3	0.8
Huntington, NY	7.7	11.1	3.3	2.9	14.3	4.5	1.1	0.8	0.7
Huntsville, AL	9.8	10.8	10.0	13.5	2.4	1.2	2.3	2.3	1.2
Indianapolis, IN	22.7	12.9	10.7	7.6	2.9	1.9	2.2	2.1	1.8
Irvine, CA	6.7	5.2	4.8	2.0	3.2	1.4	1.5	1.1	0.8
Jackson, MS	5.2	8.3	7.6	7.4	1.3	0.4	1.9	1.8	0.5
Jacksonville, FL	11.8	12.2	10.1	8.0	4.8	2.0	2.6	2.1	1.3
Jersey City, NJ	7.7	11.1	3.3	2.9	14.3	4.5	1.1	0.8	0.7
Kansas City, MO	24.7	14.6	10.8	8.3	3.6	1.8	2.8	2.1	2.0
Kenosha, WI	16.6	12.3	4.7	2.2	7.2	9.9	1.6	1.0	1.3
Las Vegas, NV	11.1	8.7	7.2	2.7	6.2	2.5	2.2	1.5	1.1
Lexington, KY	14.0	13.9	12.2	18.3	2.8	1.4	1.9	2.6	1.2
Lincoln, NE	45.1	14.0	9.8	3.6	1.7	2.7	2.5	1.7	2.7
Little Rock, AR	11.5	11.2	10.1	10.0	1.8	0.9	2.4	1.9	1.4

Table continued on next page.

Metro Area	German	Irish	English	American	Italian	Polish	French[1]	Scottish	Dutch
Los Angeles, CA	6.7	5.2	4.8	2.0	3.2	1.4	1.5	1.1	0.8
Madison, WI	41.9	14.7	9.4	2.7	3.7	5.2	2.9	1.7	2.4
Manchester, NH	8.1	22.5	14.6	3.7	10.5	4.9	17.4	3.7	0.8
Miami, FL	5.8	5.5	3.8	4.2	5.6	2.5	1.6	0.8	0.6
Minneapolis, MN	34.0	12.4	6.6	2.6	2.9	4.9	4.2	1.4	1.8
Murfreesboro, TN	11.7	12.1	11.4	12.6	2.7	1.2	2.4	2.6	1.3
Naperville, IL	16.6	12.3	4.7	2.2	7.2	9.9	1.6	1.0	1.3
Nashville, TN	11.7	12.1	11.4	12.6	2.7	1.2	2.4	2.6	1.3
New Orleans, LA	12.5	8.5	5.4	4.6	9.0	0.6	15.7	1.0	0.4
New York, NY	7.7	11.1	3.3	2.9	14.3	4.5	1.1	0.8	0.7
Norman, OK	15.8	12.7	8.8	7.8	1.9	0.9	2.2	2.0	2.0
Olathe, KS	24.7	14.6	10.8	8.3	3.6	1.8	2.8	2.1	2.0
Omaha, NE	34.7	17.0	9.3	3.6	4.5	4.1	2.9	1.5	2.0
Orlando, FL	11.1	9.4	7.8	7.0	6.0	2.3	2.5	1.6	1.2
Overland Park, KS	24.7	14.6	10.8	8.3	3.6	1.8	2.8	2.1	2.0
Oyster Bay, NY	7.7	11.1	3.3	2.9	14.3	4.5	1.1	0.8	0.7
Pembroke Pines, FL	5.8	5.5	3.8	4.2	5.6	2.5	1.6	0.8	0.6
Philadelphia, PA	17.6	20.9	8.5	2.6	14.2	5.8	1.7	1.4	1.1
Phoenix, AZ	16.0	10.5	9.3	5.1	4.9	2.8	2.7	1.9	1.5
Pittsburgh, PA	30.3	19.5	9.2	3.6	16.4	9.2	2.0	2.1	1.5
Plano, TX	11.1	8.6	8.2	6.0	2.3	1.1	2.2	1.8	1.1
Portland, OR	21.6	12.6	12.5	4.1	3.9	1.9	3.7	3.4	2.3
Providence, RI	5.6	19.6	12.6	2.3	15.7	4.1	12.7	2.0	0.5
Provo, UT	11.9	5.0	30.6	4.6	2.2	0.6	2.1	6.0	2.1
Raleigh, NC	11.4	9.9	11.5	10.8	4.9	2.3	2.0	2.8	1.1
Richmond, VA	11.0	9.6	13.4	8.5	3.5	1.7	2.0	2.4	0.9
Roseville, CA	14.1	10.9	9.8	2.6	5.8	1.5	2.8	2.3	1.5
Round Rock, TX	15.6	9.5	9.5	3.6	2.7	1.6	2.9	2.5	1.1
San Antonio, TX	12.3	6.7	5.8	3.9	2.0	1.7	2.1	1.4	0.8
San Diego, CA	12.3	9.0	8.7	2.3	4.6	2.1	2.6	1.9	1.3
San Francisco, CA	9.1	8.4	6.8	1.6	5.3	1.6	2.2	1.7	1.0
San Jose, CA	8.1	6.1	5.9	1.2	4.7	1.2	1.9	1.4	1.0
Savannah, GA	9.3	10.6	9.5	5.5	2.8	1.1	1.8	2.0	1.1
Scottsdale, AZ	16.0	10.5	9.3	5.1	4.9	2.8	2.7	1.9	1.5
Seattle, WA	18.1	11.7	11.1	3.3	3.8	2.1	3.5	3.1	2.0
Sioux Falls, SD	43.8	11.2	5.6	3.5	1.4	1.5	2.3	1.1	6.6
Stamford, CT	9.5	15.3	8.6	2.5	18.0	5.6	2.5	2.0	0.9
Sterling Hgts, MI	17.6	11.0	7.9	3.7	6.5	11.2	4.3	2.4	1.4
Sunnyvale, CA	8.1	6.1	5.9	1.2	4.7	1.2	1.9	1.4	1.0
Tampa, FL	15.4	13.4	10.3	6.4	8.6	3.4	3.4	2.1	1.4
Temecula, CA	9.6	7.1	6.5	2.5	3.7	1.3	2.1	1.3	1.3
Thousand Oaks, CA	11.9	9.4	8.7	3.6	5.2	2.3	2.5	2.0	1.3
Virginia Beach, VA	11.2	10.0	10.6	11.0	4.6	2.0	2.2	2.2	1.1
Washington, DC	11.4	9.8	8.4	3.8	4.5	2.4	2.0	1.9	0.9
U.S.	16.1	11.6	8.8	6.1	5.7	3.2	3.0	1.9	1.6

Note: Figures are the percentage of the total population reporting a particular ancestry. The nine most commonly reported ancestries in the U.S. are shown. Figures include multiple ancestries (e.g. if a person reported being Irish and Italian, they were included in both columns); Figures cover the Metropolitan Statistical Area—see Appendix B for areas included; (1) Excludes Basque
Source: U.S. Census Bureau, 2008-2010 American Community Survey 3-Year Estimates

Foreign-Born Population: City

City	Any Foreign Country	Mexico	Asia	Europe	Carribean	South America	Central America[1]	Africa	Canada
Albuquerque, NM	11.2	6.7	2.1	0.8	0.4	0.4	0.2	0.2	0.2
Alexandria, VA	24.9	1.1	6.7	2.2	0.7	2.6	4.6	6.6	0.3
Anchorage, AK	9.2	0.5	5.3	1.1	0.5	0.4	0.3	0.3	0.5
Ann Arbor, MI	17.4	0.4	10.9	3.5	0.1	0.6	0.2	0.7	0.9
Athens, GA	n/a	n/a	n/a	n/a	n/a	n/a	n/a	n/a	n/a
Atlanta, GA	7.8	1.9	2.4	1.2	0.6	0.5	0.3	0.5	0.2
Austin, TX	19.7	10.5	4.7	1.1	0.3	0.5	1.8	0.5	0.3
Baltimore, MD	7.2	0.7	1.9	1.1	1.0	0.5	0.8	1.1	0.1
Bellevue, WA	33.0	2.5	21.4	4.9	0.0	1.0	0.4	0.9	1.4
Billings, MT	n/a	n/a	n/a	n/a	n/a	n/a	n/a	n/a	n/a
Boise City, ID	n/a	n/a	n/a	n/a	n/a	n/a	n/a	n/a	n/a
Boston, MA	26.7	0.3	6.8	3.9	7.6	2.4	2.4	2.8	0.4
Boulder, CO	11.3	2.8	3.5	3.3	0.2	0.5	0.2	0.2	0.5
Broken Arrow, OK	n/a	n/a	n/a	n/a	n/a	n/a	n/a	n/a	n/a
Cambridge, MA	27.4	0.8	9.5	7.2	3.1	2.0	1.0	2.5	1.0
Cape Coral, FL	n/a	n/a	n/a	n/a	n/a	n/a	n/a	n/a	n/a
Carlsbad, CA	14.8	3.5	5.4	3.6	0.2	0.8	0.1	0.4	0.8
Cary, NC	18.3	2.7	9.6	2.1	0.6	0.7	1.3	0.8	0.5
Cedar Rapids, IA	n/a	n/a	n/a	n/a	n/a	n/a	n/a	n/a	n/a
Charleston, SC	n/a	n/a	n/a	n/a	n/a	n/a	n/a	n/a	n/a
Charlotte, NC	15.0	3.5	4.0	1.4	0.6	1.4	2.6	1.2	0.3
Chesapeake, VA	4.4	0.5	2.0	0.7	0.3	0.3	0.4	0.2	0.1
Chicago, IL	21.0	9.6	4.3	3.9	0.5	0.9	0.8	0.7	0.2
Clarksville, TN	n/a	n/a	n/a	n/a	n/a	n/a	n/a	n/a	n/a
Colorado Spgs., CO	7.9	2.2	2.3	1.7	0.2	0.2	0.4	0.3	0.5
Columbia, MD	17.9	0.9	8.8	2.2	0.6	0.8	1.9	2.5	0.3
Columbia, MO	n/a	n/a	n/a	n/a	n/a	n/a	n/a	n/a	n/a
Columbia, SC	4.6	0.3	2.0	0.8	0.3	0.3	0.1	0.5	0.2
Columbus, OH	10.6	1.8	3.7	0.8	0.4	0.4	0.5	2.9	0.1
Dallas, TX	24.7	17.1	2.6	0.7	0.2	0.4	2.4	1.1	0.1
Denver, CO	16.4	9.4	3.0	1.8	0.1	0.3	0.4	1.0	0.2
Durham, NC	14.6	4.4	4.1	1.2	0.4	0.8	2.4	0.8	0.4
Edison, NJ	40.3	0.9	31.5	2.8	1.6	1.5	0.2	1.2	0.3
El Paso, TX	25.4	22.9	1.1	0.6	0.2	0.2	0.2	0.1	0.1
Fargo, ND	n/a	n/a	n/a	n/a	n/a	n/a	n/a	n/a	n/a
Ft. Collins, CO	n/a	n/a	n/a	n/a	n/a	n/a	n/a	n/a	n/a
Ft. Worth, TX	17.8	11.9	2.9	0.8	0.2	0.4	0.8	0.6	0.1
Gilbert, AZ	8.6	1.5	3.8	0.9	0.3	0.6	0.1	0.7	0.5
Green Bay, WI	n/a	n/a	n/a	n/a	n/a	n/a	n/a	n/a	n/a
Henderson, NV	11.4	1.8	5.4	1.8	0.4	0.6	0.4	0.3	0.6
High Point, NC	n/a	n/a	n/a	n/a	n/a	n/a	n/a	n/a	n/a
Honolulu, HI	28.3	0.2	23.5	1.2	0.1	0.3	0.1	0.1	0.4
Houston, TX	28.9	13.9	5.3	1.1	0.6	1.0	5.5	1.1	0.2
Huntington, NY	14.5	0.4	4.0	3.7	1.3	1.0	3.5	0.5	0.1
Huntsville, AL	7.0	2.4	1.9	0.9	0.6	0.1	0.3	0.6	0.1
Indianapolis, IN	8.5	4.1	1.9	0.5	0.2	0.2	0.7	0.8	0.1
Irvine, CA	35.0	1.5	27.7	2.7	0.1	0.8	0.3	0.9	0.8
Jackson, MS	n/a	n/a	n/a	n/a	n/a	n/a	n/a	n/a	n/a
Jacksonville, FL	9.4	0.6	3.3	1.7	1.5	1.0	0.5	0.6	0.2
Jersey City, NJ	38.4	0.7	18.3	3.1	5.7	5.0	2.4	3.0	0.1
Kansas City, MO	8.0	2.8	2.0	0.8	0.4	0.2	0.5	1.1	0.1
Kenosha, WI	n/a	n/a	n/a	n/a	n/a	n/a	n/a	n/a	n/a
Las Vegas, NV	22.2	10.9	5.0	1.8	0.8	0.6	2.1	0.4	0.4
Lexington, KY	8.6	3.1	2.9	1.1	0.1	0.4	0.4	0.3	0.2

Table continued on next page.

City	Any Foreign Country	Mexico	Asia	Europe	Carribean	South America	Central America[1]	Africa	Canada
Lincoln, NE	7.5	1.2	3.6	0.8	0.1	0.2	0.5	0.8	0.2
Little Rock, AR	n/a	n/a	n/a	n/a	n/a	n/a	n/a	n/a	n/a
Los Angeles, CA	39.6	14.9	11.2	2.4	0.3	1.1	8.5	0.6	0.4
Madison, WI	10.0	1.6	5.3	1.3	0.1	0.7	0.2	0.6	0.3
Manchester, NH	11.9	1.1	3.1	2.7	0.5	1.1	0.5	1.7	1.1
Miami, FL	58.2	1.0	0.8	1.3	33.7	7.5	13.5	0.2	0.1
Minneapolis, MN	15.0	3.2	4.0	1.1	0.2	1.6	0.4	4.0	0.3
Murfreesboro, TN	n/a	n/a	n/a	n/a	n/a	n/a	n/a	n/a	n/a
Naperville, IL	15.9	1.3	10.1	2.3	0.1	0.8	0.1	0.6	0.5
Nashville, TN	12.3	4.0	3.4	0.8	0.4	0.3	1.3	1.9	0.1
New Orleans, LA	5.7	0.5	1.9	0.8	0.2	0.5	1.4	0.4	0.1
New York, NY	36.8	2.2	10.0	5.8	10.2	5.2	1.5	1.4	0.3
Norman, OK	n/a	n/a	n/a	n/a	n/a	n/a	n/a	n/a	n/a
Olathe, KS	n/a	n/a	n/a	n/a	n/a	n/a	n/a	n/a	n/a
Omaha, NE	9.4	4.5	2.1	0.7	0.1	0.1	0.8	0.9	0.1
Orlando, FL	18.3	1.2	2.6	1.5	6.0	5.1	0.8	0.7	0.3
Overland Park, KS	9.5	1.0	5.5	1.5	0.0	0.5	0.2	0.6	0.2
Oyster Bay, NY	14.3	0.1	6.7	3.7	0.8	1.7	0.8	0.3	0.1
Pembroke Pines, FL	36.7	0.5	4.1	1.8	15.8	11.0	2.2	0.6	0.5
Philadelphia, PA	11.4	0.4	4.6	2.3	1.9	0.7	0.3	1.1	0.1
Phoenix, AZ	21.0	14.7	2.7	1.4	0.3	0.3	0.7	0.7	0.3
Pittsburgh, PA	6.8	0.3	3.6	1.6	0.4	0.2	0.1	0.4	0.2
Plano, TX	24.1	4.9	13.1	1.6	0.3	1.2	1.1	1.3	0.4
Portland, OR	13.5	2.5	5.4	2.8	0.3	0.2	0.6	0.6	0.6
Providence, RI	28.9	0.9	4.1	1.9	10.2	1.6	6.6	3.2	0.2
Provo, UT	n/a	n/a	n/a	n/a	n/a	n/a	n/a	n/a	n/a
Raleigh, NC	14.7	4.2	3.9	1.2	0.6	0.6	1.5	2.1	0.3
Richmond, VA	7.9	1.0	1.9	1.0	0.5	0.4	2.1	0.9	0.2
Roseville, CA	n/a	n/a	n/a	n/a	n/a	n/a	n/a	n/a	n/a
Round Rock, TX	n/a	n/a	n/a	n/a	n/a	n/a	n/a	n/a	n/a
San Antonio, TX	13.8	9.6	1.9	0.7	0.2	0.3	0.6	0.3	0.1
San Diego, CA	25.8	9.5	11.3	2.3	0.2	0.6	0.5	0.7	0.5
San Francisco, CA	35.5	3.0	22.7	4.6	0.2	1.0	2.8	0.4	0.6
San Jose, CA	38.5	10.7	22.8	2.0	0.1	0.6	1.1	0.5	0.4
Savannah, GA	n/a	n/a	n/a	n/a	n/a	n/a	n/a	n/a	n/a
Scottsdale, AZ	11.2	2.1	3.2	2.6	0.2	0.7	0.3	0.5	1.7
Seattle, WA	16.8	1.3	8.9	2.4	0.1	0.4	0.3	2.0	1.0
Sioux Falls, SD	n/a	n/a	n/a	n/a	n/a	n/a	n/a	n/a	n/a
Stamford, CT	39.2	1.8	6.5	8.0	6.6	6.9	8.3	0.5	0.4
Sterling Hgts, MI	n/a	n/a	n/a	n/a	n/a	n/a	n/a	n/a	n/a
Sunnyvale, CA	43.2	5.6	30.9	3.1	0.1	1.0	1.4	0.2	0.7
Tampa, FL	15.0	1.5	2.3	1.4	5.8	1.5	1.2	0.7	0.5
Temecula, CA	n/a	n/a	n/a	n/a	n/a	n/a	n/a	n/a	n/a
Thousand Oaks, CA	19.3	4.3	7.0	4.0	0.3	0.9	1.8	0.2	0.6
Virginia Beach, VA	8.9	0.4	4.6	1.7	0.7	0.5	0.4	0.4	0.2
Washington, DC	13.1	0.6	2.6	2.2	1.3	1.0	3.1	1.9	0.3
U.S.	12.8	3.8	3.6	1.6	1.2	0.9	1.0	0.5	0.3

Note: (1) Excludes Mexico
Source: U.S. Census Bureau, 2008-2010 American Community Survey 3-Year Estimates

Foreign-Born Population: Metro Area

Metro Area	Any Foreign Country	Mexico	Asia	Europe	Carribean	South America	Central America[1]	Africa	Canada
Albuquerque, NM	10.0	6.5	1.5	0.8	0.3	0.3	0.2	0.1	0.2
Alexandria, VA	21.4	0.9	7.7	2.0	1.0	2.3	4.5	2.8	0.2
Anchorage, AK	7.7	0.4	4.3	1.1	0.4	0.4	0.2	0.2	0.5
Ann Arbor, MI	11.3	0.3	6.5	2.2	0.1	0.3	0.3	0.8	0.6
Athens, GA	8.1	3.1	2.1	0.8	0.2	0.6	0.6	0.4	0.2
Atlanta, GA	13.7	3.5	3.8	1.3	1.4	1.0	1.1	1.3	0.2
Austin, TX	14.6	7.6	3.6	1.0	0.2	0.4	1.1	0.4	0.3
Baltimore, MD	9.0	0.6	3.6	1.4	0.7	0.4	1.0	1.1	0.1
Bellevue, WA	16.4	2.7	8.0	2.7	0.1	0.4	0.4	1.1	0.8
Billings, MT	n/a	n/a	n/a	n/a	n/a	n/a	n/a	n/a	n/a
Boise City, ID	7.2	3.1	1.5	1.3	0.1	0.2	0.3	0.4	0.3
Boston, MA	16.5	0.2	5.1	3.3	2.7	1.9	1.3	1.3	0.5
Boulder, CO	11.0	3.8	3.1	2.3	0.1	0.4	0.6	0.1	0.5
Broken Arrow, OK	5.5	2.8	1.4	0.4	0.1	0.2	0.3	0.2	0.1
Cambridge, MA	16.5	0.2	5.1	3.3	2.7	1.9	1.3	1.3	0.5
Cape Coral, FL	15.4	2.4	1.3	2.2	4.5	2.3	1.7	0.1	0.8
Carlsbad, CA	23.2	10.9	8.2	1.9	0.2	0.5	0.5	0.5	0.4
Cary, NC	11.8	3.6	3.5	1.2	0.5	0.5	1.1	1.1	0.3
Cedar Rapids, IA	n/a	n/a	n/a	n/a	n/a	n/a	n/a	n/a	n/a
Charleston, SC	5.5	1.7	1.2	1.1	0.2	0.5	0.5	0.1	0.2
Charlotte, NC	10.1	2.8	2.5	1.1	0.4	1.0	1.4	0.7	0.2
Chesapeake, VA	6.2	0.4	2.7	1.1	0.5	0.3	0.6	0.4	0.2
Chicago, IL	17.6	7.2	4.5	4.0	0.3	0.6	0.5	0.4	0.2
Clarksville, TN	n/a	n/a	n/a	n/a	n/a	n/a	n/a	n/a	n/a
Colorado Spgs., CO	6.9	1.8	2.0	1.7	0.2	0.2	0.4	0.2	0.4
Columbia, MD	9.0	0.6	3.6	1.4	0.7	0.4	1.0	1.1	0.1
Columbia, MO	5.9	0.3	3.2	1.1	0.1	0.1	0.1	0.7	0.2
Columbia, SC	4.8	1.5	1.4	0.7	0.3	0.2	0.5	0.2	0.1
Columbus, OH	6.9	1.0	2.6	0.9	0.3	0.2	0.3	1.5	0.2
Dallas, TX	17.5	9.3	4.2	0.8	0.2	0.5	1.3	0.9	0.2
Denver, CO	12.2	5.7	2.8	1.6	0.1	0.3	0.5	0.7	0.3
Durham, NC	12.6	4.0	3.6	1.4	0.4	0.5	1.6	0.7	0.4
Edison, NJ	28.4	1.7	7.9	4.8	6.4	4.4	1.8	1.1	0.2
El Paso, TX	26.5	24.4	0.9	0.5	0.2	0.2	0.2	0.1	0.1
Fargo, ND	n/a	n/a	n/a	n/a	n/a	n/a	n/a	n/a	n/a
Ft. Collins, CO	5.5	1.9	1.4	1.2	0.1	0.2	0.2	0.1	0.3
Ft. Worth, TX	17.5	9.3	4.2	0.8	0.2	0.5	1.3	0.9	0.2
Gilbert, AZ	14.9	8.8	2.7	1.4	0.2	0.3	0.5	0.4	0.6
Green Bay, WI	n/a	n/a	n/a	n/a	n/a	n/a	n/a	n/a	n/a
Henderson, NV	22.0	9.4	6.5	1.9	0.8	0.6	1.7	0.7	0.4
High Point, NC	8.2	3.1	2.3	0.6	0.4	0.4	0.4	0.9	0.2
Honolulu, HI	19.9	0.2	16.0	0.8	0.2	0.3	0.1	0.1	0.3
Houston, TX	22.2	10.2	5.2	1.0	0.5	1.0	3.3	0.8	0.2
Huntington, NY	28.4	1.7	7.9	4.8	6.4	4.4	1.8	1.1	0.2
Huntsville, AL	5.3	1.7	1.6	0.7	0.3	0.1	0.2	0.3	0.2
Indianapolis, IN	6.2	2.3	1.8	0.6	0.1	0.2	0.4	0.5	0.1
Irvine, CA	34.5	13.9	12.2	1.8	0.3	0.9	4.3	0.5	0.3
Jackson, MS	2.4	0.6	0.9	0.2	0.1	0.1	0.2	0.1	0.0
Jacksonville, FL	7.9	0.5	2.6	1.6	1.2	0.9	0.4	0.4	0.2
Jersey City, NJ	28.4	1.7	7.9	4.8	6.4	4.4	1.8	1.1	0.2
Kansas City, MO	6.3	2.3	1.8	0.7	0.2	0.2	0.4	0.5	0.1
Kenosha, WI	17.6	7.2	4.5	4.0	0.3	0.6	0.5	0.4	0.2
Las Vegas, NV	22.0	9.4	6.5	1.9	0.8	0.6	1.7	0.7	0.4
Lexington, KY	6.7	2.4	2.2	0.9	0.1	0.3	0.4	0.2	0.1

Table continued on next page.

Metro Area	Any Foreign Country	Mexico	Asia	Europe	Carribean	South America	Central America[1]	Africa	Canada
Lincoln, NE	6.7	1.1	3.2	0.8	0.1	0.2	0.4	0.7	0.2
Little Rock, AR	4.3	1.8	1.3	0.5	0.1	0.1	0.3	0.1	0.1
Los Angeles, CA	34.5	13.9	12.2	1.8	0.3	0.9	4.3	0.5	0.3
Madison, WI	6.7	1.4	3.0	1.0	0.1	0.5	0.2	0.3	0.2
Manchester, NH	8.1	0.6	2.6	1.7	0.5	1.0	0.3	0.7	0.8
Miami, FL	38.1	1.2	1.9	2.2	19.6	7.7	4.5	0.3	0.6
Minneapolis, MN	9.5	1.6	3.6	1.1	0.1	0.5	0.3	1.9	0.3
Murfreesboro, TN	7.5	2.2	2.2	0.6	0.2	0.3	0.9	0.8	0.2
Naperville, IL	17.6	7.2	4.5	4.0	0.3	0.6	0.5	0.4	0.2
Nashville, TN	7.5	2.2	2.2	0.6	0.2	0.3	0.9	0.8	0.2
New Orleans, LA	7.1	0.8	2.0	0.6	0.5	0.5	2.4	0.2	0.1
New York, NY	28.4	1.7	7.9	4.8	6.4	4.4	1.8	1.1	0.2
Norman, OK	7.6	3.6	2.2	0.5	0.1	0.2	0.5	0.4	0.1
Olathe, KS	6.3	2.3	1.8	0.7	0.2	0.2	0.4	0.5	0.1
Omaha, NE	6.5	2.8	1.7	0.6	0.1	0.1	0.5	0.6	0.1
Orlando, FL	16.2	1.4	2.8	1.7	4.7	3.7	0.9	0.5	0.4
Overland Park, KS	6.3	2.3	1.8	0.7	0.2	0.2	0.4	0.5	0.1
Oyster Bay, NY	28.4	1.7	7.9	4.8	6.4	4.4	1.8	1.1	0.2
Pembroke Pines, FL	38.1	1.2	1.9	2.2	19.6	7.7	4.5	0.3	0.6
Philadelphia, PA	9.5	0.9	3.8	2.0	1.0	0.6	0.3	0.8	0.2
Phoenix, AZ	14.9	8.8	2.7	1.4	0.2	0.3	0.5	0.4	0.6
Pittsburgh, PA	3.2	0.1	1.4	1.0	0.1	0.1	0.0	0.2	0.1
Plano, TX	17.5	9.3	4.2	0.8	0.2	0.5	1.3	0.9	0.2
Portland, OR	12.6	3.5	4.3	2.6	0.2	0.3	0.5	0.4	0.5
Providence, RI	12.4	0.3	1.9	4.4	1.7	0.9	1.3	1.4	0.3
Provo, UT	7.0	2.9	0.9	0.6	0.0	1.2	0.5	0.1	0.5
Raleigh, NC	11.8	3.6	3.5	1.2	0.5	0.5	1.1	1.1	0.3
Richmond, VA	6.8	0.8	2.4	1.0	0.3	0.4	1.1	0.5	0.2
Roseville, CA	17.3	4.9	7.4	2.7	0.1	0.3	0.6	0.4	0.3
Round Rock, TX	14.6	7.6	3.6	1.0	0.2	0.4	1.1	0.4	0.3
San Antonio, TX	11.6	7.7	1.7	0.7	0.2	0.3	0.6	0.2	0.1
San Diego, CA	23.2	10.9	8.2	1.9	0.2	0.5	0.5	0.5	0.4
San Francisco, CA	30.0	6.1	16.0	2.9	0.2	0.8	2.4	0.5	0.4
San Jose, CA	36.5	8.6	22.2	2.8	0.1	0.7	1.0	0.5	0.6
Savannah, GA	5.2	1.4	1.8	0.6	0.3	0.3	0.4	0.2	0.1
Scottsdale, AZ	14.9	8.8	2.7	1.4	0.2	0.3	0.5	0.4	0.6
Seattle, WA	16.4	2.7	8.0	2.7	0.1	0.4	0.4	1.1	0.8
Sioux Falls, SD	n/a	n/a	n/a	n/a	n/a	n/a	n/a	n/a	n/a
Stamford, CT	20.4	1.1	3.7	5.1	3.1	4.2	2.1	0.6	0.4
Sterling Hgts, MI	8.6	0.8	4.2	2.3	0.1	0.1	0.1	0.3	0.6
Sunnyvale, CA	36.5	8.6	22.2	2.8	0.1	0.7	1.0	0.5	0.6
Tampa, FL	12.2	1.4	2.2	2.4	3.0	1.5	0.6	0.4	0.7
Temecula, CA	21.8	13.3	4.3	1.0	0.2	0.5	1.7	0.3	0.4
Thousand Oaks, CA	23.2	13.6	5.2	1.8	0.1	0.6	1.2	0.2	0.4
Virginia Beach, VA	6.2	0.4	2.7	1.1	0.5	0.3	0.6	0.4	0.2
Washington, DC	21.4	0.9	7.7	2.0	1.0	2.3	4.5	2.8	0.2
U.S.	12.8	3.8	3.6	1.6	1.2	0.9	1.0	0.5	0.3

Note: Figures cover the Metropolitan Statistical Area—see Appendix B for areas included; (1) Excludes Mexico
Source: U.S. Census Bureau, 2008-2010 American Community Survey 3-Year Estimates

Marital Status: City

City	Never Married	Now Married[1]	Separated	Widowed	Divorced
Albuquerque, NM	35.2	44.1	1.8	5.1	13.8
Alexandria, VA	39.9	41.6	2.5	4.5	11.6
Anchorage, AK	32.0	49.4	2.2	3.5	13.0
Ann Arbor, MI	56.4	33.6	0.6	2.8	6.6
Athens, GA	55.9	30.5	2.0	3.7	7.8
Atlanta, GA	53.5	27.6	2.4	5.5	11.0
Austin, TX	43.0	41.1	2.1	3.2	10.6
Baltimore, MD	51.2	26.6	4.1	7.3	10.9
Bellevue, WA	27.0	57.0	1.6	4.6	9.8
Billings, MT	29.4	48.4	1.6	6.3	14.3
Boise City, ID	31.7	49.1	1.5	4.5	13.3
Boston, MA	56.7	28.6	2.9	4.4	7.4
Boulder, CO	53.5	34.2	0.6	3.0	8.8
Broken Arrow, OK	23.2	61.8	0.8	4.7	9.5
Cambridge, MA	54.0	33.5	1.6	3.8	7.1
Cape Coral, FL	25.2	55.0	1.3	6.4	12.1
Carlsbad, CA	26.3	55.3	1.3	5.1	12.0
Cary, NC	25.9	61.9	1.4	3.0	7.8
Cedar Rapids, IA	33.4	47.3	1.5	5.4	12.4
Charleston, SC	44.2	38.2	2.8	5.7	9.2
Charlotte, NC	37.4	44.7	3.1	4.6	10.2
Chesapeake, VA	27.6	55.1	2.5	5.1	9.7
Chicago, IL	47.7	35.0	2.7	5.7	8.9
Clarksville, TN	29.0	50.7	3.2	4.8	12.2
Colorado Spgs., CO	28.6	51.1	2.3	4.8	13.2
Columbia, MD	29.6	55.2	2.5	4.0	8.7
Columbia, MO	49.3	36.5	1.6	3.6	9.0
Columbia, SC	54.5	28.2	3.3	5.2	8.8
Columbus, OH	42.8	37.3	2.4	4.7	12.8
Dallas, TX	39.6	40.5	3.7	5.1	11.2
Denver, CO	41.4	39.0	2.4	5.0	12.2
Durham, NC	41.9	40.3	2.9	5.1	9.8
Edison, NJ	29.9	56.2	1.4	5.8	6.7
El Paso, TX	31.9	47.7	3.6	5.7	11.0
Fargo, ND	42.6	43.2	1.1	4.5	8.6
Ft. Collins, CO	43.2	43.1	1.2	3.1	9.5
Ft. Worth, TX	32.0	48.0	3.1	4.8	12.1
Gilbert, AZ	27.5	56.9	1.5	2.5	11.5
Green Bay, WI	36.6	44.2	1.3	5.2	12.7
Henderson, NV	25.6	53.4	1.8	5.5	13.6
High Point, NC	32.6	45.5	3.9	6.6	11.5
Honolulu, HI	35.8	45.1	1.4	7.4	10.3
Houston, TX	38.1	42.8	3.5	5.1	10.4
Huntington, NY	26.8	58.4	1.8	6.3	6.6
Huntsville, AL	33.8	43.9	3.0	6.1	13.2
Indianapolis, IN	38.5	40.1	2.5	5.9	13.0
Irvine, CA	38.1	50.1	1.0	3.2	7.6
Jackson, MS	46.8	30.9	3.5	6.4	12.5
Jacksonville, FL	33.2	44.7	2.8	5.9	13.5
Jersey City, NJ	45.5	38.8	3.0	5.3	7.6
Kansas City, MO	37.4	41.2	2.6	5.6	13.1
Kenosha, WI	35.1	44.7	1.5	6.2	12.6
Las Vegas, NV	31.8	46.0	2.7	5.3	14.2
Lexington, KY	36.6	44.6	1.8	4.6	12.5
Lincoln, NE	35.5	48.0	1.3	4.2	11.0
Little Rock, AR	35.7	42.4	2.5	5.7	13.8

Table continued on next page.

City	Never Married	Now Married[1]	Separated	Widowed	Divorced
Los Angeles, CA	44.2	39.7	2.9	4.9	8.4
Madison, WI	47.1	39.3	1.2	3.7	8.8
Manchester, NH	35.3	44.3	1.7	5.6	13.1
Miami, FL	38.7	36.1	4.3	7.3	13.6
Minneapolis, MN	51.4	32.4	1.8	4.1	10.3
Murfreesboro, TN	39.5	43.9	1.7	4.7	10.3
Naperville, IL	25.2	63.4	0.7	3.7	7.0
Nashville, TN	39.3	39.8	2.6	5.3	13.0
New Orleans, LA	45.8	33.6	2.8	6.1	11.7
New York, NY	43.3	39.5	3.4	5.9	7.9
Norman, OK	41.6	40.8	1.6	5.3	10.6
Olathe, KS	24.5	61.3	1.3	3.7	9.3
Omaha, NE	37.0	44.1	2.0	5.4	11.5
Orlando, FL	43.1	35.7	3.7	4.4	13.1
Overland Park, KS	25.4	56.8	1.1	5.3	11.4
Oyster Bay, NY	26.7	59.2	1.2	7.4	5.5
Pembroke Pines, FL	29.0	48.4	2.8	7.9	12.0
Philadelphia, PA	50.2	29.9	3.7	7.5	8.7
Phoenix, AZ	37.4	44.3	1.9	4.2	12.1
Pittsburgh, PA	50.3	30.5	2.8	7.4	9.0
Plano, TX	26.6	58.7	1.6	3.5	9.6
Portland, OR	40.1	40.7	1.7	4.9	12.6
Providence, RI	53.8	28.1	4.0	5.2	8.9
Provo, UT	53.8	38.6	1.0	2.2	4.4
Raleigh, NC	41.9	41.0	3.1	4.1	10.0
Richmond, VA	51.7	26.2	3.8	6.2	12.1
Roseville, CA	25.8	55.4	2.1	5.7	10.9
Round Rock, TX	29.2	53.8	2.5	3.0	11.6
San Antonio, TX	34.5	44.5	3.1	5.6	12.3
San Diego, CA	40.5	42.9	2.1	4.5	10.0
San Francisco, CA	47.9	37.5	1.5	5.2	7.8
San Jose, CA	34.5	50.4	1.7	4.9	8.5
Savannah, GA	47.3	31.0	2.4	7.6	11.7
Scottsdale, AZ	27.6	52.0	1.0	6.4	13.0
Seattle, WA	43.6	39.4	1.4	4.4	11.2
Sioux Falls, SD	32.5	49.3	1.4	5.2	11.6
Stamford, CT	33.5	50.6	2.3	5.3	8.3
Sterling Hgts, MI	29.1	54.2	0.7	7.4	8.6
Sunnyvale, CA	29.4	57.6	1.0	4.1	7.9
Tampa, FL	39.7	37.4	3.5	5.1	14.3
Temecula, CA	29.8	54.2	1.9	3.3	10.9
Thousand Oaks, CA	27.9	56.9	1.2	4.9	9.2
Virginia Beach, VA	29.5	51.7	3.0	4.8	11.0
Washington, DC	56.7	25.6	2.9	5.2	9.6
U.S.	31.6	49.6	2.2	6.1	10.7

Note: Figures are percentages and cover the population 15 years of age and older; (1) Excludes separated
Source: U.S. Census Bureau, 2008-2010 American Community Survey 3-Year Estimates

Marital Status: Metro Area

Metro Area	Never Married	Now Married[1]	Separated	Widowed	Divorced
Albuquerque, NM	32.9	47.2	1.8	5.3	12.9
Alexandria, VA	35.4	48.9	2.4	4.6	8.8
Anchorage, AK	31.0	50.6	2.2	3.6	12.7
Ann Arbor, MI	41.0	45.0	0.9	3.9	9.2
Athens, GA	45.2	39.7	2.0	4.3	8.8
Atlanta, GA	32.7	49.6	2.3	4.6	10.9
Austin, TX	34.8	49.2	1.9	3.6	10.4
Baltimore, MD	34.6	46.7	2.7	6.4	9.7
Bellevue, WA	31.6	50.5	1.7	4.5	11.8
Billings, MT	26.8	52.6	1.3	5.9	13.4
Boise City, ID	26.2	55.6	1.7	4.4	12.1
Boston, MA	35.6	48.0	1.8	5.7	8.8
Boulder, CO	35.9	49.2	1.1	3.5	10.4
Broken Arrow, OK	25.8	53.1	2.1	6.2	12.8
Cambridge, MA	35.6	48.0	1.8	5.7	8.8
Cape Coral, FL	24.3	53.8	1.8	7.6	12.4
Carlsbad, CA	35.2	47.6	2.0	4.9	10.3
Cary, NC	30.6	53.5	2.6	4.4	9.0
Cedar Rapids, IA	28.6	53.7	1.2	5.6	10.8
Charleston, SC	33.9	47.1	3.0	5.5	10.5
Charlotte, NC	30.9	51.0	2.9	5.2	10.0
Chesapeake, VA	32.0	48.6	3.2	5.5	10.7
Chicago, IL	35.3	48.1	1.8	5.7	9.0
Clarksville, TN	25.7	54.9	2.7	5.1	11.6
Colorado Spgs., CO	27.7	53.7	2.0	4.4	12.2
Columbia, MD	34.6	46.7	2.7	6.4	9.7
Columbia, MO	40.7	44.1	1.6	4.2	9.4
Columbia, SC	34.7	46.4	3.2	5.8	9.9
Columbus, OH	32.9	48.7	1.9	5.0	11.5
Dallas, TX	30.4	51.6	2.6	4.5	10.9
Denver, CO	30.9	51.4	1.8	4.4	11.5
Durham, NC	36.5	46.6	2.7	4.8	9.4
Edison, NJ	37.0	46.5	2.6	6.2	7.7
El Paso, TX	32.1	48.3	3.7	5.5	10.3
Fargo, ND	37.0	49.1	0.7	4.6	8.7
Ft. Collins, CO	31.9	52.7	1.1	3.9	10.4
Ft. Worth, TX	30.4	51.6	2.6	4.5	10.9
Gilbert, AZ	31.8	49.9	1.6	5.0	11.7
Green Bay, WI	30.2	53.7	1.0	5.3	9.8
Henderson, NV	31.9	47.2	2.4	4.9	13.6
High Point, NC	31.3	48.1	3.2	6.5	10.9
Honolulu, HI	33.2	50.5	1.3	6.1	8.8
Houston, TX	31.5	51.0	2.8	4.7	10.0
Huntington, NY	37.0	46.5	2.6	6.2	7.7
Huntsville, AL	28.1	52.3	2.3	5.5	11.8
Indianapolis, IN	30.6	50.4	1.7	5.4	11.9
Irvine, CA	38.5	45.3	2.5	5.0	8.6
Jackson, MS	34.5	44.8	2.8	6.2	11.6
Jacksonville, FL	29.9	48.8	2.4	5.9	13.0
Jersey City, NJ	37.0	46.5	2.6	6.2	7.7
Kansas City, MO	28.6	52.2	1.8	5.5	11.9
Kenosha, WI	35.3	48.1	1.8	5.7	9.0
Las Vegas, NV	31.9	47.2	2.4	4.9	13.6
Lexington, KY	31.8	48.9	2.0	5.2	12.2
Lincoln, NE	33.8	50.5	1.2	4.3	10.2
Little Rock, AR	28.6	49.9	2.5	6.0	13.0

Table continued on next page.

Metro Area	Never Married	Now Married[1]	Separated	Widowed	Divorced
Los Angeles, CA	38.5	45.3	2.5	5.0	8.6
Madison, WI	34.8	50.2	1.0	4.4	9.6
Manchester, NH	28.6	53.1	1.4	5.3	11.6
Miami, FL	32.5	44.9	2.9	7.1	12.6
Minneapolis, MN	32.7	51.9	1.2	4.5	9.7
Murfreesboro, TN	30.3	50.8	2.0	5.2	11.8
Naperville, IL	35.3	48.1	1.8	5.7	9.0
Nashville, TN	30.3	50.8	2.0	5.2	11.8
New Orleans, LA	34.6	44.5	2.6	6.6	11.7
New York, NY	37.0	46.5	2.6	6.2	7.7
Norman, OK	28.9	50.3	2.1	5.9	12.8
Olathe, KS	28.6	52.2	1.8	5.5	11.9
Omaha, NE	30.6	52.2	1.5	5.2	10.5
Orlando, FL	32.6	48.0	2.6	5.4	11.5
Overland Park, KS	28.6	52.2	1.8	5.5	11.9
Oyster Bay, NY	37.0	46.5	2.6	6.2	7.7
Pembroke Pines, FL	32.5	44.9	2.9	7.1	12.6
Philadelphia, PA	35.8	46.5	2.3	6.7	8.6
Phoenix, AZ	31.8	49.9	1.6	5.0	11.7
Pittsburgh, PA	30.8	49.4	2.1	8.3	9.4
Plano, TX	30.4	51.6	2.6	4.5	10.9
Portland, OR	30.5	50.7	1.8	4.8	12.2
Providence, RI	34.1	46.1	2.1	7.1	10.7
Provo, UT	31.7	58.5	1.1	2.8	5.8
Raleigh, NC	30.6	53.5	2.6	4.4	9.0
Richmond, VA	33.1	48.2	2.8	5.7	10.2
Roseville, CA	32.6	48.5	2.2	5.4	11.2
Round Rock, TX	34.8	49.2	1.9	3.6	10.4
San Antonio, TX	30.8	49.7	2.7	5.4	11.3
San Diego, CA	35.2	47.6	2.0	4.9	10.3
San Francisco, CA	36.1	47.4	1.9	5.3	9.3
San Jose, CA	32.5	52.7	1.6	4.8	8.4
Savannah, GA	34.8	46.4	1.9	5.9	11.1
Scottsdale, AZ	31.8	49.9	1.6	5.0	11.7
Seattle, WA	31.6	50.5	1.7	4.5	11.8
Sioux Falls, SD	28.5	54.5	1.2	5.4	10.4
Stamford, CT	30.2	53.3	1.6	6.0	8.9
Sterling Hgts, MI	33.1	47.3	1.7	6.6	11.3
Sunnyvale, CA	32.5	52.7	1.6	4.8	8.4
Tampa, FL	29.0	47.1	2.4	7.5	14.0
Temecula, CA	33.4	49.0	2.6	5.0	10.1
Thousand Oaks, CA	31.2	51.8	1.7	5.1	10.2
Virginia Beach, VA	32.0	48.6	3.2	5.5	10.7
Washington, DC	35.4	48.9	2.4	4.6	8.8
U.S.	31.6	49.6	2.2	6.1	10.7

Note: Figures are percentages and cover the population 15 years of age and older; Figures cover the Metropolitan Statistical Area—see Appendix B for areas included; (1) Excludes separated
Source: U.S. Census Bureau, 2008-2010 American Community Survey 3-Year Estimates

Male/Female Ratio: City

City	Males	Females	Males per 100 Females
Albuquerque, NM	265,106	280,746	94.4
Alexandria, VA	67,262	72,704	92.5
Anchorage, AK	148,209	143,617	103.2
Ann Arbor, MI	56,155	57,779	97.2
Athens, GA	54,781	60,671	90.3
Atlanta, GA	208,968	211,035	99.0
Austin, TX	399,738	390,652	102.3
Baltimore, MD	292,249	328,712	88.9
Bellevue, WA	61,330	61,033	100.5
Billings, MT	50,266	53,904	93.3
Boise City, ID	101,690	103,981	97.8
Boston, MA	295,951	321,643	92.0
Boulder, CO	50,004	47,381	105.5
Broken Arrow, OK	48,048	50,802	94.6
Cambridge, MA	51,109	54,053	94.6
Cape Coral, FL	75,364	78,941	95.5
Carlsbad, CA	51,485	53,843	95.6
Cary, NC	65,819	69,415	94.8
Cedar Rapids, IA	62,065	64,261	96.6
Charleston, SC	56,741	63,342	89.6
Charlotte, NC	353,511	377,913	93.5
Chesapeake, VA	108,051	114,158	94.7
Chicago, IL	1,308,072	1,387,526	94.3
Clarksville, TN	64,768	68,161	95.0
Colorado Spgs., CO	203,944	212,483	96.0
Columbia, MD	47,891	51,724	92.6
Columbia, MO	52,458	56,042	93.6
Columbia, SC	66,532	62,740	106.0
Columbus, OH	384,265	402,768	95.4
Dallas, TX	598,962	598,854	100.0
Denver, CO	300,089	300,069	100.0
Durham, NC	108,556	119,774	90.6
Edison, NJ	48,899	51,068	95.8
El Paso, TX	311,280	337,841	92.1
Fargo, ND	53,248	52,301	101.8
Ft. Collins, CO	71,909	72,077	99.8
Ft. Worth, TX	363,896	377,310	96.4
Gilbert, AZ	102,634	105,819	97.0
Green Bay, WI	51,359	52,698	97.5
Henderson, NV	126,779	130,950	96.8
High Point, NC	49,002	55,369	88.5
Honolulu, HI	166,500	170,756	97.5
Houston, TX	1,053,517	1,045,934	100.7
Huntington, NY	100,042	103,222	96.9
Huntsville, AL	87,530	92,575	94.6
Indianapolis, IN	396,346	424,099	93.5
Irvine, CA	103,434	108,941	94.9
Jackson, MS	80,615	92,899	86.8
Jacksonville, FL	398,294	423,490	94.1
Jersey City, NJ	122,298	125,299	97.6
Kansas City, MO	223,183	236,604	94.3
Kenosha, WI	48,688	50,530	96.4
Las Vegas, NV	294,100	289,656	101.5
Lexington, KY	145,591	150,212	96.9
Lincoln, NE	129,235	129,144	100.1

Table continued on next page.

City	Males	Females	Males per 100 Females
Little Rock, AR	92,245	101,279	91.1
Los Angeles, CA	1,889,064	1,903,557	99.2
Madison, WI	114,832	118,377	97.0
Manchester, NH	54,356	55,209	98.5
Miami, FL	198,927	200,530	99.2
Minneapolis, MN	192,421	190,157	101.2
Murfreesboro, TN	53,422	55,333	96.5
Naperville, IL	68,981	72,872	94.7
Nashville, TN	291,294	309,928	94.0
New Orleans, LA	166,248	177,581	93.6
New York, NY	3,882,544	4,292,589	90.4
Norman, OK	55,172	55,753	99.0
Olathe, KS	62,358	63,514	98.2
Omaha, NE	201,063	207,895	96.7
Orlando, FL	115,883	122,417	94.7
Overland Park, KS	83,735	89,637	93.4
Oyster Bay, NY	142,056	151,158	94.0
Pembroke Pines, FL	71,515	83,235	85.9
Philadelphia, PA	719,813	806,193	89.3
Phoenix, AZ	725,020	720,612	100.6
Pittsburgh, PA	148,101	157,603	94.0
Plano, TX	127,078	132,763	95.7
Portland, OR	289,211	294,565	98.2
Providence, RI	85,802	92,240	93.0
Provo, UT	55,737	56,751	98.2
Raleigh, NC	195,143	208,749	93.5
Richmond, VA	97,331	106,883	91.1
Roseville, CA	56,894	61,894	91.9
Round Rock, TX	49,139	50,748	96.8
San Antonio, TX	647,690	679,717	95.3
San Diego, CA	660,626	646,776	102.1
San Francisco, CA	408,462	396,773	102.9
San Jose, CA	475,668	470,274	101.1
Savannah, GA	65,301	70,985	92.0
Scottsdale, AZ	104,930	112,455	93.3
Seattle, WA	304,030	304,630	99.8
Sioux Falls, SD	76,268	77,620	98.3
Stamford, CT	60,402	62,241	97.0
Sterling Hgts, MI	62,862	66,837	94.1
Sunnyvale, CA	70,560	69,521	101.5
Tampa, FL	164,061	171,648	95.6
Temecula, CA	49,002	51,095	95.9
Thousand Oaks, CA	61,989	64,694	95.8
Virginia Beach, VA	214,441	223,553	95.9
Washington, DC	284,222	317,501	89.5
U.S.	151,781,326	156,964,212	96.7

Source: U.S. Census Bureau, 2010 Census

Male/Female Ratio: Metro Area

Metro Area	Males	Females	Males per 100 Females
Albuquerque, NM	435,807	451,270	96.6
Alexandria, VA	2,716,483	2,865,687	94.8
Anchorage, AK	194,249	186,572	104.1
Ann Arbor, MI	170,132	174,659	97.4
Athens, GA	92,678	99,863	92.8
Atlanta, GA	2,563,887	2,704,973	94.8
Austin, TX	860,101	856,188	100.5
Baltimore, MD	1,304,960	1,405,529	92.8
Bellevue, WA	1,711,982	1,727,827	99.1
Billings, MT	77,490	80,560	96.2
Boise City, ID	307,856	308,705	99.7
Boston, MA	2,202,868	2,349,534	93.8
Boulder, CO	147,916	146,651	100.9
Broken Arrow, OK	460,092	477,386	96.4
Cambridge, MA	2,202,868	2,349,534	93.8
Cape Coral, FL	303,600	315,154	96.3
Carlsbad, CA	1,553,679	1,541,634	100.8
Cary, NC	552,108	578,382	95.5
Cedar Rapids, IA	127,690	130,250	98.0
Charleston, SC	324,981	339,626	95.7
Charlotte, NC	854,016	904,022	94.5
Chesapeake, VA	819,724	851,959	96.2
Chicago, IL	4,622,870	4,838,235	95.5
Clarksville, TN	135,630	138,319	98.1
Colorado Spgs., CO	322,047	323,566	99.5
Columbia, MD	1,304,960	1,405,529	92.8
Columbia, MO	83,991	88,795	94.6
Columbia, SC	374,340	393,258	95.2
Columbus, OH	901,516	935,020	96.4
Dallas, TX	3,141,634	3,230,139	97.3
Denver, CO	1,264,550	1,278,932	98.9
Durham, NC	241,401	262,956	91.8
Edison, NJ	9,099,234	9,797,875	92.9
El Paso, TX	387,876	412,771	94.0
Fargo, ND	104,688	104,089	100.6
Ft. Collins, CO	148,637	150,993	98.4
Ft. Worth, TX	3,141,634	3,230,139	97.3
Gilbert, AZ	2,085,630	2,107,257	99.0
Green Bay, WI	152,312	153,929	98.9
Henderson, NV	982,193	969,076	101.4
High Point, NC	347,487	376,314	92.3
Honolulu, HI	477,092	476,115	100.2
Houston, TX	2,957,442	2,989,358	98.9
Huntington, NY	9,099,234	9,797,875	92.9
Huntsville, AL	206,230	211,363	97.6
Indianapolis, IN	856,916	899,325	95.3
Irvine, CA	6,328,434	6,500,403	97.4
Jackson, MS	256,917	282,140	91.1
Jacksonville, FL	655,647	689,949	95.0
Jersey City, NJ	9,099,234	9,797,875	92.9
Kansas City, MO	996,319	1,039,015	95.9
Kenosha, WI	4,622,870	4,838,235	95.5
Las Vegas, NV	982,193	969,076	101.4
Lexington, KY	231,618	240,481	96.3
Lincoln, NE	151,575	150,582	100.7

Table continued on next page.

Metro Area	Males	Females	Males per 100 Females
Little Rock, AR	340,141	359,616	94.6
Los Angeles, CA	6,328,434	6,500,403	97.4
Madison, WI	282,224	286,369	98.6
Manchester, NH	198,162	202,559	97.8
Miami, FL	2,693,823	2,870,812	93.8
Minneapolis, MN	1,618,907	1,660,926	97.5
Murfreesboro, TN	777,473	812,461	95.7
Naperville, IL	4,622,870	4,838,235	95.5
Nashville, TN	777,473	812,461	95.7
New Orleans, LA	568,375	599,389	94.8
New York, NY	9,099,234	9,797,875	92.9
Norman, OK	617,347	635,640	97.1
Olathe, KS	996,319	1,039,015	95.9
Omaha, NE	426,917	438,433	97.4
Orlando, FL	1,044,696	1,089,715	95.9
Overland Park, KS	996,319	1,039,015	95.9
Oyster Bay, NY	9,099,234	9,797,875	92.9
Pembroke Pines, FL	2,693,823	2,870,812	93.8
Philadelphia, PA	2,878,862	3,086,481	93.3
Phoenix, AZ	2,085,630	2,107,257	99.0
Pittsburgh, PA	1,138,197	1,218,088	93.4
Plano, TX	3,141,634	3,230,139	97.3
Portland, OR	1,099,122	1,126,887	97.5
Providence, RI	773,916	826,936	93.6
Provo, UT	263,989	262,821	100.4
Raleigh, NC	552,108	578,382	95.5
Richmond, VA	608,491	649,760	93.6
Roseville, CA	1,053,450	1,095,677	96.1
Round Rock, TX	860,101	856,188	100.5
San Antonio, TX	1,052,485	1,090,023	96.6
San Diego, CA	1,553,679	1,541,634	100.8
San Francisco, CA	2,137,801	2,197,590	97.3
San Jose, CA	921,480	915,431	100.7
Savannah, GA	168,573	179,038	94.2
Scottsdale, AZ	2,085,630	2,107,257	99.0
Seattle, WA	1,711,982	1,727,827	99.1
Sioux Falls, SD	113,731	114,530	99.3
Stamford, CT	445,601	471,228	94.6
Sterling Hgts, MI	2,082,043	2,214,207	94.0
Sunnyvale, CA	921,480	915,431	100.7
Tampa, FL	1,347,513	1,435,730	93.9
Temecula, CA	2,101,083	2,123,768	98.9
Thousand Oaks, CA	408,969	414,349	98.7
Virginia Beach, VA	819,724	851,959	96.2
Washington, DC	2,716,483	2,865,687	94.8
U.S.	151,781,326	156,964,212	96.7

Note: Figures cover the Metropolitan Statistical Area (MSA)—see Appendix B for areas included
Source: U.S. Census Bureau, 2010 Census

Gross Metropolitan Product

MSA[1]	2007	2008	2009	2010	2010 Rank[2]
Albuquerque, NM	34.6	35.0	36.7	38.1	60
Alexandria, VA	384.3	400.0	409.6	426.1	4
Anchorage, AK	24.4	26.8	24.9	26.2	84
Ann Arbor, MI	18.2	17.4	18.0	19.0	107
Athens, GA	6.1	6.4	6.2	6.4	230
Atlanta, GA	271.9	274.2	265.2	270.6	10
Austin, TX	76.4	79.8	78.8	84.2	37
Baltimore, MD	134.0	137.6	139.1	144.4	19
Bellevue, WA	220.9	227.9	225.6	231.4	12
Billings, MT	7.4	7.2	7.1	7.2	216
Boise City, ID	25.6	25.6	24.9	25.5	87
Boston, MA	290.8	300.4	296.9	311.3	9
Boulder, CO	17.6	18.0	17.6	18.1	113
Broken Arrow, OK	43.4	46.9	43.4	44.6	55
Cambridge, MA	290.8	300.4	296.9	311.3	9
Cape Coral, FL	22.2	20.9	20.0	20.2	98
Carlsbad, CA	166.4	171.2	168.1	172.7	16
Cary, NC	51.3	53.0	53.6	56.1	49
Cedar Rapids, IA	13.1	12.8	13.3	14.0	139
Charleston, SC	26.2	26.7	26.8	27.9	78
Charlotte, NC	111.2	113.4	112.5	117.3	22
Chesapeake, VA	76.4	78.8	80.3	82.4	39
Chicago, IL	522.1	525.3	517.3	531.4	3
Clarksville, TN	9.1	9.6	10.0	10.9	163
Colorado Spgs., CO	23.9	24.5	25.2	26.4	81
Columbia, MD	134.0	137.6	139.1	144.4	19
Columbia, MO	6.2	6.4	6.6	6.9	219
Columbia, SC	30.4	30.8	31.3	32.2	69
Columbus, OH	89.3	89.7	90.5	93.9	31
Dallas, TX	358.1	370.8	358.3	376.8	6
Denver, CO	147.1	154.3	152.7	157.1	17
Durham, NC	33.5	33.8	35.0	36.3	62
Edison, NJ	1,215.9	1,242.1	1,217.4	1,282.6	1
El Paso, TX	25.3	25.7	26.5	28.7	75
Fargo, ND	9.7	10.5	10.6	11.4	158
Ft. Collins, CO	10.9	11.2	11.2	11.7	157
Ft. Worth, TX	358.1	370.8	358.3	376.8	6
Gilbert, AZ	196.4	196.0	187.4	190.6	15
Green Bay, WI	14.4	14.4	14.7	15.4	130
Henderson, NV	99.5	97.8	91.7	91.4	33
High Point, NC	32.2	32.7	32.5	34.0	65
Honolulu, HI	47.9	49.8	49.9	51.0	51
Houston, TX	373.3	396.5	364.9	378.9	5
Huntington, NY	1,215.9	1,242.1	1,217.4	1,282.6	1
Huntsville, AL	18.3	19.1	19.7	20.5	97
Indianapolis, IN	97.4	99.1	99.7	104.3	28
Irvine, CA	731.6	747.0	716.4	737.9	2
Jackson, MS	23.1	23.8	23.5	24.1	88
Jacksonville, FL	60.2	59.3	58.6	59.7	46
Jersey City, NJ	1,215.9	1,242.1	1,217.4	1,282.6	1
Kansas City, MO	101.2	103.9	103.1	105.6	26
Kenosha, WI	522.1	525.3	517.3	531.4	3
Las Vegas, NV	99.5	97.8	91.7	91.4	33
Lexington, KY	22.2	22.5	22.3	23.2	91
Lincoln, NE	13.4	13.5	14.0	14.5	137
Little Rock, AR	31.3	31.4	32.2	33.2	67

Table continued on next page.

MSA[1]	2007	2008	2009	2010	2010 Rank[2]
Los Angeles, CA	731.6	747.0	716.4	737.9	2
Madison, WI	33.0	33.6	34.9	36.4	61
Manchester, NH	20.1	21.1	20.9	21.1	95
Miami, FL	264.3	260.5	253.8	258.8	11
Minneapolis, MN	189.2	193.4	190.5	198.3	13
Murfreesboro, TN	75.4	77.9	76.4	80.3	40
Naperville, IL	522.1	525.3	517.3	531.4	3
Nashville, TN	75.4	77.9	76.4	80.3	40
New Orleans, LA	67.3	69.6	66.9	70.7	41
New York, NY	1,215.9	1,242.1	1,217.4	1,282.6	1
Norman, OK	54.4	59.4	56.4	58.6	48
Olathe, KS	101.2	103.9	103.1	105.6	26
Omaha, NE	44.7	45.4	46.6	48.0	52
Orlando, FL	104.1	103.6	101.2	103.6	29
Overland Park, KS	101.2	103.9	103.1	105.6	26
Oyster Bay, NY	1,215.9	1,242.1	1,217.4	1,282.6	1
Pembroke Pines, FL	264.3	260.5	253.8	258.8	11
Philadelphia, PA	325.3	332.0	335.7	347.7	7
Phoenix, AZ	196.4	196.0	187.4	190.6	15
Pittsburgh, PA	108.2	111.5	111.3	115.6	23
Plano, TX	358.1	370.8	358.3	376.8	6
Portland, OR	116.8	122.4	118.2	122.8	21
Providence, RI	63.8	64.8	64.3	66.8	42
Provo, UT	14.3	14.6	14.2	14.6	136
Raleigh, NC	51.3	53.0	53.6	56.1	49
Richmond, VA	60.3	61.9	62.0	63.8	45
Roseville, CA	95.3	94.7	92.5	93.5	32
Round Rock, TX	76.4	79.8	78.8	84.2	37
San Antonio, TX	75.9	78.2	78.1	82.7	38
San Diego, CA	166.4	171.2	168.1	172.7	16
San Francisco, CA	321.2	336.5	328.9	337.4	8
San Jose, CA	148.6	150.8	144.4	151.6	18
Savannah, GA	13.0	13.1	12.9	13.3	145
Scottsdale, AZ	196.4	196.0	187.4	190.6	15
Seattle, WA	220.9	227.9	225.6	231.4	12
Sioux Falls, SD	14.4	15.5	15.9	16.6	123
Stamford, CT	81.9	82.5	81.4	84.7	36
Sterling Hgts, MI	204.3	196.8	190.2	196.3	14
Sunnyvale, CA	148.6	150.8	144.4	151.6	18
Tampa, FL	114.1	112.6	111.9	113.9	24
Temecula, CA	114.8	112.9	108.4	110.8	25
Thousand Oaks, CA	36.0	34.6	34.3	35.5	63
Virginia Beach, VA	76.4	78.8	80.3	82.4	39
Washington, DC	384.3	400.0	409.6	426.1	4

Note: Figures are in billions of dollars; (1) Metropolitan Statistical Area—see Appendix B for areas included; (2) Rank ranges from 1 to 363.
Source: The U.S. Conference of Mayors, "U.S. Metro Economies: GMP and Employment Forecasts," June 2011

Income: City

City	Per Capita ($)	Median Household ($)	Average Household ($)
Albuquerque, NM	25,612	46,532	61,500
Alexandria, VA	52,547	80,173	108,615
Anchorage, AK	34,999	74,272	92,007
Ann Arbor, MI	29,404	51,783	72,710
Athens, GA	19,023	33,750	51,082
Atlanta, GA	34,475	44,771	77,979
Austin, TX	29,655	50,147	71,045
Baltimore, MD	22,975	39,113	55,603
Bellevue, WA	45,470	81,113	107,984
Billings, MT	26,556	46,065	61,537
Boise City, ID	27,221	48,506	64,930
Boston, MA	32,261	50,710	75,571
Boulder, CO	36,036	52,276	84,329
Broken Arrow, OK	29,127	64,460	79,824
Cambridge, MA	45,176	67,271	99,495
Cape Coral, FL	23,541	49,111	61,493
Carlsbad, CA	42,012	83,238	105,409
Cary, NC	41,322	88,629	110,715
Cedar Rapids, IA	27,714	50,870	65,172
Charleston, SC	30,487	48,773	69,871
Charlotte, NC	30,453	51,419	75,239
Chesapeake, VA	29,503	68,058	80,745
Chicago, IL	26,967	46,195	68,091
Clarksville, TN	20,151	45,676	53,286
Colorado Spgs., CO	27,753	52,179	68,046
Columbia, MD	44,258	93,888	110,184
Columbia, MO	23,833	40,816	58,141
Columbia, SC	23,958	36,546	58,642
Columbus, OH	22,884	42,368	54,316
Dallas, TX	26,032	41,011	66,620
Denver, CO	30,806	45,526	68,791
Durham, NC	26,282	46,556	63,483
Edison, NJ	36,223	86,282	106,245
El Paso, TX	18,119	37,836	52,689
Fargo, ND	26,851	42,144	59,185
Ft. Collins, CO	27,491	49,512	67,958
Ft. Worth, TX	23,482	48,970	64,403
Gilbert, AZ	30,005	75,895	88,751
Green Bay, WI	22,864	41,443	54,422
Henderson, NV	34,075	65,047	84,449
High Point, NC	21,447	42,587	54,636
Honolulu, HI	29,609	55,809	74,676
Houston, TX	25,700	43,349	67,252
Huntington, NY	45,590	101,495	132,016
Huntsville, AL	29,582	47,238	68,304
Indianapolis, IN	23,449	41,170	56,963
Irvine, CA	41,175	88,571	111,618
Jackson, MS	18,454	33,465	49,136
Jacksonville, FL	24,478	47,356	61,797
Jersey City, NJ	31,066	56,119	78,143
Kansas City, MO	25,666	43,587	59,427
Kenosha, WI	22,383	45,669	57,608
Las Vegas, NV	25,549	52,382	68,296
Lexington, KY	27,881	47,104	65,440
Lincoln, NE	24,981	48,203	61,452
Little Rock, AR	28,505	42,466	66,098

Table continued on next page.

City	Per Capita ($)	Median Household ($)	Average Household ($)
Los Angeles, CA	27,346	48,746	75,691
Madison, WI	29,929	51,822	67,341
Manchester, NH	26,980	51,643	64,363
Miami, FL	19,723	28,506	48,561
Minneapolis, MN	29,233	46,232	65,395
Murfreesboro, TN	24,152	47,662	61,727
Naperville, IL	44,331	99,488	126,695
Nashville, TN	26,153	44,630	61,792
New Orleans, LA	24,721	36,208	57,174
New York, NY	30,394	50,038	77,940
Norman, OK	26,485	44,634	66,513
Olathe, KS	30,311	74,320	85,603
Omaha, NE	25,872	45,115	63,175
Orlando, FL	24,643	40,669	57,840
Overland Park, KS	39,170	70,775	92,434
Oyster Bay, NY	46,295	104,110	135,820
Pembroke Pines, FL	26,976	59,968	74,235
Philadelphia, PA	21,061	35,952	50,877
Phoenix, AZ	23,626	47,187	65,034
Pittsburgh, PA	25,233	36,723	55,937
Plano, TX	39,482	80,210	104,026
Portland, OR	29,634	49,326	67,714
Providence, RI	20,513	36,831	55,831
Provo, UT	16,130	38,807	55,571
Raleigh, NC	29,216	51,173	71,402
Richmond, VA	25,814	37,236	59,299
Roseville, CA	32,249	72,857	84,691
Round Rock, TX	27,502	62,664	76,488
San Antonio, TX	21,613	42,656	58,406
San Diego, CA	31,981	61,282	83,172
San Francisco, CA	45,078	71,779	102,227
San Jose, CA	32,237	78,149	97,994
Savannah, GA	19,464	32,699	47,361
Scottsdale, AZ	49,337	71,021	106,734
Seattle, WA	40,894	60,619	85,727
Sioux Falls, SD	27,561	50,415	67,611
Stamford, CT	41,227	73,965	108,992
Sterling Hgts, MI	25,603	54,569	66,463
Sunnyvale, CA	43,937	90,701	110,963
Tampa, FL	27,186	42,359	65,617
Temecula, CA	27,706	72,433	86,415
Thousand Oaks, CA	44,263	99,980	122,170
Virginia Beach, VA	30,763	64,065	79,801
Washington, DC	42,066	59,822	92,555
U.S.	26,942	51,222	70,116

Source: U.S. Census Bureau, 2008-2010 American Community Survey 3-Year Estimates

Income: Metro Area

Metro Area	Per Capita ($)	Median Household ($)	Average Household ($)
Albuquerque, NM	25,216	48,047	63,525
Alexandria, VA	41,347	85,258	109,531
Anchorage, AK	33,461	73,412	89,351
Ann Arbor, MI	30,596	56,708	76,345
Athens, GA	21,326	40,220	59,125
Atlanta, GA	28,075	56,448	75,563
Austin, TX	29,482	56,732	76,321
Baltimore, MD	33,200	65,817	85,525
Bellevue, WA	33,755	64,821	83,560
Billings, MT	26,386	47,959	62,687
Boise City, ID	23,502	50,026	63,351
Boston, MA	36,714	69,784	93,357
Boulder, CO	37,099	64,314	89,944
Broken Arrow, OK	25,182	46,570	62,846
Cambridge, MA	36,714	69,784	93,357
Cape Coral, FL	27,392	47,232	66,948
Carlsbad, CA	29,792	61,469	82,033
Cary, NC	29,979	59,695	78,205
Cedar Rapids, IA	27,843	54,226	68,232
Charleston, SC	26,132	49,606	66,540
Charlotte, NC	28,220	52,321	72,717
Chesapeake, VA	27,943	57,262	72,109
Chicago, IL	29,963	59,707	80,417
Clarksville, TN	20,524	43,491	53,321
Colorado Spgs., CO	27,391	55,166	70,491
Columbia, MD	33,200	65,817	85,525
Columbia, MO	24,837	44,788	61,482
Columbia, SC	24,841	47,511	62,437
Columbus, OH	27,252	52,324	69,132
Dallas, TX	28,035	55,740	76,630
Denver, CO	31,829	59,919	79,382
Durham, NC	28,337	50,686	70,504
Edison, NJ	34,332	63,263	91,988
El Paso, TX	16,991	36,647	51,077
Fargo, ND	26,809	48,455	63,392
Ft. Collins, CO	29,733	55,896	73,201
Ft. Worth, TX	28,035	55,740	76,630
Gilbert, AZ	26,243	52,904	70,586
Green Bay, WI	26,427	50,989	65,233
Henderson, NV	26,211	54,458	69,877
High Point, NC	23,950	42,611	59,312
Honolulu, HI	29,303	70,356	86,269
Houston, TX	27,447	55,408	77,596
Huntington, NY	34,332	63,263	91,988
Huntsville, AL	29,179	53,974	72,853
Indianapolis, IN	27,020	51,571	69,019
Irvine, CA	28,405	59,129	83,389
Jackson, MS	23,237	45,116	61,506
Jacksonville, FL	26,678	51,663	68,189
Jersey City, NJ	34,332	63,263	91,988
Kansas City, MO	28,429	55,308	71,149
Kenosha, WI	29,963	59,707	80,417
Las Vegas, NV	26,211	54,458	69,877
Lexington, KY	26,994	48,188	65,255
Lincoln, NE	25,858	50,644	64,425
Little Rock, AR	25,016	46,076	61,616

Table continued on next page.

Metro Area	Per Capita ($)	Median Household ($)	Average Household ($)
Los Angeles, CA	28,405	59,129	83,389
Madison, WI	31,284	59,011	74,554
Manchester, NH	33,061	67,792	84,122
Miami, FL	26,283	47,086	68,986
Minneapolis, MN	32,422	63,927	82,191
Murfreesboro, TN	26,953	50,837	68,640
Naperville, IL	29,963	59,707	80,417
Nashville, TN	26,953	50,837	68,640
New Orleans, LA	25,870	46,210	64,705
New York, NY	34,332	63,263	91,988
Norman, OK	25,070	46,894	63,378
Olathe, KS	28,429	55,308	71,149
Omaha, NE	27,467	54,318	69,611
Orlando, FL	24,530	48,450	65,091
Overland Park, KS	28,429	55,308	71,149
Oyster Bay, NY	34,332	63,263	91,988
Pembroke Pines, FL	26,283	47,086	68,986
Philadelphia, PA	31,198	60,037	80,924
Phoenix, AZ	26,243	52,904	70,586
Pittsburgh, PA	27,453	47,549	64,272
Plano, TX	28,035	55,740	76,630
Portland, OR	28,651	55,618	72,200
Providence, RI	28,160	53,914	70,571
Provo, UT	20,098	56,594	70,927
Raleigh, NC	29,979	59,695	78,205
Richmond, VA	29,475	56,608	75,408
Roseville, CA	27,995	58,733	75,256
Round Rock, TX	29,482	56,732	76,321
San Antonio, TX	23,641	49,112	65,016
San Diego, CA	29,792	61,469	82,033
San Francisco, CA	39,207	74,809	102,229
San Jose, CA	38,679	85,799	111,612
Savannah, GA	24,660	47,505	62,789
Scottsdale, AZ	26,243	52,904	70,586
Seattle, WA	33,755	64,821	83,560
Sioux Falls, SD	27,502	54,069	69,244
Stamford, CT	47,283	80,122	127,756
Sterling Hgts, MI	26,370	50,439	67,151
Sunnyvale, CA	38,679	85,799	111,612
Tampa, FL	25,801	45,104	61,685
Temecula, CA	22,415	55,116	71,049
Thousand Oaks, CA	31,679	73,907	94,648
Virginia Beach, VA	27,943	57,262	72,109
Washington, DC	41,347	85,258	109,531
U.S.	26,942	51,222	70,116

Note: Figures cover the Metropolitan Statistical Area (MSA)—see Appendix B for areas included
Source: U.S. Census Bureau, 2008-2010 American Community Survey 3-Year Estimates

Household Income Distribution: City

City	Percent of Households Earning							
	Under $15,000	$15,000 -24,999	$25,000 -34,999	$35,000 -49,999	$50,000 -74,999	$75,000 -99,000	$100,000 -149,999	$150,000 and up
Albuquerque, NM	14.2	11.8	11.7	15.1	19.0	11.0	10.9	6.2
Alexandria, VA	6.4	5.7	6.2	10.0	18.5	13.8	19.5	19.8
Anchorage, AK	6.0	5.6	8.5	11.7	18.9	15.9	19.0	14.5
Ann Arbor, MI	16.3	9.0	9.3	13.2	18.3	10.3	12.4	11.2
Athens, GA	27.2	14.0	10.2	13.6	15.4	7.2	6.8	5.7
Atlanta, GA	21.0	11.0	10.2	11.4	14.7	9.0	10.4	12.3
Austin, TX	13.8	10.2	11.0	15.0	17.7	11.2	11.6	9.5
Baltimore, MD	21.5	12.5	11.7	14.1	17.6	9.2	8.1	5.2
Bellevue, WA	6.9	5.7	6.0	10.1	17.5	12.9	19.7	21.2
Billings, MT	11.4	13.4	12.2	16.9	19.9	11.5	9.9	4.9
Boise City, ID	12.9	10.7	12.0	15.6	19.3	12.0	10.7	6.8
Boston, MA	20.3	9.2	8.3	11.6	15.7	10.7	12.7	11.6
Boulder, CO	15.5	11.3	10.5	11.5	15.1	9.4	12.5	14.3
Broken Arrow, OK	5.2	7.1	8.4	14.7	22.8	16.9	16.4	8.5
Cambridge, MA	14.7	8.5	6.9	9.7	14.5	11.7	16.5	17.5
Cape Coral, FL	9.5	11.3	12.9	17.0	22.0	12.5	10.2	4.5
Carlsbad, CA	6.8	6.2	6.5	11.7	15.3	11.5	20.5	21.4
Cary, NC	4.4	5.4	7.1	9.5	16.3	12.7	21.6	23.0
Cedar Rapids, IA	10.9	11.5	11.2	15.4	21.0	12.8	11.5	5.7
Charleston, SC	16.5	10.2	9.9	14.3	17.0	12.2	11.0	8.8
Charlotte, NC	11.5	10.7	11.0	15.3	19.8	10.8	11.6	9.5
Chesapeake, VA	7.8	7.0	8.3	12.1	20.1	16.3	18.7	9.6
Chicago, IL	17.6	12.0	10.1	13.2	17.2	10.8	10.5	8.7
Clarksville, TN	14.9	10.4	11.8	18.1	22.3	11.8	8.1	2.7
Colorado Spgs., CO	11.9	11.0	10.4	14.2	20.6	11.7	13.0	7.3
Columbia, MD	5.1	4.0	5.4	7.8	16.5	14.9	21.6	24.7
Columbia, MO	19.1	12.5	11.8	13.3	18.7	9.4	9.8	5.3
Columbia, SC	20.6	14.2	13.5	14.1	14.1	8.7	8.3	6.6
Columbus, OH	17.4	12.3	11.6	16.0	19.3	10.7	8.7	4.0
Dallas, TX	16.3	13.6	13.0	15.1	16.4	8.5	8.3	8.7
Denver, CO	16.6	11.9	11.0	14.2	16.3	10.5	10.3	9.2
Durham, NC	14.5	11.8	11.0	15.6	17.3	10.8	12.1	6.9
Edison, NJ	6.5	4.6	5.9	8.9	18.3	13.3	20.8	21.8
El Paso, TX	19.0	15.0	12.6	15.3	16.6	8.9	8.5	4.1
Fargo, ND	15.9	11.4	13.7	16.3	18.0	10.0	9.0	5.6
Ft. Collins, CO	14.6	11.4	9.8	14.5	17.1	11.8	13.1	7.6
Ft. Worth, TX	13.5	12.0	11.1	14.2	19.5	12.1	11.1	6.4
Gilbert, AZ	4.7	4.9	6.6	12.5	20.6	16.6	22.6	11.5
Green Bay, WI	14.5	13.3	12.9	17.9	20.2	10.1	8.0	2.9
Henderson, NV	8.2	6.6	8.4	13.8	20.5	13.7	17.2	11.6
High Point, NC	17.7	12.8	11.3	16.1	19.0	9.2	9.3	4.7
Honolulu, HI	11.7	9.4	10.3	13.2	18.3	13.7	13.8	9.6
Houston, TX	15.4	13.4	12.3	14.3	17.0	9.6	9.4	8.6
Huntington, NY	4.4	5.3	4.7	7.7	14.2	12.4	21.0	30.4
Huntsville, AL	15.3	12.5	11.1	13.1	16.7	10.7	12.2	8.3
Indianapolis, IN	15.8	13.6	13.9	15.2	17.6	10.1	9.0	4.8
Irvine, CA	9.6	5.2	4.7	6.7	15.3	14.0	21.3	23.1
Jackson, MS	22.8	15.8	13.3	15.3	15.0	7.5	6.3	4.1
Jacksonville, FL	13.5	11.4	12.0	15.1	20.1	12.4	10.1	5.3
Jersey City, NJ	15.1	9.9	9.1	11.1	17.5	10.6	13.8	12.8
Kansas City, MO	16.5	11.8	12.8	14.9	17.2	10.5	10.9	5.2
Kenosha, WI	14.3	12.5	12.8	15.0	18.9	11.8	10.3	4.3
Las Vegas, NV	11.9	10.2	11.1	14.3	20.5	12.5	12.1	7.3
Lexington, KY	15.5	12.0	11.7	13.0	17.9	11.6	10.9	7.5

Table continued on next page.

City	Percent of Households Earning							
	Under $15,000	$15,000 -24,999	$25,000 -34,999	$35,000 -49,999	$50,000 -74,999	$75,000 -99,000	$100,000 -149,999	$150,000 and up
Lincoln, NE	13.2	12.1	11.7	14.5	20.8	12.1	10.6	5.1
Little Rock, AR	16.6	12.0	12.5	15.6	16.2	9.9	8.8	8.4
Los Angeles, CA	15.0	12.0	10.4	13.5	16.6	10.5	11.4	10.6
Madison, WI	14.6	10.2	9.6	13.7	18.6	13.7	12.0	7.5
Manchester, NH	10.7	11.5	10.6	15.5	20.3	14.8	11.3	5.4
Miami, FL	28.6	16.7	12.0	13.4	12.6	6.0	5.5	5.2
Minneapolis, MN	18.0	11.2	10.2	13.4	17.8	10.9	10.7	7.8
Murfreesboro, TN	14.7	10.7	10.2	16.4	17.8	12.9	12.3	5.1
Naperville, IL	3.9	4.0	5.3	8.0	15.6	13.4	21.5	28.4
Nashville, TN	15.2	12.0	11.9	16.4	18.7	10.5	8.9	6.4
New Orleans, LA	22.6	14.7	11.5	13.7	15.1	8.0	8.2	6.3
New York, NY	17.1	10.8	9.7	12.4	16.3	10.7	11.8	11.3
Norman, OK	15.0	13.2	11.1	15.6	15.7	11.8	10.2	7.4
Olathe, KS	5.2	6.8	7.6	10.6	20.5	17.4	20.9	11.0
Omaha, NE	13.9	12.5	12.6	15.1	18.8	11.3	9.5	6.2
Orlando, FL	14.5	13.8	13.2	18.4	17.9	8.6	7.7	6.0
Overland Park, KS	6.2	7.0	8.1	12.2	19.4	14.7	16.7	15.6
Oyster Bay, NY	4.0	5.3	5.1	8.2	12.6	12.7	21.9	30.1
Pembroke Pines, FL	9.4	9.8	8.9	13.2	18.9	14.7	15.5	9.6
Philadelphia, PA	24.2	13.5	11.3	13.9	16.2	9.2	7.3	4.4
Phoenix, AZ	14.3	11.3	11.7	15.3	17.8	11.3	11.3	7.1
Pittsburgh, PA	22.2	14.9	11.2	14.4	15.7	8.6	7.1	5.9
Plano, TX	5.7	7.1	6.7	10.5	16.9	13.6	19.7	19.8
Portland, OR	14.8	11.0	10.3	14.4	18.6	11.3	11.4	8.1
Providence, RI	24.0	12.8	10.3	14.8	16.1	8.2	7.5	6.3
Provo, UT	16.6	14.4	14.4	16.1	17.9	8.8	7.1	4.6
Raleigh, NC	10.9	11.3	10.9	15.6	18.4	12.0	11.8	9.1
Richmond, VA	21.5	14.3	11.5	15.1	15.6	8.7	6.9	6.4
Roseville, CA	7.1	6.5	8.5	12.0	17.0	15.1	20.2	13.7
Round Rock, TX	4.5	8.0	10.1	15.0	21.8	15.4	16.6	8.5
San Antonio, TX	16.7	12.8	12.0	15.0	18.0	10.7	9.1	5.5
San Diego, CA	11.2	8.9	8.3	12.8	17.6	13.4	14.7	13.2
San Francisco, CA	13.1	8.2	6.9	9.4	14.1	11.7	16.0	20.6
San Jose, CA	8.0	7.0	6.6	10.7	15.6	13.3	18.9	19.8
Savannah, GA	23.3	15.5	13.9	13.6	16.1	8.0	6.7	2.9
Scottsdale, AZ	8.2	8.4	8.2	12.0	16.0	12.3	15.1	19.9
Seattle, WA	12.0	8.5	8.4	12.9	17.4	12.5	14.5	13.9
Sioux Falls, SD	11.6	9.9	11.9	16.2	21.0	13.5	9.3	6.6
Stamford, CT	9.0	9.1	5.5	10.4	16.7	14.0	14.8	20.6
Sterling Hgts, MI	10.0	9.8	9.5	15.7	20.6	14.8	13.4	6.3
Sunnyvale, CA	6.0	5.7	5.3	8.3	14.9	14.6	20.4	25.0
Tampa, FL	17.3	13.1	11.5	15.1	16.1	9.1	9.0	8.8
Temecula, CA	7.8	6.7	7.0	10.8	19.2	14.6	21.4	12.6
Thousand Oaks, CA	5.7	5.3	5.9	8.0	12.9	12.3	22.4	27.6
Virginia Beach, VA	6.2	6.4	8.7	15.4	22.4	15.5	15.9	9.4
Washington, DC	15.9	7.9	7.7	11.6	15.6	11.2	12.9	17.3
U.S.	13.0	11.0	10.6	14.2	18.5	12.1	12.2	8.4

Source: U.S. Census Bureau, 2008-2010 American Community Survey 3-Year Estimates

Household Income Distribution: Metro Area

Metro Area	Under $15,000	$15,000 -24,999	$25,000 -34,999	$35,000 -49,999	$50,000 -74,999	$75,000 -99,000	$100,000 -149,999	$150,000 and up
				Percent of Households Earning				
Albuquerque, NM	13.7	11.6	11.1	15.2	18.9	11.6	11.4	6.6
Alexandria, VA	6.6	5.0	5.7	10.1	16.4	13.8	20.0	22.4
Anchorage, AK	6.4	6.0	8.4	11.7	18.8	16.1	19.2	13.4
Ann Arbor, MI	12.2	9.3	9.6	12.9	17.8	12.6	14.7	10.9
Athens, GA	21.3	12.6	10.3	14.0	16.1	9.5	9.1	7.0
Atlanta, GA	11.1	9.2	10.1	13.8	19.3	12.9	13.6	10.2
Austin, TX	11.0	9.0	9.7	14.2	18.9	12.9	14.0	10.2
Baltimore, MD	10.1	7.6	8.2	11.9	18.2	13.6	16.7	13.6
Bellevue, WA	9.1	7.8	8.4	12.9	18.9	14.1	16.6	12.2
Billings, MT	10.6	13.5	11.6	16.0	20.5	12.1	10.5	5.0
Boise City, ID	11.7	11.1	11.8	15.3	21.6	12.4	10.2	5.9
Boston, MA	11.1	7.6	7.3	10.8	16.5	13.1	17.5	16.1
Boulder, CO	10.0	8.7	9.2	12.3	16.5	12.1	15.9	15.2
Broken Arrow, OK	13.3	12.0	12.2	15.4	19.1	11.9	10.1	5.9
Cambridge, MA	11.1	7.6	7.3	10.8	16.5	13.1	17.5	16.1
Cape Coral, FL	11.6	12.0	11.9	17.2	18.9	11.6	10.0	6.8
Carlsbad, CA	9.9	8.8	9.0	13.4	17.7	13.5	15.3	12.5
Cary, NC	9.3	9.3	9.7	13.7	18.9	13.5	14.8	10.8
Cedar Rapids, IA	9.3	10.5	10.8	15.3	20.3	14.4	13.2	6.3
Charleston, SC	13.4	11.3	10.5	15.2	18.3	12.9	11.2	7.3
Charlotte, NC	11.4	10.4	10.6	15.1	19.2	12.0	12.3	8.9
Chesapeake, VA	9.5	9.1	9.7	14.7	20.8	14.2	14.2	7.8
Chicago, IL	10.9	9.5	9.1	12.8	18.3	13.4	14.7	11.3
Clarksville, TN	15.0	11.4	13.2	17.1	20.3	12.0	8.4	2.6
Colorado Spgs., CO	10.8	9.9	9.7	14.3	20.9	12.7	14.1	7.8
Columbia, MD	10.1	7.6	8.2	11.9	18.2	13.6	16.7	13.6
Columbia, MO	15.9	12.3	11.3	14.4	19.8	11.1	9.9	5.3
Columbia, SC	13.7	11.8	11.5	15.2	19.2	12.2	11.0	5.5
Columbus, OH	12.5	10.4	10.4	14.5	19.4	12.2	12.6	8.0
Dallas, TX	10.3	10.1	10.2	14.0	18.7	12.5	13.8	10.2
Denver, CO	10.6	9.0	9.3	13.3	18.3	13.3	15.2	11.0
Durham, NC	13.4	10.8	10.9	14.2	16.9	12.2	12.5	9.0
Edison, NJ	12.2	8.9	8.3	11.3	16.2	12.0	15.4	15.8
El Paso, TX	19.2	15.7	13.0	15.5	16.3	8.5	8.0	3.8
Fargo, ND	13.3	10.7	12.0	15.5	19.5	13.0	10.7	5.4
Ft. Collins, CO	12.2	9.7	9.3	13.8	19.0	13.0	14.1	8.8
Ft. Worth, TX	10.3	10.1	10.2	14.0	18.7	12.5	13.8	10.2
Gilbert, AZ	11.1	10.1	10.7	15.1	19.5	12.7	12.9	7.9
Green Bay, WI	10.5	11.2	10.6	16.7	20.7	14.3	10.9	5.1
Henderson, NV	10.0	9.6	11.0	14.9	21.0	13.4	12.8	7.4
High Point, NC	14.9	12.8	13.2	16.2	18.3	10.4	8.8	5.5
Honolulu, HI	8.4	7.0	7.8	11.8	18.3	15.4	18.4	12.9
Houston, TX	11.1	10.5	10.3	13.4	17.8	12.2	13.5	11.1
Huntington, NY	12.2	8.9	8.3	11.3	16.2	12.0	15.4	15.8
Huntsville, AL	11.8	10.8	10.2	13.5	17.5	12.0	14.8	9.3
Indianapolis, IN	11.4	11.1	11.2	14.7	18.7	12.7	12.7	7.4
Irvine, CA	11.1	9.9	9.2	12.7	17.5	12.3	14.4	12.7
Jackson, MS	16.1	12.6	11.1	14.8	17.7	11.6	10.2	5.9
Jacksonville, FL	11.9	10.2	11.1	14.9	20.3	12.8	11.8	7.0
Jersey City, NJ	12.2	8.9	8.3	11.3	16.2	12.0	15.4	15.8
Kansas City, MO	10.9	10.0	10.4	14.0	19.5	13.5	13.8	7.8
Kenosha, WI	10.9	9.5	9.1	12.8	18.3	13.4	14.7	11.3
Las Vegas, NV	10.0	9.6	11.0	14.9	21.0	13.4	12.8	7.4
Lexington, KY	15.0	11.2	11.5	13.8	18.9	11.4	11.2	7.0

Table continued on next page.

Metro Area	Percent of Households Earning							
	Under $15,000	$15,000 -24,999	$25,000 -34,999	$35,000 -49,999	$50,000 -74,999	$75,000 -99,000	$100,000 -149,999	$150,000 and up
Lincoln, NE	12.2	11.3	11.6	14.2	20.7	13.1	11.2	5.7
Little Rock, AR	14.1	11.8	12.0	15.8	19.0	11.5	10.2	5.6
Los Angeles, CA	11.1	9.9	9.2	12.7	17.5	12.3	14.4	12.7
Madison, WI	10.2	9.2	9.4	13.0	20.3	15.3	14.4	8.1
Manchester, NH	7.7	8.0	7.7	12.8	18.6	15.3	17.7	12.1
Miami, FL	14.7	11.9	11.3	14.5	17.7	10.7	10.9	8.4
Minneapolis, MN	9.0	8.0	8.7	12.8	19.4	15.0	15.9	11.2
Murfreesboro, TN	12.4	10.3	10.7	15.7	19.4	12.4	11.4	7.6
Naperville, IL	10.9	9.5	9.1	12.8	18.3	13.4	14.7	11.3
Nashville, TN	12.4	10.3	10.7	15.7	19.4	12.4	11.4	7.6
New Orleans, LA	15.4	12.3	11.2	14.5	17.2	11.0	11.4	7.0
New York, NY	12.2	8.9	8.3	11.3	16.2	12.0	15.4	15.8
Norman, OK	13.5	12.2	11.7	15.2	19.3	11.4	10.5	6.0
Olathe, KS	10.9	10.0	10.4	14.0	19.5	13.5	13.8	7.8
Omaha, NE	10.8	10.2	10.6	14.2	20.0	13.8	13.3	7.0
Orlando, FL	11.5	11.5	12.4	16.0	19.9	11.3	10.7	6.8
Overland Park, KS	10.9	10.0	10.4	14.0	19.5	13.5	13.8	7.8
Oyster Bay, NY	12.2	8.9	8.3	11.3	16.2	12.0	15.4	15.8
Pembroke Pines, FL	14.7	11.9	11.3	14.5	17.7	10.7	10.9	8.4
Philadelphia, PA	12.1	9.1	8.9	12.2	17.4	13.1	15.1	12.1
Phoenix, AZ	11.1	10.1	10.7	15.1	19.5	12.7	12.9	7.9
Pittsburgh, PA	13.8	12.7	11.2	14.4	18.8	11.8	10.7	6.6
Plano, TX	10.3	10.1	10.2	14.0	18.7	12.5	13.8	10.2
Portland, OR	10.7	9.6	10.0	14.5	19.9	13.4	13.6	8.4
Providence, RI	14.2	10.3	9.2	12.7	17.9	13.2	14.0	8.5
Provo, UT	8.8	9.2	9.6	15.4	22.3	14.2	13.5	7.0
Raleigh, NC	9.3	9.3	9.7	13.7	18.9	13.5	14.8	10.8
Richmond, VA	10.4	9.2	9.7	14.7	19.2	13.4	14.0	9.5
Roseville, CA	10.0	9.4	9.8	13.3	19.1	13.3	15.1	10.0
Round Rock, TX	11.0	9.0	9.7	14.2	18.9	12.9	14.0	10.2
San Antonio, TX	14.1	11.2	11.0	14.5	18.9	12.3	11.1	6.9
San Diego, CA	9.9	8.8	9.0	13.4	17.7	13.5	15.3	12.5
San Francisco, CA	9.5	7.5	7.0	10.3	15.8	12.3	17.5	20.1
San Jose, CA	7.2	6.4	6.0	9.5	14.6	12.7	19.4	24.2
Savannah, GA	14.4	11.9	11.2	14.4	19.0	11.6	11.8	5.7
Scottsdale, AZ	11.1	10.1	10.7	15.1	19.5	12.7	12.9	7.9
Seattle, WA	9.1	7.8	8.4	12.9	18.9	14.1	16.6	12.2
Sioux Falls, SD	10.2	9.1	11.2	15.8	22.1	14.8	10.6	6.2
Stamford, CT	9.0	7.0	6.7	9.7	14.9	12.0	16.8	23.9
Sterling Hgts, MI	13.8	11.1	10.6	14.1	18.2	12.3	12.4	7.6
Sunnyvale, CA	7.2	6.4	6.0	9.5	14.6	12.7	19.4	24.2
Tampa, FL	13.2	13.0	12.2	16.2	18.8	10.9	9.5	6.1
Temecula, CA	10.7	10.4	10.2	13.8	19.2	13.1	14.0	8.4
Thousand Oaks, CA	7.3	7.5	7.6	10.9	17.3	13.7	19.1	16.7
Virginia Beach, VA	9.5	9.1	9.7	14.7	20.8	14.2	14.2	7.8
Washington, DC	6.6	5.0	5.7	10.1	16.4	13.8	20.0	22.4
U.S.	13.0	11.0	10.6	14.2	18.5	12.1	12.2	8.4

Note: Figures cover the Metropolitan Statistical Area (MSA)—see Appendix B for areas included
Source: Source: U.S. Census Bureau, 2008-2010 American Community Survey 3-Year Estimates

Poverty Rate: City

City	All Ages	Under 18 Years Old	18 to 64 Years Old	65 Years and Over
Albuquerque, NM	16.3	23.5	14.6	11.0
Alexandria, VA	9.0	15.5	7.6	8.8
Anchorage, AK	7.7	10.1	7.1	4.5
Ann Arbor, MI	20.8	14.6	24.0	7.0
Athens, GA	36.2	36.3	39.1	11.6
Atlanta, GA	23.8	35.3	20.9	20.8
Austin, TX	19.2	26.1	18.0	8.7
Baltimore, MD	22.7	32.0	20.3	18.3
Bellevue, WA	5.8	4.1	6.1	6.9
Billings, MT	12.5	19.8	11.1	7.0
Boise City, ID	14.2	17.7	13.9	8.6
Boston, MA	21.1	26.7	19.8	20.7
Boulder, CO	20.1	12.5	23.4	6.3
Broken Arrow, OK	6.0	9.3	4.7	4.5
Cambridge, MA	14.6	14.5	15.2	10.3
Cape Coral, FL	12.1	18.0	10.8	8.9
Carlsbad, CA	8.0	10.3	8.1	3.3
Cary, NC	5.1	5.5	4.9	4.9
Cedar Rapids, IA	11.9	15.9	11.4	6.9
Charleston, SC	18.4	26.2	17.8	9.9
Charlotte, NC	14.9	20.9	13.6	7.5
Chesapeake, VA	6.9	9.7	5.4	8.8
Chicago, IL	21.5	31.8	18.6	17.3
Clarksville, TN	17.1	23.9	14.7	11.1
Colorado Spgs., CO	13.0	18.1	12.1	6.1
Columbia, MD	6.3	7.4	5.7	7.6
Columbia, MO	23.2	16.4	27.3	5.3
Columbia, SC	23.6	31.2	23.1	13.4
Columbus, OH	22.1	30.9	20.1	13.2
Dallas, TX	23.2	36.1	19.2	13.0
Denver, CO	19.8	30.1	17.2	15.0
Durham, NC	18.5	24.8	17.4	9.8
Edison, NJ	8.2	11.3	7.5	5.1
El Paso, TX	22.6	32.2	18.4	19.5
Fargo, ND	15.5	14.2	16.7	9.2
Ft. Collins, CO	18.4	13.2	21.4	6.6
Ft. Worth, TX	17.9	25.8	15.0	11.4
Gilbert, AZ	6.3	8.1	5.8	2.9
Green Bay, WI	14.8	19.7	14.2	6.9
Henderson, NV	8.0	10.3	7.2	7.5
High Point, NC	20.2	29.7	18.1	9.0
Honolulu, HI	11.7	14.1	12.0	8.3
Houston, TX	21.1	32.6	17.5	13.8
Huntington, NY	4.3	4.3	4.5	3.7
Huntsville, AL	16.4	24.4	15.7	7.1
Indianapolis, IN	19.4	28.7	17.4	8.8
Irvine, CA	10.9	7.1	12.4	8.2
Jackson, MS	26.9	38.8	23.3	15.4
Jacksonville, FL	15.2	22.0	13.5	9.8
Jersey City, NJ	17.4	26.7	14.8	15.4
Kansas City, MO	18.2	26.9	16.3	10.7
Kenosha, WI	15.7	22.2	13.9	9.6
Las Vegas, NV	14.6	20.3	13.3	9.1
Lexington, KY	18.1	23.3	18.0	8.6
Lincoln, NE	15.6	19.5	15.8	6.5

Table continued on next page.

City	All Ages	Under 18 Years Old	18 to 64 Years Old	65 Years and Over
Little Rock, AR	19.0	28.6	16.6	11.7
Los Angeles, CA	20.2	29.2	17.9	14.2
Madison, WI	18.5	16.2	21.0	4.4
Manchester, NH	13.6	24.0	11.1	8.6
Miami, FL	28.6	38.9	24.5	33.3
Minneapolis, MN	22.9	32.3	21.1	15.6
Murfreesboro, TN	18.3	21.5	18.8	5.5
Naperville, IL	3.7	4.4	3.2	4.9
Nashville, TN	18.8	30.3	16.3	10.4
New Orleans, LA	25.8	39.1	23.0	16.5
New York, NY	19.4	28.4	16.6	18.2
Norman, OK	17.3	16.5	19.1	5.9
Olathe, KS	6.9	8.4	6.3	6.3
Omaha, NE	15.8	22.2	14.3	9.5
Orlando, FL	17.7	24.3	16.2	13.9
Overland Park, KS	5.7	8.3	4.8	4.8
Oyster Bay, NY	3.2	3.4	3.2	2.8
Pembroke Pines, FL	7.9	9.8	6.7	10.3
Philadelphia, PA	25.6	34.6	23.7	18.4
Phoenix, AZ	20.7	29.8	18.1	9.7
Pittsburgh, PA	22.8	32.1	22.5	12.3
Plano, TX	7.9	11.1	6.7	6.9
Portland, OR	16.7	21.4	16.0	12.6
Providence, RI	27.1	35.0	24.8	21.7
Provo, UT	31.2	17.9	37.4	7.4
Raleigh, NC	16.2	21.8	15.3	7.5
Richmond, VA	27.4	42.3	25.3	14.6
Roseville, CA	8.3	10.2	7.3	8.7
Round Rock, TX	7.6	10.8	6.3	4.2
San Antonio, TX	19.7	28.4	17.0	13.9
San Diego, CA	15.2	19.6	14.9	8.4
San Francisco, CA	12.0	12.1	11.8	13.0
San Jose, CA	11.5	15.6	10.4	8.4
Savannah, GA	24.6	33.1	22.9	17.1
Scottsdale, AZ	7.7	9.6	7.9	5.7
Seattle, WA	12.6	11.1	12.9	12.4
Sioux Falls, SD	10.4	14.0	9.6	7.0
Stamford, CT	12.8	14.9	12.9	8.2
Sterling Hgts, MI	11.3	14.3	10.5	10.1
Sunnyvale, CA	6.6	7.6	6.4	5.8
Tampa, FL	19.9	30.4	16.9	15.1
Temecula, CA	9.6	12.2	8.8	5.2
Thousand Oaks, CA	5.6	6.8	5.2	5.4
Virginia Beach, VA	6.9	10.0	6.1	4.7
Washington, DC	18.7	30.0	16.5	14.3
U.S.	14.4	20.1	13.1	9.4

Note: Figures are percentage of people whose income during the past 12 months was below the poverty level;
Source: U.S. Census Bureau, 2008-2010 American Community Survey 3-Year Estimates

Poverty Rate: Metro Area

Metro Area	All Ages	Under 18 Years Old	18 to 64 Years Old	65 Years and Over
Albuquerque, NM	16.0	23.2	14.2	10.8
Alexandria, VA	7.7	9.7	7.1	6.8
Anchorage, AK	8.2	10.8	7.5	4.2
Ann Arbor, MI	13.7	13.7	14.8	6.4
Athens, GA	26.8	26.3	29.2	12.4
Atlanta, GA	13.2	18.1	11.7	9.8
Austin, TX	14.5	18.5	13.9	7.1
Baltimore, MD	10.4	13.6	9.4	9.1
Bellevue, WA	10.5	13.3	10.0	8.0
Billings, MT	12.0	18.4	10.6	7.2
Boise City, ID	14.2	18.5	13.4	7.7
Boston, MA	9.8	11.1	9.5	9.2
Boulder, CO	12.7	12.9	13.6	5.6
Broken Arrow, OK	14.1	20.9	12.4	8.4
Cambridge, MA	9.8	11.1	9.5	9.2
Cape Coral, FL	13.7	20.7	13.8	7.3
Carlsbad, CA	13.2	17.4	12.6	8.0
Cary, NC	11.6	15.0	10.7	8.1
Cedar Rapids, IA	9.2	11.4	8.9	6.6
Charleston, SC	15.4	22.5	13.7	10.2
Charlotte, NC	13.2	18.2	11.9	8.4
Chesapeake, VA	10.5	16.2	9.0	7.1
Chicago, IL	12.7	17.9	11.1	9.3
Clarksville, TN	16.5	23.3	14.2	11.3
Colorado Spgs., CO	12.1	17.0	11.0	5.7
Columbia, MD	10.4	13.6	9.4	9.1
Columbia, MO	19.2	18.5	21.4	5.7
Columbia, SC	14.2	18.4	13.4	10.0
Columbus, OH	14.8	19.8	13.9	8.4
Dallas, TX	14.0	20.1	12.0	8.7
Denver, CO	12.0	16.4	10.7	9.4
Durham, NC	16.0	20.9	15.8	7.6
Edison, NJ	13.1	18.4	11.6	11.5
El Paso, TX	24.3	34.1	19.9	20.2
Fargo, ND	12.5	12.1	13.2	8.8
Ft. Collins, CO	14.0	13.1	15.7	6.2
Ft. Worth, TX	14.0	20.1	12.0	8.7
Gilbert, AZ	14.9	21.2	13.6	7.1
Green Bay, WI	10.4	13.7	9.7	7.3
Henderson, NV	12.9	18.6	11.4	8.1
High Point, NC	16.4	23.6	15.2	9.2
Honolulu, HI	9.2	11.7	8.9	6.8
Houston, TX	15.3	22.2	12.8	10.9
Huntington, NY	13.1	18.4	11.6	11.5
Huntsville, AL	12.3	16.8	11.5	7.6
Indianapolis, IN	13.4	19.0	12.1	7.0
Irvine, CA	15.1	21.2	13.4	10.8
Jackson, MS	18.2	26.3	16.1	11.0
Jacksonville, FL	13.4	19.0	12.1	9.2
Jersey City, NJ	13.1	18.4	11.6	11.5
Kansas City, MO	11.5	16.3	10.3	7.4
Kenosha, WI	12.7	17.9	11.1	9.3
Las Vegas, NV	12.9	18.6	11.4	8.1
Lexington, KY	16.6	21.8	16.1	8.2
Lincoln, NE	14.0	17.0	14.3	6.1

Table continued on next page.

Metro Area	All Ages	Under 18 Years Old	18 to 64 Years Old	65 Years and Over
Little Rock, AR	15.1	21.9	13.7	8.6
Los Angeles, CA	15.1	21.2	13.4	10.8
Madison, WI	11.7	11.8	12.6	5.3
Manchester, NH	7.6	10.7	6.6	6.8
Miami, FL	15.5	20.7	13.8	15.0
Minneapolis, MN	10.0	13.3	9.1	7.5
Murfreesboro, TN	13.9	19.6	12.4	9.3
Naperville, IL	12.7	17.9	11.1	9.3
Nashville, TN	13.9	19.6	12.4	9.3
New Orleans, LA	16.4	23.9	14.7	11.1
New York, NY	13.1	18.4	11.6	11.5
Norman, OK	15.2	21.9	14.0	7.5
Olathe, KS	11.5	16.3	10.3	7.4
Omaha, NE	11.2	15.3	10.2	7.8
Orlando, FL	13.6	18.5	12.7	8.9
Overland Park, KS	11.5	16.3	10.3	7.4
Oyster Bay, NY	13.1	18.4	11.6	11.5
Pembroke Pines, FL	15.5	20.7	13.8	15.0
Philadelphia, PA	12.2	16.2	11.3	8.9
Phoenix, AZ	14.9	21.2	13.6	7.1
Pittsburgh, PA	12.1	17.0	11.5	8.4
Plano, TX	14.0	20.1	12.0	8.7
Portland, OR	12.4	16.3	11.7	8.4
Providence, RI	12.5	16.9	11.5	10.0
Provo, UT	13.4	11.2	15.7	5.0
Raleigh, NC	11.6	15.0	10.7	8.1
Richmond, VA	11.6	15.6	10.8	7.9
Roseville, CA	13.6	18.4	12.8	7.4
Round Rock, TX	14.5	18.5	13.9	7.1
San Antonio, TX	16.4	23.3	14.2	11.7
San Diego, CA	13.2	17.4	12.6	8.0
San Francisco, CA	10.2	12.5	9.7	8.3
San Jose, CA	9.4	12.0	8.7	7.5
Savannah, GA	15.7	21.2	14.4	10.7
Scottsdale, AZ	14.9	21.2	13.6	7.1
Seattle, WA	10.5	13.3	10.0	8.0
Sioux Falls, SD	8.7	11.3	7.7	7.8
Stamford, CT	8.9	10.4	8.7	6.9
Sterling Hgts, MI	15.4	22.1	14.1	9.1
Sunnyvale, CA	9.4	12.0	8.7	7.5
Tampa, FL	14.1	20.4	13.4	8.8
Temecula, CA	15.5	21.6	13.6	8.8
Thousand Oaks, CA	9.8	13.2	9.0	7.0
Virginia Beach, VA	10.5	16.2	9.0	7.1
Washington, DC	7.7	9.7	7.1	6.8
U.S.	14.4	20.1	13.1	9.4

Note: Figures are percentage of people whose income during the past 12 months was below the poverty level;
Figures cover the Metropolitan Statistical Area—see Appendix B for areas included
Source: U.S. Census Bureau, 2008-2010 American Community Survey 3-Year Estimates

Personal Bankruptcy Filing Rate

City	Area Covered	2006	2007	2008	2009	2010	2011
Albuquerque, NM	Bernalillo County	1.35	1.95	2.67	3.44	3.65	3.15
Alexandria, VA	Alexandria City	0.86	1.36	2.48	3.27	3.17	2.81
Anchorage, AK	Anchorage Borough	1.14	1.24	1.69	1.80	1.94	1.72
Ann Arbor, MI	Washtenaw County	2.08	3.07	3.98	4.82	4.96	4.07
Athens, GA	Clarke County	2.18	2.66	2.86	3.46	3.54	3.79
Atlanta, GA	Fulton County	3.78	4.89	5.68	7.45	8.21	7.68
Austin, TX	Travis County	1.26	1.34	1.35	1.81	1.86	1.54
Baltimore, MD	Baltimore City County	2.77	3.18	3.08	4.25	5.03	4.84
Bellevue, WA	King County	1.44	1.79	2.42	3.76	4.32	4.09
Billings, MT	Yellowstone County	1.94	2.33	2.34	2.60	3.33	3.32
Boise City, ID	Ada County	2.46	2.97	4.26	6.17	6.11	5.62
Boston, MA	Suffolk County	1.16	1.86	1.95	2.32	2.71	2.35
Boulder, CO	Boulder County	1.37	2.19	2.90	3.82	4.22	3.86
Broken Arrow, OK	Tulsa County	2.38	2.89	3.30	4.23	4.51	3.81
Cambridge, MA	Middlesex County	0.89	1.51	1.79	2.30	2.58	2.25
Cape Coral, FL	Lee County	0.89	2.27	4.92	7.38	7.32	5.33
Carlsbad, CA	San Diego County	1.40	2.55	4.46	6.50	7.23	6.48
Cary, NC	Wake County	1.86	2.35	2.66	3.45	3.08	2.89
Cedar Rapids, IA	Linn County	0.92	2.02	2.26	3.23	2.82	2.62
Charleston, SC	Charleston County	0.91	1.24	1.45	1.71	1.88	1.52
Charlotte, NC	Mecklenburg County	1.66	1.89	1.98	2.50	2.67	2.26
Chesapeake, VA	Chesapeake City	1.92	2.91	4.06	5.31	5.86	5.50
Chicago, IL	Cook County	3.24	3.34	4.72	6.40	7.44	6.69
Clarksville, TN	Montgomery County	2.84	3.29	4.14	4.65	5.03	4.53
Colorado Spgs., CO	El Paso County	1.94	3.27	4.59	5.55	6.08	5.07
Columbia, MD	Howard County	0.93	1.46	2.29	3.08	3.67	3.00
Columbia, MO	Boone County	3.82	5.14	5.43	6.39	5.70	4.75
Columbia, SC	Richland County	2.08	2.20	2.41	2.37	2.26	2.04
Columbus, OH	Franklin County	3.59	4.58	5.41	6.20	6.22	5.53
Dallas, TX	Dallas County	2.20	2.39	2.39	2.90	2.86	2.63
Denver, CO	Denver County	2.24	3.24	4.38	5.54	6.30	6.20
Durham, NC	Durham County	2.18	2.18	2.35	2.80	2.97	2.73
Edison, NJ	Middlesex County	1.04	1.62	2.30	3.27	3.86	3.56
El Paso, TX	El Paso County	2.04	2.19	2.87	3.71	3.41	3.14
Fargo, ND	Cass County	1.29	2.51	2.81	3.42	3.29	2.61
Ft. Collins, CO	Larimer County	2.37	3.49	4.30	5.39	6.26	5.31
Ft. Worth, TX	Tarrant County	2.44	2.91	3.02	3.74	3.76	3.20
Gilbert, AZ	Maricopa County	1.40	1.87	3.47	6.22	7.81	6.60
Green Bay, WI	Brown County	2.06	2.62	3.98	4.59	5.02	4.06
Henderson, NV	Clark County	2.44	4.80	8.25	12.68	12.53	10.24
High Point, NC	Guilford County	1.78	2.00	2.28	2.68	2.54	2.28
Honolulu, HI	Honolulu County	0.82	1.08	1.44	1.98	2.41	2.06
Houston, TX	Harris County	1.50	1.74	1.52	1.78	2.08	1.95
Huntington, NY	Suffolk County	1.56	2.38	3.25	4.32	4.42	4.01
Huntsville, AL	Madison County	3.19	3.65	4.45	4.94	5.11	4.81
Indianapolis, IN	Marion County	4.64	6.18	7.37	8.44	8.64	7.27
Irvine, CA	Orange County	0.88	1.61	3.03	4.93	6.26	6.03
Jackson, MS	Hinds County	5.28	6.95	5.88	6.57	6.44	6.31
Jacksonville, FL	Duval County	2.39	3.46	4.44	5.80	5.97	5.10
Jersey City, NJ	Hudson County	1.65	2.10	2.89	4.09	4.56	4.27
Kansas City, MO	Jackson County	3.98	4.69	5.21	5.89	6.43	5.44
Kenosha, WI	Kenosha County	2.41	3.03	4.13	6.06	6.97	6.05
Las Vegas, NV	Clark County	2.44	4.80	8.25	12.68	12.53	10.24
Lexington, KY	Fayette County	2.20	2.88	3.59	4.58	4.57	3.97
Lincoln, NE	Lancaster County	2.59	3.21	4.02	4.37	4.43	4.03
Little Rock, AR	Pulaski County	4.76	5.52	6.10	6.81	7.14	6.73

Table continued on next page.

City	Area Covered	2006	2007	2008	2009	2010	2011
Los Angeles, CA	Los Angeles County	1.01	1.82	3.43	5.57	7.34	6.86
Madison, WI	Dane County	1.57	2.15	2.66	3.37	3.71	3.03
Manchester, NH	Hillsborough County	1.52	2.26	3.31	3.99	4.62	3.94
Miami, FL	Miami-Dade County	n/a	n/a	n/a	n/a	n/a	n/a
Minneapolis, MN	Hennepin County	1.48	2.14	2.96	3.89	4.22	3.78
Murfreesboro, TN	Rutherford County	3.92	4.78	6.36	7.27	6.86	6.22
Naperville, IL	DuPage County	1.38	2.10	3.30	4.87	5.84	5.22
Nashville, TN	Davidson County	4.67	5.49	6.61	7.29	6.84	6.51
New Orleans, LA	Orleans Parish	1.18	1.42	1.59	2.12	2.31	2.30
New York, NY	Bronx County	1.19	1.66	2.01	2.36	2.34	2.21
New York, NY	Kings County	1.02	1.25	1.49	1.82	1.85	1.67
New York, NY	New York County	0.94	1.17	1.42	2.15	1.96	1.78
New York, NY	Queens County	1.06	1.59	1.99	2.56	2.74	2.43
New York, NY	Richmond County	0.98	1.41	1.92	2.85	3.03	2.73
Norman, OK	Cleveland County	2.04	2.78	3.38	3.86	4.26	3.80
Olathe, KS	Johnson County	1.97	2.60	3.12	4.12	4.10	3.60
Omaha, NE	Douglas County	2.99	3.57	4.39	4.43	4.65	4.04
Orlando, FL	Orange County	1.17	2.14	3.83	6.51	7.70	6.40
Overland Park, KS	Johnson County	1.97	2.60	3.12	4.12	4.10	3.60
Oyster Bay, NY	Nassau County	0.94	1.52	2.12	2.74	2.58	2.40
Pembroke Pines, FL	Broward County	1.34	2.24	3.75	5.48	6.89	5.98
Philadelphia, PA	Philadelphia County	2.11	2.19	2.02	1.88	2.32	2.05
Phoenix, AZ	Maricopa County	1.40	1.87	3.47	6.22	7.81	6.60
Pittsburgh, PA	Allegheny County	2.96	3.57	3.54	3.83	3.69	3.19
Plano, TX	Collin County	1.95	2.47	2.84	3.49	3.85	3.26
Portland, OR	Multnomah County	2.18	2.63	3.18	4.30	4.82	4.43
Providence, RI	Providence County	1.64	2.86	4.49	5.23	5.60	5.10
Provo, UT	Utah County	1.59	1.74	2.64	4.59	5.94	5.81
Raleigh, NC	Wake County	1.86	2.35	2.66	3.45	3.08	2.89
Richmond, VA	Richmond City	3.15	3.92	4.41	4.77	5.80	5.14
Roseville, CA	Placer County	1.34	2.84	5.61	8.55	9.63	8.28
Round Rock, TX	Williamson County	1.65	2.02	2.02	2.52	2.50	2.26
San Antonio, TX	Bexar County	1.46	1.73	1.91	2.39	2.32	2.05
San Diego, CA	San Diego County	1.40	2.55	4.46	6.50	7.23	6.48
San Francisco, CA	San Francisco County	0.90	1.20	1.52	2.29	2.74	2.30
San Jose, CA	Santa Clara County	0.96	1.37	2.36	3.99	4.91	4.49
Savannah, GA	Chatham County	4.85	5.26	6.33	6.98	6.53	6.28
Scottsdale, AZ	Maricopa County	1.40	1.87	3.47	6.22	7.81	6.60
Seattle, WA	King County	1.44	1.79	2.42	3.76	4.32	4.09
Sioux Falls, SD	Minnehaha County	1.72	2.51	2.84	3.22	3.57	3.23
Stamford, CT	Fairfield County	0.90	1.09	1.70	2.33	2.58	2.18
Sterling Hgts, MI	Macomb County	3.85	5.92	7.52	9.69	9.66	7.79
Sunnyvale, CA	Santa Clara County	0.96	1.37	2.36	3.99	4.91	4.49
Tampa, FL	Hillsborough County	1.80	2.76	4.09	5.55	6.26	4.92
Temecula, CA	Riverside County	1.20	2.51	5.32	8.64	10.86	9.85
Thousand Oaks, CA	Ventura County	0.77	1.68	3.17	5.04	6.37	5.94
Virginia Beach, VA	Virginia Beach City	1.72	2.64	4.06	4.99	5.46	5.01
Washington, DC	District of Columbia	n/a	n/a	n/a	n/a	n/a	n/a
U.S.	U.S.	2.00	2.73	3.53	4.61	4.97	4.37

Note: Numbers are per 1,000 population and include Chapter 7 and Chapter 13 filings; n/a not available
Source: Federal Deposit Insurance Corporation (FDIC), Regional Economic Conditions (RECON), March 9, 2012

Building Permits: City

City	Single-Family			Multi-Family			Total		
	2010	2011	Pct. Chg.	2010	2011	Pct. Chg.	2010	2011	Pct. Chg.
Albuquerque, NM	814	754	-7.4	202	270	33.7	1,016	1,024	0.8
Alexandria, VA	65	105	61.5	403	654	62.3	468	759	62.2
Anchorage, AK	381	344	-9.7	99	103	4.0	480	447	-6.9
Ann Arbor, MI	96	14	-85.4	45	277	515.6	141	291	106.4
Athens, GA	94	84	-10.6	0	87	-	94	171	81.9
Atlanta, GA	83	227	173.5	196	510	160.2	279	737	164.2
Austin, TX	1,664	1,713	2.9	1,110	2,465	122.1	2,774	4,178	50.6
Baltimore, MD	118	75	-36.4	251	914	264.1	369	989	168.0
Bellevue, WA	75	68	-9.3	129	66	-48.8	204	134	-34.3
Billings, MT	308	243	-21.1	125	10	-92.0	433	253	-41.6
Boise City, ID	352	359	2.0	0	59	-	352	418	18.8
Boston, MA	23	33	43.5	328	752	129.3	351	785	123.6
Boulder, CO	115	59	-48.7	338	56	-83.4	453	115	-74.6
Broken Arrow, OK	366	386	5.5	0	378	-	366	764	108.7
Cambridge, MA	8	14	75.0	30	20	-33.3	38	34	-10.5
Cape Coral, FL	216	269	24.5	0	8	-	216	277	28.2
Carlsbad, CA	376	267	-29.0	2	50	2,400.0	378	317	-16.1
Cary, NC	1,083	970	-10.4	276	0	-100.0	1,359	970	-28.6
Cedar Rapids, IA	342	249	-27.2	99	77	-22.2	441	326	-26.1
Charleston, SC	400	392	-2.0	164	223	36.0	564	615	9.0
Charlotte, NC	n/a	n/a	n/a	n/a	n/a	n/a	n/a	n/a	n/a
Chesapeake, VA	736	653	-11.3	349	391	12.0	1,085	1,044	-3.8
Chicago, IL	164	214	30.5	1,713	2,392	39.6	1,877	2,606	38.8
Clarksville, TN	675	996	47.6	760	510	-32.9	1,435	1,506	4.9
Colorado Spgs., CO	n/a	n/a	n/a	n/a	n/a	n/a	n/a	n/a	n/a
Columbia, MD	n/a	n/a	n/a	n/a	n/a	n/a	n/a	n/a	n/a
Columbia, MO	401	316	-21.2	50	550	1,000.0	451	866	92.0
Columbia, SC	203	199	-2.0	96	52	-45.8	299	251	-16.1
Columbus, OH	716	667	-6.8	1,391	1,642	18.0	2,107	2,309	9.6
Dallas, TX	865	809	-6.5	1,744	3,441	97.3	2,609	4,250	62.9
Denver, CO	632	703	11.2	600	1,982	230.3	1,232	2,685	117.9
Durham, NC	891	883	-0.9	296	360	21.6	1,187	1,243	4.7
Edison, NJ	28	27	-3.6	22	0	-100.0	50	27	-46.0
El Paso, TX	2,478	2,966	19.7	1,584	871	-45.0	4,062	3,837	-5.5
Fargo, ND	334	283	-15.3	497	683	37.4	831	966	16.2
Ft. Collins, CO	180	258	43.3	66	456	590.9	246	714	190.2
Ft. Worth, TX	2,759	2,426	-12.1	818	1,144	39.9	3,577	3,570	-0.2
Gilbert, AZ	1,060	1,541	45.4	0	0	-	1,060	1,541	45.4
Green Bay, WI	39	40	2.6	186	16	-91.4	225	56	-75.1
Henderson, NV	700	752	7.4	68	368	441.2	768	1,120	45.8
High Point, NC	163	169	3.7	88	0	-100.0	251	169	-32.7
Honolulu, HI	n/a	n/a	n/a	n/a	n/a	n/a	n/a	n/a	n/a
Houston, TX	2,452	2,575	5.0	2,139	5,160	141.2	4,591	7,735	68.5
Huntington, NY	62	40	-35.5	0	0	-	62	40	-35.5
Huntsville, AL	1,073	1,018	-5.1	0	4	-	1,073	1,022	-4.8
Indianapolis, IN	n/a	n/a	n/a	n/a	n/a	n/a	n/a	n/a	n/a
Irvine, CA	641	857	33.7	1,113	1,776	59.6	1,754	2,633	50.1
Jackson, MS	42	148	252.4	88	153	73.9	130	301	131.5
Jacksonville, FL	1,397	957	-31.5	68	558	720.6	1,465	1,515	3.4
Jersey City, NJ	2	0	-100.0	168	548	226.2	170	548	222.4
Kansas City, MO	68	394	479.4	212	115	-45.8	280	509	81.8
Kenosha, WI	65	36	-44.6	89	107	20.2	154	143	-7.1
Las Vegas, NV	926	814	-12.1	362	114	-68.5	1,288	928	-28.0
Lexington, KY	n/a	n/a	n/a	n/a	n/a	n/a	n/a	n/a	n/a

Table continued on next page.

City	Single-Family			Multi-Family			Total		
	2010	2011	Pct. Chg.	2010	2011	Pct. Chg.	2010	2011	Pct. Chg.
Lincoln, NE	501	544	8.6	332	379	14.2	833	923	10.8
Little Rock, AR	344	325	-5.5	84	1,004	1,095.2	428	1,329	210.5
Los Angeles, CA	636	525	-17.5	3,473	5,422	56.1	4,109	5,947	44.7
Madison, WI	186	177	-4.8	340	444	30.6	526	621	18.1
Manchester, NH	45	91	102.2	155	209	34.8	200	300	50.0
Miami, FL	27	21	-22.2	685	266	-61.2	712	287	-59.7
Minneapolis, MN	41	49	19.5	837	567	-32.3	878	616	-29.8
Murfreesboro, TN	346	400	15.6	184	8	-95.7	530	408	-23.0
Naperville, IL	94	186	97.9	0	0	-	94	186	97.9
Nashville, TN	n/a	n/a	n/a	n/a	n/a	n/a	n/a	n/a	n/a
New Orleans, LA	820	717	-12.6	260	377	45.0	1,080	1,094	1.3
New York, NY	325	264	-18.8	6,077	8,672	42.7	6,402	8,936	39.6
Norman, OK	336	350	4.2	446	39	-91.3	782	389	-50.3
Olathe, KS	364	317	-12.9	0	18	-	364	335	-8.0
Omaha, NE	1,191	1,160	-2.6	388	674	73.7	1,579	1,834	16.1
Orlando, FL	224	308	37.5	336	637	89.6	560	945	68.8
Overland Park, KS	211	274	29.9	11	462	4,100.0	222	736	231.5
Oyster Bay, NY	142	72	-49.3	0	0	-	142	72	-49.3
Pembroke Pines, FL	68	44	-35.3	0	0	-	68	44	-35.3
Philadelphia, PA	447	445	-0.4	537	1,107	106.1	984	1,552	57.7
Phoenix, AZ	1,111	952	-14.3	584	676	15.8	1,695	1,628	-4.0
Pittsburgh, PA	147	284	93.2	0	0	-	147	284	93.2
Plano, TX	311	349	12.2	303	673	122.1	614	1,022	66.4
Portland, OR	435	451	3.7	665	913	37.3	1,100	1,364	24.0
Providence, RI	8	12	50.0	13	8	-38.5	21	20	-4.8
Provo, UT	76	75	-1.3	238	28	-88.2	314	103	-67.2
Raleigh, NC	1,024	988	-3.5	226	1,319	483.6	1,250	2,307	84.6
Richmond, VA	126	92	-27.0	481	251	-47.8	607	343	-43.5
Roseville, CA	635	411	-35.3	0	0	-	635	411	-35.3
Round Rock, TX	253	259	2.4	0	0	-	253	259	2.4
San Antonio, TX	2,337	1,594	-31.8	1,237	2,476	100.2	3,574	4,070	13.9
San Diego, CA	557	451	-19.0	519	2,241	331.8	1,076	2,692	150.2
San Francisco, CA	22	31	40.9	757	1,787	136.1	779	1,818	133.4
San Jose, CA	74	83	12.2	2,348	962	-59.0	2,422	1,045	-56.9
Savannah, GA	241	197	-18.3	279	250	-10.4	520	447	-14.0
Scottsdale, AZ	160	148	-7.5	134	257	91.8	294	405	37.8
Seattle, WA	241	316	31.1	2,456	2,857	16.3	2,697	3,173	17.6
Sioux Falls, SD	546	515	-5.7	212	309	45.8	758	824	8.7
Stamford, CT	16	30	87.5	136	177	30.1	152	207	36.2
Sterling Hgts, MI	103	75	-27.2	0	0	-	103	75	-27.2
Sunnyvale, CA	112	211	88.4	744	279	-62.5	856	490	-42.8
Tampa, FL	455	590	29.7	643	104	-83.8	1,098	694	-36.8
Temecula, CA	348	288	-17.2	0	0	-	348	288	-17.2
Thousand Oaks, CA	20	18	-10.0	15	21	40.0	35	39	11.4
Virginia Beach, VA	529	535	1.1	100	944	844.0	629	1,479	135.1
Washington, DC	177	227	28.2	562	4,385	680.2	739	4,612	524.1
U.S.	447,311	418,498	-6.4	157,299	205,563	30.7	604,610	624,061	3.2

Note: Figures represent new, privately-owned housing units authorized (unadjusted data); All permit data are based on estimates with imputation
Source: U.S. Census Bureau, Manufacturing, Mining, and Construction Statistics, Building Permits, 2010, 2011

Building Permits: Metro Area

Metro Area	Single-Family			Multi-Family			Total		
	2009	2010	Pct. Chg.	2009	2010	Pct. Chg.	2009	2010	Pct. Chg.
Albuquerque, NM	1,553	1,354	-12.8	211	280	32.7	1,764	1,634	-7.4
Alexandria, VA	9,488	9,644	1.6	3,577	10,013	179.9	13,065	19,657	50.5
Anchorage, AK	424	401	-5.4	109	123	12.8	533	524	-1.7
Ann Arbor, MI	317	200	-36.9	51	277	443.1	368	477	29.6
Athens, GA	226	240	6.2	0	87	-	226	327	44.7
Atlanta, GA	6,384	6,214	-2.7	1,191	2,420	103.2	7,575	8,634	14.0
Austin, TX	6,200	6,231	0.5	2,586	4,008	55.0	8,786	10,239	16.5
Baltimore, MD	3,554	3,277	-7.8	2,040	2,876	41.0	5,594	6,153	10.0
Bellevue, WA	6,139	6,078	-1.0	3,901	5,152	32.1	10,040	11,230	11.9
Billings, MT	321	256	-20.2	136	16	-88.2	457	272	-40.5
Boise City, ID	1,630	1,578	-3.2	63	262	315.9	1,693	1,840	8.7
Boston, MA	3,748	3,394	-9.4	2,924	2,745	-6.1	6,672	6,139	-8.0
Boulder, CO	276	390	41.3	381	271	-28.9	657	661	0.6
Broken Arrow, OK	2,269	2,033	-10.4	347	1,532	341.5	2,616	3,565	36.3
Cambridge, MA	3,748	3,394	-9.4	2,924	2,745	-6.1	6,672	6,139	-8.0
Cape Coral, FL	1,175	1,262	7.4	101	325	221.8	1,276	1,587	24.4
Carlsbad, CA	2,270	2,245	-1.1	1,224	3,125	155.3	3,494	5,370	53.7
Cary, NC	4,653	4,753	2.1	560	1,613	188.0	5,213	6,366	22.1
Cedar Rapids, IA	691	577	-16.5	164	154	-6.1	855	731	-14.5
Charleston, SC	2,787	2,597	-6.8	273	1,225	348.7	3,060	3,822	24.9
Charlotte, NC	4,338	4,912	13.2	950	1,534	61.5	5,288	6,446	21.9
Chesapeake, VA	3,149	2,954	-6.2	817	2,605	218.8	3,966	5,559	40.2
Chicago, IL	4,244	4,145	-2.3	3,023	3,448	14.1	7,267	7,593	4.5
Clarksville, TN	1,092	1,427	30.7	829	574	-30.8	1,921	2,001	4.2
Colorado Spgs., CO	1,676	1,616	-3.6	84	659	684.5	1,760	2,275	29.3
Columbia, MD	3,554	3,277	-7.8	2,040	2,876	41.0	5,594	6,153	10.0
Columbia, MO	547	478	-12.6	60	574	856.7	607	1,052	73.3
Columbia, SC	2,527	2,390	-5.4	415	507	22.2	2,942	2,897	-1.5
Columbus, OH	2,887	2,420	-16.2	1,557	2,310	48.4	4,444	4,730	6.4
Dallas, TX	14,420	14,039	-2.6	5,138	10,788	110.0	19,558	24,827	26.9
Denver, CO	3,660	3,630	-0.8	1,382	3,043	120.2	5,042	6,673	32.3
Durham, NC	1,530	1,526	-0.3	383	398	3.9	1,913	1,924	0.6
Edison, NJ	7,010	6,003	-14.4	11,658	15,536	33.3	18,668	21,539	15.4
El Paso, TX	2,961	3,280	10.8	1,588	873	-45.0	4,549	4,153	-8.7
Fargo, ND	760	609	-19.9	558	927	66.1	1,318	1,536	16.5
Ft. Collins, CO	477	702	47.2	676	490	-27.5	1,153	1,192	3.4
Ft. Worth, TX	14,420	14,039	-2.6	5,138	10,788	110.0	19,558	24,827	26.9
Gilbert, AZ	7,212	7,297	1.2	1,088	1,784	64.0	8,300	9,081	9.4
Green Bay, WI	611	484	-20.8	523	396	-24.3	1,134	880	-22.4
Henderson, NV	4,623	3,817	-17.4	851	1,330	56.3	5,474	5,147	-6.0
High Point, NC	1,234	1,054	-14.6	669	993	48.4	1,903	2,047	7.6
Honolulu, HI	879	734	-16.5	1,012	990	-2.2	1,891	1,724	-8.8
Houston, TX	22,330	22,889	2.5	5,122	8,382	63.6	27,452	31,271	13.9
Huntington, NY	7,010	6,003	-14.4	11,658	15,536	33.3	18,668	21,539	15.4
Huntsville, AL	2,275	2,015	-11.4	0	4	-	2,275	2,019	-11.3
Indianapolis, IN	3,793	3,614	-4.7	2,128	1,645	-22.7	5,921	5,259	-11.2
Irvine, CA	4,008	4,097	2.2	6,386	10,150	58.9	10,394	14,247	37.1
Jackson, MS	1,303	1,207	-7.4	88	153	73.9	1,391	1,360	-2.2
Jacksonville, FL	3,387	3,245	-4.2	219	666	204.1	3,606	3,911	8.5
Jersey City, NJ	7,010	6,003	-14.4	11,658	15,536	33.3	18,668	21,539	15.4
Kansas City, MO	2,155	2,363	9.7	559	924	65.3	2,714	3,287	21.1
Kenosha, WI	4,244	4,145	-2.3	3,023	3,448	14.1	7,267	7,593	4.5
Las Vegas, NV	4,623	3,817	-17.4	851	1,330	56.3	5,474	5,147	-6.0
Lexington, KY	1,155	1,009	-12.6	206	492	138.8	1,361	1,501	10.3

Table continued on next page.

Metro Area	Single-Family			Multi-Family			Total		
	2009	2010	Pct. Chg.	2009	2010	Pct. Chg.	2009	2010	Pct. Chg.
Lincoln, NE	648	680	4.9	384	379	-1.3	1,032	1,059	2.6
Little Rock, AR	1,896	1,514	-20.1	1,663	1,716	3.2	3,559	3,230	-9.2
Los Angeles, CA	4,008	4,097	2.2	6,386	10,150	58.9	10,394	14,247	37.1
Madison, WI	794	718	-9.6	404	725	79.5	1,198	1,443	20.5
Manchester, NH	367	334	-9.0	315	368	16.8	682	702	2.9
Miami, FL	3,171	4,303	35.7	2,706	3,229	19.3	5,877	7,532	28.2
Minneapolis, MN	3,805	3,756	-1.3	1,921	1,392	-27.5	5,726	5,148	-10.1
Murfreesboro, TN	3,938	4,100	4.1	1,154	1,294	12.1	5,092	5,394	5.9
Naperville, IL	4,244	4,145	-2.3	3,023	3,448	14.1	7,267	7,593	4.5
Nashville, TN	3,938	4,100	4.1	1,154	1,294	12.1	5,092	5,394	5.9
New Orleans, LA	1,875	1,945	3.7	296	383	29.4	2,171	2,328	7.2
New York, NY	7,010	6,003	-14.4	11,658	15,536	33.3	18,668	21,539	15.4
Norman, OK	3,032	3,079	1.6	603	182	-69.8	3,635	3,261	-10.3
Olathe, KS	2,155	2,363	9.7	559	924	65.3	2,714	3,287	21.1
Omaha, NE	2,305	2,156	-6.5	918	977	6.4	3,223	3,133	-2.8
Orlando, FL	4,221	4,533	7.4	1,033	1,972	90.9	5,254	6,505	23.8
Overland Park, KS	2,155	2,363	9.7	559	924	65.3	2,714	3,287	21.1
Oyster Bay, NY	7,010	6,003	-14.4	11,658	15,536	33.3	18,668	21,539	15.4
Pembroke Pines, FL	3,171	4,303	35.7	2,706	3,229	19.3	5,877	7,532	28.2
Philadelphia, PA	5,186	4,456	-14.1	1,867	2,523	35.1	7,053	6,979	-1.0
Phoenix, AZ	7,212	7,297	1.2	1,088	1,784	64.0	8,300	9,081	9.4
Pittsburgh, PA	3,398	2,654	-21.9	217	260	19.8	3,615	2,914	-19.4
Plano, TX	14,420	14,039	-2.6	5,138	10,788	110.0	19,558	24,827	26.9
Portland, OR	3,359	3,132	-6.8	1,117	2,081	86.3	4,476	5,213	16.5
Providence, RI	1,205	963	-20.1	234	215	-8.1	1,439	1,178	-18.1
Provo, UT	1,553	1,452	-6.5	432	480	11.1	1,985	1,932	-2.7
Raleigh, NC	4,653	4,753	2.1	560	1,613	188.0	5,213	6,366	22.1
Richmond, VA	2,472	2,352	-4.9	984	357	-63.7	3,456	2,709	-21.6
Roseville, CA	2,166	1,873	-13.5	536	618	15.3	2,702	2,491	-7.8
Round Rock, TX	6,200	6,231	0.5	2,586	4,008	55.0	8,786	10,239	16.5
San Antonio, TX	5,144	4,410	-14.3	1,721	2,717	57.9	6,865	7,127	3.8
San Diego, CA	2,270	2,245	-1.1	1,224	3,125	155.3	3,494	5,370	53.7
San Francisco, CA	2,118	1,923	-9.2	2,503	3,860	54.2	4,621	5,783	25.1
San Jose, CA	861	1,002	16.4	3,318	2,095	-36.9	4,179	3,097	-25.9
Savannah, GA	1,020	1,049	2.8	281	576	105.0	1,301	1,625	24.9
Scottsdale, AZ	7,212	7,297	1.2	1,088	1,784	64.0	8,300	9,081	9.4
Seattle, WA	6,139	6,078	-1.0	3,901	5,152	32.1	10,040	11,230	11.9
Sioux Falls, SD	755	716	-5.2	326	413	26.7	1,081	1,129	4.4
Stamford, CT	546	583	6.8	380	354	-6.8	926	937	1.2
Sterling Hgts, MI	2,430	2,862	17.8	780	504	-35.4	3,210	3,366	4.9
Sunnyvale, CA	861	1,002	16.4	3,318	2,095	-36.9	4,179	3,097	-25.9
Tampa, FL	4,396	4,511	2.6	2,105	1,831	-13.0	6,501	6,342	-2.4
Temecula, CA	5,287	3,378	-36.1	1,049	1,358	29.5	6,336	4,736	-25.3
Thousand Oaks, CA	209	281	34.4	381	287	-24.7	590	568	-3.7
Virginia Beach, VA	3,149	2,954	-6.2	817	2,605	218.8	3,966	5,559	40.2
Washington, DC	9,488	9,644	1.6	3,577	10,013	179.9	13,065	19,657	50.5
U.S.	447,311	418,498	-6.4	157,299	205,563	30.7	604,610	624,061	3.2

Note: Figures cover the Metropolitan Statistical Area—see Appendix B for areas included; Figures represent new, privately-owned housing units authorized (unadjusted data); All permit data are based on estimates with imputation
Source: U.S. Census Bureau, Manufacturing, Mining, and Construction Statistics, Building Permits, 2010, 2011

Homeownership Rate

Metro Area	2005	2006	2007	2008	2009	2010	2011
Albuquerque, NM	69.2	70.0	70.5	68.2	65.7	65.5	67.1
Alexandria, VA	68.4	68.9	69.2	68.1	67.2	67.3	67.6
Anchorage, AK	n/a	n/a	n/a	n/a	n/a	n/a	n/a
Ann Arbor, MI	n/a	n/a	n/a	n/a	n/a	n/a	n/a
Athens, GA	n/a	n/a	n/a	n/a	n/a	n/a	n/a
Atlanta, GA	66.4	67.9	66.4	67.5	67.7	67.2	65.8
Austin, TX	63.9	66.7	66.4	65.5	64.0	65.8	58.4
Baltimore, MD	70.6	72.9	71.2	69.3	67.7	65.7	66.8
Bellevue, WA	64.5	63.7	62.8	61.3	61.2	60.9	60.7
Billings, MT	n/a	n/a	n/a	n/a	n/a	n/a	n/a
Boise City, ID	n/a	n/a	n/a	n/a	n/a	n/a	n/a
Boston, MA	63.0	64.7	64.8	66.2	65.5	66.0	65.5
Boulder, CO	n/a	n/a	n/a	n/a	n/a	n/a	n/a
Broken Arrow, OK	71.7	67.9	66.7	66.8	67.8	64.2	64.4
Cambridge, MA	63.0	64.7	64.8	66.2	65.5	66.0	65.5
Cape Coral, FL	n/a	n/a	n/a	n/a	n/a	n/a	n/a
Carlsbad, CA	60.5	61.2	59.6	57.1	56.4	54.4	55.2
Cary, NC	71.4	71.1	72.8	70.7	65.7	65.9	66.7
Cedar Rapids, IA	n/a	n/a	n/a	n/a	n/a	n/a	n/a
Charleston, SC	n/a	n/a	n/a	n/a	n/a	n/a	n/a
Charlotte, NC	65.8	66.1	66.5	65.4	66.1	66.1	63.6
Chesapeake, VA	68.0	68.3	66.0	63.9	63.5	61.4	62.3
Chicago, IL	70.0	69.6	69.0	68.4	69.2	68.2	67.7
Clarksville, TN	n/a	n/a	n/a	n/a	n/a	n/a	n/a
Colorado Spgs., CO	n/a	n/a	n/a	n/a	n/a	n/a	n/a
Columbia, MD	70.6	72.9	71.2	69.3	67.7	65.7	66.8
Columbia, MO	n/a	n/a	n/a	n/a	n/a	n/a	n/a
Columbia, SC	76.3	72.2	71.1	71.4	71.5	74.1	69.0
Columbus, OH	68.9	65.8	66.1	61.2	61.5	62.2	59.7
Dallas, TX	62.3	60.7	60.9	60.9	61.6	63.8	62.6
Denver, CO	70.7	70.0	69.5	66.9	65.3	65.7	63.0
Durham, NC	n/a	n/a	n/a	n/a	n/a	n/a	n/a
Edison, NJ	54.6	53.6	53.8	52.6	51.7	51.6	50.9
El Paso, TX	72.6	65.0	68.2	64.8	63.8	70.1	72.0
Fargo, ND	n/a	n/a	n/a	n/a	n/a	n/a	n/a
Ft. Collins, CO	n/a	n/a	n/a	n/a	n/a	n/a	n/a
Ft. Worth, TX	62.3	60.7	60.9	60.9	61.6	63.8	62.6
Gilbert, AZ	71.2	72.5	70.8	70.2	69.8	66.5	63.3
Green Bay, WI	n/a	n/a	n/a	n/a	n/a	n/a	n/a
Henderson, NV	61.4	63.3	60.5	60.3	59.0	55.7	52.9
High Point, NC	66.3	62.2	62.1	68.0	70.7	68.8	62.7
Honolulu, HI	58.0	58.4	58.8	57.2	57.6	54.9	54.1
Houston, TX	61.7	63.5	64.5	64.8	63.6	61.4	61.3
Huntington, NY	54.6	53.6	53.8	52.6	51.7	51.6	50.9
Huntsville, AL	n/a	n/a	n/a	n/a	n/a	n/a	n/a
Indianapolis, IN	77.1	79.0	75.9	75.0	71.0	68.8	68.3
Irvine, CA	54.6	54.4	52.3	52.1	50.4	49.7	50.1
Jackson, MS	n/a	n/a	n/a	n/a	n/a	n/a	n/a
Jacksonville, FL	67.9	70.0	70.9	72.1	72.6	70.0	68.0
Jersey City, NJ	54.6	53.6	53.8	52.6	51.7	51.6	50.9
Kansas City, MO	71.3	69.5	71.3	70.2	69.5	68.8	68.5
Kenosha, WI	70.0	69.6	69.0	68.4	69.2	68.2	67.7
Las Vegas, NV	61.4	63.3	60.5	60.3	59.0	55.7	52.9
Lexington, KY	n/a	n/a	n/a	n/a	n/a	n/a	n/a
Lincoln, NE	n/a	n/a	n/a	n/a	n/a	n/a	n/a
Little Rock, AR	n/a	n/a	n/a	n/a	n/a	n/a	n/a

Table continued on next page.

Metro Area	2005	2006	2007	2008	2009	2010	2011
Los Angeles, CA	54.6	54.4	52.3	52.1	50.4	49.7	50.1
Madison, WI	n/a	n/a	n/a	n/a	n/a	n/a	n/a
Manchester, NH	n/a	n/a	n/a	n/a	n/a	n/a	n/a
Miami, FL	69.2	67.4	66.6	66.0	67.1	63.8	64.2
Minneapolis, MN	74.9	73.4	70.7	69.9	70.9	71.2	69.1
Murfreesboro, TN	73.0	72.4	70.0	71.3	71.8	70.4	69.6
Naperville, IL	70.0	69.6	69.0	68.4	69.2	68.2	67.7
Nashville, TN	73.0	72.4	70.0	71.3	71.8	70.4	69.6
New Orleans, LA	71.2	70.3	67.8	68.0	68.2	66.9	63.9
New York, NY	54.6	53.6	53.8	52.6	51.7	51.6	50.9
Norman, OK	72.9	71.8	68.2	69.5	69.0	70.0	69.6
Olathe, KS	71.3	69.5	71.3	70.2	69.5	68.8	68.5
Omaha, NE	69.7	68.1	67.9	72.5	73.1	73.2	71.6
Orlando, FL	70.5	71.1	71.8	70.5	72.4	70.8	68.6
Overland Park, KS	71.3	69.5	71.3	70.2	69.5	68.8	68.5
Oyster Bay, NY	54.6	53.6	53.8	52.6	51.7	51.6	50.9
Pembroke Pines, FL	69.2	67.4	66.6	66.0	67.1	63.8	64.2
Philadelphia, PA	73.5	73.1	73.1	71.8	69.7	70.7	69.7
Phoenix, AZ	71.2	72.5	70.8	70.2	69.8	66.5	63.3
Pittsburgh, PA	73.1	72.2	73.6	73.2	71.7	70.4	70.3
Plano, TX	62.3	60.7	60.9	60.9	61.6	63.8	62.6
Portland, OR	68.3	66.0	61.2	62.6	64.0	63.7	63.7
Providence, RI	63.1	65.5	64.1	63.9	61.7	61.0	61.3
Provo, UT	n/a	n/a	n/a	n/a	n/a	n/a	n/a
Raleigh, NC	71.4	71.1	72.8	70.7	65.7	65.9	66.7
Richmond, VA	69.7	68.9	72.7	72.4	72.2	68.1	65.2
Roseville, CA	64.1	64.2	60.8	61.1	64.3	61.1	57.2
Round Rock, TX	63.9	66.7	66.4	65.5	64.0	65.8	58.4
San Antonio, TX	66.0	62.6	62.4	66.1	69.8	70.1	66.5
San Diego, CA	60.5	61.2	59.6	57.1	56.4	54.4	55.2
San Francisco, CA	57.8	59.4	58.0	56.4	57.3	58.0	56.1
San Jose, CA	59.2	59.4	57.6	54.6	57.2	58.9	60.4
Savannah, GA	n/a	n/a	n/a	n/a	n/a	n/a	n/a
Scottsdale, AZ	71.2	72.5	70.8	70.2	69.8	66.5	63.3
Seattle, WA	64.5	63.7	62.8	61.3	61.2	60.9	60.7
Sioux Falls, SD	n/a	n/a	n/a	n/a	n/a	n/a	n/a
Stamford, CT	68.2	70.4	70.3	72.6	70.3	71.3	71.6
Sterling Hgts, MI	75.1	75.8	76.1	75.5	73.9	73.6	73.5
Sunnyvale, CA	59.2	59.4	57.6	54.6	57.2	58.9	60.4
Tampa, FL	71.7	71.6	72.9	70.5	68.3	68.3	68.3
Temecula, CA	68.5	68.3	66.6	65.8	65.9	63.9	59.2
Thousand Oaks, CA	73.4	69.8	71.4	71.7	73.1	67.1	67.0
Virginia Beach, VA	68.0	68.3	66.0	63.9	63.5	61.4	62.3
Washington, DC	68.4	68.9	69.2	68.1	67.2	67.3	67.6
U.S.	68.9	68.8	68.1	67.8	67.4	66.9	66.1

Note: Figures are percentages and cover the Metropolitan Statistical Area—see Appendix B for areas included
Source: U.S. Census Bureau, Housing Vacancies and Homeownership Annual Statistics: 2011

Housing Vacancy Rates

Area	Gross Vacancy Rate[2] (%)			Year-Round Vacancy Rate[3] (%)			Rental Vacancy Rate[4] (%)			Homeowner Vacancy Rate[5] (%)		
	2009	2010	2011	2009	2010	2011	2009	2010	2011	2009	2010	2011
Albuquerque, NM	8.5	7.4	7.1	7.8	6.6	6.3	8.0	5.0	6.9	1.9	1.7	1.4
Alexandria, VA	10.3	10.2	9.6	10.0	10.0	9.4	10.0	8.8	7.9	2.3	2.1	1.8
Anchorage, AK	n/a	n/a	n/a	n/a	n/a	n/a	n/a	n/a	n/a	n/a	n/a	n/a
Ann Arbor, MI	n/a	n/a	n/a	n/a	n/a	n/a	n/a	n/a	n/a	n/a	n/a	n/a
Athens, GA	n/a	n/a	n/a	n/a	n/a	n/a	n/a	n/a	n/a	n/a	n/a	n/a
Atlanta, GA	13.0	11.7	12.8	12.8	11.4	12.4	16.6	13.8	11.6	4.1	3.0	4.3
Austin, TX	12.8	15.8	12.6	12.7	15.7	11.7	12.2	11.8	6.4	1.6	1.9	0.6
Baltimore, MD	12.3	11.0	11.7	12.1	10.9	11.6	13.4	11.8	10.7	1.9	2.2	2.8
Bellevue, WA	9.0	8.8	8.6	8.8	8.6	8.3	8.0	7.4	6.7	2.8	3.2	2.6
Billings, MT	n/a	n/a	n/a	n/a	n/a	n/a	n/a	n/a	n/a	n/a	n/a	n/a
Boise City, ID	n/a	n/a	n/a	n/a	n/a	n/a	n/a	n/a	n/a	n/a	n/a	n/a
Boston, MA	8.2	8.5	8.7	6.8	7.0	6.9	6.0	6.2	5.5	1.5	1.2	1.4
Boulder, CO	n/a	n/a	n/a	n/a	n/a	n/a	n/a	n/a	n/a	n/a	n/a	n/a
Broken Arrow, OK	12.7	13.3	13.2	11.8	12.7	12.7	15.1	15.9	13.0	2.4	1.4	2.5
Cambridge, MA	8.2	8.5	8.7	6.8	7.0	6.9	6.0	6.2	5.5	1.5	1.2	1.4
Cape Coral, FL	n/a	n/a	n/a	n/a	n/a	n/a	n/a	n/a	n/a	n/a	n/a	n/a
Carlsbad, CA	10.4	10.5	9.9	9.8	10.0	9.5	8.8	7.8	6.9	2.1	2.9	1.9
Cary, NC	10.5	11.0	9.2	10.5	11.0	9.1	10.3	11.4	8.9	2.8	5.0	2.9
Cedar Rapids, IA	n/a	n/a	n/a	n/a	n/a	n/a	n/a	n/a	n/a	n/a	n/a	n/a
Charleston, SC	n/a	n/a	n/a	n/a	n/a	n/a	n/a	n/a	n/a	n/a	n/a	n/a
Charlotte, NC	12.9	11.7	9.2	12.7	11.5	9.1	12.1	11.2	10.1	5.1	3.1	1.9
Chesapeake, VA	10.4	11.1	10.8	9.9	10.4	10.3	6.2	8.8	9.4	2.3	2.8	3.2
Chicago, IL	11.4	11.9	11.8	11.2	11.6	11.6	12.0	12.1	9.9	2.9	3.4	3.6
Clarksville, TN	n/a	n/a	n/a	n/a	n/a	n/a	n/a	n/a	n/a	n/a	n/a	n/a
Colorado Spgs., CO	n/a	n/a	n/a	n/a	n/a	n/a	n/a	n/a	n/a	n/a	n/a	n/a
Columbia, MD	12.3	11.0	11.7	12.1	10.9	11.6	13.4	11.8	10.7	1.9	2.2	2.8
Columbia, MO	n/a	n/a	n/a	n/a	n/a	n/a	n/a	n/a	n/a	n/a	n/a	n/a
Columbia, SC	13.3	11.1	12.4	13.0	10.9	12.4	8.4	9.4	8.7	3.1	2.5	5.1
Columbus, OH	10.8	11.7	11.8	10.2	11.7	11.7	7.6	8.0	8.2	2.0	4.2	3.2
Dallas, TX	9.4	10.5	9.8	9.3	10.4	9.6	11.7	13.5	11.8	2.1	2.3	2.0
Denver, CO	9.2	7.2	7.0	8.7	6.8	6.5	10.2	8.2	6.8	2.7	1.7	1.8
Durham, NC	n/a	n/a	n/a	n/a	n/a	n/a	n/a	n/a	n/a	n/a	n/a	n/a
Edison, NJ	9.4	9.6	10.0	8.1	8.3	8.7	5.9	6.6	6.4	2.8	2.1	2.6
El Paso, TX	8.6	7.0	6.5	8.4	6.9	5.9	9.6	5.8	9.2	2.5	1.4	1.3
Fargo, ND	n/a	n/a	n/a	n/a	n/a	n/a	n/a	n/a	n/a	n/a	n/a	n/a
Ft. Collins, CO	n/a	n/a	n/a	n/a	n/a	n/a	n/a	n/a	n/a	n/a	n/a	n/a
Ft. Worth, TX	9.4	10.5	9.8	9.3	10.4	9.6	11.7	13.5	11.8	2.1	2.3	2.0
Gilbert, AZ	18.6	18.4	16.7	13.2	12.9	10.8	18.3	16.3	10.9	3.1	2.9	3.1
Green Bay, WI	n/a	n/a	n/a	n/a	n/a	n/a	n/a	n/a	n/a	n/a	n/a	n/a
Henderson, NV	16.7	17.2	16.4	16.5	16.8	16.0	14.3	13.8	12.1	5.0	5.1	4.1
High Point, NC	13.8	12.8	12.4	13.8	12.6	12.4	15.2	12.8	11.9	6.3	4.1	3.0
Honolulu, HI	10.9	11.5	12.1	9.4	10.0	10.9	6.9	7.2	6.9	0.8	1.0	0.7
Houston, TX	12.5	12.2	11.8	12.3	11.9	11.4	15.6	16.2	16.5	1.9	2.8	2.0
Huntington, NY	9.4	9.6	10.0	8.1	8.3	8.7	5.9	6.6	6.4	2.8	2.1	2.6
Huntsville, AL	n/a	n/a	n/a	n/a	n/a	n/a	n/a	n/a	n/a	n/a	n/a	n/a
Indianapolis, IN	10.0	12.1	12.4	9.7	11.8	11.9	12.6	14.1	13.1	2.6	3.0	3.4
Irvine, CA	6.6	7.2	6.7	6.3	6.9	6.4	6.4	6.7	5.3	1.3	1.8	1.8
Jackson, MS	n/a	n/a	n/a	n/a	n/a	n/a	n/a	n/a	n/a	n/a	n/a	n/a
Jacksonville, FL	14.3	14.9	14.7	13.6	14.6	14.1	15.9	13.9	13.3	3.7	4.6	2.8
Jersey City, NJ	9.4	9.6	10.0	8.1	8.3	8.7	5.9	6.6	6.4	2.8	2.1	2.6
Kansas City, MO	11.0	10.7	11.1	10.7	10.5	10.9	14.4	14.0	12.1	3.4	2.7	2.7
Kenosha, WI	11.4	11.9	11.8	11.2	11.6	11.6	12.0	12.1	9.9	2.9	3.4	3.6
Las Vegas, NV	16.7	17.2	16.4	16.5	16.8	16.0	14.3	13.8	12.1	5.0	5.1	4.1
Lexington, KY	n/a	n/a	n/a	n/a	n/a	n/a	n/a	n/a	n/a	n/a	n/a	n/a

Table continued on next page.

Area	Gross Vacancy Rate[2] (%)			Year-Round Vacancy Rate[3] (%)			Rental Vacancy Rate[4] (%)			Homeowner Vacancy Rate[5] (%)		
	2009	2010	2011	2009	2010	2011	2009	2010	2011	2009	2010	2011
Lincoln, NE	n/a	n/a	n/a	n/a	n/a	n/a	n/a	n/a	n/a	n/a	n/a	n/a
Little Rock, AR	n/a	n/a	n/a	n/a	n/a	n/a	n/a	n/a	n/a	n/a	n/a	n/a
Los Angeles, CA	6.6	7.2	6.7	6.3	6.9	6.4	6.4	6.7	5.3	1.3	1.8	1.8
Madison, WI	n/a	n/a	n/a	n/a	n/a	n/a	n/a	n/a	n/a	n/a	n/a	n/a
Manchester, NH	n/a	n/a	n/a	n/a	n/a	n/a	n/a	n/a	n/a	n/a	n/a	n/a
Miami, FL	23.1	21.8	21.0	13.7	13.0	11.7	13.2	10.1	11.8	3.2	3.5	1.8
Minneapolis, MN	7.6	6.8	6.6	7.1	6.3	6.1	8.5	7.4	6.7	2.2	1.4	1.8
Murfreesboro, TN	8.7	10.9	9.0	8.1	10.5	8.3	8.3	8.2	8.2	1.9	2.4	2.2
Naperville, IL	11.4	11.9	11.8	11.2	11.6	11.6	12.0	12.1	9.9	2.9	3.4	3.6
Nashville, TN	8.7	10.9	9.0	8.1	10.5	8.3	8.3	8.2	8.2	1.9	2.4	2.2
New Orleans, LA	16.1	14.6	10.7	15.9	14.4	10.3	18.0	15.2	13.1	2.5	2.6	2.1
New York, NY	9.4	9.6	10.0	8.1	8.3	8.7	5.9	6.6	6.4	2.8	2.1	2.6
Norman, OK	12.6	13.3	15.1	12.2	13.2	14.8	8.3	9.6	9.9	2.8	2.7	3.9
Olathe, KS	11.0	10.7	11.1	10.7	10.5	10.9	14.4	14.0	12.1	3.4	2.7	2.7
Omaha, NE	8.3	9.6	9.3	8.2	9.1	9.0	11.7	10.1	11.1	2.0	3.3	1.9
Orlando, FL	21.2	19.9	20.1	17.5	16.6	14.0	22.8	19.0	19.0	5.8	5.9	2.5
Overland Park, KS	11.0	10.7	11.1	10.7	10.5	10.9	14.4	14.0	12.1	3.4	2.7	2.7
Oyster Bay, NY	9.4	9.6	10.0	8.1	8.3	8.7	5.9	6.6	6.4	2.8	2.1	2.6
Pembroke Pines, FL	23.1	21.8	21.0	13.7	13.0	11.7	13.2	10.1	11.8	3.2	3.5	1.8
Philadelphia, PA	8.9	9.9	10.5	8.7	9.6	10.1	11.4	11.6	12.7	1.6	1.5	1.6
Phoenix, AZ	18.6	18.4	16.7	13.2	12.9	10.8	18.3	16.3	10.9	3.1	2.9	3.1
Pittsburgh, PA	13.2	12.7	12.3	12.1	11.7	11.6	9.7	7.8	6.3	1.6	2.7	2.2
Plano, TX	9.4	10.5	9.8	9.3	10.4	9.6	11.7	13.5	11.8	2.1	2.3	2.0
Portland, OR	8.2	7.2	6.5	7.9	7.0	6.3	4.3	4.2	3.4	4.8	3.2	2.0
Providence, RI	12.8	12.7	13.7	9.2	9.4	10.8	8.5	7.5	8.8	1.7	1.3	2.2
Provo, UT	n/a	n/a	n/a	n/a	n/a	n/a	n/a	n/a	n/a	n/a	n/a	n/a
Raleigh, NC	10.5	11.0	9.2	10.5	11.0	9.1	10.3	11.4	8.9	2.8	5.0	2.9
Richmond, VA	12.7	11.7	12.4	12.0	11.2	12.0	18.5	13.5	13.7	2.2	3.1	2.4
Roseville, CA	15.2	14.0	10.5	12.7	11.3	9.2	10.6	8.4	7.1	4.0	2.9	2.4
Round Rock, TX	12.8	15.8	12.6	12.7	15.7	11.7	12.2	11.8	6.4	1.6	1.9	0.6
San Antonio, TX	10.6	11.1	11.2	10.3	10.6	10.2	12.1	14.0	9.2	1.2	1.6	1.5
San Diego, CA	10.4	10.5	9.9	9.8	10.0	9.5	8.8	7.8	6.9	2.1	2.9	1.9
San Francisco, CA	10.3	9.1	8.3	10.1	9.0	8.1	6.7	6.0	6.8	1.8	1.8	1.8
San Jose, CA	6.3	6.4	5.3	6.3	6.4	5.3	7.7	8.2	4.8	1.4	0.9	0.9
Savannah, GA	n/a	n/a	n/a	n/a	n/a	n/a	n/a	n/a	n/a	n/a	n/a	n/a
Scottsdale, AZ	18.6	18.4	16.7	13.2	12.9	10.8	18.3	16.3	10.9	3.1	2.9	3.1
Seattle, WA	9.0	8.8	8.6	8.8	8.6	8.3	8.0	7.4	6.7	2.8	3.2	2.6
Sioux Falls, SD	n/a	n/a	n/a	n/a	n/a	n/a	n/a	n/a	n/a	n/a	n/a	n/a
Stamford, CT	10.2	11.0	11.1	9.0	9.7	9.8	8.4	8.7	6.3	2.0	1.3	2.0
Sterling Hgts, MI	12.1	12.7	12.4	12.0	12.6	12.2	15.8	16.4	16.8	3.3	2.6	1.8
Sunnyvale, CA	6.3	6.4	5.3	6.3	6.4	5.3	7.7	8.2	4.8	1.4	0.9	0.9
Tampa, FL	20.5	20.2	20.4	14.7	14.2	14.5	12.4	12.6	11.7	4.1	4.0	3.8
Temecula, CA	18.7	19.9	17.7	12.2	13.9	11.4	12.3	12.3	8.4	4.0	4.7	3.5
Thousand Oaks, CA	5.9	7.3	7.1	5.5	6.6	4.7	5.0	6.4	3.2	1.5	1.1	0.5
Virginia Beach, VA	10.4	11.1	10.8	9.9	10.4	10.3	6.2	8.8	9.4	2.3	2.8	3.2
Washington, DC	10.3	10.2	9.6	10.0	10.0	9.4	10.0	8.8	7.9	2.3	2.1	1.8
U.S.	14.5	14.3	14.2	11.3	11.3	11.1	10.6	10.2	9.5	2.6	2.6	2.5

Note: (1) Metropolitan Statistical Area—see Appendix B for areas included; (2) The percentage of the total housing inventory that is vacant; (3) The percentage of the housing inventory (excluding seasonal units) that is year-round vacant; (4) The percentage of rental inventory that is vacant for rent; (5) The percentage of homeowner inventory that is vacant for sale; n/a not available
Source: U.S. Census Bureau, Housing Vacancies and Homeownership Annual Statistics: 2011

Employment by Industry

Metro Area[1]	(A)	(B)	(C)	(D)	(E)	(F)	(G)	(H)	(I)	(J)	(K)	(L)	(M)
Albuquerque, NM	n/a	15.9	4.6	22.4	2.4	9.7	4.8	n/a	3.1	14.9	11.2	2.6	3.1
Alexandria, VA[2]	n/a	12.0	4.4	24.0	2.7	9.1	1.4	n/a	6.2	23.0	8.4	2.4	1.9
Anchorage, AK	4.2	16.0	5.8	21.7	2.9	10.1	1.1	1.8	3.6	11.8	11.7	6.8	2.7
Ann Arbor, MI	n/a	12.5	3.2	37.8	2.0	6.7	7.1	n/a	3.4	13.0	8.3	1.8	2.6
Athens, GA	n/a	n/a	n/a	34.5	n/a	9.0	n/a	n/a	n/a	8.1	11.3	n/a	n/a
Atlanta, GA	3.9	12.6	5.9	13.6	3.4	9.4	6.3	0.1	3.9	17.6	11.4	5.5	6.3
Austin, TX	n/a	11.6	5.7	20.9	2.5	11.5	6.4	n/a	4.2	14.6	10.8	1.7	5.3
Baltimore, MD	n/a	19.3	5.6	18.6	1.3	8.3	4.7	n/a	4.4	14.9	10.8	3.1	3.8
Bellevue, WA[2]	4.5	12.2	5.4	14.1	6.0	9.5	11.6	<0.1	3.6	14.6	10.3	3.4	4.8
Billings, MT	n/a	17.4	n/a	12.0	n/a	12.2	n/a	n/a	n/a	13.2	n/a	n/a	n/a
Boise City, ID	n/a	15.2	5.3	16.6	1.7	8.5	9.0	n/a	3.5	15.1	12.0	3.2	4.6
Boston, MA[4]	2.9	22.2	8.3	11.9	3.3	8.9	5.6	<0.1	3.9	18.0	9.1	2.4	3.5
Boulder, CO	n/a	12.4	4.4	20.1	5.4	11.0	9.6	n/a	3.2	18.4	9.2	0.9	3.1
Broken Arrow, OK	5.0	14.9	5.3	13.6	1.9	8.9	11.5	1.9	4.0	13.3	10.9	5.0	3.7
Cambridge, MA[4]	2.9	22.2	8.3	11.9	3.3	8.9	5.6	<0.1	3.9	18.0	9.1	2.4	3.5
Cape Coral, FL	n/a	11.8	5.0	18.0	1.4	14.6	2.3	n/a	4.2	13.5	16.6	1.7	2.9
Carlsbad, CA	4.5	12.3	5.3	18.4	1.9	12.6	7.4	<0.1	3.7	17.3	11.2	2.1	3.2
Cary, NC	n/a	12.6	5.1	16.6	3.3	10.5	5.3	n/a	4.4	17.9	12.2	2.2	4.2
Cedar Rapids, IA	n/a	14.0	7.2	12.0	3.5	7.6	15.5	n/a	3.5	9.5	11.8	6.7	3.7
Charleston, SC	n/a	12.0	4.3	19.7	1.6	11.8	8.1	n/a	3.5	14.4	12.8	4.0	2.8
Charlotte, NC	n/a	10.5	8.5	14.2	2.6	9.9	8.2	n/a	3.8	16.9	11.4	4.1	5.5
Chesapeake, VA	n/a	13.3	5.1	22.1	1.5	10.3	7.0	n/a	4.7	13.2	11.9	3.3	2.8
Chicago, IL[2]	3.0	15.4	6.9	12.6	2.0	9.0	8.8	<0.1	4.5	17.4	10.2	4.8	5.4
Clarksville, TN	n/a	13.0	3.2	24.7	1.1	11.5	11.7	n/a	3.2	9.6	12.8	2.6	n/a
Colorado Spgs., CO	n/a	12.5	6.5	20.0	2.9	11.7	5.1	n/a	5.7	15.5	11.8	1.8	2.0
Columbia, MD	n/a	19.3	5.6	18.6	1.3	8.3	4.7	n/a	4.4	14.9	10.8	3.1	3.8
Columbia, MO	n/a	n/a	n/a	34.4	n/a	n/a	n/a	n/a	n/a	n/a	11.8	n/a	n/a
Columbia, SC	n/a	12.1	7.8	22.4	1.6	9.1	8.3	n/a	3.6	12.4	11.4	3.3	3.9
Columbus, OH	n/a	14.5	7.7	16.6	1.8	9.3	7.1	n/a	3.8	16.1	11.1	4.8	4.1
Dallas, TX[2]	n/a	12.2	8.9	13.2	3.1	9.6	8.0	n/a	3.4	16.9	10.4	3.8	5.8
Denver, CO	n/a	12.2	7.4	14.5	3.6	10.4	5.0	n/a	4.1	17.5	10.6	3.8	5.1
Durham, NC	n/a	22.1	4.6	20.4	1.2	7.8	12.2	n/a	3.8	12.8	8.4	1.2	2.8
Edison, NJ[2]	n/a	15.3	5.6	14.4	2.5	8.0	5.9	n/a	4.6	17.3	13.1	4.1	5.7
El Paso, TX	n/a	13.7	4.4	23.3	1.7	10.4	6.2	n/a	3.4	11.0	13.0	4.6	3.5
Fargo, ND	n/a	15.1	7.1	14.8	2.7	10.2	7.5	n/a	3.9	11.0	12.2	3.6	6.2
Ft. Collins, CO	n/a	13.7	4.1	22.1	1.8	11.8	8.1	n/a	3.7	12.9	12.8	1.9	2.2
Ft. Worth, TX[2]	n/a	12.4	6.3	13.6	1.6	11.1	10.2	n/a	3.6	11.2	12.0	7.2	4.6
Gilbert, AZ	4.7	14.6	8.2	13.5	1.6	10.3	6.4	0.2	3.6	16.2	12.5	3.6	4.7
Green Bay, WI	n/a	14.0	7.0	12.3	1.1	9.5	16.8	n/a	5.1	11.9	9.9	4.6	4.4
Henderson, NV	4.7	8.9	4.8	11.5	1.1	32.3	2.4	<0.1	2.9	12.4	12.0	4.4	2.6
High Point, NC	n/a	13.7	5.7	12.8	1.6	8.8	15.3	n/a	3.9	13.8	10.3	4.6	5.3
Honolulu, HI	n/a	13.2	4.7	22.7	1.5	14.4	2.4	n/a	4.5	13.6	10.5	4.5	3.1
Houston, TX	6.4	12.5	5.3	14.2	1.2	9.3	8.7	3.5	3.6	14.7	10.6	4.7	5.2
Huntington, NY[2]	n/a	18.8	5.7	16.7	1.9	7.9	5.8	n/a	4.3	12.8	12.9	3.1	5.4
Huntsville, AL	n/a	8.4	2.9	24.4	1.2	8.5	10.6	n/a	3.7	22.2	11.0	1.3	2.7
Indianapolis, IN	4.6	14.3	6.5	14.0	1.6	9.8	9.1	0.1	3.8	15.0	10.2	6.1	4.9
Irvine, CA[2]	4.8	11.5	7.5	10.9	1.7	12.6	11.2	<0.1	3.1	18.3	10.8	2.0	5.6
Jackson, MS	3.9	15.5	5.9	23.0	1.7	8.5	6.3	0.3	4.0	11.2	11.5	4.0	4.1
Jacksonville, FL	4.3	14.8	9.7	12.9	1.6	10.8	4.5	<0.1	3.8	16.1	12.2	5.1	4.2
Jersey City, NJ[2]	n/a	19.6	10.3	14.3	3.9	8.6	3.1	n/a	4.2	15.6	9.7	3.4	4.3
Kansas City, MO	n/a	13.5	7.1	15.4	2.8	9.6	7.7	n/a	4.5	15.6	10.8	4.5	5.0
Kenosha, WI[2]	3.4	12.7	5.3	14.1	1.1	8.7	14.7	<0.1	3.3	14.3	12.8	2.4	7.0
Las Vegas, NV	4.7	8.9	4.8	11.5	1.1	32.3	2.4	<0.1	2.9	12.4	12.0	4.4	2.6
Lexington, KY	n/a	13.2	4.0	20.0	2.3	10.5	11.3	n/a	4.0	12.5	11.2	3.6	3.6
Lincoln, NE	n/a	15.0	7.7	22.6	1.2	9.0	7.3	n/a	4.0	10.2	10.9	6.1	2.3
Little Rock, AR	n/a	14.7	5.6	21.2	2.2	8.7	5.6	n/a	4.4	12.6	11.5	3.9	4.8

Table continued on next page.

Metro Area[1]	(A)	(B)	(C)	(D)	(E)	(F)	(G)	(H)	(I)	(J)	(K)	(L)	(M)
Los Angeles, CA[2]	2.7	14.1	5.5	14.8	5.3	10.2	9.4	0.1	3.5	14.3	10.7	3.9	5.5
Madison, WI	n/a	11.9	7.5	25.3	3.2	8.2	7.8	n/a	5.4	10.7	11.1	2.4	3.5
Manchester, NH[3]	n/a	19.6	6.7	11.5	3.3	8.3	8.0	n/a	4.2	13.9	13.2	n/a	4.1
Miami, FL[2]	2.9	16.7	6.1	14.4	1.7	11.0	3.5	<0.1	3.9	13.4	13.3	6.0	7.0
Minneapolis, MN	n/a	16.2	7.9	13.4	2.2	8.4	10.3	n/a	4.6	15.8	10.2	3.6	4.6
Murfreesboro, TN	n/a	15.9	6.1	13.7	2.5	10.2	8.3	n/a	4.3	14.5	11.3	4.0	4.8
Naperville, IL[2]	3.0	15.4	6.9	12.6	2.0	9.0	8.8	<0.1	4.5	17.4	10.2	4.8	5.4
Nashville, TN	n/a	15.9	6.1	13.7	2.5	10.2	8.3	n/a	4.3	14.5	11.3	4.0	4.8
New Orleans, LA	5.3	14.9	4.7	15.6	1.4	13.8	6.0	1.3	3.5	13.1	11.1	4.9	4.4
New York, NY[2]	n/a	19.6	10.3	14.3	3.9	8.6	3.1	n/a	4.2	15.6	9.7	3.4	4.3
Norman, OK	4.3	13.9	5.6	20.9	1.7	10.1	5.8	3.1	3.9	12.8	11.2	2.7	4.1
Olathe, KS	n/a	13.5	7.1	15.4	2.8	9.6	7.7	n/a	4.5	15.6	10.8	4.5	5.0
Omaha, NE	n/a	15.9	8.8	14.1	2.4	9.1	6.9	n/a	3.7	14.2	11.2	5.9	3.7
Orlando, FL	4.2	12.1	6.3	11.5	2.3	20.4	3.7	<0.1	4.6	15.8	12.3	3.1	3.7
Overland Park, KS	n/a	13.5	7.1	15.4	2.8	9.6	7.7	n/a	4.5	15.6	10.8	4.5	5.0
Oyster Bay, NY[2]	n/a	18.8	5.7	16.7	1.9	7.9	5.8	n/a	4.3	12.8	12.9	3.1	5.4
Pembroke Pines, FL[2]	3.8	13.6	7.4	13.9	2.3	11.1	3.8	n/a	4.3	16.6	14.0	3.1	6.0
Philadelphia, PA[2]	n/a	23.0	6.9	11.3	2.0	8.2	7.0	n/a	4.5	15.8	10.3	3.2	4.4
Phoenix, AZ	4.7	14.6	8.2	13.5	1.6	10.3	6.4	0.2	3.6	16.2	12.5	3.6	4.7
Pittsburgh, PA	4.2	21.6	6.1	10.9	1.6	9.2	7.5	0.8	4.5	14.3	11.5	3.9	4.1
Plano, TX[2]	n/a	12.2	8.9	13.2	3.1	9.6	8.0	n/a	3.4	16.9	10.4	3.8	5.8
Portland, OR	5.0	14.6	6.2	14.6	2.2	9.8	11.0	0.1	3.4	13.2	10.8	3.5	5.6
Providence, RI[3]	3.4	22.2	6.1	13.2	2.1	10.5	9.6	<0.1	4.4	10.9	11.4	2.5	3.6
Provo, UT	n/a	23.1	3.3	14.8	4.4	6.9	9.3	n/a	2.2	13.5	12.4	1.5	2.7
Raleigh, NC	n/a	12.6	5.1	16.6	3.3	10.5	5.3	n/a	4.4	17.9	12.2	2.2	4.2
Richmond, VA	n/a	13.8	7.4	18.6	1.5	8.8	5.0	n/a	4.8	16.1	10.9	3.4	4.5
Roseville, CA	4.3	13.1	5.9	27.6	2.1	9.6	4.1	<0.1	3.4	12.7	11.7	2.7	2.9
Round Rock, TX	n/a	11.6	5.7	20.9	2.5	11.5	6.4	n/a	4.2	14.6	10.8	1.7	5.3
San Antonio, TX	4.7	15.5	8.1	18.7	2.1	12.2	5.4	0.4	3.7	11.7	11.7	2.5	3.4
San Diego, CA	4.5	12.3	5.3	18.4	1.9	12.6	7.4	<0.1	3.7	17.3	11.2	2.1	3.2
San Francisco, CA[2]	3.3	11.6	8.0	14.0	4.4	13.3	3.8	<0.1	4.2	21.6	9.6	3.7	2.5
San Jose, CA	3.6	13.6	3.6	10.5	5.7	8.5	17.6	<0.1	2.7	19.4	9.5	1.4	4.0
Savannah, GA	n/a	15.9	3.4	15.3	0.9	13.0	9.5	n/a	4.5	11.6	11.8	6.6	3.7
Scottsdale, AZ	4.7	14.6	8.2	13.5	1.6	10.3	6.4	0.2	3.6	16.2	12.5	3.6	4.7
Seattle, WA[2]	4.5	12.2	5.4	14.1	6.0	9.5	11.6	<0.1	3.6	14.6	10.3	3.4	4.8
Sioux Falls, SD	n/a	20.5	10.9	9.4	2.1	9.2	8.9	n/a	3.5	8.7	13.7	3.7	5.1
Stamford, CT[3]	n/a	17.4	10.3	11.6	2.7	8.2	8.8	n/a	4.1	16.0	12.1	2.8	3.5
Sterling Hgts, MI[2]	n/a	15.3	6.1	9.5	1.7	8.7	12.4	n/a	4.4	19.7	12.1	1.8	5.0
Sunnyvale, CA	3.6	13.6	3.6	10.5	5.7	8.5	17.6	<0.1	2.7	19.4	9.5	1.4	4.0
Tampa, FL	4.3	16.0	8.0	13.7	2.3	11.2	5.2	<0.1	3.8	16.6	12.7	2.3	4.0
Temecula, CA	4.9	12.2	3.4	19.7	1.3	11.3	7.5	0.1	3.5	11.3	14.3	6.1	4.4
Thousand Oaks, CA	3.8	11.4	7.9	16.3	1.8	11.6	10.9	0.4	3.2	11.8	13.9	2.2	4.7
Virginia Beach, VA	n/a	13.3	5.1	22.1	1.5	10.3	7.0	n/a	4.7	13.2	11.9	3.3	2.8
Washington, DC[2]	n/a	12.0	4.4	24.0	2.7	9.1	1.4	n/a	6.2	23.0	8.4	2.4	1.9
U.S.	4.1	15.2	5.8	16.8	2.0	9.9	8.9	0.6	4.0	13.3	11.5	3.8	4.2

Note: All figures are percentages covering non-farm employment as of December 2011 and are not seasonally adjusted;
(1) Figures cover the Metropolitan Statistical Area (MSA) except where noted. See Appendix B for areas included; (2) Metropolitan Division; (3) New England City and Town Area; (4) New England City and Town Area Division; (A) Construction; (B) Education and Health Services; (C) Financial Activities; (D) Government; (E) Information; (F) Leisure and Hospitality; (G) Manufacturing; (H) Mining and Logging; (I) Other Services; (J) Professional and Business Services; (K) Retail Trade; (L) Transportation and Utilities; (M) Wholesale Trade; n/a not available
Source: Bureau of Labor Statistics, http://stats.bls.gov

Labor Force, Employment and Job Growth: City

City	Civilian Labor Force			Workers Employed		
	Dec. 2010	Dec. 2011	% Chg.	Dec. 2010	Dec. 2011	% Chg.
Albuquerque, NM	263,601	259,931	-1.4	242,952	243,858	0.4
Alexandria, VA	96,695	99,117	2.5	92,424	94,516	2.3
Anchorage, AK	158,312	158,419	0.1	148,244	149,527	0.9
Ann Arbor, MI	63,099	62,103	-1.6	58,664	58,474	-0.3
Athens, GA	64,416	65,002	0.9	59,484	60,085	1.0
Atlanta, GA	232,329	235,446	1.3	206,028	210,598	2.2
Austin, TX	429,920	437,604	1.8	402,844	412,519	2.4
Baltimore, MD	274,017	276,429	0.9	245,658	250,713	2.1
Bellevue, WA	70,579	70,735	0.2	65,672	66,650	1.5
Billings, MT	58,498	58,675	0.3	55,316	55,995	1.2
Boise City, ID	106,962	109,041	1.9	97,521	100,874	3.4
Boston, MA	327,437	328,123	0.2	303,503	308,489	1.6
Boulder, CO	61,762	63,548	2.9	56,942	59,248	4.0
Broken Arrow, OK	47,469	47,735	0.6	44,782	45,322	1.2
Cambridge, MA	61,690	61,845	0.3	58,516	59,478	1.6
Cape Coral, FL	79,492	77,945	-1.9	69,476	70,234	1.1
Carlsbad, CA	47,115	48,251	2.4	43,939	45,410	3.3
Cary, NC	67,380	68,240	1.3	63,838	64,425	0.9
Cedar Rapids, IA	73,950	72,027	-2.6	69,600	67,747	-2.7
Charleston, SC	58,080	58,384	0.5	53,354	54,387	1.9
Charlotte, NC	344,387	344,240	0.0	315,035	314,451	-0.2
Chesapeake, VA	115,110	116,021	0.8	107,570	108,539	0.9
Chicago, IL	1,314,404	1,315,611	0.1	1,189,884	1,179,903	-0.8
Clarksville, TN	53,642	55,136	2.8	48,676	50,390	3.5
Colorado Spgs., CO	209,764	210,018	0.1	190,593	191,463	0.5
Columbia, MD	n/a	n/a	n/a	n/a	n/a	n/a
Columbia, MO	58,328	60,051	3.0	55,017	57,394	4.3
Columbia, SC	54,922	54,995	0.1	49,714	50,533	1.6
Columbus, OH	424,902	414,403	-2.5	392,390	387,740	-1.2
Dallas, TX	602,997	609,820	1.1	551,590	562,113	1.9
Denver, CO	319,329	325,874	2.0	288,061	295,836	2.7
Durham, NC	116,938	117,698	0.6	109,337	109,655	0.3
Edison, NJ	53,777	54,648	1.6	50,546	51,180	1.3
El Paso, TX	274,211	276,634	0.9	249,990	253,316	1.3
Fargo, ND	57,385	57,140	-0.4	55,304	55,356	0.1
Ft. Collins, CO	82,975	85,576	3.1	76,097	79,425	4.4
Ft. Worth, TX	338,904	342,699	1.1	311,270	317,744	2.1
Gilbert, AZ	118,345	118,842	0.4	112,626	113,586	0.9
Green Bay, WI	57,410	56,848	-1.0	51,922	51,633	-0.6
Henderson, NV	139,492	138,309	-0.8	119,913	122,019	1.8
High Point, NC	49,686	50,804	2.3	44,768	45,686	2.1
Honolulu, HI	441,056	444,744	0.8	419,892	421,022	0.3
Houston, TX	1,080,233	1,106,150	2.4	994,389	1,028,242	3.4
Huntington, NY	103,518	102,352	-1.1	97,144	95,951	-1.2
Huntsville, AL	90,774	91,862	1.2	84,297	85,874	1.9
Indianapolis, IN	403,445	410,978	1.9	366,365	373,380	1.9
Irvine, CA	81,681	83,158	1.8	76,160	78,312	2.8
Jackson, MS	82,262	83,529	1.5	74,537	75,583	1.4
Jacksonville, FL	417,935	418,417	0.1	371,136	379,176	2.2
Jersey City, NJ	116,396	118,479	1.8	104,596	106,956	2.3
Kansas City, MO	227,884	232,627	2.1	204,805	213,256	4.1
Kenosha, WI	48,638	48,381	-0.5	43,697	44,134	1.0
Las Vegas, NV	277,063	273,342	-1.3	233,762	237,867	1.8
Lexington, KY	157,131	155,894	-0.8	145,319	145,813	0.3
Lincoln, NE	142,326	147,514	3.6	137,422	142,315	3.6

Table continued on next page.

City	Civilian Labor Force			Workers Employed		
	Dec. 2010	Dec. 2011	% Chg.	Dec. 2010	Dec. 2011	% Chg.
Little Rock, AR	98,119	97,912	-0.2	91,248	91,395	0.2
Los Angeles, CA	1,920,895	1,906,816	-0.7	1,653,729	1,663,084	0.6
Madison, WI	144,027	144,473	0.3	137,726	138,351	0.5
Manchester, NH	61,974	61,913	-0.1	58,202	58,542	0.6
Miami, FL	200,338	200,590	0.1	172,181	178,782	3.8
Minneapolis, MN	213,279	214,649	0.6	200,008	203,286	1.6
Murfreesboro, TN	56,085	56,571	0.9	51,593	52,687	2.1
Naperville, IL	75,809	75,675	-0.2	71,459	70,861	-0.8
Nashville, TN	332,223	334,839	0.8	305,276	311,750	2.1
New Orleans, LA	148,131	144,947	-2.1	135,477	133,707	-1.3
New York, NY	3,927,942	3,948,044	0.5	3,583,336	3,599,448	0.4
Norman, OK	54,333	54,846	0.9	51,726	52,401	1.3
Olathe, KS	61,009	61,212	0.3	57,271	57,979	1.2
Omaha, NE	236,084	244,589	3.6	225,948	233,849	3.5
Orlando, FL	136,757	135,243	-1.1	121,383	122,868	1.2
Overland Park, KS	95,913	96,238	0.3	90,071	91,185	1.2
Oyster Bay, NY	152,818	150,530	-1.5	143,348	141,589	-1.2
Pembroke Pines, FL	82,381	81,684	-0.8	74,479	75,293	1.1
Philadelphia, PA	646,182	644,690	-0.2	578,561	579,890	0.2
Phoenix, AZ	800,878	800,658	0.0	722,214	728,367	0.9
Pittsburgh, PA	152,110	154,598	1.6	140,667	144,400	2.7
Plano, TX	147,581	149,299	1.2	137,656	140,283	1.9
Portland, OR	310,800	315,295	1.4	282,198	290,279	2.9
Providence, RI	80,643	79,067	-2.0	70,192	69,132	-1.5
Provo, UT	68,637	68,566	-0.1	63,343	64,523	1.9
Raleigh, NC	206,489	209,124	1.3	192,821	194,595	0.9
Richmond, VA	101,190	102,291	1.1	91,741	93,223	1.6
Roseville, CA	54,742	54,780	0.1	48,587	49,540	2.0
Round Rock, TX	53,943	54,845	1.7	50,395	51,605	2.4
San Antonio, TX	646,232	649,341	0.5	602,179	607,078	0.8
San Diego, CA	694,528	708,004	1.9	624,205	645,104	3.3
San Francisco, CA	456,081	463,288	1.6	414,765	428,039	3.2
San Jose, CA	458,015	466,747	1.9	405,371	421,559	4.0
Savannah, GA	63,625	64,361	1.2	56,977	57,626	1.1
Scottsdale, AZ	128,435	128,808	0.3	120,385	121,410	0.9
Seattle, WA	377,030	378,637	0.4	348,306	353,489	1.5
Sioux Falls, SD	86,840	88,314	1.7	82,385	84,389	2.4
Stamford, CT	67,654	67,672	0.0	62,891	63,288	0.6
Sterling Hgts, MI	63,730	63,483	-0.4	58,274	58,796	0.9
Sunnyvale, CA	74,400	76,170	2.4	67,784	70,491	4.0
Tampa, FL	162,264	163,252	0.6	143,133	147,016	2.7
Temecula, CA	36,269	36,869	1.7	32,733	33,729	3.0
Thousand Oaks, CA	70,198	71,202	1.4	64,388	66,037	2.6
Virginia Beach, VA	219,880	221,985	1.0	206,492	208,352	0.9
Washington, DC	340,478	342,348	0.5	307,792	308,647	0.3
U.S.	153,156,000	153,373,000	0.1	139,159,000	140,681,000	1.1

Note: Data is not seasonally adjusted and covers workers 16 years of age and older
Source: Bureau of Labor Statistics, http://stats.bls.gov

Labor Force, Employment and Job Growth: Metro Area

Metro Area[1]	Civilian Labor Force			Workers Employed		
	Dec. 2010	Dec. 2011	% Chg.	Dec. 2010	Dec. 2011	% Chg.
Albuquerque, NM	409,834	403,769	-1.5	374,929	376,326	0.4
Alexandria, VA[2]	2,417,159	2,457,806	1.7	2,277,413	2,317,235	1.7
Anchorage, AK	202,320	202,675	0.2	188,153	189,781	0.9
Ann Arbor, MI	183,061	180,313	-1.5	170,996	170,441	-0.3
Athens, GA	106,744	107,479	0.7	98,651	99,649	1.0
Atlanta, GA	2,661,869	2,697,848	1.4	2,391,846	2,444,914	2.2
Austin, TX	902,646	918,215	1.7	840,510	860,696	2.4
Baltimore, MD	1,383,128	1,401,399	1.3	1,280,277	1,306,623	2.1
Bellevue, WA[2]	1,483,979	1,492,083	0.5	1,350,324	1,383,080	2.4
Billings, MT	85,204	85,505	0.4	80,398	81,385	1.2
Boise City, ID	292,392	297,808	1.9	263,652	272,718	3.4
Boston, MA[4]	1,542,443	1,545,454	0.2	1,437,727	1,461,346	1.6
Boulder, CO	171,897	177,145	3.1	160,365	166,859	4.0
Broken Arrow, OK	434,239	435,748	0.3	402,253	407,100	1.2
Cambridge, MA[4]	1,542,443	1,545,454	0.2	1,437,727	1,461,346	1.6
Cape Coral, FL	275,835	271,425	-1.6	241,175	243,805	1.1
Carlsbad, CA	1,555,853	1,586,031	1.9	1,398,252	1,445,067	3.3
Cary, NC	557,030	563,930	1.2	514,126	518,857	0.9
Cedar Rapids, IA	148,332	144,171	-2.8	139,176	135,472	-2.7
Charleston, SC	319,849	322,117	0.7	291,009	296,646	1.9
Charlotte, NC	851,629	846,945	-0.6	760,716	760,131	-0.1
Chesapeake, VA	816,488	823,932	0.9	759,028	765,680	0.9
Chicago, IL[2]	4,026,455	4,053,839	0.7	3,657,424	3,676,824	0.5
Clarksville, TN	114,219	115,797	1.4	103,012	105,700	2.6
Colorado Spgs., CO	304,273	304,234	0.0	275,536	276,793	0.5
Columbia, MD	1,383,128	1,401,399	1.3	1,280,277	1,306,623	2.1
Columbia, MO	94,543	97,328	2.9	88,690	92,521	4.3
Columbia, SC	366,913	368,534	0.4	333,605	339,100	1.6
Columbus, OH	970,812	946,232	-2.5	895,916	885,299	-1.2
Dallas, TX[2]	2,158,513	2,180,878	1.0	1,985,464	2,023,344	1.9
Denver, CO	1,366,243	1,391,518	1.8	1,245,326	1,278,938	2.7
Durham, NC	260,016	262,346	0.9	242,064	242,767	0.3
Edison, NJ[2]	1,183,238	1,200,353	1.4	1,088,479	1,102,122	1.3
El Paso, TX	322,362	325,199	0.9	291,214	295,088	1.3
Fargo, ND	118,139	118,780	0.5	113,300	114,431	1.0
Ft. Collins, CO	173,200	178,902	3.3	160,659	167,686	4.4
Ft. Worth, TX[2]	1,072,202	1,083,608	1.1	987,399	1,007,942	2.1
Gilbert, AZ	2,125,593	2,127,867	0.1	1,944,188	1,960,752	0.9
Green Bay, WI	171,052	169,643	-0.8	159,800	158,912	-0.6
Henderson, NV	952,734	942,225	-1.1	808,526	822,726	1.8
High Point, NC	355,892	362,706	1.9	319,890	326,336	2.0
Honolulu, HI	441,056	444,744	0.8	419,892	421,022	0.3
Houston, TX	2,917,366	2,986,579	2.4	2,676,277	2,767,389	3.4
Huntington, NY[2]	1,458,781	1,439,419	-1.3	1,356,608	1,339,955	-1.2
Huntsville, AL	206,531	208,703	1.1	191,689	195,276	1.9
Indianapolis, IN	876,004	891,271	1.7	802,574	817,942	1.9
Irvine, CA[2]	1,573,923	1,597,153	1.5	1,432,760	1,473,258	2.8
Jackson, MS	269,419	273,599	1.6	248,550	252,036	1.4
Jacksonville, FL	688,236	688,514	0.0	611,911	625,167	2.2
Jersey City, NJ[2]	5,658,379	5,697,298	0.7	5,184,743	5,213,699	0.6
Kansas City, MO	1,021,911	1,037,809	1.6	934,486	961,572	2.9
Kenosha, WI[2]	450,241	443,917	-1.4	407,790	402,654	-1.3
Las Vegas, NV	952,734	942,225	-1.1	808,526	822,726	1.8
Lexington, KY	244,730	242,479	-0.9	224,961	225,726	0.3
Lincoln, NE	166,153	172,202	3.6	160,218	165,923	3.6

Table continued on next page.

Metro Area[1]	Civilian Labor Force			Workers Employed		
	Dec. 2010	Dec. 2011	% Chg.	Dec. 2010	Dec. 2011	% Chg.
Little Rock, AR	343,271	342,811	-0.1	320,094	320,610	0.2
Los Angeles, CA[2]	4,943,016	4,931,592	-0.2	4,329,943	4,358,225	0.7
Madison, WI	341,563	342,337	0.2	324,709	326,183	0.5
Manchester, NH[3]	107,716	107,839	0.1	102,028	102,624	0.6
Miami, FL[2]	1,253,036	1,279,120	2.1	1,098,081	1,148,960	4.6
Minneapolis, MN	1,824,877	1,833,108	0.5	1,705,057	1,732,939	1.6
Murfreesboro, TN	823,775	831,576	0.9	758,483	774,567	2.1
Naperville, IL[2]	4,026,455	4,053,839	0.7	3,657,424	3,676,824	0.5
Nashville, TN	823,775	831,576	0.9	758,483	774,567	2.1
New Orleans, LA	541,914	531,205	-2.0	503,787	497,205	-1.3
New York, NY[2]	5,658,379	5,697,298	0.7	5,184,743	5,213,699	0.6
Norman, OK	567,828	572,012	0.7	533,083	540,026	1.3
Olathe, KS	1,021,911	1,037,809	1.6	934,486	961,572	2.9
Omaha, NE	444,254	457,378	3.0	423,346	436,050	3.0
Orlando, FL	1,125,039	1,113,686	-1.0	996,137	1,008,325	1.2
Overland Park, KS	1,021,911	1,037,809	1.6	934,486	961,572	2.9
Oyster Bay, NY[2]	1,458,781	1,439,419	-1.3	1,356,608	1,339,955	-1.2
Pembroke Pines, FL[2]	985,607	978,951	-0.7	885,009	894,687	1.1
Philadelphia, PA[2]	1,940,214	1,933,020	-0.4	1,782,318	1,786,411	0.2
Phoenix, AZ	2,125,593	2,127,867	0.1	1,944,188	1,960,752	0.9
Pittsburgh, PA	1,208,450	1,227,585	1.6	1,117,431	1,147,086	2.7
Plano, TX[2]	2,158,513	2,180,878	1.0	1,985,464	2,023,344	1.9
Portland, OR	1,193,027	1,197,593	0.4	1,076,210	1,100,953	2.3
Providence, RI[3]	713,425	701,670	-1.6	636,018	628,393	-1.2
Provo, UT	225,671	225,769	0.0	209,836	213,746	1.9
Raleigh, NC	557,030	563,930	1.2	514,126	518,857	0.9
Richmond, VA	647,263	654,793	1.2	600,602	610,300	1.6
Roseville, CA	1,026,651	1,026,925	0.0	897,351	914,943	2.0
Round Rock, TX	902,646	918,215	1.7	840,510	860,696	2.4
San Antonio, TX	989,732	992,776	0.3	918,035	925,503	0.8
San Diego, CA	1,555,853	1,586,031	1.9	1,398,252	1,445,067	3.3
San Francisco, CA[2]	956,585	974,257	1.8	875,013	903,017	3.2
San Jose, CA	897,548	915,977	2.1	802,344	834,386	4.0
Savannah, GA	175,491	177,044	0.9	159,717	161,537	1.1
Scottsdale, AZ	2,125,593	2,127,867	0.1	1,944,188	1,960,752	0.9
Seattle, WA[2]	1,483,979	1,492,083	0.5	1,350,324	1,383,080	2.4
Sioux Falls, SD	128,476	130,762	1.8	122,169	125,141	2.4
Stamford, CT[3]	477,386	475,420	-0.4	439,033	441,807	0.6
Sterling Hgts, MI[2]	1,195,732	1,187,612	-0.7	1,071,444	1,081,037	0.9
Sunnyvale, CA	897,548	915,977	2.1	802,344	834,386	4.0
Tampa, FL	1,298,265	1,301,885	0.3	1,140,498	1,171,437	2.7
Temecula, CA	1,761,147	1,778,349	1.0	1,514,937	1,561,051	3.0
Thousand Oaks, CA	427,638	432,361	1.1	382,087	391,874	2.6
Virginia Beach, VA	816,488	823,932	0.9	759,028	765,680	0.9
Washington, DC[2]	2,417,159	2,457,806	1.7	2,277,413	2,317,235	1.7
U.S.	153,156,000	153,373,000	0.1	139,159,000	140,681,000	1.1

Note: Data is not seasonally adjusted and covers workers 16 years of age and older; (1) Figures cover the Metropolitan Statistical Area (MSA) except where noted. See Appendix B for areas included; (2) Metropolitan Division; (3) New England City and Town Area; (4) New England City and Town Area Division
Source: Bureau of Labor Statistics, http://stats.bls.gov

Unemployment Rate: City

City	\multicolumn{12}{c}{2011}
	Jan.	Feb.	Mar.	Apr.	May	Jun.	Jul.	Aug.	Sep.	Oct.	Nov.	Dec.
Albuquerque, NM	8.4	8.4	7.1	6.6	6.2	7.4	6.9	6.5	6.3	6.4	6.1	6.2
Alexandria, VA	4.9	4.7	4.5	4.1	4.5	4.8	4.5	4.8	4.8	4.5	4.3	4.6
Anchorage, AK	6.6	6.5	6.5	6.2	6.1	6.7	6.0	5.8	5.8	5.5	5.4	5.6
Ann Arbor, MI	7.4	7.0	7.5	6.6	7.2	8.2	8.3	7.7	7.0	6.1	5.5	5.8
Athens, GA	7.8	7.6	7.5	7.1	7.4	8.8	8.2	8.1	8.3	7.7	7.1	7.6
Atlanta, GA	11.5	11.2	10.7	10.5	10.6	11.7	11.5	11.7	11.5	11.0	10.3	10.6
Austin, TX	6.7	6.4	6.3	6.1	6.3	7.0	7.0	6.8	6.9	6.5	6.0	5.7
Baltimore, MD	10.8	10.2	9.9	9.5	9.9	10.8	11.1	10.9	10.3	9.9	9.2	9.3
Bellevue, WA	7.0	7.3	7.2	6.5	6.6	7.4	7.3	6.8	6.8	6.6	6.1	5.8
Billings, MT	6.1	5.6	5.6	4.8	5.0	5.9	5.5	5.5	5.2	5.0	4.6	4.6
Boise City, ID	9.5	9.3	9.0	8.6	8.1	8.5	7.9	7.9	7.8	7.7	7.7	7.5
Boston, MA	7.9	7.3	6.8	6.6	6.9	7.7	7.8	6.9	7.1	6.7	6.0	6.0
Boulder, CO	9.0	8.7	8.0	7.2	7.3	8.1	8.0	7.6	6.9	6.9	6.9	6.8
Broken Arrow, OK	5.9	6.0	4.9	4.3	4.6	5.2	5.1	4.5	5.0	5.2	4.9	5.1
Cambridge, MA	5.3	4.8	4.3	4.5	4.9	5.7	5.5	4.6	5.0	4.8	4.1	3.8
Cape Coral, FL	12.6	11.8	11.2	10.6	10.7	11.3	11.1	11.1	10.8	10.4	10.3	9.9
Carlsbad, CA	6.9	6.7	6.8	6.5	6.4	6.9	7.1	6.8	6.5	6.4	6.1	5.9
Cary, NC	5.8	5.7	5.5	5.7	5.9	6.3	6.2	6.5	6.1	5.8	5.6	5.6
Cedar Rapids, IA	6.3	6.3	6.4	6.0	5.7	6.1	5.8	6.4	5.8	5.7	5.4	5.9
Charleston, SC	7.5	7.8	7.0	7.1	7.9	9.1	8.8	8.7	7.9	7.2	6.9	6.8
Charlotte, NC	8.8	8.9	8.7	8.7	9.0	10.0	9.9	9.8	9.2	8.9	8.8	8.7
Chesapeake, VA	6.8	6.5	6.3	6.0	6.2	6.7	6.7	7.0	6.9	6.5	6.2	6.4
Chicago, IL	10.1	9.6	9.3	9.5	10.8	11.4	11.7	11.7	11.2	11.2	11.2	10.3
Clarksville, TN	10.3	10.2	9.7	9.4	9.5	10.3	9.8	9.9	9.9	9.6	9.3	8.6
Colorado Spgs., CO	10.4	10.2	9.8	8.9	9.1	9.6	9.4	9.1	8.4	8.5	8.5	8.8
Columbia, MD	n/a	n/a	n/a	n/a	n/a	n/a	n/a	n/a	n/a	n/a	n/a	n/a
Columbia, MO	6.3	5.7	5.6	5.1	5.7	6.5	6.3	6.4	5.3	5.1	4.5	4.4
Columbia, SC	8.3	8.5	8.5	8.3	10.0	11.5	11.3	10.6	9.8	9.0	8.0	8.1
Columbus, OH	8.3	8.1	7.5	7.3	7.5	8.3	8.3	8.0	7.8	7.7	6.8	6.4
Dallas, TX	9.0	8.6	8.5	8.2	8.4	9.2	9.1	8.8	8.9	8.7	8.1	7.8
Denver, CO	10.9	10.7	10.2	9.1	9.2	9.4	9.3	9.3	8.7	8.7	8.8	9.2
Durham, NC	7.1	7.0	6.8	6.9	7.1	7.8	7.7	8.0	7.7	7.2	6.9	6.8
Edison, NJ	6.6	7.0	6.7	7.0	7.2	7.9	8.0	7.0	7.1	6.8	7.0	6.3
El Paso, TX	9.5	9.2	9.2	8.9	9.1	10.0	10.1	9.8	9.7	9.4	8.7	8.4
Fargo, ND	4.3	4.1	4.0	3.3	3.1	3.8	3.1	3.3	2.9	2.9	2.9	3.1
Ft. Collins, CO	9.7	9.5	8.8	7.7	7.6	8.0	7.9	7.6	6.9	7.0	7.1	7.2
Ft. Worth, TX	8.7	8.3	8.4	8.0	8.3	9.1	9.1	8.7	8.7	8.2	7.6	7.3
Gilbert, AZ	5.3	5.0	4.9	4.6	4.5	5.1	4.9	4.8	4.5	4.5	4.3	4.4
Green Bay, WI	11.0	11.2	10.8	10.0	10.1	11.2	10.8	10.1	9.6	9.2	9.4	9.2
Henderson, NV	12.1	12.8	12.4	11.1	11.3	12.7	12.8	13.0	12.5	12.0	11.6	11.8
High Point, NC	10.1	9.8	9.6	9.3	9.9	10.6	10.7	11.0	10.5	10.5	10.1	10.1
Honolulu, HI	5.4	5.3	5.0	4.6	4.9	5.7	5.4	5.5	5.7	5.6	5.7	5.3
Houston, TX	8.4	8.1	8.0	7.7	7.9	8.8	8.7	8.4	8.5	7.9	7.3	7.0
Huntington, NY	7.2	7.0	6.4	5.8	6.1	6.4	6.2	5.8	6.0	5.9	6.0	6.3
Huntsville, AL	8.2	7.7	7.4	7.5	7.9	9.0	8.6	8.2	8.1	7.4	6.8	6.5
Indianapolis, IN	9.4	9.3	8.9	8.5	8.7	9.1	9.0	9.2	9.0	9.4	9.3	9.1
Irvine, CA	6.9	6.7	6.8	6.5	6.4	6.9	7.0	6.8	6.5	6.4	6.1	5.8
Jackson, MS	10.4	10.1	9.8	9.6	9.4	10.5	10.5	9.3	10.1	9.9	9.4	9.5
Jacksonville, FL	11.6	10.7	10.3	10.0	10.1	10.9	11.0	11.0	10.3	9.8	9.7	9.4
Jersey City, NJ	10.5	10.6	10.5	10.4	11.1	11.6	10.9	10.3	10.8	10.4	10.3	9.7
Kansas City, MO	10.9	10.1	9.6	9.3	10.0	9.7	9.7	10.4	9.6	9.1	8.5	8.3
Kenosha, WI	11.1	11.2	10.8	10.3	10.3	10.7	11.2	10.5	9.9	9.6	9.8	8.8
Las Vegas, NV	13.5	14.3	13.8	12.3	12.7	14.1	14.3	14.6	13.9	13.3	12.6	13.0
Lexington, KY	8.7	8.6	7.9	7.7	7.3	7.6	7.5	7.2	7.8	7.0	6.7	6.5
Lincoln, NE	4.1	4.1	4.0	3.8	3.6	4.1	3.8	3.6	3.5	3.3	3.1	3.5

Table continued on next page.

City	2011											
	Jan.	Feb.	Mar.	Apr.	May	Jun.	Jul.	Aug.	Sep.	Oct.	Nov.	Dec.
Little Rock, AR	7.6	7.3	7.1	6.7	7.2	8.1	7.9	7.7	7.5	6.8	6.6	6.7
Los Angeles, CA	14.4	13.5	13.4	12.9	13.0	13.6	14.6	13.9	13.4	13.1	12.7	12.8
Madison, WI	5.0	5.2	4.9	4.7	5.1	6.0	5.5	5.3	5.2	5.0	4.4	4.2
Manchester, NH	6.6	6.4	5.7	5.1	5.3	5.6	5.8	5.8	5.7	5.4	5.4	5.4
Miami, FL	13.0	12.7	13.2	14.2	14.6	14.8	13.3	13.4	12.2	11.3	10.0	10.9
Minneapolis, MN	6.5	6.2	6.1	6.0	6.3	7.4	7.5	7.2	6.3	5.8	5.4	5.3
Murfreesboro, TN	8.9	8.8	8.4	8.7	8.9	9.7	9.2	9.2	9.0	7.9	7.4	6.9
Naperville, IL	6.3	6.0	5.8	6.1	7.3	8.1	8.1	7.9	7.4	7.2	7.1	6.4
Nashville, TN	8.6	8.7	8.3	8.8	8.5	9.1	8.5	8.8	8.7	7.8	7.3	6.9
New Orleans, LA	10.0	9.0	9.1	8.4	9.3	9.6	9.7	9.1	8.6	8.7	7.8	7.8
New York, NY	9.4	9.1	8.6	8.4	8.6	8.9	9.3	9.2	9.1	9.2	8.9	8.8
Norman, OK	5.0	4.9	4.1	3.7	4.0	5.0	4.7	4.2	4.3	4.8	4.4	4.5
Olathe, KS	6.9	6.4	6.6	5.8	5.8	6.0	6.3	6.1	6.2	6.0	5.5	5.3
Omaha, NE	5.0	4.9	4.7	4.5	4.4	4.8	4.7	4.4	4.2	4.1	3.9	4.4
Orlando, FL	11.5	10.6	10.2	9.7	9.7	10.2	10.3	10.3	10.0	9.7	9.4	9.2
Overland Park, KS	6.8	6.4	6.6	5.7	5.8	6.0	6.3	6.1	6.2	6.0	5.5	5.3
Oyster Bay, NY	6.7	6.5	5.9	5.8	6.1	6.5	6.4	6.1	6.2	5.9	6.0	5.9
Pembroke Pines, FL	10.0	9.1	8.7	8.3	8.3	9.0	9.0	9.0	8.7	8.3	8.2	7.8
Philadelphia, PA	10.7	10.4	10.0	9.3	10.2	10.7	11.2	11.6	11.0	10.6	10.5	10.1
Phoenix, AZ	10.7	10.2	10.0	9.4	9.2	10.3	10.0	9.7	9.3	9.3	8.8	9.0
Pittsburgh, PA	7.6	7.4	7.3	6.7	7.3	7.7	8.1	8.4	7.4	6.9	7.0	6.6
Plano, TX	7.4	7.1	7.2	6.9	7.1	7.6	7.4	7.2	7.3	6.9	6.4	6.0
Portland, OR	9.8	9.7	9.3	8.3	8.2	9.0	8.6	8.7	8.4	8.3	7.6	7.9
Providence, RI	13.5	13.3	13.3	13.4	14.2	14.0	15.0	13.4	12.8	13.0	12.7	12.6
Provo, UT	9.1	9.1	8.4	7.7	8.3	8.7	8.8	8.7	7.5	7.0	6.0	5.9
Raleigh, NC	7.2	7.0	6.8	6.8	7.0	7.8	7.7	8.0	7.6	7.2	6.9	6.9
Richmond, VA	9.8	9.2	8.9	8.4	8.9	9.3	9.4	9.9	9.5	9.0	8.5	8.9
Roseville, CA	11.6	11.5	11.6	11.0	10.9	11.4	11.3	10.9	10.4	10.4	9.9	9.6
Round Rock, TX	7.0	6.6	6.7	6.2	6.5	7.4	7.3	6.9	7.0	6.7	6.1	5.9
San Antonio, TX	7.4	7.0	7.0	6.8	7.1	7.9	8.0	7.6	7.7	7.3	6.7	6.5
San Diego, CA	10.3	10.1	10.2	9.8	9.6	10.4	10.6	10.2	9.8	9.7	9.2	8.9
San Francisco, CA	9.5	9.1	9.2	8.5	8.4	9.0	9.1	8.8	8.3	8.1	7.8	7.6
San Jose, CA	11.7	11.4	11.4	11.0	10.8	11.4	11.4	11.0	10.7	10.5	10.1	9.7
Savannah, GA	10.7	10.3	9.9	9.5	9.8	11.4	11.3	11.4	11.2	10.6	9.9	10.5
Scottsdale, AZ	6.8	6.5	6.4	6.0	5.9	6.6	6.4	6.2	5.9	5.9	5.6	5.7
Seattle, WA	7.9	8.0	7.8	7.4	7.3	8.2	8.1	7.6	7.6	7.4	7.0	6.6
Sioux Falls, SD	5.5	5.8	5.7	5.0	4.9	4.8	4.5	4.7	4.2	4.1	3.9	4.4
Stamford, CT	7.9	8.1	7.7	7.1	7.4	7.3	7.5	7.5	7.1	7.1	6.7	6.5
Sterling Hgts, MI	9.0	9.2	9.0	8.6	8.9	9.8	11.2	9.8	9.1	8.3	7.3	7.4
Sunnyvale, CA	9.0	8.8	8.9	8.5	8.3	8.8	8.8	8.5	8.2	8.1	7.8	7.5
Tampa, FL	12.2	11.3	11.0	10.5	10.7	11.3	11.3	11.0	10.8	10.2	10.2	9.9
Temecula, CA	9.8	9.7	9.7	9.2	9.0	9.9	10.4	10.0	9.6	9.4	8.7	8.5
Thousand Oaks, CA	8.5	8.1	8.1	7.5	7.3	8.0	8.2	8.2	7.8	7.6	7.4	7.3
Virginia Beach, VA	6.5	6.1	6.0	5.6	5.6	6.0	5.9	6.3	6.4	6.1	5.8	6.1
Washington, DC	10.5	9.8	10.1	9.4	10.0	11.3	10.9	10.4	10.5	10.1	9.9	9.8
U.S.	9.8	9.5	9.2	8.7	8.7	9.3	9.3	9.1	8.8	8.5	8.2	8.3

Note: Data is not seasonally adjusted and covers workers 16 years of age and older; All figures are percentages
Source: Bureau of Labor Statistics, http://stats.bls.gov

Unemployment Rate: Metro Area

Metro Area[1]	2011											
	Jan.	Feb.	Mar.	Apr.	May	Jun.	Jul.	Aug.	Sep.	Oct.	Nov.	Dec.
Albuquerque, NM	9.0	9.1	7.7	7.2	6.8	8.2	7.7	7.2	6.9	7.0	6.7	6.8
Alexandria, VA[2]	6.2	6.0	5.9	5.5	5.8	6.3	6.2	6.2	6.2	5.8	5.5	5.7
Anchorage, AK	7.4	7.3	7.3	6.8	6.6	7.2	6.4	6.2	6.2	6.0	6.1	6.4
Ann Arbor, MI	6.9	6.5	7.0	6.2	6.8	7.7	7.8	7.2	6.6	5.7	5.1	5.5
Athens, GA	8.0	7.6	7.3	7.1	7.2	8.3	7.8	7.8	8.0	7.5	6.9	7.3
Atlanta, GA	10.4	10.2	9.8	9.6	9.7	10.5	10.3	10.3	10.2	9.9	9.2	9.4
Austin, TX	7.3	6.9	6.8	6.5	6.8	7.6	7.6	7.4	7.5	7.1	6.6	6.3
Baltimore, MD	7.9	7.7	7.4	7.0	7.3	7.8	7.9	7.8	7.6	7.1	6.6	6.8
Bellevue, WA[2]	9.3	9.3	8.8	8.1	8.3	9.0	8.7	8.0	8.2	8.1	7.7	7.3
Billings, MT	6.4	6.0	5.9	5.1	5.2	6.0	5.6	5.6	5.4	5.2	4.7	4.8
Boise City, ID	10.8	10.5	10.1	9.5	8.8	9.7	9.1	9.0	8.5	8.4	8.5	8.4
Boston, MA[4]	7.4	7.1	6.6	6.2	6.3	6.8	6.8	6.0	6.3	6.0	5.4	5.4
Boulder, CO	7.7	7.5	6.9	6.2	6.3	7.0	6.9	6.6	5.9	5.9	5.9	5.8
Broken Arrow, OK	7.7	7.8	6.6	5.6	6.0	6.7	6.4	6.0	6.4	6.7	6.4	6.6
Cambridge, MA[4]	7.4	7.1	6.6	6.2	6.3	6.8	6.8	6.0	6.3	6.0	5.4	5.4
Cape Coral, FL	12.7	11.7	11.2	10.8	10.9	11.7	11.6	11.5	11.3	10.7	10.5	10.2
Carlsbad, CA	10.4	10.1	10.2	9.8	9.6	10.4	10.6	10.2	9.8	9.7	9.2	8.9
Cary, NC	8.3	8.1	7.8	7.8	8.0	8.6	8.5	8.8	8.4	8.1	7.8	8.0
Cedar Rapids, IA	6.8	6.7	6.7	6.0	5.6	5.9	5.6	6.1	5.6	5.6	5.4	6.0
Charleston, SC	8.3	8.4	7.9	8.0	8.7	9.8	9.5	9.5	9.0	8.5	7.8	7.9
Charlotte, NC	11.2	10.9	10.5	10.3	10.6	11.3	11.3	11.3	10.7	10.3	9.9	10.3
Chesapeake, VA	7.6	7.3	7.0	6.5	6.6	7.0	6.9	7.3	7.3	7.0	6.7	7.1
Chicago, IL[2]	9.9	9.6	9.4	9.5	10.1	10.9	10.8	10.5	10.1	9.8	9.5	9.3
Clarksville, TN	11.0	10.9	10.1	10.3	10.1	10.6	10.3	10.0	10.2	9.4	9.0	8.7
Colorado Spgs., CO	10.7	10.5	10.1	9.1	9.3	9.8	9.6	9.3	8.6	8.6	8.7	9.0
Columbia, MD	7.9	7.7	7.4	7.0	7.3	7.8	7.9	7.8	7.6	7.1	6.6	6.8
Columbia, MO	6.9	6.5	6.2	5.6	6.0	6.8	6.6	6.7	5.6	5.5	4.9	4.9
Columbia, SC	8.3	8.5	8.0	8.1	8.9	10.0	9.9	9.7	9.1	8.5	7.8	8.0
Columbus, OH	8.5	8.2	7.6	7.3	7.4	8.2	8.2	7.8	7.6	7.6	6.6	6.4
Dallas, TX[2]	8.5	8.2	8.1	7.7	7.9	8.7	8.7	8.4	8.4	8.1	7.5	7.2
Denver, CO	9.9	9.8	9.3	8.3	8.5	8.8	8.6	8.5	7.9	7.8	7.9	8.1
Durham, NC	7.6	7.4	7.1	7.1	7.3	8.0	8.0	8.3	7.8	7.6	7.3	7.5
Edison, NJ[2]	9.0	9.2	8.8	8.4	8.6	9.0	9.1	8.3	8.3	8.3	8.4	8.2
El Paso, TX	10.4	10.1	10.0	9.7	10.0	10.9	10.9	10.6	10.5	10.2	9.5	9.3
Fargo, ND	4.7	4.7	4.4	3.7	3.5	4.2	3.7	3.9	3.3	3.1	3.1	3.7
Ft. Collins, CO	8.5	8.3	7.7	6.7	6.6	7.0	6.9	6.6	6.0	6.1	6.2	6.3
Ft. Worth, TX[2]	8.4	8.1	8.0	7.6	7.8	8.6	8.5	8.3	8.2	7.8	7.3	7.0
Gilbert, AZ	9.3	8.8	8.7	8.1	8.0	9.0	8.7	8.4	8.0	8.1	7.7	7.9
Green Bay, WI	7.7	8.0	7.6	7.0	7.2	7.9	7.4	7.0	6.7	6.5	6.4	6.3
Henderson, NV	13.7	13.7	13.3	12.0	12.4	13.8	14.0	14.3	13.6	13.1	12.4	12.7
High Point, NC	10.9	10.6	10.2	10.0	10.2	10.9	10.9	11.0	10.5	10.2	9.8	10.0
Honolulu, HI	5.4	5.3	5.0	4.6	4.9	5.7	5.4	5.5	5.7	5.6	5.7	5.3
Houston, TX	8.8	8.4	8.3	8.0	8.2	9.0	8.9	8.6	8.6	8.1	7.5	7.3
Huntington, NY[2]	7.9	7.7	7.1	6.6	6.7	7.1	7.1	6.8	6.9	6.6	6.7	6.9
Huntsville, AL	8.2	7.9	7.5	7.5	7.9	8.9	8.4	8.1	8.1	7.4	6.8	6.4
Indianapolis, IN	8.7	8.6	8.1	7.6	7.8	8.0	8.0	8.3	8.1	8.3	8.3	8.2
Irvine, CA[2]	9.2	8.9	9.1	8.6	8.5	9.2	9.3	9.0	8.6	8.5	8.1	7.8
Jackson, MS	8.6	8.5	8.2	8.0	7.8	8.8	8.8	7.7	8.6	8.4	7.8	7.9
Jacksonville, FL	11.5	10.6	10.2	9.8	9.7	10.4	10.5	10.4	10.0	9.6	9.5	9.2
Jersey City, NJ[2]	9.2	9.0	8.4	8.2	8.5	8.7	8.7	8.5	8.5	8.6	8.7	8.5
Kansas City, MO	9.7	9.2	8.9	8.1	8.4	8.5	8.4	8.7	8.2	7.8	7.4	7.3
Kenosha, WI[2]	10.4	10.6	10.3	8.9	8.1	8.8	9.0	9.1	8.9	9.0	8.6	9.3
Las Vegas, NV	13.7	13.7	13.3	12.0	12.4	13.8	14.0	14.3	13.6	13.1	12.4	12.7
Lexington, KY	9.4	9.2	8.4	8.1	7.8	8.0	8.1	7.4	8.0	7.4	7.0	6.9
Lincoln, NE	4.3	4.2	4.1	3.9	3.7	4.2	3.9	3.6	3.6	3.4	3.2	3.6

Table continued on next page.

Metro Area[1]	2011											
	Jan.	Feb.	Mar.	Apr.	May	Jun.	Jul.	Aug.	Sep.	Oct.	Nov.	Dec.
Little Rock, AR	7.5	7.1	6.8	6.5	7.0	7.7	7.5	7.3	7.1	6.7	6.3	6.5
Los Angeles, CA[2]	12.9	12.3	12.1	11.7	12.0	12.5	13.2	12.9	12.5	12.1	11.6	11.6
Madison, WI	5.7	6.0	5.7	5.2	5.4	6.1	5.5	5.3	5.2	5.1	4.7	4.7
Manchester, NH[3]	5.9	5.7	5.1	4.6	4.8	5.2	5.3	5.2	5.0	4.9	4.8	4.8
Miami, FL[2]	11.6	11.4	11.7	12.2	12.3	12.4	11.5	11.4	10.8	10.7	9.5	10.2
Minneapolis, MN	7.0	6.9	6.8	6.3	6.3	7.0	7.4	6.7	6.0	5.4	5.2	5.5
Murfreesboro, TN	8.8	8.8	8.3	8.6	8.4	8.9	8.4	8.5	8.5	7.6	7.2	6.9
Naperville, IL[2]	9.9	9.6	9.4	9.5	10.1	10.9	10.8	10.5	10.1	9.8	9.5	9.3
Nashville, TN	8.8	8.8	8.3	8.6	8.4	8.9	8.4	8.5	8.5	7.6	7.2	6.9
New Orleans, LA	8.4	7.8	7.9	7.2	8.0	8.0	7.8	7.3	6.9	7.1	6.5	6.4
New York, NY[2]	9.2	9.0	8.4	8.2	8.5	8.7	8.7	8.5	8.5	8.6	8.7	8.5
Norman, OK	6.3	6.2	5.2	4.6	4.9	5.7	5.5	5.0	5.5	5.8	5.4	5.6
Olathe, KS	9.7	9.2	8.9	8.1	8.4	8.5	8.4	8.7	8.2	7.8	7.4	7.3
Omaha, NE	5.5	5.4	5.2	4.8	4.6	5.0	4.8	4.6	4.5	4.3	4.1	4.7
Orlando, FL	11.8	10.8	10.4	10.0	9.9	10.4	10.5	10.4	10.2	9.8	9.7	9.5
Overland Park, KS	9.7	9.2	8.9	8.1	8.4	8.5	8.4	8.7	8.2	7.8	7.4	7.3
Oyster Bay, NY[2]	7.9	7.7	7.1	6.6	6.7	7.1	7.1	6.8	6.9	6.6	6.7	6.9
Pembroke Pines, FL[2]	10.5	9.7	9.3	8.9	9.0	9.6	9.7	9.5	9.4	8.9	8.9	8.6
Philadelphia, PA[2]	8.6	8.5	8.1	7.4	8.0	8.4	8.7	9.1	8.2	7.8	7.9	7.6
Phoenix, AZ	9.3	8.8	8.7	8.1	8.0	9.0	8.7	8.4	8.0	8.1	7.7	7.9
Pittsburgh, PA	8.1	7.9	7.4	6.6	6.9	7.4	7.5	7.8	6.8	6.4	6.6	6.6
Plano, TX[2]	8.5	8.2	8.1	7.7	7.9	8.7	8.7	8.4	8.4	8.1	7.5	7.2
Portland, OR	10.3	10.2	9.9	9.1	8.9	9.5	9.1	9.2	8.7	8.6	8.0	8.1
Providence, RI[3]	12.0	12.1	11.9	10.9	11.1	10.4	11.2	10.3	10.1	10.1	10.2	10.4
Provo, UT	8.3	8.3	7.6	7.0	7.5	7.9	8.0	7.9	6.8	6.3	5.4	5.3
Raleigh, NC	8.3	8.1	7.8	7.8	8.0	8.6	8.5	8.8	8.4	8.1	7.8	8.0
Richmond, VA	7.7	7.3	7.0	6.5	6.7	7.0	7.0	7.3	7.3	6.8	6.5	6.8
Roseville, CA	12.9	12.6	12.7	12.0	11.7	12.4	12.5	11.9	11.4	11.4	10.9	10.9
Round Rock, TX	7.3	6.9	6.8	6.5	6.8	7.6	7.6	7.4	7.5	7.1	6.6	6.3
San Antonio, TX	7.8	7.4	7.3	7.0	7.3	8.1	8.2	7.9	8.0	7.5	7.0	6.8
San Diego, CA	10.4	10.1	10.2	9.8	9.6	10.4	10.6	10.2	9.8	9.7	9.2	8.9
San Francisco, CA[2]	8.9	8.6	8.7	8.3	8.1	8.8	8.8	8.5	8.1	7.9	7.6	7.3
San Jose, CA	10.8	10.5	10.6	10.1	9.9	10.4	10.4	10.0	9.6	9.5	9.2	8.9
Savannah, GA	9.2	9.1	8.6	8.4	8.5	9.5	9.3	9.5	9.3	9.0	8.4	8.8
Scottsdale, AZ	9.3	8.8	8.7	8.1	8.0	9.0	8.7	8.4	8.0	8.1	7.7	7.9
Seattle, WA[2]	9.3	9.3	8.8	8.1	8.3	9.0	8.7	8.0	8.2	8.1	7.7	7.3
Sioux Falls, SD	5.3	5.5	5.4	4.7	4.6	4.5	4.3	4.5	4.0	3.9	3.8	4.3
Stamford, CT[3]	8.9	9.0	8.7	8.3	8.5	8.5	8.5	8.3	7.9	7.8	7.4	7.1
Sterling Hgts, MI[2]	11.1	11.2	11.1	10.5	10.8	11.6	13.0	11.9	10.8	10.0	8.8	9.0
Sunnyvale, CA	10.8	10.5	10.6	10.1	9.9	10.4	10.4	10.0	9.6	9.5	9.2	8.9
Tampa, FL	12.5	11.5	11.0	10.6	10.6	11.1	11.1	11.0	10.8	10.4	10.3	10.0
Temecula, CA	14.2	13.9	13.9	13.4	13.2	14.3	14.7	14.1	13.5	13.3	12.5	12.2
Thousand Oaks, CA	10.9	10.5	10.4	9.7	9.5	10.3	10.6	10.5	10.1	9.8	9.5	9.4
Virginia Beach, VA	7.6	7.3	7.0	6.5	6.6	7.0	6.9	7.3	7.3	7.0	6.7	7.1
Washington, DC[2]	6.2	6.0	5.9	5.5	5.8	6.3	6.2	6.2	6.2	5.8	5.5	5.7
U.S.	9.8	9.5	9.2	8.7	8.7	9.3	9.3	9.1	8.8	8.5	8.2	8.3

Note: Data is not seasonally adjusted and covers workers 16 years of age and older; All figures are percentages; (1) Figures cover the Metropolitan Statistical Area (MSA) except where noted. See Appendix B for areas included; (2) Metropolitan Division; (3) New England City and Town Area; (4) New England City and Town Area Division
Source: Bureau of Labor Statistics, http://stats.bls.gov

Average Hourly Wages: Occupations A – C

Metro Area	Accountants/ Auditors	Automotive Mechanics	Book- keepers	Carpenters	Cashiers	Clerks, Gen. Office	Clerks, Recep./Info.
Albuquerque, NM	31.32	17.27	16.78	20.00	9.94	12.22	11.83
Alexandria, VA	40.35	22.35	21.08	21.54	10.39	16.13	14.63
Anchorage, AK	33.68	25.41	19.46	29.15	11.32	17.00	14.42
Ann Arbor, MI	31.37	22.10	17.80	23.91	10.16	13.88	12.85
Athens, GA	26.19	19.21	14.55	16.56	9.40	11.01	11.62
Atlanta, GA	34.96	18.96	17.81	19.36	9.39	12.78	12.76
Austin, TX	33.31	22.03	18.23	15.60	9.71	15.47	12.65
Baltimore, MD	35.18	19.62	19.69	20.98	10.52	14.75	13.54
Bellevue, WA	33.93	19.26	19.53	25.62	12.86	16.09	14.48
Billings, MT	31.72	17.39	15.52	17.21	9.26	12.99	11.87
Boise City, ID	29.96	17.63	16.54	19.46	9.52	13.48	12.37
Boston, MA	38.02	22.17	20.63	29.24	10.44	17.04	14.75
Boulder, CO	35.82	17.99	18.53	19.50	10.87	14.83	13.63
Broken Arrow, OK	27.71	16.66	15.32	14.33	9.02	12.08	11.59
Cambridge, MA	38.02	22.17	20.63	29.24	10.44	17.04	14.75
Cape Coral, FL	31.82	18.95	16.69	19.21	9.82	12.63	12.90
Carlsbad, CA	35.75	20.90	19.21	25.56	10.68	14.81	13.88
Cary, NC	31.67	20.79	17.33	16.82	9.15	13.46	12.38
Cedar Rapids, IA	27.78	18.97	15.77	20.20	9.05	14.60	12.67
Charleston, SC	29.13	19.27	16.94	17.24	9.10	12.66	12.68
Charlotte, NC	34.36	21.08	16.96	16.80	9.43	13.44	12.88
Chesapeake, VA	30.67	19.95	16.71	18.69	9.19	12.73	12.15
Chicago, IL	35.94	18.50	18.47	25.37	9.93	14.99	13.44
Clarksville, TN	28.47	16.56	15.66	19.68	8.87	12.72	11.71
Colorado Spgs., CO	29.17	22.11	16.11	18.63	9.47	13.57	12.62
Columbia, MD	35.18	19.62	19.69	20.98	10.52	14.75	13.54
Columbia, MO	24.54	19.22	15.51	20.75	9.46	12.53	11.00
Columbia, SC	26.80	19.36	16.97	16.13	8.61	13.51	13.24
Columbus, OH	31.97	18.58	19.70	19.25	9.78	14.54	12.02
Dallas, TX	35.62	17.75	18.20	15.57	9.39	14.88	12.90
Denver, CO	36.14	19.46	17.90	19.07	10.28	16.09	14.04
Durham, NC	35.05	20.23	18.17	17.28	9.68	13.86	12.72
Edison, NJ	37.42	20.89	19.68	23.91	10.08	15.19	13.45
El Paso, TX	24.24	14.67	14.00	12.20	8.69	11.60	10.11
Fargo, ND	26.49	19.26	16.44	17.33	8.74	12.62	12.16
Ft. Collins, CO	31.89	20.64	15.91	19.26	9.79	13.91	13.25
Ft. Worth, TX	34.28	18.26	17.07	14.74	9.34	14.34	12.95
Gilbert, AZ	29.62	19.98	17.77	19.96	10.97	14.89	13.73
Green Bay, WI	29.28	18.36	16.38	21.58	9.32	14.08	13.20
Henderson, NV	30.67	19.70	17.63	28.18	10.52	14.60	13.25
High Point, NC	31.58	18.40	16.36	14.81	8.94	12.70	12.85
Honolulu, HI	30.56	22.37	17.73	33.41	10.79	14.69	14.52
Houston, TX	35.72	18.16	18.56	17.02	9.44	14.59	12.71
Huntington, NY	41.67	20.79	20.39	28.31	10.20	14.77	14.13
Huntsville, AL	31.84	18.02	15.77	15.15	8.95	10.91	11.24
Indianapolis, IN	33.54	20.10	17.39	22.19	9.25	13.29	12.55
Irvine, CA	35.34	21.61	20.04	27.99	11.00	15.22	13.65
Jackson, MS	27.11	16.41	16.10	14.11	8.86	11.51	11.33
Jacksonville, FL	32.41	19.26	16.24	16.70	9.17	13.06	12.75
Jersey City, NJ	43.13	20.02	20.67	29.57	10.28	14.44	14.33
Kansas City, MO	29.67	19.86	17.17	22.36	9.36	14.75	12.81
Kenosha, WI	34.69	21.24	18.81	27.32	9.76	14.79	13.47
Las Vegas, NV	30.67	19.70	17.63	28.18	10.52	14.60	13.25
Lexington, KY	28.79	16.08	16.29	17.06	9.06	12.88	11.97
Lincoln, NE	29.38	17.92	15.37	17.35	8.97	11.24	11.74

Table continued on next page.

Metro Area	Accountants/ Auditors	Automotive Mechanics	Book-keepers	Carpenters	Cashiers	Clerks, Gen. Office	Clerks, Recep./Info.
Little Rock, AR	28.75	16.90	15.92	17.31	9.21	11.32	11.70
Los Angeles, CA	35.72	19.00	19.14	25.79	10.84	15.06	13.54
Madison, WI	29.82	19.29	17.47	23.34	9.71	15.03	12.78
Manchester, NH	31.87	20.24	18.96	20.51	9.38	16.12	13.29
Miami, FL	35.53	17.87	16.28	17.28	9.41	12.50	11.89
Minneapolis, MN	31.31	19.76	18.66	24.09	9.82	14.74	14.14
Murfreesboro, TN	29.64	17.30	16.00	18.06	9.78	14.45	12.64
Naperville, IL	35.94	18.50	18.47	25.37	9.93	14.99	13.44
Nashville, TN	29.64	17.30	16.00	18.06	9.78	14.45	12.64
New Orleans, LA	31.66	18.89	16.95	18.29	9.24	12.09	11.64
New York, NY	43.13	20.02	20.67	29.57	10.28	14.44	14.33
Norman, OK	29.34	19.14	14.72	16.65	8.87	12.29	11.51
Olathe, KS	29.67	19.86	17.17	22.36	9.36	14.75	12.81
Omaha, NE	32.66	18.61	16.02	17.46	9.38	12.65	12.31
Orlando, FL	30.31	16.88	15.51	16.27	8.98	13.05	11.70
Overland Park, KS	29.67	19.86	17.17	22.36	9.36	14.75	12.81
Oyster Bay, NY	41.67	20.79	20.39	28.31	10.20	14.77	14.13
Pembroke Pines, FL	31.08	18.77	16.79	21.04	9.93	12.92	13.00
Philadelphia, PA	37.84	18.99	19.69	23.32	9.97	15.31	14.40
Phoenix, AZ	29.62	19.98	17.77	19.96	10.97	14.89	13.73
Pittsburgh, PA	33.23	16.76	16.45	20.63	9.10	13.75	11.81
Plano, TX	35.62	17.75	18.20	15.57	9.39	14.88	12.90
Portland, OR	30.49	20.09	18.47	22.48	11.55	15.01	13.57
Providence, RI	33.15	17.75	18.30	21.86	9.84	14.91	13.99
Provo, UT	29.78	19.84	15.32	18.97	9.14	11.72	10.73
Raleigh, NC	31.67	20.79	17.33	16.82	9.15	13.46	12.38
Richmond, VA	32.22	20.97	17.35	18.27	9.56	14.29	12.94
Roseville, CA	31.77	21.78	19.82	25.23	11.35	16.16	13.76
Round Rock, TX	33.31	22.03	18.23	15.60	9.71	15.47	12.65
San Antonio, TX	32.20	17.23	16.88	15.25	9.26	13.07	11.79
San Diego, CA	35.75	20.90	19.21	25.56	10.68	14.81	13.88
San Francisco, CA	41.46	24.38	23.01	32.26	13.13	17.76	17.53
San Jose, CA	41.15	24.15	22.09	29.61	12.05	17.82	15.92
Savannah, GA	32.41	18.85	16.56	19.40	9.20	11.24	11.80
Scottsdale, AZ	29.62	19.98	17.77	19.96	10.97	14.89	13.73
Seattle, WA	33.93	19.26	19.53	25.62	12.86	16.09	14.48
Sioux Falls, SD	28.55	18.28	14.08	16.08	9.16	11.08	11.66
Stamford, CT	37.10	23.27	21.57	28.59	10.73	16.13	16.56
Sterling Hgts, MI	32.66	21.27	17.98	21.56	10.45	14.53	12.77
Sunnyvale, CA	41.15	24.15	22.09	29.61	12.05	17.82	15.92
Tampa, FL	30.06	17.49	15.71	17.16	8.99	12.82	12.52
Temecula, CA	31.12	19.26	18.27	27.20	10.78	14.68	12.79
Thousand Oaks, CA	36.15	19.58	20.51	22.19	10.91	14.76	13.87
Virginia Beach, VA	30.67	19.95	16.71	18.69	9.19	12.73	12.15
Washington, DC	40.35	22.35	21.08	21.54	10.39	16.13	14.63

Notes: Wage data is for May 2011 and covers the Metropolitan Statistical Area—see Appendix B for areas included; n/a not available
Source: Bureau of Labor Statistics, May 2011 Metro Area Occupational Employment and Wage Estimates

Average Hourly Wages: Occupations C – E

Metro Area	Clerks, Ship./Rec.	Computer Programmers	Computer Support Specialists	Computer Systems Analysts	Cooks, Restaurant	Dentists	Electrical Engineers
Albuquerque, NM	14.07	37.22	23.38	40.34	10.13	77.32	43.52
Alexandria, VA	16.08	38.92	29.37	47.85	12.55	88.19	48.17
Anchorage, AK	19.41	35.11	25.21	37.05	14.36	82.57	48.13
Ann Arbor, MI	15.83	29.93	22.15	38.25	11.79	50.97	38.80
Athens, GA	13.80	26.38	17.43	36.33	11.61	n/a	34.22
Atlanta, GA	14.54	37.52	24.14	38.12	10.65	98.25	39.01
Austin, TX	14.00	38.53	26.47	40.99	10.93	90.89	45.14
Baltimore, MD	15.89	37.15	26.93	39.57	12.51	75.76	42.50
Bellevue, WA	17.95	45.55	28.14	43.29	12.88	106.68	45.46
Billings, MT	12.27	27.08	18.49	33.38	11.08	55.11	32.19
Boise City, ID	13.39	30.53	19.12	33.46	10.21	92.45	43.91
Boston, MA	17.12	42.32	30.29	43.41	13.05	84.70	49.22
Boulder, CO	15.53	n/a	29.14	40.69	11.39	n/a	51.95
Broken Arrow, OK	14.15	33.82	22.75	35.42	10.57	90.53	35.91
Cambridge, MA	17.12	42.32	30.29	43.41	13.05	84.70	49.22
Cape Coral, FL	11.94	32.56	22.02	36.58	11.46	42.76	36.16
Carlsbad, CA	14.82	36.63	24.22	41.73	12.22	77.88	47.72
Cary, NC	14.03	34.63	25.82	39.37	10.33	97.51	43.65
Cedar Rapids, IA	15.07	29.51	21.66	31.72	9.60	111.15	n/a
Charleston, SC	16.03	31.64	22.78	30.90	10.38	69.44	38.72
Charlotte, NC	14.59	35.56	26.91	42.34	11.24	90.62	40.18
Chesapeake, VA	14.67	29.81	24.70	38.60	12.51	103.22	38.08
Chicago, IL	14.77	37.72	27.10	34.27	10.69	59.60	42.65
Clarksville, TN	15.09	32.29	20.71	26.81	10.20	n/a	32.34
Colorado Spgs., CO	14.51	39.49	25.76	41.38	11.48	65.74	40.22
Columbia, MD	15.89	37.15	26.93	39.57	12.51	75.76	42.50
Columbia, MO	13.26	43.46	18.20	34.68	10.62	n/a	n/a
Columbia, SC	13.56	30.43	23.42	32.61	9.44	91.03	39.73
Columbus, OH	14.65	34.64	24.15	39.18	10.61	83.86	33.64
Dallas, TX	14.09	41.54	28.05	41.07	10.09	98.53	46.14
Denver, CO	15.41	38.39	28.18	42.31	10.87	66.03	40.82
Durham, NC	13.93	47.91	31.53	38.49	11.95	60.42	42.09
Edison, NJ	15.71	41.15	26.31	42.57	11.62	68.50	42.08
El Paso, TX	11.02	25.66	20.42	35.74	9.09	95.21	40.18
Fargo, ND	14.18	22.74	19.59	28.92	10.38	105.77	34.97
Ft. Collins, CO	14.16	36.07	24.55	37.49	11.09	99.42	40.34
Ft. Worth, TX	14.29	35.64	25.12	37.32	9.75	69.33	39.08
Gilbert, AZ	14.26	37.73	23.79	36.35	14.05	89.20	47.97
Green Bay, WI	15.32	30.27	22.53	34.56	9.84	85.61	38.54
Henderson, NV	14.00	33.34	22.25	39.57	14.48	69.94	41.18
High Point, NC	14.56	35.19	23.17	37.34	10.75	97.61	42.70
Honolulu, HI	15.62	32.91	24.28	33.00	13.99	71.85	39.48
Houston, TX	14.33	37.32	26.49	43.60	9.25	70.87	43.82
Huntington, NY	15.44	38.68	27.75	41.18	13.71	81.99	46.79
Huntsville, AL	14.51	38.31	21.89	42.27	11.08	84.61	49.02
Indianapolis, IN	14.38	37.17	22.44	35.44	10.67	79.81	38.43
Irvine, CA	15.39	35.93	28.47	41.41	11.68	56.38	47.12
Jackson, MS	14.60	26.73	21.39	26.99	9.43	71.38	36.57
Jacksonville, FL	14.10	34.13	21.65	36.27	11.44	79.36	40.92
Jersey City, NJ	14.89	39.81	28.83	44.33	14.27	66.79	43.62
Kansas City, MO	14.26	33.99	23.84	38.56	10.07	59.44	38.66
Kenosha, WI	15.55	34.62	27.26	37.52	10.27	41.46	36.98
Las Vegas, NV	14.00	33.34	22.25	39.57	14.48	69.94	41.18
Lexington, KY	14.34	29.44	21.11	39.30	10.12	46.44	49.64
Lincoln, NE	14.06	30.31	21.00	29.67	9.98	82.35	36.26

Table continued on next page.

Metro Area	Clerks, Ship./Rec.	Computer Programmers	Computer Support Specialists	Computer Systems Analysts	Cooks, Restaurant	Dentists	Electrical Engineers
Little Rock, AR	13.20	28.80	21.50	32.57	9.42	85.45	39.03
Los Angeles, CA	14.38	40.73	26.04	42.62	11.20	63.44	48.09
Madison, WI	14.69	35.84	25.86	34.46	10.86	84.06	36.82
Manchester, NH	15.35	34.72	26.57	39.67	11.95	n/a	39.50
Miami, FL	13.49	36.56	22.06	40.96	11.90	55.21	42.83
Minneapolis, MN	16.15	33.80	25.64	37.38	11.18	91.83	42.24
Murfreesboro, TN	13.85	35.55	23.80	34.26	11.15	70.70	39.66
Naperville, IL	14.77	37.72	27.10	34.27	10.69	59.60	42.65
Nashville, TN	13.85	35.55	23.80	34.26	11.15	70.70	39.66
New Orleans, LA	15.28	28.87	23.18	29.30	11.36	74.29	47.05
New York, NY	14.89	39.81	28.83	44.33	14.27	66.79	43.62
Norman, OK	14.52	26.49	21.03	30.74	10.31	65.63	43.62
Olathe, KS	14.26	33.99	23.84	38.56	10.07	59.44	38.66
Omaha, NE	14.20	32.18	25.63	34.93	10.92	87.54	38.13
Orlando, FL	12.62	33.08	20.38	38.82	11.78	62.52	35.26
Overland Park, KS	14.26	33.99	23.84	38.56	10.07	59.44	38.66
Oyster Bay, NY	15.44	38.68	27.75	41.18	13.71	81.99	46.79
Pembroke Pines, FL	13.55	31.99	22.73	37.90	11.70	60.26	37.94
Philadelphia, PA	16.76	35.87	25.68	40.52	14.63	78.97	46.02
Phoenix, AZ	14.26	37.73	23.79	36.35	14.05	89.20	47.97
Pittsburgh, PA	15.07	30.80	22.52	34.99	12.68	64.33	40.20
Plano, TX	14.09	41.54	28.05	41.07	10.09	98.53	46.14
Portland, OR	15.23	34.01	25.80	40.89	12.08	99.99	42.45
Providence, RI	15.00	33.98	23.71	38.52	12.81	68.14	43.91
Provo, UT	13.42	31.70	20.24	33.44	10.25	85.00	37.25
Raleigh, NC	14.03	34.63	25.82	39.37	10.33	97.51	43.65
Richmond, VA	15.25	37.03	23.92	37.80	10.44	70.36	39.87
Roseville, CA	15.59	38.33	28.76	37.48	11.39	67.02	51.08
Round Rock, TX	14.00	38.53	26.47	40.99	10.93	90.89	45.14
San Antonio, TX	13.92	37.36	24.98	41.42	9.69	93.56	39.74
San Diego, CA	14.82	36.63	24.22	41.73	12.22	77.88	47.72
San Francisco, CA	16.67	46.94	33.49	46.48	14.47	76.44	45.59
San Jose, CA	16.65	47.87	35.27	47.91	11.70	67.81	53.77
Savannah, GA	14.96	31.16	23.14	32.95	9.62	79.03	41.86
Scottsdale, AZ	14.26	37.73	23.79	36.35	14.05	89.20	47.97
Seattle, WA	17.95	45.55	28.14	43.29	12.88	106.68	45.46
Sioux Falls, SD	14.07	27.34	19.05	31.81	11.61	65.80	38.02
Stamford, CT	17.91	43.35	31.30	50.49	13.59	71.45	39.80
Sterling Hgts, MI	14.44	34.67	22.78	37.84	11.93	61.28	43.01
Sunnyvale, CA	16.65	47.87	35.27	47.91	11.70	67.81	53.77
Tampa, FL	13.17	34.50	21.13	39.51	10.45	89.88	35.43
Temecula, CA	14.48	32.65	22.98	35.24	11.58	83.02	45.72
Thousand Oaks, CA	15.02	42.78	27.22	40.19	11.33	84.35	46.54
Virginia Beach, VA	14.67	29.81	24.70	38.60	12.51	103.22	38.08
Washington, DC	16.08	38.92	29.37	47.85	12.55	88.19	48.17

Notes: Wage data is for May 2011 and covers the Metropolitan Statistical Area—see Appendix B for areas included; n/a not available
Source: Bureau of Labor Statistics, May 2011 Metro Area Occupational Employment and Wage Estimates

Average Hourly Wages: Occupations E – I

Metro Area	Electricians	Financial Managers	First-Line Supervisors/ Mgrs., Sales	Food Preparation Workers	General/ Operations Managers	Hairdressers/ Cosmetolo- gists	Internists
Albuquerque, NM	22.07	46.38	18.74	10.15	46.43	11.30	n/a
Alexandria, VA	26.66	64.81	21.51	10.83	65.53	15.65	93.95
Anchorage, AK	33.92	50.67	20.36	11.54	47.58	13.05	n/a
Ann Arbor, MI	34.11	48.63	20.53	10.48	50.08	13.82	n/a
Athens, GA	18.05	59.94	16.97	10.19	47.10	13.58	80.48
Atlanta, GA	21.62	60.72	19.34	10.24	55.36	10.88	92.73
Austin, TX	19.31	57.82	19.65	9.75	54.61	10.68	100.65
Baltimore, MD	24.69	51.58	20.74	10.83	56.53	13.66	90.93
Bellevue, WA	31.80	60.69	22.33	11.95	66.28	18.08	86.31
Billings, MT	22.32	50.49	19.12	9.48	42.76	12.15	n/a
Boise City, ID	22.03	40.93	16.90	9.04	38.37	10.45	n/a
Boston, MA	30.36	68.84	20.89	11.51	62.06	14.40	99.93
Boulder, CO	21.27	65.49	20.74	10.13	62.22	18.08	n/a
Broken Arrow, OK	23.49	45.47	16.24	9.03	44.95	10.98	113.75
Cambridge, MA	30.36	68.84	20.89	11.51	62.06	14.40	99.93
Cape Coral, FL	16.37	61.00	21.14	10.01	46.02	12.59	113.39
Carlsbad, CA	26.26	61.05	21.20	9.84	61.96	12.04	90.55
Cary, NC	19.28	56.39	19.38	9.43	62.18	14.61	76.57
Cedar Rapids, IA	26.16	53.18	20.16	8.72	50.41	10.87	n/a
Charleston, SC	19.10	49.45	19.32	9.54	52.74	19.98	n/a
Charlotte, NC	19.39	64.23	19.52	9.67	64.03	12.84	108.95
Chesapeake, VA	20.95	50.44	19.07	9.77	52.84	11.77	77.48
Chicago, IL	36.27	59.35	20.56	9.96	56.91	13.62	96.45
Clarksville, TN	19.44	37.77	16.11	9.27	37.50	12.11	n/a
Colorado Spgs., CO	23.70	55.99	18.08	9.69	49.73	12.33	n/a
Columbia, MD	24.69	51.58	20.74	10.83	56.53	13.66	90.93
Columbia, MO	19.55	45.30	16.33	9.18	35.28	13.02	n/a
Columbia, SC	19.61	49.15	19.28	9.10	49.52	13.54	104.61
Columbus, OH	21.58	56.07	19.76	10.84	56.09	11.82	70.00
Dallas, TX	21.29	59.28	20.33	9.15	59.82	14.08	79.49
Denver, CO	23.49	63.95	20.73	10.44	62.34	13.41	67.02
Durham, NC	20.47	58.70	18.10	10.28	63.12	15.09	77.08
Edison, NJ	29.60	65.85	23.40	10.12	77.01	13.94	97.46
El Paso, TX	18.17	47.49	19.16	8.46	45.95	10.47	106.28
Fargo, ND	19.52	45.32	17.27	10.91	49.52	11.82	n/a
Ft. Collins, CO	25.31	59.83	19.08	9.78	50.08	11.61	n/a
Ft. Worth, TX	20.66	52.01	19.25	9.54	52.48	12.21	89.32
Gilbert, AZ	21.37	51.98	19.48	10.57	51.63	11.42	93.77
Green Bay, WI	23.57	50.31	18.21	10.45	50.85	11.69	n/a
Henderson, NV	32.37	50.71	19.67	13.93	53.29	10.30	95.39
High Point, NC	18.81	52.54	18.30	9.58	57.40	10.42	97.21
Honolulu, HI	34.74	44.59	22.47	11.31	49.88	18.04	112.29
Houston, TX	22.37	63.28	20.04	9.73	58.09	12.77	98.23
Huntington, NY	32.39	70.09	23.90	12.02	65.75	12.12	111.13
Huntsville, AL	19.16	53.23	18.35	9.06	59.83	12.52	116.96
Indianapolis, IN	26.78	52.70	20.11	10.03	57.66	13.93	91.80
Irvine, CA	27.78	67.44	21.14	11.06	65.01	12.29	84.72
Jackson, MS	20.70	38.79	17.71	8.36	49.11	13.13	72.02
Jacksonville, FL	20.80	57.19	20.25	9.52	49.47	12.38	94.93
Jersey City, NJ	38.34	84.27	23.87	11.84	78.11	15.57	74.47
Kansas City, MO	28.23	52.94	18.47	10.02	48.38	11.98	96.76
Kenosha, WI	29.26	53.22	18.72	9.59	52.53	13.66	n/a
Las Vegas, NV	32.37	50.71	19.67	13.93	53.29	10.30	95.39
Lexington, KY	20.43	46.16	17.35	10.26	45.29	10.95	n/a
Lincoln, NE	20.25	57.13	19.01	9.66	50.03	9.47	114.01

Table continued on next page.

Metro Area	Electricians	Financial Managers	First-Line Supervisors/ Mgrs., Sales	Food Preparation Workers	General/ Operations Managers	Hairdressers/ Cosmetologists	Internists
Little Rock, AR	19.89	41.77	17.54	9.09	46.45	14.59	n/a
Los Angeles, CA	29.72	66.04	21.64	9.72	63.08	13.20	93.12
Madison, WI	27.75	49.55	19.43	9.58	51.70	10.92	n/a
Manchester, NH	24.02	47.78	20.64	10.99	55.33	11.49	n/a
Miami, FL	20.72	65.40	20.34	9.60	52.48	11.92	94.51
Minneapolis, MN	30.92	59.15	19.26	10.87	56.08	13.73	105.90
Murfreesboro, TN	20.54	51.34	19.94	10.50	47.06	12.59	82.01
Naperville, IL	36.27	59.35	20.56	9.96	56.91	13.62	96.45
Nashville, TN	20.54	51.34	19.94	10.50	47.06	12.59	82.01
New Orleans, LA	22.16	46.42	18.54	9.00	54.57	11.63	n/a
New York, NY	38.34	84.27	23.87	11.84	78.11	15.57	74.47
Norman, OK	18.96	44.79	17.12	8.65	42.74	11.99	109.00
Olathe, KS	28.23	52.94	18.47	10.02	48.38	11.98	96.76
Omaha, NE	21.89	65.54	20.63	10.40	55.65	13.85	94.83
Orlando, FL	18.63	56.61	20.19	9.67	47.91	11.18	n/a
Overland Park, KS	28.23	52.94	18.47	10.02	48.38	11.98	96.76
Oyster Bay, NY	32.39	70.09	23.90	12.02	65.75	12.12	111.13
Pembroke Pines, FL	18.76	61.20	21.21	10.13	51.16	13.47	118.93
Philadelphia, PA	34.04	63.29	24.39	11.22	63.40	13.84	51.37
Phoenix, AZ	21.37	51.98	19.48	10.57	51.63	11.42	93.77
Pittsburgh, PA	26.49	50.96	21.36	10.18	54.17	10.87	106.76
Plano, TX	21.29	59.28	20.33	9.15	59.82	14.08	79.49
Portland, OR	33.43	52.55	19.37	10.68	53.15	13.53	96.43
Providence, RI	27.19	58.42	21.68	11.61	62.44	13.62	87.42
Provo, UT	25.18	50.90	16.69	9.27	42.84	15.49	n/a
Raleigh, NC	19.28	56.39	19.38	9.43	62.18	14.61	76.57
Richmond, VA	22.12	56.66	19.61	10.51	54.37	13.98	n/a
Roseville, CA	28.49	52.89	19.67	10.48	57.72	12.55	109.55
Round Rock, TX	19.31	57.82	19.65	9.75	54.61	10.68	100.65
San Antonio, TX	20.08	56.50	20.41	9.13	49.92	11.23	111.63
San Diego, CA	26.26	61.05	21.20	9.84	61.96	12.04	90.55
San Francisco, CA	37.23	78.22	22.25	10.83	73.00	19.73	109.06
San Jose, CA	35.14	72.63	20.10	10.10	72.59	11.50	69.01
Savannah, GA	24.40	46.08	17.54	10.05	45.29	12.98	104.42
Scottsdale, AZ	21.37	51.98	19.48	10.57	51.63	11.42	93.77
Seattle, WA	31.80	60.69	22.33	11.95	66.28	18.08	86.31
Sioux Falls, SD	21.61	60.98	20.70	9.67	55.19	12.73	119.01
Stamford, CT	28.12	65.29	23.52	11.83	77.03	15.54	87.63
Sterling Hgts, MI	28.53	55.58	21.12	10.84	57.39	12.24	69.15
Sunnyvale, CA	35.14	72.63	20.10	10.10	72.59	11.50	69.01
Tampa, FL	18.16	55.17	21.18	9.37	52.79	10.53	110.77
Temecula, CA	29.14	49.84	21.05	9.95	53.62	10.14	83.72
Thousand Oaks, CA	26.84	56.18	20.41	10.02	61.47	12.36	69.01
Virginia Beach, VA	20.95	50.44	19.07	9.77	52.84	11.77	77.48
Washington, DC	26.66	64.81	21.51	10.83	65.53	15.65	93.95

Notes: Wage data is for May 2011 and covers the Metropolitan Statistical Area—see Appendix B for areas included; n/a not available
Source: Bureau of Labor Statistics, May 2011 Metro Area Occupational Employment and Wage Estimates

Average Hourly Wages: Occupations J – N

Metro Area	Janitors/ Cleaners	Landscapers	Lawyers	Maids/ House- keepers	Main- tenance Repairers	Marketing Managers	Nuclear Medicine Technologists
Albuquerque, NM	10.41	10.90	44.61	9.21	16.36	45.60	33.03
Alexandria, VA	12.11	12.72	75.86	12.02	20.52	69.78	35.51
Anchorage, AK	14.28	14.55	56.84	10.92	21.57	39.44	n/a
Ann Arbor, MI	13.09	12.69	41.29	12.15	17.35	51.06	27.88
Athens, GA	11.23	9.71	56.77	9.19	15.96	55.01	n/a
Atlanta, GA	11.33	12.62	68.30	9.18	17.74	58.21	32.61
Austin, TX	10.51	11.79	47.69	9.22	16.02	65.36	32.42
Baltimore, MD	11.62	12.20	55.89	10.42	19.26	51.62	38.86
Bellevue, WA	14.35	15.62	59.08	12.10	20.35	63.21	41.27
Billings, MT	10.47	12.16	34.89	9.30	15.01	38.80	n/a
Boise City, ID	10.74	12.31	49.86	9.47	15.69	47.44	n/a
Boston, MA	14.96	16.12	63.99	14.23	22.93	66.29	35.79
Boulder, CO	13.28	13.25	56.35	10.53	19.40	67.50	n/a
Broken Arrow, OK	10.32	10.94	63.12	8.98	16.93	40.62	32.46
Cambridge, MA	14.96	16.12	63.99	14.23	22.93	66.29	35.79
Cape Coral, FL	10.47	10.92	46.78	9.60	15.87	43.92	35.94
Carlsbad, CA	12.83	12.71	69.30	10.12	17.57	62.90	39.31
Cary, NC	10.84	11.34	55.47	9.21	17.86	60.01	31.53
Cedar Rapids, IA	11.73	12.60	50.43	9.42	18.68	49.92	n/a
Charleston, SC	10.02	10.84	53.43	9.27	15.28	49.36	31.80
Charlotte, NC	10.12	10.99	60.66	9.03	18.37	60.63	29.76
Chesapeake, VA	10.34	10.69	55.62	9.10	16.70	54.04	28.10
Chicago, IL	12.63	12.73	70.57	11.21	20.20	54.83	35.11
Clarksville, TN	10.79	10.39	45.21	9.00	16.97	37.70	n/a
Colorado Spgs., CO	12.91	12.76	49.49	9.70	17.32	53.96	33.32
Columbia, MD	11.62	12.20	55.89	10.42	19.26	51.62	38.86
Columbia, MO	11.47	10.44	52.89	9.76	14.94	40.76	n/a
Columbia, SC	10.43	9.98	53.98	9.55	16.95	45.82	29.31
Columbus, OH	11.87	11.24	55.49	9.87	17.15	63.49	31.57
Dallas, TX	10.27	10.86	68.66	9.01	16.80	62.63	31.31
Denver, CO	11.15	12.90	67.62	9.70	18.32	61.53	38.16
Durham, NC	11.04	12.35	51.08	9.24	19.89	64.87	32.80
Edison, NJ	13.58	12.45	63.89	10.48	19.78	72.38	40.48
El Paso, TX	9.87	10.09	51.70	8.92	12.47	52.13	30.81
Fargo, ND	11.26	12.20	55.02	9.59	17.22	44.27	n/a
Ft. Collins, CO	11.59	12.87	46.74	10.33	16.87	56.43	n/a
Ft. Worth, TX	11.14	11.15	56.38	9.18	16.59	54.92	34.77
Gilbert, AZ	11.50	11.12	62.72	9.60	17.63	52.33	35.95
Green Bay, WI	11.96	12.18	58.35	9.37	19.14	47.63	n/a
Henderson, NV	13.43	12.32	56.92	13.73	21.61	59.31	38.14
High Point, NC	9.71	11.67	68.09	8.88	18.08	56.11	n/a
Honolulu, HI	12.05	13.24	55.89	14.88	20.28	45.74	37.59
Houston, TX	10.09	10.78	78.76	8.73	16.98	64.43	30.60
Huntington, NY	15.04	14.38	57.39	13.45	20.73	69.03	37.67
Huntsville, AL	10.56	11.57	66.29	8.82	19.82	55.76	n/a
Indianapolis, IN	10.78	11.99	49.13	9.15	17.62	56.72	30.24
Irvine, CA	11.86	12.41	72.46	10.33	18.09	66.97	45.74
Jackson, MS	9.55	10.82	55.86	8.53	14.27	42.99	26.13
Jacksonville, FL	10.68	10.80	46.99	9.07	16.49	56.19	34.06
Jersey City, NJ	15.23	15.56	79.54	16.06	20.03	80.57	37.69
Kansas City, MO	12.11	12.09	56.96	9.43	17.83	52.56	31.32
Kenosha, WI	12.82	12.47	44.91	9.82	20.33	55.15	35.93
Las Vegas, NV	13.43	12.32	56.92	13.73	21.61	59.31	38.14
Lexington, KY	10.79	11.70	48.83	9.01	16.17	41.78	29.04
Lincoln, NE	11.34	11.65	49.92	9.05	16.99	51.29	n/a

Table continued on next page.

Metro Area	Janitors/ Cleaners	Landscapers	Lawyers	Maids/ House-keepers	Main-tenance Repairers	Marketing Managers	Nuclear Medicine Technologists
Little Rock, AR	9.61	11.43	45.17	8.67	15.28	46.19	30.49
Los Angeles, CA	12.43	13.60	80.43	10.89	19.24	63.88	42.62
Madison, WI	11.44	15.43	49.58	9.78	18.43	46.02	n/a
Manchester, NH	11.73	15.90	66.41	9.91	19.87	49.55	n/a
Miami, FL	10.12	10.62	69.52	9.24	15.63	61.78	31.68
Minneapolis, MN	12.52	14.20	60.55	11.17	20.46	58.99	34.34
Murfreesboro, TN	9.99	11.26	53.12	9.10	16.90	46.60	30.05
Naperville, IL	12.63	12.73	70.57	11.21	20.20	54.83	35.11
Nashville, TN	9.99	11.26	53.12	9.10	16.90	46.60	30.05
New Orleans, LA	10.36	10.94	55.05	9.55	17.54	42.58	32.59
New York, NY	15.23	15.56	79.54	16.06	20.03	80.57	37.69
Norman, OK	9.75	10.50	42.55	9.05	15.27	44.63	32.24
Olathe, KS	12.11	12.09	56.96	9.43	17.83	52.56	31.32
Omaha, NE	11.06	11.47	54.02	9.36	16.65	64.32	29.92
Orlando, FL	10.13	10.77	60.74	9.50	14.88	51.91	33.19
Overland Park, KS	12.11	12.09	56.96	9.43	17.83	52.56	31.32
Oyster Bay, NY	15.04	14.38	57.39	13.45	20.73	69.03	37.67
Pembroke Pines, FL	9.95	10.73	58.17	9.74	16.02	53.59	34.17
Philadelphia, PA	13.75	13.43	73.18	11.95	19.09	67.58	36.21
Phoenix, AZ	11.50	11.12	62.72	9.60	17.63	52.33	35.95
Pittsburgh, PA	12.30	12.46	65.19	9.88	17.52	61.96	25.62
Plano, TX	10.27	10.86	68.66	9.01	16.80	62.63	31.31
Portland, OR	12.36	13.43	49.96	10.92	18.72	51.57	39.20
Providence, RI	13.12	12.98	47.55	11.38	18.55	48.54	41.10
Provo, UT	10.50	12.48	52.77	9.21	16.72	47.29	n/a
Raleigh, NC	10.84	11.34	55.47	9.21	17.86	60.01	31.53
Richmond, VA	10.39	11.96	60.87	9.06	17.50	70.03	32.96
Roseville, CA	13.16	13.33	58.86	11.64	20.40	52.30	51.53
Round Rock, TX	10.51	11.79	47.69	9.22	16.02	65.36	32.42
San Antonio, TX	10.02	11.50	45.71	9.32	14.22	61.38	31.18
San Diego, CA	12.83	12.71	69.30	10.12	17.57	62.90	39.31
San Francisco, CA	13.39	17.47	84.20	15.20	23.49	81.50	39.71
San Jose, CA	13.30	15.04	89.96	11.63	23.10	77.50	53.97
Savannah, GA	10.57	12.43	52.91	8.61	15.51	49.22	n/a
Scottsdale, AZ	11.50	11.12	62.72	9.60	17.63	52.33	35.95
Seattle, WA	14.35	15.62	59.08	12.10	20.35	63.21	41.27
Sioux Falls, SD	10.90	12.35	49.87	9.57	15.63	52.97	27.27
Stamford, CT	13.77	15.87	77.33	12.35	22.39	68.28	41.12
Sterling Hgts, MI	11.95	13.55	52.10	10.96	16.71	51.84	29.23
Sunnyvale, CA	13.30	15.04	89.96	11.63	23.10	77.50	53.97
Tampa, FL	10.04	10.87	52.36	8.98	15.64	51.71	31.56
Temecula, CA	12.88	12.24	57.78	10.37	18.41	53.71	42.15
Thousand Oaks, CA	13.84	13.35	81.47	10.37	19.54	58.67	49.21
Virginia Beach, VA	10.34	10.69	55.62	9.10	16.70	54.04	28.10
Washington, DC	12.11	12.72	75.86	12.02	20.52	69.78	35.51

Notes: Wage data is for May 2011 and covers the Metropolitan Statistical Area—see Appendix B for areas included; n/a not available
Source: Bureau of Labor Statistics, May 2011 Metro Area Occupational Employment and Wage Estimates

Average Hourly Wages: Occupations N – R

Metro Area	Nurses, Licensed Practical	Nurses, Registered	Nursing Aides/ Orderlies/ Attendants	Packers/ Packagers	Physical Therapists	Postal Mail Carriers	R.E. Brokers
Albuquerque, NM	23.01	33.73	13.35	11.64	35.16	24.93	38.36
Alexandria, VA	22.67	35.92	13.65	10.83	40.55	25.00	38.67
Anchorage, AK	24.82	39.99	16.61	12.48	44.45	25.98	n/a
Ann Arbor, MI	20.97	29.78	12.70	9.20	35.03	24.62	n/a
Athens, GA	17.91	29.93	9.02	9.63	34.06	23.58	n/a
Atlanta, GA	18.73	31.13	11.18	10.67	36.50	24.66	36.66
Austin, TX	21.93	33.09	11.00	11.36	38.51	25.00	45.04
Baltimore, MD	24.45	37.14	13.64	12.00	40.03	24.89	45.63
Bellevue, WA	24.18	37.68	14.77	11.79	37.65	25.70	41.03
Billings, MT	16.95	30.66	12.41	9.36	31.15	24.77	n/a
Boise City, ID	19.60	31.49	11.32	8.98	33.98	24.47	n/a
Boston, MA	24.37	45.48	14.84	11.08	36.69	25.81	72.64
Boulder, CO	22.00	32.84	13.37	12.09	33.15	25.22	31.47
Broken Arrow, OK	17.52	26.45	10.44	9.87	35.16	24.64	n/a
Cambridge, MA	24.37	45.48	14.84	11.08	36.69	25.81	72.64
Cape Coral, FL	20.26	31.16	12.32	9.89	39.19	24.14	n/a
Carlsbad, CA	23.19	40.82	12.68	9.96	42.57	25.79	33.89
Cary, NC	20.23	28.69	11.46	10.31	33.65	24.14	30.67
Cedar Rapids, IA	16.95	23.84	12.02	12.39	35.16	24.80	n/a
Charleston, SC	20.09	32.68	11.05	10.19	33.51	23.97	25.25
Charlotte, NC	20.02	30.05	11.04	9.83	37.20	24.22	32.71
Chesapeake, VA	17.61	30.40	11.02	10.18	36.74	25.05	35.93
Chicago, IL	21.29	34.05	12.42	10.90	37.98	25.50	37.47
Clarksville, TN	19.21	28.86	10.69	11.48	34.68	23.83	n/a
Colorado Spgs., CO	20.27	31.91	12.33	10.10	34.27	25.20	24.31
Columbia, MD	24.45	37.14	13.64	12.00	40.03	24.89	45.63
Columbia, MO	18.12	27.35	10.43	8.84	32.64	24.07	n/a
Columbia, SC	19.64	28.95	11.39	11.67	37.01	24.01	26.83
Columbus, OH	20.17	30.29	11.81	10.51	36.06	24.44	37.91
Dallas, TX	21.67	32.86	11.46	10.61	45.67	25.10	49.69
Denver, CO	22.47	34.46	14.11	11.04	34.46	25.63	43.80
Durham, NC	21.12	30.91	12.81	9.85	34.94	24.39	27.11
Edison, NJ	24.95	37.07	13.21	10.76	44.91	25.53	n/a
El Paso, TX	19.64	30.75	10.19	8.82	50.67	25.05	n/a
Fargo, ND	17.52	29.06	12.76	9.83	30.26	24.33	n/a
Ft. Collins, CO	22.17	31.03	12.29	10.49	35.30	25.21	25.47
Ft. Worth, TX	20.86	31.74	11.16	9.53	41.00	25.02	n/a
Gilbert, AZ	25.14	35.74	13.23	10.78	37.94	25.15	n/a
Green Bay, WI	18.19	29.67	12.45	11.53	38.79	24.03	n/a
Henderson, NV	25.75	37.40	16.22	12.06	47.65	25.51	39.47
High Point, NC	19.43	29.35	10.81	9.11	38.46	24.13	25.93
Honolulu, HI	21.49	41.60	13.85	10.01	36.72	26.30	n/a
Houston, TX	21.93	35.63	11.44	11.31	40.26	25.24	48.78
Huntington, NY	24.27	39.67	16.90	11.03	40.95	25.69	49.57
Huntsville, AL	18.07	28.70	11.24	10.42	37.50	24.57	25.73
Indianapolis, IN	19.71	29.53	12.07	12.03	35.17	24.66	n/a
Irvine, CA	23.45	39.33	13.86	10.50	40.02	26.15	47.09
Jackson, MS	17.29	31.47	9.48	9.45	34.15	23.92	n/a
Jacksonville, FL	19.78	31.53	11.48	9.62	46.78	24.92	31.18
Jersey City, NJ	24.25	39.93	16.09	10.72	40.18	25.76	68.66
Kansas City, MO	18.99	31.89	11.80	10.34	33.08	24.74	34.16
Kenosha, WI	22.61	34.98	12.33	10.87	37.64	25.01	n/a
Las Vegas, NV	25.75	37.40	16.22	12.06	47.65	25.51	39.47
Lexington, KY	19.02	28.08	11.53	10.93	39.31	25.14	n/a
Lincoln, NE	17.88	27.45	11.86	10.14	36.58	25.07	21.00

Table continued on next page.

Metro Area	Nurses, Licensed Practical	Nurses, Registered	Nursing Aides/ Orderlies/ Attendants	Packers/ Packagers	Physical Therapists	Postal Mail Carriers	R.E. Brokers
Little Rock, AR	18.06	28.46	10.83	8.99	38.61	24.44	45.04
Los Angeles, CA	23.91	41.03	12.75	10.22	41.74	26.15	58.15
Madison, WI	20.71	35.01	13.08	15.44	35.67	24.55	n/a
Manchester, NH	21.31	32.81	14.41	10.21	36.24	25.67	n/a
Miami, FL	20.47	33.02	10.61	9.42	36.47	25.80	45.70
Minneapolis, MN	20.22	36.52	13.74	11.43	34.51	24.98	32.67
Murfreesboro, TN	18.81	30.99	11.45	9.93	35.11	24.48	28.42
Naperville, IL	21.29	34.05	12.42	10.90	37.98	25.50	37.47
Nashville, TN	18.81	30.99	11.45	9.93	35.11	24.48	28.42
New Orleans, LA	20.38	32.72	11.18	11.49	37.57	25.16	n/a
New York, NY	24.25	39.93	16.09	10.72	40.18	25.76	68.66
Norman, OK	17.73	28.19	10.47	9.07	37.21	24.52	20.67
Olathe, KS	18.99	31.89	11.80	10.34	33.08	24.74	34.16
Omaha, NE	19.20	28.72	12.12	10.10	35.39	24.82	42.69
Orlando, FL	18.83	28.25	11.78	11.28	38.75	24.96	58.00
Overland Park, KS	18.99	31.89	11.80	10.34	33.08	24.74	34.16
Oyster Bay, NY	24.27	39.67	16.90	11.03	40.95	25.69	49.57
Pembroke Pines, FL	20.12	32.78	11.94	9.51	41.16	25.81	22.28
Philadelphia, PA	24.25	35.80	13.57	11.38	36.83	25.54	65.00
Phoenix, AZ	25.14	35.74	13.23	10.78	37.94	25.15	n/a
Pittsburgh, PA	19.56	29.87	12.86	11.37	36.53	24.92	64.72
Plano, TX	21.67	32.86	11.46	10.61	45.67	25.10	49.69
Portland, OR	23.20	38.36	13.17	10.83	37.27	25.16	37.46
Providence, RI	24.57	34.53	13.47	10.47	39.32	25.29	n/a
Provo, UT	17.99	29.01	10.50	9.38	39.24	24.77	n/a
Raleigh, NC	20.23	28.69	11.46	10.31	33.65	24.14	30.67
Richmond, VA	19.43	32.30	11.49	12.18	38.53	23.96	n/a
Roseville, CA	26.08	47.71	15.40	12.45	42.79	24.88	30.05
Round Rock, TX	21.93	33.09	11.00	11.36	38.51	25.00	45.04
San Antonio, TX	20.43	33.17	11.70	10.67	45.48	24.92	29.54
San Diego, CA	23.19	40.82	12.68	9.96	42.57	25.79	33.89
San Francisco, CA	29.44	50.80	18.00	11.82	42.97	26.37	33.03
San Jose, CA	27.41	56.53	16.97	10.41	42.78	26.07	58.81
Savannah, GA	18.32	29.22	10.72	9.73	42.69	24.12	n/a
Scottsdale, AZ	25.14	35.74	13.23	10.78	37.94	25.15	n/a
Seattle, WA	24.18	37.68	14.77	11.79	37.65	25.70	41.03
Sioux Falls, SD	17.28	27.58	12.21	10.35	32.32	24.04	n/a
Stamford, CT	26.33	37.28	15.28	11.70	37.96	25.93	38.31
Sterling Hgts, MI	21.45	34.23	12.53	12.13	36.63	25.24	n/a
Sunnyvale, CA	27.41	56.53	16.97	10.41	42.78	26.07	58.81
Tampa, FL	20.00	31.80	11.52	9.58	38.77	24.78	28.72
Temecula, CA	21.99	39.09	12.30	11.12	39.91	25.31	n/a
Thousand Oaks, CA	26.90	36.89	13.50	10.39	42.71	25.44	23.53
Virginia Beach, VA	17.61	30.40	11.02	10.18	36.74	25.05	35.93
Washington, DC	22.67	35.92	13.65	10.83	40.55	25.00	38.67

Notes: Wage data is for May 2011 and covers the Metropolitan Statistical Area—see Appendix B for areas included; n/a not available
Source: Bureau of Labor Statistics, May 2011 Metro Area Occupational Employment and Wage Estimates

Average Hourly Wages: Occupations R – T

Metro Area	Retail Salespersons	Sales Reps., Except Tech./Scien.	Sales Reps., Tech./Scien.	Secretaries, Exc. Leg./ Med./Exec.	Security Guards	Surgeons	Teacher Assistants
Albuquerque, NM	12.27	27.05	38.12	13.94	11.78	n/a	10.00
Alexandria, VA	12.47	33.41	46.73	20.68	18.21	109.77	14.30
Anchorage, AK	13.13	26.16	37.99	18.95	15.02	n/a	n/a
Ann Arbor, MI	12.05	32.25	44.30	16.43	14.46	n/a	12.30
Athens, GA	10.32	25.87	33.67	14.86	13.95	107.28	9.20
Atlanta, GA	11.33	31.30	38.03	15.54	11.44	111.35	10.10
Austin, TX	12.19	33.93	39.52	15.34	11.96	n/a	12.00
Baltimore, MD	12.12	33.18	39.57	17.80	14.85	113.17	15.30
Bellevue, WA	14.24	33.18	43.02	19.27	18.98	n/a	15.40
Billings, MT	12.55	27.02	28.18	12.85	12.66	118.29	9.30
Boise City, ID	11.73	24.13	37.81	14.47	12.44	n/a	10.30
Boston, MA	12.60	41.69	47.40	20.23	14.17	115.62	14.60
Boulder, CO	13.59	36.76	42.23	17.08	13.46	88.85	13.60
Broken Arrow, OK	12.04	27.43	40.52	13.50	13.62	91.90	11.20
Cambridge, MA	12.60	41.69	47.40	20.23	14.17	115.62	14.60
Cape Coral, FL	12.20	27.71	41.79	14.85	11.15	120.15	9.40
Carlsbad, CA	12.76	29.99	41.40	18.21	13.27	92.00	13.70
Cary, NC	11.54	29.00	32.37	16.27	11.76	100.24	10.60
Cedar Rapids, IA	13.96	27.05	44.97	14.05	10.16	n/a	12.20
Charleston, SC	12.15	25.40	40.29	15.43	12.06	n/a	11.10
Charlotte, NC	11.99	28.65	39.16	16.31	13.14	115.06	11.00
Chesapeake, VA	11.18	28.00	37.11	15.64	11.60	119.02	11.40
Chicago, IL	12.39	32.65	37.38	16.68	12.12	119.74	12.00
Clarksville, TN	10.60	20.67	44.24	13.13	11.99	n/a	11.70
Colorado Spgs., CO	12.71	28.07	35.20	15.48	14.02	n/a	11.80
Columbia, MD	12.12	33.18	39.57	17.80	14.85	113.17	15.30
Columbia, MO	11.73	23.47	25.97	13.73	15.81	n/a	9.90
Columbia, SC	11.77	30.05	32.46	14.65	11.16	102.05	9.90
Columbus, OH	11.96	28.28	36.96	17.66	12.28	119.85	13.60
Dallas, TX	12.80	32.42	50.79	15.88	12.77	n/a	11.30
Denver, CO	13.31	33.23	43.23	17.43	13.73	103.52	13.80
Durham, NC	11.21	28.10	46.51	17.05	13.99	115.99	10.90
Edison, NJ	13.12	35.59	50.80	18.54	12.67	n/a	13.00
El Paso, TX	10.68	22.03	32.45	12.63	11.86	n/a	10.40
Fargo, ND	12.89	24.57	33.79	15.17	11.83	111.67	12.70
Ft. Collins, CO	11.78	30.94	37.64	15.46	10.29	108.04	12.10
Ft. Worth, TX	11.79	28.96	48.18	15.65	12.08	77.40	9.90
Gilbert, AZ	12.05	30.16	39.60	15.99	13.08	n/a	11.00
Green Bay, WI	11.35	30.90	36.26	15.79	14.29	120.35	13.90
Henderson, NV	12.51	27.10	52.63	17.96	13.25	93.59	15.30
High Point, NC	11.77	26.98	32.01	15.35	11.10	117.72	10.90
Honolulu, HI	13.11	20.99	31.88	18.51	12.01	93.71	13.20
Houston, TX	11.33	31.84	41.40	15.79	10.52	66.07	10.50
Huntington, NY	13.87	40.95	51.50	17.43	14.76	104.10	13.60
Huntsville, AL	11.31	27.28	36.21	16.22	13.18	n/a	10.90
Indianapolis, IN	11.12	30.29	38.19	16.36	12.73	118.56	11.50
Irvine, CA	13.42	32.23	43.66	18.40	14.09	86.61	15.50
Jackson, MS	12.64	26.78	n/a	13.88	11.69	88.21	8.80
Jacksonville, FL	11.67	28.67	38.14	14.83	10.26	n/a	11.10
Jersey City, NJ	13.33	38.00	48.38	18.52	14.01	82.60	13.70
Kansas City, MO	12.17	32.88	39.20	15.13	13.40	n/a	11.30
Kenosha, WI	12.04	32.95	38.93	16.79	13.93	n/a	11.60
Las Vegas, NV	12.51	27.10	52.63	17.96	13.25	93.59	15.30
Lexington, KY	11.27	23.79	39.29	14.72	10.40	119.61	13.80
Lincoln, NE	10.73	24.99	38.43	14.95	12.45	n/a	11.70

Table continued on next page.

Metro Area	Retail Salespersons	Sales Reps., Except Tech./Scien.	Sales Reps., Tech./Scien.	Secretaries, Exc. Leg./ Med./Exec.	Security Guards	Surgeons	Teacher Assistants
Little Rock, AR	10.87	26.70	31.77	13.75	11.74	109.00	10.00
Los Angeles, CA	12.42	30.78	38.68	17.76	13.10	114.00	14.30
Madison, WI	11.53	31.39	39.50	16.89	11.19	n/a	12.50
Manchester, NH	12.31	30.01	43.75	16.17	10.89	104.47	12.80
Miami, FL	11.31	27.96	40.36	14.86	11.47	116.44	11.10
Minneapolis, MN	11.40	36.26	42.33	18.91	14.53	n/a	13.70
Murfreesboro, TN	11.58	28.49	34.32	14.84	10.98	n/a	10.90
Naperville, IL	12.39	32.65	37.38	16.68	12.12	119.74	12.00
Nashville, TN	11.58	28.49	34.32	14.84	10.98	n/a	10.90
New Orleans, LA	12.01	28.99	31.55	14.64	12.18	120.03	10.70
New York, NY	13.33	38.00	48.38	18.52	14.01	82.60	13.70
Norman, OK	11.64	27.46	30.18	14.22	12.89	110.26	9.20
Olathe, KS	12.17	32.88	39.20	15.13	13.40	n/a	11.30
Omaha, NE	12.36	29.45	41.40	15.00	14.90	n/a	10.20
Orlando, FL	11.47	26.15	42.08	14.78	11.10	107.08	10.80
Overland Park, KS	12.17	32.88	39.20	15.13	13.40	n/a	11.30
Oyster Bay, NY	13.87	40.95	51.50	17.43	14.76	104.10	13.60
Pembroke Pines, FL	11.49	30.80	41.23	15.08	10.24	111.34	10.30
Philadelphia, PA	13.10	33.51	46.26	16.95	14.35	71.72	13.10
Phoenix, AZ	12.05	30.16	39.60	15.99	13.08	n/a	11.00
Pittsburgh, PA	12.70	31.74	43.12	14.52	11.93	98.95	11.10
Plano, TX	12.80	32.42	50.79	15.88	12.77	n/a	11.30
Portland, OR	12.97	30.60	49.83	16.97	13.56	n/a	14.10
Providence, RI	12.18	34.31	37.75	17.36	12.75	n/a	13.60
Provo, UT	11.81	24.32	28.32	14.47	13.63	n/a	11.30
Raleigh, NC	11.54	29.00	32.37	16.27	11.76	100.24	10.60
Richmond, VA	12.39	32.74	40.67	16.23	13.06	116.38	10.20
Roseville, CA	12.32	32.15	42.87	17.88	12.52	n/a	14.70
Round Rock, TX	12.19	33.93	39.52	15.34	11.96	n/a	12.00
San Antonio, TX	11.50	27.20	42.93	15.20	11.40	98.05	10.50
San Diego, CA	12.76	29.99	41.40	18.21	13.27	92.00	13.70
San Francisco, CA	13.43	35.39	52.68	20.80	14.96	n/a	16.00
San Jose, CA	12.12	36.81	53.90	19.87	15.84	116.76	14.90
Savannah, GA	11.37	27.05	34.62	14.67	13.87	118.18	11.60
Scottsdale, AZ	12.05	30.16	39.60	15.99	13.08	n/a	11.00
Seattle, WA	14.24	33.18	43.02	19.27	18.98	n/a	15.40
Sioux Falls, SD	12.01	27.35	49.82	12.84	12.19	n/a	10.80
Stamford, CT	13.78	42.04	46.58	20.08	15.22	n/a	13.30
Sterling Hgts, MI	12.94	33.37	46.77	16.26	12.54	112.79	12.90
Sunnyvale, CA	12.12	36.81	53.90	19.87	15.84	116.76	14.90
Tampa, FL	12.11	28.26	40.55	14.37	10.90	90.41	10.90
Temecula, CA	11.79	28.82	37.82	16.71	11.63	119.83	14.10
Thousand Oaks, CA	12.18	33.22	34.45	17.73	11.97	n/a	14.50
Virginia Beach, VA	11.18	28.00	37.11	15.64	11.60	119.02	11.40
Washington, DC	12.47	33.41	46.73	20.68	18.21	109.77	14.30

Notes: Wage data is for May 2011 and covers the Metropolitan Statistical Area—see Appendix B for areas included; hourly wages for teacher assistants were calculated by the editors from annual wage data assuming a 40 hour work week; n/a not available
Source: Bureau of Labor Statistics, May 2011 Metro Area Occupational Employment and Wage Estimates

Average Hourly Wages: Occupations T – Z

Metro Area	Teachers, Elementary School	Teachers, Secondary School	Tele- marketers	Truck Driv., Heavy/ Trac. Trail.	Truck Drivers, Light	Waiters/ Waitresses
Albuquerque, NM	22.90	23.50	n/a	18.77	15.51	10.07
Alexandria, VA	32.30	34.10	12.50	20.12	19.21	12.11
Anchorage, AK	n/a	n/a	n/a	23.41	20.42	10.88
Ann Arbor, MI	29.40	28.40	12.79	19.42	18.38	10.23
Athens, GA	27.60	25.20	10.02	18.85	16.62	8.98
Atlanta, GA	26.10	26.30	14.02	19.76	16.52	9.63
Austin, TX	24.40	25.10	15.46	16.34	16.12	8.82
Baltimore, MD	29.50	29.70	14.51	20.06	17.18	9.94
Bellevue, WA	29.00	29.50	12.43	21.25	17.47	14.87
Billings, MT	20.60	20.20	11.73	19.27	14.35	9.11
Boise City, ID	23.30	22.80	11.88	17.51	14.09	9.58
Boston, MA	32.40	32.30	16.83	22.04	18.77	14.08
Boulder, CO	25.30	n/a	13.29	19.27	15.31	11.72
Broken Arrow, OK	22.10	22.20	11.40	17.91	15.60	8.54
Cambridge, MA	32.40	32.30	16.83	22.04	18.77	14.08
Cape Coral, FL	16.60	23.50	18.47	16.80	15.29	10.07
Carlsbad, CA	31.10	32.30	12.10	19.72	17.14	9.43
Cary, NC	21.60	23.20	14.12	19.81	15.76	10.02
Cedar Rapids, IA	22.20	22.50	9.29	16.74	13.42	9.15
Charleston, SC	22.70	n/a	17.92	16.94	14.89	9.24
Charlotte, NC	22.40	22.90	13.14	19.38	15.30	9.81
Chesapeake, VA	26.90	27.40	10.50	16.76	15.61	9.90
Chicago, IL	29.70	33.40	13.54	23.08	18.28	10.68
Clarksville, TN	n/a	21.80	10.69	14.70	12.94	8.93
Colorado Spgs., CO	22.00	22.30	11.15	16.82	15.00	9.27
Columbia, MD	29.50	29.70	14.51	20.06	17.18	9.94
Columbia, MO	19.90	19.50	9.20	18.38	16.72	8.76
Columbia, SC	24.00	25.10	10.60	18.38	14.34	8.45
Columbus, OH	28.30	27.20	10.16	20.39	15.95	9.29
Dallas, TX	26.40	27.90	12.69	19.42	16.73	9.75
Denver, CO	25.40	27.00	13.58	20.43	16.74	10.21
Durham, NC	21.50	22.90	13.07	16.94	17.85	11.39
Edison, NJ	30.80	32.30	12.65	21.26	18.07	10.98
El Paso, TX	25.10	25.90	8.77	16.91	15.38	8.52
Fargo, ND	24.70	23.90	10.78	18.97	14.26	9.56
Ft. Collins, CO	n/a	n/a	n/a	19.01	14.59	9.59
Ft. Worth, TX	26.40	27.40	12.61	19.77	15.76	10.08
Gilbert, AZ	20.60	21.00	14.81	20.92	17.50	10.36
Green Bay, WI	26.50	25.70	23.32	18.88	15.41	11.50
Henderson, NV	25.10	25.20	15.49	22.68	16.25	11.09
High Point, NC	22.30	22.40	13.96	19.40	15.43	8.86
Honolulu, HI	26.40	26.00	13.11	21.19	15.58	11.68
Houston, TX	25.60	27.00	16.77	18.15	15.95	9.04
Huntington, NY	43.50	42.50	13.56	24.12	19.13	11.59
Huntsville, AL	25.30	23.80	n/a	17.13	15.28	9.23
Indianapolis, IN	24.20	24.50	12.87	19.33	15.81	9.74
Irvine, CA	33.00	35.10	16.54	22.37	16.70	10.52
Jackson, MS	20.30	20.30	14.52	17.55	14.71	9.50
Jacksonville, FL	25.90	23.10	12.03	17.52	14.95	9.39
Jersey City, NJ	33.50	36.20	14.34	22.42	17.85	12.32
Kansas City, MO	23.20	23.80	13.62	20.26	16.64	9.17
Kenosha, WI	26.60	31.70	18.51	20.63	15.76	9.63
Las Vegas, NV	25.10	25.20	15.49	22.68	16.25	11.09
Lexington, KY	23.90	25.00	n/a	17.23	16.74	9.32
Lincoln, NE	24.00	24.20	8.75	17.09	15.07	8.94

Table continued on next page.

Metro Area	Teachers, Elementary School	Teachers, Secondary School	Tele-marketers	Truck Driv., Heavy/ Trac. Trail.	Truck Drivers, Light	Waiters/ Waitresses
Little Rock, AR	22.60	24.10	12.12	19.99	14.75	8.68
Los Angeles, CA	32.30	30.80	13.04	20.25	15.97	10.20
Madison, WI	24.70	24.10	10.65	18.57	16.17	9.76
Manchester, NH	24.90	n/a	12.01	19.91	16.63	11.87
Miami, FL	21.80	24.70	11.43	19.33	14.37	9.59
Minneapolis, MN	29.20	27.70	13.35	21.15	18.54	10.18
Murfreesboro, TN	22.30	22.70	14.74	18.79	16.57	9.18
Naperville, IL	29.70	33.40	13.54	23.08	18.28	10.68
Nashville, TN	22.30	22.70	14.74	18.79	16.57	9.18
New Orleans, LA	23.60	23.80	14.84	19.44	16.87	9.55
New York, NY	33.50	36.20	14.34	22.42	17.85	12.32
Norman, OK	20.10	21.40	10.49	20.18	14.76	9.25
Olathe, KS	23.20	23.80	13.62	20.26	16.64	9.17
Omaha, NE	21.90	21.80	10.96	22.38	16.17	8.89
Orlando, FL	24.40	24.70	11.87	16.98	14.67	11.28
Overland Park, KS	23.20	23.80	13.62	20.26	16.64	9.17
Oyster Bay, NY	43.50	42.50	13.56	24.12	19.13	11.59
Pembroke Pines, FL	n/a	n/a	11.62	18.90	15.92	9.70
Philadelphia, PA	26.40	29.90	15.16	21.45	17.23	10.72
Phoenix, AZ	20.60	21.00	14.81	20.92	17.50	10.36
Pittsburgh, PA	26.60	27.50	12.13	20.16	14.78	9.89
Plano, TX	26.40	27.90	12.69	19.42	16.73	9.75
Portland, OR	27.00	27.50	13.09	19.51	18.22	12.86
Providence, RI	33.20	33.00	13.43	20.69	16.57	10.61
Provo, UT	20.50	24.60	11.22	18.38	14.00	10.76
Raleigh, NC	21.60	23.20	14.12	19.81	15.76	10.02
Richmond, VA	25.10	24.50	14.02	18.03	17.00	10.35
Roseville, CA	31.80	31.10	13.16	19.58	17.34	10.06
Round Rock, TX	24.40	25.10	15.46	16.34	16.12	8.82
San Antonio, TX	26.60	27.10	10.94	15.74	14.27	9.36
San Diego, CA	31.10	32.30	12.10	19.72	17.14	9.43
San Francisco, CA	30.60	32.50	16.04	22.23	19.77	12.19
San Jose, CA	29.80	35.00	20.43	19.47	17.06	10.45
Savannah, GA	24.10	23.50	8.97	18.62	15.26	9.05
Scottsdale, AZ	20.60	21.00	14.81	20.92	17.50	10.36
Seattle, WA	29.00	29.50	12.43	21.25	17.47	14.87
Sioux Falls, SD	19.50	19.40	10.93	18.84	15.00	8.94
Stamford, CT	33.30	34.00	17.78	21.40	17.00	10.57
Sterling Hgts, MI	28.10	29.20	11.44	18.65	14.84	9.80
Sunnyvale, CA	29.80	35.00	20.43	19.47	17.06	10.45
Tampa, FL	26.40	28.10	12.22	17.86	16.05	10.07
Temecula, CA	32.70	32.20	13.66	20.95	16.00	9.36
Thousand Oaks, CA	31.30	29.30	15.81	21.77	17.24	10.28
Virginia Beach, VA	26.90	27.40	10.50	16.76	15.61	9.90
Washington, DC	32.30	34.10	12.50	20.12	19.21	12.11

Notes: Wage data is for May 2011 and covers the Metropolitan Statistical Area—see Appendix B for areas included; hourly wages for elementary and secondary school teachers were calculated by the editors from annual wage data assuming a 40 hour work week; n/a not available
Source: Bureau of Labor Statistics, May 2011 Metro Area Occupational Employment and Wage Estimates

Means of Transportation to Work: City

City	Car/Truck/Van		Public Transportation			Bicycle	Walked	Other Means	Worked at Home
	Drove Alone	Car-pooled	Bus	Subway	Railroad				
Albuquerque, NM	79.0	10.3	2.1	0.0	0.1	1.5	1.8	1.2	4.0
Alexandria, VA	58.9	8.9	8.2	13.5	0.2	0.9	3.8	1.4	4.3
Anchorage, AK	75.7	13.7	1.5	0.0	0.0	1.1	2.6	2.2	3.3
Ann Arbor, MI	57.4	7.0	9.9	0.1	0.0	3.2	15.6	0.7	6.2
Athens, GA	73.2	10.1	3.9	0.0	0.0	1.6	5.1	1.6	4.4
Atlanta, GA	66.0	8.1	9.3	2.8	0.4	0.8	4.4	1.7	6.5
Austin, TX	71.0	11.1	4.9	0.0	0.0	1.2	2.4	3.1	6.2
Baltimore, MD	59.1	11.0	15.1	1.4	1.5	0.8	6.6	1.7	2.9
Bellevue, WA	66.5	9.8	10.9	0.0	0.0	0.7	5.1	1.2	5.8
Billings, MT	80.8	8.9	1.7	0.0	0.0	0.6	3.8	0.8	3.5
Boise City, ID	78.2	7.7	0.8	0.1	0.0	4.3	2.5	1.4	5.0
Boston, MA	38.4	7.4	12.7	17.4	1.0	1.7	15.2	2.7	3.6
Boulder, CO	52.0	6.4	9.4	0.0	0.0	10.5	9.1	1.5	11.2
Broken Arrow, OK	84.6	9.0	0.4	0.0	0.0	0.0	0.6	1.7	3.7
Cambridge, MA	30.7	4.8	6.9	18.4	0.7	7.1	23.8	1.6	6.1
Cape Coral, FL	81.6	10.1	0.4	0.0	0.0	0.3	0.7	1.6	5.4
Carlsbad, CA	77.7	6.6	0.6	0.1	1.2	0.8	1.4	1.5	10.1
Cary, NC	79.8	8.4	0.6	0.0	0.0	0.2	1.4	1.4	8.2
Cedar Rapids, IA	82.1	9.0	1.3	0.0	0.0	0.3	3.0	1.3	3.0
Charleston, SC	77.6	7.5	3.1	0.0	0.0	2.0	4.9	1.2	3.7
Charlotte, NC	76.1	11.8	3.3	0.4	0.1	0.2	2.1	0.7	5.3
Chesapeake, VA	85.8	7.0	1.0	0.0	0.0	0.2	1.2	1.2	3.5
Chicago, IL	50.4	9.9	14.5	10.1	1.9	1.2	6.1	1.7	4.3
Clarksville, TN	84.5	10.6	0.6	0.1	0.0	0.1	1.1	0.8	2.2
Colorado Spgs., CO	79.1	9.9	1.5	0.0	0.0	0.6	2.8	1.1	5.1
Columbia, MD	80.1	8.0	3.0	0.7	1.8	0.1	1.5	0.6	4.1
Columbia, MO	75.2	11.6	0.7	0.0	0.0	1.4	6.7	1.0	3.4
Columbia, SC	68.4	7.5	2.2	0.2	0.0	0.6	4.5	2.2	14.4
Columbus, OH	80.5	8.5	2.9	0.0	0.0	0.7	2.9	0.9	3.5
Dallas, TX	77.6	11.1	3.5	0.3	0.3	0.1	1.9	1.4	3.8
Denver, CO	69.1	10.3	6.5	0.8	0.3	2.0	4.0	1.3	5.7
Durham, NC	74.1	13.8	3.4	0.0	0.0	0.5	3.6	0.9	3.8
Edison, NJ	71.5	7.8	0.4	0.8	12.6	0.1	2.2	0.8	3.7
El Paso, TX	80.1	10.4	2.1	0.0	0.0	0.2	2.0	2.7	2.5
Fargo, ND	82.6	7.1	1.2	0.0	0.0	1.4	4.0	1.0	2.7
Ft. Collins, CO	72.7	8.9	1.1	0.0	0.0	7.2	3.1	1.1	5.9
Ft. Worth, TX	80.6	11.6	1.0	0.0	0.2	0.1	1.2	1.9	3.3
Gilbert, AZ	78.7	13.0	0.7	0.0	0.0	0.3	0.5	1.2	5.5
Green Bay, WI	81.1	7.7	1.7	0.0	0.0	0.5	2.7	2.7	3.4
Henderson, NV	82.1	8.5	1.2	0.0	0.0	0.1	1.4	1.6	5.1
High Point, NC	83.1	8.6	2.4	0.0	0.1	0.1	1.4	1.1	3.1
Honolulu, HI	57.0	12.7	12.6	0.0	0.0	1.8	9.7	3.2	3.0
Houston, TX	75.0	13.1	4.3	0.1	0.1	0.4	2.2	1.9	3.1
Huntington, NY	76.7	5.4	1.2	0.5	8.5	0.1	1.4	0.6	5.5
Huntsville, AL	83.5	9.9	0.7	0.0	0.0	0.1	1.1	1.5	3.1
Indianapolis, IN	81.8	10.0	2.0	0.0	0.0	0.4	2.1	0.7	3.0
Irvine, CA	76.2	7.7	0.9	0.1	0.5	2.2	5.0	1.0	6.4
Jackson, MS	82.6	10.4	1.0	0.0	0.0	0.1	1.7	0.8	3.4
Jacksonville, FL	81.0	10.7	1.6	0.0	0.0	0.4	1.8	0.9	3.6
Jersey City, NJ	34.2	7.6	16.1	23.3	4.1	0.5	8.4	3.3	2.5
Kansas City, MO	80.6	8.7	3.7	0.0	0.0	0.3	2.2	1.1	3.5
Kenosha, WI	83.6	9.4	1.0	0.0	0.5	0.3	1.8	1.1	2.2
Las Vegas, NV	77.6	11.2	4.2	0.0	0.0	0.3	2.0	1.7	3.0
Lexington, KY	80.2	10.6	1.4	0.0	0.0	0.6	3.7	0.4	3.1

Table continued on next page.

| City | Car/Truck/Van | | Public Transportation | | | Bicycle | Walked | Other Means | Worked at Home |
	Drove Alone	Car-pooled	Bus	Subway	Railroad				
Lincoln, NE	80.8	9.9	1.2	0.0	0.0	1.3	3.5	0.5	2.7
Little Rock, AR	80.6	13.1	1.1	0.0	0.0	0.0	1.5	0.7	2.9
Los Angeles, CA	66.9	10.6	10.4	0.5	0.1	1.0	3.5	1.5	5.4
Madison, WI	64.0	9.0	8.4	0.0	0.0	5.0	9.3	1.0	3.2
Manchester, NH	83.9	9.3	0.7	0.0	0.0	0.2	2.4	0.7	2.6
Miami, FL	69.4	10.4	10.4	0.6	0.3	0.6	3.7	1.2	3.6
Minneapolis, MN	61.6	7.7	13.3	0.6	0.6	4.0	6.5	1.0	4.8
Murfreesboro, TN	85.0	9.1	0.6	0.0	0.0	0.3	1.6	1.1	2.2
Naperville, IL	75.0	5.6	0.3	0.4	8.7	0.2	1.3	0.9	7.6
Nashville, TN	79.7	10.3	2.0	0.0	0.1	0.3	2.0	1.1	4.5
New Orleans, LA	68.4	12.2	6.2	0.0	0.0	1.8	5.3	2.6	3.4
New York, NY	22.9	5.2	12.1	41.0	1.7	0.7	10.3	2.2	3.9
Norman, OK	81.5	8.4	0.9	0.1	0.0	1.1	3.9	1.4	2.7
Olathe, KS	81.9	9.8	0.5	0.1	0.0	0.1	1.1	0.9	5.6
Omaha, NE	80.0	11.8	1.4	0.0	0.0	0.1	2.7	0.8	3.3
Orlando, FL	78.3	10.2	4.0	0.0	0.0	0.4	1.7	1.5	3.9
Overland Park, KS	86.1	5.7	0.5	0.0	0.0	0.3	0.9	0.8	5.6
Oyster Bay, NY	73.9	6.8	0.8	0.6	10.8	0.1	1.6	0.6	4.7
Pembroke Pines, FL	84.6	9.0	1.1	0.0	0.1	0.1	0.5	0.8	3.8
Philadelphia, PA	50.3	8.8	18.8	4.4	2.8	1.9	8.6	1.4	2.8
Phoenix, AZ	74.4	13.2	3.3	0.0	0.0	0.7	1.8	1.5	5.1
Pittsburgh, PA	53.4	10.5	18.6	0.3	0.0	1.3	11.4	1.3	3.2
Plano, TX	82.0	6.7	0.6	0.4	0.6	0.1	0.7	1.8	7.1
Portland, OR	59.9	8.8	10.1	0.6	0.2	6.1	5.6	2.1	6.6
Providence, RI	61.1	12.4	7.2	0.2	1.0	1.4	10.6	1.2	5.0
Provo, UT	61.2	12.5	2.9	0.0	0.0	2.4	15.8	0.5	4.7
Raleigh, NC	78.6	10.7	2.0	0.0	0.0	0.5	2.2	0.9	5.1
Richmond, VA	69.7	11.6	7.5	0.0	0.0	2.0	3.9	1.2	4.0
Roseville, CA	79.8	9.4	0.7	0.0	0.4	0.5	1.5	1.3	6.5
Round Rock, TX	78.5	12.6	0.1	0.0	0.0	0.4	1.3	1.0	6.2
San Antonio, TX	78.9	11.5	3.3	0.0	0.0	0.1	2.1	1.5	2.6
San Diego, CA	75.5	9.1	3.6	0.0	0.1	0.9	3.0	1.2	6.5
San Francisco, CA	37.5	8.0	22.7	6.5	1.1	3.1	9.9	4.5	6.7
San Jose, CA	77.8	10.6	2.4	0.2	0.6	0.9	1.8	1.7	3.9
Savannah, GA	75.2	11.5	4.4	0.0	0.0	0.7	3.6	1.2	3.4
Scottsdale, AZ	77.5	6.6	1.6	0.1	0.0	0.9	2.1	1.7	9.6
Seattle, WA	52.6	9.4	18.4	0.2	0.0	3.2	8.7	1.3	6.1
Sioux Falls, SD	84.4	7.9	0.5	0.0	0.0	0.5	2.3	1.1	3.2
Stamford, CT	66.5	11.6	5.0	0.3	5.9	0.2	6.7	0.8	3.3
Sterling Hgts, MI	88.3	8.0	0.5	0.0	0.0	0.2	0.5	0.5	2.2
Sunnyvale, CA	77.4	9.9	2.8	0.2	1.6	1.3	1.4	1.2	4.3
Tampa, FL	76.7	9.6	3.1	0.0	0.0	1.3	2.9	1.1	5.3
Temecula, CA	76.9	12.9	0.2	0.0	0.0	0.6	1.6	1.8	6.0
Thousand Oaks, CA	77.8	9.9	0.6	0.0	0.2	0.9	2.3	1.4	6.8
Virginia Beach, VA	82.3	9.3	0.9	0.0	0.0	0.7	1.8	1.0	3.9
Washington, DC	35.7	6.4	16.2	20.4	0.4	2.6	12.0	1.4	5.0
U.S.	76.0	10.2	2.7	1.7	0.5	0.5	2.8	1.3	4.2

Note: Figures are percentages and cover workers 16 years of age and older
Source: U.S. Census Bureau, 2008-2010 American Community Survey 3-Year Estimates

Means of Transportation to Work: Metro Area

Metro Area	Car/Truck/Van		Public Transportation			Bicycle	Walked	Other Means	Worked at Home
	Drove Alone	Car-pooled	Bus	Subway	Railroad				
Albuquerque, NM	78.6	11.0	1.5	0.0	0.3	1.0	1.7	1.3	4.5
Alexandria, VA	65.7	10.9	5.4	7.7	0.7	0.6	3.3	1.0	4.7
Anchorage, AK	74.7	13.8	1.3	0.0	0.0	0.9	2.5	2.6	4.1
Ann Arbor, MI	73.8	8.3	4.1	0.0	0.0	1.3	6.4	0.6	5.5
Athens, GA	76.0	10.8	2.4	0.0	0.0	1.0	3.6	1.2	5.0
Atlanta, GA	77.2	10.8	2.5	0.7	0.1	0.2	1.3	1.6	5.6
Austin, TX	74.9	11.4	2.6	0.0	0.0	0.7	1.8	2.2	6.5
Baltimore, MD	76.2	9.7	4.3	1.0	0.9	0.3	2.8	1.1	3.7
Bellevue, WA	69.5	11.3	7.8	0.1	0.3	1.0	3.6	1.2	5.1
Billings, MT	79.6	9.3	1.3	0.0	0.0	0.6	3.9	1.0	4.3
Boise City, ID	78.4	9.5	0.5	0.0	0.0	1.9	2.0	2.0	5.6
Boston, MA	68.9	8.0	3.8	5.7	2.0	0.8	5.2	1.3	4.3
Boulder, CO	65.9	8.1	5.1	0.0	0.0	4.2	4.3	1.2	11.1
Broken Arrow, OK	81.9	11.1	0.5	0.0	0.0	0.2	1.3	1.2	3.7
Cambridge, MA	68.9	8.0	3.8	5.7	2.0	0.8	5.2	1.3	4.3
Cape Coral, FL	75.1	14.5	1.0	0.0	0.0	0.8	0.9	1.7	6.0
Carlsbad, CA	75.4	10.4	2.7	0.0	0.3	0.7	3.0	1.4	6.1
Cary, NC	80.5	9.9	1.0	0.0	0.0	0.3	1.4	1.2	5.7
Cedar Rapids, IA	82.2	9.0	0.8	0.0	0.0	0.3	2.8	1.1	3.8
Charleston, SC	80.9	9.7	1.2	0.0	0.0	0.7	2.7	1.1	3.7
Charlotte, NC	79.4	11.0	1.8	0.2	0.1	0.1	1.5	0.8	5.1
Chesapeake, VA	80.7	9.4	1.8	0.0	0.0	0.4	3.0	1.0	3.6
Chicago, IL	70.9	8.8	4.7	3.3	3.2	0.6	3.1	1.2	4.2
Clarksville, TN	82.4	11.1	0.3	0.0	0.0	0.2	1.9	1.2	2.9
Colorado Spgs., CO	77.1	9.5	1.2	0.0	0.0	0.4	4.6	1.2	6.0
Columbia, MD	76.2	9.7	4.3	1.0	0.9	0.3	2.8	1.1	3.7
Columbia, MO	76.9	12.4	0.5	0.0	0.0	0.9	4.9	0.8	3.5
Columbia, SC	80.8	8.9	0.7	0.1	0.0	0.2	1.5	2.5	5.3
Columbus, OH	82.5	8.2	1.6	0.0	0.0	0.5	2.2	0.8	4.2
Dallas, TX	80.8	10.6	1.1	0.1	0.2	0.2	1.3	1.4	4.3
Denver, CO	75.5	9.8	3.8	0.5	0.2	0.8	2.1	1.3	6.1
Durham, NC	74.0	12.4	3.7	0.0	0.0	0.9	3.5	0.8	4.7
Edison, NJ	50.3	7.0	8.4	18.1	3.7	0.5	6.2	2.0	3.8
El Paso, TX	79.3	10.8	1.9	0.0	0.0	0.2	2.1	2.9	2.8
Fargo, ND	82.1	7.6	0.9	0.0	0.0	0.9	4.0	1.0	3.6
Ft. Collins, CO	75.6	9.4	0.8	0.0	0.0	4.1	2.3	1.1	6.6
Ft. Worth, TX	80.8	10.6	1.1	0.1	0.2	0.2	1.3	1.4	4.3
Gilbert, AZ	76.2	12.2	2.1	0.0	0.0	0.7	1.6	1.6	5.5
Green Bay, WI	82.0	8.1	0.9	0.0	0.0	0.4	2.6	1.5	4.5
Henderson, NV	78.5	11.0	3.6	0.0	0.0	0.5	1.8	1.5	3.1
High Point, NC	82.9	10.1	1.3	0.0	0.0	0.1	1.5	0.9	3.3
Honolulu, HI	64.4	14.9	8.1	0.0	0.0	1.1	5.5	2.6	3.4
Houston, TX	78.7	12.1	2.3	0.0	0.0	0.3	1.4	1.7	3.4
Huntington, NY	50.3	7.0	8.4	18.1	3.7	0.5	6.2	2.0	3.8
Huntsville, AL	85.5	9.0	0.4	0.0	0.0	0.1	1.1	1.2	2.7
Indianapolis, IN	83.4	9.0	1.1	0.0	0.0	0.3	1.7	0.9	3.8
Irvine, CA	73.3	11.0	5.6	0.3	0.2	0.8	2.6	1.3	4.8
Jackson, MS	84.4	9.6	0.5	0.0	0.0	0.1	1.3	1.0	3.2
Jacksonville, FL	81.2	10.1	1.1	0.0	0.0	0.6	1.6	1.3	4.0
Jersey City, NJ	50.3	7.0	8.4	18.1	3.7	0.5	6.2	2.0	3.8
Kansas City, MO	82.7	9.2	1.3	0.0	0.0	0.2	1.4	1.2	4.1
Kenosha, WI	70.9	8.8	4.7	3.3	3.2	0.6	3.1	1.2	4.2
Las Vegas, NV	78.5	11.0	3.6	0.0	0.0	0.5	1.8	1.5	3.1
Lexington, KY	80.6	10.8	0.9	0.0	0.0	0.4	3.3	0.5	3.4

Table continued on next page.

Metro Area	Car/Truck/Van		Public Transportation			Bicycle	Walked	Other Means	Worked at Home
	Drove Alone	Car-pooled	Bus	Subway	Railroad				
Lincoln, NE	80.7	9.9	1.1	0.0	0.0	1.2	3.3	0.6	3.3
Little Rock, AR	82.4	11.6	0.7	0.0	0.0	0.1	1.4	0.9	2.9
Los Angeles, CA	73.3	11.0	5.6	0.3	0.2	0.8	2.6	1.3	4.8
Madison, WI	73.9	9.5	4.1	0.0	0.0	2.5	5.0	1.0	4.0
Manchester, NH	83.0	7.9	0.8	0.0	0.1	0.2	1.7	0.8	5.5
Miami, FL	78.3	10.0	3.1	0.2	0.2	0.5	1.8	1.4	4.4
Minneapolis, MN	78.0	8.6	4.6	0.1	0.1	0.8	2.3	0.8	4.6
Murfreesboro, TN	81.2	10.7	1.0	0.0	0.1	0.2	1.3	1.0	4.5
Naperville, IL	70.9	8.8	4.7	3.3	3.2	0.6	3.1	1.2	4.2
Nashville, TN	81.2	10.7	1.0	0.0	0.1	0.2	1.3	1.0	4.5
New Orleans, LA	78.3	11.5	2.5	0.0	0.0	0.7	2.5	1.8	2.7
New York, NY	50.3	7.0	8.4	18.1	3.7	0.5	6.2	2.0	3.8
Norman, OK	83.1	10.4	0.4	0.0	0.0	0.3	1.6	1.0	3.1
Olathe, KS	82.7	9.2	1.3	0.0	0.0	0.2	1.4	1.2	4.1
Omaha, NE	82.3	10.2	0.8	0.0	0.0	0.2	2.1	0.8	3.6
Orlando, FL	81.4	9.3	1.7	0.0	0.0	0.4	1.1	1.7	4.6
Overland Park, KS	82.7	9.2	1.3	0.0	0.0	0.2	1.4	1.2	4.1
Oyster Bay, NY	50.3	7.0	8.4	18.1	3.7	0.5	6.2	2.0	3.8
Pembroke Pines, FL	78.3	10.0	3.1	0.2	0.2	0.5	1.8	1.4	4.4
Philadelphia, PA	73.4	8.3	5.7	1.5	2.2	0.6	3.7	0.9	3.7
Phoenix, AZ	76.2	12.2	2.1	0.0	0.0	0.7	1.6	1.6	5.5
Pittsburgh, PA	76.7	9.4	5.4	0.2	0.2	0.2	3.7	1.1	3.3
Plano, TX	80.8	10.6	1.1	0.1	0.2	0.2	1.3	1.4	4.3
Portland, OR	71.3	9.7	5.0	0.4	0.2	2.2	3.4	1.6	6.2
Providence, RI	80.9	8.8	1.7	0.1	0.8	0.4	3.0	1.0	3.3
Provo, UT	73.4	11.8	2.1	0.0	0.0	1.0	4.9	0.9	5.8
Raleigh, NC	80.5	9.9	1.0	0.0	0.0	0.3	1.4	1.2	5.7
Richmond, VA	80.8	10.1	1.9	0.0	0.1	0.4	1.3	0.8	4.6
Roseville, CA	75.2	11.7	2.0	0.2	0.3	1.7	2.0	1.6	5.3
Round Rock, TX	74.9	11.4	2.6	0.0	0.0	0.7	1.8	2.2	6.5
San Antonio, TX	79.2	11.7	2.2	0.0	0.0	0.1	2.0	1.4	3.4
San Diego, CA	75.4	10.4	2.7	0.0	0.3	0.7	3.0	1.4	6.1
San Francisco, CA	61.7	10.5	7.7	5.2	1.0	1.6	4.3	2.2	5.8
San Jose, CA	76.5	10.3	2.1	0.1	0.8	1.6	2.1	1.7	4.7
Savannah, GA	80.8	10.4	1.9	0.0	0.0	0.4	1.7	1.2	3.8
Scottsdale, AZ	76.2	12.2	2.1	0.0	0.0	0.7	1.6	1.6	5.5
Seattle, WA	69.5	11.3	7.8	0.1	0.3	1.0	3.6	1.2	5.1
Sioux Falls, SD	83.4	8.6	0.4	0.0	0.0	0.3	2.3	1.0	4.0
Stamford, CT	73.2	8.1	2.9	0.3	5.9	0.2	3.2	0.9	5.2
Sterling Hgts, MI	84.3	8.6	1.6	0.0	0.0	0.2	1.4	0.8	3.0
Sunnyvale, CA	76.5	10.3	2.1	0.1	0.8	1.6	2.1	1.7	4.7
Tampa, FL	80.3	9.4	1.4	0.0	0.0	0.7	1.5	1.4	5.2
Temecula, CA	75.7	14.8	1.2	0.1	0.5	0.4	1.9	1.2	4.3
Thousand Oaks, CA	77.0	12.6	1.0	0.0	0.2	0.6	2.1	1.1	5.3
Virginia Beach, VA	80.7	9.4	1.8	0.0	0.0	0.4	3.0	1.0	3.6
Washington, DC	65.7	10.9	5.4	7.7	0.7	0.6	3.3	1.0	4.7
U.S.	76.0	10.2	2.7	1.7	0.5	0.5	2.8	1.3	4.2

Note: Figures are percentages and cover workers 16 years of age and older; (1) Figures cover the Metropolitan Statistical Area—see Appendix B for areas included
Source: U.S. Census Bureau, 2008-2010 American Community Survey 3-Year Estimates

Travel Time to Work: City

City	Less Than 10 Minutes	10 to 19 Minutes	20 to 29 Minutes	30 to 44 Minutes	45 to 59 Minutes	60 to 89 Minutes	90 Minutes or More
Albuquerque, NM	11.3	38.1	27.1	16.3	3.2	2.2	1.7
Alexandria, VA	6.4	20.4	22.4	27.8	14.8	6.9	1.3
Anchorage, AK	16.4	44.1	22.3	12.0	2.8	1.2	1.2
Ann Arbor, MI	19.8	42.9	16.9	12.1	3.9	3.5	0.8
Athens, GA	18.1	51.0	14.2	9.1	2.8	2.9	2.0
Atlanta, GA	9.4	31.8	24.9	20.7	5.6	4.4	3.2
Austin, TX	11.1	35.5	24.8	19.2	4.6	3.1	1.6
Baltimore, MD	7.3	25.8	22.8	23.8	7.5	8.3	4.5
Bellevue, WA	12.3	34.2	24.9	20.9	4.4	2.8	0.5
Billings, MT	20.3	50.3	19.7	5.6	1.5	1.1	1.6
Boise City, ID	16.8	47.3	22.2	10.0	1.7	1.2	0.9
Boston, MA	7.8	22.5	21.7	28.9	10.6	6.7	1.7
Boulder, CO	19.5	44.9	17.3	9.6	4.9	2.7	1.1
Broken Arrow, OK	11.1	36.7	30.8	17.4	1.9	1.1	0.9
Cambridge, MA	10.2	30.1	21.3	25.8	8.4	3.2	1.0
Cape Coral, FL	7.4	29.0	25.4	26.0	6.5	3.4	2.3
Carlsbad, CA	9.4	30.2	20.3	20.5	10.7	4.9	4.0
Cary, NC	10.6	34.1	31.6	18.0	2.9	1.5	1.3
Cedar Rapids, IA	19.6	48.5	17.7	9.8	2.7	0.8	0.9
Charleston, SC	13.4	36.1	29.0	14.8	3.6	1.8	1.3
Charlotte, NC	9.4	31.2	26.4	22.7	5.5	2.9	1.9
Chesapeake, VA	9.9	28.5	25.8	25.0	7.4	1.9	1.4
Chicago, IL	5.3	18.1	17.9	29.6	14.3	11.1	3.6
Clarksville, TN	10.8	39.0	24.4	14.2	5.1	4.9	1.7
Colorado Spgs., CO	13.9	38.4	26.7	13.7	3.2	2.6	1.6
Columbia, MD	8.9	27.6	18.8	20.2	10.6	9.9	4.1
Columbia, MO	22.1	53.9	11.3	7.8	2.8	1.1	1.0
Columbia, SC	19.9	45.7	19.7	9.4	2.5	1.4	1.5
Columbus, OH	11.1	36.5	30.1	16.8	2.7	1.8	1.1
Dallas, TX	9.3	30.4	23.6	23.9	6.8	4.3	1.6
Denver, CO	9.1	29.7	26.3	21.7	7.7	3.5	2.0
Durham, NC	13.9	40.5	23.5	14.5	3.3	2.5	1.8
Edison, NJ	6.7	25.5	15.1	20.7	9.6	13.5	9.0
El Paso, TX	10.4	31.0	30.3	21.3	4.0	2.0	1.1
Fargo, ND	23.7	55.2	14.7	3.2	1.3	1.0	1.0
Ft. Collins, CO	19.1	47.0	16.9	8.7	3.5	3.1	1.8
Ft. Worth, TX	9.4	29.4	23.5	22.6	8.0	5.4	1.8
Gilbert, AZ	10.6	23.7	25.0	24.6	9.3	5.7	1.1
Green Bay, WI	18.2	48.2	19.4	7.4	3.5	2.2	1.0
Henderson, NV	9.3	29.8	33.6	21.5	3.1	1.4	1.3
High Point, NC	12.8	40.5	25.2	16.4	1.9	1.3	2.0
Honolulu, HI	10.0	34.2	22.0	25.4	4.9	2.7	0.8
Houston, TX	8.6	28.0	24.6	24.8	7.2	4.9	1.9
Huntington, NY	12.6	25.0	16.6	20.1	8.4	9.0	8.3
Huntsville, AL	16.1	43.7	25.6	10.8	1.4	1.2	1.2
Indianapolis, IN	10.7	31.8	29.1	20.4	4.2	2.5	1.2
Irvine, CA	8.8	41.1	23.6	16.1	3.9	4.9	1.5
Jackson, MS	9.7	41.0	29.5	15.7	1.8	1.3	0.9
Jacksonville, FL	9.3	30.4	29.0	22.2	5.3	2.5	1.3
Jersey City, NJ	5.0	19.2	16.6	26.6	15.9	12.6	4.1
Kansas City, MO	11.4	35.7	27.1	19.7	3.6	1.6	1.0
Kenosha, WI	18.6	32.8	16.8	15.9	7.6	6.4	1.9
Las Vegas, NV	8.2	25.9	29.5	26.5	5.3	2.9	1.8
Lexington, KY	13.9	41.2	25.2	13.5	3.1	1.9	1.2
Lincoln, NE	18.3	45.5	23.7	7.5	2.1	2.0	0.8

Table continued on next page.

City	Less Than 10 Minutes	10 to 19 Minutes	20 to 29 Minutes	30 to 44 Minutes	45 to 59 Minutes	60 to 89 Minutes	90 Minutes or More
Little Rock, AR	15.9	45.8	23.5	10.4	2.1	1.4	0.8
Los Angeles, CA	7.7	24.9	20.1	27.3	9.2	7.9	2.9
Madison, WI	14.8	42.7	25.1	12.1	2.5	1.6	1.1
Manchester, NH	13.4	37.6	21.7	15.4	5.6	4.1	2.3
Miami, FL	5.7	24.9	29.0	25.6	7.8	5.4	1.6
Minneapolis, MN	8.7	34.8	30.2	18.6	3.9	2.7	1.0
Murfreesboro, TN	14.4	33.8	16.8	17.4	10.4	5.4	1.9
Naperville, IL	8.4	24.3	16.5	20.0	10.6	14.9	5.3
Nashville, TN	9.2	31.3	29.0	22.5	5.1	1.7	1.2
New Orleans, LA	10.8	35.9	24.4	18.6	4.8	3.6	1.9
New York, NY	4.8	14.4	14.2	26.5	15.2	18.3	6.5
Norman, OK	19.8	37.7	16.5	16.9	6.6	1.5	1.2
Olathe, KS	13.5	36.7	27.0	17.2	4.2	0.8	0.7
Omaha, NE	15.9	43.8	26.1	10.5	1.6	1.2	0.7
Orlando, FL	8.4	32.3	26.3	22.1	6.1	2.9	1.8
Overland Park, KS	14.9	40.4	25.3	14.4	2.9	1.1	1.1
Oyster Bay, NY	9.6	24.9	18.3	18.8	7.6	12.6	8.2
Pembroke Pines, FL	7.1	21.2	21.5	27.7	13.9	6.7	1.9
Philadelphia, PA	6.7	21.4	20.5	27.0	12.0	8.4	4.0
Phoenix, AZ	9.9	29.5	23.9	25.2	6.6	3.6	1.3
Pittsburgh, PA	11.9	33.5	25.5	18.2	6.0	3.2	1.8
Plano, TX	9.6	28.3	22.3	24.5	9.3	5.1	1.0
Portland, OR	9.2	31.3	27.4	21.7	5.3	3.5	1.7
Providence, RI	16.0	39.6	18.8	14.0	5.5	4.4	1.8
Provo, UT	27.0	46.2	14.0	7.1	2.8	1.9	1.0
Raleigh, NC	12.2	35.4	27.4	17.7	3.4	2.2	1.6
Richmond, VA	11.9	38.3	27.5	14.3	2.7	2.8	2.5
Roseville, CA	15.7	30.1	16.9	24.1	7.0	3.1	3.1
Round Rock, TX	11.5	36.0	22.5	18.0	7.8	3.0	1.1
San Antonio, TX	10.2	32.0	26.6	22.4	4.7	2.5	1.6
San Diego, CA	10.2	36.2	27.3	19.2	3.5	2.2	1.4
San Francisco, CA	5.2	23.7	21.7	28.5	11.2	7.6	2.0
San Jose, CA	7.5	29.2	26.6	24.3	6.3	4.7	1.4
Savannah, GA	10.1	45.2	27.9	12.1	2.1	2.0	0.5
Scottsdale, AZ	14.4	31.1	23.7	23.1	4.6	1.8	1.2
Seattle, WA	8.9	29.4	25.4	24.5	6.5	4.1	1.3
Sioux Falls, SD	19.2	53.6	20.0	4.0	1.0	1.0	1.0
Stamford, CT	14.0	36.0	23.3	13.8	2.8	6.1	4.1
Sterling Hgts, MI	8.5	28.4	23.5	26.5	7.9	3.7	1.4
Sunnyvale, CA	9.4	40.0	25.4	15.2	4.8	3.2	2.1
Tampa, FL	13.6	34.8	22.7	19.9	4.6	2.9	1.5
Temecula, CA	14.3	30.3	8.3	12.0	12.7	16.8	5.6
Thousand Oaks, CA	16.1	37.0	16.6	14.2	5.5	7.4	3.3
Virginia Beach, VA	9.8	31.5	27.3	23.6	4.7	2.0	1.1
Washington, DC	5.7	21.6	23.8	29.5	10.1	7.2	2.0
U.S.	13.9	30.1	20.8	19.8	7.5	5.5	2.5

Note: Figures are percentages and include workers 16 years old and over
Source: U.S. Census Bureau, 2008-2010 American Community Survey 3-Year Estimates

Travel Time to Work: Metro Area

Metro Area	Less Than 10 Minutes	10 to 19 Minutes	20 to 29 Minutes	30 to 44 Minutes	45 to 59 Minutes	60 to 89 Minutes	90 Minutes or More
Albuquerque, NM	11.2	33.1	24.4	20.3	6.0	3.2	1.8
Alexandria, VA	6.8	19.6	18.5	25.6	13.3	12.3	3.9
Anchorage, AK	16.3	40.7	20.4	11.9	4.8	4.0	1.8
Ann Arbor, MI	13.5	34.2	22.4	17.6	6.9	4.2	1.2
Athens, GA	14.9	44.5	18.6	12.8	3.9	3.3	2.0
Atlanta, GA	8.2	23.5	20.3	24.6	11.6	8.7	3.1
Austin, TX	10.9	30.1	22.9	22.0	7.9	4.4	1.7
Baltimore, MD	8.4	24.4	21.6	23.9	10.1	8.0	3.5
Bellevue, WA	9.8	26.1	22.4	24.2	9.0	6.3	2.2
Billings, MT	20.2	43.6	22.3	8.6	2.2	1.4	1.8
Boise City, ID	14.8	35.6	23.5	17.6	4.8	2.6	1.1
Boston, MA	10.9	24.2	19.5	24.0	10.7	8.4	2.4
Boulder, CO	16.8	35.2	21.1	15.6	6.3	3.7	1.3
Broken Arrow, OK	15.1	35.0	25.6	16.5	4.2	2.2	1.3
Cambridge, MA	10.9	24.2	19.5	24.0	10.7	8.4	2.4
Cape Coral, FL	9.8	29.5	23.0	24.9	7.3	3.3	2.3
Carlsbad, CA	10.8	31.9	25.2	20.9	5.8	3.5	1.9
Cary, NC	10.3	29.0	26.1	22.7	6.8	3.4	1.6
Cedar Rapids, IA	19.0	39.4	21.2	13.4	4.2	1.6	1.3
Charleston, SC	11.2	29.1	24.9	22.1	7.4	3.7	1.6
Charlotte, NC	10.4	29.0	24.4	23.4	7.6	3.5	1.8
Chesapeake, VA	11.1	33.2	23.8	20.8	6.4	3.3	1.5
Chicago, IL	9.2	22.7	18.0	24.7	11.9	10.1	3.4
Clarksville, TN	13.2	36.3	21.8	16.2	6.1	4.4	1.9
Colorado Spgs., CO	15.0	33.3	25.8	16.6	4.5	3.0	1.8
Columbia, MD	8.4	24.4	21.6	23.9	10.1	8.0	3.5
Columbia, MO	18.3	45.7	18.2	12.2	3.1	1.5	1.0
Columbia, SC	11.9	32.2	24.3	20.9	6.2	2.8	1.6
Columbus, OH	12.2	31.4	27.3	20.1	5.4	2.4	1.3
Dallas, TX	10.2	27.1	21.4	24.5	9.5	5.6	1.7
Denver, CO	9.3	25.6	24.5	24.9	9.5	4.3	1.9
Durham, NC	12.4	35.2	24.1	18.3	5.5	3.1	1.5
Edison, NJ	8.1	20.5	16.5	23.2	11.8	13.9	5.9
El Paso, TX	10.2	29.8	29.2	22.8	4.8	2.3	1.0
Fargo, ND	22.1	49.3	17.2	7.0	2.1	1.0	1.4
Ft. Collins, CO	16.9	38.4	20.2	13.4	5.1	4.2	1.9
Ft. Worth, TX	10.2	27.1	21.4	24.5	9.5	5.6	1.7
Gilbert, AZ	10.6	27.5	21.9	24.9	8.7	4.9	1.5
Green Bay, WI	19.4	39.1	21.7	11.9	4.5	2.2	1.3
Henderson, NV	8.8	28.7	29.6	23.9	4.8	2.6	1.6
High Point, NC	12.3	37.0	24.9	17.3	4.8	2.1	1.7
Honolulu, HI	9.8	25.0	20.0	27.6	9.3	6.6	1.7
Houston, TX	8.9	25.5	20.9	25.2	10.2	7.1	2.2
Huntington, NY	8.1	20.5	16.5	23.2	11.8	13.9	5.9
Huntsville, AL	12.2	34.1	27.7	18.4	4.8	1.6	1.1
Indianapolis, IN	11.8	28.2	25.2	23.3	7.0	3.1	1.4
Irvine, CA	8.8	26.8	20.5	24.6	8.9	7.7	2.8
Jackson, MS	10.7	32.3	27.0	20.8	4.8	3.0	1.4
Jacksonville, FL	10.4	27.5	25.2	23.4	8.3	3.6	1.5
Jersey City, NJ	8.1	20.5	16.5	23.2	11.8	13.9	5.9
Kansas City, MO	13.5	31.3	25.1	20.7	5.9	2.3	1.2
Kenosha, WI	9.2	22.7	18.0	24.7	11.9	10.1	3.4
Las Vegas, NV	8.8	28.7	29.6	23.9	4.8	2.6	1.6
Lexington, KY	15.3	36.7	24.0	16.7	4.0	2.1	1.2
Lincoln, NE	18.1	42.5	24.5	9.6	2.4	1.9	1.0

Table continued on next page.

Metro Area	Less Than 10 Minutes	10 to 19 Minutes	20 to 29 Minutes	30 to 44 Minutes	45 to 59 Minutes	60 to 89 Minutes	90 Minutes or More
Little Rock, AR	14.6	33.4	22.8	19.4	6.0	2.7	1.1
Los Angeles, CA	8.8	26.8	20.5	24.6	8.9	7.7	2.8
Madison, WI	15.6	34.6	25.2	16.7	4.3	2.1	1.5
Manchester, NH	12.2	30.3	19.9	20.3	8.0	6.8	2.6
Miami, FL	8.1	25.6	22.9	26.9	8.8	5.9	1.9
Minneapolis, MN	11.6	28.8	24.9	22.2	7.5	3.7	1.3
Murfreesboro, TN	10.3	27.7	23.2	23.4	9.5	4.3	1.6
Naperville, IL	9.2	22.7	18.0	24.7	11.9	10.1	3.4
Nashville, TN	10.3	27.7	23.2	23.4	9.5	4.3	1.6
New Orleans, LA	11.0	32.2	21.2	20.6	7.5	5.2	2.4
New York, NY	8.1	20.5	16.5	23.2	11.8	13.9	5.9
Norman, OK	14.9	34.5	24.5	18.0	4.7	2.0	1.5
Olathe, KS	13.5	31.3	25.1	20.7	5.9	2.3	1.2
Omaha, NE	15.6	37.6	26.5	14.7	3.1	1.6	1.0
Orlando, FL	8.5	26.9	23.4	26.0	9.1	4.3	1.8
Overland Park, KS	13.5	31.3	25.1	20.7	5.9	2.3	1.2
Oyster Bay, NY	8.1	20.5	16.5	23.2	11.8	13.9	5.9
Pembroke Pines, FL	8.1	25.6	22.9	26.9	8.8	5.9	1.9
Philadelphia, PA	10.5	26.2	20.3	22.9	10.1	7.1	2.8
Phoenix, AZ	10.6	27.5	21.9	24.9	8.7	4.9	1.5
Pittsburgh, PA	13.6	28.0	21.2	21.2	8.8	5.3	1.9
Plano, TX	10.2	27.1	21.4	24.5	9.5	5.6	1.7
Portland, OR	11.7	29.1	23.8	21.9	7.2	4.4	1.8
Providence, RI	14.5	32.9	20.9	17.6	6.8	5.1	2.3
Provo, UT	20.5	35.8	18.5	14.8	5.5	3.2	1.6
Raleigh, NC	10.3	29.0	26.1	22.7	6.8	3.4	1.6
Richmond, VA	10.0	30.4	26.4	21.9	5.9	3.0	2.3
Roseville, CA	12.2	30.0	22.0	21.5	6.9	4.4	2.9
Round Rock, TX	10.9	30.1	22.9	22.0	7.9	4.4	1.7
San Antonio, TX	10.7	29.4	24.0	23.1	7.3	3.8	1.8
San Diego, CA	10.8	31.9	25.2	20.9	5.8	3.5	1.9
San Francisco, CA	8.4	26.5	19.6	23.9	10.6	8.5	2.3
San Jose, CA	9.0	32.1	25.4	21.5	6.1	4.4	1.5
Savannah, GA	9.5	34.6	27.4	19.9	5.4	2.2	1.0
Scottsdale, AZ	10.6	27.5	21.9	24.9	8.7	4.9	1.5
Seattle, WA	9.8	26.1	22.4	24.2	9.0	6.3	2.2
Sioux Falls, SD	18.9	44.6	23.4	8.8	1.9	1.3	1.1
Stamford, CT	12.3	31.9	19.3	16.4	7.2	7.8	5.2
Sterling Hgts, MI	10.5	27.0	23.3	23.9	8.9	4.8	1.7
Sunnyvale, CA	9.0	32.1	25.4	21.5	6.1	4.4	1.5
Tampa, FL	11.0	29.7	22.4	22.1	8.2	4.8	1.9
Temecula, CA	12.0	27.8	17.9	18.4	8.5	9.8	5.7
Thousand Oaks, CA	14.1	33.0	19.3	18.3	6.8	5.6	2.9
Virginia Beach, VA	11.1	33.2	23.8	20.8	6.4	3.3	1.5
Washington, DC	6.8	19.6	18.5	25.6	13.3	12.3	3.9
U.S.	13.9	30.1	20.8	19.8	7.5	5.5	2.5

Note: Figures are percentages and include workers 16 years old and over; Figures cover the Metropolitan Statistical Area—see Appendix B for areas included
Source: U.S. Census Bureau, 2008-2010 American Community Survey 3-Year Estimates

2008 Presidential Election Results

City	Area Covered	Obama	McCain	Nader	Other
Albuquerque, NM	Bernalillo County	60.0	38.7	0.6	0.7
Alexandria, VA	Alexandria Independent City	71.7	27.3	0.3	0.7
Anchorage, AK	Districts 18 – 32	43.0	55.9	1.0	0.0
Ann Arbor, MI	Washtenaw County	69.6	28.8	0.5	1.1
Athens, GA	Clarke County	64.8	33.6	0.1	1.5
Atlanta, GA	Fulton County	67.1	32.1	0.0	0.8
Austin, TX	Travis County	63.5	34.3	0.2	2.0
Baltimore, MD	Baltimore Independent City	87.2	11.7	0.4	0.8
Bellevue, WA	King County	70.0	28.0	0.8	1.2
Billings, MT	Yellowstone County	45.3	51.6	0.7	2.3
Boise City, ID	Ada County	45.5	51.6	1.1	1.8
Boston, MA	Suffolk County	77.5	21.1	0.7	0.7
Boulder, CO	Boulder County	72.3	26.1	0.5	1.1
Broken Arrow, OK	Tulsa County	37.8	62.2	0.0	0.0
Cambridge, MA	Middlesex County	64.0	34.3	0.8	0.9
Cape Coral, FL	Lee County	44.3	54.7	0.4	0.6
Carlsbad, CA	San Diego County	54.1	43.9	0.7	1.2
Cary, NC	Wake County	56.7	42.3	0.0	0.9
Cedar Rapids, IA	Linn County	60.0	38.5	0.4	1.1
Charleston, SC	Charleston County	53.5	45.2	0.3	1.0
Charlotte, NC	Mecklenburg County	61.8	37.4	0.0	0.7
Chesapeake, VA	Chesapeake Independent City	50.2	48.9	0.2	0.7
Chicago, IL	Cook County	76.2	22.8	0.4	0.6
Clarksville, TN	Montgomery County	45.5	53.4	0.4	0.7
Colorado Spgs., CO	El Paso County	39.9	58.7	0.4	1.0
Columbia, MD	Howard County	60.0	38.1	0.6	1.3
Columbia, MO	Boone County	55.2	43.2	0.6	1.0
Columbia, SC	Richland County	64.0	35.1	0.2	0.7
Columbus, OH	Franklin County	59.6	38.9	0.5	1.0
Dallas, TX	Dallas County	57.2	41.9	0.1	0.9
Denver, CO	Denver County	75.5	23.0	0.6	0.9
Durham, NC	Durham County	75.6	23.6	0.1	0.7
Edison, NJ	Middlesex County	60.2	38.4	0.6	0.7
El Paso, TX	El Paso County	65.7	33.3	0.1	0.9
Fargo, ND	Cass County	52.4	45.3	1.1	1.2
Ft. Collins, CO	Larimer County	54.0	44.3	0.5	1.2
Ft. Worth, TX	Tarrant County	43.7	55.4	0.1	0.8
Gilbert, AZ	Maricopa County	43.9	54.4	0.4	1.2
Green Bay, WI	Brown County	53.9	44.8	0.5	0.8
Henderson, NV	Clark County	58.5	39.5	0.6	1.4
High Point, NC	Guilford County	58.8	40.4	0.0	0.8
Honolulu, HI	Honolulu County	69.8	28.7	0.8	0.6
Houston, TX	Harris County	50.4	48.8	0.1	0.7
Huntington, NY	Suffolk County	52.5	46.5	0.5	0.5
Huntsville, AL	Madison County	41.9	56.9	0.3	0.9
Indianapolis, IN	Marion County	63.7	35.3	0.0	1.0
Irvine, CA	Orange County	47.6	50.2	0.7	1.5
Jackson, MS	Hinds County	69.2	30.3	0.1	0.4
Jacksonville, FL	Duval County	48.6	50.5	0.2	0.6
Jersey City, NJ	Hudson County	72.8	26.2	0.4	0.6
Kansas City, MO	Jackson County	62.1	36.8	0.5	0.6
Kenosha, WI	Kenosha County	58.2	40.1	0.6	1.1
Las Vegas, NV	Clark County	58.5	39.5	0.6	1.4
Lexington, KY	Fayette County	51.7	46.9	0.6	0.7
Lincoln, NE	Lancaster County	51.6	46.6	0.7	1.2
Little Rock, AR	Pulaski County	55.1	43.5	0.6	0.8

Table continued on next page.

City	Area Covered	Obama	McCain	Nader	Other
Los Angeles, CA	Los Angeles County	69.2	28.8	0.8	1.2
Madison, WI	Dane County	72.8	25.8	0.5	0.8
Manchester, NH	Hillsborough County	51.2	47.5	0.5	0.9
Miami, FL	Miami-Dade County	57.8	41.7	0.2	0.3
Minneapolis, MN	Hennepin County	63.4	34.8	0.8	1.0
Murfreesboro, TN	Rutherford County	39.8	58.9	0.5	0.9
Naperville, IL	Du Page County	54.7	43.9	0.5	0.8
Nashville, TN	Davidson County	59.9	38.9	0.4	0.8
New Orleans, LA	Orleans Parish	79.4	19.1	0.3	1.2
New York, NY	Bronx County	88.7	10.9	0.1	0.2
New York, NY	Kings County	79.4	20.0	0.2	0.4
New York, NY	New York County	85.7	13.5	0.3	0.5
New York, NY	Queens County	74.9	24.4	0.3	0.4
New York, NY	Richmond County	47.6	51.7	0.4	0.4
Norman, OK	Cleveland County	38.0	62.0	0.0	0.0
Olathe, KS	Johnson County	44.7	53.7	0.5	1.1
Omaha, NE	Douglas County	51.5	46.9	0.6	1.0
Orlando, FL	Orange County	59.0	40.4	0.2	0.4
Overland Park, KS	Johnson County	44.7	53.7	0.5	1.1
Oyster Bay, NY	Nassau County	53.8	45.4	0.4	0.4
Pembroke Pines, FL	Broward County	67.0	32.3	0.2	0.4
Philadelphia, PA	Philadelphia County	83.0	16.3	0.4	0.2
Phoenix, AZ	Maricopa County	43.9	54.4	0.4	1.2
Pittsburgh, PA	Allegheny County	57.1	41.6	0.6	0.7
Plano, TX	Collin County	36.7	62.2	0.1	1.1
Portland, OR	Multnomah County	76.7	20.6	1.1	1.6
Providence, RI	Providence County	66.3	32.1	1.0	0.6
Provo, UT	Utah County	18.8	77.7	0.7	2.8
Raleigh, NC	Wake County	56.7	42.3	0.0	0.9
Richmond, VA	Richmond Independent City	79.1	20.0	0.2	0.6
Roseville, CA	Placer County	43.2	54.5	0.7	1.6
Round Rock, TX	Williamson County	42.5	55.5	0.1	1.9
San Antonio, TX	Bexar County	52.2	46.7	0.0	1.0
San Diego, CA	San Diego County	54.1	43.9	0.7	1.2
San Francisco, CA	San Francisco County	84.2	13.7	1.0	1.2
San Jose, CA	Santa Clara County	69.4	28.6	0.7	1.3
Savannah, GA	Chatham County	56.8	42.4	0.0	0.7
Scottsdale, AZ	Maricopa County	43.9	54.4	0.4	1.2
Seattle, WA	King County	70.0	28.0	0.8	1.2
Sioux Falls, SD	Minnehaha County	49.5	48.7	0.9	0.9
Stamford, CT	Fairfield County	58.7	40.5	0.7	0.0
Sterling Hgts, MI	Macomb County	53.4	44.8	0.8	1.0
Sunnyvale, CA	Santa Clara County	69.4	28.6	0.7	1.3
Tampa, FL	Hillsborough County	53.1	45.9	0.4	0.7
Temecula, CA	Riverside County	50.2	47.9	0.7	1.1
Thousand Oaks, CA	Ventura County	55.0	42.8	0.7	1.6
Virginia Beach, VA	Virginia Beach Independent City	49.1	49.8	0.3	0.7
Washington, DC	District of Columbia	92.5	6.5	0.4	0.6
U.S.	U.S.	52.9	45.6	0.6	0.9

Note: Results are percentages and may not add to 100% due to rounding
Source: Dave Leip's Atlas of U.S. Presidential Elections, www.uselectionatlas.org

House Price Index (HPI)

Metro Area[1]	National Ranking[3]	Quarterly Change (%)	One-Year Change (%)	Five-Year Change (%)
Albuquerque, NM	201	-0.02	-3.93	-11.37
Alexandria, VA[2]	27	0.62	0.14	-21.41
Anchorage, AK	22	0.30	0.31	1.75
Ann Arbor, MI	80	0.04	-1.22	-20.92
Athens, GA	291	-3.15	-8.38	-13.77
Atlanta, GA	274	-0.43	-7.04	-19.74
Austin, TX	18	0.87	0.60	9.27
Baltimore, MD	170	0.41	-3.11	-18.40
Bellevue, WA[2]	227	-0.28	-4.64	-19.92
Billings, MT	115	-0.16	-1.90	5.84
Boise City, ID	289	2.70	-8.36	-35.65
Boston, MA[2]	89	-0.22	-1.34	-12.94
Boulder, CO	57	0.63	-0.75	1.56
Broken Arrow, OK	125	1.25	-2.04	5.19
Cambridge, MA[2]	51	0.25	-0.58	-8.62
Cape Coral, FL	187	4.51	-3.44	-51.23
Carlsbad, CA	215	-0.39	-4.25	-31.71
Cary, NC	142	-1.10	-2.57	-0.71
Cedar Rapids, IA	47	-0.35	-0.49	1.72
Charleston, SC	182	1.68	-3.29	-15.04
Charlotte, NC	180	0.57	-3.23	-5.87
Chesapeake, VA	230	0.61	-4.79	-14.57
Chicago, IL[2]	250	-0.13	-5.50	-22.86
Clarksville, TN	n/a	n/a	n/a	n/a
Colorado Spgs., CO	154	0.91	-2.72	-8.78
Columbia, MD	170	0.41	-3.11	-18.40
Columbia, MO	30	0.83	0.00	-0.17
Columbia, SC	192	-0.60	-3.60	-3.40
Columbus, OH	121	0.32	-1.98	-6.22
Dallas, TX[2]	91	-0.11	-1.44	1.58
Denver, CO	123	0.36	-1.99	-5.56
Durham, NC	79	-0.18	-1.22	-0.37
Edison, NJ[2]	210	-0.23	-4.16	-18.18
El Paso, TX	118	0.64	-1.94	-0.07
Fargo, ND	32	-0.65	-0.08	5.27
Ft. Collins, CO	6	1.10	1.49	-1.82
Ft. Worth, TX[2]	70	0.23	-1.02	0.65
Gilbert, AZ	275	2.67	-7.12	-47.78
Green Bay, WI	124	0.10	-2.01	-7.61
Henderson, NV	306	-0.37	-12.60	-59.81
High Point, NC	165	0.49	-2.96	-3.89
Honolulu, HI	24	-0.02	0.25	-5.00
Houston, TX	53	0.67	-0.67	7.03
Huntington, NY[2]	179	1.04	-3.23	-17.13
Huntsville, AL	94	0.62	-1.49	4.97
Indianapolis, IN	52	0.56	-0.65	-2.40
Irvine, CA[2]	199	-0.44	-3.89	-30.93
Jackson, MS	15	0.71	0.73	-0.07
Jacksonville, FL	276	-1.29	-7.13	-33.76
Jersey City, NJ[2]	145	-0.02	-2.62	-14.98
Kansas City, MO	157	0.46	-2.76	-8.21
Kenosha, WI[2]	253	-0.32	-5.61	-21.94
Las Vegas, NV	306	-0.37	-12.60	-59.81
Lexington, KY	90	0.26	-1.37	0.28
Lincoln, NE	21	0.20	0.47	-0.36

Table continued on next page.

Metro Area[1]	National Ranking[3]	Quarterly Change (%)	One-Year Change (%)	Five-Year Change (%)
Little Rock, AR	25	0.04	0.22	2.17
Los Angeles, CA[2]	200	-0.46	-3.92	-32.83
Madison, WI	78	0.12	-1.20	-4.18
Manchester, NH	158	0.04	-2.76	-17.37
Miami, FL[2]	251	0.74	-5.54	-43.62
Minneapolis, MN	234	0.59	-4.93	-22.61
Murfreesboro, TN	122	0.01	-1.98	-2.79
Naperville, IL[2]	250	-0.13	-5.50	-22.86
Nashville, TN	122	0.01	-1.98	-2.79
New Orleans, LA	41	0.89	-0.36	-7.18
New York, NY[2]	145	-0.02	-2.62	-14.98
Norman, OK	42	1.90	-0.37	4.51
Olathe, KS	157	0.46	-2.76	-8.21
Omaha, NE	34	0.47	-0.12	-1.56
Orlando, FL	281	0.93	-7.54	-45.20
Overland Park, KS	157	0.46	-2.76	-8.21
Oyster Bay, NY[2]	179	1.04	-3.23	-17.13
Pembroke Pines, FL[2]	203	0.71	-3.99	-44.84
Philadelphia, PA[2]	139	0.23	-2.45	-8.01
Phoenix, AZ	275	2.67	-7.12	-47.78
Pittsburgh, PA	13	0.26	0.78	6.68
Plano, TX[2]	91	-0.11	-1.44	1.58
Portland, OR	220	0.77	-4.43	-19.54
Providence, RI	198	0.39	-3.81	-21.36
Provo, UT	221	0.30	-4.46	-16.82
Raleigh, NC	142	-1.10	-2.57	-0.71
Richmond, VA	235	0.86	-4.93	-14.08
Roseville, CA	277	0.14	-7.16	-43.52
Round Rock, TX	18	0.87	0.60	9.27
San Antonio, TX	77	-0.11	-1.20	4.49
San Diego, CA	215	-0.39	-4.25	-31.71
San Francisco, CA[2]	172	-0.34	-3.14	-20.83
San Jose, CA	112	-0.44	-1.84	-23.53
Savannah, GA	205	1.61	-4.00	-15.99
Scottsdale, AZ	275	2.67	-7.12	-47.78
Seattle, WA[2]	227	-0.28	-4.64	-19.92
Sioux Falls, SD	49	0.07	-0.57	4.47
Stamford, CT	162	0.28	-2.87	-16.79
Sterling Hgts, MI[2]	46	1.07	-0.47	-30.70
Sunnyvale, CA	112	-0.44	-1.84	-23.53
Tampa, FL	236	-0.17	-4.97	-40.26
Temecula, CA	237	0.24	-4.99	-48.04
Thousand Oaks, CA	255	-0.06	-5.65	-34.87
Virginia Beach, VA	230	0.61	-4.79	-14.57
Washington, DC[2]	27	0.62	0.14	-21.41
U.S.[4]	-	-0.10	-2.43	-19.16

Note: The HPI is a weighted repeat sales index. It measures average price changes in repeat sales or refinancings on the same properties. This information is obtained by reviewing repeat mortgage transactions on single-family properties whose mortgages have been purchased or securitized by Fannie Mae or Freddie Mac in January 1975; (1) figures cover the Metropolitan Statistical Area (MSA) unless noted otherwise—see Appendix B for areas included; (2) Metropolitan Division—see Appendix B for areas included;
(3) Rankings are based on annual percentage change, for all MSAs containing at least 15,000 transactions over the last 10 years and ranges from 1 to 309; (4) figures based on a weighted division average; all figures are for the period ended December 31, 2011; n/a not available; n/r not ranked
Source: Federal Housing Finance Agency, House Price Index, February 23, 2012

Year Housing Structure Built: City

City	2005 or Later	2000 -2004	1990 -1999	1980 -1989	1970 -1979	1960 -1969	1950 -1959	Before 1950	Median Year
Albuquerque, NM	5.6	11.7	15.1	14.6	20.4	10.5	13.9	8.2	1979
Alexandria, VA	3.4	6.9	11.5	9.4	19.4	16.9	13.0	19.4	1970
Anchorage, AK	4.8	7.9	10.9	27.2	28.8	11.2	7.3	1.8	1980
Ann Arbor, MI	2.3	3.2	10.6	10.1	19.8	20.4	13.5	20.2	1968
Athens, GA	5.2	13.3	19.9	16.7	18.0	12.4	6.4	8.1	1983
Atlanta, GA	8.8	13.2	9.4	8.0	11.5	15.2	13.4	20.6	1971
Austin, TX	8.6	11.4	16.2	21.6	20.6	8.9	6.3	6.5	1984
Baltimore, MD	1.6	1.9	3.3	4.3	6.3	8.9	17.1	56.6	1946
Bellevue, WA	3.4	8.0	15.1	18.5	21.6	19.2	12.2	2.1	1978
Billings, MT	5.2	6.1	11.1	14.2	20.4	9.8	16.8	16.3	1973
Boise City, ID	3.8	9.5	21.3	15.0	22.2	7.8	8.5	11.9	1980
Boston, MA	2.6	3.4	4.0	5.0	7.1	7.8	7.0	63.0	<1940
Boulder, CO	2.7	4.9	11.3	15.7	24.1	20.0	10.4	11.0	1974
Broken Arrow, OK	8.2	14.1	18.9	21.9	25.6	5.6	3.3	2.4	1986
Cambridge, MA	3.4	4.2	4.8	7.0	8.7	6.6	4.5	60.8	<1940
Cape Coral, FL	12.6	28.3	17.1	23.1	12.4	5.3	0.6	0.6	1995
Carlsbad, CA	7.0	13.8	19.2	25.1	25.6	5.4	2.9	1.0	1986
Cary, NC	17.0	12.3	32.7	20.6	11.6	3.4	1.5	0.9	1994
Cedar Rapids, IA	4.5	8.1	13.3	6.7	14.9	16.1	13.5	22.9	1968
Charleston, SC	9.3	15.3	13.6	13.2	11.8	9.5	7.9	19.4	1981
Charlotte, NC	8.3	15.7	20.8	16.3	13.8	10.8	7.7	6.5	1987
Chesapeake, VA	5.0	8.2	22.9	22.7	16.2	11.0	8.6	5.5	1984
Chicago, IL	3.1	4.4	4.0	3.8	6.7	9.7	12.7	55.5	1945
Clarksville, TN	13.3	14.1	22.2	13.5	14.9	9.7	6.7	5.6	1990
Colorado Spgs., CO	5.4	12.0	15.5	18.5	20.6	11.4	8.3	8.3	1981
Columbia, MD	2.4	6.1	20.3	27.1	31.7	9.4	1.8	1.2	1982
Columbia, MO	10.8	13.6	19.7	14.3	12.6	11.9	7.8	9.3	1986
Columbia, SC	5.9	8.7	10.2	11.4	11.6	14.2	17.1	21.0	1968
Columbus, OH	3.4	8.6	15.4	12.7	13.9	12.3	14.1	19.7	1973
Dallas, TX	4.4	7.3	9.5	17.7	18.6	15.4	15.2	12.0	1974
Denver, CO	4.7	7.8	6.7	8.0	15.9	12.0	15.7	29.2	1964
Durham, NC	8.2	14.6	20.0	17.1	12.4	9.9	6.6	11.1	1986
Edison, NJ	2.1	3.9	7.9	26.0	14.1	15.2	20.7	9.9	1973
El Paso, TX	6.3	9.0	13.5	15.1	19.9	13.1	12.5	10.6	1977
Fargo, ND	5.8	9.5	21.6	14.6	17.1	7.3	9.6	14.4	1981
Ft. Collins, CO	5.9	13.7	20.7	17.5	22.7	7.8	4.2	7.5	1984
Ft. Worth, TX	12.6	15.0	11.0	14.1	10.9	9.3	12.1	15.0	1982
Gilbert, AZ	15.1	25.1	41.4	13.0	3.4	1.3	0.6	0.2	1998
Green Bay, WI	1.1	4.9	10.2	10.5	16.0	12.3	16.1	28.9	1964
Henderson, NV	12.1	25.3	38.5	16.5	4.4	1.1	1.4	0.7	1997
High Point, NC	7.9	12.6	18.0	12.3	16.2	10.9	10.6	11.5	1981
Honolulu, HI	3.2	2.4	8.2	9.4	27.6	23.1	13.6	12.5	1970
Houston, TX	5.5	8.0	9.0	14.3	26.7	15.4	11.6	9.4	1975
Huntington, NY	1.8	3.9	4.5	6.1	11.2	24.6	28.2	19.9	1961
Huntsville, AL	7.5	6.1	11.2	16.2	17.5	23.8	10.4	7.4	1975
Indianapolis, IN	3.0	6.8	11.7	11.6	14.1	14.9	13.9	24.0	1968
Irvine, CA	10.7	20.9	16.5	20.1	26.0	4.5	0.7	0.6	1989
Jackson, MS	2.4	2.7	6.9	13.4	24.7	22.3	17.5	10.1	1970
Jacksonville, FL	8.2	12.1	15.9	17.5	12.6	11.0	11.7	11.1	1982
Jersey City, NJ	5.3	6.9	7.2	6.1	6.0	7.3	10.2	51.0	1949
Kansas City, MO	4.3	5.6	8.9	9.6	11.9	13.3	14.6	31.8	1963
Kenosha, WI	4.5	7.2	13.5	6.1	12.7	9.4	14.2	32.3	1964
Las Vegas, NV	7.2	15.6	33.6	18.4	11.3	8.0	4.4	1.5	1992
Lexington, KY	5.8	9.7	17.1	16.7	15.8	13.6	9.9	11.6	1979
Lincoln, NE	5.1	10.3	15.5	11.0	16.4	11.4	11.8	18.4	1975

Table continued on next page.

City	2005 or Later	2000 -2004	1990 -1999	1980 -1989	1970 -1979	1960 -1969	1950 -1959	Before 1950	Median Year
Little Rock, AR	4.8	6.0	10.0	17.2	21.6	15.1	11.8	13.4	1974
Los Angeles, CA	2.2	3.0	5.5	10.2	14.1	14.7	18.4	31.9	1960
Madison, WI	5.6	10.8	12.0	9.8	16.5	13.4	11.1	20.7	1973
Manchester, NH	2.4	4.4	6.0	13.2	11.6	8.1	11.1	43.3	1956
Miami, FL	6.6	10.1	6.0	7.2	14.0	11.2	15.6	29.2	1965
Minneapolis, MN	3.4	4.0	2.8	6.5	9.6	8.0	10.0	55.9	1942
Murfreesboro, TN	13.2	19.8	24.9	13.8	11.4	8.0	4.4	4.5	1993
Naperville, IL	3.3	10.8	28.4	28.4	16.9	5.9	3.0	3.3	1987
Nashville, TN	5.9	7.6	12.2	16.6	18.9	14.7	11.7	12.5	1976
New Orleans, LA	3.3	3.2	3.8	7.5	13.7	12.7	11.6	44.2	1955
New York, NY	2.1	3.0	3.5	4.5	7.0	12.3	14.5	53.1	1947
Norman, OK	6.7	10.5	14.7	18.2	20.9	13.5	7.2	8.3	1980
Olathe, KS	8.3	17.4	25.3	19.5	16.7	5.5	3.7	3.6	1990
Omaha, NE	1.9	3.4	9.0	9.8	18.6	16.7	13.2	27.5	1966
Orlando, FL	7.7	15.0	15.8	19.8	13.8	8.9	10.9	8.1	1984
Overland Park, KS	4.0	11.3	22.7	20.9	13.9	14.0	8.9	4.3	1984
Oyster Bay, NY	1.0	2.9	3.0	5.2	6.3	14.6	49.9	17.1	1957
Pembroke Pines, FL	1.6	11.9	41.1	22.0	15.7	5.5	1.9	0.3	1991
Philadelphia, PA	1.5	1.5	2.4	3.6	6.6	10.2	17.3	56.9	1946
Phoenix, AZ	7.3	10.2	16.2	18.7	21.1	10.8	10.9	4.9	1981
Pittsburgh, PA	1.3	2.0	2.6	4.6	6.7	7.9	13.4	61.4	<1940
Plano, TX	5.1	10.7	35.9	28.0	15.7	3.3	0.8	0.6	1990
Portland, OR	4.2	6.7	8.7	5.6	11.5	10.0	13.2	40.1	1957
Providence, RI	2.0	1.9	3.3	5.4	7.2	4.6	8.1	67.4	<1940
Provo, UT	4.9	9.9	18.5	10.3	21.3	12.2	8.1	14.8	1977
Raleigh, NC	11.2	16.6	19.8	19.7	12.4	8.5	5.9	5.8	1989
Richmond, VA	3.4	3.5	3.2	6.9	12.4	11.4	15.7	43.7	1954
Roseville, CA	9.2	22.9	28.5	18.6	8.2	4.4	3.6	4.7	1994
Round Rock, TX	14.7	23.8	28.1	19.9	10.3	1.3	1.3	0.4	1996
San Antonio, TX	6.8	10.7	13.3	17.3	18.4	10.9	11.1	11.5	1979
San Diego, CA	3.1	7.1	10.4	17.7	23.3	13.2	13.2	12.0	1975
San Francisco, CA	2.0	3.5	4.4	5.3	7.3	7.9	9.3	60.3	1940
San Jose, CA	3.6	6.7	10.4	13.9	24.3	19.6	12.0	9.5	1974
Savannah, GA	6.1	4.9	7.5	10.8	16.3	15.0	15.2	24.2	1967
Scottsdale, AZ	4.0	11.0	29.1	22.6	16.4	9.9	6.2	0.8	1987
Seattle, WA	5.0	6.8	8.6	8.4	9.5	9.4	11.9	40.3	1958
Sioux Falls, SD	7.5	15.0	17.6	11.4	14.5	7.6	9.2	17.1	1981
Stamford, CT	2.0	4.9	7.2	16.7	15.9	14.4	16.2	22.7	1968
Sterling Hgts, MI	2.3	8.3	14.2	14.7	32.1	18.6	7.0	2.8	1977
Sunnyvale, CA	2.9	3.9	10.1	10.9	24.5	22.6	19.3	5.8	1971
Tampa, FL	6.0	10.3	10.3	13.2	15.1	13.1	17.0	14.9	1973
Temecula, CA	9.8	23.1	34.3	24.2	6.5	0.6	1.1	0.6	1995
Thousand Oaks, CA	2.0	8.7	12.7	17.0	33.3	21.1	4.1	1.1	1977
Virginia Beach, VA	4.2	6.5	12.2	29.0	25.3	13.5	6.7	2.7	1981
Washington, DC	3.5	3.6	2.7	3.8	7.2	12.9	15.7	50.6	1950
U.S.	5.0	8.6	14.0	14.1	16.3	11.3	11.2	19.6	1975

Note: Figures are percentages except for Median Year
Source: U.S. Census Bureau, 2008-2010 American Community Survey 3-Year Estimates

Year Housing Structure Built: Metro Area

Metro Area	2005 or Later	2000 -2004	1990 -1999	1980 -1989	1970 -1979	1960 -1969	1950 -1959	Before 1950	Median Year
Albuquerque, NM	6.8	11.9	18.2	16.1	19.3	9.3	10.8	7.6	1982
Alexandria, VA	5.2	9.5	14.4	16.6	15.5	13.4	10.7	14.8	1977
Anchorage, AK	5.6	10.0	13.0	27.8	25.8	9.8	6.3	1.8	1982
Ann Arbor, MI	3.3	9.8	16.4	10.8	17.8	14.1	10.7	16.9	1975
Athens, GA	5.1	12.1	21.9	18.6	17.7	10.4	5.3	8.9	1984
Atlanta, GA	8.8	16.8	22.1	19.0	13.8	8.6	5.4	5.5	1989
Austin, TX	12.1	16.6	20.5	19.9	15.5	5.9	4.5	5.1	1990
Baltimore, MD	3.5	6.5	13.2	14.1	13.9	10.9	14.0	23.9	1971
Bellevue, WA	5.9	9.4	16.5	15.8	16.0	11.8	8.4	16.2	1978
Billings, MT	5.0	7.2	13.6	13.8	21.3	8.9	13.2	16.9	1975
Boise City, ID	10.9	16.8	22.8	10.1	18.9	5.4	5.5	9.5	1990
Boston, MA	2.9	4.4	7.1	10.6	11.3	10.5	11.1	42.1	1957
Boulder, CO	3.3	9.6	21.0	16.1	22.5	13.0	6.0	8.6	1980
Broken Arrow, OK	5.6	8.2	12.8	15.7	21.7	11.7	11.3	12.9	1976
Cambridge, MA	2.9	4.4	7.1	10.6	11.3	10.5	11.1	42.1	1957
Cape Coral, FL	8.9	22.6	18.5	23.1	16.7	6.1	2.6	1.4	1990
Carlsbad, CA	3.8	7.9	11.7	19.0	24.9	12.8	11.4	8.3	1977
Cary, NC	12.2	17.1	25.6	17.7	10.9	6.8	4.6	5.1	1992
Cedar Rapids, IA	5.6	9.0	15.4	6.7	14.8	14.2	11.3	23.0	1971
Charleston, SC	10.2	13.4	17.5	19.0	16.2	9.2	6.5	8.2	1985
Charlotte, NC	10.2	15.4	21.4	15.6	13.0	9.2	7.3	7.8	1988
Chesapeake, VA	4.8	7.5	14.5	19.6	17.9	13.3	11.0	11.5	1978
Chicago, IL	4.1	7.4	10.6	8.8	13.8	12.1	13.7	29.5	1966
Clarksville, TN	10.3	12.1	22.1	12.8	16.1	10.9	7.2	8.4	1986
Colorado Spgs., CO	6.6	13.1	17.2	18.1	19.6	10.5	7.4	7.5	1983
Columbia, MD	3.5	6.5	13.2	14.1	13.9	10.9	14.0	23.9	1971
Columbia, MO	9.0	12.4	19.9	13.6	15.8	11.4	7.0	10.8	1984
Columbia, SC	8.1	11.8	19.5	15.4	17.6	11.1	8.4	8.1	1983
Columbus, OH	4.3	10.6	16.7	11.5	14.4	11.7	12.4	18.2	1975
Dallas, TX	8.6	13.9	16.9	20.1	15.5	10.1	8.4	6.5	1985
Denver, CO	5.6	11.4	15.8	15.1	20.7	10.6	10.1	10.7	1979
Durham, NC	7.8	13.3	19.9	17.3	14.6	10.3	7.1	9.7	1985
Edison, NJ	2.3	4.0	5.7	7.5	9.9	13.9	17.2	39.5	1956
El Paso, TX	7.5	10.1	15.0	15.8	18.9	11.9	11.2	9.7	1979
Fargo, ND	7.8	11.1	17.4	12.1	19.2	8.4	9.4	14.7	1979
Ft. Collins, CO	7.2	14.0	20.8	14.9	22.0	8.1	4.5	8.4	1985
Ft. Worth, TX	8.6	13.9	16.9	20.1	15.5	10.1	8.4	6.5	1985
Gilbert, AZ	9.6	16.4	21.6	19.1	17.4	7.4	5.8	2.5	1989
Green Bay, WI	4.5	9.7	16.0	11.8	16.3	10.2	10.3	21.2	1975
Henderson, NV	11.5	22.2	28.6	15.9	12.8	5.6	2.4	1.0	1994
High Point, NC	5.7	10.0	20.0	15.6	15.7	11.8	10.2	11.0	1981
Honolulu, HI	4.0	5.5	12.3	12.6	26.2	19.7	11.6	8.2	1974
Houston, TX	9.8	13.4	14.6	17.2	21.7	10.0	7.4	5.9	1983
Huntington, NY	2.3	4.0	5.7	7.5	9.9	13.9	17.2	39.5	1956
Huntsville, AL	9.6	10.7	18.8	18.3	14.2	15.3	7.1	6.0	1984
Indianapolis, IN	5.9	11.4	16.8	11.1	13.6	11.8	10.8	18.6	1976
Irvine, CA	2.1	3.9	7.2	12.6	17.0	16.5	19.1	21.6	1966
Jackson, MS	7.0	10.2	18.7	16.0	19.3	12.6	9.1	7.1	1981
Jacksonville, FL	9.2	14.4	18.1	18.9	13.4	8.9	8.8	8.4	1986
Jersey City, NJ	2.3	4.0	5.7	7.5	9.9	13.9	17.2	39.5	1956
Kansas City, MO	5.0	9.3	14.3	12.9	16.0	11.9	12.2	18.4	1975
Kenosha, WI	4.1	7.4	10.6	8.8	13.8	12.1	13.7	29.5	1966
Las Vegas, NV	11.5	22.2	28.6	15.9	12.8	5.6	2.4	1.0	1994
Lexington, KY	7.0	10.6	17.9	15.5	15.2	12.6	8.7	12.5	1981
Lincoln, NE	5.3	10.1	15.8	10.7	17.0	11.1	10.8	19.2	1975

Table continued on next page.

Metro Area	2005 or Later	2000 -2004	1990 -1999	1980 -1989	1970 -1979	1960 -1969	1950 -1959	Before 1950	Median Year
Little Rock, AR	8.1	10.5	17.2	16.7	19.6	11.7	8.2	8.0	1982
Los Angeles, CA	2.1	3.9	7.2	12.6	17.0	16.5	19.1	21.6	1966
Madison, WI	6.1	11.3	15.7	10.9	17.0	11.3	8.3	19.4	1977
Manchester, NH	2.9	6.4	9.6	20.0	16.6	9.9	7.7	27.0	1973
Miami, FL	3.6	9.5	14.8	19.7	23.0	13.0	10.5	5.7	1979
Minneapolis, MN	4.6	10.3	14.5	14.7	15.5	10.3	10.3	19.8	1976
Murfreesboro, TN	8.4	11.8	19.3	16.2	16.2	11.1	7.8	9.1	1984
Naperville, IL	4.1	7.4	10.6	8.8	13.8	12.1	13.7	29.5	1966
Nashville, TN	8.4	11.8	19.3	16.2	16.2	11.1	7.8	9.1	1984
New Orleans, LA	5.1	6.5	9.8	14.5	20.0	14.7	10.0	19.5	1973
New York, NY	2.3	4.0	5.7	7.5	9.9	13.9	17.2	39.5	1956
Norman, OK	6.2	8.5	11.4	16.4	19.2	13.9	11.2	13.2	1976
Olathe, KS	5.0	9.3	14.3	12.9	16.0	11.9	12.2	18.4	1975
Omaha, NE	6.0	8.8	12.9	9.9	16.9	12.9	10.3	22.3	1973
Orlando, FL	8.2	17.6	21.3	22.5	14.1	7.1	5.9	3.3	1989
Overland Park, KS	5.0	9.3	14.3	12.9	16.0	11.9	12.2	18.4	1975
Oyster Bay, NY	2.3	4.0	5.7	7.5	9.9	13.9	17.2	39.5	1956
Pembroke Pines, FL	3.6	9.5	14.8	19.7	23.0	13.0	10.5	5.7	1979
Philadelphia, PA	2.9	4.9	9.1	10.1	12.6	12.2	16.4	31.9	1961
Phoenix, AZ	9.6	16.4	21.6	19.1	17.4	7.4	5.8	2.5	1989
Pittsburgh, PA	2.1	4.1	7.3	7.5	11.9	11.2	17.2	38.7	1957
Plano, TX	8.6	13.9	16.9	20.1	15.5	10.1	8.4	6.5	1985
Portland, OR	5.5	9.8	19.5	11.7	18.3	9.4	7.7	18.1	1978
Providence, RI	2.0	3.9	7.6	10.9	12.0	10.5	11.2	41.9	1957
Provo, UT	12.2	16.9	22.4	9.8	15.8	6.1	5.9	10.9	1991
Raleigh, NC	12.2	17.1	25.6	17.7	10.9	6.8	4.6	5.1	1992
Richmond, VA	6.2	9.1	16.0	16.8	16.4	10.8	9.9	14.8	1979
Roseville, CA	5.7	12.0	14.3	16.8	19.4	11.6	11.2	8.9	1979
Round Rock, TX	12.1	16.6	20.5	19.9	15.5	5.9	4.5	5.1	1990
San Antonio, TX	10.2	12.2	15.4	16.8	17.1	9.5	8.8	10.0	1983
San Diego, CA	3.8	7.9	11.7	19.0	24.9	12.8	11.4	8.3	1977
San Francisco, CA	2.7	4.6	7.7	10.8	15.4	13.9	14.7	30.2	1964
San Jose, CA	3.5	6.1	10.4	12.9	22.7	18.9	15.6	9.8	1972
Savannah, GA	10.7	12.8	17.2	14.9	12.9	9.7	8.5	13.3	1984
Scottsdale, AZ	9.6	16.4	21.6	19.1	17.4	7.4	5.8	2.5	1989
Seattle, WA	5.9	9.4	16.5	15.8	16.0	11.8	8.4	16.2	1978
Sioux Falls, SD	7.8	13.7	17.8	9.7	14.5	7.5	8.4	20.5	1979
Stamford, CT	2.2	4.0	6.2	11.6	14.2	14.8	16.9	30.1	1962
Sterling Hgts, MI	2.2	6.2	11.0	8.9	14.3	12.5	19.9	25.0	1964
Sunnyvale, CA	3.5	6.1	10.4	12.9	22.7	18.9	15.6	9.8	1972
Tampa, FL	5.2	10.5	14.4	22.8	21.9	11.3	9.1	4.8	1981
Temecula, CA	8.1	13.1	14.7	23.2	16.3	9.5	9.0	6.0	1984
Thousand Oaks, CA	3.4	7.4	10.7	16.7	23.6	21.1	10.1	7.0	1975
Virginia Beach, VA	4.8	7.5	14.5	19.6	17.9	13.3	11.0	11.5	1978
Washington, DC	5.2	9.5	14.4	16.6	15.5	13.4	10.7	14.8	1977
U.S.	5.0	8.6	14.0	14.1	16.3	11.3	11.2	19.6	1975

Note: Figures are percentages except for Median Year; Figures cover the Metropolitan Statistical Area—see Appendix B for areas included
Source: U.S. Census Bureau, 2008-2010 American Community Survey 3-Year Estimates

Highest Level of Education: City

City	Less than H.S.	H.S. Diploma	Some College, No Deg.	Associate Degree	Bachelors Degree	Masters Degree	Profess. School Degree	Doctorate Degree
Albuquerque, NM	12.7	23.5	24.6	7.2	18.0	9.5	2.4	2.2
Alexandria, VA	9.7	13.5	14.1	4.2	30.2	18.8	6.5	3.0
Anchorage, AK	7.5	22.4	28.8	8.4	21.7	7.7	2.1	1.4
Ann Arbor, MI	3.2	8.3	13.1	4.7	30.0	24.8	6.2	9.7
Athens, GA	16.9	21.4	16.5	4.6	21.5	10.5	3.6	4.9
Atlanta, GA	13.4	21.0	16.3	3.8	27.5	11.5	4.4	2.1
Austin, TX	14.9	16.8	19.1	5.4	27.5	11.2	2.9	2.3
Baltimore, MD	21.7	30.0	19.0	4.1	13.6	7.4	2.6	1.7
Bellevue, WA	4.3	11.3	16.1	7.1	38.0	16.5	3.9	2.8
Billings, MT	7.8	29.6	23.7	7.8	22.2	5.9	2.2	0.8
Boise City, ID	6.8	22.0	26.9	7.5	24.2	8.5	2.6	1.4
Boston, MA	15.5	22.7	13.9	4.8	23.9	12.6	4.1	2.5
Boulder, CO	5.1	7.0	14.0	4.2	34.4	22.3	5.6	7.3
Broken Arrow, OK	6.7	23.3	30.2	8.6	23.1	5.9	1.6	0.7
Cambridge, MA	5.8	10.3	7.6	3.1	29.5	24.5	7.0	12.1
Cape Coral, FL	11.7	34.8	24.6	8.3	14.6	4.0	1.4	0.6
Carlsbad, CA	4.6	13.6	20.9	10.3	31.7	12.9	3.4	2.7
Cary, NC	4.8	10.3	15.3	7.3	37.4	18.4	3.0	3.4
Cedar Rapids, IA	7.3	26.8	25.2	10.3	21.9	6.5	1.4	0.7
Charleston, SC	9.2	17.7	19.7	6.5	29.4	11.3	3.9	2.2
Charlotte, NC	12.6	20.2	21.1	7.4	26.3	9.1	2.4	0.9
Chesapeake, VA	10.6	25.9	26.1	9.1	17.8	7.9	2.0	0.7
Chicago, IL	20.1	23.0	18.4	5.5	19.6	9.1	2.8	1.4
Clarksville, TN	8.8	31.2	29.8	8.4	14.9	5.2	0.8	0.9
Colorado Spgs., CO	7.6	21.1	25.7	9.4	22.1	10.7	1.9	1.4
Columbia, MD	6.1	12.9	14.9	5.9	30.0	20.4	4.9	4.9
Columbia, MO	6.8	19.2	16.3	5.5	28.5	14.6	3.5	5.6
Columbia, SC	14.6	20.7	20.1	6.1	22.1	10.7	3.7	2.0
Columbus, OH	12.3	26.9	21.8	6.6	21.8	7.2	1.9	1.4
Dallas, TX	26.9	21.6	18.3	4.4	18.5	6.8	2.5	1.0
Denver, CO	15.8	20.0	18.5	5.0	24.9	10.2	4.0	1.5
Durham, NC	14.1	16.5	16.5	6.3	25.7	12.5	3.6	4.7
Edison, NJ	7.9	22.8	12.6	5.6	29.2	17.1	2.4	2.3
El Paso, TX	25.3	23.8	22.7	6.3	14.5	5.3	1.5	0.7
Fargo, ND	5.9	20.9	24.3	10.4	26.8	8.2	2.1	1.5
Ft. Collins, CO	4.9	15.0	21.9	7.4	30.4	14.1	2.8	3.5
Ft. Worth, TX	21.7	24.3	22.4	6.0	17.7	5.6	1.4	0.9
Gilbert, AZ	4.1	18.6	28.3	11.4	25.8	8.7	1.7	1.5
Green Bay, WI	15.0	34.2	21.2	9.0	14.8	4.3	1.0	0.5
Henderson, NV	7.3	26.7	27.2	7.9	20.0	7.3	2.2	1.4
High Point, NC	14.6	28.2	21.6	7.1	20.0	6.4	1.2	0.9
Honolulu, HI	11.8	26.6	19.9	8.5	21.7	7.3	2.7	1.6
Houston, TX	25.9	22.3	19.2	4.3	17.5	6.8	2.4	1.5
Huntington, NY	7.7	21.6	14.9	8.7	25.8	14.5	4.7	2.0
Huntsville, AL	12.6	20.2	23.1	6.4	23.9	9.5	2.4	1.8
Indianapolis, IN	16.2	29.3	20.6	6.5	18.0	6.3	2.1	0.9
Irvine, CA	4.1	8.8	14.7	6.7	37.4	18.6	5.2	4.6
Jackson, MS	18.1	25.5	22.9	6.7	15.9	6.8	2.8	1.2
Jacksonville, FL	13.2	29.7	24.8	8.6	16.3	5.2	1.5	0.7
Jersey City, NJ	15.9	23.4	15.6	4.0	25.7	11.8	2.3	1.4
Kansas City, MO	13.5	26.2	23.6	6.8	18.7	8.3	2.0	0.9
Kenosha, WI	13.2	33.1	22.2	9.6	15.5	5.2	0.8	0.4
Las Vegas, NV	18.7	28.7	25.0	7.0	13.4	4.9	1.7	0.7
Lexington, KY	11.6	21.2	21.4	7.0	22.5	9.9	3.5	2.7
Lincoln, NE	7.3	23.5	23.9	10.5	23.4	7.0	2.1	2.3

Table continued on next page.

City	Less than H.S.	H.S. Diploma	Some College, No Deg.	Associate Degree	Bachelors Degree	Masters Degree	Profess. School Degree	Doctorate Degree
Little Rock, AR	12.0	21.1	23.8	6.5	21.7	9.0	4.3	1.5
Los Angeles, CA	26.3	19.2	18.1	6.1	20.2	6.3	2.7	1.2
Madison, WI	5.9	16.6	17.9	7.7	28.6	14.3	4.1	5.0
Manchester, NH	14.5	31.8	18.9	8.8	17.3	6.5	1.7	0.6
Miami, FL	32.0	28.0	10.3	7.2	14.1	4.6	2.6	1.3
Minneapolis, MN	12.2	18.8	18.9	6.4	27.4	10.2	3.7	2.3
Murfreesboro, TN	10.5	24.5	23.3	7.0	23.6	8.0	1.3	1.7
Naperville, IL	3.1	11.1	13.9	6.5	36.5	21.6	4.0	3.3
Nashville, TN	15.2	24.9	20.7	5.9	20.8	8.0	2.5	2.0
New Orleans, LA	15.3	26.4	21.9	4.2	18.5	8.0	3.7	2.0
New York, NY	21.0	24.9	14.6	6.1	19.8	9.3	3.0	1.3
Norman, OK	7.6	19.6	23.7	6.2	24.4	12.3	3.2	2.8
Olathe, KS	5.8	18.7	22.3	8.0	30.3	11.4	2.4	1.1
Omaha, NE	11.8	24.4	25.2	6.6	21.1	7.1	2.5	1.4
Orlando, FL	12.8	26.7	19.9	9.5	21.3	6.8	2.1	0.9
Overland Park, KS	3.6	13.4	19.2	6.8	36.1	15.7	3.0	2.2
Oyster Bay, NY	6.2	25.6	16.0	8.1	24.6	13.7	4.4	1.2
Pembroke Pines, FL	11.6	24.7	21.5	10.4	20.3	8.7	1.5	1.1
Philadelphia, PA	20.3	35.2	16.9	5.2	12.8	6.0	2.2	1.3
Phoenix, AZ	20.2	24.3	23.2	7.1	16.2	6.3	1.9	0.8
Pittsburgh, PA	10.8	30.1	16.9	7.6	17.9	10.0	3.8	2.8
Plano, TX	6.8	14.1	18.8	6.4	34.8	14.9	2.1	2.0
Portland, OR	10.4	18.3	22.8	6.2	26.0	10.7	3.8	1.9
Providence, RI	27.9	23.3	15.7	4.8	15.7	7.3	2.6	2.7
Provo, UT	8.1	15.3	27.7	8.9	27.8	7.1	1.7	3.2
Raleigh, NC	9.3	16.2	20.0	7.4	31.1	10.9	2.8	2.1
Richmond, VA	20.1	22.9	18.9	4.8	20.1	8.5	3.0	1.7
Roseville, CA	6.3	19.9	28.2	11.7	23.2	7.2	2.3	1.2
Round Rock, TX	10.5	19.9	26.8	8.8	23.8	8.6	0.7	0.9
San Antonio, TX	20.6	25.2	24.0	6.6	15.0	5.9	1.8	0.9
San Diego, CA	13.6	16.4	21.7	7.5	24.6	10.0	3.3	2.9
San Francisco, CA	14.5	14.0	14.8	5.4	31.2	12.5	5.0	2.6
San Jose, CA	18.1	18.8	19.2	7.6	22.7	10.3	1.8	1.6
Savannah, GA	15.8	32.7	21.4	6.7	15.7	5.7	1.0	1.0
Scottsdale, AZ	4.4	14.8	22.1	6.8	32.5	12.4	4.7	2.3
Seattle, WA	7.1	12.1	18.2	6.8	33.5	14.2	4.9	3.2
Sioux Falls, SD	9.4	27.4	22.3	9.2	21.7	6.4	2.5	1.0
Stamford, CT	14.8	23.7	14.9	5.3	23.4	13.4	3.4	1.1
Sterling Hgts, MI	15.3	28.3	21.1	9.1	17.2	7.2	1.0	0.7
Sunnyvale, CA	8.8	12.1	16.0	6.5	29.9	20.3	2.2	4.2
Tampa, FL	15.4	27.0	18.0	7.9	19.6	7.3	3.4	1.3
Temecula, CA	8.7	21.2	29.6	10.5	20.1	7.3	1.5	1.1
Thousand Oaks, CA	6.0	15.7	21.6	7.8	30.0	12.6	3.5	2.8
Virginia Beach, VA	7.2	24.3	27.2	9.9	20.8	7.7	2.0	0.8
Washington, DC	12.9	19.8	14.6	2.9	22.2	15.6	8.0	3.9
U.S.	14.7	28.4	21.3	7.6	17.6	7.2	1.9	1.2

Note: Figures cover persons age 25 and over
Source: U.S. Census Bureau, 2008-2010 American Community Survey 3-Year Estimates

Highest Level of Education: Metro Area

Metro Area	Less than H.S.	H.S. Diploma	Some College, No Deg.	Associate Degree	Bachelors Degree	Masters Degree	Profess. School Degree	Doctorate Degree
Albuquerque, NM	13.4	25.1	24.9	7.3	16.6	8.6	2.1	2.0
Alexandria, VA	10.5	19.5	17.6	5.5	24.7	15.0	4.3	2.9
Anchorage, AK	7.6	24.3	29.4	8.5	20.1	7.0	1.8	1.2
Ann Arbor, MI	6.1	16.0	20.5	6.8	25.0	16.3	4.3	5.0
Athens, GA	18.5	24.5	17.6	4.9	18.1	9.2	3.4	3.8
Atlanta, GA	12.6	25.2	21.0	6.7	22.5	8.6	2.1	1.2
Austin, TX	12.7	19.7	22.0	6.4	25.5	9.7	2.3	1.7
Baltimore, MD	12.2	26.9	20.0	6.1	19.9	10.4	2.8	1.7
Bellevue, WA	8.8	21.4	24.0	8.8	24.0	9.0	2.4	1.5
Billings, MT	8.2	32.0	22.9	7.6	21.3	5.2	2.0	0.7
Boise City, ID	11.0	25.9	27.5	7.7	19.1	6.1	1.7	1.0
Boston, MA	9.7	24.7	15.9	7.3	23.8	12.8	3.2	2.6
Boulder, CO	6.3	12.2	17.8	5.8	32.8	17.1	3.6	4.4
Broken Arrow, OK	12.1	30.1	24.7	7.9	17.3	5.3	1.7	0.8
Cambridge, MA	9.7	24.7	15.9	7.3	23.8	12.8	3.2	2.6
Cape Coral, FL	13.2	32.1	22.8	7.4	15.5	6.1	1.9	0.9
Carlsbad, CA	14.9	19.1	23.5	8.4	21.3	8.2	2.6	2.0
Cary, NC	10.2	19.8	20.0	8.4	27.9	10.0	2.1	1.8
Cedar Rapids, IA	7.1	30.0	24.2	11.0	20.1	6.0	1.2	0.6
Charleston, SC	12.5	27.0	21.8	8.3	19.7	7.5	2.0	1.3
Charlotte, NC	13.6	24.1	21.9	8.2	22.1	7.5	1.8	0.8
Chesapeake, VA	10.8	26.8	26.2	8.5	17.3	7.7	1.7	1.0
Chicago, IL	13.9	25.1	20.5	6.6	20.9	9.3	2.4	1.2
Clarksville, TN	12.2	34.0	27.2	8.1	12.0	5.1	0.9	0.6
Colorado Spgs., CO	7.0	22.1	26.1	9.6	21.6	10.6	1.7	1.3
Columbia, MD	12.2	26.9	20.0	6.1	19.9	10.4	2.8	1.7
Columbia, MO	8.5	23.8	17.6	6.0	25.0	12.0	3.0	4.1
Columbia, SC	12.3	26.8	22.4	8.5	18.8	8.0	1.8	1.3
Columbus, OH	10.3	29.3	20.6	6.9	21.7	7.8	2.1	1.3
Dallas, TX	17.1	23.0	22.7	6.4	20.9	7.4	1.6	1.0
Denver, CO	11.0	21.8	21.8	7.3	24.9	9.6	2.4	1.2
Durham, NC	13.4	20.1	16.6	6.4	23.2	12.0	3.6	4.8
Edison, NJ	15.7	26.4	15.7	6.4	21.2	10.2	3.0	1.4
El Paso, TX	28.1	24.1	22.1	6.0	13.1	4.7	1.3	0.6
Fargo, ND	6.2	24.3	23.2	11.4	24.8	6.9	1.7	1.5
Ft. Collins, CO	6.4	19.9	22.5	8.3	25.9	11.7	2.4	2.9
Ft. Worth, TX	17.1	23.0	22.7	6.4	20.9	7.4	1.6	1.0
Gilbert, AZ	14.4	24.0	25.7	8.1	18.1	7.0	1.8	1.0
Green Bay, WI	10.4	35.7	20.7	10.3	16.6	4.6	1.2	0.4
Henderson, NV	16.6	29.3	25.3	7.0	14.7	4.9	1.5	0.7
High Point, NC	16.2	29.3	21.9	6.9	17.9	5.5	1.3	0.9
Honolulu, HI	9.7	27.9	21.7	9.5	20.6	6.7	2.5	1.3
Houston, TX	19.6	23.9	22.3	5.9	18.7	6.6	1.8	1.2
Huntington, NY	15.7	26.4	15.7	6.4	21.2	10.2	3.0	1.4
Huntsville, AL	13.2	23.8	21.9	7.1	21.7	9.2	1.6	1.3
Indianapolis, IN	11.9	29.7	20.4	7.1	20.5	7.3	2.1	1.0
Irvine, CA	22.4	19.9	20.0	7.0	20.1	6.9	2.4	1.3
Jackson, MS	14.8	25.3	23.5	7.7	18.2	6.9	2.3	1.2
Jacksonville, FL	11.7	28.8	24.5	8.8	17.6	6.1	1.6	0.9
Jersey City, NJ	15.7	26.4	15.7	6.4	21.2	10.2	3.0	1.4
Kansas City, MO	10.0	27.2	23.4	6.9	20.9	8.7	2.0	1.0
Kenosha, WI	13.9	25.1	20.5	6.6	20.9	9.3	2.4	1.2
Las Vegas, NV	16.6	29.3	25.3	7.0	14.7	4.9	1.5	0.7
Lexington, KY	12.9	25.8	21.3	6.8	19.7	8.6	2.9	2.1
Lincoln, NE	6.9	24.0	23.6	10.8	23.2	7.1	2.1	2.3

Table continued on next page.

Metro Area	Less than H.S.	H.S. Diploma	Some College, No Deg.	Associate Degree	Bachelors Degree	Masters Degree	Profess. School Degree	Doctorate Degree
Little Rock, AR	12.2	30.9	24.1	6.8	17.0	6.1	1.9	1.0
Los Angeles, CA	22.4	19.9	20.0	7.0	20.1	6.9	2.4	1.3
Madison, WI	6.0	23.6	19.7	9.2	25.2	10.4	2.9	2.9
Manchester, NH	9.7	27.7	18.6	9.5	22.1	9.6	1.8	0.9
Miami, FL	17.3	27.4	18.5	8.3	18.2	6.5	2.7	1.1
Minneapolis, MN	7.4	23.8	21.9	9.2	25.4	8.6	2.4	1.3
Murfreesboro, TN	13.8	28.6	21.1	6.5	19.9	6.7	2.1	1.3
Naperville, IL	13.9	25.1	20.5	6.6	20.9	9.3	2.4	1.2
Nashville, TN	13.8	28.6	21.1	6.5	19.9	6.7	2.1	1.3
New Orleans, LA	15.4	30.2	22.9	5.3	17.0	5.7	2.3	1.1
New York, NY	15.7	26.4	15.7	6.4	21.2	10.2	3.0	1.4
Norman, OK	12.8	27.9	26.1	6.4	17.8	6.2	1.8	1.0
Olathe, KS	10.0	27.2	23.4	6.9	20.9	8.7	2.0	1.0
Omaha, NE	9.1	25.9	24.8	7.9	21.8	7.4	2.1	1.1
Orlando, FL	12.4	29.0	21.7	9.6	18.5	6.3	1.6	0.8
Overland Park, KS	10.0	27.2	23.4	6.9	20.9	8.7	2.0	1.0
Oyster Bay, NY	15.7	26.4	15.7	6.4	21.2	10.2	3.0	1.4
Pembroke Pines, FL	17.3	27.4	18.5	8.3	18.2	6.5	2.7	1.1
Philadelphia, PA	12.0	31.1	17.8	6.4	19.7	8.8	2.5	1.6
Phoenix, AZ	14.4	24.0	25.7	8.1	18.1	7.0	1.8	1.0
Pittsburgh, PA	8.9	36.8	16.7	8.9	18.0	7.6	2.0	1.2
Plano, TX	17.1	23.0	22.7	6.4	20.9	7.4	1.6	1.0
Portland, OR	9.9	22.3	26.2	8.0	21.6	8.2	2.3	1.5
Providence, RI	17.2	28.5	17.9	8.0	17.8	7.7	1.8	1.1
Provo, UT	6.4	18.0	29.9	11.0	24.1	7.4	1.6	1.6
Raleigh, NC	10.2	19.8	20.0	8.4	27.9	10.0	2.1	1.8
Richmond, VA	14.7	27.1	21.2	6.0	19.9	8.1	1.9	1.1
Roseville, CA	13.0	21.1	26.7	9.4	19.8	6.4	2.2	1.3
Round Rock, TX	12.7	19.7	22.0	6.4	25.5	9.7	2.3	1.7
San Antonio, TX	17.8	25.4	24.4	7.1	16.1	6.5	1.7	0.9
San Diego, CA	14.9	19.1	23.5	8.4	21.3	8.2	2.6	2.0
San Francisco, CA	12.9	17.7	19.0	6.9	26.6	11.0	3.5	2.5
San Jose, CA	14.1	16.2	17.9	7.3	25.1	13.8	2.6	2.9
Savannah, GA	12.4	30.5	22.9	7.0	17.8	6.7	1.7	1.0
Scottsdale, AZ	14.4	24.0	25.7	8.1	18.1	7.0	1.8	1.0
Seattle, WA	8.8	21.4	24.0	8.8	24.0	9.0	2.4	1.5
Sioux Falls, SD	8.3	29.1	22.0	10.4	21.4	5.8	2.1	0.9
Stamford, CT	11.8	23.3	15.1	6.1	24.6	14.1	3.5	1.5
Sterling Hgts, MI	12.4	28.6	24.2	7.8	16.5	7.9	1.9	0.8
Sunnyvale, CA	14.1	16.2	17.9	7.3	25.1	13.8	2.6	2.9
Tampa, FL	13.2	30.8	21.7	8.8	17.1	5.8	1.7	0.9
Temecula, CA	21.7	25.6	25.5	7.8	12.7	4.7	1.3	0.8
Thousand Oaks, CA	17.7	19.0	24.5	8.2	19.4	7.6	2.3	1.3
Virginia Beach, VA	10.8	26.8	26.2	8.5	17.3	7.7	1.7	1.0
Washington, DC	10.5	19.5	17.6	5.5	24.7	15.0	4.3	2.9
U.S.	14.7	28.4	21.3	7.6	17.6	7.2	1.9	1.2

Note: Figures cover persons age 25 and over; Figures cover the Metropolitan Statistical Area—see Appendix B for areas included
Source: U.S. Census Bureau, 2008-2010 American Community Survey 3-Year Estimates

School Enrollment by Grade and Control: City

City	Preschool (%)		Kindergarten (%)		Grades 1 - 4 (%)		Grades 5 - 8 (%)		Grades 9 - 12 (%)	
	Public	Private	Public	Private	Public	Private	Public	Private	Public	Private
Albuquerque, NM	53.5	46.5	85.4	14.6	87.4	12.6	85.8	14.2	88.7	11.3
Alexandria, VA	42.7	57.3	82.2	17.8	89.6	10.4	83.0	17.0	80.3	19.7
Anchorage, AK	48.7	51.3	91.6	8.4	93.1	6.9	91.5	8.5	93.3	6.7
Ann Arbor, MI	35.2	64.8	89.1	10.9	89.7	10.3	87.1	12.9	92.1	7.9
Athens, GA	67.7	32.3	81.3	18.7	90.5	9.5	88.0	12.0	94.4	5.6
Atlanta, GA	52.1	47.9	81.9	18.1	86.5	13.5	84.7	15.3	83.6	16.4
Austin, TX	53.7	46.3	92.7	7.3	91.4	8.6	92.5	7.5	93.2	6.8
Baltimore, MD	68.1	31.9	83.0	17.0	90.0	10.0	85.4	14.6	87.2	12.8
Bellevue, WA	25.4	74.6	82.9	17.1	83.2	16.8	87.1	12.9	89.1	10.9
Billings, MT	51.0	49.0	93.1	6.9	94.3	5.7	92.8	7.2	93.8	6.2
Boise City, ID	51.8	48.2	84.6	15.4	90.7	9.3	90.9	9.1	92.3	7.7
Boston, MA	54.7	45.3	79.5	20.5	85.1	14.9	79.5	20.5	86.6	13.4
Boulder, CO	43.8	56.2	82.9	17.1	93.5	6.5	90.0	10.0	91.9	8.1
Broken Arrow, OK	73.1	26.9	84.0	16.0	83.2	16.8	86.0	14.0	84.7	15.3
Cambridge, MA	27.9	72.1	82.1	17.9	76.5	23.5	81.0	19.0	84.3	15.7
Cape Coral, FL	72.9	27.1	90.8	9.2	92.7	7.3	92.9	7.1	94.3	5.7
Carlsbad, CA	21.3	78.7	88.7	11.3	90.7	9.3	87.7	12.3	94.9	5.1
Cary, NC	27.9	72.1	87.0	13.0	89.5	10.5	88.6	11.4	88.6	11.4
Cedar Rapids, IA	57.7	42.3	92.8	7.2	84.1	15.9	84.9	15.1	86.1	13.9
Charleston, SC	31.8	68.2	68.2	31.8	83.4	16.6	85.7	14.3	81.4	18.6
Charlotte, NC	43.0	57.0	87.1	12.9	88.5	11.5	86.5	13.5	86.9	13.1
Chesapeake, VA	36.4	63.6	83.7	16.3	87.5	12.5	87.3	12.7	93.3	6.7
Chicago, IL	63.1	36.9	82.5	17.5	86.0	14.0	87.1	12.9	85.9	14.1
Clarksville, TN	57.4	42.6	84.9	15.1	90.0	10.0	93.6	6.4	92.5	7.5
Colorado Spgs., CO	53.3	46.7	91.9	8.1	93.9	6.1	90.6	9.4	92.3	7.7
Columbia, MD	27.1	72.9	81.6	18.4	84.9	15.1	93.4	6.6	89.0	11.0
Columbia, MO	44.2	55.8	82.3	17.7	88.6	11.4	88.4	11.6	90.5	9.5
Columbia, SC	54.2	45.8	82.9	17.1	84.7	15.3	85.0	15.0	92.6	7.4
Columbus, OH	54.8	45.2	88.8	11.2	89.6	10.4	89.0	11.0	88.7	11.3
Dallas, TX	67.4	32.6	89.1	10.9	90.4	9.6	90.7	9.3	91.1	8.9
Denver, CO	53.8	46.2	89.1	10.9	88.7	11.3	89.3	10.7	90.4	9.6
Durham, NC	42.4	57.6	86.4	13.6	90.1	9.9	87.0	13.0	92.4	7.6
Edison, NJ	19.6	80.4	79.9	20.1	92.9	7.1	89.9	10.1	94.2	5.8
El Paso, TX	80.0	20.0	91.9	8.1	94.8	5.2	94.8	5.2	95.6	4.4
Fargo, ND	45.0	55.0	82.5	17.5	86.0	14.0	86.7	13.3	89.0	11.0
Ft. Collins, CO	27.2	72.8	98.7	1.3	92.2	7.8	88.2	11.8	96.3	3.7
Ft. Worth, TX	61.3	38.7	89.2	10.8	91.1	8.9	92.4	7.6	91.4	8.6
Gilbert, AZ	48.6	51.4	89.2	10.8	90.8	9.2	93.6	6.4	96.1	3.9
Green Bay, WI	69.3	30.7	89.8	10.2	92.4	7.6	92.2	7.8	92.7	7.3
Henderson, NV	51.2	48.8	85.3	14.7	91.8	8.2	96.2	3.8	94.6	5.4
High Point, NC	63.6	36.4	89.2	10.8	89.4	10.6	89.2	10.8	90.1	9.9
Honolulu, HI	36.8	63.2	71.3	28.7	79.8	20.2	75.9	24.1	76.1	23.9
Houston, TX	68.7	31.3	92.3	7.7	93.7	6.3	93.5	6.5	94.3	5.7
Huntington, NY	39.4	60.6	92.6	7.4	93.6	6.4	93.3	6.7	91.4	8.6
Huntsville, AL	44.8	55.2	83.7	16.3	88.3	11.7	84.1	15.9	89.7	10.3
Indianapolis, IN	44.0	56.0	80.7	19.3	86.2	13.8	86.6	13.4	87.3	12.7
Irvine, CA	24.1	75.9	89.2	10.8	91.0	9.0	91.9	8.1	93.9	6.1
Jackson, MS	76.3	23.7	83.1	16.9	90.3	9.7	85.8	14.2	88.4	11.6
Jacksonville, FL	48.7	51.3	80.3	19.7	85.6	14.4	82.3	17.7	83.1	16.9
Jersey City, NJ	71.6	28.4	92.7	7.3	87.6	12.4	88.7	11.3	89.2	10.8
Kansas City, MO	61.4	38.6	88.1	11.9	86.5	13.5	85.6	14.4	84.1	15.9
Kenosha, WI	63.8	36.2	94.7	5.3	87.1	12.9	91.4	8.6	94.4	5.6
Las Vegas, NV	49.9	50.1	93.6	6.4	93.3	6.7	93.5	6.5	94.4	5.6
Lexington, KY	42.1	57.9	86.2	13.8	87.4	12.6	85.7	14.3	88.7	11.3
Lincoln, NE	45.7	54.3	83.7	16.3	83.4	16.6	80.7	19.3	84.9	15.1

Table continued on next page.

City	Preschool (%)		Kindergarten (%)		Grades 1 - 4 (%)		Grades 5 - 8 (%)		Grades 9 - 12 (%)	
	Public	Private	Public	Private	Public	Private	Public	Private	Public	Private
Little Rock, AR	42.7	57.3	86.7	13.3	86.1	13.9	80.0	20.0	79.4	20.6
Los Angeles, CA	61.7	38.3	87.5	12.5	89.0	11.0	88.9	11.1	89.6	10.4
Madison, WI	27.6	72.4	90.9	9.1	87.7	12.3	87.5	12.5	90.5	9.5
Manchester, NH	52.6	47.4	72.0	28.0	87.1	12.9	88.9	11.1	94.4	5.6
Miami, FL	57.7	42.3	83.7	16.3	89.2	10.8	91.5	8.5	93.1	6.9
Minneapolis, MN	54.9	45.1	83.8	16.2	88.7	11.3	86.2	13.8	90.2	9.8
Murfreesboro, TN	45.9	54.1	90.4	9.6	95.0	5.0	94.0	6.0	97.1	2.9
Naperville, IL	36.2	63.8	86.2	13.8	94.8	5.2	95.1	4.9	92.5	7.5
Nashville, TN	50.3	49.7	78.6	21.4	84.2	15.8	80.1	19.9	81.6	18.4
New Orleans, LA	51.2	48.8	64.6	35.4	76.4	23.6	72.0	28.0	78.0	22.0
New York, NY	53.8	46.2	76.8	23.2	80.9	19.1	81.2	18.8	82.7	17.3
Norman, OK	64.9	35.1	83.3	16.7	93.0	7.0	94.0	6.0	92.9	7.1
Olathe, KS	44.8	55.2	87.3	12.7	91.0	9.0	92.7	7.3	90.6	9.4
Omaha, NE	57.1	42.9	80.2	19.8	84.2	15.8	84.7	15.3	88.3	11.7
Orlando, FL	41.4	58.6	85.3	14.7	88.5	11.5	88.0	12.0	88.3	11.7
Overland Park, KS	28.6	71.4	80.3	19.7	83.4	16.6	82.5	17.5	85.3	14.7
Oyster Bay, NY	23.4	76.6	87.5	12.5	92.9	7.1	87.7	12.3	85.8	14.2
Pembroke Pines, FL	27.6	72.4	83.2	16.8	89.6	10.4	90.9	9.1	87.6	12.4
Philadelphia, PA	59.8	40.2	75.8	24.2	80.8	19.2	78.8	21.2	81.7	18.3
Phoenix, AZ	63.1	36.9	92.5	7.5	93.6	6.4	93.9	6.1	93.7	6.3
Pittsburgh, PA	51.6	48.4	73.5	26.5	80.1	19.9	81.3	18.7	81.8	18.2
Plano, TX	43.6	56.4	86.8	13.2	89.4	10.6	89.0	11.0	91.2	8.8
Portland, OR	42.4	57.6	84.9	15.1	87.5	12.5	89.2	10.8	88.8	11.2
Providence, RI	51.2	48.8	82.7	17.3	82.8	17.2	88.7	11.3	89.0	11.0
Provo, UT	43.1	56.9	93.9	6.1	94.3	5.7	94.6	5.4	77.9	22.1
Raleigh, NC	31.5	68.5	82.9	17.1	88.3	11.7	92.1	7.9	90.7	9.3
Richmond, VA	55.5	44.5	83.9	16.1	87.2	12.8	86.0	14.0	85.8	14.2
Roseville, CA	49.7	50.3	89.4	10.6	88.7	11.3	89.6	10.4	92.7	7.3
Round Rock, TX	46.3	53.7	94.8	5.2	94.9	5.1	92.2	7.8	95.3	4.7
San Antonio, TX	68.0	32.0	89.4	10.6	93.5	6.5	92.8	7.2	93.0	7.0
San Diego, CA	54.0	46.0	90.6	9.4	91.4	8.6	91.6	8.4	92.7	7.3
San Francisco, CA	31.2	68.8	76.4	23.6	74.1	25.9	74.6	25.4	80.8	19.2
San Jose, CA	43.3	56.7	84.9	15.1	87.5	12.5	89.5	10.5	90.4	9.6
Savannah, GA	71.9	28.1	86.4	13.6	90.4	9.6	89.7	10.3	91.1	8.9
Scottsdale, AZ	31.9	68.1	86.0	14.0	87.0	13.0	88.5	11.5	87.4	12.6
Seattle, WA	29.6	70.4	75.4	24.6	78.9	21.1	73.9	26.1	78.9	21.1
Sioux Falls, SD	59.2	40.8	87.7	12.3	87.3	12.7	86.0	14.0	89.1	10.9
Stamford, CT	30.4	69.6	77.6	22.4	83.8	16.2	75.1	24.9	79.0	21.0
Sterling Hgts, MI	76.8	23.2	92.3	7.7	93.9	6.1	89.8	10.2	94.8	5.2
Sunnyvale, CA	14.1	85.9	73.1	26.9	74.0	26.0	86.6	13.4	87.2	12.8
Tampa, FL	56.3	43.7	86.9	13.1	91.4	8.6	87.4	12.6	93.5	6.5
Temecula, CA	43.5	56.5	88.1	11.9	88.7	11.3	86.8	13.2	94.3	5.7
Thousand Oaks, CA	33.1	66.9	80.0	20.0	87.2	12.8	86.3	13.7	90.4	9.6
Virginia Beach, VA	32.7	67.3	79.2	20.8	90.2	9.8	91.4	8.6	91.7	8.3
Washington, DC	67.5	32.5	79.1	20.9	84.4	15.6	79.7	20.3	84.5	15.5
U.S.	55.4	44.6	87.1	12.9	89.4	10.6	89.5	10.5	90.4	9.6

Note: Figures shown cover persons 3 years old and over
Source: U.S. Census Bureau, 2008-2010 American Community Survey 3-Year Estimates

School Enrollment by Grade and Control: Metro Area

Metro Area	Preschool (%)		Kindergarten (%)		Grades 1 - 4 (%)		Grades 5 - 8 (%)		Grades 9 - 12 (%)	
	Public	Private	Public	Private	Public	Private	Public	Private	Public	Private
Albuquerque, NM	60.0	40.0	86.4	13.6	88.5	11.5	88.0	12.0	89.6	10.4
Alexandria, VA	38.6	61.4	82.1	17.9	86.5	13.5	87.0	13.0	88.9	11.1
Anchorage, AK	49.9	50.1	91.5	8.5	91.0	9.0	89.7	10.3	91.1	8.9
Ann Arbor, MI	40.8	59.2	85.0	15.0	86.8	13.2	89.1	10.9	91.1	8.9
Athens, GA	61.0	39.0	85.4	14.6	89.5	10.5	87.7	12.3	92.8	7.2
Atlanta, GA	48.3	51.7	86.0	14.0	89.7	10.3	89.1	10.9	90.2	9.8
Austin, TX	50.0	50.0	90.8	9.2	92.4	7.6	93.0	7.0	93.2	6.8
Baltimore, MD	48.0	52.0	82.3	17.7	85.2	14.8	83.7	16.3	84.4	15.6
Bellevue, WA	39.5	60.5	84.9	15.1	89.0	11.0	88.7	11.3	89.9	10.1
Billings, MT	51.4	48.6	89.6	10.4	93.7	6.3	92.9	7.1	92.5	7.5
Boise City, ID	45.9	54.1	90.0	10.0	92.6	7.4	92.3	7.7	92.6	7.4
Boston, MA	38.1	61.9	84.2	15.8	90.0	10.0	87.6	12.4	86.3	13.7
Boulder, CO	42.6	57.4	87.3	12.7	91.0	9.0	88.9	11.1	92.5	7.5
Broken Arrow, OK	72.1	27.9	89.5	10.5	89.9	10.1	89.9	10.1	88.1	11.9
Cambridge, MA	38.1	61.9	84.2	15.8	90.0	10.0	87.6	12.4	86.3	13.7
Cape Coral, FL	62.7	37.3	90.2	9.8	91.4	8.6	90.4	9.6	91.8	8.2
Carlsbad, CA	52.5	47.5	90.2	9.8	91.5	8.5	91.6	8.4	93.0	7.0
Cary, NC	33.0	67.0	85.8	14.2	89.3	10.7	89.6	10.4	90.6	9.4
Cedar Rapids, IA	60.1	39.9	88.9	11.1	85.4	14.6	86.5	13.5	90.7	9.3
Charleston, SC	47.9	52.1	81.9	18.1	87.7	12.3	87.3	12.7	86.3	13.7
Charlotte, NC	44.4	55.6	89.2	10.8	89.7	10.3	88.4	11.6	89.4	10.6
Chesapeake, VA	49.1	50.9	84.5	15.5	89.4	10.6	89.9	10.1	92.2	7.8
Chicago, IL	55.9	44.1	84.4	15.6	88.0	12.0	88.8	11.2	90.0	10.0
Clarksville, TN	71.7	28.3	86.9	13.1	88.1	11.9	91.0	9.0	89.7	10.3
Colorado Spgs., CO	59.5	40.5	89.0	11.0	90.2	9.8	89.4	10.6	91.7	8.3
Columbia, MD	48.0	52.0	82.3	17.7	85.2	14.8	83.7	16.3	84.4	15.6
Columbia, MO	48.4	51.6	85.6	14.4	89.5	10.5	89.7	10.3	93.1	6.9
Columbia, SC	52.7	47.3	86.9	13.1	90.4	9.6	91.5	8.5	92.7	7.3
Columbus, OH	47.7	52.3	85.6	14.4	87.9	12.1	88.6	11.4	89.6	10.4
Dallas, TX	51.9	48.1	89.1	10.9	91.6	8.4	92.4	7.6	92.6	7.4
Denver, CO	52.7	47.3	87.7	12.3	91.4	8.6	91.9	8.1	91.7	8.3
Durham, NC	40.0	60.0	86.1	13.9	88.4	11.6	87.8	12.2	92.3	7.7
Edison, NJ	47.4	52.6	80.7	19.3	85.3	14.7	85.5	14.5	85.5	14.5
El Paso, TX	82.5	17.5	93.0	7.0	95.7	4.3	95.5	4.5	96.2	3.8
Fargo, ND	50.1	49.9	90.0	10.0	88.9	11.1	91.2	8.8	91.3	8.7
Ft. Collins, CO	29.7	70.3	92.8	7.2	91.2	8.8	91.3	8.7	94.9	5.1
Ft. Worth, TX	51.9	48.1	89.1	10.9	91.6	8.4	92.4	7.6	92.6	7.4
Gilbert, AZ	55.9	44.1	91.0	9.0	92.9	7.1	94.0	6.0	94.4	5.6
Green Bay, WI	65.6	34.4	88.2	11.8	87.7	12.3	89.1	10.9	93.6	6.4
Henderson, NV	56.2	43.8	92.4	7.6	93.6	6.4	95.6	4.4	95.2	4.8
High Point, NC	50.9	49.1	89.0	11.0	91.9	8.1	90.6	9.4	92.5	7.5
Honolulu, HI	30.5	69.5	79.3	20.7	83.5	16.5	78.1	21.9	76.8	23.2
Houston, TX	57.5	42.5	90.6	9.4	93.8	6.2	93.8	6.2	94.1	5.9
Huntington, NY	47.4	52.6	80.7	19.3	85.3	14.7	85.5	14.5	85.5	14.5
Huntsville, AL	45.4	54.6	88.3	11.7	87.9	12.1	84.6	15.4	88.9	11.1
Indianapolis, IN	41.3	58.7	82.1	17.9	88.0	12.0	88.9	11.1	89.2	10.8
Irvine, CA	57.7	42.3	87.4	12.6	90.2	9.8	90.3	9.7	91.8	8.2
Jackson, MS	59.9	40.1	84.3	15.7	86.1	13.9	83.3	16.7	86.2	13.8
Jacksonville, FL	47.7	52.3	85.1	14.9	86.7	13.3	84.5	15.5	87.0	13.0
Jersey City, NJ	47.4	52.6	80.7	19.3	85.3	14.7	85.5	14.5	85.5	14.5
Kansas City, MO	52.2	47.8	86.7	13.3	88.6	11.4	89.0	11.0	88.4	11.6
Kenosha, WI	55.9	44.1	84.4	15.6	88.0	12.0	88.8	11.2	90.0	10.0
Las Vegas, NV	56.2	43.8	92.4	7.6	93.6	6.4	95.6	4.4	95.2	4.8
Lexington, KY	46.8	53.2	86.6	13.4	88.2	11.8	86.9	13.1	89.0	11.0
Lincoln, NE	44.0	56.0	85.1	14.9	82.9	17.1	81.0	19.0	85.2	14.8

Table continued on next page.

Metro Area	Preschool (%) Public	Preschool (%) Private	Kindergarten (%) Public	Kindergarten (%) Private	Grades 1 - 4 (%) Public	Grades 1 - 4 (%) Private	Grades 5 - 8 (%) Public	Grades 5 - 8 (%) Private	Grades 9 - 12 (%) Public	Grades 9 - 12 (%) Private
Little Rock, AR	54.0	46.0	87.3	12.7	89.4	10.6	88.8	11.2	86.6	13.4
Los Angeles, CA	57.7	42.3	87.4	12.6	90.2	9.8	90.3	9.7	91.8	8.2
Madison, WI	45.6	54.4	88.2	11.8	88.9	11.1	91.3	8.7	93.9	6.1
Manchester, NH	34.0	66.0	66.0	34.0	91.0	9.0	89.4	10.6	91.3	8.7
Miami, FL	44.6	55.4	82.0	18.0	87.2	12.8	87.3	12.7	88.1	11.9
Minneapolis, MN	53.0	47.0	86.6	13.4	87.2	12.8	87.7	12.3	90.8	9.2
Murfreesboro, TN	44.0	56.0	84.7	15.3	87.6	12.4	85.2	14.8	84.8	15.2
Naperville, IL	55.9	44.1	84.4	15.6	88.0	12.0	88.8	11.2	90.0	10.0
Nashville, TN	44.0	56.0	84.7	15.3	87.6	12.4	85.2	14.8	84.8	15.2
New Orleans, LA	50.4	49.6	67.6	32.4	75.5	24.5	72.9	27.1	74.0	26.0
New York, NY	47.4	52.6	80.7	19.3	85.3	14.7	85.5	14.5	85.5	14.5
Norman, OK	69.1	30.9	87.6	12.4	91.2	8.8	91.4	8.6	92.1	7.9
Olathe, KS	52.2	47.8	86.7	13.3	88.6	11.4	89.0	11.0	88.4	11.6
Omaha, NE	52.3	47.7	83.9	16.1	84.4	15.6	85.1	14.9	87.6	12.4
Orlando, FL	44.9	55.1	82.3	17.7	87.4	12.6	89.1	10.9	90.2	9.8
Overland Park, KS	52.2	47.8	86.7	13.3	88.6	11.4	89.0	11.0	88.4	11.6
Oyster Bay, NY	47.4	52.6	80.7	19.3	85.3	14.7	85.5	14.5	85.5	14.5
Pembroke Pines, FL	44.6	55.4	82.0	18.0	87.2	12.8	87.3	12.7	88.1	11.9
Philadelphia, PA	42.3	57.7	76.9	23.1	83.1	16.9	82.5	17.5	83.5	16.5
Phoenix, AZ	55.9	44.1	91.0	9.0	92.9	7.1	94.0	6.0	94.4	5.6
Pittsburgh, PA	46.5	53.5	85.1	14.9	87.6	12.4	88.1	11.9	90.5	9.5
Plano, TX	51.9	48.1	89.1	10.9	91.6	8.4	92.4	7.6	92.6	7.4
Portland, OR	38.0	62.0	84.0	16.0	89.4	10.6	90.9	9.1	91.4	8.6
Providence, RI	48.7	51.3	84.2	15.8	89.2	10.8	89.3	10.7	87.7	12.3
Provo, UT	41.2	58.8	92.4	7.6	94.9	5.1	94.6	5.4	93.5	6.5
Raleigh, NC	33.0	67.0	85.8	14.2	89.3	10.7	89.6	10.4	90.6	9.4
Richmond, VA	34.8	65.2	90.7	9.3	91.6	8.4	91.1	8.9	91.6	8.4
Roseville, CA	52.9	47.1	86.9	13.1	90.6	9.4	91.8	8.2	91.5	8.5
Round Rock, TX	50.0	50.0	90.8	9.2	92.4	7.6	93.0	7.0	93.2	6.8
San Antonio, TX	64.1	35.9	89.5	10.5	92.6	7.4	92.3	7.7	93.3	6.7
San Diego, CA	52.5	47.5	90.2	9.8	91.5	8.5	91.6	8.4	93.0	7.0
San Francisco, CA	39.6	60.4	84.3	15.7	85.0	15.0	85.6	14.4	87.4	12.6
San Jose, CA	35.0	65.0	83.1	16.9	86.2	13.8	88.3	11.7	89.3	10.7
Savannah, GA	58.7	41.3	84.1	15.9	86.2	13.8	85.5	14.5	86.0	14.0
Scottsdale, AZ	55.9	44.1	91.0	9.0	92.9	7.1	94.0	6.0	94.4	5.6
Seattle, WA	39.5	60.5	84.9	15.1	89.0	11.0	88.7	11.3	89.9	10.1
Sioux Falls, SD	61.1	38.9	89.4	10.6	89.7	10.3	87.9	12.1	91.7	8.3
Stamford, CT	40.8	59.2	84.2	15.8	86.5	13.5	84.6	15.4	84.8	15.2
Sterling Hgts, MI	64.9	35.1	87.5	12.5	89.4	10.6	90.4	9.6	91.7	8.3
Sunnyvale, CA	35.0	65.0	83.1	16.9	86.2	13.8	88.3	11.7	89.3	10.7
Tampa, FL	54.8	45.2	86.4	13.6	88.7	11.3	88.6	11.4	91.6	8.4
Temecula, CA	63.5	36.5	92.3	7.7	94.1	5.9	93.7	6.3	93.9	6.1
Thousand Oaks, CA	46.9	53.1	89.9	10.1	91.2	8.8	90.2	9.8	92.4	7.6
Virginia Beach, VA	49.1	50.9	84.5	15.5	89.4	10.6	89.9	10.1	92.2	7.8
Washington, DC	38.6	61.4	82.1	17.9	86.5	13.5	87.0	13.0	88.9	11.1
U.S.	55.4	44.6	87.1	12.9	89.4	10.6	89.5	10.5	90.4	9.6

Note: Figures shown cover persons 3 years old and over; Figures cover the Metropolitan Statistical Area—see Appendix B for areas included;
Source: U.S. Census Bureau, 2008-2010 American Community Survey 3-Year Estimates

Educational Attainment by Race: City

City	High School Graduate or Higher (%)					Bachelor's Degree or Higher (%)				
	Total	White	Black	Asian	Hisp.[1]	Total	White	Black	Asian	Hisp.[1]
Albuquerque, NM	87.3	89.2	94.2	82.4	75.9	32.0	35.5	28.8	44.7	16.7
Alexandria, VA	90.3	94.5	84.1	93.3	64.6	58.5	69.8	29.2	67.6	28.1
Anchorage, AK	92.5	95.2	90.8	81.1	80.1	32.9	37.4	21.2	25.3	22.7
Ann Arbor, MI	96.8	97.6	91.5	96.1	97.4	70.8	72.7	35.7	85.4	57.0
Athens, GA	83.1	87.7	73.2	94.8	43.7	40.5	52.6	11.1	82.1	13.1
Atlanta, GA	86.6	96.3	79.0	93.8	68.8	45.5	74.0	20.5	77.0	29.2
Austin, TX	85.1	89.8	85.9	92.6	60.6	43.9	49.8	20.8	70.0	17.6
Baltimore, MD	78.3	83.7	75.2	90.7	62.6	25.2	45.4	12.5	74.4	20.2
Bellevue, WA	95.7	96.5	100.0	94.9	72.3	61.2	58.7	43.6	72.2	29.8
Billings, MT	92.2	93.2	n/a	n/a	72.6	31.0	32.2	n/a	n/a	13.9
Boise City, ID	93.2	93.9	73.3	88.8	72.5	36.8	36.7	16.0	53.6	20.4
Boston, MA	84.5	91.9	80.0	74.0	63.8	43.1	57.3	19.4	45.3	17.1
Boulder, CO	94.9	96.7	n/a	93.9	55.7	69.7	71.3	n/a	79.4	25.5
Broken Arrow, OK	93.3	94.6	91.6	85.4	77.5	31.3	31.4	35.5	43.5	22.1
Cambridge, MA	94.2	96.1	83.3	94.6	83.4	73.1	78.7	34.0	82.8	52.4
Cape Coral, FL	88.3	88.6	82.5	87.7	78.6	20.6	20.5	18.1	36.3	19.6
Carlsbad, CA	95.4	96.0	n/a	97.1	74.6	50.7	50.1	n/a	67.4	27.3
Cary, NC	95.2	96.3	98.8	95.5	63.6	62.3	63.0	45.5	81.3	16.1
Cedar Rapids, IA	92.7	93.6	80.0	88.7	81.8	30.4	30.7	18.1	57.6	16.9
Charleston, SC	90.8	95.1	78.1	91.9	72.8	46.8	55.8	19.0	60.9	20.7
Charlotte, NC	87.4	91.5	85.3	84.3	54.9	38.7	48.4	23.3	54.0	14.4
Chesapeake, VA	89.4	91.9	84.8	86.6	77.2	28.4	30.7	21.7	44.7	25.1
Chicago, IL	79.9	84.7	80.2	86.0	57.2	32.9	45.1	17.5	56.3	11.8
Clarksville, TN	91.2	91.5	91.7	89.5	84.4	21.7	23.4	16.5	30.5	18.8
Colorado Spgs., CO	92.4	93.6	90.9	86.2	75.8	36.1	38.8	19.2	36.5	13.4
Columbia, MD	93.9	95.4	93.1	92.9	66.2	60.2	64.4	44.9	75.2	34.8
Columbia, MO	93.2	94.6	82.6	93.6	84.2	52.2	55.3	19.6	74.1	39.1
Columbia, SC	85.4	94.9	74.1	n/a	90.1	38.5	57.7	14.9	n/a	23.2
Columbus, OH	87.7	89.2	84.9	89.2	65.0	32.3	36.7	16.9	62.5	14.9
Dallas, TX	73.1	76.1	81.3	85.5	42.2	28.8	38.8	13.7	58.5	7.6
Denver, CO	84.2	86.6	85.6	83.1	55.5	40.6	46.0	19.7	50.0	10.8
Durham, NC	85.9	93.7	82.9	95.3	49.7	46.5	61.3	30.1	82.9	17.8
Edison, NJ	92.1	91.7	90.2	93.3	82.3	51.1	31.8	37.1	77.2	22.4
El Paso, TX	74.7	75.2	93.7	88.2	69.1	21.9	22.3	27.0	55.5	17.3
Fargo, ND	94.1	95.3	63.5	84.1	85.4	38.6	39.2	14.5	49.4	21.9
Ft. Collins, CO	95.1	95.7	n/a	97.5	76.5	50.8	52.1	n/a	61.7	22.6
Ft. Worth, TX	78.3	82.1	83.3	84.8	47.9	25.6	30.4	16.0	41.5	8.2
Gilbert, AZ	95.9	96.5	96.1	92.0	87.7	37.6	37.6	29.3	51.0	24.7
Green Bay, WI	85.0	86.6	71.8	66.8	32.8	20.6	21.3	13.7	24.1	6.2
Henderson, NV	92.7	92.8	93.6	95.6	80.3	30.8	30.4	23.0	53.0	18.1
High Point, NC	85.4	89.4	80.6	81.5	70.2	28.5	35.0	14.7	44.7	21.9
Honolulu, HI	88.2	95.7	95.6	84.9	87.2	33.3	47.7	26.9	32.0	24.4
Houston, TX	74.1	74.2	82.6	84.1	48.7	28.2	33.5	17.2	53.4	9.6
Huntington, NY	92.3	94.5	85.9	91.9	66.2	47.0	49.0	30.5	62.0	18.5
Huntsville, AL	87.4	89.8	81.2	89.8	47.3	37.6	42.7	21.6	67.2	12.0
Indianapolis, IN	83.8	86.0	82.8	83.6	45.7	27.4	32.2	15.0	54.6	8.6
Irvine, CA	95.9	96.3	90.4	96.3	85.7	65.7	60.6	32.7	77.8	41.2
Jackson, MS	81.9	91.7	79.1	n/a	45.9	26.7	51.5	18.6	n/a	20.9
Jacksonville, FL	86.8	89.3	82.5	85.3	75.8	23.8	26.1	15.3	44.6	19.4
Jersey City, NJ	84.1	83.8	80.9	92.0	72.0	41.2	42.9	20.3	70.2	17.5
Kansas City, MO	86.5	90.9	81.4	79.4	57.6	29.9	38.4	13.2	40.2	11.1
Kenosha, WI	86.8	88.5	77.0	n/a	64.1	21.9	21.9	19.7	n/a	7.6
Las Vegas, NV	81.3	81.0	84.8	90.9	52.9	20.6	20.8	14.6	38.5	7.4
Lexington, KY	88.4	90.9	80.8	95.3	53.5	38.7	42.0	16.9	75.2	13.5
Lincoln, NE	92.7	94.3	83.1	72.6	68.6	34.8	35.0	22.5	48.4	21.1

Table continued on next page.

City	High School Graduate or Higher (%)					Bachelor's Degree or Higher (%)				
	Total	White	Black	Asian	Hisp.[1]	Total	White	Black	Asian	Hisp.[1]
Little Rock, AR	88.0	91.3	83.9	96.2	51.7	36.6	47.2	18.5	73.0	10.9
Los Angeles, CA	73.7	78.3	85.6	88.6	48.8	30.4	36.0	21.7	50.3	9.2
Madison, WI	94.1	95.8	78.4	88.3	76.7	52.0	53.8	18.3	69.8	25.4
Manchester, NH	85.5	86.8	78.7	78.3	66.8	26.1	26.5	19.9	38.0	20.1
Miami, FL	68.0	69.5	61.2	84.9	64.8	22.6	25.1	9.8	60.4	19.3
Minneapolis, MN	87.8	92.9	71.1	75.3	53.2	43.6	51.5	12.9	42.5	14.7
Murfreesboro, TN	89.5	91.7	89.4	84.3	57.2	34.7	37.1	28.3	34.4	13.8
Naperville, IL	96.9	97.3	96.3	96.4	83.3	65.5	63.4	55.4	82.6	39.1
Nashville, TN	84.8	87.3	82.0	85.2	51.2	33.3	37.8	22.6	46.8	9.6
New Orleans, LA	84.7	94.1	80.0	65.2	72.2	32.2	57.1	15.5	34.2	31.7
New York, NY	79.0	85.0	79.8	74.1	62.5	33.4	43.4	20.5	40.5	15.0
Norman, OK	92.4	92.9	91.3	94.0	80.8	42.8	42.3	42.0	75.9	27.1
Olathe, KS	94.2	94.9	97.1	87.8	69.2	45.2	46.2	27.1	60.3	21.5
Omaha, NE	88.2	90.9	85.3	88.0	45.1	32.0	35.7	12.6	58.9	8.8
Orlando, FL	87.2	91.6	79.2	82.8	78.1	31.1	38.2	15.8	42.5	18.9
Overland Park, KS	96.4	97.1	93.2	90.9	80.6	57.0	57.1	41.3	71.2	34.6
Oyster Bay, NY	93.8	94.1	88.0	93.3	85.2	44.0	42.6	43.1	64.8	24.7
Pembroke Pines, FL	88.4	88.0	89.5	87.4	84.9	31.7	29.8	33.4	52.2	29.4
Philadelphia, PA	79.7	84.2	79.3	67.4	60.0	22.4	32.2	11.8	33.4	10.2
Phoenix, AZ	79.8	80.6	86.5	85.6	54.2	25.3	26.1	19.8	52.1	7.5
Pittsburgh, PA	89.2	90.7	83.9	96.7	86.9	34.5	38.7	15.2	82.0	42.9
Plano, TX	93.2	92.6	96.6	96.1	66.3	53.9	50.7	47.4	76.1	22.6
Portland, OR	89.6	92.7	83.1	75.7	59.3	42.4	45.9	21.3	36.4	20.5
Providence, RI	72.1	79.5	73.2	67.6	53.5	28.3	40.3	19.4	35.6	7.4
Provo, UT	91.9	93.6	n/a	96.5	67.6	39.9	41.3	n/a	52.6	16.1
Raleigh, NC	90.7	93.8	88.6	86.3	57.2	47.0	55.7	29.8	59.9	14.7
Richmond, VA	79.9	87.9	73.0	79.1	31.8	33.3	55.6	12.3	58.3	8.0
Roseville, CA	93.7	94.4	89.8	92.9	79.4	33.9	32.8	29.3	48.8	17.5
Round Rock, TX	89.5	89.7	93.3	89.4	70.0	34.0	34.6	23.5	64.0	15.9
San Antonio, TX	79.4	80.7	85.5	87.6	70.0	23.6	25.1	19.9	53.1	12.8
San Diego, CA	86.4	87.5	89.4	87.5	62.4	40.8	43.0	22.8	48.2	16.5
San Francisco, CA	85.5	93.3	87.1	73.6	73.7	51.2	63.9	23.9	38.7	28.4
San Jose, CA	81.9	85.0	89.4	85.1	62.0	36.4	34.7	28.4	49.3	11.9
Savannah, GA	84.2	90.3	79.4	78.2	63.7	23.5	36.3	12.4	33.0	18.3
Scottsdale, AZ	95.6	96.0	93.9	94.5	75.1	52.0	51.6	49.7	76.4	33.7
Seattle, WA	92.9	96.1	80.9	81.9	78.6	55.8	61.5	22.3	48.9	34.7
Sioux Falls, SD	90.6	92.7	72.0	75.7	60.6	31.7	33.5	10.6	34.2	8.1
Stamford, CT	85.2	91.5	76.8	93.7	64.3	41.3	48.1	16.6	73.9	16.0
Sterling Hgts, MI	84.7	84.7	89.0	86.2	79.4	26.1	23.8	22.9	58.1	39.7
Sunnyvale, CA	91.2	93.5	97.5	95.5	60.7	56.6	49.0	21.5	75.9	16.0
Tampa, FL	84.6	87.6	78.2	84.9	71.8	31.7	37.2	13.3	59.5	16.2
Temecula, CA	91.3	92.9	97.9	86.6	75.9	30.0	31.8	27.4	31.8	19.4
Thousand Oaks, CA	94.0	95.4	94.5	95.5	73.4	48.9	48.0	59.9	72.8	23.7
Virginia Beach, VA	92.8	93.8	89.9	90.3	85.7	31.4	33.5	20.4	39.6	17.7
Washington, DC	87.1	94.1	81.8	93.7	60.3	49.8	81.2	21.9	79.2	35.1
U.S.	85.3	87.5	81.4	85.5	61.6	28.0	29.3	17.8	50.2	13.0

Note: Figures shown cover persons 25 years old and over; (1) People of Hispanic origin can be of any race
Source: U.S. Census Bureau, 2008-2010 American Community Survey 3-Year Estimates

Educational Attainment by Race: Metro Area

Metro Area	High School Graduate or Higher (%)					Bachelor's Degree or Higher (%)				
	Total	White	Black	Asian	Hisp.[1]	Total	White	Black	Asian	Hisp.[1]
Albuquerque, NM	86.6	88.9	93.6	84.1	75.4	29.3	33.1	27.9	44.3	15.1
Alexandria, VA	89.5	92.6	88.8	89.6	62.4	46.9	54.7	29.2	60.6	22.4
Anchorage, AK	92.4	94.6	90.8	80.1	80.7	30.2	33.4	20.3	25.0	22.0
Ann Arbor, MI	93.9	94.9	87.2	94.6	87.4	50.6	51.6	27.1	80.5	38.8
Athens, GA	81.5	84.9	68.6	96.0	43.8	34.5	39.8	10.3	79.8	13.3
Atlanta, GA	87.4	89.0	88.1	87.4	59.0	34.5	38.4	26.3	52.9	15.7
Austin, TX	87.3	90.5	87.9	91.6	64.5	39.2	42.5	21.8	66.4	16.9
Baltimore, MD	87.8	90.2	82.4	89.8	68.0	34.8	38.9	20.5	63.0	25.3
Bellevue, WA	91.2	93.2	87.7	85.9	67.4	37.0	37.7	20.0	48.8	17.1
Billings, MT	91.8	92.4	n/a	80.1	74.8	29.3	29.8	n/a	33.6	14.6
Boise City, ID	89.0	89.7	80.9	86.7	56.3	28.0	28.2	15.1	49.2	9.6
Boston, MA	90.3	92.9	82.3	83.2	66.4	42.4	44.4	22.9	56.9	18.4
Boulder, CO	93.7	95.6	91.0	94.0	62.0	57.9	59.5	44.1	72.0	22.2
Broken Arrow, OK	87.9	89.0	86.0	82.8	60.1	25.1	26.7	17.4	41.8	10.9
Cambridge, MA	90.3	92.9	82.3	83.2	66.4	42.4	44.4	22.9	56.9	18.4
Cape Coral, FL	86.8	89.0	73.3	86.7	65.3	24.4	25.5	13.1	41.6	13.8
Carlsbad, CA	85.1	86.1	90.1	88.0	61.9	34.1	34.9	22.8	45.8	14.5
Cary, NC	89.8	92.2	86.9	91.9	55.1	41.7	45.4	26.7	69.2	13.9
Cedar Rapids, IA	92.9	93.6	79.7	84.4	81.0	27.8	27.9	18.0	49.9	17.2
Charleston, SC	87.5	91.1	79.0	84.9	64.7	30.4	36.4	14.4	41.3	14.6
Charlotte, NC	86.4	88.7	83.6	84.6	56.8	32.2	35.4	21.5	53.1	15.8
Chesapeake, VA	89.2	91.9	83.6	88.3	83.6	27.7	31.9	17.3	39.9	20.4
Chicago, IL	86.1	89.5	83.5	90.7	60.2	33.8	37.3	19.5	62.2	12.1
Clarksville, TN	87.8	88.4	87.0	85.2	83.1	18.5	19.8	12.5	32.0	16.2
Colorado Spgs., CO	93.0	94.1	92.5	84.4	78.6	35.1	37.3	21.6	35.6	15.3
Columbia, MD	87.8	90.2	82.4	89.8	68.0	34.8	38.9	20.5	63.0	25.3
Columbia, MO	91.5	92.7	79.5	93.9	84.1	44.1	45.9	17.0	73.5	35.0
Columbia, SC	87.7	90.7	82.9	85.8	62.2	30.0	34.9	19.3	59.2	16.0
Columbus, OH	89.7	90.7	85.3	91.1	69.3	32.9	34.2	18.9	64.9	18.8
Dallas, TX	82.9	85.4	87.2	87.8	51.7	30.9	33.2	22.2	55.8	10.5
Denver, CO	89.0	91.1	87.5	84.8	62.5	38.1	40.8	22.0	46.1	12.6
Durham, NC	86.6	91.3	82.1	91.4	48.4	43.6	50.7	26.8	76.7	15.9
Edison, NJ	84.3	88.6	81.5	82.2	65.9	35.8	40.1	21.4	52.4	15.9
El Paso, TX	71.9	72.5	92.1	86.8	66.3	19.8	20.2	25.7	54.0	15.3
Fargo, ND	93.8	94.6	68.5	83.9	73.3	34.9	35.3	16.8	46.4	15.1
Ft. Collins, CO	93.6	94.3	90.1	98.0	67.8	43.0	43.8	27.4	61.6	16.3
Ft. Worth, TX	82.9	85.4	87.2	87.8	51.7	30.9	33.2	22.2	55.8	10.5
Gilbert, AZ	85.6	86.7	89.3	89.3	60.3	27.8	28.5	23.0	53.4	10.1
Green Bay, WI	89.6	90.5	75.2	78.3	41.7	22.9	23.1	16.5	30.4	7.6
Henderson, NV	83.4	83.4	87.0	89.7	57.9	21.8	21.5	16.2	38.6	8.2
High Point, NC	83.8	85.6	83.2	73.4	55.0	25.7	27.9	19.1	36.0	13.5
Honolulu, HI	90.3	96.2	97.1	87.3	89.6	31.2	44.7	26.4	31.7	21.4
Houston, TX	80.4	81.6	86.6	85.6	55.2	28.4	30.0	21.7	51.6	10.7
Huntington, NY	84.3	88.6	81.5	82.2	65.9	35.8	40.1	21.4	52.4	15.9
Huntsville, AL	86.8	87.7	83.5	90.6	53.3	33.9	35.4	25.6	60.6	15.2
Indianapolis, IN	88.1	89.7	83.6	88.8	52.7	30.9	33.1	16.8	59.6	12.6
Irvine, CA	77.6	81.4	87.7	86.6	54.8	30.7	33.4	23.2	49.0	10.2
Jackson, MS	85.2	90.6	79.1	80.3	48.9	28.7	35.5	19.4	62.0	16.0
Jacksonville, FL	88.3	90.2	82.6	86.7	77.8	26.2	28.4	15.4	45.5	20.5
Jersey City, NJ	84.3	88.6	81.5	82.2	65.9	35.8	40.1	21.4	52.4	15.9
Kansas City, MO	90.0	91.7	85.0	84.2	62.6	32.5	34.8	17.4	52.4	13.7
Kenosha, WI	86.1	89.5	83.5	90.7	60.2	33.8	37.3	19.5	62.2	12.1
Las Vegas, NV	83.4	83.4	87.0	89.7	57.9	21.8	21.5	16.2	38.6	8.2
Lexington, KY	87.1	88.7	81.0	94.8	57.2	33.3	34.9	16.8	71.3	12.0
Lincoln, NE	93.1	94.4	83.5	72.9	69.0	34.7	34.8	22.8	49.0	22.3

Table continued on next page.

Metro Area	High School Graduate or Higher (%)					Bachelor's Degree or Higher (%)				
	Total	White	Black	Asian	Hisp.[1]	Total	White	Black	Asian	Hisp.[1]
Little Rock, AR	87.8	89.1	83.6	91.1	62.8	26.0	27.9	16.7	57.4	13.4
Los Angeles, CA	77.6	81.4	87.7	86.6	54.8	30.7	33.4	23.2	49.0	10.2
Madison, WI	94.0	94.8	79.9	90.9	72.7	41.5	41.9	16.8	66.4	19.8
Manchester, NH	90.3	90.9	83.7	86.4	67.3	34.4	33.9	25.4	62.2	21.9
Miami, FL	82.7	84.6	76.4	85.9	75.0	28.5	31.1	17.3	46.7	23.6
Minneapolis, MN	92.6	94.7	80.3	80.4	62.2	37.7	39.2	19.8	43.4	16.4
Murfreesboro, TN	86.2	87.5	82.8	86.6	56.7	30.0	31.4	22.6	45.2	11.9
Naperville, IL	86.1	89.5	83.5	90.7	60.2	33.8	37.3	19.5	62.2	12.1
Nashville, TN	86.2	87.5	82.8	86.6	56.7	30.0	31.4	22.6	45.2	11.9
New Orleans, LA	84.6	88.5	79.4	70.7	71.8	26.2	31.7	14.9	31.5	20.2
New York, NY	84.3	88.6	81.5	82.2	65.9	35.8	40.1	21.4	52.4	15.9
Norman, OK	87.2	89.2	86.2	80.4	55.4	26.9	28.4	19.0	43.4	10.1
Olathe, KS	90.0	91.7	85.0	84.2	62.6	32.5	34.8	17.4	52.4	13.7
Omaha, NE	90.9	92.6	86.6	88.9	52.7	32.4	33.9	15.8	56.0	11.9
Orlando, FL	87.6	89.5	81.3	86.3	79.2	27.3	28.8	18.2	44.1	18.4
Overland Park, KS	90.0	91.7	85.0	84.2	62.6	32.5	34.8	17.4	52.4	13.7
Oyster Bay, NY	84.3	88.6	81.5	82.2	65.9	35.8	40.1	21.4	52.4	15.9
Pembroke Pines, FL	82.7	84.6	76.4	85.9	75.0	28.5	31.1	17.3	46.7	23.6
Philadelphia, PA	88.0	90.7	82.6	82.3	64.3	32.7	36.3	16.7	53.5	15.0
Phoenix, AZ	85.6	86.7	89.3	89.3	60.3	27.8	28.5	23.0	53.4	10.1
Pittsburgh, PA	91.1	91.5	86.2	91.4	84.6	28.7	29.0	15.6	71.4	33.7
Plano, TX	82.9	85.4	87.2	87.8	51.7	30.9	33.2	22.2	55.8	10.5
Portland, OR	90.1	92.2	85.0	84.7	58.8	33.6	34.4	24.0	45.5	13.5
Providence, RI	82.8	84.3	75.6	80.9	60.3	28.3	29.4	19.8	43.8	11.7
Provo, UT	93.6	94.6	88.1	92.0	73.1	34.7	35.1	35.0	46.0	18.5
Raleigh, NC	89.8	92.2	86.9	91.9	55.1	41.7	45.4	26.7	69.2	13.9
Richmond, VA	85.3	88.8	78.0	84.0	53.5	31.0	36.1	17.4	54.8	15.4
Roseville, CA	87.0	90.3	86.9	80.8	65.8	29.7	31.3	18.4	38.4	14.1
Round Rock, TX	87.3	90.5	87.9	91.6	64.5	39.2	42.5	21.8	66.4	16.9
San Antonio, TX	82.2	83.5	87.5	86.4	71.0	25.3	26.6	22.7	50.1	13.3
San Diego, CA	85.1	86.1	90.1	88.0	61.9	34.1	34.9	22.8	45.8	14.5
San Francisco, CA	87.1	90.8	87.4	83.8	66.6	43.5	47.9	23.0	48.8	16.9
San Jose, CA	85.9	88.4	91.2	89.2	62.8	44.5	42.4	29.6	59.4	13.3
Savannah, GA	87.6	90.6	82.3	80.9	70.4	27.2	33.0	14.6	31.1	19.8
Scottsdale, AZ	85.6	86.7	89.3	89.3	60.3	27.8	28.5	23.0	53.4	10.1
Seattle, WA	91.2	93.2	87.7	85.9	67.4	37.0	37.7	20.0	48.8	17.1
Sioux Falls, SD	91.7	93.2	72.8	75.0	62.8	30.1	31.3	10.9	32.7	10.0
Stamford, CT	88.2	91.1	79.4	88.9	66.0	43.7	47.9	17.9	64.4	16.0
Sterling Hgts, MI	87.6	89.6	82.2	88.1	66.6	27.0	29.0	15.5	63.0	16.0
Sunnyvale, CA	85.9	88.4	91.2	89.2	62.8	44.5	42.4	29.6	59.4	13.3
Tampa, FL	86.8	87.9	80.6	84.0	74.2	25.5	25.9	17.7	47.3	16.8
Temecula, CA	78.3	80.5	88.0	89.1	59.4	19.4	19.5	20.1	46.7	8.1
Thousand Oaks, CA	82.3	86.6	92.8	92.0	56.5	30.6	32.8	27.5	54.9	10.0
Virginia Beach, VA	89.2	91.9	83.6	88.3	83.6	27.7	31.9	17.3	39.9	20.4
Washington, DC	89.5	92.6	88.8	89.6	62.4	46.9	54.7	29.2	60.6	22.4
U.S.	85.3	87.5	81.4	85.5	61.6	28.0	29.3	17.8	50.2	13.0

Note: Figures shown cover persons 25 years old and over; Figures cover the Metropolitan Statistical Area—see Appendix B for areas included; (1) People of Hispanic origin can be of any race
Source: U.S. Census Bureau, 2008-2010 American Community Survey 3-Year Estimates

Cost of Living Index

Urban Area	Composite	Groceries	Housing	Utilities	Transp.	Health	Misc.
Albuquerque[1], NM	94.7	94.5	87.0	98.6	94.4	100.9	99.6
Alexandria[2], VA	143.5	111.4	241.2	103.9	108.1	101.0	100.7
Anchorage, AK	130.8	137.6	150.2	98.2	112.0	139.1	126.3
Ann Arbor, MI	101.0	98.8	105.4	107.7	100.4	97.3	96.4
Athens, GA	n/a	n/a	n/a	n/a	n/a	n/a	n/a
Atlanta, GA	97.4	101.7	89.4	93.4	102.1	101.0	101.8
Austin, TX	92.8	85.0	82.3	99.1	101.1	102.1	99.3
Baltimore, MD	119.2	109.4	160.3	115.3	103.9	96.5	96.5
Bellevue[3], WA	117.2	111.7	129.5	90.4	112.4	118.4	118.7
Billings, MT	n/a	n/a	n/a	n/a	n/a	n/a	n/a
Boise City, ID	96.1	101.3	83.7	97.2	101.3	101.4	102.2
Boston, MA	137.4	118.9	160.6	147.3	106.8	121.1	133.6
Boulder, CO	n/a	n/a	n/a	n/a	n/a	n/a	n/a
Broken Arrow[4], OK	90.1	92.3	69.1	96.9	101.3	99.2	100.5
Cambridge[5], MA	137.4	118.9	160.6	147.3	106.8	121.1	133.6
Cape Coral, FL	95.6	105.2	90.5	81.1	101.8	99.1	98.2
Carlsbad[6], CA	130.8	107.4	189.1	113.0	111.2	112.4	103.6
Cary[7], NC	93.8	101.4	79.9	104.5	96.6	100.3	97.8
Cedar Rapids, IA	93.7	97.4	78.9	101.3	96.7	94.5	101.6
Charleston, SC	99.8	107.6	90.3	107.5	98.3	108.7	101.7
Charlotte, NC	93.3	100.2	82.1	92.7	98.2	105.0	97.4
Chesapeake[8], VA	105.4	100.3	114.0	110.9	97.7	102.3	101.1
Chicago, IL	114.8	114.5	134.2	97.6	114.6	106.9	104.6
Clarksville, TN	97.6	90.9	89.5	93.5	93.0	99.8	110.0
Colorado Springs, CO	92.6	94.1	89.3	89.8	96.8	102.2	93.1
Columbia[9], MD	119.2	109.4	160.3	115.3	103.9	96.5	96.5
Columbia, MO	91.2	95.6	80.7	90.7	96.2	96.0	96.7
Columbia, SC	95.6	104.7	78.7	106.6	104.0	101.2	99.7
Columbus, OH	90.3	94.4	77.1	99.9	99.0	101.8	92.9
Dallas, TX	96.3	100.7	75.4	108.1	105.0	104.5	105.0
Denver, CO	105.1	102.7	113.2	90.0	95.1	106.5	106.9
Durham, NC	92.7	98.8	78.5	92.7	104.0	100.5	98.0
Edison[10], NJ	126.1	110.3	154.7	131.3	102.4	110.2	115.6
El Paso, TX	91.0	100.8	90.9	81.8	94.0	92.5	88.8
Fargo, ND	93.3	103.9	84.4	89.3	97.0	102.6	95.5
Fort Collins, CO	n/a	n/a	n/a	n/a	n/a	n/a	n/a
Fort Worth, TX	93.2	92.1	79.2	110.8	102.1	96.3	96.9
Gilbert[11], AZ	96.6	103.9	87.4	100.3	102.9	102.6	97.6
Green Bay, WI	94.9	87.4	84.3	107.3	102.3	110.1	98.7
Henderson[12], NV	100.2	105.1	92.5	91.4	103.8	106.4	105.8
High Point, NC	n/a	n/a	n/a	n/a	n/a	n/a	n/a
Honolulu, HI	168.0	155.8	252.5	161.8	125.9	123.4	120.4
Houston, TX	89.9	80.8	83.3	89.3	95.3	98.1	96.8
Huntington[13], NY	138.6	118.9	188.5	138.6	109.8	110.5	116.0
Huntsville, AL	93.7	95.9	78.7	96.2	101.8	95.0	102.4
Indianapolis, IN	n/a	n/a	n/a	n/a	n/a	n/a	n/a
Irvine[14], CA	142.9	108.2	230.3	112.8	112.0	109.0	104.4
Jackson, MS	96.7	91.3	95.1	124.3	94.9	98.4	91.7
Jacksonville, FL	94.0	100.5	82.9	101.5	106.4	88.5	95.2
Jersey City[15], NJ	131.4	106.2	171.0	135.0	103.9	103.8	118.4
Kansas City, MO	99.5	98.9	90.1	110.1	98.7	97.0	105.1
Kenosha[16], WI	99.4	94.5	104.5	109.6	101.2	110.2	91.5
Las Vegas, NV	100.2	105.1	92.5	91.4	103.8	106.4	105.8
Lexington, KY	91.9	91.9	82.8	94.5	97.1	98.8	96.6
Lincoln, NE	93.5	95.2	84.6	103.8	106.8	94.8	92.8
Little Rock, AR	95.8	94.5	89.3	105.4	95.0	90.8	99.8

Table continued on next page.

Urban Area	Composite	Groceries	Housing	Utilities	Transp.	Health	Misc.
Los Angeles, CA	133.0	107.6	197.3	112.3	109.0	110.0	104.5
Madison, WI	108.2	100.8	112.7	103.5	109.8	117.4	107.0
Manchester, NH	119.9	101.7	126.6	127.1	99.7	110.8	127.1
Miami, FL	107.2	107.4	112.0	94.3	109.0	106.3	106.4
Minneapolis, MN	110.7	108.2	119.1	100.7	104.9	102.9	110.6
Murfreesboro, TN	88.2	94.7	78.4	84.0	95.6	89.2	93.0
Naperville[17], IL	100.0	98.1	99.1	103.3	106.4	104.4	97.7
Nashville, TN	90.3	97.5	70.6	87.1	93.4	91.6	104.6
New Orleans[18], LA	95.7	95.9	95.2	89.3	99.1	91.2	97.7
New York, NY	219.2	148.8	414.6	143.6	122.9	127.7	144.1
Norman, OK	91.6	94.1	85.7	81.8	104.2	93.2	94.7
Olathe[19], KS	99.5	98.9	90.1	110.1	98.7	97.0	105.1
Omaha, NE	89.5	94.2	80.5	92.3	100.6	98.2	89.7
Orlando, FL	97.3	100.2	79.7	107.8	99.2	94.2	108.1
Overland Park[20], KS	99.5	98.9	90.1	110.1	98.7	97.0	105.1
Oyster Bay[21], NY	138.6	118.9	188.5	138.6	109.8	110.5	116.0
Pembroke Pines[22], FL	111.1	106.8	128.7	94.3	108.2	103.1	104.9
Philadelphia, PA	125.1	124.6	140.6	129.9	107.7	104.6	118.6
Phoenix, AZ	96.6	103.9	87.4	100.3	102.9	102.6	97.6
Pittsburgh, PA	94.9	104.9	76.9	100.6	111.3	93.7	99.6
Plano, TX	96.7	101.8	85.1	106.3	102.3	103.2	99.2
Portland, OR	113.7	111.3	131.0	88.3	113.7	113.7	107.6
Providence, RI	125.7	111.4	134.6	129.6	104.3	111.8	131.5
Provo, UT	90.1	89.6	82.3	82.8	93.9	89.2	98.4
Raleigh, NC	93.8	101.4	79.9	104.5	96.6	100.3	97.8
Richmond, VA	100.2	104.5	95.4	108.5	101.9	108.5	98.3
Roseville[23], CA	116.3	109.7	138.6	117.4	114.0	114.2	100.1
Round Rock, TX	88.7	82.1	76.1	104.9	88.7	93.9	96.6
San Antonio, TX	93.2	84.6	91.4	85.8	102.2	97.2	97.2
San Diego, CA	130.8	107.4	189.1	113.0	111.2	112.4	103.6
San Francisco, CA	162.9	115.9	283.8	91.2	111.5	112.3	122.4
San Jose, CA	150.5	114.7	245.3	131.9	114.6	116.2	103.9
Savannah, GA	91.6	97.1	77.2	100.6	97.7	93.2	97.1
Scottsdale[24], AZ	96.6	103.9	87.4	100.3	102.9	102.6	97.6
Seattle, WA	117.2	111.7	129.5	90.4	112.4	118.4	118.7
Sioux Falls, SD	97.2	95.0	86.2	102.4	92.5	94.4	108.1
Stamford, CT	147.5	116.5	208.0	139.7	116.5	114.4	124.2
Sterling Heights[25], MI	93.8	95.9	84.8	104.0	100.5	95.5	95.1
Sunnyvale[26], CA	150.5	114.7	245.3	131.9	114.6	116.2	103.9
Tampa, FL	91.9	98.2	79.0	96.7	102.9	93.6	95.2
Temecula[27], CA	112.5	106.7	135.9	110.2	108.9	102.6	97.5
Thousand Oaks, CA	n/a	n/a	n/a	n/a	n/a	n/a	n/a
Virginia Beach[28], VA	105.4	100.3	114.0	110.9	97.7	102.3	101.1
Washington, DC	143.5	111.4	241.2	103.9	108.1	101.0	100.7
U.S.	100.0	100.0	100.0	100.0	100.0	100.0	100.0

Note: In cases where data is not available for the city, data for the metro area or for a neighboring city has been provided and noted below; (1) Rio Rancho NM; (2) Washington-Arlington-Alexandria DC-VA; (3) Seattle WA; (4) Tulsa OK; (5) Boston MA; (6) San Diego CA; (7) Raleigh NC; (8) Hampton Roads-SE Virginia VA; (9) Baltimore MD; (10) Middlesex-Monmouth NJ; (11) Phoenix AZ; (12) Las Vegas NV; (13) Nassau County NY; (14) Orange County CA; (15) Newark-Elizabeth NJ; (16) Milwaukee-Waukesha WI; (17) Joliet-Will County IL; (18) Slidell-St. Tammany Parish LA; (19) Kansas City MO-KS; (20) Kansas City MO-KS; (21) Nassau County NY; (22) Fort Lauderdale FL; (23) Sacramento CA; (24) Phoenix AZ; (25) Detroit MI; (26) San Jose CA; (27) Riverside City CA; (28) Hampton Roads-SE Virginia VA
Source: The Council for Community and Economic Research (formerly ACCRA), Cost of Living Index, 2011

Grocery Prices

Urban Area	T-Bone Steak ($/pound)	Frying Chicken ($/pound)	Whole Milk ($/half gal.)	Eggs ($/dozen)	Orange Juice ($/64 oz.)	Coffee ($/11.5 oz.)
Albuquerque[1], NM	8.48	0.97	2.17	1.63	3.25	4.83
Alexandria[2], VA	9.73	1.53	2.54	2.28	3.40	4.57
Anchorage, AK	10.51	1.44	2.12	2.57	4.41	6.00
Ann Arbor, MI	11.43	0.91	2.03	1.70	3.09	3.99
Athens, GA	n/a	n/a	n/a	n/a	n/a	n/a
Atlanta, GA	9.79	1.16	2.12	1.65	3.35	4.30
Austin, TX	9.08	1.17	2.05	1.45	3.43	3.64
Baltimore, MD	9.69	1.67	2.54	2.26	3.46	4.33
Bellevue[3], WA	9.32	1.36	1.90	1.99	3.75	5.45
Billings, MT	n/a	n/a	n/a	n/a	n/a	n/a
Boise City, ID	8.23	1.58	1.83	1.63	3.32	4.52
Boston, MA	10.69	1.31	2.46	2.28	3.54	5.00
Boulder, CO	n/a	n/a	n/a	n/a	n/a	n/a
Broken Arrow[4], OK	7.75	0.93	2.30	1.45	2.95	3.98
Cambridge[5], MA	10.69	1.31	2.46	2.28	3.54	5.00
Cape Coral, FL	9.05	1.33	2.58	1.65	3.71	4.41
Carlsbad[6], CA	9.85	1.06	2.14	2.28	3.33	5.58
Cary[7], NC	9.39	1.17	2.49	1.61	3.03	3.99
Cedar Rapids, IA	8.61	1.04	1.92	1.58	3.22	4.70
Charleston, SC	9.33	1.32	2.59	1.71	3.26	4.49
Charlotte, NC	8.23	1.24	2.59	1.56	3.19	4.32
Chesapeake[8], VA	8.98	1.09	2.45	1.69	3.02	4.19
Chicago, IL	9.04	1.33	2.67	1.72	3.46	5.57
Clarksville, TN	8.53	0.97	2.36	1.98	3.08	3.91
Colorado Springs, CO	9.83	1.05	2.01	1.68	3.21	4.91
Columbia[9], MD	9.69	1.67	2.54	2.26	3.46	4.33
Columbia, MO	9.02	1.05	2.12	1.49	3.03	4.44
Columbia, SC	9.94	1.40	2.46	1.63	3.33	4.21
Columbus, OH	10.15	0.99	1.90	1.39	3.04	4.75
Dallas, TX	8.98	1.07	2.05	1.63	3.32	4.87
Denver, CO	9.80	1.16	1.87	1.71	3.08	5.18
Durham, NC	7.81	1.09	2.38	1.73	3.11	4.31
Edison[10], NJ	10.14	1.51	2.31	2.23	3.29	4.18
El Paso, TX	8.61	1.10	2.01	1.65	3.31	5.04
Fargo, ND	9.36	1.53	2.98	1.59	3.36	4.55
Fort Collins, CO	n/a	n/a	n/a	n/a	n/a	n/a
Fort Worth, TX	8.97	0.98	2.01	1.66	2.90	4.55
Gilbert[11], AZ	9.12	1.20	2.26	1.77	3.18	4.97
Green Bay, WI	9.71	1.31	1.77	1.30	3.04	4.38
Henderson[12], NV	9.29	1.08	2.34	1.90	3.25	4.89
High Point, NC	n/a	n/a	n/a	n/a	n/a	n/a
Honolulu, HI	8.32	1.85	3.50	3.18	4.68	6.83
Houston, TX	7.45	0.94	2.02	1.43	2.68	4.04
Huntington[13], NY	10.82	1.91	2.15	2.08	3.41	4.21
Huntsville, AL	9.94	1.24	2.30	1.55	3.13	4.45
Indianapolis, IN	n/a	n/a	n/a	n/a	n/a	n/a
Irvine[14], CA	9.34	1.08	2.23	2.26	3.30	5.48
Jackson, MS	8.82	1.04	2.47	1.60	2.98	4.16
Jacksonville, FL	9.83	1.23	2.74	1.74	3.21	4.13
Jersey City[15], NJ	9.56	1.24	2.26	2.28	3.01	4.46
Kansas City, MO	8.93	1.14	2.22	1.44	3.10	4.05
Kenosha[16], WI	9.67	1.44	1.93	1.20	3.09	4.38
Las Vegas, NV	9.29	1.08	2.34	1.90	3.25	4.89
Lexington, KY	9.31	1.06	2.07	1.53	2.93	4.13
Lincoln, NE	8.59	1.51	1.97	1.52	3.22	4.44

Table continued on next page.

Urban Area	T-Bone Steak ($/pound)	Frying Chicken ($/pound)	Whole Milk ($/half gal.)	Eggs ($/dozen)	Orange Juice ($/64 oz.)	Coffee ($/11.5 oz.)
Little Rock, AR	9.49	1.01	1.91	1.49	3.02	4.20
Los Angeles, CA	9.99	1.16	2.18	2.28	3.26	5.55
Madison, WI	8.95	1.54	2.07	1.33	3.17	4.10
Manchester, NH	10.11	1.23	2.04	1.48	2.97	4.04
Miami, FL	10.43	1.40	2.64	1.84	3.57	4.24
Minneapolis, MN	14.30	2.16	2.24	1.93	3.37	4.08
Murfreesboro, TN	8.41	1.06	1.76	1.40	2.80	4.00
Naperville[17], IL	9.23	1.02	2.52	1.66	2.96	4.86
Nashville, TN	8.40	1.33	2.54	1.39	3.14	4.26
New Orleans[18], LA	9.07	1.07	2.76	1.67	3.13	3.99
New York, NY	10.80	1.21	2.32	2.43	3.84	4.88
Norman, OK	9.14	1.01	2.18	1.52	3.08	4.13
Olathe[19], KS	8.93	1.14	2.22	1.44	3.10	4.05
Omaha, NE	8.45	1.21	2.01	1.52	3.17	4.42
Orlando, FL	9.03	1.25	2.65	1.71	3.28	4.27
Overland Park[20], KS	8.93	1.14	2.22	1.44	3.10	4.05
Oyster Bay[21], NY	10.82	1.91	2.15	2.08	3.41	4.21
Pembroke Pines[22], FL	10.38	1.40	2.69	1.87	3.16	4.20
Philadelphia, PA	10.15	1.56	2.09	2.21	3.18	4.78
Phoenix, AZ	9.12	1.20	2.26	1.77	3.18	4.97
Pittsburgh, PA	9.80	1.30	1.98	1.52	3.35	4.51
Plano, TX	8.94	1.05	2.09	1.70	3.50	4.98
Portland, OR	9.90	1.47	1.86	1.83	3.52	5.36
Providence, RI	10.38	1.07	2.44	2.22	3.22	4.57
Provo, UT	8.13	1.14	2.02	1.09	2.91	4.97
Raleigh, NC	9.39	1.17	2.49	1.61	3.03	3.99
Richmond, VA	9.15	1.09	2.50	1.71	2.88	4.42
Roseville[23], CA	10.64	1.10	2.19	2.27	2.94	4.98
Round Rock, TX	8.79	0.99	2.33	1.28	2.70	3.27
San Antonio, TX	9.00	1.03	2.08	1.35	3.01	3.51
San Diego, CA	9.85	1.06	2.14	2.28	3.33	5.58
San Francisco, CA	10.14	1.27	2.20	2.36	3.80	5.56
San Jose, CA	9.78	1.03	2.16	2.32	2.98	5.20
Savannah, GA	9.67	1.18	2.22	1.57	2.93	4.20
Scottsdale[24], AZ	9.12	1.20	2.26	1.77	3.18	4.97
Seattle, WA	9.32	1.36	1.90	1.99	3.75	5.45
Sioux Falls, SD	9.55	0.90	2.11	1.63	3.89	4.67
Stamford, CT	10.32	1.20	2.20	2.28	3.35	4.66
Sterling Heights[25], MI	10.22	0.91	2.03	1.66	3.01	3.98
Sunnyvale[26], CA	9.78	1.03	2.16	2.32	2.98	5.20
Tampa, FL	9.32	1.17	2.57	1.66	3.11	3.84
Temecula[27], CA	8.80	0.97	2.11	2.18	3.16	5.24
Thousand Oaks, CA	n/a	n/a	n/a	n/a	n/a	n/a
Virginia Beach[28], VA	8.98	1.09	2.45	1.69	3.02	4.19
Washington, DC	9.73	1.53	2.54	2.28	3.40	4.57
Average[99]	9.25	1.18	2.22	1.66	3.19	4.40
Minimum[99]	6.70	0.88	1.31	0.95	2.46	2.94
Maximum[99]	14.30	2.16	3.50	3.18	4.75	6.83

Note: **T-Bone Steak** (price per pound); **Frying Chicken** (price per pound, whole fryer); **Whole Milk** (half gallon carton); **Eggs** (price per dozen, Grade A, large); **Orange Juice** (64 oz. Tropicana or Florida Natural); **Coffee** (11.5 oz. can, vacuum-packed, Maxwell House, Hills Bros, or Folgers); (99) Values for the local area are compared with the average, minimum, and maximum values for all 331 areas in the Cost of Living Index report; n/a not available; In cases where data is not available for the city, data for the metro area or for a neighboring city has been provided and noted below;(1) Rio Rancho NM; (2) Washington-Arlington-Alexandria DC-VA; (3) Seattle WA; (4) Tulsa OK; (5) Boston MA; (6) San Diego CA; (7) Raleigh NC; (8) Hampton Roads-SE Virginia VA; (9) Baltimore MD; (10) Middlesex-Monmouth NJ; (11) Phoenix AZ; (12) Las Vegas NV; (13) Nassau County NY; (14) Orange County CA; (15) Newark-Elizabeth NJ; (16) Milwaukee-Waukesha WI; (17) Joliet-Will County IL; (18) Slidell-St. Tammany Parish LA; (19) Kansas City MO-KS; (20) Kansas City MO-KS; (21) Nassau County NY; (22) Fort Lauderdale FL; (23) Sacramento CA; (24) Phoenix AZ; (25) Detroit MI; (26) San Jose CA; (27) Riverside City CA; (28) Hampton Roads-SE Virginia VA
Source: The Council for Community and Economic Research (formerly ACCRA), Cost of Living Index, 2011

Housing and Utility Costs

Urban Area	New Home Price ($)	Apartment Rent ($/month)	All Electric ($/month)	Part Electric ($/month)	Other Energy ($/month)	Telephone ($/month)
Albuquerque[1], NM	253,971	727	-	103.95	76.48	22.15
Alexandria[2], VA	711,603	1,879	-	84.46	106.75	23.00
Anchorage, AK	422,933	1,302	-	73.24	104.51	22.55
Ann Arbor, MI	315,268	769	-	103.57	78.12	28.23
Athens, GA	n/a	n/a	n/a	n/a	n/a	n/a
Atlanta, GA	244,734	882	-	96.05	59.20	25.06
Austin, TX	222,483	878	-	92.80	79.38	24.67
Baltimore, MD	449,828	1,504	-	124.39	77.23	28.32
Bellevue[3], WA	342,917	1,473	143.76	-	-	25.99
Billings, MT	n/a	n/a	n/a	n/a	n/a	n/a
Boise City, ID	238,006	703	-	84.47	67.46	28.64
Boston, MA	437,400	1,591	-	104.49	145.16	38.25
Boulder, CO	n/a	n/a	n/a	n/a	n/a	n/a
Broken Arrow[4], OK	194,499	599	-	77.88	61.48	31.70
Cambridge[5], MA	437,400	1,591	-	104.49	145.16	38.25
Cape Coral, FL	250,980	817	149.19	-	-	17.98
Carlsbad[6], CA	525,576	1,712	-	121.58	67.99	29.85
Cary[7], NC	229,862	656	-	94.88	62.65	32.33
Cedar Rapids, IA	221,859	719	-	109.14	67.59	24.99
Charleston, SC	240,230	977	185.13	-	-	27.15
Charlotte, NC	228,128	767	141.85	-	-	28.13
Chesapeake[8], VA	313,649	1,061	-	90.31	69.61	36.17
Chicago, IL	367,442	1,369	-	87.29	65.86	28.60
Clarksville, TN	252,269	770	167.24	-	-	22.03
Colorado Springs, CO	247,964	808	-	67.47	58.34	30.25
Columbia[9], MD	449,828	1,504	-	124.39	77.23	28.32
Columbia, MO	232,638	654	-	87.59	69.65	22.62
Columbia, SC	211,375	793	-	95.48	83.90	28.01
Columbus, OH	208,376	778	-	84.44	77.22	27.99
Dallas, TX	207,192	738	-	131.03	51.86	28.15
Denver, CO	339,420	853	-	78.86	58.85	27.26
Durham, NC	216,053	751	142.15	-	-	28.00
Edison[10], NJ	442,983	1,286	-	117.56	121.47	29.75
El Paso, TX	239,227	942	-	83.02	33.89	26.95
Fargo, ND	247,098	674	-	58.85	73.12	28.32
Fort Collins, CO	n/a	n/a	n/a	n/a	n/a	n/a
Fort Worth, TX	199,901	952	-	131.65	51.86	29.95
Gilbert[11], AZ	241,396	889	184.74	-	-	22.17
Green Bay, WI	250,550	616	-	81.08	90.64	30.57
Henderson[12], NV	261,021	766	-	124.12	44.17	20.26
High Point, NC	n/a	n/a	n/a	n/a	n/a	n/a
Honolulu, HI	666,923	2,702	339.16	-	-	24.97
Houston, TX	224,736	892	-	88.47	42.02	28.69
Huntington[13], NY	551,711	1,488	-	124.59	133.23	29.99
Huntsville, AL	221,338	726	142.62	-	-	30.38
Indianapolis, IN	n/a	n/a	n/a	n/a	n/a	n/a
Irvine[14], CA	681,690	1,678	-	134.27	54.93	29.85
Jackson, MS	278,817	730	-	106.80	115.24	29.34
Jacksonville, FL	206,359	974	181.34	-	-	23.94
Jersey City[15], NJ	479,582	1,536	-	119.78	128.79	29.88
Kansas City, MO	259,295	738	-	85.30	82.44	33.57
Kenosha[16], WI	304,289	817	-	92.17	94.08	28.36
Las Vegas, NV	261,021	766	-	124.12	44.17	20.26
Lexington, KY	227,759	785	-	71.82	73.76	28.40
Lincoln, NE	243,057	678	-	65.63	79.84	34.99

Table continued on next page.

Urban Area	New Home Price ($)	Apartment Rent ($/month)	All Electric ($/month)	Part Electric ($/month)	Other Energy ($/month)	Telephone ($/month)
Little Rock, AR	253,330	719	-	82.50	73.02	33.44
Los Angeles, CA	540,850	1,863	-	125.12	62.59	29.85
Madison, WI	342,283	820	-	95.80	88.84	24.49
Manchester, NH	351,427	1,225	-	105.41	97.64	36.25
Miami, FL	290,911	1,298	152.30	-	-	26.51
Minneapolis, MN	329,223	1,103	-	89.03	86.15	24.99
Murfreesboro, TN	213,745	784	-	81.64	56.33	23.01
Naperville[17], IL	261,391	990	-	86.32	66.85	32.61
Nashville, TN	188,005	795	-	82.30	60.69	23.86
New Orleans[18], LA	252,394	988	146.02	-	-	24.58
New York, NY	972,845	2,401	-	115.77	149.07	30.33
Norman, OK	253,965	631	-	51.26	61.48	28.04
Olathe[19], KS	259,295	738	-	85.30	82.44	33.57
Omaha, NE	227,304	676	-	75.48	70.97	26.64
Orlando, FL	209,687	817	179.04	-	-	28.95
Overland Park[20], KS	259,295	738	-	85.30	82.44	33.57
Oyster Bay[21], NY	551,711	1,488	-	124.59	133.23	29.99
Pembroke Pines[22], FL	350,825	1,339	152.30	-	-	26.51
Philadelphia, PA	391,184	1,248	-	124.88	83.77	36.75
Phoenix, AZ	241,396	889	184.74	-	-	22.17
Pittsburgh, PA	208,174	797	-	96.31	86.45	22.90
Plano, TX	226,303	930	-	134.72	51.47	26.01
Portland, OR	356,341	1,289	-	71.51	80.84	22.26
Providence, RI	365,109	1,383	-	100.19	110.00	36.19
Provo, UT	230,965	838	-	55.36	63.86	27.08
Raleigh, NC	229,862	656	-	94.88	62.65	32.33
Richmond, VA	268,326	894	-	89.02	78.36	32.51
Roseville[23], CA	401,500	1,095	-	163.54	38.11	29.84
Round Rock, TX	210,266	761	-	119.07	49.29	29.72
San Antonio, TX	237,886	993	-	92.63	38.54	26.01
San Diego, CA	525,576	1,712	-	121.58	67.99	29.85
San Francisco, CA	796,762	2,518	-	87.94	66.07	23.88
San Jose, CA	713,145	1,729	-	181.97	64.31	28.30
Savannah, GA	210,203	731	165.86	-	-	27.39
Scottsdale[24], AZ	241,396	889	184.74	-	-	22.17
Seattle, WA	342,917	1,473	143.76	-	-	25.99
Sioux Falls, SD	248,539	710	-	71.54	67.18	35.73
Stamford, CT	573,093	2,004	-	112.54	154.49	28.33
Sterling Heights[25], MI	241,092	697	-	101.42	78.60	26.01
Sunnyvale[26], CA	713,145	1,729	-	181.97	64.31	28.30
Tampa, FL	212,171	790	164.70	-	-	24.95
Temecula[27], CA	385,798	1,142	-	120.75	65.28	28.81
Thousand Oaks, CA	n/a	n/a	n/a	n/a	n/a	n/a
Virginia Beach[28], VA	313,649	1,061	-	90.31	69.61	36.17
Washington, DC	711,603	1,879	-	84.46	106.75	23.00
Average[99]	285,990	839	163.23	89.00	77.52	26.92
Minimum[99]	188,005	460	125.58	45.39	33.89	17.98
Maximum[99]	1,197,028	3,244	339.16	181.97	348.69	40.01

Note: **New Home Price** (2,400 sf living area, 8,000 sf lot, in urban area with full utilities); **Apartment Rent** (950 sf 2 bedroom/1.5 or 2 bath, unfurnished, excluding all utilities except water); **All Electric** (average monthly cost for an all-electric home); **Part Electric** (average monthly cost for a part-electric home); **Other Energy** (average monthly cost for natural gas, fuel oil, coal, wood, and any other forms of energy except electricity); **Telephone** (price includes basic monthly rate for a private residential line plus additional local usage charges incurred by a family of four); (99) Values for the local area are compared with the average, minimum, and maximum values for all 331 areas in the Cost of Living Index report; n/a not available; In cases where data is not available for the city, data for the metro area or for a neighboring city has been provided and noted below;(1) Rio Rancho NM; (2) Washington-Arlington-Alexandria DC-VA; (3) Seattle WA; (4) Tulsa OK; (5) Boston MA; (6) San Diego CA; (7) Raleigh NC; (8) Hampton Roads-SE Virginia VA; (9) Baltimore MD; (10) Middlesex-Monmouth NJ; (11) Phoenix AZ; (12) Las Vegas NV; (13) Nassau County NY; (14) Orange County CA; (15) Newark-Elizabeth NJ; (16) Milwaukee-Waukesha WI; (17) Joliet-Will County IL; (18) Slidell-St. Tammany Parish LA; (19) Kansas City MO-KS; (20) Kansas City MO-KS; (21) Nassau County NY; (22) Fort Lauderdale FL; (23) Sacramento CA; (24) Phoenix AZ; (25) Detroit MI; (26) San Jose CA; (27) Riverside City CA; (28) Hampton Roads-SE Virginia VA
Source: The Council for Community and Economic Research (formerly ACCRA), Cost of Living Index, 2011

Health Care, Transportation, and Other Costs

Urban Area	Doctor ($/visit)	Dentist ($/visit)	Optometrist ($/visit)	Gasoline ($/gallon)	Beauty Salon ($/visit)	Men's Shirt ($)
Albuquerque[1], NM	92.97	89.44	90.90	3.33	35.92	24.55
Alexandria[2], VA	87.07	87.60	73.93	3.69	48.73	26.07
Anchorage, AK	154.98	127.82	156.44	3.82	40.38	27.67
Ann Arbor, MI	88.47	81.68	73.91	3.66	32.29	28.22
Athens, GA	n/a	n/a	n/a	n/a	n/a	n/a
Atlanta, GA	89.59	93.46	71.27	3.50	43.14	24.03
Austin, TX	80.31	94.25	91.08	3.38	46.67	17.99
Baltimore, MD	82.37	81.77	67.86	3.49	42.94	26.36
Bellevue[3], WA	119.29	106.93	115.25	3.65	41.48	35.93
Billings, MT	n/a	n/a	n/a	n/a	n/a	n/a
Boise City, ID	102.63	83.07	87.80	3.42	24.94	33.45
Boston, MA	149.00	109.11	99.00	3.58	45.32	40.33
Boulder, CO	n/a	n/a	n/a	n/a	n/a	n/a
Broken Arrow[4], OK	102.78	75.55	80.56	3.31	32.78	22.43
Cambridge[5], MA	149.00	109.11	99.00	3.58	45.32	40.33
Cape Coral, FL	86.37	77.36	77.14	3.58	35.30	21.93
Carlsbad[6], CA	98.80	98.60	98.80	3.83	46.67	22.25
Cary[7], NC	100.70	100.00	86.72	3.38	32.82	20.79
Cedar Rapids, IA	94.54	68.48	76.08	3.42	28.94	25.83
Charleston, SC	100.92	93.55	94.45	3.39	39.50	24.57
Charlotte, NC	88.23	97.48	113.34	3.52	34.60	17.40
Chesapeake[8], VA	100.44	85.35	97.73	3.43	31.90	21.84
Chicago, IL	87.76	99.31	99.13	3.89	39.32	27.24
Clarksville, TN	94.02	84.01	80.05	3.33	33.49	36.61
Colorado Springs, CO	96.13	87.47	93.29	3.22	35.20	28.13
Columbia[9], MD	82.37	81.77	67.86	3.49	42.94	26.36
Columbia, MO	89.45	76.70	83.52	3.40	38.51	24.67
Columbia, SC	104.50	83.33	93.94	3.32	29.53	24.13
Columbus, OH	101.33	82.50	95.03	3.45	34.87	24.92
Dallas, TX	100.25	85.21	89.17	3.46	27.60	29.72
Denver, CO	108.17	88.32	100.29	3.28	33.76	18.88
Durham, NC	93.08	79.78	104.11	3.44	40.53	18.89
Edison[10], NJ	73.68	114.41	93.38	3.44	33.65	42.73
El Paso, TX	84.25	78.17	67.17	3.36	24.15	21.49
Fargo, ND	114.50	79.75	70.33	3.41	26.27	27.00
Fort Collins, CO	n/a	n/a	n/a	n/a	n/a	n/a
Fort Worth, TX	86.80	79.10	64.56	3.46	31.61	24.89
Gilbert[11], AZ	91.10	89.66	97.16	3.32	41.43	21.20
Green Bay, WI	134.43	77.99	72.19	3.60	29.18	25.29
Henderson[12], NV	98.33	89.33	110.48	3.46	46.37	35.71
High Point, NC	n/a	n/a	n/a	n/a	n/a	n/a
Honolulu, HI	128.23	94.93	126.91	3.99	48.51	45.37
Houston, TX	92.50	79.30	88.50	3.30	41.27	20.39
Huntington[13], NY	99.33	102.25	94.67	3.76	47.00	28.40
Huntsville, AL	71.67	79.17	106.00	3.48	35.66	21.18
Indianapolis, IN	n/a	n/a	n/a	n/a	n/a	n/a
Irvine[14], CA	91.85	95.00	102.90	3.81	58.46	24.56
Jackson, MS	86.10	87.33	82.32	3.31	28.92	16.10
Jacksonville, FL	69.07	81.07	67.49	3.39	42.37	20.95
Jersey City[15], NJ	87.36	90.52	90.08	3.48	37.03	42.05
Kansas City, MO	84.43	78.00	77.58	3.38	22.43	42.51
Kenosha[16], WI	137.80	82.25	53.66	3.59	29.55	19.61
Las Vegas, NV	98.33	89.33	110.48	3.46	46.37	35.71
Lexington, KY	88.50	84.37	68.29	3.41	34.17	21.71
Lincoln, NE	110.00	62.67	103.00	3.62	25.78	27.33

Table continued on next page.

Urban Area	Doctor ($/visit)	Dentist ($/visit)	Optometrist ($/visit)	Gasoline ($/gallon)	Beauty Salon ($/visit)	Men's Shirt ($)
Little Rock, AR	94.22	66.00	82.00	3.37	41.60	25.91
Los Angeles, CA	91.20	95.47	113.07	3.83	59.53	24.52
Madison, WI	149.00	91.01	58.32	3.55	36.80	19.91
Manchester, NH	149.00	84.33	92.59	3.47	38.76	37.10
Miami, FL	100.88	89.24	82.47	3.58	46.97	22.26
Minneapolis, MN	109.71	83.18	82.60	3.45	37.85	22.44
Murfreesboro, TN	85.00	64.66	88.33	3.34	39.00	20.16
Naperville[17], IL	100.61	82.76	97.54	3.74	32.28	18.88
Nashville, TN	81.47	78.78	86.47	3.34	29.00	24.20
New Orleans[18], LA	81.57	68.39	73.40	3.39	37.95	27.58
New York, NY	113.30	106.35	63.49	3.84	53.85	33.51
Norman, OK	81.49	76.14	88.90	3.33	30.88	23.98
Olathe[19], KS	84.43	78.00	77.58	3.38	22.43	42.51
Omaha, NE	110.40	64.46	90.17	3.52	24.28	16.87
Orlando, FL	77.70	76.16	71.75	3.48	41.54	35.81
Overland Park[20], KS	84.43	78.00	77.58	3.38	22.43	42.51
Oyster Bay[21], NY	99.33	102.25	94.67	3.76	47.00	28.40
Pembroke Pines[22], FL	82.10	88.82	101.81	3.56	45.61	23.10
Philadelphia, PA	118.58	93.05	97.41	3.59	59.61	38.74
Phoenix, AZ	91.10	89.66	97.16	3.32	41.43	21.20
Pittsburgh, PA	76.19	78.97	74.77	3.60	32.77	24.63
Plano, TX	91.01	92.67	69.67	3.39	33.04	22.25
Portland, OR	122.00	93.64	112.39	3.66	38.75	23.24
Providence, RI	149.00	87.14	107.43	3.60	45.38	40.93
Provo, UT	81.73	65.71	83.88	3.22	28.53	26.75
Raleigh, NC	100.70	100.00	86.72	3.38	32.82	20.79
Richmond, VA	83.58	101.11	110.06	3.45	41.62	18.32
Roseville[23], CA	112.86	93.49	112.13	3.82	46.05	25.41
Round Rock, TX	70.96	91.23	75.69	3.36	29.33	20.61
San Antonio, TX	84.47	79.55	86.08	3.35	42.94	34.31
San Diego, CA	98.80	98.60	98.80	3.83	46.67	22.25
San Francisco, CA	121.22	94.38	110.57	3.78	63.21	42.14
San Jose, CA	103.14	105.52	139.53	3.81	57.79	23.36
Savannah, GA	87.56	71.83	74.62	3.46	37.71	19.58
Scottsdale[24], AZ	91.10	89.66	97.16	3.32	41.43	21.20
Seattle, WA	119.29	106.93	115.25	3.65	41.48	35.93
Sioux Falls, SD	79.95	73.89	95.13	3.47	27.43	22.58
Stamford, CT	113.71	101.64	97.83	3.85	52.93	27.18
Sterling Heights[25], MI	83.80	80.50	70.87	3.62	39.30	18.74
Sunnyvale[26], CA	103.14	105.52	139.53	3.81	57.79	23.36
Tampa, FL	78.56	76.67	80.19	3.46	34.23	20.20
Temecula[27], CA	82.75	86.70	86.80	3.81	36.66	28.75
Thousand Oaks, CA	n/a	n/a	n/a	n/a	n/a	n/a
Virginia Beach[28], VA	100.44	85.35	97.73	3.43	31.90	21.84
Washington, DC	87.07	87.60	73.93	3.69	48.73	26.07
Average[99]	93.88	81.72	90.54	3.48	32.65	25.06
Minimum[99]	60.00	55.33	53.66	3.18	19.78	13.44
Maximum[99]	154.98	145.97	183.72	4.31	63.21	46.00

Note: **Doctor** (general practitioners routine exam of an established patient); **Dentist** (adult teeth cleaning and periodic oral examination); **Optometrist** (full vision eye exam for established adult patient); **Gasoline** (one gallon regular unleaded, national brand, including all taxes, cash price at self-service pump if available); **Beauty Salon** (woman's shampoo, trim, and blow-dry); **Men's Shirt** (cotton/polyester dress shirt, pinpoint weave, long sleeves); (99) Values for the local area are compared with the average, minimum, and maximum values for all 331 areas in the Cost of Living Index report; n/a not available; In cases where data is not available for the city, data for the metro area or for a neighboring city has been provided and noted below;(1) Rio Rancho NM; (2) Washington-Arlington-Alexandria DC-VA; (3) Seattle WA; (4) Tulsa OK; (5) Boston MA; (6) San Diego CA; (7) Raleigh NC; (8) Hampton Roads-SE Virginia VA; (9) Baltimore MD; (10) Middlesex-Monmouth NJ; (11) Phoenix AZ; (12) Las Vegas NV; (13) Nassau County NY; (14) Orange County CA; (15) Newark-Elizabeth NJ; (16) Milwaukee-Waukesha WI; (17) Joliet-Will County IL; (18) Slidell-St. Tammany Parish LA; (19) Kansas City MO-KS; (20) Kansas City MO-KS; (21) Nassau County NY; (22) Fort Lauderdale FL; (23) Sacramento CA; (24) Phoenix AZ; (25) Detroit MI; (26) San Jose CA; (27) Riverside City CA; (28) Hampton Roads-SE Virginia VA
Source: The Council for Community and Economic Research (formerly ACCRA), Cost of Living Index, 2011

Distribution of Physicians and Dentists

City	Area Covered	Dentists[1]	D.O.[2]	M.D.[3]				
				Total	Family/General Practice	Pediatrics	Medical Specialties	Surgical Specialties
Albuquerque, NM	Bernalillo County	4.2	1.5	25.2	3.3	1.9	9.0	5.1
Alexandria, VA	Alexandria City	4.8	1.2	21.4	1.8	1.8	7.8	5.7
Anchorage, AK	Anchorage Borough	5.8	2.2	23.9	4.4	1.8	6.5	6.2
Ann Arbor, MI	Washtenaw County	9.0	3.0	47.5	2.9	3.5	19.1	9.0
Athens, GA	Clarke County	4.8	1.0	23.3	1.9	1.0	7.6	7.4
Atlanta, GA	Fulton County	5.7	0.8	31.2	1.8	2.2	11.5	8.5
Austin, TX	Travis County	4.5	1.2	22.6	2.9	1.7	7.7	5.2
Baltimore, MD	Baltimore City	3.2	1.6	29.3	1.3	1.8	12.5	6.2
Bellevue, WA	King County	7.6	1.1	29.4	4.6	1.9	10.2	5.7
Billings, MT	Yellowstone County	5.1	1.4	27.6	3.2	1.4	8.3	7.9
Boise City, ID	Ada County	6.5	1.6	22.5	3.6	1.0	6.4	6.5
Boston, MA	Suffolk County	7.8	1.1	44.4	1.1	3.0	20.4	8.2
Boulder, CO	Boulder County	6.1	2.0	28.4	5.4	2.1	8.3	6.4
Broken Arrow, OK	Tulsa County	5.1	11.2	20.4	2.4	1.3	7.6	4.9
Cambridge, MA	Middlesex County	7.4	0.6	32.2	1.5	2.9	14.4	5.7
Cape Coral, FL	Lee County	3.2	2.8	15.7	1.3	1.1	5.9	4.3
Carlsbad, CA	San Diego County	6.0	1.3	21.0	2.7	1.6	7.5	4.5
Cary, NC	Wake County	5.4	0.6	20.4	2.4	2.2	8.0	4.7
Cedar Rapids, IA	Linn County	3.4	1.4	15.7	4.2	0.9	3.8	3.4
Charleston, SC	Charleston County	7.1	2.1	40.7	3.3	2.7	13.6	10.1
Charlotte, NC	Mecklenburg County	5.4	0.7	23.2	2.4	2.0	9.1	5.6
Chesapeake, VA	Chesapeake City	3.8	1.4	17.8	3.4	1.7	6.6	4.4
Chicago, IL	Cook County	5.5	2.3	21.5	2.2	1.6	9.1	4.4
Clarksville, TN	Montgomery County	3.4	1.5	10.2	1.4	1.2	3.7	2.9
Colorado Spgs., CO	El Paso County	5.6	2.6	16.0	2.0	1.1	4.9	4.0
Columbia, MD	Howard County	9.6	1.8	41.2	3.5	4.3	18.3	6.2
Columbia, MO	Boone County	5.1	5.4	36.7	3.8	1.9	12.6	8.8
Columbia, SC	Richland County	4.9	0.6	26.1	2.9	2.0	9.9	6.3
Columbus, OH	Franklin County	5.6	5.8	22.2	2.9	1.6	8.2	5.1
Dallas, TX	Dallas County	4.5	1.8	18.7	1.5	1.2	6.8	4.6
Denver, CO	Denver County	5.4	2.6	35.3	2.9	2.3	13.2	7.7
Durham, NC	Durham County	5.4	0.9	42.5	2.8	3.3	16.9	9.3
Edison, NJ	Middlesex County	6.6	1.8	22.2	1.3	2.5	11.2	4.5
El Paso, TX	El Paso County	1.7	1.3	11.5	1.3	1.1	4.4	3.1
Fargo, ND	Cass County	5.2	0.9	29.4	4.7	1.9	10.8	6.3
Ft. Collins, CO	Larimer County	5.1	2.1	19.1	4.6	1.1	5.1	4.3
Ft. Worth, TX	Tarrant County	3.7	3.6	13.7	1.7	0.9	4.7	3.6
Gilbert, AZ	Maricopa County	4.5	3.1	16.3	1.8	1.1	6.1	3.6
Green Bay, WI	Brown County	5.3	1.5	20.0	2.5	1.2	6.4	5.7
Henderson, NV	Clark County	4.0	2.1	14.2	1.6	0.9	5.6	3.0
High Point, NC	Guilford County	4.2	0.5	21.5	2.7	1.5	8.2	5.5
Honolulu, HI	Honolulu County	6.3	1.5	24.1	2.2	2.1	9.6	5.3
Houston, TX	Harris County	4.1	0.8	18.2	1.9	1.4	6.8	4.3
Huntington, NY	Suffolk County	5.9	2.6	18.7	1.5	1.7	7.7	4.2
Huntsville, AL	Madison County	4.4	0.9	20.9	3.7	1.4	6.9	5.0
Indianapolis, IN	Marion County	4.5	1.4	24.5	2.9	1.7	9.0	5.5
Irvine, CA	Orange County	8.2	1.5	23.3	3.2	1.9	8.6	5.2
Jackson, MS	Hinds County	4.9	0.7	27.6	2.5	1.8	10.1	7.4
Jacksonville, FL	Duval County	3.7	2.0	22.1	3.2	1.5	8.0	5.0
Jersey City, NJ	Hudson County	4.8	1.0	11.3	1.0	1.4	5.6	2.5
Kansas City, MO	Jackson County	4.6	4.3	14.9	1.7	1.4	6.1	3.2
Kenosha, WI	Kenosha County	3.0	1.2	9.7	1.5	0.6	3.3	2.1
Las Vegas, NV	Clark County	4.0	2.1	14.2	1.6	0.9	5.6	3.0
Lexington, KY	Fayette County	8.1	2.6	39.4	3.7	2.2	14.0	9.8

Table continued on next page.

City	Area Covered	Dentists[1]	D.O.[2]	M.D.[3]				
				Total	Family/ General Practice	Pediatrics	Medical Specialties	Surgical Specialties
Lincoln, NE	Lancaster County	5.5	0.9	19.9	3.9	1.3	6.5	4.4
Little Rock, AR	Pulaski County	5.1	1.3	37.9	4.3	2.2	12.6	8.8
Los Angeles, CA	Los Angeles County	6.1	1.0	19.7	2.2	1.5	7.7	4.3
Madison, WI	Dane County	5.1	1.6	29.9	4.7	1.8	10.3	5.8
Manchester, NH	Hillsborough County	5.3	1.5	18.3	2.5	1.6	7.0	4.3
Miami, FL	Miami-Dade County	4.4	1.4	22.0	2.7	1.9	9.0	4.7
Minneapolis, MN	Hennepin County	5.9	1.1	31.0	4.5	2.2	10.8	6.7
Murfreesboro, TN	Rutherford County	3.4	0.2	11.1	1.3	1.0	4.3	3.1
Naperville, IL	DuPage County	7.4	3.0	32.9	3.6	2.5	13.0	6.8
Nashville, TN	Davidson County	5.7	0.7	32.8	1.7	2.4	12.9	9.0
New Orleans, LA	Orleans Parish	3.4	0.8	32.1	1.8	2.3	11.9	8.0
New York, NY	Kings County	3.8	1.1	12.4	0.8	1.4	6.5	2.3
Norman, OK	Cleveland County	3.8	3.9	10.6	1.7	0.6	3.3	1.9
Olathe, KS	Johnson County	7.1	3.6	30.4	3.6	1.9	10.4	7.0
Omaha, NE	Douglas County	5.9	2.0	29.6	3.8	2.1	10.2	7.6
Orlando, FL	Orange County	4.0	1.9	19.7	2.5	1.8	7.6	4.3
Overland Park, KS	Johnson County	7.1	3.6	30.4	3.6	1.9	10.4	7.0
Oyster Bay, NY	Nassau County	11.4	5.1	39.4	1.5	3.8	18.3	9.4
Pembroke Pines, FL	Broward County	5.0	3.4	19.5	1.6	1.6	8.3	4.5
Philadelphia, PA	Philadelphia County	4.2	5.3	17.8	1.0	1.3	7.4	3.9
Phoenix, AZ	Maricopa County	4.5	3.1	16.3	1.8	1.1	6.1	3.6
Pittsburgh, PA	Allegheny County	6.5	3.3	31.6	2.8	2.0	12.7	6.9
Plano, TX	Collin County	5.7	1.4	18.7	2.3	1.8	7.4	4.0
Portland, OR	Multnomah County	5.5	2.4	33.3	3.1	2.0	12.6	7.2
Providence, RI	Providence County	3.7	1.5	22.4	1.4	1.8	10.5	5.2
Provo, UT	Utah County	5.0	1.1	9.4	2.0	0.9	2.6	2.4
Raleigh, NC	Wake County	5.4	0.6	20.4	2.4	2.2	8.0	4.7
Richmond, VA	Richmond City	6.1	2.0	33.0	2.9	2.4	12.1	8.7
Roseville, CA	Placer County	7.9	1.3	22.7	4.0	2.0	8.1	4.8
Round Rock, TX	Williamson County	3.9	1.4	10.9	2.5	1.2	3.6	2.5
San Antonio, TX	Bexar County	4.6	1.7	20.7	2.7	1.5	7.3	4.7
San Diego, CA	San Diego County	6.0	1.3	21.0	2.7	1.6	7.5	4.5
San Francisco, CA	San Francisco County	10.2	0.8	42.4	2.8	2.9	17.2	8.4
San Jose, CA	Santa Clara County	8.7	0.6	25.1	2.1	2.6	10.9	5.4
Savannah, GA	Chatham County	4.6	1.3	26.7	2.7	1.9	9.5	7.4
Scottsdale, AZ	Maricopa County	4.5	3.1	16.3	1.8	1.1	6.1	3.6
Seattle, WA	King County	7.6	1.1	29.4	4.6	1.9	10.2	5.7
Sioux Falls, SD	Minnehaha County	3.7	2.1	23.6	4.2	1.2	7.6	5.2
Stamford, CT	Fairfield County	6.9	1.1	26.5	1.1	2.3	12.0	6.6
Sterling Hgts, MI	Macomb County	5.1	5.9	9.5	1.6	0.8	4.1	2.3
Sunnyvale, CA	Santa Clara County	8.7	0.6	25.1	2.1	2.6	10.9	5.4
Tampa, FL	Hillsborough County	4.2	2.3	22.2	1.8	1.9	8.8	5.1
Temecula, CA	Riverside County	3.1	0.9	9.8	1.7	0.7	3.3	2.3
Thousand Oaks, CA	Ventura County	5.5	0.8	17.8	3.4	1.2	6.2	4.0
Virginia Beach, VA	Virginia Beach City	5.7	0.8	19.5	3.3	1.6	6.2	4.4
Washington, DC	The District County	7.4	1.7	36.1	2.1	2.9	15.4	7.7
U.S.	U.S.	4.5	1.9	18.3	2.5	1.4	6.8	4.1

Note: All figures are rates per 100,000 population; Data as of 2008 unless noted; (1) Data as of 2007; (2) Doctor of Osteopathic Medicine; (3) Includes active, non-federal, patient-care, office-based Doctors of Medicine
Source: Area Resource File (ARF). 2009-2010 Release. U.S. Department of Health and Human Services, Health Resources and Services Administration, Bureau of Health Professions, Rockville, MD, August 2010

Crime Rate: City

City	All Crimes	Violent Crimes				Property Crimes		
		Murder	Forcible Rape	Robbery	Aggrav. Assault	Burglary	Larceny -Theft	Motor Vehicle Theft
Albuquerque, NM	5,622.2	7.7	62.0	172.4	544.7	1,002.0	3,325.0	508.4
Alexandria, VA	2,302.3	1.3	13.7	81.8	83.8	207.5	1,727.1	187.2
Anchorage, AK	4,355.7	4.5	90.9	156.4	585.9	421.2	2,816.8	280.0
Ann Arbor, MI	2,882.5	0.0	38.5	68.0	147.7	468.9	2,043.9	115.4
Athens, GA	4,698.2	4.4	25.7	97.5	201.2	1,182.1	2,923.3	264.1
Atlanta, GA	6,812.8	17.3	16.6	403.0	634.7	1,494.2	3,307.0	940.0
Austin, TX	6,230.7	4.8	33.3	154.6	283.3	1,098.7	4,373.5	282.6
Baltimore, MD	5,875.0	34.8	41.4	521.3	858.2	1,183.4	2,546.8	689.0
Bellevue, WA	3,058.7	0.0	7.8	46.2	54.0	514.3	2,274.2	162.1
Billings, MT	4,906.6	1.9	23.1	38.9	195.3	784.9	3,527.4	335.1
Boise City, ID	3,033.5	1.5	43.2	28.2	188.9	431.3	2,263.2	77.2
Boston, MA	4,106.3	11.3	39.7	299.0	553.4	556.9	2,329.6	316.3
Boulder, CO	2,954.0	4.0	33.2	29.2	145.1	481.6	2,171.2	89.7
Broken Arrow, OK	2,234.0	2.0	31.8	28.7	84.0	361.8	1,598.7	127.1
Cambridge, MA	3,422.1	0.0	20.3	157.8	261.2	445.8	2,370.9	166.1
Cape Coral, FL	2,532.5	1.9	14.3	39.9	115.9	675.1	1,617.5	67.9
Carlsbad, CA	2,005.8	0.0	19.9	40.8	133.4	397.2	1,307.0	107.5
Cary, NC	1,625.2	0.7	9.9	24.7	49.5	378.2	1,116.9	45.2
Cedar Rapids, IA	4,124.1	0.8	25.5	94.9	171.3	791.6	2,855.6	184.4
Charleston, SC	3,750.7	8.5	15.3	128.5	212.7	511.3	2,679.7	194.8
Charlotte, NC	4,963.1	7.6	30.0	225.0	350.5	1,168.9	2,846.9	334.1
Chesapeake, VA	3,705.2	4.0	11.5	122.3	246.0	523.0	2,624.7	173.7
Chicago, IL	n/a	15.2	n/a	501.6	485.5	924.7	2,638.4	673.3
Clarksville, TN	3,875.2	7.1	43.5	95.6	487.6	1,085.0	1,995.3	161.2
Colorado Springs, CO	4,712.7	5.0	80.2	132.2	274.5	867.6	3,029.5	323.7
Columbia, MD	n/a	n/a	n/a	n/a	n/a	n/a	n/a	n/a
Columbia, MO	4,202.4	2.9	35.8	126.7	347.1	533.8	3,025.6	130.5
Columbia, SC	7,053.0	12.3	56.7	264.4	667.4	1,301.9	4,236.1	514.2
Columbus, OH	7,195.5	12.2	73.2	434.6	185.3	1,970.8	3,982.5	536.9
Dallas, TX	5,608.2	11.3	38.6	343.4	307.7	1,499.4	2,766.1	641.6
Denver, CO	3,947.3	3.6	60.5	152.5	325.5	741.5	2,132.3	531.4
Durham, NC	5,548.1	9.8	25.7	281.9	373.0	1,562.1	2,988.6	307.1
Edison, NJ	1,842.7	2.0	5.0	51.8	81.7	332.7	1,215.2	154.4
El Paso, TX	3,245.9	0.8	28.7	76.7	352.1	312.8	2,226.3	248.6
Fargo, ND	3,075.4	0.0	44.1	35.1	223.7	393.2	2,211.8	167.5
Fort Collins, CO	3,597.3	0.0	46.1	36.1	233.6	463.6	2,672.2	145.6
Fort Worth, TX	5,276.2	8.4	42.6	178.2	345.9	1,252.9	3,118.0	330.1
Gilbert, AZ	1,991.0	2.3	12.1	28.3	52.5	367.5	1,456.7	71.6
Green Bay, WI	2,926.4	2.0	53.3	66.1	243.8	560.6	1,892.0	108.6
Henderson, NV	2,171.6	3.0	13.2	71.5	117.7	484.3	1,288.8	193.0
High Point, NC	5,211.9	1.9	26.6	209.0	340.1	1,247.2	3,178.3	209.0
Honolulu, HI	n/a	n/a	n/a	n/a	n/a	n/a	n/a	n/a
Houston, TX	6,042.2	11.8	31.2	414.3	528.8	1,224.3	3,269.9	561.9
Huntington, NY	n/a	n/a	n/a	n/a	n/a	n/a	n/a	n/a
Huntsville, AL	5,972.0	6.5	41.4	252.5	344.1	1,460.0	3,397.7	469.6
Indianapolis, IN	n/a	n/a	n/a	n/a	n/a	n/a	n/a	n/a
Irvine, CA	1,343.5	0.0	11.1	18.4	25.8	221.0	1,011.5	55.7
Jackson, MS	8,594.7	23.5	58.0	623.6	281.4	2,766.5	3,948.8	892.9
Jacksonville, FL	5,215.5	9.7	38.4	205.9	411.0	1,165.8	3,144.8	239.9
Jersey City, NJ	3,202.7	10.2	18.0	386.2	334.6	623.7	1,499.6	330.5
Kansas City, MO	6,710.6	21.1	48.4	336.5	733.5	1,474.4	3,440.7	656.1
Kenosha, WI	3,272.0	2.0	41.4	89.9	139.4	608.3	2,262.5	128.3
Las Vegas, NV	3,944.3	7.6	46.0	282.6	556.8	976.0	1,569.5	505.8
Lexington, KY	4,248.4	6.0	29.0	197.6	341.9	892.8	2,567.4	213.6

Table continued on next page.

City	All Crimes	Violent Crimes				Property Crimes		
		Murder	Forcible Rape	Robbery	Aggrav. Assault	Burglary	Larceny -Theft	Motor Vehicle Theft
Lincoln, NE	4,419.4	0.8	55.1	70.1	358.5	563.8	3,237.2	134.0
Little Rock, AR	9,192.3	13.0	77.2	445.3	987.4	2,198.3	4,893.2	578.0
Los Angeles, CA	2,894.2	7.6	24.0	284.4	243.2	453.2	1,438.1	443.7
Madison, WI	3,765.4	0.8	36.5	136.8	217.4	691.4	2,529.1	153.2
Manchester, NH	3,975.9	0.9	57.4	142.5	302.5	839.0	2,485.6	148.0
Miami, FL	5,924.6	15.4	10.4	421.4	660.4	1,045.2	3,215.8	556.0
Minneapolis, MN	5,798.0	9.6	113.6	413.8	516.7	1,241.1	3,009.8	493.4
Murfreesboro, TN	4,773.9	4.6	33.9	138.3	375.5	1,199.6	2,879.1	142.9
Naperville, IL	n/a	n/a	n/a	n/a	n/a	n/a	n/a	n/a
Nashville, TN	6,086.0	8.9	59.5	294.8	771.6	1,254.3	3,387.8	309.1
New Orleans, LA	4,276.5	49.1	40.4	267.5	370.7	1,037.0	1,835.4	676.4
New York, NY	2,256.5	6.4	12.4	235.2	327.6	215.0	1,336.0	123.8
Norman, OK	3,307.5	1.8	42.1	32.3	47.5	727.1	2,356.2	100.4
Olathe, KS	2,001.0	3.2	32.5	22.2	113.4	192.7	1,524.3	112.6
Omaha, NE	4,217.8	7.3	41.8	155.6	282.4	655.6	2,602.3	472.9
Orlando, FL	7,550.9	7.5	47.0	279.7	737.2	1,671.4	4,311.4	496.6
Overland Park, KS	2,504.1	0.0	22.4	20.1	119.2	274.8	1,896.8	170.7
Oyster Bay, NY	n/a	n/a	n/a	n/a	n/a	n/a	n/a	n/a
Pembroke Pines, FL	3,598.4	2.7	8.1	62.4	114.0	747.9	2,456.2	207.0
Philadelphia, PA	4,897.6	19.6	60.6	536.6	572.5	692.8	2,561.9	453.5
Phoenix, AZ	4,491.2	7.6	33.8	210.4	266.3	1,011.8	2,461.2	500.1
Pittsburgh, PA	4,506.7	17.6	21.1	380.5	479.3	943.0	2,455.1	210.1
Plano, TX	2,594.5	1.4	19.0	54.6	105.7	444.6	1,830.4	138.7
Portland, OR	5,571.0	3.9	40.8	178.1	317.9	730.0	3,725.4	575.0
Providence, RI	5,504.0	8.7	43.1	236.1	419.7	1,185.6	2,959.8	651.1
Provo, UT	2,491.2	1.7	39.1	22.9	101.1	314.3	1,924.7	87.5
Raleigh, NC	3,510.8	3.3	23.6	153.2	234.5	719.8	2,169.2	207.3
Richmond, VA	4,892.6	19.9	19.4	357.0	335.1	866.0	2,874.4	420.6
Roseville, CA	3,453.7	0.8	14.2	72.6	191.2	452.6	2,529.3	192.9
Round Rock, TX	2,819.1	0.0	23.4	31.5	49.5	417.6	2,207.0	90.0
San Antonio, TX	6,952.1	5.7	33.5	169.5	397.1	1,242.7	4,697.2	406.3
San Diego, CA	2,769.0	2.2	22.8	124.6	278.0	486.3	1,368.7	486.4
San Francisco, CA	4,655.8	5.9	16.2	388.5	291.5	556.7	2,920.3	476.8
San Jose, CA	2,607.2	2.1	26.1	100.6	202.6	406.1	1,312.0	557.7
Savannah, GA	4,766.4	9.5	14.2	215.4	160.9	1,210.9	2,859.4	296.1
Scottsdale, AZ	3,000.5	1.7	14.3	43.4	93.7	555.8	2,175.3	116.3
Seattle, WA	5,917.7	3.1	15.5	230.4	317.8	1,039.8	3,754.3	556.8
Sioux Falls, SD	3,320.9	1.9	59.7	34.2	204.1	615.5	2,263.5	141.9
Stamford, CT	1,887.2	1.6	15.5	123.6	144.8	283.1	1,162.4	156.2
Sterling Heights, MI	2,069.8	0.8	24.5	27.7	104.5	288.2	1,529.0	95.0
Sunnyvale, CA	1,787.1	0.0	19.4	44.0	62.7	303.6	1,174.0	183.5
Tampa, FL	3,916.6	7.8	13.5	196.6	405.9	900.2	2,151.6	240.9
Temecula, CA	2,366.5	2.0	2.9	41.0	26.3	522.1	1,602.4	169.8
Thousand Oaks, CA	1,753.4	0.8	12.9	40.3	58.0	288.6	1,294.7	58.0
Virginia Beach, VA	3,223.9	3.2	12.6	96.8	75.5	493.5	2,393.1	149.1
Washington, DC	5,751.2	21.9	30.6	650.5	538.1	702.0	2,999.7	808.3
U.S.	3,345.5	4.8	27.5	119.1	252.3	699.6	2,003.5	238.8

Note: Figures are crimes per 100,000 population in 2010 except where noted; n/a not available
Source: FBI Uniform Crime Reports, 2010

Crime Rate: Suburbs

Suburbs[1]	All Crimes	Violent Crimes				Property Crimes		
		Murder	Forcible Rape	Robbery	Aggrav. Assault	Burglary	Larceny -Theft	Motor Vehicle Theft
Albuquerque, NM	2,867.3	2.7	17.1	46.9	416.4	789.5	1,396.9	197.7
Alexandria, VA	3,159.7	6.4	19.4	207.3	204.1	419.6	1,954.2	348.7
Anchorage, AK	3,856.1	0.0	21.9	48.1	428.9	350.2	2,770.6	236.4
Ann Arbor, MI	3,132.8	2.1	45.5	70.6	260.3	750.3	1,801.4	202.5
Athens, GA	3,503.9	4.0	10.6	30.4	398.7	773.6	2,088.6	198.0
Atlanta, GA	3,554.7	4.9	21.3	122.0	193.5	898.1	2,007.3	307.5
Austin, TX	2,362.0	2.3	17.5	25.2	159.6	467.5	1,612.2	77.8
Baltimore, MD	3,130.3	2.7	18.1	120.0	307.5	485.3	2,009.0	187.8
Bellevue, WA	4,256.6	2.1	32.3	118.1	174.9	787.0	2,674.8	467.5
Billings, MT	2,074.6	2.0	12.2	6.1	107.8	362.0	1,436.0	148.5
Boise City, ID	1,910.1	1.7	29.0	13.3	149.8	385.1	1,251.0	80.2
Boston, MA	2,396.8	3.0	20.3	93.7	275.9	465.0	1,405.5	133.3
Boulder, CO	2,249.5	1.5	11.8	20.7	157.1	341.7	1,621.3	95.5
Broken Arrow, OK	4,256.1	7.0	43.5	172.9	426.9	1,134.0	2,112.2	359.8
Cambridge, MA	2,161.8	1.4	16.9	54.0	212.6	411.4	1,354.3	111.1
Cape Coral, FL	3,269.3	5.4	25.5	122.0	310.4	873.4	1,751.5	181.2
Carlsbad, CA	2,604.5	2.3	22.0	111.2	249.2	459.6	1,341.6	418.5
Cary, NC	2,831.7	3.8	17.0	82.3	161.4	662.6	1,701.8	202.8
Cedar Rapids, IA	1,356.7	0.8	19.1	5.3	69.4	358.4	826.7	77.0
Charleston, SC	4,165.2	5.4	28.1	121.8	390.0	803.8	2,522.8	293.1
Charlotte, NC	n/a	n/a	n/a	n/a	n/a	n/a	n/a	n/a
Chesapeake, VA	3,837.1	7.0	21.8	134.7	166.2	618.9	2,687.4	201.0
Chicago, IL	n/a	n/a	n/a	n/a	n/a	n/a	n/a	n/a
Clarksville, TN	2,416.0	4.8	33.0	44.7	127.9	641.7	1,449.7	114.2
Colorado Springs, CO	1,928.9	1.3	38.1	19.3	352.5	377.5	1,001.4	138.8
Columbia, MD	n/a	n/a	n/a	n/a	n/a	n/a	n/a	n/a
Columbia, MO	2,085.7	1.6	15.7	11.0	211.4	327.3	1,446.9	72.0
Columbia, SC	4,124.6	3.8	32.0	91.6	530.2	896.7	2,270.3	299.9
Columbus, OH	2,729.6	1.1	21.1	50.2	48.0	573.6	1,955.5	80.2
Dallas, TX	3,066.5	1.9	21.1	57.2	132.2	658.3	1,979.6	216.3
Denver, CO	2,847.3	2.2	45.3	57.2	168.5	462.2	1,895.2	216.6
Durham, NC	3,092.3	4.7	22.1	42.4	134.8	953.8	1,820.0	114.5
Edison, NJ	2,008.0	1.7	8.1	60.1	86.7	349.3	1,429.0	73.1
El Paso, TX	2,980.0	1.5	32.6	38.6	350.0	566.7	1,801.8	188.7
Fargo, ND	n/a	1.8	n/a	10.1	77.3	325.7	1,329.4	68.1
Fort Collins, CO	2,143.0	0.0	30.6	20.6	120.5	307.8	1,578.1	85.5
Fort Worth, TX	3,798.3	2.9	26.4	72.1	212.7	814.2	2,462.5	207.5
Gilbert, AZ	4,008.0	5.6	26.7	129.2	224.0	818.5	2,453.0	351.0
Green Bay, WI	1,534.7	0.5	19.4	3.9	31.1	280.8	1,158.7	40.3
Henderson, NV	3,922.4	7.3	43.9	267.1	532.5	965.5	1,625.6	480.5
High Point, NC	4,258.8	4.7	15.1	125.1	205.9	1,192.8	2,507.5	207.8
Honolulu, HI	n/a	n/a	n/a	n/a	n/a	n/a	n/a	n/a
Houston, TX	3,653.1	4.5	22.5	127.8	240.5	821.0	2,185.5	251.3
Huntington, NY	n/a	n/a	n/a	n/a	n/a	n/a	n/a	n/a
Huntsville, AL	2,326.0	4.3	17.1	43.7	139.2	586.3	1,407.3	128.1
Indianapolis, IN	n/a	n/a	n/a	n/a	n/a	n/a	n/a	n/a
Irvine, CA	2,295.4	2.4	15.0	89.7	133.1	369.6	1,475.0	210.5
Jackson, MS	2,118.5	4.3	19.9	28.8	92.2	513.6	1,326.1	133.6
Jacksonville, FL	2,948.0	3.2	19.1	57.8	308.4	534.9	1,925.7	98.9
Jersey City, NJ	2,132.2	5.3	10.9	199.6	274.7	233.8	1,288.6	119.3
Kansas City, MO	3,103.2	4.4	26.9	54.5	171.5	571.3	2,025.2	249.5
Kenosha, WI	n/a	n/a	n/a	n/a	n/a	n/a	n/a	n/a
Las Vegas, NV	3,000.0	4.5	23.2	129.5	263.4	700.1	1,607.6	271.7
Lexington, KY	3,452.1	2.3	19.8	56.5	118.0	680.5	2,474.6	100.5

Table continued on next page.

Suburbs[1]	All Crimes	Violent Crimes				Property Crimes		
		Murder	Forcible Rape	Robbery	Aggrav. Assault	Burglary	Larceny -Theft	Motor Vehicle Theft
Lincoln, NE	1,843.4	0.0	13.4	2.2	77.9	285.0	1,415.9	49.0
Little Rock, AR	4,341.6	3.8	35.9	74.8	345.9	1,107.2	2,556.8	217.2
Los Angeles, CA	2,856.6	5.4	19.0	182.0	270.5	527.1	1,415.2	437.4
Madison, WI	2,224.7	0.9	15.3	28.6	86.1	306.9	1,720.2	66.6
Manchester, NH	1,862.6	0.7	24.4	24.7	64.4	326.4	1,356.7	65.4
Miami, FL	5,303.1	7.5	23.6	196.9	426.2	888.3	3,354.8	405.9
Minneapolis, MN	n/a	1.4	n/a	49.8	104.7	403.8	2,080.7	165.1
Murfreesboro, TN	3,978.1	6.3	41.6	138.9	463.0	820.9	2,314.4	192.9
Naperville, IL	n/a	n/a	n/a	n/a	n/a	n/a	n/a	n/a
Nashville, TN	2,756.0	4.5	29.5	42.0	261.6	593.4	1,709.7	115.2
New Orleans, LA	n/a	8.9	19.3	78.9	249.2	634.3	2,145.3	n/a
New York, NY	1,900.3	2.8	7.7	124.5	147.3	308.9	1,185.6	123.4
Norman, OK	n/a	6.1	44.0	114.9	n/a	1,236.2	2,671.5	401.0
Olathe, KS	4,061.6	8.6	31.8	126.0	313.5	817.8	2,405.7	358.3
Omaha, NE	2,616.0	1.2	35.5	29.5	204.7	499.3	1,628.3	217.4
Orlando, FL	3,783.3	4.5	31.2	126.8	393.0	918.9	2,098.4	210.5
Overland Park, KS	4,071.3	9.0	32.8	129.0	318.5	827.3	2,395.1	359.6
Oyster Bay, NY	n/a	n/a	n/a	n/a	n/a	n/a	n/a	n/a
Pembroke Pines, FL	4,388.7	3.6	26.2	186.6	293.6	996.0	2,612.3	270.4
Philadelphia, PA	2,133.3	2.6	14.6	72.5	151.1	300.5	1,507.5	84.5
Phoenix, AZ	3,568.4	4.2	21.4	74.4	186.0	671.2	2,368.4	242.8
Pittsburgh, PA	1,957.2	2.7	16.2	53.2	158.9	352.9	1,304.6	68.7
Plano, TX	3,901.1	4.9	26.8	147.8	189.4	938.4	2,238.1	355.9
Portland, OR	n/a	n/a	n/a	n/a	n/a	n/a	n/a	n/a
Providence, RI	2,589.8	1.9	28.7	74.4	225.9	558.2	1,540.1	160.6
Provo, UT	2,099.1	0.9	17.6	11.8	28.9	312.5	1,658.6	68.7
Raleigh, NC	2,220.3	3.5	11.9	31.4	99.0	576.4	1,327.7	170.4
Richmond, VA	2,405.0	4.7	15.1	63.8	95.3	423.3	1,681.9	121.0
Roseville, CA	3,592.5	4.4	26.8	165.5	293.1	787.9	1,850.5	464.2
Round Rock, TX	4,207.9	3.7	24.7	87.5	227.1	777.1	2,911.6	176.3
San Antonio, TX	3,304.7	2.7	30.7	44.6	168.1	736.4	2,183.8	138.5
San Diego, CA	2,447.6	2.2	21.3	97.3	221.2	436.2	1,319.5	350.1
San Francisco, CA	2,439.8	2.5	18.6	81.3	143.0	449.0	1,490.7	254.8
San Jose, CA	2,425.6	0.7	16.9	57.5	115.7	437.3	1,587.1	210.5
Savannah, GA	2,836.9	1.6	30.8	53.7	160.5	645.0	1,784.8	160.5
Scottsdale, AZ	3,957.5	5.7	26.6	128.7	222.3	809.4	2,415.4	349.5
Seattle, WA	3,668.1	1.6	36.0	78.8	123.1	691.7	2,316.3	420.5
Sioux Falls, SD	1,176.6	0.0	11.0	3.7	83.1	372.6	646.3	59.9
Stamford, CT	2,093.4	4.1	16.0	108.5	153.3	384.9	1,236.3	190.2
Sterling Heights, MI	2,306.4	2.1	29.5	53.2	190.4	460.1	1,394.6	176.5
Sunnyvale, CA	2,578.3	1.5	21.9	82.9	169.0	430.1	1,463.7	409.1
Tampa, FL	3,883.0	3.8	28.4	115.8	334.3	840.3	2,363.5	196.8
Temecula, CA	3,080.4	4.6	20.8	117.5	233.0	752.1	1,549.4	403.1
Thousand Oaks, CA	2,283.4	2.5	13.0	84.6	135.4	393.7	1,499.9	154.3
Virginia Beach, VA	4,026.3	7.8	23.1	145.6	212.0	645.2	2,778.4	214.2
Washington, DC	2,709.2	3.7	17.4	131.1	145.6	365.7	1,777.2	268.5
U.S.	3,345.5	4.8	27.5	119.1	252.3	699.6	2,003.5	238.8

Note: Figures are crimes per 100,000 population in 2010 except where noted; n/a not available; (1) All areas within the metro area that are located outside the city limits
Source: FBI Uniform Crime Reports, 2010

Crime Rate: Metro Area

Metro Area[1]	All Crimes	Violent Crimes				Property Crimes		
		Murder	Forcible Rape	Robbery	Aggrav. Assault	Burglary	Larceny -Theft	Motor Vehicle Theft
Albuquerque, NM	4,566.6	5.8	44.8	124.3	495.6	920.6	2,586.2	389.4
Alexandria, VA[2]	3,129.6	6.2	19.2	202.9	199.8	412.2	1,946.2	343.1
Anchorage, AK	4,319.2	4.2	85.9	148.5	574.4	416.1	2,813.4	276.8
Ann Arbor, MI	3,052.1	1.4	43.2	69.8	224.0	659.7	1,879.5	174.4
Athens, GA	4,218.5	4.2	19.6	70.5	280.5	1,018.0	2,588.1	237.5
Atlanta, GA	3,876.4	6.1	20.9	149.7	237.1	957.0	2,135.7	370.0
Austin, TX	4,119.9	3.4	24.7	84.0	215.8	754.3	2,866.9	170.8
Baltimore, MD	3,776.0	10.3	23.6	214.4	437.0	649.5	2,135.5	305.7
Bellevue, WA[2]	4,198.4	2.0	31.1	114.6	169.0	773.8	2,655.3	452.6
Billings, MT	4,020.9	1.9	19.7	28.6	167.9	652.7	2,873.3	276.7
Boise City, ID	2,283.3	1.6	33.7	18.2	162.8	400.4	1,587.3	79.2
Boston, MA[2]	2,973.7	5.8	26.9	163.0	369.5	496.0	1,717.4	195.1
Boulder, CO	2,480.8	2.3	18.9	23.5	153.1	387.6	1,801.8	93.6
Broken Arrow, OK	4,047.6	6.4	42.3	158.0	391.5	1,054.3	2,059.2	335.8
Cambridge, MA[2]	2,253.3	1.3	17.1	61.6	216.1	413.9	1,428.1	115.1
Cape Coral, FL	3,073.3	4.5	22.6	100.2	258.7	820.6	1,715.8	151.1
Carlsbad, CA	2,584.9	2.2	22.0	108.9	245.4	457.6	1,340.5	408.3
Cary, NC	2,685.2	3.4	16.1	75.3	147.8	628.1	1,630.8	183.7
Cedar Rapids, IA	2,732.3	0.8	22.2	49.9	120.0	573.8	1,835.2	130.4
Charleston, SC	4,092.7	6.0	25.9	122.9	359.0	752.7	2,550.3	275.9
Charlotte, NC	n/a	n/a	n/a	n/a	n/a	n/a	n/a	n/a
Chesapeake, VA	3,819.5	6.6	20.4	133.1	176.8	606.1	2,679.1	197.4
Chicago, IL	n/a	n/a	n/a	n/a	n/a	n/a	n/a	n/a
Clarksville, TN	3,095.0	5.9	37.9	68.4	295.3	847.9	1,703.6	136.1
Colorado Springs, CO	3,697.5	3.7	64.8	91.0	302.9	688.9	2,289.9	256.3
Columbia, MD	3,776.0	10.3	23.6	214.4	437.0	649.5	2,135.5	305.7
Columbia, MO	3,394.3	2.4	28.1	82.5	295.3	454.9	2,422.9	108.2
Columbia, SC	4,630.2	5.3	36.3	121.5	553.9	966.7	2,609.8	336.9
Columbus, OH	4,628.7	5.8	43.2	213.6	106.3	1,167.8	2,817.5	274.4
Dallas, TX[2]	3,818.8	4.7	26.3	141.9	184.1	907.2	2,212.4	342.2
Denver, CO	3,108.6	2.5	48.9	79.9	205.8	528.6	1,951.5	291.4
Durham, NC	4,218.4	7.1	23.7	152.2	244.0	1,232.8	2,355.9	202.8
Edison, NJ[2]	2,001.0	1.7	8.0	59.8	86.5	348.6	1,419.9	76.6
El Paso, TX	3,199.5	0.9	29.4	70.1	351.7	357.1	2,152.2	238.1
Fargo, ND	n/a	1.0	n/a	22.1	147.3	358.0	1,751.5	115.6
Fort Collins, CO	2,817.8	0.0	37.8	27.8	173.0	380.1	2,085.8	113.4
Fort Worth, TX[2]	4,309.2	4.8	32.0	108.8	258.8	965.9	2,689.1	249.9
Gilbert, AZ	3,905.4	5.5	25.9	124.1	215.3	795.6	2,402.3	336.8
Green Bay, WI	1,993.7	1.0	30.6	24.4	101.2	373.1	1,400.6	62.8
Henderson, NV	3,685.3	6.7	39.8	240.6	476.3	900.3	1,580.0	441.6
High Point, NC	4,397.7	4.3	16.7	137.3	225.4	1,200.7	2,605.2	208.0
Honolulu, HI	3,600.7	2.0	22.9	93.8	149.4	606.1	2,315.9	410.5
Houston, TX	4,564.6	7.3	25.8	237.1	350.5	974.8	2,599.3	369.8
Huntington, NY[2]	1,845.7	2.8	5.1	67.7	88.1	262.2	1,323.7	96.1
Huntsville, AL	3,929.7	5.3	27.8	135.5	229.3	970.6	2,282.8	278.3
Indianapolis, IN	n/a	n/a	n/a	n/a	n/a	n/a	n/a	n/a
Irvine, CA[2]	2,227.4	2.2	14.8	84.6	125.5	359.0	1,441.9	199.4
Jackson, MS	4,183.9	10.4	32.0	218.5	152.5	1,232.1	2,162.5	375.8
Jacksonville, FL	4,329.3	7.2	30.9	148.0	370.9	919.2	2,668.3	184.8
Jersey City, NJ[2]	2,154.6	5.4	11.1	203.5	276.0	241.9	1,293.0	123.7
Kansas City, MO	3,937.3	8.2	31.9	119.7	301.4	780.1	2,352.5	343.5
Kenosha, WI	n/a	n/a	n/a	n/a	n/a	n/a	n/a	n/a
Las Vegas, NV	3,685.3	6.7	39.8	240.6	476.3	900.3	1,580.0	441.6
Lexington, KY	3,952.8	4.6	25.6	145.2	258.8	814.0	2,533.0	171.6

Table continued on next page.

Metro Area[1]	All Crimes	Violent Crimes				Property Crimes		
		Murder	Forcible Rape	Robbery	Aggrav. Assault	Burglary	Larceny -Theft	Motor Vehicle Theft
Lincoln, NE	4,039.5	0.7	48.9	60.1	317.1	522.7	2,968.6	121.5
Little Rock, AR	5,690.2	6.3	47.4	177.8	524.3	1,410.5	3,206.4	317.5
Los Angeles, CA[2]	2,871.3	6.3	21.0	221.8	259.9	498.3	1,424.1	439.9
Madison, WI	2,860.4	0.9	24.1	73.3	140.3	465.6	2,054.0	102.4
Manchester, NH	2,429.3	0.7	33.2	56.3	128.2	463.8	1,659.4	87.6
Miami, FL[2]	5,411.6	8.9	21.3	236.1	467.0	915.7	3,330.6	432.1
Minneapolis, MN	n/a	2.4	n/a	92.3	152.8	501.6	2,189.2	203.5
Murfreesboro, TN	4,032.1	6.2	41.0	138.9	457.0	846.7	2,352.8	189.5
Naperville, IL	n/a	n/a	n/a	n/a	n/a	n/a	n/a	n/a
Nashville, TN	4,032.1	6.2	41.0	138.9	457.0	846.7	2,352.8	189.5
New Orleans, LA	n/a	20.8	25.6	134.8	285.3	753.7	2,053.4	n/a
New York, NY[2]	2,154.6	5.4	11.1	203.5	276.0	241.9	1,293.0	123.7
Norman, OK	n/a	5.7	43.8	107.6	n/a	1,190.9	2,643.5	374.2
Olathe, KS	3,937.3	8.2	31.9	119.7	301.4	780.1	2,352.5	343.5
Omaha, NE	3,473.8	4.5	38.8	97.0	246.3	583.0	2,149.9	354.2
Orlando, FL	4,208.2	4.8	33.0	144.1	431.8	1,003.8	2,348.0	242.7
Overland Park, KS	3,937.3	8.2	31.9	119.7	301.4	780.1	2,352.5	343.5
Oyster Bay, NY[2]	1,845.7	2.8	5.1	67.7	88.1	262.2	1,323.7	96.1
Pembroke Pines, FL[2]	4,323.2	3.5	24.7	176.3	278.7	975.5	2,599.4	265.1
Philadelphia, PA[2]	3,197.2	9.1	32.3	251.2	313.3	451.5	1,913.3	226.5
Phoenix, AZ	3,905.4	5.5	25.9	124.1	215.3	795.6	2,402.3	336.8
Pittsburgh, PA	2,295.1	4.7	16.9	96.5	201.4	431.1	1,457.1	87.4
Plano, TX[2]	3,818.8	4.7	26.3	141.9	184.1	907.2	2,212.4	342.2
Portland, OR	n/a	n/a	n/a	n/a	n/a	n/a	n/a	n/a
Providence, RI	2,903.2	2.6	30.2	91.8	246.8	625.7	1,692.8	213.4
Provo, UT	2,181.5	1.1	22.1	14.1	44.1	312.9	1,714.5	72.6
Raleigh, NC	2,685.2	3.4	16.1	75.3	147.8	628.1	1,630.8	183.7
Richmond, VA	2,812.2	7.2	15.8	111.8	134.5	495.8	1,877.1	170.1
Roseville, CA	3,584.8	4.2	26.1	160.4	287.5	769.3	1,888.1	449.2
Round Rock, TX	4,119.9	3.4	24.7	84.0	215.8	754.3	2,866.9	170.8
San Antonio, TX	5,717.1	4.7	32.6	127.2	319.5	1,071.3	3,846.2	315.6
San Diego, CA	2,584.9	2.2	22.0	108.9	245.4	457.6	1,340.5	408.3
San Francisco, CA[2]	3,453.8	4.0	17.5	221.9	211.0	498.3	2,144.8	356.4
San Jose, CA	2,520.9	1.4	21.7	80.1	161.3	420.9	1,442.7	392.7
Savannah, GA	4,042.6	6.5	20.5	154.8	160.7	998.6	2,456.3	245.2
Scottsdale, AZ	3,905.4	5.5	25.9	124.1	215.3	795.6	2,402.3	336.8
Seattle, WA[2]	4,198.4	2.0	31.1	114.6	169.0	773.8	2,655.3	452.6
Sioux Falls, SD	2,597.2	1.2	43.3	23.9	163.3	533.5	1,717.7	114.2
Stamford, CT	2,065.1	3.8	16.0	110.6	152.1	370.9	1,226.2	185.5
Sterling Heights, MI[2]	2,294.3	2.0	29.3	51.9	186.0	451.2	1,401.5	172.3
Sunnyvale, CA	2,520.9	1.4	21.7	80.1	161.3	420.9	1,442.7	392.7
Tampa, FL	3,887.2	4.3	26.6	125.9	343.3	847.8	2,337.1	202.3
Temecula, CA	3,063.1	4.5	20.4	115.7	228.0	746.5	1,550.6	397.5
Thousand Oaks, CA	2,202.0	2.2	13.0	77.8	123.5	377.5	1,468.4	139.5
Virginia Beach, VA	3,819.5	6.6	20.4	133.1	176.8	606.1	2,679.1	197.4
Washington, DC[2]	3,129.6	6.2	19.2	202.9	199.8	412.2	1,946.2	343.1
U.S.	3,345.5	4.8	27.5	119.1	252.3	699.6	2,003.5	238.8

Note: Figures are crimes per 100,000 population in 2010 except where noted; n/a not available; (1) Figures cover the Metropolitan Statistical Area except where noted; (2) Metropolitan Division (MD); See Appendix B for counties included in MSAs and MDs
Source: FBI Uniform Crime Reports, 2010

Temperature & Precipitation: Yearly Averages and Extremes

City	Extreme Low (°F)	Average Low (°F)	Average Temp. (°F)	Average High (°F)	Extreme High (°F)	Average Precip. (in.)	Average Snow (in.)
Albuquerque, NM	-17	43	57	70	105	8.5	11
Alexandria, VA	-5	49	58	67	104	39.5	18
Anchorage, AK	-34	29	36	43	85	15.7	71
Ann Arbor, MI	-21	39	49	58	104	32.4	41
Athens, GA	-8	52	62	72	105	49.8	2
Atlanta, GA	-8	52	62	72	105	49.8	2
Austin, TX	-2	58	69	79	109	31.1	1
Baltimore, MD	-7	45	56	65	105	41.2	21
Bellevue, WA	0	44	52	59	99	38.4	13
Billings, MT	-32	36	47	59	105	14.6	59
Boise City, ID	-25	39	51	63	111	11.8	22
Boston, MA	-12	44	52	59	102	42.9	41
Boulder, CO	-25	37	51	64	103	15.5	63
Broken Arrow, OK	-8	50	61	71	112	38.9	10
Cambridge, MA	-12	44	52	59	102	42.9	41
Cape Coral, FL	26	65	75	84	103	53.9	0
Carlsbad, CA	29	57	64	71	111	9.5	Trace
Cary, NC	-9	48	60	71	105	42.0	8
Cedar Rapids, IA	-34	36	47	57	105	34.4	33
Charleston, SC	6	55	66	76	104	52.1	1
Charlotte, NC	-5	50	61	71	104	42.8	6
Chesapeake, VA	-3	51	60	69	104	44.8	8
Chicago, IL	-27	40	49	59	104	35.4	39
Clarksville, TN	-17	49	60	70	107	47.4	11
Colorado Springs, CO	-24	36	49	62	99	17.0	48
Columbia, MD	-7	45	56	65	105	41.2	21
Columbia, MO	-20	44	54	64	111	40.6	25
Columbia, SC	-1	51	64	75	107	48.3	2
Columbus, OH	-19	42	52	62	104	37.9	28
Dallas, TX	-2	56	67	77	112	33.9	3
Denver, CO	-25	37	51	64	103	15.5	63
Durham, NC	-9	48	60	71	105	42.0	8
Edison, NJ	-2	47	55	62	104	47.0	23
El Paso, TX	-8	50	64	78	114	8.6	6
Fargo, ND	-36	31	41	52	106	19.6	40
Fort Collins, CO	-25	37	51	64	103	15.5	63
Fort Worth, TX	-1	55	66	76	113	32.3	3
Gilbert, AZ	17	59	72	86	122	7.3	Trace
Green Bay, WI	-31	34	44	54	99	28.3	46
Henderson, NV	8	53	67	80	116	4.0	1
High Point, NC	-8	47	58	69	103	42.5	10
Honolulu, HI	52	70	77	84	94	22.4	0
Houston, TX	7	58	69	79	107	46.9	Trace
Huntington, NY	-3	48	55	62	107	42.8	24
Huntsville, AL	-11	50	61	71	104	56.8	4
Indianapolis, IN	-23	42	53	62	104	40.2	25
Irvine, CA	25	53	64	75	112	11.9	Trace
Jackson, MS	-2	53	65	76	106	55.4	1
Jacksonville, FL	7	58	69	79	103	52.0	0
Jersey City, NJ	-8	46	55	63	105	43.5	27
Kansas City, MO	-23	44	54	64	109	38.1	21
Kenosha, WI	-27	40	49	59	104	35.4	39
Las Vegas, NV	8	53	67	80	116	4.0	1
Lexington, KY	-21	45	55	65	103	45.1	17
Lincoln, NE	-33	39	51	62	108	29.1	27

Table continued on next page.

City	Extreme Low (°F)	Average Low (°F)	Average Temp. (°F)	Average High (°F)	Extreme High (°F)	Average Precip. (in.)	Average Snow (in.)
Little Rock, AR	-5	51	62	73	112	50.7	5
Los Angeles, CA	27	55	63	70	110	11.3	Trace
Madison, WI	-37	35	46	57	104	31.1	42
Manchester, NH	-33	34	46	57	102	36.9	63
Miami, FL	30	69	76	83	98	57.1	0
Minneapolis, MN	-34	35	45	54	105	27.1	52
Murfreesboro, TN	-17	49	60	70	107	47.4	11
Naperville, IL	-27	40	49	59	104	35.4	39
Nashville, TN	-17	49	60	70	107	47.4	11
New Orleans, LA	11	59	69	78	102	60.6	Trace
New York, NY	-2	47	55	62	104	47.0	23
Norman, OK	-8	49	60	71	110	32.8	10
Olathe, KS	-23	44	54	64	109	38.1	21
Omaha, NE	-23	40	51	62	110	30.1	29
Orlando, FL	19	62	72	82	100	47.7	Trace
Overland Park, KS	-23	44	54	64	109	38.1	21
Oyster Bay, NY	-3	48	55	62	107	42.8	24
Pembroke Pines, FL	30	69	76	83	98	57.1	0
Philadelphia, PA	-7	45	55	64	104	41.4	22
Phoenix, AZ	17	59	72	86	122	7.3	Trace
Pittsburgh, PA	-18	41	51	60	103	37.1	43
Plano, TX	-2	56	67	77	112	33.9	3
Portland, OR	-3	45	54	62	107	37.5	7
Providence, RI	-13	42	51	60	104	45.3	35
Provo, UT	-22	40	52	64	107	15.6	63
Raleigh, NC	-9	48	60	71	105	42.0	8
Richmond, VA	-8	48	58	69	105	43.0	13
Roseville, CA	18	48	61	73	115	17.3	Trace
Round Rock, TX	-2	58	69	79	109	31.1	1
San Antonio, TX	0	58	69	80	108	29.6	1
San Diego, CA	29	57	64	71	111	9.5	Trace
San Francisco, CA	24	49	57	65	106	19.3	Trace
San Jose, CA	21	50	59	68	105	13.5	Trace
Savannah, GA	3	56	67	77	105	50.3	Trace
Scottsdale, AZ	17	59	72	86	122	7.3	Trace
Seattle, WA	0	44	52	59	99	38.4	13
Sioux Falls, SD	-36	35	46	57	110	24.6	38
Stamford, CT	-7	44	52	60	103	41.4	25
Sterling Heights, MI	-21	39	49	58	104	32.4	41
Sunnyvale, CA	21	50	59	68	105	13.5	Trace
Tampa, FL	18	63	73	82	99	46.7	Trace
Temecula, CA	24	53	66	78	114	n/a	n/a
Thousand Oaks, CA	27	55	63	70	110	11.3	Trace
Virginia Beach, VA	-3	51	60	69	104	44.8	8
Washington, DC	-5	49	58	67	104	39.5	18

Source: National Climatic Data Center, International Station Meteorological Climate Summary, 9/96

Weather Conditions

City	Temperature			Daytime Sky			Precipitation		
	10°F & below	32°F & below	90°F & above	Clear	Partly cloudy	Cloudy	0.01 inch or more precip.	1.0 inch or more snow/ice	Thunder-storms
Albuquerque, NM	4	114	65	140	161	64	60	9	38
Alexandria, VA	2	71	34	84	144	137	112	9	30
Anchorage, AK	n/a	194	n/a	50	115	200	113	49	2
Ann Arbor, MI	n/a	136	12	74	134	157	135	38	32
Athens, GA	1	49	38	98	147	120	116	3	48
Atlanta, GA	1	49	38	98	147	120	116	3	48
Austin, TX	< 1	20	111	105	148	112	83	1	41
Baltimore, MD	6	97	31	91	143	131	113	13	27
Bellevue, WA	n/a	38	3	57	121	187	157	8	8
Billings, MT	n/a	149	29	75	163	127	97	41	27
Boise City, ID	n/a	124	45	106	133	126	91	22	14
Boston, MA	n/a	97	12	88	127	150	253	48	18
Boulder, CO	24	155	33	99	177	89	90	38	39
Broken Arrow, OK	6	78	74	117	141	107	88	8	50
Cambridge, MA	n/a	97	12	88	127	150	253	48	18
Cape Coral, FL	n/a	n/a	115	93	220	52	110	0	92
Carlsbad, CA	0	< 1	4	115	126	124	40	0	5
Cary, NC	n/a	n/a	39	98	143	124	110	3	42
Cedar Rapids, IA	n/a	156	16	89	132	144	109	28	42
Charleston, SC	< 1	33	53	89	162	114	114	1	59
Charlotte, NC	1	65	44	98	142	125	113	3	41
Chesapeake, VA	< 1	53	33	89	149	127	115	5	38
Chicago, IL	n/a	132	17	83	136	146	125	31	38
Clarksville, TN	5	76	51	98	135	132	119	8	54
Colorado Springs, CO	21	161	18	108	157	100	98	33	49
Columbia, MD	6	97	31	91	143	131	113	13	27
Columbia, MO	17	108	36	99	127	139	110	17	52
Columbia, SC	< 1	58	77	97	149	119	110	1	53
Columbus, OH	n/a	118	19	72	137	156	136	29	40
Dallas, TX	1	34	102	108	160	97	78	2	49
Denver, CO	24	155	33	99	177	89	90	38	39
Durham, NC	n/a	n/a	39	98	143	124	110	3	42
Edison, NJ	n/a	n/a	18	85	166	114	120	11	20
El Paso, TX	1	59	106	147	164	54	49	3	35
Fargo, ND	n/a	180	15	81	145	139	100	38	31
Fort Collins, CO	24	155	33	99	177	89	90	38	39
Fort Worth, TX	1	40	100	123	136	106	79	3	47
Gilbert, AZ	0	10	167	186	125	54	37	< 1	23
Green Bay, WI	n/a	163	7	86	125	154	120	40	33
Henderson, NV	< 1	37	134	185	132	48	27	2	13
High Point, NC	3	85	32	94	143	128	113	5	43
Honolulu, HI	n/a	n/a	23	25	286	54	98	0	7
Houston, TX	n/a	n/a	96	83	168	114	101	1	62
Huntington, NY	n/a	73	16	77	161	127	119	14	23
Huntsville, AL	2	66	49	70	118	177	116	2	54
Indianapolis, IN	19	119	19	83	128	154	127	24	43
Irvine, CA	0	2	18	95	192	78	41	0	4
Jackson, MS	1	50	84	103	144	118	106	2	68
Jacksonville, FL	< 1	16	83	86	181	98	114	1	65
Jersey City, NJ	n/a	90	24	80	146	139	122	16	46
Kansas City, MO	22	110	39	112	134	119	103	17	51
Kenosha, WI	n/a	132	17	83	136	146	125	31	38
Las Vegas, NV	< 1	37	134	185	132	48	27	2	13
Lexington, KY	11	96	22	86	136	143	129	17	44

Table continued on next page.

City	Temperature			Daytime Sky			Precipitation		
	10°F & below	32°F & below	90°F & above	Clear	Partly cloudy	Cloudy	0.01 inch or more precip.	1.0 inch or more snow/ice	Thunder-storms
Lincoln, NE	n/a	145	40	108	135	122	94	19	46
Little Rock, AR	1	57	73	110	142	113	104	4	57
Los Angeles, CA	0	< 1	5	131	125	109	34	0	1
Madison, WI	n/a	161	14	88	119	158	118	38	40
Manchester, NH	n/a	171	12	87	131	147	125	32	19
Miami, FL	n/a	n/a	55	48	263	54	128	0	74
Minneapolis, MN	n/a	156	16	93	125	147	113	41	37
Murfreesboro, TN	5	76	51	98	135	132	119	8	54
Naperville, IL	n/a	132	17	83	136	146	125	31	38
Nashville, TN	5	76	51	98	135	132	119	8	54
New Orleans, LA	0	13	70	90	169	106	114	1	69
New York, NY	n/a	n/a	18	85	166	114	120	11	20
Norman, OK	5	79	70	124	131	110	80	8	50
Olathe, KS	22	110	39	112	134	119	103	17	46
Omaha, NE	n/a	139	35	100	142	123	97	20	46
Orlando, FL	n/a	n/a	90	76	208	81	115	0	80
Overland Park, KS	22	110	39	112	134	119	103	17	51
Oyster Bay, NY	n/a	73	16	77	161	127	119	14	23
Pembroke Pines, FL	n/a	n/a	55	48	263	54	128	0	74
Philadelphia, PA	5	94	23	81	146	138	117	14	27
Phoenix, AZ	0	10	167	186	125	54	37	< 1	23
Pittsburgh, PA	n/a	121	8	62	137	166	154	42	35
Plano, TX	1	34	102	108	160	97	78	2	49
Portland, OR	n/a	37	11	67	116	182	152	4	7
Providence, RI	n/a	117	9	85	134	146	123	21	21
Provo, UT	n/a	128	56	94	152	119	92	38	38
Raleigh, NC	n/a	n/a	39	98	143	124	110	3	42
Richmond, VA	3	79	41	90	147	128	115	7	43
Roseville, CA	0	21	73	175	111	79	58	< 1	2
Round Rock, TX	< 1	20	111	105	148	112	83	1	41
San Antonio, TX	n/a	n/a	112	97	153	115	81	1	36
San Diego, CA	0	< 1	4	115	126	124	40	0	5
San Francisco, CA	0	6	4	136	130	99	63	< 1	5
San Jose, CA	0	5	5	106	180	79	57	< 1	6
Savannah, GA	< 1	29	70	97	155	113	111	< 1	63
Scottsdale, AZ	0	10	167	186	125	54	37	< 1	23
Seattle, WA	n/a	38	3	57	121	187	157	8	8
Sioux Falls, SD	n/a	n/a	n/a	95	136	134	n/a	n/a	n/a
Stamford, CT	n/a	n/a	7	80	146	139	118	17	22
Sterling Heights, MI	n/a	136	12	74	134	157	135	38	32
Sunnyvale, CA	0	5	5	106	180	79	57	< 1	6
Tampa, FL	n/a	n/a	85	81	204	80	107	< 1	87
Temecula, CA	0	4	82	124	178	63	n/a	n/a	5
Thousand Oaks, CA	0	< 1	5	131	125	109	34	0	1
Virginia Beach, VA	< 1	53	33	89	149	127	115	5	38
Washington, DC	2	71	34	84	144	137	112	9	30

Note: Figures are average number of days per year
Source: National Climatic Data Center, International Station Meteorological Climate Summary, 9/96

Air Quality Index

Area[1] (Days[2])	Percent of Days when Air Quality was...					AQI Statistics	
	Good	Moderate	Unhealthy for Sensitive Groups	Unhealthy	Very Unhealthy	Maximum	Median
Albuquerque, NM (365)	45.8	50.4	3.3	0.3	0.3	293	52
Alexandria, VA (365)	86.0	12.1	1.6	0.3	0.0	161	34
Anchorage, AK (365)	89.6	10.4	0.0	0.0	0.0	88	25
Ann Arbor, MI (296)	83.1	15.5	1.4	0.0	0.0	129	35
Athens, GA (365)	71.2	27.7	1.1	0.0	0.0	106	41
Atlanta, GA (365)	66.0	29.9	4.1	0.0	0.0	145	43
Austin, TX (365)	74.0	25.2	0.8	0.0	0.0	116	40
Baltimore, MD (365)	66.6	31.2	2.2	0.0	0.0	129	43
Bellevue, WA (365)	86.8	13.2	0.0	0.0	0.0	89	33
Billings, MT (365)	87.7	11.5	0.8	0.0	0.0	131	23
Boise City, ID (365)	88.2	11.2	0.5	0.0	0.0	115	38
Boston, MA (365)	75.6	23.8	0.5	0.0	0.0	108	42
Boulder, CO (365)	80.0	18.9	1.1	0.0	0.0	116	42
Broken Arrow, OK (365)	44.7	48.2	6.8	0.3	0.0	158	54
Cambridge, MA (365)	96.7	3.0	0.3	0.0	0.0	127	31
Cape Coral, FL (365)	95.1	4.9	0.0	0.0	0.0	74	34
Carlsbad, CA (365)	33.7	62.7	3.3	0.3	0.0	155	54
Cary, NC (365)	72.9	25.5	1.6	0.0	0.0	137	40
Cedar Rapids, IA (365)	78.6	21.4	0.0	0.0	0.0	84	38
Charleston, SC (365)	80.3	18.6	1.1	0.0	0.0	136	37
Charlotte, NC (365)	67.1	28.2	4.7	0.0	0.0	145	44
Chesapeake, VA (n/a)	n/a	n/a	n/a	n/a	n/a	n/a	n/a
Chicago, IL (365)	37.8	57.0	5.2	0.0	0.0	138	56
Clarksville, TN (365)	76.2	23.6	0.3	0.0	0.0	141	35
Colorado Spgs., CO (365)	74.8	24.4	0.8	0.0	0.0	119	43
Columbia, MD (n/a)	n/a	n/a	n/a	n/a	n/a	n/a	n/a
Columbia, MO (245)	91.4	8.6	0.0	0.0	0.0	97	39
Columbia, SC (365)	66.8	30.7	2.5	0.0	0.0	124	43
Columbus, OH (365)	69.9	27.9	2.2	0.0	0.0	132	42
Dallas, TX (365)	66.0	28.2	4.9	0.8	0.0	156	44
Denver, CO (365)	57.8	41.1	1.1	0.0	0.0	137	48
Durham, NC (365)	81.9	17.8	0.3	0.0	0.0	105	36
Edison, NJ (364)	83.5	13.5	3.0	0.0	0.0	142	37
El Paso, TX (365)	46.3	50.4	2.7	0.5	0.0	186	52
Fargo, ND (350)	91.7	8.3	0.0	0.0	0.0	72	31
Ft. Collins, CO (365)	60.3	36.2	3.6	0.0	0.0	127	48
Ft. Worth, TX (365)	63.3	29.0	6.6	1.1	0.0	169	45
Gilbert, AZ (365)	23.6	65.2	7.1	2.2	1.9	565	61
Green Bay, WI (365)	64.9	33.2	1.9	0.0	0.0	122	42
Henderson, NV (365)	57.5	35.9	6.6	0.0	0.0	144	47
High Point, NC (361)	78.9	19.9	1.1	0.0	0.0	116	39
Honolulu, HI (365)	92.6	7.4	0.0	0.0	0.0	91	32
Houston, TX (365)	52.9	38.6	7.4	1.1	0.0	164	49
Huntington, NY (365)	82.7	14.0	2.5	0.8	0.0	197	38
Huntsville, AL (332)	80.7	18.7	0.6	0.0	0.0	106	38
Indianapolis, IN (365)	44.1	52.6	3.3	0.0	0.0	124	53
Irvine, CA (365)	50.1	47.9	1.9	0.0	0.0	119	50
Jackson, MS (365)	68.5	30.7	0.8	0.0	0.0	124	43
Jacksonville, FL (365)	83.6	14.2	1.4	0.8	0.0	173	38
Jersey City, NJ (365)	69.0	29.6	1.4	0.0	0.0	132	41
Kansas City, MO (365)	60.8	31.0	7.7	0.5	0.0	159	43
Kenosha, WI (304)	82.9	14.8	2.0	0.3	0.0	151	36
Las Vegas, NV (365)	57.5	35.9	6.6	0.0	0.0	144	47
Lexington, KY (365)	78.1	21.1	0.8	0.0	0.0	111	39

Table continued on next page.

Area[1] (Days[2])	Percent of Days when Air Quality was...					AQI Statistics	
	Good	Moderate	Unhealthy for Sensitive Groups	Unhealthy	Very Unhealthy	Maximum	Median
Lincoln, NE (365)	96.7	3.3	0.0	0.0	0.0	78	25
Little Rock, AR (365)	64.4	32.6	3.0	0.0	0.0	122	45
Los Angeles, CA (365)	14.5	59.5	23.0	2.7	0.3	203	69
Madison, WI (359)	79.4	20.6	0.0	0.0	0.0	95	36
Manchester, NH (365)	93.4	6.0	0.5	0.0	0.0	137	35
Miami, FL (365)	89.9	9.6	0.5	0.0	0.0	109	36
Minneapolis, MN (365)	84.7	15.3	0.0	0.0	0.0	86	28
Murfreesboro, TN (243)	88.9	11.1	0.0	0.0	0.0	84	40
Naperville, IL (365)	71.8	27.9	0.3	0.0	0.0	101	40
Nashville, TN (365)	74.2	24.9	0.8	0.0	0.0	124	41
New Orleans, LA (365)	89.6	9.9	0.3	0.3	0.0	155	34
New York, NY (365)	79.7	20.3	0.0	0.0	0.0	98	32
Norman, OK (363)	66.7	30.0	3.3	0.0	0.0	127	44
Olathe, KS (365)	86.6	12.6	0.8	0.0	0.0	137	36
Omaha, NE (365)	57.8	41.6	0.5	0.0	0.0	109	45
Orlando, FL (365)	87.9	10.1	1.9	0.0	0.0	111	36
Overland Park, KS (365)	86.6	12.6	0.8	0.0	0.0	137	36
Oyster Bay, NY (365)	81.6	18.4	0.0	0.0	0.0	96	30
Pembroke Pines, FL (365)	95.9	4.1	0.0	0.0	0.0	100	34
Philadelphia, PA (365)	55.1	41.6	3.3	0.0	0.0	147	48
Phoenix, AZ (365)	23.6	65.2	7.1	2.2	1.9	565	61
Pittsburgh, PA (365)	48.2	42.7	8.2	0.8	0.0	175	52
Plano, TX (362)	78.7	14.9	6.4	0.0	0.0	150	36
Portland, OR (365)	85.5	13.7	0.8	0.0	0.0	112	31
Providence, RI (365)	82.2	16.7	1.1	0.0	0.0	108	38
Provo, UT (365)	73.2	25.5	1.4	0.0	0.0	120	43
Raleigh, NC (365)	72.9	25.5	1.6	0.0	0.0	137	40
Richmond, VA (365)	99.7	0.3	0.0	0.0	0.0	64	20
Roseville, CA (365)	75.6	18.4	6.0	0.0	0.0	147	41
Round Rock, TX (n/a)	n/a	n/a	n/a	n/a	n/a	n/a	n/a
San Antonio, TX (365)	71.8	25.2	3.0	0.0	0.0	140	40
San Diego, CA (365)	33.7	62.7	3.3	0.3	0.0	155	54
San Francisco, CA (365)	78.4	21.4	0.3	0.0	0.0	115	36
San Jose, CA (365)	71.2	28.5	0.3	0.0	0.0	121	41
Savannah, GA (365)	60.5	36.7	2.2	0.5	0.0	155	46
Scottsdale, AZ (365)	23.6	65.2	7.1	2.2	1.9	565	61
Seattle, WA (365)	86.8	13.2	0.0	0.0	0.0	89	33
Sioux Falls, SD (365)	88.5	11.5	0.0	0.0	0.0	90	36
Stamford, CT (365)	82.5	13.7	3.6	0.3	0.0	164	36
Sterling Hgts, MI (242)	78.1	18.6	3.3	0.0	0.0	135	37
Sunnyvale, CA (365)	71.2	28.5	0.3	0.0	0.0	121	41
Tampa, FL (365)	75.1	21.4	3.6	0.0	0.0	119	41
Temecula, CA (365)	11.2	55.3	27.4	5.2	0.8	320	82
Thousand Oaks, CA (365)	75.6	21.9	2.2	0.0	0.3	221	43
Virginia Beach, VA (349)	85.4	14.6	0.0	0.0	0.0	88	27
Washington, DC (365)	61.1	35.9	3.0	0.0	0.0	142	47

Note: The Air Quality Index (AQI) is an index for reporting daily air quality. EPA calculates the AQI for five major air pollutants regulated by the Clean Air Act: ground-level ozone, particle pollution (also known as particulate matter), carbon monoxide, sulfur dioxide, and nitrogen dioxide. The AQI runs from 0 to 500. The higher the AQI value, the greater the level of air pollution and the greater the health concern. There are six AQI categories: "Good" The AQI is between 0 and 50. Air quality is considered satisfactory; "Moderate" The AQI is between 51 and 100. Air quality is acceptable; "Unhealthy for Sensitive Groups" When AQI values are between 101 and 150, members of sensitive groups may experience health effects; "Unhealthy" When AQI values are between 151 and 200 everyone may begin to experience health effects; "Very Unhealthy" AQI values between 201 and 300 trigger a health alert; "Hazardous" AQI values over 300 trigger health warnings of emergency conditions; Data covers the entire county unless noted otherwise; (1) Data cover the entire county; (2) Number of days with AQI data in 2011
Source: U.S. Environmental Protection Agency, AirData Report, 2011

Air Quality Index Pollutants

Area[1] (Days[2])	Percent of Days when AQI Pollutant was...					
	Carbon Monoxide	Nitrogen Dioxide	Ozone	Sulfur Dioxide	Particulate Matter 2.5	Particulate Matter 10
Albuquerque, NM (365)	0.0	5.5	51.2	1.1	32.6	9.6
Alexandria, VA (365)	0.0	38.9	48.2	0.3	12.3	0.3
Anchorage, AK (365)	7.1	0.0	38.6	0.0	28.8	25.5
Ann Arbor, MI (296)	0.0	0.0	81.1	0.0	18.9	0.0
Athens, GA (365)	0.0	0.0	45.5	0.0	54.5	0.0
Atlanta, GA (365)	0.0	0.0	39.5	4.7	55.9	0.0
Austin, TX (365)	0.0	0.5	69.9	0.0	29.6	0.0
Baltimore, MD (365)	0.0	18.4	24.1	0.0	57.5	0.0
Bellevue, WA (365)	0.0	0.0	47.4	0.8	51.8	0.0
Billings, MT (365)	1.1	0.0	0.0	54.2	44.7	0.0
Boise City, ID (365)	0.8	2.5	81.6	0.0	7.4	7.7
Boston, MA (365)	0.0	20.0	24.4	0.8	54.8	0.0
Boulder, CO (365)	0.0	0.0	95.1	0.0	4.7	0.3
Broken Arrow, OK (365)	0.0	0.8	47.1	13.4	37.3	1.4
Cambridge, MA (365)	0.3	0.0	96.2	0.0	3.6	0.0
Cape Coral, FL (365)	0.0	0.0	73.2	0.0	26.6	0.3
Carlsbad, CA (365)	0.0	15.1	38.1	0.0	44.4	2.5
Cary, NC (365)	0.0	0.0	63.3	0.0	36.7	0.0
Cedar Rapids, IA (365)	0.0	0.0	40.0	1.1	57.5	1.4
Charleston, SC (365)	0.0	3.3	39.2	0.0	57.0	0.5
Charlotte, NC (365)	0.0	4.7	58.1	0.0	37.3	0.0
Chesapeake, VA (n/a)	n/a	n/a	n/a	n/a	n/a	n/a
Chicago, IL (365)	0.0	20.5	17.3	11.0	50.4	0.8
Clarksville, TN (365)	0.0	0.0	0.0	22.2	77.8	0.0
Colorado Spgs., CO (365)	0.0	0.0	98.4	0.0	1.4	0.3
Columbia, MD (n/a)	n/a	n/a	n/a	n/a	n/a	n/a
Columbia, MO (245)	0.0	0.0	100.0	0.0	0.0	0.0
Columbia, SC (365)	0.0	3.3	56.4	0.0	40.3	0.0
Columbus, OH (365)	1.1	0.0	35.3	0.0	62.7	0.8
Dallas, TX (365)	0.0	13.2	49.0	0.0	35.3	2.5
Denver, CO (365)	0.0	40.8	38.6	1.9	7.7	11.0
Durham, NC (365)	0.0	0.0	43.3	0.0	56.7	0.0
Edison, NJ (364)	0.0	17.9	59.9	0.0	22.3	0.0
El Paso, TX (365)	0.0	16.4	38.4	0.0	36.2	9.0
Fargo, ND (350)	0.0	2.9	56.3	0.0	29.1	11.7
Ft. Collins, CO (365)	0.0	0.0	98.9	0.0	1.1	0.0
Ft. Worth, TX (365)	0.0	12.6	59.5	0.0	27.7	0.3
Gilbert, AZ (365)	0.0	19.2	38.9	0.0	15.6	26.3
Green Bay, WI (365)	0.0	0.0	26.0	9.3	64.7	0.0
Henderson, NV (365)	0.0	2.2	78.6	0.0	15.9	3.3
High Point, NC (361)	0.0	0.0	47.9	0.0	52.1	0.0
Honolulu, HI (365)	0.0	0.0	44.7	0.3	50.1	4.9
Houston, TX (365)	0.0	10.7	32.9	5.2	44.1	7.1
Huntington, NY (365)	0.0	0.0	72.1	0.0	27.9	0.0
Huntsville, AL (332)	0.0	0.0	62.3	0.0	21.7	16.0
Indianapolis, IN (365)	0.0	0.3	15.9	5.5	78.1	0.3
Irvine, CA (365)	0.0	9.0	27.9	0.0	61.6	1.4
Jackson, MS (365)	0.0	0.0	34.8	0.0	65.2	0.0
Jacksonville, FL (365)	0.5	1.1	67.4	2.7	27.9	0.3
Jersey City, NJ (365)	1.1	33.7	24.1	2.2	36.4	2.5
Kansas City, MO (365)	0.0	21.4	0.0	22.7	54.0	1.9
Kenosha, WI (304)	0.0	0.0	65.8	0.0	34.2	0.0
Las Vegas, NV (365)	0.0	2.2	78.6	0.0	15.9	3.3
Lexington, KY (365)	0.0	9.6	32.3	1.6	56.4	0.0

Table continued on next page.

Area[1] (Days[2])	Percent of Days when AQI Pollutant was...					
	Carbon Monoxide	Nitrogen Dioxide	Ozone	Sulfur Dioxide	Particulate Matter 2.5	Particulate Matter 10
Lincoln, NE (365)	30.1	0.0	50.4	0.0	19.5	0.0
Little Rock, AR (365)	0.0	2.7	38.6	0.0	58.6	0.0
Los Angeles, CA (365)	0.0	10.1	42.7	0.3	46.3	0.5
Madison, WI (359)	0.0	0.0	39.6	0.0	60.4	0.0
Manchester, NH (365)	0.0	0.0	90.7	3.8	5.5	0.0
Miami, FL (365)	0.0	1.6	48.2	0.0	50.1	0.0
Minneapolis, MN (365)	3.3	0.0	0.0	0.0	95.1	1.6
Murfreesboro, TN (243)	0.0	0.0	100.0	0.0	0.0	0.0
Naperville, IL (365)	0.0	0.0	27.4	0.0	72.6	0.0
Nashville, TN (365)	0.0	9.9	30.4	0.0	59.5	0.3
New Orleans, LA (365)	0.0	0.0	70.1	0.0	25.8	4.1
New York, NY (365)	0.0	0.0	0.0	0.0	100.0	0.0
Norman, OK (363)	0.0	0.0	63.6	0.0	36.4	0.0
Olathe, KS (365)	0.0	0.0	90.4	0.0	9.6	0.0
Omaha, NE (365)	0.0	0.0	24.1	9.9	27.1	38.9
Orlando, FL (365)	0.0	0.5	68.8	0.0	30.7	0.0
Overland Park, KS (365)	0.0	0.0	90.4	0.0	9.6	0.0
Oyster Bay, NY (365)	0.0	0.0	0.0	6.8	93.2	0.0
Pembroke Pines, FL (365)	0.0	6.8	56.4	0.0	36.7	0.0
Philadelphia, PA (365)	0.0	16.7	35.6	0.0	47.1	0.5
Phoenix, AZ (365)	0.0	19.2	38.9	0.0	15.6	26.3
Pittsburgh, PA (365)	0.0	4.1	29.9	10.1	55.1	0.8
Plano, TX (362)	0.0	0.0	100.0	0.0	0.0	0.0
Portland, OR (365)	0.0	3.6	59.5	0.0	37.0	0.0
Providence, RI (365)	0.0	6.3	58.4	0.0	35.1	0.3
Provo, UT (365)	0.0	21.1	58.6	0.0	19.5	0.8
Raleigh, NC (365)	0.0	0.0	63.3	0.0	36.7	0.0
Richmond, VA (365)	0.3	95.9	0.0	3.8	0.0	0.0
Roseville, CA (365)	0.0	21.9	74.0	0.0	4.1	0.0
Round Rock, TX (n/a)	n/a	n/a	n/a	n/a	n/a	n/a
San Antonio, TX (365)	0.0	0.8	63.8	0.0	35.1	0.3
San Diego, CA (365)	0.0	15.1	38.1	0.0	44.4	2.5
San Francisco, CA (365)	0.0	29.6	36.7	0.0	33.7	0.0
San Jose, CA (365)	0.0	5.2	34.8	0.0	60.0	0.0
Savannah, GA (365)	0.0	0.0	23.8	27.9	48.2	0.0
Scottsdale, AZ (365)	0.0	19.2	38.9	0.0	15.6	26.3
Seattle, WA (365)	0.0	0.0	47.4	0.8	51.8	0.0
Sioux Falls, SD (365)	0.0	4.9	62.2	0.0	28.5	4.4
Stamford, CT (365)	8.8	25.5	45.2	3.3	17.3	0.0
Sterling Hgts, MI (242)	0.0	0.0	72.7	0.0	27.3	0.0
Sunnyvale, CA (365)	0.0	5.2	34.8	0.0	60.0	0.0
Tampa, FL (365)	0.0	0.0	54.0	11.8	32.6	1.6
Temecula, CA (365)	0.0	0.8	45.2	0.5	35.6	17.8
Thousand Oaks, CA (365)	0.0	3.0	91.0	0.0	5.5	0.5
Virginia Beach, VA (349)	0.0	0.0	0.0	0.0	100.0	0.0
Washington, DC (365)	0.0	11.5	30.7	0.3	57.5	0.0

Note: The Air Quality Index (AQI) is an index for reporting daily air quality. EPA calculates the AQI for five major air pollutants regulated by the Clean Air Act: ground-level ozone, particle pollution (also known as particulate matter), carbon monoxide, sulfur dioxide, and nitrogen dioxide. The AQI runs from 0 to 500. The higher the AQI value, the greater the level of air pollution and the greater the health concern; (1) Data covers the entire county; (2) Number of days with AQI data in 2011
Source: U.S. Environmental Protection Agency, AirData Report, 2011

Air Quality Index Trends

Metro Area (# trend sites)	2003	2004	2005	2006	2007	2008	2009	2010
Albuquerque, NM (22)	16	6	11	8	2	1	0	2
Alexandria, VA (50)	32	32	49	37	43	22	5	28
Anchorage, AK (n/a)	n/a	n/a	n/a	n/a	n/a	n/a	n/a	n/a
Ann Arbor, MI (n/a)	n/a	n/a	n/a	n/a	n/a	n/a	n/a	n/a
Athens, GA (n/a)	n/a	n/a	n/a	n/a	n/a	n/a	n/a	n/a
Atlanta, GA (31)	36	32	52	65	56	31	16	27
Austin, TX (5)	10	10	11	14	4	2	4	2
Baltimore, MD (18)	30	31	36	33	45	23	11	33
Bellevue, WA (16)	16	7	7	14	10	7	12	1
Billings, MT (n/a)	n/a	n/a	n/a	n/a	n/a	n/a	n/a	n/a
Boise City, ID (n/a)	n/a	n/a	n/a	n/a	n/a	n/a	n/a	n/a
Boston, MA (28)	16	9	21	10	21	9	5	3
Boulder, CO (n/a)	n/a	n/a	n/a	n/a	n/a	n/a	n/a	n/a
Broken Arrow, OK (13)	23	20	27	26	7	15	5	3
Cambridge, MA (28)	16	9	21	10	21	9	5	3
Cape Coral, FL (n/a)	n/a	n/a	n/a	n/a	n/a	n/a	n/a	n/a
Carlsbad, CA (29)	50	31	30	39	34	43	25	14
Cary, NC (7)	11	10	26	9	24	11	0	3
Cedar Rapids, IA (n/a)	n/a	n/a	n/a	n/a	n/a	n/a	n/a	n/a
Charleston, SC (8)	3	3	8	9	5	1	0	0
Charlotte, NC (13)	16	20	32	24	36	24	3	14
Chesapeake, VA (9)	10	6	12	13	11	16	0	4
Chicago, IL (81)	44	47	61	35	53	48	26	28
Clarksville, TN (n/a)	n/a	n/a	n/a	n/a	n/a	n/a	n/a	n/a
Colorado Spgs., CO (2)	4	0	6	0	1	2	0	1
Columbia, MD (18)	30	31	36	33	45	23	11	33
Columbia, MO (n/a)	n/a	n/a	n/a	n/a	n/a	n/a	n/a	n/a
Columbia, SC (10)	22	24	29	22	21	14	3	9
Columbus, OH (12)	23	13	32	11	30	10	1	6
Dallas, TX (35)	49	50	80	54	34	30	32	15
Denver, CO (23)	35	6	13	27	23	10	7	8
Durham, NC (n/a)	n/a	n/a	n/a	n/a	n/a	n/a	n/a	n/a
Edison, NJ (69)	41	40	50	40	40	31	15	37
El Paso, TX (26)	18	10	18	12	15	10	3	5
Fargo, ND (n/a)	n/a	n/a	n/a	n/a	n/a	n/a	n/a	n/a
Ft. Collins, CO (n/a)	n/a	n/a	n/a	n/a	n/a	n/a	n/a	n/a
Ft. Worth, TX (35)	49	50	80	54	34	30	32	15
Gilbert, AZ (55)	51	23	49	50	21	27	10	11
Green Bay, WI (n/a)	n/a	n/a	n/a	n/a	n/a	n/a	n/a	n/a
Henderson, NV (28)	42	22	34	35	24	12	5	2
High Point, NC (2)	11	2	4	3	9	10	5	3
Honolulu, HI (14)	2	2	2	1	0	0	0	0
Houston, TX (52)	74	66	93	64	47	24	26	33
Huntington, NY (69)	41	40	50	40	40	31	15	37
Huntsville, AL (n/a)	n/a	n/a	n/a	n/a	n/a	n/a	n/a	n/a
Indianapolis, IN (25)	38	22	49	30	42	8	10	9
Irvine, CA (66)	147	134	113	98	102	94	99	74
Jackson, MS (n/a)	n/a	n/a	n/a	n/a	n/a	n/a	n/a	n/a
Jacksonville, FL (13)	10	15	20	35	16	10	3	15
Jersey City, NJ (69)	41	40	50	40	40	31	15	37
Kansas City, MO (23)	56	35	52	74	44	39	43	22
Kenosha, WI (81)	44	47	61	35	53	48	26	28
Las Vegas, NV (28)	42	22	34	35	24	12	5	2
Lexington, KY (n/a)	n/a	n/a	n/a	n/a	n/a	n/a	n/a	n/a
Lincoln, NE (n/a)	n/a	n/a	n/a	n/a	n/a	n/a	n/a	n/a
Little Rock, AR (11)	3	0	19	11	11	2	2	2

Table continued on next page.

Metro Area (# trend sites)	2003	2004	2005	2006	2007	2008	2009	2010
Los Angeles, CA (66)	147	134	113	98	102	94	99	74
Madison, WI (3)	8	1	9	1	10	1	0	2
Manchester, NH (n/a)	n/a	n/a	n/a	n/a	n/a	n/a	n/a	n/a
Miami, FL (32)	4	11	4	12	10	5	2	4
Minneapolis, MN (29)	18	11	11	1	5	1	3	1
Murfreesboro, TN (19)	23	7	29	17	37	11	1	10
Naperville, IL (81)	44	47	61	35	53	48	26	28
Nashville, TN (19)	23	7	29	17	37	11	1	10
New Orleans, LA (7)	15	12	13	13	17	2	6	8
New York, NY (69)	41	40	50	40	40	31	15	37
Norman, OK (13)	16	6	15	33	5	5	5	3
Olathe, KS (23)	56	35	52	74	44	39	43	22
Omaha, NE (16)	4	4	16	3	7	2	4	3
Orlando, FL (15)	8	6	10	8	11	2	1	2
Overland Park, KS (23)	56	35	52	74	44	39	43	22
Oyster Bay, NY (69)	41	40	50	40	40	31	15	37
Pembroke Pines, FL (32)	4	11	4	12	10	5	2	4
Philadelphia, PA (54)	76	39	62	55	46	30	7	32
Phoenix, AZ (55)	51	23	49	50	21	27	10	11
Pittsburgh, PA (54)	129	118	123	94	97	81	58	58
Plano, TX (35)	49	50	80	54	34	30	32	15
Portland, OR (9)	2	4	4	2	5	3	5	1
Providence, RI (12)	19	10	22	16	21	6	2	14
Provo, UT (n/a)	n/a	n/a	n/a	n/a	n/a	n/a	n/a	n/a
Raleigh, NC (7)	11	10	26	9	24	11	0	3
Richmond, VA (15)	28	18	41	21	37	19	1	11
Roseville, CA (41)	79	66	62	79	53	61	43	23
Round Rock, TX (5)	10	10	11	14	4	2	4	2
San Antonio, TX (8)	21	15	15	21	3	9	3	4
San Diego, CA (29)	50	31	30	39	34	43	25	14
San Francisco, CA (46)	15	11	7	21	6	13	7	4
San Jose, CA (6)	14	8	4	14	3	13	8	6
Savannah, GA (n/a)	n/a	n/a	n/a	n/a	n/a	n/a	n/a	n/a
Scottsdale, AZ (55)	51	23	49	50	21	27	10	11
Seattle, WA (16)	16	7	7	14	10	7	12	1
Sioux Falls, SD (n/a)	n/a	n/a	n/a	n/a	n/a	n/a	n/a	n/a
Stamford, CT (14)	19	14	25	21	28	20	5	17
Sterling Hgts, MI (22)	37	37	62	38	35	24	9	23
Sunnyvale, CA (6)	14	8	4	14	3	13	8	6
Tampa, FL (30)	87	50	47	38	47	24	18	11
Temecula, CA (64)	163	157	142	133	144	131	114	115
Thousand Oaks, CA (17)	70	51	40	39	23	31	25	13
Virginia Beach, VA (9)	10	6	12	13	11	16	0	4
Washington, DC (50)	32	32	49	37	43	22	5	28

Note: Figures are the number of days the AQI value exceeded 100 in a given year. An AQI value greater than 100 indicates that air quality would have been in the unhealthful range on that day; Data from exceptional events are included; Figures cover the Metropolitan Statistical Area—see Appendix B for areas included; n/a not available.
Source: U.S. Environmental Protection Agency, Office of Air and Radiation, Air Quality Index Information, "Number of Days with Air Quality Index Values Greater than 100 at Trend Sites, 2000-2010, and at All Sites in 2010"

Maximum Air Pollutant Concentrations: Particulate Matter, Ozone, CO and Lead

Metro Aea	Particulate Matter 10 (ug/m^3)	Particulate Matter 2.5 Wtd AM (ug/m^3)	Particulate Matter 2.5 24-Hr (ug/m^3)	Ozone (ppm)	Carbon Monoxide (ppm)	Lead (ug/m^3)
Albuquerque, NM	122	5.3	18	0.069	3	n/a
Alexandria, VA	85	12.1	29	0.089	3	0
Anchorage, AK	98	5.5	38	0.045	6	n/a
Ann Arbor, MI	n/a	9.2	23	0.066	n/a	n/a
Athens, GA	n/a	11.3	23	0.073	n/a	n/a
Atlanta, GA	51	14.5	25	0.08	2	0.02
Austin, TX	34	10	19	0.074	0	n/a
Baltimore, MD	46	12.7	30	0.096	2	n/a
Bellevue, WA	n/a	7.1	24	0.068	1	n/a
Billings, MT	n/a	n/a	n/a	n/a	2	n/a
Boise City, ID	66	5.9	15	0.069	2	n/a
Boston, MA	41	10	25	0.073	2	0.01
Boulder, CO	36	7.1	23	0.072	2	n/a
Broken Arrow, OK	74	10.7	24	0.073	2	0.01
Cambridge, MA	41	10	25	0.073	2	0.01
Cape Coral, FL	67	7	13	0.065	n/a	n/a
Carlsbad, CA	101	13.3	114	0.081	2	n/a
Cary, NC	43	10.2	21	0.074	2	n/a
Cedar Rapids, IA	68	11.1	36	0.064	1	n/a
Charleston, SC	49	9.9	23	0.068	0	n/a
Charlotte, NC	48	12.1	25	0.082	2	n/a
Chesapeake, VA	37	10.2	24	0.078	2	0.01
Chicago, IL	69	14	35	0.081	2	0.24
Clarksville, TN	34	11.2	22	0.074	n/a	n/a
Colorado Spgs., CO	38	6.2	12	0.072	2	n/a
Columbia, MD	46	12.7	30	0.096	2	n/a
Columbia, MO	n/a	n/a	n/a	0.069	n/a	n/a
Columbia, SC	76	11.6	24	0.072	n/a	0
Columbus, OH	126	13.1	34	0.077	2	0.01
Dallas, TX	62	10.8	25	0.085	2	0.77
Denver, CO	68	8.6	22	0.079	2	0.01
Durham, NC	n/a	10.2	21	0.074	n/a	n/a
Edison, NJ	65	11.5	28	0.087	2	n/a
El Paso, TX	249	8.4	61	0.073	3	0.04
Fargo, ND	96	8.5	27	0.063	1	n/a
Ft. Collins, CO	43	6.5	22	0.077	2	n/a
Ft. Worth, TX	62	10.8	25	0.085	2	0.77
Gilbert, AZ	226	12.4	27	0.079	3	n/a
Green Bay, WI	n/a	10.2	36	0.078	n/a	n/a
Henderson, NV	61	7.4	22	0.079	3	n/a
High Point, NC	29	10.5	21	0.076	n/a	n/a
Honolulu, HI	70	4.7	12	0.047	1	0
Houston, TX	82	12.3	24	0.088	2	0.01
Huntington, NY	65	11.5	28	0.087	2	n/a
Huntsville, AL	37	11.6	20	0.071	n/a	n/a
Indianapolis, IN	83	14	37	0.072	3	0.08
Irvine, CA	71	12.6	32	0.09	4	0.39
Jackson, MS	n/a	11.4	22	0.067	n/a	n/a
Jacksonville, FL	62	9.4	20	0.068	2	n/a
Jersey City, NJ	65	11.5	28	0.087	2	n/a
Kansas City, MO	65	11	31	0.076	2	n/a
Kenosha, WI	69	14	35	0.081	2	0.24
Las Vegas, NV	61	7.4	22	0.079	3	n/a
Lexington, KY	35	12.2	23	0.071	n/a	n/a

Table continued on next page.

Metro Aea	Particulate Matter 10 (ug/m³)	Particulate Matter 2.5 Wtd AM (ug/m³)	Particulate Matter 2.5 24-Hr (ug/m³)	Ozone (ppm)	Carbon Monoxide (ppm)	Lead (ug/m³)
Lincoln, NE	n/a	9	26	0.05	2	n/a
Little Rock, AR	38	12.6	23	0.073	2	n/a
Los Angeles, CA	71	12.6	32	0.09	4	0.39
Madison, WI	39	10.1	30	0.063	n/a	n/a
Manchester, NH	29	8	25	0.077	2	n/a
Miami, FL	44	7.8	14	0.069	2	n/a
Minneapolis, MN	74	10	36	0.067	2	0.27
Murfreesboro, TN	42	11.8	24	0.078	2	n/a
Naperville, IL	69	14	35	0.081	2	0.24
Nashville, TN	42	11.8	24	0.081	n/a	n/a
New Orleans, LA	73	10.1	19	0.081	2	n/a
New York, NY	65	11.5	28	0.087	2	n/a
Norman, OK	41	9.2	18	0.072	1	0
Olathe, KS	65	11	31	0.076	2	n/a
Omaha, NE	249	12.2	32	0.067	2	0.26
Orlando, FL	46	7.6	14	0.071	1	n/a
Overland Park, KS	65	11	31	0.076	2	n/a
Oyster Bay, NY	65	11.5	28	0.087	2	n/a
Pembroke Pines, FL	44	7.8	14	0.069	2	0.05
Philadelphia, PA	91	13.8	35	0.088	2	n/a
Phoenix, AZ	226	12.4	27	0.079	3	0.21
Pittsburgh, PA	93	16.1	49	0.083	3	n/a
Plano, TX	62	10.8	25	0.085	2	0.77
Portland, OR	29	6.6	18	0.066	2	0.03
Providence, RI	37	9.2	26	0.079	2	n/a
Provo, UT	108	8.9	48	0.071	2	n/a
Raleigh, NC	43	10.2	21	0.074	2	n/a
Richmond, VA	33	10.2	22	0.081	2	0.01
Roseville, CA	54	8.7	27	0.096	2	n/a
Round Rock, TX	34	10	19	0.074	0	n/a
San Antonio, TX	55	8.7	16	0.078	1	n/a
San Diego, CA	101	13.3	114	0.081	2	n/a
San Francisco, CA	45	10.5	33	0.078	2	n/a
San Jose, CA	37	8.8	29	0.08	2	n/a
Savannah, GA	33	10.5	24	0.065	n/a	n/a
Scottsdale, AZ	226	12.4	27	0.079	3	n/a
Seattle, WA	n/a	7.1	24	0.068	1	n/a
Sioux Falls, SD	60	9.7	28	0.064	n/a	n/a
Stamford, CT	40	9.1	26	0.084	2	n/a
Sterling Hgts, MI	73	11.3	30	0.078	1	0.01
Sunnyvale, CA	37	8.8	29	0.08	2	n/a
Tampa, FL	62	8.1	16	0.072	1	0.73
Temecula, CA	312	15.2	36	0.109	4	0.01
Thousand Oaks, CA	45	8.7	21	0.082	n/a	n/a
Virginia Beach, VA	37	10.2	24	0.078	2	0.01
Washington, DC	85	12.1	29	0.089	3	0
NAAQS[1]	150	15	35	0.075	9	0.15

Note: Data from exceptional events are excluded; Data covers the Metropolitan Statistical Area—see Appendix B for areas included; (1) National Ambient Air Quality Standards; ppm = parts per million; ug/m³ = micrograms per cubic meter; n/a not available Concentrations: Particulate Matter 10 (coarse particulate)—highest second maximum 24-hour concentration; Particulate Matter 2.5 Wtd AM (fine particulate)—highest weighted annual mean concentration; Particulate Matter 2.5 24-Hour (fine particulate)—highest 98th percentile 24-hour concentration; Ozone—highest fourth daily maximum 8-hour concentration; Carbon Monoxide—highest second maximum non-overlapping 8-hour concentration; Lead—maximum running 3-month average
Source: U.S. Environmental Protection Agency, CBSA Factbook 2010, Air Quality Statistics by City, 2010

Maximum Air Pollutant Concentrations: Nitrogen Dioxide and Sulfur Dioxide

Metro Area	Nitrogen Dioxide AM (ppb)	Nitrogen Dioxide 1-Hr (ppb)	Sulfur Dioxide AM (ppb)	Sulfur Dioxide 1-Hr (ppb)	Sulfur Dioxide 24-Hr (ppb)
Albuquerque, NM	12.068	53	n/a	n/a	n/a
Alexandria, VA	17.595	59	3.372	21	10.5
Anchorage, AK	n/a	n/a	n/a	n/a	n/a
Ann Arbor, MI	n/a	n/a	n/a	n/a	n/a
Athens, GA	n/a	n/a	n/a	n/a	n/a
Atlanta, GA	13.657	58	1.908	33	10
Austin, TX	3.314	21.1	n/a	n/a	n/a
Baltimore, MD	17.549	61	2.152	20	7.3
Bellevue, WA	n/a	n/a	1.136	24.5	8
Billings, MT	n/a	n/a	3.876	91	23.4
Boise City, ID	9.51	45	0.366	n/a	1.1
Boston, MA	19.098	53	2.933	44.9	10.5
Boulder, CO	n/a	n/a	n/a	n/a	n/a
Broken Arrow, OK	8.311	38	5.3	63	26.2
Cambridge, MA	19.098	53	2.933	44.9	10.5
Cape Coral, FL	n/a	n/a	n/a	n/a	n/a
Carlsbad, CA	20.975	74	1.765	18	7.1
Cary, NC	n/a	n/a	1.017	12.4	5.7
Cedar Rapids, IA	n/a	n/a	0.984	28.9	8.6
Charleston, SC	7.573	n/a	1.07	21	9.5
Charlotte, NC	11.738	50	0.926	19.8	5.7
Chesapeake, VA	n/a	n/a	2.128	41	8.3
Chicago, IL	24.869	71	4.138	90	23.5
Clarksville, TN	n/a	n/a	3.654	51	12
Colorado Spgs., CO	n/a	n/a	n/a	n/a	n/a
Columbia, MD	17.549	61	2.152	20	7.3
Columbia, MO	n/a	n/a	n/a	n/a	n/a
Columbia, SC	5.345	n/a	1.974	85	12
Columbus, OH	n/a	n/a	n/a	n/a	n/a
Dallas, TX	13.186	56.9	0.808	17.3	4.5
Denver, CO	27.704	71	1.644	37	8.8
Durham, NC	n/a	n/a	n/a	n/a	n/a
Edison, NJ	22.192	71	4.829	50.2	23.6
El Paso, TX	17.067	62.7	0.756	10.3	3
Fargo, ND	5.435	44	0.293	6.1	2.5
Ft. Collins, CO	n/a	n/a	n/a	n/a	n/a
Ft. Worth, TX	13.186	56.9	0.808	17.3	4.5
Gilbert, AZ	24.524	68	1.742	10	5.3
Green Bay, WI	n/a	n/a	2.273	69	15.7
Henderson, NV	13.308	55.9	n/a	n/a	n/a
High Point, NC	n/a	n/a	n/a	n/a	n/a
Honolulu, HI	3.411	24	1.272	18	4
Houston, TX	14.941	60	2.336	45.6	13.8
Huntington, NY	22.192	71	4.829	50.2	23.6
Huntsville, AL	n/a	n/a	n/a	n/a	n/a
Indianapolis, IN	12.683	53.5	3.347	105	28.8
Irvine, CA	26.179	72.5	1.394	16.2	4.8
Jackson, MS	n/a	n/a	n/a	n/a	n/a
Jacksonville, FL	9.324	44	3.949	216	58.4
Jersey City, NJ	22.192	71	4.829	50.2	23.6
Kansas City, MO	14.93	54	5.499	49	46.5
Kenosha, WI	24.869	71	4.138	90	23.5
Las Vegas, NV	13.308	55.9	n/a	n/a	n/a
Lexington, KY	9.463	56	2.214	48	11.3
Lincoln, NE	n/a	n/a	n/a	n/a	n/a

Table continued on next page.

Metro Area	Nitrogen Dioxide AM (ppb)	Nitrogen Dioxide 1-Hr (ppb)	Sulfur Dioxide AM (ppb)	Sulfur Dioxide 1-Hr (ppb)	Sulfur Dioxide 24-Hr (ppb)
Little Rock, AR	9.982	51	1.698	9	3.7
Los Angeles, CA	26.179	72.5	1.394	16.2	4.8
Madison, WI	n/a	n/a	n/a	n/a	n/a
Manchester, NH	7.99	42.2	1.453	57.7	12
Miami, FL	9.651	49	0.831	38	5.9
Minneapolis, MN	9.673	51	0.787	29	10.2
Murfreesboro, TN	12.526	46	2.246	14	5.5
Naperville, IL	24.869	71	4.138	90	23.5
Nashville, TN	12.526	46	2.246	14	5.5
New Orleans, LA	7.759	47	7.743	248	75.6
New York, NY	22.192	71	4.829	50.2	23.6
Norman, OK	8.921	47	0.777	6	3.5
Olathe, KS	14.93	54	5.499	49	46.5
Omaha, NE	n/a	n/a	2.124	58	25.9
Orlando, FL	5.627	40	0.157	7	2.2
Overland Park, KS	14.93	54	5.499	49	46.5
Oyster Bay, NY	22.192	71	4.829	50.2	23.6
Pembroke Pines, FL	9.651	49	0.831	38	5.9
Philadelphia, PA	22.609	61.6	3.03	34	17.9
Phoenix, AZ	24.524	68	1.742	10	5.3
Pittsburgh, PA	15.254	51	7.106	161	39.6
Plano, TX	13.186	56.9	0.808	17.3	4.5
Portland, OR	8.635	33	1.35	8	3.2
Providence, RI	9.83	40	3.081	84.3	33.1
Provo, UT	14.56	50	n/a	n/a	n/a
Raleigh, NC	n/a	n/a	1.017	12.4	5.7
Richmond, VA	11.998	57	2.013	44	9.3
Roseville, CA	12.494	54	0.462	1	1.9
Round Rock, TX	3.314	21.1	n/a	n/a	n/a
San Antonio, TX	3.831	31.9	n/a	n/a	n/a
San Diego, CA	20.975	74	1.765	18	7.1
San Francisco, CA	15.598	76.6	1.188	15.3	5.7
San Jose, CA	14.394	50.7	0.352	4.1	1.6
Savannah, GA	n/a	n/a	3.42	83	33.2
Scottsdale, AZ	24.524	68	1.742	10	5.3
Seattle, WA	n/a	n/a	1.136	24.5	8
Sioux Falls, SD	6.583	48	0.247	5	1.7
Stamford, CT	10.132	50	1.529	17.8	10.4
Sterling Hgts, MI	11.96	54	3.385	107	48.8
Sunnyvale, CA	14.394	50.7	0.352	4.1	1.6
Tampa, FL	6.079	38	2.852	104	28.7
Temecula, CA	23.087	65	1.28	11	6.7
Thousand Oaks, CA	10.096	41	n/a	n/a	n/a
Virginia Beach, VA	n/a	n/a	2.128	41	8.3
Washington, DC	17.595	59	3.372	21	10.5
NAAQS[1]	53	100	30	75	140

Note: Data from exceptional events are excluded; Data covers the Metropolitan Statistical Area—see Appendix B for areas included; (1) National Ambient Air Quality Standards; ppb = parts per billion; n/a not available
Concentrations: Nitrogen Dioxide AM—highest arithmetic mean concentration; Nitrogen Dioxide 1-Hr—highest 98th percentile 1-hour daily maximum concentration; Sulfur Dioxide AM—highest annual mean concentration; Sulfur Dioxide 1-Hr—highest 99th percentile 1-hour daily maximum concentration; Sulfur Dioxide 24-Hr—highest second maximum 24-hour concentration
Source: U.S. Environmental Protection Agency, CBSA Factbook 2010, Air Quality Statistics by City, 2010

Grey House Publishing
2012 Title List

Visit **www.greyhouse.com** for Product Information, Table of Contents and Sample Pages

General Reference

America's College Museums
American Environmental Leaders: From Colonial Times to the Present
An African Biographical Dictionary
An Encyclopedia of Human Rights in the United States
Encyclopedia of African-American Writing
Encyclopedia of Gun Control & Gun Rights
Encyclopedia of Invasions & Conquests
Encyclopedia of Prisoners of War & Internment
Encyclopedia of Religion & Law in America
Encyclopedia of Rural America
Encyclopedia of the United States Cabinet, 1789-2010
Encyclopedia of War Journalism
Encyclopedia of Warrior Peoples & Fighting Groups
From Suffrage to the Senate: America's Political Women
Nations of the World
Political Corruption in America
Speakers of the House of Representatives, 1789-2009
The Environmental Debate: A Documentary History
The Evolution Wars: A Guide to the Debates
The Religious Right: A Reference Handbook
The Value of a Dollar: 1860-2009
The Value of a Dollar: Colonial Era
US Land & Natural Resource Policy
Weather America
Working Americans 1770-1869 Vol. IX: Revol. War to the Civil War
Working Americans 1880-1999 Vol. I: The Working Class
Working Americans 1880-1999 Vol. II: The Middle Class
Working Americans 1880-1999 Vol. III: The Upper Class
Working Americans 1880-1999 Vol. IV: Their Children
Working Americans 1880-2003 Vol. V: At War
Working Americans 1880-2005 Vol. VI: Women at Work
Working Americans 1880-2006 Vol. VII: Social Movements
Working Americans 1880-2007 Vol. VIII: Immigrants
Working Americans 1880-2009 Vol. X: Sports & Recreation
Working Americans 1880-2010 Vol. XI: Inventors & Entrepreneurs
Working Americans 1880-2011 Vol. XII: Our History through Music
World Cultural Leaders of the 20th & 21st Centuries

Business Information

Directory of Business Information Resources
Directory of Mail Order Catalogs
Directory of Venture Capital & Private Equity Firms
Environmental Resource Handbook
Food & Beverage Market Place
Grey House Homeland Security Directory
Grey House Performing Arts Directory
Hudson's Washington News Media Contacts Directory
New York State Directory
Sports Market Place Directory
The Rauch Guides – Industry Market Research Reports
Sweets Directory by McGraw Hill Construction

Statistics & Demographics

America's Top-Rated Cities
America's Top-Rated Small Towns & Cities
America's Top-Rated Smaller Cities
Comparative Guide to American Hospitals
Comparative Guide to American Suburbs
Profiles of... Series – State Handbooks

Health Information

Comparative Guide to American Hospitals
Complete Directory for Pediatric Disorders
Complete Directory for People with Chronic Illness
Complete Directory for People with Disabilities
Complete Mental Health Directory
Directory of Health Care Group Purchasing Organizations
Directory of Hospital Personnel
HMO/PPO Directory
Medical Device Register
Older Americans Information Directory

Education Information

Charter School Movement
Comparative Guide to American Elementary & Secondary Schools
Complete Learning Disabilities Directory
Educators Resource Directory
Special Education

Financial Ratings Series

TheStreet.com Ratings Guide to Bond & Money Market Mutual Funds
TheStreet.com Ratings Guide to Common Stocks
TheStreet.com Ratings Guide to Exchange-Traded Funds
TheStreet.com Ratings Guide to Stock Mutual Funds
TheStreet.com Ratings Ultimate Guided Tour of Stock Investing
Weiss Ratings Consumer Box Set
Weiss Ratings Guide to Banks & Thrifts
Weiss Ratings Guide to Credit Unions
Weiss Ratings Guide to Health Insurers
Weiss Ratings Guide to Life & Annuity Insurers
Weiss Ratings Guide to Property & Casualty Insurers

Bowker's Books In Print®Titles

Books In Print®
Books In Print® Supplement
American Book Publishing Record® Annual
American Book Publishing Record® Monthly
Books Out Loud™
Bowker's Complete Video Directory™
Children's Books In Print®
Complete Directory of Large Print Books & Serials™
El-Hi Textbooks & Serials In Print®
Forthcoming Books®
Law Books & Serials In Print™
Medical & Health Care Books In Print™
Publishers, Distributors & Wholesalers of the US™
Subject Guide to Books In Print®
Subject Guide to Children's Books In Print®

Canadian General Reference

Associations Canada
Canadian Almanac & Directory
Canadian Environmental Resource Guide
Canadian Parliamentary Guide
Financial Services Canada
Governments Canada
Libraries Canada
The History of Canada

Grey House Publishing
4919 Route 22, PO Box 56, Amenia NY 12501-0056 | (800) 562-2139 | www.greyhouse.com | books@greyhouse.com